HARMSWORTH
HISTORY
OF THE WORLD

BUDDHA, "THE LIGHT OF ASIA"

FROM AN INDIAN STATUE NOW IN THE BERLIN ROYAL MUSEUM

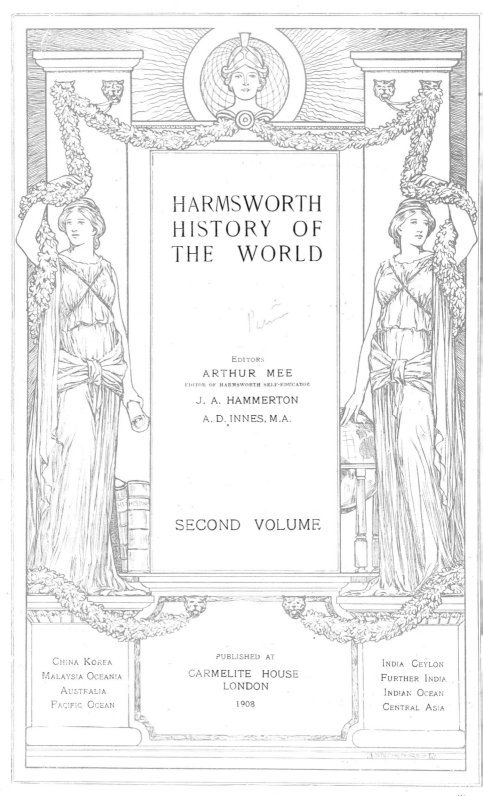

HARMSWORTH HISTORY OF THE WORLD

EDITORS

ARTHUR MEE

EDITOR OF HARMSWORTH SELF-EDUCATOR

J. A. HAMMERTON

A. D. INNES, M.A.

SECOND VOLUME

CHINA KOREA
MALAYSIA OCEANIA
AUSTRALIA
PACIFIC OCEAN

PUBLISHED AT

CARMELITE HOUSE
LONDON

1908

INDIA CEYLON
FURTHER INDIA
INDIAN OCEAN
CENTRAL ASIA

CONTENTS OF THIS VOLUME

THE DOWAGER EMPRESS OF CHINA
Painted by Stephen Reid after a Chinese drawing

LAST FIFTY YEARS IN CHINA
BY SIR ROBERT K. DOUGLAS

THE conclusion of the European Treaties of 1858 opened a new chapter in the history of China's relations with the West. Till then, foreigners can scarcely be said to have enjoyed any rights whatever in the Flowery Land. They had been allowed to trade at five ports—viz., Canton, Amoy, Foochow, Ningpo and Shanghai—but were not allowed to wander outside the limits of the foreign settlements at those centres, and were not permitted to hold any direct communication with Peking. The taking of Canton and the capture of the Taku forts altered all that, and Lord Elgin, representing Great Britain at Tientsin, found himself in a position to demand many and larger concessions from the vanquished Chinese.

After many conferences with the Chinese Plenipotentiaries a treaty was signed on June 26th, 1858, by which the Chinese agreed to accept a resident British Minister at Peking, to open to trade the ports of Newchuang, Tengchow, Taiwan in Formosa, Swatow, and Kiungchow, in addition to the old five ports, to allow British subjects to travel into the interior of the country with passports, to recognise missionary work, and to legalise the opium trade.

This treaty was to have been ratified the following year, but the Chinese re**Chinese Resume Hostilities** pented of having agreed to its terms. When, therefore, Mr. Bruce appeared at Taku in 1859 on his way to Peking, to exchange the ratifications, his ships were fired upon from the forts ; three gunboats were sunk, and 300 sailors were killed or wounded.

This rebuff was of so severe a nature, and the attitude of the Chinese was so uncompromising, that it was found necessary to wait for reinforcements from Europe. In the following year these arrived in the shape of 13,000 British soldiers and sailors under the command of Sir Hope Grant, and 7,000 Frenchmen, commanded by Gen. Montauban, whose Government had made common cause with us. The allied army soon played havoc with the Chinese defences. They landed at Peitang—seven miles north of Taku— and, meeting with no resistance, took the Taku forts in rear. Here the Chinese fought with wonderful courage, but they were speedily vanquished, and, after a vigorous assault, the fort on the north bank of the river was taken. This earthwork, as Sir Hope Grant had pointed out, **Taku Forts Again Captured** was the key to the position, and it had no sooner fallen into the hands of the Allies than the southern forts capitulated. This victory left the way open to Tientsin, where Lord Elgin, who had been reappointed Envoy Extraordinary once more found himself. After the manner of their kind, the Chinese accepted the inevitable and reserved the whole of their endeavours to reducing the terms offered by the Allies and to preventing the allied Plenipotentiaries from going to Peking. Ultimately, the Envoys refused to repeat the error of the previous year in negotiating at Tientsin, and declared their intention of proceeding at once to Tungchow in the neighbourhood of the capital, where they would be prepared to negotiate a preliminary convention preparatory to a final treaty to be signed within the walls of the capital. In order to save time, Wade (afterwards Sir Thomas Wade) and Parkes (afterwards Sir Harry Parkes) were sent forward to arrange the terms. These two officials were received to all appearances cordially by the Chinese Commissioners, the terms of the convention were drafted, and some of those who had accompanied them had returned to the allied lines when a dastardly act of treachery was committed.

The ground which had been assigned as the camping ground of the allied forces was secretly occupied by a Chinese army under Prince Sankolinsen, and on Parkes, Loch (afterwards Lord Loch), and others presenting themselves on their way to Lord Elgin's camp, they were made prisoners and carried off to Peking. Parkes and Loch were imprisoned in the Board of Punishments, while the others were incarcerated elsewhere. This violation of the rules of war was regarded very differently by the two armies. By the Chinese

Treachery and its Reward it was looked upon as putting into their hands a lever with which to extort concessions, and by Lord Elgin as an outrage which aggravated the original cause of offence. The Chinese believed that Parkes could, at a word, order the retreat of the allied armies, and that so long as they held him prisoner they could negotiate through him. Lord Elgin gave them little excuse for this fallacy. He at once replied to the emissaries who were constantly arriving in the allied camp that until the prisoners, one and all, were returned he must refuse all negotiations. And in the meantime the Allies marched on towards the capital. After gaining two victories they found themselves before the walls of Peking.

Meanwhile, the Emperor had fled to Jehol, in Mongolia, where he held his court, and indulged in those debaucheries for which he was notorious. At this safe distance he gave orders for the procedure of the war regardless of the useless sufferings he was inflicting on his subjects. At Peking a very different view was taken of the position, and the more liberally-minded officials, headed by Prince Kung, devoted their energies to procuring the release of the prisoners and of securing peace. In furtherance of these wise endeavours Prince Kung went to Jehol, and though he found the Emperor hopelessly reactionary under the influence of his entourage, yet he succeeded in forming a useful alliance with the Empress Tzu-hsi, the mother of the heir to the throne. By virtue of this alliance peace was made and those of the prisoners, including

Peace Convention Signed Parkes and Loch, who had survived the ill-usage to which they had been subjected, were released. On October 24th, 1860, conventions were signed by Lord Elgin and Baron Gros on the one hand, and Prince Kung on the other. The terms of these documents confirmed the treaties of 1858, and added indemnities for the cost of the war. These documents were no sooner signed than, with all haste, the allied Plenipotentiaries

hurried to the coast, being fearful lest they should be frozen in for the winter. It was an unfortunate climax to the campaign, and was susceptible of the version attributed to it by the mandarins, who gave out that the Allies had been defeated in battle and had taken to flight. To retire from a country at the moment of victory is so contrary to Oriental ideas that the Chinese on this occasion, as well as on others, naturally attributed Lord Elgin's hasty retreat to discomfiture.

Prince Kung, however, was under no such delusion, and having made peace, he did all he could to establish a good feeling with his quondam enemies. He recognised that the return of the Emperor to Peking was much to be desired, and he used all his power of persuasion to induce him to revisit his capital. But in this he was unsuccessful. The Emperor was surrounded by men who were interested in preventing the unfortunate Hsien-feng from learning the true position of affairs. Matters were in this condition when, to the superstitious minds of the Chinese, an evil omen, in the

Death of the Emperor shape of a comet, appeared in the sky. As if to justify the popular belief, it was announced that the Emperor was seriously ill, and almost immediately afterwards, that on August 22nd, 1861, the great Emperor had " become a guest on high." These announcements were made by the Regents, who had been appointed by the dying monarch, and who were subsequently deposed and executed by the authority of the Empress and of Princes Kung and Chun.

The signature of the treaty restored peace in the northern portion of the empire, and freed the flower of the Imperial troops for the suppression of the Taiping rebellion, which had for some years devastated the central and richest provinces of the empire. Nanking, the second city in the country, was in the hands of the rebels, as well as the important towns of Soochow, Hangchow, and a number of others, and naturally the first desire of the Emperor and Prince Kung was to recover them to the Imperial crown. With this laudable desire they thought to take advantage of the presence of foreign troops to learn something of the art of war which had made them so superior to their own armies. They eagerly accepted the loan of English drill-sergeants to

EXTERIOR OF THE INNER NORTH FORT, CAPTURED BY FRENCH AND BRITISH

INTERIOR OF OUTER NORTH FORT, SHOWING CHINESE DEFENCES

INTERIOR OF INNER NORTH FORT, AFTER THE ASSAULT

THE DESTRUCTION OF THE TAKU FORTS IN 1860

THE BRITISH FLEET LYING OFF KINTANG BEFORE THE OCCUPATION OF CHUSAN

instruct their men, and various drill-books were translated into Chinese for the benefit of their rank and file. This zeal for foreign inventions lasted as long as the Taiping rebellion endured ; but when, after the suppression of that movement by Gordon's "Ever Victorious Army," under Li Hung-chang, peace was again restored (1864), the drill-sergeants were politely dismissed, the books were put away on their shelves, and military matters were allowed to drift back to their former condition.

But there was again, before long, a call to arms. Though the storm had subsided, the waters were still disturbed, and over considerable parts of Honan and Shantung disorders prevailed. The disbanded Taipings, finding their occupation gone, spread themselves over these provinces, carrying fire and sword into the towns and villages. Naturally, in this crisis, the Emperor called on Li Hung-chang once more to take up his sword in defence of the throne. After a chequered campaign, in which victory did not always by any means rest with the Imperial forces, Li was able to report to his Imperial master

LANDING OF BRITISH TROOPS AT TALIEN-WAN ON THE 5th JULY, 1860

WEIGHING OUT THE MONEY FOR THE CHINESE WAR INDEMNITY

WAR INDEMNITY TRANSPORTED AND GUARDED INTO TIENTSIN

CHINA "PAYING THE PRICE" UNDER THE CONVENTION OF PEKING IN 1860

PRINCE KUNG
The negotiator of terms of peace with Lord Elgin, at the conclusion of the war which he had tried to avoid.

these wide regions the followers of the Prophet had thought that they had seen in the disturbed condition of China an opportunity to throw over the yoke of Confucianism and Buddhism which had so long oppressed them. For a considerable time success attended their arms, and with the allied help of Yakoob Khan, the Atalik Ghazi, they gained many important victories. But·the end came. General Tso Chung-tang was appointed commander-in-chief over a huge army, with orders to restore the rebel territories to the throne. With curious deliberation, Tso opened the campaign by turning his swords into ploughshares, and by sowing the crops which were to supply them with food for the following year. Whether or not another system would have been more expeditious, cannot be said ; but certain it is that it answered in this case. With steady perseverance Tso led his troops to victory, and in 1878 was able to report

that the Nienfei, as the rebels were called, were reduced to impotence.

There were yet, however, enemies to peace within the borders of the state. In Yunnan, the south-westerly province of the empire, there had long existed a Mohammedan population, who, for the most part, had maintained friendly relations with their fellow provincials. But this friendliness was only skin-deep, and a trifling dispute about a copper mine was the match which set the whole countryside ablaze. The strong city of Tali Fu fell into the hands of the Mohammedans, who re-established themselves there under the command of a chieftain named Tu. This man was possessed by an ambition to induce the English Government to take up his cause. With this object he sent an embassy to London to invite the co-operation of the British Cabinet. Needless to say, this was refused, and indirectly the mission proved disastrous to the rebels, for the possible interference of a foreign Power so alarmed the Chinese Government that they brought all their forces to bear against the rebels. With irresistible numbers they made themselves masters of the province, and ruthlessly massacred their crushed enemies.

Peace was not yet restored to the distracted empire. The rebellion in Yunnan had been but the reflex action of a movement which was agitating Western China and Central Asia. Through

PRINCE SANKOLINSEN
This Chinese general commanded the army that seized the British envoys, hoping thus to gain an advantage.

BARON GROS
The French representative who signed the convention with China after the march of French and British to Peking.

SIR HOPE GRANT
The commander of the British force which, acting with the French, captured the Taku forts before the march on Peking

to the throne that the Son of Heaven was once more in possession of his own.

Meanwhile, his foreign treaties were exercising a beneficent influence on the relations with China with the " outside " nations. The Chinese Government, guided by Prince Kung, learned to see that even the boasted civilisation of China was inferior to that existing in other lands, and they attempted to introduce reforms into the administration of the empire. They withdrew the management of foreign affairs from the Lifan Yamen, or Colonial Office, and established the Tsung-li-Yamen, which was to occupy the position of the Foreign Office. This was an acknowledgment of the increasing importance of foreign affairs, and though the new office served its purpose with indifferent results, it was a step in the right direction.

LORD LOCH
One of the British envoys, who, when private secretary to Lord Elgin, was taken prisoner by the Chinese army.

In military matters they showed a half hearted desire to improve their material and established arsenals at Foohow, Nanking, and Shanghai. With the continuation of peace, however, their zeal flagged and eventually dwindled away.

In another direction they attempted to impress their views of the political position on the foreign Governments and induced Mr. Burlingham, the United States Minister at Peking, to throw up his office and to undertake an advocatory mission to Washington and the capitals of Europe. His refrain was the desire of China for reform and the advisability of leaving her alone to work out her own salvation. This gospel did not get more than an acknowledgment from the Powers, and the mission was brought to an abrupt termination by the death of Mr. Burlingham at

807

AN INCIDENT IN THE FRENCH MARCH TO PEKING: THE ATTACK ON THE BRIDGE AT PA-LI-CHIAN, EIGHT MILES FROM THE CAPITAL

St. Petersburg. But even before this event occurred the value of the professions of the Peking authorities was seriously discounted: While Mr. Burlingham was proclaiming the tolerant principles of his clients, they were falsifying his words by deeds of ill-faith and cruelty. The missionary question had long been a bone of contention between China and the treaty Powers, and though by the terms of the treaties a free hand within limits was to be given to the missionaries, the native authorities never ceased to resent their presence. At Yangchou, on the Yangtse, a missionary station had been established on the faith of the promises given by the Chinese, and without the slightest provo-

capital city produced a more reasona frame of mind, and eventually the demar of the British Consul were complied wi
Shortly after this event Tseng's hostil to foreigners was again manifested connection with another and fiercer n sionary outbreak. This time the sce of the tragedy was Tientsin, in t metropolitan province of which Tse had, in the interval, been appoint viceroy. For some time (1870) sinis rumours had been current about t orphanages of the Sisters of Mercy. was said that the infantile inmates w murdered for the purpose of concocti medicine from their eyes, and a fa epidemic which broke out at that ju

A DEFENCE UPON THE WALLS OF PEKING
The guns as trained upon the advancing allies in 1860—from a photograph taken immediately after the entry

cation an attack instigated by the authorities was made on the unsuspecting missionaries, who were driven from the city with violence and whose dwellings were burnt to the ground. At this time Tseng Kwofan, the father of the Marquis Tseng, who lately represented China at the Court of St. James's, was viceroy of the province in which this outrage occurred. He had acquired favour by the suppression of the Taiping rebellion, and had preserved his anti-foreign tendencies in spite of the gratitude due for the help rendered by Gordon in that great crisis. At first he was disinclined to offer any reparation for the brutal onslaught, but the appearance of a British fleet opposite the walls of his

ture gave a certain acceptance to t report. To this ground for a riot w added the indiscretion of the Fren Consul, who used his revolver among t crowd in the street. This infuriated t mob, who broke into the orphanag murdered the sisters, and set fire to t buildings. In all, twenty foreigners we massacred, besides a number of nati Christians. Tseng was ordered to inqui into the circumstances of the riot, b as he showed plainly that his sympathi were on the side of the murderers, he w relieved of his post and Li Hung-chang w appointed in his place. The arrival of th wise administrator soon put anoth complexion on the affair, and due repar tion was made for the outrage, includir

GENERAL TSO CHUNG-TANG

This general quelled the Mohammedan rising in 1878, preceding his campaign by sowing crops to supply his troops.

...he execution of eighteen of the male-...ctors, and the despatch of a mission of ...pology to France.

This outbreak, together with several ...hich had lately disturbed the foreign ...lations of the country, induced Prince ...ung and his colleagues to raise the ...eneral question of the status of mission-...ries. It was plain that their presence ...as a cause of offence, and the Govern-...nent were quite entitled to seek for a ...emedy for the evil; but instead of ...gislating in a liberal and conciliatory ...pirit they attempted to introduce ...easures which practically would have ...et the question at rest by annihilating ...:. Their proposals were embodied in ... circular letter addressed to the foreign ...epresentatives, who, one and all, refused ...o entertain the proposals for an instant.

Another event of a politico-domestic ...haracter helped for the time being to ...vershadow all subjects of controversy. ...he whirligig of time had brought it ...bout that the Emperor had come of age ...n an imperial sense (1872). That is to ...ay that he had reached the age of sixteen, ...when it became him to assume Empire ...nd to take to himself a bride. By the

laws of the land it was necessary that the lady should be a Manchu and a daughter of a member of one of the eight military banners. As in China the bridegroom has no personal choice in the selection of his bride, it was necessary that the Dowager Empress should choose a young lady who would fulfil the requirements of the case and satisfy the taste of the Emperor. After much searchings of heart, her choice fell on Ahluta, who was the daughter of a distinguished scholar, and is said to have combined beauty with intellect. With all due ceremony the Astronomical Board fixed on the moment which the stars in their courses marked out as being the most propitious for the ceremony; and in obedience to this reckoning the midnight of October 16th, 1872, was chosen. At that instant Ahluta crossed the threshold of the Imperial Palace, and entered on her new duties.

This event did not occupy the Emperor's whole attention, and he found time to propose an improvement in the relations of the foreign representatives with his Court. Up to this time the resident representatives had never enjoyed the privilege invariably accorded by civilised states of being received in audience by

LI HUNG-CHANG

The powerful Chinese Envoy, and friend of Russia, who took such a prominent part in the foreign affairs of his country.

COMMANDING THE STORMING OF SOOCHOW IN NOVEMBER, 1863
Gordon determined on a vigorous assault on the north-east angle of the Soochow wall.

GORDON'S "MAGIC WAND OF VICTORY"
General Gordon carried only one weapon—a cane, which came to be known by this name. He frequently le
his less daring officers by the arm into the thick of the fight, exhorting them by courage and exampl

GENERAL GORDON AND THE EVER VICTORIOUS ARMY

Y-YUNG, MARQUIS TSENG
Formerly representative of China accredited to London and
the son of Tseng Kwofan, a famous anti-foreign viceroy.

he sovereign; and the excuse given was
that the Emperor, being a minor, was
not qualified to receive them. But now
that he had declared himself to be of age
the excuse was no longer valid, and no
surprise was felt, therefore, when a notice
reached the Legations that, the foreign
representatives "having implored" the
Emperor to grant them an audience, he
was graciously pleased to accede to their
request. A day was ultimately fixed for
the ceremony, which took place on
June 29th, 1873, in the Pavilion of
Purple Light. The selection of this
pavilion was a serious blot on the ceremonial since it was the hall in which the
representatives of the Mongol tribes are
commonly granted audiences. But in
spite of this drawback it was a step in
advance and has since been improved upon.

Unfortunately Tungchih's lease of power
was of short duration. Towards the end of
1874 it was rumoured that he was suffering
from an attack of smallpox. At first the
reports were favourable, and the doctors
in attendance were promoted as a reward
for their skill. Later accounts, however,
were less propitious, and on January 15th,
1875, it was announced that the Emperor
had "become a guest on high."

The succession to an Oriental throne
is always a matter of uncertainty, and in
the case of Tungchih's successor there
were manifold difficulties. An heir to the
throne should be the next in direct line,
and, as Tungchih had been as yet child-

less, the eldest son of the eldest uncle
should have been the future sovereign.
But the Dowager Empresses, having once
tasted the sweets of power, wished to
recover the regency. The infant son,
therefore, of a young uncle was selected
by these astute ladies, and eventually, at
their instigation, Prince Tsai Tien, son of
Prince Chun, was proclaimed Emperor.

In the midst of these intrigues the
Empress Ahluta was in danger of being
overlooked, and she was the one of all
others who should have been considered.
It was well-known that she was with
child, and in case the child should prove
to be a son, he would naturally succeed
to the throne, under the guidance of his
mother as regent. This was a contingency
which was utterly repugnant to the
Dowager Empresses, and it was a matter
of no surprise when an announcement was
made that Ahluta's grief at the death of
the Emperor, her husband, was so great
as to have produced a serious illness, an
ominous proclamation which prepared the
people's mind for the news of her death.
This event cleared the ground for the
Dowagers, who at once resumed power and
held it until the Emperor, coming of age,
claimed it from their hands and assumed
control. By their own seeking, therefore, they had succeeded to no bed of roses.

CHUNG HOU
The first real Chinese Ambassador to Europe, who was
resident Minister at Paris during the years 1871 and 1872.

MARKET SCENE IN TARTAR CITY

ENTRANCE TO HALL OF CLASSICS

GRAND CANAL AT CHI HWA GATE

THE DRUM TOWER

A GATE IN THE TARTAR WALL

CHIEN HEN, THE PRINCIPAL GATE

PRESENT DAY SCENES IN PEKING
H. C. White Co., London.

Already for some time the attitude of the English Government had been directed to the advisability of finding, if possible, a practicable trade route between Burma and the Chinese province of Yunnan. Independent travellers, who had risked their lives in traversing the mountain ranges which separate the two points of distance, drew gloomy pictures of the difficulties of the route. But the Government of India was hopeful of finding an easier road, and despatched a mission to make the attempt. Colonel Browne was chosen chief of the expedition, and every possible preparation was made for its successful passage through Burmese and Chinese territories. Passports were provided by the Peking authorities, and, lest there should be any difficulty in communicating with the Chinese authorities and people, Mr. Margary, of the Chinese Consular Service, was sent to meet Colonel Browne's party at Bhamo, in Burma. On his way thither he met with every courtesy from both mandarins and the people. After a short rest at Bhamo, the expedition started eastward. It had not gone far when its members were met by rumours of opposition and of threatened violence.

This attitude was so foreign to that which had been shown to Margary on his way over the same ground, that Mr. Margary refused to believe the reports, and offered to go ahead of the expedition to test their reliability. As far as the town of Manwyne, just within the Chinese frontier, he enjoyed perfect safety. On the day after his arrival there, however, he was brutally murdered, under what circumstances will never be known with certainty. But that it was a premeditated outrage is proved by the fact that at the

One of the famous " Tiger Guard "

Soldier of the Archery Corps   Officer of the Tartar Corps

TYPES OF CHINESE SOLDIERS OF THE PAST

Edwards

A GROUP OF CHINESE SOLDIERS WITH THEIR TIME-HONOURED WEAPONS
Part of the Chinese Army carries such weapons now.

Keystone Stereograph

A CHINESE SQUADRON WITH MODERN ARMS AND DRILLED BY EUROPEAN OFFICERS

THE MAKING OF THE MODERN CHINESE ARMY.

same time a Chinese force attacked Colonel Browne's party. So determined was the opposition that Colonel Browne, in face of the overwhelming forces in front of him, thought it prudent to retreat into Burmese territory. This he did, and so brought to an end this ill-omened attempt to connect the two empires. This incident was

Drought and Famine scarcely closed when a great natural misfortune overtook the empire. From September, 1875, to July, 1876, not a drop of rain fell in the provinces of Shantung and Shansi. The geological formation of these and the neighbouring districts render them singularly dependent on the fall of temperate rain. The wretched people, deprived of their fertilising supply and with quite insufficient means of importing foods, perished in their thousands. Subscription lists were opened at the treaty ports, and a sum of 36,000 taels was sent to the relief of the sufferers. A more than usually severe winter followed on this most unpropitious season, and it was reckoned that nine million persons perished from the effects of the two disasters. One result of this combination of evils was that the difficulty of carrying food to the suffering people brought home to the intelligent amongst the officials the advantage of introducing railways into the country. But the time had not arrived when such an innovation was practicable, and a short line made between Shanghai and Wusung by some enthusiasts among the foreign community of Shanghai was incontinently put an end to, and this in the face of much popular pleasure among the natives at the speed and convenience of the " fire-wheeled chariots."

By the irony of Fate, the man who had been mainly in-

THE DOWAGER EMPRESS OF CHINA
The Empress Dowager—Tzu Hsi—is the maternal aunt of the present Emperor, and is a remarkable woman. She holds the power by sheer force of personality.

strumental in opposing this railway was the first Chinese official who finally succeeded in constructing a permanent line in the country. It was at Li Hung-chang's instigation that the Wusung line was destroyed, and it was he who built the line from Tientsin to the Kaiping coal-mines, which still carries the coal, in which Li was interested, to Tientsin and Taku. Since then lines have increased and multiplied ; Peking is now in railway communication with Taku on the seacoast and Hankow in the central provinces, while throughout the empire there is everywhere a network of lines.

While these events were agitating the

War between China and France home provinces of the empire, attention was drawn to complications which had arisen in regions beyond the southern frontier of the empire. For many years France had been seeking her own in Tonquin, and had gone the length of concluding treaties with the King of Annam without having any regard for the rights of the King's suzerain, the Emperor of China. On hearing of these alliances, the Peking Government protested, and warned the French that their persistence in treating with the King of Annam would be regarded as a *casus belli*. Such threats were, however, unavailing in face of the fact that the French were determined to enlarge their borders in South-eastern Asia.

With this object in view, a survey was undertaken of the Mekong ; and Dupuis was sent to inspect the waters of the Red River and the Yang-tse Kiang. As has so often happened in Eastern complications, the two combatants drifted into an irregular war. In the first engagement Fortune declared herself on the side of

THE YOUNG EMPEROR TUNGCHIH GRANTING AN AUDIENCE

On June 29, 1873, the representatives of foreign Powers in Peking were received in audience by the Emperor in the Pavilion of Purple Light in the Palace of Peking. The next audience was granted in 1889 by the present Emperor.

China, but in most of the subsequent battles she transferred her favour to the French, and, after much exercise of diplomatic wiles and serious engagements, peace was eventually proclaimed (April, 1885). The terms of the treaty sufficiently indicated the results of the campaign. China handed over the suzerainty of Annam to France and ceded Tonquin to that Power.

No sooner was peace restored in Tonquin than occasions of quarrel arose on the north-east frontiers.

Korea has repeatedly been the cockpit of the Far East. The coast lines of **Troubles Begin in Korea** Japan and Korea are so near that it has ever been obvious to the Japanese that their safety as an island kingdom depends on the maintenance of the independence of Korea, and thus an intense jealousy has always been felt at Tōkio at the first sign of any interference in Korean affairs by China or any other Power. It happened that Korea had had the misfortune to be ruled by an ignorant and bigoted regent during the long minority of the King. The father of the sovereign, known as Taiwen Kung, was the holder of this office, and during the whole of his rule he had shown a strong anti-foreign bias; so much so that the Chinese, seeing that peace could be secured only by his removal, kidnapped him and carried him off to Paoting-fu. Unfortu- **Japanese Invade Korea** nately, they released him before he was penitent, and his return to Korea was signalised by disturbances and a fierce attack on the Japanese Legation. Fortunately, the diplomatists escaped to an English ship of war, which carried them and the news of the outrage to Tōkio. The Japanese at once despatched an army to enforce terms of reparation. As a protest against this invasion the Chinese also sent a force into Korea, and thus the two alien armies were brought face to face. The position was eminently one for negotiation, and Li Hung-chang and Count Ito drew up a treaty, by the terms of which the two Powers agreed to withdraw their forces from Korea, and for the future not to send troops into the

THE CHINO-JAPANESE WAR: CHINESE TROOPS TRYING TO SAVE THEIR ARTILLERY

disputed kingdom without giving warning of their intention.

The Franco-Chinese war and the general course of events had naturally forced on the Chinese the consciousness of their shortcomings in the face of other nations. The legations abroad had urged on the Government the necessity of having a strong army and navy as well as railways and telegraphs. In these several directions reforms were introduced. The services of foreigners were engaged to drill the armies and to command the fleets, telegraphs were constructed, and, under the influence of Li Hung-chang, a short railway from Tientsin to the Kaiping coal-mines was opened. But the trend of events was not always in the direction of progress. In the provinces of Kwang-si and Szechuen anti-foreign riots broke out, and missionaries and their churches were attacked and outraged

In the year 1889 the Emperor reached man's estate —that is to say, he had arrived at the age of sixteen—and by the law which changes not it was thereupon decreed that he should take to himself an Empress. After much cogitation a niece of the Dowager Empress, Yeh-ho-na-la by name, was chosen as his bride, and on February 26th, the august rite was performed with all due state and ceremony. In the following month the Dowager Empress, following the inevitable precedent, handed over the seals of office and retired to the Iho Park, near Peking. One of the first acts of the now emancipated Emperor was to receive the foreign Ministers in audience. In some ways this ceremony was an advance on that granted by Tungchih, but in other respects the arrangements were the same.

EMPEROR OF CHINA, TSAI-TIEN HWANG HSU
The present sovereign, Tsai-Tien, who reigns under the name of Kwang Hsu, is ninth Emperor of the Manchu dynasty. He was born in 1871, and is nephew to the Empress Regent, mother of the last Emperor, Tungchih. He succeeded in 1875.

The Ministers, instead of being received en bloc, as in 1873, were each granted a separate audience ; but the full effect of the innovation was vitiated by the place of audience again being the Tsze-kwang Pavilion, where the Emperor had been accustomed to entertain the representatives of vassal states. The resentment shown at this treatment had its effect ; and when, some time later, the newly arrived Austrian Minister asked for an audience he was received in the Cheng-kwang Hall within the Palace.

In 1894 a further recognition of the rights of the foreign representatives was evidenced by the fact that the foreign Ministers were received in audience in the Wen-hwa Hall of the Palace. This was but an indication of the general tendency of affairs. A progressive spirit seemed to have taken hold of the country. The introduction of railroads was encouraged and newspapers were introduced into a land where, until then, the "Peking Gazette" had been the solitary representative of the native Press.

Nor were the Army and Navy altogether neglected. The adoption of foreign and new weapons was sanctioned and a naval college was established at Tientsin. But while the Government was showing marked signs of a progressive spirit, an opposite disposition was evinced in parts of the empire. Anti-foreign riots broke out in various provinces, and in 1890 alarming outbreaks occurred on the Yang-tse Kiang, in the course of which two Englishmen were brutally murdered at Wuhsueh. It was proved that the prime instigator of the riots was an official named Chou Han, but though his complicity was plainly demonstrated he suffered no further

819

inconvenience than the nominal penalty of living under police surveillance. A more gratifying event which occurred about the same time was the opening to foreign trade of the port of Chung-king, on the Upper Yangtse. But neither inside nor outside the empire did matters run smoothly, and a rebellion in Korea induced a war between China **War Between** and Japan which has had far- **China and** reaching consequences. Being **Japan** unable to cope with the rebellion, the King of Korea begged for help from China, which was readily accorded, and the despatch of troops from Peking led to the arrival of a Japanese army in the neighbourhood of Seoul.

Thus, the two armies were once again face to face. The position was dangerous, and friction was created by a desire on the part of Japan to introduce reforms into the administration. As China refused to have lot or part in these proposals the Japanese undertook to enforce them themselves and presented an ultimatum to the King on the subject. The Koreans being still recalcitrant, the Japanese surrounded the palace and took possession of the King's person.

The position now became acute, and the two foreign Powers prepared for war, which broke out prematurely on July 25th. On that day two Japanese men-of-war sighted a Chinese fleet en route for the Korean coast. After a short engagement, the Chinese were defeated and put to flight, with the loss of four ships. Following up their victory, the Japanese landed on the Korean coast, and in quick succession made themselves masters of the towns of Asan and Ping-yang. The loss of these strongholds led to the withdrawal of the Chinese troops northwards from Korea. Without loss of time the Japanese followed the flying enemy, crossed the Yalu river, and virtually cleared the country of the Chinese forces. Having thus set themselves free for other enterprises they turned their attention to Port Arthur, which, after a short siege, fell into their hands (November 21st, 1894). Wei-hai-wei was the only remaining strong place left to the Chinese, and it quickly fell before Japanese prowess.

KANG YU-WEI
A reformer who in 1899 persuaded the Emperor to issue decrees that roused national opposition.

It was now obvious, even to the Chinese Government, that in their interests the time had arrived for the conclusion of peace. After several abortive efforts, Li Hung-chang was empowered to proceed to Shimonoseki, in Japan, to arrange terms. As both parties were desirous of peace, matters went smoothly, and might have gone without a hitch had it not been that a misguided native fired a revolver at Li as he was passing to a meeting of the Commissioners. Happily, the wound inflicted was not serious, and after a few days Li was able to take part in the conclusion of a treaty, which was signed, sealed, and delivered on April 17th, 1895. By the terms of this document China ceded to Japan the Liaotung peninsula, including Port Arthur, the island of Formosa, and the Pescadores group of islands. She also agreed to pay Japan an indemnity of 200,000,000 taels, and to open certain cities to Japanese trade. But, by a secret understanding, it had been agreed between the Peking representatives of Russia, France and Germany that they would use their good offices to restore the Liaotung peninsula to China, and they succeeded in inducing Japan to yield the peninsula in exchange for a further indemnity of 30,000,000 taels.

The peace had not long been concluded when a cause of offence broke out between China and Germany. On November 1st, 1897, two German missionaries were murdered in the province of Shantung. On the news of the outrage reaching the ears of the German Admiral he steamed into the port of Kiaochow in the incriminated province and occupied the island of Tsing-tao within its waters. The usual **German** explanation was demanded at **Concessions** Peking, and a half of the **in China** island of Tsing-tao, with a considerable section of the surrounding country, was granted on a long lease to Germany. The success of this negotiation encouraged Russia to propose that similar rights over Port Arthur should be granted to her. This was conceded by the Chinese Government, who also voluntarily offered to give the British Government a lease of Wei-hai-wei (July 1, 1898).

AN INCIDENT IN THE BOXER RISING: REBEL LEADER BEING EXAMINED BY OFFICERS OF THE ALLIED FORCES

These cessions of territory, coupled with the disastrous war with Japan, had induced a section of the more enlightened of the mandarins, headed by the Emperor himself, to desire such reforms in the administration of the Government as would place China on an equality with the foreign powers. As was to be expected, the reformers fell into many and great mistakes, and ranged against themselves a powerful body of public opinion. At the instigation of secret advisers, notable among whom was Kang Yu-wei, an enlightened man but an enthusiast, the Emperor issued a series of edicts which revolutionised and outraged many of the most cherished convictions of the people.

At last matters came to such a pitch that the Dowager Empress was besought to intervene to preserve the country from anarchy. Nothing loth, that redoubtable lady, who had been watching every move on the board, virtually deposed the Emperor and seized the reins of power. In quick succession edicts appeared abro-

DEFENCE OF BRITISH LEGATION AT PEKING
he scene is a balcony in the British Minister's house over-
oking the Imperial Canal and Prince Su's palace. The
ritish Marines' Nordenfeldt is in action against the Boxers.

gating the reforms ordered by the Emperor, and death warrants were issued against the native advisers who had been the instigators of the Emperor's policy. With this reversal of the order of things a strong anti-foreign spirit spread over the northern part of the empire, beginning in the province of Kiangsu and rapidly stretching over the adjacent provinces of Anhui, Shantung and Chihli. In support of the movement, there appeared an organised force known to foreigners as the Boxers, and in the country as Ihochüan, or "Patriotic Harmonious Fists." These men devoted their attention, in the first instance, to the missionaries and their converts ; but with the official support which they speedily acquired, flew at higher game, and assumed the rôle of a patriot army whose motto was "China for the Chinese." The object of this band so well harmonised with the prevailing sentiments at Peking that it received the ungrudging support of the Dowager Empress, who, in her ignorance, believed its votaries to be impervious to bullets.

Beginning of Boxer Rebellion

In April, 1900, the position of Peking had under these rapidly developed circumstances become so dangerous to foreigners that it was deemed advisable to despatch a relieving force from Tientsin, and on June 10th, Admiral Seymour, at the head of a small detachment of 1,800 marines and bluejackets, marched out towards the capital. But he had miscalculated the forces with which he had to contend, and before reaching Peking he was obliged to retreat before the Imperial troops and Boxers who stood in his way. Large reinforcements were subsequently sent from Taku, and succeeded in capturing the city of Tientsin and relieving the Legations, which had been besieged by overwhelming forces from the middle of June to August 14th.

On the arrival of the relieving force at Peking, the Dowager Empress, with the Emperor, took to flight westward, and scarcely drew rein until they reached Hsianfu, the capital of the province of Shensi. There they stayed while negotiations for peace were being conducted by Prince Ching and Li Hung-chang. As a preliminary it was determined that punishments

Elliott & Fry

SIR CLAUDE MACDONALD
Minister who commanded legation quarter during siege.

Elliott & Fry

ADMIRAL SIR EDWARD SEYMOUR
Who defeated the Boxers at Lang-Fang, June 11, 190

should be inflicted on certain officials who had taken prominent parts in the attacks on and the murder of Europeans. For such crimes Princes Tuan and Fukuo were sentenced to death, which sentence, on account of their Imperial rank, was commuted to penal servitude for life. Prince Chuang and the Presidents of the Board of Censors and Board of Punishments were condemned to commit suicide, while three other high officials were beheaded.

Justice having thus been done, the Peace Commissioners proceeded to draw up a protocol, which was signed on September 7th, 1901. The indemnity to be paid was fixed at 450,000,000 taels, on which 4 per cent. was to be charged until the capital was paid off at the end of 39 years.

The conclusion of peace brought the Emperor and Dowager Empress back to Peking, and with a return to a settled form of government arose a further desire for the material advantages of civilisation. This tendency was still further emphasised by the result of the Russo-Japanese war. The question naturally suggested itself to the Chinese : " If the Japanese were able to conquer Russia, why should we not be able to do the same ? " This mental attitude led to an inquiry as to the means by which Japan had acquired her present position, and troops of students betook themselves to the Land of the Rising Sun, while commissioners were sent to America and Europe to inquire into the systems of government in force there.

In order to enable the Chinese Govern-

ment to introduce these and other reforms Sir Robert Hart brought forward a proposal (1904) for the better collection and amendment of the Land Tax, by the adoption of which he estimated that a revenue of 400,000,000 taels would be raised This scheme would provide the means fo an improved army and navy, and fo colleges and schools throughout the empire; but the plan, though plausible, wa dismissed as impracticable in the presen condition of the country. The Govern ment took pains at the moment to expres their appreciation of Sir Robert Hart' proposals, and to assure the Empire o their desire to follow his advice. But two years later (May, 1906) they showed the true tendency of their policy by appoint ing the Ministers Tieh-liang and Tang shao-yi " to take over charge of the entire customs service, with plenary powers to reform or modify ad libitum," thus super seding Sir Robert Hart. This met with strong and united opposition from the foreign legations, and the Governmen attempted to explain away the obvious meaning of their own words.

With that vacillation which has always marked the Imperial conduct of affairs an edict was issued a few months later (September 20th, 1906) in which a genuine and beneficent reform was foreshadowed By its terms opium smoking was abolished throughout the eighteen provinces. This measure is discussed later ; and whether it succeeds or fails, it stands as an attempt to improve the condition of the people.

ROBERT K. DOUGLAS

823

1807: DR. MORRISON, THE PIONEER BRITISH MISSIONARY, TRANSLATING THE GOSPEL

1907: ARCHDEACON WOLFE AND A GROUP OF CHINESE CLERGYMEN IN FU-KIEN

A CENTURY OF PROTESTANT MISSIONS IN CHINA

CHRISTIANITY IN CHINA

CHRISTIANITY has never taken hold of the Chinese ; it has always borne an alien character. An inscription on the monument discovered in 1625 at Singan Fu, the authenticity of which was erroneously doubted in the seventeenth century, states that the first Christian missionary arrived in China in 635. Upon the monument he is known as " Olopen," which is perhaps merely a corruption of the Chinese expression for monk, and the religion, of which a somewhat vague summary is given, is called the noble law of Ta-tsin (Syria). Olopen was of the Nestorian branch of the Christian Church, a sect condemned as heretical by the orthodox body, but predominant in Asia. It is probable that the Nestorians came to China as early as 505 A.D., and that the silkworms' eggs brought by them to Constantinople in 551 A.D., if not of Khotan origin, came from China.

The books brought by Olopen were translated with the Emperor's leave, and official sanction was given to the dissemination of his teaching. The Tang Emperor Tai Tsung is said in 638 to have given his express permission to the preaching of the new doctrine, and to have allowed the building of a church on condition that his picture was placed therein. Kao Tsung (650–683) also favoured the doctrine. At a later period, however, difficulties rose; but Hsuan Tsung (712–756) again showed favour to the doctrine, and a new missionary, Kiho, is said to have entered the country. Finally the monument records its own erection in 781, under Te Tsung (780–805). The inscription is in the Chinese language, and partly in poetical form ; it contains quotations in the Syrian language, from which it appears that a large number of Nestorian priests (one reference contains sixty-seven names) were then working in China. They are said to have been organised under several episcopal vicars, the first of whom is entitled the Pope of Zinistan, or China.

Early Records of Chinese Christianity

Nestorian Strength and Influence

According to later accounts, close relations existed between the Nestorians and the Mother Church in Syria until broken off by the advance of Mohammedanism. In 845 the Christian priests, who are said to have numbered three thousand, came under the edict of Wu-tsung, which ordered them, like those of Buddha, to return to their temporal occupations. Nevertheless the Nestorians maintained their footing in China and Central Asia. They possessed a large number of parishes and churches throughout the empire, and were not without influence at the court of the Mongol princes and emperor, making many converts among the women and among some of the higher officials. They fell with the Mongol dynasty, without leaving any living trace of their existence. It was, perhaps, partly due to the belief in the existence, somewhere in the far East, of a Nestorian country under the rule of Prester John that Innocent IV., in 1245, sent envoys to the Mongol Khan in the hope of " averting the onslaughts on Christendom through fear of divine wrath."

ROMAN CATHOLICISM

At the time of the Mongol dynasty the first Roman Catholic priests arrived in China, appearing in the character of ambassadors with a diplomatic message from the Pope and temporal princes. The success of the Mongols in Western Asia and Eastern Europe, together with the growing power of Mohammedanism in Syria and Egypt, had seriously occupied the attention of the Popes who preached and the princes who took part in, the several crusades, and it was thought that an alliance might be made with the Mongols against the Mohammedans, the common enemy of both parties.

The attempts to bring about a political and military alliance of this nature led to no result, but the reports of the Papal messengers, and the emissaries of the other princes who went to Mongolia

nd China by land, offer many points of
high interest. Before the meeting of the
Council of Lyons (1245), Pope Innocent
V. sent to the East an embassy of Dominicans under Nicolas Anselm (Anselm of
Lombardy). In August, 1247, they met
he army of the general Bachu-noyan in
Khwaresm, and he sent them back with
two Tartar Mongolian envoys
with a message to the Pope
(1248). The message was conceived in a discourteous style,
and the Pope was ordered to give in his
submission ; but the general treated the
ambassadors with the greatest kindness,
in the hope of continuing further relations.

Simultaneously with the first mission,
Innocent also despatched two Franciscans,
Lorenzo of Portugal, who was appointed
Papal Legate in the East, and John of
Pian de Carpine, who started on the journey
from Breslau, in company with Benedict of Poland. These latter were the first
to reach Batu, who sent them on to the
encampment of Ogotai, where they arrived
at the moment when Kuyuk ascended
the throne in July, 1246. There they found
Russian and Hungarian priests, and a
goldsmith named Kosmos. Kuyuk was
himself the son of a Nestorian woman, and
among the women of his harem and his
high officials were many Christians, who
were allowed to practise their religion.

In November the ambassadors were dismissed with a written answer from the
Great Khan. They were diplomatic
enough to decline the company of Tartar
ambassadors, as they did not desire the
latter to be witnesses of the dissensions
existing among the Christian princes, and
so to acquire courage for further invasions.
The homeward journey through Russia,
Poland, Bohemia, and Austria proved
difficult, and they did not reach the Pope
until the end of the year 1247.

Meanwhile King Louis IX. of France
received in 1247 a demand from Batu to
tender his submission, to which
no reply was sent. In 1248, when
Louis was on his first crusade,
ambassadors from Ilchikadai,
the successor of the deceased Bachu, came
to the king in Cyprus, offering him an alliance against the Mohammedans, and in-
forming him that Ilchikadai and the Great
Khan had themselves become Christians.
Upon this information, Louis sent out an
embassy from Nicosia in 1249, consisting
of Dominicans, under Andrew of Longu-

*Papal
Emissaries
to China*

*Mission to
China during
the Crusades*

meau, to the Great Khan, to present him
with several relics and exhort him to continue in the Christian religion. The embassy
went by way of Persia, in order to
speak with Ilchi, and on arrival at the
camp of the Great Khan found Kuyuk
dead (1248). The queen regent, Ogul
Gaimish (1248–1251), accepted the gifts
as a token of tribute, and sent back the
ambassadors with presents. They were
unable to gain any more accurate information on the subject of the alleged conversion,
and returned to the king at Acre in 1251.

In spite of his dissatisfaction at the
false construction laid upon the object
of this embassy, Louis sent out, in May,
1253, new ambassadors, the Franciscan,
William of Rubruquis, and Bartholomew
of Cremona, using the supposed conversion as an excuse for their despatch.
They travelled by way of Constantinople
through the steppes between the Dnieper
and Don, and reached the encampment
of Khagatai in July, whence they were
sent on to Sartach Khan, the son of Batu,
three days' march beyond the Volga.
He, however, declined to give them leave
on his own responsibility to
remain and preach in the
country, and sent them to
Mangu. At his court, in
December, 1253, they found many Nestorian priests, who had been given
precedence over the Mohammedan imam
and the bonzes.

Mangu was present at their divine services with his family, but probably this
was a matter of indifference to him. He
himself, however, was very superstitious,
and never entered into any undertaking
without previous divination by means of
the shoulder-bones. They accompanied
Mangu to Karakorum, where they found
Guillaume Bouchier, a Parisian goldsmith.
There, at the orders of Mangu, they had
a discussion with the priests of other
religions. Mangu finally dismissed Rubruquis (Bartholomew remained behind,
as he declined to journey homeward
through the desert), with a written answer
to King Louis, in which he assumed the
titles of " Son of the heaven " and " Lord
of lords," contradicted the information
that had been given by the ambassadors
of Ilchikadai and of Ogul Gaimish, and
directed the king to act upon the orders
of Genghis Khan. After a march of two
months Rubruquis met with Sartach,
whose behaviour made Rubruquis doubt

*Second
Mission of
Louis IX.*

the truth of his reported adherence to Christianity. In September, 1254, Rubruquis reached the encampment of Batu, whom he accompanied for a month ; ultimately he returned through the Caucasus, Armenia, and Syria, and arrived at Tripoli in August, 1255, whence he sent his report to King Louis at Acre.

The Popes also were by no means idle, though their objects were now rather religious than political. In 1278 Nicholas III. sent five monks to the Great Khan, but nothing is known of the results of this embassy. The Franciscan monk, John of Montecorvino, who had started in 1289, arrived at the coast of South China in 1292 and made his way to Peking, whence he sent favourable reports in 1305 and 1306 ; in 1307 he was appointed Archbishop of Peking. In this year and in 1312 a number of suffragan bishops and other priests were sent out to him, though it seems that some failed to reach their destination. In Peking, Zaitun, and Yangchou there existed episcopal towns, churches, and, parishes, and when John of Montecorvino died, in 1328, the prospects of the Minorite mission appeared highly favourable, although Andrew of Perugia, Bishop of Zaitun, published a complaint in 1326 that no converts were made of the Mohammedans and Jews, and that many of the baptised heathen strayed from the Christian faith. On the other hand, as he himself observed, the

FIRST JESUIT MISSIONARY TO CHINA

Matteo Ricci, who arrived at Peking in 1601 and founded the Jesuit Mission.

country enjoyed full religious toleration, and no opposition was offered to the preaching of the missionaries.

Odoric of Pordenone, who arrived at the coast of China between 1320 and 1330, remained for three years in the country and returned by way of Tibet, when he drew up an exhaustive report of ♦the religious conditions prevailing in the Far East. The last communications upon the state of the country which were received from China came from John Marignolli, who resided in Peking as the Papal Legate from 1342 to 1346. Communications were

then cut off. In 1370 Urban V. attempted to improve the situation by sending out a Papal legate, an archbishop, and some eighty clergy to Peking ; but no new was ever received of any of them. The Catholic mission perished amid the disturbances which broke out upon the downfall of the Mongolian dynasty, a the Nestorians had perished before them The hostility of the national Ming dynast in China to all foreigners, the spread of Mohammedan influence in Central Asia and the conversion of rulers and people to this faith are hardly of themselves sufficient explanation for the calamities which befell the Christians popular hatred of the foreign doctrine and the foreign teachers must have materially contributed to the extermination.

THE JESUIT MISSION

The second period of Roman Catholic activit dates from the voyage t China of Francis Xavie on the conclusion of hi work in Japan. He died December 2, 1552, a Sancian, an island thirty miles from Macao, and a Portuguese Dominican Gaspard à Cruce, was th first to re-enter China After some success in preaching, he was expelled from the country, and Martin de Reda, a Spanish Augustan, who followed him in 1575, was, after three years' residence, also expelled. In 1579 the Provincial of India, acting on advice earlier given by Francis Xavier, sent two Jesuits to China, Michele Ruggiero and Matteo Ricci. They succeeded in reaching Canton from Macao in 1581, and after infinite difficulty erected mission stations in Kwangtung, Kwangsi, and afterward also in Nanking. In 1601 Ricci arrived at Peking, where he won general respect. His view was that in the work of conversion the opinions of the Chinese should be spared as much as possible. But his successor, Nichola Longobardi, whom he had himself appointed before his death in 1610, did not share these views, and laid the foundation

827

of that opposition which was to prove terribly destructive to the Catholic missions a century later.

The rapid progress of the missionaries soon excited the jealousy and hatred of the official and learned classes, and in 1616 an order was issued from Peking to imprison all missionaries. This edict was, however, executed only in that town and in Nanking. When the invasions of the Manchus began in 1618, the mis-

MISSIONARY AS CHIEF OF CHINESE ASTRONOMERS
Father Adam Schaal, of Cologne, who was so respected by the Emperor Shun Chih that in 1645 he was appointed President of the Board of Astronomy. He is here seen in his official dress of office.

sionaries were recalled to support the Government with advice and practical help, and especially to aid them by casting cannon. This was the most prosperous period of the missionaries. In 1627 they counted 13,000 converts in the seven provinces of the empire, and more than 40,000 ten years later.

The position of the missionaries was in no way affected by the downfall of the Ming dynasty. Shun Chih, the first

emperor of the Manchu dynasty, appointed the head of the mission for the time being, Adam Schaal of Cologne, to be President of the Board of Astronomy in 1645, and remained well disposed toward him until his death (1661). However, during the minority of his successor, Kang Hsi, the regents instituted measures of severe repression against missionaries. It was not until the Emperor assumed the reins of government in 1671 that the decree of banishment which had been issued against the missionaries was repealed. The revolt of Wu Sankuei in Yunnan (1673) enabled Ferdinand Verbiest, the successor of Schaal, to make himself useful by casting cannon. These and other services so increased the influence of the missionaries at the Court, that in 1691, after the provincial authorities of Che-kiang began to persecute the foreign priests and the native Christians, the Emperor issued a decree in the following year securing toleration for the Christian faith.

The downfall of the mission was brought about by French intrigue, and by the disputes of the different Christian orders and missionaries. The Pope's patronage in India, to which China was treated as belonging, had been transferred to the crown of Portugal. This monopoly, however, appeared to conflict with the growing interests of France in Further India and East Asia. The Père Alexandre de Rhodes of Avignon and the Duchesse d'Aiguillon, supported by the French Government, succeeded in obtaining a decree from Pope Alexander VII. appointing three French bishops to Siam, Tongking, and China. No foreign ship was found to take them to their destination, and this difficulty became the occasion of the foundation of the Compagnie des Indes, which was afterward succeeded (after 1698) by the various Compagnies de la Chine. At the same period the institution of the Missions Étrangères was founded in Paris, 1663, to provide a supply of clergy for the projected missions. At the wish of Colbert a number of the pupils there educated went out to China in 1685. There can be no doubt that political influence was one of the main objects which the French missionaries then proposed to themselves —a fact which explains the later animosity of the native population. It was, however, the religious dissensions of the missionaries themselves which became the occasion of the suppression of Christianity in China. Even among the Jesuits conflicting views were held as to the attitude which should be taken toward certain questions. The chief points of difference centred

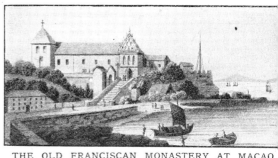

THE OLD FRANCISCAN MONASTERY AT MACAO

around the traditional worship of Confucius and of ancestors. Ricci and most of the Jesuits could see no idolatrous meanings in these customs, which they consequently permitted ; whereas the fanatical Dominicans, as afterward the Lazarists and the priests of the French missions, were entirely opposed to this view. The Popes declined to pronounce a decided opinion. Innocent X. (1644–1655) declared for the Dominicans, Alexander VII. in 1656 for the Jesuits, and Innocent XI. (1676–1689) pronounced the ceremonies permissible in so far as they were merely the expression of national veneration. Ultimately Bishop Maigrot, of the Lazarists, forbade the customs in 1693, and characterised the representations made by the Jesuits to the Pope as false in many respects. The Jesuits declined to recognise this decision, and in 1699 applied to the Emperor Kang Hsi, who made a declaration

CARDINAL DE TOURNON
Who conducted the Papal Legation to Peking in 1704, and died at Macao in 1710.

in full harmony with their views. Meanwhile at Rome the Congregation of the Inquisition had declared against the Jesuits—a decision confirmed by Clement XI. in 1704. At the same time Tournon, the Patriarch of Antioch, was sent to Peking to procure an adjustment of these differences. He did not dare to publish the Papal decree ; but Kang Hsi, whom the Jesuits perhaps used as an instrument to accomplish their designs, was informed by them of what had happened, and acted the more energetically when Maigrot declared against him and declined to recognise the Imperial authority in a matter which only the papal chair could decide. Kang Hsi banished Maigrot and ordered Tournon to leave China. The latter, being still unwilling to publish the Papal decree as such, made a summary of its contents and issued it at Nanking as his own decision. Kang Hsi replied by arresting him. He was carried to Macao where the Portuguese were obliged to place him in confinement, and there he died in 1710.

Clement XI. in 1718 issued a Bull, "Ex illa die," threatening with the greater excommunication anyone who declined to obey the Papal constitution of 1704, and sent as a new legate to Peking Mezzabarba, the Patriarch of Alexandria. Kang Hsi absolutely declined to enter into further negotiations, but stated that Mezzabarba, who had arrived in 1720 might leave the former missionaries in China, but must return to

THE OLD CHURCH OF ST. LAZARUS AT MACAO

829

Keystone Stereograph
ROMAN CATHOLIC CATHEDRAL AT PEKING

Rome with all the remainder, where the Pope was welcome to issue any orders he pleased regarding them. He was himself the sole ruler of the Chinese, and he forbade them to follow the Papal decrees. Mezzabarba then published the Papal Bull, with the additional clauses, which allowed the practice of the prohibited customs, considered merely as ceremonies of national veneration, but this

Papal Delegate Expelled compromise produced no satisfaction either in Peking or at Rome. Mezzabarba was definitely ordered by the Emperor to leave China and take with him the missionaries he had brought. Pope Benedict XIII. declined responsibility for the actions of his legate, and confirmed the decision of Clement XI. by the Bull, "Ex quo singulari," the terms of which remain in force at the present day.

Thus, in the struggle between the temporal and ecclesiastical power, the former had proved victorious and maintained its advantage throughout the following century. It is impossible to say whether the methods of the Jesuits would have ultimately proved successful or have resulted in the conversion of China. At any rate, the action of their adversaries both in China and in Japan precipitated the outbreak of the struggle and accentuated its severity. Even under Yung Cheng (1723–1735), the successor of Kang Hsi, persecution became fiercer ; and, although Chien Lung (1736–1795) showed much personal

consideration for the Jesuits who remained in Peking after the dissolution of the Order (1773), none the less, both during his reign and that of Chia Ching (1796–1820), the bloody persecutions of the native Christians and the missionaries who had secretly remained in the country continued without interruption.

The state of affairs described continued until the years 1845 and 1846, when the Emperor Tao Kuang (1821–1850) was induced by the proposals of the Imperial Commissioner Kiying, who had approached him at the desire of the French Ambassador De Lagréné, to permit the practice of the Christian religion among his subjects. He issued an order that any missionaries who might be found in the interior should be merely handed over to their authorities in the harbours open to commerce.

The conventions of 1858 and 1860 gave permission to the missionaries to visit the interior of the country and to take up residence there. Moreover, the decree of 1860, the Chinese version of which was falsified by a French interpreter, gave missionaries the right to acquire landed property in the country. From that date the Catholic missions in China have been able to develop undisturbed, apart from persecutions of a more or less local nature. Before the Boxer revolt (1900), there were about 530 European missionaries and 535,000 native Christians in thirty-one apostolic vicariates.

ROMAN CATHOLIC CATHEDRAL AT MACAO DESTROYED BY THE CHINESE

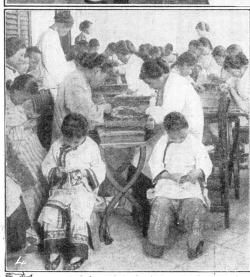

(1) The first school for deaf and dumb. (2) Athletic team of the London Missionary Society's Anglo-Chinese College. (3) Native Christians learning chemistry (photo, Edwards). (4) Chinese girls at a mission school (photo, Underwood). (5) Candidates for baptism from the Church Missionary Society Girls' Boarding School at Foo-chow.

SCENES OF PROTESTANT MISSION WORK AMONG THE PEOPLES OF CHINA

Photos. London Missionary Society, Church Missionary Society, Edwards, and Underwood & Underwood, London

CHINESE CONCEPTION OF MISSIONARIES
A notorious Chinese cartoon, by a native artist, depicting Christian missionaries gouging out the eyes of their converts.

China, and the "Variétés Sinologiques" of the present day are as valuable monographs and studies as any of those of earlier centuries when China was a book of which the pages were hardly yet cut. Among the more modern writers, P. P. David, Havret, Chevalier, and Richard have laid those interested in China under a lasting debt of gratitude to them.

PROTESTANT MISSIONS

The earliest Protestant mission was the Dutch, which, during their occupation of Formosa (1624–1662) did a good deal of missionary work, baptising thousands of natives and erecting schools. On their expulsion by Koxinga all traces of their work disappeared, with the exception of a

The scientific work done by the Jesuits in China has been of benefit to that country and the world at large. The manufacture of cannon and the correction of the Chinese calendar have been perhaps the most prominent of the benefits conferred upon China alone, while the survey of the Eighteen Provinces carried out by Kang-Hsi's command in the beginning of the eighteenth century, and the establishment of a meteorological station at Sicawei, near Shanghai, towards the close of the last century, have been a world-wide gain. In many departments of science works have been published which have secured for themselves a permanent place in the European literature on

AN ANTI-CHRISTIAN CARTOON
Christianity, represented as a hog, is being carried to the door of Confucius, who will have nothing to do with it.

translation of St. Matthew, printed in Roman letters—a style of writing with which the natives had been made familiar.

It was not until 1807 that Dr. Morrison, the first pioneer of British missions, arrived in Canton. Working practically single-handed until 1830, he produced his translation of the Bible, and assisted in the establishment of an Anglo-Chinese College at Malacca, where the Bible and other of his works were published. In 1831–1835 Gutzlaff undertook the journeys along the coast and among its islands, which, like those of later missionaries in the interior, have done so much to make China better known to the outer world. In 1830 the first missionaries from the United States

WARFARE UPON CHRISTIANITY
This anti-Christian cartoon shows the missionaries being flogged, and their Bibles being made into a bonfire.

had arrived, and about the same date Dr. Morrison had the satisfaction of making his first convert. In the absence of opportunities for work in other directions Bridgman, Williams, Legge, Medhurst, and other missionaries devoted their immense energies to writings on China, many of which are standard works at the present day. In 1835 the first missionary hospital was opened by Dr. Parker, of the American Board. With the Treaty of 1842 the isolation of foreigners in Canton came to an end, and missionaries had

NATIVE MISSIONARY PREACHING TO CHINESE
The Gospel is, by the aid of native Christian missionaries, enabled to penetrate into places that are still dangerous for European preachers.

This advance has been in spite of, and in great measure the consequence of, persecutions. The period 1890–1900 was especially marked by hostility to missions, first in the Yangtse Valley of Szechuen, then in Fukien (1895), where nine missionaries and two children were murdered, and finally, in the Boxer outbreak, when 135 missionaries and fifty-three children lost their lives. Since that date there seems to have been an entire change of feeling throughout the country, though murders of missionaries have occurred in different places. But the demands made for teaching and preaching, and

AN IRISH PRESBYTERIAN MISSION HOUSE
This was one of many mission stations burned in the Boxer rising.

opportunities of establishing themselves at Hong Kong and other ports. This encouragement had such effect that while between 1807 and 1842 there had been only fifty-seven workers in China and among the Chinese in the Straits, in 1842–1860 over 160 others were sent out. Since that time the advance has been so rapid that now (1907) there are 3,719 foreign workers with 706 stations, 366 hospitals and dispensaries, 2,139 schools, and over 154,000 communicants, and more than 10,000 native workers.

Edwards
A TYPICAL PROTESTANT MISSION STATION
The Mission Compound at Chang-pu is typical of other centres of Christian work

for the literature published by mission presses dealing with religious, economic, and scientific matters, have been on a scale for which no provision was in existence. Of the Bible alone over 2,600,000 copies were sold or distributed in 1905.

The activity of Protestant missions has not been confined to religious or medical work. The Great Famine of 1876–7 found in them the only body capable of organising the distribution of relief, and since that time no large famine has occurred without missionaries coming forward to undertake all that they could do to save those stricken by famine from starvation, and from the pestilence which generally follows, even at the cost of their own lives. An immense effort also has been made by them to lift, from the Chinese public and the official world, the veil which has prevented them from realising the nature and the advantages of European civilisation.

The Practical Result of Mission Work

The Society for the Promotion of Christian Knowledge, which has been such a powerful factor in this direction, has been dependent for its editors entirely upon missionary volunteers. The best of the so-called universities and of the schools throughout the country have owed their existence and development to missionaries.

And, finally, the movement in China towards the better administration of government, the furtherance of the principles of liberty and justice, and the elevation of the country from the low position among nations into which it has fallen, is due more to the influence of Protestant missionaries than to that of all the legations, consulates, and mercantile houses in China. The diversion of literary activity towards this direction has to a considerable extent interfered with the production of works on China such as those of Wylie, Edkins, Chalmers, and Martin in the latter half of the nineteenth century. Their place has been taken by civilians such as Bretschneider, Richthofen, Wade, Mayers, Walters, Hirth, Giles, and Bushell, while the missionary world has found in D. A. H. Smith a delineator of Chinese life and character rivalled only by Père Hèuc.

The awakening of China, which is the feature of the present hour, has revealed in Protestant missions a unity of aim which does honour to the seventy-one missionary bodies now working in the country, whose number has in itself excited the most severe criticism as tending to promote disunion and injurious rivalry. In the Conference held at Shanghai this year (1907) it was resolved that preparation should be made for a self-governing native Church, responding to the national cry of " China for the Chinese," and that missionaries should themselves federate with a view to unity of aims, economy of work, and the large spirit which would form a universal and combined effort.

Federation of Chinese Missions

The question at issue is : " Shall China be a Christian or non-Christian country ?" And to secure a satisfactory answer to this question united effort is necessary. The spirit of concord which has animated the different missions in the past encourages the hope that the realisation of what is desired may prove possible of attainment.

MAX VON BRANDT

A LITTLE PANORAMA OF CHINESE PLACES AND PEOPLE

A unique scene at the Imperial Palace of Tseaou-shan

The Imperial Travelling Palace at Hoo-kew-shan

PICTURESQUE PALACES OF THE RULERS OF CHINA

Pavilion and garden of a mandarin's house at Nanking

Mandarin's wife and family examining the goods of a travelling merchant

SCENES IN THE HOUSE OF A CHINESE MANDARIN

An important official paying a visit of ceremony in his palanquin

Dinner party at table in the house of a rich official

SCENES FROM THE LIFE OF A CHINESE MANDARIN

Emperor's state barge on the Yuho Canal   Marble bridge at the Imperial Summer Palace

A view in the vast and picturesque gardens of the Imperial Palace at Peking

Porcelain tower in the Imperial Summer Palace   Interior of Throne-room in "Forbidden City," Peking

GLIMPSES OF THE IMPERIAL SPLENDOURS AT PEKING
Photos by Underwood & Underwood, London, and H. C. White Co.

The wretched wooden shanties of the poor Chinese at Macao

The house of a rich native merchant in the suburbs of Canton

HOW THE VERY RICH AND VERY POOR OF CHINA LIVE

The cultivation, collection, and preparation of tea

One of China's most important industries: Feeding silkworms and sorting the cocoons

THE CHINESE PEOPLE AT WORK

Kite-flying at Haekwan on the ninth day of the ninth moon

Scene from the spectacle of "The Sun and Moon

THE CHINESE PEOPLE AT PLAY

Macao, a great city, which has decayed with the rise of Hong Kong, and now notorious for its gambling-dens

The mighty walls that enclose the teeming life of the great city of Peking

Outside the walls of Nanking, with a religious procession in the foreground

SOME OF THE GREAT AND POPULOUS CITIES OF CHINA

French quarter and native city of Shanghai, with an opium hulk on the left

Hong Kong, snowing the City Hall on the right and Victoria Peak in the background

Western suburb of Canton, north of the Custom House, showing a watchman's tower

VIEWS OF THE THREE GREATEST PORTS OF CHINA
Photos by Underwood & Underwood, London.

Chinamen eating with chopsticks

An itinerant barber at work in the open street of a Chinese city

Chinese tea-house at Shanghai frequented by well-to-do merchants

FAMILIAR SCENES OF DAILY LIFE IN CHINA
Photos by Underwood & Underwood, London, and Edwards, Littlehampton.

CHINA IN OUR OWN TIME

BY SIR ROBERT K. DOUGLAS

IT is always difficult to decide who wields the power in an Oriental state, and more especially is this the case in China, where the complexity of the system of government and the strange mixture of autocracy and democracy, which is so prominent in Peking, confuse the issues. Onlookers can judge only by results, and so far it would appear that the Throne is swayed by the party or person who gains the ear, even if it be only for a moment, of the Dowager Empress.

But of late the tendency of the Imperial policy has been in favour of reform. An enlightened desire for increasing knowledge has manifested itself all over the empire. Schools and colleges in which Western knowledge is taught have been opened in all large cities throughout the provinces, and outward and visible signs are not wanting to show that there is a growing impatience with the older **Reforms in Modern China** methods. Even in such matters as dress this is observable. Lads are discarding their native robes and gowns for tight-fitting jackets and wear their hair short. So long as this spirit does not become aggressive it is surely to be welcomed; but the danger is that in their ignorance and conceit they may exaggerate their powers and may be led to believe that the veneer of civilisation which they possess is enough to enable them to face with more success than in 1901 the forces of Europe. Meanwhile, every day that goes by makes any such rash act less and less likely. Every day they are being taught that the toad which lives at the bottom of the well sees only an infinitesimally small part of the sky.

That China is moving in the direction of reform there can be no question. But large bodies move slowly, and this is especially true of China in spite of Wen-hsiang's dictum that "when she begins to move she will move faster than can be foreseen." In addition to the natural diffi-

culty of getting up a momentum there are several causes in the way of rapid progress. First and foremost there is the supreme conceit of the people, who regard the rest of the world as inferior to themselves in every way. At times they are obliged **A Trait of Chinese Character** to admit a seeming superiority in the knowledge and acquirements of the "outer barbarians," but in such cases they shelter themselves behind the ingenious plea that the system involved is plainly indicated in the Confucian classics, in which all wisdom dwells.

Thus it has ever been. After the war of 1860, when the marks of the heels of the conquerors were still fresh on the neck of the empire, numerous reforms in imitation of European methods were projected, but in each case they were heralded as having been foreshadowed in the writings of the ancient philosophers, much as it might be held that Puck's boast that he would "put a girdle round the earth in forty minutes" showed a knowledge on Shakespeare's part of the electric telegraph. Prince Kung, for example, presented at that time a memorial to the Throne in which he advocated the introduction of mathematics as a subject for the competitive examinations, and served up the medicine in a wrapper bearing an authority from the classics for the suggestion.

The introduction of defensive weapons has, after each defeat of the forces of the empire, been justified in the same way; but so soon as the pressing necessity for reform has been removed by the return **Changes in Military Practice** of peace, matters have been allowed to slow down to the old level of obsolete weapons and careless drilling. Recent reforms in military matters have, so far, however, been of a more enduring nature. The Boxer riots, the advances of Russia on the north, and the victories of Japan have all conspired to bring home, not only to the mandarins, but to the people generally, the consciousness that there must be something rotten in the state of China when such events could occur.

The circumstance that Yuan Shih-kai was until the other day viceroy of the metropolitan province has tended to emphasise the position. Possibly from patriotic motives, and certainly in his own interest, this powerful satrap has been at great pains to render the troops, which are still under his command, as efficient as possible. And he has succeeded. But the decentralised system of government, by which each province provides its own army and navy, limits his exertions to the frontiers of Chih-li. Chang Chih-tung—whose celebrated philosophical book, "Exhortations to Learn," is summarised at the end of this chapter—when viceroy of the two Hu provinces, also did something in the same direction; and a year ago the forces of these two viceroys made an imposing display at the autumn manœuvres. These reforms have to be reckoned with, though their permanency is doubtful, dependent as they are on the disposition of the viceroys for the time being. The troops of one man such as Yuan Shih-kai may be next door to a ragged army armed with weapons little better than bows and arrows.

When well armed and well led, the Chinese make good soldiers, but they require a large mixture of leaven in the shape of foreign officers and non-commissioned officers. Then, like the lately disbanded Wei-hai-wei Regiment, they are capable of doing good service. One secret of the efficiency of this regiment was, equally with that of the troops which follow Yuan Shih-kai's banner, that they were regularly paid. Like the Turks, the Chinese are bad paymasters, and this forms a fatal bar to any proposed system of reform. Chinamen, like other people, will not work if they are not paid.

Reforms in the Navy have from time to time been advocated, but the same fatal bars to efficiency are existent there. Under the command of Admiral Lang

Some Progressive Chinamen

Northern China had at one time—in the early nineties—a comparatively good fleet of men-of-war. But, unfortunately for the empire, Admiral Lang was driven from the command by an intrigue promoted by native officers, and soon afterwards his ships were entirely taken and destroyed by the Japanese.

One curious instance of the anomalies likely to arise from the current system of decentralisation was afforded at the time of this catastrophe. Among the Chinese ships captured on one occasion was a ship from the southern fleet, the captain of which naively requested the Japanese commander to release her on the plea that her presence in the northern waters was due to an accident! At the present moment the Imperial Government is contemplating the creation of a new fleet, and orders have been given in Europe for the construction of a number of vessels. But a gun is useless without the man behind it; and in the same way no number of ships will avail China unless they are commanded and worked by really efficient officers and by men who are regularly paid.

Chinese Naval Policy

In municipal and social matters there are signs that the people of the large cities are becoming aware of the advantages of sanitation and of convenient and rapid movement. The changes which are apparent at Peking are conspicuous in these regards. The streets, which were a few years ago so many Sloughs of Despond, in which drownings were not unknown incidents, have now, more especially in the Legation quarter, been levelled and macadamised. The native springless carts have yielded place to jinrickshas and even to two-horse broughams, in the shapes of which is preserved, as near as may be, the form of the partly disused official sedan chair, much as the earlier railway carriages among ourselves were fashioned to resemble stage coaches. Numberless European buildings are springing into existence, and whereas, a few years ago, a bank wishing to establish itself in the

SIR ROBERT HART
A great figure in Chinese affairs since 1863, when he became Inspector-General of Customs. In 1896 he was made Inspector-General of Posts.

capital had to do so almost surreptitiously, five banks now stand out in foreign guise, naked and not ashamed. The railway from Tientsin has been advanced to the Chien Gate, while a macadamised road leads through the now historical water gate into the Tartar city.

Similar changes are observable throughout the provinces. Dr. Morrison, in a remarkable journey which he lately made from north to south throughout the empire, remarked with astonishment the number of European-built schoolhouses which he met with in all the large cities en route. These buildings were mainly erected under the genial influences of the edicts issued by the Emperor in 1898, and had escaped the storm which beset the education movement after the *coup d'état*. Nor are these buildings merely for show. They are full of students eager in the pursuit of European knowledge and fully convinced that for the purposes of getting on in life the teachings of the historians and philosophers of Europe are to be preferred to the doctrines of Confucius and Mencius. A great demand has sprung up for teachers who can impart a knowledge of English—

Spread of Education in China the language which is most sought after at the present moment by young China—and any Chinaman possessing a knowledge of it can demand his own terms. Much work has been done in the translation of standard works into Chinese. Books of history, science, and literature have been rendered into that tongue by the Society for the Diffusion of Christian Literature, among others, and through the instrumentality of these bodies Chinese students can read in their own language many of the leading works of English literature.

Translations of Sir Conan Doyle, Rider Haggard, and other authors are rapidly multiplying ; they may in some cases be a real help to the student of Chinese.

ONE OF CHINA'S GREATEST VICEROYS

Chang Chi-tung, formerly Viceroy of the provinces of Hupeh and Honan, a great leader of the new movement and author of "Exhortations to Learn."

" Ivanhoe " has been translated, and the Chinese may read in their own tongue the " Arabian Nights," " Robinson Crusoe," " The Swiss Family Robinson," " The Count of Monte Christo," " Tales from Shakespeare," " Jean Valjean," " Gulliver's Travels," " Looking Backward," and many other familiar works. The list of educational works grows year by year, says the Rev. Baring Gould, and science and philosophy each have their interpreters.

The most promising of the youths trained in the local schools and colleges are sent either to Japan or Europe to complete their education. At the present moment there are something like 8,000 students in Japan, and one or two hundred lady students, while three or four hundred youths are working at the universities of Europe and America. This system has not been unattended with difficulties in Japan, where the Chinese youths have shown themselves inclined to be riotous, being puffed up with that dangerous possession—a little learning. And on their return they do not show a much more amenable spirit. The process of pouring new wine into old bottles is proverbially ruinous, and the attempt by these youths to assimilate the constitutional liberalism of Japan with the Chinese system of government threatens many difficulties. The patriotism, loyalty and honesty they have seen displayed in Japan make the corrupt and unpatriotic system prevailing in their native land particularly abhorrent to them. In their ignorance they consider that what the

Lessons from Japan Japanese have accomplished after years spent in careful study and deliberation can be effected by their countrymen by a wave of the wand, and it will be only by hard experience and after many counterblasts that they will be convinced to the contrary.

Some estimate of the extent of know-

847

ledge required by the students educated in the native colleges can be gained by a glance at the questions set at the public examinations. " Instead of being examined on the teachings of Confucius," writes Mr. Baring Gould, " the students qualifying for Government posts are now being set such questions as—

Modernism Supplants Confucianism What is the bearing of the Siberian railway on China ? What is the bearing of the Treaty of Berlin and of the Monroe Doctrine on the Far East ? Explain Free Trade and Protection. What is Herbert Spencer's philosophy of sociology ? State how best to develop the resources of China by mines and railways. Explain how best to guard land and sea frontiers from the advance of foreign Powers. What should be the strategic points of China ? What nation has the best stamp duty ? How do foreigners regulate the Press, post office, commerce, railways, banks, taxation, and how do they get faithful men ? It has been decided that every province is to have its university, every prefecture its high school, and every village its primary school, and 250,000 teachers are required at once to meet the sudden demand for Western knowledge. Girls' schools, with gymnasia and playgrounds are about to be established."

One evidence of the effect of this spread of education is afforded by the Post Office returns. In 1901 there were 176 post-offices in China ; in 1905 there were 1,626. In 1901 10,000,000 letters were posted ; in 1905, 76,000,000.

But the most plain and palpable evidence of the change which has come over the minds of the people is furnished by the existence of railways, which now traverse the country from north to south and from east to west. It is now only about twenty years since the first effective railway was constructed by Li Hung-chang from Tientsin to the Kaiping coal-mines,

Rapid Growth of Chinese Railways and at the present time there are some thousands of miles in working order. The principal of these is the main line from Peking to Hankow, a distance of 600 miles. This railway, which was first promoted by Chang Chih-tung, was completed by a Belgian syndicate, and is remarkable not only for the extent of country through which it passes, but also for having in its course one of the longest bridges in the world—that which spans the

muddy waters of the Yellow River on the plains of Honan.

This river brings down with its current enormous quantities of loose soil, which it deposits in constant and large extents. The result is that the bottom is always silting up : and, as dredging is foreign to the Chinese system, the only alternative for the prevention of floods is to heighten

THE CHINESE SOLDIER AS HE WAS—

the banks. This the Chinese have continuously done, until in many parts of its course the bed of the stream lies higher than the surrounding country. Desolating floods are constantly the result of this mistaken system, and to avoid the evils arising from such catastrophes the builders of the railway bridge were obliged to carry their operations to a considerable distance on each bank. Five miles is the length to which it is necessary to extend the bridge over this treacherous stream, and much difficulty was experienced in getting substantial foundations for the piers. The continuation of the line from Hankow southwards to Canton was originally entrusted to an American syndicate, but in pursuance of the Monroe Doctrine of " China for the Chinese," the foreign syndicate was bought out and the work was handed over to a Chinese company. The usual results have followed ; the work languished and the completion of the line appears to be as far off as the Greek kalends. An object lesson of the delay which occurs when work of the kind is

—AND AS HE IS TO-DAY

entrusted to native capitalists is furnished by the progress made by the short line which is to span the distance between Kowloon, opposite Hong Kong, and Canton. This is a distinct line from that between Canton and Hankow. The arrangements for floating the loan were made in November 1906, but the work was begun two years ago, and only twelve miles of rails have yet been laid.

These reforms and other popular movements have been carefully watched and noted by the dominant Manchu powers at Peking, who are perfectly aware that their continued existence depends on their ability to direct the popular enthusiasms into safe channels. For some time, strong anti-Manchu feeling has been growing up in the empire, fomented by agitators such as Sun Yat-sen, of Portland Place notoriety. This man has been agitating in the southern provinces of China for a considerable time, and the recent capture of some of his correspondence has shown that there is more vitality in the movement than was at first supposed. With the establishment of the present Manchu dynasty in China in 1664, a constitution was framed under which the main army, consisting of Manchus, with their family relations and descendants, were to be provided for out of the Imperial funds. The Manchus were, by the same rule of conduct, forbidden to intermarry with Chinese, and their women were forbidden to follow the Chinese fashion of compressing the feet. Time has only added emphasis to the perpetuation of these distinctions, and the result has been that in the large garrison cities of the empire two classes have grown up side by side with little or no social intercourse. The Chinese naturally say—Why should we pay a large annual sum, amounting to considerably upwards of £1,000,000 sterling, in pensions to a body of men who have repeatedly shown themselves incapable of protecting the country against foreign invasion ? To which the Manchus reply that at present they are debarred from indulging in trade and other civil pursuits, and that if their pensions are withdrawn, these prohibitions should be likewise annulled.

So serious are these agitations that, at the bidding of the Dowager Empress, edicts have been issued abolishing some of the distinctions between the two nationalities. For instance, for the future, the preponderance at the Government Boards of Manchu presidents and vice-presidents will be abolished, and Chinese ladies will be eligible for admission to the Imperial harem. This, with the conferring of other rights, will possibly provide for a succession of Chino-Manchu sovereigns. One other mark of distinction is to be abolished. The Manchus have no surnames, at least they do not use any in China ; whereas, the Chinese attach great importance to the use and expression of

Evidences of Native Discontent

Blending of Manchus and Chinese

real surnames such as they pride themselves on possessing.

For the future it is proposed, therefore, that the Manchus should be placed on a par with the Chinese by the adoption and use of surnames. But the carrying out of these and other Governmental reforms depends so entirely on the necessities of the moment

THE OLD WAY

Prisoner in the stocks ; trussed by the thumbs and kneeling on iron chains.

PRISON REFORM IN CHINA: THE NEW WAY

Prisoners are now employed in making uniforms in well-lighted and ventilated rooms.

that it may be doubted whether they will ever be put into force. The Chinese are extreme opportunists, and act only in accordance with the pressure of the moment. This has been notably the case during the rule of the Dowager Empress. To go no further back than the Boxer movement of 1900, she adopted the principles of those fanatics under the belief that they represented the will of the nation, and no sooner found out her mistake than she veered completely round, and held out the hand of professing friendship to foreigners generally, embracing with particular fervour the ladies of the foreign legations. This consideration makes it impossible to forecast the future of the empire. We know that, with some few exceptions, the whole body of mandarins are opposed to any drastic reforms.

Their personal interests are bound up in the continuance of the present corrupt system, and it would require an effort of patriotism equal to that which transferred the territories of the Daimiyos of Japan to the Throne to make the mandarins of China acquiesce willingly in the abolition of their cherished perquisites.

The Dowager Empress has always shown her appreciation of having a large armed force at her beck and call. This she has now secured by the appointment of Yuan Shih-kai as President of the Foreign Office, or Wai-wu-pu ; and it is tolerably certain that so long as she can command the allegiance of this powerful leader, who still has the command of a large portion of the northern army, the Throne of her line is safe from the attacks of domestic enemies. Doubts have been thrown on the loyalty of Yuan ; but hitherto he has shown most pro-

AN INSTRUCTIVE GLIMPSE AT THE EDUCATIONAL METHODS OF MODERN CHINA

Teaching English vocables by comparison with Chinese symbols.

nounced good faith, and though, being Chinese, circumstances may arise which may induce him to transfer his allegiance elsewhere, there is at present no sign of his giving anything but a true-hearted support to the Throne.

One measure he has adopted in his army which has been taken up strenuously by the Empress. That is the abolition of

YUAN SHIH-KAI, THE GREAT VICEROY OF PEKING PROVINCE, REVIEWING HIS CAVALRY

This picture, drawn from photographs and sketches, gives at a glance a vivid idea of how China's army is being brought into line with the armies of the Western Powers, and how striking is the change from the obsolete armaments, still existing in the armies of other and less intelligent viceroys, to modern military practice.

opium smoking. One cause of the success of the Japanese in their late campaigns was considered to be their freedom from this vice, and Yuan at once set about following their example in the forces and populations under his control. The movement, being a popular one, was eagerly taken up by the powers that be at Peking. An Imperial edict was issued in Sept., 1906, commanding that opium smoking should be abolished throughout the empire in the course of the next ten years, and that all opium dens should at once be closed.

Whether the Government will be able to effect this remains to be seen. Certainly, in some parts, the edict has been received with enthusiasm. At Canton, one of the most populous cities of the empire, the people received the news of it gladly, and on the recent closing of the opium dens formed a procession rejoicing at the promised abolition of a practice which they had learnt, with good reason, to abhor. In the native city of Shanghai, also, the dens were closed, without any jubilation, it is true, but also without any disturbance. In other parts of the empire the reception of the edict was not so satisfactory, and it does not appear to have made any difference in the amount of acreage devoted to the growth of the poppy. These considerations account for the hesitancy of Sir John Jordan, the British Minister at Peking, in advocating the prevention of the importation of Indian opium. Let the Chinese Government, he says in effect, first show that it is in earnest in its desire to do its share in the great movement, and then it will have no reason to complain of our backwardness in carrying out our part of the programme. But in dealing with the Chinese, one is dealing with an uncertain quantity, and something more substantial than an Imperial edict is required before we can co-operate with them in this or any other political campaign.

ROBERT K. DOUGLAS

A VICEROY'S GREAT APPEAL FOR PROGRESS

A STRIKING instance of the working of the minds of Chinese statesmen during recent years is the book by Chang Chih-tung, the Viceroy of Liang-hu. The Viceroy is one of the leading men of the empire, and his book is said to have had a circulation of a million copies. The Emperor declared that the book " embodies a fair and candid statement of the facts," and that " a diligent perusal of its contents will broaden the mental scope and open up methods of far-reaching usefulness." An imperial rescript was issued, ordering copies to be distributed among the Viceroys, Governors, and Literary Examiners of China, and depositing a copy with the Grand Council of State.

This book, which has presumably had some influence on recent developments, is in twenty chapters, and the author has summarised his chapters under brief headings that may be given.

The first nine chapters have a moral note, dealing with " Radical Principles as a Means of Rectifying the Heart," and the author summarises these chapters as follows :

1. United hearts. It is plain that three things claim our attention just now—the protection of the empire, the religion, and the race. If the hands and feet are nimble, the eyes and head will be at rest, and if the constitution is robust, the purpose will be strong. The Imperial power will increase in proportion to the number of intellectual men who come forward.

2. The Inculcation of Loyalty. The moral excellence of this dynasty is so universally known that both Ministers and people should cherish an ardent patriotism in order to conserve the country.

3. The Three Moral Obligations. The sages have always taught that the true relations existing between the sovereign and the subject, father and son. and husband and wife, are of prime importance, the radix of propriety and the distinguishing feature between man and the brutes.

4. The Recognition of Class. We are grieved lest the Chinese—the descendants of the gods—should be sunk in obscurity, and we write this chapter for the protection of our race.

5. Honour due to the Classics. Some of our extra-canonical books are good, others are pernicious. Let not the bad obscure what is good. Doctrines that tend to disrupt ought not to be followed.

Before any work is approved it should be brought to the touchstone of the Holy Canons.

6. Centralisation of Power. Differentiate between officials and people, but give direction to popular thought. We denounce republicanism as rebellious.

7. The Proper Sequence of Things. That which enters first, dominates. A thorough knowledge of Chinese is necessary in order to acquire a Western education. Possessing this knowledge our ancestors will not be forgotten.

8. Attending to What is Vital. To rejoice in the new is sweet; to love the old is bitter. If we are to preserve Chinese learning, we must find out what is important and hold to it.

9. Cast out the Poison! The foreign drug (opium) is debasing the homes and sweeping away the lives of our people. Cut it off, root and branch!

The second half of the book is practical, dealing with " The Intercourse of Nations as a Means of Enlightenment," and the author's summaries of its chapters are :

1. Beneficial Knowledge. When unknown foes assail us, we are deluded and meet with disaster.

2. Travel. Discern the signs of the times, enlarge the mind, broaden the understanding, and increase the skill and knowledge of the Chinese! Without travel in foreign countries these *desiderata* cannot be obtained.

3. The Establishment of Schools. Establish schools everywhere adapted to the present time, for putting into practice the knowledge of the graduates. Rouse the stupid!

4. The Study of Regulations. The strength of Western countries is derived from their Government institutions, in which the students are required to observe stipulated rules. These have the power of conferring official rank. We should establish such institutions on the best approved method.

5. The Extensive Translation of Books. The benefits derived from the instruction of Western teachers have their limits. Those which follow the translation of foreign books are boundless.

6. Newspaper Reading. It is difficult to see one's own eyebrows and eyelashes, and hard to take bitter medicine. Be

sensible of moral corruption, and cast it out at once ! Have a knowledge of outside evil and prepare a defence !

7. Reform of Methods. Self preservation demands something more than our old inherited principles.

8. Railways. Commerce is the blood and breath of a nation.

9. Comparative Study. Know how to combine the gist of Western learning with Chinese learning, in order to enlighten dense ignorance.

10. Maintaining the Army. The despicable teaching of ease and lust is suicidal.

11. Religious Toleration. The outbreaks of petty malignity against different sects defeat great schemes, and are to be deplored.

Following upon these chapters, Chang Chih-tung draws up " Five Objects of Knowledge," which are thus stated :

1. Know the shame of not being like Japan, Turkey, Siam, and Cuba.

2. Know the fear that we will become as India, Annan, Burma, Korea, Egypt, and Poland.

3. Know that if we do not change our customs we cannot reform our methods, and if we do not reform our methods we cannot utilise the modern implements of war, etc.

4. Know what is important. The study of the old is not urgent ; the call for men of attainments in useful knowledge is pressing. Foreign education is of different kinds. Western handicraft is not in demand, but a knowledge of the methods of foreign Governments is a consummation devoutly to be wished.

5. Know what is radical. When abroad do not forget your own native country ; when you see strange customs, do not forget your parents ; and let not much wisdom and ingenuity make you forget the holy sages.

This book, quoted here from the translation by Rev. Samuel I. Woodbridge published by Messrs. Oliphant, Anderson & Ferrier under the title of " China's Only Hope," is a notable example of the means by which new ideas are being spread among the Chinese people. Our portrait of Chang Chih-tung on page 847 is also reproduced by permission from " China's Only Hope."

GREAT DATES IN THE HISTORY OF CHINA

MYTHOLOGICAL

The time that elapsed from the creation of the world till the " capture of the *lin* in the time of Confucius " was 2,267,000 years (or, according to other writers, over 3,000,000 years). The first being was Pan-ku, who was followed by a line of descendants. The period of mythology is divided into ten eras, which lasted until the opening of legendary history

LEGENDARY ·

THE THREE PRIMORDIAL SOVEREIGNS OF MIRACULOUS BIRTH

B.C.	
2852–2737	Fu-hsi or Fu-hi. Taught hunting, fishing, pasturage, established marriage and constructed musical instruments. Composed a system of written characters
2737–2697	Shen-nung (The Divine Husbandman). Invented wooden ploughs, taught agriculture, and discovered the curative properties of plants
2697–2597	Huang-ti. Invented utensils, boats, carts, a money currency, and the " tadpole " writing. Advanced astronomy and music. Mapped the empire into provinces, and his consort established the silkworm industry

HISTORICAL

2356	Yao, the first historical emperor, a model of wisdom and virtue. In his time occurred great floods which have been alleged to correspond with the Deluge of Scripture
2205	Yu establishes the Hsia dynasty
1766	Tang founds the Shang dynasty
1122	Fa, under the title of Wu Wang, founds the Chou dynasty
946-770	Frequent incursions of barbarians.
800-752	Invention of " Great Seal " characters, or writing proper
604	Birth of Lao-tse, the prophet of Taoism.
550	Birth of Confucius, or Kung-fu-tsze
371	Birth of Meng-tsze, or Mencius, follower and expounder of Confucianism
213	" Burning of the Books " by Emperor Shih-huang-ti
211	Completion of Great Wall of China
200	Invention of Li-shu, or official handwriting
179-157	The Emperor Wen Ti encourages learning
139	Communication opened between China and the Scythians of the West
129	The Chinese appear in history as aiding the Scythians against Phraates and ravaging the shores of the Caspian
126	Buddhism introduced into China
115	Regular intercourse established between China and Central Asia
A.D.	
15	Religion of Lao-tse recognised
61	Buddhist books and priests brought into China by the Emperor Ming Ti
105	Chinese made paper of bark, hemp, rags, etc.
426	Attempt to suppress Buddhism
618	Beginning of the Tang dynasty, the Augustan era of Chinese letters

A.D.	
639	Nestorians allowed to preach Christianity by the Emperor Tai-tsung, who extended the Chinese Empire to the Caspian
667	Korea subjugated by Emperor Kao-tsung
845	Nestorians extirpated and Christianity suppressed [history
932	First mention of printing in Chinese
1130–1200	China invaded and oppressed by Kitans Chu-hi, the teacher whose works form the basis of official Confucianism
1249	Louis IX. of France sends embassy to China [Khan
1264	Peking is made the capital by Kublai
1271	Mogul dynasty firmly established
1275	Missionaries introduced by Marco Polo.
1281	Kublai Khan makes unsuccessful attempt to conquer Japan. The Grand Canal extended. Kublai Khan conquers Burma
1368	Ming dynasty established by Hong Wou
1409	The Emperor Yung-lo has the first copy of his great encyclopædia
1516	Portuguese arrive at Canton
1536	Macao ceded to the Portuguese
1550	War with Japan (1550–63)
1573	Wan-li becomes Emperor, and under him ceramic and other arts flourished
1581	Jesuits come from Rome to China
1616–43	China conquered by Manchu Tartars and present dynasty established
1660	China tea introduced to England
1680	Opening of Chinese trade with East India Company
1692	Jesuit missionaries preach in China
1719-27	Commercial relations with Russia develop
1724-32	Jesuits expelled [velop
1760	War in Central Asia. Empire extended
1793	Earl Macartney received by Emperor
1812	Edict against Christianity
1816	Lord Amherst's unsuccessful embassy to China
1834	East India Company's monopoly ceases and Free Trade ships sail for England Beginning of opium dispute between Chinese and British
1842	Treaty of Nanking, whereby first war between England and China is terminated, certain treaty ports opened to trade, and Hong Kong ceded
1850	Beginning of Taiping Rebellion
1856	" Arrow " incident causes war between Britain and China
1858	Treaty of Tientsin ends the second war with China
1860	Treaty of Tientsin ratified, after Lord Elgin's march to Peking
1864	Taiping Rebellion finally crushed by General Gordon
1873	Emperor receives foreign emissaries
1876	Drought and famine in Shantung and Shansi, 9,000,000 dying
1883	War between France and China regarding Tonquin (1883–5)
1894	War between China and Japan
1895	Peace Treaty between China and Japan
1898	China grants concessions of territory to Germany, Russia, and Britain
1900	Boxer rising
1906	Edict against opium smoking

ESSENTIAL INFORMATION ABOUT CHINA

AREA. The area of the Chinese Empire is 4,277,170 square miles, and is made up of China Proper, 1,532,420; Manchuria, 363,610; Mongolia, 1,367,600; Tibet, 463,200; and Chinese Turkestan, etc., 550,340.

POPULATION. No proper census of China is taken, and the estimates of population in the several provinces vary very much. The Chinese themselves estimate that China Proper contains 407,250,000 inhabitants; Manchuria, 16,000,000; Mongolia, 2,600,000; Tibet, 6,500,000; and Chinese Turkestan, etc., 1,200,000, making an aggregate of 433,550,000. European authorities who have studied the subject consider these figures greatly over-estimated, and believe that the actual population of the Chinese Empire is well under 300,000,000. The estimated populations of the principal large cities and Treaty ports are as follows:

Peking	700,000	Chungking		620,000
Singan	1,000,000	Soochow		500,000
Siangtan	1,000,000	Hangchow		350,000
Canton	900,000	Nanking		270,000
Hankow	870,000	Ningpo		260,000
Tientsin	750,000	Changsha		230,000
Shanghai	651,000	Chinkiang		168,000
Foochow	624,000	Amoy		114,000

EMPEROR. The reigning Emperor is Tsai Tien, who was born in 1872, and under the title of Kwang Hsu succeeded his cousin Tung Chih in January, 1875. He assumed the reins of government in 1887, when he came of age, and married in 1889. He has no children, and no nominated successor. For nine years from the date of his marriage he may be said to have ruled, but his leaning towards reforms caused the Empress Dowager to assume control in 1897, since when she has been the actual ruler of the empire. The Empress Dowager—Tzu Hsi, born 1834—is the Emperor's maternal aunt.

GOVERNMENT. The Government in China is in practice an Imperial autocracy with several advisory bodies, the chief of which are the Grand Council and the recently-constituted Government Council. The functions of these Councils are not executive, the administration being now—since November, 1906—carried on by ten Boards. An Imperial edict of September 1st, 1906, promised a constitution as soon as the people are considered fit for it.

REVENUE AND EXPENDITURE. No statement of revenue and expenditure of the Chinese Government is published. An estimate by Sir Robert Hart (in 1901) places the annual revenue at 88,200,000 taels (about £13,230,000), and the expenditure at 101,120,000 taels (about £15,168,000). The chief sources of revenue are a land tax, the Government monopoly of salt, and the "likin" or toll upon goods in transit. The maritime customs and opium likin yielded in 1905, 35,111,004 Haikwan taels (£5,281,280), about one-eighth being from the opium likin. The maritime customs are security for the Public Debt, amounting to £119,755,000, the annual charges upon which now amount to £5,770,000.

COMMERCE. In 1905 the aggregate value of Chinese imports was 447,100,791 Haikwan taels (about £67,065,118), and of the exports 227,888,197 taels (about £34,183,229). The chief exports are silk—both raw and manu-factured—tea, beans, and raw cotton; the chief imports are cotton goods, metals, opium, sugar and kerosene.

REPRESENTATION IN GREAT BRITAIN. Legation, 49, Portland Place, London, W. Envoy and Minister, Li Ching-fong. Secretary, Ivan Chen. London office of Inspectorate-General of Chinese Imperial Maritime Customs, 26, Old Queen Street, Westminster, London, S.W.

CURRENCY. There is no uniform national coinage throughout the Chinese Empire. In the Treaty of September 5th, 1902, China agreed to take measures to provide one, but the promise has not yet been carried into effect. The unit and only official coinage of China is the copper cash, which is of the value of about 1·35d. The Haikwan tael (literally, customs tael) is 1⅓oz. avoird. of pure silver. Its value fluctuates with the value of the metal, and may be taken as being worth 3s. approximately. About 1,220 cash = 1 Haikwan tael. The Kuping tael, used as standard by the Chinese Government, is a few grains lighter than the Haikwan tael—100 Haikwan tael equalling 101·6 Kuping tael. The dollar (value the same as the Mexican dollar) is in extended use; and a recently-issued coin is the hundredth of a dollar with a face value of 3-10d. and an actual value of about ⅓d.

WEIGHTS AND MEASURES. The standards of weights and measures vary greatly throughout the empire, some being little more than half as much as those in use elsewhere. Those given below are in use at the Treaty ports.

WEIGHTS

10 Li	= 1 Fen	= 6 grains.
10 Fen	= 1 Chien or Mace	= 58·3 grains.
10 Chien	= 1 Liang or Tael	= 1⅓ oz. avoird.
16 Liang	= 1 Chin or Catty	= 1⅓ lb.
100 Chin	= 1 Tan or Picul	= 133⅓ lb.

1 Picul or Tan equals 1·190446 cwt.

MEASURE OF CAPACITY

10 Ko	= 1 Sheng	= from ·113 to ·163 gallons.
10 Sheng	= 1 Ton	= from 1·13 to 1·63 gallons.

The measure of capacity in China has not the commercial importance it has in other countries, because even liquids are generally sold by weight. The exact values of standards of capacity have not been fixed by treaty or regulation such as has decided the standards of weights and length.

MEASURE OF LENGTH

1 Fen	=	·141 in.
10 Fen	= 1 Tsun	= 1·41 in.
10 Tsun	= 1 Chih	= 14·1 in
10 Chih	= 1 Chang	= 141 in. (almost 12 ft.)

POSTAGE AND TELEGRAPH RATES

FROM GREAT BRITAIN TO CHINA

Letters, 2½d. per oz., and 1½d. per oz. or part of oz. over.

Postcards, 1d. Reply postcards, 2d

Printed papers, ½d. per 2 oz. Limit of weight, 4 lb.

Commercial papers, 2½d. per 10 oz., and ½d. per 2 oz. over. Limit of weight, 4 lb.

Samples, 1d. per 4 oz. or less, and ½d. per 2 oz. over. Limit of weight, 12 oz.

Registration, 2d. for each article.

Telegrams. All places except Macao, 4s. 5d. per word; or via Turkey, 4s. 2d. per word.

To Macao, 2d. per word extra.

855

A UNIQUE SPECTACLE IN ASIA

By LORD CURZON

A notable passage from Lord Curzon's prophetic chapters on
Korea in his " Problems of the Far East," written before 1896

THE spectacle of a country possessing an historical antiquity contemporaneous, as alleged, with that of Thebes and Babylon, but owning no ruins ; boasting a separate, if not an independent national existence for centuries, and yet devoid of all external symptoms of strength ; retaining latest of all the kingdoms of the East the title to successful exclusion of the foreigner, and yet animated by no real hostility to aliens ; containing beautiful natural scenery still virgin to the traveller's foot ; claiming to have given to Japan her letters, her science, her religion, and her art, and yet bereft of almost all vestiges of these herself ; inhabited by a people of physical vigour but moral inertness ; well-endowed with resources, yet crippled for want of funds—such a spectacle is one to which I know no counterpart even in Asia, the continent of contrasts, and which from a distance had long and powerfully affected my imagination.

A bridge between Japan and China, Korea is nevertheless profoundly unlike either. It has lacked the virile training of the Feudal System in Japan, and the incentives to industry supplied by the crowded existence of China. Its indifference to religion has left it without the splendid temples that adorn the former country, without the stubborn self-sufficiency of character developed by Confucianism in the latter. Japan swept it clear of all that was beautiful or ancient in the famous invasion of Hideyoshi three centuries ago—an affliction from which it has never recovered. China's policy, until interrupted by recent events, has been to keep it in a state of tutelage ever since.

Placed in an unfortunate geographical position, midway between the two nations, Korea has been, like Issachar, the strong ass couching between two burdens. Suddenly, at the end of the nineteenth century, it wakes up from its long sleep to find the alarum of the nations sounding at its gates ; the plenipotentiaries of great Powers appear in its ports to solicit or to demand reciprocal treaties ; it enters the comity of civilised peoples ; and, still half stupefied by its long repose, relaxes but slowly beneath the doubtful rays of Western civilisation.

KOREA

THE LAND OF THE MORNING CALM

BY ANGUS HAMILTON

THE CHANGING FORTUNES OF THE HERMIT KINGDOM

UNTIL the voyage of the Alceste and Lyra in 1816, men had little knowledge of the coast of Korea, of its archipelagic groups, of the shoals and reefs which made its shores the terror of all mariners. In the map of the Chinese Empire prepared by the Jesuits at Peking in the seventeenth century the space now occupied by the Korean Archipelago was covered with the drawing of an elephant—the conventional sign of ignorance with the cartographers of that time. In the absence of charts and maps the island-fringed shores of the peninsula necessarily became the scene of many shipwrecks, Dutch, American, French, and British shipping meeting in one grim and silent procession a common end : captivity on shore or death in the sea.

A Land Unknown a Century ago

Some of these unfortunate voyagers survived their experiences, leaving the records of their adventures to an incredulous posterity. In the main, although the coasts of Korea bore frequent reference in the past to these early explorers, men of science and brave sons of the high seas as they were, the lapse of time has caused European hydrographers to delete their names from modern maps. Yet, if our first knowledge of Korea is due to their efforts, now long forgotten, it is a pity to deny to their reputation a resting place among the capes and promontories, the islands and shoals, the harbours, strait and tortuous rivers which they locate The names of Broughton, Maxwell, the commander of the Alceste, Basil Ha the commander of the Lyra, are preserve as landmarks on the west, the east, and the south coasts, while Lazareli's share Broughton's Bay, and Unkoffski's linge in the waters of the bay in which foundered. Yet there were many others but what echo do we find of Duroc Schwartz, Pellisier, and the rest—what their fates and subsequent careers ?

Should not their names at least be witness to their pains and labours, to the difficulties which they faced, to the small joy of something attempted, somethin done, which was their sole consolation f many hours of cheerless and empty vigil Korea, the subject of these efforts, projec in the form of a peninsu

Physical Features of Korea

from the south-eastern corn of North-eastern Asia. Begi ning in 43° N., it extenc as far south as 34° 18', and from we to east is confined between 124° 36' ar 130° 47' E. Across the neck of the peninsu there is a mean breadth of two degrees, ar elsewhere an extreme of 135 miles. Th estimated length is 600 miles, with som 1,740 miles of coast line ; while the are is 82,000 square miles. Coterminous fo

857

even miles with the maritime province of Shestakoff ; on the south coast, Fu-san iberia, the northern boundary is separated and Ma-san-po ; on the west coast, om Manchuria and Siberia respectively by Mok-po, Chemulpo and Chi-nam-po. ie Yalu and Tumen rivers. In the south, Harbours of secondary rank on the east raits, named indifferently Broughton are Song Chin ; on the west, Kun-san ; traits, Korea Straits and Tsu-shima and in the north, the Yalu estuary. traits, divide the Hermit Kingdom, as Among the rivers are, in the north, .orea is fre- the Yalu and uently termed, Tumen ; in the om Japan ; to south, the Nak- ie east there is tong ; on the ie Sea of Japan, east the Dungan ; nd on the west on the west the ie Yellow Sea. Ta-dong, Keum, In respect to and Han. Among he general the islands of im- atures, close to portance may be he northern mentioned Quel- order there are part, Komun-do, nportant groups Port Hamilton, f mountains the Korean ith definite cen- Archipelago, and es, such as the Sir James aik-tu-san, con- Hall group. aining the Prior to 1894 ources of the the kingdom was alu and Tumen divided into vers ; while eight provinces. irther south But after the iere are the Dia- Chino - Japanese iond Mountains. war, Japan, tak- he Korean ing advantage of iountain system her newly-won is an eastern position at the ndency, and Korean Court, ivides the brought about a eninsula into reorganisation of wo unequal the internal ad-

MAP OF KOREA AND ITS SURROUNDINGS

arts. Of these ministration, arts, the eastern half is wholly moun- under which the provinces were in- inous, and in places falls sheer into the creased to thirteen. Their names to-day a. In general this littoral is precipitous are as follow : North and South Ham id rocky, unrelieved by any islands or Kyong, North and South Pyong-yang, vers of importance, and possessing few Whang-hai, Kang-won, Kyong, Keui, irbours, while the belt between the Chyung-chyong, Kyong-syang, North and ountains and the coast is narrow and South Chyol-la, and Quelpart. These, accessible, although fertile. The western again, are subdivided into 365 prefec- alf is different. Many lateral ranges tures. Seoul, the capital, and the treaty eak off from the easterly trend of the ports—Pyong-yang, Chi-nam-po, Chemul- ain cordillera, the resulting effect dis- po, Fu-san, Won-san, Kun-san, Mok-po, osing a chaos of broad-chested valleys, Ma-san-po, Wiju, Yong-am-po, and Song randed hills and long, isolated spurs. Chin—are excluded from this arrangement ivers course through the valleys, and the for purposes of individual administration. ast line, fringed with numerous groups At one time the government centred in islands and ringed with mudbanks, is the Emperor, who, assisted by various iusually indented with harbours, some officers of State, ruled as an autocrat. w of which offer valuable accommodation. With the rise of Japanese influence, the Harbours of first-class order on the east Government became decentralised, his ast are Port Lazareff, Won-san, Port Majesty, in recent years, directing affairs through the medium of a Cabinet, in which the ten principal departments of State—the Cabinet, the Home Office, the Foreign Office, the Treasury, the War Office, the Education Department, Justice, the department of Agriculture, Trade and Industry, the Household and the Privy Council—were represented.

The climate of Korea is severe, and varies between extremes of heat and cold, the fertile sheltered provinces of the south and southwest being more populated than those lying in the bleak, sparsely-peopled areas of the north. Estimates of the population fluctuate, and are sometimes as high as 20,000,000, and at other times as low as 12,000,000,

GENERAL VIEW OF THE PORT OF FUSAN

section of the Koreans, but the principa fishing grounds have been long in th possession of the Japanese who, indeed, are in econo mic ascendancy through out the country. Hithert Great Britain, America and Japan have share Korean trade, the forme supplying some 47 pe cent. of imported cottons as well as 25 per cent of the general trade. It i to be feared for the futur that the Korean marke will be the exclusiv possession of Japan, and European commerce wil suffer a considerable blow by its loss. Descended from no single stock, the Korean nation has beer

THE MAIN STREET IN OLD SEOUL, THE CAPITAL OF KOREA

with women in a majority. The pursuits of the people are similar throughout the kingdom, and largely agricultural. The area under cultivation is 6,627,000 acres. In the south, cotton, rice, tobacco, and many varieties of beans and cereals are grown; while in the north attention is paid to hunting, mining, and the lumber industry, in addition to agriculture. Beans, cotton and rice, with the development of the mineral wealth of the country, now under Japanese control and including gold, copper, iron and coal, promise the most satisfactory returns.

Coastal fisheries occupy a small

SCENE ON THE RIVER NEAR CHEMULPO

THE "INDEPENDENCE" ARCH NEAR SEOUL   THE WEST GATE OF THE CITY

THE PRINCIPAL STREET OF SEOUL

SCENES IN AND NEAR THE CITY OF SEOUL

LOOKING OVER THE CITY TOWARDS THE ROMAN CATHOLIC CATHEDRAL

THE ANCIENT OUTER WALLS AROUND THE SUBURBS OF SEOUL

GENERAL VIEW OF THE CITY OF SEOUL

DIFFERENT ASPECTS OF KOREA'S CAPITAL

ormed by the blending of many Asiatic races, including those belonging to the Mongolian and Polynesian groups. Unfortunately, the early history of Korea is far from satisfying the rigid demands of modern criticism, although it is believed that at the reputed migration of the sage Ki-tze, in 1122 B.C., from China to the peninsula the land was peopled by cave-dwellers. Ki-tze, an adherent of the last Shang sovereigns, left China with five thousand followers upon the downfall of the Third Dynasty. Appointed king by his supporters, he gave to his territories the name of Chao-hsien, or Chosen—meaning Morning Rest—and established in his new dominions the laws, polity, and etiquette of China. West of Chao-hsien lay Ma Han, and east of it Shin Han, the three Governments at this date composing the peninsula, while to each of its neighbours Chosen became a model of culture.

Settlement of Korea from China

The dynasty thus founded by Ki-tze produced altogether forty-two kings, and continued to rule over Chosen until 194 B.C. Up to about 200 B.C. a state of intermittent warfare existed between North China and Korea. In 194 B.C., as an after-effect of operations in 206 B.C. by China against the kingdom of Yen, by which name North China was described at this time, a number of Yen fugitives under Wi Man crossed the Yalu, and found asylum with Ki Jun, the king of Chosen. The following year these turned against Ki Jun, who fled to Ma Han, where he was received by the Hiaksai—a tribe whose name literally means " One hundred families "—whose chief he became, and there re-established the Ki-tze dynasty. The rule inaugurated by Wi Man lasted only some eighty-six years, for in 108 B.C. the Chinese Emperor, Wu-wang, attacked Chosen, and, after capturing the capital and killing the king, divided the kingdom into four Chinese provinces in the following year, an arrangement

which continued until 37 A.D. In 57 B.C., Yu Kio, a direct descendant of Wi Man, appeared in Shin Han, where he fashioned out of the remains of a Chinese influx in 225 B.C. the kingdom of Sinra. In 9 B.C. the fortunes of the Ki-tze dynasty were eclipsed, and the kingdom of Hiaksai—also called Kudara and Pehtsi—arose upon the ashes of Ma Han. With the dawn of the Christian era, the peninsula embraced the kingdom of Sinra, Hiaksai, and Chosen, or Korai. Later, other kingdoms—notably Fuyu, Kokorai, and Puhai—which followed it, blossomed and faded in the north, displacing the earlier divisions into which " the Land of the Morning Calm " had been cast by Wu-wang. Of them all, Hiaksai was the foremost, and in 384 A.D. extended a welcome to Buddhism, ultimately passing on to Japan a knowledge of that faith, as of Chinese letters and ethics. Centuries of internecine warfare now supervened, one or other of the little states continually appealing to China, who, wearying of these importunities, finally united with Sinra to crush Hiaksai. The peace that followed was short-lived, for a Buddhist priest, aided by Japanese, set up Hosho, son of the former king, as ruler. Hiaksai was reconquered, when the population fled to Korai, who, in turn, succumbed. Meanwhile, Sinra, having maintained close connection with China throughout the Tang dynasty, 618–907 A.D., had absorbed the whole of the eastern half of the kingdom, while Chinese influence made the capital, Chong-ju, the centre of Sinro-Korean civilisation. Indeed, it was here that the Korean Nido alphabet was discovered. In 902, however, Kung-wo, a Buddhist priest, led a revolt against the ruling power, but was himself displaced in 913 by Wang the Founder, who unified the peninsula under the name of Korai, set up his capital at Song-do, and established Buddhism as the state religion. Wang died

The Rise and Fall of Kingdoms

SIXTEENTH CENTURY ARMS
The loose decorated tunic and helmet, with the swords and maces that formed the arms and equipment of a Korean general in the sixteenth century.

A KOREAN OFFICIAL GOING TO COURT IN A MONO-WHEELED CARRIAGE

in 945 A.D. and his successor recognised the supremacy of China, united under the Northern Sung dynasty.

The territories of Korai now extended beyond the Yalu to Liao-tung, a circumstance which precipitated, early in the eleventh century, constant collisions with hordes of Khitan Tartars. Defeated in the trans-border region by these barbarians, Korea barred their further incursions by the construction of a wall, 200 miles in length, 25 ft. in height, which stretched from coast to coast across the peninsula. In addition, the king allied himself with the Kin Tartars. When that kingdom was destroyed by the Mongols in 1230, Korea made submission to the conqueror, but the murder of a Mongol ambassador in 1231 called forth an invasion by the Mongols in 1240. After prolonged resistance, the king acknowledged the supremacy of Mangu Khan in 1256, and visited his court. With peace established in Korea, Kublai Khan, the successor of Mangu Khan, made the peninsula a base of operations, between 1266–1281, for repeated expeditions against Japan. Invariably disastrous, these attacks encouraged the islanders to make reprisals, and, until the fall of the Mongol dynasty in 1368, the Korean

Incursions of the Tartars

coast was continually harried by Japanese corsairs.

With the downfall of the Mongols, there quickly came an end to the rule of the Wang dynasty. Receiving the demand of the Ming Emperor for the resumption of the payment of tribute, the Wang emperor, by way of reply, ordered General Yi Ta-jo to lead the army against the Middle Kingdom. Unfortunately, Yi Ta-jo led his forces against the throne, and, deposing the Wang, founded in 1392 the dynasty of which a minor branch still holds nominal power. The change was for the better, but the new dynasty became entirely dependent on China, although on occasion tribute was rendered to Japan. Yi Ta-jo revived the name Chao-hsien, transferred the seat of Government from Song-do to Seoul, or Han-yang, and divided the kingdom into the eight provinces—Ham-kyong, Kang-won, Kyong-syang, Chol-la, Chung - chong, Kyong - kwi, Hwang-hai, and Phyongan. Buddhism was suppressed, and its priests were forbidden to enter Seoul, while a stern Confucianism became the state religion. At the same time the custom of performing human sacrifice, of burying alive slaves and others at the funerals of famous people, was abolished.

Abolition of Human Sacrifice

At first the descendants of Yi Ta-jo were vigorous rulers who increased the centralisation of the government and advanced the welfare of the people. But when these conditions had prevailed for nearly two centuries, the Government, sapped by generations of prosperity, became neglectful and the position of the kingdom gradually dete- **Invasion of Korea by Japan** riorated. Meanwhile in Japan, long years of internal warfare and the downfall of the Ashikaga Shōgunate had brought about the complete suspension of the tribute-bearing missions from Korea. When at last peace was established under Hideyoshi, this Shōgun, ambitious to conquer China, and attracted by the weakness of Korea, demanded in 1591 the renewal of tribute and a passage through the peninsula for his armies. This demand was rejected, and in the following year Hideyoshi launched his invading hosts upon the kingdom.

Early in May, 1592, the van of a force, ultimately aggregating 250,000 men, set sail under Hideyi as commander-in-chief, with Yuki-naja Konishi, a Roman Catholic convert, in command of the Central army, Kiyomasa Kato, a Buddhist, at the head of the Eastern army, and Kuroda as the leader of the Western army. With them were 50,000 horses and 300,000 firearms, this being the first occasion of their use by the Japanese in a foreign war. Fu-san was conquered on May 25th, Seoul eighteen days later, while in July the Ta-dong was reached and Pyong-yang taken. In the meantime the Court fled from Seoul to Pyong-yang, and from that town to An-ju, when the news came that the Korean Admiral Yi Sun-sin, by means of an iron-clad, shaped like a tortoise and covered with iron plates bearing terrible spikes, had sunk the Japanese fleet, carrying supplies and some 60,000 reinforcements. The effect of this loss and the appearance of a Chinese army, 60,000 strong, in aid **Korea and China Allied Against Japan** of the Koreans, stemmed the further advance of the Japanese. The allies attacked Pyong-yang on August 27th, 1592, with equivocal success, but returned to the assault on February 10th, 1593, when the Japanese, under Konishi, were compelled to fall back upon the capital, where the forces under Kato were in position. Early in the following month a general battle was fought from which the Chinese were com-

pelled to withdraw, while the enemy was unable to pursue.

Both sides were now glad to resume the negotiations for peace which had been opened previously, and were conducted chiefly by the Chinese Chin I-kei. In spite of the opposition of the Koreans, a treaty was concluded by which Korea ceded the most southerly provinces to Japan and recognised her tributary relationship to that country. Commercial intercourse between China and Japan was to be resumed, and Hideyoshi was to marry the daughter of the Emperor of China and to be recognised as that monarch's equal. Until the completion of this convention the Japanese were to withdraw to the coast of Fusan, where they were to garrison twelve strongholds. On May 23rd, 1593, the Japanese evacuated Seoul. A little later the Chinese retired northwards and, after much fruitless negotiation, the Middle Kingdom despatched an embassy which was received in Fushimi on October 24th, 1595, by Hideyoshi. As the message from the Emperor of China with which the mission was entrusted merely recognised **Renewal of War with Japan** Hideyoshi as "King of Japan," a title which had been previously granted to the Shōguns of the Ashikaga family, war broke out again. In January, 1597, after the Japanese fleet had defeated the Korean fleet, the troops made a triumphant advance to the neighbourhood of Seoul, when the destruction of the Japanese fleet by the united Chinese and Korean squadrons compelled the Japanese army to withdraw to the sea-coast. During the operations the troops utterly devastated the country, destroying Chong-ju, the old capital of Sinra.

In the south the struggle centred round the fortress of Urusan, where the Japanese were besieged by Chinese-Korean forces until February 13th, 1598, when the town was relieved. With that success the war concluded, the port of Fusan and its fishing privileges remaining in Japanese keeping. A few months later, on September 8th, Hideyoshi, who, meanwhile, had recalled his troops, died; but it was not until 1623, when the Shōgun Iyemitsu successfully demanded the resumption of the Korean Embassy, that relations were resumed, the humiliating necessity of rendering tribute continuing until 1790, when it was discontinued.

While these events were happening in Korea, the Ming dynasty was threatened

THE EMPEROR'S RESIDENCE IN THE IMPERIAL PALACE AT SEOUL

Underwood & Underwood, London

THE IMPERIAL THRONE OF KOREA   TEMPLE WHERE THE EMPEROR WORSHIPS

GIANT STONE DOG AT THE ENTRANCE, TO GUARD THE PALACE AGAINST FIRE

IN AND ABOUT THE IMPERIAL PALACE AT SEOUL

with a Manchu invasion. Therefore, as a general precaution, in 1616 the Chinese Government agreed with the Korean Government to create a waste belt, about 62 miles broad and 298 miles long, on the right bank of the Yalu.

Neutral Belt Between China and Korea Within this zone all villages were destroyed and the inhabitants expelled; while on the Chinese side it was strengthened further by wooden palisades and a double or triple row of forts. As a consequence of the assistance now afforded to China, the Manchus invaded Korea in 1627, and, defeating the allied Chinese-Korean forces, besieged Seoul, until the

PRINCE HEUNG-SUNG, THE TAI WON KUN
Father of the Ex-Emperor of Korea and regent during his son's minority. He massacred many Christian priests in 1866, and was the enemy of progress for many years.

king, who had fled to the island of Kang-wha, gave in his submission. But no sooner had the enemy retreated than he declined to fulfil his promises, and a fresh invasion of the Manchus followed, with the result that in 1636-37 the king was forced to conclude a new convention. By the terms of this agreement Korea broke off all connection with China, and, among other things, promised to render yearly tribute to the Manchus. After the Manchu conquest of Peking, the Korean tribute was diminished until it became financially unimportant, while, further, its delivery was fixed at intervals of three years.

The modern period in the history of the peninsula coincides in some degree with the advent of Christianity, which, according to native records, took place in 1686. Between this date and 1792, when the Pope formally recognised the Church of Korea, the faith spread slowly. By 1730, in the reign of King In-jong, the two provinces of Whang-hai and Kang-won were familiar with the doctrines of Roman Catholicism, the town of Yang-geun being regarded as the actual birthplace of the movement. Fifty years later, in 1780, Kwun Chul-sin, possessed of a single copy of the scriptures, established a society for the study of Christianity; and in the same year Alexandre de Govea, the Franciscan, baptised at Peking the first of Korean colporteurs. Five years later the number of supporters had increased so much that the faith aroused opposition and the throne was memorialised, active persecution beginning in 1791, with the execution of six important converts. In 1792 the Church of Korea was entrusted to the Bishop of Peking, who despatched, as the first ordained priest to the new field, Père Tsiou, a Chinese, who, together with thirty converts, gave up his life in 1801.

A generation later Korea was detached from the diocese of North China. The first incumbent, M. Bruguière, created Bishop of Korea by Pope Gregory XVI., was detained on the northern border of the kingdom through the intrigues of Père Yu, a Chinese priest already in residence in Seoul, and died before entering his see. In 1835 Père Maubant, of the Société des Missions Etrangères, was appointed to the bishopric, and, in 1837, was given the assistance of two French priests, one of whom was Bishop Imbert. At this date there were nine thousand converts, but the imprudent zeal of their leaders gave the signal for an outburst of bloodthirsty persecution in which the three priests, together with some seventy converts, were beheaded, and sixty others strangled.

Christian Martyrs in Korea Undeterred by the fate of their predecessors, two more priests arrived in 1844. In 1846 the French Government wrote complaining of the murder of its three subjects, and despatched, in 1847, the French frigate La Gloire and the corvette La Victorieuse in support of its letter. The two vessels were wrecked, however, and the outbreak of the Revolution of

PEACE WITH JAPAN IN 1876: ARRIVAL OF THE KOREAN AMBASSADOR AT YOKOHAMA

BRITISH AND CHINESE ENVOYS SIGNING THE TREATY WITH KOREA IN 1882

1848 prevented further action. Meanwhile the King died, and in 1849 Chul Thong came to the throne, after which, until his demise in 1863, religious persecution ceased. During these fourteen years the strength of Korean Catholicism steadily increased. In 1857 there were 16,500 converts and at the close of this reign there were nearly twenty thousand adherents, many of whom were massacred by the succeeding ruler in 1866. With the death of Chul Thong, Queen Chol, the leading wife of the late monarch, seized the government and nominated to the succession a lad of twelve years of age, Heui Yi, who was deposed in 1907. On this boy's behalf a regency was proclaimed by his father, Prince Heung-sung, commonly styled the Tai Won Kun. Although no steps were taken at first to arrest the spread of the Gospel, the demand of a Russian warship for freedom of trade, in January, 1866, revived the alarm which had been created in 1860, when the boundaries of Russia and Korea had become co-terminous through the cession of the Ussuri province to Russia by China. The demand was rejected, but the Tai Won Kun, some two months later and in order to emphasise his contempt of foreign overtures, signed the death warrants of a number of French missionaries, including Bishop Berneux, Bretenieres, Beaulieu, Dorie, Petitnicolas, Pourthie, Daveluy, Aumaitre and Huin. In fact, only three priests escaped, Calais, Feron and Ridel, the latter conveying to Chifu the story of the massacre.

By this time Korea had thoroughly aroused the curiosity of the Occident and was the subject of frequent investigation. In June of this same year (1866) an American sailing ship, the Surprise, was wrecked off Whang-hai Province, the crew being safely escorted out of the kingdom; but in September the crew of the General Sherman were butchered when landing on the Ta-dong River. The massacre of the French priests and American soldiers provoked the respective Governments to demand satisfaction from China, and, with China's repudiation of responsibility for the acts of her vassal, a French squadron under Admiral Rose, on October 11th, 1866, blockaded the Han river and attacked Kang-wha; while in May, 1871, an American flotilla under Admiral Rogers, comprising

Progress of Romanism in Korea

Christian Persecutors Punished

the Colorado, Alaska, Bernicia, Monocacy, and Palos; repeated the operation. Neither fleet was very successful, and knowledge of their discomfiture spurred the Tai Won Kun' to fresh excesses, which continued until 1873, when disaffection against his policy compelled the Regent to surrender the reins of authority to their rightful holder.

Since 1866, the young king had been married to a member of the Min family, a niece of the wife of the Tai Won Kun, and under her influence conditions now rapidly improved. Unfortunate "incidents" were still to occur; but when, in September, 1875, a Korean fort fired upon a Japanese warship engaged in survey work off the coast, and in turn was seized, a treaty of peace was promptly signed with the assent of China on February 27th, 1876. By this instrument Fusan was opened forthwith to Japanese settlement, and Chemulpo and Won-san in 1880, while Ministers Plenipotentiary were to be exchanged and the independence of the kingdom specifically recognised. The first Ministers took up their respective duties in 1879, by which time there were indications of a grave crisis through a conflict of policy between the Queen's party and a reforming Opposition. The Queen's faction comprised the Min family and all other sponsors for the opening of the kingdom. On the other side was a group of Extremists, who, having imbibed in Japan an enthusiasm for reform, failed to realise that the sweeping changes already effected in the one country were unsuited to the other. While the Japanese supported the confused yearnings of the Extremists, the other faction fell back upon the counsels of China, which no longer wished to play an indecisive rôle in Korea. Thus grouped on the two sides of Korea were the future antagonists, when matters were complicated by the attempt of the Tai Won Kun to engineer a military rising in July, 1882, with a view to securing the reins of government again. Irrespective of party, both factions were attacked by the riotous soldiery, who, after killing many of the Min family and driving the queen from the capital, destroyed the Japanese Legation, killed many Japanese, and recalled the Tai Won Kun. As soon as news of the revolution reached the Chinese Government, Li Hung-chang despatched to the capital some 3,000

Opening of the Hermit Kingdom

troops, by the aid of whom the queen was restored and the Tai Won Kun deported to Tientsin, Japan receiving ample compensation. Although the revolt was suppressed, Chinese troops remained close at hand, and in October an officer of the force, Yuan-shi-kai, afterwards to become Viceroy of Pechili, was appointed Chinese Resident to the Korean Court.

China, once more established in the Peninsula, now proceeded to issue, in respect of Korea, her " Trade and Frontier Regulations, 1882," while America followed with a commercial treaty. In 1883 treaties with Great Britain and Germany were signed, Italy and Russia following suit in 1884. In this year the absolute isolation which Korea had so long preserved terminated with the opening of the capital to foreign residence and the provinces to foreign travellers. For the moment, however, the development of Korea's foreign relations was checked by a second collision between the Min faction and the Extremists, who, continuing to receive the sympathy of Japanese, were endeavouring to arrange for a Japanese man-o'-war to support a *coup de main*. Details of the plot becoming known, the leaders of the Extremists decided upon immediate action, and between nightfall of December 4th and dawn of the 5th six of the principal Korean statesmen were cut down. While these events were occurring the conspirators compelled the king to summon Japanese help, and before light had broken completely on the 5th, 400 Japanese soldiers were in possession of the Imperial Palace. Meanwhile the Koreans gathered to the attack, and, supported by Chinese troops, drove the Japanese on the 6th from the palace to their legation. On the 7th, with renewed vigour, the allies wrecked the legation, compelling the Japanese to retreat to the coast.

The collision of 1884 resulted in the payment of a second indemnity to Japan, but in April, 1885, a convention was signed at Tientsin by Count—now the Marquis—Ito and Li Hung-chang by which both Powers agreed to withdraw their military forces from Korea, each undertaking to

inform the other of any future decision to send troops there. By this arrangement tranquillity was secured to Korea for nine years, in the course of which treaties were enacted with France in 1886, and Austria in 1892, while the ports of Fu-san, Won-san and Chemulpo were opened, the telegraph introduced, a government hospital and an English language school established. At the same time the passage of these years was marked by continual rivalry between the Queen's faction and the Tai Won Kun,

THE EMPEROR HEUI HI AND THE PRESENT EMPEROR

In the spring of 1907 the Emperor Heui Hi—on the left—was deposed by the Japanese on account of his opposition to their measures, and his son, the Crown Prince, was placed on the throne.

now returned from China and secretly supported by the Japanese, as well as by the increasing domination of the Chinese Resident, a circumstance no less resented by Japan, who strove to detach Korea from her allegiance to China.

Matters drifted from year to year, until in May, 1894, the activity of some Tonghak rebels, who previously had defeated a Korean force, caused the King of Korea to appeal to China for assistance. The

LANDING JAPANESE WAR STORES AT CHEMULPO IN 1894: AMMUNITION TO THE LEFT, PONTOONS IN SEGMENTS TO THE RIGHT

THE BATTLE THAT MADE THE JAPANESE MASTERS OF KOREA: CAPTURE OF PHYONG-YANG IN 1894

In the war with China in 1894 Japan captured the important strategical point of Phyong-Yang, in North-west Korea, after a pitched battle in which 14,000 Japanese routed 13,000 Chinese.

Chinese, having notified Japan in accordance with the stipulation of the Chino-Japanese treaty of 1885, embarked 2,000 men, who, landing on June 10th, proceeded to Asan, a point some forty miles south of the capital and the centre of the disaffected area, whereupon Japan, already prepared, disembarked some 10,000 men, and took possession of Seoul, Chemulpo, and Fu-san.

In the interesting diplomatic correspondence that followed, Japan endeavoured to justify her action, but negotiations only led to a deadlock, and on July 20th the Japanese Minister in Seoul threatened the Korean Government with decisive measures unless the Chinese troops were ordered out of the country. At the request of the King of Korea, the Powers now intervened, and China had agreed to the simultaneous withdrawal of the Japanese and Chinese forces when, on July 23rd, Japanese forcibly occupied the Imperial Palace, and dispossessed the pro-Chinese party. Two days later, after three Japanese cruisers had destroyed three obsolete Chinese men-o'-war, the second-class Japanese cruiser Naniwa sank the Kowshing — an unarmed and defenceless British steamer bound for Chemulpo with 1,200 troops, the bulk of whom were drowned. On the 29th the Chinese were defeated in the first land engagement, and on August 1st war was declared.

Hostilities now proceeded apace. August and a part of September were occupied by the Japanese in moving their troops through Korea, while, in the same way, the Chinese advanced across Manchuria. By mid-September the opposing forces were in position about Phyong-yang, where, on the 15th, a general attack by the Japanese on the Chinese entrenchments resulted in victory for the Mikado. The Chinese now retired from Korea, and on

THE MURDERED QUEEN OF KOREA
On the morning of October 8th, 1905, she was murdered by a mob of Japanese and Koreans incited by Japanese agents, and was degraded after her death.

January 8th, 1895, the King, at the behest of the Japanese, solemnly renounced Chinese suzerainty. Still later, by the terms of the Treaty of Shimonoseki, April 17th, 1895, China acknowledged the independence of Korea, and withdrew from the country.

Emboldened by success, Japanese influence in Korea now began rapidly to assert itself. Japanese advisers were allotted to various departments of State, abuses were checked and reforms devised. Unfortunately, the spirit of reformation was too impetuous, and progress was blocked by the objections of the Royal Family, as well as of the Extremists, to many of the proposed changes. Opposition, however, merely aroused the irritation of the Japanese, who, disinclined to brook delay, had begun to realise that one or other of the rival domestic factions would have to be deposed. Thus, although Independence Day was celebrated on June 6th by the King and the whole nation, by the end of July an impasse had arisen during which the Japanese Minister, Count Inouyé, who was the friend of the Royal Family, retired.

Early in August another Minister arrived, in the person of Viscount Miura, who considered that the adjustment of difficulties in Korea needed only vigorous action. In this view he was supported by the Tai Won Kun, who, shortly after Viscount Miura's arrival in Seoul, appealed to the Japanese Minister for assistance in effecting a radical change. With the connivance of the Tai Won Kun and, as is generally believed, with the sanction of the Japanese Minister, a plan was formed to seize the palace, to murder the Queen, to depose the King, and to establish once again the rule of the ex-Regent. About three o'clock on the morning of October 8th, 1895, at the instigation of Viscount Miura, a mob of Japanese with a number of Koreans,

YEE YONG IK
The Korean Machiavelli, who rose
from a coolie to political power.

KIM KA CHIM
Korea's greatest politician.

HAN BIM CHUL
A Korean Foreign Minister.

PRINCE MIN YONG WHAN
This general committed suicide when his
country lost her independence in 1905.

PRINCE YI CHAY SOON
Known as "The Fat Prince."

GENERAL KWAN CHAY HUNG
Commander of the Household Troops.

MIN YONG QUAN
Korean Prince and society leader.

SOME NOTABLE FIGURES IN THE MODERN HISTORY OF KOREA

under the direction of the Tai Won Kun, gave effect to the plot. Three days later, while the monarch was a close prisoner, a spurious decree was issued, degrading the late Queen to the level of a woman of the lowest class, and applauding the fate that had befallen her Majesty as a fitting punishment for her interference in State affairs. On the following day, by a further edict and out of pity for the Crown Prince, the posthumous status of the late Queen was raised to the rank of a concubine of the first class, while on October 15th, a third edict stated that preparations for the selection of a new Royal bride were to be made.

Degradation of a Dead Queen

At this stage the Japanese Government awoke to the urgency of the situation, and recalled Viscount Miura. In the meantime, the Tai Won Kun continued to offer insults to the late Queen's memory, and to subject his Majesty to a humiliating confinement. For three months this condition of affairs prevailed, but after this the King contrived to turn the tables upon his oppressors by escaping on February 11th, 1896, to the Russian Legation, where he at once proceeded to revoke the various decrees that the Tai Won Kun had circulated.

With the return of the King the wane of Japanese influence began. In order to meet the situation, on May 14th the new Japanese Minister, Baron Komura, concluded with M. Waeber, the Russian Minister at Seoul, a Russo-Japanese Memorandum, by which the two Powers agreed to limit their respective military forces in Korea to 800 men, Japan maintaining an additional 200 police for patrolling the military telegraph line she had built between Fu-san and Seoul. The principle of this agreement was confirmed on the 9th of the following month at Moscow between Prince Lebanoff and the Marquis Yamagata, when it was agreed that the two Powers jointly should advise upon the retrenchment of superfluous expenditure,

MEMORIAL ARCH AT SEOUL TO THE MEMORY OF THE MURDERED QUEEN

and should advance any loans necessary for the execution of reforms. At the same time Russia was conceded the right of laying a telegraph line between her frontier and Seoul, where the King still remained under the protection of the Russian Minister.

Taking advantage of his presence in the Russian Legation, many Russians of high rank visited his Majesty, a curious light being thrown upon the Russian view of the Waeber-Komura-Lebanoff-Yamagata Convention by the report that M. Waeber was negotiating for the lease of the spacious harbour of Ma-san-po. At the same time the King, on July 4th, granted to French interests, which were believed to mask a Russian claim, the right to construct a railway between Seoul and Wiju, and, in the autumn of 1896, a lumber concession on the Yalu and Tumen rivers for twenty years to M. Brunner, a Russian merchant from Vladivostock, who, in point of fact, covered the identity of the Russo-Chinese Bank, the direct instrument of the Russian Government. This concession was liable to forfeiture unless work on it was begun within five years. Other concessions were also awarded, including one for the construction of the Seoul-Chemulpo Railway to an American, acting for Japanese interests. In general an era of progress had arrived, domestic development being promoted by Chief Commissioner of Customs and Financial Adviser to the Government, Mr., now Sir John, McLeavy Brown, who, possessed of large powers, applied a vigorous brush to the cleansing of the capital. By his agency many streets were widened and drained, and reforms were inaugurated. Early in 1897 the King decided to leave the Russian Legation, and in February his Majesty took up his residence in the Myung-yi Palace, which had been recently erected. The change of abode was not accompanied at first by any

Reforms by the British Commissioner

JAPAN'S POWER IN KOREA: JAPANESE ARMY PASSING THE TRIUMPHAL ARCH ERECTED NEAR SEOUL AFTER THE VICTORY AT ASAN

retrograde policy. A mining concession was granted to Germans, foreign language and missionary schools were founded, and the main commercial route of the country freed from obstructions. Still later Chi-nam-po and Mok-po were opened as treaty ports. These events, however, had hardly taken place when a reactionary movement set in, **Russian** the effect of which was ob- **Intrigues** scured in the summer of 1897 **in Seoul** by the vigorous manifestation of Russia's interest in Korea under circumstances which were dictated by the requirements of Russian policy in Manchuria. Since the eclipse of Japanese influence, owing to the events of 1895, the training of the Korean Army had reverted to Russian instructors, and, beginning in this quarter, a more decided note now appeared in the Russian policy. In August, Colonel Potiata, three officers and ten non-commissioned officers of the Russian Army came to Seoul as additional military instructors to the Korean troops, their appearance coinciding with the displacement of M. Waeber by M. de Speyer. Arriving on September 7th, M. de Speyer at once demanded the cession of a coaling station on Deer Island, near Fusan, in an effort to offset Japanese prestige at that port. Rebuffed in this direction, the Russian representative, encouraged by a certain group of Korean officials, contrived to dispossess Mr. McLeavy Brown from his dual position as Financial Adviser and Chief Commissioner of Customs, and caused M. Kir Alexieff, an official of the St. Petersburg Bureau of Finance, to be appointed the Director of the Finance Department. At the same time, in order to give colour to the magnitude of Russian financial interests in Korea, the Russo-Chinese Bank opened a branch institution under the guise of the Russo-Korean Bank. As these events were in process of evolution, the King, anxious to emphasise the independence of Korea, pronounced, on October 12th, the elevation of the kingdom to the rank of empire, and changed its official designation to Dai Han, that is, Great Han, a step eliciting immediate recognition from all the Powers.

SIR JOHN MCLEAVY BROWN
Late Financial Adviser and Commissioner of the Korean Customs.

With the dawn of 1898, the aspect of Russo-Korean intrigues against Mr. McLeavy Brown caused Great Britain to make a naval demonstration in Chemulpo Harbour, whereupon, as the moment had not arrived when the position in Korea could be forced with impunity by Russia, M. Alexieff was made to retire in March, while M. de Speyer was relieved by M. Matunine in April, when the Russo-Korean bank was closed down and the Russian military mission withdrawn. The set-back which the Russian policy in Korea now suffered was further emphasised by the conclusion of the Nishi-Rosen Convention on April 25th, by which Russia and Japan, after recognising the entire independence of Korea and mutually engaging to abstain from all interference in its affairs, pledged themselves to confer with each other before complying with any Korean requests for military or financial assistance. At the same time Russia specifically undertook not to interfere with the development of commercial and industrial relations between Japan and Korea. As if mindful of what had followed the Waeber-Komura-Lebanoff-Yamagata Convention, Japan induced the Korean Government to proclaim, in June, 1898, the opening of Ma-san-po as a treaty port. The straining of the political situation did not appreciably affect the course of domestic events, which were characterised by singular inconsistencies. Thus, at one and the same time in 1898 an edict was promulgated forbidding the granting of any further concessions, while the organisation of the Seoul Electric Light and Tramway Company, and of the Seoul **Public Works** Waterworks was authorised. **in Korea's** In September Japanese inter- **Capital** ests were given permission to build the Seoul-Fusan Railway, and in January, 1899, Japanese diplomacy brought about the surrender of the French Seoul-Wiju concession on the ground of the expiration of the time limit within which the project had to be started. Forfeiture, however, was merely nominal; and, as the Russians were anxious to prevent the construction of

EMPEROR'S GRAND MASTER OF HORSE PASSING THROUGH THE MAIN STREET OF SEOUL

COMPANY OF KOREAN SOLDIERS AT DRILL OUTSIDE THE OLD PALACE IN SEOUL

Photos Underwood & Underwood, London

WAR MINISTER PLAYING CHESS
The benign old gentleman on the left playing at So-ban, or Korean chess, was Minister of War at the time of the last Japanese invasion.

Bureau, of which Yi Yong Ik became president, undertaking that only French engineers and French materials should be employed. In regard to Ma-san-po, M. Pavlov effected, in April 1900, the Russo-Korean Convention, a secret agreement by which it was provided that, while none of the land about Ma-san-po Harbour should be disposed of in any way to any foreign Power, Russia should be permitted to establish a coaling depôt and a special settlement at this treaty port. For two years the terms of this instrument remained undisclosed, while the outbreak of the Boxer crisis in the summer of 1900 put an end for the time being to the diplomatic rivalries of Russia and Japan.

With the opening of the new century, Russia renewed her intrigues against British domination of the Korean Customs. On the

the Seoul-Wiju railway passing into the hands of the Japanese, at the request of the French Minister, M. Colin de Plancy, the concession was not revoked. Later in the year a mission of the Greek Church took up its residence in Seoul, the struggle between the respective interests of Russia and Japan advancing a step when the plans of the foreign quarter, and the regulations controlling the opening of Ma-san-po, were issued at the request of the Japanese.

With the new year, 1900, M. Pavlov, the Russian Acting Minister in Peking, arrived in Seoul, fresh from his diplomatic defeat of Sir Claude Macdonald, when two points immediately claimed his attention—the one referring to the Seoul-Wiju Railway, the other to Ma-san-po. Working in conjunction with the French Minister and Yi Yong Ik, a Korean official, afterwards Minister of Finance, the Korean Government was persuaded to take over the construction of the line, creating for the purpose a North-Western Railway

EMPEROR LEAVING THE NEW PALACE
When the Emperor goes in procession, his favourites ride veiled from the view of the populace. The new palace was built in one of the poorest parts of Seoul and made a great transformation of the quarter.

AN IMPERIAL PROCESSION PASSING THROUGH THE STREETS OF SEOUL

The imperial chair of state is canopied with yellow silk richly tasselled, screened with delicate silken panels of the same colour, and bearing wings to keep off the sun. Mr. Angus Hamilton says that an imperial procession presents " elements strangely suggestive of burlesque, romance, and the humours of a pantomime, and looks quite mediæval."

plea that Lady Om, the Emperor's principal concubine, required Mr. McLeavy Brown's house, the Chief Commissioner was given, in March, summary notice to leave his private quarters. Fortunately the British Government sharply intervened and the plan miscarried. Foiled in this, Russian diplomacy was successful in another direction, and, in April, 1901, as the five-year penalty clause in respect of M. Brunner's lumber concession had expired, M. Pavlov secured its renewal for a further three years. Meanwhile, Yi Yong Ik had not been idle, and, supported by the Korean Foreign Minister, he made the announcement that a loan of 5,000,000 yen had been arranged between the Korean Government and a French syndicate, the Yunnan Syndicate, upon the security of the Customs. As the terms were preposterous and had been designed without the authority of the Chief Commissioner, Mr. McLeavy Brown declined to sanction the arrangement, in which attitude he was supported by the Ministers of Great Britain and Japan, who strongly opposed anything which might give to France—and therefore Russia—a particular predominance in

France as Cat's paw of Russia

the affairs of the country. Mr. McLeavy Brown was at once called upon to resign his office by Yi Yong Ik, but the matter dropped before the firm front of the British Minister. By way of reply to this activity of the Russians, the first sods of the Seoul-Fusan Railway were turned, at Yong-tong-po, near Chemulpo, on August 20th, 1901, and at Fusan on September 21st.

The course of events in Korea was now attracting so much general attention that on January 30th, 1902, the momentous announcement was heralded of an offensive-defensive alliance between Great Britain and Japan, with special reference to Korea. Seven weeks later, on March 19th, communication of an additional clause to the Franco-Russian Treaty was made, by which it was no less plain that France would support Russia in the event of Great Britain assisting Japan in any Far Eastern war. External political events were now quite overshadowing the domestic situation in Korea, largely concerned with quarrels between the Extremists and Conservatives, with the Korean currency question, and with the founding of a Japanese bank. In May,

Britain Supports Japan

GROUP OF SCHOOLBOYS WITH THEIR
TEACHERS

SORCERERS CROWNING A BRIDE, WITH
PAINTED FACE

ENTRANCE TO HOME OF A WELL-TO-DO
KOREAN OFFICIAL

GENTLEMEN OUTSIDE THE TEMPLE OF
THE GOD OF WAR

FAMILIAR SCENES OF KOREAN LIFE

Photos Underwood & Underwood, London

A BUDDHIST ABBOT | KOREAN GESANG OR GEISHA | LADY'S STREET COSTUME

LADIES ATTACHED TO THE COURT | FAMILY OF THE ARISTOCRATIC CLASS

TYPES OF THE KOREAN PEOPLE

however, the formal opening of work on the Seoul-Wiju was celebrated. The following month witnessed the arrival in Seoul of Baron Gabriel de Gunsberg, a Russian secret service agent, who opened, in April, 1903, the Seoul offices of the Lumber Company, into which M. Brunner's Yalu concession had now blossomed.

During the next two months numerous lumber camps, comprising parties of **Korean Lumber Concessions** Cossack, Korean and Chinese lumbermen under Russian protection, were established on the river, while on July 20th an agreement was concluded between officials of the company and Korean frontier officers, by which the whole of the important Yong-an-po district, commanding the mouth of the great Yalu River, was leased to the company.

Government entered into direct telegraphic negotiations with St. Petersburg, the failure of which was disclosed when, on February 9th, 1904, a Japanese squadron under Admiral Uriu sank, in Chemulpo Harbour, two Russian vessels, the cruiser Variag and the gunboat and portguard ship Koreietz.

Six days later the first division of Kuroki's army disembarked at Chemulpo, and was followed a little later by the two remaining divisions and the troops which were to hold the lines of communication and to act as garrison of the peninsula.

From Chemulpo, Kuroki advanced, and the first shots of the land campaign were fired when, on February 28th, a Cossack patrol engaged a Japanese picket at Pyong-yang. A little later, on March 20th, Pyong-yang itself was occupied in

HOW THE KOREAN VILLAGES SUFFERED IN THE JAPANESE INVASION
The village of Sonkyori, burnt during the Chino-Japanese War in 1894, in the course of the battle which bears its name.

Undisturbed by the fact that the attention of the whole world, and of Japan in particular, was now focussed upon the Korean border, Russia proceeded by various devices to make good her position on the Yalu. When the several camps had been equipped with telegraphic communication, provided with defensive works, and the usual conditions of the Russo-Korean frontier had given way manifestly to military occupation, the Japanese Minister at Seoul delivered, on August 25th, 1903, an ultimatum to the Korean Foreign Office against the confirmation of the agreement in respect of Yong-an-po. In spite of the emphatic character of the Japanese protest the activity of the Russian force in the lumber camps in no wise abated, and after the lapse of a few weeks the Japanese

force, and the coastal base changed from Chemulpo to Chi-nam-po. Skirmishes were now frequent, and at Anju, as at Chong-ju on March 28th, there were encounters, while on April 6th, the van **Victorious Advance of Kuroki** of the Japanese advance occupied Wiju, Korean soil ceasing to be belligerent territory when, between April 29th and May 1st, Kuroki forced the passage of the Yalu.

The first act of the Japanese Government after the declaration of war against Russia on February 10th was to arrange a protocol with Korea. It was dated February 23rd, and comprised six articles. Briefly it may be said to have guaranteed the independence as well as the territorial integrity of the kingdom; and, after promising to ensure the safety and repose of the Imperial House, to have conferred upon Japan the responsibility of securing administrative reforms and providing for the protection of the kingdom. As a mandate from Korea, this instrument gave to Japan a free hand. While satisfaction was expressed at the prospects of Korea, there were many who found a disquieting element in the liberty exercised by Japanese subjects in various parts of the country. As the months passed without any perceptible improvement in administrative conditions, the announcement, on June 17th, 1904, that a concession of waste lands in the kingdom had been made to a Japanese subject, Mr. Nagamori, without payment and for a term of fifty years, gave rise to such a loud and long-sustained national protest that the obnoxious measure was withdrawn.

JAPANESE MARTIAL LAW IN KOREA

Three Koreans shot for pulling up rails as a protest against the seizure of land without payment by Japanese, who had obtained the concession from the Emperor.

A few weeks later, on August 22nd, Japan, still concerned with the necessity for reform, concluded a further treaty with Korea by which the financial affairs of the Government were placed in the hands of a Japanese adviser, and a foreigner, recommended by Japan, became adviser to the Foreign Office. Further, the Japanese Government was to be consulted before the Korean Government entered into any diplomatic relations with foreign Powers, granted any concessions, or allotted any contracts to foreign subjects. In spite of the control over Korean affairs granted to Japan by this Convention, general recognition of the Japanese position was not obtained from the Powers until the Treaty of Portsmouth, August 29th, 1905, put an end to the Russo-Japanese War. By this treaty the Russian Government acknowledged that Japan possessed in Korea paramount political, military, and economic interests, and engaged neither to obstruct nor to interfere with the measures of guidance, protection, and control which the Government of Japan might find it necessary to take. Less than a month later, on September 27th, a new Anglo-Japanese treaty was published, by which, so long as the principle of equal opportunity for the commerce and industry of all nations was not impaired, Great Britain similarly recognised the special position acquired and held by the Japanese in Korea.

THE JAPANESE ADMINISTRATION OF KOREA

This photographic reproduction gives a grim picture of the summary methods adopted by the Japanese officials in disposing of the inmates of a Korean gaol.

ANCIENT MONUMENTS AND FORTIFICATIONS WHICH ARE BEING DESTROYED

This photograph of the Gates of Won-ju, taken in September, 1907, illustrates how the ancient walls and gateways are being destroyed under the Japanese rule, and may be considered typical of what is happening generally in Korea.

Fortified by the action of Great Britain, Japan now proceeded to secure the assent of the Emperor of Korea to the establishment of a Japanese protectorate over his kingdom. With this purpose in view, the Japanese Government despatched the Marquis Ito to Seoul, and on November 15th, this statesman besought the Emperor's consent to the abolition of the Korean Department of Foreign Affairs in favour of a specially created Advisory Council, which was to sit at Tōkio, to the installation of the Japanese Minister at Seoul as General Superintendent of Korea, and the Japanese Consuls as Superintendents. As his Majesty did not agree with these demands, three days later, after the exercise of considerable pressure and the display of armed force, the Marquis Ito compelled the Korean Cabinet to accept a treaty by which Korea was deprived of its independence, while the future control

KOREAN VILLAGE DEVIL POSTS

On the right is "Great General of Underground"; on the left his spouse. They are supposed by the superstitious Koreans to keep the evil spirits out of the village.

THE SLEEPING GUARDIAN OF SEOUL

This stone tortoise is supposed to guard the Korean capital. The people rebelled against the electric cars on the plea that their noise would awaken the sleeping tortoise.

of its diplomatic, consular and domestic affairs was entrusted to the direction of the Japanese Government. At the same time, the Marquis Ito was appointed Resident-General to the Court of Korea, Residents were stationed at all the treaty ports and elsewhere throughout the country, and the Japanese Government undertook to maintain the dignity and welfare of the Imperial House.

While the Japanese Government lost no time in proclaiming to the Great Powers the establishment of a Japanese protectorate over Korea, an instructive light was thrown upon the methods by which the treaty had been extracted when the Emperor of Korea issued, in an Imperial letter, on January 29th, 1906, an emphatic and explicit denial of the right of the Japanese Government to make such an announcement, and invited the Great Powers to exercise a joint protectorate over his empire for a period not exceeding five years.

As the Russo-Japanese War had made the Japanese Government the sole arbiter of the destinies of Korea, his Majesty's action was of no avail. Equally ineffective protests continued to be **Repressive** made in the provinces ; and, **Measures** while scenes of anarchy were **of Japan** reported in various centres, six high officials committed suicide in the capital, where the Emperor, as the result of the publication of the Imperial letter, was practically a prisoner in his own palace. Under these circumstances, it is not surprising that the Japanese Government pushed forward the conversion of Korea into a Japanese protectorate. Since all departments of government were under

her control, one of the earliest measures was to replace the services of any foreigner employed by the Korean Government by those of Japanese, the Chief Commissioner of Customs, Mr. McLeavy Brown, being among the first to retire. Similarly, the greater part of the Korean Army was disbanded, the palace police gave way to Japanese, and thousands of Japanese settlers were brought into the country.

In spite of these indications of the futility of further resistance, the Emperor of Korea decided upon a last protest to the Powers. Influenced by the impression that the treaty of November 18th, 1905, was invalidated by the character of the **Ineffectual** measures by which it was **Protest to** extracted, early in the spring **the Powers** of 1907 his Majesty despatched Prince Yong-i Yi on a mission of appeal to the Hague Conference. Arriving on July 16th, the appearance of the envoys was the signal for immediate action on the part of the Japanese Government, and on July 19th, the Emperor was deposed in favour of the Crown Prince, while on July 26th, 1907, a final treaty was arranged. By this instrument, the authority of the Japanese Resident-General in Korea was recognised as supreme, various restrictive measures were imposed upon the Korean Government, and the immediate introduction of a number of reforms indicated. A few days later sentence of death was passed upon Prince Yong-i Yi, with which expression of vengeance Japan signalled her complete conquest of reactionary and anti-Japanese influences in the Hermit Kingdom.

ANGUS HAMILTON

GREAT DATES IN THE HISTORY OF KOREA

B.C.		A.D.		A.D.	
1122	Korea divided into three kingdoms. Ki-tze dynasty in Chosen	1686	Introduction of Christianity	1885	Korean convention between Japan and China
108	Korea broken up by the Chinese	1792	Episcopate of the Roman Catholic Bishop of Peking extended over Korea	1894	China sends troops to Korea to establish order. Japan occupies Chemulpo
A.D.	Emperor Wu Wang	1840	Persecution of Christians		
384	Buddhism introduced	1849	Toleration under Chul Thong	1895	Japanese ascendency secured by Treaty of Shimonoseki
913	Unification of Korea under Wang the Founder	1863	Accession of Heui Yi		
	Chinese suzerainty recognised	1866	Massacres of Christians and clergy	1896	Russo-Japanese agreement
1230	Submission of Korea to the Mongols		French punitory expedition	1902	Korean agreement between Japan and Great Britain
1392	Yi-ta-jo establishes his dynasty	1875	Collision with Japan. Japanese settlement	1904	Russo-Japanese war
1592	Invasion of Japanese under Hideyoshi	1882	Attack on the Japanese	1905	Japan recognised as paramount by Treaty of Portsmouth
1627	Manchu invasion	1884	Korea opened to foreign intercourse	1907	Japan assumes a more definite control

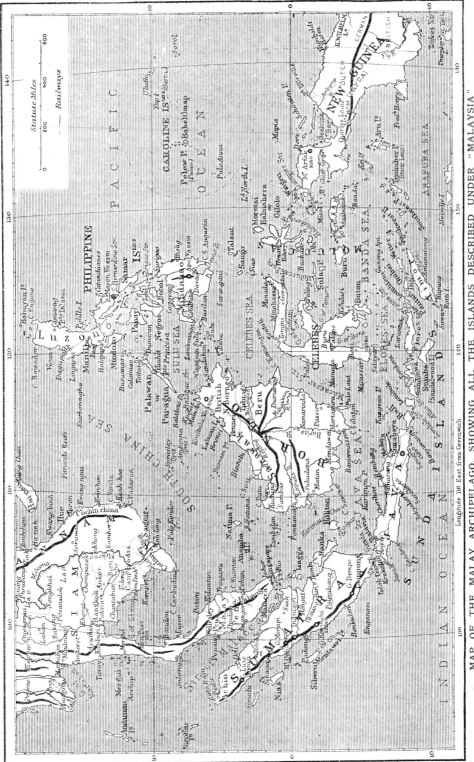

886

MAP OF THE MALAY ARCHIPELAGO, SHOWING ALL THE ISLANDS DESCRIBED UNDER "MALAYSIA"
Annam, Siam and the Malay Peninsula are dealt with in "Further India," and New Guinea in "Australia." The heavy black lines in the map represent mountain ranges

NATIVE HOUSE IN SUMATRA

MALAYSIA
THE ISLAND WORLD OF THE EASTERN SEAS
RACES OF PRIMITIVE CULTURE

MALAYSIA is the general designation of the largest group of islands in the world ; it stretches out in front of Asia to the south-east, forming the stepping-stone to the mainland of Australia on the one side, and to the Melanesian archipelagoes and the island-realm of Oceania on the other. It is known also as Indonesia, or the Indian Archipelago. The numerous members of the group include some of the most gigantic islands on the globe, with mountain ranges and navigable rivers, as well as diminutive islets, which hardly supply the sparsest population with the necessaries of life ; we find, as we go toward the east, the first traces of Australian dryness and desolation as well as regions of tropical luxuriance and splendid fertility. The term Malaysia is also extended to the Malay Peninsula, but its restricted use is adopted for convenience in these pages.

Extremes of Natural Conditions

For a long period there was no idea of any general name for all these islands and island groups, least of all among the natives themselves, who often have hardly recognised the larger islands as connected territories. Their narrow horizon, on the other hand, has completely prevented them from realising the sharp contrast which exists between their own island homes, with extensive and deeply indented coast lines, and the neighbouring continents, of which only a small part is in contact with the sea. At least they have never thought of emphasising such a distinction by collective names. The geographers of Europe, having the whole picture of the world before their eyes, were the first to mark out the two large groups of the Sunda Islands and the Philippines. The title Malaysia, of course, emphasises the purely ethnological point of view, meaning the region inhabited by that peculiar brown, straight-haired race, to which we give the name Malayan, recognised from very early times as a distinct type of mankind.

One member of the ethnological group, however, Madagascar, belongs geographically so clearly to Africa that it is treated in connection with that continent, instead of being included in the present section.

The Indian island world belongs as a whole to the tropics, and in its chief parts to the moist and warm tropical plains. Highlands, which are of incalculable importance for the culture of tropical countries, as the ancient history of America in particular shows, are found to any appreciable extent only in Sumatra, although there is no lack of mountain ranges and lofty volcanic cones on the other islands.

Physical Features of the Islands

If we recall the doctrine of Oskar Peschel that the oldest civilised countries lay nearer the tropics than those of modern times, and that, therefore, the chief zones of civilisation have withdrawn toward the Poles, it can at least be conjectured that a region so favourably situated as Malaysia was not always of

887

such trifling importance in the history of mankind as it is at present. We need not picture to ourselves a primitive highly developed culture, but one which, after reaching a certain level at an early period, remained stationary and was outstripped by the civilisation of other regions. The Dyak in Central Borneo has reached, it

Primitive Malaysian Civilisation is certain, no high grade of civilisation, but a comparison with the reindeer-hunters of the European Ice Age would certainly be to his advantage. The entire ethnological development of the country, and the influence which it once asserted over wide regions of the world, prove that at a remote period a comparatively noteworthy civilisation was actually attained in the Malay Archipelago.

Malaysia, notwithstanding its place as a connecting link between Asia and Australia, occupies from the view of ethnology an outlying position. It is true that culture could radiate outwards from it in almost every direction ; on the other hand, this region has been affected almost exclusively by movements from the north and west, from Asia, that is, and later from Europe, but hardly at all from Australia and Polynesia. These conditions find their true expression in the old racial displacements of the Malay Archipelago. The drawbacks of this geographical situation are almost balanced by the extraordinarily favourable position for purposes of intercourse which the Malay islands enjoy—a position in its kind unrivalled throughout the world.

The two greatest civilised regions of the world—the Indo-European on the one side, the East-Asiatic on the other—could come into close communication only by the route round the south-east extremity of Asia, since the Mongolian deserts constituted an almost insuperable barrier ; but there in the south-east the island-world of Indonesia offered its harbours and the riches of its soil to the seafarers

Culture Induced by Commerce wearied by the long voyage, and invited them to exchange wares and lay the foundation for prosperous trading towns. This commercial intercourse has never died away since the time when it was first started ; only the nations who maintained it have changed. The present culture of the Archipelago has grown up under the influence of this constant intercourse ; but the oldest conditions, which are so

important for the history of mankind, have nowhere been left unimpaired. We need not commit the blunder of taking the rude forest tribes of Borneo or Mindanao for surviving types of the ancient civilisation of Malaysia. The bold seamen who steered their vessels to Easter Island and Madagascar were assuredly of another stock than these degenerate denizens of the steamy primeval forests.

It is difficult to give a short sketch of Malayan history because justifiable doubts may arise as to the correct method of statement. First, we have to deal with an insular and much divided region ; and, secondly, a large, indeed the greater part of the historical events were produced and defined by external influences. The history of Malaysia is what we might expect from the insular nature of the region ; it splits up into a narrative of numerous local developments, of which the most important at all events require to be treated and estimated separately. But, on the other hand, waves of migration and civilising influences once more flood all the island-world and bring unity into

The Struggle for Individuality the whole region by ending the natural isolation of the groups. And yet this unity is only apparent ; for even if new immigrants gain a footing on the coasts of the larger islands, and foreign civilisations strike root in the maritime towns, the tribes in the interior resist the swelling tide and preserve in hostile defiance their individuality, protected now by the mountainous nature of their homes, now by the fever-haunted forests of the valleys in which they seek asylum.

Since there no longer exists any doubt that man inhabited the earth even at the beginning of the Drift Epoch, and since the opinion might be ventured that his first appearance falls into the Tertiary Age, it is no longer possible to deduce in a childlike fashion the primitive conditions of mankind from the present state of the world, and to look for its oldest home in one of the countries still existing. Least of all must we hazard hasty conclusions when we are dealing with a part of the earth so manifest'y the scene of the most tremendous shocks and transformations, and so rent and shattered by volcanic agencies, as Malaysia. In quite recent times, also, the discovery of some bones at Trinil in Java by Dr. Eugene Dubois, which Othniel Charles Marsh ascribes to a link between man and the anthropoid apes, caused a profound sensation in the scientific world and stimulated the search, in Malaysia itself, for the reg'on where man first raised himself to his present position from a lower stage of existence. However this question may be answered, it is meanwhile calculated to discourage any discussion of origins ; it especially helps us to reject those views which unhesitatingly look for the home of all Malayan nationalities on the continent of Asia, and from this standpoint build up a fanciful foundation for Malayan history. The linguistic conditions warn us against this misconception. On the mainland of Southern Asia we find monosyllabic languages ; but in the island region they are polysyllabic. There is thus a fundamental distinction between the two groups.

Two main races are represented in the Malay Archipelago, which in the number of their branches and in their distribution are extraordinarily divergent. They show in their reciprocal relations the unmistakable result of ancient historical occurrences. These are the brown, straight-haired Malays—in the wider sense — and the dark-skinned Negritos, who owe their name to their resemblance to the negro. Since the whole manner in which the Negritos are at present scattered over the islands points to a retrogression, there will always be an inclination to regard them, when compared with the Malays, as the more ancient inhabitants of at least certain parts of the Archipelago.

The Two Races of Malaysia

These Negritos form a link in the chain of those equatorial dark-skinned peoples who occupy most part of Africa, Southern India, Melanesia, and Australia, and almost everywhere, as compared with lighter-skinned races, exhibit a retrogression which certainly did not begin in modern times, and suggests the conclusion that the homes of these dark racial elements were once more extensive than they are to-day. It is doubtful, indeed, whether we are justified in assuming these negroid races to be closely connected, or whether, on the contrary, several really independent branches of the dark-skinned type of mankind are represented among them. One point is, however, established ; the Negritos of the Malay Archipelago, by their geographical distribution, and still more by

their physical characteristics, are mos closely allied to the Papuans, who inhabi New Guinea and the Melanesian group of islands.

It follows that the Papuan race once extended further to the west, and was worsted in the struggle with the Malay element. According to one view even the dark-skinned inhabitants of Madagascar would be closely akin to the Melanesians The Negritos are in no respect pure Papuans ; not only are they often so mixed with Malay tribes tha their individuality has disappeared except for a few remnants, but many indications point to the fact that there have been frequent crossings with tribes of short stature, whose relation to the Papuans may perhaps be compared with that of the African pigmies to the genuine negroes. These dwarf races cannot in any way be brought into line with the other dark peoples. Kinsfolk of the low-statured race, which has mixed with the Negritos or perhaps formed their foundation, exist on the peninsula of Malacca—especially in its northern part, on the Andamans, and in Ceylon. There were also, in all probability, representatives of this dwarf race to be found on the larger Sunda Islands, and in East Asia.

Evolution of Races in Malaysia

At any rate, it is a fact that some of the eastern islands of the Malay Archipelago, particularly the Philippines, still contain dark tribes, although, in consequence of numerous admixtures and the small numbers of these petty nations, their existence has often been doubted. Karl Semper describes the Negritos, or Antes, of the Philippines, as low-statured men, of a dark, copper-brown complexion, with flat noses and woolly black-brown hair. Where they have preserved to some degree their purity of race, they are a characteristic type, easily distinguishable from the members of the Malay race. There appear to be hardly any Negritos on the Sunda Islands proper. But in the south, on Timor, Floris, the Moluccas and Celebes, more or less distinct traces point to an admixture of a dark-skinned race with the Malay population. The same fact seems to be shown on Java Where the Negritos are more differentiated from the others—on the Philippines especially—they usually live in the inaccessible interior of the islands, far from

Physical Character of Negritos

he more densely peopled coasts, and void the civilisation that prevails there. t is sufficiently clear that these conditions)oint to a retrogression and displacement f the Negritos ; but it is difficult to arrive .t any certainty on these points.

The Papuan strain, which is so often o be found in the vicinity of the dwarf ace, may be traced to an immigration rom Melanesia, which has had its parallels ven in quite modern times. The Papuans)f Western New Guinea, who were)old navigators and robbers, penetrated o the coasts of the eastern Sunda Islands, and planted settlements there ; or possibly they immigrated to those parts as involuntary colonists, having been defeated and carried away by the Malays in their punitive expeditions. On the whole the relation of the Papuan to the Malayan civilisation is very remarkable. An explanation of it is much needed, and would prove of extreme value for the history of both races. The Papuan has not merely been receptive of Malay influences, but has also, to some slight extent, created and diffused an independent and self-developed civilisation.

THE WANDERINGS OF THE MALAYS

ALTHOUGH a certain migratory impulse which is innate in the Papuan has caused considerable migrations of the race, yet these are completely overshadowed by the wanderings of the Malay peoples, which are distinctly the most extensive known to the earlier history of mankind ; the more so because the Malays, not content with spreading over a continent, took to the sea as well, and thus became a connecting link between the four quarters of the globe.

The expression " Malays," since it is used sometimes in a narrower, sometimes in a wider sense, has given rise
What is Meant by " Malays " to many misunderstandings and unprofitable disputes. The source of the confusion lies in the circumstance that the name of the people which at the period of the European voyages of discovery seemed most vigorously engaged in war and trade has been given to the whole ethnological group, of which it formed only a single, though characteristic, part. This group, for whose accepted name it is difficult to find a substitute, is a branch of the human race easily distinguishable from its neighbours and admirably adapted to the nature of its home; its homogeneity is further attested by the affinity of the languages which are spoken by its various branches.

We may assume that it was originally an amalgamation of various primitive races. In the islands, as in Northern Asia, long-skulled (dolichocephalic) peoples appear to have spread first, but soon to have received an admixture of short-skulled (brachycephalic) immigrants.

It is an idle question to ask for the original home of these two component parts of the Malay race, in face of the incontestable fact that the kernel of the Malay nationality occupies at present, as it has occupied since early times, the island world of Melanesia ; on the other hand, comparatively small fragments of the stock, with a larger proportion of mixed peoples of partly Malay, partly Mongol, elements, are found on the continent of Asia. In this sense the region we are now surveying is the cradle of the Malay race as a separate group of mankind : it was the starting-point of those marvellous migrations which it is our immediate intention to examine more closely. The larger islands within the Malay island world have exercised an isolating and warping influence on the inhabitants, and thus have produced nations as peculiar as the Battaks on Sumatra, the Dyaks on Borneo, and the Tagales on the Philippines; but this fact must not shake our conviction that, taken as a whole, the Malay race, as we call it, is a comparatively definite idea. The later infusions of Indian and Chinese blood, which are now frequently observable, do not concern the earliest periods.

At first sight, it ought not to be a difficult task to describe the culture of those racial elements which migrated from Malaysia in various directions. Among the descendants of the emigrants there are many
The Common Factor tribes, especially in Oceania, which have found little opportunity on solitary islands to acquire new wealth of civilisation, and therefore may have preserved the old conditions in some degree of purity. It must also be possible even at the present day to determine, by the simple process of sifting and comparing the civilisations of the different branches which have differentiated themselves from the primitive stock, what was the original

inheritance which all these had in common with one another.

But the conditions are by no means so simple. Quite apart from the possible continuance of changes and further developments in remote regions, we must take into account the losses of culture which are almost inseparable from extensive migrations. Polynesia in particular is a region where a settlement without such losses is almost inconceivable ; the natural conditions are such that it is impossible to maintain some of the arts of civilisation.

If, therefore, at the present day, as we advance towards Oceania, we cross the limits within which a large number of crafts and acquisitions are known ; if on the eastern islands of Indonesia iron-smelting ends ; if on the Micronesian realm of islands the knowledge of weaving and the circulation of old East Asiatic or European beads, and on Fiji the potter's art, cease, the cause of these phenomena is not immediately clear. It is indeed possible that the inhabitants of Polynesia emigrated from their old homes at a period when smelting, weaving, and the potter's **Migrations** art were still unknown ; but it **of Primitive** is perhaps more probable that **Islanders** at least one part of the civilisation possessed by the small coral islands of the oceans has been simply forgotten and lost, or finds a faint echo in linguistic traces, as the knowledge of iron on Fiji. And, even in the first case, the question may always remain open whether the different branches of knowledge reached their present spheres of extension in the suite of migratory tribes, or whether we may assume a gradual permeation of culture from people to people, which is possible without migrations on a large scale, and may have continued to the present day.

The most valuable possession which can furnish information as to earlier times is the language, but unfortunately there is still an entire want of investigations which would be directly available for historical inquiry. This much may certainly be settled—that there are no demonstrable traces of Indian or Chinese elements in the Polynesian dialects any more than in those of Madagascar. It is thus at least clear that the great migrations must have taken place before the beginning of our era.

A proof that the islands proper in ancient times possessed a civilisation of their own, nearly independent of external influences, is given by the supply of indigenous plants useful to man which were at the disposal of the inhabitants even at the period of the migrations. Granted that the cultivation of useful growths was suggested from outside sources, still these suggestions were apparently followed out indepen- **Fruits and** dently in the islands. Rice, the **Cereals of** most valuable cereal of India **Malaysia** and South China, is not a ancient possession of the islands' culture which is acquainted instead with the taro, the yam, and sesame. Among useful trees may be mentioned the bread-fruit palm, and perhaps the coco-nut palm which are widely diffused, in the Malayo-Polynesian region at any rate. Of useful animals man appears in earlier times to have been acquainted only with the dog, possibly the pig, but not with the ox or the horse. This is again an important fact. Attention is elsewhere called to the probability that the agriculture of the Old World was older than the cattle-breeding industry, which in its developed form was introduced into India only by the Aryans. While, therefore, in ancient times the practice of agriculture may have been brought to the islands from the mainland, the knowledge of cattle-breeding at the beginning of the migration had no reached them by that road. We are no able to settle any fixed date, but these facts at least confirm the view that the years of migration fall in a comparatively early period.

The seamanship of the immigrants and the fact that even in Polynesia they continued to inhabit the coasts and peopled the interior of the islands only sparsely justify the conclusion that the mass of the migratory bands was sent out from typical maritime nations. Java, possibly which favoured the growth of population by the fertility of its soil, and where prehistoric weapons of polished **Java the** stone lead us to assume the **Base of** existence even in early times of **Migrations** a centre of some civilisation, was the chief starting-point for the migrations which split up into various subdivisions now hardly distinguishable. For the most part it would not have been a question of enormous journeys, but of an advance from island to island, where the immigrants would have been content first to occupy a part of the coast, and then, in the traditional manner, to build up a new system of life by cultivating clearings in the primeval forests, by fishing, and by profitable raids. The arts of shipbuilding and navigation must have reached a comparatively high stage; double canoes and outriggers, which enabled boats to keep out at sea even in bad weather, and to cross wide expanses of water, must have already been invented. Even at the present day the boats of the Polynesians—and of the Melanesians, who are closely connected with them in this respect—are the best which have been made by primitive races; while in the Malay Archipelago the imitation of foreign models has already changed and driven out the old style of shipbuilding. The sail must have been known to the ancient inhabitants, and it is more than probable that they understood how to steer their course by the stars and the movement of the waves, and that they possessed the rudiments of nautical cartography.

The social conditions of the early period certainly encouraged the spirit of adventure. No ethnological group in the world has shown a stronger tendency than the Malays and Polynesians to encourage the system of male associations

A CANNIBAL CHIEF OF BORNEO

as distinct from families and clans. The younger men, who usually live and sleep together in a separate bachelors' house, are everywhere organised as a military body, which is often the ruling force in the community, and, in any event, welcomes adventure and dangers in a spirit quite different from families or clans burdened with the anxiety of wives and children. These conditions create a warlike spirit in the people, which regards feuds and raids as the natural course of things, and finds

its most tangible expression in headhunting, a custom peculiar to the Malayo-Polynesian stock. Originating in the habit of erecting the skulls of ancestors as sacred relics in the men's quarter, it has led to a morbid passion for collecting, which provokes continual wars and never allows neighbouring races to remain at peace. Thus there remain even now the traces of a former state of things in which bold tribes of navigators and freebooters were produced.

We are here dealing with such remote ages that there can be no idea of assigning any precise dates to the different migrations; they can therefore be only briefly sketched, in an order which does not imply any necessary chronological sequence.

A first wave of migration flowed to the north. It is, in the first place, very probable that Malay tribes settled in the Philippines at a later period than in the great Sunda Islands, the proper home of true Malay life; but for this nation of skilful seamen it was only a step across from the Philippines to Formosa, where tribes of unmistakably Malay origin are still living. This can hardly have been the ultimate goal. There are numerous traces on the mainland of South China which point to an immigration of Malays. Again, the peculiarity of the Japanese is best explained by an admixture of Malay blood; it is indeed not inconceivable that the political evolution which began in the south was due to the seafaring Malays who first set foot on the southern islands and mixed with the existing inhabitants and with immigrants from Korea. Since this political organisation took place about 660 B.C., the migration might be assigned to a still earlier time. The first migration northward

DYAK WARRIOR NATIVES OF CERAM

GROUP OF THE COMMON PEOPLE OF BORNEO SUMATRAN

SULU ISLANDER JAVANESE HEAD-DRESS USUAL MALAY HEAD-DRESS

TYPES OF THE NATIVE RACES OF MALAYSIA

was also followed by a subsequent one, which reached at least as far as the Philippines, if not farther.

A second stream of emigrants was directed toward the east. On the Melanesian islands, which since early times were occupied by a dark-skinned race, numerous Malay colonies were founded, which exercised a marked influence on **Migration to the Pacific Islands** the Melanesians, but were gradually, and to some degree, absorbed. Even the continent of Australia must have received a strong infusion of Malay blood. The Malay migratory spirit found freer scope on the infinite island world of the Pacific, and weighty facts support the view that isolated settlers reached even the shores of North-west America. How those voyages were made and what periods of time they required is not known to us. Only the tradition of New Zealand tells us in semi-mythical fashion how the first immigrants, with their families and gods, took the dangerous voyage from Sawaii and Rarotonga to their new home, in their immense double canoes.

The third ethnological wave swept over the Indian Ocean, and bore westward to Madagascar the first germs of a Malay population ; the Arabic " Book of Miracles " relates an expedition of three hundred sails from Wakwak to Madagascar in the year 945 A.D. Possibly even the African coast was reached in this movement, although no permanent settlements were made there.

Thus we see that, at least a thousand years ago, the Malay race spread over a region which extends from the shores of America to the mainland of Africa, over almost two-thirds of the circumference of the earth. The Malayo-Polynesians have kept aloof from the continents. The oceans studded with islands are the inheritance of their race, which has had no rival in the command of the seas except **A Race that Avoided Continents** the European group of Aryan nations in our own days. If the lessons of comparative philology and ethnology supply all our knowledge of the old migrations, we have, in compensation, another ethnological movement more directly under our eyes, which also began with members of the Malay race, and forms a fitting counterpart to earlier events. The name of Malays did not originally belong to the whole race, but only

to one definite people of the Archipelago ; and it is this very people which by its migrations in more modern times has reproduced primitive history on a small scale, and thus shown itself worthy to give its name to the whole restless group. Probably, indeed, it was not even the whole stock with which we are at present concerned that bore the name of Malay, but only the most prominent subdivision of it.

The original home of this people lay on Sumatra in the district of Menangkabau. The name " Malayu " is applied to the island of Sumatra even by Ptolemy ; and in 1150 the Arabian geographer Edrisi mentions an island, Malai, which carried on a brisk trade in spices. Indian civilisation, it would seem, had considerable influence on Menangkabau, for according to the native traditions of the Malays it was Sri Turi Bumana, a prince of Indian or Japanese descent—according to the legend, he traced his lineage to Alexander the Great—who led a part of the people over the sea to the peninsula of Malacca **Europe's Early Records of Malaysia** and in 1160 founded the centre of his power in Singapore. The new state is said to have aroused the jealousy of a powerful Javanese realm, presumably Modyopahit, and Singapore was ultimately conquered in the year 1252 by the Javanese.

A new Malay capital, Malacca, was subsequently founded on the mainland. In the year 1276 the reigning chief, together with his people, were converted to Islam. The Malays, who had found on the peninsula only timid forest tribes of poor physique, multiplied in course of time so enormously that it became necessary to send out new colonies, and Malay traders and settlers appeared on all the neighbouring coast districts. Toward the close of the thirteenth century the State of Malacca was far more powerful than the old Menangkabau, and became the political and ethnological centre of Malay life. The result was that the true insular Malays apparently spread from the mainland over the island world of the East Indies. The Malay settlers played to some extent the rôle of state builders, especially in Borneo, where Brunei in the north was a genuine Malay state ; other states were formed on the west coast. The Malays mixed everywhere with the aborigines, and made their language the common dialect of intercourse for the

Sunda Islands. The Bugi on the Celebes also spread over a wide area from their original homes.

Trifling as all these modern events may be in comparison with those of old times, still they teach us to grasp the conditions prevailing in the past, and to realise the possibility of migrations as comprehensiv as those which the Malayo-Polynesian accomplished.

THE COMING OF THE ASIATICS

THE influences of the voyages and settlements were not so powerful as those foreign forces which were continually at work owing to the favourable position of the islands for purposes of intercourse. Asiatic nations had long sought out the Archipelago, had founded settlements, and had been able occasionally to exercise some political influence. The islands were, indeed, not only half-way houses for communication between Eastern Asia and the west ; they themselves offered coveted treasures. First and foremost among these were spices, the staple of the Indian trade ; gold and diamonds were found in the mines of Borneo, and there were many other valuable products. The Chinese from East Asia obtained a footing in the Malay Archipelago ; from the west came the agents of the East Asiatic commerce—the Hindus first, then the Arabs, and soon after them the first Europeans, the present rulers of the island world.

The Chinese are not a seafaring nation in the correct acceptance of the word. It was only when, after the conquest of South China, they acquired a seaboard with good harbours, and mixed at the same time with the old seafaring population, that a maritime trade with the rich tropical regions of Indonesia (*i.e.*, the Indian islands) began to flourish ; only perhaps as a continuation of an older commerce, which had been originated by the northward migration of the **Chinese Influence in Malaysia** Malayan race, and consequently lay in the hands of Malayan tribes. Since South China therefore came into the possession of China in 220 B.C., it must have been subsequent to that time, and probably much later, that the influence of the Chinese was fully felt by the inhabitants of the Archipelago. Permanent connections with Annam can hardly have been established before the Christian era.

It was not the love of a seafaring life that incited the Chinese to travel, but the commercial instinct, that appeared as soon as other nations commanded the commerce and sought out the Chinese in their own ports. The Chinese fleet the quickly dwindled, the number of voyage lessened, and the merchants of the Celestial Empire found it safer and more convenient to trade with foreigners a home than to entrust their precious live to the thin planks of a vessel. But the stream of emigration from over-populated China developed independently of these occurrences, and turned by preference whether in native or foreign ships, toward the East Indian Archipelago, in many countries of which it produced important ethnological changes.

Very contradictory views are entertained about the extent of the oldest Chinese maritime trade, and especially about the question, with which we are not here so **Early Chinese Traders** much concerned, of the distance which Chinese vessels sailed toward the west. It appears from the annals of the Liang dynasty, reigning in the first half of the sixth century of our era, that the Chinese were already acquainted with some ports on the Malacca Straits which clearly served as marts for the trade between India and the Farther East.

As early as the fifth century commercial relations had been developed with Java, stimulated perhaps by the journeys of the Buddhist missionary Fa-hien, who, driven out of his course by a storm to Java, brought back to China more precise information as to the island. The south of Sumatra also at that time maintained communications with China. The political system of Java was sufficiently well organised to facilitate the establishment of a comparatively secure and profitable trade. From these islands the Chinese obtained precious metals, tortoise-shell, ivory, coco-nuts, and sugar-cane ; and the commodities which they offered in return were mainly cotton and silk stuffs.

There are constant allusions to presents sent by island princes, on whom the Chinese Court bestowed high-sounding titles, seals of office, and occasionally diplomatic support. In the year 1129 one such prince received the title of King of Java. Disputes between the settled

Chinese merchants—who plainly showed even thus early a tendency to form state within state—and the Javanese princes ed, in later times, to not infrequent interruptions of this commercial intercourse ; indeed, after the conquest of China by the Mongols hostile complications were produced. A Mongol-Chinese army in-

Chinese invasion of Java vaded Java in the year 1293, after it had secured a strategic base on the island of Billiton, but it was forced to sail away without any tangible results. During the age of the Ming Dynasty, the trade was once more flourishing, and we can even trace some political influence exercised by China. In the years 1405–1407 a Chinese fleet was stationed in the Archipelago ; its admiral enforced the submission of a number of chieftains, and brought the ruler of Palembang prisoner to China.

The coasts of Borneo, which were touched at on every voyage to and from Java, soon attracted a similar influx of Chinese merchants, to whom the wealth of Borneo in gold and diamonds was no secret. The kingdom of Polo, in the north of the island, which appears in Chinese annals for the first time in the seventh century, was regularly visited by the Chinese in the tenth century. On the west coast, Puni, whose prince sent an embassy to China for the first time in 977, was a much-frequented town; while Banjermassin, now the most prosperous trading place, is not mentioned until 1368.

As the spread of Islam with its consequences more and more crippled the trade of the Chinese with the Sunda Islands, they turned their attention to a nearer but hitherto much-neglected sphere, the Philippines. There, too, the Malay tribes were carrying on a brisk commerce before the Chinese encroached and established themselves on different points along the coast. This step was taken in the fourteenth century at latest.

Chinese Emigration to Philippines But then the Chinese trader was already followed by emigrants, who settled in large numbers on the newly-discovered territory, mixed with the aborigines, and in this way, just as in North Borneo, called into life new Chinese-Malay tribes. When, after the interference of the Spaniards, the Chinese traders withdrew or were restricted to definite localities, these mixed tribes remained behind in the country.

To sum up, it may be said that the Chinese, both here and in Indonesia, exercised a certain amount of political influence, and produced some minor ethnological changes, and that they are even now still working in this latter direction. On the other hand, the intellectual influence of China has not been great, and cannot be compared even remotely with that of the Indians and Arabs. Chinamen and Malays clearly are not in sympathy with each other. At the present day a large share of the trade of the Archipelago once more lies in Chinese hands, the immigration has enormously increased, and the " yellow peril " is nowhere so noticeable as there. But the Malayan must not, in any way, be called for this reason an offshoot of Chinese civilisation. The Chinaman shares with the European the fate of exercising little influence on the intellectual life of the Malay. The cause in both cases is the same ; both races appeared first and foremost as traders and rulers, but kindled no flame of religious zeal. The Chinaman failed because he was indifferent to all religious questions ; the

Why Chinese Influence Failed European failed because Islam, with its geater power of enlisting followers, prevented Christianity, on which it had stolen a long march, from exerting any influence. It is possible that in earlier times the Chinese helped Buddhism to victory in the islands, but at present we possess no certain information on the subject.

The inhabitants of India have influenced their insular neighbours quite differently from the Chinese. They brought to them, together with an advanced civilisation, a new religion, or rather two religions, which were destined to strike root side by side in the Archipelago—Brahmanism and Buddhism. The Hindus and the other inhabitants of India, who have gained their civilisation from them, are as little devoted to seafaring as the Chinese, for the coasts of India are comparatively poor in good harbours. Probably the first to cross the Bay of Bengal were the sea-loving inhabitants of the Sunda Islands themselves, who, first as bold pirates like the Norwegian Vikings, ravaged the coasts, but also sowed the first seeds of commerce. But after this the inhabitants of the coasts of Nearer India, who hitherto had kept up a brisk intercourse only with Arabia and the Persian Gulf, found something very

The finest of the numerous bas-reliefs in the famous temple of Boro-Budur. Women are shown carrying vessels at a pond, where lotus flowers grow and birds disport. Bas - relief, showing a prince receiving presents.

General view of the immense temple of Boro-Budur, in Java.

Bas-relief, showing a sea-storm on one side, and a royal couple, with a child, handing gifts to certain of the mariners, who have evidently reached the shore. This is the lowest in a general scheme of four panels.

TEMPLE OF BORO-BUDUR, IN JAVA, THE FINEST EXISTING BUDDHIST MONUMENT

attractive in the intercourse with the islands, which first induced some enterprising merchants to sail thither with their store of spices, until at last an organised and profitable trade was opened. Many centuries, however, must needs have passed before the spiritual influence of Indian culture really made itself felt. Since

Influence of India on Malaysia the Hindu has as little taste for recording history as the Malay, the beginning of the intercourse between the two groups of peoples can be settled only by indirect evidence. The two articles of trade peculiar to the islands, and in earlier times procurable from no other source, were the clove and the nutmeg. The first appearance of these products on the Western markets must, accordingly, give an indication of the latest date at which the intercourse of Nearer India with the Malay Archipelago can have been systematically developed. Both these spices were named among the articles imported to Alexandria for the first time in the age of Marcus Aurelius—that is to say, about 180 A.D. ; while, a century earlier, the " Periplus of the Erythræan Sea " does not mention them.

If, then, we reflect that a certain time would have been required to familiarise the natives of India with these spices before there was any idea of shipping them further, and that perhaps on the first trading voyages, necessarily directed toward the Straits of Malacca, products of that region and of more distant parts of the Archipelago had been exchanged, we are justified in placing the beginnings of the Indian-Malay trade in the first century of our chronology. This theory is supported by the mention in the " Periplus " of voyages by the inhabitants of India to the " Golden Chersonese," by which is probably meant the peninsula of Malacca. Chinese accounts lead us to suppose that at this time Indian merchants had

Java the Centre of Early Trade even reached the south coast of China. At a later period more detailed accounts of the islands reached the Græco - Roman world. Even before cloves and nutmegs appeared in the trade-lists of Alexandria, Ptolemy, the geographer, had already inserted on his map of the world the names " Malayu " and " Java." Various other facts point to the position of the island of Java as the centre of the island civilisation, and the emporium for the commerce which

some centuries later was destined to allure even the ponderous junks of the Chinese to a voyage along their coasts.

Following in the tracks of the merchants, and perhaps themselves condescending to do a stroke of business, Indian priests gradually came to the islands and won reputation and importance there. India itself, however, at the beginning of the Christian era, was not a united country from the religious point of view. Buddhism, like an invading torrent, had destroyed the old Brahma creed, had shattered the caste system, and had then sent out its missionaries to achieve splendid success in almost all the surrounding countries.

But it had not been able to overthrow the old religion of the land ; Brahmanism once more asserted itself with an inexhaustible vitality. At the present day Buddhism has virtually disappeared in its first home, while the old creed has again obtained an almost exclusive dominion. The growth of Hindu influence in the islands falls in the transition period when the two forms of religion existed side by side, and the religious disputes with India

Importation of Hindu Religions are not without importance for this outpost of Indian culture. Buddhists and Brahmans come on the scene side by side, often avowedly as rivals, although it remains doubtful whether the schism led to any warlike complications. The fortunes of the two sects in the Malay Archipelago are remarkably like those of their co-religionists in India. In the former region Buddhism was temporarily victorious, and left its mark on the most glorious epoch of Javanese history ; but Brahmanism showed greater vitality, and has not even yet been entirely quenched, while the Buddhist faith speaks to us only from the gigantic ruins of its temples.

The thought is suggested that the Brahman and the Buddhist Hindus came from different parts of the peninsula. James Fergusson conjectured the home of the Buddhist immigrants to be in Gujerat and at the mouth of the Indus, and that of the Brahman to be in Telingana and at the mouth of the Kistna, or Krishna. The architecture of the Indian temples on Java, and the language of the Sanscrit inscriptions found there, lend colour to this view. We may mention, however, that recently it has been asserted by H. Kern and J. Groneman, great authorities on Buddhism, that the celebrated temples of Boro-Budur must have been erected (850–900) by followers of the southern Buddhists, whose sect, for example, predominated on South Sumatra in the kingdom of Sri-Bhodja. Brahmans and Buddhists certainly did not appear contemporaneously in Java.

The most ancient temples were certainly not erected by Buddhists, but by worshippers of Vishnu in the fifth century A.D. Some inscriptions found in West Java, which may also be ascribed to followers of Vishnu, date from the same century. The Chinese Buddhist Fa-hien, who visited the island about this time, mentions the Hindus, but does not appear to have found any members of his own faith there. According to this view the Indians of the Coromandel coast would have first established commercial relations with the islands ; it was only later that they were followed by the inhabitants of the north-west coast of India, who, being also connected with the civilised countries of the West, gave a great stimulus to trade, and became the leading spirits of the Indian colony in Java. This, then, explains the **Reason of Buddhist Supremacy** later predominance of Buddhism in the Malay Archipelago. In the eighth century A.D. the immigration of the Hindus, including in their number many Buddhists, seems to have increased in Java to an extraordinary extent. The construction of a Buddhist temple at Kalasan in the year 779 is recorded in inscriptions. The victory of Indian civilisation was then confirmed ; the rulers turned with enthusiasm to the new forms of belief, and spent their accumulated riches in the erection of vast temples modelled upon those of India. From Java, which was then the political centre of the Archipelago, the culture and religion of the Hindus spread to the neighbouring islands, to Sumatra, South Borneo, and other parts of the Archipelago. The most easterly points where Buddhism achieved any results were the island of Ternate and the islet of Tobi, north-east of Halmahera, which already formed a stepping-stone to Micronesia. At that time Pali was the language of the educated classes. The Indian systems of writing stimulated the creation of native scripts even among those tribes which, like the Battaks in the interior of Sumatra, were but slightly affected in other respects by the wave of civilisation. The influence of India subsequently diminished. In the fifteenth century it once more revived, a fact that may certainly be connected with the political condition of Java. Since Buddhism had at this time almost disappeared in Nearer India, this revival implies also a strengthening of the Brahman doctrine, which had survived, therefore, the fall of the Indian civilisation. In **The Coming of Islam** the meantime the victorious successors to Hinduism, the Islamitic Arabs, had appeared upon the scene. The Arabian trade to Egypt and India had flourished before the time of Mohammed, had received the products of the Archipelago from the hands of the Indian merchants, and had transmitted them to the civilised peoples of the West. It is possible that Arabian traders may have early reached Java without gaining any influence there. It was Islam which first stamped the wanderings of the Arabs with their peculiar character ; it changed harmless traders into the teachers of a new doctrine, whose simplicity stood in happy contrast to the elaborate theology of the Hindus, and to the degenerate form of Buddhism which could have retained little of its original purity in the Malay Archipelago.

The new duties which his religion now imposed on the Arabian merchant inspired him with a fresh spirit of adventure, and with a boldness that did not shrink from crossing the Indian Ocean. The rise of the Caliphate, which drew to itself all the wealth of the Orient, secured to the bold mariners and traders a market for their wares and handsome profits. Bushira then attained prosperity, and was the point from which those daring voyages were made whose fame is re-echoed in the marvellous adventures of Sindbad the Sailor in the Arabian Nights. Oman, on the Persian Gulf, became an important emporium, but even the older ports in Southern Arabia competed with their new **Arabian Merchants in Malaysia** rivals, and still retained the trade at least with Egypt. The voyages of the Arabs at the time of the Caliphate form the first stage in the connections between the Archipelago and the world of Islam, which seem at first to have been of a purely commercial character. The enterprising spirit of the Arabian merchants soon led them, after once the first steps had been taken, beyond the Malay Archipelago to the coasts of China, which, in the year 850, were already connected with Oman in the Persian Gulf by a flourishing maritime trade. This, however, necessitated the growth of stations for the transit trade in the Archipelago itself, where Arabian traders permanently settled and, as we can easily understand, endeavoured to win supporters **Decline of** for Islam. Even then conver- **Arabian** sions on a large scale might have **Trade** resulted had not the overthrow of the Caliphate gradually caused an extraordinary decline in the Arabian trade, and consequently in the influence of the Arabs throughout the islands.

A new stimulus was given to the intercourse between the states of Islam and the Malay Archipelago when, at the time of the Crusades, the Mohammedan world regained its power, and the dominion of the Saracens flourished, about 1200 A.D. Nevertheless, Islam appears to have achieved little success at that time in the islands, apart possibly from the conversion of Mohammed Shah, a Malay prince resident in Malacca. This event, however, which, according to a somewhat untrustworthy account, occurred in 1276, was of great importance for the future, since the Malays in the narrower sense became the most zealous Mohammedans of the Archipelago. The third great revival of trade, produced by the prosperity of the Turkish and Egyptian empires in the fourteenth century, prepared the way for the victory of the new doctrine, which was permanently decided by the acquisition of Java. The first unsuccessful attempt at a Mohammedan movement on Java took place in 1328 ; a second, equally futile, was made in 1391. But little by little the continuous exertions of the Arabian merchants, who soon found ready helpers among the natives, and had won sympathisers in the Malays of Malacca, prepared the ground for the final victory of the Mohammedan doctrine. The Brahmans, whose religion, as now appeared, had struck no deep roots among the people, offered a feeble and ineffectual resistance to the new creed. The fall of the kingdom of Modyopahit, which had been the refuge of the Indian religious party, completely destroyed Brahmanism in Java in the year 1478.

THE EUROPEANS IN MALAYSIA

VICTORY cheered the missionaries of Islam at the end. A few decades later the first Europeans appeared in the Archipelago. They, indeed, were fated to win the political supremacy, but their spiritual influence was not equal to that of Islam.

The Portuguese admiral, Diego Lopez de Sequeira, and his men, when they appeared in the year 1509 on the coast of Sumatra, were certainly not the first navigators of European race to set foot on the shores of the Malay Islands. Many a bold trader may have pushed his way thus far in earlier times ; and the first traveller in whom the European spirit of exploration and strength of purpose were embodied, the great Venetian, Marco Polo, had visited the islands in the year 1295, and reached home safely after a prosperous voyage. No brisk intercourse with Europe could be maintained, however, until a successful attempt had been made, in 1497–1498, to circumnavigate the southern extremity of Africa, and thus to discover the direct sea route to the East Indies. After that, the region was soon opened up.

The first expedition under Sequeira with difficulty escaped annihilation, as it was attacked, by order of the native prince, while anchoring in the harbour of Malacca. In any case the governor, Alfonso d'Albuquerque, when he was on his way to Malacca, in 1511, had a splendid excuse to hand for adopting a vigorous policy and plundering the Malay merchantmen s he passed. Since the Sultan of Malacca offered no satisfactory indemnity, war was declared with him ; the town was captured after a hard fight, and was made into a strong base for the Portuguese power. Albuquerque then attempted to establish communications with Java, and made preparations to enter into closer relations with the Spice Islands in the East, the Moluccas. After his departure repeated efforts were made to recover Malacca from the Portuguese, but the fort held out.

The Portuguese had followed on the tracks of the Arabs as far as Malacca, **Portuguese** the crossing point of the Indian **Adventures** and East Asiatic trade, and they **in Malaysia** naturally cherished the dream of advancing to China, and thus securing the trade with that country. A fleet under Fernao Perez d'Andrade sailed in the year 1516 from Malacca, and, after an unsuccessful preliminary attempt, reached Canton in 1517. Communications with the Moluccas had already been formed in 1512 through the efforts of Francisco Serrao ; and, since the Portuguese interfered in the disputes of the natives, the commander of their squadron, Antonio de Brito, soon succeeded in acquiring influence there, and in founding a fort on Ternate in 1522. They were unpleasantly disturbed in their plans by the small Spanish squadron of Ferdinand Magellan, who had himself been killed on Matan on April 27th ; this fleet, after crossing the Pacific, appeared on November 8th, 1521, off Tidor, and tried to enforce the claims of the King of Spain to the Moluccas.

Generally speaking, it was clear, even then, that the Portuguese could not possibly be in a position to make full use of the enormous tract of newly discovered territory, or even to colonise it. There was never any idea of a real conquest even of the coast districts. A large part of the available forces must have been employed in holding Malacca and keeping the small Malay predatory states in check, while the wars with China made further demands. The Malay prince of Bintang, in particular, with his large fleet, continually threatened the Portuguese possessions on the Strait of Malacca, and after 1523 caused great distress in the colony, until his capital was destroyed in 1527. The position of the Portuguese on the Moluccas was also far from secure, since the state of Tidor, which was friendly to Spain, showed intense hostility. Commercial relations had been established since 1522 with the state of Sunda in Western Java, but the permission to plant a settlement in the country itself was refused. On Sumatra, where Menangkabau was visited by the Portuguese as early as 1514, some petty states recognised the suzerainty of Portugal ; Achin, on the contrary, was able to assert its independence, while attempts to establish intercourse with Borneo were not made until 1530.

AN EARLY PORTUGUESE GOVERNOR
Alfonso d'Albuquerque, explorer, navigator and Governor of the Portuguese East Indies, who plundered the Malays in 1511.

In the same year new disturbances broke out in the Moluccas, since the encroachments of the Portuguese commanders, who had taken the King of Ternate prisoner, had incensed the subjects of this ally. When the new commander-in-chief, Gonzalo Pereira, to crown all, declared that the clove trade was the monopoly of the Portuguese Government, the indignation was so intense that the queen ordered him to be murdered, and the lives of the other Portuguese were in the greatest jeopardy. Peace was restored with the utmost difficulty. Fresh disorders were due to that corrupt mob of adventurers who ruled the islands in the name of the King of Portugal, abandoned themselves to the most licentious excesses, and undermined their own authority by dissensions among themselves. The governor, Tristao de Taide, brought matters to such a pitch that all the princes of the Moluccas combined against him (1533) ; his successor, Antonio Galvao, at last ended the war with considerable good fortune, and restored the prestige of Portugal on the Spice Islands. His administration certainly marked the most prosperous epoch of Portuguese rule in those parts. Later, the struggles began again, and finally, in 1580, led to the evacuation of Ternate by the Portuguese and their settlement in Tidor.

Thus the influence of the Portuguese was restricted to parts of the Moluccas and some places on the Strait of Malacca. The Archipelago was in most respects only the thoroughfare for the Chino-Japanese trade, which at first developed with as much promise as the East Asiatic missions. The principal station of the trade continued to be Malacca, notwithstanding its dangerous position between states of Malay pirates and the powerful Achin on Sumatra.

The history of Spanish colonisation in the Malay Archipelago is almost entirely bound up with the history of the Philippines, and is treated of in that section.

THE TOWN OF BANTAM IN THE DAYS OF THE DUTCH EAST INDIA COMPANY

The Portuguese rule in the Archipelago was as brief as in India. At the end of the sixteenth century the two nations which w_re destined to enter on the rich inheritance, the Dutch and the English, began their first attempts at commerce and colonisation in the Indian waters. The Dutch in particular, through their

Commercial Rivalry in the 16th Century
war with Spain, which crippled the hitherto prosperous trade with the American colonies, were compelled to seek new fields for their activity. Their eyes were turned to India, where Portugal, weakened rather than strengthened by the union with Spain (1580), tried in vain to enforce its influence over a vast tract of territory. Even without at once becoming hostile competitors to Portuguese trade, the Dutch merchants might hope to discover virgin lands, whose exploitation promised rich gains.

The first Dutch fleet set sail from the Texel on April 2nd, 1595, under the command of Cornelis de Houtmans, a rough adventurer, and anchored on June 2nd, 1596, off Bantam, the chief trading port of Java. This expedition did little to secure the friendship of the natives, owing to the bad qualities of the commander; but at least it paved the way for further enterprise. In the course of a few years a number of small trading companies arose, which succeeded only in interfering with each other and causing mutual ruin, until they were finally combined, through the co-operation of Oldenbarneveld and Prince

Maurice, on March 20th, 1602, into a large company, the " Universal Dutch United East India Company." This company soon obtained possessions in the Malay Archipelago, and after 1632 exercised full sovereign sway over its territory.

The company founded a permanent settlement in Bantam, whose prince made friendly overtures, and they took over the already existing trading enterprises in Ternate, Amboina, and Banda, the existence of which proves incidentally that even the Dutch had at once tried to win their share of the spice trade. Disputes in consequence arose on the Moluccas in 1603, when the natives, exasperated by the oppression of the Portuguese and Spaniards, took the side of the Dutch. The undertakings of the company were, however, first put on a systematic basis in the year 1609, when the office of a governor-general was created, at whose side the " Council of India " was placed, and thus a sort of independent government was established in the Archipelago.

The Spaniards now suffered a complete defeat. And when in their place the Eng-

Rivalry of English and Dutch
lish appeared and entered into serious competition with the company, they found themselves confronted by the Governor-General, Jan Pieterszon Coen, a man who, competent to face all dangers, finally consolidated the supremacy of the Dutch. The English tried in vain to acquire influence on Java by the help of the Sultan of Bantam. Coen defeated his opponents,

removed the Dutch settlements to Jacatra, where he founded in the year 1619 the future centre of Dutch power, Batavia, and compelled Bantam, whose trade was thus greatly damaged, to listen to terms. "We have set foot on Java and acquired power in the country," Coen wrote to the directors of the company; "see and reflect what bold courage can achieve!" To his chagrin the Dutch Government, from considerations of European policy, determined to admit the English again to the Archipelago. This proceeding led to numerous complications, and finally to the massacre of a number of Englishmen, on the pretext that they had tried to capture the Dutch ports on Amboina. Coen's whole energies were required to hold Batavia, which was besieged in 1628 by the Javanese. His death, which occurred in that same year, was a heavy blow to the Dutch power.

The influence of the company, however, was now sufficiently assured to withstand slight shocks. The Portuguese had been little by little driven back and forced almost entirely to abandon the East

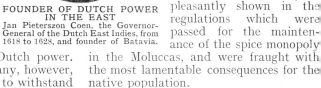

FOUNDER OF DUTCH POWER IN THE EAST
Jan Pieterszon Coen, the Governor-General of the Dutch East Indies, from 1618 to 1628, and founder of Batavia.

Asiatic trade. The English found a field for their activity in India, and the Spaniards retained the Philippines, but were compelled in 1663 definitely to waive all claim to the Moluccas. Java and the Spice Islands were the bases of the Dutch power, which reached its greatest prosperity under the Governor-General, Anton van Diemen (1636–1645). Malacca was then conquered, a friendly understanding was established with the princes of Java, and Batavia was enlarged and fortified in every way. Soon afterward the sea route to the East Indies was secured by the founding of one station at the Cape of Good Hope and another on Mauritius. But in this connection the huckstering spirit of the trading company was unpleasantly shown in the regulations which were passed for the maintenance of the spice monopoly in the Moluccas, and were fraught with the most lamentable consequences for the native population.

Greater attention was now gradually paid to the hitherto neglected islands of the Archipelago, especially as Formosa,

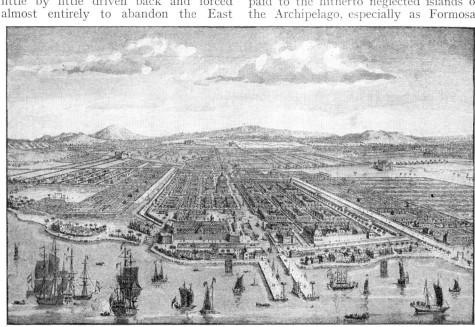

THE CAPITAL CITY OF BATAVIA IN THE SEVENTEENTH CENTURY
The headquarters of Dutch power in the East, founded by Coen in the year 1619, and then called Jacatra.

captured in 1624, was in 1662 lost to the Chinese. The attempts to set foot on Borneo met at first with little success ; on the other hand, factories were founded on different points of the coast of Sumatra, and in the year 1667 the Prince of Macassar on Celebes was conquered and compelled to conclude a treaty to the advantage of the company. In Java the **British Withdrawal from Java** influence of the Dutch continually increased ; Bantam was humbled in 1684, and the final withdrawal of the English from Java was the result. But even in later times there were many severe struggles.

Like almost all the great sovereign trading companies of the age of discovery, the Dutch East India Company enjoyed but a short period of prosperity. The old spirit of enterprise died away ; a niggardly pettiness spread more and more, and produced a demoralising effect on the servants of the company, although their dangerous posts and the tropical climate must have served as an excuse in any case for numerous excesses. In 1731 the Governor-General, Diederick Durven, had to be recalled, after barely two years of office, on account of unparalleled misconduct ; but the state of things did not improve appreciably even after his departure. The misgovernment weighed most heavily on the Chinese merchants and workmen who were settled in the towns. At last, in Java, this part of the population, which was essentially untrustworthy and had always been aiming at political influence, was driven into open revolt. Since the Chinese rendered the vicinity of Batavia insecure, the citizens armed themselves, and at the order of the Governor-General, Adrian Valckenier, massacred all the Chinese in the town in October, 1740. But it was only after a long series of fights that the insurgents, who had formed an alliance with Javanese princes, were completely defeated, and the opportunity was seized of once more extending the territory of the company.

The strength of the company was based on its jealously-guarded trade monopoly.

A CELEBRATED DUTCH GOVERNOR

Anton van Diemen, Governor-General of the Dutch East Indies (1636-45) when Dutch power was at its zenith.

A blow directed at that was necessarily keenly felt. It was observed in Holland with a justifiable anxiety that the English, whose naval power was now the first in the world, once more directed their activities to the East Indies, and came into competition with the company not only on the mainland but also on Sumatra and the Moluccas, answering all remonstrances with thinly veiled menaces. The mouldering officialism of the Dutch company was totally unable to cope with this fresh energy. While individuals amassed wealth, the income of the company diminished, and all profits on the unceasing wars with Malay pirates and similar costly undertakings had to be sacrificed.

Toward the close of the eighteenth century the States-General were compelled to aid the helpless sovereign company by sending a small fleet of warships. But when the Netherlands, after their transformation into the " Batavian Republic " on January 26th, 1795, were involved in war with England, the fate of the company was sealed ; it fell as an indirect victim of the French Revolution. The Cape settlement first went ; then Ceylon and all the possessions in India were lost. In 1795, Malacca also fell, and a year later Amboina and Banda were taken. Ternate alone offered any resistance. Java, which for the moment was not attacked by the English, was soon almost the only relic of the once wide realm of the company, which, harassed with debts and enfeebled by the political situation at home, could hold out a few years longer only by desperate means. The company was dissolved in the year 1798, and Holland took over its possessions in 1800.

The change of the Batavian republic on May 26th, 1806, into a kingdom held at **A Result of Napoleon's Wars** the will of Napoleon, and the French occupation of Holland on July 9th, 1801, involved further important consequences for the East Asiatic possessions. The British took advantage of the propitious moment to become masters of the colonies which had now become French, and in the year 1811, as a final blow, equipped an expedition against Java. Its success was complete ; Batavia fell without any resistance, and the small Dutch army, which held out for a short time in the vicinity of the capital, was forced to surrender on September 18th.

Great Britain took possession of the Dutch colonies, and proved her loyalty to those great principles which have raised her to be the first maritime and commercial power of the world by abolishing the monopolies and establishing free trade. But the precipitate introduction of these

DUTCH EAST INDIAN MERCHANT SHIP OF THE SEVENTEENTH CENTURY

colonies which had been taken from them, with the exception of the Cape and Ceylon. On June 24th, 1816, the Dutch com-

reforms and other injudicious measures soon led to all sorts of conflicts and disorders, which deprived the British Government of any advantage which might otherwise have been gained from their new possession. After the fall of Napoleon,

A MALAY VESSEL OF THE SIXTEENTH CENTURY

missioners at Batavia took over the government from the hands of the British commander. Nevertheless, the British soon afterward struck a severe blow directly at the Dutch colony, by adding to their possessions on Malacca, which had

the Netherlands, by the Treaty of London of August 13th, 1814, received back the

been held since 1786, the island of Singapore, which they acquired by purchase, and by establishing there in a short time a flourishing emporium for world trade. Batavia was the chief loser by this, and its population soon sank to one-half of what it had formerly been.

The dissolution of the company, and the British reforms, had broken down the narrow-spirited system of monopolies, and the Dutch Government had no option but to conform to the altered conditions. A small country like Holland, however, could

DUTCH EAST INDIAN WARSHIP OF THE SEVENTEENTH CENTURY UNDERGOING REPAIR

THE COLLYER QUAY AT SINGAPORE

GOVERNMENT HOUSE, SINGAPORE

SCENE FROM PENANG WHARF

ON THE RIVER AT SINGAPORE

GREAT BRITAIN IN MALAYSIA: VIEWS OF SINGAPORE AND PENANG

Photographs by G. Lambert, Singapore, and Underwood & Underwood. London

neither, from economic reasons, adhere to the British system of free trade nor waive all direct national revenue, and in its place await the indirect results of unrestricted commerce ; the colonies were compelled not only to support themselves and the colonial army which had now been formed, but also to provide for a surplus. Thus the spice mono-poly in the Moluccas, which had been successfully abolished, was reintroduced, though in a somewhat modified and less profitable form than before, since in the interval the cultivation of spices had been introduced into other parts of the tropical world. The bulk of the revenue had to be supplied by the patient population of Java, which, in accordance with a scheme drawn up by the Governor-General, Jan von den Bosch, in 1830, was employed on a large scale in forced labour on Government plantations, and was also burdened by heavy taxes.

The System of Monopoly Modified

The Dutch possessions from that time were no longer menaced by foreign enemies ; but the colonial army had to suppress many insurrections and conquer new territories for Holland. The Dutch, by slow degrees and in various ways, obtained the undisputed command of the Indian Archipelago. For a long time, in the large islands of Sumatra and Borneo, they exercised only a more or less acknow-ledged influence on the coasts, while the interior, even at the present day, does not everywhere obey their rule ; in any case the coast districts gave them much work to do, as their desperate battles with Achin, or Acheh, prove. The native princes were almost everywhere left in possession of their titles ; but on many occasions the Dutch, not reluctantly perhaps, were forced to take different districts under their immediate government The splen-did training which their colonial officials

received assured them success. A grea change in the internal conditions bega in the year 1868. The situation of th natives on Java, which had becom intolerable—and still more perhaps th knowledge that, in spite of all the force labour, the profits of the Governmen plantations did not realise expectations— led to the abolition of the *corvée* and th former unsound and extravagant method of working. The campaign which th Dutch poet and former colonial official Eduard Douwes Dekker, had conducted since 1859 against the abuses in the government, contributed to this result although for a long time no direct effect of his attacks were noticeable. The coffee monopoly, indeed, was left, though some-what modified ; so, too, the principle that the native should be left to work on his own account, and that then the results o his labour should be compulsorily bought from him at a very low price, is stil enforced, since the balance of the Indian finances must be maintained. It was possible to abandon the Javanese system of forced labour without excessive loss owing to the fact that the development of tobacco-growing on Sumatra since 1864 and of coffee-growing on Celebes opened up new sources of revenue. Accordingly, in 1873 the antiquated spice monopoly on the Moluccas was finally abolished without inflicting an insupportable blow on the State finances.

The scientific exploration of the region has been begun and carried out in a very thorough fashion. From many points of view the Dutch possessions are models for the colonial administra-tor ; and, in spite of all mistakes, the earlier development shows how a small European people can succeed in ruling an infinitely larger number of unstable Asiatics, and in making them profitable to itself.

Models for Colonial Administrators

THE FOUNDING OF BRITISH POWER IN MALAYSIA

In the year 1824 the island of Singapore was ceded to Great Britain by the Sultan of Johor by purchase, and in the hands of the British the town of Singapore speedily became the greatest port in Malaysia and one of the most important of the many centres of British trade in the Eastern seas. The picture, by Mr. Caton Woodville, illustrates the state entry of the British into Singapore in 1824.

THE ISLANDS AND THEIR STORY
JAVA: THE CENTRE OF THE DUTCH INDIES

JAVA is far from being the largest island of the Archipelago, but it is certainly the most fertile, so that it can support a very dense population ; it is also the most accessible, and consequently was the first and favourite resort of traders. It is true that culture has been able to take root easily only on the comparatively flat north coast with its abundance of harbours, while the steep south coast, looking out on a sea seldom navigated in old days, has never attained to any importance. The long, narrow island, through which a chain of lofty volcanoes runs, divides into a number of districts, in which independent political constitutions could be developed.

Apart from slight traces of a population resembling the Negritos, Java was originally inhabited by genuine Malays. No reliable early history of the island is forthcoming, since the first records, which are still untrustworthy, date from the Islamitic Age. We are thus compelled to have recourse to the accounts supplied by other nations, and to the remains of buildings and inscriptions which are still to be found plentifully on the island. In any case, Java was the focus of the Archipelago, so far as civilisation was concerned, and to some extent the political centre also, and it has retained this position down to the present day.

Our earliest information about Java can be traced to the Indian traders, who had communication with the island since, perhaps, the beginning of the Christian era. The fact that the Indians turned special attention to Java, which was by no means the nearest island of the Archipelago, must certainly be due to the existence there of rudimentary political societies whose rulers protected the traders, and whose inhabitants had already passed that primitive stage when man had no wants.

Java the Focus of Malaysia

The Indian merchants, by transplanting their culture to Java, and giving the princes an opportunity to increase their power and wealth through trade, had no small share in the work of political consolidation. We must treat as a mythical incarnation of these influences the Adyi Saka, who stands at the beginning of the native tradition, and is said to have come to Java in 78 A.D., for which reason the Javanese chronology begins with this year. He gave them their culture and religion, organised their constitution, made laws, and introduced writing. The Javanese legend mentions the names of some of the kingdoms influenced by Hindu culture. Mendang Kamulan is said to have become important at the end of the sixth or beginning of the seventh century ; in 896 the dynasty of Jangala, and in 1158 that of Pajajaram or Pajadsiran, are said to have succeeded.

Mythical Legends of Early History

The first immigrants to Java were worshippers of Vishnu, who were followed later by Buddhists ; this fact appears from the inscriptions and ruins and is confirmed by the accounts of the Chinese Fa-hien. The oldest traces of the Hindus have been discovered in West Java, not far from the modern Batavia. There must have been a kingdom in that part, between 400 and 500 A.D., whose monarch was already favourable to the new culture and religion. It is possible that the first Buddhists then appeared on the island and acquired influence. Important inscriptions dating from the beginning of the seventh century tell us of a prince of West Java, Aditya Dharma, an enthusiastic Buddhist and ruler of a kingdom which comprised parts of the neighbouring Sumatra. He conquered a Javanese prince, Siwaraga—whose name leads us to conclude that he was a supporter of the Brahman doctrines—and built a

Revelations of Ancient Inscriptions

THE MARKET PLACE IN JAVA, AS EVERYWHERE ELSE, IS THE FAVOURITE RENDEZVOUS

magnificent palace in a part of Java which can no longer be identified. It does not seem to have been any question of a religious war which led to this conflict, but merely of a political feud. We learn from Chinese sources that there was a kingdom of Java to which twenty-eight petty princes owed allegiance, and that in the year 674 a woman, Sima, was on the throne. This kingdom, whose capital lay originally farther to the east, embraced presumably the central parts of the island, and was not therefore identical with that of Aditya Dharma. Buddhism, at all events, supported by a brisk immigration from India, increased rapidly in power at this time, especially in the central parts of Java, while in the east, and perhaps in the west also, Brahmanism held its own. In the eighth and ninth centuries there were flourish-

ing Buddhist kingdoms, whose power and splendour may be conjectured from the magnificent architectural remains—above all, the ruins of temples in the centre of the island—and from numerous inscriptions. The fact that in the year 813 negro slaves from Zanzibar were sent by Java, as a present to the Chinese Court, shows the extent of Javanese commerce of that time. If we may judge of the importance of the states by the remains of the temples, the kingdom of Boro - Budur must have surpassed all others, until it fell, probably at the close of the tenth century. After the first quarter of that century hardly any more temples or inscriptions seem to have been erected in Central Java, a significant sign of the complete decay of the national forces. With this, the golden age of Buddhism came to an end.

Underwood & Underwood, London

NATIVES OF EASTERN JAVA

At the same time the centre of gravity of political power shifted to the east of the island. Inscriptions of the eleventh century tell of a king, Er-langa, whose hereditary realm must have lain in the region of the present Surabaya. By successful campaigns he brought a large part of Java under his rule, and seems to have stood at the zenith of his power in the year 1035. His purely Malay name proves that the dynasty from which he sprung was of native origin. He was, however, thoroughly imbued with Indian culture, as may be concluded from the increase of Sanscrit inscriptions in East Java after the beginning of the eleventh century. A Chinese account leads us to conjecture that about the same time a kingdom existed in the west of Java which was at war with a state in Southern Sumatra.

An Early Malay King and Warrior

The next centuries are somewhat obscure. This may be connected with a certain decline in the trade, and thus in the influence of the civilisation of India ; but it is principally due to the division and subdivision of Java into numerous petty states. But, in spite of this want of union, the attempt of the Mongol monarch Kublai Khan to seize Java proved unsuccessful ; only a part of the east was laid waste. That side of the island contained among others the states of Pasuruan, Kadiri, and Surabaya, the first of which gradually lost in importance. The states in Central Java apparently sank into insignificance compared with those of the east, this condition of things lasting until the intercourse with Nearer India once more flourished, and the kingdoms of Solo and Semarang began, in consequence, to revive.

Ths new Hinduistic age, in which Brahmanism again became prominent, had, however, a stimulating influence on the East, where the kingdom of Modyopahit rose to be a mighty power. In the west at that time the kingdom of Pajajaram was the foremost power. Javanese

records give the year 1221 (according to the Saka reckoning, 1144) as the date of the founding of Modyopahit, or, more correctly, of the preceding kingdom of Tumapel, and name as the first sovereign Ken Arok, or Angrok, who took as king the title Rayasa, and is said to have died in 1247. The kingdom of Modyopahit in the narrower sense was probably not founded before 1278 ; the first king was Kertarayasa.

Modyopahit is the best known of the earlier Javanese kingdoms, since it lasted almost to the arrival of the Europeans, and an offshoot survived destruction by Islam. A glance at the power of Modyopahit is therefore instructive, since it is typical of the peculiar conditions of the

A SCENE ON THE SOLO RIVER IN JAVA

Malay Archipelago, and all the seafaring population of the states on the coast or on the islands. Modyopahit never made an attempt to subjugate completely the island of Java and change it into a united nation, but it made its power felt on the coasts of the neighbouring islands, just as Sweden for a time ruled the shores of the Baltic without annexing Norway, or as England had long laid claim to the French coasts before Scotland joined hands to make the British realm. We may allude, in passing, to the colonies of Ancient Greece, to Carthage or Oman. In the west of Java a strong kingdom still stood, which for a time reduced Modyopahit to great straits. The advance of Modyopahit was naturally possible only when a large fleet was

Extension of Javanese Dominion

available ; this is said to have destroyed, in 1252, the Malay capital Singapore.

The kingdom attained its greatest size under the warlike king Ankawijaya, who mounted the throne in 1390, and is said to have subjugated thirty-six petty states. It is certain that the kingdom had possessions on Sumatra and settled Javanese

Zenith of Javanese Empire colonists there, also that the south coast of Borneo stood partially under its influence. It is probable that the Javanese, who, as can be proved, settled on the Moluccas, had also gained political power there. The island of Bali in the east of Java formed an integral part of Modyopahit. The kingdom seldom formed a united nation, but it exercised a suzerainty over numerous petty states, which gladly seized every opportunity of regaining independence. A great war between West and East Java, which had no decisive results, broke out in the year 1403, and led to the interference of Chinese troops.

In spite of all the brilliance of the Hindu states, the seeds of corruption had been early sown in them. The immense prosperity of the Arabian people had, centuries before, brought into the country Arab merchants, who ended by permanently settling there, as the merchants of India had already done, and had won converts for Islam in different parts of the Archipelago, chiefly among the Malays on Malacca, but also among the Chinese traders. " The Oriental merchant," says Conrad Leemans, " is a man of quite different stamp from the European. While the latter always endeavours to return to his home, the Oriental prolongs his stay, easily becomes a permanent settler, takes a wife of the country, and has no difficulty in deciding never to revisit his own land. He is assimilated to the native population, and brings into it parts of his language, religion, customs, and habits." It was characteristic of the heroic age of Islam that

Oriental Immigrants to Java the Arabian merchants had other aims beyond winning rich profits from trade; they tried to obtain political dominion by means of religious proselytism. Apparently the kingdom of Modyopahit, the bulwark of Hinduism, had early been fixed upon as the goal of their efforts.

The comparatively feeble resistance of the Buddhist and the Brahmin doctrines is partly explained by the fact that both were really comprehended by the higher classes alone, while the people clung to outward forms only. A Chinese annalist at the beginning of the fifteenth century calls the natives of Java downright devil-worshippers ; he does not therefore put them on a footing with the Buddhists of China or Further India, so familiar to him. The first victory of Islam was won in the Sumatran possessions of Modyopahit. The new doctrine found converts among the nobles of the kingdom ; of these Arya Damar, the governor in Sumatra, and, above all, his son Raden Patah, are mentioned.

The improbable Javanese account of the fall of Modyopahit only leads us to suppose that a revolt of the nobles who had been won over to Islam, probably assisted by female intrigues, cost the reigning monarch, Bromijoyo, his throne in 1478. The Brahmanists, who remained loyal, withdrew to the island of Bali, whence for a long time they commanded a part of the east coast of Java, and, when that was no longer possible, they at least hindered the advance of Islam on Bali. The victory of Islam in Modyopahit soon had its counter-

Conflict of the Creeds parts in the other states of the island. Even in 1552 the ruler of Bantam sought to obtain the protection of the Portuguese against the Mohammedans ; but it was too late. When, two years afterward, a Portuguese fleet appeared, the important trading town was in the hands of the Mohammedans. Since the conversions in the several districts of Java took place at different times, and were mostly associated with disturbances, a number of petty states soon arose, of which Pajang and Damak were the most powerful. On the island of Madura, whose destinies were always closely linked with those of Java, there were three independent kingdoms.

About a hundred years after the triumph of Islam the situation was altered. The princes of Mataram had gradually attained greater and greater power, though their country had originally been only a province of Pajang ; in the end they had subjugated most of the east and the centre of the island. In the west, on the contrary, Bantam, now Islamitic, was still the predominant power. The Dutch, after 1596, tried to negotiate an alliance with it, which could not permanently prove advantageous to Bantam. The founding of Batavia and the interference of the English soon led to hostile complications, but the attempt to expel the Dutch once more from the island did not succeed. The Dutch Trading Company, naturally, also came into conflict with the ambitious kingdom of Mataram. The Sultan, Agong of Mataram, had formed a scheme to subdue the west of Java, and had proposed an alliance to the Dutch ; but he found no response from the cautious merchants, and consequently twice, in 1628 and 1629, made an attempt to seize Batavia. After his death, his son Ingologo (1845–1670) concluded a treaty of peace and amity with the company (1646). Since the

The Dutch Preserve a Dynasty

Truna Jaya once more drew the sword against the apparently unpopular Amang Kurat, drove him out from his capital, and selected Kadiri as the capital of the kingdom which he had intended to found. But the decision rested with the Dutch, and they were resolved to keep the old dynasty on the throne, for the good reason that the expelled prince was forced to submit to quite different terms from those offered by his victorious rival. They defeated the usurper and placed on the throne the son of Amang Kurat, who had died meanwhile ; a small

The Sultan of Jokjakarta in semi-dress.

The Sultan of Solo in full dress.

THE TWO NATIVE RULERS OF JAVA IN 1864

Dutch did not for a time try to extend their possessions on Java, the peace was one of some duration. Ingologo's successor, the Sultan Amang Kurat, first invoked the help of the Dutch against a **The Dutch Trading Company** Burinese freebooter who had settled in Surabaya. The latter was expelled, and a rebellious prince, Truna Jaya, also succumbed to the attack of the Dutch fleet. The company, in the Treaty of Javara (1677), were well paid by concessions of territory and trading facilities for the help which they had rendered. But the complications were not yet ended.

Dutch garrison was left in the capital to protect him.

In the year 1703 the death of the sultan gave rise to violent disputes about the succession. Once more, naturally, Paku Buwono, the candidate who, with the help of the company, suceeded in establishing his claim to the throne, had to show his gratitude by surrenders and concessions of every kind (1705). The disputes, however, still lasted. Henceforth the sultans of Mataram could hold the sceptre and avert the fall of their feudal sovereignty only by the continuous support of the Dutch. Confusion reached its height when, by the revolt of the Chinese in the year 1740, the power of the company itself was shaken to its foundations. The reigning sultan, as well as the princes of Bantam and Cheribon, encouraged the rebellion, though they feigned devotion to the interests of the company. The result was that the sultan had to consent to fresh concessions after **Growth of Dutch Power** the defeat of the Chinese, and, what was most important, to renounce his sovereignty over the island of Madura. The kingdom of Mataram, after the loss of the coast, became more and more an inland state, and consequently was left helpless against the maritime power of the Dutch. The seat of government was then removed to Solo, or Surakarta.

But the greater the influence which the company acquired over Mataram, the more it saw itself dragged into the endless rebellions and wars of succession which had now become traditional in that kingdom. From 1749 to 1755 a war raged, which was finally decided by a partition of the kingdom. By treaties in 1755 and 1758, the Sultan Paku Buwono III. received the eastern part, with the capital Surakarta; his rival, Mangku Bumi, the western, with Jokjakarta as chief town; while a third claimant was granted some minor concessions. Besides the two states formed out of the ancient Mataram, there still remained in the west the kingdoms of Bantam and Cheribon, both entirely subject to the company.

Under the conditions thus established the more important disputes were ended; but the maladministration of the company, together with its oppression of the natives, produced their natural result in a series of petty disturbances during which robbery and pillage were carried on without a check. The final collapse of the company, and the chequered fortunes of the Netherlands in 1800, naturally increased the disorders in Java, and the reforms **Collapse of Dutch Trading Company** which General Herman Willem Daendels finally carried out in the year 1808 came too late. Britain took possession of the island in 1811, and held it till 1816. At this time the remaining territories of Bantam and Ceribon were taken away, and nothing was left to the two sultans beyond a pension and the empty title. Thus only the Susuhunan of Surakarta and the Sultan of Jokjakarta were left as semi-independent rulers; but both,

as a penalty for their resistance to the British, were once more confined to their own territory, and watched by garrisons.

With the second occupation of Java by the Dutch a new, but on the whole hardly more prosperous, era opens for the islands. The narrow-spirited monopolies and trading restrictions of the old company were, it is true, not revived, or revived only in a modified form; and since the Government devoted its attention to the widest possible cultivation of useful plants, it not only enlarged its revenue, but promoted the increase of the population and of the general welfare. But all the more heavily did the burden of the *corvée* weigh upon the natives. Insurrections were, therefore, still very frequent; one of them ended with the banishment of the discontented ex-Sultan of Bantam (1832). An earlier rebellion, which broke out in 1825 in Jokjakarta, under the leadership of the illegitimate Prince Dhigo Negoro, against the Governor-General Godard van der Capellen, had been still more dangerous. As had happened in previous cases, the troops of the princes of Madura, who **The New Régime** were loyal to the Dutch, lent efficient aid in its suppression. Although this revolt exposed many weak points in the administration of the Dutch Indies, it is only since 1868 that radical changes have been made. The *corvée* was virtually abolished in the case of the natives, and a more equitable system of government introduced. Of late years no events of importance, beyond several volcanic eruptions and a native insurrection in 1888, have to be related.

The area of Java, with the adjacent island of Madura, is 50,554 square miles, and the population 29,000,000. The whole of Dutch India is under the administration of a Governor-General—the present officer being J. B. van Heutsz—who has the power of passing laws but who must conform to the constitutional principles laid down in the " Regulations for the Government of Netherlands India." He is assisted by a council of five. The chief towns in Java are Batavia, with a population 115,887, including 8,893 Europeans; Soerabaya, with a population 146,944, including 8,906 Europeans; and Samarang, with a population 89,286, including 4,800 Europeans. The principal agricultural products are rice, maize, cotton, sugar cane, tobacco, indigo, cinchona, tea, and cacao. There are also coal and mineral oil industries.

SUMATRA: THE STEPPING STONE FROM ASIA

SUMATRA, which is far larger than Java, but of a similarly elongated shape, rises in the interior into numerous uplands possessing a comparatively cool climate ; the east coast is flatter and more accessible than the west coast, in front of which lies a row of small islands. The political attitude of Sumatra has been determined by its geographical position ; it has been connected on the one hand with the Strait of Malacca, on the other with Java. But ethnographically it is a purely Malay country, the place probably from which the ancient migrations to the west started. In the Battaks of the interior a people has been preserved which, although largely impregnated with the results of civilisation, has still retained a considerable share of its original peculiarities, and has resisted the introduction of any religious teaching from without. Sumatra, as might be expected from its position, probably came into contact with India and its culture at a somewhat earlier period than Java, since the rich pepper-growing districts on the Strait of Malacca were the first to create a systematic commerce. It is quite in harmony with these conditions that the districts on the northern extremity, the modern Achin, were the earliest which showed traces of Hindu influence, and, consequently, the beginnings of an organised national life ; thence this influence spread farther to the inland region, where signs of it are to be found even at the present day among the Battaks. The older kingdoms of the northern extremity were Poli and Sumatra; the capital of the latter, situated east of Achin, has given its name to the entire island. In Java it was the culture and the religion of the Hindus which made themselves chiefly felt, while the political power remained in

Indian Influence in Sumatra

the hands of the natives. In North Sumatra, on the contrary, the immigrants from India seemed completely to have assumed the lead in the state, and to have created a feudal kingdom quite in the Indian style. This kingdom, whose capital for many years was Pasir, held at times an extended sway, and comprised a part of the coasts of Sumatra.

While the Indian civilisation thus struck root in the north, and the political organisation of the kingdom of Menangkabau in the central districts was probably also due to its influence, it began indirectly to affect the south, where, according to Chinese accounts, a state had been formed as early as the fifth century. Southern Sumatra, by its geographical position, has always been fated to be in some degree dependent on the populous and powerful Java. In the earliest Hindu period of Java we learn of a prince whose territory lay on both sides of the Sunda Strait. It is possible that the inhabitants of Southern Sumatra enjoyed greater independence afterward, since we have no detailed accounts of the relations between the two islands, except Chinese accounts of wars between West Java and Southern Sumatra in the tenth century. In 1377 Southern Sumatra, whose ruler actually appealed to China for help, was conquered by the Javanese; for a time it belonged to Modyopahit. Palembang was then founded by Javanese colonists. We have already seen how Islam found its first adherents there, and became a menace to the kingdom of Modyopahit.

Southern Sumatra and Java

In the north, also, Islam effected the overthrow of Hinduism. At the beginning of the thirteenth century the first preachers of the new doctrine appeared in the Strait of Malacca, and at first gained influence over the Malays—in

A NATIVE RULER IN SUMATRA

The Sultan of Jambi, from a portrait taken in 1880

915

the narrower sense of the word—who came originally from Sumatra and ruled the peninsula of Malacca and the adjacent islands. In Achin itself, on the other hand, they won no success until the beginning of the sixteenth century—later, that is, than in Eastern Java. At any rate, the

PALACE OF THE SULTAN OF SIAK IN SUMATRA

political supremacy of the Hindus seems already to have broken up, and to have given place to native dynasties. Ali Moghayat Shah was, according to a credible tradition, the first Mohammedan sultan of Achin. Ala-ed-din al-Kahar (1530–1552) seems to have completely reorganised the political system; he also conquered a Battak-Hindu kingdom, which continued to resist the new doctrine in the north. In the succeeding period Achin blossomed out into a powerful state, and was naturally soon involved in the wars which raged almost without intermission on the Strait of Malacca between the Portuguese and the Malays. The fleets and armies of Achin repeatedly appeared off Malacca, and made successful attempts to capture the town from the Portuguese.

The Dutch having obtained a foothold in Java, extended their influence from that island over the south of Sumatra, and also in Lampong, which paid tribute to the Javanese kingdom of Bantam. The most important kingdom, Palembang, appears to have enjoyed a short period of independence after the destruction of Modyopahit, but it was conquered by the Geding Souro—who originally came from Demak in Java in the year 1544—and thus received a Javanese dynasty, which

reigned until 1649; after that a new line occupied the throne until 1824. A factory was set up in the vicinity of the town of Palembang by the Dutch as early as 1618, and events then took their usual course. After the natives in the year 1662 had attacked the factory and massacred almost the entire garrison, the town of Palembang was destroyed by a Dutch fleet, a favourable commercial treaty was exacted from the intimidated sultan, and this remained in force until 1811. Palembang acquired new interest for the Dutch—who meanwhile had been forced on one occasion to end a civil war by their interference—when in 1710 immensely rich tin mines were discovered on the island of Banka, belonging to that kingdom; the company promptly secured for itself a share of the profits by a separate treaty. The usually friendly relations between the Dutch and Palembang were immediately destroyed when, after the occupation of Java by the British, the whole garrison of the Dutch factory at Palembang was murdered by the sultan's order in a most horrible manner. The British undertook

DRAWING-ROOM IN PALACE OF SULTAN OF SIAK

a punitive expedition, but failed to restore order thoroughly; and the Dutch, after the restoration of their East Indian possessions in 1816, were nor more successful, until in 1823 they summarily incorporated Palembang as a province of their colonial empire.

The Dutch, on entering upon the inheritance of the Portuguese, took over their unfriendly relations with Achin. At first everything seemed to go well. The Dutch turned their attention more to Java and the Moluccas, and contented themselves with concluding a sort of commercial treaty with Achin in the year 1602, and with obtaining the concession of a strip of territory for the establishment of factories; in the meantime, also, owing to internal disorders, the power of Achin had greatly waned. But the keener the interest felt in Sumatra, the clearer it became that the originally despised Achin was a formidable and most invincible antagonist. After the middle of the nineteenth century it became the most dangerous piece on the chessboard of Dutch colonial policy. A dynasty of Arabian stock, whose first ruler, Mahmud Shah, mounted the throne in the year 1760, resolutely resumed the struggle with the Dutch. Achin

HOUSE OF A PADANG CHIEF, SUMATRA

had, it is true, been recognised as a sovereign state by the Treaty of London on March 17th, 1824; but the fact was gradually made evident that a free Malay state, with its inevitablte encouragement or tolerance of piracy, could no longer

ON THE RIVER AT PALEMBANG, SUMATRA

be allowed to exist in so dangerous a place as the Strait of Malacca.

Finally, therefore, in the year 1870, Holland, in return for a promise to resign its possessions in West Africa, received full permission to take any action it wished against Achin. Negotiations with

the sultan led to no result. The war, which began on March 25th, 1873, proved unexpectedly difficult and costly. An obstinate resistance was offered by the population on various occasions, and particularly when, on January 24th, 1874, the sultan's palace was stormed by the Dutch under Lieut.-General J. van Swieten. But this difficulty was greatly increased by the unfavourable nature of the scene of operations and the unhealthy climate. It was not until 1879 that the country could be considered subjugated; even then it still required an unusually large garrison, and occasional insurrections continue to show on how uncertain a foundation the Dutch rule in these parts is reared. No other feature in recent events requires to be noted, except the volcanic eruptions and earthquakes of 1883.

The island of Sumatra has an area of 161,612 square miles and an estimated population of 3,168,312, of whom 93,000 are Chinese. The largest town is Palembang with a population of 53,788. The mineral products are gold, petroleum, and coal, and the chief produce consists of tobacco, coffee, rubber, gum, rattan and spices, including pepper and nutmegs. As part of the Dutch East Indies, its administration is in the hands of the Governor-General, who exercises his functions through the agency of subordinate Residents.

THE FIRST BRITISH FOOTHOLD IN BORNEO

James Brooke, afterwards Rajah Brooke, making his first treaty with the Rajah of Borneo, in 1842.

BORNEO: LARGEST OF THE MALAY ISLANDS

BORNEO, the largest island of the Malay Archipelago, has not hitherto, in the course of history, attained anything like the importance to which its size should entitle it. A glance at the geographical features of this clumsily shaped island, which is surrounded on almost every side by damp, unhealthy lowlands, will satisfactorily account for this destiny ; indeed, Borneo would have probably drawn the notice of maritime nations to itself even less, had not its wealth in gold and diamonds proved so irresistibly alluring. If the physical characteristics of the huge island are unattractive to foreign visitants, they also inspire its inhabitants with little disposition for seafaring, migrations, and commerce. The Dyaks, who are the aborigines of Borneo, are mainly a genuine inland people, which in the course of history has shown little mobility and has tenaciously preserved its ancient customs. There is no trace of political societies on a large scale in the interior of the island ; the coasts alone, washed by the waves of foreign peoples, show the beginnings of national organisations, which from their position are influenced by the other islands of the Archipelago and the chief routes of maritime trade far more than by the land on which they are established. It would, for example, have been a less adventurous journey for an inhabitant of the north coast to visit the ports of China than to penetrate a dozen miles into the interior of his own island, or even to migrate as far as the south coast. Thus, the old tradition, that originally the island was divided into three large kingdoms—Borneo or Brunei, Sukadana, and Banjermassing—is untrustworthy in this form. The south coast of the island was influenced in a remarkable degree by the vicinity of Java. We have not only the

remains of buildings and idols, but also literary evidence to prove that the Hindu kingdoms of Java affected, both by conquest and by example, the adjoining parts of Borneo. Modyopahit, in particular, received tribute from the kingdom of Banjermassing and other states on the south coast ; even after the fall of the Brahman state the Islam princes of Java kept up this relation for some time. The legends of Borneo point in the same direction when they record that Banjermassing was founded by Lembong Mangkurat, a native of Nearer India, who had immigrated from Java.

At the time of the fall of Modyopahit, Banjermassing was the most powerful state in Borneo. It certainly owed its prominence to the advanced civilisation which, evoked by a large Javanese immigration, was naturally followed by the introduction of Hindu creeds. According to the legend, a son of the royal house of Modyopahit founded in the fourteenth century a Hindu dynasty which reckoned thirteen princes down to Pangeran Samatra, the first Islam ruler; the daughter of Pangeran Samatra was married to a Dyak, who became the founder of a new dynasty. The circumstance that Banjermassing became tributary to the Islam state of Demak on Java, while Sukadana and Landak, the other capitals of the south coast, were subject to Bantam, equally Islamitic, favoured the introduction of the Mohammedan faith, which first struck root in 1600. But all recollection of Modyopahit was not lost ; most of the princely families of the south coast traced their descent from its royal house.

The north, on the other hand, was considerably influenced in early times by China ; even at the present day pieces of Chinese porcelain, which evidently

SULTAN OF BORNEO IN 1880

reached the island through ancient trading transactions, are highly valued by the Dyaks of the interior. The earliest mentioned kingdoms in Borneo, Polo in the north and Puni on the west coast, may have acquired power from the trade with

RAJAH BROOKE
The venturesome Englishman who founded the British Dependency of Sarawak

China ; in the fourteenth century, certainly, Puni also was subject to Javanese influence. In addition to the Javanese, the Malays—in the stricter sense of the word—exercised great influence over Borneo, whose coasts in quite early times had become the favourite goal of their voyages and settlements. It was through them that Brunei, the chief state of the north coast, was founded, though the date cannot be accurately fixed; perhaps it was merely a continuation of the old kingdom of Polo. Malay immigrants had probably come to Brunei, even before their conversion to Islam, which took place in the middle of the thirteenth century. Modyopahit also gained a temporary influence over Brunei. When, however, the first Europeans visited the country, it was a powerful and completely independent kingdom, which for a time extended its sway over the Sulu Islands and as far as the Philippines. In the year 1577 the first war with

the Spaniards broke out, and further collisions followed later. Other Malay states on the west coast were Pontianak—probably the ancient Puni—Matan, Mongama, and others. Banjermassing, Sukadana, and Landak were also originally founded by Malays, and only subsequently brought under Javanese rule.

From the east the Bugi of Celebes sought new homes on the shores of Borneo, and also founded a number of small kingdoms, whose existence depended originally on trade and piracy. All these immigrations have naturally produced the result that the coast population of Borneo is everywhere an inextricable tangle of the most various racial elements, and that the aboriginal Dyaks have intermixed freely with Malays, Javanese, Chinese, Bugi, and others. Which racial element predominates depends on various contingencies from time to time. In the mining districts of the kingdom of Samba

TYPES OF THE INHABITANTS OF SARAWAK

in Western Borneo, for example, Chinese were settled after the second half of the eighteenth century in such large numbers that they were far too strong for the Malay sultan, and were finally suppressed by the Dutch government only in 1854.

The first Europeans who attempted to form connections with Borneo were the Portuguese, after 1521 ; they met, however, with little success, although they renewed their attempt in 1690. Meanwhile the Dutch East India Company had opened, in the year 1606, a factory in Banjermassing, whose business was to export pepper and gold dust; but, owing to the vacillating and often hostile attitude of the sultan, it was no more successful than the Portuguese settlement, and was finally abandoned, in consequence of the murder of Dutch officials and merchants at Banjermassing in 1638 and 1669. The residence of the sultan, since Banjermassing had been destroyed by the Dutch in 1612, was removed to Martapura, and remained there, although Banjermassing soon rose from its ashes. In 1698 the English appeared upon the scene, and were at first successful, until the destruction of their factory in the year 1707 thoroughly discouraged them from further undertakings. The Sultan of Banjermassing, in spite of his faithless behaviour, was in no way inclined to abandon the advantages of the European trade, but once more turned to the Dutch.

At length, then, in 1733, the Dutch resolved on a new attempt. Since that date, notwithstanding frequent misunderstandings, their relations with the island have been practically unbroken. The interference of the company in a war about the succession to the throne turned the scale and procured for it the sovereignty over Banjermassing ; and thus the greater part of the south coast of Borneo, as well as the coveted monopoly of the pepper trade, passed into its hands in 1787. During the occupation of Java by the English the reigning sultan consented to make further concessions, which after January 1st, 1817, benefited the Dutch.

To this period belongs the romantic attempt of an Englishman, William Hare, to found an independent kingdom in South Borneo. The Dutch have considerably extended and consolidated their power by new treaties and by the wars which they fought from 1850 to 1854 on the west coast, as also from 1859 to 1862 on the south-east coast. Banjermassing itself, after the interference of the Dutch in the succession to the throne in 1852 had caused a rebellion, was deprived of its dynasty in 1857 and completely annexed in 1864. A fresh rebellion in 1882 did not alter the position of affairs.

At the beginning of the nineteenth century the sultanate of Brunei had lost much of its power ; when, therefore, in the year 1839, an insurrection was raging in the province of Sarawak, the governor gladly accepted the offer of James Brooke, an Englishman, to come to his assistance.

ORIGINAL RESIDENCE OF RAJAH BROOKE AT SARAWAK

Brooke, born on April 29th, 1803, at Bandel, in Bengal, had then formed the plan of founding a colony in Borneo at his private cost ; he appeared in June, 1839, with his crew on the coast, and actually conquered the opponents of the sultan, who in gratitude entrusted the governorship of Sarawak to him in 1840, and in 1842 formally invested him with the province.

Since " Rajah " Brooke was no ordinary adventurer, but a man of noble nature and strong character, his administration proved a blessing to the disorganised country. When the sultan showed signs of suspicion, the rajah relied upon England, and compelled the sultan in the year 1846 to cede

TYPES OF MALAY HOUSES IN BORNEO

Thus the entire island of Borneo, the largest in the world except Australia and New Guinea, is divided, politically, into two parts, about three-quarters of the island being a Dutch colony, and the remaining fourth—the north and north-west portion—being British, and being composed of British North Borneo (31,106 square miles), Brunei (4,000 square miles), and Sarawak (42,000 square miles), with the contiguous island of Labuan (31 square miles). The territory of British North Borneo is adminis-

the island of Labuan to the British, and finally, after he had suppressed various risings of the Malays and Chinese, made himself absolutely independent of Brunei. Shortly before his death he offered Sarawak to the British government. But the offer was refused, and after his death in 1868 the state of Sarawak passed to his nephew, Sir Charles Brooke. Subsequently the British government reconsidered its former decision, and in 1888 both Brunei and Sarawak were received under British protection on the terms that internal administration should be left entirely in the hands of their respective rulers, but that the foreign relations of both states should be controlled by Britain. The declaration of this protectorate came as a natural sequel to the acquisition of North Borneo. This province was granted to the British North Borneo Company as its private property in the year 1881. It passed under the protection of England at the same time and on the same terms as the states of Brunei and Sarawak.

tered by the British North Borneo Company through the agency of a resident Governor, whose appointment is conditional upon the approval of the Secretary of State. The chief products of British Borneo are timber, coffee, rice, sago, tobacco, rubber, gums, and spices. There is a railway of about 120 miles and there is telegraphic cable communication with the outer world. The chief town of British North Borneo is Sandakan, with a population of 8,000, and of Sarawak the chief town is Kuching, also the capital, with a population of a little over 30,000

FAMILY TOMB OF THE RAJAH OF DINDA

A RIVERSIDE VILLAGE IN THE ISLAND OF BORNEO

CELEBES: SMALLEST OF THE LARGER ISLANDS

THE fourth large island of the Archipelago, Celebes, is of quite a different character from Borneo. Instead of the clumsy contour of Borneo, we find here a most diversified coast line. Immense plains such as we find in Borneo are wanting in Celebes, which is a land of mountainous peninsulas separated by deeply indented gulfs. If the island has not attracted commerce to its shores to the extent that might be expected from these favourable natural conditions, **A Land of Gulfs and Mountains** the reason is, doubtless, that attention has been diverted from it by the proximity of the spice-bearing Moluccas. Celebes, although fertile and not actually poor in ore and precious metals, and for that reason a valuable possession at the present day, does not contain those tempting products which hold out to the merchant the prospect of rapid and splendid profits. But although the accessibility of the island has not been thoroughly appreciated by foreigners, it has exercised great influence on the fortunes of the native population—it has sent them to the sea and turned them into wandering pirates, traders, and settlers.

Celebes has thus acquired for the eastern Malay Archipelago a significance similar to that of Malacca for the western. Celebes was not regarded by the old inhabitants of the Archipelago as a single united country. The northern peninsula with its aboriginal population of Alfur tribes had nothing in common with the southern parts, which were inhabited by the Macassars and the Bugi ; and even the Dutch have recognised this difference so far as to place the two districts under different Residencies. Celebes, on the whole, is a genuine Malay country, although there are many indications among the Alfurs that there was an admixture of dark-skinned men ; but whether we must think of these latter as stunted Negrito-like aborigines or as immigrant Papuans, is an insoluble problem for the time being. The Bugi and Macassars are pure Malays, who, in their whole life

and being, probably most resemble those bold navigators of Malay race who have peopled Polynesia and Madagascar.

In view of the fact that the bulk of the population is still divided into numerous small tribes, which show little inclination to amalgamate, we cannot venture to assign an early date for the rise of large kingdoms in Celebes. Tradition in the south can still tell how the shrines of separate localities, from which emigrants went to other parts of the island, first acted as a rallying point for small tribes or hindered the disintegration of others which were increasing in numbers and extent of territory ; the chiefs of the several localities recognised the possessor of the most ancient and most potent magic charm as their superior lord, assembled from time to time at council meetings in his village, and thus prepared the way for the erection of larger political communities. This process probably was carried out in Celebes with comparatively little interruption and without the help of foreigners. Even of Hinduism only faint traces can have reached the island, as is shown, among other instances, from the absence of Sanscrit words in the original dialects of the Bugi. The small tribes were engaged in constant feuds among themselves before any states were formed, and after that epoch these wars were continued on a larger scale, and alternated with sanguinary conflicts within the still **When Death by Violence was the Rule** incompletely organised kingdoms. The annals of Macassar relate, for example, as a noteworthy fact, that one of these princes died a natural death. The foremost power among the Macassars was Goa, later Macassar ; among the Bugi, on the contrary, the foremost power was Boni, from where the Bugi gradually spread far over the coasts of the Eastern Malay islands and to some extent founded new states.

The Portuguese opened communications with Celebes in the year 1512. The kingdoms into which the island was then divided could hardly have been long established ; for even if the annals of the Macassars enumerate 39 princes, who occupied the throne in succession down to the year 1809, the average duration of a reign during those early days of barbarism and bloodshed must have been short. Assuming, therefore, that the records are fairly trustworthy, the state of Macassar may have been founded subsequently to the year 1400. The Portuguese first tried to secure a footing on the island in 1540, when they set up a factory in Menado, and later also in the south. They obtained, however, no better results than the English and Danes at a somewhat later period. The Dutch, who had turned their attention to Celebes after 1607, alone met with ultimate success.

But meanwhile Islam had reached the island. In 1603 the Prince of Macassar, with his people, adopted the new faith. The great ideas of this world-religion were here, as in so many other places, a stimulus to the prosperity of the country, so that the influence of the kingdom of Macassar made vast strides in the next few years, until its supremacy in Southern Celebes was indisputable. It was en-

The Wars of the Petty States gaged in repeated wars with Boni, the state of the Bugi, since the people of that democratically organised kingdom refused to accept Islam, and resisted the new creed, first with their prince at their head, and then, when he was converted to the Mohammedan faith, in opposition to him. The Sultan of Macassar interfered in these quarrels, and succeeded, in the year 1640, in subduing Boni. The same fate was shared by numerous petty states. Macassar, with its naval power, partially conquered the coasts of Sumbawa and Buton ; but it was destined soon to discover that the age of large native states was past.

The destruction of a Dutch factory on Buton compelled the East India Company to take active measures ; in doing so it relied on the conquered, but still disaffected, Boni, whose royal family had found a friendly reception as fugitives among the Dutch. The Sultan of Macassar was soon compelled to abandon his conquests and resign the throne of Boni to Rajah Palaka, a protégé of the Dutch, who from the year 1672 onward raised Boni to the ruling power in South Celebes. After his death (1696) a part of his kingdom became the absolute possession of the

company. Although the Dutch always took full advantage of the inveterate hatred between Macassar and Boni, yet their attempts to extend their rule still farther led to repeated and troublesome wars, until the temporary British occupation of the island (1814–1816), and the ensuing disorders, resulted in drastic

Establishment of Dutch Supremacy modifications of the political situation. A war with the princes of South Celebes ended in 1825 with the victory of the Dutch. The independence of the native states would have then ended for ever had not the rebellion in Java diverted attention in another direction. It was only after new struggles in 1856 and 1859 that their annexation to the colonial empire of the Dutch East Indies was effected.

The history of North Celebes really belongs to that of the Moluccan Archipelago. The state of Menado may be noticed as an important political entity. When the northern peninsula, and especially the hilly district of Minahassa, had proved to be suitable for coffee plantations, European influence easily became predominant there, and all the more so since Islam had not yet won a footing. Elsewhere in the Dutch East Indies there have been few or no conversions to Christianity ; but a part of the inhabitants of Minahassa have been converted. The eastern and smallest peninsula of Celebes has also in its external life been subject to the influence of the Moluccas.

Celebes is administered, like the other islands of Dutch East Indies, by the Governor-General, with headquarters in Batavia. The area of the island is 71,470 square miles, and the population is conjectured to be under one million, but there seems to have been no authoritative basis for this estimate. The chief town and port is Vlaardingen, or Macassar, with a population of 20,000, in the extreme

Industrial Conditions in Celebes south of the island. Other trading ports are Menado and Kema on the northern peninsula. The climate of Celebes is much healthier than that of many other islands in the Malaysian group. Mining is prosecuted to some extent, valuable coal deposits existing in the northern parts. Gold has been found, and there is possibility of remunerative enterprise in its exploitation, and in the south sulphur is plentiful.

THE MOLUCCAS AND THE SUNDA ISLANDS

THE modern history of the Malay Archipelago centres in the west round Java, but in the east round the Molucca Islands. In the earlier period, when the trade in muscat nuts and cloves had not yet attracted foreign shipping to its shores, the group of the Moluccas may have been less conspicuous ; small tribes and village communities probably fought against each other, and may have extended their warlike expeditions and raids to Celebes and New Guinea, and these visits were probably returned in similar fashion. The trade in spices then raised the wealth and power of certain places to such a pitch that they were able to bring under their dominion large portions of the Archipelago. Jilolo, on the northernmost peninsula of Halmahera, is considered to be the oldest kingdom ; in 1540 it was absorbed by Ternate. It is a remarkable fact that the influence of China on the Moluccas seems to have been very slight, since the islands are hardly mentioned in the Chinese annals before the fifteenth century.

The Portuguese on their arrival found two large kingdoms, Ternate and Tidor ; both originally rose in small insular districts, their chief towns lay in close proximity, and as hostile rivals each was bent on eclipsing the other. The population of these two states was even then, probably, much mixed ; in addition to the Alfurs, presumably the oldest occupants, who, on Halmahera especially, and also on Seram, had preserved a large share of their independence, there were on the coasts Malays, Bugi, and the descendants of other nations occupied in the spice

trade. These included Javanese—who seem at first to have been almost exclusively occupied in transporting spices to their native island—Arabs, and probably also Chinese and Hindus. About Ternate we know that the seventh ruler mounted the throne in the year 1322 ; in his time Javanese and Arabs are said to have immigrated in exceptional numbers. Ternate and Tidor were maritime and insular states ; they kept closely to the coast, and while their fleets were powerful they never possessed extensive territory on Halmahera and Seram. Since their power was entirely based on the spice trade, the princes of the two states courted the favour of the Portuguese, who indeed first appeared as traders. When Ternate proved successful in this respect, the monarch of Tidor threw himself into the arms of the Spaniards, who then came forward with their claims on the Moluccas. The outrages of the Portuguese led to many rebellions and conflicts.

The Dutch first appeared on the scene in the year 1599, and planted a small settlement on Banda ; another half century elapsed, however, before they felt themselves strong enough to seize the monopoly of spice-growing and the spice trade. The sultanates of Ternate and Tidor, which had some power over the coast districts of Celebes and New Guinea, were allowed to remain ; but the spice islands proper —Amboina, after 1605, and Banda especially— were placed under Dutch administration. As it seemed impracticable to watch over all the islands, the company determined to allow the cultivation of cloves and

ENEMIES OF THE DUTCH IN BALI
These Balinese natives are said to use their wives and children as shields in battles against the Dutch

925

muscat nuts only in certain places, and everywhere else to effect a complete destruction of the spice trees.

The execution of this purpose necessitated a war, which in 1621 almost annihilated the population of the Banda Islands, so that thenceforth the company was able to introduce slaves, and thus exercise a stricter supervision. But since the seeds of the spice trees were continually being carried by birds to other islands, annual expeditions were undertaken to destroy the young plantations on prohibited soil, by force of arms if necessary; and unspeakable misery was in this way spread over the islands. These sad conditions, whose prime mover was the Governor, Arnold de Vlaming,

play the least conspicuous part in history. Devoid of any political unity, they stagnated in their isolation until foreign immigration introduced a higher type of social life, and small kingdoms sprang into existence here and there along their coasts. The interior of the islands remained unsubdued and unaffected by this change.

Bali affords a solitary exception to the general rule. This island, although profoundly influenced in ancient times by Java, frequently enjoyed political independence. When the Brahman states of East Java increased in strength towards the close of the first millennium of the Christian era, Bali also was a state with Hindu culture. Ugrasena ruled there in the year 923; in 1103 another prince,

THE DUTCH SOLDIERS IN HOLLAND'S NEVER-ENDING WAR
A Dutch fort on the island of Bali, where the inhabitants have resisted the soldiers of Holland for thirty years and are still in arms. The war has been most sanguinary and the mortality appalling.

lasted down to the British occupation in 1810, and were afterward renewed, though in a modified form. In 1824 the destructive expeditions were discontinued, but the last traces of the spice monopoly disappeared only in 1873, when the plantations were sold to private speculators. During the time when the small Spice Islands had so chequered a history, the main islands long remained neglected. The Dutch gradually succeeded in acquiring influence over the semi-civilised Alfurs, of whom those who live on Seram are organised in peculiar secret societies, which originated in the peculiar system of male associations to which reference has been made. Of all the districts of the Malay Archipelago, the "small" Sunda Islands

Jayapangu, is mentioned. Bali later formed a part of the kingdom of Modyopahit. It was impossible for Islam to convert the Balinese, who, at the time when they formed a united people, actually assumed the aggressive, oppressed the Mohammedan Sassaks on the temporarily conquered Lombok, and menaced Sumbawa. Brahmanism defied its rival in this case at least, and has lasted on Bali down to the present day. In consequence of the prevailing system of small sovereigns, complete political disintegration gradually set in. There were eight petty states in Bali in the nineteenth century, when the Dutch in the years 1846, 1848, 1849, and 1868 undertook campaigns against Balinese princes. Nevertheless, the Dutch, even recently, have

SEAPORT VILLAGE ON THE ISLAND OF CERAM

required a comparatively strong levy of troops to crush the resistance of one of the princes.

Javanese influence also temporarily touched Sumbawa, the development of which on the whole was affected by the seafaring inhabitants of Southern Celebes, the Macassars and Bugis. It was formerly split up into six small and independent states, Bima, Sumbawa, Dompo, Tambora, Sangar, and Papekat. The population of the " kingdoms " of Tambora and Papekat suffered terribly under the devastating eruption of Tambora (April 10th, 1815), as, to a somewhat less degree, did those of Sangar, Dompo, and the town of Sumbawa. In the east of Floris, or Flores, of which the capital is Larantuka, Malay and Buginese immigrants predominated ; the west, Mangerai, was dependent on Bima, one of the states on Sumbawa, and connected with it by a common language. Timor may have been mostly influenced by the Moluccas, and saw small principalities formed on its coast at a comparatively early date ; these principalities had mostly disappeared by 1600 in consequence of the advance of Timorese, in the stricter sense of the word, who inhabited the east of the island and originally, perhaps, had their homes in Seram. The most north-easterly part of Timor (Deli or Dilhi) is the last remnant of the Portuguese possessions in Indonesia ; in the south-west (Kupang) the Dutch have had a footing since 1688.

The total area of the Moluccas, or Spice Islands, is about 43,864 square miles. They consist of two main groups, the northern including Jilolo, Ternate, Tidore and the Obi group, and the southern including Buro, Ceram, Amboina and the Banda group. The total population is estimated at about 411,000. The chief town and commercial centre is Amboina, on the island of the same name, with a population of about 8,000, and an annual trade of about £85,000. The chief products are cloves and other spices, rice, sago, maize, timber, coco-nuts, and cocoa.

ATTACK OF THE OLD MALAY PIRATES

THE MANIFESTO
OF A
MODERN PATRIOT

AGUINALDO'S OATH OF ALLEGIANCE

" I HEREBY renounce all allegiance to any and all so-called Revolutionary Governments in the Philippine Islands, and recognise and accept the supreme authority of the United States of America therein. I do solemnly swear that I will bear true faith and allegiance to that Government; that I will at all times conduct myself as a faithful and law-abiding citizen of the said islands, and will not, either directly or indirectly, hold correspondence with, or give intelligence to any enemy of the United States; nor will I abet, harbour, or protect such enemy; that I impose upon myself these voluntary obligations without any mental reservations or purpose of evasion, so help me God."

AGUINALDO TO HIS COUNTRYMEN

" I BELIEVE I am not in error in presuming that the unhappy fate to which my adverse fortune has led me is not a surprise to those who have been familiar with the progress of the war. The lessons taught with a full meaning, which have recently come to my knowledge, suggest with irresistible force that a complete termination of hostilities and lasting peace are not only desirable, but absolutely essential to the welfare of the Philippine Islands.

" The Filipinos have never been dismayed at their weakness, nor have they faltered in following the path pointed out by their fortitude and courage. The time has come, however, in which they find their advance along this path to be impeded by an irresistible force, which, while it restrains them, yet enlightens their minds and opens to them another course, presenting them the cause of peace. This cause has been joyfully embraced by the majority of my fellow countrymen, who already have united around the glorious sovereign banner of the United States. In this banner they repose their trust and believe that under its protection the Filipino people will attain all those promised liberties which they are beginning to enjoy.

" The country has declared unmistakably in favour of peace. So be it. There has been enough blood, enough tears, and enough desolation. This wish cannot be ignored by the men still in arms if they are animated by a desire to serve our noble people, which has thus clearly manifested its will. So do I respect this will, now that it is known to me. After mature deliberation, I resolutely proclaim to the world that I cannot refuse to heed the voice of a people longing for peace, nor the lamentations of thousands of families yearning to see their dear ones enjoying the liberty and the promised generosity of the great American nation. By acknowledging and accepting the sovereignty of the United States throughout the Philippine Archipelago, as I now do, and without any reservation whatsoever, I believe that I am serving thee, my beloved country. May happiness by thine."

THE PHILIPPINE ISLANDS
THE STORY OF A STRUGGLE FOR NATIONALITY

THE large group of the Philippines, which comprise over 3,000 distinct islands and islets and which in a geological as well as ethnological sense represents the link connecting Indonesia to the region of Eastern Asia, forms the north-eastern portion of the Malay world of islands. Malayism is always predominant in the Philippines; it may, indeed, have prevailed in Formosa also, and thence have made further conquests. The Philippines were not always in the possession of the Malays. In the earliest historical age we find the islands inhabited by the Negritos, who were only gradually driven back to the mountains of the interior by the immigrating brown race; it was only on the north shores of Luzon that they kept their position on the sea - coast. There were probably two invasions of Malays; the tribes of the first intermixed very largely with Negritos, and on the second immigration shared their fate, since they, too, were forced to retreat to the mountainous interior of the islands, while the newcomers occupied the coasts.

The second wave of immigration, like the first, flooded chiefly the south of the Archipelago, and ethnologically changed it, while the Negritos on the coast in the north-east of Luzon once more escaped extermination. The Malays of the second migration brought to the Philippines an advanced civilisation which shows traces of the influence of India; this event may have occurred, therefore, some centuries after the Christian era. Though not absolutely convincing, many arguments support the view that the second immigrants came from Sumatra, the cradle of the Malay race; other features of resemblance point to the Dyaks of Borneo. The Tagals on the peninsula of Luzon became the representatives of the native semi-civilisation. A third immigration, which, however, was not so thoroughly carried out, is connected with the advance of Islam into the Malay island-world. The Malays of Brunei in Borneo undertook expeditions of conquest and conversion to the Philippines about 1500. They subdued Palawan and firmly established themselves on Luzon. Almost simultaneously immigrants from the Moluccas settled on Mindanao and seized the Sulu Islands. A Mohammedan pirate state arose there, while previously, as we learn from Chinese records of 1417, the group of islands was divided into three kingdoms.

The Philippines were reached, from the east, on

AGUINALDO, THE NATIONAL HERO

I

March 16th, 1521, by the Portuguese Magalhaes, who was in the Spanish service, and were called St. Lazarus Isles ; later the name Islas de Poniente was given them ; the name Philippines was not adopted until 1565. The islands excited little attention at first, while an obstinate struggle developed between the Spaniards and the Portu-

The Struggle between Spain and Portugal guese for the possession of the Moluccas. When Charles V. abandoned the Moluccas on April 22nd, 1529, the Philippines also would probably have fallen into the hands of the Portuguese if private Spaniards had not set foot on them, and if Portugal had not attached light importance to their possession. It was not until 1543 that a Spanish fleet appeared once more in the Archipelago with the commission to found a Spanish settlement. But this finally fell into the hands of the Portuguese, who theoretically still asserted their claims to the Philippines. A renewed attempt in the year 1565 met at last with success ; the Spaniards established themselves first on Sebu, then on Panay. In 1570 they turned to Luzon, and founded in the ensuing year the town of Manila.

The Spaniards, after Portugal had been united to their kingdom in 1580, found two other rivals who endangered their existence—the Mohammedans, or Moros, advancing from the south, and the Chinese, who were largely represented, especially on Luzon. These latter had long maintained commercial intercourse with the Philippines, and seem sometimes also to have won political influence. They constituted a perpetual menace to the Spanish rule, but required, nevertheless, to be treated cautiously, since the revenues of the colonies depended almost wholly on the trade with China. In the year 1603 a terrible revolt of the Chinese broke out.

It was quelled with great slaughter of the insurgents by the Spaniards with the help of the natives and of Japanese, who were also resident on Luzon for trading purposes.

A few years later, however, the number of Chinese settlers in Manila had once more risen to an alarming height. A new revolt was suppressed in 1639, and when, in 1662, the Philippines were threatened by the Chinese freebooter Cheng Ko Chuang, whose father, Koxinga, had conquered Formosa, there was once more a massacre, which, however, did not result in the total exclusion of the undesirable guests.

The Spaniards met with more success in their struggle against Islam. Christianity, thanks to the active zeal of the Spanish monks, completely outstripped Islam on Luzon, while on Mindanao and the other southern islands the progress of the Mohammedan teaching was at least checked. The task of ruling the natives was facilitated

FILIPINO INSURGENT CHIEFS

through the circumstance that no large kingdoms appear to have existed on the Philippines before the conquest. The Spanish Government was most anxiously concerned to obtain the complete monopoly of the trade of the Philippines. Commerce was permitted only with the

Spanish Trading Restrictions American colonies of Spain. A port was founded at Acapulco for the purpose of this trade, and once a year a great galleon sailed thither from the Philippines, bearing native spices and goods from China, Japan, and India. The price of this cargo was usually paid in silver dollars. A definite maximum in goods and money was fixed, which might not be exceeded. Direct trade with Europe was prohibited, notwithstanding frequent attempts by the merchants of

INTERIOR OF FORT SANTIAGO, MANILA

SCENE ON THE PASIG RIVER, MANILA

BRIDGE OF SPAIN, MANILA

CHURCH OF SAN SEBASTIAN, MANILA

MANILA'S PRINCIPAL BUSINESS STREET

ENTRANCE TO THE WALLED CITY, MANILA

931

PHILIPPINE COCO-NUT FARM

PHILIPPINE SUGAR MILL

NATIVE BATHING HOUSES IN THE NEIGHBOURHOOD OF MANILA

SCENE IN MALOLOS, AGUINALDO'S
CAPITAL

NATIVE HOUSE IN THE TOWN OF
ERMITA

THE DEFENCE OF MALOLOS, AGUINALDO'S CAPITAL, BY NATIVE TROOPS

AGUINALDO'S TROOPS ON THE DEFENSIVE IN A FIELD ENGAGEMENT

Seville. The richly laden vessels which were engaged in the commerce with America naturally tempted all the pirates and admirals of unfriendly nations, and were not unfrequently plundered, as, for example, by Anson on the coast of the island of Samar in 1743.

Plundered Galleons of Spain After 1758 the trade lay in the hands of the Real Compania de Filipinas. The harbour of Manila was first opened to all maritime nations in 1803; in 1814 free trade was introduced, and in 1834 the company was dissolved. But even then foreign competition was checked as much as possible by all kinds of vexatious customs duties; the ruinous tobacco monopoly was not done away with until 1882.

Although these ridiculous restrictions on trade and the ascendency of the clerical party hindered all progress, still the Philippines, during the union of Portugal with Spain (1580–1640), formed the centre of a splendid colonial empire. But through the competition of the Netherlands, Spain was soon restricted to the Philippines proper, which now for a long time were anything but prosperous. Nevertheless the spread of Christianity among the natives helped to consolidate the colony. When a British fleet appeared off Manila in the year 1763, and the Chinese and Indians rose against the Spaniards, the latter received the help of the Christian native population.

These allies could not save Manila from falling for the moment into the hands of the British, but the Treaty of Paris restored to the Spaniards all that had been conquered from them in the Philippines. Their power was now unchallenged, except by such rebellions as the tyranny of the monastic and mendicant orders produced among the native

FILIPINO TRENCH TAKEN BY AMERICANS
Underwood & Underwood, London

races, and by the more formidable discontent of the Malayo-Spanish half-castes, who had received a tinge of European culture, but felt themselves slighted and were eager to play a leading part. Unrest showed itself in 1824. The mutiny of the troops in 1872 might have been most dangerous had it not been smothered by prompt action. The political power of Spain seemed on the whole to have been consolidated in the course of the nineteenth century; and Spain gradually succeeded in annexing to her sovereignty a part at least of the hitherto independent districts such as Southern Mindanao and the Sulu Islands. But the ineradicable tradition of treating the colonies as sources of profit for place hunters and for the ecclesiastical orders prevented any real prosperity; it was equally impossible to treat the Tagals for all time as the Indians of Paraguay had been treated at the time of the Jesuit supremacy. The thought of freedom gradually gained ground; secret societies, resembling freemasonry, formed the rallying-point of discontented Filipinos, whose hatred was directed chiefly against the priesthood.

Though nominally a Spanish colony for 327 years, the Spanish arm did not reach over the greater part of the group. The Government was virtually subservient **Influence of Monastic Orders** to the monastic orders, who, through influence at the Court, could make or unmake the Governor-General. They absorbed all the best land in the colony, and by their intrigues and their quarrels among themselves brought the Europeans into contempt among the natives.

A revolt against the power of the monks was inevitable as soon as the natives began to acquire wealth. At first it took a

AGUINALDO AT HOME WITH HIS LITTLE SON   Keystone View Co.

SPANISH MEZTIZA GIRLS OF MANILA IN NATIVE DRESS

Underwood & Underwood, London

constitutional form. Contrary to the decrees of the Council of Trent, the monks usurped the duties of the secular clergy and acted as spies in every Christian village, procuring the deportation of any native obnoxious to them without trial. Many of the Filipinos had been ordained priests, and the natives demanded that

Discontent Among the Filipinos Mass in the country villages should be celebrated by the secular clergy, the ministration of the friars being confined to missions. In 1872 the monasteries retaliated by a Bill of Indictment against the richest and most influential native families, who were deported summarily to the Ladrone Islands, while four ringleaders of the native priests were publicly garrotted, and the native clergy were declared thenceforth to be incompetent to have the cure of souls. It was no longer a matter for constitutional methods, and the Filipinos began to talk openly of revolution. Philippine committees were founded at Madrid and Barcelona, and native scholars trained in Europe began to introduce new ideas.

The most distinguished of these was the late Dr. Rizal, who at once joined issue with the monks by disputing their legal title to the lands they occupied. It was open war, and Rizal became the idol of his fellow-countrymen. His life being unsafe, he returned to Europe, but in 1892, having received a safe-conduct from the Governor-General, he returned. He was immediately arrested, however, at the instance of the monks, on a charge of introducing seditious leaflets in his luggage. The monks demanded his execution, but the Governor took the halfway measure of banishing him to the island of Mindanao.

Filipinos in Arms Against Spain The familiar machinery of the monastic orders was now put into motion, and the procurators of the religious houses in Madrid obtained from the Government the recall of Governor-General Despujols, though he had been only eight months in office. The revolutionaries immediately planned a rising in arms, and in the desultory guerilla warfare of 1896 Emilio Aguinaldo came to the front as commander-in-chief of the rebels.

The revolt of 1896, inspired by the Filipino League, closely followed by the war between Spain and America in 1898, finally put an end to the wretched pretence of a Spanish Government, and when Manila was ceded to the Americans the real trouble began. The Filipinos were hungering for the loot of the city, and to leave the country to their tender mercies would have been an unthinkable crime. Common humanity, no less than policy, forced the hands of the American Government, and the Philippines had to be conquered from end to end. For more than two years an army of 60,000 men was kept fully occupied, and it was not until fifteen months after the capture of Aguinaldo and his lieutenant Malvar that resistance was stamped out. The Americans lost no time in substituting civil for military administration, and as soon as peace prevailed throughout the islands a legislative assembly was formed. The franchise for the Lower House was confined to property owners and persons who could speak English or Spanish. The Upper House had a majority of American members. At the same time overtures were made for buying out the hated monastic orders. The real difficulty for the Americans lay in the want of civil servants trained in colonial administration, but that is a

Philippine Policy of America difficulty which time is fast removing. The total area of the Philippine Islands is about 127,853 square miles. The largest islands are Luzon (40,969 square miles) and Mindanao (36,292 square miles). The population, according to the census returns of 1903, is 7,635,426, of whom 647,740 are uncivilised. Manila, the capital of the group, had a population of 219,941 in 1903. The islands contain about 25,000 Europeans and Americans, and about 100,000 Chinese. The legislative body consists of seven commissioners—four Americans and three Filipinos — under a Governor-General. The whole area of the islands is now under civil governors, and the country is fast settling down to industrial life and progress. The chief products of the Philippines are hemp, coffee, sugar, copra, tobacco, rice, and indigo. Before the coming of the Americans the mineral resources of the Philippines had not been investigated, but under American enterprise prospecting is being carried out. The most important minerals seem, from present indications, to be lignite, gold, iron, copper, lead and manganese. For the year 1905 the revenue was 16,110,248 dollars (about £3,222,050), and the expenditure 17,933,162 dollars (about £3,586,632).

MEN AND MANNERS IN OCEANIA

HULA GIRLS OF HAWAII, SANDWICH ISLANDS
Edwards, Littlehampton

NATIVE LADY OF FIJI

HIGH-CASTE NATIVE OF FIJI

Underwood & Underwood, London

. GROUP OF YOUNG WOMEN OF THE BETTER CLASS, TAHITI

TAHITAN FISHERMEN

YOUNG MEN OF TAHITI

WARRIORS, WOMEN, AND BOYS OF NEW CALEDONIA

MEN, WOMEN AND CHILDREN OF THE NEW HEBRIDES

YOUNG WOMAN OF TONGA AND SAMOAN "ORATOR," WITH FLY FLAPPER

SCHOOL-GIRLS OF SAMOA AND FRUITSELLERS OF NEW CALEDONIA

Kerry, Sydney

NATIVES OF THE MARQUESAS ISLANDS

FIJI WARRIORS REPRESENTING A FIGHT WITH CLUBS
Underwood & Underwood, London

"MONKEY SHAVE" IN NEW BRITAIN   NATIVES OF GERMAN NEW GUINEA

Underwood & Underwood, London

DYAK FIGHTING MEN OF NEW GUINEA

AN ELDERLY SOLOMON ISLANDER   SOLOMON MAN WITH BLEACHED HAIR

GROUP OF NATIVE MEN OF THE SOLOMON ISLANDS

MAORI MOTHER AND CHILD

TWO MAORI CHIEFS

YOUNG MAORI IN FULL DRESS

AN OLD MAORI CHIEF

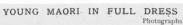

Photographs : J. Valentine, Dundee

OCEANIA

THE ISLAND NATIONS OF THE SOUTH SEAS

THE CHARACTERISTICS OF THE ISLANDS

FROM a geographical point of view Oceania is a unique feature of the surface of the globe. In the first place it is of enormous size. From the Pelew Islands in the west to Easter Island in the east it stretches over 120 degrees of longitude, that is to say, over fully a third of the circumference of the earth, and from Hawaii in the north to New Zealand in the south it covers 80 degrees of latitude. It resembles, therefore, in this respect the giant continent of Asia, while with its entire land and water area of 27,000,000 square miles it is nearly half as large again.

Enormous Extent of Oceania

The distribution of this "world of islands" within this enormous space is most uneven. Speaking generally, the islands are less densely clustered and smaller in size as one goes from west to east. Though Melanesia does not include many large islands, it includes New Guinea, a country which is not only twice as large as all the other islands of Oceania put together—320,000 square miles to 177,000 square miles—but represents the largest insular formation on the globe.

The Bismarck Archipelago and the Solomon Group contain islands which in size far exceed all the Micronesian and most of the Polynesian islands ; New Caledonia alone is in area almost twice as large as all the Polynesian islands put together, if Hawaii be omitted—7,000 square miles to 4,000 square miles. New Zealand, finally, has almost exactly ten times the area of the whole Polynesian realm of islands including Hawaii—106,000 square miles to 11,000 square miles. Melanesia forms the inner of the two great belts of island groups which curve in a thin line round the continent of Australia, while the outer belt contains all Micronesia and West Polynesia. But between the island clusters of Melanesia, in spite of their considerable area and their dense grouping on a narrow periphery, stretch broad expanses of sea. How thinly scattered, then, must be the islets of Micronesia and Polynesia, with their insignificant area, over the vast waters of the ocean ! This isolation is the main feature in their distribution. Our maps of the Pacific are always on a very small scale and cannot bring out this peculiarity. The Caroline Islands, to give an instance, do not indeed appear on them as a dense cluster, but still show clearly how close their interconnection is. Including the Pelews they comprise forty-nine islands and atolls, whose total area is six hundred square miles ; or, to give an English parallel, almost precisely the area of

Isolation of the Ocean Island Groups

Monmouthshire. This is certainly not much in itself, and how infinitely small it appears when distributed over the expanse of sea which is framed by the archipelago ! Stretching over thirty-two degrees of longitude and nine degrees of latitude it covers almost precisely the same area as the Mediterranean—namely, one hundred thousand square miles. We are, therefore, dealing with magnitudes which practically allow of no comparison; and all the more so since, of those six hundred square miles, five islands—which, it may be remarked, are the only ones of non-coralline formation—contain more than two-thirds. The small remainder is distributed over forty-four atolls, hardly rising above the level of the sea, which, with their average size of one square mile, literally disappear in that vast waste of waters. The case is the same with the majority of the Micronesian and Polynesian archipelagoes. Even if the distribution is not so thin as that of the Caroline Islands, still the insignificance of the land surface in comparison with the sea is shown by the fact that the Spaniards in the sixteenth century cruised for some decades up and down the south seas without sighting more than a few islands, which formed part of the densest clusters.

An English County in an Ocean

This distribution of its homes over so vast a region has been of the greatest importance for the inhabitants of Oceania. In the first place, they could reach their ultimate home only by navigation ; and, besides that, it was impossible to form and maintain any relations with neighbours by any other means of communication. One result of this was that the natives in general had attained a high degree of skill in seamanship at the time of the arrival of the Europeans ; another that they showed a marvellous disregard of distances and a mobility most unusual among primitive races. Not one among all the peoples of the earth can compare with the Oceanians in all these respects. The clumsy Melanesians, it is true, remain in the background ; but where can we find ships to compare in grace and seaworthiness with those of Polynesia or Micronesia, or voyages so extended as those of the Pacific races ? And what primitive people can point to colonisation so wide and so effective as the Polynesian ?

Races of Seamen and Boat-builders

Yet it must be borne in mind that all these astounding performances were exa cuted by races who knew nothing of iron until quite recent times, and were restricted to stone, wood, and shells.

The configuration of the islands in the South Sea has exercised as great an influence on the racial life as their geographical distribution and size. According to the degree of their visibility from the open sea the realm of islands is divided into high (mainly volcanic) and low (or coral) islands. There is no sharp local differentiation of the two groups within the vast region. Some archipelagoes indeed, such as the Tuamotu, Gilbert, and Marshall islands, are purely coral constructions ; others again, like all the remaining groups of East and West Polynesia, are high islands. But generally speaking, the fact remains that coralline formations, whether fringing reefs or barrier reefs, are the constant feature of the high islands. This is also the case with the five high islands of the Carolines.

This peculiar arrangement, as well as the configuration of the islands, has in various points greatly influenced the Oceanians and their historical evolution. In the first place the labour of the coral insects always increases the size of the land. This is most clearly seen in the atolls ; the reef-building capacity of those insects has produced the whole extent of those dwelling places for man. The activity of the corals, though less in itself, is more varied in its effect in the case of the high islands surrounded by reefs. First, the beach is widened and thus the entire economic position of the islanders is improved. The fertile delta of the Rewa on Vita Levu, as well as the strips of shore from half a mile to two miles broad which border the Tahiti islands, lie on old reefs. These themselves are, wherever they occur, the best fishing grounds ; besides this, they always form excellent harbours and channels—a most important point for seafarers like the Oceanians. The seamanship and bold navigation of this racial group has thus been markedly affected by the activity of diminutive molluscs.

How Coral Islands make Nations

The great poverty of the islands as a whole has been an important factor in their history. From a distance they appear like earthly Paradises, but on landing the traveller finds that even the

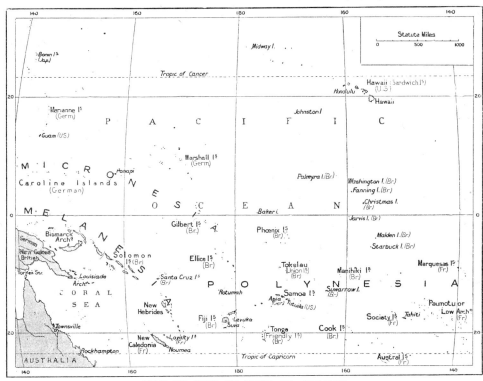

MAP OF THE ISLANDS OF OCEANIA
Showing their relationship to the Australian continent and the great island of New Guinea.

most picturesque of them offers little to man. Barely a hundredth part of the surface of the coral islands is productive ; in the majority of the larger volcanic islands the fertile soil does not amount to more than a quarter, or according to some authorities to more than an eighth, of the entire surface. There is also often an entire lack of fresh water. **Paradises of Poverty** Under such circumstances the possibility of settlement is confined within narrow limits ; if the population exceeds a definite figure there is imminent risk of death from starvation or thirst. The South Sea Islanders are therefore, in the first place, prone to wander ; in the second place they adopt the cruel custom of infanticide, in order to check the growth of the population.

A third result of the poverty of the islands, and one which is important for the geographical aspect of the settlements, is the limitation of the habitable region to the outer edge of the islands. This peculiarity is, on the atolls, a necessary consequence of their circular shape ; but it is the rule also among the high islands,

even the largest of them. Even in New Guinea itself, that immense island, with its enormous superficial development, the coast districts seem to be distinctly more densely inhabited than the interior. This is the most striking fact about the distribution of animal and vegetable life in Oceania. The land is poor ; the sea, the only means of communication, is rich in every form of life.

The poverty of this world of islands is partly connected with the nature of the soil and the enormous distances, which most organisms cannot cross, but partly also with the climate. If we leave out of consideration New Zealand, which extends into temperate latitudes, **Climatic Influences in Oceania** Oceania possesses a tropical climate tempered by the surrounding ocean. The temperatures are not excessive even for Europeans. But uniformity is their chief feature ; the diurnal and annual range is limited to a few degrees.

The differences in the rainfall are more marked. Although generally ample, in places amounting to two hundred and fifty or three hundred inches in the year, it is

947

almost completely wanting in parts of that vast region, which are so dry that extensive guano beds can be formed. The contrasts in the rainfall on the several groups and islands are the more striking, since they are confined to a smaller space. These are not, of course, noticeable on the flat coral islands, which scarcely project a couple of yards above the

Effects of Mountains on the Islands sea ; but the elevation of the high islands into the moister strata of the atmosphere presupposes a strong differentiation between the weather side and the lee side. The side sheltered from the wind escapes the rain. These two sides do not face the same points of the compass throughout the whole Pacific Ocean. Its western part, as far as the Solomons, belongs to the region of the West Pacific monsoon ; the east, however, is the definite region of the trade-winds. Hence, in the east, the most luxurious tropical vegetation covers the east and north sides of the islands in the Northern Hemisphere, and the east and south sides of those in the Southern Hemisphere ; while on their lee side the true barrenness of the soil shows itself, whereas, in the west, the conditions are almost reversed.

The effect of this climate on the development of the culture and history of the Oceanian is at once seen in the difference of temperament and character between the wild and energetic, yet politically capable, Maori on far distant New Zealand with its bracing Alpine air, and his not ungifted northern kinsmen, indolent and politically sterile, who have been unnerved by the unvarying uniformity of temperature. On the other hand the steadiness of the meteorological conditions has allowed the Oceanians to develop into the best seamen among primitive races.

Where, as in Oceania, one can be certain of the weather often for months in advance, it is easier, from inclination or necessity, to venture on an excursion

Regular Weather Conditions into the unknown than in regions where the next hour may upset all calculations. The regularity of the winds and currents of the Pacific Ocean has played a great part in the theories that have been formed about the Polynesian migrations ; in fact, most of them are absolutely based upon them.

Thanks to geographical exploration, we now know that this regularity is by no means so universal as used to be assumed ; that, on the contrary, in these regions also, the wind veers with the variations of atmospheric pressure, and the currents with the wind. Here also from time to time deviations from the usually prevailing direction—that is, from the eastern quadrants—are to be noticed. On the other hand, we are indebted to the spread of ethnographical investigation for the knowledge that the seamanship of the Polynesians not only extended to sailing with the wind, but that an occasional tacking against it was not outside the limit of their nautical skill. The ocean and its meteorology thus lose some of their value as sources furnishing an answer to the question of the origin of the Polynesians, in comparison with anthropological and ethnographical evidence ; but it would be at any rate premature to disregard them altogether. Even if skilful use of the last-mentioned methods of inquiry is likely to solve the problem of origin, the other and almost equally important question of distribution over the whole ocean can be answered

Poverty that Makes History only by giving full weight to geographical considerations. The main feature of the flora of Oceania is its dependence on the region of the south-east Asiatic monsoon. This feature is very marked in Melanesia ; but further toward the east it gradually disappears, while the number of varieties generally diminishes. Strangely enough, it is this very scantiness that has proved of such importance for the history of Oceania. The Melanesian, surrounded by a luxuriant wealth of vegetation, dreams away his existence and leaves no history ; his wants are supplied by the unfailing store of the ocean or the rich forest. We first find a historical life in the Fiji archipelago, where nature is less prodigal. The inhabitant of Polynesia or Micronesia has not been so spoilt. Scantily endowed with fertile soil and edible plants, he is confronted by the wide ocean, which he has nevertheless learnt to subdue. Although he did not possess a single tree which could furnish him with seaworthy timber, he became a craftsman, whose skill compensated for the deficiencies of Nature. But by so doing he had in one direction freed himself from the constraint of Nature, and nothing could hinder him from mastering her in another. Progress in technical skill has always been the first step toward every other form of progress, including the annihilation of distance.

Nevertheless, the Polynesians would not have been able to extend their wanderings so widely had not Nature, so niggard in everything else, given them **Importance of the Coco-nut** further support in the shape of the coco-nut palm. Its seeds, together with those of a few other plants, can cross spaces as vast as the distances between the Pacific islands without losing their germinative power ; thus these seeds have been the first condition of the diffusion of the Polynesian over the wide realm of islands. It is only recently that other food plants have become more important for the nourishment of the islanders than the coco-nuts.

This does not apply to New Zealand. Just as the country climatically is distinct from the rest of the island world, so its flora bears an essentially different stamp. It is unusually varied, and the number of species can be counted by the thousand. Only two plants, however, have proved of value to the aborigines— the rarauhe, a fern with an edible root, and the hara-keke, or New Zealand flax. The value attached to it by the first Europeans, and their consequent efforts to obtain it, led to the first friendly intercourse between the Maoris and the whites.

The characteristic of the fauna of Oceania is its poverty in mammals and animals of service to man, in the east even more than in the west. Even the dingo, which the wretched native of Australia could make his somewhat dubious companion, has not been vouchsafed by Nature to the Oceanian. It is only in quite modern times that the kindness of foreigners has supplied the old deficiency by the introduction of European domestic animals. New Zealand was once rich in the species and number of its large fauna. Many varieties of the moa,

CAPTAIN COOK

The English naval captain who circumnavigated the globe, and made important geographical surveys and discoveries.

some of gigantic size—the largest species measured thirteen feet in height—roamed the vast plains. At the present day it is one of the long extinct classes, having fallen a victim to the insatiable craving of the Maori for flesh food. It is easy to understand that the small islands are poor in animal life, for with their scanty space they could not afford the larger creatures any means of existence. On the other hand, the poverty of the fauna of New Guinea is more surprising ; notwithstanding the tropical luxuriance of its soil, its fauna is even more scanty than that of Australia. The pig alone has proved valuable to the population.

The result of this limited fauna, as reflected in an ethnographically important phenomenon, has been of much consequence in the historical development of the races of Polynesia and Micronesia. The races living principally on islands of very small size are at the present day either entirely without bows and arrows as weapons, or retain them merely as a survival. This has been traced back to the want of opportunity for practice which is more essential for the bow than for any other weapon. This opportunity could never have been very frequent even if the supply of game had been ample at the time of the immigration of the hunters. The loss of any weapon which would kill at a distance must naturally have appreciably altered the tactics of the islanders.

It is true that, on some groups of islands, fighting at close quarters, which all primitive peoples dread, **Evolution in Methods of Warfare** was avoided by the adoption of the slingstone or the throwing club in place of the arrow but, as a rule, the transition to hand-to-hand fighting with spear, axe, or club was inevitable. This always denotes an improvement in tactics, as is shown by the

949

assic examples of the Zulus in South rica, who, merely from the method of tack in close order introduced by Tchaka, id the use of the stabbing spear as the cisive weapon, won the foremost place the south-east of the Dark Continent. 1 Polynesia the new method of fighting rtainly contributed to that bloodiness of ie battles, both among the natives them-

selves and against the whites, which distinguishes its history from that of all other primitive races. The political consequences, from want of any suitable antagonist, could naturally not be so important here as in South Africa. Nevertheless, the comparatively rigid organisation of the majority of the Polynesians is certainly to a large degree the result of their tactics.

THE CHARACTERISTICS OF THE PEOPLE

ETHNOLOGY separates the population of Oceania into three large groups—ne Melanesians, who inhabit the inner belt f coast from New Guinea to New Caledonia and Fiji ; the Micronesians, on the aroline, Marianne, Pelew, Marshall, and ilbert islands ; and the Polynesians, who ihabit the rest of the great world of slands, including New Zealand.

The question of the racial position, the onnection and the origin of these three groups, has occupied scientific inquiry since the early days of their discovery, and has created a truly enormous literature, although no thoroughly satisfactory solution as hitherto been found. So far as the Melanesians are concerned, the question s indeed to be regarded as settled, since 10 one at the present day feels any doubt of their connection with the great negroid group of races. Even on the subject of the Micronesians there is a general consensus of opinion that they can no onger be contrasted with the Polynesians. They are seen to be a branch of the Polynesians, and that branch indeed which, on account of the close proximity of Melanesia, has received the largest percentage of negroid elements.

Thus it is only the Polynesian question which awaits solution. Nothing supports the view that the Polynesians grew up in their present homes. Such a theory is impossible on purely geographical grounds. We are left, therefore, with immigration from outside. The claims of America, on the one hand, and of Malaysia on the other, to be the cradle of the Polynesian race have each their supporters. Under the stress of more modern views on the penetration and wanderings of nations, the disputants have agreed in recognising a physical and linguistic connection with the latter region, without, however, denying ethnological relations with the former. The racial affinity of the

he sland aces *(margin note)*

Polynesians with the inhabitants of the Malay Archipelago is firmly established on the strength of physical and linguistic resemblances. There is more difference of opinion as to the nature and amount of the foreign admixture. As matters stand, a negroid admixture can alone enter into the question. Even those who believe in the former racial purity of the Polynesians must allow such an admixture in the case of Micronesia. As the result of numerous modern observations, it appears probable that a similar admixture exists as far as Samoa and still farther ; even remote Easter Island does not appear quite free from it.

A multitude of facts supports also the ethnological connection of Polynesia with America. The faith and religious customs in both regions rest as a whole on the same basis of animism and ancestor worship. In both we find the same rude cosmogony, the same respect for the tribal symbol, and the same cycle of myths, to say nothing of the numerous coincidences in the character of material culture possessed by them, and in the want of iron common to both. Ethnology, in face of these coincidences, is in a difficult position. Few

Origin of the Island Peoples *(margin note)* ethnologists still venture to think of any direct migration from America. It is certain that the Polynesians were bold sailors, and often covered long stretches in their wanderings, voluntary or involuntary ; but to sail over forty to sixty degrees of longitude without finding an opportunity to put into port anywhere would surely have been beyond their powers, and still more beyond the powers of their forefathers.

Under these circumstances the most satisfactory assumption is that of a large Mongoloid primitive race, whose branches have occupied the entire " East " of the inhabited world, East Asia, Oceania, and America. This theory extricates us at once from the difficulty of explaining those coincidences, but it does not directly solve the problem of the great differences in the civilisations belonging to the different branches of the Mongoloid family. It seems audacious to explain it by absorption of influences of the surrounding world, but the theory offers possibilities.

The first really historical activities of the Oceanians are their migrations. At the present day they are the most migratory people among the primitive races of the world, and voyages of more than a thousand nautical miles are nothing unusual among them. There are various incentives to such expeditions, such as the wish and the necessity of trading with neighbouring tribes, starvation, which is not infrequent on the poor islands, political disturbances, and a pronounced love of roaming. This last is the most prominent feature in the character of the Malayo-Polynesian, which has, more than anything else, scattered this ethnological group over a region of 210 degrees of longitude, from Madagascar to Easter Island, and over 80 degrees of latitude. Compared with this, the other causes of migration shrink in general significance, although locally they are often of primary importance and have had great bearing on history. The number of the journeys known to us is not great ; the interval since the opening up of the island world of Oceania is too short, and the region is too remote. Yet the number is sufficient to bring more than one characteristic of the past history of these races clearly before our eyes.

Causes of Primitive Wanderings

In the first place the frequent involuntary voyages, when the seafarers were driven far out of their course, teach us that the winds and currents have not set from east to west with that persistency which old and celebrated theories maintain, and that therefore no natural phenomena hindered the Polynesian from spreading from west to east. Under these conditions, the way from the west as far as distant Easter Island was not barred. Secondly, the frequency of these voyages allows us to understand the true character of the Pacific Ocean. It is no waste of waters, where islands and archipelagoes, like oases in a desert, lie remote and solitary ; but a sea full of life, where the constant traffic prevents any one group of islands from being absolutely cut off from the outer world.

The ocean has not presented this feature for the last few centuries only ; it has been characteristic of it since the day when the first keel touched the shores of Hawaii, New Zealand, and Easter Island. We have the evidence of the aborigines themselves for this. Their rich store of legends hinges on their old wanderings, and as it deals more particularly with the earliest voyages it gives us a welcome insight into the original relations of the islanders with one another and with the outside world ; it is thought that the question of the original home of the Polynesians might be solved in this way. The part which the land of Hawaiki under its various names—Sawaii, Hawaii, Hapai, Hevava, Awaiki and others—plays in the ancestral legends of most Polynesians is familiar even beyond the circle of ethnologists. It recurs among the Maoris of New Zealand, in Tahiti, Raiatea, Rarotonga, the Marquesas, Hawaii, and elsewhere. To see in it a definite and limited locality, from which the streams of emigration flowed at different times to the most varied directions of the ocean, appears impracticable in view of the fact that the geographical position of Hawaiki is not accurately fixed in all the traditions, but varies considerably ; it even meets us as the land of ghosts, the western land where the souls sink together with the sun into the lower world.

Legends of Ancestral Migrations

Nevertheless, the investigation of the primitive period in Polynesian history is benefited in several instances by tracing out the Hawaiki myth ; especially if this task be supplemented by a review of the anthropological, ethnographical, and geographical evidence. We may then assume with great probability that the island of Savaii, which belongs to the Samoa group, was the starting point of the migration of the Maoris to New Zealand. Under the name of Hawaii it also forms the starting point of the inhabitants of Raiatea and Tahiti. To this fact, again, point the legends of the Marquesas and the Hawaii group ; partly also of Rarotonga, which, on its side, as the " nearer Hawaiki " of tradition, served the Maoris as an intermediate station on the way to New Zealand, while it was a regular starting-place for the inhabitants of the Austral and Gambier islands. A final starting-point was the Tonga group.

Polynesia Before the Europeans

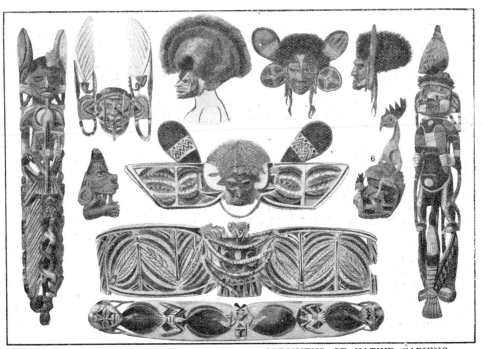

THE REMARKABLE ART OF MELANESIA: SPECIMENS OF NATIVE CARVING
The Melanesians were backward in political culture but their arts were highly developed. These examples of their carvings, chiefly from drawings made from specimens in European collections, are more graphic and realistic and display far more observation of Nature than those of the Micronesians, illustrated on the opposite page.

Not only is the number of starting-points surprisingly small in comparison with the size of the territory occupied by the Polynesians, but the original relations among the several groups appear simple to an astonishing degree. Examined in the light of ethnology and history, this simplicity cannot be maintained. It is an ascertained fact as regards the Maoris that their immigration did not occur in the form of one single wave, but that fresh batches came from the north; and a very late subsequent immigration is specially recorded. The inhabitants of the Hawaii islands are connected with Tahiti by language, customs, and legendary travels; on the other hand, the place names show the enduring recollection of Samoa. Rarotonga is the focus of the entire remotest south, while it was itself peopled with settlers almost simultaneously from Samoa and Tahiti. In the end, Tahiti seems to have sent emigrants to Rarotonga and Hawaii, also to the Southern Marquesas, as the resemblance in language and customs proves.

It is difficult to determine the date of these migrations, since these movements are a constant feature. Obviously, no reliance can be placed in the genealogical lists of the several islands, which vary from twenty to eighty-eight generations. History does not carry us very far; ethnology alone tells us that the dispersion of the Polynesians over the Pacific Ocean cannot go back to any remote period, since they have not had the time to develop any marked racial peculiarities. It can be only a question of centuries for New Zealand and many other countries. In the case of Tahiti, and perhaps Hawaii, the first settlement may be assigned possibly to an earlier date. But in no case need we go back more than a millennium and a half. The wanderings extended also to Melanesia, in the east of which, as a consequence of the distances, more settlements were planted than in the west. Fiji, in respect of social and political customs, shows almost as many Polynesian traits as its two neighbours, Tonga and Samoa, and has experienced a considerable infusion of Polynesian blood. In New Guinea, on the other hand, we find marked traces of this blood, but an almost total

Relations of the Island Groups

Comparative Lateness of Settlement

DECORATIVE ART OF MICRONESIA: SPECIMENS OF NATIVE CARVING

A comparison between the examples of Micronesian carving, illustrated above, and the Melanesian carvings shown on the opposite page gives evidence of a less free and imaginative art in the former, but a considerable feeling for decorative effect and genuine craftsmanship is to be seen by a careful inspection of the detail of these Micronesian objects.

absence of Polynesian customs and political institutions. It can hardly be shown at the present day, when the Western Pacific contains so mixed a population, in what proportion migration has been deliberate or involuntary; but, doubtless, besides the frequent driftings to east and west, there were many cases of systematic colonisation. We thus get to know an aspect of the Polynesians which is not often represented among primitive peoples.

In Africa the only examples are the Wanyamwesi of Central German East Africa, who since the middle of the nineteenth century have colonised the whole equatorial east of the continent, and advanced their settlements far into the Southern Congo basin, and the Kioto in the Western Congo State.

THE BEGINNING OF OCEANIC HISTORY

OUR knowledge of the history of Oceania goes scarcely beyond the discoveries of the island world, for the tradition of Polynesia, which goes considerably further back into the past, does not distinguish between fact and fiction. Nevertheless, even in Oceania it is possible to have a glimpse of the past. Here, as in Australia, we find remains of old buildings and sites whose nature presupposes certain definite political and social conditions then existent ; but, besides this, we have adequate data in the information which the early explorers give as to the state of things they discovered. In the case of the Polynesians and Micronesians, as in that of the Australians, it admits of no doubt that their present stage of civilisation does not denote the highest point of their development, but that in many departments of national life a distinct retrogression has taken place. In Melanesia, on the other hand, where the civilisation does not even reach the present stage of the neighbouring peoples on the east, all evidence of a previous higher culture is wanting. Melanesia is, in this respect, like a hollow between an elevation in the west, the Malay civilisation, and a second somewhat lower elevation in the east, the Polynesian civilisation.

This by no means implies that the culture possessed by its inhabitants was in itself inferior or lacked originality. On the contrary, the arts were highly developed in Melanesia ; indeed, much of the material culture, and some branches of intellectual culture, sur-

Three Degrees of Civilisation pass anything shown by the Micronesians at least. It is only in political respects that the Melanesian is behind. The cause of this is to be found primarily in the character of the negroid race, and, secondly, in the absence of any stimulus from outside. Where these causes are absent, as in Fiji, even the Melanesian has shown himself capable of political development.

The decadence of the Polynesian and Micronesian civilisation is shown in two ways—first, in buildings and works of a size, mass, and extent which preclude all idea that they could have been erected by a population at the stage in which the first Europeans found them ; and, secondly, in the political and social institutions, which bear every trace of decay. The South Sea is not poor in remains of the former class. On Pitcairn Island, which has long been deserted by all primitive inhabitants, the stone foundations of ancient temples are to be found even now ; on Rapa old fortifications crown the hills, and on Huaheine a dolmen rises near a cyclopean causeway. Under the guano layers of the Christmas Islands roads skilfully constructed of coral-rag bear witness to an age of a greater spirit of enterprise, of a higher plane of technical skill, and of a more pronounced national life. Tinian, one of the Marianne group, has its colossal stone pillars, crowned with capitals, to mark the dwelling-places of the old and more vigorous Chamorro. But all

Evidences of an Earlier Civilisation this is nothing in comparison with the ruins of Nanmatal on Ponape, and the stone images on Rapanui in Easter Island. The decadence in the political and social field is not generally so obvious as that in technical skill; but it is incontestable everywhere, and has been distinctly more disastrous to the national development of the islanders. This is shown by the loss of the old patriarchal society, in which the king was reverenced by the people as a god ; where he was the natural owner

of all the land, and where the view prevailed that all was from him and all was for him. When Captain Cook and his contemporaries appeared in the South Sea, in many places hardly any trace of such a society remained, while in others it was rapidly disappearing. The ancient dynasties had either been entirely put aside and the states dissolved, or, if they still existed, only a faint gleam of their former glory was reflected on the ancient rulers. The old organisation of the people, with its strictly defined grades, had already been destroyed, and a struggle of the upper class for property and power had taken the place of the former feudalism. This effort had been everywhere crowned with success, and had mainly contributed to break up the rigid and yet universally accepted system. Finally, even religion entirely lost its ancient character. The original gods were indeed retained ; but their number, at first limited, had been in the course of time indefinitely multiplied, since the gods created from the class of the high nobility were gradually put on a level with the older deities.

Thus the national and popular religion was changed into a superstitious worship of

Religion Becomes Superstition the individual. It is one and the same thing which destroyed the State and the religion of the Polynesians—the degradation of the old civil and religious authorities or the promotion of the formerly lower degrees. But in any case the abandonment of the old idea of a state was complete. The tokens of retrogression in Oceania, when collected, speak a clear language. They tell us, in the first place, that there must have been a time in the prehistoric period of the South Sea Islanders when an overgrowth of population on the already settled islands made it necessary to send out colonies; we learn, further, that the period of colonisation must have also been the period of the highest development of culture.

Colonisation was possible only under the government of a rigid political organisation, of which we can at most discover a reflection in the subsequent life of the South Sea races. We may not assume a growth of technical knowledge on the settled islands, such as was requisite for the erection of large buildings; so that even in the field of material culture we can suppose the existence of only an

THE NATIVE ART OF NEW ZEALAND: SPECIMENS OF MAORI CARVING
1. Carved window frame with sliding sash at Rotorua Lake, South Island: the woman is a Maori guide. 2. Maori gods. 3. Carved portal of Maori house. 4. Figure from Lake Pukaki in South Island. 5. Maori canoe.

original and more universal standard of accomplishment. We thus find the phenomenon, interesting both from the historical and the geographical point of view, that the moment of the widest dispersion of a race denotes the beginning of its decadence. This

Dispersion Promotes Decadence phenomenon is not surprising if we take into account the nature of the homes of the race. It is easier for the population of small islands to attain a higher culture and a more strict political organisation than to maintain themselves at the stage which they inherited or brought with them. The narrow limits of space make a comprehensive scheme easy and possible, but involve the danger of a conflict between opposite parties, and thus the destruction of the existing system. None of the Polynesian islands escaped this fate, especially since the character of the people shows few traits of conservatism. Quarrels and disputes have been the chief and the favourite occupation of the Polynesians as long as we have known them. The decadence is the greatest where the island communities are the smallest, and where, therefore, destructive influences are most powerful; thus in the centre of the world of islands hardly a trace of the

ancient culture has come down to us. When the Europeans appeared on the scene, marked traces of this culture—in one place a vigorous national life, in another stupendous monuments—were extant only on the outer belt, in Hawaii, New Zealand, and the remote Easter Island.

The fall of the Maoris is the best illustration of the rapidity with which the attainments of civilisation can be lost. At all times addicted to violence and intolerant of united effort, they split up the larger states of their twin islands into numerous mutually hostile and aggressive communities, from which every notion of a national unity and its effect in maintaining a civilisation has disappeared. At the same time the originally vigorous racial character lost more and more in moral restraint, and became more savage and

Evidences of Maori Decay cruel. The downfall of the ancient religion finally ensued. The old gods lost their personality, and were transformed into a multitude of forest and sea demons, unparalleled for extravagance and grotesqueness of form. Art and technical skill did not escape. As early as Captain Cook's time, it was no longer possible to produce carvings of the older kind.

955

CAPTAIN COOK'S DISCOVERIES IN THE SOUTH SEAS

The three voyages of the famous navigator, Captain James Cook, were fraught with momentous consequences to his country and the world. In his first voyage (1768-71) he circumnavigated New Zealand and surveyed the east coast of Australia. During his second voyage (1772-75) he cruised among the Pacific islands. In his last voyage (1776-79) he discovered the Sandwich and other groups of islands, and was killed in an attempt to land on Hawaii, on February 14th, 1779.

THE OCEANIC ISLANDS AND THEIR STORY

WE come now to the separate histories of the three groups of islands of which Oceania consists—Melanesia, Micronesia, and Polynesia—beginning with the first, and treating them in the order named.

MELANESIA

Melanesia, apart from Fiji, has no history properly so-called. We are acquainted merely with the treatment which the inhabitants have received at the hands of foreigners.

The chief cause of this phenomenon, which recalls the passivity of the Australians, is the slight political capacity of the negroid race. A second cause is that isolation from the outside world which can be partly attributed to the dreaded fierceness of the Melanesians. The more enterprising Polynesians have never shown any great inclination to attempt colonisation on a large scale in Central and Western Melanesia, and the whites have not entered on the task of opening up these islands with the zeal which they have shown in the rest of Oceania since the days of Cook. Exploration and missionary activity are tardy and timid in these parts, and European colonisation is still later in coming.

Notwithstanding this late beginning of serious encroachments from outside, the Melanesians came early into hostile contact with the whites. Out of the long roll of explorers, from J. Le Maire and W. Schouten (1616), past W. Dampier (1700) and J. Roggeveen (1722) to L. A. de Bougainville and De Surville (1768), there is hardly one who had not been guilty of the greatest cruelties to the natives. Even Cook, in 1774, ordered the natives of Erromango to be shot down with cannon for some trifling misconduct. But the nineteenth century has behaved still more outrageously to these islands. Their wealth in sandalwood soon attracted numerous traders, English and American in particular, but also Polynesians. All these persons, who sought merely their

Cruelties upon the Melanesians

own advantage, behaved like savages. They plundered peaceable tribes, and forced them to work as slaves on other islands ; they cut down the valuable trees, and thus caused disputes with their owners, which generally ended in the defeat of the latter.

Extortions and unprovoked bombardment of villages were matters of daily occurrence. The traders captured a chief, and only released him at a ransom of a shipload of sandalwood ; and once when the inhabitants of Fate in the New Hebrides fled from the crew of an English ship and a body of Tongan allies into a cave with wives and children, their opponents lighted a fire at the entrance and suffocated all the fugitives.

A History Written in Blood

The consequences of this treatment of the natives were soon seen. The warlike and able-bodied Melanesians returned blow for blow, and avenged the outrages committed by the whites upon their fellows when and where they could. Whoever was imprudent enough to land upon their coasts was murdered. It thus comes about that the history of the exploration of Melanesia down to present day has been written in blood. Even missions have met with greater initial difficulties here, and found a harder task than anywhere else in the South Sea.

The long duration of racial struggles has produced the result that the national characteristics of Melanesia are no longer in their primitive integrity. New Guinea, where little more than the fringe of the island has been explored, has, indeed, suffered little, and the inhabitants of the Bismarck Archipelago and the Solomons have hitherto successfully repulsed any serious attack on their modes of life and thought or their material possessions. The state of things is less favourable in the more easterly archipelagoes, Santa Cruz, New Hebrides, New Caledonia, and Fiji. Here, undoubtedly, the stronger infusion of Polynesian blood has weakened the

957

Underwood & Underwood, London

A TYPE OF MELANESIAN CANOE
These strangely constructed Reef Island canoes sail incredible distances among the Melanesian group, trading fish and coco-nuts for the products of the larger islands.

powers of resistance of the population, while these groups have also been longest exposed to the brunt of the attacks of the whites. The result, as is always the case where the barbarian comes into touch with civilisation, has been a decline in the numbers, physique, and morals of the native population. This is most marked in New Caledonia, where the natives, under the influence of the French system of transportation, have sunk from a war-like and honour-loving nation, endowed with high intellectual gifts, into a ragged mob. It is difficult to form an idea of the numerical shrinkage, since the older accounts are mere estimates. Nevertheless, the inhabitants of the New Hebrides and Santa Cruz have undoubtedly much diminished in numbers, a change which in Fiji can be proved by actual statistics.

FIJI

The great political capacity, judging by a Melanesian standard, of the Fiji Islanders can be traced to the strong admixture of Polynesian elements and the position of the archipelago, which lies advanced toward the east. Their history begins with those feuds which have played a part in all the Polynesian islands for centuries. In these wars, unimportant enough in themselves, the Europeans interfered about the beginning

of the nineteenth century, without any political intentions at first. In 1804 twenty-seven convicts, escaped from Norfolk Island, took sides, sometimes with one, sometimes with another chief; but the crew of the slaver Eliza, which was wrecked on the cliffs of Nairi in 1808, had a still more decisive share in the course of events, since they possessed muskets. Their choice fell on the chief Naulivau of Mbau, who thus was enabled to overthrow the head of the "State" of Verata in Great Fiji, or Viti Levu. His successors remained in possession of the supreme power until 1874. After a reign full of military successes, which won him the surname Vuni Valu, meaning "root of war," Naulivau died in the year 1829. He was followed by his brother, Tanoa, one of the most ferocious cannibals whom Fiji ever knew.

Under his son, Seru, better known by the name of Kakobau or Thakombau (1852-1883), the kingdom founded by the first Vuni Valu reached its greatest prosperity and extent, comprising almost the entire archipelago. His accession occurred at a time when the Fiji Archipelago had attracted, in more than one respect, the attention of the whites. The Wesleyan mission had obtained a footing here since 1835; in 1844 the Catholic mission also. Principally through the

Underwood & Underwood, London

THE WORK OF AN EARTHQUAKE
This beautiful rock in Blanche Bay, New Britain, was thrown up by volcanic disturbance thirty years ago.

SCENES OF VILLAGE LIFE IN THE ISLANDS OF MELANESIA

1. "Tambo" House, Laembay, Utupua, Santa Cruz.   2. Native houses, in the Bismarck Archipelago.
3. Aerial house in the New Hebrides.   4. Native house in the Fiji Islands.   5. Native village in New Caledonia.
6. Hurricane-proof house in Port Vila, Santa Cruz.   Chiefly from photos by Underwood & Underwood.

activity of the former the old feuds had stopped, at any rate in the coast districts of Great Fiji; British, American, and other white traders were able to settle there in complete security. In 1847 the United States of America, in order to express their appreciation of the newly discovered field, established a consular agency there.

At the same time artful aspersions were cast on the Wesleyan mission in order to weaken British influence. In 1849, when the house of the consul, Williams, was burnt, the natives stole some of his property. Williams demanded from Thakombau compensation to the amount of "three thousand dollars, twelve and a half cents." An unprejudiced witness informs us this "exact" sum was not justified,

THAKOMBAU, A FAMOUS KING OF FIJI
He ruled over the greater part of the Fiji Islands from 1852 to 1883, and was nominally Christian. Under him, the islands reached their greatest prosperity, and he voluntarily ceded his country to the British Government in the year 1871.

and was not paid. In the next year, in consequence of other thefts, it had mounted to five thousand and one dollars and thirty-eight cents. Williams laid this demand before the commanders of two American warships, with a request for support, but it was rejected. In 1855, however, Captain Boutwell, who had been sent to Fiji for a renewed inquiry, ordered Thakombau to pay capital and interest forthwith. The sum to be paid was fixed in a second letter at 30,000 dollars, and threats of force were held out. Finally, Boutwell sent for the chief on board his ship, demanded 45,000 dollars, and threatened to hang him. Thakombau then signed the agreement.

Complications, also, were threatened with France. Fourteen years after the

unsuccessful attempt at settlement in 1844, French Catholic missionaries tried once more to gain a footing on Viti Levu. Since Thakombau, who in 1854 had adopted Christianity, partly from conviction, but mostly on political grounds, felt the impossibility of any longer maintaining his position, especially as his relations with Tonga were very strained at that time, he determined to escape from his difficulties and cede his land to England. On October 12th, 1858, he made a treaty with the British Consul, Pritchard, to which all the chiefs of the island subsequently agreed, to the following effect : Thakombau, who wished to become a British subject but to retain his title and suzerainty, promised 200,000 acres of land ; in return, Britain was to take over the American debt. The British Government, from the wish not to cause unpleasantness with America, refused the offer. Now, not only did the Americans immediately press their claims, but Tonga demanded a large sum of money for the assistance which it professed to have previously rendered. The monarch in his difficulty accepted the proposal of the Melbourne Polynesian Company in 1868, which promised to satisfy the claims of America in return for the grant of the land offered to the British Government. The flourishing condition of the German trading firms, which had been active in the country since 1860, had drawn public attention to Fiji. On conclusion of the treaty, the company paid the Americans £9,000. In return, it at once received 110,000 acres.

During these negotiations there had been incessant disputes among the natives themselves ; at the same time there had been quarrels between them and the numerous white immigrants. In order to put an end to this state of things, Thakombau in 1871 formed a constitutional government, with a Ministry composed of twelve chiefs, a legislative council chosen by the whites, and a supreme court. So long as the interests of the Government and the colonists coincided, this artifice, frequently tried in the South Sea, was

SUVA, THE CAPITAL OF THE FIJI ISLANDS   Underwood & Underwood

This, the chief town of Fiji, is on the south coast of Viti Levu, the largest island in the group.   It is the centre of trade, and in 1906 had a population of 1,121 Europeans.   It is extremely healthy, the temperature varying from 93° to 61°.

harmless in results ; but when the whites were required to pay taxes, they simply ignored the laws. The public debt soon grew to £80,000. Thakombau saw no alternative left him but to renew the offer of his land to Great Britain, but this time as a gift. England at first refused it again, and only changed her purpose from the fear that other Powers—America, or Germany, which was interested just then in the enterprise of the Godeffroys—might close with the offer. On September 30th, 1874, England accepted Thakombau's offer, which had actually in the interval been made to the German Empire and declined by it. Fiji became a British Crown colony. England took over all the debts, and paid Thakombau a yearly allowance until his death in 1883. The sales of land completed before the British annexation were not at once recognised, but gradually tested ; in 1885, more than ten years later, the Germans concerned were compensated with a small solatium of £10,620.

Fiji Islands become British Crown Colony

Settlement of German Claims

In the spring of 1902 Fiji concluded a separate federal treaty with New Zealand. The individual islands in the Fiji group number over 200, and of these some 80 are inhabited. The total area of the islands is 7,435 square miles. The population is estimated at 122,000, of whom 2,500 are Europeans, and over 17,000 Indians. The largest islands are Viti Levu (4,250 square miles) and Vanua Levu (2,600 square miles). The government is in the hands of a governor appointed by the British Crown, and assisted by an Executive Council. There is also a Legislative Council consisting of ten official members, six elected members, and two native members. For native government the colony is divided into provinces, which are administered through native chiefs. In 1905 the revenue was £192,974, and the expenditure £132,043. The chief products of the islands consist of sugar cane, coco-nuts, bananas, maize, tea, tobacco, and rice, and

FIJIAN TEMPLE, FORMERLY A SCENE OF CANNIBALISM

there are several sugar mills, a tea factory, a soap manufactory, and some saw mills. There is regular communication with Australia, New Zealand, Tonga and Samoa, Honolulu and Canada.

MICRONESIA

The small average size of the Micronesian islands has not prevented the inhabitants from developing a peculiar, and, in many respects, a higher, culture than their kinsfolk in the east and south. The several localities have, indeed, proved too limited for any development of political importance. The only events to be recorded are the usual feuds between the hostile village communities, although, judging by the ancient buildings and terraces on the Pelews, on Ponape, and the Marianne Islands, the conditions for a politically organised activity must have been far more favourable in earlier times than at the present day. It is at present impossible to determine whether the decadence of the Pelews and the Carolines is due to other reasons than the antagonism of conflicting interests produced by the cramped space.

Village Feuds and Decadence

On the other hand, the process of disintegration on the Marianne Islands can be accurately traced. All accounts from the period anterior to the beginning of the Spanish conquest and conversion speak in the highest terms of the condition of the islands, their high stage of civilisation and large population. Guam was compared to an immense garden, and in 1668, at the beginning of the Jesuit mission, contained 180 splendid villages. The total number of the Chamorro, as the aborigines were called by the Spaniards, is reckoned variously ; a favourite estimate is 200,000, but even 600,000 has been given; the lowest calculation does not sink below 40,000.

In addition to an advanced agriculture, which, notwithstanding primitive tools, could boast of cultivating rice, we find an excellently developed art of navigation, a knowledge of pottery, a regulated calendar, and so forth. The Spaniards destroyed all this in a few years. According to an accurate calculation, in 1710,

forty-two years after the arrival of the Jesuit father Sanvitores, there were 3,539 Chamorro still left ; in 1741 there were 1,816. Their rapid diminution was caused by the fierce fights which broke out so soon as the freedom-loving inhabitants perceived that conversion in the ultimate resort aimed at subjecting them to the Spanish yoke. The census of 1741 brought home to the Spaniards the magnitude of the devastation wrought by them. In order to make up for the alarming mortality they introduced Tagals from the Philippines. The number of the inhabitants after that increased ; in 1783 it amounted to 3,231 souls ; in 1803 to 4,303 ; in 1815 to 5,406 ; and in 1850 to more than 9,000. But an epidemic of smallpox swept off the population in 1856. It had risen again to 5,610 only in 1864, and at the present day it reaches to about double that figure. The reckless extermination of the people is almost the least evil which the Spaniards perpetrated on the Chamorro ; the annihilation of the national characteristics was still worse. At the present day no more traces are left of the old culture, with its buildings, its navigation, its agriculture, and technical skill, than of the old strong and proud physique of the inhabitants. In

A YOUNG KING AND QUEEN
OF THE MARQUESAS

place of a love of freedom the miserable half-caste people of to-day show a dull indifference, while lethargy has taken the place of industry, and an unthinking use of Christian customs is substituted for a frank paganism. Next to the Tasmanians no people in the South Sea can have felt more deeply the curse of contact with the Europeans than the Chamorro. An account of the history of the Polynesians presents difficulties, in so far as every separate group has its own history. It is the exception to find any points of connection between neighbouring archipelagoes. This necessitates the separate treatment of the larger and more important groups, at any rate, although certain broad characteristics recur regularly. Since this phenomenon is still more marked in the case of the smaller and

The Curse of the White Man

less densely peopled archipelagoes, whose importance is slight, we shall abandon the task of any detailed description, and refer the reader for their most interesting features to the chapter on missionary work.

Within the region of Polynesia t h e Hervey, T u b u a i, Society, Tuamotu and M a r q u e s a s Islands form a mass which stands out apart from the other clusters. This purely external grouping has, it is true, no geological foundation, but justifies the inclusion of the archipelagoes under the general title of East Polynesia, although the relations of the groups among themselves belong mostly to prehistoric or very early times.

TAHITI

The history of East Polynesia, whether native or colonial, is connected m a i n l y with the double island of Tahiti. It is the only focus of an independent development, and also the natural starting-point and centre of the French Colonial Empire in East Polynesia. When Samuel Wallace finally discovered the

QUEEN POMARE AND HER HUSBAND
This queen of Tahiti assumed power in 1827, and reigned for fifty years. In her time the French took possession.

island on June 19th, 1767, he found three states there, which were fighting savagely for the upper hand. The Spaniards took possession of the island on January 1st, 1775 ; but they soon abandoned it again after the death of their captain, Domingo de Bonechea, on January 26th. In 1789, the mutineers of the Bounty landed on Tahiti. Some preferred to remain there, took the side of the king, Otu, or Pomare, as he preferred to call himself, and thus enabled him to extend his sovereignty over the other islands of the archipelago.

The first English missionaries landed there on March 7th, 1797, and were destined soon to play a large part in the political life of Tahiti. In 1802 Pomare carried away the sacred Oro figure from the Marae at Atahuru, the possession of which was fiercely contested, and which he was compelled to surrender. He died suddenly on September 3rd, 1803, and his son, Pomare II., born in 1780, was

PALACE OF QUEEN POMARE IV. AT PAPEETE, THE CAPITAL OF TAHITI, IN THE YEAR 1876
The residence of the French Governor is seen immediately beyond the Royal Palace

forced to fly. He took up his abode on Murea, the headquarters of the Christian mission. In July, 1807, he crossed with a number of Christians over to Tahiti, surprised his enemies, and massacred them so relentlessly that the whole island rose against him and the missionaries, and drove them back to Huahine and Murea. But in the battle

Massacre by a "Christian King" at Narii—November 12th, 1815—King Pomare II., who had become a Christian on July 12th, 1812, completely defeated his enemies; the other islands of the archipelago adopted Christianity in consequence. Pomare crushed the power of the nobles, and gave the islands at the end of 1818 a new and written constitution. He died on November 30th, 1821. Pomare's infant son died on January 11th, 1827. His sister Aimata, a girl of seventeen, then mounted the throne as Pomare IV.—or Pomare Wahine I.— while her aunt, Ariipaia, remained regent, in accordance with custom.

The reign of Aimata is marked by an overflowing tide of calamity, which soon burst on Tahiti, and ended in the loss of its independence. It began with the attempt of the Catholic Church—made in November, 1836, from the Gambier Islands—to gain a footing in Tahiti. In consequence of a law introduced by the British preachers of the Gospel, the French missionaries were forbidden to land; they therefore appealed to France for aid. On August 27th, 1838, Captain Abel Dupetit-Thouars appeared off Papeete with the frigate Venus, in order to demand satisfaction. He insisted upon an apology under the sign manual of the queen, and 2,000 piastres in Spanish money. The queen was forced to comply. In April, 1839, Captain Laplace demanded that the Catholic Church should be granted equal privileges with the Protestant, and that a building site for a church should be conceded.

Aggression by France, and Its Results In September, 1842, Dupetit-Thouars, who had returned, once more expressed extravagant "wishes" to the Government, and, when they could not be granted, proclaimed a French protectorate in defiance of the protests of the queen and the English missionaries.

When a Tahitian popular assembly, relying on the intervention of the British Captain Nicholas, declared for Britain and Pomare IV. (1843), Dupetit-Thouars on November 6th deposed the queen, and threw into prison the British Consul Pritchard, in whose house she had taken refuge. The storm of indignation roused in England by this procedure forced France in 1844 to reinstate Queen Pomare IV. ; but the protectorate over the island was retained. It was only after a three years' war, waged with great fury on both sides, that the Tahitians submitted, on February 6th, 1847, and the queen returned from Murea to Papeete.

Pomare IV. died, after a reign of fifty years, on September 17th, 1877. Her son, Pomare V., abandoned all his imaginary sovereign rights to France on June 19th, 1880, in return for an annuity of £1,000, and died in 1891.

The political development has not been favourable in any way to the preservation of the national existence. In Cook's time the inhabitants were estimated at 120,000, a figure far too high, but one which in any case denotes an unusual density of population ; in 1892 the numbers hardly reached 10,000. The

"Blessings" Attending Civilisation introduction of disease, immorality, and drunkenness has taught the Tahitians a bitter lesson about the "blessings" of civilisation. Tahiti, as one of the French colonies in the Eastern Pacific, is administered by a governor assisted by a Privy Council and an Administrative Council. The island has an area of about 600 square miles. The chief town is Papeete, with a population of 4,282, of whom 2,490 are French. The chief products are copra, sugar, rum, pearls and mother of pearl. Coco-nuts, bananas, oranges, and sugar cane grow luxuriantly, especially near the coast. There is regular steamer communication with San Francisco, New Zealand, and Australia. In 1905 the imports were of the value of about £121,000, and the exports of £123,000.

THE ISLAND GROUPS AROUND TAHITI

The history of the island groups which cluster round Tahiti, the Society, Tuamotu, Marquesas, the Cook, and Tubuai, or Austral, Islands, is not without some anthropological, political, and religious interest. The picture presented to the discoverers was everywhere the same ; war and discord prevailed, limited usually to the separate islands and groups. The warlike inhabitants of the Tuamotu Islands

THE FAMOUS STONE IMAGES AT RONORORAKA IN EASTER ISLAND

undertook, even at the beginning of the nineteenth century, bold expeditions to other islands, plundering and carrying off the inhabitants as captives, until a stop was put to their proceedings by the influence of Tahiti.

The relations between the natives and the Europeans in these parts were every-**Difficulties** where due to the instrument-**of Religious** ality of the missions. It would **Workers** have been well if the matter had rested with the introduction of one denomination only. But the Protestant missionaries were soon followed on every group by Catholics under the protection of France. The inevitable result was an effort on the Protestant side to keep the intruders off, and on the side of the French Catholics to gain a religious and political footing. In all this the native was the scapegoat. Any infectious diseases which the traders had not introduced were communicated by the crews of men-of-war. The French tricolour now floats over the whole large group of islands, and the Romish propaganda has succeeded, though not to the full extent desired, in breaking down the undisputed power of Protestantism. European civilisation has diminished the number of inhabitants and has put a mere caricature in the place of a nationality which, despite many dark traits, was primitive and vigorous.

EASTER ISLAND

Easter Island, or Rapanui, as the Polynesians call the most remote islet of the vast island world, is, with its area of forty-five square miles, one of the smallest high islands of the Pacific Ocean. Nevertheless, it draws our attention on account of one of the weightiest problems of ethnology and thus of the history of mankind. If any connection at all exists between Polynesians and Americans, we must regard Easter Island as the most easterly pier in the bridge. There is nothing in the ethnography of Easter Island which supports such a theory, Salmon, the Tahitian who accompanied the German Hyena expedition of 1882 under Lieutenant-Captain Geiseler, and the American Mohican expedition of 1886, reported a story of the natives of Easter Island, according to which they are supposed to have come in a large **Peopling** boat from one of the Galapagos **of Easter** Islands with the trade-wind and **Island** to have landed at Anakena in the north of the island; but he did not disguise the fact that this tradition was contrary to the ideas of other natives, who maintained that there had been an immigration from the west. The architecture of the island is supposed to show resemblances to buildings in Central and South America; but the simple huts of the Easter Islanders are not

965

to be compared with those colossal erections. Again, the construction of the famous stone images, some fifteen feet high and made of lava, extends to comparatively recent periods, when there can be no possible idea of America's influence ; besides this, productions of similar size, although not of quite the same character, were nothing extraordinary among the other Oceanians, at least in earlier times. For this reason the modern relations between Easter Island and America are all the more frequent. Intercourse with the whites generally has, indeed, only brought the islanders misery and destruction hitherto. The beginning of the " mission of civilisation " is marked by the landing, on April 6th, 1722, of the Dutchman, Jacob Roggeween, who ordered the natives to be fired upon without any reason whatever. He found the island then most prosperous and densely populated, an appearance which it has long since lost. The natives were possibly too friendly and yielding to the whites. In 1805 the ship Nancy, from New London, which had been engaged in seal fishery at Mas-a-fuera, south-west of Juan Fernandez, came to Rapanui and carried away twelve men and ten women after a desperate fight. The men, when, three days after, they were released from their chains on the open sea, sprang overboard immediately, in order to reach their home by swimming ; but the women were carried to Mas-a-fuera. The crew of the Nancy is said to have made several subsequent attempts at robbery. The American ship Pindos later carried away as many girls as there were men on board, and on the next morning as a pastime fired at the natives collected on the beach.

The most calamitous period began in 1863. Peruvian slave dealers then established a depôt on Easter Island in order to impress labourers to work the guano works in Peru from the surrounding archipelagoes ; for this purpose they carried away the majority of the inhabitants of the island. Most of them were, however, brought back at the representations of the French Government ; but, unfortunately, smallpox was introduced by them and caused great ravages. In 1866 Catholic missionaries began their work, but they left the island after a few years, accompanied by

Coming of the Dutch

Slavery and Smallpox

some faithful followers, and went to Mangarewa. The last reduction in the number of the population was effected by the deportation of 400 Easter Islanders by a Tahitian firm to Tahiti and Murea, where they were employed as plantation labourers.

The population has not been able to bear such frequent and heavy drains on its vitality. Estimated by Cook at 700 souls, by later travellers at 1,500, and numbering before 1860 some 3,000, it has dwindled at the present day to 150, whose absorption in the mass of the immigrant Tahitians, Chilians, and others is only a question of time. Since 1888 Easter Island has been used by Chili as a penal colony.

PITCAIRN

The history of Pitcairn, an isolated island lying far to the south-west of the Tuamotu, is, during the period which we can survey, detached from the framework of native history ; its personages are almost entirely European immigrants. Pitcairn is one of the few islands which were uninhabited when the Europeans discovered them, although numerous remains in the form of stone images, relics of Marae, stone axes, and graves with skeletons, attest that the island was once populated.

Evidences of Earlier Inhabitants

The modern history of the island begins with the mutiny of the crew of the Bounty against their captain, Bligh, 1779, as related in the story of Australia. While the latter steered with his eighteen companions in his open boat to Batavia, the twenty-four mutineers sailed first to Tahiti. A number of them remained behind there, while eight men, under the leadership of the helmsman Christian, accompanied by six Tahitian men and twelve women, set sail in January, 1790, for the uninhabited island of Pitcairn. In order to prevent any escape from the island, Christian burnt the Bounty, whose tall masts might have betrayed the refuge of the mutineers. The beginning of the community was at once marked by disputes and quarrels ; the men were killed in fighting, and in 1801, John Adams, aged thirty-six—who died in March, 1829—was the only man on the island, with some women and twenty children.

Adams, realising by the previous course of affairs the danger which threatened the little society, struck out other paths. By his care in educating the young generation a tribal community was

966

developed which united many of the good qualities of the Europeans with the virtues of the Polynesians, and by its sterling character and high morality, won the sympathies of Great Britain to no small extent, especially since these colonists regarded themselves as Englishmen and spoke English as familiarly as Tahitian. Great Britain has always watched over the welfare of this little society. The limited water supply of the island having threatened to prove insufficient for the growing numbers, the eighty-seven inhabitants then living were removed by the British Government to Tahiti in 1831; but most of them soon returned to Pitcairn. When, in 1856, in consequence of hurricanes, it became difficult to find food for the once more rapidly increasing population, 187 of the 194 settlers were removed to the then uninhabited Norfolk Island. The majority remained there, and increased and prospered. In 1871 the number had risen to 340 souls; in 1891 it reached 738 souls; and, according to the last account, it is now about 900 souls. Some, however, this time also, could not live in a strange island, and returned to Pitcairn, where their number in 1879 had

CHILDREN OF THE BOUNTY MUTINEERS

George Young, son of Young the midshipman, with his child and wife, Hannah Adams, daughter of John Adams.

again risen to 79 souls. The population of Pitcairn at various periods was as follows: 1800, 29; 1825, 66; 1831, 87; 1837, 92; 1841, 114; 1856, 194; 1864, 43; 1873, 76; 1879, 93; 1884, 104; 1898, 142; 1901, 126; 1904, 169. Contrary to the disquieting rumours circulated in 1896, to the effect that Pitcairn no longer supplied the requirements of human inhabitants, the population is thriving at the present day.

The size of the island is not more than three miles long from east to west and two miles broad from north to south. There is a range of steep hills, the highest being Outlook Ridge, which is 1,008 feet high. The village of Adamstown is on a plateau about 400 feet above sea-level. Bounty Bay is the best of the three landing places, but even it is dangerous by reason of the violence of the sea and the currents. The climate is rainy but somewhat uncertain, hence the danger of drought. The chief food of the islanders is the sweet potato, but pineapples, bananas and yams grow abundantly.

The chief of the remaining islands of Polynesia — Hawaii, Samoa, Tonga, and New Zealand—are treated independently at greater length in the following chapters.

HOME OF JOHN ADAMS ON PITCAIRN ISLAND

HAWAII: BEGINNING AND END OF A KINGDOM

THE Hawaiian group of islands, otherwise called the Sandwich Islands, have a total area of 6,449 square miles. The chief members of the group are Hawaii (4,015 square miles), Maui (728 square miles), Oahu (598 square miles), Kauai (547 square miles), Molokai (261 square miles), Lanai (139 square miles), Niihau (97 square miles), and Kahoslawe (69 square miles).

The history of Hawaii begins for us with its discovery by Captain Cook; all that took place on it previously bears the impress of myth. The legends mention sixty-seven ancestors of Kamehameha I., and place therefore the beginning of the settlement of Hawaii at a period which would approximately correspond to the sixth century of the Christian era. As a matter of fact, human bones have been discovered under old strata of coral and lava streams; in any case, with such a system of chronology a large margin of error must be allowed for. Far more important is the exceptional evidence for the solution of the question of the origin of the native people. A large mass of the traditions point to the Samoan Sawaii as the chief point of emigration, without necessarily ex-cluding accretions from other groups of Polynesia. The recurrence of Samoan geographical names in Hawaii is an argument in favour of the legends. If we may judge by the frequent mention which they make of Tahiti and the Marquesas, the main route seems to have led over these islands.

How Hawaii was Peopled

It seems probable that some twenty generations after the first immigration—*i.e.*, about the eleventh century—a new wave of nations touched Hawaii, produced by a general movement in the island worlds of the South Sea, which, again, was due to the expulsion of Polynesian immigrants from the Fiji Islands. Into this period, therefore, fall, according to legend, the journeys of famous chiefs and priests to distant isles, rendered possible by the greater enterprise of the ancient races and the higher perfection of navigation at that time. The first and only attempt at oversea expansion gave way to a fresh period of isolation, which lasted at least into the sixteenth century, probably down to the date of Cook's landing. During this long period the Hawaiian people developed all its peculiar characteristics; then it was that those numerous states and societies were founded, which were mutually hostile.

Coming of the Europeans

The waves of war surged high in the fourteenth century, when King Kalaunuiohua tried for the first time to unite all the islands under his sceptre. The first intercourse with Europeans dates from the sixteenth century. In 1527 one of the three vessels of Don Alvarado de Saavedra is said to have been wrecked on the cliffs of South Kona, and in 1555 the Spanish navigator Juan Gaëtano is supposed to have discovered the Hawaiian Islands. This intercourse, even if it is based on fact, produced no results on the external and internal history of the country.

James Cook, on his landing (1778), found three states—Hawaii and Maui, both of which were governed by one ruler (Taraiopu, or Terriobu), since the ruler of Hawaii had married the queen-widow of Maui; and, thirdly, Oahu, to which Kauai and Niihau belonged. Not only were Oahu and Hawaii at war with each other, but all these states were riddled with internal dissensions. The task of reducing this chaos to order was reserved for Kamehameha I., or Tamea-Mea (1789–1819), who not only won more foreign successes than any other Polynesian ruler, but in intellectual gifts towered above the average of his race. He had distinguished himself in war as a young man, and national bards prophesied of him that he would one day unite the people. A few years after Cook's murder (February 14th, 1779) he began to put into practice his bold plans, on Hawaii at first, and afterwards on Maui (1781) and the other islands. Partly by his personal valour, partly with an army disciplined by the help of Europeans—to which after 1804 a fleet of twenty-one ships was joined—he attained his object in 1795. After storming the fort "Pali" on Oahu, to which island Kamehameha is said to have crossed with 16,000 men, he proclaimed himself sole monarch of the Hawaiian Isles. The two northwest islands, Kauai and Niihau, then voluntarily submitted.

Like the Zulu king, Tchaka, and the Wanyamwesi leader, Mirambo, Kamehameha has been compared to great rulers of the Mediterranean sphere of civilisation. Turnbull places him by the side of Philip of Macedon, and Jarves calls him the Napoleon of the South Sea ; to others he has suggested Peter the Great. He must have been a powerful personality. Adalbert de Chamisso was proud of the fact that he had shaken hands not only with General Marquis de Lafayette and Sir Joseph Banks, but also with the great Hawaiian. Kamehameha I. was great not merely in intellectual capacity, he was still greater by his moral strength and the power and purity of his will. If we take into

SANDWICH ISLANDER WITH MASK

account also his majestic bearing, which commanded respect, the vastness of his influence is at once accounted for.

The course of Kamehameha's reign, after he had united his kingdom, was peaceful. It was for the Hawaiians an era of revolution in every field, though least so in that of social life. Kamehameha made no changes in the relations of the several classes of the people to each other and to the monarch. The lower class remained then, as formerly, in its strictly dependent and subservient condition, and he had further weakened the power of the nobility, which even before his time had been slight. A new feature was the external reputation gained by political union, and the growth of the people into a power unprecedented in the Pacific. This, at an early period for Oceania, had quickly turned the attention of the European Powers and of North America to the north of the Pacific Ocean, as is shown by the numerous British, Russian, American, and French expeditions.

DOUBLE CANOE OF THE SANDWICH ISLANDS WITH MASKED ROWERS
Reproduced from an engraving accompanying the original edition of Captain Cook's "Voyages"

969

KING KAMEHAMEHA I. AND HAWAIIAN WARRIORS IN 1815

prosperity by transmarine commercial enterprise and a policy of tariffs ; but at the same time their intimate relations with the natives were destined to destroy the old religion, the stronghold of Hawaiian nationality.

As long as Kamehameha held the reigns of government with the strong hand, the crash was delayed. Kamehameha was all his life a firm supporter of paganism, for only through a strict observance of the traditional doctrines was it possible in those times of ferment to retain the respect of the people for the person and power of the godlike monarch. His death, which occurred on May 8th, 1819, changed the situation. Liholiho, his son, who mounted the throne as Kamehameha II., immediately sank to be a puppet in the hands of his nobles, and especially of his co-regent Kaahumanu, the favourite wife of the late king, and his aged chief counsellor, Kaleimoku, the " Pitt of the South Sea." By their advice he abolished the ancient and revered custom of Taboo, and compelled women to share a large public banquet and to eat the pork which was forbidden them. The majority of the people gladly welcomed this step. The minority, who, under the lead of Kekuaokalani, a cousin of the king, remained true to paganism, were defeated in the sanguinary battle of Kuamoo ; Kekuaokalani fell, together with his heroic wife, Manona. The destruction of the old temples and images, already initiated, was carried out with renewed zeal ; nevertheless idolatry had many supporters in secret. The half-heartedness of the reforming policy was more unfortunate ; the Hawaiians had been deprived of paganism, but nothing tangible was put into its place.

The visits of European and American

The changes in the domain of culture and economics involved more momentous consequences for the future of the Hawaiian people. Only the higher classes of the people were materially Europeanised ; the masses had to continue for some time in the old paganism and the ancient Polynesian semi-culture. Nevertheless it could not be long before the whole nation was subject to this change. Kamehameha neither intended nor suspected that it should take the form of a complete disintegration of the old national life. This decline was mainly produced by the introduction of European immigrants, who made their way into all the influential posts, and produced a temporary economic

squadrons during this period induced the monarch to seek an alliance with Great Britain, particularly since Russia and the United States had already shown signs of establishing themselves permanently in the archipelago. Kamehameha I., in order to increase his dignity at home by the support of the great world power, had made over his kingdom to Britain in February, 1794, but his offer did not meet with any cordial response. In 1823, Liholiho and his consort, Kamamalo, went to London, in order in this way to anticipate the wishes of others. They both died in 1824 in England, but were buried in their native country. Liholiho's successor, his brother Keaukeauouli, was only nine when placed on the throne under the name of Kamehameha III. The regency during his minority was held by Kaahumanu and the old and tried Kaleimoku. Both found work enough in the succeeding years. It is true that Protestant missionaries had laboured since 1820 with good results ; but all their efforts were stultified by a faction of morally and physically corrupt white immigrants, whose numbers grew from year to year. Drunkenness and immorality became so rampant that no improvement of the conditions could be hoped for except by legislation. Toward the end of the " twenties " the contest of the Christian missions for supremacy began on Hawaii. The Protestant mission was under the protection of the Americans ; the Catholic gained ground only after threats from French warships. In the year 1837 the French extorted a declaration of universal religious liberty, which put an end to the violent persecutions often suffered by the Catholic Christians.

The wise Kaleimoku died in 1827, and the death of the energetic queen-regent,

KING KAMEHAMEHA V. AND HAWAIIAN NOBLES IN 1870

Kaahumanu, followed in 1832. Kamehameha III. declared himself of full age in 1833, when he chose another woman, Kinau, for his co-regent, and nominated her son, Alexander Liholiho, heir to the throne.

The first newspapers printed in the Hawaiian language appeared in 1834. Churches and schools of every sort were erected in large numbers. At the same time the first sugar plantations were laid out, and silkworm breeding was introduced by the British. Soon cotton-growing was added as a new branch of industry. In October, 1840, the kingdom received its first constitution. It was drawn up by the American, Richards, and

971

presented a strange mixture of ancient feudalism and Anglo-American forms. The ministry consisted entirely of foreigners. Richards became Minister of Public Instruction ; Wylie, a Scottish doctor, represented the Foreign Office. The finances were administered after 1842 by Dr. Judd, under whom the public revenue increased from 41,000 dollars in the year 1842, to 284,000 dollars in 1852.

In spite of religious toleration the disputes between the Protestant and **Hawaii Under a Constitution** Catholic clergy continued until the year 1837. They were often exploited by the French Consul in order to put strong pressure on the Hawaiian Government in favour of the Catholic mission. At the same time the British Consul took steps which seemed to point to an annexation of the islands by Great Britain. This induced the Hawaiian Government to obtain a guarantee of the independence of the kingdom from the United States of America in December, 1842, from France at the beginning of 1843, and from England on July 26th, 1843. The action of Lord Paulet, commander of the frigate Carys, in taking possession of the island (February 25th, 1843), on his own responsibility, was not recognised by the British Government.

The constitution of 1840 was changed in 1852, 1864, and on July 6th, 1887 ; with every revision it resembled more and more the usual European constitutional forms, especially when, in 1864, the old institution of the queen-regent was abolished. A privy council, consisting of the Ministers and a number of members nominated by the king, stood next to the sovereign. The Cabinet contained first five, and later four, members ; the Parliament was com-posed of a House of Nobles and a House of Representatives. The most important offices have always been filled by foreigners. Kamehameha III. died in December, 1854. His successor, Alexander Liholiho —Kamehameha IV., married to Queen Emma—then aged twenty, lost no time in placing himself on better terms with France, which, in defiance of the independence guaranteed in 1843, had overwhelmed the kingdom with difficulties and had repeatedly humiliated it. A final treaty between the two countries was effected in 1858. On the death of Kamehameha IV. in 1864, his elder brother, who had something of Kamehameha I. in him, succeeded to the crown. The first act of Kamehameha V. was to alter the constitution of 1864. In the next year an immigration bureau was instituted as a check on the constant shrinkage in the population ; 500 Chinese were brought into the country, to be followed by the first Japanese in 1868. Finally, measures were taken to check the leprosy which had been introduced from China in 1853, and had **Shrinkage in the Population** spread alarmingly. Kamehameha V. died suddenly in 1872, the last of his family. For some months Lunalilo, a kinsman of the Kamehamehas, held the sceptre. After his death, which occurred on February 3rd, 1874, Colonel David Kalakaua, born on November 16th, 1836, in Honolulu, was elected king. In spite of his somewhat frivolous nature, he was a far-sighted monarch ; in 1875 he concluded a commercial treaty with the United States of North America, which secured for his kingdom the most favourable tariffs and greatly promoted the prosperity of the islands. The cultivation of sugar and rice, the two

H. C. White Co.
GENERAL VIEW OF HONOLULU, CAPITAL OF HAWAII, SANDWICH ISLANDS
Showing in the inset the former palace of Queen Liliuokalani, now the United States Executive Office.

King Kamehameha V.

King Kalakaua I.

Queen Liliuokalani.

Ellis & Walery

THE LAST THREE NOTABLE RULERS OF HAWAII

principal exports, increased enormously, and indeed there was a general increase both in exports and in imports. But this revival of trade benefited only the whites. Want of labourers made it once more necessary to introduce foreigners. In 1877 the first Portuguese came into the country from the Azores; in 1884 there were some 10,000. At the same time increasing streams of Chinese and Japanese flooded the land; in 1890 there were counted 15,301, and 17,360.

The numerical proportion of these ethnologically undesirable Mongols to the native population has, up to the beginning of the twentieth century, steadily increased. In moving forward to the conquest of the Pacific, the yellow races have found Hawaii the best point of attack. The growth of economic and political relations with America during the reign of Kalakaua (1874–1891) has been as rapid and continuous as the Mongol immigration.

Concession to the Americans As long ago as the winter of 1873–1874, Pearl Harbour, near Honolulu, was offered by Lunalilo to the Americans by way of compensation for commercial concessions. When the treaty of 1875 required to be renewed in 1887, the United States of North America claimed this place as a permanent possession; further, Hawaii was not to venture to conclude treaties with any other foreign Power without their consent, while they claimed the right to land troops in Hawaii at all times. The influence of the British residents prevented Kalakaua from conceding these humiliating conditions. The refusal of

the American proposals signified, from an economic aspect, the beginning of a financial crisis, by which the Hawaiian dynasty was ruined.

Kalakaua died on January 20th, 1891, at San Francisco. The seventeen years of his reign had been outwardly rich in " progress." He had a small standing army at his disposition ; Hawaii had obtained lines of railroads and steamships ; palaces and lighthouses had been built and Honolulu lighted by electricity. Waterworks and **Record of a Reign** telegraph lines had been constructed, and large stretches of barren country had been made cultivable by irrigation works. The stage of European civilisation began, it must be confessed, with an enormous load of debt, attributable to the frivolity and the extravagance of the popularly beloved king, who had been married since 1863 to Kapiolani, but had no issue.

He was succeeded by his sister, Lydia Kamakaeha Liliuokalani, a woman of fifty-two, who was proclaimed Queen on January 29th, 1891. Her short reign ended with the downfall of the Hawaiian monarchy and the annexation of the island by the United States. Under the dominion of the new American tariff laws, which secured considerable export bounties to native sugar producers, Hawaii could no longer compete in the world market ; exports rapidly fell off, and the national prosperity flagged. The foreign section of the population, which was dependent chiefly on the American trade, found this a reasonable cause for supporting more

973

boldly the idea of close connection with the United States. The results were dissensions in the Government, an over-rapid change in the constitution, which was intended to weaken the influence of the foreigners, and a threatened *coup d'etat* on the queen's part. The end was the deposition of the queen and the proclamation of Hawaii as a republic on January 17th, 1893. The efforts of the victorious Americans of Honolulu toward a close connection with the United States were at first unsuccessful. President Harrison, shortly before the expiration of his term of office, which ended on March 4th, 1893, advocated annexation in a message to the Senate ; but his successor, President Cleveland, was opposed to it. The kingdom thereupon was declared to be changed into the Republic of Hawaii on July 4th, 1894, and a constitution was framed, which provided a Legislative Assembly, a Senate, and a House of Representatives. The constitution, however, hardly lasted long enough to become an actuality ; after President McKinley's entrance on office in the spring of 1897 the incorporation with the Union was effected without any difficulty. The constitutional position of the island group was settled on June 14th, 1900. Hawaii now forms a territory of the United States ; the popular element in its government consists of a Senate with fifteen members and a House of Representatives with thirty members. The first election of a representative to Congress took place on November 6th, 1900. The Governor, a secretary, and the three Judges of the Supreme Court are nominated by the President of the United States, the other officials by the Governor.

Republic that was Still-born

The planting of the Stars and Stripes in the middle of the Northern Pacific Ocean is not the first step which American Imperialism has taken since 1898, but it is one of the most momentous. Tutuila in the Samoan group and Guam in the Marianne Islands are both like feelers which are stretched out far towards the south-west in the direction of Melanesia and Australia ; the broad surfaces of the Philippines flank the important international trade route from Europe to the eastern margin of Asia. In the case of Hawaii a higher standard must be applied. When the Isthmus of Panama has been cut through, and the United States really

Value of Hawaii to United States

becomes a power in the Pacific, then Hawaii, apart from its trade, will be indispensable as a strategic base commanding the northern half of the Pacific. It will be the only intermediate station on the long route from the Central American canal and from San Francisco to Eastern and Southern Asia. The annexation of Hawaii by America is a particularly hard blow for Japan, which had itself been forced to see a similar attempt fail.

Only remnants are now left of the native race, and only traces of the nationality of Hawaii. There has been an uninterrupted decline in the native population since the discovery of the islands. In 1778 there were estimated—though the calculation is certainly excessive—to be 400,000 souls ; in 1832 the first actual census gave 130,313 natives. Four years later there were only 108,579 ; in 1860, 71,019 ; 1884, 40,014 ; 1896, 30,019. At the present day it is extremely difficult to fix the number of pure natives, on account of the numerous half-castes, whose numbers were put at 6,186 in 1890, and 8,485 in 1896, an increase of more than 33 per cent. in six years. At the same time the full-blooded Hawaiians have diminished by 10 per cent. We cannot make the Europeans entirely responsible for the alarmingly rapid retrogression of the Hawaiians. Besides the diseases introduced by the former, the original laxity of morals, the drunkenness, various epidemics, and more than all the traditional practice of infanticide, have been the chief causes. In place of the natives there will soon be only Chinese, Japanese, Europeans, and Americans in Hawaii.

The Death of a Nation

The Hawaiian islands are extremely fertile, and export sugar, rice, coffee, wool, hides, bananas, pineapples, and sisal. During the fiscal year 1905-6 the imports, were of the value of over £3,000,000— three-quarters being from America, and therefore duty free—and the exports to the United States, consisting nearly entirely of sugar, aggregated £5,400,000, and to other countries only £11,300. So entirely is Hawaii imbued with the modern American spirit that Honolulu, the capital, is lighted by electricity, has its electric tramway, and nearly every family has a telephone installation, while the Marconi system of wireless telegraphy is in commercial use between the islands.

974

SAMOA & ITS SETTLEMENT BY THE POWERS

MORE labour has been devoted of recent times to the investigation of the history of Samoa than to that of all the other Polynesian island groups put together. The results obtained are hardly proportionate. The long list of proud genealogies with an infinity of names tells of the vigorous life of the petty states on the several islands and their divisions; tradition also records various invasions from Fiji and Tonga. But we do not obtain the slightest information about the date of the various events to which the legends refer. The investigations go to prove that the general condition of Samoa in the periods before its discovery by Europeans was hardly distinguished from that of other archipelagoes. Its political organisation, and to some degree its stage of social institutions, had alone been somewhat more fully developed. The vendettas and disputes between different influential families, which are also recorded, are of little importance to the world, although they have naturally been exaggerated to great events from the perspective of the Polynesians.

The traditions of Samoa do not run back very far; we need not assume more than 500 years for its inhabitants as a historical nation; how far before that date their immigration must be placed, it is impossible to calculate. The chief event of early history is the subjugation by the Tongans and the Samoan war of liberation which was connected with that—according to one authority about 1600 A.D., according to another about 1200 A.D. That was their heroic age. *Malie tau, molie toa* —" Well fought, brave warriors "—was, according to legend, the admiring shout of the Tongan king to two young chiefs as he pushed off from shore on his return journey. This title, which then passed to the elder of the two brothers, Savea, has been hereditary in his family down to the present day.

Samoa is the land of titles. Above the common people stand the nobles, at the head of whom are the village chief, Alii, and the district governor, Tui, while the highest

Heroic Age of Samoa

chief, or king, bears the title of Tupu. Little inferior to him are the Tulafale, or orators, whose political position, generally, depends entirely on their personal abilities. Besides this, titles taken from certain districts or places, in commemoration of certain persons or events, are conferred as honourable distinctions, whose possession is a preliminary condition for the attainment of the political headship. The most famous of these titles is the above-mentioned " Malietoa," which the township of Malie, lying nine miles to the west of Apia, has the right to confer; a second and hardly less renowned is " Mataafa," which is bestowed by the village of Faleata. On the other hand, the claim to the sovereignty rests on the lawfully conferred right to four names, Tuiatua and Tuiaana, Gatoaitele and Tamasoalii, the last two of which are traced to the names of two princesses

Where Titles are Cheap

Shortly before Jean François Count Lapérouse landed on Samoa in 1787, Galumalemana, a chief of the Tupua family, had, after fierce civil wars, usurped the sovereignty of the whole island. On his death, about 1790, violent struggles broke out between the brothers entitled to the inheritance, from which at first Nofoasaefa, an ancestor of Tamasese, emerged victorious. He could not, however, permanently maintain his position, but retired to his ancestral home, Asau, on Savaii, and once more revived the cannibalism which had almost been forgotten in Samoa. Galumalemana's posthumous son, Jamafana, who even before his birth had been called by the dying father prophetically the uniter of the kingdom, finally inherited the throne. He was succeeded, after 1800, by Mataafa Filisounuu, who was at once involved in serious wars with the Malietoas. The victory rested with the Malietoa Vaiinupo, an ally of the ruler of Manono, who seized the power on the same day of August in the year 1830 on which John Williams set foot on Savaii as the first missionary. Malietoa assumed in consequence the title " Tupu," which has since been customary in Samoa. He also was converted to Christianity, and received the name of Tavita, or David; he died on May 11, 1841. The two decades after his death were in Samoa once more a war of all against all. Out of the number of claimants to the throne, Malietoa Laupepa and his uncle Pea, or Talavou, finally held the power jointly for some years. But, influenced by the foreigners in the country, the Samoans, in 1868, resolved to put only one chief at the head of affairs, and to assemble the estates of the realm no longer in Manono, but in Mulinuu, near Apia. Manono, jealous of its ancient precedence, declared Pea king, and conquered Malietoa Laupepa and his followers. Finally, in 1873, through the intervention of the foreign consuls, who had been appointed in the interval, a treaty was concluded by which the ruling power was put into the hands of the seven members of the Taimua, an Upper House, by the side of which the meetings of the district governors, the Fai Pule, or Lower House, still continued. But in 1875 disorders were renewed, and this time the impulse came from outside.

As far back as 1872 the enterprising New Zealanders had advocated a British annexation of Samoa, and had offered to equip a ship for that purpose. At the same time the United States had obtained, on February 17th, 1872, the concession of the harbour Pango-Pango on Tutuila, the

State of General Warfare

best of the group. The annexation of all Tutuila, proclaimed by a sea captain on his own responsibility, was not sanctioned in Washington. About the middle of 1873, the American "Colonel" Steinberger, a German Jew by descent, appeared as a commissioner in Samoa, in order to study the resources of the island group. This cunning and ambitious man soon raised himself to the most influential position, and induced the natives to ask for a protectorate of the United States. Steinberger himself conveyed the petition to Washington; he returned on April 1st, 1875, to Samoa, but only with presents and a letter of introduction from the President, Ulysses S. Grant. Steinberger gave the country a simple constitution, appointed Malietoa Laupepa nominal king, while he himself modestly assumed the title of Prime Minister. He settled the succession, arranged the system of jurisdiction, and established order and peace throughout the land. But in December, 1875, at the instance of the jealous missionaries and the English population, he was carried off by an English man-of-war, after a bloody battle, and taken to New Zealand. He died in New York toward the end of the century.

The intentions of the United States toward Samoa were now more apparent. In 1887, the American Consul hoisted his flag, and only the energetic remonstrances of Germany and Great Britain hindered the

Peace and a Constitution

NATIVE HOUSE AT APIA IN THE SAMOAN ISLANDS   Kerry, Sydney

GENERAL VIEW OF THE TOWN OF APIA, THE CAPITAL OF GERMAN SAMOA Edward,
The mountain in the middle distance is Vaëa, on the top of which Robert Louis Stevenson, the famous novelist, is buried

Americans from firmly establishing themselves. In June of that year the German Government concluded a treaty with the Samoans, by which they were prevented from giving any foreign government special privileges to the prejudice of Germany. On January 17th, 1878, the Americans, for their part, entered into a treaty to secure friendly relations and promote trade with Malietoa Laupepa ; at the same time the harbour of Pango-Pango was definitely given over to them.

On January 24, 1879, Germany was assigned the harbour of Saluafata, on Upolu, as a naval station ; Great Britain also, by a treaty of August 28th, 1879, secured for herself the use of all these waters, and the right to choose a coaling station. On September 2nd, by a treaty between Germany, Great Britain, the United States, and Malietoa, the district of Apia was declared neutral territory, and placed under a municipal council to be appointed by the three Powers in turn. Finally, on December 23rd, on board the German ship Bismarck, Malietoa Talavou was elected, by numerous chiefs, to the dignity of king for life, with Laupepa as regent.

Since the middle of the 'fifties the Hamburg merchant house of Johann Cesar Godeffroy and Son had made the South Sea the chief sphere of its enterprises, and, a decade and a half later, had monopolised the trade with the central and eastern group of islands ; it had also acquired large estates on the Carolines and the three large Samoan islands, Savaii, Upolu, and Tutuila. Misfortunes on the stock exchange placed the firm, toward the end of the 'seventies, in so precarious a position that, in view of the Anglo-Australian movement to occupy all the unappropriated South Sea Islands, Prince Bismarck abandoned his colonial policy of inaction, and, at the beginning of 1880, introduced the " Samoan proposition," by which the empire was to interfere and undertake to guarantee the small tribute due from the Godeffroys. But the German Reich stag rejected the proposition on the third reading on April 29th, 1880,

King Malietoa Talavou died on November 8th, 1880. His nephew, Malietoa Laupepa, was totally unable to check the renewed outbreak of civil war among the natives ; in fact, at the beginning of 1886 one party chose the chief Tamasese as king. He found support from the Germans, because Laupepa, in November, 1885, had secretly offered the sovereignty to England. Continued injury to German interests, and insults and outrages inflicted by Laupepa's adherents on German civil servants, led, in August, 1887, to Laupepa being arrested by German marines, and taken first to the Cameroons and then to the Marshall Islands.

Tamasese's rule was also brief. On September 9th, 1888, the adherents of Malietoa Laupepa proclaimed the

renowned Mataafa king, and defeated
Tamasese. When his people ventured on
outrages against the Germans, the two
German warships lying off Apia, at the
request of the
German Consul
Knappe, landed
their crews; but
through trea-
chery they fell
into an ambush
on December
18th, and were
almost annihi-
lated. Stronger
German detach-
ments were re-
quired before
the rebels were
repulsed. In ad-
dition to this, a

RIVAL KINGS IN THE CIVIL WAR OF 1889
King Tamasese, the candidate
chosen by the German officials.
King Mataafa, the candidate
chosen by the Samoan people.

hurricane, on March 19th, 1889, wrecked
the two German gunboats, Eber and Adler,
in the harbour of Apia, and ninety-five
brave sailors lost their
lives. The English ship,
H.M.S. Calliope, escaped
by steaming out, and the
captain, Kane, displayed
the greatest skill and
seamanship. The Ameri-
cans suffered nearly as
heavily as the Germans.

A settlement of Samoan
affairs was the result of
a conference held in
Berlin during the sum-
mer of 1889, to which
Germany, England and
the United States sent
representatives. In the
final protocol of June
14th, the island group
was declared independent
and neutral under the
joint protection of the
three Powers. Tamasese
and Mataafa were de-
posed, and Malietoa
Laupepa, who had been
brought back to Samoa
in late autumn, was
reinstated on the throne.
Mataafa, however, was
soon re-elected king by
his party, but in 1893 was conquered
on Manono and banished by the Powers
who signed the treaty. Tamasese the
Younger took his place, and the civil

KING OF SAMOA
Wearing his royal head-dress

war continued. Malietoa Laupepa then
died on August 22nd, 1898. Only two
candidates for the succession were seriously
to be considered—the banished but popular Mataafa, and
Tanu Mafili, the
son of Laupepa,
aged sixteen, a
protégé of the
English mission,
and thus of the
British and
American Go-
vernments.
Tamasese the
Younger was
kept by the
British in re-
serve merely as
a substitute for
Tanu.

The subject of the drama, which was un-
folded in the winter of 1898-1899 in the
distant South Sea archipelago, was not
merely the welfare of the
few Samoans or the possession of the small islands.
There were far weightier
conflicting interests. No
words need be wasted
about the causes of the
intense Anglo-Australian
longing for the islands.
The United States, who
had obtained Hawaii
and the Philippines
immediately before this,
thus possessed magnifi-
cent strategic and com-
mercial bases for the
northern part of the
Pacific, but not for the
south. The interests of
Germany, finally, were
based on economics. In
production and trade it
considerably surpassed
both parties; and it was
a point of honour with
the German Government
not to let the prize which
had once been grasped
escape in the end from
their fingers.

The Samoans chose
Mataafa by an overwhelming majority.
At the same time the American Chief
Justice Chambers, on December 21st,
declared that the young Tanu was elected

with his approval, and that Mataafa could not come into the question, since he was excluded by the Berlin protocol, although a clause to that effect proposed by Prince Bismarck had not been adopted in the final version. The remonstrances of the German Consul Rose, and the German municipal councillor, Dr. Raffel, were disregarded. Mataafa then took the matter into his own hands and drove the supporters of Tanu out of Apia down to the sea and the ships of the allied Powers. After repeated bombardments of the coast villages by the British and American war vessels in the second half of March, a joint committee of inquiry was instituted in the spring of 1899 at the suggestion of Germany, and this, in July, transferred the rights of the abolished monarchy temporarily to the consuls of the three Powers. On November 14th, Germany and Britain came to an agreement, and in the Washington protocol of December 2nd the United States also gave their assent.

Withdrawal of Great Britain

Great Britian under this treaty entirely renounced all claim to the Samoan Islands. By the repeal of the Samoa Act, Upolu and Savaii, with the adjacent small islands, became the absolute property of Germany, while Tutuila and the other Samoan Islands east of 171° W. longitude fell to the United States. Germany in return renounced her claims to the Tonga Islands and Savage Island in favour of Britain, and ceded to the same Power the two Solomon Islands, Choiseul and Isabel. The German Reichstag approved the treaty on February 13th, 1900. On March 1st the newly nominated German governor, Solf, took formal possession of the islands. On August 14th, finally, the wisely conceded self-government of the natives came into force again. Mataafa bore, instead of the former title of king, that of high chief.

The German islands, Savaii and Upolu, have an area of 660 and 340 square miles respectively, with populations of 13,201 and 18,341. The white population is under 500, rather more than one-half being German. The exports are chiefly copra and cocoa beans. In 1905 the imports were of the value of £169,350 and the exports £101,450. The chief island in American Samoa is Tutuila, with an area of 54 square miles and a population of 3,800. Manua and the smaller islands under the Stars and Stripes have a total area of 25 square miles and 2,000 inhabitants. The harbour of Paga Paga, in Tutuila, is an American naval station, and is the only good harbour in the islands. The chief product is copra, in which commodity the natives usually pay their taxes. In 1905 the import trade was under £19,000 and the export trade under £10,000.

Resources of Samoan Islands

THE DISASTROUS HURRICANE AT APIA IN 1889
This memorable storm wrecked two German gunboats, and ninety-five German sailors were drowned. The British ship H.M.S. Calliope escaped only by a feat of seamanship by its captain, who steamed out to sea.

979

SURRENDER OF THE TONGA OR FRIENDLY ISLANDS
The arrival of the British Fleet at Tonga on May 19th, 1901, to receive from Germany formal possession of the islands under the treaty of 1899, whereby Germany abandoned all claims to the group in exchange for half of the island of Samoa.

TONGA : THE LAST SOUTH SEA KINGDOM

OF the islands in the central part of Oceania, only the Tonga Archipelago or Friendly Islands, in addition to Fiji and Samoa, has a noteworthy history. We know little of its course before the arrival of Captain Cook, with the exception of its social conditions.

At the head of the constitution stood the Tuitonga, monarch and god in one, with absolute power over persons and property. Of less importance in reputation and sanctity was the Tui Ardeo, said to be the descendant of a dethroned royal family, which had still retained a minor chieftancy. The Tuitonga had to show peculiar honours to the Tui Ardeo on different occasions. The king and his family composed the first class (Hau) of the nobility. The second (the Eiki or Egi, who also bore the title Tui, or lord) furnished the highest officials in the kingdom and the district governors, and was appointed by the king, although the dignity was hereditary. The first of the second class was in pre-European times the Tui Hatakalawa, the Minister of the Interior ; in Mariner's time (1810) he came in precedence after the Tui Kanakabolo, or War Minister.

Since in the nineteenth century the Tuitonga was excluded from all share in the wars, the War Minister easily attained to greater influence than the monarch himself ; indeed, the Minister has been taken by more than one traveller for **Grades of Tonga Nobility** the king. The last class of nobility, or Matabule, furnished councillors and servants of the Eiki and the Tuitonga, district governors, public teachers, and representatives of the most honourable crafts, such as shipbuilding and the making of weapons. The three classes of nobility were the sole possessors of the soil, as well as of the power of Taboo. The common people had no share in either ; they possessed only personal freedom, and supported themselves merely by the cultivation of the lands of the nobles, by handicrafts, or by fishing. Among handicrafts those requiring superior skill were reserved for the higher class of the commons, the Mua, while agriculture and the profession of cooking were assigned to the lower class, or Tua.

Captain Cook, in 1773 and 1777, found that the Tubou nobles, had secured all the important offices of State. The kings apparently took their wives only from the family of Tubou. Toward the end of the eighteenth century this concentration of power had increased to the extent of denying the authority of the royal house. This roused other Eiki families to imitate the example of the Tubou. The regents of **The Little Wars of Tonga** Hapai and Vavau first revolted ; those of Tongatabu followed. After long struggles the victory rested with Finau, the Eiki of Hapai, although he could no longer force the whole archipelago to obey his rule. At the beginning of the nineteenth century he shifted the political centre of gravity to Vavau. In 1830 Taufaahau, the lord of Hapai, and Tubou, the Eiki of Tongatabu, adopted Christianity ; and when the Finau died out in 1833, Vavau fell to the former. In this way Taufaahau governed over the same kingdom as Finau I. had done thirty years earlier. In 1845 Tubou, or, as he was called after his conversion, Josiah of Tongatabu, died also. Taufaahau, as King George Tubou I., now united the whole archipelago into one kingdom. This state bore from the first the stamp of European influence. The Wesleyan mission had soon extended its activity to political and social matters. In 1839 George issued an edict for Hapai and Vavau, which established a court of justice of four members and a written code, and abolished the old customs, according to which each chief administered justice at his own discretion. The legislation of 1862 finally raised the existing serfs to the position of free farmers of the soil, from which they could not be ousted so long as they paid their rent. The taxes, 25s. a year, were uniformly imposed on all male inhabitants over sixteen years of age.

After 1838 on Tonga also there were quarrels between the Catholic and Protestant missions. In December, 1841, threats of a French warship caused the ruler of Tongatabu to seek an English protectorate, which was not granted him. The Catholic missionaries, however, obtained admission. Their success in the religious field was never important ; but in the political field they had, even in 1847, so great an influence over Tongatabu, that the chiefs of that part created opposition to the rule of George I., which was repressed in 1852 by the storming of the fortresses Houma and Bea, defended by French missionaries. Although the chiefs were reinstated in their former posts, and the missionaries received no injury to life or property, France felt herself aggrieved. She extorted in 1858 an official permission for the Catholic teaching, and put various Catholic chiefs in the place of Protestants.

King George, notwithstanding, found time to make expeditions to other countries. The Tongans had at all times, owing to their great nautical skill, undertaken campaigns against Samoa and Nuka Hiwa, and had caused panic especially in the neighbouring archipelagoes. The, people of Fiji had thus a strong tinge of the Polynesian in them. A few years after Cook's second visit (1777), a Tongan adventurer played a great part in the Fijian disorders. In 1854 King George appeared with a large fleet, avowedly to

KING OF THE FRIENDLY ISLANDS
Poulaho, of whom this portrait is given by Captain Cook, was the ruler of the Friendly Islands at the time of his visits in 1773 and 1777.

support Thakombau in his difficulties. George Tubou I. completed the internal reforms of his island kingdom by the constitution of November 4th, 1875. This was partly the creation of the king himself, partly that of his old and loyal councillor, the Wesleyan missionary Shirley Baker. Its contents kept closely to English forms ; in its ultimate shape, as settled by the chambers and printed in the English language in 1877, it provided for a legislative assembly, which met every three years. Half of its members belonged to the hereditary nobility and were nominated by the king ; the rest were elected by the people. The executive power lay in the hands of a ministry of four, who, together with the governors of the four provinces and the higher law officers, composed the Privy Council. The administration of justice was put on an independent footing, and comprised a supreme court, jury courts, and police courts. Education was superintended by the missionaries, who had erected well-attended schools on all the islands. An industrial school and a seminary, which was called Tubou College in honour of the king, were founded. The prohibition against the sale of land to foreigners, which was inserted in the constitution at Baker's advice—" the Tongans are not to be driven into the

A NIGHT DANCE BY TONGA WOMEN AT HAPAI IN THE FRIENDLY ISLANDS
Reproduced from a plate accompanying the original account of the voyages of Captain Cook.

sea "—was important for the economic future of the Tongans; even leases of land were allowed only after notice had been given to the Government.

In view of the increased interest which the European Powers in the 'seventies took in the South Sea Islands, Tonga, with its favourable situation, could not permanently be neglected. King George and his chancellor, Baker, were on terms of open friendship with Germany. On November 1st, 1876, this " good feeling " took the form of a commercial treaty, establishing friendly relations with the German Empire, according to which the harbour of Taulanga on Vavau was ceded as a coaling station. On November 29th, 1879, Tonga concluded a similar treaty of amity with Britain. By an agreement of April 6th, 1886, Germany and Britain decided that Tonga should remain neutral territory. On August 1st, 1888, a treaty was made with the United States.

KING GEORGE I. OF TONGA

In 1890 Shirley Baker had become so unpopular with the chiefs and people that the British High Com-missioner removed him from the group, replacing him, at the king's request, with Mr. Basil Thomson, who was commissioned to reorganise the adminis-tration and finances, and to draft the penal code which became law in 1891.

King George Tubou I. died on February 18th, 1893, at his capital, Nukualofa, aged ninety-five years. He was suc-ceeded by his great-grandson, George Tubou II., a timid youth of nine-teen. English trade had been steadily displacing German trade in spite of a monthly subsidised ser-vice of the North German Lloyd to Tonga and Samoa, and when, in March, 1899, the German warship Falke appeared off Tongatabu, nominally with orders to occupy the harbour of Taulanga until Tongan debtors had paid the sum due

LAST NATIVE SOVEREIGN
IN OCEANIA
George Tubou II., King of Tonga.

of £20,000—according to another state-ment merely with orders to induce the king to open the Tongan courts to the recovery of debts to foreigners—an English warship from the Australian station sailed in on April 10, and paid George II. £25,000 on the sole condition that the king made no concessions whatever of landed rights to any foreign Power. In return for this Britain renewed her guarantee of independence for Tonga. Since that time the group of islands has been valuable to Germany only as the object of an exchange; in the treaty of November 8th, 1899, she abandoned all claims in exchange for half of Samoa. Thus Tonga and the adjoining Savage Island were, in spite of the protest of King George II., placed under a British protectorate on May 19th, 1900.

With the Tongan kingdom, the last of the native states of Oceania disappeared. It is true that the constitution, formulated on a European model, was in many details unadapted to the Polynesian nature. But Tonga preserved many other points which recalled the old nation-ality. These relics of an indigenous development are fated soon to die away.

The kingdom of Tonga consists of three island groups—Tonga, Hapai, and Vavau—with an area of 390 square miles, and a population of 21,763, of whom 240 are British or European. The chief articles of produce are copra, green fruit, and fungus, and the trade is chiefly with New Zealand and New South Wales. In 1905 the imports were of the value of £70,868, and the exports of the value of £110,729. Ac-counts are kept in dollars, shillings and pence, and the only legal tender is now British coin. The weights and measures used are as in the United Kingdom. There is regular steamer communication with Australia and New Zealand.

THE PICTURESQUE SCENERY OF NEW ZEALAND

New Zealand is rich in natural beauty; parts, such as the Milford Sound, seen in our first view, suggest the Norway Fiords, while falls such as those of Waitakerei, illustrated above, or the Waiau River, lower, recall scenes in the British Isles; but the geysers or hot springs, and the giant fern gullies, are peculiar to the country.

Photos by Valentine, Dundee, and H. C. White Co. London

NEW ZEALAND
THE BRITISH DOMINION FARTHEST SOUTH

NEW ZEALAND, which, on geographical and ethnological grounds, may be considered here rather than in connection with Australia, occupies a geographical position reminding one strongly of that of the neighbouring island continent. To the south and east of New Zealand the ocean is quite free from any considerable islands; only toward the north and west are relations possible with the habitable world—on the one side with Australia and Tasmania, on the other with New Caledonia, Fiji, Tonga, and the Cook Islands. New Zealand is situated as regards all these countries so that the lines of communication with it are almost radii of a circle, a fact important geographically and historically. It was merely a consequence of the inferior seamanship of the inhabitants of Australia, New Caledonia, and Fiji that the original immigration to New Zealand did not take place from these places.

New Zealand lies about twelve hundred and fifty miles from the islands just mentioned. This distance, in spite of their advanced nautical skill, was too far for the navigation of the Polynesians, and thus must have prevented any permanent and systematic expansion of the Maoris; their naval expeditions did not go beyond one or two voyages to the Hawaiki of legend, and the occupation of the neighbouring Chatham Islands, which was effected in 1834 with the help of a European captain.

Coming of the Maoris

The case was otherwise for the New Zealand of the Europeans. Two or three generations ago its proximity to Australia and Tasmania enabled a thorough and rapid scheme of colonisation to be carried out thence; at the present day, when it feels itself strong in the number of its inhabitants and its resources, it lies far enough off to be able to entertain the idea of an independent national existence by the side of the Australian Commonwealth. A feeling in favour of independence was discernible as early as 1860 or 1870, hardly a generation after the beginning of the colonisation proper. The interference of New Zealand in Samoan affairs in the year 1872 was followed by the annexation of the Kermadec Isles to New Zealand, in 1887, and of the Cook Islands and Manihikis in 1900; Fiji appears nearing the same destiny now. The influential circles of New Zealand are universally of opinion that all the island groups of Polynesia belong to it as naturally as, according to the idea of the Australians, the Western Pacific Ocean falls within their magic circle. Each of the two countries feels itself a leading power in the Southern Hemisphere; hence the grandiose phrase, " the position to which this land is entitled in the concert of the Powers," used in 1900 by Richard Seddon, the Prime Minister of New Zealand, who died on June 10, 1906.

Aspirations After National Independence

Although the population of New Zealand, according to the census of 1906, amounted to only 888,578 it would be unwise to ignore its pretensions. Apart from their advantageous position for the command of the Southern Pacific Ocean, the two islands possess a coastline so greatly indented that it surpasses Italy itself in the number of its bays. Besides this, it now produces gold and coal in considerable quantities, while copper, silver, iron-ore, sulphur, platinum, and antimony are also plentiful.

New Zealand, lying entirely within the temperate zone, possesses a further advantage in its climate, which, judging by the physical and intellectual qualities of the Maoris, must be credited with a considerable power of modifying racial types for the better, unless it be indeed the case, as is sometimes asserted, that it has a bad effect on the physique of Europeans.

985

Agriculture in New Zealand, as in Australia, is rapidly increasing; although the climate is temperate, there are cold nights in summer, making the produce of the harvests very variable. Nevertheless there are more than 14,000,000 acres of land under cultivation at present. According to rough calculations 40,000,000 acres — nearly 70,000 square miles, or two-thirds of the entire surface—are suitable for agriculture and grazing, though at present one-third of the country is covered with forests. The backbone of the industries of New Zealand, as of Tasmania, which in many respects enjoys the same climatic conditions, is the breeding of cattle and sheep. This industry is steadily growing, as cattle can remain out in the open and find sufficient food the whole year through. Of the exports for the year 1905, amount-ing to nearly £16,000,000, not less than £11,000,000 came from animal products; gold produced £2,094,000, and agriculture only £1,635,000.

The area of New Zealand equals that of Great Britain plus half of Ireland. The Dominion consists of three islands, of which the southernmost, Stewart Island, is the same size as Hertfordshire, and sparsely settled. North Island is half as large again as Scotland; Middle Island is just the size of England and Wales with their islets. New Zealand has for dependencies the Cook Islands, the Chathams, and several uninhabited islands, south or south-east of Stewart Island.

The original inhabitants of New Zealand, the Maoris, were benefited by the advantages of their country only to a certain degree; their physique indeed was improved there, but industrially they were unable to profit by the green fields or the splendid forests of Kauri pine. They made use of the native fauna only so long as there were creatures to hunt and eat; even yet the heroic ballads of the Maoris tell of conflicts with the gigantic moa, the first species of the fauna, which had lived on for thousands of years unmolested, to fall a victim to the intrusion of man.

The first Maoris immigrated into the two islands, then uninhabited, fully 500 years ago; in the course of time batches of fresh immigrants followed them, the last perhaps in the eighteenth century. The point from which the migration started was Hawaiki, the theme of so many legends, the Savaii of the Samoan Islands; the intermediate station, and for some Maoris the actual starting point, was Rarotonga.

According to the legend, the chief Ngahue, with 800 vassals in twelve ships, whose names are still kept

MAP OF THE DOMINION OF NEW ZEALAND

A MAORI MIGRATION IN THE EARLY COLONIAL DAYS
The Maoris were formerly migratory, but are now settled and pursuing the peaceful paths of agricultural industry.
The illustration shows a family on the march accompanied by all its worldly wealth—pigs, dogs, spears, and babies.

sacred, landed in the Bay of Plenty on North Island. When the British began to colonise, the population was estimated at 100,000 to 200,000 souls. Such an increase in a comparatively short time could be the result only of periods of undisturbed tranquillity. The beasts and birds—above all, the numerous gigantic species of moa, reaching thirteen feet in height—did not enjoy this peace. The inhabitants, accustomed to a flesh diet and ever increasing in numbers, looked for a substitute, and were driven in desperation to cannibalism. With this momentous step, the first crisis in the history of the Maoris, the prosperous time of peace was irrevocably past ; the ensuing period was one of continuous murder and slaughter, tribe against tribe, man against man.

Beginning of Cannibalism

During the centuries immediately after the first immigration, all evidence points to the existence of large states, which occasionally were subject to one common head. There seems also to have been a religious centre. This was the period of the national prosperity of the Maoris, when their workmanship also attained its highest perfection. Europeans had only a passing knowledge of them in this advanced stage ; Abel Tasman saw in 1642 large and splendid double canoes in use among them. Such canoes the Maoris of the eighteenth century were no longer able to build. The decadence was universal. The ancient kingdoms broke up into small communities of bold incendiaries and robbers, who recognised no political centre, but were engaged in fierce feuds one against another. The belief in the old gods gave way to a superstitious belief in guardian spirits, charms, and counter-charms. The national character, always inclined to pride and tyranny, ended by becoming more and more bloodthirsty, revengeful, and cruel.

The intercourse of the Maoris with the Europeans at the end of the eighteenth and the beginning of the nineteenth century rendered the incessant civil wars only more fierce by the introduction of firearms. In the year 1820 the chief Hongi, accompanied by the missionary Kendall, visited England, and was presented to King George IV., who received him with marked attention and showered presents upon him. Having soon learnt the political condition of Europe, and being

Intercourse with Europeans

dazzled by the still brilliant reputation of the victorious career of Napoleon, he exchanged most of his presents in Sydney for weapons and ammunition, armed his tribe, and filled the North Island until 1828 with all the horrors of war. Thousands of Maoris were shot or made slaves, and

A Maori Would-be Napoleon hundreds eaten. Hongi, having neglected to wear in some battle in 1827 the cuirass which the King of England had given him, received a shot in the lungs, from the effects of which he died fifteen months afterward.

The diminution of the native population owing to such protracted wars was an advantage to the whites already settled in the country. Ever since the year 1800, there had been a large number of " pioneers of culture "—runaway sailors, escaped convicts from New South Wales, and other adventurers. Their relations with the Maoris had at first been restricted to a barter of New Zealand flax and timber for rum, iron, and other European products ; later, a trade in tattooed Maori heads sprang up, to which, even at the present day, European and American museums give testimony.

In 1814 the Anglican mission under Samuel Marsden began its labours in the Bay of Islands, and soon obtained such an influence among the natives that it seemed in 1820 as if the North Island would develop into a Christian Maori state. The horrors enacted on the island by Hongi stopped this movement only temporarily ; after Marsden's death not only did the work of conversion proceed rapidly, but the idea of a Maori state under Anglican guidance was approaching its realisation. There was at that time in England little inclination to organise a state colonisation of New Zealand ; Australia lay nearer and had a less dangerous population. But when, in 1831, a French warship anchored in the Bay of Islands the missionaries induced

French and British Competition thirteen leading chiefs of that district to petition King William IV. for protection for New Zealand. The Government consented, and nominated, in 1833, James Busby, a colonist from New South Wales, as Resident, entrusting him with a jurisdiction over the British settlers which was backed up by no force at all. Busby's first act was to grant a national flag to New Zealand, which was officially recognised by Great Britain toward the end of 1834.

The missionaries thus obtained the object for which they had so perseveringly striven, a Maori state apparently self-governing, but in reality dependent on them. At Busby's instigation, this state, represented by thirty-five chiefs of the North, was called, after the autumn of 1835, the United Tribes of New Zealand. At the same time the chiefs declared that they would annually hold an assembly, and there pass the necessary laws. Busby himself wished to conduct the Government with the help of a council consisting of natives, for which, after a definite interval, representatives were to be elected. The preliminary costs of this new constitution should, he proposed, be defrayed by Great Britain, which was to be petitioned not only for a loan, but also for the further protection of the whole scheme.

Busby's plan, which was ridiculed by all who were acquainted with the conditions of New Zealand, had been suggested by another fantastic undertaking, that of Baron Thierry. This adventurer had commissioned Kendall, the missionary, to obtain large tracts of land for him

40,000 Acres of Land for 36 Hatchets in New Zealand, and Kendall had bought, in 1822, 40,000 acres on the Hokianga, from three chiefs, whom he paid for them with thirty-six hatchets. But Thierry, without entering on his property, roamed about in South America, in order to become the " sovereign " of some people, even if it were the smallest Indian tribe. Later, he pursued the same aims on the South Sea Islands, and was finally chosen by the island of Nukahiwa in the Marquesas to be its head. As " Sovereign Chief in New Zealand and King of Nukahiwa," he announced to the British Resident in North New Zealand his speedy arrival from Tahiti (1835). The kings of Great Britain and France, he declared, as well as the President of the United States, had consented to the founding of an independent state on Hokianga Bay, and he was waiting only for the arrival of a suitably equipped warship sent from Panama to sail to the Bay of Islands.

Busby's counter-measure was the founding of the United Tribes of New Zealand. Strange to relate, this step was taken seriously in Great Britain, though not in Australia, and every protection was guaranteed to the chiefs. There was a strictly correct exchange of notes between Thierry and Busby, until Thierry, at the close of

988

1. Houses of Parliament, which were destroyed by fire in December, 1907 ; 2. Customs House ; 3. Queen's Wharf ; 4. The port in the year 1843 ; 5. General view of the town, showing Government House, Cathedral, and Houses of Parliament.

VIEWS OF WELLINGTON. NEW ZEALAND, PAST AND PRESENT

1837, accompanied by ninety-three European adventurers, appeared in person on the North Island. At first amicably received by some of the chiefs, he soon perceived that the British settlers, as well as the missionaries, were working against him. When it appeared that his announcement that hundreds of his subjects would soon follow him was idle talk, Thierry became the laughing-stock of whites and Maoris, was deserted by everyone, and thenceforward eked out a scanty existence as a pauper.

From King to Pauper

Thierry's French name, the founding of French companies for the colonisation of the east side of the South Island, and finally the settlement of the French missionary Pompallier in New Zealand—all this gradually aroused a keen interest in the two islands among private circles in Britain. Captain Cook, who had explored the islands in 1769-70, 1773-74, and 1777, had always advocated an occupation of the country, and even Benjamin Franklin had proposed to found a company for the colonisation of New Zealand, but both without results. It is true that in 1825 a New Zealand Company was formed, and some emigrants were sent to New Zealand, but the behaviour of the natives alarmed the new-comers so that, with the exception of the four most stout-hearted, who remained in the country, all returned to Australia or England. The attempt, which had swallowed up £10,000, was a failure. In 1837, the idea of colonisation was again taken up by Edward Gibbon Wakefield, the founder of the Colony of South Australia, by Lord Durham, the leader of the attempt of 1825, and by other representatives of the British Parliament ; but since the Association for the Colonisation of New Zealand could not break down the opposition of the missionary societies, of the Government, and of the two Houses of Parliament, it was broken up. At the end of 1838 the New Zealand Land Company, also founded by Wakefield and Lord Durham, took its place. This wished to acquire land from the Maoris, in order to resell it to English emigrants. The price was to be adjusted so that not only a surplus should be produced for the construction of roads, schools, and churches, but also an ade-

Attempts towards Colonisation

quate profit for the shareholders. When the company, on June 1st, 1839, publicly put up to auction 110,000 acres of New Zealand land, so many bidders were forthcoming that very soon £100,000 was received.

In view of the fact that a vigorous colonisation of New Zealand was unavoidable, the Colonial Minister, the Marquis of Normanby, now tried to anticipate the New Zealand Land Company and to secure for the Government the expected profits. Under the influence of the Wakefield agitators, Lord Glenelg, the predecessor of Normanby in office, had planned the appointment of a British consul to New Zealand and the annexation of districts already occupied by whites under the Government of New South Wales. On June 15th, 1839, Captain Hobson was nominated by Normanby consul for New Zealand, with a commission to induce the natives to recognise the sovereignty of the Queen of England. He was to administer the island group belonging to New South Wales, in the capacity of a deputy Governor. In order to nip the plans of the company in the bud, Hobson was further instructed to bind the Maori chiefs to sell land exclusively to the Crown, and to suppress the speculation in land which was raging in New Zealand, by requiring that all purchases of land effected by British subjects should be investigated by a special committee.

Action by the British Government

But the Government came forward too late with their measures. An expedition of the New Zealand Land Company, under the guidance of a brother of Wakefield, had already landed in Queen Charlotte's Sound on August 16th, 1839, had obtained an immense territory from the natives for a few articles of merchandise, in spite of all the efforts of the missionaries, and had lost no time in founding the town of Wellington on Port Nicholson. The capital of the " Britain of the South Sea " was thus created. One out of every eleven acres of the purchased land was to remain reserved for the natives as an inviolable possession.

Since also a French company was well on its way to secure a strong footing in New Zealand, Hobson, who had landed on the North Island on January 29th, 1840, concluded—with the support of the missionaries, who saw in a Crown

1. General view of the town in 1850; 2. Scene from the wharf to-day; 3. Heart of the town of Auckland fifty years ago; 4. The principal street of Auckland during the ceremonies on the occasion of the Duke of York's visit, 1891.

VIEWS OF AUCKLAND, NEW ZEALAND, PAST AND PRESENT

Colony the smaller evil—the Treaty of Waitangi with a number of the more important chiefs, in which they absolutely and for ever resigned the sovereignty of their land to the Crown of England. The Crown in return guaranteed to the Maoris the royal protection, all the privileges of British subjects, and all their rights to land and property, but reserved the right of pre-emption of every district which the natives should be willing to sell. The few dozens who first signed were soon joined by other chiefs, so that the number of signatures shortly before the middle of the year 1840 reached 512. In June, therefore, the British sovereignty could also be proclaimed over the South Island and Stewart Island " on the basis of the right of Cook's discovery." On September 19th, Hobson hoisted the British flag in Auckland. Finally, on November 6th, 1840, New Zealand was declared a Crown Colony. Hobson was nominated Governor, and Auckland became temporarily the seat of government.

Treaty with the Maoris

The Treaty of Waitangi is in various respects an event of historical importance. For the first time a European nation laid down the fundamental principle that the natives, even of an uncultivated country, have full possessory rights over their own land. We may contrast with this the conduct adopted by the Government and the settlers toward the neighbouring Australians and Tasmanians ! Now, for the first time, " savages " were officially put on a level with colonists—that is to say, were treated as men.

The treaty is also important politically. Great Britain, by firmly establishing herself in front of the broad expanse of the Pacific Ocean, secured a commanding position in the entire Central and Southern Oceanic world. This was an exceptionally hard blow for France, since, after the total failure of her Australian and Tasmanian schemes of colonisation, there was no other considerable tract of territory to be found

NEW ZEALAND'S FIRST GOVERNOR
Captain Hobson, who was appointed Governor of New Zealand in 1839, and who executed the Treaty of Waitangi with the Maori chiefs.

which could serve as a strong base within her widely distributed colonial empire in the South Pacific. The French ships which arrived off New Zealand in July, 1840, were compelled to return without having effected their purpose.

Who will prove victorious in the fight for the supremacy in the Pacific Ocean ? The answer is difficult. At the present day the Pacific is a stage trodden by many actors ; in a possibly not distant future it may become the theatre of war for the United States, Russia, Great Britain, and possibly Japan. In any case, New Zealand will possess great value, owing to her geographical position. Strategically she forms a splendid flanking outpost for Australia, which is otherwise exposed defenceless to every attack from north or east ; and as far as industries go she is at least as well dowered as her larger neighbour. Inferiority of size is compensated by more favourable climatic conditions.

The Treaty of Waitangi soon involved momentous consequences for the colony itself. The British Government, which had never recognised the New Zealand Land Company, reduced its claims— 20,000,000 of the 46,000,000 acres of land " bought " by Europeans —first to 997,000, and after a more exact investigation in 1843, to 282,000 acres. To the Englishmen who claimed the remaining 26,000,000 acres, only 100,000 were awarded ; to the London Mission only 66,000 instead of 216,000 acres. The rest in all cases, instead of being given back to the natives, was declared to be Crown land and bought by the Government. From that time the natives had quite a different notion of the value of their land, which they had hitherto unsuspectingly sold for muskets, rum, tobacco, blankets, and toys. They began more and more frequently to dispute the old bargains, first by complaints and protests, then by blows, and finally by war and murder. After the Maoris had murdered several Europeans in 1843, and repeatedly torn down the

Beginning of Maori Discontent

1. Port Chalmers, Otago; 2. Napier, "the Garden City of New Zealand"; 3. High Street of Christchurch;
4. Dunedin from North-east Valley : 5. Nelson from Britannia Height.

SOME OF THE PROSPEROUS CITIES IN THE DOMINION OF NEW ZEALAND

Photos H. C. White Co., Edwards, and Underwood & Underwood, London

British flag, Britain was obliged to consider herself at war with the islanders. The successor of Hobson, who died in 1842, was Robert Fitzroy, known as the commander of the Beagle, which had carried Charles Darwin on his voyage round the world. Fitzroy was, however, incompetent for his post, and by all sorts of concessions, such as remissions of entrance-tolls and restitution of land sold by the Maoris to the immigrants, he prompted the natives to make renewed demands. His measures with this view rapidly emptied the colonial coffers. The New Zealand Land Company, in consequence of the perpetual disturbances, also fell into difficulties and temporarily suspended its operations. Besides this, the British forces, from want of artillery, did very little against the brave Maori warriors.

A too Supine Governor

In November, 1845, Sir George Grey, who had won his spurs as the first Governor of South Australia, arrived in New Zealand. Since the attempt to quiet the insurgents by peaceful methods was unsuccessful, the Governor prohibited the importation of arms and ammunition, and rapidly defeated the chiefs Heki and Kawiri. He was able to conclude peace by the end of January, 1846. Isolated subsequent outbreaks were suppressed with equal promptness. Grey's next object was to prevent the recurrence of civil wars by a system of suitable reforms. Besides the above mentioned reduction of the landed property of the missions, he put an officer into the native secretaryship, which had been hitherto administered by a missionary, and settled the land question in the interests of the natives.

The new constitution, recommended by the British Government, which gave the colony complete self government, appeared premature to him, and was not therefore put into force; he contented himself by dividing the colony into two provinces. In order to revive immigration, which had almost ceased, steps were taken to advance to the New Zealand

SIR GEORGE GREY
One of Britain's great Colonial administrators. He rescued South Australia from panic and pacified New Zealand by his vigorous policy.

Company in 1846 and 1847 a sum of £236,000 free of interest, and the Crown lands of the district of New Munster were assigned to it until July, 1850. The minimum price for an acre was fixed at £1 sterling. With the company's co-operation, the Free Church of Scotland founded the Colony of Otago on the South Island in 1847, and the Church of England settled Canterbury in 1849. These were the last acts of the company, whose directors were compelled to suspend the business finally in 1850 from want of funds, a fortunate turn for the development of the Colony of New Zealand, which had suffered only from the juxtaposition of the company and Government. For this reason the Government remitted the payment by the company of the sum advanced, and assigned to the shareholders, in 1852, £268,000 sterling as compensation for their landed rights.

Sir George Grey's term of office ended on December 31st, 1853; after a short furlough at home he was transferred to Cape Colony. But, in 1852, before leaving, he had obtained for the two islands that same privilege of self-government which had been granted by the mother country to the Australian colonies —that is, a responsible government. The constitution, which was largely due to Grey himself, provided for six provinces with separate administration under a separate council and an elected superintendent. The provinces composed a Federal State with a Parliament, which, consisting of an elected lower house of representatives and a nominated legislative council, met for the first time in 1854 at Auckland, the seat of the Governor and of the central Government. Simultaneously with the final settlement of the Australian constitutional question in general, the forms of responsible government were extended to New Zealand in all its parts. In the matter of the native question alone the Home Government reserved the right of interference until 1862. The colonial

The First New Zealand Parliament

Scene on a North Island stock farm.

Freezing works in Canterbury district.

New Zealand's chief industry—Loading wool for export.

Sheep fair at Ohaupo, in North Island, an important stock centre.

NEW ZEALAND'S GREAT LIVESTOCK INDUSTRY

COMMANDING OFFICER'S HUT DURING THE MAORI RISING OF 1846

Cabinet included a native Minister, but his powers were slight ; all matters relating to the natives and their lands were really settled by the Governor and an Imperial official known as the native secretary.

The departure of Sir George Grey was followed by a cycle of years of external tranquillity, and of visible prosperity for the colony. Nevertheless they contained the germ of fresh troubles. From fear lest the chambers, in which they were not represented, should weaken the power of the central Government, which had been greeted with confidence, the natives of the North Isl nd, in 1856, combined into the "Land League," which was intended to check completely the further sale of land to the Government. In 1857 matters culminated in a national combination, which was intended to block the growth of the foreign element. The centre of the

movement 'ay on the shores of Lake Taupo in North Island, a region in which the natives still kept their lands. South Island had by this time passed completely into European hands, and therefore did not come within the sphere of war. The lead in the struggle was taken by the chiefs of the Waikato Valley, who proclaimed the old chief Potatau as their king. But Potatau was of a conciliating temper, and the leading spirit of the whole agitation was the young and vigorous Wocemu Kingi, or William Thompson, of the tr be of the Ngatiawa, called the king-maker, who had the support of the younger chiefs. As long as the "King of Peace," Potatau I., lived, the Maoris kept quiet.

SCENE OF THE MAORI TROUBLE IN 1845
A view of the town of Korarika, better known to-day as Russell, in the Bay of Islands, North Island. It was partially destroyed by the Maoris in March, 1845.

Under his successor, Potatau II., hostilities to the whites broke out in 1860, and soon assumed such proportions that the British Government sent out Sir George Grey to New Zealand for the second time. In spite of all the respect which the natives entertained for him, and of the constitution which he gave them, he was unable to procure more than a brief suspension of hostilities. The question now to be answered was which race should remain in the country. The great Maori war lasted fully ten years, if several interruptions owing to the exhaustion of both sides are included. The Maoris showed a courage and endurance which places them in the first rank of all primitive peoples ; on the other hand, the British operat ons were hampered by continual friction between the Colonial

TOMB OF POTATAU, THE FIRST MAORI KING
Potatau was elected king of the confederated Maori tribes in 1857, and died in 1860 at his capital, Nagaruwahia, where he is buried. He was a lover of peace.

THE EARLIEST GOLD DISCOVERY IN NEW ZEALAND
Conference between Lieut.-Governor Wynyard and Maori Chiefs at Coromandel in 1853, concerning gold discoveries.

Government, the Governor, and the commanders of the military forces sent from home. These dissensions were not the less disastrous because the blame for them lay rather with the system of dual control itself than with the individuals who were fated to work it.

One defeat of the British followed another; troops after troops were sent across from England and Australia as time went on. At length, in 1866, William Thompson, the chief of the Waikato confederacy, made his submission; a last effort on the part of his more irreconcilable supporters was crushed in 1868 and 1869 by the colonial troops, the British regiments having left the island. Practically the war was at an end by 1867. In that year an agreement was made that the Maoris should have four seats in the Lower House. In 1870 peace was completely restored. The war had cost the colony and the mother country a large sum of money, had imposed a heavy burden of debt, of which the effect was to be felt for the next fifteen years, and had

MAORI PEACE-MAKER
The peace-maker was formerly an honoured institution. His sole occupation was to carry messages between hostile chiefs, and to bring about peace. His person was sacred.

sacrificed the lives of a considerable proportion of the colonists.

The natives, their pride crushed, and they themselves deprived of all hope of maintaining their nationality or even their race, withdrew into Kingsland, a district some 1,600 square miles in size, to the north-west of Lake Taupo, where they were left unmolested for a time. The last three decades have not been entirely free from collisions with the whites; but, on the whole, the Maoris have resigned themselves to the situation. They have cultivated a considerable part of Kingsland on a sensible system, and they possess more than 3,000,000 sheep, 50,000 cattle, and 100,000 pigs. Almost all can speak and write English, and all have been baptised; they eagerly vote for Parliament, where they are represented by four members in the Lower House and two in the Upper House. It is true that here, too, the old nationality is gone irrevocably; the 40,000 Maoris—for such is the figure to which the nation numbering 150,000 in its palmy days has shrunk—hardly resemble their ancestors in any one respect. They have not, for two generations, practised cannibalism, but, on the other hand, they have become addicted to drunkenness ; and consumption, asthma, and scrofula have followed in the wake of this vice.

Almost a century had elapsed since Captain Cook had hoisted the flag of Great Britain on its shores, and there were not yet 100,000 European colonists in the country. The causes of this slow movement, as compared with the rapid development of New South Wales and Victoria, were not to be found in the nature of the country; the South Island, which was almost entirely spared

mandel on the North Island and at Nelson on the South Island in 1852 remained solitary instances until, in 1861, the discovery of the rich alluvial deposits at Otago produced a veritable gold fever. After they were exhausted, the productive fields on the west coast were worked. Otago exported in 1863 gold to the value of more than £2,000,000, the west coast, in 1866, rather more. Toward the end of the 'sixties the production and export from the North Island increased. Owing to this the confidence of the Mother Country in the future of New Zealand was immensely strengthened ; the London money market shows a long list of loans made during the last thirty years for the development of the resources of the country. New Zealand at the present day has the largest public debt per head of population of any country in the world. On March 31st, 1906, it was £59,670,471 sterling, equivalent to £67 0s. 11d. per h ad.

The administration has undergone very few alterations in the course of the last half-century. At the beginning of the 'sixties it was certain that the union of the provinces, which in

AN EPISODE IN THE MAORI WAR OF 1863
The 57th Regiment taking a redoubt on the Katikara River

from disturbances, developed during those first decades considerably faster than the North Island, where war was raging. The squatters and shepherds who immigrated from New South Wales and Tasmania, soon perceived that the South Island was very suitable for sheep farming, and a few years after the founding of the Church Colonies, Otago and Canterbury, almost the entire centre and east of the island were divided into pasture lands. In 1861 the island exported roughly 8,000,000 lb. of wool of the value of £500,000 sterling ; in 1905 wool was by far the chief export of New Zealand, standing at £5,381,333.

The South Island also gained much from the discovery of gold. The finds at Coro-

course of time had increased by three and were working independently side by side, was on y a question of time. After Wellington, which lies in the centre and on Cook Strait, had been chosen for the federal capital, the privileges of the provinces were abolished in 1875. Since then New Zealand has consisted of eighty-one counties, which send their representatives to Parliament at Wellington. On the question of foreign policy, and the decision regarding federation with the Australian Commonwealth, the reader can refer to another part of this work.

Decentralisation is the striking feature of contrast between New Zealand and

Australia. There is no overshadowing city, such as Sydney or Melbourne. Auckland, Christchurch, Dunedin, and Wellington are the four chief towns. Auckland, the largest, has about 70,000 inhabitants; Dunedin, the smallest, about 56,000. None of them exercises any special political influence, the reasons being in part geographical, in part historical. The means of communication in

FRIENDLY NEGOTIATIONS WITH THE NATIVES
A large conference between settlers and Maoris held near Napier, Hawkes Bay, in 1863.

New Zealand were, until recently, by sea, and Auckland was a four-days' voyage from Dunedin. The North and South Islands were also parted by a wide and stormy strait. Naturally, under such circumstances, intercourse between the coastal towns was difficult. Each city, too, except Auckland, which is more of a trading centre, owed its existence to the pastures of its hinterland. Their spheres of influence were rather from east to west than from north to south. The historical reason for this comparative isolation is to be found in the character of the early settlements. The South, or rather the Middle Island of New Zealand was colonised systematically by settlers who were connected with each other by the strong ties of religion or race. Christ-

church was settled by a company, in which shares could be held only by members of the Church of England. Dunedin in the same way was the home of a Scotch settlement. Until 1864 the Home Government recognised the character of New Zealand settlement by giving each province an independent constitution. The provincial governments were abolished in 1864, and a centralised Government established at Wellington. Living in the happy islands of New Zealand is probably the easiest in the world. The climate is singularly favourable to agriculture, and the surface of the earth is broken into numberless hills and vales, giving a variety to New Zealand scenery which is wanting on the Australian plains. The Government has resumed land freely for closer settlement, so that the rent of a holding is very low; Government departments grade the farmer's wheat, freeze lambs, and generally tend to smooth difficulties from the path of agriculture. The result is a community without great inequalities of wealth. New Zealand has no millionaires, but she need have no paupers. The line of life is that of an English town to which parents have been attracted by a great school, where all have about the same income and the same interests

A MAORI HOUSE OR "WHARE"

NEW ZEALAND'S TIMBER INDUSTRY
Woodmen felling a Kauri tree in North Island. These trees often grow 160 feet high and up to 15 feet thick.

But if it were necessary to sum up in one word the dominant love of New Zealand life, "wholesomeness" would be the word of choice. There is something in the climate, soil, and water of New Zealand which gives physical vigour to man and beast. The sheep and lambs of the far-famed Canterbury plains are without any question the best in the world. Trout, introduced from Europe into the rivers and lakes of New Zealand, without losing any of their gameness, reach a size and weight which would be regarded as impossible in their native haunts. Indeed, many anglers now vis t New Zealand instead of Norway, attracted also, no doubt, by the prospect of deer-stalking in the South Island. The hot springs are found in both North and Middle Island, but the world-famed hot spring of Rotorua have given the North Island a special distinction in this

respect. The curative effect. of these springs, and the healthiness of the climate in their vicinity, is best indicated by the attraction the district possessed for the Maoris.

New Zealand, after some hesitation, has decided to hold aloof from the Commonwealth of Australia. As one of their statesmen said: "The 1,200 miles of sea between Auckland and Sydney furnishes us with 1,200 reasons for keeping to ourselves." In effect, as the High Commissioner points out, New Zealanders are insular and self-contained. Like all islanders, "they have a special objection to interference by outsiders in their wn affairs, and absorption in these, with entire indifference to the politics of other countries, and an excellent conceit of themselves. Nine-tenths of them know almost as little about ordinary Australian politics as do Englishmen. They have no animosity towards, or jealousy of, the big island continent; but their interest, their pride, their hopes, are centred in their own islands."

Federation, indeed, held out to them a practical inducement — namely, that they should be included within the ring fence of the Australian tariff. But this was not sufficient; for the eyes of New Zealanders look eastward, and their dream is to be the head of a Pacific Federation, which leaves them

ONE OF THE GREAT SAW MILLS ON THE WAIROA RIVER
The Kauri pine yields a valuable gum which is employed in varnish manufacture, and the timber is used for ship masts, paving blocks, and other purposes.

indifferent to the Commonwealth in the West. For a generation at least New Zealand wil pursue her course alone, connected with England, in spite of the distance, more closely than with Australia —because the national spirit is not yet awakened and she is too weak to stand alone—she will always be the purest jewel in the Crown of Empire. Though Australia's future may be greater, New Zealand's, at any rate, will be great and bright enough for the people—so they think. It may be that the distinguishing title of "Dominion," bestowed on it in 1907, will tend to encourage this inclination to political separation.

New Zealand was the first British community to make a serious and systematic attempt at improving the lot of the people by means of legislation. The Land question first presented itself, and was met by a bold and, on the whole, successful series of measures to break up the big private estates and to give an opportunity for the closer settlement of the small farmer. In fact, the Land Law of New Zealand aims at preventing any but small or middling farmers from acquiring agricultural land from the Crown. The methods are a progressive land tax, an absentee tax, and the levying of rates upon unimproved values.

Equal consideration was shown to the town workers. Beginning with the Industrial Arbitration Act—introduced by the Hon. Wm. Pember Reeves—it provided a tribunal with coercive powers to hear and determine every class of industrial dispute. It did not, however, like the New South Wales Act, make it

RICHARD SEDDON

He was born in Lancashire and went to New Zealand as a mechanical engineer. He entered politics, and by his force of character and intense national patriotism soon took a commanding position in New Zealand affairs.

a misdemeanour to lock-out or strike without submitting the dispute to this Court. There followed a whole code of labour laws providing for fair working conditions not only in factories, workshops, and mines, but also in open-air industries. Encouragement was given to the formation of unions both of employer and of employed. Old Age Pensions were granted to the aged poor, and the State took upon itself the whole burden of public charity— outdoor relief, hospitals, and lunatic asylums. Of course, there are carpers at such free-handed largess from the State ; but, on the whole, it appears that these measures have not produced the fatal consequences which should have followed such a daring violation of the "laws of political economy"! It is alleged that prices have risen ; but there is nothing to show that the rise in New Zealand is greater than that which has occurred everywhere during the last few years. It will be safer to take Mr. Reeves' appreciation of these measures. "The notion that New Zealanders, as a people, have as an ideal some elaborate State Socialism may be dismissed . . . They are not even—curiously—Fabian Socialists, but they find in practice that by collective actions they can do many things which they wish to do. They are, so far, satisfied with the chief experiments they have tried . . . The competent farmer, skilled mechanic, and able-bodied labourer, have usually a more hopeful life than in other countries. . . . The contentment of the man of small means is nowhere disturbed by the contrast of flaunting wealth."

ESSENTIAL INFORMATION ABOUT NEW ZEALAND

AREA. The Dominion of New Zealand consists of two principal islands—North Island and South Island—a smaller island known as Stewart Island, and several smaller islands, the whole forming a group 1,000 miles long, and at the broadest part 180 miles broad. In 1901 Cook Islands and a few less important Pacific islands were included within the colony of New Zealand, which has since been raised to the dignity of a Dominion. The coast line of New Zealand is over 4,300 miles long, and the distance from Australia is 1,200 miles. The total estimated area is 104,751 square miles, the three largest islands being as follows: North Island, 44,468; South Island, 58,525; and Stewart Island, 665 square miles. The following islands are included in the Dominion of New Zealand : Auckland Islands (200 miles south of Stewart Island, with 330 square miles and uninhabited); Chatham Islands (536 miles east of New Zealand, and consisting of 375 square miles, with a population of 399, about half being Europeans and the remainder Maoris); Cook Islands and adjacent small islands (total area about 280 square miles, and population about 13,000) ; and Kermadec Islands (about 600 miles north-east of New Zealand, with an area of 15 square miles, and a population of five). There are also a few detached uninhabited islands of small size.

POPULATION. The population of New Zealand in 1906 was as follows : Males, 471,008 ; females, 417,570 ; total, 888,578, not including aborigines, but including 2,570 Chinese (2,515 males and 55 females). Maori population : Males, 25,587 ; females, 22,248 ; total, 47,835. Grand total, 936,413. The chief towns with their populations (including the suburban populations), are as follow : Auckland, 82,101 ; Wellington, 63,807 ; Christchurch, 67,878 ; Dunedin, 56,020 ; Palmerston North, 10,239.

CONSTITUTION. The legislative power is vested by statute of 1852 in a governor and a general assembly composed of two chambers, the Legislative Council and the House of Representatives. The Upper House, or Legislative Council, has 38 members, who receive payment at the rate of £200 per annum. Those who were appointed before September 17th, 1891, are life members ; the remainder hold office for 7 years, but may be re-appointed. Since 1900 the House of Representatives has consisted of 80 members, who are elected for 3 years, and who receive £300 per annum. There is adult suffrage, women having the vote as well as men. There are four Maori members, representing the four Maori electoral districts, and every native—male and female—residing in these districts has the franchise.

GOVERNOR AND ADMINISTRATION. The Governor is appointed by the King of England. The present Governor is the Rt. Hon. William Lee, Baron Plunket, K.C.V.O., who assumed office in June, 1904. The administration consists of eight Ministers, the present Prime Minister—who also holds several other portfolios—being the Hon. Sir J. G. Ward, K.C.M.G.

REPRESENTATION IN LONDON. The Hon. W. P. Reeves, High Commissioner for New Zealand, 13, Victoria Street, Westminster, London, S.W. Secretary, Mr. Walter Kennaway, C.M.G.

REVENUE AND EXPENDITURE. The total revenue for the financial year ended March 31st, 1907, was £8,399,075, the chief sources of income being Customs, Railway Receipts, Post Office and Land and Income Taxes. The expenditure for the same year was £7,774,926. The net Public Debt of New Zealand on March 31st, 1907, was £61,276,547, with an annual charge (interest and sinking fund) of £2,457,285, the principal being equal to almost £70 per head of the population, the highest per capita national debt in the world.

COMMERCE. The value of New Zealand exports for the year 1906 was £18,095,137, consisting chiefly of wool (£6,765,655), frozen meat (£2,877,031), gold (£2,270,904), butter and cheese (£1,901,237), hides and leather (£868,651), phormium fibre (£776,106), and Kauri gum (£522,486). The imports totalled £15,211,403. About four-fifths of New Zealand's exports were purchased by Great Britain and one-seventh by Australia, leaving about £1,200,000 to be taken by other nations Of New Zealand imports, Great Britain supplied over £9,000,000, and other British possessions almost £4,000,000. In the year 1903, New Zealand adopted a scheme of preferential tariffs whereby certain goods of British manufacture are admitted at lower rates of duty than goods from competing foreign countries. The duties payable by competing foreign goods are subject to increased duties ranging from 20 per cent. to 100 per cent. of the scheduled duties.

CURRENCY AND WEIGHTS AND MEASURES. These are the same as in Great Britain.

POSTAGE AND TELEGRAPH RATES
GREAT BRITAIN TO NEW ZEALAND

Letters, 1d. per oz.
Postcards, 1d. Reply postcards, 2d.
Printed papers, ½d. per 2 oz. Weight limit, 5 lb.
Commercial papers, 2½d. for 10 oz., and ½d. per 2 oz. over. Weight limit, 5 lb.
Samples, 1d. for 4 oz. and ½d. per 2 oz. over. Weight limit, 5 lb.
Parcels, under 3 lb. 1s. ; under 7 lb., 2s. ; under 11 lb., 3s. If over 4 ft. and under 6 ft. in length and girth combined, 1s. per parcel extra. Limit of size, 6 ft. combined length and girth.
Registration, 2d. for each article.
Telegrams, 3s. per word, or via Turkey, 2s. 9d. per word.

PATENTS. New Zealand patents may be applied for within one year of application in Great Britain. Fees are 10s. on provisional application, 10s. on complete application, and £2 on sealing. Renewal fees are £5 before end of fourth year, and £10 before end of seventh year. Time limit is 14 years.

TRADE MARKS. Classification as in Great Britain. Duration 14 years, and renewable every 14 years. Fees, 5s. on application for each class, and 20s. on registration. Five copies of mark necessary, and wood-cut or electro.

DESIGNS. Conditions exactly as in Great Britain. Term, five years.

THE WESTERN POWERS IN THE SOUTH SEAS

OCEANIA, at the present day, is in its full extent colonial territory ; the few land surfaces on which as yet no white power flies its flags are uninhabited or barren rocks and reefs. The New Hebrides alone are not yet disposed of. The value attached to Oceania by the Western Powers, which is expressed in its **The Modern** political annexation, dates from **Value of** recent times. Apart from the **Oceania** Marianne Isles, on which the beginnings of Spanish colonisation go back to the sixteenth century, no group of islands found favour in the eyes of European governments before the close of the eighteenth century. The reason was the deficiency of Oceania in precious metals, valuable spices, and rich stuffs. This deficiency made the region valueless to the leading colonisers of early times, Spain and Portugal ; the others, however, Holland, France, and England, had their hands full with the development of their Indian, African, and American colonial possessions.

The first steps toward the colonisation of Oceania in the nineteenth century were taken by the French. Since the conquest of Algeria was not enough to prop his tottering throne, Louis Philippe had, after the middle of the 'thirties, issued the programme of a Polynesian colonial empire. The plan succeeded only in East Polynesia, where a really compact region could be brought under French suzerainty ; elsewhere France had already opponents of her schemes to contend against, and these were found not only in the ranks of the Protestant missionaries, but also in the Cabinets of London, Washington, and St. Petersburg. She was thus able to annex only the south-east wing of West Melanesia, New Caledonia, and its vicinity.

Great Britain has had to take over a large part of her present Oceanic possessions, even New Zealand, under compulsion, not from choice. In earlier times the constantly recurring fear of French rivalry was the moving cause. As German trade relations with the South Sea developed, there was the additional anxiety of German encroachment, and in this connection the Australian Colonies and New Zealand, now conscious of their place in history, had become the representative of the British idea of colonisation. When the German Empire stepped on to the colonial world stage, the annexation of new territories to the British colonial empire ceased to be half-hearted and became the natural event. At the present day Great Britain regards Central Melanesia, Central Polynesia, and South-east Micronesia as her sphere of interests. The " free " New Hebrides, French New Caledonia, and German Samoa make little difference to this.

Germany has become a colonial Power in consequence of long-standing commercial relations. In this way it could partly occupy unclaimed countries ; partly also, following the American example, it has entered upon the inheritance of the oldest Pacific Power, the Spaniards. At the present time Germany rules a compact territory, important both by its extent and wealth, which comprises a large part of Melanesia, and almost all Micronesia, but, like the French possessions, it suffers **Germany's** from its excessive remoteness **Portion of** from the mother country. **Oceania** Besides this, Germany has rivals, which are formidable both industrially and politically, in the new American colonies of Hawaii and the Philippines, and still more in Australia. Samoa, which lies in front, may prove more of a trouble than a blessing to the empire.

The Power which has appeared last in order of time on the Pacific stage is the United States of America, whose right of entry has been bought by the expulsion of Spain. The firm footing of America on the Philippines, Hawaii, Mariannes, and Samoa (Tutuila)—that is, on four places distributed over the whole range

1003

of islands—becomes important from the change in the political situation thus produced ; America, which hitherto has turned its face merely toward the east, now looks to the Pacific. At the same time it is preparing to cut through the only obstacle to the development of its power on the west, the Central-American isthmus.

The total effect of this American movement is that the possession of Oceania is valued more highly than before, and that the Pacific Ocean has become the focus of interest. Recent events on the east coast of Asia furnish the best proof of this. Oceania has room for colonisation only by the Great Powers. Spain has been compelled to leave it, since it has been blotted out from the list of living world Powers. Portugal, following the decisive sentence of a pope, has never set foot on it. Holland, at the most easterly extremity of its colonial kingdom, just touches the Pacific with Dutch New Guinea ; but it has not yet been active there. Chili possesses Easter Island merely for show. Japan, finally, has found the doors closed to her on Hawaii. The whites acquired influence over the destinies of the Australians and Oceanians, as over the majority of primitive peoples, in two ways—by taking possession of their territory politically and exploiting its industries, and by introducing Christianity into the national paganism. It is a characteristic feature in Oceania that the impression produced by the missions far surpassed the other in permanence and to some degree in results. This is not the case with the Australian continent, where missionary attempts have always remained occasional and, in comparison with the gigantic area, of trifling extent ; they were timidly begun and achieved no important results. Much indeed is told us of the achievements of native pupils in reading, writing, and arithmetic, but that says less for the general success of the mission than for the intellectual gifts of the race. The love of the Australian black-fellow for an irregular, hand-to-mouth, hunter's life has been ineradicable.

Better prospects were open to the missionary in Oceania. In the first place, the confined area allowed a concentration of all available forces ; and, in the next place, the national disunion of the Oceanians prepared the ground for the

The Powers in the Pacific

missionaries, as the conversions of Thakombau, Pomare, and Kamehameha II. show. The prospect of the political support of the white preachers of the Gospel was too alluring, and many availed themselves of the easy method of an almost always superficial change of faith. The real results of conversion are, nevertheless, generally unimportant. The very promising beginning made in Tahiti suffered a severe set-back after the interference of the missionaries in the disputes for the throne. In New Zealand the disorders under Hongi brought the work of conversion to a standstill for years, as was the case in Hawaii from the struggle of the Kamehameha dynasty for the political headship in the archipelago. It was only on Tonga that the conversion of the entire north was completed within ten years of missionary work, from 1830 to 1840. The kings Taufaahau and Tubou lent it valuable aid ; and, besides that, the field was then left exclusively to the Protestant Church. From the moment when the French bishop Pompallier set foot on the soil of Tongatabu in 1841 we have presented to us that picture of denominational discord and intense jealousy among the disciples of the different schools of religion which only too easily poisoned other phases of national life.

Mission Work in the South Seas

This hostility between the denominations is one of the greatest hindrances to missionary work in Oceania, and prevents any disinterested feeling of joy being felt when a whole group of peoples is won for Christianity. It is difficult to decide on whom the chief blame rests, since the accounts of individual efforts, as well as of the combined result, vary according to the denominations. But in the great majority of cases the Catholic missions, which came too late, were the disturbing element. Since they enjoyed the protection of France everywhere, they made up for their tardiness by unscrupulous action, of which the events on Tahiti, the Marquesas, Tuamotu in Hawaii, and, above all, in the Loyalty Isles, supply us with examples. In the Loyalty Isles, the English missionary Murray had won over the greater part of three islands to Protestantism. In 1864 the group of islands was occupied by the French, at the instigation of Catholic missionaries, and Protestant were replaced by Catholic

Catholic versus Protestant

services. The French soldiers treated the natives so harshly that various Powers lodged protests with the Government of Napoleon III. But this interference became disastrous only in 1872, 1873, and 1880, when regular religious wars occurred between the members of the two Churches, in which even women and children were not spared. On the other hand,

Religious Factions at War

the Protestant missions must be made responsible to a large degree for having often combined the functions of missionary and trader. This practice, which had been adopted by John Williams, the apostle of the South Sea, has not been discontinued, in spite of frequent prohibitions by Great Britain. The co-operation of all whites, which is an essential condition for an effective mission of civilisation, was thus destroyed ; the professional trader had no motive for supporting the Church whose labourers were obnoxious to him as competitors.

There was also a second reason. While the Catholic missionary sharply defined the exterior boundaries of his community, and then devoted himself exclusively to it—the success of the Jesuits in building up large communities, upon which practice the increase of Catholics on Hawaii followed— the Protestant was distracted by reason of his business as a trader. Both Churches were equally open to the reproach of having interfered in the political affairs of the Oceanias as long as any territory was still to be obtained. It is true that the missionaries, working alone in the middle of turbulent tribes, were often forced to take one side or the other if they did not wish to risk both their lives and the success of their missions ; but just as frequently we find no apparent cause. In New Zealand there had been an attempt to found a separate Maori kingdom under ecclesiastical rule, a counterpart of the Jesuit state in Paraguay.

Value of Missions in Oceania

What did missions do for the Oceanians ? In the controversy as to the value of missions in the South Sea, many voices entirely condemned their line of action. Charles Darwin, on the other hand, has pointed out that, apart from other progress, missionary activity had the noteworthy result of creating a network of stations over the wide South Sea, before the value of that proceeding was realised by the Western Powers, and by so doing indis-

putably civilised the habits of the native. We have only to compare the little-visited Solomon islanders with the formerly savage and now quite peaceful Fijians. The credit of this does not belong entirely to the missions, however. So long as they alone represented Europeanism, there was, on the contrary, much bloodshed in Oceania. It was only when the strong hands of the Colonial Governments, which were more concerned with the undisturbed possession of the country than the welfare of the inhabitants, guided the helm that these improvements in culture were evident.

The mixture of good and evil in the achievements of the missionaries is visible in the domain of knowledge. It must not be forgotten with what zeal the more enlightened of them identified themselves from the first with the national feelings of the Oceanic peoples, and how much they collected which has been essential for our later comprehension of the subject. But it is none the less to be remembered that in the complete—although possibly inevitable—destruction of the national

Destruction of National Character

characteristics of Oceania, no persons took part more ignorantly than these very missionaries. They unscrupulously invaded every branch of the national life in order to adapt them to their own views. They even substituted, in many parts, the ugly calicoes of Europe for the time-honoured dress, at once tasteful and practical, of Oceania ; they introduced fashions which were bound to jar on the native sense of beauty, and which, by their total disregard of hygienic laws, have promoted the increase of various chronic diseases.

Now, when the island world of Oceania is divided, missions with their thoroughly successful enterprises have played their historical part. The history of mankind takes broader strides ; its wide paths surround even the islands of the Pacific. What can we say of the future of the Oceanic islands ? Apportioned as they are among the Great Powers of the world, they will probably develop a history more industrial than political. In great measure they will become overrun by European and Asiatic immigrants. " Civilisation " has done for these natives its worst ; education and scientific political systems hereafter may atone for what has gone before.

OCEANIA AND MALAYSIA IN OUR OWN TIME

BY BASIL THOMSON

BROADLY speaking, the inhabitants of all the scattered islands lying between the east point of New Guinea and the west coast of South America are divided between three races, called for convenience the Malayo-Polynesians, the Micronesians, and the Melanesians. The Polynesians inhabit all the large groups lying east of Fiji, including Hawaii, Tahiti, Rarotonga, Tonga, Samoa, and New Zealand ; the Micronesians, the small atolls about the Equator which form the Gilbert and Ellice groups ; and the Melanesians all the groups lying west of Fiji—namely, the Solomons, Loyalty, New Hebrides, New Britain, and New Ireland. Fiji is the meeting ground of the two great races. None of these are of unmixed blood. Throughout the Polynesian Islands there are individuals of almost negroid characteristics, and, as the prevailing wind blows from the south-east, Polynesians have for centuries drifted into the Melanesian groups and been cast away there. The latest suggestion—that of Dr. A. H. Keane and others —is that the substratum of the Polynesian race is Caucasian ; that the islands were peopled by a stream of immigrants from Asia still in the Neolithic period of culture, whose progress is marked by Megalithic remains, such as are to be found in Western Europe and in the Malay Peninsula, and that after they had been settled in the islands for long ages, a stream of negroid marauders from the westward conquered them,

BASIL THOMSON

The writer of this chapter was for some years Prime Minister of Tonga, and is recognised as one of the foremost authorities on Oceania.

taught them the masculine arts of war and navigation, intermarried with their women, and founded the present mixed race. Thus they would account for the backwardness of the feminine arts, such as pottery and weaving, and the comparatively advanced quality of the masculine arts of shipbuilding and fortification.

Almost all the Polynesian tribes speak of Bulotu, a place in the Far West, as the land of their origin and the place to which their spirits will return after death. Bulotu has been identified with various places in the Malay Archipelago, but such identifications must always be purely conjectural.

In physique the Polynesians are muscular, tall and well-proportioned ; of an olive complexion, inclined to reddish-yellow, that may be best compared with café-au-lait. Their limbs are fleshy, though well-proportioned, and the chiefs of both sexes are prone to corpulency. Their hair is naturally wavy and black, but frequent smearing with lime dyes it a tawny brown, like sealskin. Their faces are generally open and pleasant, and sometimes even beautiful, especially in the men, who might be used as models by a sculptor.

The political institutions were generally governed by hereditary chiefs, subject to the checks which a powerful aristocracy might put upon their power. In some of the islands the hereditary chief was regarded as the incarnation of a deified ancestor, and sometimes evolution of this idea had produced a dual monarchy, the one spiritual and the other temporal, like the Mikado and the Shōgun of Japan. Among no people in the world does noble birth carry so much prestige. In Tonga a plebeian had no soul, and nowhere in the islands cou'd a man rise above the station to which he was born. In Hawaii, as in Siam and in ancient Egypt, the k ng sometimes married his half-sister in order that the royal blood might not be diluted. Rank derived from the mother counts for more than that inherited from the father; but this is less a relic of matr archal institutions than an acknowledgment, in a race of dissolute habits, of the uncertain paternity of a child.

Prestige of Blue Blood

The religion of the Polynesians was remote ancestor worship; but there was no powerful priesthood, and in practice the religion was nothing but a regard for the *taboo* and the occasional propitiation of chiefs lately dead. Certain acts were permanently taboo, or forbidden. The Marquesan women must not enter a canoe, but must swim whenever they had to cross water. A taboo, or prohibition, was laid upon some article of food that was growing scarce, and until the ban was removed none could use it. Those who touched a corpse were taboo until they had cleansed themselves by expiation; and contact with a chief would in itself bring sickness unless it was removed by pressing his feet against the abdomen—a custom which became so irksome to the Tongan chiefs that one of them consecrated a vessel given him by Tasman to be a substitute for his feet.

The Polynesian picked his way through life in dread of infringing the taboo. It was in the air he breathed, in the things he touched and ate, and not until he was safe in the grave was he freed from its dangers. It was the fountain of the chief's power and his engine of government. The chief was believed to have a sort of spiritual exhalation, called *Mana*, that invested his every word and deed with power, and withered up the plebeian who incautiously approached him. The penalty for an infringement of the taboo was death by disease of the liver; and in Tonga it was a common practice to open the bodies of the slain to see whether they had been virtuous. Christianity has swept away

Potency of the Taboo

all these beliefs, and the power of the chiefs has waned. Most of the Polynesian tribes are decreasing, but not very rapidly; and they have shown so much readiness to adopt European customs that it is probable that they will eventually be absorbed, and that the population of the islands in the distant future will be a hybrid race with a strong admixture of European blood.

The Melanesian varies a good deal in the different groups. As the name implies, his complexion is dark, inclined to be black, with a dull, sooty tinge under the skin. His hair is frizzy and matted. He is muscular, but shorter and more thickset than the Polynesian. His language, though derived from a common source, is split into an infinite number of dialects, varying so widely that they are almost unintelligible beyond the limits of the tribe.

In some parts of Melanesia there are hereditary chiefs, but their influence is small. There are no powerful confederations, and they govern through a council in which every warrior has a voice. In other parts each little tribal unit is a miniature republic, with manhood suffrage. They are more warlike and savage than the Polynesians, and infintely more primitive. To go from Samoa to the New Hebrides is to travel back through the centuries; to pass from the society of men into the society of schoolboys. The Melanesians have little pride of birth, and whereas few Polynesians will indenture themselves as labourers for Europeans, Melanesians are always ready to leave the islands for the plantations of Fiji and Queensland. After working for three years and adopting European habits and dress, they come back to their islands, distribute their clothes, and revert to their original savagery. Familiarity with Europeans has not made intercourse with them easier. It is now unsafe to explore islands where Cook was received with friendliness. Outrages upon unarmed vessels, which have long been impossible in Polynesia, still occur occasionally in the western groups.

Differences between the Races

No argument as to the origin of these races can be founded upon their arts. Artistic skill seems to be sporadic and accidental. Whereas the Maoris have much decorative skill in sculpture and carving, other Polynesian tribes, such as the Samoans and Tongans, have none at all. Decorative art is more developed in Melanesia, and in the island of New Georgia, in the Solomons, it rises to a very high pitch of excellence. The Melanesians are very industrious both as planters and artificers. They have got beyond the outrigger in canoe-building. Their women are more moral than the Polynesian women ; their men show greater aptitude for acquiring foreign handicrafts, but they are decreasing even more rapidly than the Polynesians, partly from the former depopulation of their islands by the labour trade, partly from the European diseases introduced by returning labourers.

The population of the islands before the arrival of Europeans is difficult to estimate. The Marquesans and the Fijians were apparently decreasing when they first came under observation. Like the Aztecs at the time of the Spanish conquest, they seemed recently to have developed intertribal warfare to a pitch unknown before. As far as can be judged it seems probable that the inhabitants of all the islands, including Hawaii and New Zealand, never numbered more than two **Estimates** millions. They have shrunk **Regarding** now to something less than **Population** half a million. The Micronesians, on the other hand, are not decreasing. The islands lie so low that the water in the wells is always brackish, and the soil is so unproductive that fish and a certain kind of taro are the staple foods. Mindful of the danger of having a population too large for the food supply, the increase is artificially limited, and popular opinion does not permit a woman to have more than five children. Their physical type is distinct. The skin is light brown, like the Polynesians ; the hair is coarse, black, and rather straight. The eyes are sometimes oblique, like the Mongolian's. The body is long and the legs short, thick, and muscular. At first sight one would take the Micronesian to be a hybrid between the Mongol and the Polynesian.

All the Polynesian and many of the Melanesian tribes are now nominally Christian. Beginning with the voyage of the ship Duff, sent out by the London Missionary Society in 1797, mission enterprise has had an astonishing success. Hawaii went to the American missionaries, the eastern groups to the London society, disputed at various points by French

Roman Catholics ; Tonga and Fiji fell to the Wesleyans, who have since sent out emissaries to New Britain and the d'Entrecasteaux group ; the Presbyterians and the Church of England divide Melanesia between them.

The tendency of the missions in some of the islands was to become political **Political** organisations. Great chiefs **Work of** became Christian from political **Missions** motives, and their people followed them like a flock of sheep. Often when professing Christianity, the natives do not at first believe their own gods to be false gods—rather that it is convenient to discontinue worshipping them for a season. How could they be false gods when they are their own ancestors, of whose existence upon earth there could be no shadow of doubt ? Nevertheless, conversions continued to be rapid, and apostates rare. The Polynesians are born orators, and here was a field that permitted the meanest of them to declaim from the pulpit, though under the old order they had been born to silence. For this reason the Wesleyans, with their hierarchy of native ministers, catechists, and local preachers, have been more prosperous than the Roman Catholics, who may not delegate the functions of their priests. There are signs that the influence of the missionaries is now waning. From time to time there have been symptoms of a craving for a native Church, free from the trammels of a European priesthood, and it is impossible to foretell what form of religion the future may bring forth in Polynesia.

Most of the South Sea Islands have now been appropriated. Tahiti, the Marquesas and New Caledonia belong to the French. Germany holds the Marshalls, most of Samoa, an island in the Solomons, New Britain, and a strip on the northern coast of New Guinea. The Americans have Hawaii and an island in Samoa. **Ownership** Fiji, the Ellice and Gilbert **of the** groups, Rarotonga, the remain- **Islands** der of the Solomons, South Eastern New Guinea, Norfolk Island, and a number of small islands, annexed with a view to future cable stations, belong to Britain, which also has a protectorate over Tonga. The New Hebrides are not yet actually appropriated owing to the opposition of the Australians to any French penal colony so near their shores.

There is now settled government throughout Polynesia, but in some of the Melanesian groups the protectorate is nominal. The European population of these islands can almost be counted on the fingers, and where there is no European settlement it is impossible to make the government self-supporting. Most of the Melanesian islands are malarious, whereas Fiji and the islands to the eastward are healthy; and though the climate is hotter than an English summer and the damp heat of the rainy season is trying, Europeans are able to do any kind of work except field labour. The future of the islands is bound up with that of Australasia. Every kind of tropical produce thrives luxuriantly, but the market is overstocked. Fiji and Hawaii, where enormous sums have been invested in the latest machinery for producing sugar, have been hampered by the necessity of importing labourers, the former from India, the latter from Japan. The second great staple, copra, or dried coco-nut, from which oil is pressed for soap and candle making, has to compete with plantations nearer the European market. Coffee has been nearly destroyed by the leaf disease. Tobacco and tea, though both are of excellent quality, have not yet become known to European buyers. When the population of Australia attains ten millions, the market difficulties will vanish.

Nature of the Climate

Great Britain is the only Power that as yet has succeeded in establishing a self-supporting colony in the South Seas, and in governing and training the natives of Fiji without a single soldier or ship of war in the islands. In the time to come it is probable that all the islands will be politically dependent upon Australasia.

For many generations perhaps the islands will be holiday resorts. Europeans will conduct the business of the towns and manage the plantations and the mines, and the country trade will be in the hands of coloured people, Indians, natives and Chinese. The labouring population will undergo great changes. Little by little the natives will disappear as a distinct race, and a mixed people, a blend between all the races that now inhabit the islands, will take their place. The process has already begun, and prosperity, attracting men of other races to the centres of commerce, will accelerate it enormously.

The Coming of Hybrid Races

Speaking geographically and ethnologically, the Philippines do not belong to the islands of the South Seas, though one of the three races inhabiting them, called for want of a better title, Indonesians, may be nearly related to the Polynesians. Probably the original inhabitants of this important group were the Negritos, a negroid people of low stature and dark skins, flat noses, thick lips, and woolly hair. They are a timid, nomadic people who seldom emerge from the forests on the mountain slopes of Luzon, Panay, Negros and Mindanao, where they live by hunting and on the wild fruits of the forest. The Indonesians are confined to the island of Mindanao. Physically they are not unlike the Malayo-Polynesians. All their tribes are pagan, and some of them are very warlike. But the great majority of the Filipinos are of Malayan origin, though the type has been modified by intermarriage with other peoples. Of the forty-seven Malayan tribes seven are Christian, seven Mohammedan, and the remainder pagan; but the Christians and Mohammedan tribes together form the bulk of the population. Among them is to be found every stage of social development, from the highly educated, Christianised native to the almost primitive savage. The total native population of the group is thought to exceed 6,000,000, but accurate figures of the nomad tribes are almost impossible to procure.

Filipinos of the Present Day

The Philippines contain enormous undeveloped wealth in copper, coal, and gold, and as the mines are developed by American capital and wealth pours into the islands, education and peaceful settlement will do something towards welding the diverse human material into a homogeneous whole. Even if public opinion in America should oppose colonial expansion, it is quite impossible for American government to relinquish the islands. The Filipinos would accept no other rulers, and for the time they are quite incapable of ruling themselves. It is not a country where Europeans can do outdoor labour, and for many generations will it be unsafe to place the balance of power in the hands of the natives. America has, in fact, blundered into Empire against her will, just as England had responsibilities forced upon her in the days when Empire was regarded as a burden.

BASIL THOMSON

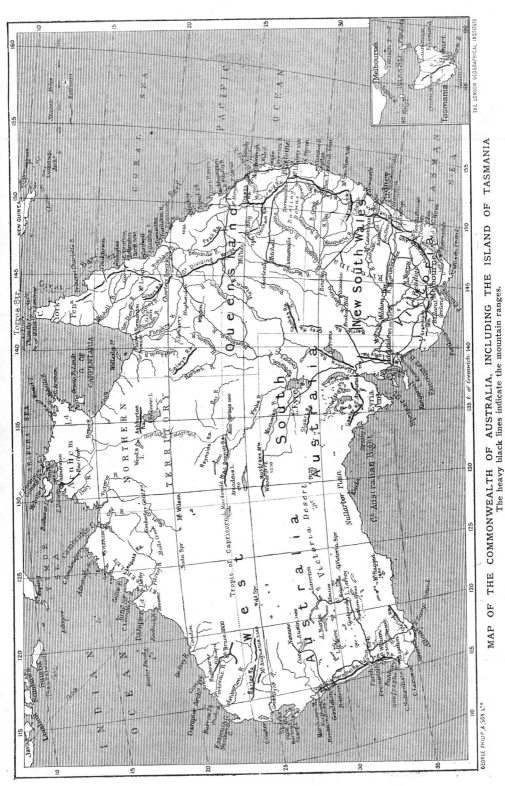

MAP OF THE COMMONWEALTH OF AUSTRALIA, INCLUDING THE ISLAND OF TASMANIA
The heavy black lines indicate the mountain ranges.

GEORGE PHILIP & SON LTᴰ

THE LONDON GEOGRAPHICAL INSTITUTE

AUSTRALIA

THE ONLY CONTINENT-STATE
THE NATURE OF THE COUNTRY

THE position of Australia, from the standpoint of the history of the world and of civilisation, is best described as terminal or marginal. In this respect it has many features in common with Africa, and especially with the southern half of Africa. Just as the African continent runs out toward the west into the narrow but almost landless Atlantic, and toward the south into the desolate and inhospitable Antarctic Ocean, so the mighty waste of waters of the Southern Indian and Southern Pacific Oceans spreads round the western and southern halves of Australia.

Australia is shut off from the open sea only upon the east; we there find large clusters of islands, which, on the map at least, produce the impression of a dense mass. But, in reality the area **Geographical Features of Australia** of these eastern islands is nothing in comparison with the expanse of ocean and the continent; and leaving New Zealand out of the question, they cannot, with their diminutive superficial size, be considered as having influenced Australia in the past.

Australia is thus the most insular of all continents. It would appear completely free and detached from the other continental land masses were it not for the dense Malaysian group which lies to the north-west, and forms a connecting link with the south-east coast of Asia. This group contains larger islands than its Oceanic continuation; it is also more densely packed, so that it seems admirably adapted as a bridge for migrations. And it has undoubtedly served such purpose. In the case of certain plants and animals, the migration from Asia to Australia can be proved, and it is extremely probable that the ancestors of the Australian native tribes crossed the Indonesian bridge.

If we consider Australia, under these circumstances, as part of the Old World, we **Australia an Old World Country** are certainly treating the question rightly; only, this conclusion is less frequently based by historians on the facts of geography, zoölogy, and botany than upon the evidence of native culture and institutions, which are entirely borrowed from the civilisation of the Old World. But the first argument is more interesting and historically more far-reaching, since it brings into our field of view not only Australia, but also all Oceania, which is, much more obviously than Australia, connected with the Asiatic continent. The path from Asia to both regions is almost precisely the same.

The marginal situation of Australia has produced on its aboriginal inhabitants all the effects which we find in every primitive nation in the same or a similar position. The whole development of their culture bears the stamp of isolation. The disadvantageous position of the continent is by no means balanced by variety of internal conformation. The coast line compares favourably in extent with those of South America and Africa when the greater superficial area of these two continents is taken into account. So with the number of its peninsulas, Australia **Desolate** fares better than those two **Coast** continents. But what profit **Districts** could the natives derive from these very slight advantages if the islands and peninsulas are as sterile, inaccessible, and desolate as most of the coast districts, and the greater part of the interior itself ?

The Australian continent, according to its vertical configuration, is a vast plateau, rising in the east, and sinking in the west, which slopes away from north to south. This tableland is only fringed by mountain ranges on its edges. A chain of mountains runs along the east coast from the southern extremity, and follows the coast line at a varying though never great distance, until it ends in Cape York. From this great watershed the land gradually slopes away in a south-westerly direction to the Indian Ocean, seamed by a few detached ranges and mountains, which rise to a considerable height in isolated masses.

The western coast range is not so high as the eastern ; but, in contrast to the latter, it is prolonged into the interior as a tableland, which, abounding in mineral wealth and furnishing good pasture, stretches far into the centre of the country. On the south and north there is no such high ground bordering the coast and turning inwards. Some half century ago, this non-existent high ground played an important part in the current theories as to the interior ; since its existence was assumed, necessitating the belief that the interior was an enormous basin, in which the rivers from all sides united their waters in a large inland sea. We know now that the **The Myth** north rises so gradually from **of an** the sea to the interior that the **Inland Sea** rivers, in consequence of their gentle and uniform fall, overflow their banks far and wide after every heavy downpour of tropical rain. There is still less difference of height observable between the interior and the south coast. The lake district, which runs in a long line from Spencer Gulf to the north and north-west, lies almost on the level of the sea.

Except in the south-eastern district of

New South Wales, where the Murray rises, none of the Australian mountains is high enough to form among perpetual snows a reservoir for the constant supply of the rivers ; but the principal, and, from its position, the most important, range—that of the east coast—is high enough to divert the atmospheric moisture from the remaining parts of the continent. The existing conditions are precisely similar to those in South Africa, which, geographically and ethnographically, has many points of affinity with Australia. Just as the curving ranges of the east coast of Africa collect on their wild and rugged flanks all the aqueous vapour of the south-east trade-winds blowing from the Indian Ocean, so the moisture contained by the Pacific south-east trade-winds does not go beyond the limits of the high grounds of East Australia.

As a result of this restricted area of rainfall, there is no river system of importance except that of the Murray and its tributary the Darling, on the east of the continent. This testifies to the absence of any watershed in the interior, in so far as its sources **Australia's** comprise the whole western **Lack of** slopes of the East Australian **Water** coast range from New South Wales to Queensland. We are concerned, therefore, only in its eastern, northern and western parts with measurements such as Europe can show. The real value both of these rivers and of most of the others in Australia, whether rapid or stagnant, lies in the facilities they offer for navigation and irrigation by the free use of dams, locks and weirs. The Darling is by far the longer but shallower arm, which, even without artificial works, becomes navigable after floods, and can then be ascended by steamers of small

BRITAIN CONTRASTED WITH AUSTRALIA
Area of Great Britain, 88,729 ; that of Australia, 2,946,358 square miles.

MAP OF SOUTH-EAST AUSTRALIA, INDICATING PRODUCTS OF THE DIFFERENT DISTRICTS

draught as far as the point where it cuts the thirtieth degree of southern latitude. The Murrumbidgee, the right tributary of the Murray, is open to navigation for six months in the year. The Murray is now available at all times for the objects of commerce.

In the north and north-east, owing to the heavier rainfall, there is less scarcity of water. We find there numerous watercourses of considerable breadth, of which quite a number are navigable for a short distance inland. They open up the interior of the country up to the foot of the coastal ranges. Only the still little known streams of the northern territory, the Roper, the Daly, and the Victoria can be ascended by large vessels for a very considerable distance.

In the west and the south, and in the interior, during the greater part of the year the channels of the rivers either lie quite dry, or consist of a chain of broad ponds, which are divided by banks and never connected after their formation. These beds, however, become real watercourses at the time of the summer rains, when they swell to such a size that their overflow fertilises huge tracts of apparently barren country. Even the water which disappears in the ever-thirsty ground forms great underground reservoirs, which are tapped by artesian bores. The south coast, again, as far as the mouth of the Murray, is entirely devoid of any river worth mentioning. It is sufficiently obvious that such a lack of uniformity in the water supply of the continent must have the most far-reaching effects on all its

1013

THE SCENERY OF AUSTRALIA: BY MOUNTAIN, LAKE, AND SEA-SHORE.

The two upper pictures represent Weatherboard Falls, N. S. W.; and the south end ox Tasman's Island; the lower two subjects show the north-east view from Mount Kosciusko, N. S. W., and the crater of Mount Gambier, South Australia; the centre picture is Castle Rock, Cape Schanck.

THE SCENERY OF AUSTRALIA: GLIMPSES OF ITS WONDERFUL FOREST LANDS

The first two illustrations show the forest of the Cape Otway Range, and Fern Tree Gully, in the Dandenong Range, Victoria; the lower pictures are of Cabbage Tree Forest, American Creek, N. S. W., and the junction of the Buchan and Snowy Rivers, Gippsland; the centre showing one of the famous "bottle" or baobab trees.

phenomena of life. Ethnographically, the uncertainty of the rainfall in the interior has compelled the natives to be continually migrating if they wish to find sufficient food ; it is one reason why these unsettled migratory bands can never attain any size, if, indeed, the scanty supplies of the soil are to be enough to feed them.

Native Races of Australia This, however, will not suffice to explain the splitting up of the aborigines into a number of small tribes, which do not cohere, since this feature of their polity is similarly characteristic of the races in the coast districts, where food and water are plentiful. It may rank, no doubt, as a contributory cause ; their gradual disappearance without leaving any mark on history is a necessary sequel. This main feature of the hydrography of Australia is not limited in its effects to the natives only ; it has, on the contrary, exercised a marked influence on the density of colonisation by the whites. In the parts of the country remote from the coast, the colonist, precisely as in sub-tropical South Africa, required ample room, and it is no mere coincidence that the colonies of Australia were everywhere founded in the more fertile coast districts.

The characteristic feature of the climate of the interior of Australia is its dryness. The country, from its position between the tenth and fortieth degrees of southern latitude, is for the most part, and throughout its whole length, included in the region of the southern trade-winds. In addition to this there is the disadvantage which we have already mentioned, that the highest ranges of mountains are found on the weather side of the continent, the result of which is that the main portion of the country is sheltered from wind and rain. Under these circumstances, there is in the interior excessive heating of the soil, which also receives the tropical rains of the north coast. The former produces, especially in summer, an extensive Central **Climatic Conditions of Australia** Australian zone of low pressure, which gives rise to a rain-bringing north-west monsoon, and draws it far into the continent, sometimes even to the south coast. Unfortunately this wind, in the extent of the regions over which it passes and in its effect on the climate, is far inferior to the southeast trade-wind, under the dominion of which many tracts are for months without any rain whatever. The west, which it reaches after all moisture has been deposited, suffers peculiarly from this drawback. It must always, however, be remembered that the arid portion occupies a comparatively small portion of the continent, and that every year lands which were considered desert are found to be suitable for cattle and sheep.

The conditions of the rainfall in Australia go by extremes. " It never rains but it pours " aptly characterises the manner in which the water pours down from the clouds ; in Sydney, on one occasion, ten inches of rain—a quarter, that is to say, of the annual rainfall—fell in two hours and a half. The vegetation of the country is nowhere sufficient to store up such volumes of water, but every year of settlement sees an increasing portion of this precious surplus stored by artificial means.

Except on the coast, where there is a subtropical richness of vegetable growth, the vegetation of his native soil greatly assists the Australian in his struggle for existence. The Australian flora of the interior, like that of all steppe regions, is rich in varieties, of which it affords, for example, more than **Nature of the Vegetation** Europe ; but in its general characteristics of dryness, stiffness, and want of sap, it is quite in keeping with the pervading nature of the country. Australia is, however, productive of a variety of grasses and salt-bush, which furnish nutritive food for sheep and cattle. The characteristic of stiffness and dryness is found in every blade of the notorious Australian spinifex or porcupine-grass plains with their dry, sharp-edged grasses ; and we find it most conspicuously in those districts seamed with sandhills, salt plains, and stony tracts, where the steppe becomes a desert, and where only the extraordinary abundance of certain grasses and thorns succeeds in keeping the soil from being absolutely bare. These features, however, are found only in a small area and not at all in the inhabited portion of the continent, which, except in the tropical jungle of the northern districts, presents few obstacles to a settler.

The forest, or, as it would be more correctly called, the Australian heath, with its tree trunks standing far apart and its want of underwood, has never interfered with the wanderings of the natives or the whites. On the contrary, with the vigorous growth of grass which has been able to spring up unchecked everywhere between the smooth, branchless stems, it has formed a carpet over which the settler could march to the tempting pasture grounds of the hinterland. The economic centre of gravity of the continent lies, even at the present day, in these open forests and meadow-like districts, which are general in all parts of the interior.

For some time very successful

COLONISTS HUNTING THE KANGAROO

attempts have been made to increase the value of the drier districts by a system of wells, and the labour expended has already repaid itself many times. With food plants of all kinds the native has not been so stingily provided by the continent as the older accounts seem to assert. The bulbs so characteristic of steppe countries are indeed insignificant in Australia; but in their place the native, who is certainly not fastidious, has at his disposal numerous other roots, various wild kinds of corn, mushrooms, berries, and blossoms, so that there can be no question of any actual lack of food.

The Australian has been most inadequately endowed with a native fauna. As one might expect from the general physical features of the continent, it is limited ; so much so, that it has not provided the aborigines with a single domestic or useful animal. The few animals that might be thought of for such purposes are all considered too wild. The dingo, the only mammal available for domestication, was, in all probability, introduced in a domesticated state and has since become wild. In addition to this, hunting, owing to the fleetness of all animals of the chase, is a very difficult undertaking for the aborigine armed with inadequate weapons; none even of the numerous well-equipped European expeditions have ever been able to provide themselves with food by this means. The nocturnal habits of an unusually large number of animals greatly increase the difficulty of catching them. These difficulties, insuperable for the aborigines, the European has met in the best possible way by introducing European domestic animals. They have all succeeded admirably, have multiplied to an astounding degree, and now represent a most valuable part of the national property ; in fact, together with the mineral output, sheepbreeding has contributed the largest share to the marvellously rapid development of the colonies. Even the mineral wealth of the country has entirely failed to affect the position of the native. He, like the Bushman of South Africa, has never gone so far as to employ any metal in its crude state, but meets the European as a fully

Fauna of the Continent

AUSTRALIAN NATIVES HUNTING WALLABIES

1017

developed man of the Stone Age, or of a yet earlier stage. The whites have set about all the more vigorously to make use of the mineral treasures of Australia. The opening of the gold-fields about the middle of the nineteenth century certainly marks the

only the range of a genial and temperate maritime climate. There is an abundant and perpetual supply of water both running and stagnant, and Tasmanian vegetation is of a luxuriance such as on the mainland is found only in the more favoured parts of Victoria, or on the northern rivers of New South Wales and Queensland. Tasmania really deserves the name of " Australia Felix," which was formerly given to the south-eastern portion of the mainland.

It may appear at first sight astonishing that from such a favourable foundation the aborigine has not mounted to any higher stage of culture than the Australian, but the explanation is not far to seek. There appears to be no affinity of the Tasmanian and the Australian, yet the intellectual abilities of the two races are on a par. Even in the domain of ethnical psychology, the law of inertia holds good ; the better conditions of life enjoyed by the Tasmanian are balanced by the greater isolation and seclusion of his country. The forest and the sea, which runs far inland in numerous creeks, have furnished the native with a more ample diet ; but an opposite coast, which might be the transmitter or source of new achievements in culture, was more completely wanting there than even in the case of Australia. The coasts of the mainland were out of the question as promoters of culture ; and the Tasmanian navigated the sea only to the most modest extent ; longer voyages would merely have brought him to an unprofitable wilderness of water.

AUSTRALIAN BIRDS: THE EMU AND THE LYRE BIRD

most crucial chapter in the history of the Colonies. Even now, when the " gold fever " has long since given way to a normal temperature, the mining industry has all the greater importance for the development of Australia and its position in the great future which we may anticipate for the Pacific Ocean, because its wealth in other useful minerals, especially in coal and iron, is undisputed.

The natural features of Tasmania call for little remark. In the conformation of its surface, a direct continuation of the coast range of East Australia, it resembles in its flora and fauna also the south-east of the continent. On these and, above all, on geological grounds it cannot be separated from the mainland, in comparison with which, however, it is singularly favoured by climate. Tasmania has neither abrupt contrasts of heat and cold nor an uncertain supply of water ; a large rainfall is distributed over the whole year, and the temperature has

AUSTRALIAN ANIMALS: THE DINGO AND THE PLATYPUS

NATIVE PEOPLES OF AUSTRALIA

AND THE TRAGEDY OF THE TASMANIANS

WHAT, then, is the state of the inhabitants of these countries, whose external conditions have just been sketched as guides to the historical development, and what is the state of the makers of their history ? What place do the primitive inhabitants take in the circle of mankind ? Are they autochthonous in their land, or have they immigrated ? Have they kinsmen, and, if so, where ? And what, lastly, is the composition of the modern non-native population of the continent ? We will endeavour to answer these questions.

A satisfactory consensus of opinion now prevails as to the anthropological position of the Australians. The similarity of their methods of life, the uniformity of their attainments in culture and of their habits, and to some degree the identity of the languages, might lead to the erroneous view that they are a homogeneous race, which cannot be grouped with the Malayan or Papuan. Anthropological investigation has now proved that this homogeneousness does not exist, and that the native population of Australia represents, on the contrary, a mixture of at least two very distinct elements. This view finds corroboration in the differences of the colour of the skin and the formation of the hair, and also of the shape of the face.

The colour of the skin varies from a true yellow to a velvety black with numerous **Types of Australian Aborigines** intermediate degrees, among which the dark-brown tint is far the most common colouring. The hair, too, with a prevalent tendency to curl, ranges from the true straight-haired type to the complete woolly-haired type of the negro. The shape of the face and skull, finally, shows a multiplicity of differences, such as cannot be greater even in nations proved to have a large admixture of foreign blood. The flat negro nose, on the one side, and the typical Semitic nose on the other, form the extremes here. It is thus clearly established that a dark, woolly-haired race and a light, straight-haired race shared in the ancestry of the Australian. But where, then, was their original home ? Both races obviously could not be autochthonous at the same time ; indeed, the nature of the continent seems to exclude the possibility that it was the cradle even of one race. **Origin of the Natives** Whence, therefore, did the two elements of admixture come, and which is the earlier on the new soil ? A key to this problem we find even at the present day on the north coast of Australia, in the still existing trade of the Malays with the north-west, and in the immediate vicinity of New Guinea with a Papuan population, which also has a predilection for crossing the group of islands of the Torres Straits to the south. For the migration of the Papuan-Melanesian, or, in more general terms, of the negroid element, no other path than that by New Guinea can be thought of. But two roads were open to the Malayan—the direct road from the Indian archipelago, which even at the present day maintains a connection with Australia, and the detour by Polynesia. We have no evidence that this second one was used ; but we know now from the ethnography of New Guinea that its population had a distinct infusion of Malayan-Polynesian blood. But what in the case of New Guinea is demonstrable fact lies in the case of Australia within the range of probability, since the conditions of access to both countries from Polynesia are practically identical.

The question of priority sinks into the background compared with the solution of the main problem. An answer also is barely possible, since the migration from both sides to Australia must not be regarded as an isolated event but as a continuous or frequently recurring movement. A certain coincidence of time is, under the circumstances, to be assumed.

From another standpoint also the question of priority gives way before that of the predominance of the one or the other element. The point, briefly put, is to ascertain clearly the causes of the wonderful inability of the modern Australian to navigate the sea—a peculiar defect, which has prevented him from settling not only on the more remote of the coasts which face Australia, but even on the neighbouring islands. When we see how the negroes and all the dusky remnants of nations on the southern margin of Africa feel the same dread of the sea, and when we reflect that the nature of his present home has induced the Melanesian to become a navigator, although he is far removed from being a true seaman, we must at once entertain the conjecture that it is the negroid blood in his veins that fetters the Australian so firmly to the sod. Up to a certain point this conjecture is doubtless correct, for the law of heredity holds good in the domain of ethnical psychology. It is impossible, however, to make Papuan ancestry alone responsible for this peculiarity ; it has not hindered the Melanesians from arriving, under favourable circumstances, at a fair degree of proficiency in navigation. If the Australian has failed to do the same, it is partly because his circumstances have made him unfamiliar with the sea.

Native Dread of the Sea

The full force of this second cause is apparent when we consider the nature of the country, and the extent to which the economic basis of the Australian native's life is narrowed by the poverty and inhospitable character of his surroundings. He who must devote every moment in the day to the task of providing food and drink for his body, and is forced to roam unceasingly as he follows his fleeting quarry from place to place, has neither the time nor the inclination to retain or to develop an accomplishment like navigation, which requires constant practice, and which does not at first seem necessary in a new country. And even if the ancestral Malayan blood had transmitted to the young race any nautical skill, such as we admire to-day among the Polynesians and western Malays, the Australian continent would have put an end to it, for it has always been the country of material

The Primal Struggle for Subsistence

anxiety, and, as a consequence, the country of continual decadence.

The loss of seamanship is in reality only a sign of this. The aloofness from the outer world engendered thereby was the first step toward that complete disappearance of Australia from history throughout the millenniums that have elapsed since its first colonisation. But other completely remote races have developed a history and a civilisation. It was not only the absolute seclusion from the rest of the world and the unbroken quiet in which Australia reposed, as the corner pillar of the Old World between the Indian Ocean and the Pacific, that the entire absence of any historical development of its own was due, but also to the total impossibility of creating a true national life on its niggard soil. The attempts to do so, which the Europeans found on their arrival, can at best be termed a caricature of political organisation.

The Tasmanian has also not progressed far in the field of political development. Since the nature of his country is richer in resources than Australia, economic considerations must be excluded from the list of possible causes. The same remark applies to the small proficiency in navigation, which we noticed also in Australia. The explanation can be found only in that close affinity of the Tasmanian to the Melanesian ethnical group, upon which all observers have insisted. This is primarily shown in the physical characteristics ; but, secondarily, it appears in the inability of the Papuan to rise higher than the stage of village communities. New Guinea offers the closest parallel.

Political Backwardness of Aborigines

The whites do not belong to the continent, but have made it commercially subject to them, and have thus, in contrast to the aborigines, who have never succeeded in breaking the strong fetters of nature, become the true makers of its history. This history even now looks back on barely a century, a period of time that hardly counts in the life of a people. Yet it has already been full of vicissitudes, even if, in this respect, it has been greatly surpassed by the outwardly similar history of the United States of America.

In contrast with America, which for centuries has been a crucible for almost all the races and peoples of the globe, the immigrant population of Australia, Tasmania, and New Zealand is unusually

AUSTRALIAN ABORIGINES: YOUNG MEN

YOUNG AND OLD AUSTRALIAN NATIVES

homogeneous. It is composed almost exclusively of Britons, by the side of whom the members of other nationalities practically disappear. Even the hundred thousand Germans who have settled there hardly affect the result, especially since their absorption into the rest of the population is merely a question of time. The Chinese, since they never make their home in the country, may be disregarded as factors in the growth of national life.

The ethnical unity of the white population of Australia is of extreme importance for the British Empire. England's dominant position on the Indian Ocean may appear most favourable ; but in view of the efforts made by the colonial Powers of continental Europe to strengthen their recently acquired possessions in those parts and to increase their influence generally, this position may grow less tenable. The same turn of fortune is in prospect for England, and all other European colonial Powers, on the Pacific. There it is the cutting of the Central American isthmus which is to the advantage, both strategically and economically, of the United

YOUNG NATIVE WOMAN

States, above all other Powers, and threatens to give them in the South Seas a great superiority over all rivals. The interests of England are, from the position of affairs, most at stake. It is for this reason a great stroke of good fortune for her that the corner pillar, which both supports the dominions on the Indian Ocean, and is, on the other side, the chief agent of British interests in the Pacific Ocean, is, as it were, a part of England itself. In thought and action, customs and habits, mother and daughter exactly resemble each other. Even in the matter of dress the daughter country has not found it necessary to consider the change of climate.

This feeling of complete sympathy gives ground for great confidence in the future. The similarity between Australia and Great Britain justifies the assumption that the same community of feeling must reign in every other department of life. This feeling is so strong that even the latest and boldest of all the political steps of the Australian Colonies, their union into the Commonwealth of Australia, which was proclaimed on September

17th, 1900, is regarded in England and Australia alike as taken entirely in the interests of union. Indeed, as the newest conception of the British Empire—as an alliance of self-governing nations united by the ties of kinship—tends to replace the old ideas of headship and subordination, the cohesion of all the parts becomes greater as each independently develops its own resources.

One of the greatest achievements of the nineteenth century in the field of ethnology, the art of reconstructing from prehistoric finds the natural history of long-past years, which lie beyond all tradition and written record, fails in Australia.

This does not imply that discoveries of the kind might not be made ; quite the reverse. The continent has its *mirnjongs*, or ash-heaps, measuring sometimes ten feet in height, and often several hundred yards in circumference, and containing pieces of bone and stone axes ; these are very common in South Australia and Victoria, particularly on Lake Conne-warren, and form an exact counterpart of the " kitchen middens " of Denmark. Great heaps of mussel-shells are also found in the vicinity of the sea-shore ; there is even one really artistic erection dating from prehistoric times. This ancient monument, as we may fairly call it, is the stone labyrinth of Brewarrina on the upper Darling, some sixty miles above Bourke. It consists of a stone weir a hundred yards or so long, which, built on a rocky foundation, stretches diagonally through the river. From this transverse dam a labyrinth of stone walls reaching some ninety yards up stream has been constructed, which is intended to facilitate the catching of the fish which swim up or down stream. The walls form for this purpose circular basins of from 2 ft. to 4 ft. in diameter ; some are connected together by intricate passages, while others possess only one entrance. These walls are so firmly built of ponderous masses of rock that the mighty floods, which some-

times poured down with a depth of 20 ft., were able at best only to dislodge the topmost layers of the stones.

The conclusions which we can draw from the existence of the mirnjongs and the shell mounds, but especially from the Brewarrina Labyrinth, throw some little light on the ancient Australians. Each of the three constructions presupposes in the first place that the population, at least in the south-east, was considerably denser in early times than at the time of the landing of the Europeans ; otherwise the piling up of the refuse mounds would imply periods of whose length we could form no conception. The building of the labyrinth also can be explained only by the employment of large masses of men, especially since the materials had to be brought from a considerable distance. But, besides this, it can have been erected only by an organised population.

GROUP OF FEMALE AUSTRALIAN ABORIGINES

CIVILISED AUSTRALIAN NATIVES

Australian hordes of the present day would be incapable of such combined efforts.

Another circumstance confirms our assumption of the retrogression of the Australians both in numbers and in culture. The boats, whether they consist of nothing better than a piece of bark tied together at both ends, and kept apart in the middle by pieces of inserted wood, or appear in the shape of simple rafts, carry in the middle on a little pile of clay a fire, the modern object of which is merely the immediate cooking of the fish that are caught ; but its invariable presence there suggests the thought that it is a survival from former regular sea voyages, when the custom was justified.

This proof by probability that the Australians have retrograded in numbers and in civilisation is all that can be derived from the evidence of the country and the national life. This is no great achievement ; but it shows how completely unfavourable natural conditions have overwhelmed the energies and capabilities of the natives. It is, for the time being,

impossible to judge the length of the periods with which we have to reckon, or to determine whether a deterioration of the climate has contributed to this decline ; such a contingency is not impossible.

After all, we can follow the history of the Australians and Tasmanians only from the moment of their intercourse with the white men. There is no question here of a true development, such as can be traced in all nations except a few border nations in the north and south of the globe. The expression " history " really connotes too much in this case ; for all the European civilisation and the white men brought to them tended to one and the same result ultimately —the slow but sure extinction of the whole race. The methods of extermination may differ, but the end is always the same.

In physical geography the expression "geographical homologies" is constantly employed. It is borrowed from comparative anatomy and signifies the recurrence of the same configuration, whether in the horizontal outlines or in the elevation of the surface, which we find in the countries of our globe. The best known of these homologies is the striking similarity in the contours of South America, Africa, and Australia, which, in the words of Oskar Peschel, display as great a uniformity of shape as if they had been constructed after a model. It is not our intention to examine this similarity closely ; but we must consider for a few moments that exact correspondence of the southern extremities of those continents, which goes far beyond a mere linear resemblance.

The tapering away into a wedge-like point, facing the Antarctic, which is a feature peculiar to the three continents— if the island of Tasmania is reckoned as part of Australia—is, so far as its shape goes, an excrescence breaking through the general scheme on which their outlines are modelled. The meaning and cause of this precise contour have remained a mystery to men like Humboldt and Peschel. But there is no doubt as to the influence which these vast and lonely promontories, tapering away into the ocean, have exercised on physical geography and the distribution of culture. From the first point of view, their position and shape determine the course of the entire circulation of the seas of the Southern Hemisphere. The character of the climatic conditions is influenced by them, and the greater or less degree to which the land masses of the Southern Hemisphere can be inhabited is in the last resort decided by them. On civilisation the effect of this wedge-like shape is exclusively negative. It places the inhabitant of those promontories on the remote, southern edge of the habitable world, cuts him off to the north from the centres of civilisation, and confines him to regions which are continually narrowing. Still more momentous are the consequences on the art of navigation. The vast ocean, limitless and islandless, surrounds each of the three extremities. How, then, should primitive people venture on the high seas when even a highly developed navigation cannot flourish without some opposite coast which can be reached ?

The Southern Promontories of the World

But the homology goes still further for Africa and Australia in a large degree, and in a more restricted degree for South America. It shows itself this time in the destiny of the natives during intercourse with the whites. The Bushmen, the Hottentots, and the Australian aborigines at the present time can hardly be called even the fragments of a nation. The aborigine of southern South America has hitherto fared better. Neither Patagonians nor Araucos have, it is true, emerged unscathed from intercourse with the white intruders ; but they have been able to retain the characteristics of their race, and have remained free and independent. No careful observer will imagine that this is a consequence of creole courage ; what has preserved the Indian hitherto from destruction is merely the political immaturity of his opponents and the insufficiency of their numbers to people the vast territory of South America. The Australians and Tasmanians did not fare so well as the Indians. The Tasmanians have been for a quarter of a century blotted out from the list of living peoples ; the same fate impends upon the Australians, and is, to all appearance, inevitable. The Tasmanian tragedy is not only the most gloomy from its dénouement, but has a sad pre-eminence for the large number of sensational details. It opens on May 4th, 1804, when the natives, on approaching the new settlement of Hobart in a friendly spirit, were, through an unfortunate misunderstanding of their intentions, greeted by the English garrison with a volley of bullets ; or we can, if we prefer, take the date June 13th, 1803, when the first batch of English convicts landed on the spot where the present capital of the country, Hobart, stands. This year saw the birth of the Tasmanian woman, Trukanini, or Lalla Rookh, who was destined to survive all her tribesfolk. She died in London in 1876. The death struggle of the whole people had thus lasted precisely a lifetime.

Contrast with South America

The destruction of the Tasmanians was not accomplished without vigorous resistance on their part. By natural disposition peaceable, harmless, and contented, they had endured for many years the ill-treatment of the transported convicts and the colonists without transgressing the laws of self-defence. It was only after 1826 that, driven to frantic desperation, they amply revenged the treatment they had suffered, and murdered all their tormentors who fell into their hands. The twenty-two years that had intervened do not add fresh laurels to the history of English colonisation, or redound to the honour of mankind generally. In the very first years of the settlement, the hostilities, which, according to the official admission, were always begun by the whites, assumed such proportions, and the oppression of the natives was so harsh, that in 1810 a special law had to be passed which proposed to punish the murder of an aborigine as an actual crime. This remained a dead letter, since it was impossible to obtain legal evidence in the case of blacks, who were despised and possessed no rights. The relation between whites and natives resolved itself into a perpetual series of outrages and reprisals.

The Tragedy of the Tasmanians

It was not only by these persecutions that the growth of the English colony exercised an adverse influence on the fortunes of the natives. Until the landing of the whites, the sea, with its inexhaustible store of fish, molluscs, and other living creatures, had supplied all their food ; but in proportion as the colony increased, with the growth and prosperity of the towns, the advance of the colonists, and

AUSTRALIAN ABORIGINES DANCING AT A CORROBOREE OR NATIVE GATHERING

the multiplication and extension of their pasture grounds, the region where the natives could live was curtailed ; above all, they were driven away from the coast. But this was a vital question for the Tasmanians, since the rough and wild interior was absolutely wanting in all the means of life. We now understand how these originally timid natives became veritable heroes from desperation, and waged unceasing war upon the whites when and how they could.

The victory of the English was not lightly won. The natives, driven by force into the interior, soon acquired so accurate a knowledge of the country, covered with dense forest and intersected by ravines, that it was difficult to get at them. As Charles Darwin tells us, they often escaped their pursuers by throwing themselves flat upon the black ground, or by standing rigidly still, when, even at a short distance, they were indistinguishable from a dead tree trunk. Unable to control the natives while they lived at large, the English finally resorted to other measures. By a proclamation they forbade the natives to cross a certain boundary. They then, in 1828, offered them also a reservation where the persecuted and pursued might collect and live in peace. Both measures proved futile. The first would never have

NIGHT SCENE OF NATIVE AUSTRALIAN LIFE NEAR SYDNEY A HUNDRED YEARS AGO
Reproduced from an engraving of the year 1804

been really understood by the people, even if they had grasped the sense of the words. For the second, the time was already past : the natives were no longer susceptible to a fair treatment, and the Europeans were not disposed to maintain a pacific attitude. The old order of things continued. Finally, the Governor, Colonel Arthur, endeavoured to sweep the natives into one district by drawing a cordon across the island. The attempt failed ignominiously. An expenditure of £30,000 resulted in the capture of two natives !

Native versus Colonist

With the failure of this last attempt at suppression, the tragedy of the Tasmanians enters on another phase. This was free from bloodshed, but was not less disastrous than the former, and is inseparably connected with the name of George Augustus Robinson. This extraordinary man, by trade a simple carpenter at Hobart, and unable to write English correctly, offered, when all warlike measures were ineffective against the natives, to induce them by peaceful overtures to emigrate. We know how thoroughly he accomplished his self-imposed task. Unarmed and single-handed, he attained by pacific negotiations a result which a whole populous colony had failed to achieve in decades of bloody warfare.

Through the mediation of Robinson, one tribe was assigned to Swan Island, three others to Gun Carriage Island. Later, in 1843, all the natives were united on Flinders Island. These " tribes " were by this time not very numerous : powder and shot, smallpox, and other diseases had caused too great ravages during the last forty years. In 1804 the native population was put at 8,000 souls roughly ; in 1815 some 5,000 were still estimated to exist. Their number in 1830 reached some 700, and in 1835 had dwindled to 250. In 1845, when the survivors were taken across to Oyster Cove in the D'Entrecasteaux Channel, only 45, and in 1861 only 18, were left. The last male Tasmanian, King Billy, or William Lanne, died in 1869 at Hobart, aged thirty-four, and in 1876 the race of the Tasmanians became entirely extinct on the death of Trukanini—the fate that awaits all primitive races from intercourse with civilisation.

Extinction of the Tasmanian

It is idle at the present day to load the parties concerned with reproaches. No nation, vigorously engaged in colonisation,

has yet been destined to keep the shield of humanity spotless and pure. It must also be admitted that in later years earnest attempts were made to atone for the wrongs done to the natives in the earlier period. That the wrong methods were chosen is another consideration, which does not do away with the crime, but may be pleaded as an extenuating circumstance.

The knell of the Australians has not yet sounded. The restless race still roams the vast steppes, still hunts here and there the nimble kangaroo, and throws with strength and skill the spear and the boomerang. But how cooped in its once wide domain ! The whole of the east, fairly rich in resources even for the rude savage, the north-east and south-east, have long been taken by the white man. Now, in most recent times, the latter is making vast strides from the west into the interior, and the north is being more and more encroached upon. The aborigine is faced by the alternatives of retiring into the desert-like interior, or of being forced to capitulate to civilisation and become the servant of the European. Neither alternative is calculated to perpetuate either him or his peculiar nature.

Australian Aborigines at Bay

The tragic history of the Australians is distinguished from that of the Tasmanians in two respects : it was of longer duration, and covered an incomparably larger area. Anyone who knows that the political organisation of ancient Australia found practically its only expression in the claim of each single tribe to one definite territory—within the tribe itself the land was at times divided between the various families—will also understand that the rude encroachments of the first Europeans, whether convicts or free colonists, could not fail to provoke grave disputes. Among the natives themselves violation of territory ranked as the most flagrant breach of the peace.

Next to this the class of human beings who were first brought to those shores greatly influenced the form which subsequent conditions assumed. There may be a division of opinions about the value of transportation as a means of punishment or as a measure for colonisation, but there can be no doubt that it has been ruinous to native races, whose fine qualities might have been turned to good account. Tasmania, to give an example in our own field, has proved this ; so, too, New Caledonia and South-west Africa under German rule in the twentieth century; and it was patent in Australia. That shiploads of convicts were disembarked without precautions, and were still more carelessly looked after, is admitted even by the official reports of the time; in 1803 complaints were made that the number of guards was insufficient. Under the circumstances it was very easy for the prisoners to escape into the bush, and they did not fail to use the opportunity. The consequences for the unfortunate blacks were soon apparent. The first gifts to them consisted of smallpox and liver diseases, brandy and tobacco; and they soon learned to be immoral, foul-mouthed, beggars and thieves. And while the natives were at first peaceable and friendly, the coarseness and brutality of the convicts soon led to their becoming more and more hostile, until they, on their part, began that guerilla warfare which has lingered on for over a century. There has, how-

Influence of the Convict ever, been no lack of good intentions on the Australian continent. The energies of the Government have been more than once directed toward the object of gaining over the natives; the term of office of the first governor, Phillip, was full of such praiseworthy efforts; but there could be no idea of any success unless all the immigrants radically changed their behaviour towards the natives, and the settlers, whose immigration began in 1790, did their honest best to fill the cup to overflowing.

English Governments, however, have always endeavoured to mitigate the inevitable cruelties and misunderstandings which result from a collision between settlers and aborigines in a new country.

Nor was this spirit of humanity lacking even in the convict settlement of New South Wales. In 1839 a voluntary society was founded for the protection of the aborigines, and by its influence a law was passed which provided for the appointment of commissioners who should be responsible for the care of the natives. And now in all the states blacks and half-castes within the settled districts are fed, clothed, housed and taught at the public expense. They also have the privilege of travelling without charge on the Government railways.

The number of the Australian natives has never been actually determined. The highest estimate allows for more than 1,100,000 Australians at the beginning of the European immigration. This figure is certainly far too high, and is universally rejected. Other calculations range from 100,000 to 200,000 for the pre-European period. Beyond doubt the continent was sparsely peopled. So far as aborigines are concerned, it is incomparably more so now; 50,000 is certainly too high an estimate. The diminution of the native population has therefore proceeded at an alarmingly rapid rate. In Victoria in 1836 they were counted to be some 5,000 souls; in 1881 they had sunk to 770. The shrinkage has not been so great in all districts, but it is universal. The birth rate among the natives is nowhere equal to the death rate.

Decline of Australian Aborigines

According to the census of 1901 the total number of aborigines on the continent was 20,758, the distribution throughout the various states being as follows: New South Wales, 4,287; Victoria 652; Queensland, 6,670; South Australia, 3,888; West Australia, 5,261. The number would be considerably higher if the half-castes were included.

Beattie, Hobart

LAST TWO MEMBERS OF A VANISHED RACE
King Billy, or William Lanne, the last male Tasmanian aborigine, who died in 1869, and Trukanini, the last native woman, who died in 1876.

CAPTAIN COOK LANDING AT ADVENTURE BAY, VAN DIEMEN'S LAND, IN 1777

A graphic representation of the reception of the famous navigator by the Tasmanian aborigines, who regarded the white men with mingled dread and veneration. The last native Tasmanian died several decades ago, chiefly as a result of the convict settlement of the island, and the race is now quite extinct.

THE BRITISH IN AUSTRALIA
AND THE FOUNDING OF NEW SOUTH WALES

THE efforts of the Europeans of Australasia in the field of economics and politics have been crowned with great success. From a corner of the world which Europe during a whole century and a half, from its discovery by Abel Tasman in 1642 to the landing of Phillip in Botany Bay in 1788, had not deemed worthy of any notice, they have conjured forth a state which at the present day needs only a sufficient period of development, independence, and a more considerable population in order to be reckoned as one of the important factors in the making of the history of mankind. These deficiencies are such as will repair themselves in course of time.

The history of the discovery of Australia is deeply interesting, both as regards the history of civilisation and of international trade, because its effects have **Discovery** been parallel in many ways to **of the Island** those produced by the discovery **Continent** of America—both continents required to be twice discovered by the civilised world before it appreciated their value and occupied them permanently. This similarity is expressed even in the intervals of time between the old and new discoveries, which are to some extent proportional to the size of the two land masses. In the case of America, the period that elapsed between the voyage of the Northmen and the voyage of Columbus was 500 years ; in the case of Australia little more than a century and a half elapsed between the voyage of Quiros in 1606 through the Torres Strait and the discovery of the east coast by James Cook in 1770. If we consider Abel Tasman's voyages in 1642 and 1644 as the first proper discovery, the interval is considerably diminished.

The abandonment of the first discovery was no accident in the case of the two continents ; no necessity then existed for bringing the new worlds into the sphere of civilised activity, At the period of the first finding of America, as in the centuries preceding, the centre of gravity of Europe inclined one way—toward the East, which had long supplied all its needs, both material and spiritual. Europe therefore neither understood nor valued the new discovery, and let it sink into complete oblivion.

At the second and final revealing of America the position of affairs was quite **A Parallel** altered ; in fact, it may be said **from** that the discovery itself was a **America** consequence of the very alteration. Europe, after the year 1000, had gravitated strongly to the East as the Crusades and the prosperity of the city-states of the Mediterranean prove ; but since the appearance of the Ottoman Turks the centre of gravity had been considerably shifted, and men felt more and more urgently the necessity of freeing themselves at least from the necessity of trading through Egypt, Syria, and Pontus, and of securing the communication with the south and east coast of Asia by a direct route. There was no cause to abandon this goal, which was at first supposed to have been reached in the voyages of Columbus and his contemporaries, even after it was recognised that the lands reached were a new world.

Such important economic considerations do not concern the first visits to and subsequent neglect of Australia. The whole story of its discovery comes rather under the head of the search for the great unknown southern continent, which lasted 2,000 years. The search originated with an assumption that the great continents of the Northern Hemisphere must be balanced by similar masses of land in the south. The hypothetical southern continent always excited an interest which was purely theoretic ; and herein lies the explanation why in the sixteenth and seventeenth centuries, that age of practical tendencies, so little attention was paid to the problem. The explorers of the southern seas hoped to demonstrate the existence of this country ; but the idea of making full use of it crossed no one's mind. Australia, after the first glimpses of her shores, was allowed to relapse into oblivion. Tasman's first voyage had proved that the ocean was landless for many degrees of southern latitude— that is to say, the presumed continent did not exist in that region. Although Dutch ships had touched or sighted points of the west and north coast of Australia several times since 1606, no one guessed that in this winding course Tasman had circumnavigated a continent. Scientific curiosity was satisfied with the negative conclusions established by his voyage.

ABEL TASMAN
The famous Dutch navigator, who, in seeking for the supposed circumpolar continent of the Southern Hemisphere, unwittingly sailed round the continent of Australia.

It is not easy for those who know the great natural wealth of Australia and the beauty of its landscape to realise the **First Impressions of Australia** disappointment of those navigators who first landed on its shores. It was, indeed, a marvellous misfortune for the continent that the majority of the numerous navigators who set foot on the shore before James Cook were fated to land on spots which were especially bleak, sterile, and inhospitable. This was the case of the Dutchman, Dirk Hartog, who landed on the shores of Shark Bay in 1616 ; and such were the experiences of the numerous other Dutchmen who in the first half of the seventeenth century set foot on the west, north, and south coasts, Abel Tasman among their number.

The opinion of the Englishman, William Dampier, was, however, fraught with consequences for the continent. This navigator, as successful in piracy as exploration, who, with a mind full of the discoveries of Cortes and Pizarro, in two voyages (1689–1699) at the end of the seventeenth century surveyed a considerable part of the west coast, penetrated to some distance into the interior in search of the rich cities of an antique civilisation. His verdict was crushing enough ; according to him the country was the poorest in the world, far

inferior to the coast of Portuguese South Africa. No corn grew there, no roots, no pod fruits or vegetables from which food could be got. The miserable aborigines had neither clothing nor houses, and were the most wretched creatures in the world. Compared with these blacks the very Hottentots seemed gentlemen. The results of this report by Dampier, which was unfortunately—as to the part which he visited—only too much based on fact, show themselves in the entire cessation of voyages of discovery to Australia for more than two-thirds of a century, apart from some attempts at colonisation in the country, such as had already been made by the Dutch in 1628.

Even the final and lasting discovery of Australia by James Cook in 1770 did not immediately lead to the exploration of the continent. That far-sighted explorer certainly had such a goal before his eyes when he took possession of the whole east coast, from the thirty-eighth degree of southern latitude as far as Cape York, in the name of his king, for England ; certainly the glowing accounts which his companion Banks, the botanist, brought back of the magnificent scenery and the splendid climate were calculated to attract the attention of governments to the possibility of colonising this new earthly paradise. But the political situation was not favourable to such plans. England stood on the eve of her tedious war with the united colonies of North America ; she required to guard her position on the near Atlantic, and could not **Birth of the Colonies** possibly think of following out any plans in a remote corner of the southern seas. And yet the birth of the Australian Colonies dates from the War of Independence in America.

England had, since 1600, transported a large number of her criminals to the Atlantic colonies, where their hard labour was welcome. The convicts were bought by the colonists at sums ranging from £8 upwards, and they became a source of considerable profit to the Government at home. The War of Independence brought this arrangement to an abrupt end in 1779, and England, whose prisons were soon overcrowded, was compelled to look round for some other locality. Of the districts proposed in Parliament in 1783— namely, Gibraltar, the Gambia territory, and the region of Botany Bay in New South Wales, only the last, from reasons easy to explain, could be seriously considered. Gibraltar did not offer room enough, the transportation to Gambia would have simply meant "the execution of capital punishment by malaria," as the phrase in the Parliamentary report ran. The objections to Australia were only the enormous distance and the difficulties attending the transport of such numbers. In any case the decision of Parliament, in spite of the Royal assent, was not put into action soon enough to anticipate the plan of a certain Mr. Matra, subsequently English Consul in Tangiers. He proposed to settle in New South Wales the numerous families who had been expelled from North America on account of their support of the mother country, and at the same time to improve

System of Penal Colonies

appreciably the position of England in the trade of Europe by the increase in production which might be looked for. Matra also failed to carry his plan then. The Secretary of State, Lord Sydney, certainly favoured the scheme in 1784, but he finally recurred to the idea of transportation.

In August, 1786, Lord Sydney submitted a memorandum to the Admiralty requesting that arrangements should be made for the transport and convoy of "at least seven or eight hundred convicts." The new settlement was intended to be something more than a prison. It was hoped that it would supply flax, hemp, and timber for naval purposes, and that it would grow a sufficient quantity of "Asiatic products" as "may render our recourse to our European neighbours unnecessary." One ship was to be set apart for women, and a tender was to be employed in conveying to the new settlement a large number of women from the Friendly Islands, New Caledonia, and other parts which are contiguous thereto, where any number might be procured without difficulty.

Hopes Regarding Botany Bay

The text of this memorandum, together with the protests and criticisms of Captain Arthur Phillip, R.N., who was appointed the first Governor, and to whose foresight, energy, and humanity Australia owes a deep debt, are printed in the series of historical records published by the Government of New South Wales. Had Phillip's advice been followed and a shipload of free mechanics and agriculturists sent out six months in advance of the main expedition, most of the difficulties which beset the early settlement would have been avoided. But then, as now, the demands of the " man on the spot" were ignored by a British Government ; and only the heroism and patience of Governor Phillip extricated the young colony from the starvation and other evils which he had predicted before leaving England as a necessary consequence of faulty arrangements. And even Phillip would have failed had he not left behind him a powerful and devoted believer in the future of Australia — Sir Joseph Banks,

DAMPIER'S FIRST SIGHT OF THE BOOMERANG
One of the exploits of William Dampier, seaman and buccaneer, was the exploration of part of Australia. He afterwards rescued Alexander Selkirk, " Robinson Crusoe," from his island prison.

President of the Royal Society, who had sailed with Cook on his voyage and given the name to Botany Bay on account of its varied flora. Next to Phillip, Sir Joseph Banks is the man to whom Australia owes most.

First landing at Sydney Harbour A frigate and a tender of the Royal Navy, six transports, and three store ships, having on board, all told, 1,163 souls, of whom 443 were free, sailed from England on May 13th, 1787. They arrived in Botany Bay between January 18th and 20th, 1788. As, however, the anchorage was bad, and water scarce, Phillip did not disembark his convoy—in fact, no convict ever landed at Botany Bay—but pushed along the coast in search of a better site. His seaman's instinct led him to select Port Jackson, where, as he writes to Lord Sydney, "I had the satisfaction of finding the finest harbour in the world, in which a thousand sail of the line may ride in the most perfect security." Sydney Cove was selected as most suitable for landing, and on January 26th this was occupied as the site of the new colony. It was none too soon. Two days after the arrival of the fleet at Botany Bay, and during Phillip's absence, two sail were announced off Botany Heads, and standing for the entrance to the bay. They turned out to be the Boussole and Astrolabe, under Admiral la Perouse. Thus narrowly did the French miss becoming owners of Australia !

In February, 1788, the Governor removed a small number of convicts, under the superintendence of Lieutenant King and some soldiers, to Norfolk Island, which lies almost halfway between NewZealand and New Caledonia. The duty of this minor colony was to manufacture the flax which Cook had found there in large quantities, in order to supply the main colony cheaply and conveniently with material for clothing. King set to work with zeal, planted corn and vegetables, and devoted himself to the manufacture of flax.

But in spite of all efforts it was not possible either here or on the mainland to feed the colony from its own products. The need for some help in the way of provisions was most urgently felt by both countries during the early years. The same need had been felt by some of the early colonists on different parts of the east coast of America, in Virginia and Carolina ; and this was the cause of the failure of the great French scheme of colonisation in Cayenne in 1763. Virgin soil is not at once in a condition to feed large masses of inhabitants, especially when it is treated with as little technical knowledge as was shown by the settlers **Difficulties of Early Settlement** of Phillip and King, no one of whom understood anything of agriculture ; besides, the soil of Sydney is not fertile. Again, the criminals, who preponderated in numbers, felt little desire to work. According to Phillip, twenty-three men did more than a thousand convicts. The leading thought of the whole of Phillip's term of office was to increase the number of free settlers and to bring over skilled agriculturists. But when Phillip voluntarily resigned his post in December, 1792, through shattered health, the number of free immigrants was still insignificant. The bulk of private holdings were in the hands of " emancipists," or time-expired convicts, who were hardly more industrious than the convicts themselves.

Under the prevailing circumstances, the internal conditions of the colony were terribly disorganised during the first years. The want of provisions, which was felt soon after landing, became so acute in 1790 that for months only half rations or less could be distributed; the cattle that had been brought with the settlers escaped or died, and the first fields which were sown produced nothing. In

TWO GREAT FIGURES IN AUSTRALIA'S EARLY HISTORY
Sir Joseph Banks—on the left—accompanied Captain Cook, and afterwards, from his knowledge of Australia, he was able to support in England the policy of Governor Arthur Phillip—on the right—in the latter's heroic efforts on behalf of the settlement of the new colony.

addition to this, scurvy broke out from want of fresh meat. The soldiers were disobedient and mutinous, and drunkenness became a besetting vice. Robbery, murder and arson were daily occurrences. In February, 1790, the distress became so acute that the Governor found himself compelled to send 200 prisoners to the Norfo'k Islands, although there was anything but a superabundance of food there. Meanwhile, fresh transports kept arriving from England with prisoners, masses of poor wretches crowded together, more than half of whom frequently died on the long voyage. The survivors were then often so weak that, half dead, they had to be unloaded at Port Jackson in slings like bales of merchandise. On the other hand, provisions, seed corn, and cattle did not arrive.

Governor Phillip, in the midst of all this misery, which often forced him to live on half rations like the convicts, never lost heart for an instant. With prophetic instinct, he declared in the colony's darkest hour, "This country will prove the most valuable acquisition Great Britain ever made." Amid the mass of duties which devolved on him in the way of constructing houses, laying out gardens and fields, and continually battling with famine and mutiny, he found the time to interest himself in the exploration of the interior ; he was desirous of forming amicable relations also with the natives. One thing alone was calculated to fill this patient, dogged man with distaste for his post, and that was the opposition, passive indeed, but all the more obstinate, which his own troops showed to all his measures. As a matter of fact, up to the end of 1790, the Marines, and then the New South Wales Corps, a regiment specially organised for Australia, thwarted every one of his regulations. The soldiers disregarded the Acts of Parliament, in virtue of which Phillip exercised his office, and submitted to military laws only.

A successor to Governor Phillip was finally appointed at the end of 1795 in the person of Hunter, also a sailor, who had accompanied the expedition of 1787.

The Man Who Made Australia

A SCENE FROM SYDNEY'S EARLY DAYS
Inspection of the convicts, upon their landing at Sydney, by Governor Phillip, the first and greatest Governor of the penal settlement.

The interval of nearly three years was filled by the government of two officers of the New South Wales Corps, Major Grose and Captain Paterson. The administration of both is conspicuous for the enormous growth of the abuses against which Phillip had vainly contended. Above all, the general vice of drunkenness had assumed most dangerous dimensions, being chiefly encouraged by the increased trade in spirits, which the soldiers of the militia as well as their officers made their chief business, from want of military duties. The name " Rum Corps " that was soon given to these troops has perpetuated this strange conception of military service. For the colony itself, it clearly involved great losses. The convicts, instead of being educated to be peaceable and industrious families of farmers, were being ruined by the vilest alcohol. As a result, the coarsest immorality, blood-curdling outrages, and inhuman cruelty were the order of the day.

A Period of Vice and Outrage

Captain Hunter, the second Governor, was unable to check these evils during the term of his office, which he held from September, 1795, to 1800. He certainly put an end to the tyranny of the military, and re-established the civil courts which had long been in abeyance. He also, as far as possible, suppressed the distilling of spirits in the colony, and checked the general immorality. But the evils were by this time too deeply rooted to be eradicated so quickly by a somewhat imprudent man like Hunter. Drunkenness therefore continued rife, as did the ordinary quarrels of the whites among themselves and with the natives. Even the enormous tracts of country which Hunter's predecessors had distributed to civil servants and military officers remained in their possession, as well as the excessive number of convicts, whom they ruled despotically like slaves.

THE SECOND GOVERNOR
Captain Hunter, who tried, with some success, to reduce the early convict colony to law and order.

It would, however, be unjust if we judged Hunter's administration by this one side of it; on the contrary, it distinctly promoted the development of the colony in more than one department. The cultivation of large tracts, which was compulsorily enforced by the owners, did much to relieve the scarcity of food—the chief misfortune of the colony up to the nineteenth century; but, on the other hand, it placed the monopoly of all economic advantages in the hands of a few. These were indeed the two objects that Major Grose had contemplated when he made similar regulations in his time.

The two new achievements by which Hunter's term of office was honourably distinguished are more partial, but not less important in results. Firstly, under him the knowledge of the geography of the continent was widened. This was due to the voyage of Mr. Bass, a naval surgeon, which proved clearly that Van Diemen's Land was an island ; to the first explora-

ORIGINATOR OF SHEEP-FARMING
John MacArthur, who established Australia's chief industry.

tion of the Blue Mountains ; and to the discovery of coal seams near Point Solander. It was also found that the cattle which had run away in the early days of the colonisation had begun to multiply into large herds of half-wild animals ; and in this way it was proved that the supposed impossibility of acclimatising cattle did not in fact exist.

The introduction of systematic sheep farming with a view to the wool, which is now one of the most important branches of industry on the continent, is inseparably connected with the name of John MacArthur. During the whole of the unedifying struggle between the Governor and the military, this officer had been the most vigorous representative of the movement in favour of making and selling spirits. He was altogether a shrewd and practical man, to whom among other things the Australian wine trade owes its origin. In 1794 MacArthur procured sixty Bengal sheep from Calcutta, to which he shortly added some Irish sheep. By crossing, he created a breed whose fleeces were a mixture of hair and wool. In 1797, in order to produce a finer wool, he obtained, through the agency of some friendly naval officers, a few sheep from Cape Town. These were, as it happened, fine merinos, a God-send to the continent, for these few animals, and some ordinary Cape sheep, which were subsequently added, were the progenitors of immense flocks, and the foundation of the present wealth of Australia.

The results of MacArthur's breeding were prodigious. When in 1801, in consequence of a duel with a fellow officer, he was ordered to England, he took back specimens of the wool he had grown himself and put them before experts in London. Their verdict was most favourable. MacArthur's proposal, that land and convicts should be assigned him in Australia with the definite object of providing the English woollen industry with Australian material on a wholesale scale, was favourably answered in October, 1804. Lord Camden, the new Secretary of State, instructed the Governor of New South Wales to concede to MacArthur 5,000 acres in perpetuity for grazing purposes, to give him convicts as shepherds, and to afford him generally every possible assistance. The Governor thereupon issued a proclamation, in which the concession of tracts for sheep farming or cattle breeding was publicly announced. MacArthur himself received the land he selected in the best part of the colony, on Mount Taurus in the cow pasture district, where the half-wild herds of cattle had been found in 1795. There with his original

State Help to Encourage Sheep-farming

The New South Wales Corps was more powerful than ever in the country, and had just given a proof of its influence in London by effecting the recall of his predecessor. As might be expected, the brandy trade was in full swing ; not less than 20,000 gallons were stored in Sydney alone. Even of other wares the civil and military officers had a practical monopoly, which was exceedingly remunerative to them, though it did not bring in the 1,200 per cent. which the spirits paid. King's first step was to check this abuse. Empowered by the Government in London to make the landing of spirits in Port Jackson dependent on his consent, he prohibited, in the autumn of 1800, their importation and sale without a special permission. All that came by ship in defiance of this order

PORT JACKSON, THE HARBOUR OF SYDNEY, FIFTY YEARS AGO
One of the finest natural ports in the world, the first Governor, Phillip, having truthfully reported that in it "a thousand sail of the line may ride in the most perfect security."

flock, augmented by purchases in England and Australia, he established his breeding farm, which he called Camden Estate, in honour of the Secretary of State. This became the centre of the new and rapidly flourishing wool-growing industry.

Since 1800 the Governor had been Philip Gidley King, a man who seemed more qualified than anyone else to rescue from the quicksands the misdirected fortunes of the Australian colonisation. King is the same man whom we have already met with as Vice-governor of Norfolk Island, where he had had displayed excellent qualities in his ten years' struggle against the deficiencies of Nature and the insubordination of his charges. The inheritance to which he succeeded was not hopeful.

was either sent back again—in one year, according to Zimmerman, no less than 32,000 gallons of spirits and 22,000 gallons of wine, although the number of adults in the colony was only 4,200—or was bought by King and sold again at a cheap price. The cheapness ensured only that the usurious trading profits ceased. It is easy to conceive the reception which the measures of King found among the members of the New South Wales Corps, especially when we consider what a strong backing they had in London. Owing to the perpetual European wars the import of Spanish wool to London had come to a standstill, so that the proposals of MacArthur to provide the industry with raw material from Australia

Energetic Suppression of Abuses

were thankfully adopted. MacArthur himself obtained a splendid position at home through it, as did the entire New South Wales Corps, whose most influential member he was. Notwithstanding the exasperation of the corps, things did not go so far as open hostility to the Governor. The corps certainly made the Governor's life as unpleasant as possible through the infringement of his regulations in a thousand ways, while King retaliated by limiting the authority of the regiment to purely military affairs. But this did not prevent the Governor from honourably and honestly helping MacArthur in his efforts in wool-growing. Nevertheless the perpetual friction was quite enough to induce King to resign his responsible post in July, 1805. He retired without expecting or receiving thanks from the Home Government, which had always listened to his opponents more attentively than to him. He might, however, take the consciousness with him that he had done good service to the colony.

Suppressing Military Monopolies The survey of the western part of the south and east coasts between Cape Stephens (33° S.) and Cape Palmerston (22° S.) which was carried out during King's term of office, as well as the exploration of the Gulf of Carpentaria by Matthew Flinders, were valuable additions to geography, and important for later colonisation. The formal annexation of the continent by means of extensive schemes of settlement was his work. This step was necessitated by the unceasing efforts of the French to gain a firm footing in Australia. King, indeed, impressed upon the French explorers the prescriptive rights of England, but at the same time he thought it expedient to make these rights patent to all by an immediate colonisation of different places. In 1803 Van Diemen's Land was occupied, while, simul-

GOVERNOR KING
One of the capable early Governors of the penal colony, whose tenure of office was beset with difficulties.

taneously with the removal of the convicts, who constituted a common danger, two settlements were founded at Restdown, or Risdon, on the left bank, and Hobart Town on the right bank, of the Derwent. At the same time the first, but unsuccessful, attempt at colonisation from London was made at Port Phillip, the great bay on which Melbourne now lies ; and, lastly, the foundations were laid of Launceston, on the north coast of Van Diemen's Land, and of Newcastle, now the second harbour of New South Wales.

King might also be satisfied with the results of national industries at the end of his career. On the departure of Phillip in 1792, about 1,700 acres were under permanent cultivation, and the number of domestic animals could hardly be reckoned in dozens. In 1796, a year after Hunter's arrival, the number of such animals had reached 5,000, and there were 5,400 acres under the plough. In August, 1798, the figures were 6,000 acres and 10,000 head of cattle ; for August, 1799, 8,000 acres and 11,000 head. The white population had amounted to 4,000 souls when Hunter entered on office. On his retirement in 1800, their number was, according to Mossman, 6,000. Under King's five years of government this inheritance had developed into the following dimensions. In 1806, according to Zimmerman, 165,882 acres had been given

RESIDENCE OF GOVERNOR KING IN 1804
The Governor's house was situated on Rose Hill in the township of Parramatta. In the foreground on the right of the picture the stocks may be seen.

GENERAL VIEW OF THE TOWN OF SYDNEY AS IT WAS IN THE YEAR 1800

away in estates or reserved for the Crown ; of these, 20,000 acres were cleared ; 6,000 acres were planted with wheat, 4,000 with maize, 1,000 with barley, 185 with potatoes, 433 served as garden ground. Of the districts allotted, 15,620 acres were held by civil officials, 20,697 by officers ; 18,666 acres were the property of 405 " emancipists." There were 112 free settlers ; in addition, there were 80 discharged sailors and soldiers, and 13 persons born in the colony. The number of stock was as follows : 566 horses, 4,790 cattle, 23,110 sheep, 2,283 goats, 7,019 pigs ; altogether, 37,768 head. The white population amounted to 9,462 persons in 1806. Of these there were 5,172 men, 1,701 women, and 2,589 children.

The successor of King, nominated in 1805, was William Bligh, long well known in geographical circles for the wonderful voyage in the course of which he traversed **Captain of the Bounty** in an open boat large portions of the Pacific and Indian oceans. Being commissioned, as captain of the ship Bounty, to transplant the bread-fruit tree from Tahiti to the West Indies, he had caused such discontent among the crew by his terrible severity that in the middle of the voyage they placed him with eighteen companions in a boat, in which he eventually reached Batavia, while the rest of the crew either returned to Tahiti or founded on Pitcairn Island the small community which has been so often described.

Bligh's marvellous rescue had not deprived his character of any of its original roughness. As commander of a man-of-war he had provoked a mutiny of the crew by his tyranny, and in New South Wales, also, where he arrived in the middle of August, 1806, he contrived to make himself unpopular from the first by his inhuman severity. He was not, indeed, deficient in an honourable intention of **Tyranny of the Governor** promoting the interests of the colony, which now showed such promise ; but he lacked a proper comprehension of his duties. Caprice of every sort, brutal floggings even of free settlers, the razing of houses of which the position dissatisfied him, the compulsory removal of colonists in 1807 from Norfolk Island to Van Diemen's Land—all these were measures which made the new Governor hated. He also by such acts repelled the better class of people, so that he was surrounded with persons of ill-repute in their place.

The episode which brought the ill-feeling to a head is, as Mr. Jenks expresses it in his " History of the Australasian Colonies," " the most picturesque incident in the early history of the colony." In accordance with his instructions, which required him to continue the measures directed by King against the excessive power of the New South Wales Corps, and, above all, to proceed against the still flourishing brandy trade, Bligh had issued an edict in February, 1807, which absolutely

1037

prohibited the making and sale of spirits, and forbade the erection of distilling apparatus on private property.

Now, MacArthur had ordered some distilling apparatus from England, in connection with his attempts at vine culture. This was taken from him and sent back by the orders of the Governor. The **Historic Australian Quarrel** strained relations thus produced between the two men were aggravated by Bligh's accusation that MacArthur had received his 5,000 acres of pasture land by supplying false information. MacArthur's self-justification by reference to the order of the Privy Council was finally answered by Bligh with a command to appear in court, because a convict had fled to one of the breeder's ships. MacArthur refused to pay the fine, and the Governor seized his schooner. MacArthur desisted from supplying the crew with food. The unfortunate sailors therefore landed in defiance of a port regulation. This was enough for Bligh, who at once arrested the crew, and MacArthur for "causing them to commit an illegal act." Even if Bligh had law upon his side, yet his sharp procedure was unwise in view of MacArthur's honourable position.

The indignation of the New South Wales Corps at once vented itself in action. At the instigation of the officers, Major Johnston liberated the prisoner on January 26th, 1808, occupied Government House, and, agreeably to the wish of MacArthur and other prominent colonists, declared the Governor deposed, and sent him as a prisoner on board a ship lying in the harbour. All the executive officials who had supported the Governor were dismissed or arrested, the colony was put under martial law, and, for almost two years, until the arrival of the new Governor on December 31st, 1809, was administered by Johnston and the members of his corps. MacArthur himself, on a fresh hearing of the case, was unanimously acquitted.

The attitude of the British Government toward the unpleasant incident was long in making itself known. The tidings of what had happened had reached England by the end of the year, but there every-one was so occupied with the Napoleonic wars that another year elapsed before any steps against the rebels were decided upon. Lachlan Macquarie was entrusted with the mission. Johnston was brought back to England under strict arrest on a charge of mutiny. All the appointments and assignments of land which had been made after Bligh's arrest were declared null and void, and all the old officials were reinstated. Bligh, who was still living on his ship in Australia, was recognised as Governor, but immediately recalled and replaced by Macquarie. MacArthur was finally expelled from the country. He thus had the hardest lot ; keenly interested in its industrial welfare, he was compelled to remain for years far away from the country and his undertakings. It was not until 1817 that he was allowed to return to his Camden Estate. Johnston fared better, since, thanks to the representations made by Macquarie to the proper quarters as to Bligh's character and method of governing, he was merely cashiered. Honours were finally showered upon Bligh himself in England. He became Vice-admiral of the Blue, and a Fellow of the Royal Society. He died on December 7th, 1817.

GOVERNOR BLIGH
The captain of the Bounty and the most tyrannous governor of the early Australian settlements.

Macquarie had not come across from England alone. On the contrary, he brought a whole line regiment of soldiers with him. This meant nothing less than a complete change of system. The New South Wales Corps was incorporated into the English Army and withdrawn from Australia for ever ; the Governor henceforth had at his disposal disciplined Regulars instead of a corps which had been **Military Problem Solved** ruined by twenty years' sojourn in a penal colony. Macquarie had generally a much easier position than any of his predecessors. Twenty years of work had produced valuable results, notwithstanding all hindrances and cessations, and after King's careful tenure of office the colony had made great advances in prosperity. In 1810 there were already 11,590 white colonists ; 7,615 acres were under the plough ; the number of cattle reached 12,442, that of sheep 25,888 ; the taxes brought in nearly £8,000 annually.

Under these favourable conditions the energy of Macquarie could be principally devoted to matters of a positive and executive nature, as was most in keeping with his disposition. In this respect he was the direct opposite of Bligh, whose abilities were merely directed toward the repression of abuses, while he displayed no sort of talent for organisation. Macquarie's first care was to establish well-regulated conditions in Sydney. He nearly rebuilt the town ; the construction of new streets, the organisation of police, the erection of public buildings, especially schools and churches, the laying out of promenades—all this is his work. In 1816 the first bank was set up, followed three years later by a savings bank. He made it his object to construct good roads in the vicinity of the town, as well as to regulate the courses of the rivers. He especially encouraged the cultivation of the soil in every direction, and not least so by extreme liberality in grants of land. This liberality, coupled with the extensive demands for public— that is to say, home—assistance for his reforms, exposed him even then to much censure, both in England and Australia.

Macquarie's efforts to extend the range of colonisation were not less meritorious than his attempts to raise the moral tone and develop the industries within the colony itself. His four predecessors had all been sailors, whose interest in geography was exhausted by voyages of discovery along the coast. The contour and shape of the Australian continent had, it is true, been definitely ascertained by them, but **Exploration of the Interior** for a full quarter of a century after the landing in Botany Bay nothing more was known of the interior than the narrow strip of land between the coast and the Blue Mountains looming in the west, which had always been considered impassable. Macquarie urged the colonists to new efforts, and finally, in 1813, Wentworth, Blaxland, and Lawson discovered a way through the mountains, and found beyond them immense plains of fertile

country. Macquarie, in spite of the hundreds of miles of most difficult ground between Sydney and the new territory, at once set about constructing a road, which was ready to be opened in 1815. At the same time the town of Bathurst was founded as the centre of the newly opened up country, which soon became **Swelling Tide of Prosperity** the seat of a brisk wheat-growing industry and the source of the rapid prosperity of the colony. New South Wales owed this renewed prosperity largely to the favourable period at which its discovery and exploitation had taken place. With the close of the Napoleonic wars, England's hands were untied ; even private persons revived their interest in the oversea possessions. New South Wales now became the goal of a continuously swelling stream of emigration, which added to the existing settlers a large percentage of free colonists, who were either time-expired soldiers or discharged convicts.

Macquarie himself was by no means friendly to the newcomers. From the very first he supported the view " Australia for the convict," and tried by every means to check the influx of free immigrants. In 1818 he actually carried a measure by which these latter were deprived of the free passage which had been customary since the founding of the colony. The results turned out quite otherwise from what Macquarie expected. The small man indeed kept away, but not the man of means. The latter, however, could at once set to work on a large scale. He required only to buy sheep, the Government supplied him with land and with convicts as shepherds. Thus he became a large landed proprietor ; but the convict was not the least helped by Macquarie's measures. In spite of all his popularity, the obvious favour which he showed to the emancipists provoked a feeling against him among the free settlers.

A special commissioner, Mr. Bigge, was sent from England in 1818 to make an inquiry into the condition of the colony and the administration of the government, and on the receipt of his report in 1821—

GOVERNOR MACQUARIE
One of the wisest Governors of the early colony and the maker and organiser of Sydney as a town.

which still remains the best authority for the condition of the colony since the departure of Governor Bligh—Governor Macquarie was recalled. The unfavourable attitude of the Government towards him was intensified by the outcry of the great landed proprietors. These claimed wide tracts of land for their grazing farms ; but

Recall of a Governor the Governor was pledged to support the small proprietors who had been convicts previously. This was sufficient incentive to the now powerful wool industry to advocate the recall of Macquarie, which took place in 1821.

Macquarie had still more reason to be satisfied with his results than King. Even the statistics presented a quite different aspect. In 1821 the white population of the colony was estimated roughly at 39,000 souls ; 32,267 acres were under cultivation ; there were 103,000 head of cattle, 4,564 horses, and more than 250,000 sheep. The annual revenue of the community was £30,000 sterling. Besides this, internal affairs were splendidly organised, and there was confident hope that the stream of immigration would not dry up. In short, the departing Governor might fairly feel that it was his own diligent activity for eleven years that had extricated Australia from her seemingly hopeless position in the swamp of corruption.

Macquarie's entrance into office had brought with it a change of system in the administration, and a similar change signalised his departure. The former had substituted the civil administration for the military ; the latter put the beginnings of a constitution in the place of the autocracy. All the governors of the colony had been hitherto practically despotic ; they had marked out the methods of colonisation according to their own judgment, and embodied in themselves the legislative power ; they were indeed the ultimate court of appeal. They were, it is true, responsible to the British Secre-

Beginning of a Constitution tary of State for War and the Colonies ; but London was far away, and the political situation in Europe guaranteed sufficiently that too much notice would not be taken of Australia. Bligh's motto, " My will is the law," is characteristic of this view. So long as the majority of the population consisted of convicts or was descended from them, unlimited authority might be concentrated in one hand ; but as soon

as the free population predominated, this situation was impossible. Even in 1812 the creation of a board of assessors, composed of officials and colonists, had been suggested, but Macquarie had considered that such an institution, which had proved its value in all other English colonies, was unsuitable for Australia.

After his departure, the limitation of the power of the Governor was an accomplished fact. The New South Wales Judiciary Act, which received the Royal Assent on July 19th, 1823, adopted most of the recommendations of Bigge's report. A Legislative Council of not more than seven or less than five members, nominated by the Governor, was created, but its functions were purely advisory, although the Governor's power to impose taxes was limited to taxes for local purposes. If the Council disapproved of the Governor's action, its objections were submitted to England, where the Colonial Office gave a final decision. In the one case of a rebellion the Governor had dictatorial power.

On the legal side, the reforms were also extensive. Hitherto the Governor had been

Legal Reforms Introduced the highest court of appeal in all questions of law ; now these were absolutely withdrawn from his decision in favour of a supreme court of judicature on the English model, and the jury system was introduced. The only right retained by the Governor was the remission of sentences on criminals, subject to the approval of the English Government. The first Governor who ruled under these new forms was Sir Thomas Brisbane (1821–1825), but that they were strictly adhered to and achieved the results intended was entirely due to the accident which caused the appointment to the first Chief Justiceship to be in favour of a sound and fearless constitutional lawyer. To Francis Forbes is due the subordination of the executive to the law, and the firm application of the British legal principle that a wrongdoer cannot plead in justification the command of a superior officer. Thanks to Forbes, the administration of Sir Thomas Brisbane kept strictly within the limits imposed on the Governor ; but, in compensation, he devoted his chief attention to the further exploration and opening up of the country. The course of the Murray and Murrumbidgee was now traced ; the country was traversed diagonally as far as the south coast in the vicinity of modern Melbourne, the shores of

Queensland and North Australia were explored, and the continent secured from the renewed designs of the French by settlements on various outlying points. The first observatory on Australian soil was constructed by Brisbane at Parramatta.

Brisbane gave the perpetually increasing number of free immigrants the land for grazing purposes free, and conceded to the Australian Agricultural Company, founded in England in 1824 with a capital of £1,000,000, not less than 1,000,000 acres of land near Port Stephens and in the Liverpool Plains. He encouraged production and trade in every way; in 1825 there were 45,514 acres under cultivation; more than 4,000 cwt. of wool was exported, and some thirty Australian ships were engaged in fishery and commerce. The incomings (over £70,000 sterling) had more than doubled since 1821.

Two other important and essentially different events fall into the term of Brisbane's office: the separation of the island of Van Diemen's Land from New South Wales, and the official declaration of the freedom of the Press. The former was decreed in 1823, and took effect in 1825; the latter was announced in 1824, but its actual application was postponed until the administration of Bourke.

Brisbane's successor was another military officer, Sir Ralph Darling, who ruled the destinies of the colony from 1825–1831. His lot was not cast in easy times. As a legacy from his predecessor he inherited a difficulty with the colonial Press, which was unrestrained in its attacks upon the measures of Government, and exercised a dangerous influence upon the convicts. By the Constitution of 1823 it was provided that no Bill should become law

without the certificate of the Chief Justice that it was not repugnant to the laws of England. Immediately upon his arrival Governor Darling, acting upon instructions from England, carried a measure imposing an annual licence upon newspapers. Forbes, who sympathised with the views of the paper principally aimed at by the measure in favour of an extension of popular government, refused his certificate. Darling retaliated by a measure imposing penalties for the publication of seditious or blasphemous matter and another putting a duty upon newspapers. Forbes again refused his certificate. The dispute was ended by the new Constitution of 1828, which gave wider legislative powers to the Council established in 1823 and increased its numbers to fifteen. The necessity for the Chief Justice's certificate was abolished.

Darling at once reintroduced a Newspaper Bill, the harsher provisions of which were subsequently modified at the instance of the British Government. The new Council also dealt with the jury question and a law passed excluding emancipists from serving on criminal juries. By a Rule of Court of the same year the professions of barrister and attorney were formally divided, and regulations drawn up governing admission to them. This Constitution Act also abolished the Grand Jury and substituted in its place the Attorney-General, "in whose name all offenders should be prosecuted by information."

This system continues to the present day. Darling's recall was due to an unfounded attack upon him, engineered by the Press. The charges were investigated in Sydney and by a Parliamentary Committee in London, and Darling was absolutely acquitted of all wrongdoing. But before his character was thus cleared he had quitted Australia.

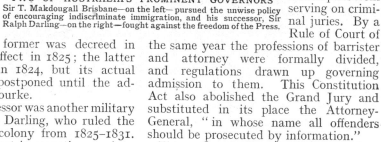

TWO OF AUSTRALIA'S PROMINENT GOVERNORS
Sir T. Makdougall Brisbane—on the left—pursued the unwise policy of encouraging indiscriminate immigration, and his successor, Sir Ralph Darling—on the right—fought against the freedom of the Press.

THE DAWN OF A NATION
AND DEVELOPMENT OF NEW SOUTH WALES

THE period 1831–43 marks a transition from the old to the new in the history of the colony. The abuses of officialdom are curbed. Free settlers are already more numerous than bond. The country is settling into the normal conditions of English life. Capital in abundance has flowed into the country ; and merchants share with pastoralists the responsibility for public affairs which is felt instinctively by the leaders of society in any British community. Consequently we read less of squabbles with the Governor, and more of movements and policies.

The first sign of national self-consciousness was a demand to control the public lands. Previously to 1824 lands had been practically given away at the Governor's will, the only incumbrance being an insignificant quit rent and the obligation to employ one convict to every hundred acres. Governor Brisbane had made these conditions more stringent and had abolished free grants. But the demand for land increased, as Bigge's report made the favourable conditions of Colonial life more widely known. In 1824 the Colonial Office directed that 5s. per acre should be the upset price of land and that no one person should be allowed to purchase more than 9,600 acres.

The object of this limitation was to suppress the speculation in land which was then rampant. The land was to be reserved for bonâ fide settlers, and, further, only so much was to be cultivated as the needs of the colony required. The object finally was to look to the future with its growing claims for land. The results did not correspond to the unwearying solicitude of the Government. On Darling's departure, the area of the land sold or leased amounted to 3,422,000 acres, which obviously could not be kept entirely under cultivation by the 51,155 white colonists. In the short period from 1831 to 1835, this number

The Land Question

Evils of Squatting on the Land

increased by no less than 585,000 acres, which had been purchased by auction. The Government had realised by this sale the sum of £202,600 ; but it could not fail to see that only the smaller part of these estates had been bought with the immediate object of cultivation ; the vast majority were merely bought as a speculation. This applied to the 1,548,700 acres, which had been publicly sold in the years 1836 to 1840.

The area expressed by these figures was far too gigantic to be required by the real demand for land, notwithstanding the brisk immigration of those years. Nevertheless these figures testify to the enormous impetus which was then given to the prosperity of the colony, a prosperity which was indeed interrupted at the opening of the " forties " by a disastrous industrial crisis. Its beginnings were foreshadowed in the figures for the years 1839 and 1840 : 1836, 389,500 ; 1837, 368,600 ; 1838, 315,300 ; 1839, 285,900 ; 1840, 189,400 acres.

Hardly less than the trouble caused by the speculative purchaser of land was that which arose from the common practice of " squatting." This is a word which originally came from North America; but the practice designated by the word proved more important for the development of Australia than for the history of the United States. This process of squatting was extremely simple ; sheep or cattle breeders, on their own responsibility, without any authorisation, and without payment of purchase money or quit-rent, took possession of tracts of country for grazing purposes, and thus withdrew them from any possibility of being legally divided among later candidates.

It was in the first place essential for the squatter's trade of stock breeding that the " run " which he appropriated should cover a large extent of country.

Moreover, if endless quarrels and disputes were to be prevented among the owners of the herds, no other expedient was left for them except that of all pastoral societies under simple conditions, indeed of all primitive farming generally; that is to say, since the country offered no natural boundaries, and there was no inclination, time or means to erect artificial boundaries, a clear demarcation was obtained by leaving broad tracts unused between the separate estates. There was in fact a reversion to the most primitive type of boundary; that which consists of a strip or border of land. It is a type still to be found in the case of African village communities, which are often surrounded by zones of wilderness or forest; it was prevalent in Europe of the Dark Ages, and some German villages had boundaries of this kind down to the time of the Hohenstaufen dynasty.

The most complicated difficulties were thus produced for the Government. It had declared at home that the whole continent was its property, and all land belonged to the Crown. In this way it possessed the incontestable right to dispose of the land at pleasure; but, on the other hand, the equally incontestable obligation was imposed on it of directing its distribution in such a way that all who shared in the most important duty of developing the colony—mother country, Colonial Government, and settlers alike—might have their rights secured. This was, however, no easy task, owing to the conflict of interests between large landed proprietors and small farmers, between cattle breeding and agriculture, which had rapidly been produced under the squatter system.

The " squatting " difficulty presented itself to Sir Richard Bourke (1831–1838) **Attempt to Settle the Land Question** as that which pressed most urgently for a solution. Unwitting that Australia had not reached that stage in her development when small holdings were desirable, and that the carrying capacity of unimproved land for sheep—which had now become the mainstay of the colony—was not more than a sheep to five acres, he

SIR RICHARD BOURKE
This Governor's unfortunate attempt to solve the land question contributed to the grant of a constitution in 1842.

endeavoured to discourage the holding of large " runs." Undoubtedly the system had led to abuses; but in the absence of a plentiful supply of labour pastoral occupation is practicable only over large **An Unwise Decree** tracts. As a beginning to clear his path the Governor issued a decree declaring that no one could acquire or had acquired any title to Crown Lands by mere occupancy; and, in 1837, made the right to squat dependent on the payment of a fee of £10 annually. Whoever paid it had a right to settle on any unoccupied lands. This was resented by the party of self-government as being arbitrary taxation, and was one of the causes which led to the Constitution of 1842.

One of the measures adopted by Sir Richard Bourke, on the recommendation of his Council, had a disastrous effect in encouraging speculation in land. Possessed of the Old World idea that men would not go far to occupy land if they could own a freehold nearer the capital, the Governor was persuaded that the upset price of 5s. per acre was too high and induced squatting. He was, therefore, empowered to reduce this to any lower minimum he thought fit.

As might be expected, even these arrangements did not remove all the deficiencies which are connected with a young pastoral industry. Stock, indeed, flourished, and their profits were enormous. In 1839 there were reckoned to be a quarter of a million of cattle and more than a million sheep. The revenue of the colony was also materially increased by the grazing tax, then fixed at £10 annually, to which were added payments of one penny for every sheep, threepence for every ox, and sixpence for every horse; and the enterprising spirit of the sheep farmers alone had made the colony economically independent. Of the export trade, which had risen in 1840 to £5,000,000 sterling, by far the greater part was due to the wool industry.

But two drawbacks of the system are incontestable: firstly, the uniformity of the tax brought great grievances with it; and, secondly, pastoral enterprise on a large scale, the form of industry which alone was encouraged by it, exercised a far-reaching, but not beneficial influence on the entire social development of the white population of the continent. The right to occupy land thus depended on the payment of the fee, but after that the choice of locality as well as the quantity **Enormous** of land were entirely in the **Land** discretion of the colonist. **Holdings** Under these circumstances, most of the estates were far larger than was required to graze the stock of the owner, even if full weight is given to the often pleaded excuse of the growth of the herds ; and properties as large as a German principality were not uncommon. This mattered little, so long as free land was available and to spare. But when the supply grew limited these enormous estates were felt to be hindrances on colonisation, and the more oppressively so since the gross disproportion between the holdings was now obvious to all.

A few instances show for what the proclamation of 1837 is responsible in this respect. Apart from the inconsiderately large assignment of land to the Australian Agricultural Company—one million acres—and the gifts to the officers and the officials of the New South Wales Corps, the concessions of land in the first decades of the century had been confined within very modest limits. Even the most wealthy man could not call more than a few hundred acres his own. How different was the position of the pastoral kings of the 'forties and 'fifties ! When Governor Gipps, in 1845, made a searching inquiry into the property of some colonists, he ascertained that in one district eight persons with eight licences occupied 1,747,000 acres, while in the same part nine others with nine licences had only (!) 311,000 acres. The four largest stock breeders of the colony owned 7,750,000 acres—that is to say, they were masters of a territory nearly twice the size of Yorkshire.

The colossal size of such tracts of property could not but be harmful to the community. The pastoral industry requires, on the one hand, immense tracts ; on the other, and especially under the favourable climatic conditions of Australia, it has no use for a large supply of labour ; even the largest sheep farmers retain very few hands in permanent employment. The immediate result is a twofold **Australian** loss to the entire population. **Economic** The wool clip brings large sums **Conditions** of money into the country, which, instead of circulating, remain in the hands of a few, and thus encourages capitalism. Closely connected with this is the impossibility of raising the density of the population above a certain minimum rate. Where hardly a dozen hands are employed on hundreds of square miles, and where, further, the settlement of other independent colonists would diminish

CHARACTERISTIC SCENE ON THE PASTURE LANDS OF NEW SOUTH WALES

the profits of the sheep owner, it is impossible for the population to become dense. As a matter of fact, even at the present day, the rural population of the interior is trifling in comparison with that of the towns on the coast.

Still more serious, however, than all these defects in the Regulations of 1837 was the immunity of the greater part of the land to which claim was laid from the payment of the grazing tax, since it inevitably jarred upon the popular idea of justice. A man who was fortunate, or sufficiently unscrupulous, could acquire a kingdom for his £10, while his neighbour could call only a few clods his own. As a matter of fact, the owner of the above-mentioned gigantic tracts had not paid a penny more than any other colonist who had obtained land after the promulgation of the regulations. Sir George Gipps, who had been at the head of affairs in Sydney since 1838, attempted to check the extension of squatting, and issued a proclamation with retrospective force, by which every squatter was bound, for the purpose of

THE HOME OF AN EARLY SQUATTER

at a time when there was no labour for intension culture. The only result was to stimulate the purchase of land, in which too much of the colony's capital was already locked up. Sir George Gipps, however, carried the day. He impressed upon the Home Government that the continuance of the practice which had hitherto obtained would soon deprive the Crown of all available land; and by this argument, and by proving that the greatest outcry was made by the largest landed proprietors, he succeeded in upholding his enactments; only in small points was any consideration shown to the squatters. In 1892, a new law was promulgated which fixed the minimum price for an acre at £1 sterling. The sales of land fell off still more. In 1843, 4,800 acres, and in 1844 only 4,200 acres, were sold. It was only when the crisis ended that these figures improved once more to 7,200 acres in 1845, and 7,000 acres in 1846.

The change for the better coincides with the fall of the Ministry of Peel on June 26th, 1846. The

LATER STYLE OF SQUATTER'S RESIDENCE

maintaining his existing title to his property, to buy at least 320 acres of land by auction; any improvement to the land would be taken into consideration. If he did not do this, he exposed himself to the risk of being ousted from his position by any other squatter who had conformed to the prescribed conditions.

This proclamation met with the worst possible reception from the people. Three hundred and twenty acres, which form a large farm in Europe, could not in most parts of Australia support a single family

new Colonial Secretary, Earl Grey, at once returned to the old paths and allowed the concession of pasturage rights for fourteen years, with the right of pre-emption. At the same time the regulations as to the recovery of the quit-rent were considerably modified. The land legislation in the succeeding year went still farther in this direction, since, on March 9, 1847, the Governor of New South Wales received authority to let, in the uncolonised districts, tracts of 16,000 or 32,000 acres for eight or fourteen years. Each lessee received with his contract the right to acquire 640 acres at the fixed price of £640 sterling as a homestead, and to have the lease renewed after the expiration of the fourteen years for a further term of five years. The rent was based on the number of the head of stock; a run which **Conditions** was large enough for 4,000 **of Land** sheep was to cost £10 sterling. **Acquisition** The lease at the same time gave the lessee the right of pre-emption. The land question in New South Wales thus obtained its definite settlement for a decade and a half. On the whole, it cannot be denied that the proclamation of 1844 was bound to injure the colony if we reflect on the bad economic conditions of Australia. This was intimately connected with another question, the difficulty of obtaining labour.

During the first four decades of Australian history the demand for labour was adequately satisfied by the assignment of convicts to settlers. But in 1822, in consequence of the publication of Bigge's Report, the immigration of freemen began to assume large proportions; but the increased demand for land more than absorbed the additional supply. Wages, which had been a matter for Government regulation, began to be determined by the market rate. The distance from Europe had acted as a protective duty, and led to the establishment of manufacturing of woollen cloth, hats, earthenware, pipes, salt, candles, soap, beer, leather, and many other articles in common use, so that Wentworth, writing in 1819, and not foreseeing the cheapening of freights, anticipated that the time was near when the necessity of importing manufactured goods from England would cease. Mr. Tregarthen, who writes upon this subject with special knowledge, estimates that "previous to 1836 the average daily wage of mechanics in building trades was almost 6s. 6d., and farm and other labourers, taking one year with another, were paid at the rate of about £18 per annum, with food and lodging."

During the years following 1836, larger numbers of free immigrants came to Australia, bringing with them a higher standard

SIR GEORGE GIPPS
This Governor's efforts to settle the question of land tenure were ill-advised and caused great discontent.

of living, and consequently a desire for better wage than that previously paid. Competition with convict labour had hitherto so degraded the free workers that, as a rule, they were willing to live upon a wage so small as compared with the current prices of commodities as to render it impossible for them to maintain even a semblance of decency, to say nothing of comfort, and even after the class of assigned servants had been largely diluted by free immigration, the convicts, emancipated or bond, comprised one-third of the total population, and had a proportionate influence on the labour market. But as the colony grew, and the demands of the settlers for assigned servants became far in excess of the supply, the influence of the convict element was to a great extent removed. Wages rapidly rose, and about four years after the arrival of the first assisted settlers the prospects of the working classes greatly improved.

The commercial crisis of 1843, which shook the very foundations of the new settlement, was, like all such crises, the sign of a legitimate but over-strained prosperity. The success of the colony in attracting immigrants proved for a time its undoing. By the advice of his Council, Sir Richard Bourke set apart the proceeds of land sales as a fund for paying the expenses of free immigrants, who, in consequence, entered the colony in a steady flow after 1837.

" The new arrivals were greedily looked for and warmly welcomed by the settlers, and all industrial pursuits revived amazingly. With the increase of enterprise, wages rose, and the standard of living was greatly improved. The thrifty and industrious found that, with the expenditure of the same amount of energy which was **The Influx** required at home to keep the **of Labour** wolf from the door, they could **and Capital** earn sufficient to live in comparative comfort and luxury. Glowing accounts went to England of the magnificent prospects of the colony, while the demands of the increased and more industrious population caused a rapid expansion of trade and commerce. The eyes of European capitalists were attracted to Australia as a possible field for the profitable investment of their money, and capital soon began to flow into the country with a stream relatively greater than even the stream of immigration. There were already two large banks in existence, the Bank of New South Wales and the Bank of Australia ; now four new banks were established, to say nothing of other loan and trust companies. With increased facilities for borrowing came an increased desire to borrow, and enormous transactions in land and live-stock took place all over the country, payment usually being made by long-dated bills on one or other of the banks. The prospects of the colony seemed excellent and fascinating, dreams of rapidly acquired fortunes began to float before the eyes of farmer, pastoralist, and merchant alike."

In this feverish condition of affairs the Government policy of restricting land sales proved an additional factor of disturbance. Australia cannot be a country of small holdings, and English ideas on the proper size of an estate were ludicrously inadequate. The Secretary of State, no doubt, considered that a holding limited to 320 acres was a liberal allowance to any settler; while the Governor, not appreciating the almost unlimited extent of good land in the colony, feared to exhaust the Crown's domains. The consequence of this limitation of sales was to increase the price of private lands. In the meantime money was abundant ; four new banks had been established, making six in all, and each was eager for business. Advances were freely made—in many cases far in excess of the value of the mortgaged property. Mr. Tregarthen quotes an instance in which £10,000 had been lent by one bank, which only returned **Beginning of Financial Crisis** £100 per annum when taken over by the mortgagees. Meantime, wages increased and notes were replacing gold in currency. Finally, in 1843, the whole unsubstantial fabric collapsed.

"The men who had been living luxuriously on other people's money" —again we quote Tregarthen, because the passage describes equally well the

WILLIAM CHARLES WENTWORTH

A native of Australia and chief agitator for a constitution.

later crisis of 1892—" found themselves brought up with a round turn, and at once tried to realise what they could. Property upon property was forced into a market in which all were sellers and none buyers, and prices fell to ridiculous figures. The rebound was even more **A Time of Great Panic** unreasonable than the inflation. Sheep were sold by the sheriff's officer for sixpence per head, and large stations near Yass and on the Hunter River sold, land and all, at the price of about three shillings per head for the sheep which were on them ; cattle bought at six guineas each were parted with for three-and-sixpence per head. Houses and personal property all went the same way. Carriages, which in the prosperous days had cost £140, sold for £3, and were run as cabs by the servants of the late owners."

The national self-consciousness which found expressions in the effort to resume the use of Crown lands for the people generally was also manifested in a movement for constitutional reform. The party was headed by a young native of the colony, William Charles Wentworth, who had returned to Sydney upon taking his degree at Cambridge. Governor Bourke yielded one important step to Wentworth's demands in 1831 by consenting to place the estimates of expenditure before his Council. But he roused the ire of the reformers by his licence fee on squatters. Wentworth, at a public meeting in 1833, denounced this in correct style as " taxation without representation," and became president of a Patriotic Association, which was formed to secure self-government for the colony, and to that end petitioned the House of Commons and maintained a parliamentary agent in London. These representations so far prevailed that in 1842 the English Parliament passed a new Constitution for New South Wales. The Council was increased to thirty-six members, twenty-four of whom were to be elected, and District Councils were formed to administer the funds for the police and local works.

The new Council, which met in August, 1843, soon came into conflict with the

Governor, Sir George Gipps, over his Land Regulations. Wentworth declared the collection of licences to be "taxation by prerogative." Gipps, however, held to his own scheme and the dispute was still unsettled when he handed over the Governorship to Sir Charles Fitzroy (1846–1851), under whose rule the struggle for free institutions continued.

Agitation for a Constitution But before recounting the details of this struggle it will be convenient to group together the events connected with the successful opposition to convict importation, which was closely connected with the movement for self-government.

During the first four decades of the colonial development of Australia, the question whether the introduction of English convicts was useful or harmful did not come forward. It was only at the time when the free settlers began to outnumber the others, and the influx of respectable English countrymen produced an adequate supply of free labour, that a movement made itself felt in favour of checking or diverting the still numerous arrivals of criminals from the Old Country. In favour of this agitation was the noticeable fact that the presence of so many persons of low morality in the country had a most detrimental effect on the characters of both old and young. Out of 60,794 inhabitants of New South Wales, there were, in the year 1833, no fewer than 16,151 convicts, and in 1836, 27,831. Many of these, however, would return to England at the expiry of their sentence. The number of crimes and misdemeanours committed by these convicts reached an alarming figure. The colony received an annual subsidy of £200,000 to defray the cost of maintaining the convicts, and out of the subsidy there was a substantial balance available for public works. The system also meant cheap labour. But these were poor set-offs to the moral degradation for which the system was responsible—so at least thought one party of the colonists.

Evils of Convict Settlement At the same time, it had been observed that transportation was to blame for an increase of crimes. While the population of England had increased between 1805 and 1841 by 79 per cent., the number of crimes had risen by 482 per cent.; and from 1834 to 1845 as many as 38,844 prisoners were transported. Transportation, however, was not reckoned as a punishment in the circles which it concerned. It was owing to this movement that a commission appointed by the lower house recommended that the transportation of criminals to New South Wales and Van Diemen's Land should at once be discontinued, and expressed its opinion that it was desirable to facilitate the emigration of prisoners to other countries when they had served their sentences. These resolutions went too far for some Australians, although they had so often petitioned for the discontinuance of transportation. They feared to lose the cheap labour hitherto available, and begged, therefore, but without success, that the existing arrangement should be continued. The penal colony of Moreton Bay, established in 1826, was done away with in 1839; and on May 22nd, 1840, New South Wales was struck out from the list of countries to which prisoners could be transported. Only Van Diemen's Land and Norfolk Island retained temporarily their old character.

The new regulations did not, indeed, meet with universal assent; on the contrary, in consequence of the **Changes in the Penal System** renewed outbreak of wild speculation in land, and the loss suffered by the already permanently settled districts, violent demonstrations were made in these latter. The Government, however, had neither inclination nor time to destroy the work so laboriously brought to a close and to begin again; so the cries for alteration died away unheard.

But the Mother Country soon found a difficulty in obtaining room for her criminals when transportation to New South Wales was abolished. Van Diemen's Land was quickly overcrowded, and the plan of founding a new convict settlement in North Australia was shown to be impracticable. At the same time the thought of once more stocking with convicts the districts of East Australia, which had been so capable of receiving them for more than half a century, forced itself forward; and all the more so as the colony of Port Phillip, now Victoria, which had arisen meanwhile in the south, cried out loudly for cheap labour, and in New South Wales there were still land-owners who earnestly desired to see the restoration of the old condition of things, with its abundance of workers. Both encouraged the Home Government (1848)

THE DEVELOPMENT OF NEW SOUTH WALES

to resume the old policy. The Act of 1840 was repealed, and the institution of new penal colonies was contemplated.

Foremost in the movement against transportation was a young ivory-turner, who afterwards, as Sir Harry Parkes, was the founder of Parliamentary institutions in Australia, and subsequently of the Commonwealth. Public meetings of protest were held in Sydney; but Mr. Gladstone, then Secretary of State, was regardless of expressions of Colonial feeling. Two shiploads of convicts were sent over in 1849. The one ship was allowed to land her freight at Sydney, when the convicts were at once secretly hired by private persons and sent up country; the other, which tried to land at Melbourne, had to return with all on board. The vigorous opposition of the people did not prove ineffective in the sequel. In 1851, New South Wales finally ceased to be considered as a sphere of transportation. The prospects for Victoria were hardly less favourable; and in 1853 Van Diemen's Land gained exemption for the future from any further influx. After 1853 only Western Australia was still employed as a transportation district; and since South Australia from the first had been constituted on a different principle, the institution did not last much longer. It was abolished there also in 1868.

Closely connected with the popular movement for the abolition of transportation was the agitation for self-government. The Constitution of 1842, which had given the Council a modified control over public expenditure, had also whetted the popular appetite by accustoming the people to elections. A persistent pressure was brought to bear in England for an extension of Parliamentary Government, which was only too acceptable to the pedants of the Colonial Office, who at that time were obsessed with the amazing notion that separatism was a source of strength and the maintenance of an empire a danger to Great Britain.

British Opinion of Colonies

The prevalent sentiment of the "Intellectuals" of that day was thus expressed by Richard Cobden: "The Colonial system,

SIR CHARLES A. FITZROY
Governor of New South Wales, 1846-1851, under whom the struggle for free institutions continued.

with all its dazzling appeals to the passions of the people, can never be got rid of except by the indirect process of Free Trade, which will gradually and imperceptibly loose the bands which unite our Colonies to us by a mistaken notion of self-interest." Earl Grey, in 1847, made an attempt to grant a constitution which would make a Customs Union and a Federal Government inevitable. This was denounced by Wentworth as an interference with political liberty. The English Government had abolished the preferences to Colonial products in British markets. Australia had therefore nothing to gain by submitting to any limitation to her powers of self-government. The terms of the Constitution will be more fittingly dealt with in discussing the development of the several colonies.

Constitution with Certain Obligations

The internal development of New South Wales, which was shown conspicuously during the 'forties and 'fifties by the treatment of the land question and the transportation question, was accompanied by a corresponding widening of the sphere of colonisation. But while the land question hinged chiefly on the distribution of the districts which lay roughly within the boundaries of modern New South Wales, this territorial expansion went far beyond such limits. In the first enthusiasm of early colonisation, attempts were made to cover the whole continent at once; but when the deficiency of their powers was recognised, the settlers were content to occupy some few districts, which were very unequally distributed along the coast of the continent; for while they were numerous in the south-east and east, the distant west lay isolated, and the north was entirely uncolonised.

This peculiar distribution is very closely connected with the history of the rise of the different daughter colonies of New South Wales; this again was strongly influenced by the course of the geographical exploration of Australia. As a general rule, exploration came first, and colonisation followed. This order of things was reversed only in the founding of Western Australia; there colonisation began in one part which had long been known; but the exploration of the hinterland was the concern of later decades.

The successful expedition of Wentworth, Blaxland, and Lawson, in the year 1812, across the Blue Mountains into the interior, had fired the zeal for exploration. The years 1817 and 1818 saw the discovery by J. Oxley of the extensive grazing grounds known as the Liverpool Plains. In 1824, two young colonists, Hamilton Hume and William Hovell, were the first to reach the vicinity of Geelong, near modern Melbourne, from Sydney, having traversed the whole southeast of the continent, past the sources of the Murrumbidgee and the Murray. At the same time Allan Cunningham, the botanist, continued the explorations of Oxley in the north as far as the Darling Downs (1827). Finally, in the years 1828 and 1829, came the important journeys of Charles Sturt in the district watered by the Darling and Murray Rivers. These journeys not only threw new light on the river system of the country, but also guided the colonial expansion of Australia into other paths. In this respect particularly all these travels were rich in results.

Exploration of the Interior

The first successful founding of Port Phillip was the direct consequence of the journey of Hume and Hovell. Various sheep farmers of the interior followed Allan Cunningham's tracks, and thus laid the real foundation of the later Queensland. The favourable report by Sturt on the district between the Lower Murray and the Gulf of St. Vincent was entirely responsible for the colonisation of South Australia. The travels of later years did not, with one exception, produce any political results when once the foundation of the new states had been laid. Geographically they are not, for the most part, inferior to the early essays in exploration, and certainly brought more definite information as to the industrial value or worthlessness of the soil than the first rapid journeys.

Laying the Keels of Other States

This applies particularly to the expeditions which took as their object the accurate investigation of the river system of the Darling-Murray, the travels, that is to say, of Major Thomas Livingstone Mitchell, who succeeded in accomplishing his survey after six years of strenuous effort. It also applies to the discovery of the interior of Victoria—" Australia Felix "—by the same traveller, and not less to the enterprises of the brave Edward John Eyre—born 1815, died January, 1902—on the soil of inland South Australia, in the low-lying lake region, and on the terribly barren south coast as far as King George's Sound (1839–1841).

Finally, similar results were achieved by numerous exploring parties in the heart of Western Australia. The majority of these travellers could not bring back very pleasant reports. Apart from Victoria, all accounts of the industrial value of the country were discouraging or absolutely deterrent. The north-east alone formed a striking exception; there, later travels accomplished results which, to some degree, are comparable to those of the first explorers. It was the journeys of Ludwig Leichhardt which can claim this marvellous effect, and Queensland and North Australia are the regions which owe their real discovery and opening up to a German. It is not too much to say that Leichhardt's splendid expedition from Darling Downs to Port Essington (1844-1846) increased the possible area of colonisation by about a million square miles, or one-third of the whole continent. The colonists required only to follow the steps of the explorer in order to come into possession of an almost incalculable expanse of profitable land.

Australia's Debt to a German

A peculiar feature of all Australian exploration before the middle of the nineteenth century was its restriction to the edge of the continent; the centre was not reached. The explanation is found in the novelty of the sphere of work. Until the broad strip of territory along the edge was thoroughly explored in most of its parts, there was no motive to attack the real heart of the country. Even when, in the second half of the nineteenth century, the centre was chosen as a goal, the want of any tangible attraction greatly checked the course of exploration.

TEAM OF OXEN TRANSPORTING GIANT TIMBER

HARVESTING THE PINEAPPLES ON A GREAT FRUIT FARM

STORING THE SUGAR CANE PREPARATORY TO THE CRUSHING

ONE OF AUSTRALIA'S LEADING INDUSTRIES: SHEEP-SHEARING

SCENES FROM THE COUNTRY LIFE OF AUSTRALIA
Photos by Underwood & Underwood, London

THE EARLY HISTORY OF THE COLONIES
TASMANIA: THE GARDEN COLONY

OF the six colonies which compose the Commonwealth of Australia, only three—Tasmania, Victoria, and Queensland—are offshoots from New South Wales; South Australia and Western Australia—like New Zealand also—were, on the contrary, founded by direct colonisation from England. Considering the enormous difficulties with which New South Wales had continually to contend, this circumstance is not surprising. In the case of Western Australia, the mere distance from the east coast of the continent was sufficient to restrain enterprise from the eastern side. But South Australia was, in its origin, so hazardous an experiment that the Government in Sydney did well to play the part of an unconcerned spectator. In other respects even there, east of the Great Australian Bight, the question of distance was not devoid of importance. It is, at least, no accident that the three daughter colonies lie in one zone with their mother colony ; that Van Diemen's Land, an island comparatively far away from Sydney, was colonised as the first offshoot, to the complete neglect of the neighbouring parts of the mainland ; and that even the first steps toward founding Victoria were taken not from Sydney, but from Van Diemen's Land. Seldom has the natural advantage which attaches to the position of an island facing a wide stretch of opposite coast been so clearly shown as here.

The first step of the Australian mother colony towards the establishment of independent offshoots was the founding of the penal colony of Van Diemen's Land in the year 1803. The cause of this settlement was primarily the fear of French schemes of annexation, which more than once had given rise to the erection of military posts on the coast of Australia. In the next place, the English Government did not think it advisable to concentrate too large a number of criminals in any one place. A small convict settlement on Norfolk Island had already been founded under the influence of this idea, but had not proved successful. Van Diemen's Land seemed, both in point of size and of remoteness from the continent, a more desirable place than Norfolk Island for the confinement of dangerous criminals. To carry out these intentions, Governor King sent Lieutenant Bowen with a detachment of soldiers and some convicts to Van Diemen's Land in June, 1803. A settlement called Restdown, a name later corrupted into Risdon, was founded on the left shore of the estuary of the Derwent.

About this same time the plan had been formed in England of colonising the shores of the recently discovered Port Phillip on the south-east corner of the mainland. The execution of the plan was entrusted to Colonel Collins, a man who had gone to Port Jackson as a judge in the first convict ship, had been Advocate-General of New South Wales for a long time, and happened then to be in London. The expedition, consisting of two ships with four hundred convicts and the necessary warders, landed on the south side of Port Phillip, near the site of the modern Sorrento. Small excursions into the country soon showed it to be bare and inhospitable, and as Collins also, after prolonged search, found no water, he abandoned the district on January 27th, 1804, in order to take his people over to Van Diemen's Land, a course which Governor King sanctioned at his request. He sailed directly for the estuary of the Derwent, broke up the colony of Bowen there, and founded a new joint settlement on the right bank of the river at the foot of Mount Wellington. He called the place, in honour of Lord Hobart, the Colonial

Founding the Various Colonies

First Attempt to Colonise Victoria

Minister of the day, Hobart Town, a name abbreviated in 1881 to Hobart. The north of the island was also occupied. Simultaneously with Collins's expedition, and again owing to the fear of a French occupation, Colonel Paterson conducted another troop of convicts from Sydney to Van Diemen's Land, where, on the west shore of Port Dalrymple, Yorktown was immediately founded. Its first inhabitants could not make themselves at home there, and in 1808 they were taken further into the interior and settled in a locality called Launceston, after King's native town in Cornwall.

The occupation of this new field for colonisation from opposite sides had greatly hastened the exploration of the island, and, with it, the knowledge of its economic advantages; but the first steps had been taken without the orders of the Home Government and by no means to its satisfaction. The permanent shortage in provisions, which had shown itself in the early days of colonisation in New South Wales and Norfolk Island, was soon felt in the newly-planted colony. The cause was primarily the strict embargo on the landing of any except convict ships; and next the complete economic dependence on New South Wales. Under ordinary conditions this would not have led to inconvenience; but when, as happened in the year 1806, owing to the great floods of the River Hawkesbury, supplies ran short in the mother colony, the position of all the settlers could not but be the more precarious, since about that time (1807) the number of the inhabitants of Van Diemen's Land was increased · by the entire population of

GOVERNOR DAVEY'S PROCLAMATION
This pictorial proclamation was intended to teach the natives that British justice is even-handed, and that punishment would follow bad treatment of the natives on the part of white men as well as criminal acts on the part of the natives themselves.

Norfolk Island, where settlement had always proved somewhat of a failure. The conditions of life in Van Diemen's Land under these circumstances did not for the moment appear hopeful. For a long time the Government was forced to leave it to every convict to find his own food, clothing, and shelter. Since the flesh of the kangaroo was known to be a suitable article of food, the convicts at once scattered over the whole interior. This was advantageous for the exploration of the country, but not calculated to produce law and order among the colonists, and still less to maintain good relations with the aborigines.

The mutual relations of the whites gave rise to many difficulties. To many a convict who had been given leave for a kangaroo hunt, but especially to the numerous prisoners who had escaped from the gaols, it did not occur to return from their rovings in the interior to the yoke of servitude. They soon acquired a taste for the free life of the bush, formed themselves into bands, which lived by plundering the white settlers, and with this comfortable vocation, which was disastrous to the prosperity of the colony, laid the foundation for that wild bushranging which up to 1830 was such a curse to Van Diemen's Land, and spread later to the mainland. The energetic Governor Arthur at last succeeded, by a rapid campaign, in checking the evil—for a time at least (1825-1826). Twenty years later, under Governor Wilmot, it revived with much greater force.

Considering all the misery which the bushrangers brought upon the island, it was fortunate that the outrages by which they thoroughly intimidated the settlers were confined mostly to the interior; the south and north coasts remained, on the whole, free from such calamities, and were therefore able to develop steadily though slowly. Collins himself, who died at Hobart Town in 1810, did not live to see much of this progress. He had laid the foundations for it when he began, in 1807, to construct the marvellous road from Launceston to Hobart Town, but, under the prevailing conditions, it had not lain in his power to develop it farther. Lieutenant-Colonel Davey, his successor, arrived at Hobart Town only at the beginning of 1813. In the interval, Governor Macquarie had paid his first visit (November, 1811), which was an important event for Van Diemen's Land, since Macquarie with characteristic energy flooded the island with an infinity of new schemes, urged the construction of roads, public buildings, even whole towns, and, what was most essential, succeeded in awakening the public spirit of the better classes.

Enterprise in the New Colony

Now, for the first time, a systematic organisation was noticeable, which soon showed itself in the proclamation of Hobart Town as the capital of the country in the year 1812. Davey's term of office, which lasted until 1817, hardly carried out the extensive plans of Macquarie. Mr. Jenks says of him: "Davey seems to have treated his office more or less as a joke. He was totally without ceremony and would drink and jest with anyone." Bushranging alone was an eyesore to him, and the wish to suppress it finally led him to exercise his office. His first act was to place the whole island under martial law; but besides this he forbade any inhabitant to leave his house at night without permission. If, under this régime, there was any progress at all, it was entirely due to private persons. In 1815 the colony was already in a position to export wheat, and in the following year salted meat, to Sydney. In 1816, the first newspaper was started in Hobart Town. When Davey left, the white population counted quite

LIEUT.-GOVERNOR COLLINS
Who attempted to settle Port Phillip and finally founded Hobart Town.

3,000 souls, and about 3,000 acres were under cultivation.

But there was as yet no cattle breeding or sheep farming. These industries were introduced in the succeeding years. Davey's place was filled by William Sorell, an able man, whose chief concern was not to place free and respectable immigrants among a population composed of convicts; he next turned his attention to the economic development of the island as well as to the suppression of bushranging. He, like Davey, was unable to achieve great results in that field; on the other hand, he had attracted settlers in large masses, thanks to the favourable terms which he offered. Not only did the Government grant free allotments of land, but it also supplied food for six months, lent the entire stock of cattle required at the outset as well as the first seed corn, and, besides this, guaranteed a minimum price for the entire produce in grain and meat. When, in 1821, Governor Macquarie set foot for the second and last time on the soil of Van Diemen's Land after an interval of ten years, the white population amounted to 7,400 souls, who had 14,000 acres under cultivation and 180,000 sheep with 35,000 cattle on their pasturages.

The introduction of systematic sheep farming coincided indeed with Sorell's governorship, but the credit belongs to Colonel Paterson, who induced the experienced sheep breeder, MacArthur, to send him over a shipload of his famous flock. An attempt, made in 1819, to put wool on the English market failed lamentably; in 1822, however, 794 bales were exported and received gladly by the market. At the present time the wool trade has long been one of the most important industries.

First Wool Exports from Tasmania

It is easy to understand that under these circumstances the colonists regretted the departure of the Governor, who was also personally popular. When he was recalled in 1823, the Home Government was actually petitioned to appoint him for a second term.

Sorell's successor, Arthur (1823–1836), did not do so well, in spite of a long

administration and great
services. His personal character was partly to blame
for this ; partly, also, his
stiff official bearing toward
the free settlers. Arthur's
entrance on office was connected with important
changes in the constitu-
tional position of Van
Diemen's Land. The rapid
growth of the white popu-
lat on during the last few
years had made the want
of an independent govern-
ment widely felt. Not only
were all questions touch-
ing the common interest

GENERAL VIEW OF HOBART TOWN FIFTY YEARS AGO

dependent upon Sydney, but even the
matters of daily occurrence were decided
there. Even though Macquarie tried to
check this evil by conferring larger powers

GOVERNMENT HOUSE, HOBART

on the Lieutenant-Governor, the position
was bound to become intolerable. This
view was held in London; the same Act
of Parliament, in 1823,
which limited the powers
of the Governor of New
South Wales entirely
severed Van Diemen's
Land from the parent
colony and put it on the
same footing as New South
Wales.

Colonel Arthur was ap-
pointed the first Governor.
His twelve years' tenure of
office was the most eventful
in the whole history of
Van Diemen's Land. The
settlement of the convict
question which met him

at the outset, demanded all his energies.
Soon after his arrival a band of more
than one hundred criminals had escaped
from Port Macquarie and pillaged the
island. The strengthened military force
proved sufficient to check their excesses,
and 103 of the culprits were executed
by the orders of the Governor.
Clemency towards criminals was not a
characteristic of Arthur, although he
thought his island was intended only
for them, an opinion which Macquarie
in his day had held about Australia.
Arthur regarded the free settlers as
a necessary evil. The outcome of this
biassed attitude was an unremitting,
if not exactly paternal, solicitude for
the prisoners. When, in 1832, Macquarie
Harbour, on the west coast, had to be
given up on account of the excessive
density of the population, he established a new settlement at Port Arthur
on the south-east, where the prison
system was raised to a veritable science.

THE BUSY PORT OF HOBART TO-DAY

The second task of Arthur was the native question. Notwithstanding all the unrest which the struggles with the convicts as well as with the aborigines, produced in the island, they were not serious enough to check the growth of the colony in any sensible degree; there was a surprising increase during Arthur's term **Rapid Growth of Tasmania** of office both in the population and the area of cultivated land. At his arrival the population had amounted to something over 10,000 souls; when he left, in 1836, this total was quadrupled, and the area of cultivation had similarly increased. The number of sheep then reached nearly a million; and the exports, which in 1823 had amounted to approximately £25,000 sterling, had risen to over £500,000.

In order to open up the industries of the island on a large scale, the Van Diemen's Land Company had been formed in England, which obtained a concession first of 250,000 acres, and then of 100,000 acres more. It exercised an influence on the development of the colony up to quite recent times. For educational purposes there were twenty-nine schools, while religious needs were provided for by eighteen churches. Peace was at last concluded between the Government and the newspaper Press, with which Arthur for years had waged as bitter a war as Sir Ralph Darling in Australia; after 1828 complete freedom of the Press prevailed. On the whole, Arthur and the colony could be satisfied with the results.

The subsequent fortunes of Van Diemen's Land up to the beginning of the second period in Australian development, which began in the same way and about the same time for all the Colonies, can be given in a few lines. Arthur's successor was Sir John Franklin (1836–1843), who had already gained renown by his exploration of the North Polar regions. Fitted **A Scientist as Colonial Governor** by his whole disposition for scientific pursuits, he was the less competent to face the numerous difficulties of his responsible position, since the decline of Australian industries began in his time. Yet he too did good service to the island. The organisation of the educational system was entirely his work. He was further the founder of the Tasmanian Society, now known as the Royal

Society of Tasmania; he enabled William Jackson Hooker to complete his work on the flora of Tasmania, and finally initiated the study of the geology and natural history of the island by encouraging numerous travellers. His administration was the scientific era in Van Diemen's Land.

The brief administration of his successor, Sir Eardley Wilmot (1843–1846) was occupied with the struggle between the colonists and the English Government about the abolition of transportation. Van Diemen's Land had always enjoyed the dubious advantage of being provided with large masses of criminals in proportion to its area. The detrimental effects of penal colonisation in its moral and economic bearings had therefore been most noticeable there, and in 1835 there began a systematic agitation of which the object was to prevent convicts from being landed on the island for the future.

This agitation did not completely stop even in the succeeding years, and when, at the beginning of the 'forties, the **Suppression of Penal Colonisation** prisoners of Moreton Bay were taken across to the island, it immediately flared up again brightly. Fuel was added to the flames when, under Wilmot's government, 2,000 prisoners were brought over from Norfolk Island, which after 1825 had once more become a penal settlement, and when it was seen that new batches were constantly arriving from England. Up to 1844 the number of criminals sent to Van Diemen's Land amounted to 40,000. The most worthless of these were the Norfolk Islanders, many of whom escaped to the bush, where they combined in marauding gangs of from 100 to 500 men, and waged guerilla warfare on everyone. They burnt the houses, killed the inhabitants, drove away the cattle, and revived the worst features of the old bushranging. This was the climax. The agitation against the system of penal colonisation became general. A great league against it was founded, and in the government of Sir William Denison, who had succeeded Wilmot in 1846, after several years of effort, transportation to Van Diemen's Land was finally abolished in 1853. This reform was accompanied by a change in the name of the colony, which has since then been known as Tasmania.

THE FIRST LEADERS OF THE
AUSTRALIAN COMMONWEALTH

Sir EDMUND BARTON
Premier

Sir JOHN FORREST
Minister for Defence

Sir WILLIAM LYNE
Minister for Home Affairs

LORD HOPETOUN
Governor-General

Hon. JAMES G. DRAKE
Postmaster-General

Rt. Hon. CHAS. KINGSTON
Trade and Customs

Sir GEORGE TURNER
Treasurer

Rt. Hon. G. H. REID
Opposition Leader

Sir RICHARD BAKER
President of Senate

Sir EDWARD BRADDON
Senior Member for Tasmania

Hon. ALFRED DEAKIN
First Attorney-General
and present Premier

Sir J. R. DICKSON
Minister for Defence

Photographs by British Australasian, Ltd.; Russell & Sons, Elliott & Fry, London; Newman, Sydney; and Hammer & Co., Adelaide

VICTORIA AND QUEENSLAND
DAUGHTER STATES OF NEW SOUTH WALES

"THE colony of Victoria might, with some justice, be spoken of as a granddaughter rather than a daughter of New South Wales," says Mr. Jenks. It was finally founded by settlers from Van Diemen's Land; it was purely Australian only in the period before it was definitely colonised. This begins with the attempt of Colonel Collins, which we have already noticed, to establish a penal settlement on the shores of Port Phillip in 1803. The plan failed, with the result that no one for more than twenty years troubled about a country which was considered "unproductive and unpromising." In 1825 the attempt was renewed, in consequence of the favourable reports of Hume and Hovell, and also with the object of forestalling the French. The penal station of Dumaresq was founded on Westernport, which was mistaken for Port Phillip; no water, however, could be found, and the settlement was discontinued in 1828.

This concludes the preliminary stage in the history of the colony. The real founding of Port Phillip, as modern Victoria was called until 1851, was due to private enterprise. The few fishermen and sailors who in the first half of the nineteenth century led a half-savage existence on the eastern parts of the south coast of Australia, were joined in 1834 by a family named Henty, which settled in Portland Bay. The members of it had already taken part in the unlucky enterprise in Western Australia, had afterwards hoped to find free land in Van Diemen's Land, and now, since they were at the end of their resources, ventured on a bold plunge into the unknown. The special permission to settle for which they applied was at first refused by the authorities, but subse-

quently granted, in consideration of the dreaded encroachment of the French. Henty's success prompted further enterprise, which was once more directed toward Port Phillip. The leader of this attempt was John Batman, a wealthy sheep farmer of Van Diemen's Land. He started in May, 1835, with several companions for the south coast of Australia, inspected the country, and "bought," on June 6th, 1835, for a couple of dozen axes, knives, and scissors, some blankets, 30 mirrors, and 200 handkerchiefs, with the stipulation of a yearly payment of about £200 sterling in goods, two vast territories comprising together 600,000 acres, an area more than the size of Cambridgeshire. The consequence was the founding of an association of various settlers of Van Diemen's Land, the Port Phillip Association, and the planting of the first settlement in Geelong. The contract of sale was sent to England; the Government naturally termed it worthless. If the country was English, the natives had no right to alienate the land without the Governor's sanction; if it was not English, the association had no claim on the protection of England. The association, realising in the end that it had no case, was content with 20,000 acres, worth then some £7,500. In 1836 it was dissolved. In England there was at first little inclination to allow a new colony to be founded. Circumstances were, however, stronger than the will of the Government. Even on August 26th, 1835, Governor Bourke of New South Wales had prohibited the occupation of land round Port Phillip without his permission; but only a year later, in September, 1836, he and the English Government saw

THOMAS HENTY
The Founder of Victoria

R   24   G

VICTORIA'S CAPITAL SEVENTY YEARS AGO: MELBOURNE IN 1837

ten shillings a day and upward were not considered high. An ox cost from £12 to £15, a horse £100 or more, a sheep up to £3. The inevitable reaction followed. The over-production of corn and cattle, which very soon appeared, led in every department to a collapse of prices, ending in a regular bankruptcy. Wages rapidly sank ; the price of an ox was hardly as many shillings as it had fetched pounds in the past, and hundreds of businesses suspended payment. The crisis was violent but short ; it was ended by the middle of the " forties." Since that time, apart from the gold fever, which set in a little later, and the declaration of the independence of the colony, no event of great importance has disturbed the development of Port Phillip. It made continuous but rapid progress. In 1840 Melbourne was declared a free port ; in 1843 the trade of the colony amounted to £341,000 ; in 1848 it had reached £1,049,000. The proceeds of the sales of land increased in proportion. Of the £250,000 which composed the whole revenue of the colony in the year 1850, more than half came from that source alone. The outgoings were 30 per cent. less than the incomings.

themselves compelled by an unexpectedly large influx of immigrants to open the country to colonisation.

After this concession, development was rapid. The administration had in 1835 started with a single Government official, a Captain Lonsdale. In the following year it was enlarged by a regular police force, with whom three land surveyors were associated. In 1837 Sir Robert Bourke himself laid the foundation of Melbourne and Williamstown, and in 1842 the former received a municipal government. In June, 1836, there were calculated to be 177 colonists with 26,000 sheep ; two years later both figures were tripled or quadrupled. At the same time the exports of the young colony amounted to £12,000 sterling, while the imports reached £115,000. As in New South Wales, the Crown lands were sold by public auction, except for the period 1840–1842, when the plan of allotment at a fixed price was tried.

It is pleasant to record that good relations existed from the first between the colonists and natives. This is partly

Owing to the strong tide of immigration, by the end of 1841 no fewer than 205,748 acres had been transferred to fixed proprietors, and in return £394,300 had been paid to the land fund, from which source the expenses of government were defrayed. This large sum illustrates the superabundance of money in the country at the time. Owing to the scarcity of workmen, wages of

THE GOLD-FIELDS OF BALLARAT FIFTY YEARS AGO

Market Square, Castlemaine

Sandhurst, now included in Bendigo

General View of Bendigo

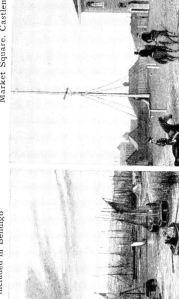

The Government Offices, Melbourne

The Approach to Melbourne

The Centre of Ballarat

THE BEGINNINGS OF VICTORIA'S THRIVING TOWNS HALF A CENTURY AGO

traceable to the sensible behaviour of the early settlers ; it is partly due to the services of William Buckley, whose romantic adventures are well known. He had been a convict, and had escaped from Collins's expedition in 1804. He then lived thirty-two years among the natives, and now was the mediator between the two races. We hear of hardly any outrages, fights with the blacks, or similar occurrences, in the history of Port Phillip. The settlers could extend their sheep runs farther and farther into the interior without molestation. In 1849 Port Phillip owned more than a million sheep ; the export of wool amounted to nearly 13,000,000 lb.

This splendid growth brought up as early as 1842 the question of the political severance of the colony from New South Wales. Nevertheless, a whole series of representations to the English Government on the subject produced no effect. The colonists then, in July, 1848, resolved on a step as bold as it was original. Six representatives should have been elected to the Legislative Council which sat at Sydney. The candidates were requested to withdraw their applications, and the English Secretary of State for the Colonies, Earl Grey, was chosen as their solitary representative. The scheme was, of course, apparent. At the subsequent election in October the Government insisted on the

nomination of proper deputies. But the object of the colonists was so far attained that the separation of the two colonies was now seriously considered in England. The Board of Trade took up the question, the Ministry gave way, and in the Constitution Act of 1850 the settlement, numbering 77,000 souls, was raised to an independent colony under the name of Victoria. The news of this decision reached Melbourne in November, 1850 ; but it was not until July 1st, 1851, that the new order of things came into force.

QUEENSLAND

The expedition which had been made by Oxley along the east coast north of Sydney had prompted several attempts at colonisation. Settlements had been founded at Port Essington, on Melville Island, and at other points, but no results had been obtained. When, a little later, the maintenance of the convicts in Van Diemen's Land began to cause difficulties, the expedient of founding a penal station on Moreton Bay was adopted. This lasted until 1840, and has, under the name of Brisbane, remained to the present day the seat of government of the later Queensland. But it must not be regarded as the true nucleus of the colony. In the first place, the presence of the penal station deterred all free settlers from going there ; and next, the land in its

EARLY PIONEERS ON THE BUSH TRACK IN QUEENSLAND

AN EPISODE OF EARLY COLONIAL LIFE IN QUEENSLAND

Native police under English officer preparing for an engagement with the blacks.

neighbourhood was not offered for sale. Queensland thus, at least for its first beginnings, showed a unique development from the standpoint of political geography. It developed from the interior toward the coast.

Queensland's real origin is traceable to the squatters who followed the track of Allan Cunningham from New South Wales to the north. They continually drove their flocks on further from the Liverpool Plains to the New England district and the Darling Downs. These districts were even then the best pasture grounds in the world, but suffered much from want of access to the sea, since owing to the intervening chain of mountains the long détour by New South Wales had to be taken before the value of the products could be realised. Even the discovery of a difficult mountain path to Moreton Bay was of no use, since the authorities absolutely prohibited the squatters from any communications with the place. A change was first made in 1859 after the abolition of the penal station. Practicable roads were now constructed over the mountains, public sale of land was introduced in 1842, and the fresh stream of immigration was diverted into the newly opened districts. Yet there was not at once a marked development; good land was abundant, but the labour was not forthcoming. In nine years less than 2,500 acres had been disposed of,

Efforts were soon made to obtain political separation from New South Wales. The request was granted in 1859; the north-east corner of Australia was proclaimed an independent colony under the name of Queensland.

The aspect of Queensland at the moment when it received independence was essentially different from that of the other Australian colonies at the same stage in their career. The entire white population amounted in 1859 to only 30,000 souls, who were equally distributed between the town and the country. There were some twenty towns, of which Brisbane then contained 4,000 inhabitants, while others of them boasted only of some hundreds. The so-called town of Allora had only fifty-five inhabitants. These settlements were mere villages, not only from the small number of their inhabitants, but in their essential nature; they did not show a trace of organised municipal government. The greater credit is thus due to the certainty and rapidity with which all the authorities adapted themselves to the new conditions suddenly burst upon them. The example of Queensland proves the high capacity of the Anglo-Saxon to adapt himself to any form of polity, for the Queenslanders entered upon self-government without any such preliminary training as all the other Australian colonies had enjoyed in their gradual process of development.

Travelling to the diggings in the days of the gold "rush."

An old quartz crusher.

Scientific mining: Battery of 105 stampers at Bendigo.

A Ballarat gold-mine to-day.

Diggers engaged in surface mining.

In the old days: Military escort accompanying the transport of gold from the mines.

SCENES IN THE LAND OF GOLD: OLD METHODS AND NEW

Photos Underwood & Underwood, London

THE
AUSTRALIAN
COLONIES-III

THEIR
EARLY
HISTORY

WESTERN AUSTRALIA: THE YOUNGEST STATE

WESTERN Australia was founded directly from England. It is true that a number of convicts had been sent in 1826 from Sydney to the west coast of the continent in order to counteract any French schemes; but the establishment of the stations of Albany and Rockingham can hardly be termed a colonisation in the proper sense of the word. The first real settlement was in 1829. In the previous year a Captain Stirling had published a glowing account of the district at the mouth of the Swan River, which induced the Government to order Captain Fremantle to hoist the English flag there. But further measures of the Government failed from want of means.

The moving spirit of the private enterprise which first started the colonisation was Thomas Peel. In combination with others he offered to send in the course of four years 10,000 free emigrants to the Swan River on condition that, in return for the cost, which he estimated at £300,000, an area of 4,000,000 acres should be assigned to him. When the Government did not accept this offer, Peel considerably reduced the scale of his scheme, and this time was successful. Under the guidance of Captain Stirling, destined to be the Governor of the new colony, to whom 100,000 acres of land had been promised, the first band of emigrants sailed from England in the spring of 1829, arrived in June on the Swan River, and founded at its mouth the town of Fremantle, and higher up stream the town of Perth. In the course of the next year and a half thirty-nine emigrant ships, with 1,125 colonists, attracted by eulogistic descriptions, followed the first party to Western Australia. Fortune did not smile on the attempt; there was land enough and to spare, but there was a lack of working men, of roads, and of markets.

Peel's plan had been to cultivate tobacco and cotton, sugar and flax, to breed horses for India, and by fattening oxen and swine, to provide the English

Private Scheme of Settlement

fleet with salted meat. All this came to nothing; the colonists themselves had hardly enough to eat, and the larger their landed property the greater their helplessness and distress. Many settlers, and among them the Henty family, left the ungrateful soil of the colony; others lost all they possessed; Peel himself, who had settled with 200 colonists, is said to have lost £50,000. The founders had, from the very beginning, never given a thought to the support of the new-comers, nor had anyone troubled about dividing the land even roughly, to say nothing of a proper survey. It was nothing unusual for the settlers to lie for months after their arrival shelterless on the shore, exposed without protection to the scorching Australian sun, to sandstorms, and to violent downpours of rain. Thus much of the labour that had been expended on the soil was wasted, while the health of the people suffered. If they were finally in a position to occupy the tract assigned to them, difficulties of another sort began.

Hardships of Early Settlers

From the very first hour the relations between the settlers and the aborigines were most hostile; and the aid of a troop of mounted police was required for the protection of the former. Under these circumstances there could be no idea of progress in the sense in which it can be recorded of the majority of other Australian colonies in their early days. Everything went on very slowly, especially as immigration, after the first wave, absolutely came to a standstill. The few settlers left in the land certainly did their utmost; they most energetically set about breeding sheep and horses, laid the foundation of some other towns, and settled King George's Sound. Development in the first six years did not go beyond this; of 1,600,000 acres distributed to the colonists as such, in 1834, only 564 acres were under cultivation. Some stimulus was given to development by the Western Australian Association,

Slow Progress of the New Colony

founded by Major Irwin in 1835, which was intended to encourage emigration to Western Australia and safeguard its interests in other countries. Among its members, besides English gentlemen, were included some residents of Calcutta, who contemplated the establishment of a health resort as well as a trading settle-**Development by Capital Enterprise** ment. The company benefited the colony in many ways; but in spite of all agitation it could not alter the slow course of the economic growth. In 1840 the population had amounted to only 2,300 souls; two years before, the colonists had received the privilege of sending four members to the Legislative Council.

The year 1841 saw the formation of some large undertakings to exploit Western Australia. One was a limited company, founded by the Western Australian Association with the object of buying up cheaply the land once assigned to Captain Stirling, and then disposing of it in small lots. One pound sterling was to be paid down for each acre. This plan never came into execution. The other undertakings of the same Western Australian Association promised greater success. At the suggestion of the traveller, George Grey, of whom we shall hear more, a settlement, which received the name of Australind, was founded in the Leschenault district on the north coast of Geographe Bay, some hundred miles south of Perth. It was flourishing splendidly when the company broke up; the small town still exists.

The want of labourers, which became more urgent from year to year, drove the colony to follow the example of Queensland. In 1845 the Council seriously contemplated inviting German settlers, under the impression that the harsh treatment of German immigrants in the United States would make it easy to divert the stream. At the same time the advisa-**Convict Settlers Admitted** bility of admitting pauper immigrants was considered. The most momentous resolution, however, was the introduction of transportation. According to a resolution of the Council of 1846, a certain number of convicts, whose passage was to be provided at the cost of the mother country, were to be admitted annually, in order to be employed on road-making and other public works. The English Government accepted the proposal only

too willingly. While it did nothing at all to help the execution of the two other schemes, it lost no time in disembarking shipload after shipload óf convicts on the welcome new transportation territory, as Western Australia was officially declared to be on May 1st, 1849. After 1850 " ticket-of-leave " men were sent out, and allowed freedom of movement within the colony, subject to the obligation of periodically reporting themselves to the police.

In contrast to New South Wales and Van Diemen's Land, the Colony of Western Australia was greatly assisted by the introduction of penal colonisation. By April, 1852, there were 1,500 transportees in the country, half of whom were ticket-of-leave men. This number implied a large staff of officials, and a stronger military force; it also necessitated the construction of large buildings, for which the sum of £86,000 was granted by England alone. Thus money and life were brought into the colony. The old colonists took heart again, a new stream of free settlers flowed in, more and more land was bought and **Colony Saved by Convicts** cultivated, and the land fund grew in an encouraging fashion. Coal-fields were also discovered, guano beds were exploited, and sandalwood exported; the Madras Cavalry began to obtain their remounts from Western Australia, and a pearl fishery was started in Shark Bay. Under these circumstances it is not wonderful that the white population, which had only amounted to 5,000 in 1850, was now trebled. The number of sheep and cattle, as well as the volume of trade, showed a corresponding increase.

There was, however, a dark side to this bright picture. In spite of the increase in sales of land, the incomings did not cover the expenditure. In order to make good this deficit, an arrangement had been made by which the ticket-of-leave men should be able to buy their liberty at a price varying from £7 to £25, according to the length of their sentence. But in spite of the extensive use which the transportees, who in Western Australia belonged exclusively to the male sex, made of this privilege, the measure was ineffectual; the colony was more than ever dependent on liberal subsidies from the mother country. This had an important effect on political development, since this financial dependence, in

THE IMPORTANT MANUFACTURING TOWN OF FREMANTLE

MUNDARING WEIR ON THE GREAT WATER SYSTEM OF COOLGARDIE

GENERAL VIEW OF PERTH, THE CAPITAL OF THE COLONY

SCENES IN WESTERN AUSTRALIA TO-DAY
Photos Greenham & Evans, Perth

MUSTERING CATTLE ON AN AUSTRALIAN STATION

caused bad blood in the adjoining colonies, as well as the circumstance that many convicts from Western Australia, on serving their sentence, turned their steps toward the east. In 1864, Victoria raised a violent protest against the continuance of penal colonisation in the far west of the continent, and demanded measures of repression. Finally, in 1868, the English Government struck Western Australia out of the list of penal colonies, after it had received in all 9,718 transportees. The

connection with the transportation which suited England, was the chief reason why Western Australia was absolutely ignored when a responsible government was granted to the other colonies. A third reason was the composition of the inhabitants and their stage of civilisation in 1850. Even in 1859, 41 per cent. of the male population were actual or former convicts, and in most localities these convicts outnumbered the free colonists. The number of illiterate persons, excluding the actual convicts, reached $37\frac{1}{2}$ per cent. It was absolutely impossible to place a community so constituted on an independent footing.

Western Australia was long in making up for its original inferiority to the sister colonies. It lost, however, its character of a penal colony quicker than was acceptable to the free and the emancipated colonists, who were spoilt by the cheap price of labour and the sums of money spent by the mother country on transportation. The continuous influx of escaped criminals soon

complete ruin of the colony, which the colonists who had been enriched by convict labour prophesied, did not occur.

It is only recently that it has been able to meet its outgoings from its own resources, and not until 1890 did it receive self-government and attain the same footing as the other colonies. But the discovery and working of large goldfields in the interior guarantee to it, however, perhaps the most successful course of any of the Australian colonies.

"RUNNING IN" HORSES FROM THE BUSH

SOUTH AUSTRALIA IN DEVELOPMENT

THE founding of South Australia, which, like Western Australia, was colonised from England, was really due to the favourable accounts brought back by the explorer Sturt as to the country seen by him at the mouth of the Murray, and to the report of Captain Collet Barker, who was entrusted with the exploration of the Gulf of St. Vincent. In consequence of this, the South Australian Land Company, which included, besides a number of members of Parliament, Edward Gibbon Wakefield, was formed in London in 1831. Wakefield had learned from personal experience the defects of English prison life ; he saw the only remedy in a systematically conducted removal of the superfluous English population, which, in his opinion, plunged the masses into distress and misery and assisted crime, to new scenes, such, for example, as South Australia, just then coming into notice. According to his plan, large uncultivated **A Scheme of** tracts of land should be **Emigration** assigned to a colonisation **Praised by Mill** company provided with sufficient means, on the understanding that it founded settled communities. The company was to indemnify itself for all initial expenditure by the sale of land at fixed prices ; the profits above that were to be applied to the cost of bringing over English workmen to the colony. This idea of an emigration fund raised by sales of land originated with Wakefield, and was the essential feature of his system. It is discussed and warmly praised by Mill in the last chapter of his " Political Economy." In every colony there were to be neither more nor less hands available than required.

The Government at first took up almost the same attitude toward Wakefield's plans and the proposals of the South Australian Land Company as toward the founders of Port Phillip. There was a reluctance to sap existing settlements by establishing new ones ; and, further, it seemed impolitic to confer legislative rights on a private company. On the other hand, the influence of the Wakefield family was strong, and possibly this new system might prove more lasting than those previously adopted. The Government therefore, in 1834, resolved to make an attempt on the lines of Wakefield's plan. The means for the undertaking were to be furnished by the company. **Emigration** The direction of land sales and **and Sales** emigration was placed in the **of Land** hands of three commissioners in London ; in the colony itself the Government reserved the right to nominate a Governor and some other officials, while the rest were to be nominated by the company. It was definitely promised that no convicts should be transported from the United Kingdom to the colony. The first three ships sailed from England in February, 1836. Two landed in July on Kangaroo Island, where the passengers immediately began to establish themselves on Nepean Bay ; the third ship, which did not arrive until August, sailed to the coast of the mainland and the banks of the River Torrens. The choice of this landing-place by Colonel Light seemed to most of the new-comers as unsuitable as the choice by them of Nepean Bay appeared to him. In the next year, the votes of the colonists were finally given in favour of the spot chosen by Light ; and the building of a town, which, at the wish of King William IV., was called Adelaide, after his consort, was at once begun.

The development of the young colony shows a bright and a gloomy side. The **Friction** existence of two sets of officials, **in the Early** and the numerous restrictions **Settlement** which were imposed on the officials of the company, soon led to such friction that the majority of both parties had to be recalled. These measures exercised little influence on the purely economic development. In 1837 alone more than 60,000 acres of land were sold, from which £43,151 accrued to the company. Up to the middle of 1839 a quarter of a million acres had been sold, bringing in £230,000. In 1840 there were 10,000 settlers, who owned 200,000 sheep and 15,000 head of cattle.

The rapid and brilliant rise of South Australia, like that of Victoria, was followed by a great financial crash. The frenzy for speculation in land had grown to a prodigious extent ; and, although **Speculation and its Results** wages reached a giddy height (skilled workmen earned up to fifty shillings a day), the profits to be made by speculation proved a greater attraction and distracted many from industrial enterprise. In addition to this, the second Governor of the colony, Colonel Gawler, allowed himself to be led into constructing large public buildings and parks, although the mother country had expressly refused to bind herself to any contributions. The colony had very soon to deal with a debt of £405,000. The South Australian Company was equally to blame with Colonel Gawler for this turn of affairs. The head of the company, Angas, had also speculated in a manner quite contrary to the objects which Wakefield had in view. He invested half the company's capital in land, engaged in whale fishery, trading, and banking, and induced the colonists, by guaranteeing them an excessively high interest on deposits, to entrust him with their cash. The commissioners also did not rightly understand their duties. The price which had been fixed for land before the founding of the colony was £1 an acre ; huge tracts had been disposed of at that figure. But instead of raising the price, they took the astonishing step of reducing it to twelve shillings.

Some improvement of the situation was finally effected by the appointment of George Grey to guide the colony. His name will always be conspicuous in the history of the British colonies, but it is also famous in the field of ethnography. On his return from his two journeys through Western Australia in 1837 to 1839 he had prepared a memorandum,

showing the methods by which the British possessions in the South Seas and in South Africa should be administered. When South Australia declared itself bankrupt in 1841 the opportunity was offered him of putting his theory into practice. By his appointment to be Governor in Adelaide the administration of the Colonies practically was transferred to the English Government.

Grey found a heavy task awaiting him. The treasury was empty ; a host of officials had eaten up the revenue of the colony, and the burden of debt was crushing, notwithstanding that some of the bills drawn by Gawler upon the Home Government, which had been dishonoured on presentation, were ultimately paid by the British Parliament. Grey's first step was to discontinue all building not imperatively urgent, to dismiss superfluous officials, and to lower the salaries of the rest. An improvement was soon apparent. In 1841, out of 299,077 acres sold, only 2,503 had been under cultivation ; at the end of 1842 there **The Task of a great Pro-Consul** were more than 20,000 cultivated, and that with an increase in the population from 14,600 to 17,000 souls. Unfortunately for the colony, the mother country was not willing to take over the rest of the old burden of debt. Grey was neither able nor willing simply to break with the existing financial methods ; he issued bills drawn on the Home Government, but only a small part of them were paid. This caused ill-feeling in South Australia, where the financial crisis reached its height in 1843. Meanwhile the situation grew more tolerable as rich veins of copper were discovered and worked. From that time South Australia has developed regularly with a few trifling fluctuations, easily explicable from the youth of the undertaking. The population amounted in 1848 to 38,600 whites, against 3,700 natives ; the trade, in 1839 only £427,000, reached in 1849

VIEW OF ADELAIDE FIFTY YEARS AGO

Photos. Edwards and Exclusive News Agency.

PRESENT-DAY SCENES IN ADELAIDE, THE CAPITAL OF SOUTH AUSTRALIA
1. Parliament House; 2. Town Hall; 3. University; 4. The principal street.

the sum of £888,000, of which £504,000 came from exports.

The term of office of George Grey, so fraught with blessing for South Australia, ended in 1845—it was his fortune always to be placed in a position where a keen sight and a tight grip were necessary—for he was then removed to New Zealand. The history of his unimportant successors is featureless except for the efforts of the colonists to win political self-government. When the colony was founded, the English Government had intended to give it a constitution as soon as the number of inhabitants reached 50,000. In 1842, when the system of commissioners was abolished, a council of eight members, four of whom were officials and four

colonists selected by the Governor, was placed under the Governor. In spite of the growing prosperity of South Australia, some years had yet to elapse before the Home Government would make any further concession, although the interests of the colonists were insufficiently represented by the new institution. It then happened that in 1849 the population, contrary to expectation, amounted to 52,000. The Government kept faith, and in 1850 South Australia became a recognised colony. On August 20th, 1851, a council of twenty-four members met for the first time; of these, two-thirds were elected by the colonists, eight—but of these only four might be officials—were nominated by the Governor.

Matthew Flinders

Robert O'Hara Burke

Sir Thomas Mitchell

The Burial of Burke

Egerton Warburton

William John Wills

Charles Sturt

SOME OF THE LEADING EXPLORERS OF THE AUSTRALIAN CONTINENT

Flinders circumnavigated Australia in 1801 and charted much of the north coast. Burke and Wills were the first to cross the continent from south to north, but died of starvation on their way back (1860). Sir Thomas Mitchell, in the thirties, made four expeditions into the interior, and his labours were extremely valuable. Warburton crossed to Western Australia from the east ; Sturt was another of the chief explorers, and explored South Australia and the interior in 1845.

THE MODERN DEVELOPMENT OF AUSTRALIA
AND THE BIRTH OF THE COMMONWEALTH

THE favourable and rapid development of the younger Australian Colonies in the second half of the " forties " had fostered, among those English statesmen who were interested in the colonies, the idea that the same measure of self-government should be granted them that New South Wales had enjoyed since 1842. Van Diemen's Land and Port Phillip, which were in a position to meet their outgoings entirely from their own resources, had the foremost claim to the independent control of their revenues ; but South Australia also was rapidly approaching this same consummation. Western Australia alone lagged behind.

In 1847 these ideas took some tangible shape. Earl Grey, then Secretary of State for War and the Colonies, openly expressed to the Governor of New South Wales his intention of granting to the young colonies the constitution of 1842 ; in fact, he wished to take a further step, and to establish in all Australian Colonies, by the side of the Legislative Council, an Upper House, whose members should be drawn from the town communities. Since a vigorous protest against the last two heads of the plan was raised in Australia, he abandoned them, but put the matter before the Committee of the Privy Council for Trade and Foreign Plantations. As the result of their deliberations the committee recommended the introduction of **Proposals for New Constitutions** a constitution, modelled on that of New South Wales, for Van Diemen's Land, South Australia, and Port Phillip, and the last-named was to be separated from New South Wales.

The elaboration of details was to be entrusted to the various parliaments ; but the committee expressed their expectation that the Customs duties and Excise would at first require to be administered by the British Parliament. At the same time the committee advised the introduction of a uniform tariff for all the colonies. The Bill, which was drafted in accordance with the suggestions of the committee, became **Uniform Fiscal Policy** law on August 5th, 1850, under the title, " An Act for the Better Government of Her Majesty's Australian Colonies." Van Diemen's Land, South Australia, and Victoria—hitherto Port Phillip—received the constitution recommended by the committee. Western Australia had the prospect of obtaining it so soon as it was able to defray the cost of its civil administration. Every proprietor of land of the value of £100, who was at least twenty-one years of age, had the franchise, as had everyone who occupied a house or rented a farm at the annual value of £10. The customs and excise were settled on the understanding that the colonial Governments decided their amount ; but no differential duties were to be imposed. At the same time goods intended for the use of English troops were not dutiable, and existing commercial contracts were not to be prejudiced.

With the Act of August 5th, 1850, the chief step toward the alteration of the constitution of the Australian Colonies was taken ; but it did not signify any final settlement. It is true that the receipts from the customs were guaranteed to the colonies, but they were still collected by officials nominated from England. Again, the profits from the sale of the Crown lands were not entirely at the disposal of the Australians, since half was applied by the mother country to the encouragement of emigration. Finally, the nomination of the higher officials rested completely with the Home Government. A general agitation against the retention of these powers was raised directly after the introduction of the new constitution. Absolute self-government, without any restrictions, was demanded, and the English Government did not delay to concede this clamorous demand. In April, 1851, the entire management of the Customs was put into the hands of the colonies ; the following year the application of the proceeds of the digger's licences was entrusted to them, and at the same time it was left to their discretion to bring before the English Government their further wishes as to the completion of the constitution. At the end of 1854, the colonies submitted their propositions to the Government. Those of South Australia and Tasmania received the Royal assent at once, while those of Victoria and New South Wales were reserved to be confirmed by Act of Parliament, on the ground that they involved concessions which the Crown by itself was powerless to make. The confirmation of Parliament was granted, after some slight amendments had been made, in the year 1855.

The contents of the new constitutions may be briefly recapitulated as follows.

Government without Restrictions

The most essential innovation, which was common to all four colonies, was the transition from the single-chamber system to the dual-chamber system. By the side of the former Legislative Council, which was thenceforth the First Chamber, or Upper House, came in each case an Assembly, or Lower House. In New South Wales the former consisted of twenty-one members nominated by the Crown for life, while the Lower House, according to the scheme, numbered fifty-four representatives, who were chosen from the well-to-do classes of electors possessing a certain income. At the present day the number of members of the Upper House is unlimited, while that of the Lower House amounts to ninety ; these are elected for three years. The Council of Victoria comprised, after the law of 1855, thirty members—at the present day forty-eight ; the Assembly, seventy-five (now ninety-five). Both Houses are elective in this colony. The members hold office for six and three years. In South Australia the Council, nominated by the Crown, consisted of twelve ; the Assembly, elected by votes, comprised thirty-six members ; but in 1856 voting was introduced for the Upper House also, and the number of its members was fixed at eighteen. The number in the Upper

Details of the New Constitutions

IN THE EARLY DAYS OF THE GOLD RUSH : A BUSY SCENE AT BENDIGO

GOLD-SEEKERS: THE PIONEERS WHO HAVE FOUNDED SO MANY AUSTRALIAN COMMUNITIES

House was raised later to twenty-four, sitting for twelve years, and in the Lower House to fifty-four members, elected for three years, who were well paid. In 1902, however, the number of representatives was lowered to eighteen and forty-two. In Tasmania, finally, the Council has always numbered eighteen, and the Assembly thirty-seven representatives, who are all elected.

In each colony there is a Governor, nominated by the Crown, but paid by the colony. The usual term of office is six years. The position of the Governor with regard to the legislature and the Cabinet is that of a constitutional sovereign. But his power is also limited by the instructions which he receives from the Colonial Office. His assent is necessary to all Colonial Legislation; but a Bill which has received his assent, though it is then **Powers** provisionally enforced as law, **of the** may be disallowed by the **Governors** Colonial Office. It would not be possible to discuss within the limits of our space the question as to the real influence which the Governor exercises in virtue of these legal powers. Indeed, his influence, which in the case of a man of strong character may be very great, is, like that of the King, rather personal and extra-legal.

The highest executive officials are the Ministers, whose number varies from six in Tasmania to nine in New South Wales. **The New** The grant of full self-govern- **Colony of** ment to the Australian Colonies **Queensland** in the middle of the nineteenth century, and the separation of Victoria as an independent colony from New South Wales, did not complete the organisation and the external enlargement of this Colonial system. Since gold had been found in large quantities in the district of Moreton Bay, in 1858, at the petition of the inhabitants this also was separated from New South Wales, and, under the name of Queensland, was provided with the same self-government as the elder sister colonies. The Legislative Council contains forty-one members nominated by the Crown, the Assembly seventy-two members elected for three years. Seven Ministers are associated with the Governor, who is nominated by the Crown.

The growth of Queensland has been as steady as that of most of the other colonies. The year 1866 brought drought and great mortality among the cattle, involving the ruin of many businesses and private individuals ; the financial crisis also, at the beginning of the " nineties " struck the colony with great force. But in spite of these blows the population has grown comparatively rapidly and prosperity has increased. The number of inhabitants, which in 1861 hardly amounted to 35,000, had reached 147,000 in 1873 ; on **Queensland's Material Prosperity** January 1, 1900, it amounted to 512,604 souls. This growth, which is due principally to large immigration, has been much helped by the policy of subsidising the immigrants, adopted since 1871. The rich gold-fields, of which some twenty-five are being worked at the present day, attracted large multitudes. The immense size of Queensland, stretching through eighteen degrees of latitude, and the consequent variety of industries—in the sparsely-peopled north all the tropical products are grown, while in the densely-inhabited south the crops of the temperate zone are cultivated—led some years ago to the idea of its division into two provinces with separate governments, but a common central administration. The twenty-first degree of southern latitude was suggested as the boundary line.

Western Australia was the last of the Australian Colonies to receive self-government. The system of transportation was in force there until the year 1868. Its discontinuance did not alter the relations to the mother country. The year 1870 saw the introduction of a Legislative Council composed of members partly nominated, partly elected ; but it was not until October 21, 1890, that the previous Crown Colony joined the ranks of the other colonies on equal terms. Its Council contains twenty-four members, the Assembly forty-four, all of whom are elected. The development of Western Australia has only recently been more rapid, since large gold-fields of great extent were discovered in 1887. The population, **Grant of Self-Government** numbering in 1881 barely 30,000 souls, has increased, almost entirely through immigration, to nearly 200,000. The internal development of the Colonies was early accompanied by the effort to spread the power of Australia beyond the limits of the continent. This was noticeable as far back as 1869 in the opening of the Fiji question ; but no real oversea expansion took place before 1883. Notwithstanding the position of New

Guinea in the immediate vicinity of Australia, neither the Colonies nor England itself had ever shown any inclination to acquire territory there. It was only about the middle of the 'seventies, when rumours of Germany's intentions on the immense island were prevalent, that the Australians remembered its proximity, and New South Wales suggested off hand the incorporation of that part of New Guinea which was not subject to Dutch suzerainty. England assented, on the stipulation that the Australians bore the cost of administration ; that they refused. The question, however, was still discussed in Australia, and when the Germans really threatened to take steps, the Premier of Queensland, on his own responsibility, declared that he had taken possession of the eastern portion of the island in March, 1883. England then shrank from placing the destiny of so large a territory in the hands of the small population of Queensland, although the Australian Colonial Conference in December was in favour of the acquisition. Meanwhile Germany actually took possession of the north of **The British Flag in New Guinea** the island, and England was obliged to content herself, on November 6, 1884, with the south-east alone. At the present day British New Guinea is governed by the Commonwealth as a separate colony. A Governor and a Chief Justice have been appointed by the Federal Government and the island is a dependency of Australia.

The solution of the question of self-government would certainly not have been so quickly reached had not all the conditions in Australia at the beginning of the 'fifties been suddenly and radically altered by the discovery of rich gold-fields in various districts. Gold had already been found during the construction of the road over the Blue Mountains (1814). The Government had hushed up the discovery from fear that it would be unable to control the excitement which would assuredly be caused by its publication. It was only when the opening of the Californian mines in 1848 had attracted the attention of the world that serious attention was paid to the precious metal in Australia. An Australian blacksmith, Hargreaves, who had spent some years in California, carefully examined the mountains near Bathurst, in February, 1851, and on the 12th of that month he found quantities of alluvial gold in Lewes Pond Creek.

HOISTING THE BRITISH FLAG IN NEW GUINEA

Fearing that the Germans would take over the island of New Guinea, the Premier of Queensland took formal possession of the eastern portion in March, 1883. Germany took over the northern portion.

This discovery did not remain a secret like the former one. The whole continent rang with the news, and by May dense crowds of colonists were flocking to the place. A few weeks later gold was also found near Ballarat in Victoria ; then in October also near Mount Alexander, north of Melbourne. A few months later the veins of gold at Bendigo to the south were also discovered. In Queensland, gold was not found until 1858, and in Western Australia not until 1886-1887.

The Gold Fever

The effect of these discoveries upon the world was indescribable. In the first place the whole population of Australia caught the gold fever. Every man who could work or move, whether labourer, seaman, or clerk, rushed to the gold washings. The old settlements were so emptied of their inhabitants that Melbourne for a long time had only one policeman available. South Australia produced the impression of a country inhabited merely by women and children. The situation was the same in Tasmania, and even in New Zealand. Afterward, when the news of the discoveries reached America and the Old World, a new wave of immigrants flooded the country, and the whole overflow of the population streamed into the gold-fields.

Under these circumstances the population of Australia rapidly increased. In Victoria, where the influx was the greatest, the population had numbered 70,000 souls in July, 1851 ; nine months later that number was living on the gold-fields alone, and in 1861 the whole population of the colony amounted to 541,800 souls. New South Wales then reckoned 358,200 inhabitants; South Australia 126,800; Tasmania 90,200 ; Queensland had 34,800, and Western Australia 15,600. This rise in the figures of the population was encouraging to the economic development of Colonies, but it put the Government which was suddenly confronted with these occurrences in a very difficult position. The exodus of civil servants from their recently created posts was so universal that the administration threatened to come to · a standstill. Salaries were doubled, but to no purpose ; the attraction of the gold-fields was too potent. The Governor of Victoria found himself finally compelled to apply to England for a regiment of soldiers, who could not run away without

Difficulties Caused by the Influx

being liable to a court-martial. The Government offices were at the same time filled by two hundred pensioned prison warders, brought over from England.

The Government was soon faced by another class of difficulties arising from its legal position toward the new branch of industry. According to the view of the legal advisers of the Government all mines of precious metals, whether on Crown land or private property, belonged to the Crown. They advised the Governors therefore to prohibit gold-mining absolutely, in order not to disturb the peaceful development of the Colonies. Under the prevailing conditions this counsel was as superfluous as it was foolish, since the means at the disposal of the authorities were absolutely insufficient to enforce it. Sir Charles Fitzroy, the Governor of New South Wales, contented himself with issuing a proclamation, as soon as the first find of gold was publicly announced, which permitted gold-mining on Crown land only on payment of a fixed prospecting tax of thirty shillings a month ; and on the discovery of rock gold claimed for the Government ten per cent. of the proceeds of working the quartz. This order naturally met with little response from the gold-diggers, however much in other respects it was calculated to aid the development of the colony by increasing the public resources. It is true that they agreed to it in New South Wales, where the political situation had not been so violently disturbed, but not so in Victoria, where the Governor had also adopted the enactment of Sydney. For one thing, the Government was not so firmly established there as in the mother colony ; and Victoria had also received a very high percentage of the roughest and most lawless people as new members of the population. Not every one of them was so fortunate as to find gold ; they could not pay the high fee, and began to agitate, first, against the amount of the impost ; secondly, against the institution itself. The ill-feeling was soon universal, not only in the gold-fields, but also in the old settlements and towns.

Laws to Regulate Gold-mining

The prevalent idea was that the application of the large sums derived from the licences and imposts merely to the payment of the costs of the administration did not meet the interests of the population, and that the system should be

PROCESSION OF THE GOVERNORS OF AUSTRALIA AT THE MELBOURNE EXHIBITION OF 1888

changed. A reduction of the tax did not satisfy anybody; on the contrary, disturbances in the camps became more and more frequent. A murder had been committed in October, 1854, in Eureka Camp near Ballarat. The feeble police force made some blunders in following up the case, and consequently disturbances broke out among the gold-diggers,
Disturbances on the Gold-fields which were soon aimed at the hated prospecting licence; and, finally, when the Governor had sent all the troops at his disposal into the riotous district, a regular battle was fought on December 3 between thirty gold-diggers and a body of soldiers. Out of the 120 rioters who were captured, the ringleaders were sent to Melbourne to be tried, but there was no court to be found which, in spite of the overwhelming evidence of guilt, would pronounce a verdict against them.

The tax question was settled only in 1855. A gold-digger's licence, costing £1 for the year, was substituted for the monthly prospecting tax, which was abolished. In order to cover the loss of revenue to the colonial exchequer, an export duty of half a crown on every ounce of gold was imposed. This wise measure laid the imposts primarily on the successful gold-digger, a policy which secured a good reception for the law and satisfied all parties. Before the end of the year the Governor of Victoria was able to report to London that quiet prevailed in every camp.

It is not necessary to follow in detail the respective histories of each colony, because each has followed, in the main, along the same lines of political and economic development. The turning-point with all was the discovery of gold, which caused a rush of population from Great Britain that entirely shifted the political centre of gravity.

The first use which every state made
Votes for Women of its new powers was in the direction of democratising political institutions. The franchise was gradually reduced until all disabilities from poverty were removed; and, since 1900, universal adult suffrage, without distinction of sex, has been established in every state except Victoria. Every colony also has had its conflicts between the elective Assembly and the nominated Council, which have resulted either in a lessening of the money qualifica-

tion of the councillor, or, as in Victoria and South Australia, in the replacement of the nominee by the elective system.

It has been found by experience that those Upper Chambers which rest upon an elective basis are more powerful than those whose members are nominated. Thus, the Legislative Council of Victoria has always been able to assert its will in opposition to the Assembly; while the Legislative Council of New South Wales, like the House of Lords, having always the fear of " swamping " before its eyes, has always yielded to the ascertained wish of the majority of electors. Disputes between the two Houses have generally arisen over money Bills, the Assembly claiming that the Upper House has only the powers of the House of Lords with regard to these—that is to say, that it may reject but not amend them, the Council insisting that it has every power of a legislative chamber, of which it has not been expressly deprived by the Constitution Act. Usage has confirmed the claim of the Assembly in this respect until it has become a part of the unwritten
The Upper Houses and Finance constitution. The constitution of Victoria expressly prohibits the Council from amending a money Bill. This led to the two gravest political disputes in Australian history.

In 1863, the McCulloch Ministry imposed protective duties. The measure was rejected by the Upper House. The Customs Duties Bill was then tacked to the Appropriation Bill. The Council refused to be tricked in this way, and rejected the Appropriation Bill. An appeal to the electors returned a large majority in favour of the new duties. Meantime, in the absence of an Appropriation Bill, public servants could not be paid their salaries, and all creditors of the Crown had to wait for their money. The ingenious device was then resorted to of drawing money from a bank to pay the State creditors and immediately confessing judgment when the bank sued for its recovery. The order of the Supreme Court thus became a warrant to repay the money to the bank, by whom it was immediately lent again to the Government and the same process repeated. In order to prevent Parliamentary proceedings from being reduced to a farce, the Council, after a conference, yielded. But a similar difficulty arose again in 1873, when, Sir

AUSTRALIAN BANK CRISIS OF 1892: SCENE OUTSIDE THE UNION BANK, MELBOURNE

Graham Berry being Premier, the Council rejected a Bill for the payment of Members. This was again tacked to the Appropriation Bill, which was again rejected by the Council. The Government on this occasion simply deferred the payment of its debts and dismissed most of the public servants.

The situation thus created was so impossible that the two Houses soon agreed to terms. The Appropriation Bill was passed without the sums for the payment of Members, and the dispute was referred to the Secretary of State in London. Sir Graham Berry and Professor Charles Pearson, a member of his Cabinet, personally preferred a request to the British Government to provide a means of escape from constitutional deadlocks. The Secretary of State, however, refused to interfere, and thus finally estab-

Several Constitutional Deadlocks

lished the principle that the Colonies are absolute masters in their own household. In 1880 the Council passed the Bill for payment of Members.

Simultaneously with the agitation for greater political powers, and for the same reason—namely, the influx of population—the eternal land question entered upon a new phase in all the colonies. Not all

of the many thousands of immigrants could be employed in gold-mining, and many of the diggers were unsuccessful. Few matters caused the authorities of those days more anxiety than the task of

Employment Difficulties for New Settlers

finding employment for the new settlers. The private companies which, both in Victoria and New South Wales, had undertaken the construction of railways proved in every case unable to complete their task. The Governments of the two colonies took over the undertakings. But every extension of the railways into more fertile districts increased the demand for land and strengthened the antagonism between the small settler, who required a freehold, and the pastoral lessee. The interests of the two classes were at that time irreconcilable ; but obviously it was to the interest of the country to encourage the small settler, even at the expense of the squatter. Unfortunately, heated passions were aroused, and the leaders of neither side foresaw that the difficulties would solve themselves by the mere increase of population. Consequently, a measure was passed in 1861 by Sir John Robertson which showed too plainly an animus against the squatters.

The result was a class warfare which distracted New South Wales for more than twenty years. The principle of the measure—which was copied, with modifications, by every other colony—was the permission to any man of full age to enter upon and mark out—or, as it was called, "select"—an area ultimately fixed at 640 acres of Crown lands, whether **A Law that** these were vacant or in the **Encouraged** occupation of a squatter, and, **Blackmail** by residence and the payment of £1 per acre, by annual instalments of one shilling, to become its owner. While this measure was a measure of justice when the agricultural districts near the coast were occupied as sheep-runs, it worked great hardship in the more remote districts, which at that time, in the absence of means of transport, were unsuitable to agriculture. A class of blackmailers grew up, who travelled the country "selecting" a few picked spots of a run—e.g., the paddocks containing water—picking out the eyes like a cockatoo, as it was called—whose only object was to be bought out by the squatter. The squatters, in self-defence, were forced to purchase all the strategic portions of their run, and by thus "peacocking" it they prevented settlement.

Another device of self-protection was the employment of "friendly" selectors, who would be supplied by the squatter with funds to make the necessary "improvements," and at the end of his term of residence would sell to the station. Selections of this sort were called "Dummies," and such a proceeding was made a misdemeanour. Yet, so powerless are laws when they make offences of what the community regard as legitimate methods of self-defence, that though "dummying" has been notoriously practised on almost every large station in New South Wales, only one person has been convicted of the offence, and he by his own confession. The **Recurrence** difficulties of the situation were **of Land** increased by the selector being **Difficulties** allowed to bring action for trespass in respect of his holding before it was fenced. The selector alleged that the squatter drove his sheep on to his holding; the squatter, in his turn, said that they were driven there by the selector, who wanted to make out of a lawsuit the money which he would never get out of his land.

By 1884 the situation had become intolerable. The climatic conditions and

the potentialities of the different portions of the colony had become better known, and the railways had been driven far into the interior. It was seen that while 640 acres were an excessive holding in the rich agricultural districts of the seaboard, they were wholly insufficient to provide a living in the pastoral districts. The colony was consequently divided into three districts—eastern, central, and western—which were placed under the charge of local boards, and a special tribunal was appointed to settle disputes. The pastoralists in the eastern and central divisions were given a fifteen-years tenure of half their runs, while the other half was thrown open to selection. New tenures were introduced in the form of long leaseholds, under varying conditions, and conditional purchases of the freehold were forbidden in the western district. This measure was amended in 1895 and 1897, when the old feud between selector and squatter may be said to have died out.

The wool industry is still the mainstay of Australia, but pastoralists have learnt the value of agriculture, and experience has proved that even the un- **Evils of** likely lands of the western **Large Land** district can be made to grow **Holdings** wheat profitably. The demand for land, however, in the richer districts of each colony, which were naturally the first to be held in freehold by the early settlers, is still beyond the supply, and every Government has had to consider measures for breaking up the excessive estates held by private owners whose wealth makes them indifferent to using them most profitably.

The other states avoided the principal evils of the New South Wales Land Act by throwing open only specified areas for free selection, or providing that only surveyed lands should be open to this form of acquisition. No other state, however, has the same variety or extent of good lands as New South Wales.

The fiscal question divided parties in all the Australian states within a few years of the grant of responsible government. The cause was again the number of new immigrants and the necessity of finding employment for men who were tired of gold-digging. Professor Rabbeno has observed that the movement towards Protection is synchronous with the absorption of the more fertile public lands by private owners. This was certainly the

THE AUSTRALIAN LABOUR TROUBLE OF 1890

The most memorable of Australia's industrial crises was the Labour and Shipping Strike at Melbourne in 1890. The illustrations represent : 1. Troopers escorting non-union men to the Melbourne gas-works. 2. Pickets trying to stop men from going to Gas Company's office for employment. 3. Mounted infantry arriving at Spencer Street Station from the country to preserve order. 4. Mass meeting of strikers in Flinders Park, Melbourne, on August 31.

case in Victoria, where the good agricultural land is comparatively a small area, the freehold of which had passed into the hands of a few very wealthy men. At first employment was found on public works, which were constructed out of **Beginning** Government loans and the pro- **of Protective** ceeds of the sale of public lands. **Policy** Victoria entered the London money market first and sold her lands earlier than the other colonies. She was thus the first to be compelled to adopt a protective policy. New South Wales lived longer on loan money and sold more acres of land. She had also a low tariff, which was only incidentally protective.

The relative progress of the two states was for a long time the classic example used by Free Traders and Protectionists alike, although they did not quote the same figures, to prove the superiority of a Free Trade policy. Now, however, that since 1900 New South Wales has come under the protective tariff of the Commonwealth, her progress has been so much more rapid that it is evident that her apparent superiority over Victoria in the early days was due to natural causes, and not to her fiscal policy. The controversy has ceased to be a live issue in Australia since the Commonwealth definitely adopted a protective tariff, which has been approved by the people in two General Elections, and

has, on the public admission of Free Traders, " come to stay." One result has been to stimulate immigration by the establishment of new industries. Every year sees the establishment of branches of European or foreign factories to supply the goods which, previous to the tariff were imported.

All State aid to religion was withdrawn in New South Wales immediately upon responsible government. In the other colonies it never existed. In every colony education is compulsory. Religious teaching is given in New South Wales upon the Irish national system. In Victoria it does not form part of the curriculum. A right of entry is given to the clergy of any denomination during school hours to give religious instruction to the pupils of his persuasion ; but this is rarely availed of except by the Church of England. Secondary and technical schools exist in all the capitals and in some of the large towns. The State gives bursaries, which take a **Conditions** child from the State school, **of State** through the intermediate, to **Education** the university. The system of teaching, and the curriculum of the State schools, is antiquated, and could be much improved. From motives of economy, the pupil teacher system is encouraged, and its evils are apparent. The Roman Catholics have established separate

King, Sydney

A RED-LETTER DAY FOR THE AUSTRALIAN COLONIES
Federal Procession of February 1, 1901, passing Sydney Post Office, where an illuminated map of Australia was exhibited.

schools, and their alleged desire to get State assistance, either directly or by the system of payment by results, has led to strong sectarian divisions, which have always to be reckoned with in an election, though they are not much spoken of.

From 1877 to 1890 large sums were spent by all the states in assisting immigration. Employment was found for the newcomers on railways and other public works, which were constructed out of moneys borrowed in London. The period was one of immense prosperity, and large sums of English money were invested, on deposit at call, or for short periods, with the Colonial banks, at rates of interest from 5 per cent. to 7 per cent., which were lent again by the banks on mortgage for fixed terms to squatters who required money for improvements or for the purchase of their runs for protection against selectors. So long as loan moneys were plentiful, there was no danger in this process ; but when borrowing was reduced and there came a cycle of bad seasons, the banking resources of the colony were unequal to the strain, and a crisis occurred in 1892, from the effects of which Australia is only now recovering.

Simultaneously with this shock to the credit of Australia, a portent appeared in the political horizon which was at first sight no less terrifying to foreign capitalists. Australia had always been democratic—she had introduced the ballot, triennial Parliaments, and Universal Suffrage — but it was not till 1892 that a distinctive "Labour Party" appeared in the New South Wales Parliament. This political organisation was

London Stereoscopic Co.

SIR HENRY PARKES
Formerly Premier of New South Wales and the father of Australian Federation, which was consummated Jan. 1, 1901.

the outcome of an unsuccessful strike, which, beginning with the refusal of a shipowner to reinstate an officer, spread sympathetically throughout the ranks of organised labour.

It was met and defeated by an equally extensive organisation of employers. Beaten, defeated in the strike, the labourers sought their revenge in politics. It must, however, be admitted, looking back over a period of sixteen years, that the work of the party has been inadequate, by comparison with the excessive hopes of its members and the undignified alarm of its opponents. The Labour Party, indeed, was never a party of revolution, and is, indeed, opposed at the elections by the Socialists. Its influence certainly quickened the passage of a measure establishing old age pensions of ten shillings a week to every person over sixty-five (1899); and Women's Suffrage (1901) also owes much to its support. But for the most part it has advocated measures which found place in the programme of one or other of the established parties.

The chief merit of the Labour Party lies not so much in what it has accomplished as in the spirit of greater earnestness and sincerity which it has introduced in Australian politics. Among the measures which owe much to its support is the Industrial Arbitration Act (1901), which provides a tribunal which is empowered to deal with all matters affecting the condition of any industry, whenever a dispute arises between employer and employed. This court can declare a minimum wage, and, under certain circumstances, direct that preference be given to unionists ; an order affecting the particular dispute may be made a common rule of the whole trade,

MELBOURNE EXHIBITION, WHERE THE FIRST FEDERAL PARLIAMENT MET, ON MAY 9, 1901

It was first intended to hold the ceremony in the Melbourne Parliament building, but owing to space and other reasons the Exhibition Buildings were finally selected. The landing of the Heir Apparent on the soil of federated Australia was the occasion of a memorable outburst of united welcome from the six colonies, all petty colonial jealousies being forgotten. Receptions at Parliament House and the opening of the first Federal Parliament followed.

in order to prevent any employer obtaining an advantage by methods which the court may have declared unfair. This measure, which depends largely for its success upon sympathetic administration, has, since 1904, been administered by a ministry of **Arbitration in Labour Disputes** professed enemies—who have not, however, ventured to repeal or amend it—and it has been clipped of much of its usefulness by the judicial decisions of a court, some members of which have not hesitated to forget their judicial position and denounce its principles and methods. The Act has, however, been thoroughly successful in putting down sweating, and, even in its crippled condition, has prevented strikes. By one of its clauses, to strike or lock out before invoking the jurisdiction of a court is made a misdemeanour. It has not been found in New South Wales that the workmen refuse to obey the order of the court.

In 1885, at the request of all the colonies but New South Wales, the Imperial Parliament passed an Act establishing a Federal Council consisting of delegates from the several colonies who were empowered to legislate on certain matters of common interest, and also had a limited authority in respect of internal affairs.

This council, which met annually, never fulfilled the hopes of its founders,

among whom Mr. James Service (Victoria) and Sir Samuel Griffith (Queensland) were the chief. New South Wales, under the guidance of its great statesman, Sir Henry Parkes, refused to join the movement, on the ground that the powerlessness of the council to enforce its decrees would have one of two results—either only trival matters would be brought before it, or it would come into conflict with the states. In either case the council would excite prejudice against the more complete union which was always before Sir Henry's eyes. In 1891 Sir H. Parkes, in the face of great obstacles caused by the antagonism of the Victorian Ministers, who resented his holding aloof from the Federal Council, assembled the representatives of all the colonies, including New Zealand, to Sydney, and obtained their agreement to present proposals for federation to their several Parliaments. The main principles **Father of Federal Movement** of the proposed union were discussed by the assembled Ministers in open debate, and upon the resolutions so arrived at a measure was drafted by Sir Samuel Griffith and Mr. A. Ingles Clark (Tasmania) which has remained the substance of the present constitution. Various untoward circumstances prevented this measure being discussed in the New South Wales

Parliament, and the other colonies waited upon New South Wales. Sir H. Parkes went out of office, and the Ministries which followed were opposed to union. But the popular interest in the movement had been kept alive through the unflagging exertions of Sir Edmund Barton, and Sir Henry Parkes announced his intention (1894) of moving in the matter in Parliament. Mr. Reid, the leader of the Provincialists, was then in office. He cleverly anticipated Sir Henry's attack by adopting a suggestion which had been made by Sir John Quick that a constituent convention should be elected to frame a draft constitution. Sir Henry Parkes was not elected to the Parliament of 1895, and Mr. Reid was in no hurry to hasten the federal movement.

Convention in Favour of Federation The Convention, which consisted of ten representatives elected from each state, met in Adelaide in April, 1897, and was adjourned to Sydney, and again to Melbourne, where its labours were finally completed in May, 1898. The measure, thus passed, had to be adopted by a plebiscite in every state. The Provincialist Parliament of New South Wales endeavoured to secure its rejection by requiring that if there were not 80,000 affirmative votes, the measure should be considered lost. As the total number of anticipated voters was between 170,000 to 200,000, it was thought that this device—which was a flagrant breach of the agreement made by New South Wales and the other states that the question should be decided by a majority—would finally stifle the movement towards union. However, in spite of the bitter opposition of Mr. Reid and the Free Trade party, a majority of votes were cast for the Bill, though the number was 5,000 short of the required minimum. Some trifling alterations were then made in the text of the draft Bill, and in 1899 it was again submitted to the popular vote. On this occasion the majority exceeded the statutory minimum, and New South Wales fell into line with the other states, to the deep resentment of the provincial Free Traders. The Commonwealth thus formed was proclaimed on January 1, 1900, and the history of the several states has from that date merely a local interest.

Federation Finally Secured

King, Sydney

BIRTH OF THE AUSTRALIAN COMMONWEALTH: THE SWEARING-IN CEREMONY

Standing beside what are now priceless memorials to the Australian people, the table and the inkstand used by Queen Victoria when she signed the Commonwealth Act, Lord Hopetoun, the first Governor-General of the Commonwealth, swore: " I, John Adrian Louis, Earl of Hopetoun, do swear I will well and truly serve our Sovereign Lady Queen Victoria in the office of Governor-General of the Commonwealth of Australia, and that I will do right to all manner of people after the laws and usages of this Commonwealth without fear or favour, affection, or regard. So help me God."

King, Sydney

THE BIRTH OF THE AUSTRALIAN COMMONWEALTH: SWEARING-IN CEREMONY IN THE CENTENNIAL PARK, SYDNEY, JANUARY 1, 1901

This photograph shows the natural amphitheatre in which the swearing-in pavilion stood. A quarter of a million people obtained excellent views of the ceremony. The air and space of the continent were thus typified in the inaugural ceremony. Lord Hopetoun and the new Ministry took the oaths of fealty and office at the actual table used by Queen Victoria when she signed the Commonwealth Act in July, 1900. This present of the great Queen to the new Australia was placed for the occasion in the beautiful pavilion.

AUSTRALIA IN OUR OWN TIME

BY THE HON. BERNHARD R. WISE

NOT only is the island continent of Australia equal in size, and as varied in climate, as Europe without Siberia, or as the United States without Alaska, but the wide distances are already developing different types in the several states. Nevertheless, beneath this diversity there is an underlying unity.

In no country in the world is there less admixture of races. Australia is completely British. Of the total population taken at the census of 1901—3,782,443—only 148,801 were born outside the British Empire; 2,933,274 were born within the Commonwealth. Contrast this with Canada and her million Frenchmen, or with South Africa, where the English are outnumbered by the Dutch. This homogeneity of race, together with its geographical situation, give Australia its great importance as a unit of the empire.

Dominant British Element By its position it commands the trade route between America and Asia, and is the frontier of the empire on its most vulnerable side—the Far East—where, under its improved military system, it could land a fully-equipped military unit within thirty days of the outbreak of disturbance. Australia's place in the line of the empire's defence must depend, inevitably, upon the temper of her people. The first or second or third generation of native-born Australians may be, as they are now, British in every instinct; but account must always be taken, in considering the future, of the disintegrating influences of time and distance. As Australians outgrow the somewhat depressing idea of dependency they are taking to the newer and more stimulating idea of Nationalism.

In this mood, and having this ideal, they aim first, as being their immediate duty, to develop Australia. They would have an Australian navy. Already—thanks to the exertions of the Labour Party—they are forming a citizen army, based on universal service. They frame their tariffs solely in order to develop Australian industries, to maintain the Australian market for Australian workmen. The Australian holds that in thus strengthening Australia he helps the empire.

It is often said that Australia neglects her responsibilities by discouraging the growth of population. It is true that an occasional and irresponsible working-class speaker may, at times, **Growth of National Ideals** exhort his fellows to "keep the good thing for themselves"; but it is not true that there is any general tendency among Australians either to check population or to discourage immigration. Critics should remember the immensity of the continent, and that its physical characteristics have prevented the spread of settlement. There were three stages of settlement in Australia—first, of the fertile lands between the mountains and the sea; secondly, of the uplands; thirdly, of the great plains beyond. Each new stage was rendered possible only by a long experience. The western plains, on which the best wheat now grows, were thought for many years to be unsuitable for settlement; and two generations elapsed before it was discovered that salt-bush was food for sheep. Even now the immense distance of the interior from the seaboard practically blocks it from settlers, so that the full capacity of Australia will never be known until the Commonwealth completes two transcontinental railways—from east to west, and from north to south.

Accordingly, if we would estimate Australia in respect of increase of population we should bear in mind the slow and gradual shifting of agriculture from the coast towards the west. More than half, or 56 per cent., of Australia is still empty and in the larger states, such as South Australia and West Australia, the proportion of permanent to temporary occupation is very small. Taking Australia as a whole, the average population to the square mile is only 1·27. Victoria, being the smallest, is the most densely populated state ; but she had in 1901 only a population of 13·67 to the square mile. The charge against Australia of her unduly small birth-rate is not yet proved. Not that the rate has fallen off in comparison with the years from 1850–1880 ; but even in 1905 it was at the rate of 24·43 per thousand, which does not compare unfavourably with other countries of a similar standard of civilisation. Probably the apparent decline is due to the earlier rates being abnormal, owing to the rapid influx of young emigrants.

Sparseness of the Population

Until 1887 all the colonies assisted immigrants. The large influx of newcomers, and the construction of public works out of loan money, led to great speculations in land, with English money deposited at call. In consequence, first the building societies (1889–1891), and secondly the banks, with few exceptions, stopped payment. Public works were stopped and private expenditure curtailed. The distress led to labour troubles, which were no sooner ended than Australia entered upon the worst and most protracted drought ever known. In 1900, for the first time since the bank failures, there was an excess of arrivals over departures, and with the return of good seasons efforts are being made by all the states to encourage settlement and immigration.

And, indeed, there is no country which holds out better prospects to the immigrant. The climate is as various as that of Europe, but it has no extremes of heat or cold. It ranges for the most part from sub-tropical to temperate ; from the land of the mango and grenadilla in the far north, through the sugar-cane regions on the eastern coast, to the potato fields of Victoria, and the snow of the Australian Alps. There is no industry connected with the land in older countries which cannot be carried on profitably in Australia. Whatever an immigrant has done in other lands he may do in some part of Australia. Nor need he be frightened by the bogey of drought.

Attractions Offered to Immigrants

Experience is teaching that drought can be fought by the storage of water and ensilage. The destructiveness of drought in the past has been mainly due to overstocking and the recklessness engendered by good seasons. Further, drought chiefly affects the interior and the coastal regions.

It is true that the population of Australia is too much concentrated in the capital cities. Of the 3,782,943 people numbered in the 1901 census, 1,482,304 lived in the capitals. The causes of this abnormal concentration are, first, the centralised administration of the several states, which grew out of a military command, and not, as in the United States, out of a town-meeting ; secondly, the economic condition of the country. The primary industries are still the principal industries of all the states, and their products are exported. The sea-borne trade of Australia is out of all proportion to the average of other countries, so that it is inevitable that the population should crowd into the cities when the bulk of the people live by exports and imports. As manufacturing competes with the extractive industries, the proportion between town and country population will become more reasonable. It must also be remembered that it was the policy of every State Government to draw all trade to the capital city.

Australian Industrial Conditions

It has been aptly remarked that, " strictly speaking, Australian states never resembled distinct states. Trade, geography, England, and ' the crimson thread of kinship ' made them one from the first." Obviously, too, the barriers of intercolonial trade, of six distinct tariffs, and the need for defence against foreign aggression, were strong motive towards union. But they were not sufficiently powerful to overcome state jealousies. It was left to Sir Henry Parkes, by the battle cry, " Australia for the Australians," finally to rouse the people to a sense of their responsibilities. This cry, like Sir Edmond Barton's " A continent for a nation, and a nation for a continent," was idealistic without being visionary, and in inculcating respect for a larger self, made men think more kindly of their past lives and of the great future which lay before them. The provincialists showed that they felt instinctively that they were fighting the new spirit of nationalism by the title of Colonists' Defence League, which they gave their organisation. Colonial dependency was, indeed, dying in the last ditch, and a new idea of empire, almost unnoticed at the time, was springing into life.

The opposition was naturally greatest in New South Wales, as being the oldest colony, and was increased by the attitude of the Free Trade Party, who, placing their fiscal dogma before all else, refused to join the union except on the impossible terms that the smaller colonies—which, unlike New South Wales, had long used up their revenue from waste lands—should abolish their tariff. In the meantime a convention of ten delegates from each state had prepared a Constitution for submission to a referendum. The Bill was approved by a majority in every state after the difficulties, already described, which it met in New South Wales. But at the elections for the following year, New South Wales returned only three Federalists out of sixteen members, and had henceforward, under the influence of its Press and politicians,

Opposition to Scheme of Federation maintained a consistently anti-federal attitude. This inter-state jealousy, which is unfortunately felt more or less in other states, though nowhere to the same degree as in New South Wales, determined the form of the Constitution. In the choice between the American and the Canadian forms, the American was necessarily adopted to meet the susceptibilities of the different states. Consequently, the Commonwealth has only those powers which are expressly conferred upon it by the Constitution, while all the reserve powers remain with the states.

This leads to curious conflicts. The Commonwealth is empowered to deal with immigration ; but it cannot take a step to settle immigrants on the lands, because these are under the sole control of the states. The Commonwealth also deals with such matters of general interest as : (1) laws relating to customs and excise ; (2) trade and commerce ; (3) banking ; (4) quarantine ; (5) industrial disputes extending beyond the limits of one state ; (6) navigation and shipping, and other subjects of legislation, making forty-nine in all. A High Court has been established, consisting of five judges, to serve as a much-needed Court of Appeal from the State Courts,

and to interpret and protect the Constitution. Any law passed by a State Parliament, in conflict with a federal law or with a constitution, is to that extent void ; but in other respects the states retain full power of legislation. The Federal Parliament has two Houses. The franchise in each state for either

Composition of Federal Parliament House is that for the Lower House of the state. The Federal Senate is elected by the state voting as one constituency ; is small, sexennial, and has six members from each state. The Federal House of Representatives is triennial, is twice the size of the Senate, and contains representatives from each state proportionately to its population. The original ten or twelve topics of common interest are expanded into forty-nine, and include relations with Pacific islands, laws as to special races—if not aborigines of federating states—and laws to prevent strikes. Inter-state duties and preferences are abrogated. Provision is made for accepting and governing surrendered and acquired territory, and for carving new states out of old states with the consent of the latter. Appeal to the judicial committee of the Privy Council is maintained, but modified.

The financial clauses of the Constitution are the least satisfactory, and are, for the moment, causing great friction. The problem before the framers of the Constitution was to ensure inter-state free trade—which involved a common tariff under the control of the Commonwealth—with the financial requirements of each state.

It was evident that the customs receipts from a federal tariff would amount to much more than the federal expenditure. At the same time, each state would find itself deprived of the customs duties, which formed a large, but unequal proportion of their revenues. The logical

Jealousy of Federal Powers solution would have been for the Commonwealth to take over sufficient of the State debts, that the interest on these should absorb the surplus. But the provincialists feared that such a power would give the Commonwealth a handle to check future borrowing by the states, and the Constitution finally empowered the Commonwealth only to take over the debts of the states incurred previously to 1900. The Commonwealth Government has offered to propose

T   27   G

an amendment to the Constitution which would enable the states to be relieved of the debts incurred subsequently to 1900; but this proposal to " rob " them of their " debts " has been indignantly rejected.

Deprived of this method of disposing of the federal surplus, and compelled to satisfy the demands of provincialists, that the states should have some **State and** security that they would **Federal** receive their portions, the **Revenue** framers of the Constitution, at the suggestion of the late Sir Edward Braddon, adopted a clause providing that the Commonwealth should return to each state at least three-quarters of the receipts from customs and excise duties. The operation of this clause was limited to ten years. The Commonwealth, in fact, has always returned to the states more than the legal three-quarters ; and the provincialists, who at first denounced this clause as " The Braddon Blot," are now demanding that it should be continued for another twenty years. The clause, however, is calculated in the future to hamper any Federal Government, so that this proposal is not likely to be accepted. The Commonwealth in its turn has renewed its offer to take over the State debts. Matters at present are in a deadlock ; but under the Constitution the Commonwealth has power to levy taxes and deal with the customs surplus as it pleases.

At present the revenue of the Commonwealth is derived entirely from customs and excise ; but if no arrangement can be come to with the states, it will be necessary to impose some form of federal, direct taxation in order to fulfil ministerial promises to grant Old Age Pensions.

The expenditure of the Commonwealth is mainly in respect of the services which have been taken over by the Commonwealth from the states—e.g., the post office and telegraphs, defence and, in the immediate future, quarantine. This is **State and** called in Federal Budgets **Federal** " transferred expenditure." **Expenditure** The " other expenditure "— as it is called—is the expenditure by the Commonwealth for purely Commonwealth purposes—e.g., the cost of Parliament.

It is obvious that, being relieved of such large items of expenditure as defence, postal services, the collection of customs and excise, and at the same time entitled to receive back from the Commonwealth not less than three-fourths of the proceeds of customs and excise, the states have been, since 1900, in a position to effect great economies. New South Wales, for instance, receives as its share of the Commonwealth surplus nearly a million a year, and has also been relieved of annual expenditure amounting to £750,000. The last three years also have been years of abounding prosperity, yet the Government of New South Wales during this period has increased the public indebtedness, while at the same time following the vicious practice of treating the proceeds of land sales—which amount to £900,000 per annum—as revenue instead of regarding them as a capital fund for public works. No other colony has been so extravagant as New South Wales, though none, except Queensland, has utilised to the full the opportunities for economy which federation has afforded.

The friction between the states and the Commonwealth need cause no alarm as to the future. Every federation has experienced the same difficulty, and Provincialism dies of its own pettiness. **Parish** In Sydney, for instance, the **Pump** Ministry of the day—1907— **Politics** has threatened to change the site of the observatory, and thus destroy the value of seventy years' astronomical observations, rather than allow it to pass to the Commonwealth under the clause of the Constitution which empowers them to take over the Astronomical and Meteorological departments of the State. The internal opposition to other federations has been far more formidable. There was the same discontent in the early days of the United States, which found expression in the now half-forgotten rising known to history as the " Whisky Rebellion " ; and contemporary observers have related of Canada that during the first ten years of the Dominion not 30 per cent. of Canadians would have voted for its continuance had any opportunity been offered to them of expressing an opinion.

It was the same in the case of the Scottish union with Great Britain, which Lockhart, a contemporary, declared to be " a base betrayal and mean giving up of the sovereignty, independence, liberty, laws, interest and honour of Scotland," and with regard to which he was as thoroughly convinced as any New South Wales Provincialist that " if Scotland had only stood out,

RESIDENCE OF GOVERNOR

HOUSES OF PARLIAMENT

GENERAL VIEW FROM THE POST-OFFICE BUILDINGS

NEW LAW COURTS

GOVERNMENT OFFICES

Photos: Edwards and E. N. A.

PRESENT-DAY PICTURES OF MELBOURNE

She would have made her own terms," so satisfied was he that England would not have lost "a good thing." "Had the Scots," he says, "stood their ground, "I have good reason to affirm that the English would have allowed a much greater number of representatives. The English saw too plainly the advantage that would **History** accrue to England by a union **Repeats** of the two kingdoms upon his **Itself** scheme, and would never have stuck at any terms to obtain it."

It is not at present easy to forecast the political future of Australia. Much depends upon the calibre of Federal members, in which each successive Parliament shows a decline. The salary of a member is too small for a livelihood, and too much for subsistence. Attendance in Parliament involves the abandonment of all business which cannot be carried on in the capital. For this the present salary—£600—gives no compensation; so that there is a growing tendency for Parliament to be composed of rich, old men, and those to whom the salary is the principal attraction. It would have been better if the proposal made at the Convention had been carried, fixing the salary at £1,000 a year.

Assuming, however, that Parliament maintains its prestige relatively to the State Parliaments, the probability is that there will be a considerable strengthening and extension of Federal power. The history of America shows that the influence of a central authority increases inevitably and insensibly; and in Australia this tendency will be much increased by the influence of the Labour Party, who, curiously enough, bitterly opposed the establishment of Federation. The levelling up of the conditions of industry in the various states is a principal object of the Party; but this involves the equalisation of the conditions in each state. It would be unfair, for example, if the Industrial **Strengthening** Arbitration Court in Sydney **of Federal** were to establish a minimum **Control** wage in New South Wales which was not paid by trade competitors in other states. Consequently an amendment of the Constitution may be looked for which, in some form or another, will give the Federal Parliament control over all industrial relations within the Commonwealth.

It was said by a Federal speaker during the Federal campaign, that Federation

would not cost the people of New South Wales two-and-sixpence per head—just the cost of registering a dog! In fact, it has not exceeded eighteenpence per head. Yet the enemies of Federation denounce its extravagance, and declare that its cost is enormous. Each party is looking at a different side of the shield. The expenditure of Federation is, as has been explained, partly on the "transferred services" and partly on matters which are purely Federal, which are called "other expenditure."

The total expenditure of the Commonwealth is large on account of the cost of running and keeping up the transferred departments; but Parliament is absolutely penurious in dealing with Federal services. Sir John Forrest, in his Budget speech of 1906, dealt with this matter very tersely: "It will be remembered that at the Adelaide Conference it was stated that the extra cost of Federation would amount to £300,000. Last year ' the other expenditure,' as distinguished from transferred expenditure, amounted to £827,355. If we deduct from that amount the provision **Economy** made for new works in **in Federal** the transferred departments, **Expenditure** £318,488; New Guinea, £20,000; sugar bounties and expenses of £154,706, and the Queen Victoria Memorial, £25,000; we arrive at a net amount of £309,161—equal to one-and-sixpence per head of the population." It illustrates the economical bent of Federal members that since its existence the Commonwealth has issued no loan.

The spirit which carried to success the Federal movement—"Australia for the Australians"—soon found expression in legislation.

Two features strike the English observer of Australian politics—first, the reliance on the State; secondly, the apparent recklessness of the legislation. The former is explicable by the history of Australia, and the second is largely the result of a misunderstanding. In order to understand the legislation in detail, some general observations are necessary.

Few contrasts in history are more striking than the differences between the development of the two British democracies which margin the Pacific—that of Australia and that of the United States. Localism and individualism are the breath of life in the policy of the United States. Australia from the first has regarded the citizen rather than the individual, and has known no dread of Government action. The differences between the two countries is in their origin. The United States sprang from the town meeting ; Australia, from the first, was centralised. The Government was an earthly providence from the beginning—dispensing food, controlling industries, and fixing the rate of wages. Nor did the influx of free settlers materially change the situation, because these spread themselves too quickly over the vast area of waste land to acquire that sentiment of localism which became instinctive in the concentrated settlements of New England. There came, indeed, to be a strong provincial jealousy between the several colonies which has even defied Federation. But this was never incompatible with a very wide exercise of the functions of government within each colony. In no part of the world has the doctrine of " Laisser faire " fewer adherents. The " administrative nihilism " (to use Professor Huxley's phrase) which would confine the action of a Government to preserving order **Functions of the Government** would have seemed treason to the busy settlers, who depended upon the Government to overcome the natural obstacles to settlement and provide those conveniences of civilisation which, in such a country, individuals would be powerless to obtain unaided.

Thus, in Australia, the Governments of the several states construct and own railways, tramways, and ferry-boats. They do their own printing, and make clothes for the police and military. They maintain agricultural farms, own and let out bulls and stallions, supply seed-wheat, sell frozen meat and dairy produce, export wines, and maintain cellars for its storage in London, provide hospitals and parks, subsidise agricultural shows and other forms of popular amusement, run mining batteries and grant aid to prospectors, send commercial agents to foreign countries, undertake the storage and shipment of meat and butter for export, and generally endeavour in every way to improve the means of communication and transport, and to aid in the development of the resources of the country. The Government, indeed, is expected to take the risk of testing new processes of production, and a Government department is always at hand to supply any citizen, without

charge, with the latest results of agricultural or industrial experiments in other countries. In no country does a settler on the land find more ready or abundant assistance from the organised power of the State.

This tendency to rely upon the Government has been strengthened by the **The Labour Party** collectivism of the Labour Party, who hold the faith that laws can regulate industries, and that the mere removal of social inequalities does little good unless the weaker are protected by law against the tyranny of the strong. To the Australian Labour Party, " private enterprise," " freedom of contract," " the law of supply and demand," and the other shibboleths of individual economics, are merely other expressions for " individual anarchy." Yet Australians are not lacking in enterprise. They take certain things from the Government as a matter of right—on the northern rivers of New South Wales the settlers have from the Government boats in which to save their own lives and property in time of flood—but they are certainly not remiss in the pursuit of their individual interests. At the worst there is a certain lack of public spirit and an unwillingness to give personal service to the state. This, however, is characteristic of any country whose leisured class has no traditional responsibility, and where the greater part of the community is occupied in the absorbing conquest of new lands. It was not until 1906 that New South Wales was given even a meagre form of local self-government.

Australians thus have swallowed all economic formulæ, and, Socialists without a creed, are pressing into their service every social instrument and agency. The contrast with the United States is startling. Indeed, the motto of the Labour Party might be " To make Australia everything **Fight against the Rule of Wealth** America is not " — so strenuously is it striving to protect Australia against the rule of wealth, and to practise the lessons which have been taught by the recent disclosures of social anarchy in United States.

In considering the charge brought against Australian legislators of being reckless, it must also be remembered that Australia is the Cinderella of modern nations, whom Democracy has just claimed for her own. It is a land of political faith and ideals, where the dreams of the study are soon translated into laws. Every adult has a vote; nowhere is there more unity of purpose, or freedom from distracting cares. Thus, whatever Democracy can accomplish will be accomplished in Australia, for good or ill; and its **The Coming Triumph of Democracy** qualities are soon determined in such a testing ground of politics. At present, all goes well. Material prosperity, the buoyancy of youth, the novelty of political power, combine to dissipate misgivings; and the day of disillusionment—if it should ever come—is still far distant. But, as yet, other countries hardly understand; and even in England there is jealousy and some suspicion of the bold, new ways. The capitalist class is timid, and others are doubtful. But no Act has yet been passed which in any way threatens property or which disregards the larger interests of the Empire.

The Labour Party, indeed, is neither Anarchist nor Socialist. Socialists, indeed, run candidates against nominees of the caucus. It is composed of level-headed men, representatives of trade-unions and the more intelligent labourers. Its members are, however, not confined to the artisan or labouring class, but are recruited from the majority of farmers and by a number of the younger professional men and clerks. It is supported because it is the only party with clear principles which have never been abandoned; and its leaders command the respect of all classes of the community. The Australian Labour Party is, indeed, on most essential points, opposed to the principles of the same party in England. The Australian labour men think so well of their country, and are so convinced that a country which is worth living in is worth fighting for, that they are pressing for universal military service. And instead of being indifferent to **Aims of Labour Party** the Empire, they are eager to strengthen it, because they know by experience that, on the whole, British rule makes for justice and freedom. But the apologia for Australian legislation should now come to detail.

The chief misapprehension exists upon the question of a " White " Australia. One of the first Acts of the Commonwealth Parliament, to whom the control of immigration is given by the Constitution, was a measure which was intended to exclude the coloured races from Australia. The ideal of a " White " Australia is held with passionate conviction by the vast majority of the Australian-born, who believe it to be a duty which they owe to civilisation to preserve Australia for the white races. The Parliament desired to enact the direct exclusion of coloured aliens; but the Colonial Office would permit this result to be effected only indirectly, by the use of a language test— i.e., the writing from dictation of fifty words in any European language. This provision exists in the law of Natal, where it is used for the same purpose, and Canada has an Act of equal stringency. The Australian Act also prohibited the importation of labour under contracts made abroad, partly in order to protect the intending emigrant from being trapped into improvident contracts, from ignorance of Australian conditions, and partly to prevent the importation of " strike-breakers " in the event of a labour dispute. This law has been wickedly **Laws to Regulate Labour** misrepresented by the provincialists, who detest the Commonwealth, and others who are interested in diverting the stream of immigration to other places than Australia. Harrowing tales have been told and believed of " Six Hatters " who have been prevented from landing in Australia by the greedy desire of the Labour Party to avoid competition. Without exception, all these tales are false. *No single white man or woman has ever been prevented from landing in Australia since the law has been passed.* Its provisions have been applied only to the objects for which they were intended—viz., the exclusion of coloured alien labourers; and during the tenure of office of the Labour Party permission was freely granted to any respectable coloured merchant, student, or traveller, who obtained a passport from his Government, to enter and travel in Australia. In 1905 the text of the section dealing with contract labour was altered so as to remove the possibility of any honest misapprehension, by expressing in clear terms the kind of contracts which were aimed at. The present difficulty in the way of immigration is the jealousy between the several states and their unwillingness to co-operate with the Commonwealth. The

1. General view of Brisbane.   2. Government House, Sydney.   3. General view of Sydney.

BRISBANE AND SYDNEY IN OUR OWN TIME
Photos Edwards and E. N. A.

Commonwealth has offered to provide and assist European emigrants of the right stamp, if the states will place at its disposal information as to the lands which each has for settlement, and the opportunities which each offers to new-comers of obtaining work. It illustrates the pettiness of provincial feeling that none of the states has made a reply to this communication. In the same spirit the Postal Act enacts that "no agreement for the carriage of mails shall be entered into on behalf of the Commonwealth unless it contains a condition that only white labour shall be employed."

A Federal Proposal Ignored

It was inevitable, by the Constitution of the Commonwealth, that a sufficient revenue must be raised through the Customs House at least to equal the proceeds of the tariffs of the federating states. Two of these, Victoria and South Australia, had already protective tariffs. It was obvious that the Federal Tariff could not destroy industries already protected. There was, however, a strong Free Trade feeling in New South Wales— existing chiefly, it must be admitted, among those classes who were protected by items in the so-called Free Trade Tariff of that colony, that a compromise tariff was passed after two years' struggle. In effect, this was a low protective tariff. It was not, however, high enough to prevent importers' rings from dropping prices of imported articles to cut-rates, which would stifle any infant industry. This was particularly noticeable in the case of agricultural machinery, and at the last General Election an overwhelming majority was cast in favour of a higher tariff.

The new tariff contains concessions in favour of Great Britain, although, of course, it has been framed mainly in the interests of Australia, because experience proves that there will be no immigration unless the immigrants can find industries to work at. Even the low tariff of the first Parliament caused some half-dozen large English and American firms to produce in Australia the goods which were formerly imported, and thus provide new employment for Australian workmen. In those industries, however, which cannot yet be established in Australia the new tariff gives to Great Britain a preference of from

Australia's New Tariff

5 to 10 per cent. Altogether the subsidy to Great Britain is officially estimated to be at least £1,250,000.

Two measures must be mentioned as completing the tariff policy of the Commonwealth. The first was designed to prevent the importation of "dumped" goods, and of goods which are made by trusts—the principle being to prohibit the import of competing goods which are not made under similar conditions as to wages, etc., as in Australia. The Minister for Customs has power to seize any goods at the Custom House suspected of infringing this law, and the burden of proving the contrary is thrown on the importer. At present the Commonwealth is engaged in a contest with an American agricultural implement trust, alleged to be an offshoot of the Standard Oil Company, with reference to the importation of harvesting machines, which were dropped 50 per cent. in price immediately upon the introduction of the tariff.

The second measure connected with the tariff policy is designed to prevent the benefit of protection going wholly to the manufacturers, and to require a just division of the profits. On proof that any protected manufacturer is making exceptional profits by means of a monopoly created in his favour by the tariff, an excise duty may be imposed upon his products, of such amount as will prevent the tariff from unduly raising prices. Such a person would be required, in the first instance, to work his factory according to highest industrial standards.

Objects of Tariff Policy

It is premature to judge of the effect of laws which have been so short a time in operation ; but it may be questioned whether these are not too complicated to prove effective. Nevertheless, they are a notable attempt to escape from the possible evils of a protective system.

It should be mentioned that tribunals exist in all the states for the purpose of determining rates of wages and other industrial conditions. The process in New South Wales is for an Industrial Court, presided over by a Judge of the Supreme Court, who is assisted by elected representatives of employers and employed. The essential feature of the Act is that it deals only with organised labour, whether this be a trade union or an industrial union specially organised under the Act. Thus, only a union can bring a complaint before a Court, and the collective funds of the union are a security for obedience to an award. The Act has worked with great success, although, unfortunately, it has become a battle sign of political partisanship. Passed by the Progressive Party, it has incurred the bitter hostility of the party calling itself Liberal, whose representatives during the last three years have put every obstacle in the way of its successful working, and are now proposing to substitute for it the Victoria system of Wages Boards.

During its five years' currency, the Act has stopped sweating in the clothing trade, and every important trade, in all about 110, is working under it. During the whole of this period there has been no industrial disturbances, and no strike, until the ill-organised union of wharf labourers went on strike this year (1907). For, as the author of the Act has repeatedly said, " it could not always prevent strikes, any more than diplomacy could always prevent war." There has been no instance of a union disobeying the award of a Court, and after an award **Laws that** has been made, no employer **Regulate** has come before the Court to **Wages** complain of its working. The Act was modelled upon that which has been so successful in the Dominion of New Zealand. The Wages Board serves the purpose in Victoria of an Industrial Court. Its weakness its inability effectively to enforce the penalties against individual workmen. Also, there is a want of harmony between the several awards. The wages of one trade may be fixed without regard to any dependent industry. For each trade has its own Board, consisting of an equal number of employers and employed presided over by an elected chairman, or, in default of an election, appointed by the Government. The Boards can take evidence, and make awards ; but, not being permanent bodies, they have no power to enforce penalties, and there is reason to believe that the evasion of awards is frequent. To remedy these weaknesses, Victoria is now establishing an Industrial Court, to serve as a court of appeal from the Boards, and to enforce penalties. Such a Court will inevitably be compelled to assume gradually the powers of the Industrial Court which New South Wales is now abandoning. For, it will be impossible to deal with an appeal

from the Wages Board of any trade without, in effect, regulating all the industrial conditions of the trade in question, and incidentally affecting others. The success or failure of any Wages Board has been found by experience to depend entirely on the good sense and capacity of its chairman. Passing now from politics and legislation, **Conditions** something may be said about **of Life in** Australian life and its charac- **Australia** teristics. The first thought of the incomer from the Old World, when once he has left the cities behind him, is that of limitless space. Boundless space, unlimited opportunities for human enterprise, with Nature waiting to be tamed by man's industry and ingenuity, to give a rich recompense in return—that is the first impression given by the hinterland of the cities.

This is not an impression of the eye only, but is strengthened a hundredfold by knowledge acquired concerning the mineral and agricultural wealth of Australia, and one soon learns that Australia can produce wheat crops of thirty bushels an acre, far surpassing the scanty yield of the Manitoban prairies, almost before he has left the first city with which he makes acquaintance. In that city, among the men whom he is sure to meet, he also will recognise the influence of life in boundless space. Inhabitants of a continent whose riches have so far been but slightly tapped, peculiarly blessed with climates of many varieties, from the tropical heat of Northern Queensland and of the northern part of South Australia, which is a geographical contradiction in terms, to the usually temperate but never frigid air of New South Wales and of Victoria, their hopes, their ambitions, and their confidence in themselves and in Australia, are as generous and as exhilarating as the air itself. Hence come two peculiarities, the first likely to puzzle and the second calculated in some measure to repel a new arrival. The first **Spirit of** is a courage in matters of busi- **Industrial** ness and in setting forth upon **Enterprise** grand undertakings apt to disconcert a man nurtured in less elastic surroundings. This is due not so much to the fact that the possibility of failure never presents itself to an Australian mind, or to a well-grounded belief that ultimate failure is out of the question. No real man can fail always in a country so bounteously endowed, and temporary failure does not depress a man when he knows that he can, and most likely will, rise to the surface again soon. The courage of the Australian is elastic; his hopeful spirit will brook no denial. From this comes an arrogance of manner and tone which are, at first acquaintance, rather disconcerting to the English mind, and the English mind is rather too apt to counter it by a certain air of superciliousness. Such, at any rate, is the Australian impression generally; but it is a wrong impression, having, like most fallacies, a historical origin. In the past, far too many ne'er-do-wells of gentle birth were sent to Australia, nominally to seek their fortunes in a new land, really in order that their degradation might continue out of sight and out of hearing of their relatives. They were incompetent and really supercilious. The Australian of to-day is, therefore, naturally prone to suspect the fresh arrival from England of both these faults, and to meet him more than half-way by boastful proclamation of his own capacity.

Mutual Suspicion and Regard

What, apart from work, can sociable and vigorous men do in Australia ? What is the manner of life, what are the social opportunities in the rural districts and in the cities ? These are questions to which the answers are both general and particular. The great cities—especially Sydney and Melbourne—are at least as well furnished with the comforts of life and with the means of communication as any in the world. Better than most, in this last respect, for the State undertakes the business and does it well. The hotels, judged from a cosmopolitan point of view, are fair ; the clubs are as good as any clubs can be, and much more hospitable than those of any other country. There are first-class theatrical and musical entertainments, and French restaurants nearly equal to any out of Paris.

Society receives the visitor with a frank readiness, to which the Old World—to say nothing of the American world—is a complete stranger ; and it is a society of keen wits working in the brains of eager men, and of lively, attractive, and sensible women. Does a globe-trotter desire to see cricket or to play it ? He can see the very best to be seen on the face of the globe, and, if he be anywhere near its standard, he will be a welcome recruit. Nowhere will he see better horseracing, and should the newcomer be a yachts-

Australia the Home of Sport

man he will nowhere find better sailing than on the enclosed waters of Sydney's beautiful harbour. Hunting, in the English sense, can hardly be said to amount to much, but riding over the soft " bush " tracks is a glorious exercise, and a drive across country an exhilarating revelation to an Englishman.

What shall be said of life in the " back-blocks " ? That of the small and independent farmers, the " cockies," as they are called, is lonely to a degree. A typical story, which necessarily suffers by condensation, is told of two of these. A rides across, ten miles perhaps, to B, his nearest neighbour, and remarks : " Say, my horse is ill. What did you give yours when he was ? " B (without looking up from his work) : " Kerosene." A (next morning) : " Say, I gave my horse kerosene, and he died." B (still engrossed in his work) : " So did mine."

Boundary riders on the big stations have a dull life, too, seldom seeing another human being, except their fellow-workers, at breakfast-time. But for those who can enjoy a wholesome open-air life there are many compensations. Stock must be attended to, the more important parts being done by the pastoralist and his sons, but there is a fair amount of shooting for keen sportsmen ; while joint picnics and dances, in the company of other pastoralists, serve to make the time pass pleasantly enough.

Charms of Australia's Daughters

In a land where distance daunts no one, visits to the towns are fairly frequent, and girls will come from the back-blocks who prove themselves as refined in thought, as cultivated in mind, as easy and graceful in carriage as any that the Old World produces. Remember, too, when you see those lissom figures gliding smoothly to strains of dance music at a Government House ball, that they can sit a horse to perfection, and that those slender hands can do hard and useful work, and have probably made the fashionable and becoming dresses they are wearing.

" Advance, Australia ! " is a true watchword, for Australia has advanced, is advancing, and will advance, not merely in the confident eyes of her sons and daughters, but in deed and in truth. As Mr. Frank Bullen noted in his travels, " Australia is by far the richest of the Colonies, as Canada is the most astute."

BERNHARD R. WISE

GREAT DATES IN THE HISTORY OF AUSTRALIA

1601	Alleged Discovery by the Portuguese
1606	Discovery by the Dutch
1627	Coast surveys by Dutch navigators
1642	Tasman's voyages in Australian waters
1665	The Dutch apply name of New Holland to Western Australia
1686	William Dampier lands in Australia
1763-6	Explorations of Willis and Cartaret
1770	Captain Cook lands at Botany Bay, and names the country New South Wales
1788	Phillip founds penal colony at Sydney
1793	First church erected in Australia. First free emigrant ship arrives at Sydney
1798	Bass and Flinders discover Bass's Straits
1801-5	Grant and Flinders survey coasts
1804	Colonel Collins tries to found settlement in Victoria, but leaves for Van Diemen's Land or Tasmania
1808	Governor Bligh deposed
1809	Governor Macquarie appointed
1813-23	Interior exploration by Wentworth, Lawson, and other travellers
1829	Province of Western Australia formed
1828-31	Exploration of South Australia by Sturt
1831-6	Expeditions of Sir T. Mitchell into East Australia
1834	Province of South Australia formed
1835	Edward Henty settles in Portland Bay, Victoria
1836-7	South Australia made into a colony. Eyre crosses from Adelaide to King George's Sound
1837-9	Founding of Melbourne. Captain Grey's explorations in North-West Australia
1839	Discovery of Gold at Bathurst. Transportation suspended. The colony of Victoria receives its name
1840	Exploration of Eastern Australia by Strzelecki, and of Western Australia by Eyre
1842	Industrial depression. Sydney incorporated as a city. First Constitution Act passed
1843	Western Australia explored by Landor and Lefroy
1845	Exploration of interior by Sturt
1848-58	Gregory and Mueller explore northern portion
1849	Agitation against revival of transportation
1850	Province of Victoria created
1851	Gold rushes after discovery of gold by Hargreaves
1853	Transportation stopped except in Western Australia
1859	Province of Queensland created
1860	Landells's expedition into interior
1861	Burke and Wills cross the continent and perish in the return journey
1861-2	The continent crossed from sea to sea by the expeditions of Stuart, McKinley and Landsborough

1865	Entire cessation of transportation to Australia decided upon
1866	Royal Society of New South Wales founded
1867	Exploration of South Australia by Cadell
1869	Duke of Edinburgh visits Australia
1871	Protest by Australian colonies regarding home interference in fiscal arrangements
1882	Morrison walks from Gulf of Carpentaria to Melbourne
1883	Melbourne and Sydney united by direct railway. British New Guinea founded by Queensland
1884	Victoria, Queensland and Tasmania agree to the principle of federation, which is opposed by New South Wales
1885	Exclusion of Chinese from Victoria. First despatch of Australian troops (to the Soudan)
1887	Chinese Restriction Bill passed in New South Wales
1888	Australian protest against Chinese immigration
1890	Melbourne Conference of State Premiers adopts federation motion. Great strikes begin
1891	Earl of Kintore, Governor of South Australia, travels overland to Port Darwin. Federal Council meets in Hobart, and Federal Constitution adopted
1893	Australian Bank crash Australian Federation Conference
1896	The Horn scientific expedition to interior
1897	Great heat and drought. Commonwealth Bill passed in Victoria
1899	Australian Naval Conference at Melbourne
1900	Federal delegates received by Queen Victoria at Windsor, and Constitution Act receives Royal Assent. Old Age Pension Bill passed in Victoria
1901	Federation formally accomplished, with Lord Hopetoun Governor-General (January 1), and first Parliament meets (May 21). Visit of Duke and Duchess of York to open Parliament. Old Age Pensions in New South Wales
1902	Lord Hopetoun resigns and is succeeded by Lord Tennyson. Drought in Australia. Commonwealth Tariff Bill passed
1903	Lord Northcote succeeds Lord Tennyson as Governor-General. High Court established. Election of second Parliament, where strength of Labour Party increased
1904	Labour Arbitration Bill becomes law
1905	New Cabinet formed with Mr. Deakin as Prime Minister
1906	Importation of opium prohibited
1907	New Customs Tariff, giving preferential treatment to British goods. Declaration of the Government foreshadowing Conscription

ESSENTIAL FACTS ABOUT AUSTRALIA

AREA. The total area of the six colonies comprised in the Commonwealth of Australia is 2,972,573 square miles, the areas of the respective states being: New South Wales, 310,367; Victoria, 87,884; Queensland, 668,497; South Australia, 903,670; Western Australia, 975,920; and Tasmania, 26,215 square miles.

POPULATION. The population of Australia—not including aborigines—was, according to the census returns of 1901, 3,773,248, and at the rate of normal increase it ought to be now between 300,000 and 400,000 higher than these figures. The population of the various states was as follows: New South Wales, 1,354,846; Victoria, 1,201,070; Queensland, 498,129; South Australia, 362,604; Western Australia, 184,124; and Tasmania, 172,475. The number of aborigines in the various states are as follows: New South Wales, 4,287; Victoria, 652; Queensland, 6,670; South Australia, 3,888; and Western Australia, 6,212. The aborigines of Tasmania are extinct. The populations of the chief cities of Australia are (in New South Wales): Sydney, 481,830; Broken Hill, 27,500; Newcastle, 12,988; Parramatta, 12,560; Maitland, 10,073; (in Victoria): Melbourne, 515,350; Ballarat, 49,648; Bendigo, 43,660; Geelong, 26,672; (in Queensland): Brisbane, 119,428; Charters Towers, 20,976; Rockhampton, 19,691; Townsville, 15,506; Ipswich, 15,246; (in South Australia): Adelaide, 173,235; (in Western Australia): Perth, 27,553; Fremantle, 14,704; (in Tasmania): Hobart, 24,655; Launceston, 18,077.

GOVERNMENT. Power is vested in the Federal Parliament, which consists of the King—represented by a Governor-General—a Senate or Upper House and a House of Representatives. The Senate has 36 members, six from each original state. The first House of Representatives has 75 members—26 from New South Wales, 23 from Victoria, nine from Queensland, seven from South Australia, five from Western Australia, five from Tasmania. The present seat of the Federal Government is Melbourne, but it is intended to neutralise a site within the borders of New South Wales, and to establish a new federal capital.

EXECUTIVE. The present Governor-General is Lord Northcote, G.C.M.G., C.B., who succeeded Lord Tennyson in 1903, and the present Prime Minister of the Federal Parliament is the Hon. Alfred Deakin.

STATE GOVERNMENTS. The Commonwealth Constitution reserves to the six original states considerable powers, and in every state the two-chamber system of government prevails, under a governor representing the King of England. In New South Wales the present Governor is Sir Harry Holdsworth Rawson, R.N., G.C.B., and the Premier is the Hon. C. G. Wade, K.C. In Victoria the Governor is Major-General the Hon. Sir Reginald Talbot, K.C.B., and the Premier is the Hon. T. Bent. The Governor of Queensland is the Right Hon. Lord Chelmsford, and the Premier is the Hon. Robert Philp. The Governor of South Australia is Sir George Ruthven Le Hunte, K.C.M.G., and the Premier is the Hon. T. Price. In Western Australia the Governor is Admiral Sir F. G. D. Bedford, G.C.B., and the Premier is the Hon N. J. Moore. The Governor of Tasmania is Sir Gerald Strickland, K.C.M.G., and the Premier is the Hon. J. W. Evans, C.M.G.

REPRESENTATION IN ENGLAND. The Commonwealth has not yet established an Agency-General in London, but this step will doubtless be taken in time. The present London office of the Commonwealth is at 72, Victoria Street, Westminster, and the officer in charge is Captain R. Muirhead Collins, C.M.G. The various states maintain agents-general in London: New South Wales, T. A. Coghlan, I.S.O., 123, Cannon Street, E.C.; Victoria, Hon. J. W. Taverner, 142, Queen Victoria Street, E.C.; Queensland, Hon. Sir Horace Tozer, K.C.M.G., 1, Victoria Street, Westminster, S.W.; South Australia, Hon. J. G. Jenkins, Threadneedle House, E.C.; Western Australia, Hon. C. H. Rason, 15, Victoria Street, Westminster, S.W.; and Tasmania, Hon. Alfred Dobson, C.M.G., 5, Victoria Street, Westminster, S.W. Queensland has a commercial branch at the City offices of the Board of Trade in Basinghall Street, E.C.

FINANCES. The Commonwealth revenue for the year 1905-6 was £31,206,128, and the expenditure was £29,532,397. By the Constitution the Commonwealth must pay to each state not less than three-fourths of the customs revenue collected within that state. The total public debt of Australia on December 31st, 1906, was £237,813,166, with an annual interest charge of £8,572,294, and represents £58 10s. per head of the population.

COMMERCE. The Australian imports for the fiscal year 1906 were of the value of £87,669,988, and the exports were of the value of £112,680,421. Three-quarters of the imports were purchased from countries within the British Empire—three-fifths of the grand total from Great Britain—while the remaining quarter was divided among foreign nations, of whom the United States and Germany were the largest contributors. Of Australian exports—chiefly wool, wheat, gold, meat and dairy produce—quite two-thirds were purchased by countries within the British Empire—the United Kingdom accounting for about one-half of the grand total—while France, Germany and Belgium, in the order given, were the chief foreign purchasers.

WEIGHTS AND MEASURES. These are the same as in Great Britain.

POSTAGE AND TELEGRAMS (Great Britain to Australia). The conditions and rates are the same as for New Zealand—see page 1002.

PATENTS. Application must be made before the invention has been published or become known in Australia. Specification in duplicate. Fee 20s. on application and 40s. on acceptance of complete specification. Sealing fee, £5, payable within 16 months of application. Renewal fee of £5 on expiration of seventh year. Extreme life of patent, 14 years.

TRADE MARKS AND DESIGNS. A Federal Act of 1905 superseded the varying conditions in the different states. Conditions are similar to British practice.

IMPORTANCE OF THE PACIFIC
THE ROMANCE AND ADVENTURE
OF THE GREAT WORLD-OCEAN

BEFORE MAGELLAN'S VOYAGES

IN considering the importance of the great world-ocean from the standpoint of universal history, nothing at the present day more forcibly arrests our attention than the phenomenon of the manifold relations which, through the intermediary of its various parts, are established between the inhabitants of different continents.

From north to south, from east to west, the paths in which the political, intellectual, and commercial life of humanity rolls majestically onward stretch in a dense network from continent to continent. What an immense expanse is presented here as compared with the ancient sphere of civilisation, or even with that of the days before Columbus, confined as this was to the countries around the Mediterranean and the seas which encircle Europe ! The Pacific Ocean has played a noticeable part in the course of human **Historical** history. Of the three-quarters **Rôle of the** of the earth's surface which is **Pacific** covered by the ocean, it forms very nearly half. In conformity with its vast extent and its other natural and geographical features we find that the history of the Pacific Ocean bears the mark of grandeur, while, at the same time, owing to its distribution over such an enormous area, this history is lacking in intensity.

Professor Ratzel has aptly described the shape of the Pacific Ocean by calling attention to its widely-sundered margins, a distance of three or four times the length of the Atlantic separating its Asiatic from its American shores. Its wide opening on the south is occupied by Australia and Oceania, whereby the Pacific acquires its most peculiar features—namely, the presence of a third island continent in the Southern Hemisphere, and the richest island formation to be found anywhere on the earth. Both the narrowing in of the ocean toward the north, and the bridge of islands in the south, besides imparting a special character to its shape and surface, also form, in a primary degree, the paths along which the history of the Pacific pursues its course.

So far as our experience goes backward, we cannot discover that Bering Strait **Value of** has ever been of greater im-**Bering** portance historically than any **Strait** other Arctic channel bordered by two inhabited shores. Leaving out of consideration the long but still time-limited occupation of Alaska by the Russians, Bering Sea has as a means of commercial intercourse never attained more than an insignificant importance.

Thus, in spite of its convenience, our beautiful bridge is left unused, because the masses for whose crossing it might serve are wanting. On the other hand, as we pass southward toward temperate and tropical climes and more habitable coasts, the dividing expanse of water widens out in measureless breadth, and the opposite shore recedes farther and farther alike from the material and the ideal horizon.

Nor is the conformation of the coast of the two great continents bordering the Pacific everywhere of such a kind as to attract their populations to the sea. This especially applies to America. From its farthest north to its southern extremity that continent throughout its whole **Pacific** length is traversed close to the **Coast of** Pacific coast by a steep and **America** rugged mountain chain, forming an almost insurmountable barrier between the coast and the interior, interrupted by only a few rivers in the northern continent but entirely unbroken in the southern portion. The Pacific side, in fact, represents the backward side of America from the historical standpoint ; the front of the continent is turned toward the Atlantic.

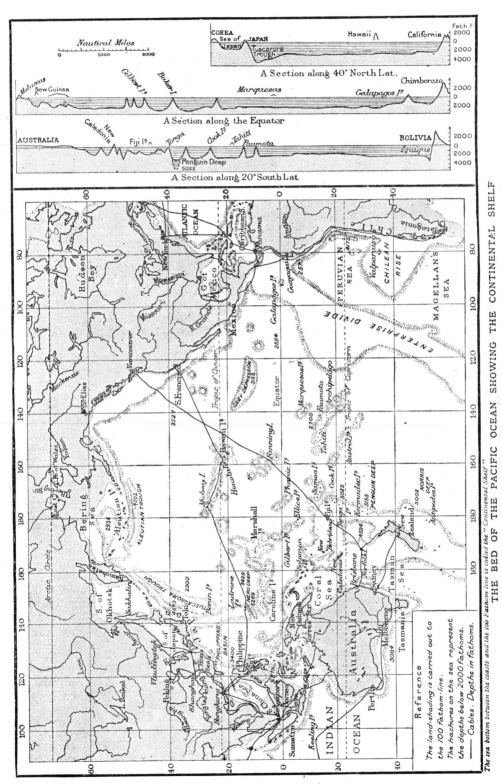

THE BED OF THE PACIFIC OCEAN SHOWING THE CONTINENTAL SHELF

The western shore of the Pacific Ocean has a much more favourable aspect. Numerous large and powerful streams hasten toward it from the interior of Asia, thus intimately connecting the latter with the ocean. The surface of contact is still further increased by the series of island groups which, like a band, fringe the eastern shore of Asia and provide the first halting-place to its inland population on venturing forth upon the sea. Thus, while on the one side these island groups invite the inland dwellers out to sea, on the other they intercept the migrating populations on their outward course and retain them for prolonged periods.

According to the view of Darwin, which deserves the fullest consideration, the islands of Polynesia were not populated until a few centuries before their discovery by Europeans ; on the other hand, the traditional, mythical history of Japan traces back the existence of the population of that country to periods so immeasurably remote as to surpass the boldest flights of our imagination. Now, though the millions of years to which the son of the **Age of Pacific Peoples** distant empire proudly ventures to look back may not be able to stand the test of modern criticism, there is nevertheless usually a small grain of truth buried among the chaff of national vanity. At any rate this contradiction furnishes a kind of scale or measure for estimating the age of the history of the Pacific Ocean.

Historians have as yet failed to answer the question as to when Man first came to occupy the coasts of the Pacific. In all probability this important event occurred in prehistoric ages. It is equally impossible to determine what race of men, still less what particular people, first arose on the coasts of this ocean. From palæontological reasons there is some ground for assuming that America was originally peopled by immigration from without; such an immigration would most easily take place from Northern Asia, owing to the close proximity of that part of the Old World, and its effect would be the spreading of the Mongol type of population over America.

Whatever views may be entertained as to the usual division of the races of mankind, whether we recognise three or five or even more separate races, no one will any longer deny that the answer given to the question as to the origin of the human race is inclining more and more to the view of a primary unity of type from which an apparent plurality of type has arisen by differentiation. In this fashion, from a Mongoloid ancestral type common to the old Asiatic and the new American branches, the red American race may have been developed ; while **Development of National Types** a remnant of the same primitive type may, under the specific influences of Asia, have produced the Mongol race. In a similar manner we may ascribe to the Indian Ocean the formation of the Malay race, although the Pacific Ocean also may have had a share in this, at least so far as the peculiar racial variety of the Polynesians is concerned. Finally, both oceans conjointly conveyed to the Australian continent, which was originally peopled by a Negroid race, immigrants of Malay and Polynesian descent, from the intermixture of which with the primitive inhabitants we get a new, sharply demarcated type—that of the Australian race. The latter next continues to spread eastward over a portion of the island world of the Pacific Ocean, or Melanesia.

Whether the Mongoloid type of the north-temperate or the Negroid type of the equatorial zone was the first to make its appearance on the shores of the Pacific Ocean must be left undecided. We know, at any rate, that in prehistoric times the margins of the Pacific, as well as its immeasurable island world, were still peopled by four distinct races, yellow, red, brown and black. Only the white race is absent. Through indefinite periods the destinies of these four principal types of the human race pursue their course side by side without definitely crossing or influencing each other. Each of them more or less pursues a separate, independent course of development within the limits of its own domain, because mutual contact is prevented by the immense **Segregation of the Four Races** expanse of the separating tracts of water. Their entrance, too, into the sphere of historic apprehension is marked by the widest differences. While the densely crowded populations of the Pacific coasts of Asia, pushing and being pushed onward in a continuous stream, have early arrived at a high state of culture and are therefore among the first to acquire historic importance, the isolated continent of America forms a world by itself, which for a long time appears wrapped in darkness and presents problems no less difficult to the historian than to the anthropologist. Even the key for the comprehension of undoubtedly historic characters has been irrecoverably lost. Hence America forms a very late addition, and one very difficult of comprehension, in the scheme of universal history. This remark applies still more forcibly to Australia, which, though less isolated, is still less favourable to human development, owing to its physical and climatic peculiarities. In spite of the fact that the sea renders them close neighbours to the progressive Malays, the Australian aborigines are content with playing a passive, merely receptive part.

Quite apart from anthropological and ethnographical reasons, we are more and more led to adopt the view according to which the gradual occupation of the island world of the Pacific Ocean by the human race could have proceeded originally only from the west. Thus, the sea first made its civilising influence felt in a direction from west to east. In subsequent times, however, after the white race, with

Occupation from West to East

its remarkable capacity for expansion, had gained the ascendency in America, this condition of things was changed. Those peculiarities of the Pacific Ocean which favour navigation in an opposite direction from that mentioned above were now brought into action, so that, since then the influence of the Pacific as a promoter of civilisation has proceeded in a direction from east to west.

As regards the time when the gradual settlement of the Pacific island world had its beginning, Friedrich Müller assumes it to date back to about the year 1000 B.C. According to the views of later anthropologists this colonisation was not completed until a few centuries before the discovery of Polynesia by the white races, by whom the inhabitants of these islands were regarded as a race sharply distinct from the Malays. There is a sharp line of demarcation between the dark-skinned, frizzly or woolly-haired Melanesian and the lighter-coloured, yellowish-brown, sleek or curly-haired Polynesian or Micronesian. The only feature common to all is that, in spite of many intellectual endowments, they for the most part remained a people in a state of nature, who probably never dreamed of regarding themselves as one

people, or conceived the notion of forming a state. The almost interminable subdivision and insular isolation of their separate racial divisions, the wholly tropical situation of their homes, in which the presence of the coco-palm, the breadfruit tree, and an abundance of fish and shellfish entirely relieved them from the

Why the Islanders Stagnated

necessity of labouring for a living, a climate which makes little or no demand for houses or clothing—all these conditions could not do otherwise than generate a certain ease of living and absence of care which are impediments to the development of a higher civilisation, in the sense in which we conceive it in the case of a firmly-settled continental people. In spite of this, the Polynesians, though they knew nothing of iron, and were only slightly acquainted with other metals, display a remarkable ability, combined with artistic skill, in the manufacture of different implements, which capacity reaches its culminating point in the shipbuilding art. To this advanced condition of their seamanship we must finally trace back the expansion of the race over the whole immense breadth of the ocean.

It is, in fact, in the form of these involuntary migrations of its inhabitants that the Pacific Ocean plays so important a part in this remote domain of the history of mankind. In opposition to the view which traces back the Polynesian race to the island world of South-Eastern Asia, William Ellis asserts with conviction that America was the point of departure of the population of the Pacific island world. He denies that it is possible for the Polynesians to have originated from the west, since the prevailing winds and currents tend in this direction, and, apart from this, because common ethnographic features between the Polynesians and the aboriginal inhabitants of America are by no means wanting. Now it is true that

Theories Caused by the Winds

within a small area winds and currents often exercise a considerable influence ; on the wide expanse of the Pacific Ocean, however, they have long since ceased permanently to determine the distribution of mankind. On the contrary, we have actually a series of observations extending over several hundreds of years which lead to the conclusion that extended migrations, whether voluntary or otherwise, have on a large scale taken place in a direction contrary to that of the prevailing winds and currents. At the same time we must constantly bear in mind that sudden unexpected storms are at least as efficacious in driving the most expert sailor out of his course as the constant regular currents of air and water which the skill of the navigator is capable of conquering. Im-

Storms that Peopled the Islands portant to the ethnologist as is this phenomenon—which in the course of thousands of years has extended a dense network from land to land—it is equally so to the history of Polynesia, which is entirely taken up by the mutual relations of different groups and the fusion of races which has resulted therefrom. In the majority of cases, probably, these unpremeditated voyages were the precursors of planned-out migrations, which, on the one hand, led to the permanent settlement of new islands, and on the other were followed by the establishment of colonies in districts long previously occupied. This series of later migrations and colonisations forms, as Ratzel justly points out, the sole fact which indicates the stage of civilisation reached by the Stone Age. On this account it cannot be easily understood, since it is impossible to compare it with other achievements of a similar character. The area which was thus brought within the sphere of colonisation many times exceeds the empire of Alexander the Great or of the Roman Emperors. In the sphere of territorial domination it represents the greatest achievement before the discovery of America.

Intimately connected with the abundant intercourse of which the Pacific has been the scene from times immemorial stands the fact that nowhere has it supplied time or space for the development of an independent civilisation. Neither the immense island of New Guinea, with its thinly scattered, idle population, nor the still more remote New Zealand, has

Lack of Independent Civilisations been capable of becoming the centre of a new civilisation, to say nothing of the other innumerable smaller islands. Only a few isolated elements within the domain of civilisation have under specially favourable circumstances been able to undergo an independent development. Apart from this the Pacific Ocean presents merely variations of one and the same fundamental theme. In this the absence of a real political formation or state

structure is constantly repeated; it was only in the Hawaiian Islands that, at the time of their discovery by Europeans, three states existed, which afterward, under the native king Kamehameha, united into a single state. In all other cases the community or society, even when under monarchical sway, was limited to a single island, and hence remained quite insignificant in extent and influence. In all the larger islands, such as New Guinea and New Zealand, we fail to find even the slightest trace of a centralised political organisation.

Hence there can scarcely be a question of a real history of Oceania before its discovery. Nevertheless we ought not on that account to speak of the Polynesians as a people without a history; for tradition plays no small part in their social life. They have also an idea of chronology, in which the Creation forms the basis or starting-point; in the absence of written signs they make use of notched sticks, the so-called "history-rods," as aids for remembering names and periods of time. As one might expect, these tra-

History from Island Legends ditions sometimes go back to a very remote past. At Nukahiwa, in the Marquesas Archipelago, eighty-eight generations are said to have been established, which would mean a period of about twenty-five hundred years; at Baratongo the more modest number of thirty generations is claimed; and the Maoris of New Zealand limit themselves to twenty. On the other hand the Hawaiian king Kamehameha claimed a descent in direct line from a series of sixty-six generations of ancestors. Of course no real historical value can be attached to legends of this kind; but they nevertheless give evidence of a strongly-rooted feeling of autochthonous descent, which must have originated in a fairly long period of residence on the soil, and accordingly have been preceded by a certain degree of civilisation. Apart from this, according to generally accepted views, the civilisation of Polynesia had, at the time of its discovery, sunk to a very low level as compared with the development it had reached in earlier times.

To the question whether the conditions of national life in the Pacific were affected by influences emanating from the eastern shores of the American continent, it is difficult to give a decisive answer either in the negative or in the affirmative. In the dissemination of the Mongoloid race over the continents of the Northern Hemisphere, America, according to the prevalent view, seems to have played the part of receiver—that is, the movement took place in a direction from Asia to America ; while the view of a reflux current in the opposite direction can with difficulty be accepted. On the other hand, some of the island groups of the Pacific display so much analogy with the North-west of America in their flora and fauna, as well as in the ethnological characters of their population, that the idea of a casual connection between the two regions easily suggests itself ; while, on the contrary, there is no lack of theories according to which the Polynesian population of the Pacific must be traced back to North America, or of others which, instead of a single former movement in one direction, assume several movements in either direction, and which, in Ratzel's words, " would substitute for the artificial theory of a former single migration and of a simple descent, the idea of a diffusion and stratification of the different races, *inter se.*" However, no such influence on the part of America is discernible in historic times, and hence, from our standpoint, we are justified in regarding America as the passively receptive, not as the actively radiating or disseminating element.

America and the South Sea Islands

We have already pointed out the obstacles which stand in the way of the existence of any mutual relations between the west coast of America and the Pacific Ocean. Native American civilisation adopted a decidedly continental course, and did not take at all kindly to the sea, even in places where—as in that great Mediterranean Sea of America, the Gulf of Mexico and the Caribbean Sea—the natural conditions were most favourable to a seafaring life.

A comprehensive historical glance at the immense border regions of the Pacific Ocean enables us to recognise the beginning of a period in which its historical formative influence has for its basis, as it were, the human race itself— a period which may be described as the typically continental period. Both the border regions and the island areas are now occupied. All the energies of their inhabitants, however, are centred upon their own internal organisation and development, and there is an almost complete absence of mutual relations ; even the knowledge of their existence in the case of widely-separated areas vanishes completely from the memory of man. Thus we see how the civilised nations of Eastern Asia gradually succumb politically, socially, and intellectually to a rigid paralysing formalism ; how the States of America, soon discarding the sea, consume and speedily exhaust their energies in the struggle with a somewhat chary Nature ; how finally they and the natural populations of Polynesia and Australia lose touch with the rest of mankind and relapse into the condition of isolated, degenerating units.

Relapse into Isolation

THE PACIFIC OCEAN IN MODERN TIMES

THE first impulse to the enormous expansion of the white race through navigation undoubtedly originated from the Mediterranean. The prosperity which its seafaring nations derived from the profitable commerce of the East impelled the western Europeans of the Atlantic coast to emulate their example and to seek unknown sea roads to the Far East ; for it was only by such roads that that region was accessible to Europeans. The idea of an overland route across the gigantic continent of Asia seems to have been allowed to drop ; that it was not feasible had been amply demonstrated by many

Early Maritime Adventure

fruitless attempts dating from the time of Alexander the Great down to that of Frederic Barbarossa and Saint Louis. Moreover, Asia was still, at irregular intervals, pouring forth its devastating hordes toward the West, as in the Great Mongol invasion which as recently as the beginning of the eighteenth century was still surging in Eastern Europe.

Of course, a small continent like Europe, with its comparatively small populations, could not cope by land with the enormous populations of Asia. Hence, since a road to the East had to be found somehow or other, it could be found only by sea.

The history of geographical discoveries does not fall within the scope of this work; it will therefore suffice to mention that the immediate object in the search for a direct sea-route from Western Europe to India was the rediscovery of the two countries Cathay and Zipangu, which had vanished from the intellectual horizon, but were thought to be, as it were, neighbours of India, their existence having been proved by Marco Polo. The later and wider aims were merely the gradual outcome of the enormous and quite unexpected extent of the original discoveries. In the natural order of things the first attempts, undertaken chiefly by the Portuguese, were made in an easterly direction; their most important result was the circumnavigation of the Cape of Good Hope, accomplished in 1486 by Bartolomeo Diaz. About the same time, however, the conception of the spherical shape of the earth, which was rapidly gaining ground, led to similar enterprises being undertaken in a westerly direction also.

It was in the pursuit of such attempts that Christopher Columbus discovered the Bahamas and Antilles for Spain in 1492, and that John Cabot discovered the North American continent for England in 1494. Both discoverers imagined themselves to have really found what they had sought—the east coast of Asia, a belief in which they persisted to the end of their lives. Nor did Pedralvarez Cabral, who in 1500, while attempting to reach India by an eastern route, was driven by a western drift current to the coast of Brazil, recognise the importance of his discovery. He, in fact, believed he had found only an island of no special attraction, and, altering his course, made haste to return with all speed to the coast of Africa. **A Great Portuguese Navigator** For shortly before (1497–1498), Vasco da Gama had succeeded, by rounding the Cape of Good Hope, in reaching India, being the first European navigator who had done so, and in forming there connections of the utmost advantage to his native country, Portugal. Inspired by this success, so important in a practical sense, the Portuguese now turned their attention exclusively to the route discovered by Vasco da Gama. **Spain Emulates Portugal** On the other hand, the Spaniards, who on their side pursued further the road first mapped out by Columbus, soon became convinced that the countries discovered in the west could not be part of Asia. Driven by a passionate longing for the gold which had been found during the early explorations, they followed the westward-pointing track of the yellow metal, and soon obtained from the natives of Central America the knowledge of the existence of that " other sea " on the coasts of which gold was to be found in superabundance.

In the search for the precious metal, Nuñez de Balboa crossed the Cordilleras of the Isthmus of Panama, and was the first European who from their heights set eyes on the Pacific Ocean, which he did on September 25th, 1513. He applied to it the name of the " South Sea," and took possession of its coasts in the name of the King of Spain. This event forms an important landmark in history. Henceforth the newly discovered continental area was recognised as a portion of a large and independent continent. Further, the existence of the greatest ocean of the earth was made known and turned to advantage. The still existing civilised states of the New World were annihilated and extinguished almost at one blow, and the development of the human populations of the Western Hemisphere was thus turned into an entirely new channel. Finally, this discovery also led to a fundamental change in the political structure of the civilised states of the Western Hemisphere. The discovery of the Pacific Ocean by Europeans had a double immediate effect. First, it led to a definite general knowledge of the true shape and size of the earth—a knowledge which has had immense results in the domains of civilisation, commerce, and politics.

VASCO DA GAMA
The first voyager to reach India by sailing round the Cape of Good Hope.

Secondly it led up directly to the incredibly rapid conquest of the Pacific coasts by Spain. The lamentable helplessness with which the densely populated and civilised native states of Central and South America fell to pieces before the onslaught of a few hundreds of European adventurers, like the Aztec Empire of Mexico before the small band of Cortes, and the Empire of the Incas in Peru before Pizarro, remains one of the most remarkable phenomena in history. The discovery of an unexplored ocean separated from the Atlantic by the whole length of the American continent led to a series of zealous endeavours to find the connection between these two great masses of water. It was of importance to the Spaniards, first of all, who had been anticipated by the Portuguese in reaching India by the eastern route, not to be misled by the obstacle which had unexpectedly barred their course to the west. It was soon recognised that Central America, which had been the first portion of the continent they had become acquainted with, possessed no strait connecting the

FIRST EUROPEAN TO SEE THE PACIFIC
The Spanish explorer, Vasco Nunez de Balboa, saw the Pacific Ocean on September 25, 1513, after crossing the Isthmus of Panama. He called it the South Sea, and took possession of its coasts for his native country, Spain.

two oceans ; hence the problem for solution was to find one elsewhere. In the hope of discovering such a passage farther south, voyages of exploration were made along the eastern coast of Brazil, and in 1515 Diaz de Solis advanced as far as the mouth of the La Plata, where, however, he met his death.

In 1520 Ferdinand Magellan, a Portuguese in the Spanish service, succeeded in discovering the strait called after his name, between the South American continent and Tierra del Fuego. Through this strait he entered the Pacific Ocean, in which he at once vigorously pursued his course. After a voyage of more than

three months Magellan reached the Ladrones, and, later on, the Philippine Islands ; and though he was not fated to enjoy the triumph of a successful return, he at all events is incontestably entitled to the distinction of being the first navigator and the first European who traversed the Pacific along its entire breadth. Magellan's companions continued the voyage after the death of their leader, and reached the Moluccas. Here, on the island of Tidor, they fell in with Portuguese who had previously arrived there by the opposite route, and who were not a little astonished to see white men arriving from the east. Here, then, two advance columns, which had set out from opposite directions, for the first time joined hands. It was here that the great girdle of knowledge which had been laid round the earth was made complete, and thus European energy and intelligence achieved in the course of some decades a result which the aboriginal inhabitants of the Pacific Ocean had never attained for as many thousands of years. Within a short time the whole Pacific and the Pacific coasts of America were discovered. California was reached even before the middle of the sixteenth century, and as early as 1527 a regular navigation route was established between the coasts of Mexico and the far distant Moluccas.

In the meantime the Portuguese also had advanced farther eastward from the Indian Ocean. This advance, however, was of a quite different character from the conquest of America by the Spaniards. The Portuguese did not make their appearance in India as " conquistadores "; in fact, to do so would have scarcely been possible when we take into account the much more ancient and advanced civilisation of that country, its well-established political system, and the greater density

NUNEZ DE BALBOA FIGHTING HIS WAY TO THE CORDILLERAS

and numbers of its population. They accordingly did not indulge the ambition of subjecting the newly-discovered territories and adding them as provinces to their own small and remote kingdom, but contented themselves with establishing trading-stations on the coasts and with acquiring and fortifying for the protection of the latter several points on **Policy** the coast, as well as maintain-**of the** ing in constant readiness a **Portuguese** capable fleet of warships. In other respects the sphere of Portuguese colonisation falls chiefly within the region of the Indian Ocean. The latter, however, served, after all, merely as a first step towards its greater neighbour, inasmuch as the Portuguese extended their explorations from the Indian Ocean more and more towards the East as far as the coasts of China, where they founded settlements, and to Japan, which they reached by accident in 1543.

For exactly one hundred years Japan was opened up to the outer world, a period forming but a small fraction in the history of the island empire, but one which was fraught with important consequences in the grouping and position of the European sea Powers. About the middle of the sixteenth century Japan began eagerly and zealously to open its gates to Western civilisation and the teaching of Christianity; for three generations, however, it was the unwilling spectator of a jealous rivalry between the Portuguese and the Dutch, who had arrived in the country in the year 1600—a contest rendered the more discreditable by the unscrupulous choice of the weapons with which it was carried on. This state of things the Japanese finally decided to terminate by what seemed to them the only possible solution—namely, by simply shutting their door in the face of the unruly strangers. By this step, which, indeed, is quite at variance with the character of **The Closed** its people, Japan for more than **Door of** two centuries disappears com-**Japan** pletely from history, and ceases to exercise any influence whatever on the development of affairs on and upon the Pacific Ocean.

It is a remarkable phenomenon that the immense increase in power and wealth which the era of geographical discovery brought to Europeans fell much less to the share of the real discoverers than to others. The discoveries made between

1486 and the middle of the sixteenth century, with the sole exception of those of the two Cabots, were placed entirely to the political account of Spain and Portugal. Both these kingdoms suddenly came into possession of immense territories from which they drew undreamed-of wealth and treasure. The populations of these territories—at least of those in America—became the pliant and feeble tools of their conquerors.

The real fruits of geographical discovery were to fall into the hands of those who had participated in the competition, not with precipitate haste and with the sole object of enriching themselves suddenly and without effort, but with far-seeing deliberation and with silent but untiring efforts—the Dutch and the English. The Dutch, a small people, subject to the powerful monarchy of Spain, had boldly risen against their political and religious oppressors, and, in spite of the enormous disproportion between their own resources and those of the suzerain Power, and chiefly on account of their excellence in seamanship, had carried out **Dutch** a successful resistance. They in **Competition** part transferred the seat of **with Spain** war across the Indian Ocean, established themselves in the Spanish-Portuguese possessions, destroyed Portuguese influence in important localities, as they had done since 1600 in Japan, and gradually succeeded in getting the trade of India almost entirely into their own hands. But the activity of the English assumed still grander proportions.

At the time of the discovery of America, England had lost all her Continental dominions with the exception of Calais, and found herself restricted to her island possessions. Even her dominion over Ireland had at that time almost slipped from her grasp, and Scotland formed an independent kingdom. England possessed no territories outside of Europe, and she had fallen from her high rank as a great European Power, while outside of Europe her influence was virtually nil. It was at this time that the discoveries of the sea route to India and of America first turned the attention of this healthy and energetic people towards lands far distant; and the prudent sovereigns of the then reigning House of Tudor kept the eyes of their subjects fixed in this direction.

The inborn love of this island nation for maritime adventure then, as if by magic,

MAGELLAN'S SHIPS PASSING THROUGH THE STRAITS THAT NOW BEAR HIS NAME
From the painting by J. Fraser, by permission of Mr. A. H. E. Wood.

suddenly blossomed forth in luxuriant growth and drove its people with irresistible force across the sea. It was not, however, merely for the quest of gold, as had been the case with Spain, that England entered upon the career of territorial exploration and colonisation ; nor, like the Portuguese, with the object of making the profitable trade in spices a monopoly in their own hands, but with a nobler, more far-seeing purpose in which the overthrow of the newly-found native populations and civilisations formed no part.

England Enters the Competition

Thus,· from the moment when the existence of the Pacific Ocean was ascertained, it engaged the attention of the English. They quietly allowed the Spaniards and Portuguese to push forward their discoveries and conquests in the East and West Indies without, for the time being, entering into competition with them. On the other hand, they concentrated their efforts upon finding a route into the Pacific Ocean unknown to the Spaniards and Portuguese, but available for themselves, establishing themselves in this route, and in this way spreading and developing their rule in, as it were, the opposite direction.

The efforts of the English found a visible expression in the search for the North-west Passage, which was pursued with an iron persistency, and has proved of the utmost importance in history. That the newly-discovered continent in the north was bounded by the sea, like that in the south, appeared beyond question.

Accordingly, it was thought that there must exist a northern route leading from the Atlantic into the Pacific Ocean. Such a passage being situated nearer to England than any other, the problem was to find it. Though the attempts made in this direction did not at once lead to the expected result—nor, indeed, did they produce any result of practical value later on—they were nevertheless accompanied by effects of extraordinary significance. They acquired importance not only in a geographical sense, by leading to a true comprehension of the nature of the earth, but also in

The North-west Passage

a political direction ; for as a result of numerous enterprises the northern part of the American continent passed into the possession of England, which made much better use of it than the Spaniards had done of its central and southern portions.

The first reports of the success of Columbus had, as early as 1494, instigated John Cabot, a Portuguese in the English service, as well as his son Sebastian, to undertake a voyage by which even at that time they hoped to reach the land of Cathay, or China, and the Spice Islands by the shortest route—that is, by a north-west passage. In the course of this voyage, however, they discovered the northern coast of the North American continent, and took possession of it in the name of England. In a second voyage, undertaken in 1497, they enlarged the discoveries of their first expedition, and the same result was attained by a third voyage made by Sebastian Cabot alone in 1498.

Voyages of the Cabots The actual search for the much-longed-for North-west Passage was not, however, begun until the year 1517, when the younger Cabot discovered Hudson Bay, and very probably penetrated into Davis Strait and within the Arctic Circle.

The first attempt towards the solution of the problem was, however, soon forgotten in the beginning of the Reformation, which absorbed the entire attention of the English people. It was not until after the death, in 1547, of the Royal theologian, Henry VIII., that the transoceanic movement was once more revived, and attracted a much more general and lively interest than on the first occasion. Its special feature lay in the fact that the movement proceeded not so much from the State as from individuals and corporations, and that, although it was favoured and supported by the Government, it was neither initiated nor directed thereby ; indeed, up to the time of Henry VIII. (1509–47) a Royal Navy had not even existed. A few wealthy and influential and private individuals and merchant guilds

THOMAS CAVENDISH
English navigator who spoiled the Spaniards and sailed round the world in 1586-88

fitted out, at their own cost, whole fleets which, according to circumstances, engaged in commerce or made voyages of exploration, or, on their own responsibility, sailed in quest of warlike adventures, which in many instances had a strong savour of piracy.

At the beginning of this new period an expedition left England mainly for purposes of exploration, but with an object diametrically the opposite of the voyages which had been set on foot at the beginning of the century for the discovery of the North-west Passage ; for it was now proposed to discover the nearest route to China in an easterly direction and along the north coasts of Europe, or, in other words, to find a north-east passage, which, it was hoped by the English commercial world of that time, would lead to a fresh development of their trade, then in a very depressed condition. On May 10th, 1553, Sir Hugh Willoughby sailed from London with this object ; but neither his expedition nor those of later English navigators were successful in this sphere of exploration, in which they had to yield the palm to the more fortunate Dutch and Russians.

Hence English explorers once more turned their attention to the North-west Passage. Frobisher's voyage of discovery in 1576 was followed by a large number of others, such as those of Davis, Hudson, Bylot, Baffin, and others. Although from **The Work of English Explorers** natural causes these expeditions did not obtain the desired object, they nevertheless proved of infinite importance in considerably advancing the colonisation of North America, of which the beginnings had been attempted by Humphrey Gilbert and Sir Walter Raleigh in 1583 and 1584. This was not a colonisation after the fashion of Spanish conquistadores or Portuguese spice-merchants, but a slow, gradual, tranquil, and thoughtful immigration of industrious, energetic Northern Europeans, who did not go with the sole aim of rapidly gaining treasures, but in order to find a livelihood founded on enduring and arduous labour ; who, while wresting the virgin soil from its native hunting population and bringing it under cultivation, became intimately attached to it, and thus laid the firm foundation of a political system, which grew with surprising rapidity and was full of the hardiest energy. Simultaneously with the bold explorers of North America

Excursions Against the Spaniards a number of naval heroes left England in search of adventures, whose main object, however, was to inflict the greatest possible damage on the Spaniards, who were detested on account of political and religious antagonism, and thereby also to enrich themselves. Besides such names as Hawkins, Raleigh, and Cavendish, that of Francis Drake shines forth with special lustre. Drake combined the hero with the explorer. So great was his boldness that he was no longer satisfied with attacking the Atlantic possessions of Spain ; indeed, the West India islands and the coasts of the Gulf of Mexico had been already so much harassed by the English corsairs that the Spaniards in these possessions now kept a good look-out. On the coasts of Chili and Peru, on the other hand, they considered themselves perfectly secure and unassailable. Relying on their sense of security and consequent unguardedness, Drake, who was morally and materially supported by the Queen, at the end of 1577 left England with five ships, well equipped by himself, sailed through the Straits of Magellan, and, without encountering any resistance, began a private war against the Spaniards in the Pacific Ocean. He was entirely successful, and set out on his homeward voyage richly laden with spoil. He tried to turn the voyage to account by searching for the North-West Passage from the Pacific Ocean—that is, in the reverse direction. However, after sailing along the West Coast of America up to the forty-eighth degree of north

Memorable Voyages of Drake latitude without finding a sign of the desired passage, he decided on the voyage across the ocean, and returned to England, after having touched at the Moluccas and sailed around the Cape of Good Hope.

Drake's circumnavigation of the world, which had more or less the character of a warlike expedition, marks the first conscious and deliberate step on the part of England towards a policy of universal expansion and the sovereignty of the seas, a policy the surprising results of which not only produced a great change in the distribution of power in Europe, but also subsequently, and in a manner entirely unpremeditated, brought into the foreground a new and important factor in international life—America.

In this way, moreover, was laid the foundation of the predominance of the white race over the whole globe. For the Pacific Ocean and its place in history generally, Drake's voyage had a special significance ; for by it, at one stroke, as it were, that ocean became the centre of public interest and the scene of the struggle for the sovereignty of the seas.

Here was displayed for the first time in a striking manner the internal hollowness and weakness of the apparently gigantic strength of Spanish dominion ; for, as seems only natural, numerous other piratical enterprises, not only English, but also Dutch, followed in Drake's successful track, and all of them, with more or less impunity, managed to harass and plunder the Spanish possessions and

England's Maritime Supremacy Spanish ships in the Pacific Ocean. True, the maritime war between England and Spain was not finally decided in European waters until 1588 (the destruction of the Armada), but we may safely assert that the issue was prepared by the events which took place in the Pacific Ocean, and that it was here that England found the key to her maritime supremacy.

About the year 1600 the third continent washed by the Pacific Ocean—Australia— also began to rise from the mist which had hitherto enveloped it. Its discovery, however, at first attracted but little notice, and had no immediate practical results. This was due to several causes : the natural features of the country were not very inviting, the climate was not favourable, and its native population was scanty and in a low grade of development. There was further a dearth of all desirable productions, and the coasts of the continent were difficult of access owing to the presence of barrier reefs. Meanwhile, Britain had lost her American colonies, which now enter upon the stage of history as an independent political entity under the name of the United States of America ; and besides this she was under the necessity of maintaining the deportation of criminals, who had formerly been sent to the American continent. She was thus obliged, in the year 1788, nearly two hundred years after its discovery, to take possession of the Australian continent in earnest.

This enforced settlement had, however, to yield to one of a voluntary character as soon as the real value of the formerly despised country became known. Immigrants, after a time, poured into the country and furnished ample proof that in Australia Britain had obtained an acquisition of extraordinary value. Owing to the fact that the new immigrants were almost exclusively of British nation-

SIR FRANCIS DRAKE
The first Englishman to sail the waters of the Pacific. His momentous work and the example he set laid the foundations of Great Britain's colonial empire.

ality, the continent acquired a homogeneous population, and Britain a colony which kept up very close ties with the mother country. Especially were those elements wanting which had driven the Americans into a political—indeed, almost national—opposition to Britain. Accordingly the population of Australia had made this youngest of continents into a second antipodean edition of " Old England," a daughterland which furthers the policy of " Rule, Britannia " on the Pacific Ocean with no less pride than her great prototype at home. In the colonisation of Australia its native aboriginal population is even of less import than the Indians of North

America ; politically it is of no account whatever, its scanty remnants having been forced back into the inhospitable interior parts of the continent. The acquisition of the Pacific Ocean by

Britain's Pacific Acquisitions England, which was begun since Cook's discoveries, has not stopped at the Australian continent, but has been extended to numerous parts of Melanesia, Micronesia, and Polynesia. It is a remarkable fact that in their numerous voyages from the Mexican harbours to the Moluccas and Philippines, and, since 1565, in the opposite direction also, the Spaniards discovered so very few of the innumerable island groups which stud the intervening seas. Even the few of the archipelagoes they did discover—the Marshall, Bonin, Solomon, and Paumotu Islands, and others—were not considered by them worth acquisition or colonisation ; only the Mariana, Caroline, and Pelew groups were in course of time taken possession of or laid claim to in order to serve as points of support for their colonies in the Philippines. The Portuguese and Dutch took still less interest in the acquisition of territory in the Pacific ; they left that ocean entirely out of the sphere of their commercial policy, and, in fact, formed no settlements in it at all. Thus it came about that during the voyages of the English and French in the latter third of the eighteenth century—those of Cook, Bougainville, La Pérouse, D'Entrecasteaux, and others—numerous island groups were discovered which were not yet occupied by Europeans, and were therefore owner-less or unclaimed territory. Of course, the crews of the ships composing these expeditions were not sufficiently numerous to spare any of their men for the permanent occupation of these islands ; but they were soon followed by compatriots in the shape of adventurers, explorers, merchants, and missionaries.

Rapidly the islands of the South Sea, about whose inhabitants, products, and climate the most favourable reports were

White Men in South Sea Islands spread abroad, became centres of attraction for immigrants. In this manner the white race, represented chiefly by Englishmen and Frenchmen, later also by North Americans and Germans, spread over the Island world of the Pacific Ocean. The English especially, who had just obtained a footing on the Australian continent, were

THE FIRST ENGLISH SHIP IN THE PACIFIC: DRAKE'S "GOLDEN HIND" AT LIMA

in the vanguard of this movement. Besides settling in Tasmania and New Zealand, they also established themselves in Polynesia and Melanesia, and in the course of the present century have succeeded in acquiring a considerable portion of the Pacific island area. The French, too, have secured for themselves a considerable portion, more especially in the Polynesian groups, as well as New Caledonia. Later on, the North Americans also entered into the competition, and since 1885 the German Empire, by the adoption of a vigorous colonial policy, has also acquired possessions in Melanesia and Micronesia.

The Powers in the South Seas

Nor must we omit to mention here another European Power which, although it did not participate in the division of the Pacific island area, nevertheless, by a vigorous advance towards the ocean, early entered upon a path by which it gradually developed into one of the most powerful and determinant factors in modern history —namely, Russia. Recognising that its strength existed in its continental character, the mighty Slav Empire by degrees withdrew from the ocean ; it sold Alaska and the Aleutian islands to America, and exchanged the Kuriles for the pseudo-island of Saghalin ; but, on the other hand, it cleverly managed to extend its zone of contact with the ocean by a series of brilliant moves, vitally important to its own interests, towards the south. In the twentieth century that movement brought her into direct conflict with Japan, resulting in a set-back to the encroachments of the European Power, which still lacks effective command of a warm-water port. If and when she becomes secure mistress of such a position, her power on the Pacific will take a new aspect.

The occupation of the whole expanse of the Pacific by the white race requires, like the advance of Russia to the shores of that ocean, to be regarded from a higher vantage-ground. It is, in fact, more than a political event ; it is a fact of the utmost importance in universal history, an energetic step forward on the road which seems to have for its final goal the reunification of the divided human race, an issue not to be controlled by and scarcely patent to human consciousness, but one which is regarded by many as inevitable. Nowhere on the earth has this levelling influence of the white race

Ultimate Fusion of World Races

operated more energetically than in Oceania, but of course always at the expense of the aboriginal population.

In general, the Polynesians showed themselves very accessible to "white" influences ; they approached the white immigrants sympathetically, and adopted with ease their manners and customs and their modes of life and thought ; but in the acquisition of these foreign elements their own original structure became undermined. Wherever the influx of white elements is strong enough, mixed races are produced with greater rapidity, and in these the white influence is always the determinative factor. Thus in New Zealand the pure native Maoris are fast approaching extinction ; and the Sandwich Islands are nothing more than an appendage of the North American Union. On the other hand, where this influx is not sufficient to produce a rapid anthropological transformation, the native element is injured by a mere superficial contact with European culture or by what we may rather call its shady side. Men who as naked savages have led a true amphibious life, half on land, half on sea, die off prematurely when turned into civilised Christians. The white race, though it forms the determinant factor, does not, however, stand alone in this filling up of the gaps of defunct Pacific populations. Side by side with it the yellow race is engaged in a similar task. Of course, the motives from which the Chinese set out in this process are fundamentally different from those of Europeans and North Americans, and consequently their effect, too, is widely different ; nevertheless, to a certain extent at least, the latter has a similar tendency in both cases.

Effect Upon the Natives

It is neither love of adventure, lust for gain, nor political or scientific interests which drive the Chinaman to seek a home in foreign countries, but mainly the difficulty of obtaining a living in his own over-populated empire. According to natural laws the efflux of this surplus population takes place in the direction of least resistance ; but since Japan, till very recently, was closed to foreigners, while both divisions of India were themselves suffering from over-population, and the large islands of the Indian Ocean were very soon satiated with Chinese, the stream of Chinese emigration overflowed to Australia, America, and the island

DRAKE'S FIRST SIGHT OF THE PACIFIC OCEAN

world which stretches between these two continents. These latter, owing to the great disproportion between their extent and population, seemed specially adapted for receiving it.

Nevertheless, even there, the " yellow " invasion has not met with a very welcome reception. Nor is this a matter for surprise. First, we have to deal with the apparently unbridgeable gulf which exists between the white and yellow races. Neither the white man nor the Chinaman considers himself as the one and absolute superior of the other—in the way, that is, that both look on themselves in relation to all other native races ; but they recognise and fear each other as formidable rivals, without being able—owing to a total difference in mental outlook— to find some common ground of agreement. Fear without respect is the character of their mutual relations, combined with a repugnance reaching almost to disgust of the one nature toward the other, which prevents any direct intermixture of the two races, and consequently

The Yellow Invasion

removes the most effectual means toward the levelling of racial differences. In addition to this the Chinaman is a dangerous industrial opponent to the white man, whom he excels as an indefatigable, unpretentious, and at the same time intelligent workman, thereby lowering the value of white labour and depreciating wages.

Accordingly the policy of Australia and America is directed toward the prevention of Chinese immigration by all possible means, as much from the subjective standpoint of justifiable self-defence as from an inborn instinct. We must not, however, shut our eyes to the fact that the Chinaman might put forward the same claims on his side—if he had the power. It is therefore with the white race a simple question of self-help in the hard struggle for existence. When we consider the profound differences of the forces brought into play in the contact of the spheres of expansion of the yellow and white races upon the Pacific Ocean, a final solution of this difficult

The Side of the Chinaman

problem must appear still very remote. On the other hand, it becomes more and more evident that the part which the island world shut in by the Pacific Ocean has played in the shaping of the history of the world is not yet concluded, but, on the contrary, is destined to produce even greater effects in the future. The island **Stream of Chinese Emigration** groups of Polynesia, Micronesia, and Melanesia, in which new half-caste populations are being developed from the intermixture of white men and Polynesians, seem adapted for intercepting such part of the Chinese stream of emigration as is not mainly directed to the gold-fields of Australia and North America ; and it is probable that, owing to the extensive subdivision which of necessity goes on in these localities, this portion may become absorbed in the other racial elements.

The eastern margin of the Pacific—the American continent—seems specially designed for co-operating in this gradual work of unification. This view will probably meet with as little favour in the United States as will the suggestion that that country, still exuberant in its youthful strength, can expect to exercise its influence for ever. It looks, in fact, as if America were the continent which, after being for a long time inhabited by a single race, is suddenly about to collect all races upon its soil. We have no more striking proof of the force of oceanic influence and the historical importance of navigation. The mutual relations of the different races of America toward each other are very variable. The Indians of Central and South America, who led a settled, agricultural, and—according to their light—civilised kind of life in states of their own formation, were naturally unable to withdraw themselves from the influences of the white man to the same extent as the nomad hunting populations of North America and the wild tribes of the **Natives of America** South. The civilised Indians suffered the consequences of subjection, and hence furnished rich material for the formation of mixed races. The hunting and primitive races, on the other hand, avoided all contact with the white man except in a hostile sense ; they have accordingly suffered annihilation in the unequal combat, and have had to leave their settlements in the hands of those who have supplanted them. The whites, in their turn, especially in

the tropical zone, have shown themselves neither willing nor able to bear the heavy burden of bodily labour on their own shoulders, and have therefore fastened it upon those of the subjected races. Where the latter were not present in sufficient abundance, or where their physical strength was not equal to the performance of the hard task demanded of them, other means of obtaining the necessary relief were resorted to. The institution of negro slavery in America forms one of the saddest chapters in the otherwise brilliant history of the white race ; and though the nineteenth century may rest with the consciousness of having removed this shameful institution from the New World, and of having thus—at least partially—atoned for the sins of its fathers, this does not furnish any justification for letting pride at this act of civilisation banish our feeling of shame for the old moral wrong.

As things are to-day, America forms the centre whither stream the surplus populations of all the continents. It cannot resist this tide of immigration, inasmuch as there is still plenty of **Crucible of the Nations** space for its reception. " In this crucible," says Friedrich Ratzel, "all the different races of mankind will become intermingled ; there will, of course, be cases of retrogression or ' throwing back ' in this process, but bastard races, when they are preponderant, have a considerable advantage over pure races." At the time of its discovery by Europeans, America was inhabited by a single race about whose numbers we have no information ; but they certainly cannot have been very great. The densely populated Indian States of Central and South America formed mere oases within unpopulated deserts. At the present day, of its 100,000,000 inhabitants, 60,000,000 belong to the white race, 10,000,000 to the black, 9,000,000 to the red, 200,000 to the yellow, and some 20,000,000 to different mixed races. In this calculation are comprised the negro half-castes, to whom the pure negroes, however, are as one to four. Since this considerably increases the total of the mixed races, we may assume that about a fourth of the total population of America consists of mixed races. Now, every pure race can furnish the material for the formation of a mixed race, while the reverse is impossible ; farther, every mixed race, in the gradual crumbling away of neighbouring races, grows at their expense by absorbing the fragments. From these considerations it would appear that America is likely, in the near future, to be the scene of a great and general fusion of races. While the eastern margin of the Pacific basin appears in a state of active fermentation pregnant with events, its western margin also is being aroused into fresh activity. We have already remarked on the appearance on the Pacific coasts of Asia of the greatest continental Power in the world ; we have seen how Australia has become an excellent point of support to the greatest naval Power ; we are daily watching the interesting efforts at colonisation made by France, by the United States, and by the German Empire. It is therefore of special importance to consider the peculiar attitude assumed by the ancient civilised nations, the hereditary possessors of Eastern Asia, toward the successful invasion of the Pacific by the white race, which has now become a matter of history. In Japan, about the middle of the nineteenth century, a complete revolution was effected with surprising suddenness. Since that time the Japanese —or at least the influential classes among them—have been seized with a veritable passion for adopting all the institutions and customs of the white nations, even to the extent of imitating their external appearance in dress. The conditions are different in China. There, in spite of the multiplication of points of contact, we meet as yet with little comprehension of, and response to, European methods. On the contrary, it opposes to the invasion of the white race the mechanical obstacles of its immense superiority in number and density of population ; and, more than this, it meets this invasion **Attitude of Yellow Races** by an expansion on its own side, which, in spite of its apparently pacific character, forms, for the very reason of its being unavoidable, an extremely menacing factor. The waves of Chinese emigration radiate in all directions, but farthest to the side of least resistance— that is, across the Pacific Ocean. Here

DE BOUGAINVILLE
Who commanded the first French expedition round the world.

will of necessity be performed the first act of the inevitable struggle between the white and yellow races—a struggle viewed with much dread and fraught with much danger from the standpoint of **Coming Conflict of Races** ethnological history. Thus, if we cast a final backward glance over the Pacific, it appears at first as an element of separation and differentiation, assigning local limits to the various divisions or branches of the human race and providing them with the opportunity of accentuating and perpetuating peculiarities of type. Since this task has been completed, the ocean slowly and gradually, reversing its purpose, is destroying its own work, and tends in an opposite direction as an element of union, thus presenting us with a true image of the eternal circulating stream of Nature. The same glance reveals to us yellow, red, brown, and black races settling upon the coasts and islands of the ocean, stretching their limbs and extending themselves, supplanting or tolerating one another ; soon, however, arriving at a certain pause from which only the yellow races emerge, owing to their great numbers and multiplying powers, while the rest degenerate in every direction.

At the present day we see only two important elements as natural antagonists upon the shores of the Pacific, each prepared and ready for the fray : they are the ancient indigenous yellow race and the newly arrived white race. Both are ably and well represented : the yellow by the Japanese and Chinese, the white by the English and North American.

In the recent war the West declined to recognise the struggle as the beginning of a battle for supremacy between the white and the yellow races ; on the contrary, it showed its readiness to admit Japan into the comity of nations, rejecting the theory of inherent antagonism. If the time should come when the yellow and the white rise up against each other in a death grapple, Europe will repent of her standing aloof in the Russo-Japanese War. Whether she was wise in acting on the higher hope, time alone can show.

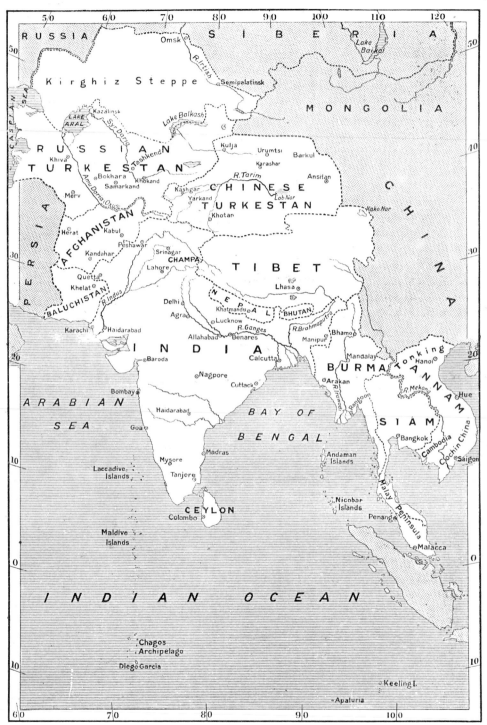

THE MIDDLE EAST DIVISION OF THE HARMSWORTH HISTORY OF THE WORLD

Following our progress westward we proceed now to the history of the Asiatic countries on the north of the Indian Ocean. These include India and Ceylon and the great peninsula which is best described as Further India : Burma, Siam, Annam, and contiguous countries. The Indian Ocean itself and the lands which border on India to the north and west—Tibet, Turkestan, Afghanistan and Baluchistan—also come within this division.

HARMSWORTH HISTORY OF THE WORLD

THIRD GRAND DIVISION

THE MIDDLE EAST

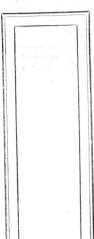

THIRD GRAND DIVISION
THE MIDDLE EAST

The regions included under the heading of the Middle East embrace the Indian Ocean, with so much of the Asiatic Continent as lies east of the Caspian Sea and the Persian Gulf, excepting what has already been treated under the heading of the Far East.

In this region, interest attaches primarily to the great Indian peninsula, which, like China, has a recorded history reaching back for nearly five thousand years, but, also like China, remained to Europeans a land of myth and marvel, hidden behind a curtain, of which a corner was raised at rare intervals, until the sixteenth century of our era.

Eastward of India proper lies the great double peninsula of Further India or Indo-China, half Indian and half Chinese in its associations. North lies the mysterious hidden land of Tibet, and beyond that—with Siberia on its northern and China on its eastern boundary—the vast Central Asian territory which bears the general name of Turkestan, the home of nomad hordes that, from time to time, have conquered and devastated half Europe as well as all Asia.

Finally, our division includes Afghanistan and Baluchistan, lands whose history is in part bound up with the Nearer East and the Empire of Persia, but whose most intimate connection is with Turkestan and India.

PLAN

THE INTEREST & IMPORTANCE OF THE MIDDLE EAST
Angus Hamilton

INDIA
Sir William Lee=Warner, Professor Emil Schmidt, and Arthur D. Innes, M.A.

CEYLON
Professor Emil Schmidt and Arthur D. Innes, M.A.

FURTHER INDIA
J. G. D. Campbell, M.A., Arthur D. Innes, M.A., and other writers

THE INDIAN OCEAN
Professor Karl Weule

CENTRAL ASIA
Francis H. Skrine, Dr. H. Schurtz and other writers

For full contents and page numbers see Index

LANDS & PEOPLES

OF THE MIDDLE EAST

THE INTEREST AND IMPORTANCE
OF THE MIDDLE EAST

BY ANGUS HAMILTON

ALTHOUGH the boundaries of the Middle East are well known, for the purposes of this history they may be regarded as including (a) Central Asia : Afghanistan, Baluchistan, Turkestan, and Tibet ; (b) Further India : Siam, Annam, Burma, Tonquin, Cochin China, and Cambodia ; (c) India, with the little independent states of Nepal and Bhutan, and the island of Ceylon. Within this region the physiography of Asia nowhere shows to such advantage as in the elevated uplands, where a central tableland, at once the loftiest and most extensive in the world, is buttressed by stupendous orological development. Covering some 3,000,000 square miles, the central tableland is intersected by high ranges which enclose a number of plateaus, while it is also marked in the Gobi Desert and in the Lob Nor basin by extensive depressions. Towering above these uplands, which reach in the Tibetan plateau a height of from 14,000 feet to 15,000 feet, in the Pamir plateau 9,000 feet to 12,000 feet, and in the Iranian plateau 6,000 feet above sea-level, are the lofty crests of the Himalayas, Tian-shan, Kun Lun, Altai and Mustagh Ata.

Radiating from the Great Pamir, as the pivot of several converging systems, are the Hindu Kush and the Mustagh Ata or Kara Koram Mountains from the south-west and south-east, the Kun Lun from the east and the Tian-shan from the north-east. The Pamir plateau covers some 30,000 square miles and in its southern limits connects the Mustagh Ata with the Hindu Kush by a ridge which serves as the water parting between the basins of the Upper Oxus and the Indus. To the north it acts as the water divide between the Zarafshan and the Syr-daria. The Tibetan tableland is no less intimately identified with the orography of the Middle East, but, lying between the Himalayas and the Kun Lun Mountains, it is the least accessible portion of this highland region.

The dominating feature of the mountain system of Mid-Asia is found in the gigantic mass which, in the shape of the Hindu Kush, Kara Koram, and Himalayas, forms the true water parting between the inland and seaward drainage of the Middle East. Divided into a western, central, and eastern section, the mountains constitute themselves the southern scarp of the central tableland and extend some 2,000 miles in one uninterrupted curve, from the eastern extremity of Assam to the low hills which lie to the north of Bokhara, varying in width throughout from 100 to 500 miles. The eastern section of the great divide contributes the Nepal highlands as well as Sikkim and Bhutan to the general rise of the Indian frontier, and maintains a mean elevation of 16,000 feet.

These three purely frontier territories, Nepal, Sikkim, and Bhutan, of which Sikkim long since has been incorporated with the dominions of India, nestle high up on the southern slopes of the inner range of the Himalayas. As may be imagined they are wholly mountainous. Their primitive and rugged character, too, is quite uninfluenced by Indian civilisation. Nepal, the largest, is a mere strip, some 500 miles in length and 160 miles broad, descending from **States of the** the heights of the Himalayas **Himalayan** to the Indian plain in five **Ranges** contracting terraces. At the same time the Nepal highlands are crowned by the highest elevations on the face of the globe. A right-angle ridge, 12,000 feet in height, separates Nepal from Sikkim, while the most easterly of the three, as also the most exposed, is Bhutan. Four hundred miles in extent and extremely elevated, it is at once the bleakest and the most beautiful part of the Himalaya region.

Throughout the line of the Himalaya system the serried continuity of the various parallel chains and ridges composing it is broken occasionally by some signal peak of marvellous altitude. The extreme westerly sections of the Hindu Kush do not disclose this irruptive grandeur in any great degree, and it is not until the Tirieh Mir, near the Nuksan Pass, now fixed at 25,000 feet, is reached that a really formidable height presents itself. Tengri Khan, the central point of the Tian-shan, however, records an identical elevation. Unlike the Hindu Kush, the Kara Koram chain offers quite a selection of lofty peaks; but then the mean elevation of the Mustagh Ata, by which name the eastern extension of the Hindu Kush is more precisely described, is rarely less than 18,000 feet. The highest points occur close within the angles formed by the convergence of the Hindu Kush and the Mustagh Ata, and between the Gilgit valley and the Kara Koram Pass. In connection with the former, Sven Hedin **The Lofty** fixed the highest point on **Peaks of** the Mustagh Ata itself at **Central Asia** 25,000 feet, while in the latter there are the Dapsang, 28,000 feet, and Peak K², 28,278 feet. In the Himalayas proper there is even a greater wealth of distinctive elevation, and no less than forty peaks are known to exceed 24,000 feet.

If the mountain systems of the northern part of the Middle East appear to belong to a single family, no such idiosyncrasy may be said to distinguish its rivers, and, whether the area concerned is the steppe of Eastern and Western Turkestan, the Iranian plateau, the elevated tablelands of the Himalayas, or the Great Plain and Deccan plateau of the Indian peninsula, there is very little reciprocity between the respective systems of drainage. In connection with the former the Tarim River constitutes Lob Nor the basin of Chinese Turkestan by draining the northern watershed of the Tian-shan, Mustagh, and Kun Lun mountains, much as the Aral Sea receives through the Amu-daria and the Syr-daria the drainage of Russian and Afghan Turkestan. At the same time, while the flow from the northern slopes of the Pamir plateau, the Hindu Kush and the Paropamisus goes to the Aral, the southern slopes of the Hindu Kush drain to the Arabian Sea through the Indus river, in the drainage system of which North-eastern Afghanistan is embodied.

Afghanistan boasts a three-fold system of drainage. Although the areas already mentioned drain to the Aral and to the **The Great** Indus, a much larger proportion **Watersheds** of the country, at least 200,000 **of Asia** square miles in extent, drains into the Seistan Lake, in the main through the Helmund river. Unlike Afghanistan, Baluchistan possesses no particular system, inland or seawards, and in many respects is as waterless as the Sahara. East of the Hindu Kush, at its meeting with the Mustagh, the presence of the water parting is manifested by the southern flow that is here given to the drainage of the watershed. From this point the main conduit southwards to the Arabian Sea is the Indus; further east the Ganges carries the drainage of the Himalayas, and the Brahmaputra that of the Tibetan highlands and their more remote hinterland, to the Bay of Bengal.

From the base of the Himalayan slopes a triangular peninsula projects southwards to Cape Comorin, possessing, between the delta of the Ganges-Brahmaputra on the east, and the delta of the Indus on the west, a length of 1,900 miles on each face. Breaking away from the foot of the mountains is the Great Plain of India, with an extreme elevation of 1,000 feet and an area of 500,000 square miles, but draining entirely to the Indus and the Ganges. South of this plain there rises the Deccan tableland, with a general level of about 2,000 feet and of a vast dimension. There is much that is distinctive about these two features of the Indian peninsula. The deltaic area is conspicuous for its richness and size, while the plateau is no less remarkable from the manner in which it preserves a continuity of character undisturbed by the encroachments of various containing hills. But the Ghats, which enclose the Deccan on the eastern and western sides, and the Nilgiris, which fulfil a similar purpose at its southern extremity, do not complete the mountain system of Southern India.

Beyond the Nilgiris the orographic formation of the peninsula is carried on by the Palni Hills, while the highest elevations that are to be found south of the Himalayas exist in the Anamalai Hills, 9,700 feet. Occupying the apex of the Indian triangle, by means of Adam's Bridge, these hills link together the Indian and Cingalese mountain systems. The most remarkable feature of the Southern upland, however, is the pronounced individualism which characterises its fluvial drainage. Unlike the central tableland in the north,

Character of River Systems which drains seawards only through the three rivers, Indus, Ganges, and Brahmaputra, the Deccan is scored by no less than fifty separate systems. In spite of this, the central tableland dismisses to the Arabian Sea and the Bay of Bengal respectively a greater volume of water in any one of its three streams than the Deccan discharges to any source throughout its entire system. In this connection, too, it should be borne in mind that the Indian peninsula drains always to the sea, an inland—to the Aral Sea and Lob Nor—as well as a seaward flow, describing the systems of Mid-Asia.

Although Eastern Assam has been indicated as the termination of the main water divide of the northern part of the Middle East, there is such an appreciable watershed connection between the Himalayas and Further India that the orographic influence of the mainland can be said to have penetrated the Indo-Chinese peninsula for some considerable distance. In a strictly scientific sense it has yet to be shown whether Further India possesses an independent highland system. If there is any doubt about the precise connection between the ranges of the Indo-Chinese and those of the Tibetan mass, there is no doubt that the rivers of Northern India

and Indo-China, as well as the Yangtse and Hoang-ho of China Proper, find their origin in the Tibetan plateau.

In a region as vast as the Middle East, there is necessarily much diversity in the systems of natural economy that apply to it. Extremes are touched in so many directions, and under such a variety of **Climatic Influences in the Region** subjects, that comparison is liable to beget confusion rather than to add to our general knowledge of this division of the Asiatic continent. None the less, the salient features of the Middle East present an attractive study and in many places disclose considerable unsuspected uniformity throughout vast areas. An example of this is to be noticed in the similarity of the climatic influences which affect the Aral basin on the one hand, and the Pamir, Tibetan, and Tian-shan uplands in another direction. Although the former is only slightly raised above sea-level, and the altitude of the latter varies between 12,000 feet and 18,000 feet, the climatic conditions of either area preserve the same fierce heat, identical periods of protracted drought, and the same intense cold.

India and Further India naturally respond to a different set of circumstances in the composition of their climates. India particularly is held at a disadvantage, since, although retaining the phenomena which produce a brisk climate, the benefit of possession is destroyed by the conflicting physical conditions of the peninsula. While the effects of tropical latitude, therefore, are tempered by the elevation of the Deccan tableland, great heat prevails everywhere because through their extreme altitude the Himalaya highlands intercept the cooling currents from the northern tablelands and, reflecting the solar rays, intensify the fiery blasts which proceed from the furnaces of the Indian deserts. In spite of an all-pervading heat, there is an even **Heat and Rain in India** distribution of humidity over the entire peninsula. Arising from the Indian Ocean during the incidence of the monsoon, neither the Deccan plateau nor its circumambient ranges are high enough to arrest the passage of the rainclouds, which, spreading farther and farther inland, ultimately precipitate their contents against the southern slopes of the main continental divide.

Save in the extreme north, on the uplands of the Burmo-Chinese frontier, Further India is subject wholly to tropical conditions, exaggerated rather than improved by the oceanic environment of the Indo-Chinese peninsula. Unendowed with sufficiently modifying elevation, an excess of moisture is accompanied by enervating heat, while the absence of a cold-weather season, resembling that which bestows such a boon upon India, renders the climate of Indo-China peculiarly trying. Examination of the climatic conditions of the Middle East would not be complete without a brief glance at the countries affected by the Iranian plateau. Although extremes of temperature distinguish both Afghanistan and Baluchistan, by reason of the proximity of the Arabian Sea there is much greater humidity in Biluchistan than in Afghanistan. At the same time, while the heat of Afghanistan is more intense than that which prevails in many parts of Bengal, no district of Asia is hotter than certain parts of Baluchistan. Yet, so long as terrific heat is unaccompanied by moisture, the prevailing conditions of climate are usually salubrious, although the heat of Baluchistan is aggravated by devastating sand storms. In this connection it is only in the lowland districts between the Oxus and the northern slope of the Hindu Kush that fevers are endemic in this part of the Middle East.

Climatic Conditions Around India

The orological traverse formed by the three systems, Hindu Kush, Mustagh, and the Himalayas, establishes not only the water parting of this section of the Asiatic continent, but the line of demarcation between the northern and southern flora, fauna and ornithology. Although the bleakness of the Asiatic highlands and their accompanying expanses of barren plain precludes a plentiful arboreal growth from distinguishing the heart of the Middle East, the region is by no means unproductive. The extreme altitudes are necessarily destitute; the valleys are stony and the mountain sides denuded of vegetation, but plateaux of 12,000 ft. are covered with rank grasses, while the secondary elevations are marked by an extensive distribution of mountain ash, poplar, pine, and larch. It is impossible to observe a definite line between tropical and non-tropical flora in Central Asiatic highland areas since, owing to the vagaries of the climate of the Middle East, subtropical life occasionally breaks out in the so-called temperate zones.

Vegetation in High Altitudes

It is not until the mountain systems of the north have been exchanged for the sweltering plains of the Indian peninsula or the deltaic valleys of Indo-China, that a genuinely distinctive element appears in Mid-Asian vegetation. Although signal success attends in the almost tropical areas of the Great Plain of India, the cultivation of cereals, vegetables, and plants, that are characteristic of a cooler region, the main interests centre in the growing of crops of a distinctly tropical complexion—rice, tea, coffee, jute, indigo, cinchona, betel, poppy, oilseeds, in addition to a variety of aromatic products, eliciting indiscriminately the attentions of the *ryots*. No less notable is the change to be found in the trees and palms which, as indigenous to the Indian peninsula, and ignoring the species common to temperate as well as torrid zones, include ebony, teak, sandal-wood, mango, banyan, date, palmyra, and bamboo. Unlike the Indian peninsula, less than half of which actually lies within the tropics, Indo-China or Further India is entirely tropical, a fact which an exuberant vegetation quickly makes patent. Vanilla, sugarcane, cloves, pepper, sago, ginger, cinnamon, cotton, rice, tobacco, tea and coffee, besides products everywhere interchangeable, flourish in the cultivated lands; while in the primeval forests eagle-wood, teak, gum, gutta-percha, cardamum, coco-nut, and bamboo abound.

The Tropical Vegetation of Further India

As comprehensive in its flora as it is in the character of its mountain systems and in the nature of its rivers, plains, and climate, it is only in its fauna and ornithology that the Middle East allocates to itself a number of specific types. Prominent among the species of the central uplands and along the line of the water parting there are in wild state the yak in Tibet; the ass, the camel, and the dromedary in Eastern Turkestan. Further to the south there are the elephant, lion, tiger, leopard, rhinoceros and crocodile in India and Indo-China; the lion, tiger, leopard and wolf in Afghanistan and Baluchistan. Common to the entire area are the usual domestic animals — buffalo, horse, ox, sheep, and dog; while, in addition, the dromedary, camel, elephant, the water buffalo, the ass, and the yak have been reduced to the service of man.

Although the Middle East itself is not concerned with all the philological and racial distinctions of Asia, a very confused ethnic distribution does fall within its narrow limits. Roughly divided between Mongolo-Tatars and Aryan-Caucasic peoples by the line of the water parting, the first fusion of the two races took place within the western limits of the Aralo-Caspian and Lob Nor basins, when an intimacy arose between the Turki, who frequented the unarable steppes of Eastern and Western Turkestan, and the Tajik, who tilled the western cultivable zone, which so modified the Mongolic features of the Turki that the race now resembles the Aryan Tajik in everything but speech. In the east and south of Lob Nor, continuing along the northern slopes of the watershed, a more Mongolic caste prevailed, which now betrays itself in Bhutan and on the Tibetan plateau ; while in Further India it is represented by the assortment of Tibeto-Burman, Tai, and Chinese-Annamitic tribes that now occupy **The Races** the northern and north-**of the** eastern frontiers of the **Middle East** peninsula. Although the presence of the mountains prevented a Mongolic descent upon the plains of India from the east from taking place, frequent Mongolic irruptions broke over the west, the residue of which has added so much to the ethnographic perplexities of the Middle East. In this direction the line of mountains was pierced by two passages, the Kabul Valley on the north-west, and Makran on the west, with the result that Mongolo-Tatar stock predominates in Northern Afghanistan. In Afghan-Turkestan the Hazaras, although now a Persian-speaking people, are marked out by their physiognomy as of Mongolic ancestry ; while the Kizzil Bashis of Kabul are Persian-speaking, and the Ghilzais Pushtu-speaking, Turki tribes. In addition, there are the Usbegs and the Turkomans, equally possessing Turki descent. In Baluchistan, too, the Brahuis, an aboriginal and numerous race occupying the eastern highlands, whose identity was long mysterious, are now believed to spring from Mongolic or Dravidian progenitors.

Excluding the Baluchistan highlands, Afghan-Turkestan represents the extreme limit of Mongolic movement towards India. South of the Hindu Kush, an Aryan element prevails in the tribes forming the population in Afghanistan and Baluchistan, as well as towards Persia and the northern plains of India. It is, however, in no way surprising that Aryan stock should underlie the ethnography of the southern areas of the Middle East, since the **The Peopling** earliest habitat of this great **of the** racial division were the **Middle East** valleys and mountains of the Oxus watershed. Retiring before the pressure of the Mongols, the Aryan peoples crossed over the main divide of Asia into the Peninsula. Although the last to arrive from the north-west, they did not penetrate much beyond the northern plains, remaining principally within the region covered by the basins of the Indus and Ganges. Elsewhere, indeed, were other races—the Dravidian in the Deccan and Ceylon, and the Kolarian about the central ranges, the latter being either the absolute aborigines or the first arrivals in the country. These latter branches of the human family represent, in point of fact, the only distinctive stock that India has produced, the Tibeto-Burman, Chinese-Annamitic, and other Mongoloid reductions along the Himalaya system, the Assam highlands and the Indo-China frontier being even more alien to India than the Aryan tribes themselves.

While the Kolarians belonged to the lowest grade of human culture, and were wholly unresponsive, the Dravidians were susceptible to the elevating influences of the Aryans, who ultimately applied to their own purpose the Dravidian alphabet. To-day, moreover, the Dravidian and Aryan peoples of India are unified in a common system of caste that extended throughout Southern Asia, the ethics and principles of which were devised originally by the Aryan leaders as a precaution against their numerical inferiority **The** in the face of the more numer-**Caste** ous indigenous element. To **System** the four original degrees of caste at first proclaimed an infinite variety has been added until the institution, which in its earliest conception referred to colour, now possesses hardly any relation to its original form.

Following their invasion of India, the Aryans passed into Persia, where they imposed their own forms upon the Semitic structure of civilisation already there.

Much as the Aryan language developed into Sanscrit in India, so in Persia it gave birth to Pehlevi, in which the Zend Avesta of the Zoroastrians is written. In Baluchistan, the Baluchis, as opposed to the Brahuis, are Aryan ; and, north of Baluchistan, extending from the axis of the mountain system in an indefinite westerly direction across Afghanistan and Persia, are areas in which the Aryan races exercise, if not unchallenged, at least uninterrupted, sway. Many subdivisions
Descent of the Afghans of the Aryan family exist in Afghanistan under the guise of Afghans, Galchas, and Tajiks. Of these the Afghans, or Pathans as they are called in India, are the most important. Claiming to be Ben-i-Israel, and insisting on descent from the tribes who were carried into captivity by Nebuchadnezzar, they are a Pushtu-speaking people, possessing, with all Pathans, the bond of a common speech, although they do not admit other Pushtu people to be Afghan. Further east, along the crests of the watershed, an Aryan population occupies Nepal, while there are Caucasic-Aryan indications among the tribes in Southern Siam and Cambodia.

Although the races of the Middle East may be classified broadly under one or other of the four branches, Caucasic-Aryan Mongolo-Tatar, Dravidian, and Kolarian, each group is divisible into several subsections. In many cases, too, these subsections, while physiologically in harmony, have developed complete linguistic independence. In this way, and considering each division as a complete racial unit, the Caucasic-Aryan peoples are affiliated with six stock tongues : (1) Kartveli ; (2) Cherkess ; (3) Chechenz ; (4) Lesghian ; (5) Aryan ; (6) Semitic—the first four of which appertain solely to the Caucasus region ; while the Mongolo-Tatar races are identified with eight : (1) Tibeto-Burman ; (2) Khasi ; (3) Mon ; (4) Tai ; (5) Chinese-Annamitic ; (6) Koreo-
Languages of the Middle East Japanese ; (7) Ural-Altaic ; (8) Malayan. The affinities with Dravidian and Kolarian are more doubtful ; but it is held by those most competent to judge that, owing to constant fusion of the species, there is now only a slight philological disparity between many Dravidian and Aryan dialects.

The existence of so much linguistic difference among races now forming the branches of a single racial family should not be astonishing when the divergent characters of the original tribes are borne in mind, nor is it remarkable that the Aryan peoples should produce greater evidence of common linguistic origin than the Mongolic or even the Caucasic races. Less subject to conditions which necessarily imposed changes upon speech than the nomadic northerners or the more polyglot communities from the Caucasus, the Aryans rapidly evolved a state of civilisation in which language, manners, customs and race type were identical, and through which Aryan domination over Southern Asia was established long before Mongolic peoples began to play havoc with the Middle East. It was, of course, by reason of this ascendancy that the Aryan language became a mother tongue to so large a part of primitive mankind. In many ways, therefore, the rise of these areas to their present importance dates back to the earliest age. Ever the cradle of the human race, they have aroused in turn the attentions of brown, yellow, and fair peoples, while their possession has stimulated the ambitions alike of the Moslem,
Commercial and Political Factors Christian, and Hindu. The further consideration of the Middle East concerns the commercial and political aspect of the region more than its general structure. At present the rights of three Powers—Russia in Central Asia, France and Great Britain in Further India, and Great Britain in India as throughout the areas lying to the south of the main water divide—prevail in the several sections appropriated to them. France in Further India, however, is committed to a policy which aims at the annexation of the whole of Indo-China, while Russia is no less intent upon the absorption of Chinese Turkestan. The complexion which the Middle East will wear for the future promises to be of unusual interest, for the realisation of their aims by Russia and France foreshadows a considerable alteration in the *locus standi* of Great Britain. Moreover, it should not be forgotten that trade, no less than prestige, would be affected by any modification of the traditional powers which Great Britain has so long exercised there, since, if Russia and France were confirmed in a paramountcy over Chinese Turkestan and Further India, the transfer would probably presage our exclusion from the markets of the region.

ANGUS HAMILTON

THE SUPREME LAND OF MARVELS

BEAUTIES OF NATURE AND
TRIUMPHS OF ART IN INDIA

AN ANCIENT HINDU TEMPLE AT HULWUD IN GUJERAT

THE GREAT MOSQUE ERECTED BY SHAH AHMED AT AHMEDABAD

ENTRANCE TO THE GREAT CAVE OF ELEPHANTA, NEAR BOMBAY

THE GREAT HINDU TRIAD IN THE CAVE TEMPLE OF ELEPHANTA

THE FAR-FAMED ROCK TEMPLE OF ELEPHANTA

TEMPLE ON THE ISLAND OF SALSETTE   INTERIOR OF THE TEMPLE OF INDRA

THE GREAT EXCAVATED TEMPLE OF ELLORA

THE CAVE TEMPLES AT ELLORA AND SALSETTE

HINDU TEMPLES AT BINDRABUND   KASHMIR TEMPLE OVER 2,000 YEARS OLD

A FAMOUS HINDU TEMPLE AT BENARES ON THE GANGES

NOTABLE EXAMPLES OF HINDU ARCHITECTURE

TOMBS OF THE KINGS OF GOLCONDA

THE MAUSOLEUM OF ZUFDIR JUNGE AT DELHI

THE TOMB OF IBRAHIM PADSHAH AT BEJAPORE

TYPES OF MOHAMMEDAN ARCHITECTURE IN INDIA

MOSQUE OF A SLAVE OF SHAH AHMED   MOSQUE OF SHAH AHMED'S WIFE

THE JUMMA MOSQUE, WITH HINDU PORCH IN CENTRE OF THE SOUTHERN COLONNADE

THE MOSQUES AND TOMBS OF AHMEDABAD

THE TOMB OF HYDER ALI AT SERINGAPATAM

SULTAN MAHMUD SHAH'S TOMB AT BEJAPORE

THE TOMB OF AKBAR, INDIA'S GREATEST EMPEROR, AT SECUNDRA

TOMBS OF THREE GREAT INDIAN RULERS

THE MOSQUE AT FATTEPUR SIKRI, NEAR AGRA, BUILT BY AKBAR

THE MOSQUE OF AURANGZIB AT BENARES

THE JUMMA MUSJID, OR GREAT MOSQUE, AT AGRA

THREE OF INDIA'S MOST FAMOUS MOSQUES

THE KUTUB MINAR AT DELHI   THE FAKIR'S ROCK ON THE GANGES

AURUNGABAD SEEN FROM THE RUINS OF AURANGZIB'S PALACE

SOME PALATIAL MONUMENTS OF THE PAST

LOG-PIER BRIDGE, WITH HOUSES, NEAR SRINAGAR, KASHMIR

WOODEN BRIDGE AT BHURKOTE IN THE HIMALAYAS

ROPE BRIDGE AT SRINAGAR, THE CAPITAL OF KASHMIR

TYPES OF NATIVE BRIDGES IN NORTHERN INDIA

FISHING BOATS IN THE MONSOON NORTH OF BOMBAY HARBOUR

PILGRIMS ON THE GHAT, OR LANDING-PLACE, AT HARDWAR ON THE GANGES

BY SEA-SHORE AND RIVER IN INDIA

GANGOOTRI, THE SACRED SOURCE OF THE GANGES

THE SACRED SOURCE OF THE RIVER JUMNA IN THE HIMALAYAS

SOURCES OF INDIA'S TWO GREAT SACRED RIVERS

VIEW IN THE BORE GHAT, NEAR BOMBAY

VIEW FROM TOP OF THE BORE GHAT, NEAR BOMBAY

THE SPLENDID MOUNTAIN SCENERY OF THE EASTERN GHATS

VIEW IN THE KOA-NULLAH

THE FALLS OF DHUAH KOONDE

BETWEEN NATAN AND TAKA CA MUNDA IN THE SRINAGAR MOUNTAINS

THE MOUNTAINS AND GORGES OF KASHMIR

1. Jag Deo and Warrangur, in the Barramahal.　2. Ryacotta in the Barramahal.　3. Daulutabad, the ancient Deo Gurh.

HILL FORTS IN SOUTH AND CENTRAL INDIA

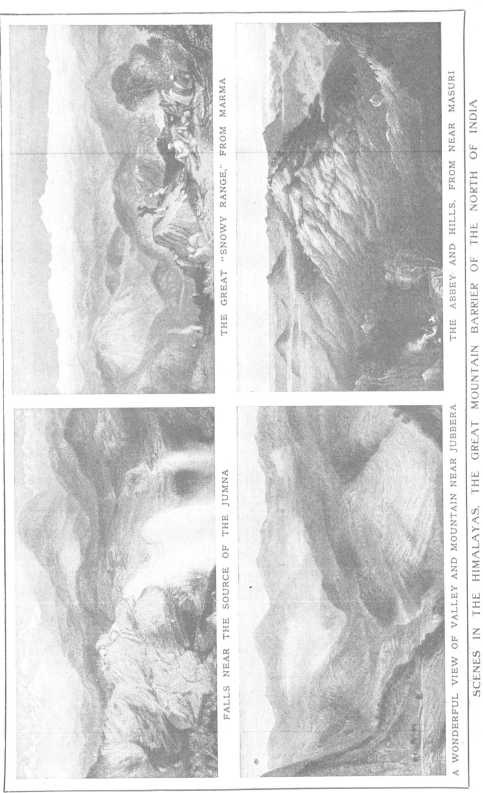

THE GREAT "SNOWY RANGE," FROM MARMA

THE ABBEY AND HILLS, FROM NEAR MASURI

FALLS NEAR THE SOURCE OF THE JUMNA

A WONDERFUL VIEW OF VALLEY AND MOUNTAIN NEAR JUBBERA

SCENES IN THE HIMALAYAS. THE GREAT MOUNTAIN BARRIER OF THE NORTH OF INDIA

INDIA

THE SUPREME LAND OF MARVELS

BY SIR WILLIAM LEE - WARNER, DR. E. SCHMIDT AND A. D. INNES

THE LAND AND THE PEOPLE

THERE is no tract of the earth's surface whose story appeals to the imagination so vividly, so intensely, as that of India. India is the supreme land of marvels, of mystery, of the supernatural ; of miracles which appeal to us not as the figments of superstitious ignorance, but as mani-festations of the incomprehen-sible. A land vast, unknown, unknowable, where the keenest of Western minds, after a lifetime of endeavour, profess that they know no more of the inner being of the people than they did at the beginning. A land full of the grotesque, yet whose grotesqueness has a terrific quality— fantastic, yet solemn. A land of countless revolutions, where yet there seems to brood, changeless, eternal, the spirit of an imme-morial past.

The Land of Myth and Mystery

Utterly remote from the ideas and the civilisation of the conquering races of the West, India is, nevertheless, the first recorded home of a vast migratory wave of that same Aryan stock from which, in later ages, those conquering races sprang. Rome and Athens were yet in the womb of a far-off future, Troy and Mycenæ were unborn, the great Sheikh Abraham had not founded his race, when the fair Aryan folk were sweeping over the plains of Hindustan. Before David sang, or Homer, their ballads were commemorating the deeds of their national heroes ; in the Land of the Five Rivers mothers were telling their children tales which sprang from the same sources as Grecian mytho-logy, Celtic folk-lore, and Teutonic legend. The ancient language of the conquerors was the eldest branch of that primal stock which in other regions and ages developed distinctive perfections in the utterance of Plato, of Virgil, or of Shakespeare.

But through the ages those Eastern Aryans were severed from their Western kinsfolk ; they worked out their own development apart. Once, East and West clashed when Alexander pierced the bar-rier, and led his victorious army into the Punjab ; but the contact was brief. Again the veil fell. The centuries rolled on, Imperial Rome rose and crumbled, a second Rome achieved and held a spiritual domination which was already tottering, ere Europe traced out the untrodden high-way of the ocean, and the veil was raised. In the interval—a period of some eighteen hun-dred years—all that Europe knew of India was derived from hearsay among the peoples of Western Asia, and the reports of an occasional enterprising tra-veller ; fabulous tales, for the most part, of splendour indescribable and wealth incalculable ; tales which were the magnet that drew Columbus along the ocean path

Lifting of the Veil

that led to an unknown continent instead of to the Indies he sought; and took Vasco da Gama by another way round Africa to the very shores of India. Yet all but two and a half centuries were still to pass before the Europeans were to be anything more than traders, with groups of offices and warehouses here and there on the fringe of the great peninsula. For almost simultaneous with the coming of the Europeans was the coming of the Mughals, or Moguls, who established over all the northern portion, or Hindustan, an empire perhaps the most gorgeous the world has known, which was presently extended over the southern portion, or Deccan. It was the disintegration of that great empire which gave the British an opportunity of establishing a territorial dominion in two provinces; which, once founded, they were soon compelled, in self-defence, to expand into a general ascendancy, and then a practically universal supremacy. The rule of the British in India has been a unique experiment, without precedent or parallel in the world's history.

Mogul and European Inroads

Thus, before the sixteenth century of the Christian era India had dwelt apart, like China, as far as Europe was concerned, untouched by her influence, save for one brief moment; and with a civilisation of her own, already advanced and highly organised before any appreciable culture began to leave its records in Europe. In those early centuries an Aryan race acquired a complete domination over all the primitive peoples of the lowlands, and an ascendancy even in most of the highland regions which could not be effectively conquered. The previous occupants were not wiped out, but survived—here and there in separation almost complete even to the present day—for the most part as subjects, but also intermixing largely with the newcomers. Over the whole great area a common religion and a common social organisation prevailed, though with immense local modifications; and these led to a hereditary and permanent differentiation between those social groups or castes which, comparatively at least, preserved their purity of blood—the sacerdotal and military castes, the Brahmans and Rajputs—and the rest. Everywhere all the castes were to be found, though Brahmans in one district and Rajputs in another might be numerically preponderant.

Early Aryan Civilisation

But this system did not involve the development of an organic Indian state, or of Brahman states, or Rajput states. Instead, it produced an aggregate of kingdoms with ever varying boundaries and without individual sense of nationality, the masses of the population passing under the lordship of alternate conquerors without other interest in the change of rulers than depended on the accident of their personal characters. But throughout all, the Rajput retained his prestige and the Brahman his spiritual ascendancy.

The old religious conceptions became degraded, absorbing into themselves the baser superstitions of the primitive inhabitants. Hence, for some centuries the new moral scheme of Buddhism became dominant; but this in turn became corrupted and degraded, and lost its hold utterly. Hinduism revived, but for the most part in a baser form than of old; filled, as concerned the common people, with gross and often hideous superstitions.

Upon this India broke, about the year 1000 A.D., the storm of Mohammedan invasion. Islam had gripped both the Iranian Aryans and Semites beyond the mountains, and the Mongolian Turkomans of Central Asia; Turkish and Pathan or Afghan conquerors swept over the northern plains; Moslem empires and kingdoms were established, and planted new empires and kingdoms in the Deccan also. Rajput princes struggled to maintain a precarious independence often lost and often more or less recovered; but the Mohammedan aliens, always a minority, dominated the peninsula as a whole, as a ruling race. Yet still the old principle prevailed. There was bitter race antagonism between the Moslem and the infidel, the Hindu and the foreigner; but no national organisation, no Indian State, no countries having political unity, presenting an object for patriotic sentiment. Though an empire might extend its temporary sway over a vast area, it never attained an organic homogeneity.

The Islam Invasion

A conqueror from beyond the mountains, the so-called Mogul Babar, founded the Mogul dominion just when Europe was in the first throes of the Reformation. His grandson, Akbar, made the empire a mighty reality, and adopted within it a policy more enlightened than any of his European contemporaries could compass. While the Spanish Inquisition was at the height of its power, Akbar, virtual head of Eastern Mohammedanism, was ruling on principles of universal toleration, and treating Mussulmans and Hindus with complete impartiality. His son and grandson neither altogether maintained nor entirely deserted that policy; but a Mohammedan supremacy was definitely re-established. Their successor, Aurangzib, was a fanatical Mohammedan, and in his day the old hatred between the rival faiths was fully restored. The possibility of educating Moslems and Hindus into one nationality was lost for ever. With his death, the break up of the Mogul Empire was already assured. Hindu Powers were already coming into being who would soon grasp at dominion, and the great provincial governors were on the verge of turning themselves into virtually independent sovereigns.

Before forty years had passed the French and British mercantile settlements were vieing with each other to obtain ascendancy at native courts. Fifteen years saw the decisive end of that contest, and the British, almost by an accident, masters of Bengal. India was no more **British Power in India** one than the Teutonic or the Latin nations of Europe are one. The Sikh, the Mahratta, and the Bengali are as far apart as the Portuguese, the Italian, and the Frenchman. The Mohammedan, indeed, was not and is not more akin to the Hindu than the Spaniard is to the German. But to both Hindu and Mohammedan the European is alien, as the Turk is alien alike to the Spaniard and the German, who, for the purposes of resisting Turkish domination, would feel themselves akin. In India, more than nine-tenths of the population are either Hindus of one kind or another, or else Mohammedans. There are computed to be about four Hindus to every Mohammedan, and rather more Mohammedans than the whole number of subjects of British race in the entire British Empire outside of India. Yet for more than a hundred years the alien ascendancy has been acknowledged, and for fifty it has been unchallenged. That it has been welcome is as questionable as that it has brought incalculable benefits to the masses in India is indisputable. The ruling race has felt the responsibility of dominion; it has accepted the white man's burden. The schoolboy said of a certain famous headmaster—his natural enemy—" He is a beast, but he is a just beast."

It would take a very hostile critic to refuse that measure of praise to the British dominion in India.

Few countries in the world contain within well-defined boundaries a greater diversity of geographical, anthropological, and ethnographical conditions than those displayed by the Indian peninsula. India **Natural Conditions of India** is indeed a world in miniature; those natural conditions which modify the progress of civilisation are varied in the extreme, and the civilisation of the inhabitants of this country is characterised by divergences which are the inevitable result of conformation to so varied an environment.

The points of contrast are intensified by their mutual proximity; broad alluvial plains are followed by the highest mountains in the world, burning tropical heat by the everlasting frost of the snow-clad peaks, the extremity of drought by the greatest rainfall in the world, tropical luxuriance by appalling desolation. Side by side with savages living entirely on the products of the chase, and by agriculture of the most primitive character, we find Brahmans devoted to the contemplation of the deepest problems of human existence. Black Dravidians, yellow-skinned Mongols, brown Asiatic Aryans, Hindu or Afghan, representatives of the white European races—all are parts of the population of India. Her history is a history of the struggles for predominance between these different peoples and races.

Nearer India owes its name to the river upon its north-west frontier, the " rushing " Sindhu of the Aryans, a name which was extended to include all the territory beyond the river by the old civilisations of Europe when they first came into contact with this distant land. India is the central of the great peninsulas which project southward from the continent of Asia. The southern portion of the country **India's Geographical Position** lies within the tropic zone, while its northern regions advance into the temperate zone beyond latitude 35°. Its frontier position has separated it from immediate communication with the steppes and deserts upon the boundaries of Asia proper except upon the north, the north-east and north-west; its coasts, running south-west and south-east, are bounded by broad seas impassable to peoples in the lower stages of civilisation. Upon the

1147

extreme south the island of Ceylon lies so close to the mainland that the intervening straits are rather a means of communication than an osbtacle to intercourse.

Extent and Population of India
The area of India is nearly equivalent to that of Western Europe, if a line of division be drawn passing through the eastern frontiers of Norway, Denmark, Germany and Austria. In respect of population, it considerably surpasses the district thus defined (293,000,000 as compared with 240,000,000); while its population is more than double that of East Europe (125,000,000).

Configuration of the Country
The configuration of the country in horizontal section is simple; its long coasts are broken by but few capes or gulfs, and these are of little importance. The largest gulf is that of Cambay, or Khambat, which was of high importance at an early period as a commercial centre. Good harbours, such as Bombay and Goa, are comparatively few in number. Upon the west coast, landing is a difficult operation, as the Western Ghats descend abruptly to the sea; while on the east, the coast, though flat, is lashed by formidable seas during the monsoon season. Lagoons have been formed only in the south of the peninsula on each side of its extremity. These facilitate communication along the coast even during the unfavourable monsoon season. On the north-east and north-west of the coast line, the Indus, the Ganges, and the Brahmaputra, which bring down large quantities of sediment, have pushed out formidable deltas into the sea, communication through which is impeded by the constant changes in the course of the various mouths and the heavy deposits of silt. One arm of the Ganges alone has attained to political and commercial importance during the last 150 years. The Indian frontier with respect to the rest of Asia is defined with no less simplicity than the coast line. The configuration of the country, considered in vertical sections, is more complicated. Here we meet with three great districts characterised by sharply contrasting features, the great mountain range on the north of India, the lowlands in the north of the peninsula, and the tableland in the south.

The northern frontier of India, which divides the country from the tablelands of Central Asia, is formed by the highest mountain range in the world, the "home of snows," the Himalayas. Bounded on the east and on the west by the openings made respectively by the Brahmaputra and the Indus, this range has a length of 1,500 miles, with a nearly uniform breadth of 137 miles; its area is almost equivalent to that of Germany. Its importance for India consists in the climatic protection it affords against the influence of the waterless districts of Asia, in the large rainfall which it collects, in the supply which it affords to the great fertilising streams of Northern India, and in the protection it gives to the country against the invasions of the restless inhabitants of the steppes. Not only does the range contain the highest peaks in the world, but it is as a whole almost impassable for large bodies of men. Never has there been an invasion of India from Tibet across the Himalayas by great armies or large bodies of people. The mad attempt of the Sultan Mohammed ibn-Tughlak to attack China by land ended with the total destruction of the army of Hindustan in the mountain snow-fields (1337).

The Great Mountain Barrier
The few passes which exist can be traversed only at rare intervals and by small bodies; the merchant and the missionary make their way across them. From a remote period a certain number of Mongol immigrants have very gradually trickled into Northern India by this route—Bhutan, Sikkim, Nepal—by which also Buddhism made its way to the north.

Mountain systems join the Himalaya at each end, completely excluding India from the rest of Asia. On the north-west we have the mountains dividing India from Afghanistan and Baluchistan, which run from north to south, decreasing in height as they advance southward, and broken by several important passes. These long, narrow valleys have provided the route for all those foreign invaders, Aryans, Greeks, Scythians, Afghans, Mongols, Persians, who from earliest times have acted as modifying forces upon the historical development of the Indian populations.

On the eastern side, the Himalaya range is joined by a number of high, steep mountain chains running north and south, divided by deep valleys, through which the rivers of the Irawadi, Salwén, Mekong, Yangtse Kiang, flow southward, a barrier of extraordinary strength preventing any communication eastward. The most westerly member of this mountain system sends one of its spurs south-east to the Bay of Bengal, the Patkai Mountains, 5,666 feet in height. Thus, upon the east, India is also shut off by a mountain wall surrounding the low-lying plains of the lower Brahmaputra in the shape of a horseshoe. This wall is passable only upon the south, and by this route has undoubtedly entered that infusion of Hindu-Chinese blood which is plainly recognisable to the anthropologist in the mixed races of Assam, Lower Bengal and Orissa.

The second great region of India is composed of two great river systems, those of the Indus and of the Ganges-Brahmaputra. The Indus turns at right-angles to the mountain range, taking the shortest route to the sea, which it reaches in a rapid descent—a fact of no less importance for the nature and the inhabitants of its valley than the fact that the long channels of the Ganges and the Brahmaputra run parallel to the mountain range. While the Indus passes the spurs **India's** of the Himalaya, and is fed by **Great** tributaries from these sources, **Rivers** a sufficient supply of moisture is available for the cultivation of the ground. The earth then showers her gifts upon mankind with such lavish bounty that the Punjab, the district of the Five Rivers, even in the grey dawn of history, was the goal of the ambitions of the nomad tribes inhabiting the dry steppes of Afghanistan and Central Asia. On the other hand, in the valley of the lower Indus the arable land is restricted to a narrow belt on each bank of the stream, which here runs so rapidly that navigation is almost impossible ; while it brings down such heavy deposits of silt that its delta is continually changing, and the arms of the delta, and the sea in their neighbourhood, are with difficulty accessible on account of the outlying banks of sediment. Eastwards from this arable country, upon the Indus, stretches the Great Desert, across which communication is almost impossible. It extends southwards to the sea, and northwards almost to the foot of the Himalayas, at which point alone a narrow strip of land makes communication between the two river systems possible. Hence it was at this spot that peoples advancing into India from the west came into collision

with the inhabitants already settled in the valley of the Ganges. This district has repeatedly been the scene of those decisive battles which predetermined the history of India for long periods.

The eastern, which is the larger portion of the plains of North India, is far more favourably situated than the western. **The** The Ganges and Brahmaputra **Ganges** run parallel to the mountains, **Valley** though they are so far apart from the Himalayas, from the heights of the Deccan on the south, and from the frontier mountain range about Burma, that on each side a wide declivity is available for copious irrigation by artificial means. The whole river valley is alluvial land ; but a distinction must be made between the earlier and the later deposits. The line of demarcation between these begins at the Ganges delta. Up to that point the land falls away so rapidly from the west that the soil is dry and fruitful. Everywhere irrigation can be provided in sufficient measure to satisfy the most zealous cultivator of the soil, which also receives new deposits of rich manure from the silt-laden waters of the rivers. Navigable streams cross this district, which is more suitable than any other in India for the development of important towns. The characteristics the eastern portion of the river valley are wholly different ; in the delta of the Ganges, and in the whole of Assam, the deposits of silt have been so recently made, and the ground in consequence lies so low, that drainage works are impossible. The country is almost everywhere in a swampy condition, and the malaria of the district is dangerous to human occupants. Navigation is difficult, as also is communication by land, for the ground is not sufficiently firm to permit the laying down of roads. Hence the civilisation of this part of the Ganges-Brahmaputra valley was in a comparatively backward **Civilisation** condition before the rise of the **of the** English power in India; Aryan **Ganges Delta** and Mussulman influences made themselves felt comparatively late, and it is only during the last one hundred and fifty years that the greater intellectual power and energy of Europeans has brought prosperity to the delta of the Ganges.

In the southern part of India the table-land known as the " South Land," the Deccan of the Aryans of North India, rises in isolation. It forms a great elevated highland with steep walls, which fall sheer into the Arabian Sea at the Western Ghats ; on the eastern side the plateau is somewhat lower and lies at some distance from the Bay of Bengal, from which it retires gradually as it advances southward. In this district between the highlands and the sea rise individual isolated plateaus and numerous single peaks, by which the plains are diversified. The tableland attains its greatest height on the west coast with the mountains of Anamalai, 8,977 feet high, and of Nilgiri, 8,477 feet high, falling gradually away to the eastward. Hence, most of the rivers of the Deccan run eastward—for example, the Son, Mahanadi, Godavari, Kistna, Kaveri, Tanghabadra ; two streams only, the Narbada and the Tapti, have worn out deep gorges in their westward career. These, together with the mountain ranges of the Vindhya and Satpura running parallel to them, divide the highlands into the great southern section, or Deccan, and the northern, or Central India ; which for a long time proved an obstacle to the advance of the Aryans, more by reason of its malarial swamps and its jungle vegetation than because of its mountainous nature. All the above-mentioned streams are unimportant as means of navigation and communication, on account of the variable water supply and the rapids and waterfalls by which they are broken when they reach the precipitous edge of the highland. The line of the Narbada, or Nerbudda, carried across the peninsula, is commonly held to be the boundary between Hindustan and the Deccan.

Features of the Deccan

Friedrich Ratzel has laid great emphasis upon the importance of geographical position to natural history ; the position of India has exercised a most decisive influence upon the whole course of development of the natural products of the country and also of its population. The position of this central peninsula of Southern Asia, situated as it is with reference to the enormous dry, waterless districts of the desert and the steppes on the one hand, and on the other hand to the tropical sea with its moisture-laden atmosphere, determines the amount of the rainfall and its distribution, and therefore also the fertility of different parts of the

Importance of Geographical Position

land, which again influences the population. In the spring and summer the great deserts and steppes of Central Asia are scorched by the sun, which then attains its greatest altitude ; the barometrical pressure is low and the currents of air with their burden of moisture from the tropic Indian seas travel in a north-easterly direction across India, a deviation due to the revolution of the earth. In the southern portion of the country these clouds then meet the steep wall of the Western Ghats and deliver a large proportion of their moisture, breaking in violent thunderstorms upon the mountain wall, to return again to the sea in rushing torrents and streams.

The air currents, however, after crossing the watershed of the Ghats, become drier, and provide but a scanty rainfall for the eastern district where the highlands slope away. Not until they reach the giant wall of the Himalaya do they drop all the moisture which they have retained. For this reason the mountains of Assam can boast the heaviest rainfall upon the earth ; the rainfall of Cherra Punji in the Hsia Mountains of Assam amounts to 444 inches during the summer and 520 inches for the whole of the year. On the other hand, during the winter months a high barometrical maximum prevails over Central Asia, while South Africa and the Indian Ocean, which are then scorched by the sun, show a low average barometrical pressure. The currents take a backward movement, and blow from the great dry continent as the north-east monsoon, bringing to India but little moisture, and that at uncertain intervals. Consequently the wide districts to the east of the Ghats as far as the Himalaya Mountains suffer greatly from droughts, and, should the rains of the east monsoon fail, are confronted with terrible famines.

Heaviest Rainfall in The World

The fertility of the country depends upon the amount of natural or artificial irrigation which it receives. Vegetation, apart from human agency, flourishes most luxuriantly on the Malabar coast. Beyond the range of the Western Ghats different conditions prevail. A forest country is first met with, where the deciduous nature of the trees is a protection against the excessive drought of the dry season. Vegetation then conforms to the character of the steppes in general, and agriculture is restricted to the immediate neighbourhood of springs or tanks, to the river banks, or to the river deltas. The steep wall of the Western Ghats ends upon the north with the river Tapti, so that at this point the moisture-laden currents penetrate more deeply into the country. The remoter heights of Central India produce a heavier rainfall; though the forests are more extensive in that district, the prevalence of malaria is an obstacle to human occupation. The great plains in the north of India receive a diminishing rainfall in proportion as they are removed from the delta of the Ganges on the west; compensation is, however, afforded by the works of artificial irrigation which distribute the streams falling from the Himalaya, and, in some degree, those which rise on the north wall of the Deccan. The delta of the Ganges and the lower ground in the valley of the Brahmaputra suffer from an excess of rainfall and ground moisture.

The cultivation of the country, especially as regards the growth of cereals, is primarily conditioned by the existing facilities for irrigation. Where copious **Variety of India's Cereals** supplies of water are to be had, rice is the staple product of agriculture, as it is on the whole of the Malabar coast, on the deltas of the Deccan rivers, of the Indus and the Ganges, and in Assam. Under proper irrigation, land containing less moisture will produce a heavy yield of wheat, as is the case in the Punjab, the British North-west Provinces, Oudh, the Central Provinces, and certain favoured parts of the presidency of Bombay. Where irrigation is difficult, several kinds of cereals and other subsidiary products flourish. Where the land is too dry for these plants, as is the case in large districts of the southern Deccan, stock breeding enables mankind to make a living at the expense of some hardship; the caste of the shepherds (Kurumbas), which is now scattered and decayed, played an important part at an early period.

The population of India is distributed according to the fertility of the soil. The mineral wealth of the country is comparatively small. Coal is by no means common and has only recently been worked upon any large scale; iron ore is widely distributed, but was used by the natives only to a very small extent, and the importance of this industry has been practically extinguished by the competition of the

great European undertakings. The riches of India in precious metals and stones have been considerably exaggerated; the real wealth of the country does not lie within the soil, but grows upon it. Consequently the population is almost entirely of a peasant character; the last census, before the opening of the twentieth century, showed only 2,035 towns **Distribution of India's Population** properly so-called among 717,549 settlements; of this number, 1,401 had less than 1,000 inhabitants, 407 had between 10,000 and 20,000, and 227 had a population above 20,000. Only twenty-six towns had more than 100,000 inhabitants, and only four—Calcutta, Bombay, Madras, and Haidarabad—more than 300,000. In England, 53 per cent. of the population live in 182 towns of more than 20,000 inhabitants, whereas in India this holds good only of 4·84 per cent., distributed in 227 towns of 20,000 inhabitants. The collective population of the country—287,133,481 inhabitants upon 1,560,080 square miles, excluding Burma—gives an average of 184 inhabitants to the square mile. In individual districts of some size this average varies between 24 and 1,395; it is larger in British India than in the native states, a fact apparently due to European influence upon the country and still more to the circumstance that England has occupied all those states where the soil is more than usually fertile.

A systematic ethnographical examination of the population of India is an extremely difficult task; no universal lines of division can be drawn including all the most important phenomena of divergent nationality. The differences, moreover, by no means run in parallel lines. The most important points to be noted are physical characteristics, language, religion, and social peculiarities, together with the characteristic signs of national feeling which these differences imply. The many changes in Indian history pre-suppose the **Introduction of Alien Blood** impossibility of any physical uniformity throughout the population. Apart from the infusions of Portuguese, Dutch, and English blood during the last four centuries, foreign representatives of the white or yellow races have frequently invaded the country through the north-west passes. However, as far as the Mongol princes are concerned, almost every trace of their existence has disappeared from the ethnological characteristics of the modern Indian. The white races have, however, exercised a permanent modifying influence, and their descendants form one of the main racial elements of the country. From a remote period vigorous commercial relations were maintained on the west coast with the western continents, which have left their traces upon the physical characteristics of the coast dwellers ; the Semitic type of countenance common among the Mohammedans of the Malabar coast is derived from the Arabs. Fugitive Jews have repeatedly entered the country in bodies, such as the Jews of Cochin (now 1,300 in number), who, according to their traditions, left their country after the destruction of their great sanctuary by Titus (70 A.D.) ; another instance is the Jewish colony in Bombay, which was expelled from its former settlements by Mohammedan fanaticism. Similarly, a large number of fire worshippers fled from Persia in the year 1717 before the zeal of the Mohammedans, and the coast of Bombay is now inhabted by 90,000 Parsees who remain true to the religion of Zarathustra. In many cases their Semitic cast of features recalls the representations of the kings in ancient Nineveh, whereas others remind us of the modern representatives of the white races in the Armenian highlands.

Jewish Colonies in India

The east coast has been peopled rather by Indian migrations directed especially towards the opposite coast of Burma than by immigration from abroad. A strong infusion of Mongolian blood has, however, entered from the north and north-east. The southern slopes of the Himalaya to the east of Dardistan are peopled by a mixed race of Mongol Indians apparently formed by the slow infusion of Mongols from Tibet over the extremely difficult mountain passes. A similar population is to be found in Assam and in many of the tribes inhabiting East Bengal and Orissa ; though here the Mongol element probably entered the country by the easier route through Burma rather than by crossing the extremely difficult mountain ranges which run in parallel lines to the east of Assam.

The Mongol Element

All these infusions of foreign blood, however, excluding the mixed Indo-Mongolian population, form a very small and almost unappreciable element in the racial composition of the country. The two main component elements are the representatives of a white race, which entered the country from the north-west at a comparatively early period, more than four or five thousand years ago, and a dark race, which may be considered as directly descended from the original population. This race is recognisable by the dark colouring of the hair, eyes, and skin ; it is of universal distribution, and is often intensified into the deepest shades of dark brown ; a further characteristic point, reminding us of the black negro races of Africa, is the moderate size of the skull and the short, broad nose. The race, however, is differentiated from the negro type by the shorter and more upright stature, and especially by the hair, which, though black, is but moderately crisp, and while often found in curls or waves, is never of a woolly nature. The representative types of this race usually attain a stature which is considerably less than the average height of the Teutonic stock. Races living under very unfavourable conditions, with an insufficiency of nourishment, such as many of the dwellers in the mountains and jungles, and the slave castes, are so far below this average stature that they may be considered as dwarf tribes, though it is impossible to make this characteristic a line of demarcation between them and the other dark races of India.

The Dwarf Tribes of India

The white races in India are distinguished from the dark especially by their complexion, which in pure-blooded types is no deeper than that of the Europeans about the Mediterranean. Their average stature is considerably higher, while their features are smaller, and their noses, with higher bridges, are more prominent than in the case of the black races.

An examination of the geographical distribution of the different Indian races will begin with what are, comparatively speaking, pure representatives of the fair races of the north-west, immediately adjoining the population of Afghanistan and Baluchistan, which has been more or less modified by infusions of Semitic blood. Such influence is less prominent in Kashmir, in the hill country, and in the Punjab, as far as the upper course of the Ganges ; on the other hand, further eastward, in the centre, and especially in the lower course of the Ganges, a deeper complexion may be observed in many of the subordinate grades of caste and settlement. Further east again, in Assam, the characteristics of the fair race disappear by degrees, and are but moderately pronounced among the higher castes ; the chief element of the population is formed by the fusion of the black and yellow races.

Of similar composition are the numerous small mountain tribes of the Himalaya as far as Dardistan. Southward the fusion of black and yellow come to an end about the frontiers of Orissa ; at this point the characteristics of the fair race are again strongly marked in the higher Brahman castes. In Central India is found a belt of almost purely dark-complexioned population ; further south again, in the Deccan and the plains upon its frontier, the black races are greatly preponderant, though in individual castes varying infusions of white blood may be observed. On the west coast, on the other hand, besides the small colonies of foreigners—Jews and Parsees—closely united bodies of white inhabitants are to be found concentrated among the dark population. Individual branches of the Brahman caste—the Konkanath, Nambutiri, and Haiga Brahmans — zealously preserve the purity of their caste and race ; a warrior caste of the Nair and the caste of the Temple Maidens are distinguished from the surrounding population by their fairer complexions.

Purity of Caste and Race

Indian languages display the utmost variety. Philology has distinguished three typical forms of language—the isolating, the agglutinative, and the inflectional. These three types are represented in India, and, in general, coincide with the three racial types there represented—the mixed Mongolian and dark-skinned races (Hindu-Chinese), the unmixed dark races (the Dravidians) and the white race (the Aryans). If a straight line be drawn from Goa in a north-westerly direction to the beginning of the Ganges delta, the agglutinative languages will lie chiefly to the south-east of this line, the district of the inflectional languages extending on the north-west into the Ganges delta and the valley of the Brahmaputra, while the isolating languages are found at the edge of the southern slopes of the Himalayas and the mountains of Southern Assam.

The boundary between the Aryan and Dravidian languages is not to be conceived as a sharp line of demarcation ; the Dravidian languages are sporadically found within the district of the Aryan tongues. The early disruption of the Dravidian peoples has naturally brought about great differences of grammatical form, and many dialects have borrowed numbers of foreign words from neighbouring languages. These isolated Dravidian tribes invariably live hard lives upon a low plane of civilisation ; they include the Khonds, in the mountain districts of Orissa, Ganjam and Cuttack ; the Gonds, a tribe which has been broken into several isolated linguistic units, between the Narbada and Godavari ; the Oraon in Chota Nagpur ; and finally the most northerly representative of this division, the Mal Paharia, established upon the lower Ganges in the mountains of Rajmahal, whose language, though greatly differing from the other Dravidian tongues, must none the less be included within the Dravidian family. Whether the Brahui, who inhabit the district from the lower Indus to Baluchistan, should be added to the Dravidian family is an unsettled question. Assuming that they are members of this family, the strong differences between their language and that of related tribes may easily be explained as the effect of the different migrations which had passed over their country. Philologically their language resembles in such respects the Dravidian languages of South India.

The Languages of India

The Kolarians, about 3,000,000 in number, in the Presidencies of Bengal, Madras, and the Central Provinces, are an ethnological puzzle ; they have been broken into isolated communities, and their language, which was undoubtedly widely distributed at an early period, has been broken up and confined by the advance of the Aryan and Dravidian languages. Their language is to be distinguished from the Dravidian tongues — though physically they closely resemble the Dravidian type—by an entirely different vocabulary, and by an embryonic inflectional system. As yet, however, very little is known of them, and further research will no doubt modify the views now held upon their philological position and dialectical division. It has been said, but by no means proved, that they are philologically related to certain tribes of Further India.

A Tribe that Puzzles Scientists

The construction of a scheme to illustrate the distribution of the different religions is by no means facilitated by the fact that sharp distinction between them is often impossible. The simple conception of a divine being, inherited and obstinately retained from the earliest periods of tribal development, is in every case the primitive underlying idea, and is manifest even in the most advanced religious systems. While the Hindus assert their faith now in Vishnu, now in Siva, at the same time none are found to deny the existence of demons, upon whom the religious fears and veneration of lower tribes are entirely concentrated; and these powers have also been recognised within the Hindu heaven. Consequently, statistics of the adherents of the various religions are extremely unreliable ; their variations as compared with the known populations of different nationalities frequently show the lines of religious demarcation to be extremely vague and unstable. For the lowest of these faiths, the demon worship, the census of 1890 gives a percentage of 2·64 of the whole population of British India, and of 5·20 for the other parts of the country.

The greater proportion of the inhabitants of India (72⅓ per cent.) are worshippers of one or other of the great divinities of the Hindus. Where this average is not attained we find that Hinduism has had to struggle with Mohammedanism, and also with demon worship, or other special forms of religion. Such cases are shown in this table, giving the percentage of adherents of the two religions.

Province	Hindus	Mohammedans
Punjab ..	37·1	55·7
Kashmir ..	27·2	70·5
Assam ..	54·7	27·0
Bengal ..	63·4	32·8

The whole number of the followers of Mohammed has been estimated at 243,000,000 ; and of this total 57,000,000— that is, almost a quarter (23·5 per cent.), belong to India. This belief is represented in every part of India ; the tolerance displayed by the Mohammedans toward the caste system gives them the advantage of being able to maintain commercial relations with every branch of society in the country, though naturally to a larger extent in the older Mohammedan towns.

Consequently, the North-west Provinces and states, where Islam entered the country, are most thickly populated with Mohammedans or Mussulmans. In the south, the numbers of the Mohammedans diminish considerably. The faith is practically unknown to the tribes of the Central Provinces, and a very small percentage is found in Mysore and Haidarabad.

Buddhism, at one time so widespread in India, has now degenerated into Hindu-polytheism in the mountainous countries of the north—the Himalaya and Kashmir valleys ; and on the north-east—the frontiers of Tibet and Burma. Few adherents survive of the northern branch of this religion, and in Kashmir alone they scarcely amount to one per cent. of the whole population. The Jain religion, which is related to Buddhism, is better represented in certain provinces, though nowhere has it retained a higher average than five per cent. of the whole population.

Of other religions we may mention that of the Sikhs, which is almost exclusively confined to the Punjab (1,900,000, two-thirds per cent. of the whole population). They form a Hindu sect, which has rejected various restrictive principles such as that of caste, and has developed rites peculiar to itself. Other religions which have entered India from abroad are very weakly represented ; such are the Parsees, on the west coast of India, with Bombay as their centre, and with 90,000 adherents— that is, 0·03 per cent. ; the Jews, early colonists in Bombay and Cochin, together with scattered Jews of various origin throughout India, numbering 17,200 souls (0·006 per cent.), and the Christians with 2,300,000 (0·8 per cent.). Of these last 2,036,600, that is, 89 per cent., are converted natives, while 80,000, that is, 3·5 per cent., are half-breed Indians, and 168,000, that is, 7·4 per cent., are Europeans. More than half of these Europeans are soldiers with their relatives. The caste system has exercised so deep an influence, is so characteristic a phenomenon of Indian social life, and is, moreover, an institution of such infinite diversity in its details that its true nature can be understood only in connection with its historical development as a part of the national history.

ANCIENT INDIA
THE ARYAN INVASION AND THE CONQUEST
OF THE NATIVE RACES

THE history of India is a drama in three great acts. The first of these is occupied by the struggles of two races for predominance ; the second, by the struggles of two religions ; and the third, by the conflict for the economic exploitation of the country. In the first period, Aryans are opposed to Dravidians. The result of their struggle is a development of a mixed race of people whose political, social, and religious institutions are to be explained partly as the result of fusion, and partly as due to the predominant influence of one or the other element. The mixed people which was thus developed supported the Hindu religion and theory of existence. The Semitic, Turanian, and Mongol tribes who entered the country from the north-west brought the Mohammedan faith with them ; the struggle of these two religions forms the second period. In the third act Europeans appear upon the scene, and the economic struggle for the wealth of the country ends with the total collapse both of Mohammedan and Hindu independence, victory remaining with the side that possessed superior intellectual power, clearer foresight, and greater strength. From the prehistoric period to the end of the first thousand years after Christ forms the period of native Aryan - Dravidian development, the period of ancient India. For about 700 years the struggle of Hinduism with the foreign religion continued, and forms the " mediæval " period ; while the " modern " period covers little more than the last 150 years, in which, however, the whole people has undergone far more fundamental changes than any that all previous centuries have brought to pass.

The Great Drama of India

We have first of all to consider the two races whose struggle composed the first period of Indian history, together with the mutual influence which they exercise upon each other.

The original inhabitants of India have left us neither written nor traditional records of their existence during the pre-historic period. Traces of human agency during this period have, however, been discovered in India. As in Europe, discoveries of stone implements, of lance and arrow heads, of knives, razors, hammers, made of jasper, agate, and chalcedony—flint proper not occurring in India—show that an earlier age of human development preceded the time when metals were employed. Whether this period goes back to the Tertiary Age, as many investigators suppose, is still a doubtful question.

Traces of Early Indian Development

The most ancient tombs contain no examples of metal work ; those, however, that are found in sepulchres of later date display high technical skill, and enable us to infer a considerable advance of civilisation in general, such objects being revealed as iron arrow-heads, knives, lamps, tripods, stirrups. In many cases women or men were beheaded at the funeral of a dignitary and buried with him. Rarely has any definite tradition of the person buried in the grave been preserved. The earliest literature, Dravidian and Sanscrit alike, has not a word to say upon the subject of these graves.

On the other hand, the poems of the Aryans, who were making their victorious invasion of India at the dawn of history proper, provide us with much information upon the life of the original inhabitants, who are naturally described from a hostile point of view. They are contemptuously known as " slaves," " low class," " people talking an unintelligible jargon." They are described as being of black complexion, their figures small and ugly, in spite of their heavy ornaments of gold and precious stones, their noses broad, and their eyes small. They were indeed a complete contrast to the Aryans, who must have been particularly impressed with these points of difference in the enemy, as their own stature was tall and proud,

Records of Invading Enemies their complexion fair, their noses boldly formed. " With beautiful noses " is the title which they give to the images modelled in their own likeness. The enemy are said to have been driven back into the mountains, whence they made reprisals, attacking the herds and the property of their oppressors as " robbers " without harm to themselves. Magical arts were attributed to them, including the power of drying up the streams and rivers which bring fertility and verdure to the plains. Mysterious also is the power of the gods to whom they prayed ; hence these were soon considered as demons, or " Yakshu," who disturbed the fire of the Aryan sacrifices, and for whom no sacred flame was ever kindled.

This description of the original inhabitants in the old Aryan poems entirely corresponds with the appearance of the mountain and jungle tribes of the present day, and also with that of the lowest castes of the population in modern India. Like their savage ancestors, the tribes of the present day carry on their existence under conditions of the greatest difficulty, and their general civilisation is as low as their environment is rough. In many cases their sole agricultural implement is a stick with the point hardened in the fire, with which they grub up the scanty roots and bulbs of the jungle ; at a somewhat higher stage of development, agriculture is carried on by burning down a portion of the forest every year and planting in the fructifying ashes the seeds of the native cereals or tubrous plants,

Primitive Conditions Surviving a scanty harvest which ripens rapidly. The tribe then sets out upon its wanderings to choose a new piece of forest for its next harvest. A few goats or sheep and the small pariah dog alone accompany it ; from the climbing plants or the bark of the trees nets are woven, the waters of the tanks or pools are poisoned with leaves or fruits, and the tribe thereby obtains a meal of fish. The arrows of the savage wanderers lay low the forest game which fall into their traps and snares ; wild honey provides them with the sweets of their meal. They roast their food at a fire which is kindled by the rotary friction of two sticks ; comparatively few of the forest tribes have learned the art of pottery. A roof of leaves or an overhanging rock is their shelter, an apron of grass or leaves or of tree-bark is their clothing, the scantiness of which serves to emphasise the weight of the ornaments with which they load every possible part of their bodies.

Though the poverty of the life of these tribes may arouse our sympathy, yet their character demands our hearty respect. All who have come into contact with them and learned their habits, praise their independent spirit, their fearless bravery, their truth, honour, and fidelity. They are true to their plighted word, true to their wives and to their race. The arrow of an absent chief, given by his wife as a means of recommendation into the hands of an English ambassador, secured for this emissary security and

Family Life Among the Modern Tribes hospitality among all the members of this wild tribe, even in the remotest districts. Family life has often developed upon other lines than among modern civilised peoples ; but however much the form of marriage may have changed, man and wife yet remain true to one another within the limits of that family life which custom has consecrated, and woe to him who would break faith or attempt to seduce another's wife. Both patriarchal and matriarchal organisations occur ; that is to say, either the father or the mother may be considered as the centre of the family and tribe. In the latter case, relationships are reckoned through the female line. Under the patriarchal system monogamy prevails, and marriage continues until dissolved by the death of one or other of the parties. A man acquires his wife by purchase or capture, though the latter is only conventional in form. Only in rare cases does the man take a second or several wives. In many cases it certainly happens that upon the completion of a marriage the husband's brothers become *ipso facto* husbands of his wife—as in Kurg among the Todas and the Kurumbas. To be distinguished from this kind of polyandry, where the

THE LIVING REPRESENTATIVES OF THE PRIMITIVE PEOPLES OF INDIA

The types of natives seen in this page are living representatives of the earliest known indigenous peoples of the country, over whom the incoming Aryans prevailed. 1. Kurumbars, or hill people of the Nilgherries. 2. Forest people, or Yenadies. 3. Bedur, or Veda, of Southern India. 4 and 5. Toda men and women, hill people of the Nilgherries.

man always remains head of the family, is the primeval custom, still prevalent among certain castes on the Malabar coast, which allows the wife to choose her own husband, to dismiss him at pleasure, and to take another without thereby incurring any stigma. Marriages which can thus be dissolved are entirely legitimate, as also are the children of them. The man, however, remains a stranger to the wife's family, and the children reckon their descent from the mother. Consequently, in these cases descent is reckoned through the female line, whereas in the patriarchal system descent in the male line is the fundamental principle of those larger social organisms, the hordes, consisting of several families, which again may develop into a tribe at a later period. In the latter case, the head of a tribe is sometimes a hereditary chieftain, and at other times is chosen by the heads of families. He is the representative of the tribe and directs its general policy. The tribe forms an exceedingly close corporation in its dealings with the outer world ; attacks made by strangers often lead to blood feuds, and peaceful intercourse and barter of goods is conducted, as among the Vedda in Ceylon, by the so-called silent trade.

Recognition of Maternal Descent *(left margin)*

The mountain and jungle tribes are obliged to carry on a hard struggle for existence. The climate alternates between seasons of burning heat and terrible rain storms, and a tribe driven into the jungle or on to the thirsty plains of the steppes obtains but scanty nourishment ; often enough, even those tribes which enjoy more favourable conditions of life are hard pressed by the extremities of famine. In the jungle the tiger and the poisonous snake lie in wait for them ; their scanty crops are destroyed by wild animals, elephants, pigs, and porcupines ; leprosy, malaria, cholera, and other diseases make their way to the remotest settlements, and Death plies his scythe with ruthless power. Encompassed as he is by hostile powers, how could the savage conceive of the supreme Beings which guide human destinies as being friendly to man? Evil demons pursue him from his birth to his grave, thirsting for his blood. Everywhere they lie in wait for him, in earth, in water, and in air ;

Hardships of Jungle Tribes *(left margin)*

in the rocks, in the darkness of the forests, upon the dry steppes ; at night they rush through the darkness to destroy whomsoever they may meet. They thirst for blood and can therefore be temporarily appeased by bloody sacrifices of fowls, goats, or even of men ; their anger can also be averted by those magic arts which the Shaman priests employ against them in their frenzied dances. Can we be surprised that such men were considered as demons, as Yakshu, as Rakshasa, by the Aryans, whose bright and heavenly gods were their stay and counsel ?

The most ancient Aryan poems do not, however, display to us these miserable savages as the only opponents of the invaders ; we gain information upon other tribes in higher stages of civilisation. Together with the unsettled and nomadic Kikata settled tribes also existed, the Nishada, who lived under a regular social organisation, and were even envied and hated by the Aryans for their wealth. The gods, and especially Indra, the destroyer of cities Purandara, are constantly praised for overthrowing hundreds of cities of the Black Dasyu ; these latter indeed are said to have possessed not only fortifications to protect them against the enemy, but also " winter retreats," autumn rain and cloud castles on their mountains, where they might take refuge from inundations in the plains or from dangerous miasmas. The tribes of the Naga, who worshipped snakes, were to be destroyed on account of their wealth and valuable possessions. Their capital, in which their prince, Wasuki, rules, is said to abound in treasures and fair women ; the prince possesses a talisman which can even bring the dead to life. " The treasure chambers in the rocky ground are full of cattle, horses, and good things ; the warders, the Pani, are faithful watchmen."

War Gods of Indian Peoples *(margin)*

At the same time, these tribes are represented as cunning traders, ever ready to take advantage, and bringing to the Aryans for barter the products of Nature's bounty or of their own skill in handicrafts. The trade indeed is welcome, but hateful are the traders, the " hateful misers," the men " without faith, without honour, without victims," and Indra is called upon to stamp down the greedy merchants with his feet. Upon the further advance of the Aryans we learn that there were important native kingdoms in the country and that the conquerors entered into friendly relations with these. When the conquerors made their way into the central district between the Jumna and the Ganges, they appointed the King of Nishadi, a vassal of the kingdom of Ayodhya, to guard the sacred district of the confluence of these two streams ; at a later date Aryan Brahman missionaries came upon the flourishing Pandya kingdom in the south of the peninsula.

The old Aryan songs and myths provide no further information upon the civilisation of the more advanced native tribes ; the language, however, of the dark races who belong to the Dravidian family enables us to draw many further conclusions as to the civilisation to which they had attained.

This language is certainly modified by Aryan elements (Sanscrit), but the non-Aryan portion of its vocabulary provides an accurate picture of the pre-Aryan civilisation of those races. According to Bishop R. Caldwell, who lived among the black population and devoted more than a generation to the study of their language, **Historical Evidence of Languages** the original vocabulary of the Dravidian races enables us to conclude that before they came into contact with the Aryans they possessed kings who lived in permanent dwellings and ruled over small districts. They had bards who sang songs at their feasts, and it also appears that they were in possession of an alphabet, and that they were accustomed to write upon palm leaves with a stylus. A bundle of these leaves formed a book.

There were no idols, no hereditary priesthood, and the primitive Dravidians appear to have been entirely unacquainted with the ideas of Heaven or Hell, of sin, or of the soul ; they believed, however, in the existence of gods, which they named ko (king), an absolutely non-Aryan word. Temples were erected in their honour, known as ko-il (house of god) ; no conclusions as to the nature of their divine service can be drawn from their language. The Dravidians of that period possessed laws, but no judges ; doubtful cases were decided by precedent. Marriage was a permanent institution among them. The most important metals were known to them with the exception of tin, lead, and zinc, as also were the greater planets, with the exception of Mercury and Saturn. They could count up to a hundred, and in

some cases to a thousand ; higher numbers such as the Aryan lakh (100,000) or crore (10,000,000). were unknown to them.

Medicine was practised among them, though medical science or doctors were unknown. Hamlets and villages existed, but no large towns. Boats, great and small, and even decked ships able to keep the **Early Dravidian Life** sea, were employed ; these, however, did not cross the ocean, consequently, foreign countries, with the exception of Ceylon, were unknown to them, and their language appears not to recognise the difference between continent and island. Agriculture was a professional occupation, while war was their chief delight, their arms being bows and arrows, swords and shields. Manufactures were highly developed, especially the arts of spinning, weaving, and dyeing ; and their pottery had been highly perfected, as is indeed plain from the examples found in the graves. Little was known of the higher arts and sciences ; no word exists to signify sculpture or architecture, astronomy or astrology, philosophy or grammar. Indeed, their vocabulary is singularly lacking in words which imply intellectual pursuits ; their only word for spirit is " diaphragm " or " the inside " ; there certainly exists a Dravidian word for " think," but no special words for thought, judgment, consciousness, or will.

As against this last sentence, however, we must not forget that the overpowering influence of the Brahmans and their highly developed terminology for abstract mental operations may very well have superseded many native expressions. Comparative philology does not provide wholly conclusive results, even in religious matters ; and a comparison of those elements common to the early Vedda and to all Dravidian races, even to those at a high stage of civilisation, plainly shows that the fundamental beliefs and religious **Limitations of Dravidian Vocabulary** conceptions of the jungle tribes were not confined to those we have mentioned, but were the common property of Dravidian religious thought and practice from the very outset. Whatever view may be taken of the prehistoric period in India, the fact remains that the dark-complexioned inhabitants of the country, of whom the Dravidians were by far the strongest element, formed the original population of India.

In the year 1833, Franz Bopp, observing the close connection of Sanscrit, the language of the Brahmans, with most of the ancient and modern languages of Europe, was able to establish the affinity of these languages beyond all dispute. He pointed out that Sanscrit was closely related not only to the old Persian (Zend), but also to almost all the other lang-

Relationship in Tongue and Blood uages of Europe, the only exceptions being the Basque and certain isolated groups of Ural-Altaic languages in the north and east of Europe. How was this similarity to be explained ? Peoples thus connected by the tie of language might easily be conceived as connected by the tie of blood —that is, as descended from a common ancestral tribe. The Grimms and others lent their support to the theory that this primitive people had lived in Asia, a supposition which became almost an article of faith. The ancestral tribe there settled was said to have been gradually broken up, the component parts migrating in different directions, for the most part westward, even as the solar system is conceived to have been formed by the separation of the planets and their satellites from the primal nebula. At a later period the influence of the Darwinian theory made the genealogical table illustrating these descents somewhat more complex. The idea, however, that Asia has been the common cradle of these Indo-Germanic or Aryan families of peoples continued to maintain its ground. In more recent times philological and anthropological evidence has led investigators to place the common origin of all these peoples in one or another part of Europe, but there is no real consensus of judgment on the point.

We may, indeed, doubt the intrinsic probability of the fact that any single district of the enormous steppe country extending from Central Asia to the North Sea could have been the

Where is the Cradle of the Indian Races ? cradle of so large a family of peoples. Natural boundaries are unknown upon the steppes, and the peoples inhabiting them spread outward without let or hindrance. The nomads inhabiting those districts prefer to follow the natural changes of season, climate, and consequently of vegetation, wandering abroad at their will and pleasure. The language of the Yakuts in the north-east of Siberia is closely connected with that of the Ottomans in the extreme south-west of that great continent.

It is waste of time to inquire at what point the first immigrants entered the steppe district. It is highly probable that as soon as a tribe had secured a footing there, it did not confine its movements to a small district, but, finding no barriers to oppose its passage, rapidly extended its settlements over a wide area uniform in development, though sporadic in distribution. Not until then did isolation of position, difference of environment, and foreign influence, begin to produce divergences in physical characteristics, language and customs. Thus in different provinces similar peoples, occupying widely distributed settlements, developed into individual tribes more or less strongly differentiated. In 1872 Johannes Schmidt conceived the development of the Indo-Germanic languages in the following manner : " I should like to replace the genealogical tree by a diagram of waves expanding in concentric circles at a distance from a central point, the rings

How Languages Spread from one Centre becoming weaker in proportion to the distance to which they spread from the central point." With some such theory the facts as known to us most nearly coincide, in so far as the peoples and the languages in close local connection show stronger mutual affinity than those at a remoter distance.

The westerly development of the wave circles after radiation from the central point does not concern us here, and we need follow only the history of the most eastern, or Indo-Iranian group. Our investigation into the date, locality, and the mode of life of this original circle depends upon information derived from comparative philology, and from the traditions and the earliest literature of the peoples which have proceeded from this centre. Such an investigation will show that the two peoples of the Iranians and Indians, between whom all outward connection has now disappeared, broke away from their common centre only a few thousand years before the outset of historical chronology. The comparatively late date of this separation is proved not only by the close similarity of the old Iranian language Zend) to the language of the earliest Indian hymns, but also by the wide similarities existing in manners and

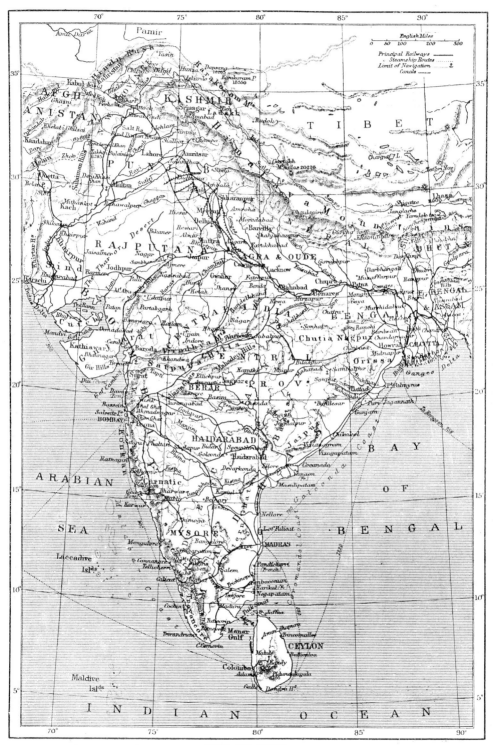

MAP OF INDIA

customs, especially those concerned with religion, language, mythology, and worship. Both peoples are called by the same proud name of Aryans, the noble, or the lofty ; in both peoples the arrival of the youth at man's estate was marked by the custom of girding him with a string. Both religions contain the same names for

Lessons from Manners and Customs

the deities worshipped— Mitra, Indra, Siva, Yama, Asura. However, the deep gulf dividing the two peoples is apparent in the different manner in which these beliefs have developed ; the gods worshipped by the Indian branch as the chief deities have sunk to low estate and lost their sanctity among the Iranians ; the bright, shining, glorious, all-helping Indra of the old Indian faith and the great god Siva became in the Persian pantheon evil-minded gods or hostile demons, as does Asura in India. The figures of the gods have remained unchanged, and only the faces have been altered, while to the highest deities the same sacrificial drink, the soma, is still offered.

The traditions and the language of the two peoples point to a former common settlement in the north, and there is good reason for accepting the generally received theory which considers their early home as situated in the land watered by the Oxus and the Jaxartes. The civilisation of this early settlement can be inferred in its general features from the vocabulary in use by its descendants. As might be expected in a country of steppes, the chief food supply depended upon cattle breeding. The wealth of the population consisted in herds of cattle, sheep, and goats, and in the keeping of these flocks the dog was the faithful companion of man. The horse was also bred, but only for traction, not for riding purposes. War chariots drawn by horses played an important part in the struggles of the Aryans upon their immigration to India. The possession of

Wealth in Flocks and Herds

waggons enables us to conclude that the Indo-Iranians were not exclusively a shepherd people. The fact that they were able to build houses of wood, and that their animals were driven into permanent courtyards, justifies the conclusion that they were to some extent a settled race. The cultivation of cereal plants, barley, wheat, and millet was common throughout the Indo-Germanic family in primitive times. Most probably,

when the Aryans entered the fertile district of the Five Rivers they had already acquired the knowledge and practice of regular irrigation from experience on the banks of the Oxus and Jaxartes. Cattle breeding provided their chief sustenance of milk and flesh, as also their clothing of wool and skins. Of metals, copper and bronze were known, while iron is rarely mentioned. Horn was used more often than bronze for the arrowheads, which the Aryans smeared with poison. Besides the bow and arrow their offensive weapons included the club, the axe, the sword, and the spear.

There must have been a considerable amount of peaceful intercourse. Straight roads existed traversed by waggons drawn by horses, while rafts and rowing boats passed over the rivers ; commerce by barter was established, and hospitality readily granted to the stranger who came in peace. Generally speaking, the morality of the Indo-Iranians reached a high pitch of perfection. Family life was pure ; the relations of the members of the race among themselves were regulated by estab-

Conditions of Primitive Morality

lished custom, which insisted upon truthfulness and good faith ; in their dealings with foes the race were high-spirited, bold, and warlike. The father was the head of the family, but the wife also was highly respected and honoured. At the head of the tribe or community, the chief was placed not only to conduct the temporal affairs of his tribe, but also to represent the tribe before the powers of heaven. There was no special priestly class, but the whole people was inspired with a profound religious feeling.

We have no knowledge of those causes which induced the Indian Aryans to migrate from their original settlements. Increase of the population above the number that the land could permanently support ; the hostile attacks of other steppe tribes, either of remote Indo-Germanic peoples from the west or of nomadic Mongolian tribes from the east and north ; those internal dissensions which ultimately led to the definite separation of the Iranian and Indian branches ; possibly also the reports of the fabulous fertility of a great land on the south—any or all of these causes may have led to a great national movement. For this, of course, no accurate date can be given ; modern experts are inclined to place it about the middle of the third millennium B.C., or considerably earlier. The route followed by the migrating people led southward. Here, indeed, they were confronted by a high mountain wall—the Hindu-Kush and the Pamirs ; but these districts could easily be traversed by a hardy, mountain-bred shepherd people, who would be able to drive their flocks over these chains and to reach the plains beyond, the fertility of which must have seemed an attractive paradise to a people of the steppes, hard pressed by the stern necessities of existence.

It is by no means improbable that the Indian Aryans may have entered the country both by the Pamirs and the Hindu-Kush. At a point further eastward they could without difficulty have crossed by Chitral or Gilgit to the Indus and the lovely district of Kashmir, as well as to the upper Punjab. The western road over the Hindu-Kush led them into the Kabul district of Northern Afghanistan. Here the earliest of their extant sacred hymns seem to have been composed ; here also the last links between the Iranian and Indian branches of the Aryans may have been severed. From the frontiers of the Afghan highland the spectator could behold the fruitful plains of the Five River Land, and an advance to the plains through the natural passes of the mountain wall was easy. It was, no doubt, by this route that the main branch of the race reached its new home ; not, however, in one great column, but in detachments, tribe following tribe at long intervals. Powerful was the impression made upon those who crossed the mountain range reaching to the heavens, and long did the recollection of those snow-clad peaks remain among the people ; they alone were considered worthy to support the throne of the gods on high. Magnificent also were the results of the migration when the Aryans arrived in the Punjab, that district watered, with what was to them an inconceivable abundance, by streams swollen with rain and melting snow—a guarantee of inexhaustible fertility. The poets sang the praises of these rivers with high enthusiasm.

Not without a struggle did this fair land fall into the hands of the immigrants ; the dark-skinned inhabitants whom they found in possession did not tamely surrender. The Vedas, the Sagas of that

Gateways of Early Immigration

Hymns of Historical Import

period, ring with the din of battle and the cry of victory ; the great gods of the Aryan heaven are called upon to strike down the wicked Dasyu, and are praised with cheerful thanks for overthrowing hundreds of the cities of the despised and miserable slaves, the Dasa. Serious friction occasionally occurred between different tribes of the same race when newcomers demanded their share of the conquered territory. The Aryan masses pressed successively further eastward. We can trace their advance from their resting-place on the heights of the Afghan frontier to the Jumna, the most western of the Ganges streams, across Five River Land. This river is often named in the later Vedas, but the Ganges not more than once or twice. Such an upheaval of the different tribes, and so great a rivalry for the possession of the fertile soil, must necessarily have led to collisions. Many tribes and their kings are mentioned by name, especially the federation of the " Five Peoples " in the north of the Punjab, the Yalu and Turvasa, the Druhyu and Anu, together with the Puru, who were situated farthest inland on the banks of the main stream, and headed the confederacy, which originally included the two first-named tribes, and afterwards the third and fourth. Beyond the boundaries of these five confederate peoples who inhabited Arya Varta, or Aryan land proper, the Tritsu, a branch of the powerful ambitious warrior tribe of the Bharata, advanced eastward, and bloody conflicts arose between them and the western peoples of the Punjab. The allied tribes were driven back, were confined henceforward to Five River Land, and gradually lost their common interests and the consciousness of their kinship with those of the Aryans who extended further eastward. Most of them disappear from our view ; only the Puru (King Porus) held out for a long time on the Indus. In the general civilisation of those Aryans who migrated into the land of the Five Rivers, that progress may everywhere be observed which is connected with a higher development of agriculture and results in greater prosperity, greater security, and greater expansion in other directions. The Aryans now no longer lived a nomadic life on the boundary steppes, but were settled in permanent

Echoes from Remote Battlefields

habitations upon arable territory, with well-defined boundaries.

Cattle breeding continued to be vigorously pursued ; the ox was the unit of value, not only for the purposes of trade, but also for estimating the rank of individuals. The title of a tribal chief was even then " Possessor of Cows," and battle is still called " desire for cows." Milk, either fresh or in the form of butter-milk, cream, butter, and curds, was still the staple article of food ; the flesh of domestic animals was rarely eaten ; and hunting was carried on chiefly as a sport, or for protection against wild beasts ; while fish as an article of food was still despised. A flesh diet was replaced by the use of corn, chiefly of barley, to a less extent of wheat, while rice is not yet mentioned. The plough and sickle were more important implements than of yore. Corn was threshed, pounded in the hand mill by the women, and made into bread, cakes, or porridge.

Settlement Supersedes Nomadism

The house was now a permanent habitation, and built on a new and stronger plan. A roof of vegetable fibres, tree bark, or straw kept out the rain ; in the centre of the main room blazed the hearth, round which seats were arranged— probably of earth, as at present ; these were covered with animal skins and served as sleeping-places. Earthenware pots, brazen caldrons, and hand mills for the corn were the most important kitchen utensils. Close to the house stood the fenced yard where the herds were penned, and in which the threshing-floor was laid out. The house was the special care of the woman. Here she cooked food for the whole family, spun the wool for thread, and wove artistic fabrics ; here she made beautifully adorned cloaks of the skins of the animals killed ; here under her care grew up the daughters and small boys. The man's business lay outside in the field, on the pasture and the corn land, at hunting or in war. It was his part to ply the handicrafts which were now increasing in number and rising to a higher level of skill ; the waggon builder made strong vehicles ; the smith blew up his fire with a fan made of birds' feathers, and wrought not only bronze, but also the iron which the original inhabitants probably brought to him in its raw condition, after smelting it out of

Conditions of Life and Industry

the ore (the native Indian form of pocket bellows does not seem to have been in use among the Aryans) ; the goldsmith produced bright decorations, artistic plates, bracelets, and rings to be worn in the ears, round the neck, and upon the wrists and ankles of the women.

The relations of man and wife were regulated by sound moral principles. To bring forth sons, worthy members of a tribe and an honour to the parents, was the highest ambition and the greatest pride of the father and mother. Respected, and on an equality with her husband, the woman was mistress of the house, though the man as being the stronger was the natural head, protector, and leader of the family. The man wooed the maiden on whom his choice had fallen through friends and relations ; if his suit was approved by the girl's parents, the marriage took place before the hearth of the house in which the maiden had lived hitherto under the protection of her parents. The bridegroom took the girl's hand and led her three times round the hearth ; the newly-married pair were then conveyed to their new home in a chariot drawn by white steers, the former ceremony was repeated, and a meal in common concluded the festival. Polygamy was exceedingly rare, while polyandry was utterly unknown to the ancient Aryans. If a death took place in a house, the body was buried or burnt— interment in both forms is mentioned in the early Vedas—widows never followed their dead husbands to death, either voluntarily or as a matter of social custom.

Early Marriage Customs

The houses stood in groups, forming separate hamlets or villages. Some of these places were fortified against hostile attacks by walls of earth or stone (place names ending in *pur* meaning " fortified "). Men and animals were often obliged to flee into fortified settlements, which were usually uninhabited, before the outbreak of floods or hostile incursions. A group of villages formed a larger community, while several of these latter became a district. The district belonging to one tribe formed a corporate whole, each of these groups having its own special chief, while at the head of the whole stood the king (Rajan, the " reigning."). The title was hereditary, or the king might be elected, but in either case a new king must be recognised in the general assembly of all men capable of bearing arms. In the samiti were discussed all those matters which affected the whole tribe, especially questions of war and peace. The inhabitants of the district or the village met together in special halls, which served not only - for purposes of discussion and judgment, but also for conversation, and for social amusements, such as dice playing. As the race was thus organised for the purposes of peace, so also the army, composed of all men capable of bearing arms, was made up of divisions corresponding to the family, village, and district group, each under its own leader. Famous warriors fought in their own war chariots harnessed with two horses and driven by a charioteer, while the main body of the people fought on foot.

The king was the leader in war ; he was also the representative of his people before the gods ; in the name of the people he asked for help or offered praise and sacrifice. He was allowed in certain cases to be represented by a Purohita, who conducted the sacrifice, while anyone who possessed high poetical gifts and a dignified appearance might permanently occupy **The Rise** this position. Other nobles, **of the** princes of districts, etc., might **Kingship** appoint Purohitas, whose influence was increased in proportion as formal prayer took the place of extempore petitions, and worship became stereotyped by the growth of special uses and a fixed ceremonial. Here we have in embryo the separate classes of king and priesthood, an opposition which was to exercise the most far-reaching influence upon the further development of the Aryan people.

The Aryan people brought from their primal home one precious possession—a deep, religious feeling, a thankful reverence for the high powers presiding over Nature, who afforded them a secure and peaceful existence by assuring the continued welfare of the flocks and of the crops planted by man. The good and kindly gods were those who sent to man the fertilising rain and sunshine, bringing growth and produce, and to them, as to high and kindly friends, man offered his faithful prayers and pious vows. To them he prayed that his flocks might thrive, and that he might be victorious in battle, that he might be given sons and have long life ; they, the bright, the all-knowing, and the pure, were the protectors of morality and the wardens of the house, of the district,

and of the whole tribe. Certain gods belonging to primeval times appeared in the Pantheon of the Aryans who conquered the Five River district, bright figures worshipped in common by the Iranians and the Indian Aryans. But among these latter they grow pale and lose their firm outlines, like the misty figures of dim remembrance ; **Pantheon** they become many - sided, **of the** secret, uncanny, diabolical, and **Aryans** other gods of more definite character come into prominence. Three gods are of special importance —Indra, Surya, and Agni. Together they form the early Indian Trinity (Trimurti). In the hymns which have come down to us, Indra is most frequently mentioned ; he was the atmospherical god, especially favourable to the Aryans, who gave the rain and the harvest, and governed the winter and the thunderstorm. We can easily understand how the god of the atmosphere became the chief Aryan divinity ; as the Aryans learnt upon Indian soil to observe the regular recurrence of atmospherical phenomena, especially that of the monsoon winds and the thunderstorms upon which their prosperity depended, the deeper and stronger became their gratitude and reverence to this god. It is Indra who sends down the water of the heaven, who divides the clouds with the lightning flash before which blow the roaring winds, the Maruts, especially the fierce Rudra, the hurricane, which rushes immediately before the thunder clouds.

The second of the three chief gods is Surya, the bright sun god, giving light, warmth, and life, an object of high veneration. Ushas, the morning dawn, opens for him the doors through which he passes to traverse the heavens in his chariot with its seven red horses. After these two gods the third of importance is Agni, the fire born from sticks when rubbed together ; this god lights and warms the hearth of the house, drives away all things evil and **The** impure, and watches over the **Chief** morality of the household. As **Gods** the sacrificial flame upon the altars, he is the means of communication between mankind and the other gods ; in his destructive character he devastates the settlements of the enemy and the hiding-places of their demons in the depths of the forest.

The worship of these gods is characterised by a feeling of lofty independence. Not only does man receive gifts from them, but he also gives them what they need. They, indeed, prepare for themselves the draught of immortality, the Amrita ; but they **Minor Gods of Aryan Mythology** hunger for sacrifices and cannot do without them. Especially do the gods love the honey-sweet draught of Soma drink. Almost presumptuous appears to us the prayer in which Indra is invited to partake of the Soma offering :

" Ready is the summer draught, O Indra, for thee ; may it fill thee with strength ! drink the excellent draught which cheers the soul and conveys immortality ! hither, O Indra, tu drink with joy of the juice which has been pressed for thee ; intoxicate thyself, O hero, for the slaughter of thy foes ! sit thou upon my seat ! here, O good one, is juice expressed ; drink thyself full, for to thee, dread lord, do we make offering."

Though Indra is here invited in person, yet the personifications of early Indian mythology were much less definite than those of the Greeks. Imagination and expression vary between the terms of human existence and the abstract conceptions of the natural powers of fire, thunder, sunshine, etc. Consequently the god as such is somewhat vague and intangible in the mythology of the old Aryans of India ; the characteristics of one deity are confused with those of another, and the different attributes of

any one god often reappear as separate personifications.

A large number of the hymns to the gods have been preserved to us (1,017 in all) ; these form the earliest body of evidence upon Indian life, thought, and feeling. The earliest of these songs were undoubtedly sung by the Aryans upon their migrations. At first the unpremeditated outpourings of a pious heart, they gradually became formal prayers ; thus these hymns were preserved in families of bards and faithfully handed down from generation to generation until at a much later period they were reduced to writing. In many of the Vedas belonging to the earliest period we find a deep longing for truth, a struggle for the solution of the deepest mysteries of existence—in short, a speculative spirit of that nature which marks a later stage of Brahman development ; other songs, however, are **How Aryan Hymns have been Preserved** pure and simple prayers for victory, children, and long life, while others, again, contain promises of sacrifice and praise if the help of the gods should be granted. The general collection of all these hymns was made at a considerably later period, subsequently to the occupation of the Ganges territory, and not before the seventh century before our era.

SCENE IN THE PUNJAB, OR "LAND OF THE FIVE RIVERS"
The Punjab was the first part of India to come under Aryan civilisation, and the Sutlej, one of the five rivers, is seen in the middle distance of the picture, which also shows the "Persian wheel," used for irrigating fields, being turned by a couple of bullocks, the driver seated at the end of a beam supported over a horizontal wheel.

THE ARYAN EXPANSION
AND THE GROWTH OF BRAHMANISM
BRAHMANISM IN THE NORTH

THE most important events at the conclusion of the Vedic age took place on the frontier line between the Indus and the Ganges. Here was developed the opposition between the warrior and priestly classes which was afterwards to lead to important results. At the head of the allied tribes in the Punjab stands the proud King Visivamitra, who combines the functions of king and priest in his own person and invokes the help of the gods for his people. Among his adversaries, however, the King Sudas no longer commits the duties of prayer and sacrifice to his own priests, but to a special class, the white-clothed, long-haired priests of the Vasishtha family, and their prayers are more effectual than those of the priest-king. This event is typical of the second stage of early Indian development, which ends in the complete victory of the priests **The Rise** over the warrior class and the **of the** establishment of a rigid hier-**Hierarchy** archy. The date of this social change coincides with that of the expansion and establishment of the Aryans in the Ganges territory.

The sacred books are of less value for the external history of this period than are the songs of the Rig-Veda for the preceding age; nevertheless, many of them, such as the Brahmanas, contain important evidence concerning individual tribes, their settlements and history. A large body of historical evidence is, however, contained in the second great epic poems of this period, the Mahabharata and the Ramayana; the riotous imagination of the composers has given a strong poetical colouring to the whole, and the lack of definite purpose which is apparent in their construction makes careful and minute criticism imperative.

The Mahabharata in its present state is the longest poem of any people or age.

It contains 110,000 double lines, and each one of its eighteen books is enough to fill a large volume. The historical basis of the great poem of the Bharata rests upon early tradition. The enthusiasm inspired by heroic deeds found its vent in poetical composition, and the praise of heroes was passed from mouth to mouth. This epic poem in embryo may be earlier than the first thousand years B.C.; but **Longest** when that period of turmoil **Epic in the** and confusion was followed by **World** an age of more peaceful development, the memories of these exploits grew fainter in the minds of successive generations. The old songs and ballads were collected and worked into one great epos; many of the events and figures are the additions of later poets, such as the story of the Five Pandu brothers, while the whole poem is marked by the brilliant overflow of a luxuriant imagination and by ruthless compression of the historical facts; the histories of nations become the victories or defeats of individual heroes; long years of struggle with warlike tribes are reduced to one lengthy battle. To this quasi-historical part of the Mahabharata were added at a later time a series of lays more extensive than the original poem and written from the Brahman point of view. If the non-epic elements be removed from the poem the following story remains.

At the point where the two streams of the Jumna and the Ganges leave the mountains and flow through the plains, the powerful Bharata tribe of the Kuru had established themselves upon their eastern and western banks; even to-day the district on the right bank of the Jumna is known as the Kuru-kshetra, the sacred Kuru land. This royal tribe divided into two branches. Of the two sons of King Santanu, the elder, Dhritarashtra, was born blind, and the royal power was therefore conferred upon his younger brother Pandu. To the latter five sons were born, and to the former a hundred ; and the struggles of these two groups of cousins formed the substratum of the epic.

All these brothers were admirably instructed in knightly pursuits by the Brahman Drona, "in the use of the bow and club, of the battleaxe and the throwing spear, of the sword and dagger, in the chase of the horse and elephant, in conflicts from chariots or on foot, man to man or in combination." In the elder line, Duryodhana, the eldest of the one hundred brothers, was especially distinguished for his skill in the use of the club ; Bhima, the second son of Pandu, was famous for his superhuman strength. The third son of Pandu, the beautiful long-haired Arjuna, excelled with all arms, but especially in the use of the bow and arrow. In one of the tournaments which concluded the education of the princes he outstripped all competitors ; after a contest with many other princes, he won the hand of the beautiful Krishna, the daughter of Drupad, King of Pantshala. By his victory she also became the wife of the other four brothers, a polyandric marriage which is represented by the Brahman poet as the result of a misunderstanding with the mother of the Pandu brothers.

Duryodhana, who had meanwhile been crowned king, dreading the military power of his cousins and of the Pantshala, with whom they had allied themselves by marriage, divided his kingdom with the eldest of the Pandu brothers, Prince Yudhishthira. At the moment of his coronation Yudhishthira played a game of dice with the enemies of his house, the Kaurawas, at which he lost not only his crown, but also the freedom of himself and his brothers, and the wife whom they possessed in common But by the decision of the blind old prince Dhritarashtra, the forfeit was commuted for a banishment of thirteen years. The Pandu brothers, with their wife, spent this period in solitude, need and misery in the forests, and then demanded their share of the kingdom. To this proposition the Kaurawas declined to agree, and both parties secured the support of numerous powerful allies. The Kaurawas were joined by Karna

When Knighthood was in Flower

Gambling for a Kingdom

(another Siegfried or Achilles), who distinguished himself in these battles by his splendid bravery and military prowess ; the Pandawas enjoyed the advantage of the cunning advice of the Yadawa prince, Krishna, who placed his services as charioteer at the disposal of Arjuna. A fearful battle ensued of eighteen days' duration, in which, after marvellous deeds of heroism, all the warriors were slain with the exception of the five Pandu brothers. From this time onward the whole of the kingdom was in their power, and Yudhishthira ruled for a long period after the manner of an ideal Brahman prince. Thereafter they retired from all earthly splendour and became ascetics with no temporal needs, wandering from one holy shrine to another, until at length they entered the heaven of the gods opposite the holy Mountain of Meru.

However large an element of the Mahabharata may be purely poetical, none the less the poem enables us to localise with some accuracy a number of the tribes which were actively or passively involved in the struggle of the two royal houses, and the overthrow of the warrior class to which that struggle led. Of the warrior class the chief representatives are the Kuru, who are represented as settled on the upper course of the Jumna and Ganges, Hastinapura being their capital town ; they were also in occupation of the sacred Kuru land to the west of the Jumna as far as the point where the Saraswati disappears in the sands of the desert. The poem places the Pandu and their capital of Indraprastha—the modern Delhi on the Jumna—in the central *Doab* (*i.e.*, the land lying between two converging rivers, above their confluence), the central district between the Jumna and the Ganges. In the lower Doab is settled a federation of five tribes, the Pantshala. Opposite these on the western bank of the Jumna dwell the Surasena, while to the east beyond the Ganges are the Kosala, with the capital town of Gogra, who extended their power after the destruction of the Kuru and Pandu, their later capital of Ayodhya becoming a focus of Brahman civilisation. Below the confluence of the Jumna and Ganges, the sacred Prayaga, where at an earlier period Allahabad had become a centre for pilgrimages, the northern bank of the main stream was occupied by the Bharata

Historical Facts in the Great Epic

tribe of the Matsya, while to the south-east of these, in the district of the modern Benares, lived the Kasi ; on the southern bank the native tribe of the Nishada formed a defence against the Aryan tribes in the north. East and north of the Ganges, together with the Kosala, were also settled the mountain tribes of the Kirata, who were in alliance with the Kuru, while further to the south were the Pundra Banga and Anga, the Mᵗhila, the Wideha and Magadha.

The action of the great epic poem is laid within the district of these various tribes. Several centuries must have elapsed since the battle of King Sudas, during which the Aryans had formed states in the fruitful central district, the Madhyadesa, and had extended to that tributary of the Ganges now known as the Garuti. In the earlier period of Indian antiquity, the chief historical events take place in the country between the Ganges and its great western tributary the Jumna ; whereas at a later period pure Brahman civilisation is developed in the kingdoms formed further to the east— namely, north of the Ganges in Wideha **Great National Movements** (capital town Mithila, the modern Muzaffarpur), and upon the southern bank of the great river, in Magadha and Wihara (the modern Behar ; capital town Patali-putra, the modern Patna). During this period at any rate the eastern frontier of these states was also the eastward limit of Aryan occupation. That national move-ment ceased at the point where the first arms of the great delta of the Ganges diverge from the southern bank of the river behind the mountains of Rajmahal ; the almost impenetrable malarial swamp districts which then composed the whole delta remained for a long period in the undisputed possession of the wild jungle tribes and noxious and poisonous animals. However, the last offshoots of the stream of Aryan immigration turned southward to the fertile districts of Orissa from Magadha at the period when Brahmanism had reached its culminating point. Here the north-eastern arms of the Mahanadi delta mark the extreme limit of the territory then in Aryan occupation, which consequently extended to the sea upon the east.

At a yet earlier period the Aryans had reached the Western or Arabian Sea. Immediately after the occupation of the Punjab, the waves of the migration passed down the Indus valley, and the Aryans became acquainted with the dis-tricts at the mouth of the river, to which also they gave its name (Sindhu). Their settlements in that district did not, however, become a point of departure for transmarine migration. The coast was **The Line of Least Resistance** ill-suited for the navigators of the period, and a far more favourable spot was found further to the south-west in the Gulf of Cambay ; settlements were made here at a period considerably subsequent to the arrival at the mouth of the Indus. The Great Desert and the unhealthy swamps which intervene between this gulf and the Indus district prevented any advance in that direction ; moreover an easier route was discovered by the tribes advancing from the Punjab to the Ganges district along the narrow frontier between the two territories. Consequently, new arrivals found the land already occupied by settlers who had taken this route, and bloody conflicts may have been of repeated occurrence. Driven on by tribes advanc-ing in their rear, hemmed in before by earlier settlers, they found a favourable opening of escape in the strip of fertile territory which extended southward be-tween the desert and the north-western slopes of the Central Indian highlands, the Aravalli Hills. This path could not fail to bring them to the Gulf of Cambay, which here runs far inland ; and, on its western shores, the rich districts of Gujerat and those at the mouth of the Narbada and the Tapti lay spread before them. This was the most southerly point on the western side of India at which the Aryans made any permanent settlement.

Hence, during this period Aryan India included the whole of the north-western plains extending in a south-westerly direction as far as Gujerat, and eastward as far as the Ganges delta, its extreme **Extent of Aryan India** south-easterly point being the delta of Orissa. The highlands of Central India formed a sharp line of demarcation between the Aryan and Dravidian races. The district was, however, not entirely secluded from Aryan influence, which at the outset of that period had begun to put out feelers across the frontier line. The Aryans had already become acquainted with the sea, which was for them rather a means than a hindrance to communication ; the fact is proved by the similes occurring in the old battle songs, wherein the hard-pressed warrior is compared to a sailor upon a ship staggering under a heavy storm upon the open sea. The Aryan colonisation of Ceylon took place before the power of the warrior class had been broken and the social organism stamped with the impress of Brahman-ism. On comparing this period **Settled Political Systems** with that during which the Aryans advanced into the Punjab, we find a fundamental change in the conditions of Aryan life as they are displayed in all these struggles and settlements. Nomadic life under the patriarchal system is replaced by feudal principalities surrounded with all the splendour of chivalry. Changes in other conditions of life had necessarily effected a fundamental transformation in the political and social condition of the people. A more settled life, and the advance of agriculture at the expense of cattle breeding, led to a more comprehensive sub-division of labour ; though, when occasion demanded, the peasant left the plough-share for the sword, yet it was no doubt at an early period that that warrior nobility arose which made war its business and profession. The leadership of the tribe as the latter flourished and increased became rather a professional post ; in place of the tribal elder appears the king in possession of full royal powers and standing high above and apart from his people. The position of both king and noble must have advanced to more brilliant development in the greater area of the Ganges territory. In the Maha-bharata the battles and the names con-nected with them are no doubt in large part the result of poetical invention ; but the description of the civilisation then existent cannot be wholly imaginary, and the royal courts with their knightly organisation, however romantic in appear-ance and akin to the insti- **Influence of the Priesthood** tutions of mediæval Europe, may be considered as definite historical facts. No greater change can be imagined than that apparent in the latter condition of those peoples whose history we have traced throughout this proud and warlike period. Gone is the energy of youth ; gone, too, the sparkling joys of life and struggle ; the green verdure of the Aryan spring has faded, the people has grown old. The

nobility has yielded the pride of place to the priesthood, whose ordinances shackle all movement toward freedom and inde-pendence. The new power appears in the garb of the deepest poverty, but its spiritual influence is all the more profound ; the ambition of the priests was not to be kings, but to rule kings.

The origins of this great social change go back to a remote period. Even during that period when the Aryan power was confined to the Punjab, the seeds of opposition between the temporal and spiritual powers are found in existence ; in the great battle in which King Sudas conquered the confederacy of the Punjab, the opposition becomes prominent for the first time. At an earlier period it was the natural duty of the tribal chieftain to stand as mediator between his people and their gods. But it was not every powerful prince or general who possessed the gift of the inspired poets and musician, and many kings therefore entrusted this sacred public duty to their Purohita. His repu-tation was increased by his power of clothing lofty thoughts in inspiring form, and the position passed from father to son together with the more **Order of Hereditary Minstrels** stirring hymns which were orally transmitted. Thus priestly families arose of high reputa-tion whose efforts were naturally entirely directed to secure the permanence of their position ; the most certain means to this end was the creation of a compli-cated ritual for prayer and sacrifice which could be performed only by a priesthood with a special training. The scene of sacrifice was prepared with great attention to minutiæ, the altars were specially adorned on every opportunity, and the different sacrifices were offered with scrupulous respect to ceremonial detail ; there were priests who recited only the prayers from the Rig-Veda, others who sang hymns from the Samaveda ; a high-priest stood at the head of the whole organisation.

Consequently the character of prayer, sacrifice, and indeed the whole body of theology underwent a fundamental trans-formation. Originally the victim had been the pure offering of a thankful heart, while prayer had been the fervent yet humble expression of those desires which man in his weakness laid before the almighty powers of heaven. Gradually, however, the idea of sacrifice had been

Siva, the Destroyer, the second of the Hindu deities

Ganesha, the god of success, invoked on every necessity of daily life

Agni, the guardian deity of the south-east part of the earth

Surya, the sun god, one of the gods of the early Indian Trinity

Indra, the king of heaven and one of the ten guardian deities of the earth

Lakshmi, the goddess of prosperity, wife of Vishnu

Vishnu, one of the three principal Hindu deities

Saraswati, goddess of learning, Vishnu's second wife

THE CHIEF BRAHMAN AND HINDU DIVINITIES

modified by the theory that human offerings to the gods were not only welcome but also necessary and indispensable to those powers. In the sacred writings of a later date passages repeatedly occur, stating that the gods are growing weak because the pious priests have been hindered by evil spirits from making the necessary sacrifices. Indeed, it was only by means of the sacrifices that the gods, who had formerly been subject to death like men, had acquired immortality. " The Gods lived in the fear of death, the strong Ender, and therefore they underwent severe penance and made many offerings until they became immortal."

Growth of the Idea of Sacrifice

Hence was developed the further idea that by means of sacrifice man could gain a certain power over the gods themselves and thereby extort gifts and services from them ; and ultimately the sacrifice was conceived to be a thing of immense magical power before which all the other gods must bow. The all-compelling power of the sacrifice was in the hands of the priests, the Brahmans, and became the firm foundation of their increasing predominance. An Indian proverb says : " The universe depends upon the gods, the gods upon the Mantra (the formula of sacrifice), the Mantra upon the Brahmans, and therefore the Brahmans are our gods."

Tradition is silent upon the details of the process by which the dominant power passed from the hands of the nobility to the priesthood. It was to the interests of the priests to obliterate historical facts as rapidly and completely as possible from popular memory, and to inculcate the belief that the high position of the Brahmans had been theirs from the outset. The history of the period has been thus designedly obscured, and only at rare intervals is some feeble light thrown upon it. The epos of the fall of the great race of the Bharata shows us how the power of the nobility was worn away in bitter struggles ; many priestly figures, such as Drona and his son Aswatthaman, take up arms and join in the destruction of the nobility.

A fact throwing special light upon the acerbity of the contest between the two struggling powers is the appearance in the poem of the mythical figure of Rama, who was considered an incarnation of Vishnu at a later period, a Brahman by birth, and armed with the axe. The balance of fortune did not, however, invariably incline in favour of the Brahmans, as is plain from the many maxims in their ritual and philosophical writings conceived in a very humble tone : " None is greater than the Kshatriya (the warrior), wherefore the Brahman also makes sacrifices together with the royal offerings to the Kshatriya." The issue of the struggle began to prove doubtful from the Brahman point of view, and therefore the myth claimed the personal interference of the powerful god Vishnu, who usually became incarnate in times of greatest need, and therefore descends for this reason to the aid of his special favourites, the Brahmans. After an infinite series of bloody conflicts, he gains for them a brilliant victory ; thrice seven times did Parasurama purify the earth of the Kshatriya.

Help of the Gods in Battle

THE BRAHMAN SYSTEM AT WORK

NOTWITHSTANDING their military capacity and their personal strength, the nobles had been defeated, and the priests, armed with the mysterious magical power of the sacrifice, had gained a spiritual dominion over the people. This power the priesthood at once proceeded to secure permanently and irrevocably by arrogating to themselves the monopoly of all religious and philosophical thought, by the strict and detailed regulation of public and private life in its every particular, by forcing the mind, the feelings, and the will of every individual into fixed grooves prescribed by the priests. The legal books, the earliest of which belong to the course of literature of the old Vedic schools, explain the high ideal which the Brahmans proposed to themselves as the true realisation of national life ; an ideal, however, which was hardly ever attained in its reality, or at the most only within the narrow areas of individual petty states.

The position of the priests is defined with the greatest precision and detail in the Dharmasastra of Manawa, a work afterward ascribed to Manu. In order to make this work yet more authoritative, its composers assigned to the personality of its author an age almost amounting to immortality (30,000,000 years) and divine origin ; attempting to identify him with the first ancestor of the Aryans, the mythical Manu. In reality it was not until shortly before the middle of the first millennium B.C. that the Brahman code had developed so large a quantity of precepts defined with such exactitude ; in its present form the work of Manu seems to be the result of later re-editing, and to date from the period between the first century B.C. and the fifth century A.D. Buddhist precepts are plainly apparent in it, and many prohibitions of the earlier and later periods are brought together in spite of their discrepancy, as, for instance, the slaughter of animals and the eating of flesh, side by side with the religious avoidance of animal food. Buddhist terms of expression are also found, such as the mention of female anchorites, "an apostate sect," which are evidence in favour of a later date. The book consists of a collection of proverbial sayings which were intended to fix the customary law, as established by the Brahmans, for a district of

TYPES OF THE ANCIENT BRAHMANS

These figures from frescoes of the second century B.C. are taken from the cave X at Ajantâ (after James Burgess). They bear the Nâma of the Brahman divinities upon their foreheads, and the type of face is rather Aryan than Dravidian ; but the ornaments and umbrella are not, as Fergusson and Burgess suppose, signs of low caste.

Northern India of limited area. The work contains 2,685 double lines divided into twelve books ; of these books, five are concerned with the rights and duties of the Brahmans, whereas only two books are devoted to the warrior caste, and only one to all the other castes put **A Book of Ancient Proverbs** together. Manu expressly proclaims the existence of four castes only : " The Brahmans, Kshatriyas, and Vaisyas form the classes in a second state of existence ; the Sudra is in the first state of existence and forms the fourth class ; a fifth does not exist." In this division the first point of note is the contrast between those in a first and those in a second state of existence, the " twice-born," a contrast which coincides with the racial contrast between

the Aryans and the original inhabitants ; within the Aryan group a principle of tripartition is again apparent, which, in modern language, amounts to the separate existence of a learned, a military, and a productive class.

Manu here speaks of only four divisions of society ; elsewhere he recognises the **The Four Divisions of Society** existence of other caste subdivisions : the castes of the physicians, astrologers, handicraftsmen, oil manufacturers, leather workers, musical performers, etc., are subdivisions of the fourth class. Properly speaking, however, the origin of these castes is, according to Manu, different from that of the main groups ; these latter are of primeval origin, created together with the world and—an important factor—by the purpose of the Creator. A famous hymn of the Rig-Veda, which is a later interpolation, describes the origin of the castes : " The sacrifice Purusha, those who were born at the very first (the first men), they offered it upon sacrificial grass ; to it the gods made offering, the Sadhyas and the Rishis. When they divided Purusha, into how many pieces was he cleft ? What did his mouth become, and what his arms, what his legs and his feet ? His mouth became the Brahman, the Rajanya came forth from his arm, the Vaisya from his thighs, the Sudra from his feet. The world was born from his soul, the sun from his eyes, Indra and Agni from his mouth, Wayu from his breath. From his navel came forth air, from his head the heaven, from his feet the earth, from his ear the districts of the world. In this manner did the gods create the world."

Symbolically, the Brahmans were formed from the same member of the body as the great gods of early India, Indra, and Agni—namely, from the mouth, which speaks " sanctity and truth " ; the military

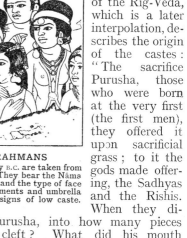

were formed from the arms, whence they received their "power and strength." The thigh bones were the means of mechanical progress, the lowly toil of life ; from these, therefore, were the Vaisya formed who go behind the plough and gain material "riches and possessions" by their industry. From the feet, however, **Theories of Caste Divisions** which ever tread in the dust of earth, is formed the lowly Sudra, who, from the very beginning, is "destined to service and obedience." Thus, according to Manu, by means of the sacrificial power of the gods and of the sacred primeval Brahmans, were formed the four great classes of human society.

The Brahmans have another theory to account for 'he subdivisions within the Sudra class, which was explained as mixed castes proceeding from the alliance of members of different castes. It is important to notice that position within these mixed castes is dependent upon the higher or lower caste to which the man or the woman belonged at the time of procreation. Alliances of men of higher castes, and even of the Brahmans themselves, with low-caste women, are legally permissible ; the children, however, of such a marriage do not take the father's caste, but sink to the lowest castes. Wholly different is the punishment of breaking caste incurred when a woman has children by a man of lower caste than herself ; not only is she expelled from her own caste with ignominy and disgrace, but the higher the caste to which she belonged by birth, the lower is the social depth to which she and her children sink ; indeed, the lowest of all castes, that of the Tshandala, is considered by the Brahmans to have been formed by the alliance of Brahman women with Sudra men. On the other hand, the children begotten by a Brahman of a Sudra woman belong to the higher gradations of the Sudra group, **Penalties of Inter-caste Marriage** while the father in no way loses his own permanent position. Such is the teaching of the Brahmans as laid down in the book of Manu upon the origin of mixed castes. The investigator, however, who leaves the Sanscrit writings, examines Indian society for himself, and judges the facts before him without prejudice, cannot resist the impression that this theory upon the origin of mixed castes is as impossible as that of

the creation of the four main castes from the sacrifice. The only mixed caste in the proper sense of the words is that of the temple women, and their children ; among these, daughters become temple women, sons temple musicians, or inferior temple servants, etc. But in all other cases where there is no very great difference of caste between the parents, the child takes the lower caste and a new mixed caste never arises. However, in the very rare cases in which a woman of extremely high caste has a child by a man of very low caste, abortion is invariably procured, or the mother commits suicide. The Brahman doctrine upon the origin of the lowest castes is an intentional perversion of the facts.

One of the most skilful investigators of the caste system, W. R. Cornish, says that the whole chapter of Manu upon mixed castes is so childishly conceived and displays so much class prejudice and intolerance, so appalling a punishment awaiting the Brahman woman who should err, while at the same time the Brahman is allowed so much freedom of communication with other castes without injury to **Reasons for Caste Restrictions** his position, that the intentions of the author become forthwith obvious. These intentions were to maintain purity of blood in the higher castes and especially in that of the Brahmans, by appointing the heaviest of all punishments upon any woman who should prove unfaithful to her caste. It was not thus that the lower social groups of which we have spoken originated ; they are earlier than the laws of Manu. The legislator, however, employed the fear inspired by the prospect of sinking to their degraded position as a powerful instrument whereby he might attain his object, the preservation of racial purity among the Brahmans.

The truth is that castes have arisen from different origins. Differences of race and racial prejudice form a first line of cleavage. Noteworthy in this connection is the old Aryan name for caste, *warna*—that is, colour. The white and the black, the Aryan and the original inhabitant, the "best," the "first" (because the most successful and powerful) in contrast with the low and the common, the Dasyu—these oppositions form the first sharp line of demarcation. At their first meeting the latter class were naturally not allowed the privilege of conforming to the institutions

The figures grouped on this page are representative of the Brahmans of to-day, the first being that of a Brahman priest, or "pundit," and the next a fakir, or devotee, while the young Brahman in the centre displays the mysterious caste marks and is wearing the sacred thread. The lower figures represent, on the left, a Hindu jogi, or mendicant, posing in the attitude of one of the gods, and the last is another Brahman type.

BRAHMAN TYPES OF THE PRESENT TIME

of Aryan society; extermination was the sole method of dealing with them. At a later period, however, as the conquerors became more prosperous and settled, it was found advantageous to employ prisoners or subject races as serfs for the purpose of menial duties. The original inhabitants of the country were

Rise of a Warrior Nobility
thus adopted into the Aryan society, and in that social order the first deep line of cleavage was made. Other differences then developed within the Aryan population. It was only natural that the man who displayed a special bravery in battle should be more highly honoured and receive a larger share of booty, of territory, and of slaves to cultivate that territory. Thus, in course of time, a warrior nobility was formed, the Kshatriya, who rose to power as we have seen in the struggles of the Mahabharata. We have already seen the manner in which a further social division was brought about by the formation of a hereditary priesthood, the Brahmana. In proportion, however, as these two classes became exclusive hereditary castes, so did they rise above the great mass of the people, the farmers, the shepherds, and the handicraftsmen whose occupations were now considered as professions lacking in dignity. The Kshatriya proudly called themselves Rajana, Rajwansi, the Royal, or the Rajputs, the men of royal race, and thought themselves high above the common people.

Thus the great castes appointed by Manu had been formed. Further differences arose within these. Only the Brahmans and warriors were able for any length of time to prevent the rise of subdivisions within their own groups. Their narrow and well-defined profession, and also, among the Brahmans at any rate, their jealously preserved racial purity, protected them from disruption. But in the two remaining groups, the Vaisya and

Subdivision of the Castes
the Sudra, who had now entered the social organism of the Aryans, a different set of circumstances prevailed; the development of larger political bodies resulted in subdivision within these classes. As existence grew more secure and prosperity increased, the necessities of life increased proportionately. In the simple times of the primeval Aryan period, every tribe was able to satisfy such demands for skilled labour as might

arise within it; in the more complex organisation of society within the Ganges states such simplicity was no longer possible. Undertakings demanding technical skill called forth by the claims of a higher civilisation necessarily brought about the subdivision of labour and the creation of technical professions; manual labour in its several branches became hereditary among individual families of the lower castes, as other professions had become hereditary among the Brahmans and Kshatriyas.

It is possible that similar caste divisions corresponding to the various professions may have existed among the original inhabitants of the country before they came into contact with the Aryans. The natives were by no means, in every case, uncivilised savages; some of their tribes were superior in technical skill to the Aryans themselves, and bartered the products of their higher knowledge with the Aryans through merchants. The existence of caste divisions among them at an earlier period is supported by the enumeration in the code of Manu of the manufacturing castes in the lower divisions

Division According to Occupation
of the Sudra—astrologers, oil makers, leather workers, musical performers, and so on. It is inconceivable that the Brahmans, when formulating the rules of Indian society, should have troubled to arrange these numerous subdivisions of the many castes of the Sudra, the more so as they were accustomed to avoid any possible connection with this unclean stratum of society; far more probable is it that those differences of caste within the Sudra which coincide with professions existed before the Aryan period.

The political relations of the Aryans to the non-Aryan natives also contributed to the development of the Aryan caste system. The deadly hatred of the black, snub-nosed people which inspires the hymns of the Rig-Veda was laid to rest; during the struggles between the several Aryan princes and states political necessities often led to acquaintances, alliance, and friendship, even to racial fusion with the native tribes. In the Mahabharata we find a Nishada prince appointed guardian of the important river ford at Prayaga; we find Dravidian races fighting side by side as the equal allies of pure Aryan tribes, while the names of certain personalities famous in the great epos, together with peculiarities of character and custom, are evidence for the close connection between the distinguished Aryan warrior and the native inhabitant. Krishna, " the Black," is the name given to the Yadawa prince who appears as the firm ally and friend of Pandawas.

The attempt has been made to explain this name by the hypothesis that his tribe had entered India earlier than the other Aryans, and had therefore been more deeply burned by the sun ; to this, however, it may be replied that the complexion of a tribe may be deepened rather by fusion with a black race than by exposure to the sun. In character also Krishna appears unlike the Aryans ; he is full of treachery and deceit, gives deceitful counsel, and justifies ignoble deeds by equivocation methods wholly foreign to the knightly character of the Aryan warrior. The Pantshala princess is also entitled Krishna, " the Black "; the fact that she lived in true Dravidian style with the five Aryan princes in a polyandric marriage shows the close relations existing between the Aryans and the native peoples.

Progress of Race Fusion

Similar relations are also apparent in the history of the colonisation of Ceylon ; the Aryan ancestor Vijayas had married a Dravidian Kalinga princess, and his grandson, together with many of his companions, took native women to wife without any exhibition of racial prejudice. Thus, since the time of the Aryan immigration, an important change had taken place in the relations of the two races The rapidity with which the racial fusion was carried out is apparent at the present time in the physical contrast between the peoples of the North-west and the Ganges territory; in the Punjab, in Kashmir, and to some extent in Rajputana, hardly a trace of the black population is to be found, a result of the deadly animosity with which the war of conquest was prosecuted ; further to the east the mixed races re-appear, and the evidence of darker complexion, broader features and noses, increases proportionately from this point. Such a fusion, and particularly the incorporation of whole races of the native inhabitants within the Aryan society, must obviously have increased the subdivisions within the castes.

The Brahmans, who took the utmost precaution to preserve their caste purity, were least affected by the entrance of foreign racial elements ; at any rate, in Northern India their caste, even at the present day, has changed but little from the Aryan type. In Orissa, however, and to a greater extent further southwards, even this exclusive sect considered it expedient on different occasions to admit individuals or even whole tribes of the black race within their caste, if they could thereby attain any external advantage ; thus at the present day in the Deccan many more dark than fair Brahmans are to be met.

Marriage in the Caste of Warriors

In the warrior caste, purity of blood was thought of less vital importance ; among this caste there even existed a legal form of marriage, the " Rakshasa " marriage, which provided that the bride should be taken by force from a hostile, often dark-complexioned, tribe. The nobles thus being by no means averse from marriage with the natives, the common people naturally had the less inducement to preserve the purity of their Aryan blood. At the same time, however, such connections often led to disruption within the caste ; the orthodox members refused to recognise the mixed families as pure Kshatriya or Vaisya, avoided communication with them, and by this process a group which had been originally uniform was gradually broken into an increasing number of disconnected castes. The infusion of foreign blood thus acquired seems to have modified by slow degrees the larger part of the Kshatriya and practically the whole of the Vaisya. Thus we have an intelligible explanation of the fact that only in comparatively few districts, as for instance, Rajputana, could particular castes retrace their origin with any clearness to the old Aryan warrior nobility, their proud title of Kshatriya resting in many cases upon fictitious genealogies. At the present day there is absolutely no caste of the Vaisya which can prove its connection with the early Vaisya of the Aryan Ganges states. The modern caste system of India is broken up into many hundreds or thousands of separate groups. However, in early Brahman times the four main divisions of society appointed by the legal codes had an actual existence. Of these the Sudra led lives that can scarcely be qualified as human. Considered as once-born, a great gulf was fixed between them

Modification of Caste Purity

and those who had advanced to a higher state by virtue of a second birth. To them was forbidden the use of the sacred band with which the youth of the three higher castes were girded as a sign of manhood upon their coming of age (two threads of wool which passed over the left shoulder and the right hip). It was a mortal crime for any of the upper classes to teach a Sudra anything of the sacred proverbs or prayers. A great gulf divided the Sudra from the Vaisya. Upon this latter the two high castes of the priests and the warriors looked disdainfully. The Vaisya was, however, a twice-born, wore the sacred band, and the knowledge of the Vedas was not forbidden to him. It was the common and monotonous nature of his calling that degraded him in comparison with the higher caste. He was not allowed to devote himself to the proud service of arms, or to deep spiritual and religious questions and interests. His lot was to till the soil throughout his life, and upon that level he remained. He was the peasant, the shepherd, the lower-class citizen in the flourishing towns, the manufacturer, the merchant, the money-changer. He often attained to high prosperity, but could never pass the barrier which the stern laws of caste had set against his further progress.

The Peasant Caste

Higher than the Vaisya stood the warrior, the Kshatriya, in the social organism of the Brahmans. The splendour of his profession and of his influence was but the shadow of that which it had been during the first centuries of the settlement upon the Ganges. Moreover, in the more peaceful times which succeeded the period of establishment within that district, the profession of the warrior nobles decayed considerably. The more, however, his real importance decreased, the more anxious were the Brahmans that he should make a brilliant figure before the mass of the people, in order that he might thus become a valuable ally to themselves for the attainment of their own purposes. Thus the nobility continued to enjoy a predominant and honourable position. Their freedom was great compared with that of other castes, and large possessions in landed property secured to them the enjoyments of life, as well as respect and consideration. If the Kshatriya exhausted all the pleasures of his high position and

Decay of Warrior Caste

was overcome by weariness of the world, he was allowed to join the company of hermits and to devote the remainder of his life to inward contemplation.

The Brahmans belonged to the same group of twice-born, and wore the same sacred band as the other high castes, but had succeeded none the less in securing for themselves a position that was infinitely the highest in the country. The tremendous principle that they were beings endowed with a special and divine wisdom, and differing in kind from all other men, that they possessed divine power and corresponding privileges, is pushed in their legal books to its uttermost extreme.

The outward appearance of the Brahman in no way represented the power of his caste, in which respect he is to be contrasted with the Kshatriya. Modesty, indeed poverty, characterised his appearance and his mode of life. Lucrative professions, which were in his eyes derogatory, were closed to him. On the other hand, it was the duty of every Brahman to found a family, and his great ambition was to beget sons, who should revere his memory after his death, and provide prayer and sacrifice for his spirit. Consequently, the material possessions of the Brahmans became more and more divided. Moreover, the whole Brahman theory of existence was opposed to the temporal point of view. Not only physical existence, but also material possessions were considered by him as so many obstacles in the way to felicity which his soul would tread when, after purification, it became reunited with the universal element.

Priests that Scorn Wealth

Hence in the eyes of the Brahman the mendicant profession was in no way derogatory, since the whole world already belonged to him. Begging, on the contrary, seemed to him the loftiest of all professions, as it implied the least amount of hindrance in the prosecution of his high tasks. It is true that voluntary offerings, even when the Brahman power was at its height, by no means invariably sufficed to maintain the caste, many members of which were obliged for this reason to adopt one of the lucrative professions. Many gifts were made to them as payment for relief from spiritual duties, for religious instruction, prayer, sacrifice, and judicial pronouncements. If the income from these sources proved insufficient, the Brahman was allowed to plough the fields or to tend the herds. He might also learn the arts of war and practise them, or carry on commercial business, though money-lending upon interest, the sale of intoxicating liquors, or of milk and butter, the products of the sacred cow, were forbidden to him. It was as impossible for a Brahman to get his living by the practice of the lower arts of music and song, or by unclean occupations, as by the practice of leather working, or any other degrading trade.

The life of a Brahman as a whole included several grades, that of the neophyte, the patriarch, the hermit, and the ascetic. Upon his coming of age the youth of this caste was girded with the sacred band and received into the community of the twice-born. His education was passed under the supervision of a spiritual teacher, the Guru, whom he was to reverence more highly than his own father. " If a Brahman pupil should blame his teacher, even though with justice, he will be born again as an ass ; should he betray him falsely, as a dog ; should he take his property without leave, he will be born as a small worm, and should he refuse him service, as an insect." Under the Guru the young Brahman learned during the long course

Education of the Brahman

of his education the sacred books, all the prayers, offerings, and ceremonial connected therewith, and all the laws governing Brahman society. Then came the stage of family life, a burden laid upon him as a member of the earth to maintain the prosperity of his tribe and caste by begetting sons. This task accomplished, the rest of his life was to be devoted to the highest and most beautiful task, the work of redemption and purification of the soul from earthly elements. The Brahman, often accompanied by his wife, leaves his home and becomes a hermit in the forest. There he lives only upon such fruits or roots as his surroundings afford, or upon the scanty gifts of pious devotees, being entirely occupied with the fulfilment of religious precepts and with deep introspective speculation upon the evils of existence and the means of purification.

The highest task of the Brahman's existence is pure and untroubled thought,

Underwood & Underwood, London

SACRED COWS OF THE BRAHMANS

These mild-eyed beasts are deferentially allowed to do as they please, while the bullocks are used as draught animals. A Hindu would not think of striking a Brahman cow to make her move—it would be a horrid impiety, punishable by the gods with all sorts of personal misfortune.

far removed from all worldly interests, upon the deepest questions which can occupy the human mind. Brahmans of similar interests often united for pious practices ; spiritual orders were formed, with rulers to regulate their behaviour, and with the common object of entirely forgetting the world around them and devoting themselves to introspection. Others were not content with such intellectual submergence in the divine, and also sought to suppress and to destroy the earthly element, the flesh, while they still lived. The most ingenious tortures and penances were devised, and the universal ordinances of Manu did not leave this subject untouched : " The penitent is to roll upon the ground, to stand upon tip-toe all day, or to stand up and sit down alternately with-

Penances of Brahman Devotees

out cessation. During the hot season he is to sit under the burning rays of the sun between four fires ; in time of rain he shall expose himself naked to the downpour, and wear wet clothes during the cold season. By increasing severity of his penance, he is gradually to wear away the temporal element. And when he is sick unto death, he is to rise and walk directly north-east with air and water for his sole nourishment, until his mortal powers give way and his soul is united with Brahma."

The Brahman philosophy has been reduced to writing in the Upanishads, the " mystical teaching of that which lies concealed beneath the surface." These also are considered as sacred writings, but are the exclusive possession of the highest castes, whereas the Vedas were open to the people. Their teaching is spiritual pantheism ; the cosmos is one being, a world-soul, Atman or Brahman. The teaching of the Upanishads is explained in detail in the philosophic system of the Vedanta.

Teaching of Brahman Philosophy

The world-soul in its original form, and in its ultimate condition, the " self," is impersonal, without consciousness, in absolute tranquillity, infinite, without beginning or end, and existing by and for itself. As soon, however, as the desire for activity arises within it, it becomes the personal creator—Brahma ; this it is which creates the world perceptible to the senses. Everything in the world, the heaven and the foundations of the earth, fire and water, air and earth, suns, plants and all living beings, animals, men and gods are the emanation of that all-pervading spirit, the Brahman, conceived as personally operative. When this latter desires to become creative, its objective appearance in the world implies the production of spirit—apperception, thought and will—and of bodily form, which varies in the case of different living beings, consisting of a material body, which disappears upon death, and a more immaterial form in which the soul remains upon the departure of the body ; this latter survives until the soul which it clothes is again absorbed into the impersonal and unconscious Brahman. During the period of earthly existence the universal being by objectifying itself abandons that state of absolute passivity which is its highest form ; it sinks, that is, from the highest stage of perfection. Hence is derived the suffering inseparable from earthly existence, and return to the ideal condition of passivity enjoyed by the world soul is the great longing of every creature.

Redemption from the Sin of Existence

The path of redemption is by no means easy. By the iron laws of causation, the operation of the world-soul becomes a curse permanently imposed upon every physical being. Every act, bad or good, leads to some new act, to further separation from the highest existence, and hence to further unhappiness. Every death is followed by a new birth, the soul entering a higher or a lower plane of existence according to the merits of its previous life, becoming a god, a Brahman or a Sudra, a four-footed animal, an insect or a worm. The more practical doctrine for popular consumption also inserted promises of purifactory fires and the punishments of hell, which were painted by Indian imagination in the liveliest possible colours. The chain of transmigrations which the soul may thus undergo is of endless duration, including millions of new births. None the less, a definite goal is set before it, and the reunion or absorption of the personal soul into the absolute passivity and unconsciousness of the primal Brahman is a definite possibility. The way leading to this end is the way of knowledge, the way of understanding, which can be attained only by absolute self-absorption. This pantheistic teaching of the Brahmans emphasises the width of the distinction between the purely spiritual nature of the original Brahman and that of the existing world. Several philosophical systems and schools—six of which have found general recognition— have attempted to solve the great problem by different methods. Of these, two are of especial importance for the further development of Indian thought, the Samkhya philosophy and the already mentioned Vedanta philosophy, the end or perfection of the Vedas. The former considers the external world as having an objective reality under certain aspects, a reality derived from the creative power of the world-soul ; whereas to the Vedanta philosophy material existence is purely illusory, and has no value as such. According to this latter, as soon as the Brahman acquires consciousness and personality, it also assumes an imaginary physical form. In its most refined form it appears as the chief divine personality, Iswara. But all such forms are necessarily subject to the conditions of activity, of goodness, and of imperturbability or darkness, so that this highest god appears as a trinity. He is the personally active creator, Brahma ; the all-helping, ever operative Vishnu, or the Rudra Siva, the agent of dissolution and destruction

Different Brahman Systems

At the same time, however, these and all the other gods, together with mankind and the whole of the material world, are merely a dream, an idea of the world-soul which is itself the sole existing reality.

It was not easy to appreciate all the difficulties which beset every Indian philosophical system, much less to pass judgment upon the results. The text of the sacred Vedas, the basis of all knowledge, was with the utmost difficulty harmonised with the philosophy. The interpreter was obliged to take refuge in comments and explanations which are refinements of hair-splitting and miracles of ingenuity. Commentators were invariably anxious to surpass one another in learning and erudition, in readiness and brilliancy of exposition. The methodic and the formal finally strangled the material content of the system, and Indian philosophy was thus degraded into a scholasticism with every characteristic of that current in the thought of mediæval Europe.

Conflict of Brahman Authority

The teaching of Brahman philosophy was fully calculated to satisfy the introspective spirit of the Brahman weary of life and tormented by doubt. To him, bound fast in the chains of asceticism, this teaching appeared as truth of the highest and most indisputable order. To the great mass of the people, however, such teaching was unintelligible, and would in any case have proved unsatisfactory. The worker for his daily bread demands other spiritual food than the philosophic thinker. A popular divinity must be almighty and at the same time intelligible to mankind. If the Brahmans did not wish to lose their influence upon the people, a danger threatened by the appearance of Buddhism with its powerful spiritual influence, they were forced to offer to the people gods more definitely comprehensible to the ordinary mind.

The gods of the old Vedas of the military period had lost their splendour and power upon the downfall of the nobility. They had developed under other circumstances, and were unable to conform to the new conditions of life. But in legend and poetry other ideal figures had arisen, the heroes of the flourishing period of the Aryan domination in the west of the Ganges valley. Mythology provided them with a genealogy, bringing them into connection with those forms of Nature which had ever been objects of especial reverence—the Sun and Moon dynasties. The Indian heroic period, however, was historically too near in date to the development of Brahmanism for its figures to attain the position of supreme gods. Other divinities came forward from other directions. The diminution and the importance of the old Vedic gods was largely due to the conjunction and partial fusion of the two races which had originally opposed one another as deadly foes. At that period the Aryan gods had been primarily gods of battle and slaughter. Circumstances now had become more peaceful and tranquil. As, however, under Brahman influence the people lost the proud consciousness of their strength, as they also became penetrated with the sense of the miseries of existence, so did they become more inclined to receive the mysterious and repellent forms of the primeval Indian demonology, which had formed the shadowy spirit world of the original inhabitants.

This change in the belief of the great mass of the people was by no means unwelcome to the Brahmans. In the worship of these gods, in their magic formulæ and incantations, their objective representations, they found a great deal which corresponded to their own worship; and they had, therefore, the less scruple in forming an alliance with the demon world of the Dravidians. Hence it

Degradation of Brahman Doctrines

is that in the later sacred books of the Brahmans, even in the Atharva Veda, the latest in date of the Vedas, numbers of alien and evil spirits leer upon us, of which the earlier books, the Rig-Veda especially, knew nothing. For the Brahmans it was perfectly easy to include these spirits within their own pantheon, for their theory of immanence and emanation enabled them to incorporate within their own system elements the most contrary to the divine nature.

BRAHMANISM IN THE SOUTH

AS the Aryan states on the Ganges flourished and extended, as life became more highly organised, so did the Brahmans become ever more inclined to the solitary life. In countries as yet untouched by Brahman teaching, in the jungle deserts and beyond the boundaries of foreign native states, whole colonies of hermits arose, living either in isolation or under some organised constitution. Often, indeed, they had to struggle with the attacks of hostile races. We hear a great deal of the evil Rakshasa, who harassed or disturbed the pious hermits. But they also met with more civilised and kindlier treatment, and men were found who would gladly make small offerings to the more highly educated foreigners, receiving instruction and stimulus in exchange.

These men thus became the pioneers of Brahmanism, and their monasticism and influence steadily extended southward. The Mahabharata describes how Arjuna, during his pilgrimage from hermitage to hermitage, at length reached the maidens' baths of Komarya at Cape Comorin. Similarly Rama meets hermits everywhere. The name, however, that constantly recurs in all these reports, the man who is ever ready to help all Aryan-Brahman kinsmen with counsel and assistance, the man who possesses the greatest influence in the whole of the south is Agastya. In the myths he appears as one of the greatest sages of the primeval period, the son of Mitra and Varuna, the strong helper in the necessity of the old Aryan gods when they were threatened with conquest by the evil demons, the Asuras. In the south, he is the incarnation of the victorious advance of Brahman culture. The Vindhya Mountains, hitherto uncrossed, bend before him. He is the sworn enemy of the evil demons, the gods of the original inhabitants, and the bringer of civilisation to the Dravidian kingdoms, and consequently the Tamir Muni, the sage of the Tamils.

The history of the south before the Brahman period is hidden for us in darkness, penetrated only here and there by the feeblest rays of light. Native legends consider the starting-point of the general development of civilisation and politics to be Korkay (the Greek Colchi) at the mouth of the sacred River Tambraparni in the Gulf of Manaar. This district, sheltered upon the east by the bridge of Adam from the inhospitable Sea of Bengal with its dangerous cyclones, forms a connection between the two rich lands of India and Ceylon on the north and south. Korkay was an old town even when the Greeks first visited it and brought news of its excellence to the West. It owes its origin and its prosperity to the product of that gulf, the pearls, which were highly prized in antiquity, in which this Bay of Colchi has proved richer than any other part of the earth at any period of history. The age of that old trading station is

A Great Figure in Brahmanism

An Ancient Metropolis

probably identical with the date of the use of pearls for ornamentation among the peoples of antiquity. The ancient ruins of Korkay have been discovered at a distance of several miles from the present coast line, buried in the alluvial soil which the Tambraparni brings down, advancing its delta ever further into the sea, not far from the modern harbour of Tutikorin. The legend relates that Korkay was founded by three brothers, who lived in unity for a considerable period, afterward separating and founding three kingdoms—the Pandya kingdom in the extreme south, the Chola kingdom in the north-east, and the Chera kingdom in the north and north-west.

Of these the most important was the Pandya kingdom, which for a long period held the harbour of Korkay as its capital. The totem sign or insignia of its kings was the Fish (carp), a fact confirming the legend, which states that the centre from which further civilisation was developed lay upon the sea. At a later period the capital was placed more in the centre of the country at Mathura. When the first Aryan-Brahman hermits advanced into that distant territory, they found flourishing and well-organised states in existence. The later introductions of northern civilisation were collectively attributed to the name of Agastya. He arrived at the court of King Kulasekha, was well received, and wrote books in the language of the country, treating of every branch of science and culture.

An Early Aryan Kingdom

Utterly different from its northern development is the history of the expansion of Aryan civilisation in the south. In the north, it had led to a racial struggle. The rude strength of races more powerful intellectually and physically had been pitted against backward tribes, the consequence being that the latter had disappeared or had been reduced to the lowest stage in the social organism ; whereas in the south the struggle was fought with intellectual weapons, the higher knowledge and power of pre-eminent individuals. Brahmanism creeps in quietly and insinuatingly, makes concessions, leaves the people in possession of their language, increasing their vocabulary with elements of the sacred Brahman language (Sanscrit) only where it is incapable of expressing the terms of abstract thought and religious teaching.

THE GREAT HINDU TEMPLE OF MADURA
Showing the court of the sacred tank used for ablutions, which is an important feature of all Hindu temples.

But even then this language is so highly respected that kings and towns consider it an honour to bear a Sanscrit together with their old Dravidian name, which former are known to us only from the later accounts of the Greeks. Moreover, the native name Pandya, indicating the sap of a palm-tree, one of the staple products of the country, so closely resembled the Pandava of Aryan legend that the two were considered identical; and the Pandya dynasty of the southern kingdom was identified with the Aryan gods who had sprung from the Pandu dynasty in the north. The Brahmans even left the people their system of writing. The original native Vattezhat alphabet, a wholly original creation, maintained its ground in the three kingdoms of Southern India until the end of the first millennium A.D., when it was replaced by a more modern system which may be traced back to the Southern Asoka inscriptions.

Results of Brahman Influence

We may, perhaps, assume that the conversion of the south to Brahmanism took place between 1000 B.C. and 500 B.C.

The earliest historical mention of the Pandya kingdom of Southern India occurs in the Buddhist chronicles of Ceylon. The forerunners of the Aryans under Vijaya had already encountered a strong kingdom in that district, to which the north of Ceylon was probably tributary, and it appears that the new Aryan arrivals who took wives from that country were obliged to send the regular tribute of pearls and conchs to the Pandya princes. The reports of Megasthenes at the end of the fourth or beginning of the third century B.C. mention the Pandya kingdom as lying at the extreme south of the Indian peninsula, adding a word upon its productiveness in pearls. Roman coins are occasionally found in this southern portion of India, and confirm Strabo's references to the commercial relations existing between the Romans and the Pandya kingdom and of the embassy sent by the latter to the Emperor Augustus. The boundaries of this kingdom coincide upon the south and south-east with the north coast of the Gulf of Manaar and the Palk Straits. From the north end of these the frontier line advances in a westerly direction to the Palni hills. Upon the west the power of the Pandya king often extended to the Arabian Sea; and even at the present day the language of the east, Tamil, is spoken in the southernmost districts of the Malabar coast. During the

Historical Records of the South

1183

whole of its existence, the Pandya kingdom was distinguished by a brave and war-like spirit. It was continually at variance with its southern neighbours, the Singhalese, and also with the Chola in the north. Generally speaking, its civilisation was far in advance of that possessed by any other state of Southern India.

Early Kingdoms of the South The north-eastern neighbour of this most southerly state was the state of the Chola, a tribe of almost equal antiquity with the Pandya. Ptolemy speaks of the nomadic Sorai of this district, of the wandering Chola. The chief tribe was that of the Kumruba, a nomadic race of shepherds, and their restless life, perhaps, explains those warlike tendencies which brought them into continual discord with neighbouring tribes. They were also constantly involved in hostile undertakings against the more distant Ceylon. Their capital has often changed its position ; Comba, Trichinopoly, Tanjore, now occupy the sites of their earlier capitals.

In the south of the peninsula the kingdom of the Chera, the third of the Dravidian kingdoms, occupied the coast of Malabar from about Calicut to Cape Comorin, though its frontiers at different periods extended eastward beyond the Ghats—Mysore, Coimbatore, Salem—while during other periods portions even of the district on the Malabar coast were occupied by the Pandya kings. On the whole, this branch of the Dravidian States was more peacefully inclined than its eastern neighbours. The fertile character of the Malabar coast favoured a more restful course of development, and rather inclined the inhabitants to tranquillity. The vernacular diverged from the Tamil as lately as one thousand years ago, and must now be considered a special language, though the old Tamil alphabet, the Vattezhat, still remains in use. Upon

Southern India Before the Brahmans the north of the Chera kingdom the Brahman civilisation at an early period exercised a deeper influence upon the inhabitants of the Malabar coast than in any other part of Southern India. While the age of chivalry was at its height, the Aryans had advanced as far as Gujerat on the Gulf of Cambay ; from this point Aryan influence extended eastward. Between the native independent states of the Bhils, colonists were con-

tinually advancing, and Aryan manners were extended over the west of Central India, reaching the land of the Mahrattas in course of time. The triumphant colonisation of the west coast, known by the Sanscrit name of Kerala, the land of the Chera, belongs to the later period of Brahman predominance. In the northern half of this district, especially in the modern Kanara and Malabar, a federation of sixty-four cantons seems to have existed before the Brahmans entered the country.

When the Brahmans pressed into this fruitful territory in greater numbers, they maintained the existing constitutional forms while securing their own recognition as the royal masters of the country. A legend of Brahman origin ascribes their arrival to the help of the Brahman god, Vishnu, incarnate as Rama, with the battleaxe. The legend represents him as a son of the Brahman sage, Jamadagni. During the absence of this latter, a sacrificial calf was stolen from his cell by the Kshatriya Prince Kartavirya, and the son avenged his father by killing the Kshatriya.

How the Brahmans Won Power In the feud which resulted, Jamadagni fell a victim, and Rama swore vengeance upon the whole order of the Kshatriya, and exterminated them—" He purified the earth thrice seven several times of the Kshatriya." The gods rewarded him for his piety with a promise that the country should be his as far as he could hurl his battleaxe. The weapon flew from Gokama to Cape Comorin. Thus the whole of the Malabar coast was gained and settled by the Brahmans, to whom Parasu Rama presented the district. At the present day the Malabar chronology begins with that throwing of the axe and the creation of the country, which is dated 1176 B.C. The legend was invented as a foundation for the claims which the Brahmans raised upon entering the country. Their theory was that they were the actual possessors of the land, which they had restored to its old masters only upon lease, and that therefore the warriors must reverence them and swear to them oaths of allegiance. Even at the present day the superior Brahman castes on the whole of the Malabar coast enjoy a far higher position than those upon the east coasts of the peninsula.

The Colour of India

THE PICTURESQUE ARCHITECTURE
OF PALACE,
MOSQUE, AND TEMPLE

i

THE PEERLESS GEM OF MOHAMMEDAN ARCHITECTURE: THE TAJ MAHAL AT AGRA

THE SACRED CITY OF THE HINDUS: BENARES ON THE GANGES

VIEW OF THE TEMPLES AND MOSQUES OF SASSUR, NEAR POONA, IN THE DECCAN

A HINDU CUSTOM NOW SUPPRESSED: PREPARATIONS FOR A "SUTTEE"

A RULING PRINCE OF WESTERN INDIA WITH HIS VASSALS

TRAVELLERS WITH ESCORT IN THE ANCIENT PROVINCE OF KATTYWAR

THE FOUNDING OF BUDDHISM
AND DECLINE OF THE ANCIENT RELIGION
BUDDHA AND HIS TEACHING

AN examination of the state of India about the sixth century B.C. shows the prevailing conditions to have been as follows. The Aryans had risen to a high prosperity, their social life had rapidly developed, states large and small had been formed, populous towns were adorned by the splendour of their royal courts and by the wealth of the inhabitants; agriculture, industry, and trade were flourishing. National feeling among the ruling race had also undergone a change, and in some respects a change for the worse; the bright spirit of youth, the sense of power, the pride of freedom, were things of the past. Society was divided or cleft asunder by the institution of caste. Any feeling of equality had given way to the spirit of caste, which induces the lofty to look down with contempt upon the humble, precludes all possibility of common action for the public good, and therefore makes national feeling impossible. For every caste its every action was accurately prescribed, while the highest activities, those of thought, were monopolised by the Brahmans. The latter claimed to have sprung from the head of the first man, and in actual practice were the head of society. But speculation had undergone a fundamental change since the period of Aryan immigration. The priests continued to offer formal prayers to the old gods in which no one any more believed. A deep sense of the futility of existence penetrated every thinking mind, while opinions were divided as to the means which should be adopted to gain release from existence. Schools and orders multiplied continually. It was as if one of the fierce cyclones of Bengal had burst upon the forest. The giant forms of the ancient gods lay dead upon the ground, and from this devastation new cults were rising,

each struggling with the other for air, light, and space. Of these, one alone was fated to become a mighty tree, collecting almost the whole of Central and Eastern Asia beneath its branches—Buddhism.

The centres of Indo-Aryan development slowly changed in the course of ages from west to east. Advancing over the north-west passes in the third millennium B.C., the Aryans occupied the Punjab, the Land of the Five Rivers, during the second millennium; about the middle of this period may have occurred those struggles on the frontier between the Punjab and the Ganges district, when King Sudas defeated the allied tribes of the west. The end of the period may be considered to include the flourishing times of the principalities on the Jumna and the upper Ganges, whose struggles have provided a foundation of historical legend for the great heroic poem of the Bharata. Another 500 years and the centre of gravity has again moved eastward to the countries which end where the Ganges delta begins and where the town of Benares rises. Here about this period were formed a number of principalities and free states, among them the powerful kingdom of Magadha with the old capital of Rajagriha, in that district of the modern Behar which lies to the south of the Ganges.

We should know exceedingly little of the different petty states lying on the northern side of the Ganges opposite Magadha were it not for the fact that here was the home of that religious teacher Buddha, whose doctrine is to-day accepted by hundreds of millions of men. Upon the spurs of the Himalaya, on the stream of the Rohini, the modern Kohani, had settled the tribe of the Sakya, within which the Kshatriya nobility still played an important part in the continual friction that occurred with the neighbouring petty states. To this class belonged the chieftain of the tribe, Suddhodana of the Gautama family, the father of Buddha, who resided in the capital of the country, Kapilavatthu—in its Sanscrit form, Kapilavastu. According to the Buddhist legend, Suddhodana had married two daughters of the neighbouring **Birth of Buddha** Koyla prince, on the other bank of the Rohini, who was also a Kshatriya. For a long time he remained childless, but in his forty-fifth year the elder of his wives, Maya, became with child. As, according to the custom of the period and of her order, she was journeying homeward to her father's house, there to await her confinement, she was surprised on the way in the grove of Lumbini by the birth of a son, who was named Siddhartha. This is the personal name of Buddha, who is often known by his family name of Gautama. All his other titles are additional names, the number of which is proportionate to the reverence and admiration of his devotees. In every case, like the titles of Redeemer, Christ, applied to Jesus, they are merely descriptions of his personal characteristics. For instance, Sakya Muni means the sage of the Sakya family; Bhagavat means the reverend; Sattha, the teacher; Jina, the conqueror. Buddha also is but one of these titles, meaning " The Enlightened."

The birth of Siddhartha is placed with some probability between the years 560 and 557, and his death between 480 and 477 B.C. On the seventh day after his birth his mother died, the child being then carefully tended and brought up by his aunt, Prajapati. According to the custom of the time, the young Siddhartha was married in his nineteenth year to his cousin, Wasodhara, a daughter of the Kolya prince, and their union was blessed after ten years by the birth of a son, Rahula. Any other man would probably have been contented and happy in the position of Siddhartha. He had everything and

was everything which a noble Kshatriya could desire to have or to be. But in his twenty-ninth year a sense of dissatisfaction came upon him. Amid all his external prosperity, his lofty and serious mind could not refrain from the contemplation of the futility of existence.

His thoughts on the woe of the world and the means of liberation therefrom take in the legend a personal and objective figure. A god appears to him first as an old man in his second childhood, then as a stern tyrant, again as a corrupting corpse, and finally as a reverend hermit. It was the birth of his son which determined him to put into execution a long preconceived resolve. He saw in the child a new bond which would fetter him to the **Flight of Buddha** world. The story of Siddhartha's flight is the most moving picture in the whole legend of his life. Only once was he willing to look upon that which is the dearest thing in this world, only once would he press his new-born son to his heart. Quietly he glided into the bed-room where his wife and child were resting; but the mother's hand lay upon her child's head, and he could not take the child in his arms without waking her.

Thus he left wife and child without a word and went out into the night with no companion but his charioteer, whom he presented with all his ornaments and ordered to inform his family of his resolve. He then cut his hair short, exchanged his rich garments for the rags of a passing beggar, and made his way alone to the capital of the Magadha kingdom, Rajagriha, near which pious hermits had settled in the caves of the rock. To these he joined himself, hoping to learn from them the solution of the great riddle of existence. But Brahman metaphysics brought no consolation to his soul. Neither from Alara Kalana nor from Uddaka Ramaputta could he obtain the object of his search—the path to freedom from the pain of existence. He left both teachers and turned to the forests of

AN EARLY INDIAN BUDDHA
The image of the Buddha here reproduced is from a very ancient Indian sculpture in clay.

A FAMOUS STATUE GROUP OF BUDDHA AND HIS PUPILS

This unique representation in stone of the great Indian sage, seated amidst his pupils, is one of the most famous religious curiosities of Siam, and is to be seen in the great pagoda of Vat Suthat at Bangkok.

Uruvela, near the modern Buddha-gaya, in which five Brahman hermits were already living a life of asceticism. For six years he surpassed them all in the cruelty of his penances until his former powerful and beautiful frame had been worn to a shadow. The reputation of his extraordinary self-torture spread far and wide, but he himself became the more unhappy in proportion as others esteemed him far advanced upon the road to salvation.

He fell in a swoon from weakness, but on his restoration to consciousness he had found strength to leave the path of error. When he again began to take food like other men he lost the belief and respect of his five companions. They departed and turned to the holy town of Benares to accomplish their purification in more sacred surroundings. The man they left behind had now to undergo a severe **Buddha's Mental Conflict** mental struggle. Buddhist legend represents the conflict between his intellect and his sympathies as a battle between bright and dark spirits who struggled in conflict so that the world trembled and was almost moved from its foundation. Siddhartha was left alone, wrestling for enlightenment by the banks of the Nairanjara. The prospect cleared and the mysteries of suffering and of the road

to salvation were laid open before him. He had now become the "Buddha," the Enlightened, who had attained knowledge of redemption not only for himself but for the whole world. For seven days Buddha remained in extreme exaltation of mind, in holy glorification under the **The First Converts to Buddhism** sacred fig tree. A pair of benevolent men brought him rice cakes and honey, and he in return gave them his greatest gift, his teaching. These two men, Tapussa and Bhallika, were his first converts, who took "refuge with Buddha and knowledge." Doubt then came upon the enlightened sage as to whether the coarse mind of the masses was capable of realising the great truths he taught. But the world god Brahma urged him to preach his doctrine, and Buddha gave way. He went to that very forest where the five companions of his former penance were staying and explained the main features of his doctrine, to them in the "Sermon of Benares." Neither a life of pleasure nor the extirpation of all pleasure could lead to the goal, the true way lying midway between these extremes. In broad outline he shows them the truth upon the question of suffering and the eight-fold road to liberation.

From this point onward the life of Buddha is entirely occupied with the

1187

teaching and conversion of the people, The persuasion of five nobles of Benares brought about a rapid increase in his scanty congregation, to which fifty adherents were shortly added. The reputation of the new doctrine spread far and wide; the people thronged from every direction and from distant settlements to hear his teaching. Buddha **The Rapid** sent out his sixty disciples as **Spread of** apostles: "Go forth, ye mendi-**Buddhism** cants, upon your way, for the salvation of the people, for the good of the people, for the salvation, the advantage, and the prosperity both of gods and men." The Enlightened One did not remain alone after despatching his apostles. Shortly afterward thirty rich youths accepted his doctrine; they were followed by one thousand fire worshippers. The most important convert, however, was Bimbisara, king of the great Magadha kingdom. In him Buddhism gained a powerful patron, and the conversions of lay brothers immediately due to this success were numbered by tens of thousands. Even more important converts were the two most famous pupils of the master, Sariputta and Mogallana.

The conversion of King Bimbisara marks the first step of that policy which was characteristic of this religion in its later developments— that of entering into relations with the ruling powers and invoking their protection. Henceforward Buddhism rises and falls in the several states as their ruling dynasties prosper or decay. The same phenomenon appears in Ceylon, where the Buddhist communities attained to extraordinary prosperity under powerful and fortunate kings, while the political disasters resulting from the war with the Dravidians repeatedly brought the doctrine to the point of annihilation. Toward its patrons Buddhism invariably displayed a considerable amount of adaptability. Its first chief patron, Bimbisara,

secured the introduction into the monastic communities of the monthly penances formerly practised by many Brahman monks, the strict observance of the four quarters of the moon, the Poya days of the modern Singhalese, and also of the Uposadha days.

When Buddha returned, during his later wanderings, to his native town, where his son Rahula entered the community, at the request of the old prince he added to the rules of the community the regulation that no son should become a monk without his father's consent. The fundamental objections of Buddha to the institution of orders of nuns were overcome only by the influence of his foster mother, Prajapati, **The Rise of** who was of royal race and de-**Buddhist** sired to found such an order. **Monasticism** On the other hand, the new doctrine thus powerfully supported gained not only popular approval but also material help. Poverty was, as a rule, obligatory only upon individual monks, and from the outset the order was always glad to receive rich presents. The first of such foundations was that of the Bamboo Grove, near the capital of Magadha; and even during the lifetime of the master, princes and rich men rivalled one another in making similar offerings. A long list of large gardens and parks were even then assigned to the order, one of the most famous of these being the garden of Jetawana at Sawatthi. In Ceylon, where the history of Buddhism is more easily followed, the larger and more valuable part of all the arable land eventually fell into the hands of the order.

Among the pupils who gathered round the person of Buddha, one of the most

MAYA AND THE CHILD BUDDHA
After an Indian drawing.

human figures is his cousin Ananda, who, though not distinguished for intellectual power, engages our sympathy by his loving devotion to his master. But even in that narrow circle which gathered round the Enlightened One, the element of evil

THE CITY OF BENARES, WHERE BUDDHA PREACHED HIS GREAT SERMON

was to be found, even as in the apostolic band of Jesus. Devadatta, a personality swollen with pride and dominated by immeasurable ambition, is, during the time of Buddha, a type of that sectarian spirit which resulted in the repeated schisms of later years ; even during the master's lifetime many believers were led astray by him. And as at a later period one sect invariably abuses and maligns another, so here legend even reproaches the ambitious disciple with attempts upon his master s life.

For forty-five years after his " enlightenment," Buddha traversed the country, preaching his doctrine and making thousands of converts ; at length a severe illness reminded him that the end of his life was approaching. In deep anxiety his congregation asked who was to follow **Last Days of the Prophet** him as their leader. But the master refers them to their knowledge : " Be your own illumination ; be yourselves your refuge, have no other refuge ; for the doctrine shall be your light, the doctrine shall be your refuge, and have no other refuge." By sheer will-power the sick man was cured for the time ; but he himself prophesied his death at the end of three months. The last days of Buddha are related by the legend with details so realistic that it is probable they contain some substratum of historical truth. He is said to have gone to Pawa with his favourite pupil Ananda, where, with other monks, he received hospitality from Kunda the smith. Tainted pork was set upon the table at their meal, and after partaking of this he fell ill. However, he continued his journey. But in the neighbourhood of Kusinara his strength failed him, and, lying down under two beautiful amyris trees, he awaited death. He thanks his faithful Ananda for all his love and devotion, asks the monks gathered round him three times whether any feels doubt, and, when all have asserted their faith, **Death of the Buddha** he speaks his last words, " Of a truth, O monks, I say unto you, all that is must decay ; strive for perfection and faint not." Then his life passed into Nirvana. " As the mortal remains of the King ot kings are treated, so shall one treat the remains of him who has been perfected," so runs the saying of Ananda when the. Mallers of Kusinara questioned him upon the form of burial. The preparations lasted six days, after which the funeral pyre was lighted with the utmost pomp. The ashes of the great departed were collected. Constant demands for relics came in, with proposals to guard them in fitting memorials ; and it was at last arranged that the remains should be divided into eight parts and presented to the eight most important states in which Buddha had lived and worked.

Later tradition relates that immediately after the funeral the most important monks met together in Rajagaha, under the presidency of Kasyapa, who defined as accurately as possible the formulæ of the doctrine (the first council of Rajagaha). It is said that the sayings of Buddha relating to the discipline of the order were set forth by Upali, while the general teaching upon the daily life of all, including the lay adherents, was recited by Ananda. This teaching was then committed to memory by 500 monks, and by them handed down to tradition. Exactly 200 years after the death of the master it became necessary to call a second council at Vesali. As a number of monks had supported views which diverged in detail from the original doctrine, a committee met at Vesali and determined the direction of Buddhist doctrine for the future.

Transmission of Buddhist Doctrines

The first council of historical authenticity is the third, that of Patna, about 250 B.C. Dipawamsa, the earliest chronicle of Ceylon, reports upon this as follows : " With the object of destroying infidelity, many of the pupils of Buddha, 60,000 sons of Jina, met together in council. Over this assembly presided Tissa Mogalliputta, son of Mogalli. For the purpose of purifying the faith and formulating the doctrine for the future, the president, Tissa, appointed 1,000 Arahats, choosing the best members of the assembly, and held a synod. The third council was brought to an end after a space of nine months in the monastery of Asokarama, built by King Dhammasoka." In order that the doctrines of the master might be the better transmitted to the disciples, the council formulated his teaching in the canonical books of the Tripitaka, " the three baskets." This council was also responsible for the despatch of numerous missionaries, who introduced Buddhism into Ceylon among other places ; from this period begin the monastic annals of the Singhalese, which, at a later period, were worked into the chronicles. In these there is mention made of the names of some of the missionaries who were then despatched, and the credibility of the chronicles has been considerably strengthened by the discovery of the tomb of one of those missionaries in North India.

Despatch of Buddhist Missionaries

Granted that the council of Patna is historically authentic, the same can by no means be said of the two preceding councils. It is indeed true that the council of Vesali was held 200 years after the death of Buddha

—that is to say, less than fifty years before the conversion of Ceylon ; and we may therefore suppose that later tradition was upon the whole well informed of the events of that time. But the narratives of Ceylon make it plain that that council was not called to formulate the doctrines of Buddhism, but was merely a gathering of Buddhist monks from a limited area to settle certain points of detail concerning monastic morality. Individual monks had put questions to the meeting, for instance, whether it were lawful to eat solid food only at midday, or also in the afternoon until the sun had cast a shadow two ells in length ; whether it was lawful to keep salt in buffalo horns ; whether it was lawful to sit upon a chair covered with a plain cloth.

We can readily understand that such a gathering of monks may have grown to be considered a council, remembering

A GEM OF BUDDHIST ART
This wonderful carved gateway at Bhilsa dates back to at least 250 years before the Christian era and is considered one of the finest specimens of Buddhist art. It is here reproduced from Fergusson's "History of Indian Architecture," by permission of Mr. John Murray.

the Buddhist method of emphasising important facts by the multiplication of them. Thus, according to later legends, there was not one Buddha only but as many as twenty-four before him ; the Buddha of the present age had not visited Ceylon once, but three times, and so on. Hence the canonical teaching required not one, but several formulations, and it was not enough to magnify the synod of Vesali into a council ; it was necessary to presuppose another council held immediately after the death of Buddha—that of Rajagaha. This council, indeed, is mentioned only in appendices, which were apparently added to the canonical writings at a much later date.

As the history of the Buddha doctrine previous to Asoka is thus uncertain, we are justified in asking what amount of historical truth is contained in the legends upon the personality of its founder. The attempt has been made to deny the personal existence of Buddha ; and this view has been justified by the allegorical meaning of the chief names in the personal history of Gautama. Suddhodana, his

Did Buddha Live ? father's name, means " The man whose food is pure " ; Maya means illusion ; Kapilavastu means the town of Kapila, the founder of the Sankhya philosophy ; Siddhartha means " He who has fulfilled his task." Such scepticism is, however, far too sweeping. In March, 1895, in the Terai of Nepal, near the village of Nigliwa, in the neighbourhood of Gorakhpur, about ten miles distant from the ruins of a memorial mound, an inscription of King Piyadasi, the " Pious," was discovered upon a pillar. This inscription states that Asoka, in the fifteenth year of his reign, had set up for the second time the memorial of the Konagamana Buddha, the mythical predecessor of the historical Buddha, and in the twenty-first year of his reign had himself visited the spot and there performed his devotions. The Chinese Hiuen Tsang (Yen Tsung), who visited the shrines of the Buddhists about 636 A.D., mentions the memorial and the inscription on the pillar. Moreover, on December 1st, 1896,

Underwood & Underwood, London.

A BUDDHIST TOPE, OR SACRED PLACE

There are many of these huge mounds in India, but their precise use is a matter of conjecture. They are flat on the top and surrounded with a wide platform at the foot, while elaborate gateways and enclosing walls encircle the whole. One of the gateways is shown in detail on the opposite page.

a pillar was examined near the village of Padeira, thirteen miles from Nigliwa. This pillar had also been seen by Hiuen Tsang. It rose nine feet above the ground, was covered with inscriptions made by pilgrims, while upon the three feet of it below the level of the ground was found an inscription written in very ancient characters in the " Brahmi "—formerly and erroneously known as the Maurya or Asoka—alphabet, dating at least from the year 800 A.D.

The purport of the inscription was that Priyadarsin, after a reign of twenty years, here makes his prayer in person, expressly designates the spot a birthplace of Buddha, and makes the fact known by the erection of a stone pillar. At the same time, he

Evidences of Buddha's Personality remits the taxes due from the village of Lummini (the modern Rumin-dei), and makes presents to the inhabitants. Finally, William Caxton Peppé, while making excavations in January, 1898, on his property at Piprawa, in the Terai— that is to say, in the immediate neighbourhood of Kapilavastu, opened an ancient memorial, and discovered a finely-worked sandstone chest covered by a giant slab, which, together with other objects, contained bone fragments in an urn, and bore the following inscription : " This resting-place for the remains of the exalted Buddha is the pious offering of the Sakyas, the brother with his sisters, children, and wives." There is no reason whatever for casting doubt upon the authenticity of the inscription, and there-fore we may consider that this

The Bones of Buddha latter discovery—the objects are now in the museum of Calcutta, while the bone fragments were given to the King of Siam—included the actual remnants of Buddha him-self—that is to say, one of the eight parts into which the carefully preserved remnants of the Enlightened One were divided, which was handed over to the Sakyas of Kapilavastu after the death of Buddha and the cremation of his corpse. It is but a few years since methodical investigation into the field of Indian epigraphy was begun, and researches in this direction will no doubt speedily bring yet more valuable information to light.

For the rest of the life of Buddha we are forced to depend upon the internal probability of the legendary stories. Of these, the main features are far too simple and natural to have been evolved by the riotous imagination of later times. Espe-cially is this true of the stories of his birth from a noble family, his education, his early marriage, his sympathy with the general sense of the futility of life, his retirement from the world, the penances which he underwent, his renunciation of Brahmanism, and his death. His person-ality is undoubtedly to be conceived in strict accordance with tradition, for to that personality the new doctrine undoubt-edly owed a great deal of its success. Especially credible is that part of the legend which tells us of his dignified bear-ing, of his high intellectual endowments, of his penetrating glance, the firmness of his convictions, his oratorical power, his gentle-

Character of the Great Teacher ness, kindness, and liberality, and the attractiveness of his character. When Ananda in-formed his master of the fact that the Maller Roya was an influential man whose conversion would be highly advantageous to their party," He poured such a flow of love upon the Maller that he could not but follow the teacher as the calf follows the cow."

The benevolence of Buddha's character more than anything else drew the hearts

of mankind towards him. He had, no doubt, a carefully thought-out metaphysical system of his own ; he made many rules to govern the life of his apostles, which were either borrowed from Brahman orders or were innovations of his own, but it was not to these that he owed his success. The great difference between him and the Brahmans was the deep, warm love which he bore for his neighbours. In his system under its later form, which still continues in Ceylon, we see only the lifeless labours of his successors. In Buddha himself lived and worked the originality of a high and lofty mind, coupled with the benevo-lent power of purity and warmth of heart. The influence of these characteristics con-tinued for at least a century after his death, as is proved by the edicts of Asoka.

Asoka was not a Buddhist when he assumed the government of the powerful kingdom of Magadha (269 B.C.). About 261 he was converted, though he did not make public profession of his faith before 259. The humanitarianism of the master finds a strong echo in the decrees dictated by the glowing enthusiasm of his royal

A Great Royal Convert convert. Asoka gives expression of his warm love for the whole of humanity. " All men are to me as my children. As I wish my children welfare and prosperity in this and the next world, so I do to men." Many of his numerous inscriptions on rocks or pillars are intended for the instruction of his people upon the nature of true religion. " What is Dhamma ? It is to flee from the evil and do the good ; to be loving, true, patient, and pure in life." The king forgets none of the essential virtues—moral purity, truth, nobility of heart, kindness in word and deed, goodness to all, respect and obedience to parents, love to children, tenderness to the weak, kindness to all creatures, reverence to the priests, the utmost toleration for other faiths, liberality in almsgiving, the avoid-ance of anger, passion, and cruelty. How changed is Buddha's teaching in the dead conventionalism of its modern form !

One of Asoka's edicts, perhaps the last, gives us some indication of the date when Buddha's doctrines first became stereotyped. This is the inscription of Bairat, or Bhabra, discovered in 1840 and assigned by Edmund Hardy to the year 249 B.C. Here the later teaching first makes itself heard, and in this in-scription occur only the later expressions concerning Buddha, his doctrine and the community of his believers, together with the phrase, "Everything that has been said by the exalted Buddha is well said." Here alone is there any reference to the articles of a legal code. The decree of Bhabra was issued after the council of Patna, by which it was influenced, and in this council Buddhist teaching was definitely formulated. The theory is further supported by the despatch of many missionaries shortly after the conclusion of the council. A probable cause of this step was the reformulation of the doctrine. Thanks to this mission, and especially to that of Mahinda, the son of Asoka himself, to Ceylon, where the doctrine had remained unchanged in all essentials, later Buddhism and its history are fairly plain to us.

THE INFLUENCE OF BUDDHISM
AND THE CONTEMPORARY RELIGION OF JAINISM

BUDDHISM after Asoka, like the doctrines of the Brahmans, is founded upon a metaphysical basis. The fundamental principle of every Buddhist doctrine is Bodhi (knowledge). The connotation, however, of this term is in no way profound or comprehensive. The Buddhist philosophy, unlike the Brahman, does not seek to probe the reason of all existence, but while recognising that all life is suffering, and that every act of suffering involves fresh suffering, it confines itself to the discovery of release from suffering. The fundamental pessimism thus characteristic of Buddhism is the natural product of the age. The doctrine, however, is content with the fact of suffering as it is. It does not seek to advance to the conception of a supreme being, or even to the thought of an original world-soul in a state of passivity. It does not seek to explain suffering, as did the Brahmans, by supposing a descent on the part of the supreme being to the lower levels of action. Questions of this kind

The Great Problem of Life are beyond the sphere of that knowledge which it desires. Hence there is for Buddhism no supreme divinity. Gods certainly exist, but, far from being able to help men, they suffer as men suffer. Thus for Buddha there are no thanks to be paid to God, no prayers or requests, and consequently no mediator between God and man, no priest, no sacrifice, no worship. The fact of a divine existence has been banished from the philosophy of this religion. The problem of life none the less remains to its adherents. What is the individual life ? What is the process of its continuance by reincarnation ? How can the suffering of life come to an end ?

At this point Buddhist philosophy diverges from the Brahman system, which posited an actual existence for the individual soul. According to Buddhism, there is no being which passes into another upon death. Personal existence is brought about by the conjuncture of a number of different elements which in themselves, and separately, have no personality or soul. These five elements of life are matter, feeling, imagination, will, and consciousness. The union of these is life, the division of them death. Upon death, one thing alone survives, the moral consequence, the final account of the good and the bad that has been done during life, the Kamma, an element of impulse

Life and Death driving the other elements to reunite after death and form another life. Like the beam of the scales, according to the nature of the final reckoning the reunited elements rise and fall to the formation of higher or lower beings. Thus, not to be born again implies the extinction of that yearning for existence. The Kamma being the consequence of actions performed in life, it can be destroyed only if during life man avoids all temptation to action ; that is, renounces all desire.

At this point knowledge comes by her own. Only he who has this perfect insight into the true connection of life and suffering can reach this height. Ignorance at the other end of the scale leads to continued action, to reincarnation and further suffering. Thus the most important point is, according to the Buddhist formula, the knowledge of the " four sacred truths." These embrace all that Buddha meant by knowledge. They are most concisely stated in the sermon of Benares :

" This, ye monks, is the sacred truth of suffering ; birth is suffering, age is suffering, sickness is suffering, death is suffering ; to be joined to one thou doest not love is suffering, to be divided from thy love is suffering, to fail of thy desire is suffering ; in short, the fivefold bonds that unite us to earth—those of the five elements—are suffering ; it is a yearning for existence which leads from new birth to new birth, which finds its desire in different directions, the desire for pleasure, the desire for existence, the desire for power. This, ye monks, **The** is the sacred truth concerning **Buddhist** the release from suffering ; this **Creed** desire must be extirpated by the entire destruction of inclination, which must be avoided, put away, left behind, and driven out. This, ye monks, is the sacred truth concerning the way to release from suffering ; it is this sacred eight-fold path of right belief, right resolve, right speech, right action, right life, right desire, right thought, and right self-absorption."

He who seeks relief in " Enlightenment " must first of all be convinced of the truth about suffering, and must abhor all temporal attractions. Typical for him must be the horror which seized Buddha upon his flight from the world at the appearance of the old and broken man, of the man with a deadly disease, and of the putrefying corpse. This feeling the Buddhist must carefully cherish. He must cultivate the habit of introspection by contemplation of the thirty-two elements in the human body which arouse disgust, and by meditation on death and corruption, for by these means only will he be brought to that frame of mind for which temporal affairs have no attraction. He alone who retires from the world— that is to say, the monk—can become a perfect Buddhist.

Buddhist monasticism is in immediate connection with the Brahman monastic system. As in the latter case a band of learners gathers round a famous hermit, so also in the former. The yellow garment, the shaven head, the alms pot, are borrowings from an earlier period ; as also are the days of strict retirement during the **System of** phases of the moon, together **Buddhist** with the solemn penances and **Monasticism** the cessation from activity during the three months of the rainy season. However, from the very first the organisation of the order was as weak and loosely connected as that of Brahman monasticism. Here, too, the master left his pupils to their own resources, a process which might prove successful provided that some clear mind or powerful intellect could be found to command universal respect. This, however, was by no means invariably the case, and the looseness with which the order was organised resulted not only in schism, the chronic weakness of Buddhism, but also in its ultimate defeat upon the revival of Indian Brahmanism.

A necessary preliminary to the constitution of a monastic order was the existence of non-monastic friends of the Buddhist teaching—the Upasakas. Any form of human activity was in some way a contradiction of the command to leave the Kamma in complete passivity The laity could thus never become Buddhists in the full sense of the term, and belonged only to the second class of the order ; the community properly so called consisted only of mendicant monks, who depended for a living upon the benevolence of others, and who considered their name of beggar, or Bhikshu, as a laudatory title. In the course of time certain rules of conduct were formulated for this class and stereotyped according to the usual Buddhist method ; they are characterised by a spirit wholly alien to the **Rules** strong humanitarianism which **for** pervades the teaching of **Monks** Buddha himself. Ten chief commands were binding upon the monk. It was unlawful to kill any living thing—" either worm or ant " ; nothing should be taken except what was given—" not even a blade of grass " ; falsehood was forbidden and the use of intoxicating liquors ; family ties were to be renounced as " a hateful thing " ; food was not to be taken at the wrong time or at night ; wreaths or scents were not to be used, and the monk was to sleep upon a mat spread upon the ground ; dancing, music, singing or theatrical performances were to be avoided, and gold and silver were not to be used.

The order was open to any who desired to enter it. Disqualifications were infectious diseases, such as leprosy, etc., slavery, official posts, the lack of parental consent. The would-be monk must be more than twelve years old ; he was obliged to pass a novitiate and receive full instruction upon the doctrine and morality under a monk in full orders ; ordination could not be undergone before the twentieth year. The discipline imposed upon the monk the " Middle way," as Buddha had already taught in the sermon of Benares ; that is to say, his life was not to be a course of mortification, but everything was to be excluded which passed the satisfaction of the simplest needs, or could in any way lead to strengthen the ties binding the monk to the world.

The habitation was not to be placed too near villages or towns, the noise of which might disturb contemplation, though at the same time it was to be near enough to enable the mendicants to gain what they required. It was but rarely that a monk dwelt alone in a " Pansala " ; in most cases several monks lived together. During the flourishing period of the order great monasteries

sions of Buddha's commands. In these assemblies new monks were ordained and business questions discussed. During the three months of the rainy season the monk was not to wander about, but to remain quietly in one place, either in his monastery or with some prosperous patron.

Female Monastic Orders Gautama consented with much unwillingness to the foundation of a female order, considering that it involved great dangers to his doctrine. The supervision of the nuns and the ordinances binding upon them were much stricter than in the case of the monks, who exercised a certain authority over the nuns. The

THE SPLENDID JAIN TEMPLE OF SHET HUTTISING AT AHMEDABAD
Dedicated to Dhurmanath, one of the deified mortals whom the Jains reverence as rulers of the world.

often sheltered a considerable number of Bhikkhus within their walls. The clothing—the upper garment of yellow—was to be entirely simple, and food was to be received in the alms dish from those who **The Life of the Monks** were benevolent enough to give to the beggar. The first half of the day was to be occupied in the task of mendicancy, and for the rest of the time the monk was to devote himself to introspection and pious exercises. Twice during the month, at the full and the new moon, the monks living within any one district collected for their solemn confession ; the articles of confession were then read aloud, and an opportunity was thus given to individuals to confess their transgres-

inscriptions of Asoka make mention of many nuns, and under his government the female order was transferred to Ceylon by his daughter Samghamitta. However, it attained to no great importance, either in Ceylon or in India. According to the Singhalese chronicles, it seems to have entirely disappeared from the island as early as the end of the first millennium A.D.

An attempt to estimate accurately the importance of Buddhism with reference to Indian civilisation must begin by answering these two questions : Has this doctrine satisfied the religious requirements of the people ? What has been the influence of its moral teaching ? The Buddhist doctrine of liberation could bring complete satisfaction only to a few

1195

Underwood & Underwood, London

THE JAIN TEMPLE OF MEMNATH ON MOUNT ABU
Built entirely of carved marble, this is an edifice of unrivalled beauty.

the last of which was Kasyapa; and five thousand years after the passing of Buddha into Nirvana a new Buddha, Maitreya, will arise. Of these personalities legends innumerable exist. The worshipper demands to see them in concrete form, and hence every Buddhist temple and palace is adorned with their likenesses and portraits, and especially with reproductions of Gautama. This desire for some tangible object of veneration appeared immediately upon the death of the master. A general demand arose for some sacred relic of the deceased, and his earthly remains were collected from the ashes of the funeral pyre and divided. In course of time the demand for relics increased in proportion to the distribution of the doctrine, and in every country of Buddhist faith there arose many thousands of shrines containing relics, stupas, or Dagobas, the goal of millions of pious pilgrims.

These relics were, however, purely symbolical. Buddha himself had entered the Nirvana—Nothingness; the people, however, demanded living gods, and Buddha himself had not denied the existence of these. The people, as a whole, were not so penetrated with the sense of the great suffering of existence as were the philosophical monks, although they suffered more than these from the petty cares of life, and their daily occurrence. Their old gods were called in to help in this department. The Buddhist mechanically repeats his formula of refuge; but in practice that refuge is made with the Aryan, Brahman, and Dravidian gods, including the sacred fig-tree and the Naga snake, the sun and the stars, the evil demons of the Dravidian faith, and the bright forms of Vishnu or Siva. All of these deities, together with Gautama, find a place in the broad creed of the Buddhist devotee, and during a solemn procession their grotesque images are carried side by side with the benevolent features of the Enlightened. In reality the earthly fate of the Buddhist is still guided by those old gods whom the master thought to set aside as of secondary importance. They are, no doubt, mere mechanical additions to the Buddhist faith in the southern

dominant minds. It is a doctrine of cold and unsympathetic nature, inasmuch as it offers no recompense for the infinite suffering of which the true Buddhist must feel the sway. It offers no supreme being which can sympathise with and relieve the miseries of human existence; it can promise no state of beatitude where man will be recompensed for his sufferings upon earth; it can promise only mere annihilation and nonentity. The doctrine was of too abstract a character to satisfy the great mass of the people, who desire gods made in the image of man, and yearn for some supreme object of adoration which is at least comprehensible to mankind. The immediate consequence of these desires was the transformation and elaboration of the legend concerning Buddha's life. It *Legends* was not enough to attribute *of Many* to Buddha supreme wisdom, *Buddhas* almighty power, and thousands of miracles; his personality was also multiplied. When the true doctrines have fallen into decay, and mankind has become evil, there appears at long intervals a new Buddha to resume the teaching of the same doctrines of salvation. The Buddha Siddhartha is said to have been preceded by as many as twenty-four Buddhas,

The Gods of the Buddhists

districts of Buddhism, as, for instance, in Southern India about the year 1000 A.D., and in Ceylon, Burma, and Siam at the present day; on the other hand, in northern Buddhism in Tibet and Mongolia the doctrine with which they have been incorporated has been so entirely transformed by their influence **Ethical Teaching of Buddhism** that the original system of Gautama is scarcely recognisable. The ethical teaching of Buddhism is not based upon divine authority, but upon individual egoism; moral duties or virtues as such are nonexistent, utilitarianism being the guiding principle. This principle, indeed, inspires the commands respecting personal behaviour, self-restraint, the government of the senses, self-sufficiency, vigilance. Indeed, every command explaining a man's duty to his neighbour, such as the exaggerated care against the taking even of animal life, or the exhortations to sympathy, kindness, and benevolence,

spring not from the ground of the heart, but from the purely selfish desire to advance by their fulfilment toward the ultimate goal of liberation. The moral teaching of Buddha, as regards the manner in which it makes kindness and love binding upon all men, is high above the ethical system of the Brahmans and far below the purity and nobility of Christianity. Especially is it lacking in moral force. How, indeed, could a religion provide a strong and energetic ethical system when its chief duties consisted in **The Grand Error of Buddhism** the entire avoidance of action and its highest aim in total extinction—Nirvana. The indolence of the system has been stamped upon the whole Buddhist world; stricken with fear at the thought of suffering, its strength lies rather in endurance and passivity than in action. In a people enervated by such beliefs it is impossible to expect any powerful bond of union, any feeling for the greatness of race or state, any sense of patriotism. We do not forget what the princes did for their people, but at the same time this could be only a drop in the ocean; they cared for the poor and the sick, planted fruit trees on the roads, constructed great works of irrigation, were liberal, especially toward the monastic orders. But this very liberality was a cause of further weakness; the best and the richest districts fell into the hands of the orders, and many strong arms were thereby condemned to inactivity. Meanwhile the people became impoverished, and bore their sad existence with resignation or indifference.

The caste system Buddha no more attempted to set aside than the gods; in his view both of these were necessary institutions as existing from the creation of the world. The great difference between his teaching and that of the Brahmans consists in the fact that he meant his precepts of humanitarianism to be binding upon all the castes. His followers were to be kind and benevolent even to the low-born Sudra, and were not forbidden even to accept food from him. At the same time a caste feeling was deeply rooted in

Underwood & Underwood, London

A LITANY IN STONE: INTERIOR OF A JAIN TEMPLE

In Western Hindustan Mount Abu rises 6,000 feet abruptly from the desert, and on its top, in the 11th and 12th centuries, the Jains built the exquisitely carved marble temple of Vimala Sah, of which this is an interior view. The marble must have been quarried 300 miles away. The temple is dedicated to a prophet, Parsvanatha, whose image is repeated again and again in the carvings of the temple; indeed, this curious structure is a sort of litany in stone.

Buddha and the whole of his order ; though we often hear of the reception of distinguished members of the higher and the highest castes by the master during his lifetime, instances of such treatment of the Sudra Buddhists do not occur. Even at the present day the collective Buddhist sects of Ceylon are recruited solely from the highest castes. Buddhism is also open to the further reproach of having done nothing to raise the social position of woman. The founder showed the greatest reluctance, and was induced only by a strong pressure from without, to admit the woman within his community, and even then she was not placed upon an equality with the man. Generally speaking, the only consolation he had to give to the woman in her subordinate position was that she must bear her burden, because it was appointed by the order of things, in the same way as the burden of a Sudra or of a worm.

Severe but true is Bishop Copleston's criticism of Buddhism—that it lowers mankind by the very assertion of man's supremacy.

Buddhism, though the most successful, was not the only religious system which rose during that period of intellectual movement. Contemporary with Gautama was that personality to whom the now existing sect of the Jains refers the origin of its religion ; his name was Nataputta, though he was known by his adherents as Mahavira Wardhamana, the revered Jina or world-conqueror. He, too, had his origin in that centre of intellectual movement on the lower Ganges, and his life and teaching are marked by many points of resemblance to his more important contemporary. Like Buddha, he was the son, born in 599 B.C., of a distinguished Kshatriya, by name Siddhartha, who was apparently governor of the outlying town of Kandapura, of Vesali, where the feudal aristocracy was as predominant as among the Sakya. On his mother's side he was related to King Bimbisara of Magadha, and, like Gautama, he found in this king a patron of his doctrine ; indeed, these two religious systems owe their prosperity primarily to the existence of that great kingdom and its ruler. Until his twenty-eighth year Nataputta lived with his parents ; then, however, like Gautama, he joined the Brahman

Buddhism and Woman

The Founder of Jainism

ascetics and lived for twelve years under their rules, surpassing all but one of these in the severest penances as a naked ascetic. Thus he arrived at supreme knowledge or Kewala, and so acquired for his soul freedom from its earthly trammels. The last thirty years of his life (until 527) were devoted to the dissemination of his teaching and to the organisation of the community he founded.

His honorary title of Jina has been taken by the sect which he founded, the Jains. They believe in a great number of prophets of their faith anterior to Nataputta, and pay special reverence to this last of these, Parsva, or Parsvanatha. Herein they are correct, in so far as the latter personality is more than mythical. He was indeed the royal founder of Jainism (776 ?), while his successor, Mahavira, was younger by many generations, and can be considered only as a reformer. As early as the time of Gautama, the religious confraternity founded by Parsva, and known as the Nigantha, was a formally established sect, and, according to the Buddhist chronicles, threw numerous difficulties in the way of the rising Buddhism. The numerous points of correspondence between Buddhism and Jainism are sufficiently explained by the fact that both systems originated in Brahman teaching and practice. The formation of the Jain canon dates from the fifth century A.D., during which period the " holy " scriptures were established at the Council of Valabhi, under the presidency of Devarddhiganin. But this council has been put as early as 154 ; and according to one authority the writings from which the canon has been formed are as early as the first, and perhaps the second or third centuries B.C.

The Jains, like the Buddhists, accept the Brahman theory of the misery of existence and the necessity for liberation. Where, however, the Buddhist philosophy diverges from the Brahman, they follow the older creed. According to their system, the soul has a real and self-contained existence ; during life it is fettered to the base elements of the material body, which it leaves upon death. The soul is then enclosed in a form of ethereal lightness until the Karma—the ethical resultant of the actions performed in life—obliges it to become reincarnate and to resume the burden of suffering.

Doctrines Taught by the Jains

Buddhist philosophy culminates in the release from this necessity of reincarnation —that is to say, in nonentity—whereas the Jains assumed the existence of an elaborate system of higher and highest beings which claim veneration from mankind. In the different regions occupied by these divine personalities, the Jina, or all-conquerors, take the highest place. They alone, released from death and from new birth, live in eternal and absolute purity. They are the souls, freed from all earthly trammels, of the great prophets, who are far more numerous in this religion

Underwood & Underwood, London

THE RICHEST TEMPLE IN CALCUTTA
This Jain temple is one of the most magnificent in all India. It was built by a rich merchant, who lives in a palatial house near the temple. The chief material used is white marble, and every square foot of the surface is set with jewels.

than in Buddhism. Time is divided into three parts—present, past, and future ; and in each of these divisions twenty-four Jinas appear at long intervals to bring knowledge to the world of those lofty truths leading to salvation. The twenty-third Jina of the present earthly period was Parsvanatha, and the twenty-fourth Mahavira. All of these Jinas, alike by their precept and example, have shown to the world the path to liberation, which consists in purity of faith, in true insight, and in virtue undefiled.

True faith consists in belief in the Jina and in the whole system of higher beings ; true insight is provided by the philosophical system of the Jains. According to this system, both the world and the soul have an eternal objective existence. The misfortune of the soul consists in its connection with the body, and when its desire for action is extinguished it becomes free. The precepts of pure virtue coincide almost entirely with those of the Buddhist teaching.

The five fundamental precepts of the Jain monks are the same as the first four of the Brahmans, and run as follows : Thou shalt not kill any living being ; thou shalt not lie ; thou shalt not take what has not been given to thee ; thou shalt refrain from intercourse with worldly relations. The fifth precept includes within itself the remaining precepts of the Buddhist monks : thou shalt renounce all earthly possessions, and chieflysha lt call nothing thine own.

While insisting upon the importance of these commandments, the Jain teaching also recognises the value of asceticism in its severest form as an aid to liberation. About the year 80 A.D. this point led to the schism between the two main sects of this religion, which, however, agree upon fundamental principles—the Digambara, " those who are clothed with the vault of heaven "—that is, the naked—and the Svetambara, " those clothed in white."

Centres and objects of worship are numerous, as might be expected from the high importance attached to the divine beings. All Jain temples are placed by preference upon lofty mountains, such as Mount Abu, Mount Girnar, in Gujerat, etc. These buildings are adorned with rich decoration, and with a wealth of designs representing the different Jinas with their tokens—the ox, the ape, the fish, etc.

Everywhere the Jains enjoy the reputation of honourable and capable men ; their reliability and commercial industry has enabled them to acquire prosperity and often great wealth. Their benevolence is not without a somewhat comic side, as in some of the hospitals for animals which they have founded, and in their custom of wearing a respirator and carrying a small broom to avoid killing even insects involuntarily.

1199

AN INDIAN NAWAB WITH HIS RETAINERS SETTING OUT FOR THE CHASE

INDIA FROM ALEXANDER TO THE MOHAMMEDAN CONQUESTS

RECORDS OF THE ANCIENT DYNASTIES

FROM the earliest times the inexhaustible natural riches of the great plains of the Ganges have been a source of prosperity and of misfortune to India. In every age this district has proved a strong attraction to foreign peoples.

The great Aryan immigration was the first movement of the kind of which we hear, but by no means the last. Legends speak of the invasion of Assyrian rulers, of Ninus and Semiramis ; and though these may be purely mythical figures, yet those legends undoubtedly rest upon some historical foundation. Diodorus quotes the name of an Indian king, Stabrobates, "the lord of draught animals." It is true that this name appears rather Iranian than Indian. However, upon Assyrian monuments—as, for example, the obelisk of Salmanassar II., belonging to the year 842 B.C.—are representations of the Indian elephant and the rhinoceros, which were led before the victorious king, together with his prisoners. At a later period the Persian Cyrus is said to have undertaken a fruitless campaign to India, and upon his defeat to have retired to the same desert of Gedrosia through which Alexander retreated with his Macedonians. There is no **Persian & Assyrian Invaders** doubt that Darius subdued the races north of the Kabul River and west of the Indus, and explored the course of this latter stream about 510 B.C. Those tribes formed a special satrapy of Persia, and their contingents are said by Herodotus to have fought under Xerxes against the Greeks.

The Indian expedition of Alexander the Great is the earliest established chronological fact in the history of India. In the year 327 B.C. he started from Sogdiana and Bactria with about 100,000 warriors. Advancing along the Kabul River he was repeatedly obliged to wage desperate

conflicts with the bold mountain races and to destroy many of their fortified posts, but he arrived in the spring of the following year at the Indus frontier of the rich district of the Punjab.

The peoples there settled had changed but little since the time when their brothers had marched eastward into the Ganges district, had there founded states, and had struggled with the rising power of Brahmanism, with which they had eventually compromised. At that time the population was divided into a number of smaller tribes, the warrior caste holding the predominant position. Here Alexander met with a wholly unexpected resistance. Plutarch says of the Indians that the bravest and most warlike of them were the "mercenaries, who marched from one town to another defending each position to the last, and inflicting great **March of Alexander to India** loss upon Alexander." So intense was the animosity of the conqueror to this caste that, after promising unmolested retirement to the Kshatriya defenders of a town, he laid an ambush for them and destroyed them during their retreat. And "no less was the vexation caused him by the Indian philosophers, who reviled the kings who joined him and stirred up the free populations ; for this cause he hanged many of them."

Though the old bravery remained, the old tribal feuds had by no means died out, and Alexander was greatly helped by the strained relations subsisting between the Gandhara and their eastern neighbours, the Puru, the most important race in the Punjab. The Gandhara king, Taxiles, joined with other chiefs in doing homage to the invader, and supported Alexander's army with his own troops. In the spring of 326 the Greeks crossed the Indus near the modern Attok, and, after receiving the homage of the people, marched against the Puru prince, Porus. This monarch awaited the Greek advance on the eastern bank of the Hydaspes. The Kshatriya fought with the courage of despair, and the greater portion of the Puru warriors were left upon the field of battle. The aged and heroic prince upon his war elephant retreated only when he found his army destroyed, his two **Check to** sons slain, and himself seriously **Alexander's** wounded. Not only did the **Progress** Macedonians leave him his kingdom, but they added to it a number of conquered districts.

After a rest of thirty days Alexander advanced upon a fresh campaign; he had received trustworthy information concerning the peoples of the fruitful Ganges district, their populous towns and splendid capitals. However, his army failed him at the Hyphasis in the year 325, and the world-conqueror had come to the end of his victorious career. In boats and rafts he sailed down stream to the mouth of the Indus, and there divided his army into two parts. One of these returned to Persia by sea under Nearchus, while he himself was forced to retreat through the waterless desert of Gedrosia, under a burning August sun, and saved but a few remnants of the other half. Shortly afterward Alexander succumbed to his fatigues, his excesses, and the effects of the climate, in the year 323.

Alexander's Indian campaign had been of short duration, but the irresistible nature of his onset was equalled only by the importance of its consequences to the country; from the various tribes who had resisted the foreigners was formed the powerful Magadha kingdom. Among those who had been brought over to Alexander's side by the hope of personal advantage was an adventurer known as Chandragupta. A Sudra by birth—from his mother Mura, a low-caste woman, the royal family succeeding the Nanda was known as the Maurya dyn- **Results of** asty—his position upon the **the Greek** lower Ganges had become un- **Invasion** tenable for him by reason of his intrigues. The confusion caused by the advance of Alexander into the Punjab seemed to him a favourable occasion for the realisation of his ambitions, and he contrived to maintain connection with both of the two parties.

After the retreat and death of Alexander dissensions broke out among the Greek party remaining in the country; Porus was murdered by a Greek leader, Eudemus, and the Diadochi—the rivals in the succession to Alexander—began a series of quarrels over the division of the empire. Chandragupta then placed himself at the head of the Indian movement, secured predominance in the Punjab in 316 B.C., and in the following year gained possession of the Magadha kingdom, which, under his rule, extended, in 296 B.C., from the mouth of the Indus to the mouth of the Ganges. Seleucus Nicator found Magadha so powerful in 303 that he considered it prudent to secure the alliance of his eastern neighbour by giving him his daughter in marriage and renouncing his claim to Eastern Gedrosia, Aracho-sia, and Paropamisus. The excellent terms upon which these two princes lived is evidenced by their mutual despatch of ambassadors to the courts of Babylon and Pataliputra.

The first detailed description composed by an eye-witness of India and its people is that for which we have to thank the Greek Megasthenes. Only a few frag- **A Greek** ments remain to us of his work **Picture of** entitled "Indica"; but even **Early India** from these we may learn many important details of the conditions of life in the Magadha kingdom. From a Greek point of view the description is highly prepossessing. Megasthenes praises the population for their honesty, uprightness, strength, moderation, and peaceful inclinations, though they are ready to repel invaders by force of arms. The prosperity of the state rested upon agriculture; this occupation was considered so sacred that it was not to be interrupted even in time of war, and the farmer could peacefully till his land while bloody battles were proceeding in the immediate neighbourhood. The kingdom was defended by a numerous well-organised, and highly-trained warrior class—one of the seven classes, or castes, of the people, between which so sharp a line of demarcation existed that they could not even eat together. The land was common property, and one-fourth of the produce was paid to the State to meet government expenses. The Buddhist ascetics were then considered a subdivision of the Brahmans.

The grandson of Chandragupta, the son and successor of Bindusara, Asoka (269 to 232 B.C.), was the most powerful ruler of ancient India; his kingdom

SCENE IN MODERN PATNA: THE ANCIENT CAPITAL OF THE GREAT MAGADHA KINGDOM

The city of Patna was founded over 2,000 years ago, and was the capital of the ancient Magadha kingdom. Its most famous king was Asoka, the grandson of its founder, the convert of Buddha and the great protagonist of Buddhism.

extended over the greater half of the peninsula, and his influence far beyond these limits. After thousands of years no king has received such deep veneration as this Magadha ruler, whose name even to-day is deeply honoured from the shores of the Black Sea to the furthest islands of Eastern Asia, and from the shores of **The Greatest** the polar ice to the equator. It **of India's** is not to the greatness of his **Early Rulers** political power that he owes his fame, but to the gospel of human love, which he substituted for the teaching of Gautama.

The Magadha kingdom, with its capital of Pataliputra, or Patna, founded by Chandragupta in 315 B.C., was not destined to exist long; its most brilliant period is the reign of Asoka, the grandson of its founder, under whom it extended over all North and Central India, and the Northern Deccan. Less than a century after the accession of the great king, and 137 years after the founding of the Maurya dynasty, the last ruler, the tenth of the dynasty, was overthrown by his general, Brihadratha. The succeeding dynasty of the Shunga lasted only 112 years—178 to 66 B.C. ; the kingdom of the Kanwa, who succeeded, gradually diminished as the Scythians gained in power.

The natural conditions of the Asiatic Highlands impose a nomadic life upon the inhabitants. Mongolian, Turco-Tartar, and Scythian peoples were continually struggling for the possession of the grass steppes and pasture lands after the immigration of the Aryans. Race collided with race, and, like a wave driven before the stormy blast, confusion reached the uttermost limits of the country. An unusually strong upheaval of this nature had disturbed these nomadic tribes in the second century B.C.

The Mongolian tribe of the Hiung Nu—progenitors of the Huns—living east of the Oxus district in the steppes between Khiva and Khotan, had attacked the Tibetan Yue Tshi, who are, no doubt, to be identified with the Scythian Issedones upon their western frontier. This tribe they had **Struggle** defeated and forced to emigrate. **for the** The conquered nation then **Steppes** advanced upon the Græco-Bactrian kingdom, founded about 250 B.C. by Diodotus, a kingdom which had now advanced beyond the Indus into the Punjab. Before the onslaught of these invaders the predominance of the Greeks in Bactria Proper came to an end shortly after the year 140 B.C. A Scythian offshoot, the Sakæ, under the leadership of the king Maues in 100 B.C. and Azes in 70 B.C., turned toward the Indus, and, following the course of this river southward to Sindh, ultimately arrived at Gujerat.

Another tribe, the Kushana, followed the Kabul River into the Punjab under the prince Kozulo Kadphises. H re they destroyed the last remnants of the Greek supremacy in th year 25 B.C., and the following king, Huemo Kadphises, extended his power over the larger part of North-West India.

The most important ruler of this dynasty was the next king, Kanishka, whose kingdom extended from Yarkand and Khokand to Gujerat, and from Afghanistan as far as the Jumna. From his anointing, on March 15th, 78 A.D., dates the Saka Chronology. Nahapana is sometimes regarded as the founder of this kingdom. Upon their advance into India the Scythian hordes came into contact with Buddhism, and enthusiastically embraced this new religion. Like Asoka, Kani hka called a special council at Kashmir to reformulate the doctrine of Buddha. Supplementary exp'anations were then added to the three Pitakas of the Council of Patna. From this council it appears that even at that time the old doctrines of Buddhism had not been preserved in their original purity in Northern India, but had undergone considerable changes under the influence of Brahman and Dravidian ideas. At the same time, it is probable that the deities introduced by the Scythians were not entirely without influence upon the conclusions drawn up by the council of the mighty Scythian ruler.

Scythians Embrace Buddhism

The kingdom founded by Kadphises, like that of Chandragupta, reached its most flourishing period under the second successor of th founder, while its importance begins to decrease after the third centu y A.D., when other dynasties and states became more prominent. However, the history of India during the first millennium A.D. appears to the modern inquirer like a great mosaic picture, in which only individual or small related groups of stones are now recognisable. Coins, casual reports from travellers, especially Chinese, and inscriptions show us movement and counter movement, rise and decay among states both small and great, but in no case is it possible to reconstruct the history in detail. In many cases, we have only the most scanty sources of information, a few isolated names and events, while other states

History Seen in Patches

certainly existed and have left behind not a trace of their career.

The famous Maurya dynasty began to decay shortly after the time of Asoka, but the old splendour reappeared for a moment under the dynasty founded by Gupta in 290 A.D. This king, who had formerly been a vassal of Magadha, made himself independent, and under his grandson Chandragupta I. and his immediate successors the prosperity of the kingdom advanced so rapidly that it included all the territory between Nepal and the Narbada, between Cutch and the Ganges delta. During the sixth century, however, the prosperity of the realm was shattered by the attack of the "White Huns" in 515. These invaders were utterly defeated about 530 near Kahror by Yasodharma, a vassal of the Gupta kingdom. He himself assumed the supremacy and further extended the boundaries of the kingdom, though its history from this point is known to us only by a number of royal titles.

A kingdom of larger extent further to the south was also formed during the struggle with the White Huns, who had left their habitations on the Oxus after the year 435 A.D. and had invaded India. In the struggle against their king, Mihirakula, Yasodharma had been anticipated by another vassal of the Gupta kingdom, Sanapati Bhatarka, in 495. This prince was the founder of the Valabhi dynasty and kingdom, which attained a high measure of prosperity under his sixth successor, Dhruwasena. It included Gujerat, extending to the Narbada. The rulers at one time showed special favour to Buddhism, and at another transferred their preference to the Brahmans or to the Jains, who still count many adherents in the old Valabhi district. The canons of this latter doctrine were definitely formulated at the Council of Valabhi.

Invasion by the White Huns

To the second half of the first millennium A.D. belongs the development of an important Hindu kingdom in the Deccan, that of the Chalukya. This race is considered to have come from Northern India, and the founder of the dynasty, Jayasimha I., established himself about 500 A.D. in the Deccan at the expense of the Dravidian Pallavas. The new Hindu kingdom rapidly increased in size and power, and in the following millennium embraced the greater portion of the Deccan.

In the year 630 it was divided into an eastern and a western kingdom. The Chalukya prince, Vishnuwardhana, obtained the kingdom on the east coast, which included the coast line between the mouths of the Krishna and Godaveri. For a long period he was at war with the Chola on the south, and eventually succumbed to their attacks in 1060. The western Chalukya constituted a flourishing kingdom until the year 747, and were then conquered and reduced to great weakness by the Rashtrakuta. After a long period of depression, Tailapa Deva, the son of Vikramaditya IV., conquered the Rashtrakuta of Malkhed, and also Malava and the Chola, in 973, and became the founder of the later Chalukya dynasty, whose kingdom disappears towards the end of the twelfth century, when it was divided among a number of branch dynasties.

This period of political change and complete racial fusion had gradually obliterated the points of c o n t r a s t existing between the original races and peoples. The unity of the Indian people, Hinduism as it is in modern times, had been slowly formed from this former ethnical dualism. Its character is marked by two special peculiarities, religious belief and social institutions or castes.

During the time of Asoka we find great points of difference existing within the sphere of religious belief. The Brahman doctrine of the nature of the world and the Deity was a purely esoteric system of belief, the other castes, and particularly the great mass of the Sudra, believing in the power of demons. Within the Brahman school of thought a third faith had arisen—Buddhism. This had been at first tolerated by the Brahmans, as they had failed to recognise the points of opposition to their system which its teaching involved. It has largely to thank Asoka for the vigour of its advance. It

Extent of Buddhist Dominion

Early Indian Religions

MONUMENT OF AN ANCIENT KING
This temple, on the hill of Takt-i-Suliman, near Srinagar, is believed by the Brahmans to have been erected by Jaloka, the son of Asoka, who reigned about 220 B.C.

was preached throughout India by the royal missionaries, and was introduced into Ceylon immediately after the Council of Patna. It also penetrated far beyond the boundaries of its Indian birthplace. During the first century of our era it reached China, where it was recognised as the State religion during the fourth century. In 372 it was introduced from China into Korea, reaching, in the fourth and fifth centuries, Cochin China, Ava, Formosa, Mongolia, and Japan during the sixth century. At an even earlier period that form of it established in the Pali canon had passed from Ceylon to Burma in 450, and afterward became the dominant faith of Siam in 638 ; it was brought to Java from the Indian continent in the sixth or seventh century. We have a striking example of the powerful influence which its teaching of liberation and its humanitarianism exercised even upon uncivilised nations in the case of the Scythian Kanishka. At the Council of Kashmir the doctrines formulated at Patna were reasserted.

But even at that time in the North of India a schismatic movement had begun, due to the introduction of a barren system of dialectic, and also to the perversion of the doctrine and worship by the Dravidian belief in demons. At a later period the belief underwent so great a transformation among the Tartar and Mongolian peoples that the northern Buddhism of the present day is merely a frightful caricature of the pure Buddhist doctrine. The soul, to which Gautama had denied an objective existence, was reintroduced as an element of belief. The souls of the future Buddhas, the Bodhisattwas, especially those of the Manjusri and the Avalokitesvara, were accorded divine veneration, becoming personifications of the mystical religious knowledge and of the spirit of the Buddhist churches; while almighty power was

1205

typified in a third divinity, Vajradhara. Thus the heaven of this Buddhist sect was provided with a trinity, and to this were attributed the most abhorrent characteristics of the lower gods; and Shamanist customs and incantations, together with bloody sacrifices, were introduced into the worship. This incorporation of Indian Dravidian ideas and customs with Buddhism is chiefly the work of the Indian monk Asanga, who lived at Peshawar, in the Punjab, during the sixth century A.D. The resulting doctrine, called by the northern Buddhists the Great Chariot, to distinguish it from that which they contemptuously termed the Little Chariot—the earlier Buddhism—together with the conception that the spirit of the Churches became incarnate in one temporal head, eventually led to the development of Lamaism in the countries to the north of India.

Blending of Religious Beliefs

Next to the Asoka inscriptions the most important sources of information upon Indian Buddhism are the accounts of the Chinese Buddhists who made pilgrimages to the sacred shrines of their religion, especially the reports of Fa Hien (400–414) and of Hiuen Tsang (629–645). From Fa Hien we learn that in the whole of Nearer India the two doctrines, the Great Chariot, or Mahayana and the Little Chariot, or Hinayana, existed side by side, though at the same time the Brahman teaching counted numerous adherents. At the time of Hiuen Tsang, Kashmir was entirely given up to northern Buddhism, while the Little Chariot was predominant in Western and Southern India; in the Ganges district Buddhism suffered greatly from the competition of Brahmanism. Hiuen Tsang was present at the Council of Kanauj, where the doctrines of the northern sect were formulated. Buddha's birthplace was at that time in ruins, but his religion was even then firmly established in those countries in which he had himself been personally active. In the rest of India the old doctrine was still highly flourishing, and only in Kalinga had it been driven back by the rise of Brahmanism throughout that district.

Shortly after the pilgrimage of Hiuen Tsang serious misfortunes came upon the Buddhists. These are most probably to be explained by persecutions, which were at most purely local; Indian Buddhism collapsed more from internal weakness and diversity of growth than from the open hostility of other religions. Soon after the conclusion of the first millennium A.D.—about 1200—it had ceased to exist almost throughout India. The princes of Kashmir and Orissa supported it for a time; but about 1340 its last stronghold, Kashmir, also fell, and when the first Mohammedan kingdom of India was founded, nearly the whole population, with the exception of some few adherents in Bengal and Orissa, together with the Jains, acknowledged the gods of Hinduism.

THE STORY OF LATER HINDUISM

THOSE long-continued political disturbances which we have described proved unfavourable to the strengthening of religious conviction. Among the Brahmans a period of deep metaphysical speculation had been succeeded by a period of repose, while the lowest gods and the rudest forms of worship had been gradually accepted by the people at large. It was not until the eighth century that the reaction began. Tradition names Kumarila, who lived in the first half of that century, as at once the deadly enemy of the Buddhists and the reviver of the Brahman religion. But the first great reformer so called was probably Sankara Acharya. He was born in the Deccan in 788, was chiefly active in Northern India, and died in the Himalayas in 820. He revived the Vedanta philosophy and created the new popular Hindu religion. The esoteric portion of his doctrine acknowledges one unique supreme god, the Brahma Para Brahma, the creator and governor of the world, who is to be worshipped by mystical introspection; the elements of religious thought extant in the people as a whole he united and inspired in the figure of Siva. The great apostle of the worship of Vishnu, on the other hand, was Ramanuja, who lived in the first half of the twelfth century. His doctrines were preached by Kabir (1380–1420) in Bengal, and Chaitanya (born 1485) in Orissa. From the time of those reformers onward, Siva and Vishnu have been the corner-stones in the system of Hindu worship. In the popular religion Brahma retires into the background. The fundamental element in the philo-

Popular Hindu Religions

sophical conception of Vishnu is immanence, so that this kindly helping god becomes properly the god of incarnations, of Avatars. His being permeates all things, and hence he may appear in most different forms. Whenever gods or men are reduced to the extremities of need, Vishnu brings them help in one or another of his manifestations. Legend num-

A God of Many Incarnations bers many of these incarnations, in all twenty-two, but the generally accepted number is ten. In the first three the god appears as the fish, the tortoise, the boar; in the fourth, as the male lion; and in the later incarnations in human form, first as a dwarf; afterward, in the sixth, seventh, and eighth as Parasurama, as Ramatshandra, and as Krishna—that is, in forms taken from the heroic legends of Indian antiquity. Of these incarnations Krishna has become the most popular, the people recognising a national characteristic in the amusing tricks assigned to K r i s h n a by the legend. The representation of Buddha as the ninth incarnation of Vishnu no doubt belongs to a period when an attempt was made to unite Buddhism with the Hindu religion. A later theory also considers Buddha under this incarnation as an agent who tempts the wicked to scorn the Vedas and the laws of caste in order to secure their eventual destruction, and so to free the world of them. Finally, the last incarnation of Vishnu belongs to the future; at the end of the present age the god will appear as Kalki and found a new kingdom of purity.

In the conception of Siva, Brahman ideas of " darkness " meet the demon beliefs of the Dravidians. It is among the mountain tribes of the Himalaya that the figure of Siva, the " mountain spirit," originates, borrowed from Kiraata, a divinity given over to sensual pleasures, drinking, and dancing, and followed by a train of lower spirits. The fundamental conception of the Dravidian races of divinity as evil in nature is commingled with the Brahman ideas of darkness in the

BRAHMA WITH HIS CONSORT SARASWAT
In Indian mythology, after a god was personified, he was given a consort. Saraswati is the goddess of learning.

person of Siva, the god of destruction. As Rudra he personifies the destructive forces of nature; as Mahakala, the dissolving power of time; as Bahirava, he is the destroyer, or destruction as such; and as Bhuteswara, adorned with a garland of snakes and death's-heads, he is the supreme deity of all the demons of the Dravidian belief. Thus Siva is rather a Dravidian Vishnu than an Aryan creation; as, indeed, is manifested by the distribution of their several worships, the devotees of Siva being more numerous in the south and those of Vishnu in the north.

Thus in the northern districts of the Madras presidency the worshippers of Vishnu preponderate by a number varying from ten to one to four to one; while in the central districts of the presidency the number of adherents of each faith is almost equal. In the south, the worshippers of Siva surpass those of Vishnu by a number varying from four to one to sixty-seven to one. In the loftier conception of Siva, Brahman thought becomes more prominent; from death springs up fresh life, from destruction the new and more beautiful is restored. Thus the " destroyer " becomes a benefactor, Sada, Siva, Sankara, Sambhu; he personifies the reproductive forces of Nature, and as such is worshipped under the name Mahadeva, the great god; Isvara, the chief lord. No image is of more frequent occurrence in India than his symbol. Yet more definitely Brahman is the idea of the power of the sacrifice and of asceticism, and in this connection Siva appears in the form of the " Great Penitent," Mahayogin. Per-

Gods of the Hindu Pantheon sonification has not extended so far among the Hindu deities as it did among those of Greece and Rome; consequently, the Hindu pantheon is not composed of one great family of grandparents, fathers mothers and children. Brahma and Vishnu had no son, and only two sons exist loosely connected with Siva—known as Subrahmanya, or Skanda, the god of war, and Ganesa, the god of cunning

ORIGINAL TYPE OF THE CAR OF JUGGERNAUT
An ancient stone temple, built in imitation of the original type of the Car of Juggernaut, which, in many different forms, has so long figured and still figures in Hindu processions.

female side of his existence plays a more important part, owing to the fact that the god himself occupies a position of greater activity, and has absorbed a larger proportion of Dravidian deities who were essentially feminine. Each of the chief forms, under which Siva appears, has been intensified by the addition of a wife.

To the narrow circle of the supreme gods is added a number of superior beings, partly drawn from prehistoric legend, such, for instance, as the sacred singers of the Vedas, the Rishis, the Pandu brothers of the Bharata battles, and others drawn from the numerous band of lower deities worshipped by individual tribes. The Hindu heaven is spacious enough to contain any deity of the smallest importance or mystery, and includes stones and mountains, rivers and tanks, weeds and trees, useful and dangerous animals, spirits of the deceased, individual demons, and every variety of atmospherical phenomenon.

The wide differences—in fact, the oppositions—which characterise the manifestations of the divine element are reflected in the worship; the lowest fetish worship exists side by side with the veneration of the purer and higher powers of heaven. Hinduism is particularly distinguished from all monotheistic religion by the fact that its votaries do not constitute a Church, or, indeed, possess a universally accepted creed. A Hindu may worship Vishnu or Siva in one or other of their different forms, as also Ganesa, or one of the many Saktis; his choice depends entirely on the forms of prayer and incantation which he has received from his spiritual tutor and adviser, the Guru. These formulæ vary in the case of individual gods, and any god can be transformed into the patron deity of the Hindu who bears upon his forehead the sign of this special god. Under these circumstances common worship is impossible. Worship, like faith, is purely personal, and is composed of formulæ and spells of magic power, of purificatory rites and sacrifices which the worshipper offers to the gods or induces his priest to offer for him.

and success, who is invoked upon every necessity of daily life, and whose deformed, stumpy figure with the elephant's head is everywhere to be found.

Consorts are assigned to all the more important deities; yet the conception of wifehood has in this case been overshadowed by the personal attributes of the deity, might or power. According to Brahman philosophy, as soon as a supreme being becomes personal, his attributes coalesce into male and female divisions, the latter of which, contrary to our conceptions, is the more operative of the two. In the case of the less active gods, Brahma and Vishnu, this opposition is by no means so prominent. The consort of Brahma, Saraswati, is the goddess of learning and knowledge; while Lakshmi, the wife of Vishnu, is the goddess of supreme good and beauty. However, in the worship of Siva the

CELEBRATION OF THE FEAST OF GANESA AT BENARES

The image of Ganesa, the God of Success, who has the head of an elephant, may be seen in one of the vessels.

Worship of this kind, therefore, demands no great space or building where the congregation may meet together before their god ; the sanctuary proper is never more than a small shrine or an unimportant chapel with the symbol or image of the god. The temples, which have increased to enormous size, especially in Southern India, owe their dimensions to the addition of subordinate rooms such as pilgrim halls, side galleries, or tanks surrounded by steps.

Divine worship is carried on under three main different forms. Vishnu, of all the supreme gods, is most like man in shape. Consequently, his statue is tended like a human being by priests specially appointed for the purpose. The worship of his image may be compared to the playing of a small child with its doll, and the offerings made to him are those things which delight the Hindu

IDOLS IN A TEMPLE OF JUGGERNAUT

heart—rice, coraco, pastry, and flowers or decorations of pearls and precious stones. Siva, on the other hand, the lofty and often terrible god, dwells at heights unattainable by humanity. It is exceptional for his temple to contain a statue. However, worship is rendered everywhere to his symbol, the lingam, which is bathed in holy water, smeared with butter or covered with flowers. The worship of the third group of gods, Dravidian in origin, necessitates a bloody sacrifice. Goats are slaughtered before the altars, and the images and temple floor are sprinkled with the blood of the animal. Poorer people offer a cock to these, or to other lower divinities. The human sacrifices prevalent at an earlier period are now practically abolished, though survivals in a milder form occur even at the present day.

To these forms of daily worship, prayer and sacrifice, must be added the religious festivals which occur upon the days dedicated to numerous individual gods. Scarce a people or a religion can be found which celebrates so many pious festivals as the Hindus. Specially meritorious is a pilgrimage carried out under circumstances of unusual difficulty to the source of some holy stream—such as the Ganges or the Narbada—or to one of the great sanctuaries of Siva or Vishnu. As Brahmanism had already sowed the seed which was to develop into Hinduism and its religion, so upon the social side the Brahman caste regulations provided a practical basis for organisation. The caste system has been promoted by many influences and checked by many others. Even Buddhism showed a tendency to equalise and level the sharp barriers existing between the castes.

Religions and Caste System When at a later period Mohammedanism was introduced, its adherents declined to recognise caste, and many Hindu sects in imitation laid down the social equality of all men as a fundamental principle.

On the other side influences existed which furthered the persistence and multiplication of the castes. During antiquity the incorporation of members of foreign races must have produced subdivisions within the several castes; newcomers would be regarded with some contempt by the older members, and differences of this nature grew in course of time to absolute division. Within the warrior caste this process was constantly repeated; and in the same way deep schisms often arose within the Brahman caste, especially in the south. It was a common occurrence for a caste or some part of it to claim and acquire a higher position by means of falsified genealogies or other evidence, though without obtaining absolute recognition. Local separation of the members of one and the same caste naturally results in a multiplication of castes. The divided parts mistrust one another, especially on the point of purity of descent, and ultimately the sense of their common unity is lost, and that which had been one caste becomes two. Caste divisions of this nature are especially common among nomadic shepherd tribes or trading and agricultural castes, which are driven from time to time by outbreaks of famine to change their dwelling-place and to divide their forces; divisions may also be brought about by war and the shifting of political boundaries.

Increase of Caste Divisions A man who has arrived at high prosperity often attempts, and with success, to break away from his caste brothers, and to assume the name and the special customs of a higher caste. Religious divisions are also a frequent cause of caste disruption.

One of the commonest causes of caste increase is change of profession, which often results in a change of circumstances or social conditions. Under European supremacy it is a phenomenon of daily occurrence that the Hindu who enters the service of a white man thinks himself better than his former caste brothers, and new castes of coachmen, water-bringers, grass-cutters are constantly arising in this way. At the present time separation of profession is the main characteristic of the caste system, profession being invariably hereditary. This custom tends to preserve the purity of blood; no one who belongs to one caste may marry with the member of another caste. Among the higher castes mere contact defiles, or the breath of a low-born man even at a considerable distance. Eating with a member of another caste is absolutely forbidden. Stern precepts thus regulate individual behaviour. Castes have their own presidents and inspectors, appoint pecuniary fines or expulsion as punishment for grievous offences, and also watch over the welfare of the whole, by maintaining the rate of wages and the hours of labour, by organising strikes upon occasion, and by supporting the poor and maintaining widows and orphans. Almost as great

Position of Women in India an obstacle to national development as caste influence has been the low position held by the woman. Among the Aryans and also among the lower native tribes the woman was respected and honoured. During the epic period she was the central point of interest in the brilliant tournaments of the Kshatriya, and was the equal companion of man for the poets of the succeeding age, whereas now she is but a miserable creature, an oppressed and hard-worked slave.

Here, too, Brahman influence is to be traced in the repression of the woman. The Brahmans considered that the safest means of securing racial purity, the fundamental precept of their social organisation, was to limit the freedom of the woman to the closest possible regulations. The only task left to her was to present her husband with descendants of pure blood, and to this task everything that may raise the esteem in which woman is held was ruthlessly sacrificed. Contempt and stern compulsion accompany her from birth to death. Should a son be born to a Hindu the festival conch-shell is blown, and the friends bring congratulations and cheerful offerings; but when the child is a girl, the father looks upon the ground in embarrassment, while his friends offer him condolences instead of congratulations. Special festivals are arranged only in honour of boys and never of girls. After the birth of a son the mother remains unclean for three weeks, but for four weeks after the birth of a daughter. The boy is instructed by his spiritual tutor in accordance with his father's position ; the girl receives no instruction at all. Whatever she learns she learns from her mother, who knows nothing more than a few texts and prayers for the possession of a faithful husband, and a few curses against polygamy and infidelity.

At the age of seven to nine years old the girl is married to a boy of from twelve to fourteen years of age, or even to an old widower, without any attempt being made to consult her inclination ; often she meets her husband at the ceremony for the first time. After the ceremony is concluded she remains for the moment in her parents' house, to be transferred to her husband upon the first signs of puberty.

Practice of Child Marriage Mothers of thirteen and fourteen years of age are by no means exceptional in India. How unfavourable an influence must be exercised by early marriages of this kind upon the physical and intellectual welfare of the nation is sufficiently obvious. Upon her marriage a girl begins a miserable life of slavery within the prison of the woman's apartments ; she must cover her face before every male member of the family, she may not speak to her husband for days together, she may not call him by name or eat with him ; her existence is passed in deadly monotony. Before the period of the English supremacy the woman's ideal was to be cremated with her dead husband. These suttees are now a thing of the past, but the lot of the widow is almost worse than death by fire. The death of her husband is ascribed to her ill deeds committed in a former state of existence, and her remaining days are weighted down by hatred, severe penance, mortification, and the burden of the heaviest tasks.

Such is the lot of woman in those strata of society which profess to fulfil the ideal of Hindu existence. In reality, these severities are often tempered by mildness and affection. Among the poorer Hindus of the lower castes the wife is obliged to share the task of procuring sustenance for the family, and thus rises to be the equal of the man, and gains self-respect by the consciousness of being of some use in the world, though at the same time even in this class of society the wife is considered an inferior being.

In the subordination of civil society as arranged by themselves, the **Brahman Claims to Learning** Brahmans retained learning and science as their prerogative, and were themselves under the special protection of the goddess of learning, Saraswati, the chief wife of Brahma.

The Brahmans have left their special mark upon the whole religious, scientific, and artistic literature of India by the creation of a learned language, Sanscrit. The earliest hymns of the Vedas, dating perhaps from the third millennium B.C., are written in an ancient but highly-developed language ; from this the popular tongue gradually diverged as in course of time it was broken into different dialects. The priests considered it of high importance that the language in which they spoke to the gods should be higher and more perfect than the vulgar tongue. As they gradually rose above the common people to power and influence they transformed the language of religious thought and worship by a strictly logical and scientific procedure into the Samskrita, the " perfect language," as distinguished from the vulgar tongue or " original " language, the Prakrita. They can pride themselves upon including in their number the greatest grammarian of all time, Panini, who flourished apparently about the middle of the fourth century B.C. The contrast between the esoteric lore of the Brahmans and the more popular teaching of Buddha is expressed in the fact that Buddha and his disciples preached to the people in their own tongue in every country which they visited. It **Sacred Languages of India** was not until Buddhaghosha (410–430) had transcribed the commentaries of the great Buddhist Mahinda into the sacred books that this language, the Pali, became the sacred tongue of southern Buddhism. Brahman influence is also apparent in the formation of the southern branch in so far as this latter chose Sanscrit and not Pali for the purposes of religious writing.

The most important part of Brahman literature is concerned with religious questions. The Vedas are the foundation of all later religious and philosophical developments. Of the four collections of the Vedas, the Rig Veda belongs to a remote period of antiquity, parts of it undoubtedly dating from the third millennium B.C., while two later collections, the Sama and Yajur Vedas, belong to the period when the ritual had been formulated. The Vedas are collections of hymns and texts which the priest had to repeat during the performance of sacrifice. There were three orders of priests, and each of the three collections which we have mentioned was for the use of a particular order. To the Hohis, or highest of the three orders, belonged the Rig Veda, which they were required to recite in a loud voice. Next to them came the Udgahi priests ; they used the Sama Vedas, which they sang in chorus. The Yajur Vedas were for the use of the Adhwaryu priests, who were allowed only to mutter in a low voice. The fourth Veda, the Athar, contains magical formulæ against sickness and the attacks of enemies, together with extracts from the Rig Veda. The Brahmanas also belong to pre-Buddhist times ; these are prose compositions containing a substratum of historical truth interwoven with legendary narratives, and consist primarily of a description of the ritual employed in the great sacrifices as performed by the different priests. The Upanishads are works of a different character, and contain the results of Brahman philosophical speculation, together with religious and philosophical teaching upon the nature of the world and the world-soul from a monotheistic point of view. They are marked by a profundity of speculation and richness of thought which are evidence of the serious prosecution of the truth for its own sake. Wholly different are the Tantras, which belong to a much later period ; these are a collection of mystical religious precepts, prayers, and magic formulæ for the service of Siva in his more esoteric character and female personification.

Sacred Hymns of Hinduism

Hindu Religious Literature

Though these writings were composed at a later date than those previously mentioned, they are none the less considerably older than the extant version of the eighteen Puranas, with their eighteen appendices, amounting in all to about 400,000 double lines, and dealing with the legends of Vishnu. These were also included by the Brahmans among the "Scriptures of Antiquity," though their age cannot certainly be determined. In their present form they are a later edition, but their fundamental elements exist in part in the Mahabharata.

Together with religious writings the Sanscrit literature includes all other departments of Brahman thought. The historical is their weakest side. In this respect the Brahmans are in strong contrast to the Mohammedans, who were ever ready to write the histories of their age and their rulers ; and also to the Buddhists, in whose chronicles all important events affecting the monasteries were transmitted to later generations. These chronicles have entirely disappeared in the general ruin of Buddhist monasteries in India ; in Kashmir alone, where Buddhism maintained its ground to a late date, the historical sense has not entirely vanished with the monasteries. The book of the kings there written, the Rajatarangini, carries on the history of this district into the post-Buddhist period. In Ceylon, where Buddhism remains the dominant religion, the chronicles have been continued from the earliest period to the dissolution of the Singhalese kingdom and the British occupation.

Poverty in Historical Literature

Brahman thought was unequal to the task of scientific investigation into natural causes ; in this department inquiry was checked by the conception of a divine element, which penetrated the vegetable and animal worlds, and was even immanent in the stone. At the same time the duty of sacrifice gave them a certain knowledge of the parts of the body and their surgical treatment ; indeed, this was a good school for empirical surgery, in which native practitioners acquired a high degree of skill. Even such difficult operations as those for cataract, stone, reconstruction of the nose, removal of the fœtus, were successfully and skilfuly performed; and the medical treatises of the Brahmans make mention of no less than 127 different surgical instruments. At a later date, when the Arabs became acquainted with Indian surgery they gave full recognition to their superior knowledge. The treatment of internal disease rested upon purely empirical methods ; a large collection of specific remedies existed, and the chemists

THE DEVELOPMENT OF HINDU ARCHITECTURE

Hindu architecture became monumental after stone had been introduced as a material by Greek influence. It found its highest expression in religious buildings. In the earliest period, temples were hewn out of the living rock and left open. Then came an era of primitive shrines, such as the smaller picture on the right. The later ages rose to an oppressive wealth of decoration of which the pyramid tower at the top of the page is typical. The temples grew to immense size, tower being added to tower, while courts and ablution tanks were added for the use of worshippers.

employed in the preparation of medicines had acquired scientific knowledge of a number of important chemical bodies.

Astronomy was a science in closest connection with the priestly calling ; indeed, the primeval religion of the Aryans had consisted in prayers to those powers which were manifested in heavenly phenomena, in the movements of the sun,

Astronomy in Early India the planets, and the fixed stars. Thus even in the earlier Vedas the solar year is calculated with a high degree of accuracy, the year consisting of twelve months of thirty days, an intercalary month being added to every fifth year. Religious sacrifices and festivals were also performed on dates previously fixed by means of astronomical calculation. Still, in the period of Alexander the Great astronomy as an exact science was at a comparatively low level, and much help was given by foreigners who had made further advances in these studies. Towards the middle of the first century A.D., however, the science made a great advance, though it relapsed during the period of the formation of the great Mohammedan states. Only by individual princes—for example, those of Jaipur—has astronomy been studied in modern times with any degree of interest. Side by side with this science stands that of mathematics, for which the Brahmans showed high capacity. They developed independently the decimal system of notation, and the Arabs undoubtedly learnt very much from the mathematical studies of the Brahmans. The study of algebra reached its highest point in the person of Aryabhata —born in 476 A.D.

The sacred hymns of the Indians are admirable compositions ; of no less importance are the epic poems composed under Brahman influence, the Mahabharata and Ramayana. Epic materials have also been incorporated with the Brahmanas.

The Early Literature of India The development of the fable with characters from the animal world by the Indians is well known. One of the earliest collections of this nature, the Panchatantra, probably goes back to the second century B.C., and is, at any rate, earlier than the sixth century B.C., when it was translated into Persian ; in another form this collection enjoys greater popularity as the Hitopadesa. The Indian fable has made its way over the whole world, and Æsop's fables, together with the story of Reynard the Fox, are but an echo of Indian poetry. Of dramatic works the Indians have about sixty pieces of ancient date, almost all of which are comedies rather than tragedies.

Painting and sculpture hardly rose above the level of decorative art ; the breath of pure beauty observable in the representations of Buddha is due to Greek influence. Both arts were subordinated to architecture, and are characterised by the fantastical conjunction of human and animal forms, the multiplication of individual members of the body, by exaggeration of movement, a total lack of proportion, the desire to fill up space, and an ignorance of the laws of perspective.

Architecture produced more successful results and became monumental after stone had been introduced as a material by Greek influence. For more than a thousand years this art was confined to the erection of religious buildings ; palaces of any size or splendour do not appear until the rise of the Mohammedan kingdoms. Hinduism in religion and worship has left

Religion and Indian Architecture its stamp upon architectural style ; there being no congregations, the sanctuary proper is but a narrow space to contain the statue or the symbol of the god. But round about the sanctuary, for the convenience of the pilgrims who arrived to make their offerings and to perform their pious vows, were erected long corridors, great pillared halls, and large tanks approached by flights of steps for ablution.

In this way temples which enjoyed a high reputation and were visited by tens of thousands of pilgrims during the year often grew to enormous size. Especially is this true of the Dravidian temples, which are distinguished by their size and massiveness and by their towered gates with richly adorned pyramidal roofs rising in terraces. The buildings of the Chalukya kingdom are characterised by delicacy of decoration, and those of the Jains by an oppressive wealth of ornament. To the earlier Buddhist period belong the huge temples, hewn out of the natural rock and left open, of Karli, Adjanta, Ellora, and other places. Noticeable in Buddhist architecture are the numerous buildings containing relics of enormous size, which are especially common in Ceylon. The famous mosques belong to the later Mohammedan period.

THE MOHAMMEDAN SUPREMACY IN INDIA

THE DYNASTIES BEFORE THE MOGUL EMPIRE

HISTORIANS are accustomed to detail the events of the Mohammedan period of India according to the succession of dynasties. This long period, however, upon a more careful examination of its content, falls into two main divisions which end and begin respectively with the year 1526. The first of these periods is characterised by continual ferment and confusion. Hindus and Mohammedans are in a state of uninterrupted and fierce struggle, kingdoms are founded and overthrown, dynasties rise and fall. During **War** the second period, however, a **Between** greater stability prevails; the **Religions** opposition between the two peoples gradually disappears, and for more than three hundred years India is dominated by seventeen monarchs of one and the same dynasty, that of the Moguls in unbroken succession.

During the first period the supremacy passed through the hands of these dynasties :

Dynasty	Years of Reign
House of Ghazni	1001–1186
House of Ghor	1186–1206
The Slave Dynasty	1206–1290
House of Khilji	1290–1321
House of Tughlak	1321–1412
The Seiads	1416–1451
Bahlul Lodhi	1451–1526

The first of these dynasties was confined to the Punjab; that of the Ghors extended the Mohammedan supremacy over the whole lowland district of Northern India ; the Slave rulers advanced to the Vindhya Mountains, and the second of the Khilji rulers governed the whole of India almost to the southern point. The Mohammedan power in India then reached its first period of greatest prosperity. Then began the downfall ; the Tughlak rulers lost the

Deccan and Bengal, and under the two last dynasties the frontiers of the kingdom often extended but a few miles beyond the walls of the capital at Delhi.

This period of five hundred years was a time of severe oppression for the Hindus, a time of cruel murder and bitter struggle. As the lightning flash announces the oncoming storm, so also a warning movement preceded that convulsion which burst upon the unhappy land, the impulse to which was given by India herself. In the year 979 A.D., Jaipal, the Prince of Lahore, in the Punjab, considered that the growing power of his western neighbour, Nasir ed-din Sabuktegin, lord of Ghazni, threatened danger to himself. He sought to reduce this prince by means of an incursion into Afghanistan ; this effort resulted in a friendly settlement. When, however, Jaipal, supported by the princes of Delhi, Ajmir, and Kanauj, resumed the offensive in 988 he was utterly defeated at Lamgan. Turco-Afghan hordes marched through his country murdering and plundering ; Sabuktegin established himself at the confluence of the Kabul and the Indus, and thus got possession of the **Brother** obvious base for an invasion of **Against** India. He was succeeded by **Brother** his son Ismail, who, however, was dethroned in 998 by his brother, the famous Mahmud of Ghazni.

Mahmud (998–1030), also known as Bhut Shikan, or the Iconoclast, was the most important ruler of the Ghazni dynasty. From his Tartar father he had inherited tenacity and military prowess, while his mother, a Persian woman, had given him a feeling for higher civilisation. He was a clever, energetic, and enterprising man, and also a zealous patron of science and

1215

art. Magnificent mosques and palaces arose within his capital; famous poets and scholars were the adornment of his brilliant court—among them Firdusi, the chronologist el-Beruni and the universal historian Abu Ali el-Hussein, known as ibn-Sina or Avicenna. He founded and richly endowed a university in Ghazni; education was also supported **Scholar,** by a museum of natural history. **Warrior,** Splendid foundations were **and King** created by him to provide for men of high intellectual gifts. Although military operations almost constantly kept him away from his country, no internal disturbance took place during the thirty-three years of his reign.

As a matter of fact, Mahmud had no comprehensive political insight. His Indian operations were by no means undertaken with the object of conquering the magnificent country and furthering the development of its material resources, but were mere raids and forays for the purpose of capturing gold, jewels, and slaves. The Mohammedan world is inclined to consider Mahmud of Ghazni one of the greatest rulers of all time, and his co-religionists and contemporaries regard his military achievements as unequalled by those of any ruler; but this belief is founded not so much upon his military achievements as upon the religious fanaticism which overthrew the idols of hostile peoples and destroyed the temples of the un-believers. In this respect also they overestimate their hero and his intentions; the devastation of the Indian temples was undertaken by Mahmud chiefly with the object of plundering the enormous treasures which had been gathered there in the course of centuries.

The first years of the new ruler were occupied by struggles with his smaller

neighbours. Then he turned his face to India. In the year 1001 Jaipal was defeated for the second time and ended his life upon the funeral pyre, the Western Punjab, with Lahore, falling into the hands of the conqueror. This, Mahmud's first Indian campaign, was succeeded by sixteen furious raids upon Kashmir, Multan, the Ganges, and even the southern point of the peninsula of Gujerat; especially rich was the booty gained by the plunder of the temples of Nagarcot, Tanesar, Somnath and Mattra; yet the boundaries of the Ghazni kingdom extended no further than the Western Punjab. Its extension upon the west and north was far greater, for Mahmud found time in the intervals of these campaigns to conquer the countries **Plunder** of Ghor, or West Afghanistan, **from the** Transoxania and Persia. When **Shrines** Mahmud died in 1030 at the age of sixty-three he left a powerful kingdom behind him. His fourteen successors, however, were unable to preserve it unimpaired; the quarrels of pretenders to the throne, internal revolts, and the attacks of enemies upon the west and north (the Seljuks) resulted in eventual disruption. In 1150 Ghazni fell into the hands of the princes of Ghor; its numerous and magnificent buildings were utterly devastated, and only the tombs of Mahmud and of two other princes remained intact. The last two members of the Ghazni house, Moizz ed-dowlet Khusru Shah, 1152–1160, and Khusru Malik, 1160–1186, maintained an uncertain sovereignty in Lahore until this last remnant of the once powerful Ghazni kingdom was swept away by the princes of Ghor.

Since the date of its subjugation by Mahmud (1010), Western Afghanistan had played a subordinate part; but in 1163, when Ghiyas

GATE LOOTED BY MAHMUD OF GHAZNI

One of the famous sandalwood gates of the Hindu temple at Somnath which were carried off by Mahmud of Ghazni in 1024, but which, in 1842, were brought from Afghanistan to Delhi by Lord Ellenborough

A SCENE IN THE ANCIENT CITY OF LAHORE

The old city of Lahore was the capital of the Western Punjab. The period of its highest splendour was in the reign of Akbar, about the end of the sixteenth century. Its carpets, its silks and woollen fabrics, have long been noted.

ed-din Mohammed ibn-Sam ascended the throne, the power of Ghor rapidly increased. The new ruler appointed his brother, Moizz ed-din Ghori, as co-regent, an unusual proceeding in a Mohammedan state, and upon the death of Ghiyas (December 10th, 1203), the regent became sole ruler.

In 1186 the Ghaznavid monarch, Khusru Malik, was attacked, conquered, imprisoned, and ultimately murdered along with his sons in 1192. With their death, the dynasty of the Ghazni princes became extinct, and the Western Punjab, with its capital of Lahore, was added to the kingdom of Moizz ed-din. The acquisition of these territories advanced the boundaries of Ghor to the immediate neighbourhood of the Rajput states ; in particular, the kingdom reached the frontiers of Ajmir, which was governed by Pithora Rai. This state became the object of the next operations of Moizz ed-din. A battle was fought at Thanesvara within the narrow space between the desert and the mountains, and **Expansion of** between the streams of the **Mohammedan** Sarasvati and the Jumna **Power** Tarain, in which the Afghan cavalry was utterly defeated by the Indian warrior castes (1191). In the next year, however, Moizz ed-din conquered Ajmir and the Hindu states attached to that kingdom. Pithora Rai was captured in flight and slain. Shortly afterward Ajmir fell into the hands of the conqueror, who displayed even greater cruelty than

Mahmud of Ghazni, and massacred the inhabitants or sold them into slavery. He then advanced upon Delhi. This town, after its capture by his field-marshal, Kutb ed-din, in 1193, remained henceforward the chief centre of the Mohammedan power in Hindustan. In 1194 Moizz ed-din defeated the prince Jei Chendra, of **A Great** Benares and Kanauj, thus ex-**Mohammedan** tending his frontiers to the **Kingdom** borders of Behar. In the following years he was occupied with his brother in Merv, Kharizm, and Herat, until the death of the latter left him the sole ruler of the great kingdom. In the meantime, Kutb ed-din and the second in command, the Khilji chieftain, Mohammed ibn-Bachtyar, had subdued Behar (1194) and Upper Bengal (1195), Gwalior (1196), Gujerat and Oudh. The dynasty of Ghor then attained the zenith of its power. A defeat suffered by Moizz ed-din in the course of an undertaking against Kharizm in 1204 broke up the western part of the empire as far as the Punjab. The sultan, indeed, succeeded in suppressing the revolts of his governors in those provinces ; but he himself fell a victim on the Indus in 1206 to the dagger of an assassin.

Moizz ed-din Ghori left no male descendants, and had made no arrangements for the succession, the immediate consequence being great disorder. One of his nephews, Ghiyas ed-din Mahmud, was, indeed, set up as heir to the throne, but four of his governors in the chief provinces made themselves practically independent. In India the experienced general and governor, Kutb ed-din Ibak, immediately grasped the reins of government (June 26th), while civil war continued for nine years (1206–1215) in the other provinces of the empire, until their incorporation with Kharizm. When Kutb declared himself independent, Hindustan—in its narrower sense, the district watered by the Ganges and Jumna—which had hitherto been merely a province of the kingdoms of Ghazni and Ghor, became independent also. The new ruler had originally been a Turkish slave of Moizz ed-din. From a subordinate position he had gradually risen to become commander-in-chief and governor, a career that was typical of the rise of many rulers in succeeding times. Though many of these ascended the throne by hereditary right, yet the whole of this line of rulers has received the common name of the Slave Dynasty (1206–1290).

A Slave who became a King

Kutb had enjoyed his power for only four years when an accident at polo caused his death at Lahore in 1210. His character has been thus well described by a Mohammedan historian : " The kingdom was full of the honourable and cleansed from the rebellious ; his benevolence was as unceasing as his bloodshed." His religious zeal is evidenced at the present day by the splendid mosques and the proud minaret in Old Delhi, which still bears his name, Kutub Minar. His son, Aram Shah, was a weak-minded prince, and in the very year of his accession (1210) was defeated and apparently murdered by the revolted Shams ed-din Altamsh, who also had been a Turkish slave, and had found favour with Kutb, who had given him his daughter, Malikah Jihan, in marriage, and entrusted him with the governorship of Budaun. Altamsh did not immediately get the whole country into his power ; a brother-in-law of Kutb had made himself independent in Sindh, Multan, Bhakor, and Sivistan. The Punjab also revolted from him, and in Behar and Bengal in 1219 the governor, Hasan ed-din, of the family of the Khilji, laid claim to the territory. Before Altamsh was able to turn upon him, the invading armies of Genghis Khan burst upon Western Hindustan.

A Period of Revolt and War

This conqueror had utterly devastated the kingdom of Kharizm, and when the fugitive monarch, Jelal ed-din Mankburni, sought shelter in the Punjab, he was pursued by Genghis Khan, who devastated the provinces of Multan, Lahore, Peshawar and Malikpur (1221–1222). The fugitive prince of Kharizm had begged Altamsh for assistance ; the latter, however, was careful not to irritate the Mongol bands, and remained inactive in Delhi until at length the thunder clouds rolled away as rapidly as they had come. Thereupon Altamsh subjugated Bengal and Behar in 1225. In 1228 he got the Punjab and Sindh into his power, and also subdued the kingdom of Malwa in the south after a long struggle (1226–1232). Those Hindu states which had not appeared against him in open hostility were treated mildly and made dependent upon the kingdom under certain conditions. On the death of Altamsh (1236), his kingdom extended from the Indus to the Brahmaputra, and from the Himalaya to the Vindhya Mountains. His government was well organised, a spirit of vigorous intellectualism prevailed in his court, and the ruins of Ra Pithira, or Old Delhi, are evidence not only of the wealth, but also of the artistic taste of this highly-gifted monarch. A time of disturbance followed. In the next eleven years no less than five descendants of Altamsh sat upon the throne of Delhi. All the Slave princes were threatened by danger on three sides—from the Hindus, who were the more reluctant to submit to a foreign yoke in proportion to the pressure laid upon them by the fanatical Mohammedans ; from the generals and governors who were attracted by the success which had attended the rise of the first Slave princes ; and from the Mongols, whose devastating campaigns were continually and rapidly repeated after the first advance of Genghis Khan.

Records of the Slave Dynasty

The immediate successor of Altamsh was his second son, Feroz Shah Rukn ed-din, whose government (1236) came to an end after seven months in a palace revolution. His place was taken by his sister, Raziyah Begum, a woman admirably fitted for supreme power, and the only Mohammedan queen who reigned upon the throne of Hindustan (1236–1239). Her powerful and masculine intellect, her strength and sense of justice, her spirit and courage, enabled her to fulfil the heavy responsibilities of her position ; and she did not shrink from riding into battle upon her war elephant in male clothing. However, as says the historian, Mohammed Kasim Hindushah Firishtah (about 1600), her only fault was that she was a woman. Her love for an Abyssinian slave made her unpopular among the people, and a series of revolts began, which ended in her downfall. The country was further disturbed both by internal dissensions and by Mongol invasions during the short reigns of the two following rulers (Bahram Shah and Mastud, 1240–1246).

Protection from these dangers was not forthcoming until the reign of the serious and upright Nasir ed-din Mahmud Shah (1246–1266), the sixth son of Altamsh, who left almost the entire business of government to his brother-in-law and father-in-law, the Grand Vizir or Wazir, Ghiyas ed-din Balban. The Mongols were defeated in 1247. They had meanwhile overthrown the Abbassid kingdom of Bagdad. Hulagu confined his power to **A Mongol** Persia, and expressed his **Embassy** friendly intentions by sending **at Delhi** an embassy to the court of Delhi. The spirit of those times and the character of the all-powerful wazir can be inferred from the fact that on the entrance of that embassy the city gate of Delhi was decorated with the corpses of Hindu rebels. Of these there was indeed no lack. Hardly had a revolt been suppressed in one quarter when new disturbances broke out elsewhere, and it became necessary to crush the Hindus with measures of the sternest repression in the Jumna Doab, in Bandelkand, in Mewar, Malwa, Utsh, Karrak, and Manikpur successively.

On February 18th, 1266, Mahmud died, and was succeeded by the wazir Ghiyas ed-din Balban, who had previously been the virtual ruler of the empire. He, too, had begun his career as a Turcoman slave. He inflicted severe punishment upon the bands of rebels in the north-east and upon the Hindus of Mewat, Behar, and Bengal, and is said to have slaughtered 100,000 men during his conquest of the Rajputs of Mewar. Among military operations against foreign enemies, we must mention an incursion of the Mongols into the Punjab. They were defeated in two battles by the sultan's son, Mohammed

Khan, who was, however, himself slain. Balban was especially distinguished for his fanaticism ; and if Delhi under his rule gained a reputation as a centre of art and science, this is due not so much to the ruler as to the disturbances of the period, when every intellectually gifted man fled to the place of greatest security. The capital thus **A Centre** became a refuge for numbers **of Science** of deposed princes and high **and Art** dignitaries, and for a long time streets and squares were named after countries from which those rulers had been expelled. Balban died at the age of eighty in 1287. He was succeeded by his grandson, Moizz ed-din Kei Kobad, a youth of eighteen, who had inherited his father's sternness and cruelty without his strength. He plunged into a life of dissipation and soon became a tool in the hands of his wazir, Nizam ed-din. In 1290 he regained his freedom of action by poisoning the wazir, but shortly afterward was himself murdered in his palace by the new wazir, Jelal ed-din.

Even under the rule of Balban a transformation had been taking place. This monarch had abandoned the guiding principle of his predecessors of placing upstarts from among the slaves in the most important offices, and had given them to men of distinguished families of Afghan or Turco-Tartar origin. Of these families one of the most important had long been that of the Khilji, which had been settled partly in the district at the sources of the Amu Daria during the tenth century, while other branches had advanced to Afghanistan. There, while retaining their Turkish dialect, they had embraced Mohammedanism, and gradually adopted the Turkish civilisation.

Their tribal chieftain, Jelal ed-din Khilji, was seventy years of age when the above-mentioned palace revolution gave him the supreme power in Delhi in the year 1290. His dynastic title was Feroz Shah **A Prince** II. To secure his position he put **of Afghan** out of the way the son of Kei **Descent** Kobad, by name Gayomarth. In other respects, however, he was a man of mild character, well disposed to all men, moderate to weakness, even against his foes, a friend to the learned classes and the priests. He was soon forced to turn his attention to the Mongols. These he successfully overthrew in person in the Punjab (1292), while his nephew, Ala ed-din Mohammed, whom he

1219

had appointed governor of the Doab, between the Jumna and the Ganges, suppressed a revolt in Bundelkand and Malwa (1293). Ala ed-din then advanced, on his own responsibility, in 1294, with 6,000 horse, upon a mad raid through the pathless mountains and forests of the Vindhya Mountains, 700 miles southward. On the way he plundered the temple of Somnath. But the greatest booty he found in the well-watched fortress of Devagiri, which he captured by treachery. Before the southern princes were able to collect their troops, he had returned to his own province by another road. Under the pretext of asking pardon from his uncle for his independent action, he enticed the aged Feroz Shah into his own province, and there had him assassinated (July 19th, 1295).

Treachery that won a Throne

This deed is entirely characteristic of Ala ed-din Mohammed Shah I., who seized the government in 1296, after expelling his cousin, Ibrahim Shah I., the lawful successor. Cruel, false, and treacherous, with a ruthless tenacity which made him secure of his object in every undertaking, he was an entire contrast to his benevolent uncle. To his subjects he was invariably a terror, although he won general popularity by his splendid court, his liberality, and good order. Conspiracies and revolts of relations, wazirs and Hindus continued throughout the twenty years of his rule, but were always suppressed with fearful severity. The kingdom was also disturbed by three Mongol invasions. The first of these was vigorously repulsed in 1297, while the other two (1298 and 1303) created but a small impression, and were the last of their kind for a long period. It was not until 1310 that Mohammed Shah was able to realise the desires he had formed, on his incursion to Devagiri, of extending his power upon the south.

Rise and Fall of Kingdoms

The history of the Deccan during the first Mohammedan century of North India is occupied by struggles between the Rajputs and Dravidians, and by the foundation and disappearance of Aryan-Dravidian kingdoms in the Central Deccan, such as the Southern Mahratta kingdom, that of the Eastern Chalukya in Kalinga, and that of the Western Chalukya in the Northern Konkan. To these must be added from the thirteenth century the kingdoms of Ganpati and Bellala; further to the south that of Mysore, and the earlier kingdom of the Pandya, Chola, and Chera.

Mohammed Shah I. entrusted the conquest of the Deccan to his favourite, Malik Kasur, a former Hindu slave, who had renounced his religion, embraced Mohammedanism, and risen to the highest offices in the kingdom. He overran the Mahratta country in a rapid series of victories; the capital of the Bellala, Dvarasamudra, was captured and plundered (1311); the kingdoms of Chola and Pandya were subjugated; and in two years the whole of India, as far as Cape Comorin, was subject to the rule of Delhi. The conquered princes became tributary vassals, though only when they revolted or declined to pay tribute were they deposed and their territory incorporated with the empire.

This brilliant success in no way diminished the number of revolts which were called into existence by the universal unpopularity of the sultan and his favourite. Mohammed Shah contracted the vice of drunkenness, and after suffering from dropsy, died on December 19th, 1316, perhaps from poison given him by Kasur. The latter was, however, overthrown in the same year. After the eldest son, Shihab ed-din, or Omar Shah, had reigned for a short period, Mubarek Shah, the third son of Ala ed-din, ascended the throne on March 21st, 1317, and immediately secured his position by blinding his brother. Some statesmanlike regulations aroused general hopes of a good reign, but shortly afterward the young and voluptuous sultan left all State business to a Hindu renegade from the despised Parvari caste, by name Nasir ed-din Khusru Khan. On March 24th, 1321, the sultan, with all the members of his family, was murdered by his emir, who became sultan of Delhi, under the title of Khusru Shah. Unpopular as he had been while grand wazir, the animosity against him was raised to the highest point by the shameless outrages upon Hindu and Mohammedan religious feeling which he committed in giving the wives of the murdered sultan to his favourites in marriage, setting up images of the Hindu gods in the mosques, and so forth. Failing a legitimate heir to the throne, a revolt was headed by the Mohammedan governor of the Punjab, Ghiyis ed-din Tughlak; he attacked and slew the

A Line of Vicious Rulers

One of the splendid tombs of antiquity. The domed structure is the tomb proper, and the round tower in front is one of several such towers that stood around it. The monument stands about a mile from modern Delhi.

A general view of a scene of desolation and of the shadow of departed glory. The old capital of the Mogul Emperors stands in a barren plain, snakes and other reptiles finding harbour in the crevices of the ruins.

RUINS OF ANCIENT DELHI, THE CAPITAL OF THE MOGUL EMPERORS

unpopular ruler at Delhi, after a reign of little more than four months.

The supremacy of the Khilji had seen only three generations ; and of this period of thirty years two-thirds belong to the reign of Mohammed Shah I. Under his strong government the king-

Fusion of Hindu and Mohammedan

dom had undergone a great transformation. The heredi-tary enemies of the country, the Mongols, had been driven back for a long period, and, after their conversion to Mohammedanism, had retired to the Asiatic highlands. Many of those who had remained behind embraced Mohammedan-ism and took service in the army, though in 1311 they were all put to death in consequence of a conspiracy. The Khilji showed themselves largely tolerant in religious questions, and the frequent revolts of the Hindus were inspired rather by race-hatred than by religious oppression. Gradually the points of difference between the peoples began to disappear. The Mohammedans adopted many Hindu customs, and the latter also began to conform to those of the ruling race, as is proved by the case of the Hindu favourites, whose influence was constantly an important factor in the Indian history of that period. From this gradual fusion arose the commercial dialect of the country, Hindustani, or Urdu, the language of the camp. The different elements composing the vocabulary of this dialect indicate the extent of the racial fusion which then took place.

Under Mohammed Shah I., the kingdom had attained its greatest extent abroad. A decree issued in Delhi was valid as far as the southernmost point of India, and only a few Rajput princes continued to maintain their independence. The acquisitions, however, which had been made thus rapidly were never united by any firm bond of union, and even during

Mohammed's time that process of disruption began which made terribly rapid progress under the following dynasties.

Ghiyas ed-din Tughlak, the son of a Turcoman slave belonging to the sultan Balban, and of a Hindu mother, had risen by his own merits to the position of a governor in the Punjab, and showed himself no less capable during the short period of his sultanate (1321–1325). He directed his attention to the improvement of the country, to the security of the western frontier, to the recovery of those parts of the kingdom which had fallen away, and to the suppression of a rebellion at Tirhat. Upon his return from Tirhat he and his eldest son were killed by the collapse of a pavilion erected for a festival, a catastrophe which had perhaps been brought

The Rule of the Son of a Slave

about by his second son, Fakhr ed-din Junah Khan, who succeeded him in the government as Mohammed Tughlak (1325–1351). His government was marked by the infinite misery which he brought upon the country. He was a man of high intellectual capacity and had enjoyed an excellent education, was learned as few were, a distinguished author and a patron of learning ; at the same time he carefully observed all the precepts of his religion, was liberal to extravagance, and founded hospitals, alms-houses, and other benevolent institutions. But all these good qualities were entirely overshadowed by the madness which characterised his every political action. His eccentricity

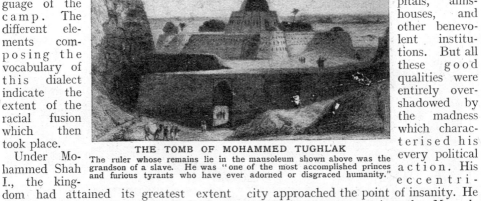

THE TOMB OF MOHAMMED TUGHLAK
The ruler whose remains lie in the mausoleum shown above was the grandson of a slave. He was "one of the most accomplished princes and furious tyrants who have ever adorned or disgraced humanity."

city approached the point of insanity. He led a huge army against the Mongols with the object of inducing them to buy his retreat for an enormous sum, before swords had been so much as drawn on either side (1327). One hundred thousand men were sent to China, across the Tibetan passes of the Himalayas, which were utterly impassable for an army on this scale ; they perished almost to the last man in ice and snow (1337). A third army was sent to Persia, but disbanded before operations began, and the soldiers dispersed plundering over their own country.

In 1339 a decree was suddenly issued to the effect that all the inhabitants of Delhi should emigrate to Devagiri, which was henceforward called Daulatabad ; twice they were allowed to return and twice was the emigration decree reissued, on one occasion during a fearful famine which carried off many thousands. The obligatory use of copper currency, instead of silver, brought financial disaster upon the country. At the monarch's pleasure man-hunting parties were organised throughout whole provinces ; his own subjects were the quarry, and they were killed like beasts. The taxes were raised to an impossible extent and extorted with such cruelty that large masses of the peasants fled to the forests and formed robber bands. The natural result was that revolts broke out in every direction against this mad ruler, and that the provinces strove their utmost to secure their independence. The empire, which had embraced almost the whole of India upon the accession of Mohammed ibn Tughlak, was diminished, at the time of his death in the fever swamps of Sindh, by the loss of Bengal, the coasts of Coromandel, Devagiri, Gujerat, Sindh, and all the southern provinces ; of twenty-three provinces scarce half were left to him. Mohammed ibn Tughlak, says Mountstuart

Miseries of a Mad Reign Elphinstone, "left behind him the reputation of one of the most accomplished princes and furious tyrants who have ever adorned or disgraced humanity." The damage which Mohammed had inflicted upon the empire could not be repaired even by the upright government of his successor, Feroz Shah III., who was born about 1300 and reigned from 1351 to 1388. His attempts to recover the re-

TIMUR, THE MONGOL INVADER

The Mongol prince and general whose warriors invaded India and captured Delhi in 1398.

volted provinces ended with the acquirement of only a nominal supremacy. The country was, however, largely benefited by his domestic policy, and he enabled the kingdom to recover its prosperity by a sensible and upright system of taxation, by the honesty of his judicial administration, by his regulations for military service, for which purpose he earmarked the revenue of certain districts, by the completion of useful public works such as irrigation, channels, reservoirs, dams, and canals—for instance, the great Jumna canal, which the British have recently restored in part —and by the foundation of schools and hospitals.

The last five representatives of the house of Tughlak followed one another in rapid succession after the death of Feroz. The period from 1388 to 1394 was one of incessant civil war ; ultimately the once powerful kingdom was reduced to a few districts in the immediate neighbourhood of Delhi. At this juncture the Mongols made an invasion in larger numbers and with greater ferocity than they had ever previously attempted. They were no longer the undisciplined hordes of Genghis Khan, but the well-drilled bands of Timur. While the last of the Tughlak princes, Mahmud Shah II.,

A Dynasty Becomes Extinct found a safe refuge in Gujerat, the grey-haired conqueror advanced to Delhi, which opened its gates to him upon a promise of protection (December 18th, 1398). But one of those "misunderstandings" which often occurred during the campaigns of Timur resulted in a fearful massacre of the population. The conqueror, laden with booty, returned to Samarkand in 1399, and Mahmud Tughlak then reappeared from his hiding-place. With his death, which closed an inglorious reign over an empire which was almost non-existent (February, 1412), the dynasty of Tughlak became extinct.

After the Afghan Daulat Khan Lodi had ruled for a short period (1413–1414), Khizr Khan, who had formerly been a

1223

governor and then a revolted emir of Multan, seized what was left of Hindustan. His own province speedily revolted, and his attempts to recover the Punjab before his death in 1421 proved fruitless, as did those of his three descendants, Mubarek Shah II., who ruled till January 28th, 1435, Mohammed Shah IV., until 1445, and

Remnant of an Empire Alim Shah; their dominion was practically confined to the town of Delhi. These rulers—Shiites, reputed to be of the house of Ali—are collectively known as the dynasty of the Seiads (1414–1415). Under Alim Shah the boundaries of the empire were distant about an English mile from the capital, and at no time did they extend further than a distance of twelve miles.

In the year 1451 Bahlul Lodi, who ruled over the Punjab in Lahore, took possession of the town of Delhi. He died in 1488, but his son Nizam Iskander, who died in 1517, succeeded in extending the boundaries of the kingdom westward beyond Lahore and eastward beyond Benares. However, under the grandson of Bahlul, Ibrahim (1517–1526), a proud and tyrannical ruler, serious revolts broke out. The eastern districts were entirely separated from the kingdom, and his governors in the Punjab rose against him and called in his powerful neighbour Babar from Kabul to their assistance. These shocks put an end to the feeble rule of the Lodi princes, and a new period of brilliant prosperity then began for Hindustan.

Mohammed ibn Tughlak had undergone the mortification of seeing the southern province with its capital of Daulatabad secede during his lifetime, in spite of the partiality he had shown for it. The Viceroy of the district, Hasan Gangu, a Shiite Afghan, declared himself independent in 1347, transferred the capital to Kulbarga on the west of Haidarabad, and became the founder of the Bahmani dynasty. His frontiers extended from Berar to Kistna, and from the Sea of Bengal to that of

Secession of a Province Arabia; to this empire were added Konkan, Khandesh, and Gujerat by his great-grandson, Ala ed-din Ahmed Shah II. (1435–1457). The Bahmani dynasty attained its greatest power at the outset of the reign of Mahmud Shah II. (1482–1518), who ruled over the whole of the Deccan north of Mysore. This rapid rise was followed by an equally rapid fall; by the revolts of the provincial governors, the

north was broken into five minor Mohammedan states between 1484 and 1512, while in the south the kingdom of Bijanagar rapidly rose to high prosperity.

Of these revolted governors the first was Fatteh Ullah Imad Shah, of Berar, a converted Hindu of Bijanagar; his empire, which was founded in 1484, continued until 1568, when it was absorbed by Akbar. In rapid succession followed the governors, Adil Shah of Bijapur, whose empire lasted from 1489 to 1686, and Nizam Shah of Ahmednagar, from 1490 to 1595. Two years later the governor, Barid Shah, of Bedar, made himself independent, his dynasty lasting until 1609, as did finally in 1512 Kutb Shah of Golconda, his dynasty lasting until 1687. None of these petty Mohammedan states were able to secure predominance, and after a varying period of prosperity all were re-absorbed into that Delhi kingdom from which they had originated.

In this rivalry of the Mohammedan Deccan states the greatest success was attained by a Hindu state in the south, the kingdom of Bijanagar, which was founded in 1326 by two fugitives from the

Short Life of a Hindu State low caste tribe of the shepherds, though it was unable to attain any considerable importance in view of the overwhelming strength of its Mohammedan neighbours on the north. The first dynasty of Bijanagar became extinct in 1479; the second, a side branch of Narasinha, founded about 1450, rapidly rose to prosperity. The Chola had long since lost their former importance, and the power of the Pandya was then broken. At the end of the fifteenth century Bijanagar was indisputably the predominant Hindu power in the south of the peninsula; the petty Hindu states from Kattak, or Cuttack, to Travancore were dependent upon this kingdom. At the beginning of the sixteenth century it was in possession of the whole of the east coast.

The importance of this great Hindu state and of its artistic rulers is evidenced by the magnificent ruins which are now buried in the jungles of Bellary. Bijanagar was under no apprehension of attack from the Mohammedan states in the north, which held one another in check until the middle of the sixteenth century; when, however, they joined in common action against the Hindu state, the latter inevitably collapsed.

MOHAM-
MEDAN
INDIA—II

PROFESSOR
EMIL
SCHMIDT

THE MOGUL EMPIRE
IN THE HEIGHT OF ITS POWER AND GLORY

THE series of the so-called Mogul or Mongol emperors begins with one of the most brilliant and attractive figures in the whole of Asiatic history, the sultan Mohammed Babar, who earned the title of "the Lion." In fact, his race was Turk rather than Mongol. He was the son of Omar—four generations removed from Timur in direct descent —one of the small princes in the magnificent mountain country of Ferghana in the upper Oxus district, his mother being a Mongolian woman. On the death of his father in 1493 he found himself surrounded by danger on every side. In 1494 he took up the reins of government in person, and the following ten years of his life are full of battles and dangers, bold exploits and severe defeats, brilliant successes and heavy losses ; now he was on the throne of a great kingdom, and again an almost **The First** abandoned fugitive in the **Mogul** inaccessible gorges of his **Emperor** native mountains ; his adventures during that period would themselves suffice to make up the most eventful life that man could possibly desire. At the end of 1504 he was obliged to yield before the superior power of the Uzbegs, and, giving up all hope of territory from that side of the Hindu Kush, he fled across the mountains to Afghanistan. Two months later (1505) he had taken Kabul, which remained henceforward in his possession, but even then his life was a constant series of desperate efforts and remarkable changes of fortune. At the same time his personality is most human, and for that reason most attractive ; he was a man of pure and deep feeling, his love for his mother and his relations was as remarkable as his kindness to his conquered foes. The depth and the warmth of these sympathies he has expressed with every elaboration of style in Turkish and Persian songs, and his memoirs, written in East Turkish, reflect

an extraordinary character and certainly form one of the most remarkable works in the literary history of any nation.

The defeats which Babar had suffered in Transoxania and Bactria induced him to turn his gaze to India ; he was able to claim the Punjab as the heir of Timur, and the invitation of Daulat Khan, the **Babar** rebel Lodi governor in Lahore, **Invades** gave him both a pretext and a **India** motive for attacking the neighbouring kingdom in 1524. He found no difficulty in overcoming such resistance as was offered in the Punjab. He was especially superior to his opponents in artillery, and crossed the Sutlej at the end of 1525. At Panipat, between the Sutlej and the Jumna, ten miles north of Delhi, Ibrahim Lodi took up a position on April 21st, 1526, with a force whose numbers are reported as 100,000 soldiers and 1,000 war elephants to oppose the 25,000 warriors of Babar, and lost both his throne and his life. Delhi and Agra, which had been the residence of the Hindustan Afghans from 1503 to 1504, immediately fell into the hands of the conqueror, who divided the rich imperial treasures among his warriors, including the famous diamond, the Kohinoor, "the mountain of light." This jewel, which had previously been taken from the Khilji Mohammed Shah, now fell to the lot of Humayun, the son of Babar ; after many vicissitudes, it ultimately became the **Spoils of** glory of the British Crown **a Great** jewels. The victory of Panipat **Victory** gave Babar possession of North India to the north-east of Delhi and also the small strip of land along the Jumna as far as Agra.

Shortly before the end of 1526 he was also master of the district south of the Jumna as far as Gwalior. He was now opposed by the Hindus. The princes of Rajputana, led by Rana Sanka, marched against him with a powerful army to a point seven miles west of Agra. A battle was fought at Fattehpur Sikri, or Kanwa, on March 16th, 1527, where the Rajputs were utterly defeated; Mewar fell into the hands of the conqueror, who immediately proceeded to reorganise the administration of his new acquisitions. How the Rajputs could fight with the courage of despair, Babar was to learn in the following year when he besieged one of the princes who had escaped from the battle of Sikri, in his fortress of Chanderi. As his troops were storming the walls on the second day the enemies set fire to the town with their wives and children after the manner of the old Kshatriyas, and then rushed upon the foe with drawn swords; the bodyguard of the prince killed one another, each man struggling for the first blow. In 1529 Mahmud Lodi, a brother of Ibrahim, was expelled from Oudh, the southern part of Behar on the right bank of the Ganges was captured, and the Raja Nasir ed-din Nasrat Shah of Bengal was forced to lay down his arms.

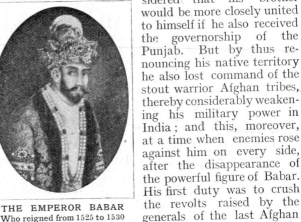

THE EMPEROR BABAR
Who reigned from 1525 to 1530

In three years Babar had conquered in a series of brilliant victories the whole of the plains of Northern India as far as Bengal. Now, however, his health, which had been undermined by the extraordinary privations of his life, began to fail. On December 26, 1530, Babar the Lion died before he had reached the age of fifty; his last words to his son and heir, Humayun, were "Do not kill your brothers, but watch over them tenderly."

BABAR REVIEWING HIS TROOPS
This great Mogul emperor was a man of strong character, wide tolerance and warm sympathy.

Babar was succeeded by his son, Nasir ed-din Mohammed Humayun, who was born in 1507; he, however, had not inherited either his father's iron will or his pertinacity, much less his firm principles,

his high ambition, his warmth of heart, and his unchanging fidelity. Babar had intended Humayun to become ruler of the kingdom, and had destined the governorship of Kabul and Kandahar for his second son, Kamran. Humayun considered that his brother would be more closely united to himself if he also received the governorship of the Punjab. But by thus renouncing his native territory he also lost command of the stout warrior Afghan tribes, thereby considerably weakening his military power in India; and this, moreover, at a time when enemies rose against him on every side, after the disappearance of the powerful figure of Babar. His first duty was to crush the revolts raised by the generals of the last Afghan rulers, and then to punish Bahadur Shah, the Raja of Gujerat, for his intrigues. Bahadur was expelled by the emperor in person; hardly, however, had he returned to his capital to deal with an outbreak in Bengal, when the troops he had left in Gujerat were driven out and he was even obliged to renounce his claims to Malwa.

Meanwhile, upon the east, in Bengal, a heavy storm was threatening the Mogul power. Ferid Khan, a Mohammedan of high talent, who apparently belonged to the Afghan royal family of the Suri, had assumed the leadership of all the enemies of the Mogul rule, and was speedily able to secure the possession of Bihar. Humayun was forced to besiege the strong fortress of Chunar, an operation which detained him for many months at Benares; meanwhile, Bengal was conquered by his cunning opponent, who had in the meantime adopted the title of Sher, or "Lion," Shah. He then defeated the descendant of Timur in two battles in 1539 and 1540; after these misfortunes Humayun was obliged to abandon his kingdom and take refuge with his brother Kamran at Lahore.

Here, however, his position was equally unstable. Kamran was terror-stricken at the unexpected success of Sher Shah, with whom he concluded peace, the price being the cession of the Punjab, while the deposed emperor was forced to spend a period of disappointment, terrible privation, and constant flight in Rajputana; on October 14th, 1542, his son Akbar was born to him in the desert of Thar at the time of his greatest need. In 1543 he turned to Kandahar. Sher Shah, who had been master of the whole Ganges district since his decisive

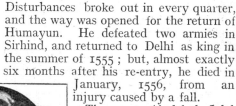

THE EMPEROR HUMAYUN
Who reigned from 1530 to 1556.

victories over Humayun, now turned his attention to the improvement of domestic organisation, and did his best to foster the progress of agriculture, to provide for public peace and security, to improve communication by making long roads, and to reorganise the bureaucracy, the taxation system, and the administration of justice. He met with a violent death on May 22nd, 1545, during the siege of a hostile fortress.

His successor, Selim Shah, attempted to continue his father's administration; his short reign (1545-1553) was largely occupied with the suppression of different revolts. Under the government of his incompetent or vicious successors, Feroz (1553), Mohammed (1553), Ibrahim (1554) and Secander (1555), the empire rapidly fell to pieces.

Disturbances broke out in every quarter, and the way was opened for the return of Humayun. He defeated two armies in Sirhind, and returned to Delhi as king in the summer of 1555; but, almost exactly six months after his re-entry, he died in January, 1556, from an injury caused by a fall.

The young Abul-fath Jelal ed-din Akbar, who ascended the throne of Hindustan on February 23rd, 1556, had been entrusted by his father to the care of the faithful Turcoman Bairam Khan, whose bold action had in the meantime inflicted a total defeat upon the armies of the Lodis, under Hemu, on November 5th, 1556, in a second battle of Panipat, and had advanced beyond Delhi and Agra. State administration was for four years carried on also by Bairam, who made himself unpopular by his jealousy for the prestige of his title of Khan Babu, or royal father. However, during a hunting expedition Akbar suddenly returned to the capital, and in 1560 issued a decree to the effect that he would henceforward take all State business under his own control. Bairam in surprise attempted a revolt, but, lacking adherents, was obliged to submit to the young emperor, who received him with all honour. In the same year Bairam was murdered by one of his enemies when on the point of making a pilgrimage to Mecca. Akbar was then obliged to confront the task of uniting into one powerful kingdom the whole of Hindustan, which had been devasted by centuries of war and was broken into hundreds of petty principalities. Before

THE TOMB OF HUMAYUN AT DELHI
Humayun was the son of the great emperor Babar, and the father of Akbar; he possessed none of the great qualities of these rulers, and his reign was interrupted by a usurpation while he was a fugitive.

his time every conqueror had been the ruler of a foreign land, whence he had drawn suppor and strength; Akbar at the age of eighteen was obliged to rely upon himself alone. The character of Babar had been inherited by his grandson; Akbar possessed his grandfather's intellectual powers, his iron will, and his great heart with all its kindness and benevolence.

TOMB OF ONE OF HUMAYUN'S MINISTERS AT DELHI

Humayun's Minister, Tardi Beg Khan, was Governor of Delhi when it was taken by the army of the Lodis, during the minority of Akbar, Humayun's son and successor. He was beheaded, and is said to be buried in this tomb, although this is questioned.

The son of a fugitive emperor, born in the desert, brought up in nominal confinement, he had known the bitter side of life from his youth up. Fortune had given him a powerful frame, which he trained to support the extremities of exertion. Physical exercise was with him a passion; he was devoted to the chase, and especially to the fierce excitement of catching the wild horse or elephant or slaying the dangerous tiger. On one occasion, when it was necessary to persuade the Raja of Jodpur to abandon his intention of forcing the widow of his deceased son to mount the funeral pyre, Akbar rode 220 miles in two days. In battle he displayed the utmost bravery. He led his troops in person during the dangerous part of a campaign, leaving to his generals the lighter task of finishing the war. In every victory he displayed humanity to the conquered, and decisively opposed any exhibition of cruelty. Free from all those prejudices which separate society and create dissension, tolerant to men of other beliefs, impartial to men of other races,

Greatest Mogul Emperor

whether Hindu or Dravidian, he was a man obviously marked out to weld the conflicting elements of his kingdom into a strong and prosperous whole.

In all seriousness he devoted himself to the work of peace. Moderate in all pleasures, needing but little sleep, and accustomed to divide his time with the utmost accuracy, he found leisure to devote himself to science and art after the completion of his State duties. The famous personages and scholars who adorned his capital were at the same time his friends; every Thursday evening a circle of these was collected for intellectual conversation and philosophical discussion. His closest friends were two highly talented brothers, Shekh Feizi and Abul Fazl, the sons of a learned free - thinker. The elder of these was a famous scholar in Hindu literature; with his help, and under his direction, Akbar had the most important of the Sanscrit works translated into Persian. Fazl, on the other hand, who was an especially close friend of Akbar, was a general, a statesman, and an organiser, and to his activity Akbar's kingdom largely owed the solidarity of its internal organisation. For a long period in India, central authority of any description had been unknown, and the years of Humayun's exile had proved unfavourable to the introduction of a stricter system among the Moguls. Under Akbar, also, many generals, after he had reduced a revolted province to order, attempted to keep back the taxes payable to Delhi and to claim the district for themselves, as in Oudh, Malwa, and Bengal. Some were overthrown with a strong hand, others the emperor was able to bring over to himself by clemency. His own brother, Mohammed Hakim, who attempted to occupy the Punjab in 1566, was expelled from the country. Akbar won over the Rajput princes by a display

A Royal Mæcenas

1228

of kindness and concession. He himself married the two princesses of Ambur and Marwar; and his eldest son, Selim or Jehangir, had a princess of Ambur to wife. The princes of those petty states who were treated by the powerful Emperor as equals gladly forgot that their ruler was an alien both by his creed and his **A Policy that Made Friends** descent, and considered it an honour to occupy high positions in Akbar's army. Of these one only, the Prince of Chitor, maintained an attitude of hostility. His capital was besieged by Akbar in 1567, and the bold commander was shot by the emperor himself upon the walls. After the old Rajput custom, the garrison first killed their wives and children, and then themselves; but the prince, who had fled, still declined to submit. At a later period, during Akbar's lifetime, the son of this expelled monarch succeeded in founding a new state in Udipur, whose rulers still pride themselves upon the fact that their genealogy remains unstained by any trace of connection with the emperors of Delhi.

The remnants of the last Mohammedan dynasty offered a yet more vigorous resistance to Akbar than the Rajputs had done. In 1559 these "Afghans" were expelled from Oudh and from Malwa. In Gujerat various pretenders to the throne were quarrelling among themselves. One of these called in Akbar to his help. Akbar adopted a strong policy and expelled the combatants collectively, reconstituting the country as a province in the years 1572–1573. In 1581 fresh disturbances broke out, and an indecisive struggle was continued for a long period, until peace was at last secured by the death of Mozaffar III. Habib in 1593. Similarly, much time elapsed before Bengal was definitely conquered. With the exception of the son of Suleiman Khan Kararani, Daud Shah, who had surrendered in 1576, neither the Mogul generals nor the Afghans were definitely pacified until 1592. Orissa also fell into the power of the ruler of Delhi. In Sindh military adventurers, stragglers left from the Afghan supremacy, also continued their intrigues; they were subdued in 1592, and pacified by the gift of high positions within the empire. A short campaign against Prince Yusuf of Kashmir, belonging to the Chak dynasty, led, in 1586–1587, to the incorporation of that province, which now became a favourite summer residence of the Mogul emperors. A harder struggle was fought with the Yusufzai tribes of the almost inaccessible Kafiristan. Even at the present day the configuration of their district has enabled them to maintain **Extent of Akbar's Empire** their independence. The last conquest in the extreme west was Kandahar, which had been already occupied by Humayun, but had been retaken by the Persians in the first years of Akbar's reign. The emperor recovered this district in 1593–1594.

Thus the kingdom of Akbar extended from Afghanistan to Orissa, and from the Himalaya to the Narbada. Beyond this latter boundary the confusion was no less

THE TOMB OF SHER SHAH AT SASSERAM
Ferid Khan, a Mohammedan of high talent, deposed Humayun, the son and successor of Babar, and, under the name of Sher Shah, reigned until his own death in 1545.

than it had previously been in the north. Akbar was called in by one of the disputants, and his army quickly got possession of Berar, with its capital, Ellichpur. An unexpected resistance was, however, encountered before Ahmednagar, the central point of the Mohammedan states of the Deccan. A woman of unusually strong

IN THE ROYAL CITY OF AKBAR: RUINS OF AGRA

These different views of the ruins of the palaces of Fattepur Sikri at Agra represent buildings dating from
1556–1605, and are thus monuments of the days of Akbar, perhaps the greatest emperor who ever held sway in India.

character, by name Chand Bibi, who was regent for her great-nephew Bahadur Nizam Shah during his minority, united several of the disputing princes before the approaching danger. When besieged in her capital, she succeeded in inspiring her adherents with so fierce a spirit of resistance that the Moguls were glad, in 1596, to conclude peace on the condition that the claims of Chand Bibi to Berar should be given up. Fresh disturbances led to a renewed invasion of the Moguls. After an indecisive battle, Akbar himself, in 1599, took command of his troops, but Ahmednagar resisted until Chand Bibi was murdered by her own troops in 1600. Akbar now set up a nominal ruler, Morteda II., whose dynasty came to an end in 1637 under Shah Jehan.

The last years of Akbar's life were troubled by severe domestic misfortunes and by his sorrow at the death of his friend, Abul Fazl. The Prince Selim, or Jehangir, who had been appointed his successor, was addicted to the pleasures of drink and opium, and was of a passionate temper and a deadly enemy of his father's chief counsellor, Fazl. Akbar had appointed his son as Viceroy of Ajmir; that, however, proved insufficient to satisfy his ambition. He aimed at the possession of the Imperial throne, took possession of the State treasury, assumed the title of King, and occupied Oudh and Behar. Akbar, however, treated him kindly, and Selim made a show of submission, but revenged himself by a cowardly stroke. He incited one of the petty princes in Bandelkand to murder Abul Fazl by treachery in 1602. This calamity was followed by the loss of Danial, the third prince, who succumbed to an attack of dropsy on April 8, 1605, a disease which had already carried off his elder brother Murad in 1599. By these heavy blows of adversity the emperor's

INDIA'S GREATEST NATIVE EMPEROR
The strength and wisdom of Akbar, his measures of reform, his equal treatment of all races and creeds, and the nobility of his character amply justify his title of " The Great."

powers were broken. After a long illness his condition rapidly grew worse, and on October 15, 1605, died Akbar, the greatest ruler who ever sat upon the throne of India.

Under the rule of every Mohammedan conqueror who had invaded India from the north-west, the land had suffered by reason of the twofold antagonisms of religion and race. The Hindus, who formed the majority of the population, were considered of no account; they repaid with their hatred the pride and scorn with which they were treated, and prosperity for India was obviously impossible under such rulers. History has justly honoured Akbar with the title of " The Great," but the honour is due less to his military successes, great as they were, than to the insight with which he furthered the internal welfare of the country and to the manner in which he softened the antagonisms of religion and race by gradually obliterating the most salient differences.

At the time of his accession Akbar was a good Mohammedan, and in 1576 he projected a pilgrimage to Mecca to the grave of the Prophet. Shortly afterwards, however, the interchange of philosophical ideas at his evening gatherings was stimulated by the presence not only of the Mohammedan mollah, but also of the learned Brahman priest, and even the Roman missionary. No one of these religions appeared to him as absolutely true. Under their influence, and in the conversation of his confidential friends that conception of the jealous God which Mohammed had borrowed from Moses was transformed to the idea of a Supreme Being watching over all men with equal love ; while the doctrine of the God incarnate became in him a pure belief, high above all material conceptions, to the effect that the Deity can be apprehended not through any revelation in human

1231

shape, but only by the exercise of reason and understanding; that He is to be served not by all kinds of ceremonies and empty forms, but by moral purity of life. If weak humanity desires material symbols of the Supreme Being, then the **Religious** loftiest to be found are the **Views** sun, the constellations, or the **of Akbar** fire. Akbar's conception of God left no place for ritual precepts, for prophets or priests. To support his dignity, however, in the eyes of the people, he issued decrees announcing that the king was the head of the Church, his formula of confession being as follows: "There is no God but God, and Akbar is his Caliph." At the same time, he never employed force to impose his religious views upon dissentients. These views, indeed, were too abstract and profound for popular consumption, and were unintelligible except to a small circle of philosophical adherents. Toleration was a fundamental principle in his character, and he was never anxious to convert the members of other religions. Every Mussulman was allowed the free exercise of his religious principles; but, on the other hand, such principles were binding upon no one else. Thus he was opposed to those many forms of compulsion which Mohammedanism lays upon public and private life. Akbar did nothing to further the study of the language of the Koran, and showed no preference for Arabic names such as Mohammed, or Ahmed. The formula of greeting, " Peace be with you," was replaced by the sentence, " God is great."

Thus to a certain extent Akbar curtailed the privileges of his native religion. At the same time he removed many of the disabilities which burdened the Hindus and their religious practices. The poll-

JEHANGIR, THE SON OF AKBAR
Mohammed Selim, the son whom Akbar appointed his successor, and who reigned as Jehangir, or "the World's Conqueror," undid much of his father's work and proved a most unworthy successor.

tax upon unbelievers, a source of deep dissatisfaction among the Hindus, and the dues levied upon pilgrims during their journeys, were entirely remitted. Their religious practice was interfered with only in cases where the pronouncements of the priests were totally opposed to the principles of humanity—as, for instance, in cases of trial by ordeal, child marriage, compulsory death upon the funeral pyre, and the enforced celibacy of widows. The civil rights of Mohammedans and Hindus in no way differed, and every position in the state, high or low, was open to members of either religion.

In the domestic administration of his great kingdom Akbar displayed the greatest foresight and energy. Former rulers had been accustomed to collect the taxes by methods inconceivably disastrous. The revenues of important districts had been appropriated to individual generals, who were allowed to extort the utmost possible amount from the inhabitants, and for this purpose large masses of troops were permanently kept on foot. The Imperial taxes properly so-called were collected by an army of officials who were accessible to influence of every kind, and appropriated no small portion of the receipts as they passed through their hands. Sher Shah had been the only ruler to introduce a more equitable system of taxation, and the regulations made during his short reign were swept away in the confusion of the following years. In its main details Akbar's system was a further development and extension of that **Reform** of Sher Shah. He was fortunate **of** in finding in the Hindu Todar **Taxation** Mal a man of stainless probity and admirable capacity for organisation, who did more than anyone else to renovate the administration and especially the taxation system. Todar Mal was the first official to make a complete and exact census of the whole territory north of the Narbada. A survey was taken of all arable land, an accurate estimate made of the products, and taxation was calculated from these data, the amount being established at one-third of the average produce for the previous ten years. Undue severity was thus avoided as far as possible, and in times of famine or failure of the crops taxes were remi'ted and advances made of gold or corn. Sher Shah had, indeed, appointed only one-fourth of the yearly produce as the unit of taxation. Akbar's regulations, however, proved more advantageous both for the State and for the agricultural population, as speculation was prevented by a strict system of bookkeeping and by the possibility of appeal to higher officials; while the fixity of the regulations enabled one-half of the revenue officials to be dispensed with. All officials, officers and soldiers included, received a fixed and liberal salary, and were no longer obliged to depend upon incomes drawn legally or illegally from subsidiary sources.

Trade and commerce were promoted, a strong impulse in this direction being given by the introduction of a uniform currency. The hundreds of different currencies which had hitherto been in circulation were called in, and an Imperial coinage was struck in the mints of every province. The empire was divided into fifteen provinces —three of which were in the Deccan — and these were governed under Imperial direction by governors, who were invested with civil and military powers. The administration of justice as far as the Mohammedans were concerned, lay in the hands of a supreme judge, Mir-i-adl, whose decision was final. He was assisted by a Kasi, who undertook preliminary investigations and produced the legal codes bearing upon the case. The Hindus were judged by Brahmans with a legal training. The organisation of the army was,

SIR THOMAS ROE
Ambassador from King James I. to the Court of the Emperor of India between 1615 and 1618.

comparatively speaking, less vigorous and consistent. On the whole, however, the internal organisation of the state, which was laid down to the smallest detail in the ordinances of Akbar, marked a great step in advance, and proved a blessing to the country, which enjoyed a prosperity hitherto unexampled.

When Akbar died, he had appointed as his successor his son, Nur-ed-din Mohammed Selim, who took the Imperial title of Jehangir—that is, World Conqueror. In previous years he had often been a sore anxiety to his father, chiefly by reason of his drunkenness and furious temper, which provoked him to acts of cruelty and frequently broke out during his reign. When his chief general, Mahabat Khan, had married his daughter without previously announcing his intention, he had the newly-wed couple flogged with thorns, and deprived the general of the dowry and of his private possessions. After the revolt of his son Khusru, he had 700 of his adherents impaled along the road before the gates of Lahore, while his son was conducted in chains upon an elephant through this avenue.

Sir Thomas Roe made some stay at the Indian court from 1615 to 1618 as the ambassador of King James I., and has given us an account of the brilliancy of the court life, of the Emperor's love for splendour and display, of his kindness to Europeans, numbers of whom came to his court, of his tolerance to other religions and especially to Christianity. Two pearls in his crown were considered by him as representing the heads of Christ and Mary, and two of his nephews were allowed to embrace Christianity. The same ambassador, however, also relates accounts of banquets that lasted through the night, of which drunkenness was the invariable result, the orgies being led by the Emperor himself. At the same time the Emperor attempted to play the part of a stern Mohammedan; when during the day one

SHAH JEHAN I.
Who reigned from 1627 to 1668

RUINS OF OLD AGRA WITH THE TAJ MAHAL IN THE DISTANCE

of the initiated allowed a thoughtless reference to one of these orgies to escape him, the Emperor asked seriously who had been guilty of such an offence against the law, and inflicted so severe a bastinado upon those who had been his guests at the forbidden entertainment that one of them died. Of the general condition of the empire, Roe gives a description **An English** which compares unfavourably **Ambassador** with the state of affairs under **in India** Akbar. He praises the financial arrangements, but characterises the administration as loose, the officials as tyrannical and corrupt, and mentions the decay of militarism in the army, the backbone of which was now the Rajput and Afghan contingents. "The time will come," he wrote, "when all in these kingdoms will be in great combustion." However, the reign of Jehangir passed without any great collapse ; Akbar's institutions had been too firmly rooted to fall by the maladministration of one government only.

Jehangir had been already, in 1586, married at an early age to a daughter of Rai Singh of Amber ; a Persian woman, however, by name Nur Jehan,. "The Light of the World," gained complete influence over him. Her grandfather had occupied an important position in Teheran ; her father, however, was so impoverished that the future Empress upon her birth was exposed in the street, where a rich merchant found her, adopted her, and called in her own mother as foster nurse. Nur Jehan received a good education, and by her wit and beauty she won the heart of Jehangir, then Crown Prince, whose attentions became so pressing that upon Akbar's advice a young Persian was given her hand together with an estate in Bengal. Hardly had Jehangir been a year upon the throne when he made proposals to the husband, which the latter answered by killing the emissaries who brought them and was himself cut to pieces in consequence. In 1611 Nur Jehan gave way, and henceforward her influence over the Emperor was complete. As long as her excellent father, who had been made wazir of the empire, was alive, she exerted that influence for good ; Jehangir restrained his drunkenness, and ceased those inhumanities which had stained the imperial title in previous years.

A war with Udipur was rapidly brought to an end in 1614 by the second prince, Shihab ed-din Mohammed Khurram, or Shah Jehan ; his bold action also brought the war against the Mohammedan Deccan, which had opened unfavour- **Power of** ably, to a successful conclusion. **a Royal** The Emperor hated his eldest **Consort** son, Khusru, who died in imprisonment in 1622 ; but the second was both his favourite and that of the Empress, who gave him her niece in marriage; he was publicly appointed successor to the throne. Nur Jehan, however, had consulted no one's pleasure but her own after her father's death, and she now gave her favour to the youngest of the princes, who was closely connected with herself by his marriage with her daughter.

When his father fell seriously ill, Shah Jehan, who had been placed in the background, marched upon Delhi, but was obliged to retreat to Telingana and Bengal, where he was defeated by Mahabat Khan. The latter then suddenly incurred the displeasure of the Empress, and with a view of anticipating any act of hostility on her part, he seized the persons both of the Emperor and the Empress. They succeeded in escaping from imprisonment and in concluding a compact with Mahabat which provided that he should once more take the field against Shah Jehan ; but the general was afraid of the later vengeance of Nur Jehan and deserted to the prince. There was no further collision between the two parties; the Emperor died in 1627, while upon a journey from Kashmir to Lahore. Nur Jehan was treated with respect by the successor to the throne ; she survived her husband by nineteen years, which she spent in dignified seclusion, winning universal affection by her benevolence.

Shah Jehan I., after the slaying of his brother Shahriyar, who had formed an alliance with two sons of Danial, and the suppression of a revolt in Bandelkand, put an end to the short rule of his nephew Dawarbakhsh, the son of Khusru, and found himself in undisputed possession of the throne in 1628 ; under his rule the Mogul Empire attained the zenith of its wealth and prosperity. The Emperor displayed great perspicacity in the choice of capable officials, exercised a strong personal supervision over the administration, introduced many improvements, and in the course of twenty years extended the system of territorial occupation and taxation which had been created by Todar Mal to the districts on

NUR MAHAL, "LIGHT OF THE HAREM"
The Taj Mahal, the richest mausoleum in all the world, was built by the Emperor Jehan in memory of his wife, Nur Mahal, who is here represented in an engraving from Dapper's "Asia," published in 1672.

the far side of the Narbada. Though he is described as reserved and exclusive before his accession, he afterwards appeared kindly, courteous, and paternally benevolent to his subjects, and succeeded in winning over those Mohammedans whom Akbar had formerly affronted, without losing the good-will of the Hindus.

The best evidences for the brilliance of this period are the numberless private and public buildings which arose under the government, not only in the two capitals of Delhi and Agra, but also in all other important centres in the kingdom, even in places which are now abandoned. Under Shah Jehan, Delhi was as entirely transformed as Rome under Nero or Paris under Napoleon III. The palaces of his period, with their reception rooms, their marble pillared halls, their courts and private rooms, together with the mosques and mausoleums, marked the zenith of Mohammedan art in India. Of these monuments the most famous is the mausoleum called the Taj Mahal, "Crown of the Harem," the grave of Nur Mahal, "Light of the Harem," a favourite consort of the Emperor.

Opposite the imperial fortress of Agar rises this building, one of the most delicate constructions in the world, its outline clear and simple as crystal, built in marble of wonderfully delicate colouring, with decorations which bear the mark of a fine and restrained taste. Symbolical of court life and splendour was the famous peacock throne, a decoration for the imperial chair, made of diamonds, emeralds, rubies, sapphires, and other jewels, which represented in its form and colours a peacock's tail fully extended. The traveller Jean Baptiste Tavernier (1605–1689), a jeweller by profession, estimates the collective value of the precious stones employed in this ornament

1235

at £160,500,000. Though such works of architecture and artistic skill must have cost enormous sums, and though many lives were sacrificed in the numerous wars of Shah Jehan, the people enjoyed high prosperity under his rule ; and the Emperor, surpassing in this respect the Medicean Lorenzo " the Magnificent,"

A Period of High Prosperity left a vast quantity of State treasures behind him at his death. Those disturbances which had broken out in the Deccan in 1629 were speedily suppressed by the Emperor, who forced the State of Ahmednagar to conclude a peace favourable to Delhi. After a fresh outbreak four years later this province was incorporated with the Delhi kingdom in 1637, and Abdallah of Golconda, an ally of Ahmednagar, was forced to pay tribute. Affairs beyond the Afghan frontier ran a less favourable course. The Uzbegs, who had penetrated into Kabul, were at first driven back from Balkh ; in 1637, Kandahar, which had been occupied by the Persians, was also reconquered. When, however, the Uzbegs renewed their advance in 1618, the Emperor's third son, Mohammed Muhi ed-din Aurangzib, was forced to retreat during the winter of 1647 over the Hindu Kush, and lost the greater part of his army in consequence ; Kandahar was reconquered by the Persians in 1648, and remained in their possession, Shah Jehan definitely renouncing the idea of reconquest in 1653. In the year 1655 fresh compli-cations broke out in the Deccan. Au-rangzib, who had been sent there as gov-ernor, made a treacherous incursion into Golconda ; the capital was stormed, plun-dered, and burnt, and in 1656 Abdal-lah was forced to conclude peace under conditions of great severity. Bijapur was

then surprised on some trivial pretext. But before the subjugation of this district could be carried out, Aurangzib received news of his father's sudden illness, and was obliged, in 1657, to conclude a treaty with Moham-med of Bijapur, on conditions favourable to the latter, in order that he might march northward with his army.

Shah Jehan had been prostrated by uræmia. Four of the Emperor's sons, who were equally brave but different in position and character, immediately appeared as rival claimants for the throne. Dara Shu-koh, born in 1613, was a man of Akbar's type, talented, liberal, well disposed to the Hindus, and friendly to Europeans and Christians. His manner, however, was against him ; he was passionate, often insolent, had no personal following, and was especially unpopular among the Mohammedans. The second prince, Shoja, was a drunkard, and was hated by the Mohammedans for his leanings to the Shiite doctrine. On the other hand, Aurangzib was a fanatical Mohammedan,

Rivals for the Throne beloved for his affability, with a halo of glory from his recent exploits, but ambitious and treacherous. The fourth prince, Murad Baksh was of a noble disposition. but was intellectually of no account, and was marked by a leaning to sensuality. Aurangzib, who was at the head of a well-tried army, allowed his two elder brothers to destroy one another, while he gained over the short-sighted Murad by exaggerated praise and flattery, and by promises of the succes-sion. With the help of Murad he then de-feated Dara, who had emerged vic-torious from the struggle with Shoja, and invited the unsuspi-cious man, under a pre-text of cele-brating his victory, to a feast. On the next morning Murad awoke from his

CAVALRY SOLDIER OF THE MOGUL EMPIRE

debauch to find himself a prisoner in the citadel of Delhi, but was afterwards transferred to the State prison of Gwalior. Meanwhile Shah Jehan I. had recovered and again assumed the government. As, however, he favoured his eldest son, Aurangzib made him prisoner in 1658, and kept him under honourable restraint in the citadel of Agra until his death in 1666. Shortly afterwards Aurangzib succeeded in seizing the person of his eldest brother ; and in 1659 Dara was condemned to death on a pretended charge of apostasy from the Mohammedan faith. Murad met the same fate in 1661, as a result of an attempt to escape from his imprisonment. Shoja fled to Bengal, and perished in 1660 in the malarial district of Arakan, while his sons were kept prisoners until their death in Gwalior. Thus no rival except Aurangzib remained to the successor of Shah Jehan among his brothers or relations.

EMPEROR AURANGZIB
The third of four brothers, he obtained the throne by treachery in 1658. His oppression hastened the disruption of the empire.

Aurangzib, or Alamgir I. (1658–1707) had inherited none of the great talents of Babar and Akbar, neither their statesmanlike foresight nor their humanitarian disposition, and still less that religious tolerance which had made the people prosperous and the state powerful. Those

Religious Bigot on the Throne famous monarchs had been creative minds, capable of finding the right measures to deal with every difficulty; whereas Aurangzib was a narrow-minded monarch who displayed his good qualities invariably at the wrong time and in the wrong place. His actions were dictated, not by love for his subjects, but by ambition, mistrust, and religious fanaticism. No one was ever better able to conceal his true feelings ; no means were too contemptible or too arbitrary which could enable him to reach the goal of his ambition. His effort was to promote the one true faith of the Sunnah, and his ambition was to be the type of a true Mohammedan monarch. To his co-religionists he displayed a leniency which was a direct invitation to mismanagement, intrigue, and disobedience, while his hand was heavy upon the hated Hindus who formed the majority of his subjects. He was well read, especially in the Koran, and his private life was marked by moderation and simplicity; his public appearances were characterised by an excess of splendour and by painful observance of every religious duty.

At the beginning of his reign the Emperor seemed inclined to model his behaviour upon the religious tolerance of his ancestor Akbar, and married his son Mohammed Muazzem to the daughter of a Hindu prince. But after a short interval his fanatical hostility to the alien religion made itself felt, and discord between the Emperor and his subjects was the natural result. The tax upon all saleable articles, which was only $2\frac{1}{2}$ per cent. for the Mohammedans, was doubled by Aurangzib in the case of the Hindus ; the hated poll-tax, which Akbar had abolished, was again imposed upon the Hindus, and while preference was shown to the Mohammedans, a double burden was laid upon the Hindus, who were also excluded from the administration and the army. In 1679 Aurangzib pulled down the three most sacred temples of the Hindus in Multan, Mattra, and Benares, and erected a mosque upon the site of the temple of Krishna. In Rajputana alone the Brahman sanctuaries which were devastated by his fanaticism might be counted by hundreds ; the priests were killed, and the temple treasures transferred to Delhi.

The Satnami, a purist Hindu sect on the left bank of the Sutlej, were the first to revolt against such oppression—a movement that was repressed only with difficulty. Their example was followed by the Rajput tribes, and the struggle was carried on with varying success and

Revolts Against Oppression with such bitter cruelty that from that date the Rajputs have displayed a deadly hatred to every later ruler of Delhi. Aurangzib's own son, Mohammed Akbar, the fourth prince, enraged at the inhumanity of the imperial orders given him, joined the side of the oppressed, but was forced to flee ; he first turned to the Mahrattas, who were at war with his father, and afterwards retired to Persia, where he died a few years later, in 1706.

MOHAM-
MEDAN
INDIA—III

PROFESSOR
EMIL
SCHMIDT

THE DISRUPTION OF THE EMPIRE

AURANGZIB had successfully led the army of Shah Jehan against the Mohammedan states in the Deccan, and had inflicted severe losses upon Golconda and Bijapur ; but independent rulers were still powerful in that district. In the meantime a third state founded upon the basis of national religion had grown from insignificance to a power more formidable and coherent than any of the surrounding states This was the Mahratta people, a powerful tribe inhabiting the district of Maharashtra and the country to the south ; from this centre **Rise of** capable men had for many years **Mahratta** migrated to the neighbouring **Power** Mohammedan principalities, especially to Bijapur, where they had occupied important positions in the administration and in the army.

The head of one of these immigrant families, Shaj Bhonsla, had distinguished himself as a cavalry commander, and had been rewarded by the Mohammedan Sultan of Bijapur with the military fief of Puna, and later with a more important district in the modern Mysore. From his marriage with a woman of noble birth sprang the founder of the Mahratta power, Sivaji. National and religious sentiment inspired him with deep hatred for Mohammedanism. During his father's absence in the southern parts of his fief the son, with the help of the troops under his command and other Mahratta allies, seized a number of the strongest fortresses, confiscated the taxes, and plundered the lands of his lord far beyond the boundaries of his own district ; his father was then suspected of complicity and imprisoned by the Sultan of Bijapur. Sivaji entered into negotiations with the powerful Emperor of Delhi, Shah Jehan, and the fear of this mighty monarch procured the release of his father ; the son then displayed even greater insolence to Bijapur. Ultimately an army was sent against him under Afzal Khan ; Sivaji induced the hostile commander to agree to a friendly meeting before the fort of Pratapgad, where he murdered him ; the army was

taken by surprise and massacred in large part. Ultimately he secured the cession of additional territory and the right of maintaining a standing army of 50,000 infantry and 7,000 cavalry.

These events had taken place shortly before the accession of Aurangzib. The upstart now directed his attacks against the empire itself. His marauding bands advanced into the neighbourhood of Surat in 1662, and an imperial army retreated before him with disgraceful cowardice. A new expedition succeeded in inducing Sivaji to appear in person at the court of the powerful emperor. Aurangzib received the Hindu with almost contemptuous coldness, and proposed to confine him forcibly in Delhi. However, the cunning Mahratta and his son made good their escape, hidden in two provision-hampers. In the year 1674 Sivaji declared himself independent, assumed the title of Maharaja, and proceeded to strike a coinage in his own name. Had Aurangzib been a far-seeing ruler, he could not have failed to recognise a dangerous enemy in **The Mogul** this rising Hindu state on the **Dominion** south-west, and would have **Threatened** entered into an alliance with the Mohammedan states in the Deccan. But he hoped to secure sole supremacy over all the Mohammedans in India, and even furthered the action of the new Hindu prince when he extorted from Bijapur one-fourth of its yearly revenue as payment for freedom from his plundering raids—a tax known as the Chaut, which was later, under the name of the "Mahratta tribute," to be a source of sore vexation to the Delhi kingdom.

The far-seeing opponent of the two Mohammedan powers availed himself of his favourable position to develop, as far as possible, the internal organisation of his Hindu state. Society was organised on the pattern supplied by the old traditions ; the Brahmans, whose intellectual training and higher education had been developed through long generations, were the born counsellors of the nation ; the chief official posts were occupied by members of noble Brahman families, who saw that the administration was properly conducted. The warriors, claiming a doubtful descent from the old Kshatriya immigrants, formed the professional officers and the well-drilled and regularly-paid army. The agricultural class, or Kunbis, not only devoted their energies to production, but also formed the guerilla reserve of the standing army. All remaining handicraftsmen or merchants formed collectively the fourth class, or Shankardachi.

The state thus organised had a small standing army of cavalry armed with lances which, when necessity arose, could be rapidly increased to a powerful force by calling out the militia, and could as rapidly be reduced to its former dimensions. The Mahratta army was a highly mobile force, and consequently far superior to the slow-moving troops of the Mogul Emperor; when these latter appeared in overwhelming strength, they found only peaceful peasants tilling their fields; the moment the enemy divided his forces he was immediately attacked unawares.

Mobile Mahratta Army Plundering raids and the Mahratta tribute imposed upon neighbouring states brought in a large yearly revenue; the booty taken in war was in part divided among the soldiers and the militia, but the larger part was distributed among the small and almost impregnable mountain fortresses which guarded the State chest and military treasuries. Thus Sivaji had at his command a strong army ever ready for action and self-supporting, while the expensive and incapable troops of his opponent devoured the riches of the empire; the Mahrattas had no lack of recruits to swell their ranks, while the Mogul army had great difficulty in maintaining its strength, though enlistment proceeded far and wide. Such was the opponent that Aurangzib thought he could play off against the sultans of the Deccan; in reality the Mahratta power, joining now one and now another of these opponents, inflicted injury upon both and aggrandised itself at their expense.

In the year 1672, Sivaji surprised an imperial army, and inflicted so severe a defeat that for a long time the Mogul troops were forced to confine themselves to the defence of their headquarters in Aurangabad. Revolts in the north and the north-west of the empire had made it impossible to unite all the imperial forces for action upon the south. A favourable opportunity seemed, however, to have arisen in 1680, when Sivaji died and was succeeded by his son Sambaji, who was nearly his equal in energy. This was the date of the secession of Prince Akbar. The Emperor, who was by nature suspicious, now declined to trust anybody, and placed himself at the head of his southern army with the object of crushing his Mohammedan opponents, Ali of Bijapur and Abul Hasan of Golconda, intending afterwards to overthrow the Mahrattas. In 1683 he marched to the Deccan; in 1686 Bijapur was taken, and Golconda fell the next year. The last independent Mohammedan states in the Deccan thus disappeared.

Overthrow of the Mohammedans

In 1689 Sambaji and his son, who was six years of age, were captured by Aurangzib; the father was killed after the most cruel tortures, and the child kept in strict confinement. This action, however, aroused the obstinate Mahratta race to yet more irresistible efforts. Aurangzib was utterly defeated at Berampur, and his youngest son, Mohammed Kambaksh, with his commander-in-chief, Zulfikar, suffered such heavy losses on the east coast that the prince was forced to withdraw and unite his troops with his father's. Other imperial armies were repeatedly beaten or forced to surrender. The very forces of Nature seemed to be conspiring with the enemy; a sudden inundation of the River Bhima cost Aurangzib the whole of his baggage and 12,000 cavalry. The Mogul emperor gathered all his forces for a final effort; strong citadels were captured and Mahratta troops scattered. But fresh fortresses were occupied, and the Mahrattas dispersed only to reunite at some other centre. Ultimately, the queen regent, Tara Bai, the widow of Raja Ram, the brother of Sambaji, had recourse to desperate measures, and devastated the whole country in order to deprive the enemy of his supplies. At this moment the bodily powers of the old emperor gave way, and in 1707 Aurangzib, or Alamgir I., died in a fainting fit.

Confusion of Mogul Power

On the death of Aurangzib the finances of Delhi were in utter confusion; the greater proportion of the revenue existed only on paper, and had been diminished by embezzlement, by revolts, and by the generally impoverished condition of the nation, while the expenditure had risen enormously during the long-continued war. The Hindu population, who were considered as subjects of the second class only, were inspired with deeper hatred for the Mohammedan dynasty. The strong foundations of the State had been shaken; a state of ferment existed at home, the south was threatened by the Mahratta power which Aurangzib's blind policy had aggrandised, and the states on the north-west beheld these anxieties with delight. Moreover, the dynasty upon the peacock throne of Delhi had degenerated; the power of the house of Timur had spent itself in a short succession of brilliant rulers, and the emperors of succeeding years were but miserable shadows of their great predecessors.

SHAH ALAM

He reigned from 1707 to 1712, but was unequal to the task of keeping the empire together.

In the next twelve years no fewer than eight rulers succeeded one another on the throne. The first, Muazzem Shah Alam Bahadur Shah I. (1707–1712) displayed much tolerance, but his strength was unequal to the task of restoring the broken organisation. His vicious successor, Moizz ed-din Jihandar Shah (1712–1713), was an utterly insignificant figure. He was succeeded by Farokhsir, 1713–1719, a weakling who surrounded himself with foolish counsellors, and vainly attempted to curb the growing power of the nobles by clumsy intrigues; he was murdered in the palace. Two children were then placed in succession upon the throne; both succumbed to consumption, Rafi ed-darajat after three months, and Rafi ed-daula Shah Tehan, in an even shorter time. The rule of Roshen-akhtar Mohammed Shah (1719–1748) was of somewhat longer duration. He, however, was a voluptuary who cared only for his own pleasure, and handed over the imperial seal to his chief wife to use as

MOSQUE OF SHAH ALAM AT AHMEDABAD

she pleased. His son, Ahmed Shah (1748–1754), was taken prisoner and blinded with his mother; he died in 1774. Even shorter was the rule of his aged successor, Aziz ed-din Alamgir, who was murdered by his grand wazir in 1759.

Such, during the first half-century after Aurangzib's death, were the "wielders of the sceptre" in Hindustan, with the exception of a few unsuccessful candidates for the throne, such as Azin Shah (1707), Kambakhsh (1707–1708), Nekusiyar (1719–1723), and Ibrahim (1720). The royal power was in the hands of ambitious Ministers, of harem favourites, of flatterers, and of parasites who pandered to the excesses and debauches of the rulers. Shah Alam Bahadur suffered greatly from dependence upon Zulfikar, one of Aurangzib's bravest generals during his wars in the Deccan, and Jehandar Shah was but a tool in the hands of this man; after the latter's accession, during a revolt of Zulfikar, he was handed over to the rebels, who killed both him and his betrayer. The next four rulers were elevated to the throne by the "king makers," two brothers who gave themselves out to be descendants of the Prophet; these were the Seiads, Hussein Ali and Abdullah, who murdered Farokhsir, made two children emperors, and were finally suppressed a year after the accession of Mohammed Shah. Hussein Ali fell under the dagger of an emissary of the Emperor, while Abdullah was defeated with his army; his rank saved him from death, but he was kept in life-long imprisonment. Henceforward the business of State was conducted by women and parasites. Ahmed Shah and Alamgir II. were pure nonentities compared with their ambitious, faithless, and despotic commander-in-chief and Minister, Ghazi ed-din, grandson of Asaf Jah of Haidarabad.

Such were the hands that steered the ship of State, which was now tossed by wild waves amid dangerous reefs and began to strain in all its joints. The degenerate bureaucracy had but one desire—to turn the weakness of the Government to their own advantage ; taxation became extortion and robbery, while bribery and corruption took the place of justice. Princes and vassals, generals and wazirs tore away provinces from the empire, while warlike Hindu tribes threw off the Mohammedan yoke. Thus the Bhartpur Jats in Rajputana gained their independence, and the principality of Jaipur seceded. The Jaipur rulers—Jey Singh II. in particular—were distinguished for their devotion to astronomy. Jaipur itself was built as a capital in 1728, the splendid town of Ambur having been previously abandoned at the order of the above-named Jey Singh. In Oudh the Shiite Persian Sadat founded the kingdom of Lucknow, while a converted Brahman, Murshid Kuli Khan, formed a kingdom of Bengal, Orissa, and Behar. Malwa fell into the hands of the Mahrattas, and in the south Asaf Jah seized the whole province of the Hindustan Deccan.

To the many difficulties and troubles of the empire was added the outbreak of fanatical religious wars. In the extreme north-west of India, in the Punjab, Nanak (1469-1538), who had been under the influence of Kabir, preached, about 1500, a new doctrine of general peace and brotherly love. He made an attempt to obliterate the differences between Brahmanism and Mohammedanism by representing all the points of divergence as **Origin of the Sikhs** matters of no importance, and emphasising the immanence of the Divine Being as the one material point. It was a pure reform, dissociated as far as possible from any sensualism of theory or practice. All men were equal before God according to this theory, which did not recognise divisions of caste. The adherents of Nanak, whose numbers were at first but small, called themselves Sikhs—that is, disciples or scholars. During the next 150 years they organised themselves as a federation of districts united by religious and political ties.

It was only to be expected that the denial of the authority of the Vedas should please the Hindus as little as the refusal to accept the Koran pleased the Mohammedans. One of the Sikh gurus, or spiritual **The Sikhs Become Warriors** leaders, Arjun, was accused under Jehangir of being implicated in a revolt ; he was thrown into prison in 1616 and so cruelly tortured that he died. From this moment the character of the religious movement entirely changed. Hur Govind, the son of Arjun, thirsting for revenge, issued new proclamations and gave a new character to the sect in 1638 ; the disciples of peace now became warriors of fanatical fierceness. The movement would perhaps have died out if the fanatical Aurangzib had not executed the guru Tegh Bahadur in 1675. Hatred of the Mohammedans immediately flamed up afresh. Govind II., the son of the murdered man, declared himself the son of God sent by his Father to drive and extirpate evil from the world ; warrior and Sikh were henceforth to be equivalent terms. " Ye shall no longer be called Sikh (disciples), but Singh (lions)." Govind maintained his ground with varying success against Aurangzib, who was then occupied with the Mahrattas in the south. Shah Alam Bahadur attempted to win over the Sikhs by conciliation ; in 1708, however, Govind was murdered by a Mohammedan Afghan, and the anger of the Sikhs was boundless.

Pillaging and murdering with appalling cruelty all who declined to accept their faith, they advanced upon Delhi, but were utterly defeated by Bahadur, and forced to retire to inaccessible hiding-places. The emperor, however, died suddenly at Lahore in 1712, perhaps from poison. The sect grew powerful during the disturbances which then broke out, and, under Farokhsir, reoccupied a large part of the Punjab. Led by their chief, Bandah, they again advanced in 1716, marking every step in their advance by ruthless devastations ; Lahore was captured, the governor defeated, and an

FAROKHṢIR AND MOHAMMED SHAH
Both of these rulers were weaklings, and allowed the decay of the empire to proceed apace, Farokhsir reigning from 1713 to 1719 and Mohammed from 1719 to 1748.

imperial army driven back. Fortune then declared against them; they were repeatedly beaten by the imperial troops and driven back with Bandah into one of the northern fortresses, where they were starved out and killed. Bandah escaped, owing to the devotion of a Hindu convert, who personated his leader, and succeeded in duping his captors for some **Decline** time. But of the once formid-
of Sikh able sect there remained only **Power** a few scattered bands, who gained a scanty livelihood in the inaccessible mountain valleys of the Punjab. At this period a foreign Power swept over Hindustan like a scourge from heaven. Nadir Shah, the son of a Turcoman, though born in Persia, had begun his career as leader of a band of freebooters, and had seized the throne of the Safavi dynasty on March 20, 1736. The lack of ceremony with which the Persian Ambassador was treated in Delhi gave him an excuse for invading Hindustan in 1738. After conquering the Mogul army, which had been reinforced by the troops of Sadat, Wazir of Oudh, and of Asaf Jah, Nizam of Haidarabad, he marched into the capital in 1739. Strict discipline was preserved among the troops. A report suddenly spread among the Hindus that the Persian king was dead; the inhabitants then threw themselves upon the soldiers, who had dispersed throughout the town, and slaughtered 700. Nadir Shah attempted to restore order, but was himself attacked, and then commanded a general massacre of the inhabitants. From sunrise to sunset the town was given over to pillage, fire, and murder, 30,000 victims falling before the Persian thirst for vengeance. All the treasures and jewels of the royal treasury, including the peacock throne, the pride of Delhi, were carried off, the bullion belonging to the empire, to the higher officials, and to private individuals was confiscated, and heavy war indemnities were laid upon the governors of the provinces.
Massacre The sum total of the booty **and** which Nadir carried off from **Pillage** Hindustan has been estimated at £50,000,000. Eight years later Nadir Shah was murdered, on June 20, 1747; his kingdom immediately fell into a state of disruption. In Afghanistan the power was seized by Ahmed Khan Abdali, who styled himself Shah Durani, adopting as his own the name of his tribe; he was strongly attracted by the rich booty which Nadir

had carried off from Hindustan. In six marauding raids between the years 1747 and 1761 he devastated the unhappy land and its capital. The massacre of Mattra, the sacred town of Krishna, which took place during the third invasion of Ahmed Shah, was a terrible repetition of Nadir's massacre at Delhi; during a festival of the inhabitants a detachment of Ahmed's army attacked the throng of harmless pilgrims in the defenceless town and slaughtered them by thousands.

In less than a century after the death of Shah Jehan the once powerful Mogul Empire had sunk to the lowest point of misery and weakness; it would undoubtedly have disappeared altogether had not the British become predominant in India. Meanwhile, important events had taken place in the south during the first half of the eighteenth century. Saho, the grandson of the Mahratta prince Sivaji, was released shortly after the death of Aurangzib; he was—and in this respect he became a pattern for the treatment of young Indian heirs to the throne— wholly estranged from the national interests of the Mahrattas. He **Ebb Tide** had grown up in a harem under **of Mogul** the influences of the Mohamme- **Fortunes** danism with which he had been surrounded, and his thoughts and feelings were rather Mohammedan than Hindu; his first act as king was to make a pilgrimage to the grave of his father's murderer.

Previous to the accession of Saho, the Mahratta government had been in good hands. When Sambaji had been captured and killed, his young son, who was also a prisoner, had been declared king; meanwhile, the government had been carried on by the brother of Sambaji, Raja Ram, and after his death by his no less capable widow, the kingdom suffering no deterioration, notwithstanding the imprisonment of the monarch. When, however, Saho took up the power in person a change occurred for the worst. Enervated in body and mind, he left all State business to the care of his prudent Minister, Balaji Wiswanath, officially known as the Peshwa; and it was to the efforts of this man that he owed the establishment of his position with reference to the Mogul kingdom, though he would himself have been well content to become a vassal of Delhi. The chief work of the Peshwa was to reduce to order the whole organisation of the Mahratta state with its peculiar military basis. During the reigns of Hussein Ali and Abdullah he marched upon Delhi and procured not only the recognition of the sovereignty of the Mahratta princes but also the formal right of levying upon the whole of the Deccan the Mahratta tax, one-fourth of the whole state revenue. Thus, under Saho, the power practically fell into the hands of the Peshwa ; and when his post became recognised as hereditary, the new Brahman Mahratta dynasty of the Peshwas grew up side by side with, and rapidly overshadowed, the dynasty of Sivaji.

Baji Rao (1720–1740), the son of Balaji Wiswanath, who united the intellect of a Brahman with the energy of a warrior, raised the Mahratta kingdom to its highest point. He was forced by the prince and his adherents to establish the power of the constitution upon a territorial basis. But he saw that the strength of his people consisted primarily in their military organisation ; his country would be more powerful if its sphere of interest was marked by no fixed boundaries, and if it could gradually extend its claims to the **Extension of Mahratta Influence** Mahratta tribute over the whole of the fallen Mogul Empire, and even further. In matters of domestic policy, the Peshwa conducted State business entirely upon his own responsibility, without consulting the prince, who had become a merely nominal ruler. A refusal to pay the Mahratta tribute, and the murder of the Mahratta general, Pilaji Gaekwar, gave Baji Rao the opportunity of subjugating Gujerat. In 1723 he captured the province of Malwa, and in the negotiations with Delhi he secured not only all the country south of the Chambal, but also gained the cession of the three most sacred towns of the Hindus, Mattra, Allahabad, and Benares. When the Mogul Emperor raised objections, Baji Rao advanced to the walls of Delhi in 1737 ; at the beginning of 1738 he forced Asaf Jah of Haidarabad, the plenipotentiary of the Grand Mogul, to cede all the country south of the Chambal. But before the agreement could be confirmed by Mohammed Shah, the devastating invasion of Nadir Shah burst upon the country, and even the Mahrattas shrank back in dismay. It was not until after the death of Baji Rao, in 1740, that his successor, Balaji, the third Peshwa, secured the formal completion by Delhi in 1743 of

the contract proposed in 1738. About the same period (1741–1743) the Mahrattas repeatedly advanced north-eastwa·d against Bengal, the last of these movements being under the leadership of Raghuji Bhonsla ; from this district they extort d the Mahratta tax and the cession of Kattak, a part of Orissa, in 1743. **Zenith of Mahratta Power** Called in by Delhi to bring help against the revolted Rohillas in Rohilkand, they completed the subjugation of this tribe, and were rewarded with new concessions as to tribute ; after the third invasion of the Afghan Ahmed Shah, they penetrated to the north-west corner of India, captured Lahore, and drove the scanty Afghan garrison out of the Punjab. They had now reached the zenith of their power ; wherever the Mogul kingdom had exercised dominion during the period of its prosperity, the Mahrattas now interposed upon all possible occasions ; though not the recognised dominant power, they exacted their tribute almost everywhere.

They met their match, however, in Ahmed Shah. The Mahratta general, Sindhia, was defeated, and two-thirds of his troops slain, while the army of the general, Holkar, who succeeded him, was shattered. Thereupon, a new and greater army advanced against the Afghans, under the cousin of the Peshwa. The decisive battle was fought on January 6th, 1761, at Panipat; the Mahrattas were utterly defeated, 200,000 falling in the battle or in flight, including the general, a son of the Peshwa, and a number of important leaders.

The Peshwa survived this disaster but a short time. The Mahrattas were obliged to withdraw from Hindustan, and never again did the Peshwas recover their former importance ; the Mahratta kingdom was now transformed into a loosely united confederacy. The later successes of this people were gained by individual and almost independent Mahratta princes with the help of European officers and soldiers. The policy of Baji Rao had exactly suited the nature of the Mahratta state ; the position of the Prince had sunk to unimportance, and the Peshwa had been raised to the highest point. At the same time, however, individual commanders had tended to become more and more independent. The principle of rewarding the chief general with the Mahratta tax levied f·om a rich province, and thus enabling him to keep on foot a considerable body of troops, proved utterly destructive of the unity of the state; these commanders ultimately became provincial lords supported by the troops under their command. The independence thus acquired was also favoured by internal dissensions within the nominally ruling family and by political discord with Haidarabad, Delhi, Oudh, and Bengal. Under the third Peshwa, Balaji (1740–1761), this process of disruption had made rapid strides, and the landed nobility, which had hitherto been purposely kept in the background, now reasserted itself to the detriment of the body politic. The king's power had decreased so much under the influence of the Peshwa, that his influence was gradually confined to the provinces of Satara and Kholapur; so also the actual power of the Peshwa ultimately coincided with the province of Puna. For the first time under Baji Rao appear various Mahratta princes whose ancestors had previously held for the most part wholly subordinate positions; they now formed a confederacy, at the head of which the Peshwa was barely tolerated. About 1738 Raghuji Bhonsla, who had led the invasions of Bengal and Orissa, was recognised as the rival of the Peshwa, and attained almost complete independence in the province of Nagpur, which nearly corresponds to the modern Central Provinces, until his death in 1755. The general Sindhia, who, though of good family, had once filled a menial position under Baji Rao, and Rao Holkar, who was originally a shepherd, became lords of the two principalities of Indur and Gwalior, formed from the newly won province of Malwa. On the north-west the Gaekwar became chief of the province of Baroda. Thus, the once powerful Mahratta kingdom had been broken into five great and several smaller principalities under the purely nominal supremacy of the Peshwa. On the other hand, the former Mogul province of the Deccan, to gain which Aurangzib had sacrificed the welfare of his kingdom, gradually rose to an independent state of considerable importance. In the year 1713, Chin Kilikh Khan, better known by his earlier title of Asaf Jah, the son of a Turcoman general in the Mogul army, in which he had himself been

A Divided State

Splitting of a Kingdom

an officer, was sent to the Deccan as governor (Nizam ul mulk), but was speedily recalled by the jealous Seiads. He then turned to his former province, and defeated two armies which were sent out against him, and this success was speedily followed by the deaths of Hussein and Abdullah. Recalled to Delhi as grand wazir by Farokhsir, he found the imperial court and the whole body politic in a hopeless condition of degeneracy, and he immediately resigned. Asaf Jah was dismissed by Farokhsir, with every mark of consideration and respect; but he was preceded by mounted messengers to Mobariz, who had taken his place as governor in the Deccan, with orders to depose the viceroy upon his return. This intrigue failed utterly. Mobariz was defeated in 1724, and Asaf Jah sent his head to Delhi with congratulations on the rapid suppression of the "revolt." To preserve some show of dependence, the Nizam repeatedly sent presents to the capital, but in reality his independence was complete. He was able to maintain his position against the Mahrattas; the chaut could not be refused, but he lightened the burden of this tribute by despatching his own officials to collect it, and transmit it personally to the Mahrattas. While the Mogul kingdom was hurrying ever more rapidly to its fall, this province rose to considerable importance and prosperity under Asaf Jah. When the Mahrattas made their advance, Mohammed Shah appointed the capable Nizam as dictator in 1737; the weakness of the empire, however, was so great that even Asaf Jah was unable to bring help either against the Mahrattas or against Nadir Shah. In 1741 he returned to his own country. On his death in 1748, he left behind to his dynasty a flourishing kingdom of the size of Spain.

In the east, the Carnatic—that is to say, the lowland beneath the precipices of the Ghats—formed one of the states under the supremacy of the Nizam, and was governed by the Nawab of Arcot. The smaller principality of Tanjore to the south of Arcot was governed by a d scendant of Sivaji, and to the north-west of this district Mysore began to develop as an independent state. To these must be added a number of petty principalities, for the most part feudal holdings or independent creations of adventurous Naiks or generals.

Kingdom of the Nizam

PRINCES & PEOPLE
OF
MODERN INDIA

A RAJAH ON HIS STATE ELEPHANT

A PRINCE OF THE PUNJAB

A YOUNG HILL RAJA

THE RAJA HINDU RAO, A MAHRATTA PRINCE OF DELHI

DANCING WOMAN OF KASHMIR   MOHAMMEDAN WOMAN OF DELHI

A NAUTCH DANCE IN THE PALACE OF A NATIVE PRINCE

ZEMINDAR, OR FARMER, AND A PATHAN

JEMADAR, OR HEAD SERVANT

SERVANTS WITH DOGS AND HAWKS, BELONGING TO THE KING OF OUDH

HINDU FAKIR, OR HOLY MAN   MOHAMMEDAN AT HIS PRAYERS

A GROUP OF THE EDUCATED BRAHMAN CLASS

THE BEGINNING OF BRITISH INFLUENCE IN INDIA

In 1599 Queen Elizabeth sent Sir John Mildenhall to the Great Mogul, the renowned Akbar, with an application for trading privileges for an English company to which she wished to grant a charter; the commissioner was successful, and in 1600 a company was incorporated under the style of "The Governor and Company of Merchants of London trading to the East Indies."

MODERN INDIA
THE FOUNDATION OF BRITISH DOMINION
BY ARTHUR D. INNES

THE Persian smote Delhi; the Afghan shattered the Mahratta hosts on the field where, two hundred years before, young Akbar's generals had won Hindustan for the Moguls. But the dominion of India was destined neither for Persian nor for Afghan. Not through the mountain passes, as of old, but by the new highway of the ocean the new invader came—by the waters that linked together the East and West, which the land-barriers held asunder. Between the invasion of Nadir Shah and the last great raid of the Durani a new conquering Power had suddenly revealed itself on the east; a power mightier than Mogul or Mahratta, Afghan or Turcoman.

In spite of the early invasion of India by Alexander the Great, continuous intercourse between India and Europe was never established until Vasco da Gama, in 1497-8, showed the Westerns a new road to reach the semi-mythical lands of the East, by sailing round the Cape of Good Hope. The Portuguese led the way, and maintained their lead for a century. In the Indian seas they contested the supremacy of the Arabs. Under the great Albuquerque they secured a footing— bases of naval operations—at Ormuz, on the Persian Gulf, and at Goa, on the west coast of the Indian peninsula. Between **The First Europeans in India** 1515—the year of Albuquerque's death—and 1580—the year in which Philip II. of Spain annexed the Portuguese crown—Portuguese fleets were supreme in the Indian seas, and though Portugal had not taken possession of territories, she had established numerous trading and naval stations. She absorbed the European trade of the East. Then she was herself absorbed by Spain for a time. But Spain was already engaged in the early stages of her maritime struggle with England: the united Netherlands, in revolt against her dominion, were emerging to take their own place as a sea-going, trading, and colonising power of the first rank. If the English, like the Spaniards, gave their main attention to the New World, still, English and Dutch alike resolved to take **Spanish Supremacy Challenged** their share in exploiting the re-opened East. On the last day of the last year of the sixteenth century the British East India Company received its charter from Elizabeth. Within two years the Dutch East India Company was incorporated. When Albuquerque died, the Mogul dynasty had not yet come into existence; Akbar was still reigning when the merchant adventurers of England and Holland began to take the lion's share in the trade which had been a Portuguese monopoly.

For Portugal and Spain, the oceanic commerce was, so to speak, in the pocket of the Crown. It was regulated and governed with a single eye to the filling of the royal treasury. For Dutch and English it was a speculation of private adventurers, from whom the Government was satisfied to receive payment in return for privileges granted. The Spanish system throttled personal enterprise; the English system fostered it. But personal enterprise could not have thought of coping with the power of the Mogul Empire in its most magnificent period. By a tacit accommodation the Dutch company turned mainly to the Spice Islands and the English increasingly towards India; but the English sought settlements on the Indian littoral frankly as traders with no ulterior political designs.

In 1613 the English were allowed to set up their first trading station or factory, under the protection of the native Government, at Surat, in what is now the Bombay Presidency. Seven years later they were permitted to establish themselves, in very tentative sort, in Bengal. In **English Trading Stations** 1532 the Portuguese, between whom and the natives there was no love lost, had a collision with the Empire and were wiped out. The English, partly owing to the successful services rendered by an English surgeon at the Imperial court and also at the viceregal court in Bengal, were granted a settlement at Hugli, on the mouth of the Ganges, and extensive trade privileges. In 1639 a southern potentate, not yet a subject of the Moguls, granted them similar rights on the Coromandel coast, where their factory of Fort St. George developed into Madras. The nucleus of each of the three future presidencies was thus established. A few years later Bombay superseded Surat. It had remained hitherto in the hands of the Portuguese. In the middle of the seventeenth century Portugal broke free from Spain; Charles II., immediately after the restoration, married a Portuguese princess. Bombay was ceded as part of her dower, and was transferred by the Crown to the East India Company. The whole transaction was aimed against Spain and Holland, English commercial rivalry with Holland being at its height, while both the dead Lord Protector and the living Charles Stuart favoured alliance with France.

In Eastern waters, however, neither Spain nor Portugal counted materially any longer, and the conflict of interests tended more and more to restrict England and Holland to separate spheres. On the other hand, the relations between Charles II. and Louis XIV. were favourable to the development of French enterprise within the British area; and the French Minister Colbert grasped the idea of French colonial and maritime expansion. His **English and French Interests** policy gave France a navy which, until the battle of La Hogue, in 1692, showed promise of challenging English and Dutch supremacy on the seas; and it created a French East India Company which, during the same period, established itself as firmly as the English at

THE FIRST SMALL BEGINNING OF THE BRITISH EMPIRE IN INDIA

In 1613 the English were allowed to set up their first trading station or factory at Surat in what is now the Bombay Presidency. In the picture of the station reproduced above, the figures 1 indicate the church, 2, the residence and 3, the warehouse. The illustration is taken from the "Voyages" of Mandelslo, published in 1727.

FORT ST. GEORGE, WHICH DEVELOPED INTO THE CITY OF MADRAS

In 1639 a southern potentate, not yet a subject of the Moguls, granted the English trading rights on the Coromandel coast, where their factory of Fort St. George was built in 1641, and afterwards developed into Madras.

points not far distant from the chief English stations. It was in 1690 that Hugli was superseded by the new factory and fort called Fort William, which became a portion of Calcutta.

In spite of the wars between France and England—which was merged in Great Britain in 1707—during the reigns of William III. and Anne, the French and English companies confined themselves to commercial rivalries; and during the half-century between 1690 and 1740 it became increasingly probable that there would some day be a struggle *à outrance* to decide whether French or British should hold the field and expel the competitor. What did not present itself to the minds either of directors or politicians in England or France was that the commercial struggle would develop into a contest for political ascendancy on Indian territory.

In fact, so long as the power of the Mogul was or seemed to be a reality, political ascendancy was an unattainable dream. A shrewd observer here and there might perceive that the colossus was brittle, and that what Babar had done with an army of 12,000 men might be done again by a European general. After the death of Aurangzib, it required less acuteness to perceive that the fabric of the empire was breaking up into a congeries of states, having no homogeneity, which could be dealt with piecemeal—to which the maxim *divide et*

European Political Ascendancy

impera might be applied. But, again, the condition of such a programme for ambitious Europeans was that there should be no European rival, and, as between European rivals, the determining factor would be maritime superiority. The man who did perceive these things, and deliberately constructed a policy of which they were the foundation, was not an Englishman, but a Frenchman. Unfortunately for him, the fundamental facts were not realised in France. The ends he had in view were disapproved; the means to obtain them were ignored. The eyes of the French Government were turned to the European continent. It never realised that trans-oceanic ascendancy depends on maritime supremacy; it never realised that political ascendancy in India was a rational aim for practical politicians.

A French Empire Builder

Dupleix toiled and planned; the British did not toil and plan. But all that Dupleix could do was of no avail when British squadrons controlled Indian waters and his victories in India were cancelled by British successes in North America. His rivals appreciated and adopted the methods which his ingenuity devised; he taught them to forge the weapons which were to give them the prize he had sought to win himself. But in 1740 the most audacious prophet would hardly have predicted the change in the situation which was to develop during the succeeding twenty years.

For in 1740 nearly the whole of India still professed allegiance to the Mogul. Nadir Shah had indeed smitten, but after smiting had retired. The Mogul's dominions were in the hands of satraps, but these had huge armies at their command. A British and a French company **The Eve** of traders had some half-dozen **of India's** moderately fortified stations **Conquest** apiece at remote points of the vast peninsula, with a few hundred white soldiers scattered among them. Neither Britain nor France had any idea of turning her energies to conquests in India. In 1760 the British were masters of Bengal and Bihar, masters of the Carnatic, dominant at Haidara-bad ; the French were on the verge of losing their last foothold at Pondichery; the great Mahratta Power was on the verge of its huge disaster at Panipat.

How that change came about we shall presently trace. Why it was possible we can point out at once. French and British strove in the first in-stance for mastery over each other, not over natives ; their strife in India was merged in a strife all over the world, in which victory was determined pri-marily by naval pre-ponderance. The British, dominating the French, acquired terri-torial power, not by challenging and over-throwing native states, but by supporting the successful claimants to native thrones in the south, and by helping to overthrow in Bengal a dynasty which was the object of a great native conspiracy. It was not even needful to divide and then conquer ; the division was there, ready made. If the British found a leader with the requisite initiative, audacity, and foresight, conquest was almost inevitable.

In 1740 Great Britain, technically at peace with France, had entered upon a war with the second Bourbon Power, Spain. Sooner or later, it was tolerably certain

that she would be at war with the sister country of France also.

The French governor in India, François Dupleix, promoted in 1741 from Chander-nagore to Pondichery, hoped, with the expected declaration of war, to find his opportunity, in spite of pacific instruc-tions from home. With the help of a capable naval commander stationed at the Mauritius, and the goodwill of the Indian potentate most nearly concerned—the Nawab of Arcot, or the Carnatic—he would wipe out the English from Southern India. Once freed from European rivalry, diplomacy and tact should procure for the representatives of France an in-valuable influence at the native courts. Tact and diplomacy would be supplemented, not, indeed, by huge armies, but by small forces so disciplined, organised, and led that they would be more than a match for ten times their number of the undisciplined levies at the disposal of the native princes. The white soldiery would no doubt be a mere handful ; but Dupleix relied on training Indian soldiers under European discipline with Euro-pean commanders to a European standard of efficiency.

The British at Madras also had it in their minds that a war between Great Britain and France might be turned to account on Indian soil ; but Dupleix, the diplomatist, was beforehand with them. When war was actually declared in 1744, Anwar-ud-din, the Nawab of the Carnatic, **Dupleix** warned them that no hostilities **Develops** would be permitted. Two years **his Plans** had almost elapsed when La Bourdonnais arrived with a squadron to help Dupleix. Anwar-ud-din declined to interfere ; the French attacked and captured Madras. Dupleix repudiated the terms of ransom, arranged with La Bourdonnais, under which Madras had surrendered. La Bourdonnais, insulted

DUPLEIX, THE FRENCH GOVERNOR
François Dupleix, the French Governor in India, was a soldier statesman whose policy would have changed the whole course of Indian history if his home government had supported him in his designs.

and mortified, withdrew, and was almost immediately recalled. Until 1782, French ships ceased to be a factor in the situation. Dupleix kept his grip on Madras. This did not accord with the views of Anwarud-din, who intended to take possession himself. Dupleix defied the Nawab's summons to surrender the town; the Nawab sent 10,000 men to enforce his demand. Dupleix's experiment was put to the test. The garrison, some 500 men, sallied forth, and scattered the 10,000 in ignominious rout. Reinforcements, numbering under 1,000, of whom three-fourths were sepoys (*sipahis*), natives drilled and officered by Europeans, re-

doubtless have had an exceedingly different result, but it was not renewed. The treaty of Aix-la-Chapelle had ended the war between France and England. The peace did not deprive Dupleix of his

A Peace that was no Peace prestige, a valuable asset; but it robbed him of the tangible prize he had won. Madras, under the treaty, was restored to the British, in exchange for Louisburg, on the St. Lawrence, which had been taken from the French during the war.

France and England might be at peace, but French and British in India were minded to carry their conflict to a decisive conclusion. They found their opportunity in the chaos of the native governments.

PONDICHERY, THE HEADQUARTERS OF FRENCH POWER IN INDIA
This view of the Governor's Palace at Pondichery is taken from Laplace's "Voyage Autour du Monde," published in 1835.

peated the success. Dupleix's military theory was converted into a demonstrated truth. Dupleix himself at once became a recognised power.

A hundred miles southward, however, at Fort St. David, the British, under Stringer Lawrence, maintained a stubborn **Hostilities of French and British** resistance. In 1748, a British squadron appeared and besieged Pondichery for seven weeks, at the end of which it was compelled to retire, baffled by the approach of the monsoons, the gales which made it impossible for a fleet to keep the sea. The siege only served to raise French prestige. Its renewal next year would

A double dynastic contest was on the tapis. Anwar-ud-din had been made Nawab, or Lieut-Governor of the Carnatic, by the superior Nizam, or Viceroy of the Deccan, only so lately as 1740. Chanda Sahib, representative of the popular family which had held the nawabship before Anwar-ud-din, was ransomed from captivity with Mahrattas by Dupleix. Being free, Chanda Sahib claimed the nawabship, with the support of Dupleix. But the old Nizam himself also died in 1748. A son, Nadir Jang, seized the throne; a grandson, Muzaffar Jang, claimed it. The two claimants, supported by Dupleix, made common cause against the two *de facto* rulers. The latter naturally appealed for British support; so that French and British carried on their struggle in the character of auxiliaries or allies of the native dynastic competitors.

Dupleix was prompt; the British were slow. In 1749, it seemed as if the French were assured of victory all along the line. Anwar-ud-din was killed; his son, Mohammed Ali, who claimed to succeed him, was shut up in Trichinopoli by Chanda Sahib. Nadir Jang, the victim of a conspiracy, was assassinated, and Muzaffar Jang was acclaimed Nizam. The two French candidates appeared practically to have won. The fall of Muzaffar Jang in a skirmish made no difference, since another French nominee, Salabat Jang, took his place. Virtually the French general, Bussy, was Nizam.

Brief French Success

Now, however, the tide turned. A vigorous governor, Saunders, arrived at Madras, who promptly sent all the apparently available assistance to Mohammed Ali at Trichinopoli, and then accepted the immense risk of denuding Madras of practically eve·y fighting man in order to effect a diversion. The scheme

THE ROCK AND FORTRESS OF TRICHINOPOLI
Here Mohammed Ali, son of Anwar-ud-din, was held by Chanda Sahib in 1749.

was Robert Clive's, and to him its execution was entrusted. Saunders staked all on his confidence in the genius of a young man of five and twenty who had shown distinguished courage as a volunteer, but had held no sort of command. Clive's plan was to seize the Nawab's capital at Arcot, and so compel Chanda Sahib to

detach a large portion of the force at Trichinopoli, to prevent the organisation of hostile forces in the northern district.

The plan proved a triumphant success. Clive's force consisted of 200 British and 300 sepoys, with eight officers, of whom only two had been in action. The little force appeared suddenly before Arcot. The garrison, seized with panic, fled. Clive took possession, and laboured strenuously to make the fortifications defensible. Also, in a night attack, he inflicted heavy losses on the ex-garrison, which had reassembled and encamped in the neighbourhood. The news alarmed Chanda Sahib; in a short time 10,000 of his troops were investing Arcot. For seven weeks the little garrison maintained a desperate resistance; then the besiegers resolved on a grand assault in force. By desperate fighting, the assault was repulsed. The besiegers began to retire. Clive sallied from Arcot, fell upon them, and shattered them. The amazing exploit fired the imagination of the natives. Bands of Mahratta and other soldiery, which had hitherto held aloof, rallied to the standard of so brilliant a leader. Before the midsummer of 1752, Mohammed Ali was relieved, and Chanda Sahib's force was in its turn besieged and finally compelled to surrender.

Clive's First Great Success

So long as Dupleix remained in India, it could not be said that there was no hope of a French recovery. But his proceedings, which had involved enormous outlay, found no favour with the French Government. In 1754 he was recalled, and replaced by a governor whose outlook was exclusively commercial. His ablest coadjutor, Bussy, remained, indeed, at Haidarabad; but the prestige had passed from the French to the British, the natives looked upon the latter as the successful Power, and it was certain that if a fresh conflict should arise the French would be beaten unless the Home Government gave them a real and energetic support—which was not promised by its treatment of the recalled governor, Dupleix.

The conflict was renewed. In 1756 Great Britain and France again went to war. In a very short time British ships were again controlling the Indian waters ; no strong reinforcement had a chance of reaching the French. Bussy was occupied in maintaining his position at Haidarabad. Circumstances to which we shall presently advert took Clive to Bengal.

Failure of Dupleix's Successor The struggle was carried on in the Carnatic by the French under the leadership of Lally, who arrived to conduct operations. But his instructions expressly forbade him to play Dupleix's game of intriguing with the country Powers. An able soldier, he did not understand the natives, whom he enraged by ignoring religious and social ideas which were sacrosanct in their eyes ; his own officers were frequently on the verge of mutiny. He had no resources to fall back on ; the district known as the Northern Sarkars was ceded to the French by the Nizam, but was seized by a British force despatched by Clive from Bengal. His military operations were twice disconcerted, and a victory was snatched from him by the appearance of a British squadron. He summoned Bussy from Haidarabad to his aid ; the Nizam transferred his alliance to the British. On January 21st, 1760, the decisive battle was fought at Wandewash, Eyre Coote commanding the British. The engagement was between European troops almost equally matched in numbers ; large native contingents which were present confined themselves to the rôle of admiring spectators. Coote's victory was complete. For another twelve months the French struggled on, till their only foothold was in Pondichery itself. Then, a year after Wandewash, Pondichery, too, was obliged to surrender. When the Peace of Paris was signed in 1763, nothing was left to France in India but trading

Release of French Hold Upon India stations dismantled of fortifications, and held upon terms which precluded the maintenance of any effective drilled forces. The British were established in the peninsula without possibility of a European competitor so long as they could maintain control of the seas—at least, until such time as a European Power should be able to extend its borders across Central Asia.

During the last phase of the Anglo-French rivalry in the Carnatic—which we date from the recall of Dupleix in 1754 —Robert Clive was laying the foundations of actual territorial dominion in Bengal, where hitherto the French and British traders had abstained from hostilities.

LORD CLIVE, FOUNDER OF BRITISH INDIA
Clive was a clerk in the service of the East India Company, and opportunity enabled him to display his genius for arms and administration. He is the father of British dominion in India.

Under the dominion of an able Nawab, Ali Vardi Khan, Bengal and Bihar, in 1740, formed another of the great practically independent satrapies of the empire. In 1756 Ali Vardi Khan died. His successor was a vicious, bloodthirsty, and half-crazy youth named Suraj ud Daulah. In mere self-defence, the incompetent British Governor at Fort William (Calcutta) was just engaged in strengthening his very inefficient fortifications. Suraj ud Daulah took offence and ordered the British to desist. When they protested, he marched an army on Calcutta. The Governor and most of the British fled. Those who remained at their post were seized, men and women, and packed for the night into a cellar with no ventilation but a small grating. When the door was opened in the morning, of the 147 captives, only 23 were still living. Such was the tragedy of the notorious Black Hole of Calcutta.

News of the declaration of war between France and England had not arrived at Madras when the authorities learned the ghastly story of Calcutta. This was the intelligence which greeted Clive on his return to India after an absence in England. British warships were at Madras under Admiral Watson. It was resolved forthwith to send an expedition to Bengal to bring the Nawab to book, under the joint command of Clive, as general, and Watson as admiral. In December the force entered the Hugli ; in January it was in possession of Fort William. The Nawab's garrison collapsed before it. Suraj ud Daulah gathered an army ; Clive sallied from Fort William and scattered it. The Nawab toppled from the heights of arrogance to the depths of fright. But while his tone to the English changed, he tried surreptitiously to invoke the aid of the French. Then came the news from Europe that Great Britain and France were at war again ; Clive swooped on Chandarnagur ; French intervention was paralysed.

Events that led to Plassey

Still the British had a serious problem to face. The Nawab of Bengal had been humiliated ; but if the expeditionary force withdrew from Bengal at this stage in order to concentrate in the Carnatic, where a renewal of the struggle with the French was certain, there would be no security for Calcutta. The problem was simplified when it was notified to Clive that certain of the Nawab's Ministers were anxious to dethrone him, and set up in his place the commander-in-chief, Mir Jaffar. The conspirators invited the co-operation of the British. The British were willing. Terms were settled between the contracting parties ; the principal go-between was tricked by an Oriental device to which Watson refused to be a party—a difficulty which Clive got over by forging the admiral's signature. Watson accepted the situation, and Clive always maintained that his own action in the circumstances was absolutely justified, though this was the sole occasion in his career in which he stooped to fraud. The treaty with the conspirators being

From " Glimpses of Bengal " by permission
SURAJ UD DAULAH
The Nawab whose name lives as the perpetrator of the awful tragedy of the Black Hole of Calcutta.

duly signed, Clive announced to Suraj ud Daulah that he was coming to the capital, Murshidabad, with his army, to demand reparation and security in respect of British grievances. He followed up his despatch by advancing with his whole force—some 3,000 men, of whom two-thirds were sepoys. The Nawab marched against him, with 50,000 men, including fifty French. But Mir Jaffar was pledged to desert with half of them, though no one knew whether he would keep his promise when the time came. Nevertheless, Clive risked the engagement at Plassey. The Nawab's army was scattered like chaff ; Suraj ud Daulah fled to Murshidabad, and, while attempting to escape in disguise, was caught and murdered by Mir Jaffar's son. The victor of Plassey made Mir Jaffar Nawab ; but no one, least of all the new Nawab himself, dreamed of supposing that he was anything but a puppet in the hands of Clive, whose arms were thenceforth regarded by the natives as irresistible.

The appointment of Mir Jaffar was formally confirmed by the Mogul. The Company, Clive himself, and sundry other officers received immense rewards from the new Nawab—rewards which might have been enormously increased if Clive had spoken the word. They were made zemindars, or landlords, of vast districts, of which they practically enjoyed the revenue. Mir Jaffar would now have adopted the normal course of oppressive and capricious Oriental despots ; but Clive was his master, and Clive acted as the protector of the people. His success in this capacity ranks among his most remarkable achievements.

While Clive was in Bengal controlling the new administration, the French were making their last effort in the Carnatic. Despite the obviously critical position on the Ganges, the Englishman dared, in 1758, to despatch to the south the troops which, under Colonel Forde, stormed Masulipatam, and secured the Northern Sarkars for the British instead of the French. In 1759 the Wazir of Oudh, along with the heir of the Mogul, thought to make conquest of Bengal, and besieged

Success of a Bold Movement

Patna. Clive made an extraordinary forced march to its relief, and the invading army melted before the mere terror of his name. For reward, he was given his *jaghir*—the quit rents of the district where Mir Jaffar had appointed the Company as zemindar.

In the same year, 1759, the Dutch appeared—and disappeared—as interveners in Indian affairs. Called in by Mir Jaffar, restive under the restraint imposed by the British, Dutch ships entered the Hugli. Their proceedings were suspicious, but there was no warrant for locating them as hostile till they seized some English vessels. That was enough for Clive; he had three ships, which promptly engaged and overcame the seven Dutchmen, and he occupied the Dutch factory at Chinsurah, and dictated terms. The Dutch admitted their own aggression, and virtually undertook to maintain no troops in Bengal.

In 1760, Clive sailed for England, a few days after Coote's victory at Wandewash. In 1761 the Mahratta Power, which was threatening to dominate the peninsula, met with its disastrous check at Panipat, at the hands of Ahmed Shah. A year later, a new Power arose in the south, where a Mohammedan soldier, known to history as Haidar Ali, seized the throne of Mysore, and rapidly organised an aggressive military state.

Thus it befell that a company of London merchants suddenly found themselves effective lords of the whole of the Carnatic and of the whole of Bengal—seeing that in each of these provinces there reigned a Nawab who had won his throne by **Merchant Lords of an Empire** British arms and retained it in virtue of their support— while the natives accounted them virtually masters of the Nizam of Haidarabad also. The meagrely paid servants of a trading concern cannot, in the nature of things, be expected suddenly to develop the statesmanlike qualities necessary for organising government on a huge scale under unprecedented conditions, especially where unlimited opportunity makes the temptation to exploit the new

dominions for their own private personal advantage all but irresistible. When the strong restraining hand of Clive was withdrawn, there followed in Bengal an evil era of extortion and misrule. The prestige of British arms, however, suffered no eclipse under the officers whom Clive had trained. Mir Jaffar was deposed for **Abuses in Clive's Absence** failing to meet the financial demands made on him; a new Nawab, Mir Casim, was set up. Mir Casim prepared to organise resistance, came into armed conflict with the British, and had to flee to Shujah Daulah, the Nawab or Wazir of Oudh. Mir Jaffar was reinstated, and was presently succeeded at his death by his son. The Wazir again proposed to eject the new Power from Bengal in 1764; but Clive himself could not have routed him more decisively than Hector Munro, at the battle of Baksar or Buxar, in October. A few months later, Clive himself reappeared in India, with full powers to deal with the maladministration which had arisen in his absence.

SHAH ALAMGHIR
Who during the period from 1753 to 1760 was the titular "Mogul."

Manifestly it was impossible that the British should continue to evade actual responsibility for the government in Bengal; yet they had, in the first place, no official status, and in the second, the organisation which was adapted for the mercantile management of a "factory" was not adapted for the political administration of a province as large as France. Official status Clive obtained by a treaty with the titular Mogul, Shah Alamghir, whose technical authority was still recognised over most of India. The *Diwani* of Bengal and Bihar was conferred on the Company, the Diwani meaning in effect the entire business of administration. Under the same treaty the Sarkars were bestowed on the British as from the Mogul, instead of merely as from the Nizam, his titular viceroy in the south; and the Carnatic was separated from the titular over-lordship of the Nizam.

Meanwhile, Clive reorganised the Company's system. The authorised practice by which the Company's servants were permitted to carry on private trading was abolished, but the impossibly meagre

OPENING OF THE TRIAL OF WARREN HASTINGS IN WESTMINSTER HALL, FEBRUARY 12, 1788

The seven years' trial of Warren Hastings was one of the most memorable in British history, the leaders of the impeachment being Burke, Fox, Sheridan, Windham, and Grey. The trial resulted in acquittal, but it cost Hastings £70,000. Before his death in 1818 the immense value of his services had begun to be recognised, and is now universally acknowledged.

salaries which had made private trading a necessity were increased. Hitherto no one had hesitated to accept the most substantial presents in return for services, actual or potential ; the custom had been developed into an engine of corruption and extortion ; it was now peremptorily forbidden. The army officers were annoyed by finding their extra pay—known as "double batta"—cut off. They resigned *en bloc*. Clive accepted the resignations and arrested the ringleaders.

Finally, he laid down the lines of foreign policy. There was to be no endeavour to extend dominion —the Company had as much on its hands as it could manage. Friendly relations were to be maintained with the great Mahratta rulers; but Oudh on the north, and Haidarabad in the south, were themselves to be maintained as a check on the Mahrattas— although, according to all Indian precedent, the conquerors at Buxar were quite entitled to take possession of Oudh. At the beginning of 1767, Clive left India finally. In England he became the object of fierce obloquy. But the House of Commons, invited to condemn him, recorded instead its sense of the great services he had rendered to his country. Later, the man who had won an empire for Great Britain, and had ruled in India with a justice and a restraint unprecedented for a hundred years, died by his own hand.

Clive's reforms were only partially sustained by the Company's directors in London. Neither private trading nor the rece.ving of presents cea;ed ; the old evils were diminished, but not destroyed ; the men at the head of affairs were not competent to carry out properly a task

which would have taxed the highest administrative ability to the uttermost. The governing bodies at Madras and Bombay muddled their conduct of foreign affairs, were weak when they meant to be firm, and irritating when they meant to be conciliatory. Consequently they failed to secure the confidence of the Mahrattas or of the Nizam, or of Haidar Ali, either in their good faith or in their vigour. In Bengal, matters improved when Warren Hastings became Governor in 1770. But the British Parliament was awaking to a sense of its responsibilities. Amid the excitement of Middlesex elections and of recalcitrant colonists in America, Lord North found time to devise a Regulating Act for the better government of India. As an experiment in constitution-making, it was sufficiently inadequate ; but it was a clumsy move in the right direction. It meant that Great Britain was becoming aware that in the long run the nation, not a company, would be accountable for the welfare of the newly acquired territories. The experiment lasted for eleven years —years during which the British Empire was being rent in twain, and for a short time Britain's place among the nations was at stake. But for one man, who triumphed in spite of the experiment, her position in India must have been lost. But the Regulating Act had one fortunate feature—it nominated Warren Hastings as Governor-General of the Company's Indian territories, though it hampered him desperately by nominating at the same time a council with the will and the power to thwart him at every turn, and an independent judiciary, whose legal theories were quite unintelligible to the native population of the country.

From the painting by Sir Joshua Reynolds

WARREN HASTINGS

This great English administrator laid India and the Empire under his debt. In spite of the opposition of his council, his policy in directing Indian affairs was brilliantly successful.

To understand the course of events during the rule of Warren Hastings, we must begin by marking out the years in which he held real control, and noting the bearing on Indian affairs of occurrences elsewhere. In 1772, Hastings became Governor of Bengal. In 1774, North's Regulating Act came into force. Hastings became Governor General, and the new Members of Council and the new judges came to India. From the end of 1774 till 1777, Hastings was overruled by an antagonistic majority in the Council. From 1777 to 1782 Hastings was dominant. After 1782 he was again seriously hampered by opponents effectively countenanced by the directors at home. From 1775 to 1782, Great Britain was engaged in the war with the American colonies. In 1778, France ; in 1779, Spain ; and in 1780, Holland were added to her enemies ; and until 1782, when Rodney crushed the French fleet in the West Indies, she was by no means supreme on the seas. Therefore, Hastings had to secure the British in India in a position newly won, under unprecedented conditions, against the rivalry of great native Powers, entirely out of his own resources without support from England, under perpetual pressure from the directors for money when he was in need of every available penny. And all this for some years, in the face of a cabal in his Council which had both the will and the power habitually at once to thwart his policy and to attack him personally.

Difficult Task of Hastings

Experience has taught us that when a higher and a lower civilisation are in contact, the more advanced race will act wisely in persistently maintaining its own ethical standards. When the great Indian experiment began, it was believed that expediency might on occasion justify a policy not openly admissible as between European peoples, but in perfect accordance with the Oriental rules of the game. An example occurred while Hastings was still only Governor of Bengal. On the north-west of Oudh lay Rohilkhand, a district occupied mainly by a peaceful Hindu population, over whom, within the last half century, an Afghan tribe of Mohammedan hill-men, known as the Rohillas, had established their domination. The Oudh wazir coveted Rohilkhand, and he had reason to believe that the Rohillas were intriguing with

Duplicity Versus Honesty

the Mahrattas. He appealed to the British to aid him in bringing them into subjection, to forestall a combined attack of Rohillas and Mahrattas upon Oudh. He backed the appeal by promise of a very substantial reward for assistance. The maintenance of Oudh as a buffer between Bengal and the Mahrattas was a principle of policy laid down by Clive. Hastings gave the assistance ; the Company received the reward. Hastings had omitted to make conditions as to the conduct of the campaign ; and the Wazir's troops behaved in the usual Oriental fashion, in spite of the protests of British officers. The action of Hastings in the matter did not interfere with his being appointed Governor-General.

Already complications were arising in a new quarter. The recognised head of the Mahratta confederacy was the Peshwa, a hereditary Minister, or "Mayor of the palace," at Puna. The Gaekwar at Baroda, Holkar at Indur, Sindhia at Gwalior, and the Bhonsla at Nagpur, were the other princes of importance. The death of the Peshwa led to a disputed succession ; the Bombay Government gave its active support to one of the candidates, Ragoba or Ragonath Rao. In 1775 it made a treaty with him, though the power to do so was vested in the Governor-General, not in the Governor of Bombay. Policy, however, demanded that Bombay should be supported from Calcutta ; whereas the antagonistic cabal in the Council negotiated with the Regency which had established itself as the *de facto* government at Puna. Sindhia, Holkar, and the rest, took or changed sides as suited them. When at last Hastings got the upper hand at Calcutta, he renewed the treaty with Ragoba, and prepared to send an expedition across India to support him. Bombay, in a hurry to show its own vigour, tried to strike without waiting, and met with disaster. The effect was fortunately minimised by the brilliant operations and rapid movements of the Bengal expeditionary force. Meanwhile, at Madras, successive governors had been giving umbrage both to the Nizam and to Haidar Ali. The Nizam was meditating an anti-British confederacy. When France declared war against Great Britain in 1778, Haidar found fresh cause of offence in the British seizure of the French port of Mahé, which

A Much Disputed Succession

was in Mysore territory. In 1780, the Nizam, Haidar, and the leading Mahrattas came to terms among themselves; the British seemed to have their hands full with the Mahratta business in the Bombay quarter. Haidar Ali suddenly fell on the Carnatic, sweeping it with fire and sword. The blunderers at Madras were quite unprepared, and their forces were either cut up or driven behind fortifications. British prestige was recovered, however, by a brilliant diversion in the North Mahratta territory, where the fortress of Gwalior, supposed to be impregnable, was captured by a daring surprise. The Mahrattas became divided in mind, and the next year found them holding back from the contest. Before the end of 1781, Eyre Coote, the victor of Wandewash, was in command in the Carnatic, and had thrice routed the armies of Haidar Ali. In 1782, the position of the British was again made extremely perilous by the appearance in Indian seas of the French Admiral Suffren, who proved himself, on the whole, rather more than a match for the English Admiral Hughes. But, most opportunely, the very able Haidar Ali died; and though his son Tippu Sahib carried on the war, the other native Powers fell away from him. The French fleet was neutralised by the peace of Versailles, and would probably in any case have been paralysed very shortly, as Rodney's victory in the West Indies had restored British Naval supremacy; and Tippu would by himself have been unable to maintain a successful struggle. Now, however, Hastings was again fettered by opposition at home; and the Madras Government made peace with Mysore on their own account, on terms which almost appeared to have been dictated by a victorious foe. For the successful phases of the whole struggle, the credit belongs to Warren Hastings; for its unsuccessful phases the discredit rests with the Calcutta cabal, and the Bombay and Madras Governments. As a total result, while Great Britain had been waging a war all over the world, in which she acquired nothing and lost half a continent, Warren Hastings had succeeded in maintaining her position in India, not only unimpaired, but, on the whole, strengthened, even in the south and west, as well as in Bengal and Oudh.

It is in connection with his administration in Bengal and Oudh that Hastings has been so frequently held up to obloquy—with what degree of justice in the Rohilla affair, the reader will have judged already. On his assuming the Governorship of Bengal, it became the first business of Hastings to organise the collection of revenue and the administration of justice. It was not possible to adopt measures which were more than tentative. The establishment of English district magistrates laid the basis of future organisation in the one field; in the other, a definite working system was set up, pending a

HAIDAR ALI, AN ENEMY OF THE BRITISH

This commander of the Mysore army had initial success against the British, but was defeated by Sir Eyre Coote.

THE MAHRATTA FORTRESS OF GWALIOR

This Mahratta stronghold, supposed to be impregnable, was, in 1780, captured by the British, under General Popham, by a daring surprise.

fresh assessment of the land from which the revenue was drawn.

This material improvement was followed by the arrival of the three new members of the Council from England, who, forming a majority, proceeded so far as possible to reverse all the Governor-General's arrangements. Of this period, the most striking event was the affair of Nanda **Trial on** Kumar, or Nuncomar, a Brah- **a Charge** man who, having a grudge **of Forgery** against Hastings, brought sundry charges against him on evidence which was probably forged. The Council took Nuncomar's part; but a native who, in his turn, had a grudge against Nuncomar, brought a perfectly independent charge of forgery against him. The case was fairly tried before the newly constituted High Court. Nuncomar was proved guilty, and was executed. It is practically certain that Hastings had nothing to do with the matter, but the removal of his accuser was so exceedingly opportune for him that the world has generally attributed the whole business to a conspiracy between Hastings, the Chief Justice, and a useful native.

When the successive deaths of two of the opposition cabal gave Hastings control, he established that board for the examination of land tenures and for re-assessment which formed a part of his scheme of reorganisation which had recently been reversed. Also he initiated the system of " subsidiary alliances " which was to be a leading feature of the rule of Lord Wellesley; arranging by treaty to maintain the army in Oudh under British control for the support of the Wazir out of revenues to be drawn from districts ceded by the Wazir to the Company for that purpose. Further, he got rid of the most unworkable feature of the Regulating Act. The judges were independent of the Administration, recognised no superior authority but the Crown in England, and claimed to exercise jurisdic- **The Judges** tion over the Council and the **and the** Governor-General. The Execu- **Executive** tive found itself paralysed. In order to bring the Executive and Judiciary into harmonious relations, Hastings proposed to establish at Calcutta a court of appeal from the district courts, and to appoint the Chief Justice head of this court, as a servant of the Company, with extensive supervisory powers over the system. Nothing but a compromise could

possibly have removed the deadlock, and the comprom'se arrived at proved effective. This affair, like t1at of Nuncomar, has been treated as if it attached some extraordinary discredit to the Chief Justice, Sir Elijah Impey; with singularly little reason.

It remains to note the two matters which, along with the Rohilla war and the execution of Nuncomar, have been used—and with little more justification—for the vilification of the great Governor-General. First was that of the Oudh Begums. When Shujah Daulah, Wazir of Oudh, died, the Begums, or Royal ladies, claimed that he had left most of his treasure to them personally. The Calcutta Council, in opposition to Hastings, maintained their claim as against the succeeding Wazir, Asaf ud Daulah. The latter, with his treasury thus depleted, naturally found himself unable to meet his obligations to the British. When Hastings got the upper hand, the Wazir declared his sincere desire to keep the promises made, but pointed out that the British, instead of helping him, were deliberately making it impossible. The Begums would not surrender **Affair of** the treasure, nor could he **the Oudh** recover it from them without **Begums** British assistance. The Wazir had the better claim, but the British were pledged to the Begums. On the other hand, these ladies had certainly been fostering antagonism to the British, who, it was argued, were thereby released from any obligations to them. Hastings, in dire need of money, was not difficult to satisfy as to the proofs, and gave Asaf ud Daulah active aid in recovering the property—a process carried out, as in the case of the Rohilla war, in accordance with Oriental rather than Western ideas of permissible severity.

There remains the affair of Cheyt Singh, Raja of Benares. In the course of various transactions with Oudh, this province was handed over to the British—that is, the Company, instead of the Oudh Wazir, became the over-lord of the Raja, who was under normal circumstances liable for a normal tribute or rent, and for further contribution in time of war. It was a matter of course that such vassal princes submitted to their over-lords precisely so long as they thought resistance or evasion would be dangerous. In 1778 and the following years, under pressure of the wars with the Mahrattas and with Haidar Ali, Hastings made heavy demands for extra

THE OLD COURT HOUSE AT CALCUTTA IN THE TIME OF WARREN HASTINGS

contributions. Cheyt Singh began to evade payment, probably under the impression that the power of the British was tottering and that he would be able to get free. Hastings declared him recalcitrant—in which he was probably quite correct—imposed a very heavy fine by way of penalty, and came with a small escort to Benares to enforce his demand. Benares rose in support of the Raja, and cut up the sepoys. The district, however, was brought into subjection promptly enough, Cheyt Singh was deposed, and a new Raja reigned at Benares. In 1784 North's Regulating Act was superseded by Pitt's India Act, which introduced a new system. Warren Hastings returned to England in 1785. Personal animosities, party exigencies, and an honest misapprehension both of what he had done and the conditions under which he had done it, led to his impeachment ; and, although seven years later he was fully acquitted on every count, it is only in recent years that his character has begun to be reinstated in the eyes of the public. But when he left India in 1785 at least the Province of Bengal recognised him as the best ruler it had known.

MEMORIAL OF THE TRAGEDY OF THE "BLACK HOLE OF CALCUTTA"
The view illustrates the Writers' Building in Calcutta at the end of the eighteenth century and the monument, surmounted by an obelisk, which was erected to commemorate the victims of Suraj ud Daulah.

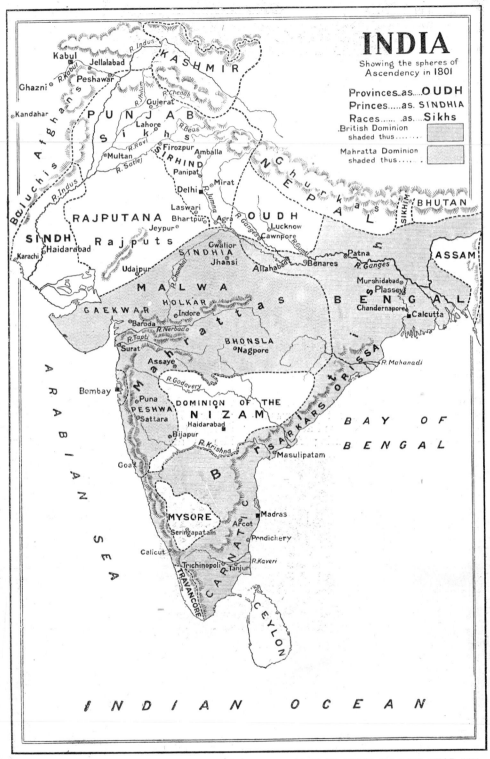

MAP SHOWING THE EXPANSION OF BRITISH DOMINION IN INDIA TO THE YEAR 1801

THE EXPANSION OF BRITISH DOMINION

THE retirement of Warren Hastings was immediately followed by the inauguration of the new British governmental system, which lasted, with slight modification, till 1858, a period during which the whole of India came under British supremacy, though large portions were not, and still are not, under direct British rule. It will be convenient, therefore, to take a survey of the position of the various Indian Powers in 1785.

At Delhi abode the Mogul, the phantom of an emperor. Westward of Delhi lie Sirhind and Rajputana, peopled chiefly by high-caste Rajputs or by Sikhs; westward again is the great Indus basin, comprising Sindh and the Punjab. Throughout these districts there existed no powerful state until the rise of Ranjit Singh at Lahore, when the nineteenth century began. Eastward, the Ganges basin was in effect divided between Oudh and Bengal, the latter under direct British rule, the former under practical British control. The whole of the eastern coastal territory, with slight exception, from Ganges mouth to the extreme south of the peninsula—Orissa, the Sarkars, the Carnatic —was British, though a nominal sovereignty was still exercised by the Nawab of Arcot. West of the British line comes first the great group of Mahratta states, dominating the rest of the peninsula, with the exception of Tippu Sahib's sultanate of Mysore, the Nizam's dominions, and the small British district of Bombay. Of the Mahratta groups, there were five chiefs: on the south—west of the Nizam—the Peshwa at Puna, the nominal head of the whole; in the north at Gwalior, dominating Delhi, the Sindhia dynasty; between Sindhia and the Peshwa, from west to east, the Gaekwar at Baroda,

MARQUESS WELLESLEY
Who, as Lord Mornington, rendered distinguished service when Governor-General, 1798-1805, and checked the efforts of Tippu Sahib.

Holkar at Indur, and the Bhonsla at Nagpur, enclosing the Nizam on the north. South of the Nizam and west of the British was Mysore.

Thus the militant Powers were Mysore, the Nizam, and the Mahratta confederacy. Of these, the Nizam was not strong enough to cope single-handed with either Mysore or a Mahratta combination. The Mahrattas, overwhelmingly strong in combination, could not rely on each other for mutual support. Mysore had been organised as a military state by a military adventurer, the father of the reigning sultan, and the hostility of its ruler to the British was ingrained. The fourth militant Power was the British. Not one of the ruling dynasties had been in possession for more than three-quarters of a century. The boundaries of every state or province expanded or contracted from decade to decade. From the time when Clive left India to the time when Mornington landed it was the intention of the British Government to work on European principles, to avoid extension of territory, and to preserve the balance between the native states. But such a conception was foreign to the native mind. Consequently, Cornwallis found himself, with great reluctance, forced to act in a manner very little less aggressive than Mornington, who had no reluctance whatever about it.

To meet such conditions, a strong central government was required within the British territories. In times when twelve months might easily elapse between the sending of a despatch from Calcutta and the receipt of the reply it was manifestly necessary for Calcutta to be free to act on its own responsibility, subject only to very general instructions from home. It was manifest also that the governing body must not be one with divided powers which could be paralysed by internal disagreements. Further, the dominion had been acquired by the East India Company, consistently with its charter, so that the claims and responsibilities of three parties had to be adjusted—the Government on the spot, the Sovereign at Westminster, and the Company. The adjustment was effected by Pitt's India Act in 1784. Bengal, Bombay, and Madras were each to have its own Governor, Commander-in-Chief, and Council, of two additional members, but Bengal was supreme over the others. Its Governor was Governor-General; if one member of his Council supported him he could take his own way; on emergency he could act independently of his Council. The general rule was adopted—to be set aside only in one instance before the end of the East India Company—that the Governor - General himself should be a man of European experience, while his Council should be Indian experts. The responsibility accepted by the Directors and by the Home Government consisted in their selection of a Governor-General, in their laying down the general lines of policy, with the consequent necessity for the Indian Government to justify itself if it deserted the lines laid down, and in their exercise of patronage. As between Company and Parliament, a Parliamentary Board of Control was established— changing with changes of Ministry—which had a general power of supervising, if it thought fit, and overruling the appointments made, the despatches sent, and the policy laid down by the Company. The new system was inaugurated by the selection of a Governor-General whose sound sense and military capacity had been thoroughly tested, whose integrity was unimpeachable, and whose fearless independence was absolutely secure. Lord Cornwallis reached India in 1786, the functions of his

Difficulty of Long-distance Government

MARQUESS CORNWALLIS
He subdued Tippu Sahib and did good work as commander in India. Appointed to India again in 1805, he died soon after his arrival.

office having been discharged in the interval by Sir John Macpherson, an experienced Indian official.

We shall find it convenient to defer our account of the British Administration and its development, and to proceed here with the story of the relations between the British *Raj* and the native Powers, down to the Victorian period.

At the moment when Cornwallis reached India, the aggressive Moslem fanaticism, and the generally arrogant attitude of Tippu Sahib—elated by the peace recently accepted by Madras—caused the Puna Mahrattas and the Nizam to dread his activities more than those of the British. The astute Madhoji Sindhia of Gwalior had already come to the conclusion that unless very exceptional circumstances arose it would be wise to maintain friendly relations with the British. His main object was to secure a personal ascendancy within the Mahratta confederacy and on the north and west. Sindhia's attitude, on the whole, decided that of Nagpur and Indur, while Baroda was not aggressive. Cornwallis, in thorough accord, *a priori*, with the policy of non-intervention favoured at home, found it unnecessary to do more in the south than reorganise military arrangements so as to ensure that, if necessary, he could intervene with effect. Tippu, not being anxious to unite the Mahrattas, the Nizam, and the British against himself, composed his quarrels with the two former; and for some time Cornwallis was free to occupy himself with administrative reforms. Cornwallis was well aware that Tippu was only waiting his opportunity to attempt the overthrow of the British; but the circumstances which forced on the collision were curious. When the Nizam had made his peace with Tippu, the Governor-General—in accordance with instructions from home—invited him, in 1788, to carry out the terms of a treaty made twenty years before, and to complete the cession of a district known as the

Moslem Hostility to British

CORNWALLIS RECEIVING THE SONS OF TIPPU SAHIB AS HOSTAGES OF PEACE

The result of the victories of Lord Cornwallis against Tippu Sahib was a peace by which much territory was ceded, and Tippu's sons were handed over to the British as hostages for the peaceful behaviour of their father, the Sultan of Mysore.

Gantur Sarkars. The Nizam replied by inviting the British to give effect to another clause in that treaty and aid him in the recovery of certain other districts which had been appropriated by Haidar Ali. Cornwallis, while declining to commit himself, was unable in his answer wholly to repudiate the obligation. Tippu concluded that a combined attack was imminent, and forestalled it by himself attacking a British protectorate, Travancore; and thus war began.

Causes of a War

The Nizam and Puna professedly supported the British, to whom, however, both intended to leave the hard work. The campaign of 1790 was ineffective, partly owing to the culpable neglect of the Madras Governor. In 1791, Cornwallis himself took the field. He captured Bangalur, whereupon the Nizam's troops joined him. Supplies ran short, and Cornwallis had to fall back. Then the Mahrattas appeared—not to assist in the campaign, but to ask for funds. The final effect was to stultify the scheme of the year's operations. Before the following spring, however, the Governor-General was able to perfect his arrangements, to bring Tippu to bay almost at the gates of his capital, Seringapatam, and to force him to submission, which involved, as a necessity of Oriental warfare, the cession of nearly half Mysore. Of the ceded districts, Cornwallis retained only about one-third, transferring the rest to his nominal allies, the Nizam and the Mahrattas. But those he retained were of strategical importance. There was no other way of materially curtailing Tippu's power of aggression in the future; to have left his territories intact would have been a direct incitement for him to seek a fresh opportunity for attack, and for the Nizam and the Mahrattas to transfer their alliance to him. There is no manner of doubt that Cornwallis would have avoided extending the British territories if it had been possible, or that both the Company and the Government in London were anxious not to expand, but to concentrate. But Cornwallis saw that there was no choice, and London ratified his judgment.

Partition of Tippu's Territory

We defer the discussion of the large administrative measures which marked his rule. In 1793 he retired, at the moment when the French Republic had just declared war upon England—a war which was to last, with two intervals of a few months, till 1815, affecting in no small degree the policy of the successors of Cornwallis and of the native **Effect of** Powers. This, however, does **European** not become conspicuous, as **Wars** concerns the British, during the rule of the next Governor-General, Sir John Shore, who, later, became Lord Teignmouth. Between Warren Hastings and John Lawrence—for a period, that is, of nearly eighty years—Shore was the only Governor-General appointed with an exclusively Indian record. He was an official of great capacity, an excellent counsellor, as Cornwallis knew by experience; but usually lacking in the vigour and decision of character which the circumstances demanded in the ruler of British India.

Hence, Shore's anxiety to maintain an attitude of non-interference threatened to bring about a serious crisis in Southern India. With Cornwallis, the great principle had been to keep the peace between the southern Powers; with Shore, it was to avoid entanglement in their quarrels. The Mahrattas took immediate advantage of the situation to attack the Nizam and to wrest territory from him.

The Nizam was aggrieved, because a firm attitude on Shore's part would have protected him; he felt himself deserted, and began to organise his troops under the command of French officers, while both the Mahrattas and Tippu formed the hasty conclusion that the British power was on the verge of collapsing. It was fortunate for the British that the Mahratta states and dynasties were plunged, by a series of deaths, into a state of factions and rivalries which effectively prevented concerted aggression. The great Madhoji Sindhia died; it was some years before **British** the new Sindhia, Daulat Rao, **Power** secured ascendancy; and the **in Peril** same thing happened with the new Peshwa, Baji Rao, at Puna. The same lack of firmness shook the prestige of the Governor-General in Bengal itself, where there was for a moment a real danger that the army

CAPTURE OF BANGALUR AND DEATH OF COLONEL MOORHOUSE

When Cornwallis reached India he found a state of unrest that demanded strong action; and he took the field against Tippu Sahib, soon capturing Bangalur, the Mysore capital. One of the chief incidents in the assult is depicted above.

THE EMBASSY OF A NATIVE RULER TO THE GOVERNOR-GENERAL
The painting by Zoffany, from which our illustration is taken, represents the progress of a great embassy from the Wazir of Oudh to Calcutta, proceeding by way of Patna, to meet Lord Cornwallis, the Governor-General, in 1788.

would seize control of the Government. The British Raj was upheld partly by white troops of the King's Army, partly by sepoy regiments forming the Company's army. There was intense jealousy between the officers of these two branches, and also between the Company's military officers and their civil officers. The two military branches united to formulate common demands, which would have resulted in a military domination. It was evident that a much stronger man than Shore, who in effect surrendered to the mutineers, was required to cope with the situation, and Lord Mornington was appointed to replace him. Nevertheless, in one field Shore had displayed a firmness and a personal courage which went far to counterbalance his failures. In the dependent State of Oudh misgovernment was rampant. On the death of the Nawab, a reputed son, Wazir Ali, succeeded him, with every intention of following in his predecessor's footsteps. But when it was ascertained that Wazir Ali's title was bad, the British Government refused to recognise him, and gave its support to the late Nawab's brother —on terms recognising the British right of control. A British force was to be maintained by a subsidy, secured by

Attempted Military Dominion

the Allahabad territory. Shore arranged matters himself, remaining unprotected at Lucknow, the Oudh capital, in the midst of a population which seemed on the verge of a violent outbreak; refusing, though in hourly risk of his life, to call up British troops, since to do so might have precipitated a sanguinary struggle. His coolness and courage won the day. Saadat Ali was established on the throne of Oudh without bloodshed. Critics of British methods in India are apt to forget that if in such a case Shore had abstained from insisting on British control, the British would in a few years' time inevitably have been compelled to annex Oudh altogether.

Lord Mornington, elder brother of Arthur Wellesley afterwards Duke of Wellington, initiated a new era in Indian policy. Hitherto the British aim had been to maintain a balance of power among the native potentates, after the European model. But the theory of balanced powers was altogether foreign to native conceptions. From time immemorial India has been a field in which rival thrones strove for supremacy, until the Moguls had achieved a general sovereignty, which exercised some check over the aggressive tendencies of individual principalities.

Brother of the "Iron Duke"

For the preservation of any modicum of general security and order, it was necessary that some power should be recognised as paramount ; and the Mogul sovereignty had now for a long time been the merest fiction. The balancing scheme would not serve as a substitute. If, then,* the re-establishment of a paramount Power was a necessity, it was clear enough that, in the interest of the Indian population in general, as well as in that of the British, the ascendancy must be secured not to a native Power, but to the British. For the British themselves it was essential that no Power other than their own should be paramount. The necessity was accentuated by the state of affairs in Europe, where Bonaparte was now the leading figure. No one yet knew what his precise designs might be. But he had proved himself unmistakably the first of living generals ; and though Britain

Need for the British Paramountcy

had proved herself the strongest of the naval powers, her actual supremacy on the seas was by no means secured in 1797.

Only fifteen years before a French admiral in Indian waters had almost enabled Mysore to overthrow the British in the Carnatic. Half the native Powers now had armies organised by French officers, and were hoping for French aid to free them from the British incubus ; and, in fact, Bonaparte meant the recovery of French ascendancy in India to play its part in his scheme of an Asiatic dominion as a means to the subjugation of Europe. To the French menace was added at the moment an alarm lest the Mohammedan ruler at Kabul, Zeman Shah, who was supposed to be extremely powerful, should make alliance with the zealot Tippu in Mysore and aim at re-establishing a great Mohammedan dominion in India.

Mornington then, who was thoroughly conversant with Indian affairs, arrived at Calcutta, with the intention of making the British paramount. He had hardly landed when proof came that Tippu Sahib was intriguing with the French at Mauritius. Mornington made immediate preparation for a duel with Tippu, in case it should prove necessary. For the moment, the Mahrattas were too much taken up with their internal feuds to be dangerous. The Governor-General turned at once on the Nizam, and pressed upon him the immediate dismissal of the French corps organised in Shore's time, and the substitution of a British contingent—since the Nizam knew that he could hardly stand alone with the Mahrattas on one side of him and Tippu on the other. The Nizam accepted the situation.

Meanwhile, negotiations were on foot with Mysore. But as the British demands involved terms which would deprive

SIR DAVID BAIRD DISCOVERING THE BODY OF TIPPU SAHIB
Tippu Sahib, the " Tiger of Mysore," tried by intrigue and arms to crush British power in India, but was killed in the assault upon Seringapatam on May 4, 1799.

ASSAULT UPON SERINGAPATAM, WHERE TIPPU MADE HIS LAST STAND

The storming and capture of Seringapatam, the capital of Mysore, in 1799, ended the hostilities and machinations of its Sultan, Tippu Sahib, a dangerous enemy of British supremacy in India. He was killed in the final assault.

Tippu of French assistance in any shape, and would make him as dependent as the Nizam on the British, Tippu would make no agreement. He continued his intrigues, in spite of reports of French reverses in Egypt, where Nelson annihilated the Mediterranean fleet at the Battle of the Nile.. In the early spring of 1799, the British advance on Mysore began. In April, Tippu was at bay in Seringapatam; in May the defences were stormed, and the Sultan was killed in the fight. Mornington restored the old Hindu dynasty—which had been dethroned forty years before by Haidar Ali—under British protection, and with greatly reduced territories. Of the lands of which Mysore was shorn, a portion was offered to the Mahrattas on terms which they rejected. Another portion was bestowed on the Nizam, and promptly ceded back to the British as security for the maintenance of the British contingent at Haidarabad. The practical result was that more than half of Tippu's dominion was brought under direct British government, and the rest under British protection.

Death of Tippu Sahib

Disputed successions in minor districts, but notably in the Carnatic, enabled the Governor-General to carry on the business of establishing British supremacy by refusing recognition to claimants who would not accept his terms—which in effect transferred entire political and administrative control to the British : an arrangement displeasing to the dynasties, but indubitably of immense advantage to the population. Oudh was treated in even more high-handed fashion, the Nawab being required to dismiss most of his own army, and greatly increase the British contingent, ceding for their maintenance a belt of provinces—known from this time as the North-West Provinces—which enclosed the entire frontier of Oudh. Wellesley—the conquest of Mysore had brought the Governor-General his marquisate—now found himself face to face with the Mahrattas, the only Power which really had in it the possibilities of challenging the British for supremacy in India.

British Supremacy Extended

The three chiefs who had recently succeeded—Daulat Rao Sindhia, Jeswant Rao Holkar, and Baji Rao Peshwa—occupied in a struggle between themselves for ascendancy, had made no attack on the British. But they had been equally resolute in refusing overtures for subsidiary alliances which would have brought them under Wellesley's control.

In 1802, however, the Peshwa suffered a grave defeat from Holkar. Seeing his chance of supremacy vanish, he thought it better to seek British protection, like the Nizam, than to be wiped out by Holkar; and he accepted Wellesley's terms. Now, it was admitted in theory that the Peshwa was the head of the Mahrattas. If, then, the great confederacy ac-

Mahrattas Accept British Suzerainty knowledged Baji Rao's treaty with Wellesley, they would be formally admit-

ting British paramountcy. Baji Rao had hardly been re-established at Puna under the ægis of the British when he began to repent. Hence, in August, 1803, the disappointed Holkar standing aside, the attitude of Sindhia and the fourth chief, the Bhonsla of Nagpur, forced the British to a virtual de-claration of war. Sindhia and the Bhonsla acted in conjunction in the north of the Deccan. North, in the neighbourhood of Gwalior, Sindhia's own main army was set in motion, under command of the French officers, whose dismissal Wellesley had failed to procure. The campaigns were not prolonged. In the Deccan, Arthur Wellesley routed Sindhia and the Bhonsla at the bloody battle of Assaye, in September, losing one-third of his men. Two months later he repeated his success at Argaon; and between

"THE TIGER OF MYSORE"
Tippu Sahib, the son of Haidar Ali, carried on hostilities against the British, and, at one time, threatened to kill the East India Company.

these two victories Lake shattered Sindhia's northern army at Laswari. By the end of the year both the chiefs submitted, accepted the British suzerainty, dismissed their French officers, and ceded extensive districts to the British, portions of which were transferred to the Nizam.

Holkar, however, now bethought himself of offering an independent resistance. The remarkable success of his tactics at the outset created a panic, and almost set the whole body of the Mahrattas in motion again; but despite opening disasters, the tide turned in a few months, and British superiority was asserted with sufficient effect to prevent any general rising. Nevertheless, enough had been done to alarm the home authorities, to

whom it appeared that Wellesley was plunging into a reckless and very dangerous course of aggression in open defiance of instructions; and in 1805 the great Governor-General found himself superseded, while Holkar was still in arms.

Since the time of Clive there have been two Governors-General, and only two, whose policy was controlled by the firm conviction that Britain ought not to let slip any legitimate opportunity for bringing fresh territories in India under her direct control. Yet scarcely one escaped the necessity of adding something to the Company's dominion. Failure to extend active protection to an ally, failure to answer defiance by chastisement, omission to demand cession of territory as the reward of victory—each and all of these were invariably and universally regarded by native Powers as marks not of moderation or magnanimity, but of weakness, inviting fresh defiance, which, in its turn, involved a heavier penalty than would have sufficed in the first instance. The most pacific declarations have only led the way to annexations; hence, neither the Indian potentates on the borders of the British dominion, nor European critics, have ever been able to divest themselves of the conviction that denials of aggressive intention have been merely expressions of systematic hypocrisy.

In the cases of Wellesley and Dalhousie, there is no room for the charge of hypocrisy—unless the argument that British domination is best for the native population be regarded as hypocritical. For

Reluctant Makers of the Empire neither of those two expanders of empire ever made the slightest pretence that their annexations were made with

reluctance; they hailed opportunities. Lord Hastings also accepted them without regret. But there was probably no other Governor-General who would not have preferred to be able to say at the end of his tenure of office that he had added no fresh territories to the British dominion in India.

Yet the impossibility of standing still was immediately exemplified on Wellesley's departure. His place was taken by the veteran Cornwallis, who would soon have found, as he had found before, that facts were too strong for theories, and would doubtless have displayed the same common-sense as before in dealing with them. But the old chief died **A Few** before he had realised the situa**Years of** tion; Sir George Barlow held **Leniency** the reins of office *ad interim* till the new Governor-General should be appointed. The theory of non-intervention was given full play. The terms of Wellesley's treaty with Sindhia were modified in favour of the latter ; Holkar was forced to sue for peace, and got it on terms of which he had never dreamed. The British declined to intervene for the

the treaty of Tilsit. Nelson had broken the French naval power at the Nile in 1798, and shattered it at Trafalgar in 1805. All that it was now capable of was to raid British commerce from its station at Mauritius. But a union of France and Russia threatened an overland advance against India. Hence negotiations with the intervening Power of Persia, which Wellesley had inaugurated, were renewed, and an attempt was made to establish friendly relations with the ruler of Afghanistan at Kabul, with little effective result in either case. The matter ceased to be urgent, as friendship cooled between Napoleon and the Tsar.

Within India, Minto found occupation in reducing to tolerable order the district of Bandelkhand, on the south of the Jumna, which the Peshwa had transferred

EARL OF MINTO   MARQUESS OF DALHOUSIE   MARQUESS OF HASTINGS
The first Earl of Minto was Governor-General of India during 1807–13 ; he made many frontier treaties, and success crowned his administration. The tenth Earl and first Marquess of Dalhousie was Governor-General during 1847–56, and added Lower Burma to British dominions. The first Marquess of Hastings was made Governor-General of Bengal and Commander-in-Chief of India in 1813 ; his victories and diplomacy extended British dominions, and he founded Singapore.

protection of the States of Rajputana against Mahratta aggression ; bands of Mohammedans and Hindu mercenaries were allowed to accumulate in Holkar's territories under the names of Pathans or Pindaris—freebooting hordes, who ravaged and robbed unchecked ; Rajputana was filled with anarchy. Before a decade was passed, the Mahrattas were preparing to make another bid for ascendancy as against the British.

In 1807, Barlow's acting appointment was closed by the arrival of Lord Minto, whose rule was signalised by the capture of Mauritius from the French and of Java from the Dutch, nominally the allies and actually the subjects of Napoleon. The moment of Minto's appearance in India was also that of the rapprochement between Napoleon and the Tsar which issued in

to the British in exchange for some territory in the Deccan. But beyond this it was becoming clear that the theory of non-intervention was breaking down. Hitherto the whole of the north-west— roughly, everything west of the Jumna and the Chambal above their junction— had stood outside British interference. **Rise of** Recently one of the Sikh chiefs, **Punjab** Ranjit Singh, had established **Power** his own supremacy at Lahore, and constructed a very powerful military monarchy in the Punjab. He now sought to extend his rule eastwards over the Sikh principalities of Sirhind between the Satlej and the Jumna. These Cis-Satlej Sikhs appealed to British protection. Diplomatic relations were consequently opened with the Punjab, whose very astute monarch was quick to realise that British friendship was much more desirable than British hostility. He resigned his Cis-Satlej claims under protest, and on a promise that within the Punjab there should be no interference. The loyalty of the Punjab ally, as well as that of the Sirhind protectorate, remained unbroken till 1845. Finally,

Lord Minto's Policy Holkar having died, the activities of the Pathan chief, Amir Khan, became so exceedingly aggressive that Minto was obliged to threaten intervention on behalf of Nagpur, which Amir Khan was endeavouring to master. The threat drove the Pathan adventurer back to Indur, and the struggle with the Pathans and Pindaris was deferred for Minto's successor to carry through.

Minto's policy created a somewhat inexplicable uneasiness at home, and in 1813 he was replaced by Lord Moira, afterwards Marquess of Hastings, a politician and soldier of considerable experience, who was already nearly sixty. He went to India looking upon Wellesley's policy as pernicious and dangerous. Very soon he became his great predecessor's disciple. In plain terms, he found a vigorous anti-British aggression afoot on every side ; and he recognised that the British must either be paramount or cease to count. His choice between the alternatives was not in doubt.

The first move came from a new quarter. North of the Ganges, in Oudh, lie the rich lands known as the Terai. Beyond the Terai are the mountains of Nepal, occupied by the Ghurka highlanders, soldiers unsurpassed, hardy, daring, staunch, though small of stature and few in number. The Ghurkas were dissatisfied with their mountains, and began to lay claim to the Terai. Hastings required them to retire, and sent troops to occupy the districts. The Ghurkas replied by themselves occupying them. There was no alternative to war.

The opening campaign was more disastrous than usual. Neither officers nor men had any experience of hill-fighting, which the stout little Ghurkas understood to

RANJIT SINGH
This was the Sikh who rose to power in Lahore. He was ignorant but able ; in 1809 he made an alliance with the Earl of Minto, and the British afterwards supported him.

perfection. Only one British column, commanded by Ochterlony, on the west of the extended frontier, met with any success. The rest met with repulses of varying severity, despite the very small forces of the Nepalese. Every antagonistic or potentially antagonistic force in India was on the alert at once, and preparing either to strike at the British or to strike into the turmoil which would be occasioned by their overthrow. But Moira was prompt and energetic ; the hostile Powers, lacking organisation, did not declare themselves at once. Time was given for Ochterlony to turn the tide in Nepal. Skilfully led, the British overwhelmed the valiant foe. Territory, of course, was ceded, but the terms were honourable to both parties, and, on the one hand, established a lasting amity between the British and the independent Nepal State, while, on the other, the new territories supplied the British with some of the finest regiments in their service. Moreover, the immediate effect was to damp completely the ardour of the disaffected princes.

Moira, thenceforth to be known as Marquess of Hastings, had by this time thoroughly adopted for himself Wellesley's fundamental idea of establishing ascendancy by means of subsidiary alliances—that is, of maintaining under treaty in the native states, in return for a subsidy which might or might not be secured by a cession of territory, a force which should at once protect the prince and the state from native aggression, or from revolt, and practically ensure British control. At

A Strong Policy Resumed an auspicious moment for him, the vigorous George Canning became President of the Board of Control in London, so that his measures were not hampered. Further, the outrages of which the hordes of Pathans and Pindaris were guilty—with the undoubted connivance of Indur and Gwalior—made British activity not merely plausible but absolutely imperative. The death of the Nagpur Bhonsla in

1816 induced his successor to accept that subsidiary alliance which the dead prince had resolutely declined. But mischief was obviously brewing among the three greater Mahratta principalities of the west. In 1817, the British movement, primarily for the suppression of the Pindaris, began. Hastings had avoided the common mistake; he had a huge force organised, to take the field at several points simultaneously. By these dispositions, Sindhia was paralysed for hostile action, as was Indur. The Peshwa and the Bhonsla each attempted to capture

Vigour Brings Peace the British "Residents" and destroy the escorts at Puna and Nagpur; each was brilliantly foiled. Thereafter, the converging British forces were far too strong to meet with any serious resistance. All the Mahratta chiefs, except the Peshwa, came to terms, as did Amir Khan himself, by the beginning of 1818; the Peshwa, too, was forced to surrender before long; nothing was left but the capture of some isolated garrisons, the last of which fell in 1819. At Kirki (Puna), Sitabaldi (Nagpur), and near Sirur, there were characteristic engagements in which small British bodies repulsed an apparently overwhelming enemy. But for the most part, this war

SIKH WARRIOR TRIBESMEN

was one in which the British forces were palpably too powerful to be faced in the field. Beginning as a war in the simple interest of public order, for the suppression of brigandage on a huge scale, it developed into the overthrow of the Mahratta Confederacy, every one of whose chiefs, except Sindhia and the Gaekwar had attacked the British; while conclusive proof was forthcoming that Sindhia was hand-in-glove with the enemy, and was restrained only by the paralysing British column which held him under surveillance. It could not, then, be said that the terms imposed were harsh. As concerned Sindhia, the British did little more than assert the right from which Barlow had debarred them, of extending protection to Rajputana. The Bhonsla was deposed and replaced by a minor, till whose majority

Overthrow of Mahratta Confederacy the British took over the administration. Holkar accepted a subsidiary alliance. The Peshwa's territories, on the other hand, were annexed, and his office abolished, while he himself was allowed to retire to British territory on a handsome pension; and the small state of Sattara was cut out of his dominion, and bestowed on the heir of tne house of Sivaji.

Hastings had been allowed to follow out his policy; when the work was done, the Directors were, as usual, pained by the great outlay it had involved, and

SIKH ARMOUR AND WEAPONS

alarmed at the responsibilities imposed on the Company by the accession of territory. In India, sundry ruling houses had been discomposed, a marauding swarm of brigands dispersed, some thousands of soldiers deprived of opportunities for loot, protection extended to a number of minor chiefs, and an unprecedented security bestowed on vast populations.

The Work of Lord Hastings The man who had done these things was in effect censured and superseded, though not in form. Nevertheless, his successor, Lord Amherst (1823), was as little able as his predecessors to abstain from expansion. Hastings had brought the whole Indian peninsula into the compass of British ascendancy, except for the Indus basin, which remained independent. While Ranjit Singh ruled at Lahore there was no danger of troubles in that quarter. But Amherst was assailed on a new side. Across the great Bay of Bengal, the ruler of Burma thought fit to throw down the gage to the British.

In the course of the last thirty years Burma had suffered from an illusory belief in its own overwhelming power and the feebleness of the British, chiefly because the latter, while giving an asylum to Burmese subjects, had not resented the menaces of the monarch at Ava by force of arms. The latter had, in the time of

Lord Hastings, gone so far as to demand the " restoration " of Lower Bengal, as though it had been a Burmese province. Now, the Burmese took possession of an island off Chittagong, which the British claimed as their own. Amherst turned out the Burmese force, and warned Burma that the limit of British forbearance had been reached. Burma replied by, in effect, announcing an invasion. Whereupon Amherst declared war.

First Burmese War The weary campaigns of the first Burmese War demand brief relation. In 1824, an army was sent over sea which occupied Rangoon. There it remained inactive, owing to deficient supplies. In December the Burmese were driven from their entrenchments before Rangoon. As the next spring advanced, the British advanced up the Irawaddi as far as Prome. Then they were stopped by rains. A second expedition through Arakan was also checked by rains and by disease. It was not till the beginning of 1826 that the Burmese king was forced to come to terms, paying a substantial indemnity, and ceding the districts of Assam, Arakan, and Tenasserim—to the great satisfaction of the inhabitants, who had no love for their Burmese rulers.

The prolongation of the Burma War— which ought to have been carried through

THE BRITISH EXPEDITION GOING UP THE IRAWADDI TO RANGOON IN JULY, 1824.

in six months, whereas it occupied two years—again gave occasion for a small native state in the heart of India to make an experiment in ignoring British authority. This was Bhartpur, whose main fortress had successfully defied the assault of Lord Lake in 1805, and was supposed to be impregnable. Blunders and misunderstandings between Ochterlony, the commandant in the north - west, and the Governor-General, encouraged the reviving impression of British weakness. But when Metcalfe was sent to replace Ochterlony, he recognised the necessity for asserting British strength. Amherst yielded to Metcalfe's opinion, and placed troops at his disposal. The defiance of Bhartpur was met by an Engineers' attack on the " impregnable " fort which proved completely successful. The brief excitement which had begun to stir the native mind was promptly allayed. The fall of Bhartpur seemed conclusive proof of irresistible power.

It was not till after 1840 that the British again had to resort to arms to quell an Indian foe, or to emphasise the reality of their ascendancy by requiring further cessions of territory. The period of expansion was closed by the Burmese War, which lay altogether outside of India itself. The next period of expansion was inaugurated by intervention in another state beyond the borders of India. The period from 1826 to 1839 was occupied

LORD METCALFE AND LORD WILLIAM BENTINCK
The first Baron Metcalfe was provisional Governor-General of India in 1835–6; his abilities lay in civil administration. Lord William Bentinck was Governor-General from 1828 to 1835, and is noted as having suppressed suttee, infanticide and dacoity.

A Few Years of Peace almost entirely with organisation and reconstruction in the dominions directly subject to the British, and in those wherein the minority of a prince placed administration temporarily in the hands of the British. For what was done during those years, and notably under the rule of Lord William Bentinck, much credit is due to the Government. It is open to question, however, whether Government was equally wise in its inaction. The pressure from

home was strong to prevent intervention in the internal affairs of native states. It was the time of the Reform movement in England, and reformers in all countries are slow to believe that the principles applicable under the conditions with which they are familiar are not equally valid under conditions with which they are unfamiliar. Non-intervention was carried to extremes, with the result that in the Gwalior State the army acquired a dangerous predominance, and in Oudh misgovernment was allowed to reach such a pitch that even the authorities in London began to fear that annexation might be forced upon them.

Bentinck succeeded Amherst in 1828, and retired himself in 1835. Even his rule was not wholly devoid of additions to the British dominion, since the two minor states of Kurg in the south, and **British System in India** Kachar on the north-east, were annexed—but by their own expressed desire. After a year, during which the very able Governor of the North-west Provinces, Sir Charles Metcalfe, held the Governor-Generalship ad interim, Lord Auckland was sent out. Before we proceed to the record of his tenure of office we shall turn to examine the other aspect of the great British experiment in India—the conduct of administration by Westerns among Orientals.

The constitution of the Government laid down for the British dominions in India by the India Act of 1784 remained in force, with some modifications, until 1858. The ruler of British India was the Governor-General in council. The only limitation to his power lay in the two facts, that he was removable at the will of a supreme body in England, and that he might be severely called to account if he transgressed their instructions; he need not obey, but if he did not he must be prepared to justify his disobedience. He disobeyed at his own peril. His council could help him, and might hamper him, but could never actually thwart him. The supreme powers in London were responsible for appointing to the post a capable man, and one whose views, at the outset at least, were in harmony with their own. That responsibility was shared between the nation, as represented by the Ministerial Board of Control, and the directors of the East India Company—the Company being the subordinate of the two. The instructions issued to the Governor-General, which he could disobey only at his peril, were laid down on the initiative or with the sanction of the Board of Control.

Responsibility for Indian Government

The Governor-General was usually, but not always, a person whose actual knowledge of the East was at secondhand; who was, however, versed in the business of administration, diplomacy, or war— possibly of all three; while his advisers on the Council were Indian experts. At home, the tendency of directors to subordinate political to commercial considerations was increasingly counteracted by the trained politicians on the Board of Control. The most noteworthy changes in the system took place on the renewal of the Company's charter in 1833, when certain powers which had been left to the Governors-in-Council of the minor presidencies were transferred to the central or supreme Government in Bengal.

On the acquisition of fresh territories, those which lay in Northern or Central India were normally joined to the Bengal Presidency; those on the west of the Nizam's dominions, to Bombay; those on the south and east, to Madras. With the extension of dominion, those territories which had been in touch with the British were usually brought under the same system of government as the first presidencies to which they were attached; those which lay further afield were usually known as non-regulation provinces, and were controlled on somewhat different lines, their governors being allowed a larger latitude. As the ascendancy was established, a British Resident or Agent was appointed to the court of each state, whose functions were partly ambassadorial, partly advisory, while his advice might on occasion be of a peremptory character. The ascendancy, as we have seen, was usually supported by the maintenance of

Treatment of New Territory

a considerable "contingent" or sepoy force, under British officers, who further protected the native Government against either disturbance from within or aggression from without, while restraining it from becoming aggressive itself.

The British power, then, was maintained by the three Company's armies in the three presidencies, composed not quite exclusively of native regiments under British officers, natives holding only non-commissioned appointments. In the Bengal army, these natives, it is to be noted, were mainly high-caste Hindus, either Brahmans or Rajputs, with a strong admixture of Mussulmans, who adhered to the Mogul traditions, while the Hindus were specially sensitive about all matters which touched their caste. The Bombay and Madras armies, recruited from districts where few of the population belonged to the higher castes, were much less sensitive —facts which bore fruit in the time of the Mutiny. Besides the Company's armies, there were a certain number of King's troops or white regiments of the Regular Army serving in India in rotation. The officers of the Company's armies were the servants of the Company; the two main branches of the ordinary administration—magisterial and revenue work— were in the hands of the Company's civil service. But in the non-regulation provinces the highest posts were often in the hands of soldiers, who were also extensively employed in what is known in India as "political" work, a term applied generally to the business of foreign, diplomatic, and quasi-diplomatic affairs.

The Fighting Force

In general, the aim of government was not to impose upon the natives European customs or laws, except where Europeans were concerned, but to systematise the existing indigenous laws and customs, so far as they were ascertainable, and to apply them in accordance with native sentiment, except where they were palpably productive of serious evils.

Now, the great bulk of the revenue was derived from land, and the history of the land settlements illustrates the honest, if not always perfectly successful, efforts of the British Government to regulate matters with justice. The beginning was made in Bengal, as being the first territory under direct British government. Here the issue of the attempt was the "Permanent Settlement" of Cornwallis. The measures taken by Warren Hastings had been avowedly of a temporary character, pending a full investigation of the system of land tenure. Lack of experience, coupled with Western preconceptions, which British commissioners naturally read into the conditions they found, led Cornwallis somewhat astray.

The Moguls and their Nawabs had farmed out the districts to revenue officers, whose business it was to collect the amount of revenue at which the district was assessed. Primarily, these zemindars became landlords, in so far as the money they collected might be termed rent. They were the receivers of rent from the cultivator, and they might collect a great

provements in cultivation. On this theory, the great object was to encourage the zemindar to improve cultivation by giving him security of tenure. The districts were assessed, the amounts the zemindars were to pay were fixed in permanence, and their full proprietary rights were confirmed to them and to their heirs. By degrees, however, the true relation of the zemindars to the soil became apparent. In the South of India they had never acquired the same outward likeness of landed proprietors as in Bengal. The investigations conducted there in connection with the territories annexed after the Mysore wars led to the conclusion that the actual peasantry were the

DURBAR OF THE RULER OF THE MAHRATTA STATES AT PUNA
The Peshwa at Puna was the nominal head of the five Mahratta chiefs. His support of the British action against Tippu Sahib was secured by treaty in 1790, and the ceremonial attending the ratification of the treaty is depicted above.

deal more than ever reached the Treasury. They had no legal security of tenure or of succession to a zemindari, but if they paid what was expected, and behaved themselves, they were not likely to be dispossessed, and their sons were normally appointed to succeed them. It may be remarked that they were usually Hindus, the Mohammedans seeking rather military employment. Sundry of the great zemindars had received the title of raja. With western analogies in their minds, the British regarded the zemindars as landlords, proprietors of the soil, like the landed gentry in England, with the peasantry as their tenants, as the persons who would reap most benefit from im-

true proprietors, or else the " village communities," of which they were members. Hence, the land settlement in the south was for the most part made on the basis of the direct payment of the rent or land tax by the *ryot* or peasant cultivator to the Government, without intervention of any zemindar. The peasant got his fair rent, fixity of tenure, and right of transfer, subject to his payment of the Government claim. Here, however, the Bengal error of making the assessment permanent, was avoided. The valuation, subject to certain modifications, was extended over a term of years long enough to give the cultivator security that he would get full benefit for all improvements ;

but after the term of years, the valuation was to be revised.

A third form of land settlement was necessary in the provinces of the Upper Ganges. Here a large proportion of the inhabitants belonged to Rajput clans. In the old days, the chief of the clan had often been looked upon as the proprietor of the soil, and under the Mogul Government these chiefs, or *talukdars*, had frequently been appointed to collect the revenue for their districts, like the zemindars of Lower Bengal, as far as government was concerned, but with a much closer approximation to the position of English or Scottish landowners. But besides the talukdars with traditional rights, there was much of the land which had undoubtedly been held by peasant cultivators and village communities. In these regions the " Thomasonian " settlement was a very careful attempt to adjust the several claims of talukdars, ryots, and village communities, to be regarded as the true proprietors under Government. Some authorities are of opinion that the ideas then current in England led in this case to the claims of talukdars being unduly overridden in favour of peasant proprietary—to the economic advantage of the peasant, but to the irritation not only of the chiefs, but of the clan sentiment of the population.

With wars perpetually on hand, it was not till the period of expansion was closed by the Burmese War that the Government was able to undertake very much beyond the ordinary business of administering the law, collecting the revenue, and carrying through the land settlements in Bengal and the Deccan. The Thomasonian settlement in the North-West Provinces came later. But the period which followed—in England, the era of the great Reform Bill and of reaction against the old Toryism— was filled with earnest efforts to improve the condition of the peoples of India. These efforts, largely, though by no means exclusively, connected with the rule of Lord William Bentinck, were of two kinds—those directed to the introduction of positive improvements, and those aiming at the suppression of evil but traditional customs and institutions. Among the former the two most noteworthy were, perhaps, the development of education among the natives by the aid

The Land Question

Efforts for Reform

of the State, and the gradual creation of a system of irrigation by canals, to cope with the recurrence of droughts and famines which periodically devastated the whole peninsula.

Participating in the character of both classes of reform was the control established over the primitive pre-Aryan races of certain hill-districts. Hall among the Mers of Merwara, and Outram among the Bhils of Kandesh, won among these peoples—who had never been brought into real subjection either by Mohammedan or Mahratta conquerors—a personal ascendancy, which gave them an extraordinary influence, where hitherto both coercion and conciliation had failed. In both cases the wild folk learned to look upon the Englishmen with an overmastering admiration and trust which led them to an unprecedented docility; so that they were taught for the first time in their history to desire peace and order among themselves, to give up savageries which had held sway from time immemorial, and to develop themselves into a well-conducted, if decidedly primitive, agricultural folk. Of very much the same character were the proceedings of Charters Macpherson among the Khonds in Orissa. In this district, the ghastly practice of offering human sacrifices still prevailed among a people who believed that wise men propitiate the Evil Spirit who is too strong for the Good Spirit. Hence the Khonds argued that if you want a good harvest you must sacrifice human victims to the powers of evil. Macpherson acquired sufficient ascendancy over them to induce them to try the experiment of omitting the propitiatory sacrifice, and telling the goddess to hold the British responsible for their neglect of her interests. The harvest was particularly good, and the British were manifestly none the worse. From this the Khonds inferred that the British were more powerful than the goddess, and the practice of human sacrifices ceased.

Personal Influence with Natives

Human sacrifices were peculiar to the primitive Dravidian districts. But among the Hindus the practice of " suttee " (*sati*, dedicated), the self-immolation of widows on the husband's funeral pyre, was almost universal. It had, in the course of centuries, acquired a powerful religious sanction, although it was not authorised by the Hindu scriptures; so much so that

Government long hesitated before venturing on a measure so antagonistic to popular sentiment as its suppression, contenting themselves with the Mohammedan rule that the act of the widow must be voluntary in fact, as it always was in theory. Proof of compulsion, however, was hard to obtain, though there could be no doubt that compulsion was habitually applied. Bentinck, on his arrival, made up his mind that total suppression must be risked, and, to the general surprise, the edict was accepted without any signs of popular excitement. The native potentates took example from the British, and suttee disappeared.

Brigandage on a gigantic scale was crushed with the suppression of the Pindaris. It remained on a smaller but still sufficiently serious scale in the form of dacoity. India was infested with bands

by strangulation. The natives believed them to be under divine, or rather diabolic, protection ; and it was only the curious counter-superstition that the *ikbal* (the luck) of the Company was stronger than the Thug demon that gradually brought the populace to venture on giving evidence. Every conviction of a Thug weakened the popular superstition in their favour. Presently some of the Thugs themselves began to reveal the secrets of their organisation, and Bentinck's administration has the credit of the suppression of the whole gruesome system, its success therein being mainly due to the abilities and energy of Major Sleeman.

The repression of one more evil practice remains to be noted. The mortality among girl-infants was enormous. No one doubted that it was due to infanticide, but to prove

SUTTEE, OR SACRIFICE OF A WIDOW UPON HER HUSBAND'S FUNERAL PYRE
The British Governors long hesitated to attempt the suppression of this practice, but Lord William Bentinck, Governor-General from 1828 to 1835, issued an edict making the practice criminal, and obedience followed without resistance.

of Dakaits or Dacoits, who wrought pillage and slaughter and vanished. It was gradually ascertained that there was a regular hereditary caste of Dacoits, members of which formed the nucleus of most of these bands, often in league or association with eminently respectable members of society. Such was the popular fear of these brigands that immense difficulty was experienced in collecting evidence against them. They flourished most in the districts where Western doctrines of evidence prevented summary methods of punishment, and it was only by very slow degrees that the evil was reduced materially, and finally practically stamped out.

Quite distinct from the bands of Dacoits were the Thugs—another hereditary caste which carried out its murderous operations against individuals, without bloodshed,

that a baby had not died a natural death was next to impossible. The cause was clear. The Hindu was bound by his religion to see that his daughters got married. Conventions had made the cost of marrying a daughter into a crushing expense for a poor man ; therefore a poor man could not afford to bring up daughters —and his daughters did not grow up. Merely to penalise a crime which could hardly ever be proved was a hopelessly inadequate remedy. Government set a limit to the expenditure on weddings, and penalised the " religious " beggars whose attendance in swarms—demanding in the name of religion a hospitality which the Hindu dared not refuse—had created a very substantial portion of the cost. The result was that in a very few years the balance of the sexes was restored.

EXPEDITION TO KANDAHAR GOING THROUGH THE BOLAN PASS IN 1838

The main route to Afghanistan by Peshawar and the Khaibar Pass could not be taken owing to the refusal of permission by Ranjit Singh, and the route by Quetta through the Bolan Pass had to be followed. The expedition was successful in its immediate object, and placed Shah Shuja on the throne of Afghanistan in place of Dost Mohammed, but the final result was the tragedy of the march from Kabul, a disaster unparalleled in the history of British arms in India.

1284

THE COMPLETION OF BRITISH DOMINION

THE chapter in the history of the British expansion in India which opens with the governor-generalship of Lord Auckland is very largely concerned with regions and peoples that had hitherto lain beyond the area wherein British activities had mainly been exercised.

Of these countries, two—the Punjab and Sindh—lie within the borders of India proper. Beyond the Punjab is Afghanistan ; beyond Afghanistan, Persia ; and beyond Persia, Russia. And we must now examine the history of all these during the half-century following the retirement of Warren Hastings, with more or less detail, according as it belongs to or bears upon the history of India herself.

Russia was destined to take the place, formerly held by France, of the one European Power which might attempt to challenge British supremacy in India. That place was lost by France from the day when British naval supremacy was **Russia as a Rival for India** finally established. For Russia alone the overland route might conceivably become some day practicable. In any case, the expansion of Russia must be Asiatic. Geographical conditions made it sure that her boundaries would gradually shift nearer and nearer to the Indian frontier.

But Russia was remote. In effect, Persia and Afghanistan lay between her and the mountain-barriers of India. It was not till Palmerston ruled in the Foreign Office that English statesmen began seriously to feel in her more than in France the Power against whose aggression Great Britain must be on guard. Persia, however, began to feel the Russian pressure at an early date. She felt that she must be overwhelmed by Russia unless she had British support. In the eyes of the British, she stood as a buffer against France rather than Russia. When the Tsar was in alliance with Napoleon, in the first decade of the nineteenth century, Britain was ready to support Persia. Hence, Persian treaties were inaugurated in the time of Lord Minto. When France

had ceased to be dangerous, diplomatic arrangements with Persia were in the hands of the home authorities, and they ceased to interest themselves in Persia. Hence, when trouble arose between Russia and Persia in 1826, Britain did not intervene. Thereupon Persia, unprotected, placed herself virtually at Russia's disposal. **Persia at the Feet of Russia** Beyond that was the fact that half the Mohammedans in India regarded the Shah as the head of Islam. Persia began to dream of an Indian empire, to be acquired with Russian support. What Russia dreamed of is a matter for conjecture.

Persia could not approach India without first absorbing Afghanistan. At times Persia and Afghanistan had been under one ruler ; but since the days of Ahmed Shah Durani—who had triumphed over the Mahrattas at Panipat in 1761— Afghanistan had been independent under the rule of his offspring. When Wellesley reached India in 1798, the Kabul state was credited with great strength and aggressive intentions. It was rent, however, by dissensions and rivalries for the rulership. A powerful family, the Barakzai brothers, became dominant, and set up and deposed the nominal kings of the Durani dynasty. In 1810 the then king, Shah Shuja, was driven from the country, and took up his abode under British protection. After various vicissitudes, Afghanistan was in effect parcelled out among the Barakzai brothers, except Herat, which remained in the hands of one of the Durani family—to whom the **The Buffer State** Barakzais still professed allegiance. From 1826, one of the brotherhood, at Kabul, Dost Mohammed, was the real monarch, at first with the title of Wazir, and later with that, familiar to British ears, of Amir.

More than once during these years there had been menaces of Persian aggression in the direction of Herat ; but the Barakzais had been largely occupied by alternate feuds and alliances with their

Indian neighbour, the Sikh ruler of the Punjab, Maharajah Ranjit Singh of Lahore. The reader may be reminded that the Sikhs had come into being as a reformed Hindu sect early in the sixteenth century. Primarily a heterodox religious body, their disregard of caste separated them from the orthodox Hindus, while they were in even worse odour with the Mussulmans. Hence, forming a close community, they were not long in acquiring the characteristics of a distinct race, while the circumstance compelled them to adopt a military organisation, under a series of leaders or prophets called Gurus, of whom the last, Govind Singh, was killed in 1708. The Sikhs—" disciples "—all bore the name of Singh (lion) ; in their military capacity they were known as the *Khalsa*, the " army of the free."

Occupying mainly the Punjab and Sirhind, between the upper Jumna and the Sutlej rivers, the Sikhs were perpetually exposed to persecution from the Moguls at Delhi, and to the attack of Afghan invaders. Yet they were not crushed. They formed a sort of confederacy of territorial groups known as *Misls*, whose power was quite out of proportion to their numbers, since they were in a considerable minority among Hindus and Mohammedans. But they did not

Rise of Sikh Power achieve dominion until the chief of one of the Misls, young Ranjit Singh, just when the eighteenth century was passing into the nineteenth, began to get himself recognised as the head of the whole Sikh body in the Punjab.

Among the native princes with whom the British came into contact, Ranjit Singh—with two others, Haidar Ali and Madhoji Sindhia—stands out as of altogether exceptional ability. Under his guidance, the Sikhs gradually dominated the entire Punjab, in course of time mastering Multan on the south-west ; wresting Peshawar and Kashmir from the Barakzais. With the help of European officers, he so organised the Khalsa that it became —in proportion to its numbers—by far the most powerful and best disciplined army that any Indian monarch had controlled. In nothing, however, did his shrewdness

EARL OF AUCKLAND
The first Earl of Auckland originated the policy that led to the tragedy of the disastrous march from Kabul in January, 1842.

approve itself more thoroughly than in his relations with the British. With keen eyes he watched the progress of affairs in India ; he was under no illusions when Holkar seemed for a moment to have bidden successful defiance to the victors of Assaye and Laswari. The initial failures of the Ghurka War set him on the alert for possibilities ; but after that he was fully convinced that Fate would one day bring all India under British dominion, and he was steadily resolved to do nothing which should draw the Punjab into collision with the British during his lifetime.

The territory of the Sindh Amirs was formed by the districts of the Indus basin below the Punjab. The population was chiefly Mohammedan ; the state or states were not highly organised, or aggressive ; and they paid tribute to the Durani monarchy.

About the year 1808, the British opened diplomatic relations, as we saw before, with Persia, with Kabul, with Lahore, and also with Sindh ; in the last case, mainly for the purpose of opening up the Indus for commerce. When fear of French aggression ceased, the Government of India in turn ceased to interest itself much in Persia or Afghanistan. A friendly Punjab was a secure barrier against the invasion of Afghans or Persians which hardly amounted to a serious menace ; and Sindh was in no way a source of anxiety. In that quarter, the only difficulties likely to arise would spring from Ranjit Singh's desire to extend his dominions, that astute ruler being determined to acquire everything which the British did not peremptorily forbid, as they had vetoed his proposal to claim sovereignty in Sirhind ; and further, to make a great favour of acceding to their wishes, in return

The Astute Policy of Ranjit Singh for which concessions in other directions might fairly be claimed. Sindh itself did not come within the range of his aggressive ambitions until after 1818, when he had made himself master of Multan, which had hitherto been subject to Kabul.

By 1836, commercial treaties had been arranged with the Sindh Amirs ; Ranjit Singh was still living, and at the height of his power, in the Punjab ; Shah Shuja was dwelling at Ludhiana in Sirhind, a futile pretender to the Afghan throne ; Dost Mohammed was the *de facto* ruler of Afghanistan ; and Mohammed Shah, who had recently succeeded to the Persian throne, was meditating vast schemes— to be carried out with Russia at his back— of which the first stage was to be the reconquest of Afghanistan, and the first step the capture of Herat.

Lord Auckland had hardly arrived in India when it became obvious that the affairs of Afghanistan and Persia required serious attention, a necessity due to the fact that everyone was perfectly satisfied that Russia was at the back of Persia in **Fears of** her aggressive designs, and that **Russian** the Shah was merely the **Designs** catspaw of the Tsar. Dost Mohammed was anxious. He did not like Russia ; but he did not like the Sikhs. The new Governor-General was politely indisposed to intervene in favour of Kabul against Lahore, and the Amir hoped to change his attitude by a show of friendliness to Russia. Diplomacy should have been able to reconcile Ranjit Singh and Dost Mohammed, whereby the designs of Persia would have been frustrated. But Auckland's advisers were too successfully beguiled by the Dost's assumption of friendliness to Russia, and were superfluously anxious to propitiate Ranjit. When they found that the shrewd Sikh had no desire to be presented with Kabul, they bethought themselves of ejecting Dost Mohammed in favour of Shah Shuja, a measure which could be carried out only by the employment of a large British force.

Now, in 1837 the scheme, though exceedingly wrong-headed, had the excuse that Persian armies were actually moving on Herat, and had begun the siege before the end of the year. But Herat held out stoutly, under the leadership of a young English officer, Eldred Pottinger, who had made his way thither. The months passed, the besiegers made no impression, Persia realised that Russia was satisfied to egg her on without taking risks herself, and by the autumn of 1838 the siege broke up, and the whole movement of aggression collapsed. The only possible pretext for direct intervention in Afghanistan had vanished.

Nevertheless, Auckland and his advisers, in defiance of all competent opinion, **Movement** pressed on with their design. **Against the** Ranjit Singh did not refuse **Afghans** assistance, but declined to allow British troops to march through his territory. Hence, the main route by Peshawar and the Khaibar Pass was barred. The second route, across Sindh and Baluchistan, and by Quetta through the Bolan Pass, was adopted, the Khaibar being left to the Sikhs. Thus, not Kabul but Kandahar in the south of Afghanistan became the primary objective of the British expedition.

The Amirs, or chiefs of the Sindh confederacy, and the Baluchi chiefs of Kelat, though theoretically friendly, raised as many obstacles as they dared, openly or secretly, but did not venture on a display of palpable hostility. By the end of March, 1839, the British had gained possession of Kandahar, without meeting active resistance, and Shah Shuja was duly proclaimed. Some three months later, the army proceeded against Ghazni, a very strong fort, *en route* for Kabul. One of the gates which had not been properly secured, was blown up, enabling the place to be successfully stormed—an operation which caused great elation. Dost Mohammed's followers at Kabul were not prepared to face an engagement, and the Dost himself had no alternative but to flee precipitately across the border, A year later, having redeemed his honour as a soldier by valiant conduct in a skirmish, and feeling his cause to be helpless, he showed his appreciation of

HYDER KHAN AND DOST MOHAMMED
Hyder was Governor of Ghazni in the troubles of 1838–41, and Dost Mohammed was the real ruler of Afghanistan from 1826 to 1863.

British honour by voluntarily surrendering himself, and retiring to honourable custody in British territory.

If Shah Shuja had been restored at the cost of comparatively little bloodshed, it was still obvious that the acquiescence of his subjects was only skin-deep, and that his throne could be secured only by the presence of the British bayonets which had won it for him— at least during the months between the flight and the surrender of Dost Mohammed. Five thousand men were left at Kabul, and smaller garrisons at Kandahar and other points. Macnaghten remained at the capital with Shah Shuja, to control the government.

Surrender of Dost Mohammed

When the Dost surrendered, the quiescence of the Afghans did not lead Auckland to remove his troops, but to withdraw another hardly less important factor in the quiescence —the subsidies to native chiefs and tribes, which had tranquillised them. This form of economy was not appreciated by the Afghans, who were very soon seething with hostility, embittered by the misconduct of some of the troops in the Kabul garrison, which, to make matters more dangerous, had been placed in very inadequately fortified cantonments outside the city, while the general who commanded them was painfully incompetent.

The event might easily have been prophesied. Shah Shuja had entered Kabul in August, 1839. In November, 1841, a riot broke out, and one of the British political officers, Sir Alexander Burnes, was murdered. The troops lay passive in the cantonments while the riot expanded into a general rising. Messages for reinforcements were despatched to Kandahar and Gandamak ; but the troops at Gandamak themselves had to fall back on Jellalabad to cover the Khaibars, and the winter weather soon made any advance from Kandahar impossible.

A son of Dost Mohammed, Akbar Khan, was recognised as the leader of the rebel-

SHAH SHUJA
The Amir of Afghanistan who was restored to his throne by the help of British arms in 1838.

lion. Macnaghten, absolutely paralysed by the utter incompetence of the military management, very soon found that annihilation would be the only alternative to acceptance of the most ignominious terms of surrender. The conditions were, that the British should retire, bag and baggage, from Afghanistan, leaving hostages ; the Afghans were to facilitate their departure. But Akbar Khan, instead of providing the promised facilities, began to seize stores and to demand more hostages. Macnaghten made a last desperate attempt at a personal negotiation with Akbar, who seized and shot him dead—probably an unpremeditated *dénouement*.

Even now, the military authorities, on whom the control devolved, could see nothing better than to ratify the convention. The garrisons, however, at Kandahar, Ghazni, and Jellalabad, refused to obey the orders for evacuation. On January 6, all the British subjects at Kabul—some 15,000 souls, soldiers, civilians, and camp-followers, men, women, and children—began their disastrous march, through tempests and snowstorms, towards Jellalabad—all except the hostages. On the 14th, a single survivor reached the goal. None other, save a few who had been added to the hostages, were left alive. All had fallen victims to the merciless weather or the more merciless Afghans.

The disaster was without parallel in the history of the British in India. It originated in an inexcusable attempt to carry out a policy of interference which was in itself a reversal of the principles on which even the most aggressive of Governors-General had acted hitherto. The policy had been carried out with a blind disregard for the most ordinary military precautions, and for the sentiments of the population. When the crisis, thus rendered inevitable, arrived, it was faced with paralytic despair. There were native chiefs—Dost Mohammed was one such, and Ranjit Singh, who died in 1839, had been another—who knew

A Great British Disaster

1288

THE BRITISH FORCES IN POSSESSION OF KANDAHAR IN MARCH, 1838

that these things did not arise from essential decay in the might of the British ; but such men were the exception. In the native mind, British prestige had received a blow from which it would not easily recover.

Auckland was replaced by Ellenborough, whose erratic self-confidence was hardly less dangerous than the feeble dependence of his predecessor. The redemption of British honour lay not with the chiefs of the Government, but with the subordinates. At Jellalabad, the small British garrison maintained a brilliant defence. At Ghazni, on the other hand, the commandant failed to hold his own ; but at Kandahar, General Nott soon proved himself master of the district. A relief force from India, under Pollock, made its way to Jellalabad. Nevertheless, the orders from headquarters were that both Kandahar and Jellalabad should be evacuated, though the British hostages were still in the hands of the Afghans. Both Nott and Pollock, however, succeeded in finding excuses for evading the order. It was very soon realised that the recovery of the hostages and a decisive demonstra-

GUNS ABANDONED BY DOST MOHAMMED AT URGHUNDEE IN THE CAMPAIGN OF 1838

tion of British military superiority were imperative conditions precedent of retirement ; and Lord Ellenborough saved the face of the Government by suggesting that the withdrawal of both garrisons should be effected via Kabul.

Summer was now well advanced. Neither Nott nor Pollock had any hesitation about accepting the Governor-General's suggestion. Nott marched on Ghazni, and recaptured it. Pollock advanced on Kabul direct, routed Akbar Khan, and entered the capital on September 15. Next day he was joined by Nott. Within a week, the hostages, alive and well, were once more free. Resistance to the British, under competent commanders, was palpably hopeless. British prestige, though weakened, was still saved ; yet it was

to threatened, if not to actual, attacks by the several native Powers on the British. The annexation of Sindh was, on the contrary, deliberately engineered by Sir Charles Napier, who himself described it beforehand as a piece of rascality which would be beneficent to Sindh and advantageous to the British. It is extremely unlikely that it would have taken place if the recent blow to British prestige had not called for a conspicuous demonstration of British vigour, still more striking than the retrieval of the disaster in Afghanistan.

The Sindh Amirs were not dangerous, or aggressive. The British were entitled to some gratitude for preserving them from the attack of Ranjit Singh ; but that debt had been repaid by their acquiescence, however reluctant, in the high-handed demands made upon them when the Afghan expedition first set out. Then, however, the course of events in Afghanistan produced a natural tendency to kick against the practical domination which was being exercised over them. It was just at the time when Nott and Pollock were reasserting British power in Afghanistan that Napier was sent to control the restive princes in Sindh. Sir

BALUCHI AMBUSH IN THE SIRI KAJOOR PASS

manifest that the whole policy of a military occupation of Afghanistan was a false one, and that annexation was out of the question. In the course of the troubles, the puppet Shah Shuja had been assassinated. The British Government, resolved on evacuation, had the courage to restore Dost Mohammed himself to the throne ; and it is to the credit of that shrewd and capable chief that he proved himself fully deserving of the confidence thus late displayed in his loyalty.

The grim blunder of the Afghan episode supplied the motive for the one act of inexcusable aggression in the story of the British expansion in India. The overthrow of the French, of Suraj ud Daulah, of Tippu Sahib, of the Mahrattas, had in every case been clearly attributable

Charles, then, was ready enough to seize any plausible excuse for a campaign.

The opportunity was given by the ambitions and intrigues of Ali Murad, a chief who desired for himself a supreme position instead of a subordinate one. In effect, this man frightened his brother Rustam, one of the actual heads of the confederacy, into evading a meeting with Napier. This " contumacy " was punished by a demand for a treaty which would have meant in effect a surrender of independence. The natives became excited, and attacked the British Residency at Haidarabad on the Indus. Napier thereupon marched on Haidarabad. At Miani he met, and completely routed, with less than 3,000 men, a Baluchi army of 20,000. A week later, resistance was ended by

SIR WILLIAM MACNAGHTEN AT THE HEAD OF THE EXPEDITION TO KABUL IN 1838

another fight at Daba. Before the actual outbreak of hostilities, there would have been no serious difficulty in securing as much control of Sindh as was at all demanded by public policy. After war broke out, it could at least be plausibly maintained that anything short of annexation would be attributed by every native in India to the consciousness of weakness on the part of the British Government. To question the fact that Sindh itself was all the better for the change of rule would be absurd ; but the change itself was effected, on this one occasion, very much on the principles on which the thirsty lamb in the fable was annexed by the hungry wolf. The moralist may note that it bore fruit, incidentally, in the mutiny of several regiments of sepoys, who had hitherto received pay for service in Sindh as on a foreign station. Sindh could in no case have either

SURRENDER OF DOST MOHAMMED TO SIR WILLIAM MACNAGHTEN BEFORE KABUL

offered a prolonged resistance to the British, if aggressively inclined, or have rendered effective aid in a hostile combination. But the Kabul affair had excited both the Sikhs of the Punjab and the most powerful native army outside the Punjab. In the Mahratta War, in the time of Lord Hastings, the Sindhia dynasty at Gwalior had suffered the least. The will to attack the British had not been wanting, but it had so befallen that the disposition of the British troops, when the Pindari War began, had paralysed the Sindhia of the day for hostile action. Hence, when the war was ended, he alone of the Mahratta chiefs had been allowed to retain practical independence. In 1843 the succession devolved upon an heir by adoption, who was eight years old; and the effective government passed to Tara Bai, the youthful widow of his predecessor. In accordance with precedent, the British Government intervened to impose its own nominee as regent during the minority. Tara Bai threw herself on the support of the army, which dominated the situation.

Maull and Fox

LORD ELLENBOROUGH
Governor-General from 1841 to 1844, during the Afghan troubles.

AKBAR KHAN
A son of Dost Mohammed and the leader of the Afghan rebels in 1841; he shot Sir William Macnaghten, on December 23, 1841.

Now at this moment the Khalsa, the Sikh army in the Punjab, also dominated the government in that great district. The army of Gwalior and that of the Punjab were both Hindu. Concerted action between the two might lead to a general movement for the establishment of a Hindu supremacy in India. As yet affairs in the Punjab were too unsettled for such a plan to be put into immediate

GENERAL POLLOCK
He persuaded Ellenborough to permit an advance upon Kabul, and successfully carried it out, entering the city on September 15, 1842.

execution. As things stood, it was imperative to place the powerful Gwalior army hors de combat before concerted action should become possible. That Tara Bai intended to bid defiance to the British was obvious when the regent nominated by them was driven from the Gwalior territory. Troops were collected at Agra to emphasise a demand for the reduction of the Gwalior army and the increase of the British subsidiary contingent. Tara Bai resolved to defy the British, and her army proceeded to occupy an entrenched position at Maharajpur, while a second force covered Gwalior on the south-west.

The campaign was short and sharp. On the next day Sir Hugh Gough advanced from Agra, and shattered the force at Maharajpur, after sharp hand to hand fighting. At Puniar, a second column, advancing from Jhansi, defeated the other army. Native troops could never rally after a rout, and Sindhia's dominion lay at the mercy of the British. Tara Bai's army was reduced to 9,000 men, and a somewhat larger force of sepoys under British officers was subsidised. The State was placed under the effective control of the British Resident, but only until the young Sindhia should be of age. The point of immediate importance was secured—that Gwalior as a hostile military power ceased to be dangerous; whereof the value was very soon to become apparent. For another fierce struggle was at hand, under another Governor-General—

Ellenborough's erratic and bombastic methods created so much uneasiness that, shortly after Maharajpur, he was replaced by the experienced soldier and administrator, Sir Henry Hardinge.

We have remarked that the Sikh portion of the Punjab population had long been organised as an army of co-religionists, known as the Khalsa. The genius of Ranjit Singh, during his forty years' ascendancy, had made the Sikhs masters of the whole Punjab, and had developed the Khalsa into a very powerful and highly organised army. While Ranjit lived, the Khalsa was as loyal to him as the English Army of the Commonwealth was to Oliver Cromwell. On his death, at the beginning of the

troops to the north-west, to meet the emergency when it should come ; but his necessary measures of precaution were inevitably suspected of having an aggressive intent.

By the autumn of 1845 it was patent that the Punjab Government was in the hands of the Khalsa, and that the Court was powerless to control it. In December the news came that the Sikhs were advancing in force upon the Sutlej—that they had crossed the river, and invaded British territory, at a point some way above the British advanced post on its southern bank at Firozpur.

There the force of 7,000 men would be able to hold its own, but it was isolated. If

BATTLE OF MIANI ON FEB. 17, 1843, BETWEEN NAPIER'S FORCE AND THE BALUCHIS

Afghan troubles, that army began to realise its own potentialities of political power, the more keenly as it found intriguers for the succession bidding for its support. But it was still like Cromwell's army when Cromwell was gone ; it lacked a head and hand to control and direct ; it was at first inert. Its record of victories, however, disposed it instinctively to foreign aggression ; the disasters in Afghanistan imbued it with a belief that it was a match for the British. The Gwalior campaign checked its arrogance, but only for a time. It was increasingly obvious that, unless a new Ranjit Singh should arise, it would presently force a struggle. Hardinge gradually brought up

this force were "contained" by a sufficient body, the main Sikh army would advance through Sirhind. If it did so successfully the British might find themselves face to face with a general Hindu rising. But, although it had been impossible to bring up to the north-west anything like an overwhelming force, Hardinge and the Commander-in-Chief, Sir Hugh Gough, were prepared for the emergency. A week after the Sikhs crossed the Sutlej converging British columns to the number of 10,000 men had advanced and formed a junction at Mudki. There, on December 18, was fought the first battle, with the advance column of the Sikhs, numbering probably from 20,000 to 30,000. The Sikhs were defeated and fell back, leaving seventeen guns ; the victors lost nearly 1,000 men.

The object now was to effect a junction with a force from Firozpur, but the Sikhs occupied a very strong entrenched position at Firozshah, on the line of march between Mudki and Firozpur. Here they were found by Gough and Hardinge on the morning of December 21. The former wished to attack at once. He was overruled by Hardinge, who felt that failure would mean annihilation, and elected to await the arrival of the contingent from Firozpur. Hence the attack was not opened till four o'clock in the afternoon of the shortest day in the year. When darkness fell, the Sikhs still held their entrenchments, and there was great risk that in the morning they would be reinforced. But when, in the morning, the assault was renewed, it was found that the Sikhs were already in full retreat. Their expected reinforcements appeared, but followed the example of the main body ; which was well for the exhausted British troops. Firozshah was by no means the most signal victory, but was probably the most critical of British battles in India since Plassey and Buxar. After it, the overthrow of the Khalsa was a certainty. The Sikhs, however, who believed that their leaders had betrayed them at Firozshah, were not yet beaten, though forced back to the line of the Sutlej. Even their power of acting on

VISCOUNT GOUGH AND VISCOUNT HARDINGE

Viscount Gough was commander-in-Chief in India, 1843–9, and won the battles of Mudki, Firozshah, Sobraon and Chillianwalla. Viscount Hardinge was Governor-General, 1844–7, and himself took the field as second in command to Sir Hugh, afterwards Viscount Gough.

SHER SINGH

The leader of the Sikhs whom Gough defeated in the hard-fought battle of Chillianwalla.

the offensive was not broken till they met with a severe defeat at the hands of Sir Harry Smith at Aliwal, a month after Firozshah. The decisive blow was not struck till February 10th, when, in a furious conflict at Sobraon, where they held the passage of the river, the Khalsa was completely routed, beyond all hope of rallying. The struggle from first to last had been desperately contested. On the night of Firozshah, its issue had even been extremely doubtful. But for the Maharajpur campaign, two years earlier, a great hostile force would have been lying at Gwalior on the British flank. Had it been there to strike when the Sikhs crossed the Sutlej !

After a conflict so provoked and so terminated on Indian soil, annexation would have followed as a matter of course had the victors been any one except the British Government. But the Sindh affair was unique in British annals. Hardinge, like nearly all his predecessors, very much preferred maintaining native governments to absorbing territories, and he made it his aim now to restore a native government in the Punjab. Yet merely to retire and leave anarchy behind was out of the question. The self-seeking court, and the patriotic sirdars or chiefs, had alike found themselves unable to control the Khalsa. It was a condition of government on which the sirdars themselves insisted that British troops should remain to preserve order. The result was that here again a provisional government was set up until the boy Maharaja, Dhulip Singh, should be of age. A Council of Regency was appointed. Henry Lawrence was made British Resident and virtually Dictator ; the Khalsa was reduced to 30,000 men, the rest being disbanded ; no fewer than 250 guns were surrendered, including those captured in the campaign ; there was the inevitable indemnity, and cession of some territory. British troops were to remain in the Punjab for a year. At the end of the year the sirdars once more declared that, if they were withdrawn, the country would again be plunged into anarchy.; and they stayed.

The indigenous notion of the meaning of a central government is aptly summed up in the remark of a Sikh sirdar—that

General perhaps the most remarkable of the whole series, but as yet untried and new to his post. The double change precipitated a new crisis.

The resignation of Mulraj, the native governor of Multan, led to two British officers being sent thither to take temporary charge On their arrival, Mulraj's troops rose, and the officers were murdered. Multan was in revolt against the constituted government, but proclaimed its defiance of the British domination—which the British themselves were exercising only temporarily and with reluctance, as admittedly the only alternative to anarchy. But the domination was displeasing to the Khalsa—which was convinced that its previous overthrow had

BATTLE OF FIROZSHAH, ONE OF THE MOST CRITICAL IN BRITISH INDIAN HISTORY

a certain district " has not paid its tribute for three years ; it is time to send an army." Under the vigorous but sympathetic rule of Lawrence and the officers whom he posted to the frontier districts, a different order of ideas began to be instilled into the native mind. Had that wise and energetic rule been continued, it is possible that Hardinge's aim might have been achieved, and a strong and public-spirited native administration have been established. But all too soon Lawrence's health broke down, and he was replaced in January, 1848, by a Resident who, though an able man, lacked the unique genius which gave Lawrence an influence so extraordinary ; and at the same moment Hardinge himself was replaced by Lord Dalhousie, a Governor-

been due not to its own military inferiority, but to the treachery of its commanders— and to many of the sirdars who found anarchy profitable. The British adopted the technically correct course of requiring the Punjab Government and troops to restore order and avenge the murder of the British officers who had been acting in its service. In the opinion of Lord Gough the commander-in-chief, either the Punjab Government was loyal and could and would suppress the revolt, or it was disloyal, and the revolt would inevitably develop into a conflagration which could be dealt with only by an army of conquest. The despatch of small columns would only precipitate the conflagration, and bring about immediate disaster. The Punjab Government professed

DEFEAT OF THE SIKHS AT THE BATTLE OF ALIWAL BY SIR HARRY SMITH, JANUARY 28, 1846

loyalty, but did not hasten to strike. A young frontier officer, Herbert Edwardes, at the head of a few loyal Pathans and by no means loyal Sikhs, on his own responsibility made a dash for Multan, and drove Mulraj's troops within the walls in June. He was joined by the Government forces under Sher Singh, and soon after by a British column from **Operations** Lahore; but it was matter of **Against the** doubt whether Sher Singh and **Punjab** his Sikhs would remain loyal. In fact, in September, they declared in favour of the rebels, and withdrew from the siege; and Sher Singh set about calling the Khalsa to arms to recover the independence of the Punjab. The British force remained before Multan, but there was now no prospect of its early capture. By this time Lord Gough's preparations for a great invasion—should it prove necessary —were almost completed. The rising of the Khalsa put the necessity beyond doubt. The nearer districts of the Punjab were under control; Sher Singh concentrated his forces beyond the River Chenab. On its banks at Ramnagar there was a sharp skirmish, but the Sikh position was too strong for the passage to be forced. A few days later, however, a column effected the passage higher up the river, and engaged the enemy at Sadulapur; the result of which was that Sher Singh fell

back on a strong position at Rassul, and Gough carried his whole force over the Chenab.

Gough wished to await the fall of Multan and the arrival of the British column which would then be released; but, under pressure from headquarters, he presently resolved to advance on Sher Singh. The two armies met at Chillianwalla on January 13, 1849. Here was fought another of those desperate and sanguinary battles which distinguish the campaigns against the Sikhs—a battle which was so far a victory that the British remained masters of the field, and the Sikhs fell back on their entrenched position at Rassul, which could neither be turned nor stormed.

Meanwhile, the force before Multan had been reinforced by a column from Bombay, and Multan was captured. Sher Singh **Rout of** resolved to march on Lahore, **the Sikh** and evacuated Rassul, evading **Army** Gough, who fell back, to intercept his advance, on the Chenab near Gujerat. There the British were joined by the column from Multan, and the decisive battle of the campaign was fought, the Sikh army being completely and decisively shattered.

Except Henry Lawrence, there was probably no competent authority in India who doubted that annexation had now become a sheer necessity ; since, except Henry Lawrence, there was no one capable of asserting the personal ascendancy which might ultimately have reconciled the conflicting factors in the Punjab, and have welded them into a stable governing force. The young Maharaja was pensioned off. The Khalsa, conscious at last that it had been squarely beaten in a square fight, acquiesced in the fate it had brought upon itself ; the sirdars sombrely bowed to the inevitable. The Punjab became a British province, and very soon a recruiting ground for the staunchest native regiments, and a training field for the best British officers, military and civil, in the service of the Company, and ultimately of the Crown. Last, and hardest to vanquish of the native Powers which have challenged British supremacy, the Sikh state was transformed into the strongest buttress of the supremacy which it had challenged. To effect **British Annexation of Punjab** the transformation, the best brains and the best troops were concentrated in the new province ; which was well for the province, but not so well for the security of the great dependency in general, though the injurious results did not become evident till after the withdrawal of Dalhousie's master-hand.

Thus Dalhousie's governorship opened with a fierce war, conducted to a triumphant issue, and closed by the absorption of the Punjab under British rule, even as Wellesley had begun by overthrowing the Sultan of Mysore.

One other military conquest marks Dalhousie's era—a conquest for which, as of the Punjab, it cannot be said that any aggressiveness of the Governor-General was responsible. It has been observed in **Trouble with the Burmese** a previous chapter that the infantile ignorance and inflated insolence of the Burmese monarchy forced the British into war and annexation beyond the Bay of Bengal in the time of Lord Amherst. For the second, but not the last time, the same thing happened now. The Burmese authorities habitually ignored the treaty they had entered upon, and subjected the British mercantile community in Rangoon and on the coast to persecution which threatened to drive them from the country. Protests were disregarded ; British envoys were deliberately insulted. An ultimatum was at last sent to Ava at the beginning of 1852, by no means unreasonable in its terms.

The ultimatum was ignored. An expedition was swiftly and thoroughly organised. A fortnight after the time limit named in the ultimatum, Rangoon was captured. Six months later, when the dangerous summer season was over, the army advanced to Prome, on the way to Ava, and took it, as well as the town of Pegu in the south. Dalhousie did not

BRITISH VICTORY OVER SHER SINGH AT CHILLIANWALLA ON JANUARY 13, 1849

wish to extend the borders of the Indian dominion beyond India proper. He stayed the advance ; he made no treaty with a Power to which treaties were waste paper. But nine-tenths of the population hailed the prospect of the substitution of British rule for that of Ava—having before them as an object lesson the prosperity of the previously ceded provinces—

Extending the Empire in Burma and policy, in the Governor-General's eyes, forbade the restoration to an Oriental potentate of districts in which the British flag was flying. Accordingly, he announced by proclamation, that the province of Pegu was annexed to the British Dominions, and proceeded, without further hindrance from Ava, to establish the British Government therein.

Dalhousie's conquests, important as they were, were unsought. The same thing cannot be said of his annexations by legal process, unless we except Oudh. He was the first Governor-General who deliberately laid it down that if a native state could lawfully be brought under direct British rule, the presumption was in favour of annexation. The principle hitherto acted upon—apart from Sindh—had been, that so long as the maintenance of a decent and unaggressive native government in a state was practicable, the presumption was against annexation.

Now, since Wellesley's time, the British had claimed that status of general suzerainty which had previously been recognised as an attribute of the Moguls. According to Indian precedent, expressed in terms of Western law, the throne and the rule of a native state escheated to the suzerain on the lapse of legitimate heirs. By Hindu law, springing from the religious doctrine that for the welfare of a man's soul it was necessary that his offspring should perform certain religious functions when he was dead, a man who had no heirs of his body might adopt an heir, who thereby acquired all the rights

Native Rules Regarding Succession which ordinarily passed to the natural heir. The Mohammedan over-lords, however, had declined to allow political status to be thus passed on without qualification, refusing to recognise an adoption to which their assent had not been obtained, sometimes granting the assent on terms, sometimes refusing it absolutely. Hitherto, the British had not, in practice, exercised the right of refusing assent altogether, but

it was impossible to question that they were legally entitled to do so if they thought fit.

Now, it was an obvious fact that order, justice, law, and material prosperity, prevailed much more under British than under the best native administration. Therefore, Dalhousie held that when the law warranted him in substituting a British for a native administration, the change ought to be carried out in the best interests of the people : provided always that no special considerations existed which, in a particular case, might outweigh the general principle. And as it befell, the years of his rule provided an exceptional series of important cases in which the lapse of natural heirs involved an escheat, if the suzerain should decline to recognise an heir by adoption. By the free exercise of a legal right, undisputed but hitherto rarely enforced, extensive territories might be given the benefits of direct British rule. In judging Dalhousie's principle, however, it should be remarked that the rule had been formally laid down, five-and-twenty years before, that adoptions were not to be recognised as a matter

Dalhousie's Pretext for Annexation of right, but only as a matter of grace. Dalhousie did not refuse to sanction adoption as a matter of course. When the question arose in regard to Kerauli, a small but very ancient state in Rajputana, the adoption was recognised ; mainly, indeed, on the plea that Kerauli was not a dependent principality, but a protected ally. But in two important instances considerable ill-feeling was engendered by the refusal of the privilege, in both of which Dalhousie had a very strong technical case. The first was that of Sattara. When Lord Hastings annexed the Peshwa's dominions, he had bestowed the principality of Sattara on the heir of the house of Sivaji, the founder of the Mahratta Power. Twenty-one years later, it had been found necessary to remove the Raja, whose throne was transferred to his brother. Repeated applications on the part of this prince for permission to adopt an heir had been consistently refused. When he adopted an heir without permission, the Governor-General was quite obviously within his rights in refusing recognition. Not quite so clear was the case of Jhansi, in Bandelkhand, ceded to the British by the Peshwa in an exchange of territory a few years earlier. Here, inheritance by adoption had already been once refused ; but a kinsman of the deceased Raja had been allowed to succeed. When the throne again fell vacant in 1853, adoption was refused, and Jhansi was absorbed—to the wrath of the Rani, the deceased ruler's widow.

Different from these was the case of the great Mahratta State of Nagpur. For many years it had been badly ruled. The Bhonsla, who died in 1853, left no son, and had himself declined to adopt an heir. Dalhousie had the alternatives of selecting a successor or accepting the lapse ; he chose the latter course. The importance of the Nagpur affair lay in the fact that this was one of the great semi-independent principalities, and its absorption by the British could hardly fail to be interpreted as a first step in the policy of extending the practice of annexation on a technical plea to 'the greater as well as to the minor states — a prospect peculiarly alarming to Gwalior, owing to the singular fact that no Sindhia, since the first, had been the heir of his predecessor's body ; every one had been an adoptive son. The justice of the annexation cannot be disputed, but it filled every native court in India with alarm. The series culminated with the annexation of Oudh, one of the two great Mohammedan principalities still in existence, the second being that of the Nizam. From the days of Warren Hastings, the Nawabs had been consistently loyal to the British, who had later rewarded them with the Royal title. But whether as Nawabs or kings, they had traded on their services and misgoverned persistently, in happy confidence that, however much the British might threaten, they would

Two More Native States Annexed never take the final step of abolishing the dynasty—much as the Turk at Constantinople treats the European Powers. Matters, however, at length reached such a pass that a merely formal retention of status by the king became the only alternative to his deposition and the annexation of the province. Dalhousie personally favoured the former course, but was sufficiently doubtful to refer the case home. The home authorities decided in

SIR JOHN LAWRENCE
Whose viceroyalty in India, 1863-9, was the culmination of a brilliantly successful administrative career.

favour of annexation. But the process had alarmed the native governing classes throughout India, since they saw their own ascendancy endangered, alike in the Hindu and the Mussulman districts. Dalhousie was conscious of the risks, but the Home Government, absorbed in the Crimean War, was oblivious of the fact that an emergency was being created.

Rousing of Native Alarm

The organisation of the Punjab, first under the rule of the brothers Henry and John Lawrence and later under John without Henry—whose theories were too independent for a chief so masterful as Dalhousie—bore splendid fruit when the crisis arrived, in the loyalty both of the actual Sikh regiments and of the frontier levies of hill-men. The benefits of British rule came home more forcibly in that province to the mass of the population. The Governor-General's progressive energy was exercised with great advantage to the peaceful classes throughout the British dominion. · Education was vigorously advanced ; roads were built ; irrigation by canals was pressed forward ; railways were planned, though their active construction received sanction from home hardly in time for much to be done before Dalhousie's retirement ; the same thing may be said of the telegraph. It is worth noting that in both these last cases, the immediate effect was damaging to the British Government ; the superstitious terrors of the population being aroused, and the most grotesque suspicions prevailing as to the deep and dark designs of the Government.

But the brilliant achievements were patent to intelligent eyes ; the alarm and irritation, unreasonable and reasonable, were hidden beneath the surface. When Dalhousie retired at the beginning of 1856, worn out by his own ceaseless and exhausting energy, he was under the firm conviction that a period of peace, progress, and prosperity was secured. History presents not a few instances of such hopes and convictions proving the precursors of a cataclysm ; rarely, if ever, has the cataclysm been more sudden, more unexpected, more startling.

SIR JOHN INGLIS   SIR COLIN CAMPBELL   COLONEL NEILL

SIR HENRY LAWRENCE   SIR JAMES OUTRAM   SIR HENRY HAVELOCK

EARL CANNING   NANA SAHIB

Sir Colin Campbell, the son of a Glasgow carpenter, became Lord Clyde, and was Commander-in-chief in India and suppressed the Mutiny. Inglis succeeded Sir Henry Lawrence in command at Lucknow, which he defended during the siege. Neill defended Cawnpore, and was shot in the advance to relieve Lucknow, in the defence of which Lawrence met his death. Outram defended Lucknow during the second period of its siege, and Havelock was the hero of the first relief. During Canning's Governor-Generalship the Mutiny occurred, and Nana Sahib was its chief instigator.

NOTABLE FIGURES IN THE INDIAN MUTINY

THE STORY OF THE MUTINY

BEFORE we enter upon the account of the cataclysm itself, we shall do well to call to mind the very peculiar conditions under which the British Empire in India had been acquired. Here was a vast territory, the size of Europe without Russia and Turkey, where the great majority of the inhabitants had for many centuries been Hindus by religion, parcelled out into kingdoms which had never been touched by the European conception of political nationality. Over a great part of these kingdoms Mohammedan invaders, largely of Tartar origin, had established military supremacies. Finally, a Tartar Mohammedan dynasty had acquired a formal sovereignty over the whole peninsula. At the moment when disintegration had set in, and the Mogul Empire was again breaking up into a congeries of independent states—sometimes of Hindus free from the Mussulman yoke, sometimes under Mussulman domina-

The Eve of the Mutiny tion—a European Power, utterly alien to Hindu and Mussulman alike, almost by accident and without premeditation made itself master of two great provinces, Bengal and the Carnatic, where its dominion was maintained chiefly by means of sepoy armies—native soldiers commanded by the alien officers. The new Power came into collision with one after another of the native states; every collision resulted in a greater or less acquisition of territory, till half the peninsula was under its direct administration and the other half acknowledged it as legally paramount. The alternative to this alien domination was chaos. The Europeans treated all sections of the population with even-handed justice, sternly curbing the predatory classes, fostering material prosperity, and honestly striving to rule sympathetically, subject always to the necessity of maintaining its own paramountcy, but always with a consciousness that the mental and moral attitudes of the Oriental and the Occidental are mutually unintelligible. But on the native mind British policy did not produce the impression of that disinterestedness on which the dominant race prided itself. Of what use were professions that the British had no desire to extend their dominions, when almost every decade found fresh provinces absorbed into British territory? Moham-

Native Attitude to Britain medans and Mahrattas saw in the new lords of India only their own lust of conquest carried to a more successful issue; saw only that their own dominion, or hope of dominion, was rent from them by the alien—that they were subjects where they might have been masters. The Brahman found himself shut out from the political career which even under Mohammedan princes had been open to him. The military classes had to be content with their pay as sepoys, unsupplemented by miscellaneous looting. The benefits of British rule applied mostly to the helpless masses who had no choice but to acquiesce in any rule, good or bad, which might be imposed upon them; and even to them the new rule was alien, unintelligible, suspect, because it did not square with their traditions.

Beyond all this, the whole number of members of the ruling race formed but an infinitesimal fraction of the entire population. Even in the British provinces the sepoys outnumbered the white soldiers by five to one. The dependent provinces were protected, and controlled, partly by their own native levies, partly by more sepoy regiments, the British "contingents." The whole highly artificial fabric of the **The Basis of British Dominion** alien dominion rested primarily on the active loyalty, or, at least, on the quiescence, of these great masses of native soldiery which, trained to fight by the aliens themselves, had learnt to believe in their own efficiency.

It is obvious, then, that there were a number of great separate Interests to which British rule was, or seemed to be unfavourable. The strength of the position lay in the fact that the separate

SCENES OF THE MASSACRE AT CAWNPORE

The view at the top of the page is that of the house in which the women and children were massacred; the well into which many of the victims were thrown is now surmounted by the memorial seen on the right. The centre picture shows the entrenchments of Sir Hugh Wheeler, and the fourth represents the interior of the building after the massacre, the floor strewn with clothing, books, and other articles, while everything was soaked in blood.

interests were mutually antagonistic. The condition of a movement, with any chance of success, against the British *Raj* was the provision of an apparently common aim which should unite those Interests. No such unifying aim was producible, and hence the British power survived the attack.

But with so many elements of unrest in existence, it was possible for one interest or another to believe that it could take advantage of a general destructive movement, and of the general scramble which would follow, to come by what it considered its own—provided that the destructive movement could be made sufficiently general. The first thing to be done for bringing this about was to foster the spirit of animosity against the British, and, above all, to kindle the flame of revolt in the sepoy army.

Now, Dalhousie's annexations had raised the alarm of the governing classes in the dependent states to the highest pitch. Out of the dangerously small number of white troops a dangerously large proportion was absorbed by the most recently **Alarm of** conquered province in the far **the Native** north-west. Never had the **Potentates** country lain so much at the mercy of the sepoys. There was a new Governor-General, Lord Canning, in the saddle. British officialdom was sublimely unconscious of danger. Most of its chiefs had learnt to depend on orders from headquarters. Nine-tenths of the officers of the Army were pathetically confident in the loyalty of their own regiments. Canning's accession to office was almost immediately followed by a quarrel with Persia, and an expedition which withdrew some of the best officers, and still further reduced the number of white troops. It remained only to provide the sepoys with an adequate grievance which could be used by astute intriguers as a lever to set them in motion.

The lever was duly provided. The great bulk of the sepoys in Hindustan were high-caste Hindus, more sensitive on the subject of caste than any other. The obligations of caste were very inconvenient for purposes of military service —e.g., a man suffered heavy caste penalties if he crossed the sea. From time immemorial agitators had periodically taught the sepoys to believe that the British intended to Christianise them by forcing them to lose caste. Now, Canning's

advisers persuaded him to issue the General Service Enlistment Act, which required the sepoy to enlist for service overseas as well as in the Peninsula—a measure dictated by the demand for troops to serve in Pegu. At a stroke, the Hindustani sepoys, soldiers from generation to generation, saw their sons either **Beginning** debarred from their hereditary **of the** career or doomed to loss of **Ferment** caste. Now, the event showed clearly that a revolutionary Mussulman organisation was at work which hoped by means of a general revolt to snatch a restoration of the Mogul supremacy. But this faction could not afford to let its own purposes be known, since the Hindus generally, and the Mahrattas in particular, would have had no inclination to overthrow the British Raj merely to replace it by a Mohammedan dominion. What is tolerably apparent is this—that the organisation existed, that it had a definite policy, and that it sought to precipitate a general revolution in order to give its policy an opportunity. It meant to make a catspaw of the Hindustani sepoy; whereas the disaffected Hindus had no policy at all, and no organisation.

When the explosion came, the premature announcement of the Mogul policy went far to check the dependent Hindu states from throwing in their lots with the revolution, giving the British time to recover from the first sudden shock, and limiting the actual area of the struggle mainly, though not quite exclusively, to Hindustan proper. But the Hindustani sepoy had already committed himself before the Mogul plot was exposed.

Still one more touch was required to bring the sepoys up to mutiny point. It was provided by an inexcusable departmental blunder, the incident of the greased cartridges. The troops were armed with a new rifle, which required **Caste** greased cartridges, the ends of **and** which had to be bitten off **Cartridges** before use. A rumour spread that the grease employed was the fat of oxen and swine. Swine's flesh is unclean to the Mohammedans; the cow is sacred to the Hindu, who would lose caste by tasting its flesh. Whether true or not, there was enough evidence in support of the rumour to give it universal credence in the ranks. The mischief was done, though no more of

ADVANCE OF THE SIEGE TRAIN FROM FIROZPUR

the offending consignment of cartridges were issued.

Still the outbreak was delayed, and still the authorities in general declined to believe that any special precautions were necessary. The story of the cartridges was spread abroad in January, 1857. In February, one regiment refused to handle the cartridges issued to it. In March another regiment mutinied for the same reason, and was soon after disbanded. In April, there was another mutiny, this time at Mirat, a great military station in the Delhi district, where the heir of the Moguls still held court. The mutineers were imprisoned.

Then the storm burst—probably earlier than the agitators had intended. On May 10, the sepoys at Mirat rose *en masse*, shot their officers, killed every European on whom they could lay hands, marched on Delhi, and proclaimed the restoration of

TROOPS OF THE NATIVE ALLIES ON THE MARCH DURING THE MUTINY

FIRST BENGAL FUSILIERS MARCHING DOWN FROM DAGSHAI IN THE PUNJAB

the Mogul Empire. From Delhi, down the Ganges basin, through Oudh to Benares, the flame spread. Bengal proper, from Patna to the coast, was tolerably secure. Bihar, the district from Benares to Patna, at first remained quiet. Outside the district where the Mogul and Mohammedan tradition was strongest, the troops of the dependent princes were ready to make common cause with the mutineers ; the princes themselves, whether from loyalty or from distrust of a Mogul programme, were not. In the Punjab, by the prompt and vigorous action of the officers, sometimes supported by white troops, the doubtful regiments were disarmed, while the irregular frontier levies were devoted to their British officers, and shared with the Sikhs themselves an intense aversion from the Hindustani sepoys.

But between Delhi and Patna there were only five white regiments and a few

MUTINEERS SURPRISED BY HER MAJESTY'S 9TH LANCERS

artillerymen, distributed at Mirat, Agra, Cawnpore, Lucknow, and Dinapur, at each of which there were three or four times the number of sepoys; while at sundry other stations there were sepoys, but no European soldiers. During the month following the outbreak at Mirat, practically all those regiments, except at Dinapur, had declared against the British. The main points of the mutineer concentration were Delhi, Cawnpore, and Lucknow, the last being the capital of the recently annexed kingdom of Oudh. At Gwalior, Sindhia found himself unable to maintain control of the troops, which set off to

Growth of the Mutiny

Delhi, in which there were some 30,000 sepoys. At the end of the same month the small Lucknow force of British and loyal sepoys was shut up in the Residency, which Henry Lawrence, with exceptional prescience, had carefully prepared for a defence. Lower down the Ganges, Benares and Allahabad were already secured by Neill and Brasyer.

At Cawnpore, as at Lucknow, the garrisons included a large number of women and children, and at the former post a desperate resistance was maintained for a while in an almost indefensible position. It had already fallen before the actual siege of the Lucknow Residency

THE RE-TAKING OF DELHI BY COLONEL HODSON ON SEPTEMBER 20, 1857

operate on their own account. Jhansi also revolted; and the siege of Cawnpore was mainly the work of Nana Sahib, the adopted son of the last Mahratta Peshwa, Baji Rao, whom Lord Hastings had dethroned and pensioned very handsomely nearly forty years before. The Nana chose to entertain a bitter grudge against the British because, though he succeeded to Baji Rao's great estates, the cash pension was not also continued to him, although it had been very expressly granted to the ex-Peshwa for the term of his own life only.

By the middle of June a small British force, increased by the end of the month to over 6,000 men by troops from the Punjab, had planted itself on the Ridge before

began. The garrison, with no prospect of holding out long, or of early relief, accepted the terms under which Nana Sahib promised to convey them in safety down the river to Allahabad. They were no sooner embarked than they were massacred by volleys from the banks, followed up by a general slaughter of the men, except the very few who managed to escape. The women and children were taken back prisoners to Cawnpore, and the bulk of the sepoys marched to join their comrades before Lucknow.

Tragedy of Cawnpore

From this point, then, we have to observe first the siege of Delhi with its great native army by the small but

HODSON KILLING THE BLOODTHIRSTY SONS AND GRANDSON OF THE KING OF DELHI

increasing British force; the siege of the Lucknow Residency by a second great sepoy army; and the operations of Havelock, who, arriving to take command at Allahabad, was about to lead a force of 2,000 men through the heart of the disturbed districts to the relief of Lucknow. With regard to the last, it may be remarked that the mutiny very shortly spread to Dinapur, whereby for the time communica-

tions were interrupted between Allahabad and Bengal.

The relation between these three centres or spheres should be noted. The crucial point was Delhi. If the British on the Ridge should be overwhelmed, the revolt would certainly become universal; if they succeeded in capturing Delhi, the blow would prevent that catastrophe. Lucknow, less important in itself, detained a great

STORMING THE BATTERIES AT BADLE-SERAI ON THE HEIGHTS ROUND DELHI

LOYAL SEPOYS AT RIFLE DRILL

mutineer army from marching on Delhi; and its fall would also be the signal for the Oudh clansmen, as distinct from the sepoys, to join the rising. If it fell before Delhi were captured, the British on the Ridge could hardly escape annihilation. How long Lucknow would be able to hold out would depend very largely on the success of Havelock's relief operations.

The loyalty of the Sikh princes of Sirhind kept open the communications between the Punjab and Delhi; but John Lawrence was for some while too anxious as to the condition of the new province to allow any quantity of troops to move from it. Before the middle of August, four attacks on the Ridge were made in force, and repulsed. The British were then strengthened by the arrival from the Punjab of Nicholson with a flying column; at the beginning of September, the long awaited and very much needed siege-train arrived

CHIEF OF THE SIKHS
Who remained staunch to the British

from Firozpur, an attempt to intercept it having been brilliantly frustrated. By a series of skilful and daring engineer operations, the work of Baird Smith and Alexander Taylor, breaching batteries were brought to bear, on the 11th, and the cannonade went on for two days. On the morning of the 14th, by an act of desperate courage, Home and Salkeld succeeded in blowing up the Kashmir Gate. Three out of four assaulting columns stormed the ramparts, and made their footing good; then by degrees, on the ensuing days, the British forced their way into the city; on the 21st they were masters of the whole of it, and held the Mogul himself a prisoner. A portion of the mutineer army made good its retreat or flight towards Lucknow.

During these three months the garrison of the Residency in the Oudh capital had held out stubbornly. Nearly half the fighting force were loyal sepoys, many of them Sikhs; the non-combatants were nearly as numerous as the

MUTINOUS SEPOYS WITHIN THEIR DEFENCES

combatants. The skilful preparations made the ramparts secure against assault, provided that they could be adequately manned ; while the great army of besiegers did not know how to use their artillery effectively for breaching. There was ample store of grain. The dangers from which the garrison suffered were : the immense strain on every member of the garrison, owing to the fact that the enemy were in immense force, under shelter, at many points only a few yards from the walls, while the defenders could take only brief spells of rest ; and the almost overwhelming risk of breaches being effected by

Terrible Days of Lucknow

reached such a point that some of the loyal sepoys actually gave warning that, unless relief arrived, or was certainly at hand at the end of September, they would not indeed surrender the place, but would march out and make terms for themselves.

While the British were grimly holding grip before Delhi, and exploding the enemy's mines at Lucknow, Havelock, with his 2,000 men—of these, too, nearly a fourth were Sikhs—was making desperate efforts first to rescue the captives at Cawnpore, and then to fight his way through Oudh to Lucknow. The insurgents —sepoys, or followers of Nana Sahib—

MEETING OF HAVELOCK, OUTRAM, AND COLIN CAMPBELL AT THE RELIEF OF LUCKNOW

mines. The vigilance of the engineers was such that no fewer than twenty-five mines were countered and destroyed in sixty-five days ; others were mis-directed or exploded harmlessly. Only one accomplished its purpose, and created a breach ; but the mutineers seem to have been so surprised at this success that the breach itself was once again made defensible before they attempted to rush it. Perhaps the greatest of all the dangers lay in the strain on the nerves of the defenders owing to the extreme difficulty of obtaining from outside any news on which reliance could be placed. Matters

faced him repeatedly, to be repeatedly routed. On one day he fought two separate engagements ; on another, three. Nothing could stay the pauseless advance till he reached Cawnpore—to find a ghastly shambles. At the last moment, the Nana had ordered the women and children to be butchered in cold blood. That appalling crime aroused such a passion of vengeful rage as has, perhaps, no parallel in British history.

Brilliant Advance of Havelock

A few days later, Havelock crossed the river ; but cholera was ravaging his now greatly reduced force. Wherever the mutineers faced him, he smote them—only to find fresh forces barring the way. Report came that the Gwalior army was moving to threaten his rear. Dinapur had mutinied. He found himself with no choice but to fall back again across the Oudh border to Cawnpore. The Oudh *talukdars*, or chiefs, thought he had abandoned that province, and now allowed their retainers to join the mutineers, which they had not hitherto done. On the other hand, the rising between Allahabad and Dinapur was checked and suppressed. Presently Sir James Outram was advancing with fresh regiments to join Havelock. The junction was effected on September 15, at the moment when the Delhi force was storming the Mogul capital. The advance through Oudh was renewed, the force now numbering 3,000 men. On the 23rd it was four miles from the Residency, with the mutineer army between. On the 25th it fought its way in. There was no question now that, thus reinforced, the place could hold out till a technical "relief" should be effected, though the siege was not yet raised, nor any part of its garrison able to be removed.

The revolt had started with one chance, or two, of succeeding—that either the whole British community should have been overpowered, or the whole native community have risen in arms, before reinforcements arrived from England. Neither of these results had been achieved.

Turning of the Tide — Within a large but restricted area almost every native regiment had mutinied; but detachments had remained loyal, and the landowners had sat still and, to a great extent, kept their clansmen sitting still. Outside that area, in places where there were no white regiments, sepoy battalions had declared in favour of the mutineers without moving to join them. Even the Gwalior army had only threatened. Four months after the proclamation

HAVELOCK'S GRAVE AND ALAM BAGH PICKET-HOUSE

of the Mogul, his own city was being stormed. Before another fortnight the British in the Oudh capital had been reinforced. New troops and new commanders were reaching Calcutta. There were no more fears about the Punjab, where fresh native regiments were being levied in secure confidence of their loyalty.

Final Relief of Lucknow — Six weeks after Outram and Havelock reached Lucknow, Sir Colin Campbell was in Oudh leading the army which was not to check, but to crush the revolt. In November, Lucknow was effectively relieved, the non-combatants were withdrawn, and a strong force left under Outram to hold the Alam Bagh fort. At this moment the Gwalior army, under an able leader named Tantia Topi, joined in the fray, but was eventually driven back in rout across the Jumna.

In the first three months of 1858, Sir Hugh Rose advanced from Bombay, crushed the insurgents in outlying districts, laid siege to Jhansi, fought a pitched battle with Tantia Topi, shattering his forces completely, and captured Jhansi itself on April 3, though the Rani escaped. Meanwhile other columns converged on Oudh, including a contingent of Ghurkas from Nepal, and on March 17th drove the mutineers headlong from Lucknow.

Resistance was not over, for the Oudh talukdars, who had hitherto abstained from taking an active part, were alarmed by a proclamation of Lord Canning's, and, thinking that their fate was already sealed, resolved to take it fighting. Moreover, the Jhansi Rani, Tantia Topi, and Nana Sahib, were not disposed to submit ; the first, from a spirit akin to that which tradition ascribes to Boadicea ; the other two because they knew their share in the Cawnpore massacres had placed them beyond reach of pardon. But the crisis was passed when Campbell effected the final relief of the

THE BRITISH RESIDENCY AT LUCKNOW AFTER THE SIEGE

The top picture shows the ruins of the Residency as drawn by a British officer after the siege; the telegraph apparatus was in the high tower to the left. The centre oval is a picture of the Residency from the Water Gate, the verandah having been shot away; the appearance of the billiard room gives an idea of the general destruction.

INTERIOR OF ALAM BAGH FORT AT LUCKNOW AFTER THE SIEGE

Lucknow Residency. The issue was placed beyond all doubt when he drove the mutineers from Lucknow itself, and Sir Hugh Rose captured Jhansi. The Rani was killed in action in June; the taluk-dars submitted in December ; Nana Sahib vanished ; a few months later, Tantia Topi was caught and hanged, since nothing could transform the hideous butchery of Cawnpore into a legitimate operation of war.

The Mutiny had brought home in England the conviction that the anomaly of governing a dependency so vast as India through the medium of a commercial company must be brought to an end. The prophecy, passed from mouth to mouth among the natives, as an incentive to rebellion, that the rule of the Company was to last a hundred years, and no more, was fulfilled almost to the year. It had begun with Clive's victory at Plassey ; it

was ended by the proclamation which transferred the government to the British Crown, in accordance with the India Act passed by Lord Derby in August, 1858.

The spirit of compromise which pervades British institutions has produced a system which is theoretically crowded with contradictions. Nothing could well be more indefensible on paper than the old compromise between the Company and the Crown in India. But the illogicalities of the Constitution serve their turn ; and the Honourable East India Company served its turn, too— better, probably very much better, than a system which would have better satisfied a political theorist. But a stage had been reached at which it had become cumbrous and unworkable. Thenceforth the responsibility for the Indian Empire was to rest undivided upon the British nation.

ARTHUR D. INNES

RUINS OF THE CLOCK TOWER GATEWAY AT LUCKNOW AFTER THE SIEGE

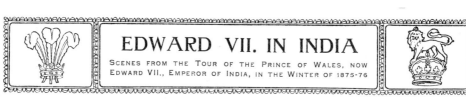

ARRIVAL OF THE PRINCE OF WALES AT BOMBAY ON NOVEMBER 8, 1875

ENTRY OF THE PRINCE OF WALES INTO BARODA ON NOVEMBER 9, 1875

THE PRINCE PRESIDING AT A GRAND CHAPTER OF THE STAR OF INDIA AT CALCUTTA

RECEPTION OF THE SURVIVORS OF THE DEFENCE OF LUCKNOW IN JANUARY, 1876

STATE ENTRY OF THE PRINCE OF WALES INTO LAHORE IN FEBRUARY, 1876

ARRIVAL OF THE PRINCE OF WALES AT AGRA IN MARCH, 1876

THE GRAND STATE RECEPTION OF INDIAN POTENTATES BY THE PRINCE OF WALES AT CALCUTTA ON DECEMBER 23, 1875

AFTER THE MUTINY
THE RECONSTRUCTION OF INDIA
BY SIR WILLIAM LEE-WARNER

BY the end of October, 1858, military operations had almost ceased ; peace and order were fast taking the place of confusion and violence, and the transfer of government from the Company to the Crown, with Lord Canning as first Viceroy, had been completed. Anarchy was, of course, still rife in outlying districts ; marauders were here and there prowling about at large ; fugitive bodies of mutineers showed more or less cohesion. Public business throughout the North-west Provinces and Oudh, with some parts of Bengal and the Punjab, had been so completely disorganised that many months would have to pass before the civil power could assert itself to the full. But the great cities of Delhi, Agra, Cawnpore, Allahabad, were held in force ; the populace knew that rebellion had missed its mark ; while the native chiefs, almost without exception, had been splendidly loyal.

The Peace that Followed the Mutiny Lord Canning was, therefore, able to gather up the tangled threads of government and to ponder constructive measures that in no very long time were to tranquillise the country and give uniformity of rule throughout its vast area.

Among his earliest acts was the issue of a proclamation drawn up by the Ministry in England, and revised by Her Majesty, whereby an amnesty was granted " to all offenders, save and except those who have been, or shall be, convicted of having directly taken part in the murder of British subjects. . . . To those who have willingly given asylum to murderers, knowing them to be such, or who may have acted as leaders or instigators in the Revolt, their lives alone can be guaranteed. . . . To all others in Arms against the Government, We hereby promise unconditional pardon, amnesty, and oblivion of all Offences against Our-

selves, Our Crown and Dignity, on their return to their homes and peaceful pursuits. . . ." Impartial protection of the law, freedom from interference with religious belief, admission to all offices for which qualification might be proved,

Pardon for the Rebels protection of the rights of the native princes, and other boons to the people at large, were graciously authorised.

Among those to whom leniency was to be extended were the turbulent landowners, or talukdars, of Oudh. On the final capture of Lucknow, the proclamation by the Viceroy, previously mentioned, had in its first draft confiscated their estates, though, upon Outram's remonstrance, a clause had been inserted which gave hopes that something less than the full pound of flesh would be exacted, if only complete submission were promptly rendered. On a visit to Lucknow, Lord Canning assembled the chief of these barons, as they have been styled, and, accepting their profession of repentance, restored to them the possession of their forfeited fiefs, with a permanent and hereditary proprietary title—an act of grace which has since that time borne fruit in their active loyalty and the orderly control of their vassals ; while it at once gave rest to the most dangerously disaffected portion of the country, and was welcome evidence to the remainder that vindictive retribution does not always fall upon the conquered. But

Leniency that Bred Loyalty while Lord Canning's worst anxieties were now at an end, and the calm courage with which he confronted all difficulties had its reward in the assurance of a security far greater than had prevailed before the rebellion, the task before him was one of vast magnitude. Among the demands made by the new order of things, two stood out as primarily importunate. These were the re-establishment of financial equilibrium and the reorganisation of the Army, native and European.

Changes in the system of public accounts render comparisons between the expenditure of India at one period and another a task of no little difficulty. But the final report of the Royal Commission on the administration of the expenditure of India, published in 1900, throws a clear light upon the financial position with which Canning had to deal. The year 1860–61 saw the ebb mark of the tide of Indian finance. A chronic deficit, continued almost without intermission for a period of twenty years, had already added £50,000,000 sterling to its national debt. The outbreak of the Mutiny in 1857 entailed a loss of revenue which averaged £12,000,000 for that and the succeeding two years. All the efforts of the Government, aided by the imposition of taxes which convulsed society, availed only to reduce the annual deficit by £6,000,000. There was no course open to Canning and his financial advisers—Wilson, who died in August, 1860, and Laing, who succeeded him—save to supplement additional taxation by a severe reduction of expenditure. The military, naval, and civil outlay of 1860–61 had been cut down to £29,500,000, and now, with a bold hand, it was reduced by nearly four millions.

The returning prosperity of the country gave buoyancy to the public receipts, and in 1861–62 the tide had turned. Equilibrium was practically restored, and the Government escaped the necessity of levying the unpopular licence tax. From that time forward, further relief was afforded in the gradual reduction of the income tax, and of the additional duty on cotton-twist and yarn, and the reform of the salt duties. The stamp duties and the excise on spirits and opium continued at their enhanced rates to sustain the burden of administration; and by the exercise of a prudent policy in all departments, Canning added to his success, in restoring peace and order, the further merit of placing the national finance upon a safe and enduring basis. The land revenue in 1862 yielded £2,500,000 more than before the Mutiny, and when in that year Lord Canning laid down office, all

Need for Financial Economy

Measures of Financial Reform

doubt as to ultimate financial prosperity had passed away.

While treating of the measures taken during this viceroy's time for the reorganisation of the army, it will be convenient to extend the inquiry so as to carry the account of the more important changes in its constitution up to the present day.

When the Mutiny broke out the ratio of the British forces to the native armies of Bengal, Madras, and Bombay, together with the local levies and contingents, was about one to eight, or 39,000 to 311,038. Independent of financial considerations such a disproportion was one that events so soon to follow showed to be dangerous to the last degree. But not only had it to be determined what a safe ratio would be; the very form of the British armament must first be settled. This had hitherto consisted partly of Europeans enlisted in England for the Company's service, and partly of royal regiments of cavalry and infantry sent out to India, but liable to be withdrawn for service elsewhere on the outbreak of war. It was now debated whether under the Crown a local European army should be placed at the exclusive disposal of the Government of India, or whether the forces deemed necessary should be part and parcel of the Queen's army. After much discussion it was decided that the Company's European forces should be transferred to the Crown and be supplemented by royal regiments. Further, a Commission appointed to advise on these changes laid it down that the British forces should be 80,000 strong, and that the native troops should not exceed them by more than two to one in the Bengal army and three to one in those of Madras and Bombay. In Bengal the native army had to be re-formed almost *de novo*. Eighty-six entire regiments had mutinied, and only a few had remained loyal, or, at all events, inactive. These last were not disbanded; but in the main the new force consisted of Sikh, Gurkha, Pathan, and Rajput levies. The Madras and Bombay armies, the Haidarabad contingent, and the Punjab Frontier Force, had taken no part in the rebellion. These, therefore, were left intact, though to them also were applied the principles of reorganisation now found necessary. When, in 1864, that reorganisation was complete, the three armies in India had an aggregate

Remaking of the Indian Army

SOLDIERS OF NATIVE REGIMENTS IN INDIA

The first group is a number of the 18th Bengal Lancers; the middle picture shows a parade of Sikhs, that warlike tribe whose rise began as a religious sect and who soon developed into active militants and threatened British supremacy; the third group are Gurkhas, the northern hill tribesmen, who exhibit as much courage and steadiness as the best white regiments within the bounds of our empire.

Photos Gregory & Co., London

strength of 205,000 men, of whom 65,000 were British soldiers. The artillery, except a few mountain batteries, were wholly British.

Between 1860 and 1878 there were no field operations on a large scale. But the Afghan war of 1878-80 brought to light many important defects; and a Commission was appointed by Lord Lytton not only to devise means for the reduction of army expenditure, but to test how far the existing system had been found adapted to the requirements of troops on active service. The immediate outcome of the inquiry was the reduction of four regiments of native cavalry and eighteen of native infantry; though, as the strength of each regiment was raised from 499 to 550 of all ranks in the cavalry, and from 712 to 832 in the infantry, the total strength remained much what it was before. There was also a reduction of eleven batteries of British artillery. In 1885 threatenings of war with Russia led to considerable additions throughout the army. In the British forces the increase amounted to 10,600 men; in the native armies to 20,000. The grand total then reached 226,694 men of all ranks, the British numbering 73,602. In 1886 the battalions of the native armies were linked together; in 1888 regimental centres were fixed upon for these groups, and at the same period a reserve was formed for the native army in general. During the next five years various changes and improvements took place. The Imperial Service troops, voluntarily supplied by some of the leading native states, came into being; military works, hitherto carried out by the Civil Department, were transferred to a Military Service Department; amalgamation of the Presidency Commissariats was taken in hand; the Punjab Frontier Force passed from the control of the Punjab Government to that of the Commander-in-Chief; in lieu of three staff corps one was organised for the whole of India; in the Bombay army a large infusion of better material replaced men of inferior physique; the native army was supplied with the Martini-Henry rifle; the sixteen Hindustani regiments of the Bengal army became " class " regiments, composed severally of Brahmans, Rajputs, Mohammedans, Jats, and Gurkhas; the Intelli-

Defects in the Army System

Progress of Army Reform

gence Branch of the Quartermaster-General's Department was reorganised and strengthened.

With the year 1895 we come to a measure of importance affecting the whole of India, the abolition of the separate Presidency armies. By this arrangement India was now divided into four territorial commands, named after the Punjab, Bengal, Madras, and Bombay, each command being vested in a lieutenant-general. The whole army thus came under the direct control of the Government of India and the Commander-in-Chief, whereas formerly the armies of Bombay and Madras were under local commanders-in-chief controlled by the Presidential Governments. Later on certain local corps, hitherto under the Foreign Department, were also brought under the Commander-in-Chief and allotted to the divisional commands according to their geographical situation.

Upon this general reconstitution of the army there followed, between 1895 and 1903, many changes in the composition of commands and regiments. The mountain batteries were strengthened; the Haidarabad contingent disappeared; the Presidency medical services were amalgamated under a Director-General; military factories came under the administration of the Director-General of Ordnance. The years 1899-1901 witnessed special activity in remodelling and improving armament, mobilisation, equipment, and defences, while many measures then resolved upon were carried out in 1902 and 1903. Thus, in 1900, the reorganisation of the transport system was finally authorised; in 1900-1 the native army received the ·303 magazine rifle, while the rearmament of the regular army was completed in 1902-3. Between the years 1900 and 1904 about 400 British officers were added to the native army; the field artillery and the commissariat service received special attention; transport organisation was more fully developed; and a thorough investigation dealt with sanitary arrangements, the system of clothing, opportunities for recreation, and numerous other details.

Series of Regimental Changes

The total number of regular troops in the five commands, including Burma, was, in 1903, 232,111, of which 74,170 were British and 157,941 native soldiers. The reserve of the native army numbered about

25,000, and the auxiliary forces about an additional 76,000 men. A new scheme of military organisation is now, however, in course of development, and, in place of four territorial commands, there will be three complete army corps and ten divisional commands.

The present administration of the army may be described in a few words. While, subject to the control of the Crown, the supreme authority is vested in the Governor-General in Council. One of the members of Council, commonly called the " Military Member," formerly dealt with administration and finance. Since March, 1906, this arrangement has been recast, and military affairs are now in the hands of two departments—the Army Department and the Department of Military Supply. This latter department, which is in charge of an ordinary member of Council, has the management of all matters connected with important Army contracts, and the supply and registration of transport animals ; it also controls the working of the departments of Ordnance, Remounts, Military Works, Army Clothing, and the Royal Marine, as well **Present** as the military work of the **Military** Indian Medical Service; while **System** military accounts have become a branch of the Finance Department. The Army Department is under the immediate charge of the Commander-in-Chief, subject to the control of the Governor-General in Council, and while his powers have been largely extended, he has been relieved from a good deal of petty business. Immediately subordinate to him are the Chief of the Staff, the Quartermaster-General, the Adjutant-General, the Principal Medical Officer of His Majesty's Forces, and the Military Secretary.

From this account of Army reorganisation inaugurated by Canning and completed by his successors, we may now return to the other acts of his administration. The loyalty during the Mutiny of nearly all the great native princes has already been noted. Conspicuous among these were the Cis-Sutlej chiefs, Patiala, Jhind, Nabha, and Kapurthala ; the Rajas of Jaipur, Udaipur, and Kerauli ; Sindhia and the Nizam ; the Begam of Bhopal, the Gaekwar of Baroda, the Maharaja of Kashmir, and many smaller magnates. Gratitude dictated that none of these should go unrewarded, and Lord Canning determined that no stint should be shown in the bestowal of such acknowledgments as would best be prized. Titles of honour, remission of debts, enlargement of territory, guarantees of succession, large money grants, *sanads* of adoption, reductions of annual tribute, an increase in the number of guns of salute, jewelled swords, and various privileges, were showered with lavish hand on all who had **Loyalty** deserved well of the British **and its** Government; and nobly since **Rewards** that time has such munificence been repaid. The immediate anxieties of the Mutiny being now over, Canning was free to devise measures of internal improvement. Early among these was the passing, in 1859, of the Bengal Rent Act. By the Permanent Settlement of 1793, while the Government surrendered to the zemindars its right to take the produce of the soil, it had been endeavoured to secure the ryots in their ancestral holdings. This endeavour had met with but small measure of success. The promised leases at customary rates had been withheld, rents were constantly raised, illegal cesses were levied, and by 1859 the ryots could hardly keep body and soul together. Act X. of that year, though often evaded, and though it did nothing for tenants-at-will, proved a considerable boon to the agriculturist by recognising occupancy rights and fixity of tenure, and its deficiencies have to some extent been made good by later enactments.

In 1860, the Viceroy's Executive Council was strengthened by admission of its legal member to the full status of an ordinary member of Council, while the Legislative Council was remodelled, and certain native members added to it. Similar councils on a smaller scale were established in Bengal, Madras, and Bombay. In the same year came the amalgamation of the supreme and Sadr courts, whereby each presidency had its high court ; and before Canning left the country the penal code drafted **Legislative** by Macaulay and completed by **and Legal** Sir B. Peacocke, became law **Reforms** throughout India. Consolidation of British territory had been so prominent a part of Dalhousie's policy that little in this direction remained for his successor. But in 1860 the three provinces of British Burma were combined under a Chief Commissioner, and the Central Provinces formed by the union of Nagpur with the Sagar and Narbada districts were raised to the same status.

Between 1859 and 1862 much was accomplished in the way of material progress. Of 1,300 miles of railway open at the latter date, more than half had been laid out during the preceding two years, while 3,000 more miles were in course of making ; the Grand Trunk Road extended from Calcutta to Peshawar, a distance of 1,500 miles ; new branches of **Civil and** the Ganges Canal had been **Industrial** thrown out and the Eastern **Progress** and Western Jumna Canals were already at work ; the cultivation of tea, coffee, and cinchona received encouragement ; the foundations were laid of a Forest Department ; and partly as a consequence of all this enterprise trade was now reviving.

The creation, in 1857, of universities at Calcutta, Madras, and Bombay stimulated education, the number of schools of all classes rose rapidly, a medical college was opened at Lahore, English newspapers conducted by natives appeared in considerable numbers, and a new literature in Hindi and Urdu was springing up.

In the midst of his beneficent projects Canning had, in 1861, to face a famine which, in spite of all efforts, carried off nearly half a million of the poorer classes in the northern provinces, and brought severe distress upon many millions more. This was followed by the scourge of cholera and by torrential rains, which flooded vast tracts of country, sweeping away roads, bridges, and crops.

Lord Canning had hardly completed his last tour in India when a terrible blow befell him in the death of his gifted wife. A few months later he laid down the office which for six years he had held with such serene courage amid unexampled difficulties, and returned to England. But the strain, mental and physical, had been enough to sap a more vigorous constitution, and on the 17th of the following January, he, like Dalhousie. passed away in the prime of life. His suc- **Canning's** cessor, Lord Elgin, landed in **Policy** March, 1862, and the first **Continued** year of his Viceroyalty was passed at Calcutta, where he made himself acquainted with the machinery and problems of Indian government. Closely following his predecessor's policy, he aimed at the peaceful development of industry, avoiding the introduction of novel and vexatious taxation, setting his face against interference with native chiefs, doing his best to keep down military expenditure, and steering clear of frontier complications. Of these last there was some danger, arising from the proceedings of Dost Mohammed, who was bent on an expedition to curb the refractory governor of Herat, Sultan Jan. Though urged to counsel the Amir against this undertaking, lest Persia should side with the Governor and Russia should back up Persia, Elgin refused in any way to embroil himself in the quarrel, and even withdrew his Vakil from Kabul in order to avoid all appearance of countenancing the Amir's designs. The death of the Dost in the following summer eventually placed Sher Ali on the throne, but in the struggle for its possession which ensued between the two brothers, the Viceroy contented himself with congratulations to the successful claimant at whose court the British Vakil was to assume his place.

In February, 1863, Lord Elgin made a tour through Northern India, settling down at Simla for the hot season. At Benares he held his first durbar, and at the opening of a new section of the East **A Viceroy** Indian Railway looked forward **Who Died** to the day when private enter- **in Harness** prise should supplement, if it did not take the place of, official activity in the extension of lines throughout the country. At Cawnpore, he was present at the consecration by the Bishop of Calcutta of the spot that marked the graves of those whom Nana Sahib's treachery had done to death. This was followed by a grand durbar at Agra to which there thronged the chiefs of Rajputana and Central India. Addressing them in a dignified speech the Viceroy declared the principles by which the Government of India was actuated, and the measures by which it was in their power to second its endeavours to secure peace and general prosperity. Passing on to Ambela, he received a large gathering of the Sikh princes, whose behaviour during the Mutiny he warmly eulogised, at the same time offering wise counsels for their future guidance. Till the end of September Lord Elgin remained at Simla further familiarising himself with the task that seemed to lie before him in the coming years. He then set out to visit the Kangra Valley and its neighbourhood. The journey across the hills west of Simla in the keen mountain air severely taxed his powers. At one point he had to cross the Chandra on a frail bridge of twigs which swayed from side to side at every step, and this effort perilously tried his heart, already, apparently, in an unhealthy condition. When, after some days of further travel, he reached Dharmsala, it was only to find a grave there.

One military undertaking had alone disturbed the quiet of his two years' rule. To the north of Peshawar a colony of Wahabi fanatics had their abode at a place called Sitana. Here preparations had been made for a raid upon British territory, and in time these became of so threatening a character that the Viceroy was strongly urged by the Lieutenant-Governor of the Punjab to fit out a punitive expedition. To this he at last reluctantly assented, and in October, 1863, a force of 6,000 men moved out from Peshawar towards the Ambela Pass. Here, however, it was found that the Buner tribe had joined the Wahabis, and these, with the men of Swat, made further progress impossible for the time. From day to day further clans swelled the enemy's numbers, and Neville Chamberlain was hard set to repulse their **Successful** combined attacks. After Lord **Punitive** Elgin's death the Council at **Expedition** Calcutta had ordered the withdrawal of Chamberlain's force so soon as this could be prudently done. Sir W. Denison, however, who had come up from Madras to take up temporary charge of the duties of Governor-General, promptly cancelled this order and directed the despatch of reinforcements. Thus strengthened, Garvock, now in command in place of Chamberlain disabled by a wound, drove the enemy out of Ambela. The Buners came to terms and, acting as guides to a British detachment, assisted in destroying the headquarters of the fanatics at Malka. This brought the campaign to an end.

When the news of Lord Elgin's death reached England it was universally felt that no one could so fitly fill the post of Viceroy as Sir John Lawrence, then a member of the Secretary of State's Indian Council. With his usual readiness Sir John sailed by the next mail steamer and arrived in Calcutta on January 12, 1864. His biographer, Mr. Bosworth Smith, has said that "a succinct history of India during the viceroyalty of Sir John Lawrence would require at least a volume to itself." Within our narrow limits it will

not be possible to give more than an outline of the various problems of government with which he was called upon to deal.

No one knew better than Lawrence what were the pressing needs of internal administration. Although his predecessors had restored the financial equilibrium, it was only by starving the spending **Lightening** departments and by recourse **the Burden** to taxes which strained the **of the Poor** loyalty of the people. Lawrence did all that was possible to relieve the tax-payer from these burdens. In 1862 the additional duty of 50 per cent. on cotton piece-goods was repealed, and in 1864 the remaining enhanced duties of customs were reduced from 10 to 7½ per cent., a further reduction being carried out in 1867. The unpopular income-tax, imposed in 1860, had been taken off incomes under £50 a year, and Lawrence proposed to replace it altogether by duties on exports, but public opinion would not permit this change. The salt duty and increased stamp dues he was constrained to leave alone ; but much was done by wise administration to increase the revenues and provide funds for education and public works. In particular, a new policy of far-reaching consequence, first suggested by Dalhousie, was adopted in 1867-68. The public debt was divided into productive and unproductive, the expenditure upon irrigation and railways being charged to a capital account under its proper head. By stern adherence to a policy of non-intervention across the borders, military expenditure was kept low ; and fortunately the fall in the gold value of the rupee, which, after 1875, dislocated the finances, had not yet occurred to increase the home charges.

Of public works involving enormous outlay, the more important may here be mentioned. Sanitation, especially in military cantonments, had hitherto been left almost to itself, with a consequently heavy **Attention to** mortality. Lawrence saw that **Sanitary** further neglect was unbear- **Requirements** able. A Commission resulted in the establishment of a Sanitary Department in each Presidency, and later of sanitary committees in every cantonment. Secondary, if secondary, to sanitation was the building of suitable barracks and hospitals. Here the expenditure from first to last amounted to more than ten millions. A large extension of railway lines had become imperative for both strategic and commercial purposes. Adequate schemes were framed to meet this demand, and no less than £26,000,000 were expended in this direction during Lawrence's time. Canals, whether as a means of watering the cultivator's fields or of carrying traffic, admitted of no delay. Agreeing with **Canal and Irrigation Schemes** Lawrence that their cost should be defrayed by loans, Lord Cranbourne sent out Colonel Strachey as Superintendent of Irrigation, authorising their construction wherever urgent need called for them. If anything had been wanted to emphasise the importance of easy communication by land and water, the two famines with which Sir John had to grapple were more than sufficient. A shortage of the monsoon in 1865, followed in the next year by terrible inundations, plunged Orissa into the direst distress. Had not the Lieutenant-Governor of Bengal shut his eyes to what was going on around him, the disaster might have been greatly modified. When at length the real state of things came to the Viceroy's knowledge, vigorous measures of every kind were taken. Relief works did something to check the mortality, and large sums of money were advanced by the Government of India. But it was food, not money that was wanted, for money had no purchasing power where no crops existed.

Importation by steamships was then attempted. This expedient came too late. The monsoon had now burst on the coast, and it was with the greatest difficulty that even a small portion of the freights could be landed. When the famine ceased, it was calculated that the deaths amounted to nearly a million. Two years later, the failure of the rains in the North-western Provinces preluded a similar calamity. The lesson learnt in Orissa was not neglected. Relief works, distribution of **Period of Great Famines** alms and food, remissions of land revenue, and advances made for the purchase of seed corn modified the evil; while the Ganges and Jumna Canals watered the thirsty soil and abundant harvests in Oudh helped to keep life in the millions of the neighbouring provinces. Yet, in spite of every effort, some 60,000 souls are said to have perished. Nor was it only in British India that the stress was felt. Rajputana, Indur,

Gwalior, Marwar, Malwa, Bikanir and Gujerat suffered equally. To their honour, the native chiefs followed the example of the Indian Government, and were aided by it in their endeavour to ward off starvation. But starvation was followed by disease, and in some parts of these provinces scarcity continued to prevail for nearly two years. The tale of deaths exacted it is impossible to compute.

From this story of woe it is pleasant to turn to Lawrence's determination to win the confidence of the native states by explaining the desires of the British Government, and by allaying the fears to which not even the Sanads of adoption granted by Canning had put an end. For this purpose he not only abstained from interference with their internal government, but by personal intercourse sought to draw closer the ties by which they were bound to the supreme Power. To a durbar held at Lahore in 1864 he welcomed some 600 of the nobility of the Punjab, prominent among whom were the Phulkian princes, whose aid in the Mutiny stood us in such stead. **Native Co-operation Secured** Addressing the assemblage in Hindustani, and in terms which, avoiding self-exaltation, won the ready attention of his hearers, the Viceroy adverted to the warm interest taken by the Queen in all her Indian subjects, enumerated some of the blessings that British rule had given the country, eulogised the conspicuous loyalty shown in the troublous days so lately passed, and urged upon the chiefs the advantages to be gained by the spread of English education. The public ceremonial was supplemented by private visits to and from the Viceroy. In these Sir John discussed the condition of the several states, and mingled with approval for the past advice and encouragement for the future. Coming from a man whose sincerity of purpose was so fully recognised, such words were not allowed to fall to the ground. At the second of these impressive scenes he, in 1866, received at Agra the principal chiefs of Rajputana and Central India. To these also Lawrence delivered a weighty speech in Hindustani, dwelling upon the principles by which he hoped they would be guided in dealing with their subjects, and pointing out that those who did most in developing the resources of their dominions would find most favour in the

DURBAR OF SIR JOHN LAWRENCE AND 604 NATIVE PRINCES AT LAHORE, OCTOBER 18, 1864

SIR JOHN LAWRENCE'S GRAND DURBAR HELD AT LUCKNOW, NOVEMBER 9—17, 1867

eyes of a Government that valued such endeavours above long descent and extensive sway. Once more, in 1867, a similar pageant was enacted at Lucknow, where Lawrence received the talukdars of Oudh, who assembled in all their splendour of retinue to greet for the last time the man to whom their country owed so much. But if Law-

Native Treachery Punished rence was eager to engage the goodwill of the native nobility by such policy as would best commend itself to them, he did not hesitate to punish tyranny and bad faith. One flagrant outrage, committed by the Nawab of Tonk, came to his notice in 1867. This chief had been at enmity with one of the tributaries, the Thakur of Lawa. Under the pretence of reconciliation the Nawab summoned the Thakur to receive a *khilat*. The latter, attended by his uncle and a small retinue, duly presented himself at court. By-and-by the Thakur's uncle, Rewat Sing, with his son and fourteen adherents, were invited to the house of the Nawab's Minister, and there treacherously murdered, one man alone escaping, and the Thakur himself being held a prisoner. Subsequent inquiry proved beyond doubt that this atrocity had been contrived by the Nawab. He was therefore deposed in favour of his eldest son, his Minister being imprisoned at Chunar. The avarice and oppression of another chief, the Maharaja of Jodhpur, provoked an appeal by his subjects to the Viceroy. A severe reprimand warned him that deposition would follow unless he mended his ways.

Though Lawrence's face was firmly set against annexation, there was one act of the authorities in England to which, while yielding loyal obedience, he was unable to reconcile himself. This was the restitution of Mysore to native rule. For the third of a century this kingdom had been administered by British officials. On the death, in 1868, of the titular

Mysore Restored to Native Rule Maharaja, it was decided to proclaim his infant son as successor, and to hand over the government of the country to him if at the age of eighteen he should show himself qualified for its duties.

Legislation in Lawrence's time bore a fruitful crop of Acts; and two of these, dealing with tenant right, specially belonged to his initiation. When, after the Mutiny, Canning reinstated the talukdars of Oudh in their possessions and gave them a heritable title, the grants were declared "subject to any measure which the Government may think proper to take for the purpose of protecting the inferior zemindars and village occupants from extortion, and of upholding their rights in the soil."

Since that time the talukdars, in fancied security from interference, had failed to heed this proviso. The cry of the oppressed went to Lawrence's heart. Determining upon a complete investigation of the matter, he entered into correspondence with the Chief Commissioner, Sir C. Wingfield, whose championship of the talukdars had already been the subject of remonstrances from Lord Elgin. Wingfield's opposition to interference on behalf of the sufferers was supported by an outcry in the Press ; friends of the talukdars in their own province in Bengal, and even in England, swelled the clamour ; certain members of the Supreme Council were on the same side, and others of the Secretary of State's Council recorded minutes of dissent from the Viceroy's proposals. Lawrence, however,

Problems of Land Tenure stood firm, and sending Mr. Davies as special commissioner to Oudh, empowered him to direct the proceedings of the settlement officers and to decide all questions of tenant right. A report furnished by Davies showed that while proprietary rights had practically disappeared during the long supremacy of the talukdars, tenancy rights still survived. These it was resolved to maintain, and in 1868 the Oudh Tenancy Bill became law. By it, while the landlords were confirmed in all the rights granted in 1859, the occupancy rights of the cultivators received definition, rents could be enhanced only under certain restrictions, and compensation for improvement of holdings was decreed to tenants who might be evicted after occupancy for a fixed term of years.

A similar fight had to be waged in the Punjab. When, early in Lawrence's time, the period for reviewing the settlements came round, many of the zemindars who, on the annexation of the province, had neglected to register their names as superior landlords, now claimed to do so. Had this been allowed, the result would have been to degrade to the status of tenants-at-will no less than 46,000 out of 60,000 heads of families in one district alone, who had become entitled to their tenancies at beneficial rates. In the Viceroy's eyes such a proceeding would have been monstrous. Accordingly, in 1868, he introduced and carried through the Legislative Council a Bill whereby much the same safeguards as in Oudh protected the occupancy tenants in the Punjab.

If no great wars occurred between 1864 and 1869, several small military expeditions had to be undertaken. The most important of these was against Bhutan. On the Bengal frontier were certain lands, known as the Assam Duars, and comprising 1,600 square miles, which the Indian Government rented from the Bhutanese. As a punishment for repeated raids and outrages, Lord Canning withheld payment of the rents due on these lands. Fresh outrages were the result, and in 1863 Lord Elgin was persuaded to send a mission under Mr. Ashley Eden to the Deb Raja, nominal ruler of Bhutan. The members of it met with the grossest contumely, and Eden, under threat of imprisonment, was compelled to sign a treaty ceding the Assam Duars. On his return this treaty was, of course, repudiated by the Indian Government, an ultimatum being sent to the Deb Raja threatening war unless full reparation was made within three months. The term of grace having expired, four columns entered the Bengal Duars, and the forts commanding the passes into Bhutan were captured. The easternmost of these, Diwangiri, was held by Colonel Campbell with 500 men, who, a few months later, taken by surprise, had to abandon their position and retreat. Fresh troops being hurried up, Diwangiri was re-taken, and the enemy sued for peace. This was granted them upon terms that were generally considered unnecessarily lenient. Among other expeditions may be mentioned that against the Bhils in the centre of India, and another on the north-west frontier against the Hasanzai Pathans in the neighbourhood of the Black Mountain, who had swept down upon Oghi, a frontier station of the Punjab police. Two strong

A Little War with Bhutan

columns moved up to Abbotabad, and thence on to Oghi. The main position on the Black Mountain was captured with little loss, and, the headmen tendering their submission, hostages were taken from them for the fulfilment of the terms imposed. The Government of India was also called upon to take part in a war which did not concern it— namely, that against Theodore, King of Abyssinia. Sir R. Napier, afterwards Lord Napier of Magdala, commanded this expedition, with the result so well known and so creditable to his skill and energy. What was less creditable was the decision of the Government in England that the expenses of the campaign were to be borne by India.

Indian Operations in Africa

Anything like a detailed account of the encouragement given by Lawrence to education is impossible here. It must suffice to say that from the universities downwards to the primary schools, public instruction received a strong impetus, and in the last year of his rule more than three-quarters of a million sterling was allotted to the support of Government and aided institutions.

While Lawrence's domestic administration met generally with public approval, his foreign policy gave rise to vigorous opposition. The keynote of it was " masterly inactivity," the avoidance of all interference in Afghan affairs. This attitude was justified by its results, but it led to awkward situations while the numerous sons of Dost Mohammed, who died in 1863, were fighting for the throne. At first Sher Ali Khan, the eldest son, was recognised by the Viceroy as Amir of Afghanistan ; but when, in 1867, after a long struggle, Mohammed Afzal Khan made himself master of Kabul and Kandahar, he in his turn was accepted as de facto ruler. On his death shortly afterwards, similar recognition was accorded to his brother, Azim Khan. Later on again, Sher Ali, with the aid of his son, Yakub Khan, recovered possession of Kandahar, and entered Kabul in triumph in September, 1868.

Lawrence had not been indifferent to the distractions that had weakened a country which he desired to be both strong

EARL OF MAYO
The sixth Earl of Mayo was Viceroy of India from 1868 till his assassination at Port Blair in 1872.

London Stereoscopic

and friendly. He therefore so far modified his attitude of neutrality as to give Sher Ali six lakhs of rupees and 6,000 stands of arms. He also encouraged the Amir's proposal to pay him a visit in India, but the rebellion of Abdurrahman in Turkestan caused this to be postponed until Lord Mayo's arrival in the following year.

Lawrence's Legacy of Peace When, in January, 1869, Lawrence laid down his high office, he could say with a clear conscience that he had "handed over the Government to his successor efficient in all departments, with no arrears, and with all open questions in a fair way towards settlement." His services were rewarded by elevation to the peerage, with a pension of £2,000 a year for his own life and that of his immediate heir.

Lord Mayo, who was chosen by Mr. Disraeli to succeed Sir John Lawrence, took charge of his post on January 12, 1869. India was at peace throughout, and his predecessor had, to a very large extent, obliterated the traces of the Mutiny. There was, however, much scope for the energies of even so untiring a worker as Lord Mayo. Above every other question towered that of finance, and his inheritance in that direction was a deficit of £3,250,000 sterling.

To establish an equilibrium was the fixed resolve of the new Viceroy, whatever the cost might be. In his budget for the year, Sir R. Temple had calculated on being able to pay his way without loans. But estimates are one thing and actuals another, as had been revealed in the previous year when, in place of £2,000,000 to his credit, Mr. Massey had to face the same amount on the wrong side of the ledger. So when Temple's budget, framed upon the actual figures for nine months out of the twelve came to be checked by the full and final accounts of the past year, it presently appeared that a deficit more than double that for which provision had been made awaited the Government. The **Important Fiscal Problems** immediate difficulty was tided over by two expedients. Retrenching the projected outlay on public works, education, and other services, Lord Mayo obtained £1,150,000. Another £500,000 accrued from doubling the income tax for the last six months of the current year, and by raising the salt duties in Madras and Bombay. It was therefore possible to declare a small surplus.

But Mayo was bent upon reforms which, in ordinary circumstances, should render deficits impossible. An enhanced income tax could not be persisted in ; nor could he safely have recourse again to sudden curtailments of outlay. His first measure was to reorganise the mechanism of the Financial Department, so that it should no longer be at the mercy of imperfect and unpunctual estimates submitted by the local governments. A much more important one dealt with the funds for provincial expenditure. Hitherto, the Government of India had doled out money to meet the wants of local governments, which, although they collected the greater part of the revenue, had no responsibility for financial administration. In 1870, Lord Mayo gave to each of the larger provinces a fixed grant out of the revenues collected by it. From this the charges for services affecting the province were paid, any deficit being met by revenue raised locally.

Reorganisation was also possible in the Public Works Department, in railways, and in the Army. In the first of these, Lord Mayo adopted his predecessor's **Mayo's Financial Policy** proposal that new lines of railway should be undertaken by the State, the cost being defrayed by loan. It was also decided that the public works debt should be separated from the ordinary debt, and capital expenditure on productive works treated as borrowed by the Public Works Department. Military charges were reduced by £500,000, many needless posts in the Army Department and the Staff being abolished. The net result of these measures was, for the three years between 1870 and 1873, a total surplus close upon £6,000,000 sterling.

In his foreign policy Lord Mayo addressed himself to those problems which had engrossed so much of Sir John Lawrence's attention during the later years of his Viceroyalty. Shortly before the latter's retirement, Sher Ali had made up his mind that a visit to India would help to consolidate his rule. As already stated, internal disturbances delayed the execution of this project ; but in March, 1869, he was received by Lord Mayo at Ambala in the Punjab. In addition to the general idea of securing the Viceroy's goodwill, the Amir set his heart upon certain definite objects. These were a formal treaty with the British Power, a fixed annual subsidy, assistance in arms or men whenever he

WILD AFRIDIS AND KHAIBARIES AT PESHAWAR DURING LORD MAYO'S VISIT IN MAY, 1870

Lord Mayo, during his viceroyalty, from 1869 to 1872, visited outlying parts of the territory under his charge, including Peshawar, which is illustrated above. and Burma, on his return from which he met his death by assassination at Port Blair.

might think it necessary, the promise of support to himself and his descendants in all emergencies and against all rivals ; and lastly, an acknowledgment of his younger son as heir to the throne in exclusion of Yakub Khan, his eldest son, to whom he owed his restoration at Kabul. The

Visit of the Amir
last of these proposals was, of course, untenable, and the Amir was made to understand that it was contrary to our standing policy to interfere in the internal affairs of Afghanistan. For the rest, Lord Mayo could do no more than promise the moral support, with occasional supplies of money and material, already guaranteed by his predecessor. To oral assurances of interest in the welfare of Afghanistan, and of readiness to enter into correspondence with the Amir on all matters about which advice might be useful, Lord Mayo, two days after the conference, added a letter, intimating that the Viceroy's Government would view with the utmost displeasure any attempt on the part of the Amir's rivals to create disturbances at Kabul, and would endeavour from time to time, as circumstances might require, to strengthen

his position and enable him to exercise his rightful rule with equity and justice. Sher Ali could not but be a good deal disappointed at failing to obtain explicit promises on the points so near his heart. Nevertheless, the visit was not without the effect of confirming the friendly feeling on both sides, and impressing the Amir with the power and resources of the Government of India. As a corollary to the policy which it had been determined to maintain in regard to the frontier nations, including Afghanistan, Lord Mayo was no less desirous than Lawrence to come to an understanding with Russia. The Government in England were of like mind, and interviews between Prince Gortchakoff and

The Path to Anglo-Russian Agreement
Lord Granville helped to smooth the way to an accord. A joint Commission for defining Afghan and Russian territories was not appointed until 1884 ; but the first steps towards it were made by a formal statement regarding Afghanistan which was given to Russia, and is known as the Clarendon-Gortchakoff agreement of 1872-73. Progress was also made in settling the boundaries of Persia. For

some years the Shah had been encroaching upon Southern Baluchistan, or Kelat, the Khan of which country was under British protection. Pressed by Lord Mayo, the S ah agreed to arbitration, and Co onel Goldsmid was deputed by the Government of India to inquire into the respective rights of the disputants. The **Arbitration on Persian Questions** result was a convention satisfactory to both parties. At the same time, Lord Mayo took the opportunity of trying to compose the quarrels betweeen the Khan and his unruly Sirdars, and by the adroit management of Sir W. Merewether, the Commissioner in Sindh, this end was attained. About one other question of boundary, that of Sistan on both sides of the Helmund, Sher Ali and the Shah of Persia were still at variance. On its settlement Colonel Goldsmid was engaged when summoned to the more urgent business regarding Kelat. This done, he completed his earlier task by an award which stood good for thirty years when, the river altering its course, a revision became necessary.

With the frontier tribes on the north-west no collision occurred during Lord Mayo's time, their inclination to raids being checked by the vigilant outlook kept by a strong police force. But in the country between Assam and Burma an inroad of Lushais had to be chastised by moving up two columns under General Bouchier and Brownlow in November, 1871. The advance was a toilsome one through swamps and jungle. Opposition, however, was quickly overcome, the headmen of the tribes yielded at discretion, and hostages being taken for future good behaviour, the campaign came to an end in February, 1872.

With the native states in India Lord Mayo's relations were very similar to those of his predecessor. Avoidance of annexation, punishment of the individual **Relations with Native States** offender and not of the state, the lightest possible control where things were going well, with the education of native minors by British officers, were the cardinal points of his policy. He was, however, obliged to take notice of an act of discourtesy on the part of the Maharaja of Jodhpur, who objected to the seat assigned to him in durbar, and to punish more severely the Maharao Raja of Alwar, whose extravagance and misgovernment

led, in 1870, to his supersession by a council of its nobles under the presidency of a British officer. For the training of the sons of chiefs two colleges, somewhat after the pattern of Eton, were founded, the one at Ajmir, the other in Kathiawar. Both have flourished, and their outcome testifies to their founder's wisdom.

Turning to legislation, we find a large number of valuable enactments. Among these were the Evidence Act, the Contract Act, an Act embodying various amendments in the Criminal Code, an Act for legalising marriages of a certain class, an Act aiming at the prevention of murder of girl-children, the Punjab Revenue Act an Act dealing with encumbered estates in Oudh, and many others of greater or less importance.

In the matter of education, Lord Mayo's endeavours were chiefly confined to the extension of primary schools and to encouraging Mussulmans to take advantage of opportunities hitherto neglected by them. The improvement of agriculture was a matter upon which he set much store. For this purpose he planned a **Education and Agriculture** separate department, with a director-general at its head. But financial difficulties stood in the way, and when the new department sanctioned by the Secretary of State came into being it was made to embrace also revenue and commerce. So multifarious were the branches of each that agriculture profited but little, and after an existence of ten years the whole scheme was dropped.

At the close of his third year Lord Mayo paid a visit to Burma, and on his voyage back to Calcutta called in at Port Blair to inspect the convict settlement there. When the day's work was done, he insisted on climbing Mount Harriet, which he thought might be made to serve as a health resort for sick prisoners. Before the descent was made darkness had come on, and just as he was about to embark upon the launch that should convey him to the steamer in the offing a fanatical Mussulman, who had been released on a ticket-of-leave, eluded the guards, leapt upon the Viceroy's back, and with a sharp knife dealt him two fatal blows between the shoulders. Death followed a few minutes later. The body was taken on board the Glasgow for Calcutta, and ultimately to Ireland, where it found its last resting-place in a village churchyard in County Mayo. The assassin was, of course, hanged.

Pending the arrival of Lord Northbrook as Viceroy, the Governor of Madras, Lord Napier of Ettrick, proceeded to Calcutta to assume the office of Governor-General. The only matter of importance that came before him was the publication in March of the budget for the coming year. Lord Mayo had hoped to see the discontinuance of the income tax, and Lord Napier's views were in the same direction. But Temple was in favour of its renewal, and the acting Governor-General felt that he ought not to impose his wish upon a colleague whose province was finance. The tax was, therefore, reimposed for a year at the current rate of one per cent. The following year saw its abolition; nor was it again put into force during Lord Northbrook's viceroyalty. For in spite of the Bengal famine, for which some £4,000,000 sterling had to be provided in 1873-4, the deficit was a small one. In the following year this was converted into a surplus which in 1875-76 reached a handsome figure.

The famine referred to was the one serious difficulty that crossed Lord Northbrook's path. In 1873 the rainfall was so deficient in Bengal and Bihar that autumn sowings were impossible. Sir G. Campbell, Lieutenant-Governor of the Provinces, warned the Viceroy of the impending calamity, and the latter at once came down from Simla to concert measures for meeting it. With the help of the Lieutenant-Governor and Sir R. Temple an elaborate but somewhat extravagant scheme of famine relief was worked out in the minutest detail. Fortunately the rice crop of 1873 in Burma proved to be an unusually heavy one, and thence 300,000 tons were purchased, smaller supplies from various other localities bringing up the total to nearly 480,000 tons. The stores from Burma were shipped to Calcutta, and the whole amount was carried by rail to the neighbourhood of the afflicted districts. The railway, however, did not penetrate to the actual seat of the famine, nor could the Ganges be

Relieving a Great Famine

London Stereoscopic
EARL OF NORTHBROOK
Lord Northbrook was Viceroy of India from 1872 to 1876, and resigned because of differences with the Government of Lord Salisbury.

utilised for transport during the dry season. Transport trains of carts, horses, mules, and camels had to be organised, and Temple, now in charge of operations, decided to build a railway fifty miles in length which, while serving as a relief work, should be an asset for the future. When, therefore, in the following May the famine set in in all its rigour the Government was fully prepared to meet it. The accumulated stores were opened for sale at little more than nominal rates, the relief works swarmed with thousands eager to obtain supplies on such favourable terms, while those too weak to earn a wage, or unable for other reasons to leave their homes, had food distributed to them. In the middle of June the monsoon broke. This was followed by an abundant harvest, Government having advanced to the cultivators the money needed for the purchase of seed. The failure in Orissa was not repeated, the loss of life being trivial. But the operations cost £6,000,000 sterling, of which more than three-fourths were provided by the State.

Generous Distribution of Food

Foreign politics at the time were quiescent. Russia honourably adhered to her engagements regarding Afghanistan, and Persia had no grievance against us. Sher Ali, it is true, was in a less amiable mood than when under the spell of Lord Mayo's genial influence. Still nervous as to the imagined designs of Russia, and hankering after a definite agreement with the Government of India for the protection of his country, he tried to wring from Lord Northbrook promises which even Lord Mayo had refused to give. He also for a time showed much soreness as to the Sistan boundary award. The Viceroy did his best to allay all uneasiness in regard to Russia, but would not go further than to assure the Amir that, in case of wanton invasion of his territories, help in money, arms, and troops should be forthcoming. By way of solace for the losses which the Amir's subjects had endured from the Persian raids, a sum of five lakhs of rupees was placed to his credit. Later on Sher Ali found a fresh pretext for resentment in the displeasure which Lord Northbrook, perhaps unwisely, felt constrained to express at the treacherous imprisonment of Yakub Khan, invited by his father to a friendly interview at Kabul. Yet, though disappointed and sullen, he refrained from anything at which the Government of India could **Minor Native Revolts** take umbrage, and, had the Ministry in England been content to leave things as they were, the relations with Afghanistan, if not actively cordial, would have remained sufficiently tranquil. Of frontier disturbances there were few. Just before Lord Northbrook's arrival the Kukas, a new Sikh sect, attempted two incursions, the one in Sirhind and the other near Nabha. These were easily put down. On the north-eastern border the Dafla tribes had to be chastised in 1874 for their frequent raids, and in the following year the Nagas, to the east of Kachai, caused some trouble.

In one native state alone was interference found necessary. For some time past the misrule of the Gaekwar of Baroda had become too flagrant to pass unnoticed. In 1873 a Commission was appointed to inquire fully into the condition of the state, with the result that the chief was warned that unless within eighteen months things had greatly changed for the better, he would be deposed. It was by Colonel Phayre, Resident at the Gaekwar's court, that this ruler's misdemeanours had been brought before the Viceroy, and six months afterwards that officer reported an attempt to poison him. Evidence pointed to the Gaekwar's instigation to this crime. It was decided to put him on his trial before a Commission made up of the Maharajas of Jaipur and Gwalior, with the latter's late Minister, Dinkar Rao, and three British officers. The accused was ably defended by Sergeant Ballantyne, of the English Bar, and after a month's trial the verdict was inconclusive, the British Commissioners being unanimous as to complicity, while Jaipur voted not guilty, and Sindhia, with Dinkar Rao, held the charge not proven. The matter was referred to the Secretary of State, who ordered the deposition oi the Gaekwar, not on the result of the inquiry, but as a punishment for general maladministration. At the same time, without annexation of the State, a very distant connection of the Gaekwar's family was found living in comparative poverty in British India, and him the Maharani of the late ruler was allowed to adopt with a view to his education and succession to the throne.

Education was fostered in every branch, primary schools in Bengal receiving especial attention. And by this time so large was the supply of qualified natives that Lord Northbrook found it feasible to open to them many of the better-paid posts in the local civil services. But the most important educational movement of the period was due to Sir Sayyid Ahmad Khan, who opened an Anglo-Mohammedan college at Aligarh, in the North-western Provinces. This institution has continued to flourish, extending its operations until at the present it at least vies with the best efforts of the Imperial Government.

The visit of the Prince of Wales in the autumn of 1875 came as a pleasant diversion from more serious matters.

Early in 1876 Lord Northbrook found himself entirely out of harmony with the Cabinet at home. Distrusting Sher Ali and apprehensive of Russian designs, the Conservative Ministry had in the previous year pressed upon the Viceroy the advisability of obtaining the Amir's permission to establish an agency at Herat, and thereafter at Kandahar, as a means of obtaining more certain information of the trend of matters in those parts. Lord Northbrook, was unanimously supported by his Council in returning a strong remonstrance. His arguments were treated with scant respect, and in the following year Lord Salisbury insisted upon a Mission being sent to Kabul, the real object of which, however carefully wrapped up, was to pave the way for a permanent agency there also. Again Lord Northbrook endeavoured to dissuade from such a project. The Ministry was obdurate, and the Viceroy resigned.

Maull & Fox

SIR RICHARD TEMPLE
Governor-General of Bombay from 1877 to 1880, who rendered good service in the famine of 1874 and during the Afghan war of 1878-80.

The Wonder of India

THE empire which Babar and his Moguls reared in the sixteenth century was long one of the most extensive and splendid in the world. In no European kingdom was so large a population subject to a single prince, or so large a revenue poured into the treasury. The beauty and magnificence of the buildings erected by the sovereigns of Hindustan amazed even travellers who had seen St. Peter's.

The innumerable retinues and gorgeous decorations which surrounded the throne of Delhi dazzled even eyes which were accustomed to the pomp of Versailles. Some of the great viceroys, who held their posts by virtue of commissions from the Mogul, ruled as many subjects as the King of France or the Emperor of Germany. Even the deputies of these deputies might well rank, as to extent of territory and amount of revenue, with the Grand Duke of Tuscany, or the Elector of Saxony.

There can be little doubt that this great empire, powerful and prosperous as it appears on a superficial view, was yet, even in its best days, far worse governed than the worst governed parts of Europe now are. The administration was tainted with all the vices of Oriental despotism and with all the vices inseparable from the domination of race over race. The conflicting pretensions of the princes of the royal house produced a long series of crimes and public disasters.

Ambitious lieutenants of the sovereign sometimes aspired to independence. Fierce tribes of Hindus, impatient of a foreign yoke, frequently withheld tribute, repelled the armies of the Government from the mountain fastnesses, and poured down in arms on the cultivated plains. In spite, however, of much constant maladministration, in spite of occasional convulsions which shook the whole frame of society, this great monarchy, on the whole, retained, during some generations, an outward appearance of unity, majesty, and energy.

By Lord Macaulay

THE IMPERIAL DURBAR AT DELHI ON JANUARY 1, 1877: PROCLAMATION OF QUEEN VICTORIA AS EMPRESS OF INDIA

THE NEW EMPIRE OF INDIA

BY SIR WILLIAM LEE-WARNER

THE sequel to the "forward policy" which Lord Northbrook had so vainly resisted was not long delayed. Arriving in April, 1876, Lord Lytton lost no time in giving effect to the wishes of the Cabinet in England. His first proposal to the Amir was that he should receive a friendly mission under Sir L. Pelly. Scenting in this some sinister design, Sher Ali, with more or less valid excuses, declined the intended honour, suggesting in his turn that he should send an envoy to confer with the Viceroy on all matters needing discussion. This was met by a flat refusal, the original proposal being again insisted upon.

At a loss how to meet the danger to his independence which he felt to be imminent, the Amir then despatched the Viceroy's Vakil at his own Court to represent the grievances he considered himself to have against the Government of India, and to explain how he was situated. For answer, the Vakil was informed that the Viceroy would assent to a conference at Peshawar or elsewhere, between the Amir's Minister and Sir L. Pelly, on the one condition that the residence of British officers in Afghanistan should be permitted. At the end of January, 1877, the respective envoys met, Pelly reaffirming the conditions upon which the Government would undertake the defence of Afghanistan. In vain did Nur Mohammed urge the inability of the Amir to ensure the safety of a British agent in his capital; in vain did he appeal to the agreements sanctioned by Lawrence, Mayo, and Northbrook; in vain was it asked what new circumstances had arisen to render necessary the new demand so insistently pressed. Pelly, bound by his instructions, was inexorable, and to a fresh appeal made by Nur Mohammed, no answer had arrived when, after a short illness, the much-tried Minister died. Before his successor, bearing conciliatory messages from the Amir, could take up the negotiations, Lord Lytton closed the conference, and the British Vakil was withdrawn from Kabul.

Meanwhile, irritated by England's action in reference to the war in Turkey, Russia, as a counter stroke, determined on a mission to Kabul, and by June, 1878, Colonel Stoletoff was on his way to that capital. Without awaiting proof as to whether this proceeding was invited, or even welcomed by the Amir, the British Government decided to resent the presence of a Russian mission following upon the rebuff with which its own proposals had been met. In August, therefore, Lytton despatched a letter calling upon Sher Ali to make arrangements to receive a special embassy about to be sent under Sir Neville Chamberlain. The Amir naturally protested against so imperious a message, explaining that the Russian mission had been forced upon him, and that he was anxious to get rid of it; also promising in good time to receive Chamberlain, and appealing to the friendship which had so long existed between himself and the Government of India. Nevertheless, the mission went forward.

On reaching the mouth of the Khaibar, Chamberlain sent on Major Cavagnari to arrange with the commandant of Ali Musjid for his further advance. That officer courteously replied that without orders from the Amir this could not be permitted. Such refusal was deemed intolerable, and when, to a

EARL OF LYTTON
The son of the great novelist was Viceroy from 1876 to 1880, and represented Disraeli's forward policy.

1335

letter demanding ample apology, together with an undertaking to accept a permanent British mission, no answer within the brief interval allowed was forthcoming, Lord Lytton, supported by the Cabinet, declared war. Three columns, under Generals Stewart, Roberts, and Browne, at once advanced towards Afghanistan.

A Short Afghan War Ali Musjid was captured, Stewart and Browne respectively occupied Kandahar and Jellalabad, while Roberts prepared to invest Kabul. Terrified by these rapid movements, and much broken by the death of his favourite son, the Amir made over the defence of his capital to Yakub Khan, and fled to Mazar-i-Sharif, where he died shortly afterwards. Yakub, now acknowledged as Amir, soon found that armed resistance would be useless. He therefore entered into negotiations, and in May a treaty was signed at Gandamak, whereby the presence of a British Resident at Kabul was accepted, the foreign relations of Afghanistan came under British control, and certain positions of the country necessary for Lord Beaconsfield's " new scientific frontier " were ceded, England in return undertaking to safeguard Afghanistan from foreign invasion. Towards the end of July, the newly appointed Resident, Cavagnari, arrived at Kabul with his staff and escort, and was splendidly received, the Bala Hissar being assigned to them for residence.

EARL ROBERTS IN 1880
When Sir Frederick Roberts, he made his famous forced march from Kandahar to Kabul, October, 1880.

Till the beginning of September, everything seemed to be going well. But on the 3rd of that month certain of the Amir's troops, long kept out of their pay, broke into revolt. Failing to obtain more than a month's arrears, they appealed to the Resident, who, of course, could do no more than refer them to their own master. A second application in that quarter being met by no redress, they turned their fury upon the Residency. A stout resistance was offered by the small force under Cavagnari, but after an attack of some hours the insurgents succeeded in setting fire to the building. The Resident fell, crushed by a beam of the roof, and all with him were put to the sword. The Amir at once telegraphed to Roberts, who, pushing

forward from his camp on the Shuib Gardan, quickly occupied Kabul, Yakub taking refuge with the British. Of the military operations the most remarkable incident was the brilliant forced march of General Sir Frederick Roberts from Kabul to Kandahar, which concluded with the decisive defeat and overthrow of the Afghan Ayub. The upshot as regards Afghanistan was that, Sher Ali being dead, and Yakub having abdicated, Abdurrahman, a grandson of Dost Mohammed, was installed as Amir by General Stewart in July, 1880, and the army of occupation withdrew. The new ruler was informed by letter that so long as he was guided in the conduct of his foreign relations by the advice of the Government of India, unprovoked aggression by any foreign Power would be met by such assistance from the British Government as circumstances might require. While Lord Lytton was sailing through troublous seas in the course laid down for him in foreign policy, he was not exempt from the calamities to which the internal administration in India is always exposed from the malignant forces of Nature. First of these was a storm-wave which, at the end of October, 1876, swept down upon Lower Bengal, destroying the crops, turning the fields into salt marshes, wrecking homesteads, and filling the banks with corpses over an area of nearly 3,000 square miles. Pestilence followed cyclone, and in spite of every effort in behalf of the wretched sufferers, more than 100,000 human beings perished from one cause or another, to say nothing of the loss of cattle and the ruin to agriculture.

This, however, was but a small matter compared with the famine which shortly afterwards came upon Western and Southern India, and to a **Another Great Famine** less degree upon the North-Western Provinces and the Punjab. The usual measures of relief works—of importation of rice, remissions of revenue, house to house visitation, suspension of the import duty on food grain—were promptly adopted. The Duke of Buckingham in Madras, Sir P. Wodehouse in Bombay, and Sir R. Temple, as Famine Commissioner in both presidencies, strove with untiring

THE FORT OF ALI MUSJID IN THE KHAIBAR PASS

The fort itself is on the summit of the hill, 1, and the pickets of Ali Musjid are at 2; the spot where Major Cavagnari met the commandant of Ali Musjid is at 3 and 4 is the Khaibar River. The pass converges to 40 ft. wide near this point.

energy to minimise the distress that surrounded them on every side. Warned by the enormous outlay upon the recent famine in Bengal, Lord Lytton's Government was compelled to insist upon economy, especially as the area to be dealt with was now so much more extensive. It was, moreover, impossible to fight the battle on the same terms as before in tracts of land where there were no railways and where the death of cattle from want of fodder rendered transport unavailable. Accordingly, when in 1878 the awful conflict came to an end it was computed that some 7,000,000 of the inhabitants owed their death, directly and indirectly, to famine, while the cost to the State amounted to £11,000,000 sterling. Out of this twofold evil there at all events came the negative good that the Government showed itself more keenly alive to the urgent necessity of extending its system of railways and of supplementing them by irrigation works. A Famine Commission was also appointed to explore the afflicted districts, to gather information as to the causes of past famines, and to lay down a plan for fighting a like calamity in the future.

The shadow of the visitation described—for in the autumn of 1876 it was already evident that a fierce struggle was at hand—did not deter the Viceroy from carrying out his programme of Imperial rejoicings in view of the addition of the title of Empress to Her Majesty's style. At Delhi a splendid camp was laid out for himself, his subordinate governors and lieutenant-governors; a force of 15,000 troops was cantoned in the immediate neighbourhood; pavilions for the chiefs and princes formed a semicircle in front of that from which the proclamation was to be read. Lord Lytton, with a long train of elephants, made a triumphant entry, and on the 1st of January, 1877, addressed the assembled feudatories, conveying to them a gracious message from their Empress. The Maharajas of Kashmir and Gwalior were made generals of the British Army; other princes had guns added to their salutes; honours for good service were conferred upon European and native gentlemen. A review of the troops took place on the following day, and various entertainments filled up the week. Similar festivities on a smaller scale enlivened the provincial stations, and 15,000 prisoners had their sentences remitted.

Two remedial measures on behalf of the cultivators of the soil were set on foot during Lord Lytton's viceroyalty. The Deccan Agriculturists' Relief Act, which led to further legislation of this kind, enabled courts of law to review usurious transactions of moneylenders which had provoked agrarian disturbances in the Western Presidency, while in Bengal the Act of 1859 was amended so as to give further protection to the ryot from the oppression of the landholder. Another measure by which it was sought to afford scope to the ambition of the more advanced classes was the reservation of a number of posts in the covenanted Civil Service for native probationers selected by the Government of India. These, termed "Statutory Civilians," were, after a two years' training, to receive appointments hitherto filled by civilians selected by public competition, at a slight reduction of the ordinary salary. The scheme seemed a hopeful one, but a twenty years' experience resulted in the establishment in its place of the provincial services. One other Act, intended to curb the licence of the native Press, had a still shorter life. By the Liberal Ministry so soon to come into power such restriction was viewed as indefensible. Yet it cannot be said that a free Press has yet given to India the benefits expected from it.

MAJOR CAVAGNARI
The leader of Sir Neville Chamberlain's advance party, which was refused passage before Ali Musjid.

Elliott & Fry
SIR DONALD STEWART
General Sir Donald Stewart, when British commander in Kabul in 1880, installed Abdurrahman as Amir.

When, in 1880, Lord Beaconsfield gave place to Mr. Gladstone, Lord Lytton at once resigned office, and Lord Ripon sailed for India.

Sent out with the special purpose of reversing his predecessor's foreign policy, the new Viceroy promptly handed back to Afghanistan Kandahar and certain other portions of its territory that had been occupied by us, while nothing more was said as to the residence of British agents at Kabul and elsewhere, or of the scientific frontier on which so much stress had been laid. The result was to allay Abdurrahman's suspicions and ultimately to win his loyal friendship. But though no further complications involved us with Afghanistan itself, there was danger of our being brought into collision with Russia in behalf of that ill-defined country. To avert any such evil, Lord Ripon and his Government proposed an arrangement by which the frontier between Afghan and Russian territory in Central Asia should be defined. The Cabinet in England concurring, negotiations were opened with St. Petersburg, which issued in the despatch of a joint British and Russian Commission to the scene of the debatable territory, there to devise a boundary acceptable by both parties; and before the end of the year the commissioners had begun their work. While, however, to Lord Ripon belongs the credit of suggesting arbitration, the final solution was not arrived at in his time. An account of its incidents must, therefore, be reserved until we come to the viceroyalty of his successor. Besides the instructions which Lord Ripon received as to foreign politics, he was pledged by Mr. Gladstone's Ministry to reforms in various directions upon a more liberal basis. We have seen that Lord Lytton's Vernacular Press Act was speedily repealed, reliance being placed upon the ordinary penalties of the law for the correction of seditious writings.

MAJOR CAVAGNARI AT A CONFERENCE WITH OFFICERS OF THE AMIR
Sir Louis Cavagnari was appointed British Resident at Kabul in 1879; three weeks after his arrival some mutinous Afghan regiments besieged the Residency and, aided by the populace, massacred Cavagnari and his companions.

From this removal of disabilities Lord Ripon proceeded to two constructive measures, one of which gave rise to a considerable enlargement of the policy initiated by Lord Mayo, while the other evoked a fierce outcry from the British Indian public at large.

The former was an extension of municipal and local boards throughout the country with the special object of enlisting the co-operation of the Indian people in matters of education, sanitation, and local works of public utility.

The latter was the introduction, in 1883, of a Criminal Procedure Amendment Bill, generally known as the " Ilbert Bill," from the name of the member in charge of it, Mr. C. P. Ilbert. Hitherto, except in the Presidency towns, no charge against a European British subject could be entertained by a magistrate or a sessions judge who was not of such birth. The new Bill, which aimed at removing this restriction, at once raised a violent outburst of anger and alarm from all ranks of the British community. Europeans valued the privilege of being tried by one of their own blood, and feared that racial prejudice or even mis-appreciation of evidence would prejudice their trial before native magistrates. Meetings throughout the country denounced the project, associations formed themselves at various centres to bring pressure upon the Government, protests poured in upon Lord Ripon, a hot debate raged in the Legislative Council Chamber, and vigorous representations were made to the Secretary of State. In Calcutta the excitement was at its fiercest, and fears were even entertained that personal insult might be offered to the Viceroy on his return to the capital. After many months of this agitation the Government, though refusing to withdraw its Bill, assented to a compromise whereby all Englishmen were enabled to claim trial by jury throughout the country. Whether it was worth while to awaken dormant animosities for the sake of change in a procedure that had hitherto worked so smoothly has been much debated, but it must be admitted that the law as finally passed has created no well-grounded grievance.

From a matter so contentious we may pass to more pleasant things. General prosperity smiled upon the land. Surpluses

1339

took the place of deficits ; from railways, canals, and other public works the returns increased year by year ; thanks to a series of good seasons the foreign trade of the country steadily rose ; it was found possible to lower the salt tax and to abolish the customs duties on the importation of foreign piece-goods. With the native states no interference was found necessary ; but in 1881 the trans-

and drew up a syllabus of recommendations for the guidance of the Departments of Public Instruction in the various provinces.

One cloud alone was visible on the horizon. During his visit to Burma, at the end of 1880, Lord Ripon received a deputation of mercantile residents at Mandalay complaining of the king's arbitrary interference with the course of trade. On his return to Calcutta the Governor-General made representations to the Court of Ava, which it was hoped would check the abuse of monopolies, which formed the chief grievance. A discontinuance of the system was promised, and a mission sent to India accepted a treaty that, if carried out, would have removed all friction between the two Governments. Thebaw, however, refused to ratify his envoy's concessions, with the result that measures of a serious nature had to be taken in Lord Dufferin's time.

In December, 1884, Lord Ripon left India, and, except that in 1882 he was called upon to furnish a contingent of troops for Egypt, his rule was not vexed by any military operations or by internal disturbances that demanded forcible repression.

Shortly after his arrival, Lord Dufferin invited Abdurrahman to pay him a visit in India for the purpose of discussing all outstanding questions in reference to Afghanistan. The Amir cordially responded, and in the following March arrived at Rawal Pindi in the Punjab, where he was welcomed with every honour. For some months past the Boundary Commission had been at work, when an incident occurred which threatened to put an end to the undertaking. On the left bank of the River Kushk was a place called Panjdeh, to which both Russians and Afghans laid claim. Here, on March 31, a collision took place between

A TROOP OF INDIAN CAVALRY IN THE KHAIBAR PASS
This gateway between India and Afghanistan is the only pass on the north-west frontier suitable for artillery ; it is 33 miles long and is overhung by mountains which sometimes rise sheer from 1,400 to 3,000 feet above the pass.

ference of rule in Mysore to the young Raja came into force, and an important instrument, or Sanad, recorded in full detail the obligations under which the state's internal independence was to be guaranteed by the paramount power. Education was stimulated by the appointment of a Commission, which reviewed the whole subject from the date of the Despatch of 1854, classified the schools of all kinds, overhauled the Grant-in-Aid rules,

A SCENE IN THE BAZAAR AT KABUL, THE CAPITAL OF AFGHANISTAN

The chief merchandise sold consists of fruit, which is grown locally, also carpets, shawls, and silk and cotton goods.

GENERAL VIEW OF KABUL, WITH THE BALA HISSAR IN THE FOREGROUND

The Bala Hissar dominates the city and is a former palace of the Amir ; it was the British Residency in 1879, and in it Major Sir Louis Cavagnari and several companions, with about 75 natives, were murdered by mutinous Afghans.

SCENES IN THE CAPITAL CITY OF THE AMIR

the troops of the respective nations, in which the Afghans were worsted. For the moment it seemed likely that this event would kindle a war between England and Russia.

The Amir, however, who was then being entertained as the Viceroy's guest, attached but little importance to the possession of Panjdeh, and negotiations between the Courts of St. Petersburg and St. James's ended in the neutralisation of the disputed territory until the demarcation should be completed. Meanwhile the conference at Rawal Pindi went on. Lord Dufferin's courtesy and tact were met by frankness on the part of the Amir, the gist of whose policy was a determination not to admit either Russian or Englishman within his dominions. Satisfied by assur-

ABDURRAHMAN
This grandson of Dost Mohammed was proclaimed Amir by the British under General Stewart in 1880.

ances that the British had no thought of interference in his domestic affairs— assurances backed by promises of arms and money—the Amir returned to Kabul, henceforth to remain a loyal friend. Demarcation, interrupted for a while, was pushed forward, Sir P. Lumsden being replaced by Colonel Ridgeway, who, deputed in 1886 to St. Petersburg, brought matters to so successful a close that in July, 1887, an agreement was signed which embraced the whole of the frontier in dispute.

Concurrently with these negotiations ending in so friendly a manner, foreign politics had to deal with the hostile attitude of the Burman king. Reference has already been made to his treatment of commercial residents at Mandalay, and to the abortive mission of 1882. In 1885 it was suspected that Thebaw was preparing to throw himself into the arms of France as a prospective ally in case of

pressure being put upon him from India. An ultimatum was therefore sent demanding that he should receive a permanent British Resident at his court, and defer to the advice of the British Government in regard to his foreign relations. The answer from Ava was a distinct defiance. Thereupon a force of 10,000 troops marched upon Mandalay, which was occupied in ten days, the king surrendering himself a prisoner.

After a full consideration of the different courses open to him in order to ensure stable government, and having himself visited the country, Lord Dufferin decided that annexation pure and simple, and the direct administration of the province by British officers, offered the best prospects of securing the peace and prosperity of Upper Burma and our own Imperial and commercial interests. A complete administrative system was therefore drawn up by which the two provinces were gradually assimilated to each other. The task, however, of pacifying a country infested by robber gangs, and both unaccustomed to, and intolerant of, any form of regular government, was one that at first taxed all the energies of the new administration. Yet within two years peace and order reigned throughout, and each succeeding year has witnessed increasing prosperity with a cheerful acceptance of British rule.

While political complications were thus successfully met, legislative enactments dealt with some vexatious questions. Succinctly told, the object and result of the three great Tenancy Bills passed in Lord Dufferin's time were the settlement of disputes between the zemindar and the ryot, with especial reference to the protection of the

Russell
MARQUESS OF RIPON   MARQUESS OF DUFFERIN
The first Marquess of Ripon was Governor-General of India from 1880 to 1884, and the Marquess of Dufferin and Ava, who added Burma to the British dominions, was Viceroy from 1884 to 1888.

Elliot & Fry

latter. The matter as regards Bengal had already been under the consideration of Lord Ripon's Government without any definite arrangement being come to. While the landlords contended **Dufferin's** that by Act X. of 1859 **Tenancy** partiality had been shown to **Bills** their tenants, these, on the other hand, emphasised the disabilities under which they laboured by refusing in many parts to pay rent. Act VIII. of 1885 reviewed the whole rent-law of the province, establishing a fixity of tenure whereby, while the landlord was entitled to a fair share of the increased value of the produce of the soil, the tenant obtained the same security in his holding that he had enjoyed under the old customary law.

In Oudh, again taking up the work begun by Lord Ripon, Lord Dufferin carried through his Legislative Council a Rent Act which largely curtailed the powers of eviction and enhancement of rent that the taluk-dars claimed. Whereas hitherto the cultivator's tenure held good by law for a year only, the new Act declared the tenant-at-will entitled to retain his holding for a period of seven years from the date of his rent being settled in accordance with provisions therein laid down, and, further, to claim compensation on ejection for improvements made within thirty years previously.

Reference has already been made to a compromise in 1886 which had sought to adjust somewhat similar difficulties in the Punjab. But by 1886 these had considerably increased, and further steps were necessary to define existing rights.

KING THEBAW IN STATE

The last native King of Burma, whose misrule and arrogance drew upon him repeated remonstrances and protests from successive Governors-General of India, until the climax when Dufferin deposed him and annexed Burma.

The result was a Bill, in 1887, which, as in Bengal and Oudh, gave relief to the tenantry, and was accepted by both parties as a satisfactory settlement of their dispute.

Though not carried through in Lord Dufferin's time, two important measures of internal policy were initiated by him. The one was an enlargement of the powers of legislative councils; the other, the admission of natives of India to a larger share of the civil appointments until then reserved for the "competition-wallah." These proposals synchronised with the formation of a body styling itself the "National Congress," which, under the fostering care of Mr. Hume, a retired English civilian, had been originally organised to promote self-government and representative institutions. The party soon fell into the hands of pleaders and the privileged classes of Hindu society, such as Brahmans, Khatris, and Bengali Babus, who gradually gained control of the native Press, receiving financial support from large landowners and others desirous of securing their interest. Mohammedans held aloof form the Congress, and the masses of the cultivators were indifferent to it. As years advanced, professional agitators and the less scrupulous adherents of the party captured the machinery, and professing to speak the voice of India, entered upon an open **Concerted** campaign of sedition and mis- **Native** representation which led to **Agitation** serious trouble in 1907. Lord Dufferin foresaw the probable course of events, and courageously took the opportunity of a farewell dinner given to him on

1343

St. Andrew's Day to declare the limits within which a further share of power could alone be conceded to the educated classes.

In military matters Lord Dufferin's Government advocated a far-reaching organic reform entailing the abolition of the Presidency commands—a measure that had to wait for its fulfilment till Lord Elgin's time. Among minor events may be mentioned the rendition to Sindhia of the fortress of Gwalior, whereby the long-cherished desire of that chief was at last gratified ; the foundation of the " Countess of Dufferin's Fund," out of which hospitals and dispensaries were opened for the treatment of native women by members of their own sex ; the establishment of a university at Allahabad; and the gift of a Legislative Council to the North-western Provinces.

Dufferin's Military Policy

In September, 1888, Lord Dufferin was created Marquess of Dufferin and Ava, and on December 10 he made over his vice-royalty to Lord Lansdowne. It was by his own wish that his term of office had been shortened by one year, for advancing age warned him that energies tried by so many burdensome offices must seek relief in retirement from public life, or, at all events, in duties of a less exacting nature.

Apart from certain minor expeditions, Lord Lansdowne's viceroyalty was free from the scourge of war. But many difficulties in regard to frontier states awaited his attention. Barbarous tribes had to be brought into subjection and predatory outbreaks chastised ; feuds between neighbouring tribes demanded intervention ; tedious negotiations were necessary for the opening up of roads for commercial enterprise ; various boundaries called for definition, as, for instance, between the Shan States and Siam, between Burma and China, between Sikkim and Tibet. Here a British Agency had to be established, there the disputed succession of a chief could be settled only by our recognition ; and in one state—that of Manipur, on the borders of Assam—stern measures were necessary in retribution of the treacherous murder of British officials. But no problem of foreign policy was so important as the settlement of our relations with Afghanistan. From time to time projected missions to Kabul had been abandoned for one reason or another, and

Problems of Lord Lansdowne

THE DEPARTURE OF KING THEBAW OF BURMA FROM HIS CAPITAL OF MANDALAY

especially because of internal dissensions, which Abdurrahman had to quell before he could safely engage in foreign diplomacy. However, in September, 1893, a mission under Sir H. M. Durand set out for Kabul, and was there cordially welcomed by the Amir. The result was eminently satisfactory, all questions as to respective spheres of influence being amicably decided, while an agreement was entered into for the demarcation of the whole frontier between Afghanistan and India. In return for concessions made by the Amir, his subsidy was largely increased, and the Government of India agreed to permit the importation of arms and ammunition.

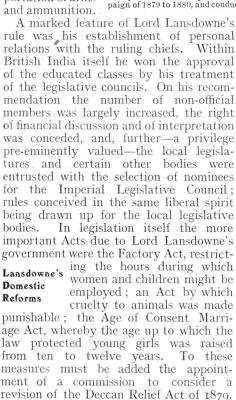

Russell

MARQUESS OF LANSDOWNE

Elliott & Fry

SIR H. M. DURAND

The fifth Marquess of Lansdowne was Governor-General of India from 1888 to 1893, and materially strengthened the friendliness of the ruling chiefs for the British Crown. Sir Henry Mortimer Durand was political secretary to Lord Roberts during the Afghan campaign of 1879 to 1880, and conducted the mission to the Amir in 1893.

A marked feature of Lord Lansdowne's rule was his establishment of personal relations with the ruling chiefs. Within British India itself he won the approval of the educated classes by his treatment of the legislative councils. On his recommendation the number of non-official members was largely increased, the right of financial discussion and of interpretation was conceded, and, further—a privilege pre-eminently valued—the local legislatures and certain other bodies were entrusted with the selection of nominees for the Imperial Legislative Council; rules conceived in the same liberal spirit being drawn up for the local legislative bodies. In legislation itself the more important Acts due to Lord Lansdowne's government were the Factory Act, restricting the hours during which women and children might be employed; an Act by which cruelty to animals was made punishable; the Age of Consent Marriage Act, whereby the age up to which the law protected young girls was raised from ten to twelve years. To these measures must be added the appointment of a commission to consider a revision of the Deccan Relief Act of 1879.

Lansdowne's Domestic Reforms

To economics and public works Lord Lansdowne gave the closest attention. Thus, in accordance with the recommendations of the Famine Commission of 1881, an Imperial Department of Revenue and Agriculture was created with provincial Departments organised upon a similar basis. Steps followed for a more scientific and more moderate assessment of the land revenue, one, too, which should tend towards relieving indebted and distressed landowners. The area brought under irrigation increased by nearly 2,000,000 acres, while close upon 4,000 miles of new railway lines were opened between 1888 and 1893. With a people so wedded to custom, perhaps no reform is more difficult than that of sanitation. Something, however, has been done by the establishment of provincial sanitary boards, and the system of waterworks introduced during Lord Lansdowne's viceroyalty bids fair to be of inestimable benefit. As with so many previous Viceroys, financial disturbance troubled Lord Lansdowne. Though between 1889 and 1892 he had been favoured with considerable surpluses, deficits again made their unwelcome appearance. These were mainly due to the rapid and continuous decline in the value of silver. So great was the embarrassment thus created that the Ministry in England determined to appoint a committee to consider proposals made by the Government of India for restricting the coinage of silver at the Indian mints and making sovereigns legal tender at a rate not exceeding 1s. 6d. for the rupee. These proposals, though modified by the committee, resulted in fixing the ratio between gold and silver at 1s. 4d. for the rupee, and with this standard to work upon, Indian finance is now free from the oscillations that had so long vexed it from a fall in the rate of exchange.

Falling Price of Silver

In military affairs many important steps were taken. Among them were the abolition of the Presidential Army system, the amalgamation of the three separate staff corps, the recruitments from more warlike classes in many of the native regiments, the equipment of the Imperial service troops offered by the feudatory chiefs at the instance of Lord Dufferin, and large measures for the more prompt mobilisation of the army and the defence of the harbours and frontiers of India. Lord Lansdowne also laid the foundations of police reorganisation on which Lord Curzon was to build, instituted an inquiry into the administration of gaols, founded an Imperial library, and collected valuable statistics by means of the Imperial census.

On January 24, 1894, he handed over charge of his office to Lord Elgin with the consciousness that the measures taken during the five years of its tenure had contributed towards the greater security and increased wellbeing of the country at large, more active co-operation on the part of the native princes, and friendlier relations with foreign states. His successor brought to the task of governing India those qualities of common-sense and high principles which ensure success to their possessor if willing to profit by the experience of others. His judgment and courage were soon put to the test by a succession of unlooked-for calamities. The first trouble was a legacy from events occurring towards the close of his predecessor's reign. In 1892 the Mehtar of Chitral, who received a subsidy from the Government of India, suddenly died. His second son, Afzal-ul-Mulk, thereupon seized the reins of State to the

EARL OF ELGIN
The ninth Earl of Elgin, the present Secretary of State for the Colonies, was Governor-General of India 1894-99, and pursued a cautious and conservative policy.

Russell

exclusion of his elder brother, Nizam-ul-Mulk, who took refuge with the British at Gilgit. Hardly had Afzul established himself on the throne when he was attacked by his uncle, Sher Afzul, and fell in the struggle. In his turn Sher Afzul had to yield to the old Mehtar's eldest son, whose right was recognised by Lord Lansdowne, a British officer being appointed to reside in Chitral as representative of the Indian Government. In 1895, fresh complications arose. Umra Khan, chief of Jandol, invaded Chitral, and at his instigation Nizam-ul-Mulk was treacherously murdered by a younger brother, Amir-ul-Mulk, who called upon the Viceroy to recognise him as Mehtar. This demand was refused, and in the confusion Sher Afzul again descended from Afghanistan, like Amir-ul-Mulk, claiming and being denied recognition. A collision shortly afterwards occurred between his troops and a body of Indian sepoys, under the command of a British officer, which was driven into the fort of Chitral, and there besieged by a large force of Chitralis. Two British columns, speedily despatched, relieved the fort, order was restored, and the invader fled the country.

Everything now gave promise of quiet times, when once again famine loomed large. So general, indeed, was the failure of the monsoon in 1896 that distress more or less acute threatened nearly the whole of India. Every measure that previous experience had dictated was at once set in operation, yet at one period nearly 5,000,000 of half-starved human beings were earning a scanty subsistence on the relief works, while the death-rate increased by leaps and bounds. Charitable contributions from various quarters reached the high figure of some £3,000,000

Russell
LORD CURZON
Lord Curzon of Kedleston was Viceroy of India from 1899 to 1905, and followed an energetic policy of reform in every direction. The fourth Earl of Minto succeeded Lord Curzon after a term of service as Governor-General of Canada, and is the present Governor-General.

Eliott & Fry
EARL OF MINTO

sterling, and the loss to the Government of India in one shape or another was computed at not less than £17,000,000. On the top of famine came bubonic plague in Bombay, which eventually spread over the greater part of the country. Endeavours to stamp it out by isolation and **Plague that Follows Famine** sanitary precautions have been baffled as much by the caste and religious habits of the people as by our ignorance of its cause, and now, after ten years, it appears to have become endemic.

To crown the anxiety with which the Viceroy and his councillors were beset in these directions, a general and apparently concerted rising of border tribes along the north-western frontier necessitated extensive military operations. Afridis, Mohmands, Orakzais, Buners, Waziris, and others poured down into British territory, capturing forts, beleaguering posts, and overwhelming native garrisons. For

their punishment, two expeditions were fitted out—the one against the Afridis under Sir W. Lockhart, the other, commanded by Sir Bindon Blood, against the other tribes. Throughout the winter of 1897 these forces were engaged in a bitter struggle, and though in the end the insurgents were vanquished, victory was bought at a heavy cost of life and large expenditure of money. Apart from the measures demanded by famine and plague, which absorbed so much of the energies of civil governments, nothing of striking importance marked **Work of Lord Elgin's Viceroyalty** Lord Elgin's rule. Progress was made in the way of opening up a wider career to educated natives by enlarging the number of posts to which they were accounted eligible, and in developing the provincial, as distinguished from the Imperial, system; something also was done towards improving municipal administration. In 1899 Lord Elgin was succeeded by Lord Curzon of Kedleston.

It would be difficult to imagine a greater contrast than that between the brilliant Englishman who now took up office and the cautious Scotsman who had just laid it down— between the steady determination of the one to follow in the footsteps of his predecessors and the bold energy of the other intent upon regenerating India in every direction. During the seven years of his rule Lord Curzon pushed his inquiries into every nook and corner of the administration, completing some useful reforms and originating a variety of schemes upon the value of which time alone can pronounce. It is impossible here even to summarise the multifarious projects on which his active mind busied itself. Nor can we treat in much detail the more prominent occurrences of his rule.

Of frontier questions, those most perplexing to successive Viceroys have had reference to the North-

THE FORT OF CHITRAL: SCENE OF A MINOR SIEGE
In the fort of Chitral, in the native state of Chitral on tne north-west frontier of Kashmir, Sir George Robertson (then Surgeon-Major Robertson) was besieged in 1895, and relieved by Colonel Kelly after a forced march from Gilghit.

west. Till lately, the territory contiguous with the border was under the administration of the Punjab Government. This involved a great deal of work which, if not of any Imperial character, seemed to Lord Curzon to demand special arrangements. These he proposed to make by carving out of the Punjab a frontier

Several Frontier Problems province under the rule of a commissioner, subject to the Government of India. Though meeting with much opposition, the scheme was ultimately sanctioned by the Secretary of State. Cognate with it was the question of protecting the frontier. Hitherto this duty had been in the hands of Imperial troops, whose neighbourhood was thought at times likely to provoke collision with the frontier clans. It was therefore decided to substitute tribal levies under the command of carefully-selected British officers. After the severe castigation which the tribes had recently received, it was not to be expected that renewed outbursts would occur in the near future, and thus

Protection of the Frontier these two experiments were launched at the most favourable time. So far they seem to have been successful, but it would be rash to draw conclusions from so short an experience of their working.

Another measure which roused still greater opposition was the subdivision or " partition " of Bengal. In this there was no novelty of procedure. As Lord Dalhousie had found it necessary to sever Bengal from the Governor - Generalship, as the North-western Provinces and the Punjab became distinct provinces, and Assam a Chief-Commissionership, in each case because it was found impossible for a single officer to administer so wide an extent of country, so now Bengal required relief of a similar nature. The idea, however, roused the Bengal pleaders and the newspaper proprietors to a frenzy of wrath, and the agitation against it was active. Meetings of protest were organised throughout the province ; the native Press teemed with vituperation of the most rancorous character ; English goods were boycotted, and the " Friends of India," as they style themselves, still continue their outcry in the House of Commons. But the change once carried out has been maintained, and it may safely be predicted

ENTRY OF THE BRITISH MISSION INTO LHASA
During the viceroyalty of Lord Curzon, in 1903, a British mission under Colonel Younghusband entered Tibet to compel observance of the provisions of the treaty of 1887 ; a few minor engagements took place, and Lhasa was reached on August 3, 1904.

1348

that the administrative advantages of the redistribution of charges will soon be recognised. In financial matters Lord Curzon reaped what others had sown. Thanks largely to Lord Lansdowne's treatment of the exchange difficulty, he enjoyed a succession of surpluses averaging about three millions sterling. But if the funds at his disposal were large, the demands upon the public purse kept pace with the incomings. Famine, the equipment of the army, and the need of civil administrations, all helped to swallow up what might otherwise have been devoted to the remission of taxes. Not till 1903, therefore, was it possible to move in this direction. In that year, however, the salt tax was reduced by eight annas per maund, and the limit of exemption from income tax was raised, two measures involving an annual sacrifice of revenue to the amount of two and a half millions.

THE SIGNING OF THE TREATY OF LHASA

The Treaty of Lhasa, which was signed in the apartments of the Dalai Lama at the Potala in Lhasa on September 7, 1904, permitted trade between India and Tibet; it engaged Tibet not to sell or lease any Tibetan territory to any foreign Power without the consent of Great Britain and to pay an indemnity of £500,000 in 75 yearly instalments.

The famine of 1899-1900 affected a population of 25,000,000 in British India, and more than 30,000,000 in native states. For weeks together, upwards of 6,000,000 of human beings were dependent upon the charity of Government. The expenditure exceeded £6,000,000 sterling, besides liberal advances made to agriculturists, loans to native states whose finances were unequal to measures of relief, and large remissions of arrears of revenue. At the end of 1902, remissions to the extent of over £1,000,000 sterling were granted to clear off the arrears that had accumulated during the time of distress, and so to give the rural population of the affected tracts a fresh start in life. Each previous visitation had added to the experience gained by Government in respect to the treatment of famine, but much credit was due to the Viceroy's personal energy in coping with so far-reaching a calamity.

In the existing state of education, Lord Curzon found a scope for his reforming energies. To consider the subject generally, a conference was held at Simla, in 1901, at which the views of those most competent to advise were fully stated, the result being a series of resolutions embodying a programme of reconstruction. The most urgent question was that of extending elementary education, the provincial fund for which had long been insufficient. Ultimately an annual grant of thirty-five lakhs of rupees for this purpose was accepted as a permanent charge upon the Imperial Exchequer. Something was also done for training colleges, industrial schools, and female education. The universities presented a more thorny problem. In the absence of a general inspection of the affiliated institutions, many of the so-called colleges were no better than "cramming" establishments of an unsatisfactory character, with a direct interest in lowering the university standards. This desire was tacitly encouraged by the Senates, in which a superabundance of members with no practical knowledge of education made it their object to attract the largest number of students and to glorify themselves by an

Reform of Indian Colleges

General's complaints no heed was paid, his letters being returned unopened. In 1902 a conference at Yatung was arranged with China as the suzerain of Tibet. The Chinese envoys, however, arrived too late, and nothing was done. Later on, with the consent of the Chinese, Khamba Jong, just across the Tibetan frontier, was fixed upon as the place of meeting, the Dalai Lama accepting the proposal, only to decline all negotiation when the mission arrived. It was now felt by the Governments of India that no further delay could be allowed in settling the matter. A British force, therefore, pushed on to Lhasa, which it occupied after some fighting. A treaty, subsequently revised

Edwards

GENERAL VIEW OF LHASA, THE METROPOLIS OF LAMAITE BUDDHISM
Lhasa, which means "the abode of divine intelligence," is the capital of Tibet, and has only recently been entered by foreigners. Towards the left of the picture is the Potala, the palace of the Dalai Lama, and there was signed the treaty of September 7, 1904, by which non-British interference in the affairs of Tibet was made impossible.

increasing out-turn of graduates. By a Bill passed into law in 1894, the universities were provided with new Senates, mainly composed of teachers, and leave was given to each to frame its own regulations and to inspect its own colleges. This step, which ought to have been taken long before, was received with a storm of obloquy, on the ground that it was intended to "officialise" the universities and, by insisting upon an impossible standard of efficiency, to crush the weaker colleges out of existence.

Among foreign matters was the mission to Lhasa, provoked by the failure of the Tibetan Government to observe the treaty made with it in 1887. To the Governor-

by the Secretary of State, was exacted, the Dalai Lama fled, and the Tashi Lama, his successor, has since shown himself ready to accept British friendship. Another mission, this time to Afghanistan, was despatched in 1904, its object being to draw closer the relations between the two countries, and so persuade the new Amir, Habibulla Khan, to take measures for opening up his dominions to free commercial intercourse. A treaty was, after some delay, concluded which merely reaffirmed existing arrangements.

Tibetan and Afghan Relations

Lord Curzon, having taken leave to England in April, 1904, was reappointed Governor-General on his return to India

THE PRINCE AND PRINCESS OF WALES IN INDIA

In December, 1905, the Prince and Princess of Wales arrived in Calcutta. Their three months' tour was a pageant of Oriental magnificence, and brought much benefit to India on account of their reception by the native princes and people.

in the following December. He took an active part in the great scheme of military reorganisation to which the Commander-in-Chief, Lord Kitchener, had devoted his energies. The Governor-General persuaded himself that the direct participation of the Commander-in-Chief, as a member of Council, in the disposal of military business that came before the Government of India would weaken the control of the civil authorities over the military affairs of India. Neither the Government of Mr. Balfour, nor that of the Liberal Party which at a later date succeeded it, shared these fears. Before, therefore, another year was over he relinquished his post in India in favour of Lord Minto, who assumed office in November, 1905.

The new Governor-General at once attended to two matters of great importance which his predecessor had nearly brought to a final issue. A Police Commission had reported upon the various forces throughout India, recommending substantial increases of pay and the introduction of much-needed reforms of system. The necessary changes were at once carried out in this department. In the extension of irrigation, the late Viceroy had provided further important safeguards against famine, and Lord Minto actively followed the lead given him.

As soon as he had settled the outstanding questions which awaited his arrival, Lord Minto strove to allay the feelings of unrest and discontent which recent changes had increased, and even proceeded to consider how far it might be possible to associate the natural leaders of Indian society in the guardianship of common and imperial interests. The formation of councils of notables, the enlargement of legislative councils, and the increase of facilities for discussion of the budget, were some of the schemes which he contemplated. Unfortunately, the Hindu Press in all parts of India, and the opposition to the division of Bengal, with the popular movement in favour of boycotting European goods, had already inflamed racial animosity; and he was obliged to turn aside for the moment from the task of reform to that of repression and the preservation of the public peace. It may be noted that during this period of unrest the Mohammedans, who have always realised that the programme of the Congress party is not in their interest, have displayed loyalty to British rule.

The tour of their Royal Highnesses the Prince and the Princess of Wales in the winter of 1905–6 was a success in every way and exercised a most salutary effect upon all ranks of Indian society.

THE PRINCE OF WALES REVIEWING THE INDIAN ARMY
The drawing from which the illustration is taken is the work of an artist present at the military review at Rawal Pindi where 25,000 troops were on parade. In the picture the Prince of Wales is the front figure on horseback Lord Kitchener is immediately behind him, and the Princess of Wales occupies the front position in the carriage.

INDIA IN OUR OWN TIME
BY SIR WILLIAM LEE-WARNER

HAVING now traversed the dusty road of Indian history, and marked the stages along it indicated by the terms of office held by the Viceroys down to the present time, we may pause and take a general survey of the country.

India consists of two parts—British India, comprising, with Berar, which is administered by the Nizam, 1,097,900 square miles, with 232,000,000 of British subjects ; and native states, under British protection, covering 675,267 square miles, with 62,000,000 of people, subject to the laws of their own ruling chiefs. The former is divided into thirteen Provinces, of which the following are the largest in matter of area : Burma, Madras, Bombay, Bengal, the United Provinces of Agra and Oudh, Eastern Bengal and Assam, the Central Provinces and the Punjab. Of these, Bengal is **Area and Population of India** the most populous, with over 50,000,000 ; the United Provinces, with nearly 48 ; Madras, with 38 ; and Eastern Bengal with 31 millions, following in the order stated.

The Boards of three members, known as the Governor-in-Council in the Presidencies of Madras and Bombay, conduct the affairs of those Provinces ; but elsewhere one Lieutenant-Governor or Chief Commissioner is the executive head of the administration. Beneath these higher authorities Commissioners, except in Madras, where there is a Board of Revenue, exercise authority over divisions, and collectors under them have charge of Districts. The 259 districts are the real units of administration in British India, being in turn subdivided into *talukas*, or *tahsils*, over which a native officer has control.

The law, whether of Parliament or of India, lays down in detail the powers which the supreme Government of India, consisting of a Governor-General and six members of Council, to which is added the Commander-in-Chief as an extraordinary member, must retain in their own hands. The Provincial Governments exercise all authority not specially reserved by the Government of India, and in turn distribute a share of their powers among the Commissioners, the **How Great Britain Rules India** collectors—who are also magistrates—and the sub-divisional officers. Throughout, the whole administration business is divided into departments, such as judicial, revenue, military, financial, public works, political, and legislative ; and as the streams of work pour in from the villages through the districts into the provincial offices, they are conducted into the proper department of the secretariat or provincial offices, whence orders issue to the part affected, or else a reference is made to the supreme Government.

The Indian Civil Service, to which natives of India as well as other subjects of the King gain access by open competition, supplies the upper layer of the official classes, and is so thin that the average of civilians actually at work at any time is about one for every quarter of a million of the Indian population. Including this thin crust, mainly composed of British officers, there are some 22,000 natives of India holding public posts on monthly salaries of 75 rupees and upwards, thus forming 77 per cent. of the entire staff of officials employed in India on the salaries stated.

Part of the work of Government in British India is, however, performed by **Local Governing Bodies** municipal and local boards. Of the former, there are 749 dealing with an urban population of 17,000,000 ; of the latter, 1,089, administering an expenditure of nearly £3,000,000 sterling on education, civil works, and sanitation.

But the real field open in India to the application of indigenous principles of government consists in the 670 native states under their own ruling chiefs, who apply a public revenue of 24,000,000 of rupees to their own uses and the wants of more than 60,000,000 of their subjects. Some of these chiefs rule over considerable states, while others govern mere jurisdictory estates. Five—viz., Nepal, Haidarabad, Mysore, Baroda and Kashmir—are in direct relations with the supreme Government, in addition to 148 states, in Central India, twenty in Rajputana, and two in Baluchistan. The rest are under the control of the Provincial Governments, those under Bombay numbering 354 large and small states. But none of

co-operation in time of Imperial need; it settles successions, and preserves their integrity; but it does not interfere in the local affairs of those which are large enough to exercise internal sovereignty, except in cases of gross misrule.

The economic condition of British India, for which the British Governments are responsible, depends mainly upon the following facts. The population, in the main rural, is scattered among 551,490 villages. Only 5,000,000 are attending schools, of whom 505,000 are studying English. And in the whole of India, including the native states, not 16,000,000 out

SIMLA: THE SUMMER HEADQUARTERS OF THE INDIAN GOVERNMENT
Frith
Simla is beautifully situated amid magnificent scenery on the southern slopes of the Himalayas; it is a sanatorium as well as the seat of the Government during the hot summer months, and during the winter it is deserted.

these states are subject to British law, the principle of autocracy pervading the whole. The ruling chief promulgates laws without the intervention of a legislative council. He is supreme alike in executive and judicial matters; he spends the revenues as he thinks proper, and tolerates no free Press or political agitation. The tie which unites such states to the paramount Power is light. The British Government acts for one and all of them in their foreign relations. It regulates the extent of their armed forces, and claims their military

of 293,000,000 have ever learnt to read or write. The people are divided by religion, caste, and language, no less than 147 vernaculars being spoken in the empire. Two-thirds of the population depend on agriculture, and many more on labour or industries connected with it. Yet more than half of the empire is subject to failure of the annual rains, and therefore to a cessation of the work from which its inhabitants derive their livelihood.

The prevention and mitigation of famine therefore demand constant forethought, and in a less degree sanitary measures

The General Post Office, which is built on the site of the Black Hole.

General view of the city as seen from the Ochterlony Monument.

The Town Hall and the High Court, showing the statue of Lord William Bentinck.

VIEWS IN CALCUTTA, THE CAPITAL OF BRITISH INDIA

are urgent, in view of the habits of life which favour the spread of plague, cholera, and fever. Much has been done by the extension of irrigation to prevent famine, and about one-seventh of the cropped area in British India is now fertilised by means of canals. The annual value of the crops on irrigated areas is **Canal and Irrigation Schemes** at present equivalent to 87 per cent. of the total capital outlay, or about £28,000,000. In Sindh and the Punjab, irrigation colonies have been recently planted out on a grand scale. Railways have been extended so as to bring relief to all parts, there being now 30,000 miles of line open to traffic.

The material improvement effected by these measures is reflected in the extension of cultivation, the expansion of trade, and the increase of revenue. In the last ten years imports have risen over 50 per cent., and exports nearly as greatly, no less than £100,000,000 sterling of gold and silver having been absorbed in that period. The salt tax, reduced from 2½ rupees to 1 rupee, brings in less than formerly, and opium receipts are falling as a result of other causes. But the increased receipts from land, stamps, and excise, and the earnings of railways, produce a larger revenue. The net revenue of British India is about £49,000,000, and for the last six years substantial surpluses have accrued. The burden of taxation proper is less than two shillings a head, or if land revenue, which is not taxation, be added, it is three shillings and sixpence a head. Of the total Indian debt, £234,000,000, no less than three-fourths is productive debt, representing capital borrowed at low rates for the construction of railways and canals yielding large returns, which are therefore excluded from the net revenue mentioned above, while the country's other liabilities are covered by reserves, loans, and other assets. It **Sources of Indian Revenue** may be added that the post office and telegraphs are worked at a low profit, and the country therefore escapes payment of charges which in the United Kingdom are pitched high enough to produce a substantial revenue.

Despite, therefore, the losses due to failure of the rains, which no human foresight can avert, the risk of frontier wars, and outbreaks of devastating plague, the material condition of India is sound.

It possesses a free Press, and 600 vernacular newspapers testify to the activity of its political organisations. The Government, secure in its intentions, and confident of the results which it has achieved, has hitherto taken no steps to correct the misstatements of fact which are disseminated by these organs; but the question must arise whether a foreign Government, employing a large native army and reducing its civil servants of European extraction to a minimum, can afford to allow the credulous masses of its subjects to be daily seduced from their allegiance by falsehood and seditious writing. Current events seem to indicate the necessity of educating the people more rapidly than has been the case in the past, and of placing before them the true facts relating to themselves and their governors.

At this point inquiry suggests itself as to the part which India is playing in the history of mankind. What does its possession mean to the United Kingdom? And what does British dominion mean to the Indian Empire with its vast population? The India of to-day is in every respect **Progress of a Century** different from India at the beginning of the last century. Then desolation still impressed its fresh traces on the land. Internal wars and the competition of rival claimants for native states had not ceased. Forests and hill tracts witnessed human sacrifices and the most degrading superstitions. Property in slaves was recognised. The open country was exposed to gang robberies and the detestable practices of Thugs. The patient cultivator, oppressed by his landlord, was squeezed by the robber, and if a horde of Pindaris passed through his district, fire and sword worked havoc in his village. All this has been changed, and even clean forgotten by the present generation; changed not by the gradual progress of a people righting their own wrongs step by step, but by the sudden grasp of the reins by a foreign ruler, lifting up the weak, establishing courts of justice, suppressing disorder with a firm hand, and organising the military forces of India for the maintenance of peace and order. To the work of pacification succeeded the rapid application of foreign science to human needs, improving by leaps and bounds the moral and material condition of the people. Even the physical features of the country have been altered. The conservation

INDIAN BULLOCK CARRIAGE, OR REET   SNAKE CHARMER IN PUBLIC STREET

KASHMIR WOMEN SHELLING RICE   20-WOMAN TEAM WITH ROAD ROLLER

SCENES IN LIVING INDIA

Photographs by H. C. White Co. and Underwood & Underwood, London

and restoration of forests have reclaimed large tracts from sterility due to want of rain. The rainless tracts of desert have been converted into popular colonies of busy cultivators.

The Indian, who rarely left the limits of his village, is now a frequent traveller by road or rail. New markets have been opened to his products, foreign capital is brought from distant lands to his service, and a variety of new occupations is offered to him both above and beneath the surface of the land. The revenue returns show that in the last thirty years the proportion borne by land revenue to the gross public income has fallen

all its watertight compartments of caste. is moving forward, and Mohammedans are no longer content to look only backwards on the glories of the past with longing, lingering looks. They have taken their education into their own hands. The minds as well as the bodies of all classes are stirred by new desires, and although the masses still lay behind their leaders, they feel the ferment of a new civilisation. Religion has not escaped the universal change. When his river gods have yielded their freedom to the engineer and the dreaded goddess of smallpox has been defrauded of her victims by the doctor, the priest must shift his ground; and

THE FINEST RAILWAY STATION IN THE WORLD: VICTORIA TERMINUS, BOMBAY
This elaborate edifice, in Italian Gothic style, with Oriental modifications in the domes, was completed in 1888 at a cost of £300,000; it is certainly the finest railway station in India, and is said to be unequalled in any country.

from 39 to 22 per cent., thus indicating the progress of industrial enterprise. The increasing volume of trade, the absorption of the precious metals, the style of domestic architecture, the clothing of the people, their staying power, and their rapid recovery from the effects of bad monsoons or disastrous floods—all tell a tale of material progress. A moral advancement is equally visible. The East, which in olden times regarded Western methods with " patient deep disdain," now sends her sons over the seas to learn the secret of European machinery and commercial success. Hindu society, with

although European missionaries may not win many converts, railways, public works, and hospitals have turned the world upside down, and given new courage and hopes to even uneducated masses of mankind.

India on her part, lifted from the despond and helplessness of ages by her improved communications with the West, has rendered and will render a still larger return for the services received by her. Her contributions in corn, tea, cotton, and other products to countries in which the growth of population has outstripped production, are of the highest value. Her

THE TRADE OF THE EAST: AFGHAN CAMEL TRAIN CROSSING THE INDUS WITH MERCHANDISE FOR THE MARKETS OF INDIA

This ancient means of transport for long distances is still used by certain Afghan tribes, who, on the approach of cold weather, collect their belongings, consisting chiefly of hides, fruit, and grain, which they take to the cities of India and transport from one commercial centre to another until disposal, afterwards returning to Afghanistan in the spring.

religious books, philosophic works, and languages are of great help to scientific inquirers, and there is no reason why her sons should not be enrolled in the lists of great inventors. Her fighting power and her resources may assist to promote the cause of peace, and give her neighbours a chance of acquiring that freedom and peace which she herself enjoys. The fact that the Convention of August 31st, 1907, between Great Britain and Russia includes three Asiatic countries, Afghanistan, Tibet, and Persia, and is actuated by a sincere desire "to prevent all cause of

British Columbia must to some extent accommodate their local interests in the labour market to the obligations of the central authority towards the Indian subjects of His Majesty. Problems of public administration, a free Press, representation, and self-government, must be looked at from another side when applied to a population composed mainly of uneducated men, divided by sharp lines of religion and caste, upon whose patriotism—if that term means allegiance to an alien rule—too great a strain must not be placed. Questions of free trade, or

DEVIL-DANCING BEFORE THE PRINCE OF WALES DURING HIS VISIT TO INDIA IN 1906

misunderstanding between Great Britain and Russia," shows how the politics of East and West are intertwined. The maintenance of peace, the development of commerce, and promotion of moral progress are the objects of British Imperial policy, and it is well that India should join hands with the United Kingdom in the attempt to secure them for her neighbours.

In the narrower sphere of the relations between the two countries, abundant testimony is afforded as to the far-reaching effects of their mutual interdependence. The distant dominions of the Crown in South Africa, America, and

tariff reform cannot be settled without thought of India's feelings and wants. The difficult internal problems of the unemployed invite inquiry into the Indian plan of campaign against famine, and economists must ask themselves how it is that there is no Poor Law relief in India. These and other instances may be cited to illustrate the extent to which the internal as well as the external politics of the United Kingdom and the Indian Empire are interwoven, emphasising the oneness of mankind and the claims of universal history to the consideration of statesmen.

WILLIAM LEE-WARNER

GREAT DATES IN THE HISTORY OF INDIA

DATE	B.C.
3000	India occupied by Dravidian Peoples
2500	Aryan domination of Upper India
2000	The Laws of Manu
1000	The Mahabharata
500	Gautama (Buddha) institutes BUDDHISM
322	Invasion of India by Alexander the Great
250	Asoka rules in Hindustan
	A.D.
500	Buddhism displaced by the later Hinduism
664	Saracen incursions begin

1000–1500

DATE	
1001	MAHMUD OF GHAZNI begins series of Mohammedan invasions
1176	First Mohammedan Dynasty ("Ghori") established in Hindustan by Shahab-ud-Din
1206	Turkish "Slave" Dynasty established at Delhi
1288	Afghan Khilji Dynasty at Delhi
1321	Turkish "Tughlak" Dynasty at Delhi conquers the Deccan
1350	Bengal and the Deccan throw off the Delhi supremacy. Bahmani (Mohammedan) Dynasty in the Deccan
1398	TAMERLANE devastates Upper India
1414	Seiad (Arab) Dynasty at Delhi
1450	Lodi (Afghan) Dynasty at Delhi Five main kingdoms in the Deccan
1498	VASCO DA GAMA reaches India by the Ocean route. The Sikh sect founded in the Punjab by Nanuk

1501–1600

DATE	
1507	Portuguese established at Goa by Albuquerque
1526	BABAR the Turk conquers Hindustan. BEGINNING OF THE MUGHAL OR MOGUL SUPREMACY
1530	Humayun succeeds Babar
1540	Humayun expelled by Sher Shah (Afghan)
1556	Return and death of Humayun. The empire won back for his young son AKBAR at Panipat
1561	Akbar assumes the government. Period of toleration, Hindus and Mohammedans being appointed impartially to the Imperial service. Organisation of the Mogul Empire over North India. The great Deccan kingdoms remain independent
1600	Charter of the English East India Company

1601–1700

DATE	
1605	Jehan Gir succeeds Akbar
1613	FIRST ENGLISH FACTORY IN INDIA AT SURAT
1620	First English settlement in Bengal, at Hugli
1627	Shah Jehan succeeds Jehan Gir. The Mogul Empire partly absorbs the Deccan
1632	FALL OF THE PORTUGUESE POWER
1630	English settlement at Madras
1658	Aurangzib deposes Shah Jehan. Beginnings of the Mahratta power under Sivaji
1662	Portugal cedes Bombay
1679	Aurangzib begins conquest of the Deccan
1687	Fall of the Deccan kingdoms
1700	Govind, the last Sikh guru

1701–1750

DATE	
1701	François Martin, French Governor in the Carnatic
1707	Death of Aurangzib, followed by gradual DISINTEGRATION OF MOGUL EMPIRE
1717	Development of Mahratta power under the Peshwa or Minister Balaji Wiswanath, at Puna
1724	Asaf Jah (Nizam), Viceroy of the Deccan, assumes virtual independence
1735	Extension of Mahratta ascendancy over Malwa
1739	Invasion of NADIR SHAH. Sack of Delhi
1740	Oudh and Bengal establish virtual independence under viceroys
1741	Dupleix Governor at Pondichery
1746	France and Britain being at war, DUPLEIX ATTACKS MADRAS, captures it, and employs sepoys to rout the forces of the Nawab of Arcot
1748	Restoration of French and English conquests
1749	Renewed Anglo-French hostilities in support of rival claimants to the thrones of Haidarabad and Arcot
1750	Predominance of the French

1751–1800

DATE	
1751	CLIVE AT ARCOT: BEGINNING OF BRITISH ASCENDANCY
1752	Surrender of French at Trichinopoli
1756	Black Hole of Calcutta
1757	BATTLE OF PLASSEY ESTABLISHES BRITISH POWER IN BENGAL
1760	Lally decisively defeated by Eyre Coote at Wandewash
1761	END OF FRENCH POWER IN INDIA. Overthrow of Mahrattas by Ahmed Shah at Panipat
1764	Bengal secured by Munro's victory over the Oudh Nawab at Buxar
1765	CLIVE ACCEPTS THE DIWANI OF BENGAL FOR THE COMPANY FROM THE MOGUL
1773	Suppression of the Rohillas. North's Regulating Act
1774	WARREN HASTINGS, Governor-General
1780	First Mahratta war; capture of Gwalior. Invasion of Carnatic by Haidar Ali of Mysore
1782-3	The French admiral Suffren in Indian waters. The crisis ended by the death of Haidar, and the treaty of Versailles
1784	PITT'S INDIA ACT
1786	Cornwallis, Governor-General
1790	War with Tippu Sahib of Mysore
1792	Partial annexation of Mysore
1793	The permanent settlement (of land) in Bengal. Sir John Shore (Lord Teignmouth), Governor-General
1798	Lord Mornington (MARQUESS WELLESLEY), Governor-General
1799	CONQUEST OF MYSORE
1800	"Subsidiary alliance" with the Nizam

1801–1850

DATE	
1803	Second Mahratta war. British victories of Assaye and Laswari
1805	Barlow, Governor-General ad interim. Mahratta treaties

DATE	
1807	Minto, Governor-General. Missions to Persia, Afghanistan, the Punjab, and Sindh
1808	
1809	Treaty with RANJIT SINGH
1813	Lord Moira (Lord Hastings), Governor-General
1814-5	GHURKA OR NEPAL WAR. Treaty with Nepal
1817-8	PINDARI WAR, developing into third Mahratta war. Annexation of Peshwa's territories
1820	Extension of (the Sikh) Ranjit Singh's power in the Punjab
1823-6	Lord Amherst, Governor-General. First Burmese war. Annexation of Assam, Arakan, and Tennasserin
1828	BENTINCK, Governor-General
1829	Abolition of Suttee
1830	Suppression of Thuggee
1835	Establishment of educational system. Liberty of the Press
1836	Auckland, Governor-General
1839	Shah Shuja restored at Kabul by British arms. Death of Ranjit Singh. Growing power of the Khalsa in the Punjab
1841	DISASTER OF KABUL
1842	Afghan war. Kabul recaptured. Dost Mohammed restored. Lord Ellenborough, Governor-General
1843	Annexation of Sindh. Gwalior repressed in the MAHARAJPUR campaign
1844	Hardinge, Governor-General
1845	Sikhs invade British territory. SUTLEJ CAMPAIGN concluded by battle of Sobraon
1848-9	Dalhousie, Governor-General. Beginning of second Sikh war, ended by battle of GUJERAT. ANNEXATION OF PUNJAB

1851–1907

DATE	
1852	Second Burmese war. Annexation of Pegu
1853	Annexation of Nagpur
1856	Annexation of Oudh. Canning, Governor-General
1857	OUTBREAK OF THE MUTINY (May). Storming of Delhi and reinforcement of Lucknow (Sept.). Relief of Lucknow (Nov.)
1858	Suppression of Mutiny. TRANSFER OF GOVERNMENT FROM THE COMPANY TO THE BRITISH CROWN. Canning first Viceroy
1862	Lord Elgin, Viceroy
1863	Ambela Campaign
1864	Sir John Lawrence, Viceroy
1869	Lord Mayo, Viceroy
1872	Lord Mayo assassinated. Lord Northbrook, Viceroy
1875	Visit of the Prince of Wales (Edward VII.)
1876	Lord Lytton, Viceroy
1877	Queen proclaimed Empress of India
1879	Afghan War
1880	Lord Ripon, Viceroy
1881	British withdrawal from Afghanistan
1885	Lord Dufferin, Viceroy
1886	Panjdeh incident. Burma annexed. First Meeting of National Congress
1887	Agreement between Russia and Britain regarding Afghan frontier
1888	Lord Lansdowne, Viceroy
1893	Lord Elgin, Viceroy
1898	Lord Curzon, Viceroy
1905	Lord Minto, Viceroy

STREET PIGEONS IN THE CITY OF JAIPUR SACRED MONKEYS AT GALTA NEAR JAIPUR

SECURING A MONSTER ELEPHANT   FLAMINGOES IN A GARDEN AT JAIPUR

SCENES OF ANIMAL LIFE IN INDIA
Photographs by H. C. White Co. and Underwood & Underwood, London

ESSENTIAL INFORMATION ABOUT INDIA

AREA. The area of British India—that is, the districts under direct British rule—is 1,097,900 square miles, and of the feudatory or native states 675,267 square miles, making a total of 1,773,167 square miles.

POPULATION. The population of British India proper, at the census of 1901, was 232,072,832, and of the feudatory or native states 62,964,349, making a total of 294,361,056. The total number of persons not born in India was 641,854, of whom 96,653 claimed the United Kingdom as their place of birth. India contains 31 towns with a population of over 100,000, of which the chief are as follow: Calcutta, 1,026,987 ; Lucknow, 264,049 ; Lahore, 202,964 ; Bombay, 776,006 ; Rangoon, 234,881 ; Cawnpore, 197,170 ; Madras, 509,346 ; Benares, 209,331 ; Agra, 188,022 ; Haidarabad, 448,466 ; Delhi, 208,575 ; Ahmedabad, 185,889.

GOVERNMENT. India being a British Crown Colony, the government is vested in the King of England, who is titulary Emperor of India. The government is based upon the Government of India Act of 1858. The administration is entrusted to the Secretary of State for India—the present holder of the office being Mr. John Morley—assisted by a council of not fewer then ten members, nine of whom must have resided for not less than ten years in India and have left India not more than ten years before their appointment. The executive authority in India is vested in the Governor-General in Council, who is also Viceroy, the present holder of office being the Earl of Minto. The Council consists of the Governor-General, the Commander-in-Chief, and six ordinary members, who usually hold office for five years. For administrative purposes India is divided into nine provinces—Madras, Bombay, Bengal, Eastern Bengal with Assam, Agra and Oudh, the Punjab, Burma, the Central Provinces, and the North-West Province—each under a Governor, Lieutenant-Governor, or Chief Commissioner.

REVENUE AND EXPENDITURE. Indian finances are calculated in rupees, the value of which fluctuates ; but for Budget estimates the value of the rupee has, for some years, been reckoned as 15 to £1 sterling. In 1905, the revenue of India was Rs.1,272,194,569, and the total expenditure Rs.1,220,353,583. The chief source of revenue is the Indian State railways, and the chief scurces by taxation are the taxes on land, excise, opium, salt, customs, and stamps.

NATIONAL DEBT. The permanent Debt in India, at December 31st, 1906, was £84,054,041, and the permanent in England was £146,457,439.

COMMERCE. The imports of India for the financial year 1906-7 were of the value of Rs.1,618,220,082 ; and the exports for the same period reached a value of Rs.1,823,925,759. Great Britain supplied almost half of the imports, and took about one-fourth of the exports. The chief articles of Indian produce exported are raw and manufactured cotton and jute, rice, seeds, skins and hides, opium, wheat, tea, lac, wool, and coffee, the order of importance being the order given. During the last few decades

Government has devoted considerable attention to the development of Indian agriculture, with gratifying results. Experimental farms have been established, and colleges for teaching the scientific side of agriculture. Irrigation works have helped materially to the improvement. A recent census showed that India possesses 205 cotton-mills, employing 212,720 hands ; 39 jute-mills, with 144,879 hands ; 6 woollen-mills ; 7 paper-mills ; and 279 collieries, with an output of about 9,000,000 tons annually, and giving employment to about 90,000 persons.

CURRENCY. The rupee is the standard of Indian currency, but, being a silver standard, its value fluctuates considerably. The value was formerly about 2s., but, after many fluctuations, it has remained steady at about 1s. 4d. for the last decade, and this may now be accepted as a safe basis of reckoning. This basis gives the following equivalents for the Indian coinage :

1 pie	=			=	⅓ farthing
3 pies	=	1 pice		=	1 ,,
4 pice	=	1 anna		=	1 penny
16 annas	=	1 rupee		=	1s. 4d.
15 rupees	=			=	£1

A lac is 100,000 rupees, and a crore is 100 lacs.

WEIGHTS AND MEASURES.—An Act of 1871 provided for a uniform system of weights and measures, based on the French kilogramme—the Indian equivalent of which was to be a ser, but the Act has never been carried into effective operation. Thus varying local values are found throughout India. The maund is equivalent to about 25 lb. in Madras, to 28 lb. in Bombay, and 82⅔ lb. in Bengal. The Imperial weights are as follows :

1 tola	=		= 180 grains
5 tolas		= 1 chittack	= 2 oz. avoird. (about)
16 chittacks		= 1 seer	= 2 $\frac{1}{10}$ lb. (about)
40 seers		= 1 maund	= 82⅔ lb.

In linear measure the gaz = 36 inches, and the kos = about 2 miles, but these vary very much. The bigha = ⅝ acre.

POSTAGE RATES. Great Britain to India.—Conditions and rates are as for New Zealand. (See page 1002.)

TELEGRAMS. Great Britain to India. —Charge, per word, is 2s. ; or, if via Turkey, 1s. 10d. per word.

PATENTS. An invention may be patented only if within one year from the date of application in another country, if a patent has been taken out in another country. Government fee on petition is Rs.10, and the specification, of which eight copies are required, must be filed within six months of date of order giving permission to file with fee of Rs.30. Renewal fees are Rs.50 at end of each year from fourth to eighth years and Rs.100 at end of each year from ninth to thirteenth year. Limit of patent life is fourteen years.

TRADE MARKS. There is no Trade Mark Registration Act in India, but a mark for which protection is desired may be advertised in " The Government Gazette" and proceedings taken thereafter under Common Law, or a copy may be filed under the Act for Registration of Assurances.

DESIGNS. Designs may be registered as copyright for a period of five years, four copies of the design being required.

1363

The Ruanweli Dagoba, a Buddhist monument dating from about 200 B.C.

Thuparamaya Dagoba, the shrine of Buddha's jawbone, erected about 250 B.C.

The Abayahagiriyn Pagoda, completed in 87 B.C. over a relic of Buddha.

The ruins of a nine-storey palace built about 200 B.C., and set with precious stones.

RUINS OF CEYLON'S ANCIENT CAPITAL CITY OF ANURADHAPURA

Photographs by H. C. White Co. and Underwood & Underwood, London

CEYLON
THE LAND, THE PEOPLE, AND THE LEGENDARY PERIOD

THE history of India at the very earliest times known to us has been influenced by its position on the southern boundary of a great continent. Its frontier mountain ranges, apparently impassable, have been repeatedly crossed by foreign nations, and these invasions constantly transformed the history of the country so richly dowered by Nature. The case of Ceylon is wholly different. As the most southerly outpost of India, it is so far removed from the rest of Asia that no races have penetrated the island from the interior of the continent.

Every invasion within historical times started from the peninsula itself, from which Ceylon is divided by a narrow strait little broader than a river. As regards its general characteristics, therefore, it is practically a continuation of India. The Eastern and Western Ghats form an abrupt boundary to the Deccan. On the south lie the plains of the Carnatic, broken by several isolated plateaus—the Sivaroy, Palni, and other mountains— and by numerous small islands of granite and gneiss rock. This plain **Position of the Island** gradually sinks away southward to fall below the sea at the Coromandel coast. Beyond the narrow Palk Straits, Ceylon gradually rises again above the sea-level, the north of the island being almost entirely flat coral soil, while in general outline the whole is formed like a shield. The centre of this immense shield, the highlands of Malaya, are crowned by the central mountain range of Ceylon, the most

southerly and the greatest of those isolated mountain systems in Southern India. The narrow straits are interrupted by numerous islands placed like the pillars of a bridge, and form rather a link of communication between the island and the mainland than an obstacle to intercourse, the characteristics of both countries being almost identical **Physical Features of Ceylon** in consequence of this connection. In Ceylon, as in India, the rocky foundations of the soil consist of the same primeval stone, and on each side of the Palk Strait the characteristics of rocks and mountains are identical. The same winds blow upon both countries ; in the summer the rainy south-west monsoon bringing a bountiful supply of moisture to the steep and mountainous west, while in winter the dry north-east monsoon refreshes the eastern side of the island.

The vegetable world of Ceylon is therefore a repetition of that of India. The west of each country is marked by luxuriant growth and inexhaustible fertility, while the east shows a poorer vegetation and a more niggardly soil ; in the east, as in the flat north of the island, the population attains to any density only when the industry of man has succeeded by scientific works of irrigation in collecting the fertilising moisture against the times of long drought. The fauna of Southern India and of the island are again, generally speaking, identical. In both cases the

1365

forests are inhabited by the elephant, the great cats—the Bengal tiger alone has not crossed the straits—apes, snakes, white ants, and leeches. The scanty means of livelihood produce the same epidemics in the dwellers of both countries; sickness and death are **Plants and** due to cholera, and especially **Animals** to malaria, which is prevalent **of Ceylon** at the foot of the mountain ranges and of the many isolated peaks, with their blocks of stone thrown in wild confusion one upon another, as also in the jungles of the river beds.

It would be astonishing if this identity of natural characteristics were not observable also in the population which has inhabited the island from the remotest antiquity. At the present day Ceylon, like India, is inhabited by two main types anthropologically and ethnologically different, a dark and a fair race, of whom the latter immigrated at a comparatively late time, and were not the original inhabitants of the island.

In primeval times India, like Ceylon, was the home of one race only, characterised by dark colouring, wavy hair, and small or even diminutive stature.

The facts of geology, and of the distribution of plants and animals, prove that the continent and the island must have formed a continuous whole at no very remote epoch. Assuming, however, that the Palk Straits have always been situated where they are now, it would have been an easy task for people, even in the lower stage of civilisation, to have crossed from the plains of Southern India by the Adam's Bridge to the attractive districts of the island. It can be historically demonstrated that Tamil invasions took place at least two thousand years ago,

and the plantations of Ceylon at the present day annually attract from the continent a Dravidian population which is to be numbered by thousands. It is, however, certain that before the first historical immigration the island was inhabited by tribes standing in the closest possible relation, anthropologically and ethnologically, to the Dravidian peoples. The legendary woodland tribes of the wild Wakka are undoubtedly to be identified as the ancestors of the modern Veddas; while, in all probability, the first Aryan immigrants into Ceylon found other Dravidian races in possession who had risen to a higher state of civilisation in more favourably situated habitations. The "Tamils of Ceylon," who now inhabit the north and the east coasts of the island, are undoubtedly for the most part descendants of those Dravidians who overran the island from the north in numerous campaigns.

Together with this dark race of primeval Indian origin, the island is inhabited in the more fertile southwest portion chiefly by the Singhalese, an entirely different race, both in civilisation and physique. These were originally strangers to the country, with totally different physical characteristics, language, religion, manners, and customs. Where was the home of these strangers? Certainly not in the south of India, which was then inhabited by pure **Races** Dravidians. The geographical position of Ceylon obviously points to **Island** North India as the most probable point of departure for a migration of this nature. The southern part of the island is confronted by no country whatever, while in the east and west the mainland is far distant and is divided from Ceylon by broad oceans, to be

H. C. White Co.
GROUP OF YOUNG SINGHALESE WOMEN

traversed only by the children of a highly-developed civilisation. On the other hand, the coasts of Nearer India, curving inwards from the north-west and north-east, plainly point the mariner towards Ceylon. With the exception of a few Malays introduced within the last century, the island exhibits no trace of Indonesian or Malay blood which might in any way remind us of the African races. On the other hand, the nearest relations of the Singhalese are to be found along the line of the coast routes followed by those Aryans who crossed the mountain frontier and entered India in the third millennium B.C., and in the mixed tribes of the North Indian plains descended from them; physical characteristics, language, customs, and social organisation alike point to this origin. Evidence of this nature even enables us to define with some precision the date at which these immigrants entered the island and the road by which they came. The highest castes of the Singhalese have always been the Goiwansa or Handuruwo — that is to say, those of noble birth ; Brahmans have never found a place among their various castes. Where they are mentioned by tradition, or in historical records, we have to deal with pure invention on the part of the chronicler, or with foreign Brahmans, references to whom occur, for example, in the accounts of the introduction of Buddhism into Ceylon ; in no case, however, **The Castes of the Singhalese** do the Brahmans appear as an essential element in Singhalese society. Thus the Singhalese branch must have broken away from the Aryan-Indian group of peoples at a time when the Brahmans had not yet secured their supremacy over social order, justice, and morality, popular feeling, thought,

and action—that is to say, before the period of the formation of the great states of the central Ganges. Hence the Singhalese migration cannot have started from the east of India, from the mouths of the Ganges, or from Orissa ; for it was not until the Brahman's supremacy had been assured that the Aryans advanced into those districts. **Advance of the Aryans** At a much earlier period the Aryans on the west had advanced to the sea, starting from the Punjab and following the Indus to the mouths of that river, while at a later period they followed the Aravalli Mountains to Gujerat. But the Indus was of very little importance as a trade route for transmarine commerce ; its current was too strong, its delta too soft and shifting, while the sea coast offered no protection against storms. On the other hand, an admirable base for transmarine enterprise was afforded by the sheltered Gulf of Cambay, running far into the country with its rich hinterland. This was the point where the Aryans took the sea, during the flourishing period of the great Aryan states on the Ganges ; and during the whole of the Mohammedan period it formed the chief harbour of India. The inference that earlier Aryan marine migrations started from Cambay is irresistible.

This conclusion is well supported by tradition. In Ceylon, human memory has been more tenacious than on the Indian continent, and has preserved a reliable historical record for more than 2,000 years. It is true that the epic of Ramayana, which in its Singhalese form is a shorter imitation of the great work of Walmiki, a glorification of the mythical conqueror of Ceylon, is pure poetical

Underwood & Underwood

SINGHALESE CRAFTSMEN AT WORK

invention. Unhistorical are all the legends there related of the expedition of Rama, of the seduction of his faithful wife Sita, of his alliance with the apes—the black races of the Southern Deccan—of his enemies the Rakshasa, of his bridge over the straits, his wonderful exploits, and his ultimate return to India. Rama is a model of virtue from the Brahman **Legends &** point of view, and the many **Traditions** exploits related of him are **of Ceylon** only the scaffolding used by the artists in constructing the ideal of a Brahman royal prince.

We have, however, more valuable historical sources. The monarchy lasted for more than 2,000 years, as did the Buddhism which it protected, a course of development more favourable to the muse of history than the political and religious revolutions which disturbed the history of India proper. In the monastic libraries everything was recorded which concerned the order itself and its patrons the kings ; and the annals thus collected were from time to time condensed into literary works.

Thus the oldest of the Ceylon monasteries, the Mahawira, or Great Monastery in Anuradhapura, has preserved the tradition of the introduction of Buddhism, and the history of the " Great Family " of 174 kings, in its chronicle, called the Mahawansa. Two Pali books, the Dipawansa, or History of the Island, and the Mahawansa, which is later by 150 years, are works diverging but little from the original, and, like that original, both are continued until the death of King Dhatusena in 479 A.D. At a later period, however, continuations were constantly added to the Mahawansa, which were carried on to the end of the Singhalese monarchy and till the English occupation in 1816. For a long period these and similar works lay forgotten in the libraries of the monasteries, until, in 1836, George Turnour made the first part of the Mahawansa known by a faithful **Ancient** translation, throwing a flood **Historical** of light upon the early history **Records** of Buddhism. Other chronicles display divergences from the original source, which explain the difference between the views of the several monasteries to which they belong ; they are shorter, less accurate, and, moreover, inadequately translated. A third class of documents is still hidden in the collections of manuscripts within the Buddhist monasteries.

In the case of every chronicle the light of history dawns only with the introduction of Buddhism into the island—that is, with the time of Asoka, in the third century B.C. The accounts given of earlier events in Ceylon are chiefly pure Buddhist invention, which attempted to increase the sanctity of the sacred places in the island by asserting the presence therein of Buddha or of his twenty-three predecessors. These improbabilities apart, the prehistoric portions of the chronicles contain secular stories of far greater importance for us. Here we find reduced to writing that tradition which for centuries had been handed down by the people ; transformed and decorated, no doubt, the work of whole epochs being assigned to individual personalities, but, on the whole, plain and recognisable in its main features. The very first figure of Singhalese history can be supported from the evidence of historical ethnology. Wijaya—or *Victory*—led the foreign tribes across the straits, and his characteristics can be recognised in the Aryans who advanced to the sea before the era of Brahman supremacy. **Story** In the country of Lala, or **of a Royal** Gujerat, so runs the legend in **Exile** chapter seven of the Mahawansa, a lion surprised a caravan which was escorting the daughter of the King of Wanga and of a Kalinga princess ; the lion carried off the king's daughter to his cave, and from their marriage was born a son, Sihabahu, and a daughter, Sihasiwali. Mother and children fled from the captivity of the lion ; the lion's son grew up and, after killing his father, became the successor of his maternal grandfather, the King of Wanga. At a later period, however, he returned to his native country of Lala, and built towns and villages in the wilderness, in spots where irrigation was possible. His eldest son, Wijaya, was made viceroy when he came of age ; but he developed into an enemy of law, and his associates committed innumerable acts of treachery and violence. Ultimately the people grew angry and complained to the king. He threw the blame on the friends of the prince, but censured his son severely. The offences were repeated, and upon the third occasion the people called out, " Punish thy son with death." The king then half shaved the heads of Wijaya and his 700 retainers, and put them on board a ship, which was driven forth into the open sea. Wijaya first landed in the harbour of Supparaka, in India ; fearing, however, that the reckless immorality of his followers would arouse the animosity of the natives, he continued his voyage. This prince, by name Wijaya, who then became wise by experience, landed in the district of Tambapanni, of the country of Lanka, or Ceylon. As the King Sihabahu had killed the lion, his sons and descendants were called Sihala—that is, lion slayers ; and as this island of Lanka was conquered and colonised by a Sihala, it was given the name of Sihala—Europeanised as Ceylon—that is, Lion Island.

The historical foundation of this legend carries us back to the starting-point of the Singhalese settlement, the country of Lala ; the name survived in the Greek Larike, the modern Gujerat ; the solitary lion, who at the very outset inhabited the country and attacked and plundered the neighbours, is to be explained as an early Aryan settlement on the Gulf of Cambay. The nickname of "lion" was a favourite designation for all the warrior Aryans and their leaders. In Gujerat itself a famous dynasty, known as "the Lions," continued till recent date ; while all Sikhs bear the name of Singh—i.e., Lion. At that period the Aryan conquerors had not been subjected to the stern caste regulations of the Brahmans, and had no scruples of conscience in contracting alliances with native wives—e.g., the Kalinga princess. The migration to Ceylon belongs to a somewhat later time. The lion prince made the former desert a populous country, with towns and villages ; then further disturbances broke out. According to the Buddhists, who followed the Brahman version of Indian history, the lawlessness of Wijaya and his adherents consisted merely in resistance to the Brahman claims. The rulers attempted to use compulsion. However, the bold

Underwood & Underwood, London

SITE OF THE CITY OF ANURADHAPURA

The growth of the jungle is so rapid that sites of the old towns in Ceylon are soon overgrown ; even the once great city of Anuradhapura, the capital before our era, is now, as this picture shows, overgrown with the jungle.

spirit of the warlike part of the Aryans continually revolted against Brahman predominance, until the warriors were defeated and sailed away to seek intellectual freedom in a new country. Driven back from the Malabar coast, where Brahman influence seems to have penetrated at an earlier period, they found what they required on the north-east coast of Ceylon, an arable district untroubled by Brahmans.

Wijaya landed with his adherents, apparently about 543 B.C., at Tambapanni—according to the Sanscrit name of the river, Tamraparni, the Taprobane of the Greeks. His later history is adorned by tradition with features familiar in the legends of Odysseus, and perhaps appropriated thence, owing to the intercourse of early European civilisations with the Spice Islands. The strangers first fall into the hands of an enchantress, Kuweni, who kept them fast in an underground place ; they are then freed, as in Homer, by Wijaya, who is helped by a god well disposed to man—in this case, Vishnu. He marries the princess enchantress, and with her help becomes supreme over the country ; then, however, he divorces her and marries the daughter of the powerful neighbouring King Pandu of Madura, while his comrades take wives from the daughters of distinguished families in the Pandu kingdom.

The death of Wijaya, who left no legitimate descendant, was followed by a short interregnum—the country of Lanka was without a king for a year ; however, a new influx of the Aryans arrived from Lala, and Wijaya's nephew, Panduwasudewa, seized the throne of the Singhalese king. After the death of his son Abhaya, the succession was interrupted for seventeen years by disputes about the kingship. Then, however, after the defeat and slaughter of an uncle, the most important of the legendary rulers ascended the throne, by name Pandukabhaya. Under his governorship the Singhalese State rose to considerable power ; the different races of the island were reconciled, and **Building of a Mighty Capital** lived peacefully together in the capital of Anuradhapura. This town had been founded by the first settlers ; now, however, the tank which had been previously built was extended to form a great lake, and by the construction of a palace and shrines for the different religions and sects the settlement became highly important, and is spoken of by the chronicler as " delightful and well built." The oldest of the king's uncles, the former Prince Abhaya, was installed as governor of the town ; two Yakkas were appointed as overseers for every two of the four quarters into which the town was divided, another Yakka being made sentinel of the southern gate. The despised races, such as the Chandalas, were settled in the suburbs, where they were employed in street-cleaning, police work at night, and burials ; outside the town, cemeteries and places for torture and execution were constructed. The royal hunters—the Veddas, who now dwell apart from the other inhabitants—had a street of their own. The king appears in the character of a benevolent monarch. Hospitals are erected for the sick, and the ruler attempts to meet the views of the various religious sects by assigning quarters to them, building them houses, and erecting temples. The Singhalese rulers thus mentioned by tradition cannot be

H. C. White Co.

ANCIENT SHRINE OF BUDDHISM IN CEYLON

The Temple of Isurumuniya at Anuradhapura, dating from 300 B.C., and attributed to King Tissa, is hewn from the living rock on a lake surrounded by lotus plants but infested with crocodiles.

considered in any degree historical personages. Wijaya is as vague a personality as the founder of Rome, and Pandukabhaya was no more a legislator than Numa. It is probable that the characteristics of famous generals were interwoven with the picture of those legendary kings ; the most we can say is that they represented successive stages of civilisation. Wijaya is the personification of the first Aryan emigration, as Panduwasudewa is of a second ; his successor, Abhaya, represents the struggle of the princes for supremacy, while Pandukabhaya personifies the final victory of one individual over his rivals, and the introduction of social order, the reconciliation of the natives to the immigrants, the rise of general prosperity, and the development of the kingdom. Generally speaking, the Aryan development in Ceylon advanced on parallel lines with the development of the kindred tribes in the Ganges territory. The victorious conquest of the original inhabitants and the occupation of the country, the struggles of princes with one another, and the final formation of certain great towns, supported by the many natural products produced by cutivation or by a bountiful Nature, and advanced by the peaceful **Development of Settled Government** incorporation of the subject tribes into the body politic —such is the general course of development. In one respect only was the development of the island Aryans essentially different from that of their brothers on the mainland—the Brahmans never asserted their fatal influence upon the intellectual development.

CEYLON IN THE HISTORICAL PERIOD

THE early history of Ceylon assumes a more reliable character about the year 300 B.C. It is characterised by three main movements—Buddhism, internal struggles for the succession, and foreign wars with the Dravidians on the continent.

The first human figure in Singhalese history is Dewanampiya Tissa, the contemporary of King Asoka. In the Singhalese chronicles his date is not yet accurately determined. While his own history is written in full detail, the scantiest account is given of his three successors, of whom we know little more than the facts that they were all younger brothers of Tissa, that each of them reigned ten years, and that they endowed many pious foundations to support the monks. Similarly, King Asela, who is distinguished from the above-mentioned rulers by the first entrance of the Tamils into the succession, is said to have reigned ten years. He is stated to be the son of King Mutasiwa, **Beginning of Buddhism in Ceylon** who had died a century earlier! These accounts of the different reigns have often received wholly arbitrary additions. Consequently the great event in Ceylon, the introduction of Buddhism under Tissa, is to be placed at a later date than that assigned by the chronicles. The chroniclers supposed Tissa to have accepted the new doctrine shortly after his accession, which is stated to have occured in 307, the actual date being 251 B.C., and placed his death in 267 B.C., whereas the despatch of Buddhist monks to Ceylon by Asoka did not take place before 250 B.C.

The monarch who gave the monks so hearty a reception was naturally painted by them in most brilliant colours. Tissa is placed at an equal height of piety to Asoka, who had extended his kingdom from Afghanistan to the modern Mysore, and legend is even ready to retrace the friendship of the two monarchs to their association in a previous state of existence in which the kings were said to have been brothers. But all this brilliant description cannot entirely hide the truth that the Ceylon king was dependent in some degree upon Asoka. In his thirteenth rock inscription, Asoka prides himself on the fact that he had disseminated the Dhamma " as far as Tambapanni " ; moreover, Tissa, who ascended the throne amid great festivities in 251 B.C., represents him **Ceylon Subject to Asoka** self as being again crowned by special deputies of Asoka after the exchange of rich presents destined for coronation purposes. The surprising liberality with which the exponents of the new doctrine were received was probably due in part to the dependent position of Ceylon. Mahinda, the son of Asoka by a woman of inferior birth, the daughter of a merchant in Wedisa, was most kindly received by Tissa with six other missionaries a month after his second coronation.

Magnificent endowments of land, such as the splendid park of Magamega in the capital, together with the mountain of Chetya, were the first gifts to the missionaries ; the transference was made with the greatest pomp, and dwellings for the monks were immediately erected upon the lands. On the very first day the king and six thousand of his subjects were converted to the new teaching, which had long before lost its original simplicity, and in which the worship of relics was an important element. Hence almost immediately two of the greatest objects of veneration were brought by special ambassadors from the country of the founder ; these were the collar-bone of the " Enlightened One," and a branch of the sacred Bo tree. At the present day upon the island the shrines built for such relics with their cupola-shaped thupas or stupas, in some cases of enormous size, are to be found by **Shrines and Relics of Buddha** thousands, and are a characteristic feature in the landscape. The relics were accompanied by the order of nuns of Samghamitta, who also found many adherents.

The introduction of Buddhism was fraught with the most important consequences to the whole development of the Singhalese people. The Indian Brahmans had attained their high position at the price of severe struggles ; the Buddhist monks received theirs as a present from the Singhalese kings, and henceforward the people were under their spell. At the moment the order merely acquired sites for the erection of monasteries, of summer resorts, and of shrines for relics. In other respects, the command of complete poverty which Buddha had laid upon his bikkhus, or beggars, was strictly followed, and the monks obtained the necessaries of life as alms, and in no other way ; but after a little more than one hundred years this rule was broken, first by the king Duttha Gamani, who was celebrated for his services to the order, and afterwards by his grandson Wattha. Successive kings assigned the best land, the canals and tanks, and, indeed, whole villages with their inhabitants, to the monks. By degrees, if not the whole, at any rate the best part, of all arable and cultivated land passed into their possession.

Growth of Monastic Wealth

Meanwhile the inhabitants became impoverished. The population increased in proportion to the land recovered for cultivation by means of irrigation, but the products of such land chiefly went to support the idle monks. Many villages were in a state of serfdom to the monasteries ; the remainder, oppressed by the royal taxes and the alms which they were obliged to place in the pots of the yellow-robed mendicants, were cut off from all hope of prosperity. A considerable proportion of the growing youth disappeared into the monasteries of monks and nuns ; those who remained upon the land were oppressed by the teaching that activity in any form was an obstacle to true happiness ; while intellectual growth became impossible, and freedom or self-respect were unknown.

The pious king who had introduced Buddhism to the island, with many of his successors, might well look with satisfaction upon the wealth of the country, the increase of agriculture, the growth of the population, and the boundless piety of his subjects. To the splendour of the capital, even in later times, testimony is borne not only by the admiring accounts of the Singhalese historians and Chinese pilgrims, but still more by the miles of ruins, now hidden in the primeval forest, which alone mark the sites of former temporal and ecclesiastical palaces. The extent of the arable land and the thickness of the population are shown by the enormous tanks—now dry—almost as large as lakes ; while the slavish subjugation of the people is evidenced by the gigantic shrines and the many miles of irrigation works which were constructed by the forced labour of the villages and districts. But the apparent greatness of the royal power was at the same time its weakness ; the people over whom the king ruled was a people of subservient slaves. In the mountains only did a remnant of the former population survive ;

Remains of Former Splendours

H. C. White Co.

THE MOST SACRED TEMPLE OF BUDDHA'S TOOTH
This temple was built in Kandy in the fourteenth century to contain an alleged tooth of Buddha, which speedily caused the city to become an important centre of Buddhist power and influence throughout Ceylon.

even there small ruins of monasteries are to be found ; but there also lived strong and independent men. When a Tamil invasion overran " the royal domains " on the great northern plains and compelled the king to flee from his capital, the wave of conquest was broken upon the mountains.

Almost all the kings were good rulers according to Buddhist ideas ; but their praise depends entirely upon the extent of the gifts with which they endowed the order. Mahawansa in one and the same breath relates that Asoka, the great friend of the order, was the wisest and best of princes, and that he killed his ninety-nine brothers to secure his sole power in Jambudipa, or India. Similarly, later the murderers of brothers and kings are described as "men who devoted themselves to works of love and piety," or as men "who after their death enter the community of the king of the gods," provided only that they were benevolent to the order during their reigns. The numbers, the riches, and the influence of the order increased with extraordinary rapidity. Purity of life and doctrine, however, deteriorated no less speedily. The history of the order is a history of violent schisms. From the time of King Wattha Gamani, the brotherhoods of the monasteries of Mahawihara and Abhayagiri were separated by bitter jealousy and hatred ; the tension increased with the value of the possessions which the kings assigned to one or other of the parties, and bloody struggles broke out the moment the king definitely declared for either of the two rivals. Energetic rulers made attempts at reunion, which appeared successful for the moment ; but the old hatred invariably broke out sooner or later, and seriously impaired the prestige of the Church. The disconnected nature of the doctrine itself was reflected in the looseness of monastic morality. Mahawansa complains, " In the villages which have been presented to the order, purity of life for the monks consists solely in taking wives and begetting children." The people gradually grew more indifferent to the order, for which their respect had long since ceased ;

Priestly Wars and Vices

and the order itself was so shattered by the long, weary Tamil wars that from 1065 A.D. onward scarce four monks in full orders could be found throughout the island. Since this was the number required by the laws of the Church for the formation of a legal chapter and the creation of new members, monks had

A HERMITAGE IN THE MOUNTAINS OF CEYLON
The chief Buddhist cave temples of Ceylon are in the mountainous district about 60 miles north-east of Colombo ; their date is said by tradition to be about 100 B.C.

to be imported from India or Burma. The list of successors to Dewanampiya Tissa provides a more intelligible but a far less pleasing picture than the obscurer figures of that monarch's predecessors. After the reigns of three kings, who appear but shadowy personalities in the chronicles, the Tamils invaded the country in the year 237 B.C., according to the Mahawansa, under the leadership of two young princes, who possessed numerous ships and a strong force of cavalry. After killing the king, Sura Tissa, they ruled over the kingdom for twenty years. The Buddhist historians describe them as righteous, and we may therefore assume them to have been tolerant. They were defeated and killed by Asela.

Tale of the Tamil Invasion

In 205 B.C., however, after the lapse of the usual ten years, the Tamil Elara invaded Ceylon from the north, " a man of the famous tribe of the Uju " ; he slew the king, and held the supremacy for forty-four years impartially against friend and foe. The only province that did not bow to the foreign yoke was the mountainous Rohana in the extreme south of the island ; from that point a descendant of the great family, Duttha Gamani, again expelled the Tamils. One Tamil fortress after another fell into his hands ; and finally in 161 B.C., in a battle at Anuradhapura, he killed the Tamil king Elara himself in single combat, and immediately afterward Elara's nephew, Bhalluka, who had brought up a fresh army too late from Malabar. This portion of the Mahawansa reads like a stirring epic. The monks had every reason to praise the pious and liberal conqueror of the Tamils. He refounded numerous monasteries and erected permanent memorials in the Palace of the Thousand Pillars of Lohapasada in the Marikawatti and the Ruwanweli dagobas.

An Epic of Ancient Ceylon

Laji Tissa, a grandson of Duttha Gamani, killed his uncle, Saddha Tissa, in 119 B.C. to secure the power for himself ; his successor and younger brother, Khallata Naga, was murdered by his Minister, Maharattaka, in 109 B.C. Hardly had Wattha Gamani Abhaya, the youngest grandson of Duttha Gamani, avenged this treachery, when the Tamils, attracted by these quarrels about the succession, again invaded the country under seven leaders, and forced the young king to seek refuge in the mountains. At that time purity of blood among the Aryan Singhalese kings had long been lost. Scornfully the Brahman Giri called after the flying king, " The great Black Sihala is flying ! " Like his grandfather, Wattha Gamani in 88 B.C. raised in the highlands a force which succeeded in liberating the throne of Wijaya from the hereditary foe ; afterwards, during his reign of twelve years he built many monasteries, and assigned large districts for the support of the monks, who had hitherto lived on the alms they gained by begging.

During the Tamil supremacy the population had been so impoverished, and the contributions of alms had grown so scanty, that the very existence of the order would have been endangered if forced to depend on this source. At the point where he had been insulted by the Brahman Giri, Gamani founded a monastery which he called Abhaya Giri, after his own name and that of the Brahman. The elder monastery of Mahawihara, inspired by jealousy, soon found an excuse for quarreling with its younger sister foundation. The dispute led to one good result—the reduction to writing of the sacred doctrine which had hitherto been orally transmitted from generation to generation. The three Pitakas and the commentaries to these, the Atthakathas, were written in the Singhalese language, and a wound was consequently inflicted upon the Buddhist Church which has never since been healed. Melancholy is the picture which the

Quarrels of Monastic Orders

H. C. White Co.

TEA-PICKING AT NUWARA ELIYA, CEYLON

This photograph of a characteristic Singhalese tea-garden was taken at Nuwara Eliya, the Governor's summer residence, which is 6,210 feet above sea-level.

historians of the monastery of Mahawihara have drawn of the immediate successors of Wattha Gamani. His son, Chola Naga, is described as a robber and brigand from the very moment of his accession, and afterwards as a cruel persecutor of the monks ; apparently he had declared against the brotherhood. However, his wife, Anula, from 47 B.C. to 42 B.C. seems to have been a disgrace to the royal throne, and to have rivalled Messalina by her poisonings and voluptuousness. She poisoned her husband's successor to secure the throne for herself and to gain full license for her unbounded avarice. Henceforward death was active in the royal palace : Anula herself was killed in 42 B.C., while twelve years later Amanda Gamani was assassinated by his younger brother, as was Chandamukha Siva in the year 44 B.C. The last of the great family, Yasalalaka Tissa, who had murdered his predecessor, had a favourite

Underwood & Underwood, London
THE TROPICAL FRUITS OF SUNNY CEYLON
The produce of Ceylon includes coconuts, cinnamon, coffee, tea, plantains, tamarinds, grapes, cinchona, cacao, cardamoms areca-nuts, and other fruits.

warder, by name Subha, who bore a very close resemblance to himself. The king would amuse himself by clothing his servant in the royal robes and setting him on the throne, while he himself took the post of doorkeeper. Once, however, when he joked

Jest that Became a Tragedy

with the false king arrayed in his royal robes, the latter called out, " How can this slave dare to laugh in my presence ! " Yasalalaka was punished with death, and Subha continued to play the part of legitimate king ; however, after a year, he was killed by Wasabha, a member of the Lambakanna caste, who seized the throne. The Lambakanna caste had displayed rebellious tendencies at an earlier period. Their caste pride had been wounded by King Ilanaga, who reigned 38–44 A.D. ; they had revolted and expelled this monarch for three years. On the present occasion they maintained their possession of the throne for three generations. Then ensued a period of rebellion and murder, and the power passed into different hands, until in 248 A.D. three of the Lambakanna murdered the king, Wijaya II., and seized the power.

In the country generally times were hard, and the prevalence of robber bands made life and property alike uncertain ; the royal prestige was greatly impaired, and the order was weakened by the dissensions of the two chief brotherhoods. The last of the three above-mentioned Lambakanna, by name Gothabhaya, vigorously attacked the Abhayagiri sect, and expelled from the Church and banished

Monastic Sect Expelled

from the island some sixty monks who " had adopted the false Wetula doctrine, and were like thorns to the conqueror's religion." At a later period, however, he was persuaded to change his mind by Samghamitta, a pupil of the banished high-priest, to whom he entrusted the education of his sons. In the case of the elder, Jettha Tissa I., this education proved unsuccessful ; upon reaching the throne he sternly oppressed the Abhayagiri monks, and persecuted his tutor in particular, who was forced to flee to the mainland. Twelve years later he was succeeded by his younger brother Mahasena, who ruled from 277 to 304 A.D. This king was persuaded by his tutor, who had now returned, to begin a severe persecution of the Mahawihara brotherhood. He prohibited these monks from receiving alms, and thereby made it impossible for them to remain in the "royal domains"; they were forced to flee to the mountains. For nine years the venerable mother monastery remained entirely abandoned ; proposals were brought forward to dismantle it, and to use the valuable materials for the improvement of the hostile Abhayagiri monastery, when at length the king revoked his decision against the persecuted monks. His adviser, Samghamitta, was killed in the course of a popular rising, the expelled monks were recalled, and their monastery was splendidly restored. Henceforward the king attempted to make amends to the brotherhood for the wrong which he had done to them by a special display of liberality.

A King who Persecuted the Priests

The next four kings were good Buddhists, liberal to the Church and benevolent to their subjects. Sirimeghawanna, from 304 to 332, the son of Mahasena, is lauded for the complete restoration of the Mahawihara monastery, and also as being the ruler under whom a princess of Dantapura, the capital of Kalinga, brought to Kandy in Ceylon the most sacred relic of the Buddhists, the tooth of Buddha. Among the following monarchs Shettha Tissa II., from 332 to 341, is distinguished as a sculptor and a painter, while his son Buddhadasa, from 341 to 370, was famous as a physician and the author of a Compendium of the Whole Science of Medicine. Then followed Upatissa II., from 370 to 412, who was murdered by his brother Mahanama. Under the latter, from 412 to 434, an event took place of high importance to southern Buddhism—the translation into the Pali language of the Atthakathas, emanating from Mahinda, which had hitherto existed only in Singhalese and were unknown in India. The monk Buddhaghosha was sent from Magadha to Ceylon by his teacher Rewata to translate this work "according to the rules of Magadha, the root of all

Rise of the Arts

languages"; in the seclusion of the Ganthakara monastery at Anuradhapura he completed this great work.

In the year 1893, on the occasion of the twenty-fifth anniversary of his coronation, King Chulalongkorn of Siam issued a new edition of it in thirty-nine volumes.

The example set by Mahanama in murdering his brother was rapidly followed. Then the Tamils reappeared under their king Pandu and his sons, occupying the northern part of the island from 416 to 463 ; they were ultimately driven out of the country by Dhatusena, a great landed proprietor and apparently a descendant of the family of Asoka—the Maurya dynasty. "He gave the country peace, and restored to religion those rights which the strangers had abolished"; however, he was imprisoned by his own son Kassapa, and buried alive in the year 479.

This scandalous deed opened another period of misery for the country. In the next two centuries, from 479 to 691, no fewer than twelve rulers died violent deaths. Fratricide and the revolts of generals produced a rapid series of changes in the succession to the throne. The provincial viceroys tended to independence, and the sectarian warfare within the Buddhist Church continued undiminished. The Tamils, who had formerly invaded the country for plunder and conquest upon their own initiative, were now constantly brought in by the Singhalese princes or generals to overthrow the legitimate occupants of the throne. Temples and royal treasuries were plundered, religion was oppressed, and the people grew more and more impoverished. During the fifth and sixth centuries, however, the period of the king Kumara Dasa, from 515 to 524, to whom is ascribed the Sanscrit translation of the Ramayana, which remains only in the Singhalese translation, and of Agrabhi I., from 564 to 598, who was famous as a poet, Chinese pilgrims describe the capital as a brilliant town ; even at the outset of the seventh century a Singhalese historical work speaks of the beauty of Anuradhapura.

Period of Crime and Disorder

Nevertheless, under Aggabodhi IV., from 673 to 689, the capital could no longer hold out against the hereditary enemy; the royal residence was removed to Polonnaruwa, or Pulathi, at a greater distance from the point of Tamil invasion, the harbour of Mantotte on the Gulf of Manaar. This change became permanent about 846 A.D. The island gained some occasional relief from the internal wars of the different Dravidian races on the mainland. Nevertheless, Sena I. (846 to 866) was obliged to take refuge in the inaccessible recesses of the highlands ; the northern part of the island was cruelly devastated, the capital plundered, and its treasures carried off to India. Now, however, attracted by the rich booty, the Chola began war with their Tamil neighbours. Thus, under Sena I., the Singhalese crossed the Palk Straits ; the Pandya king was killed, the hostile capital of Madura plundered, and the booty taken from Ceylon recovered. Under Kassapa IV., from 912 to 929, a Singhalese army went to

Rohana, the last, though not the inviolate, bulwark of the Singhalese kingdom. His successor, Vijaya Bahu I., also known as Sirasanghabodhi (1065–1120), though at first defeated, repeatedly advanced into the lowlands, where he overthrew three Chola armies, captured their fortresses, **Invaders Finally Expelled** recovered Anuradhapura, and shattered the last resistance of the enemy in a bloody conflict under the walls of Polonnaruwa ; this victory permanently freed the country from the Chola.

The power of Ceylon was not yet, however, definitely established. When Vijaya Bahu endeavoured to enter into friendly relations with the enemy, and sent special ambassadors to the Chola king with rich presents, the noses and the ears of the

Underwood & Underwood, London
VIEWS OF KANDY, THE FORMER SEAT OF THE TYRANNICAL KANDYAN KINGS

the help of the Pandya king, though with little effect, and the Tamil ruler was forced to take refuge in Ceylon.

This rapid rise of Singhalese prosperity was of no long duration. Under Udaya III. (964–72) and Mahinda IV. (975–91) Ceylon was invaded by the Cholas ; under the leadership of their king, Para-kesariwarman (1052–61), they **Invasion by the Cholas** overran the island to its southern-most extremity, the province of Rohana, carried away two sons of the king Manabharana, and killed the king Wira-Salamega about 1056. The plundering extortions and the religious animosity of this Malabar people reduced the country to an awful state of desolation. It was not until 1059 that a brave noble, Loka, succeeded in driving the Chola from his native province of

emissaries were cut off. Further, when he ordered his troops to march against the Cholas, a mutiny broke out, and the whole of the south rose against the king, who had much difficulty in crushing the rebellion. The country was utterly exhausted, and the Buddhist order was in so feeble a state that not a single monk in full orders was to be found anywhere in the island ; monks, accordingly, had to be brought over from Ramanya or Martaban in lower Burma.

Under Vikkama Bahu I., the southern provinces broke away entirely and were divided among different rulers. The king had the utmost difficulty in driving out an Aryan adventurer from North India, who had blockaded him in a mountain fortress, and in recovering Polonnaruwa. The population was completely exhausted, and the taxes were collected by measures of the severest oppression, " as the sugar mill presses the juice from the cane." To meet his necessities, Vikkama Bahu was forced to appropriate Church property, and thus made the monks his deadly enemies. They emigrated to Rohana, taking with **Oppression** them Buddha's tooth and his **Causes** alms-dish. During the many **Desolation** wars the irrigation canals had been destroyed, and the once fruitful land had become a malarial desert. Towns and villages were abandoned, and had grown so desolate " that their sites were undiscoverable."

Parrakkama Bahu I., or Parakrama, from 1164 to 1197, was the greatest monarch who ever sat upon the Singhalese throne. Only by realising the misery under which the country almost succumbed during his youth can we estimate the results achieved by the intellectual force and patriotism of this ruler, whom history rightly names " the Great."

After the death of Vijaya Bahu I. the Singhalese monarchy had almost entirely collapsed. The nominal ruler was still resident in Polonnaruwa, but the greater part of the country was broken into petty principalities. In the province of Rohana alone four such princes were to be found, including Manabharana, who laid claim to the little district " of the twelve thousand villages," and was the father of Parrakkama the Great. This ruler spent his youth in the mountains ; " he received a thorough instruction in religion, in the different legal systems, in rhetoric and poetry, dancing and music, in writing and in the use of sword and bow, and in these exercises he attained the highest degree of perfection." Upon the death of his uncle he became ruler of his principality.

Parrakkama's administration was in every respect admirable ; he introduced **Ceylon's** a properly organised system of **Greatest** taxation, and endeavoured to **Ruler** make the utmost possible use of streams and rainfall for the irrigation of the soil. At the same time he drilled those of the male inhabitants capable of bearing arms, with a view to the reunion of his country as a whole. His first expedition was directed against the highland of Malaya, which he subdued with the support of a general of King Gaja Bahu IV. The court at Polon-

naruwa was entirely denationalised ; it was thronged by crowds of foreigners, including princes from the mainland, who disseminated foreign influence, foreign customs, foreign religion, and " filled the land of the king like thorns in a bed." For this reason he declared war upon Gaja Bahu, and advanced by a rapid series of victories to the land of pearls, " the coast of the Gulf of Manaar." Ultimately the king and the princes were captured. After thus attaining his object, the conqueror restored their country to his defeated foes. A chieftain of Rohana, Manabharana the younger, had attempted to turn the war between Parrakkama and Gaja Bahu to its own advantage ; he was conquered in like manner, and also left in possession of his land. Both of these conquered princes appointed the victor as their successor. Thus Parrakkama became master of the whole island, although at first he was obliged sternly to suppress repeated revolts, especially among the freedom-loving inhabitants of the south and in the western province of Mahatittha.

The king's strong hand soon made itself felt beyond the boundaries of his kingdom. **Relations** For a long period he had been in **of Ceylon** friendly relations with Ramanya **and Burma** or Lower Burma. Vijaya I. had invited Burmese monks to Ceylon, and the two countres were united by peaceful commercial relations. However, during the gloomy period of the last Singhalese king, Arimaddana, the ruler of Ramanya had attempted to profit by the unfavourable condition of Ceylon. A tax was laid upon the exportation of elephants, which made the purchase of these animals almost impossible for the impoverished Singhalese. The usual presents were withheld from the Singhalese ambassadors, the ships of Ceylon were forbidden to land in Burma, and the emissaries sent from Polonnaruwa were finally robbed and imprisoned. Parrakkama then sent a strong expedition to Ramanya ; his ships were greatly damaged by a storm, but the army succeeded in defeating the Burmese troops, storming the capital, and killing the king. Parrakkama's supremacy was proclaimed, and peace was granted only upon condition of an indemnity to compensate for former vexations, to which was added the obligation of a yearly tribute.

In Southern India also, Parrakkama avenged the wrongs that had been committed against Ceylon in former years.

The struggles between the Cholas and the Pandyas had continued since the time of Vijaya Bahu I. Under their king Kulasekhara the Cholas had fiercely besieged King Pandu in his capital of Madura. It was not to the interest of Ceylon to see a great Dravidian kingdom in place of the numerous petty states, who might wear one another out by internal struggles ; Parrakkama therefore sent to the help of the Tamil king a strong army under Lankapura and Jagad Vijaya Nayaka. Before the arrival of this force, Madura had fallen and King Pandu had been killed ; however, the Singhalese had **Singhalese Invasion of India** defeated the Cholas and devastated their country. King Kulasekhara was besieged in his fortress of Rajina and was barely able to save himself by flight. He was forced to conclude peace upon terms highly disadvantageous to himself. The Pandya kingdom was restored, Prince Vira Pandu was installed in Madura as king, and a Tamil coinage, with the head of Parrakkama, was struck to commemorate the campaign. The captured Cholas were sent to Ceylon, where they were forced to work at the restoration of those same religious buildings which their forefathers had destroyed in their plundering raids. True to the proverb of his choice, " What is there in the world that a persevering man cannot perform ? " Parrakkama gave his devastated island

NATIVE FARMING IN CEYLON
The elephant is frequently used for ploughing and other purposes on the " paddy," or rice farm, and he is here seen harnessed to a primitive Singhalese wooden plough.

Underwood & Underwood, London
ELEPHANT CARRYING A HALF-TON LOG
The intelligence and great strength of the trained elephant give him a high industrial value, which is nowhere more apparent than it is in the teak forests of Further India.

a fresh lease of prosperity. As chieftain of a small district, he had once observed, " In a country like this not the least drop of water that falls from heaven should **Schemes of Irrigation** be allowed to run into the sea until it has first done good service to mankind." This principle was now vigorously put into practice throughout his great kingdom. He had tanks built or restored by thousands ; the greatest of these, for example, the " Sea of Parrakkama," was equal in extent to the lake of the Four Forest Cantons. More than five hundred new canals were made, and several thousand ruined waterways were reconstructed. Malarious swamps and impenetrable jungles were transformed into miles of flourishing rice fields and orchards ; towns and villages arose from their ruins, with a dense and prosperous population.

The decaying capital of Polonnaruwa rose to new splendour and was provided with everything that could conduce to comfort and luxury. The ruler was not forgetful of the old and famous capital of Anuradhapura, the palaces which the founder of the empire had erected, the shrines consecrated by Mahinda and his successors ; and the monasteries and relic shrines were cleared of their jungle overgrowth and restored. The administration of the country was reorganised, and a mild and equable system of taxation introduced. The disorders which had

1379

broken out in the Church were checked, and the morality of the priesthood improved. Parrakkama even succeeded in reconciling that feud between the chief sects which had lasted for a thousand years, and in unifying the doctrine; "the attempt to bring about this union seemed no less desperate than an attempt to raise the mountain of Meru from its foundations." Parrakkama the Great was succeeded by his nephew Vijaya Bahu II. (1197-8), a weakling characterised by the monks as a great scholar and poet; after a reign of one year he was assassinated. Then began a period of the greatest confusion. During the eighteen years immediately following the death of the great king the empire saw no less than fifteen different rulers, with reigns of one, nine, and seventeen days, three, seven, nine, and twelve months. At least five were murdered; six were deposed, and in some cases blinded. A motley row of figures passes before us, Singhalese, Kalingas, Cholas, and Pandyas. The Kalinga prince Magha, who reigned from 1215 to 1236, seized the island with an army of twenty thousand warriors, was the first ruler able to secure his position upon the throne; at the same time his rule proved a devastating scourge to the unfortunate country which had never yet been subjected to so fearful a visitation.

In the south alone a few capable leaders were able to maintain their independence in the mountain fortresses defended alike by Nature and by art. Of these petty principalities, the most important was Dambadenya, where Vijaya Bahu III. (1236-40), who traced his descent from Vijaya Bahu I., had established himself; from this base of operations he was able to subdue the province of Malaya. His son Parrakkama Bahu III. (1240-75), drove out the Dravidians in 1255, almost annihilating them, together with the Chola king, Someswara; still,

Malay Raids in Ceylon he was forced to struggle with other enemies, for the weakness of Ceylon had attracted the Malays, who were especially active at that period. Their leader, Chandrabhanu, twice invaded the country and devasted "the whole of Lanka"; the Malays, however, never succeeded in permanently establishing themselves on the island.

In the works of peace, Parrakkama II. rivalled his great predecessor. During the

Religious Enemies Reconciled

Dravidian rule proprietary titles had been lost or confused, and a redistribution of the country among laity and monks was now undertaken. Roads were laid down, tanks and canals restored, and Polonnaruwa, which had been almost entirely ruined, was rebuilt; in Anuradhapura works of restoration were begun upon the main buildings, which had been severely damaged. Meanwhile, the so-called monks had plunged into every kind of vice, and the old quarrel between the brotherhoods broke out with renewed fury. Here, too, the king's action improved the situation.

Vijaya Bahu IV., the successor of Parrakkama II., was murdered by one of his generals two years later, though the murderer also received short shrift. In default of a powerful ruler, the people quickly relapsed into their former state of misery, and, to complete the tale of their suffering, a terrible famine broke out. A Pandu army invaded the country so suddenly that even the greatest relic of the Buddhist world, the tooth of Buddha, could not be hidden, but was carried off to Madura with other booty. The tooth

A Great National Relapse was not recovered until the reign of Parrakkama Bahu III. (1288-93). This raid of the Pandyas seems to have been the last Dravidian invasion of Ceylon; a few years later, in 1311, the Mohammedans under Kafur advanced from the north to the Palk Straits, and from the middle of the fourteenth century the Pandyas became tributary to the kingdom of Bijanagar, in the Deccan. The Singhalese chronicles make no reference to wars with the Dravidians later than the year 1290. In consequence of the incessant civil wars, the ruling kings removed their capitals further within the mountains, and Buddhism hardly existed even in name. Hence, even up to the time of Parrakkama IV., about 1300, only the very scantiest historical record was kept in the monasteries, and from that date until the middle of the eighteenth century historical writing ceased entirely. The records became somewhat more definite at the time of Raja Simha I. (1586-92), who secured the throne by murdering his father. But it was not until the time of Kirti Sri raja Simha (1747-80) that the gaps were filled up with the scanty material to hand and with the aid of tradition.

THE EUROPEANS IN CEYLON

" IN those days certain merchants carried on trade in the harbour of Kolamba, which they continued until, in the course of time, they had grown very powerful. The Parangi, or Portuguese, were collectively base unbelievers, cruel, and hardhearted." In the year 1498 Vasco da Gama had cast anchor before Calicut ; seventeen years later came the destruction of the Arab trade, which had hitherto monopolised the valuable products of Asia, especially the spice exports ; Ormuz, Malacca, and Goa became the foundations of the Portuguese power in the Indian seas. Portuguese ships had visited Ceylon as early as 1505 ; in 1515 a fleet sailed to the island from Calicut under Lopez Soarez, and the Singhalese monarch in Kotta gave permission to the admiral to found a permanent trading station in the harbour of Colombo, near his residence. If the king hoped to gain powerful friends by this means, he was soon bitterly undeceived. He was forced to **Aggression by the Portuguese** become a Portuguese vassal, and to agree to the payment of a yearly tribute of cinnamon, precious stones, and elephants. Hostilities were the early and the natural result. The kings removed their capitals to the mountains of the interior, first to Sitawaka, then to Kandy. But in vain ; the war continued without interruption, and every Portuguese campaign penetrated further into the country.

By degrees, however, the difficulties afforded by the precipitous highland slopes, the jungles of the primeval forest, the dangers of the climate, and the military strength of the highlanders increased. The latter learnt the arts of strategy, tactics, and the use of weapons from their enemies ; they had of old been famous for their skill in metal-working, and were able to keep their guns and cannons in better repair. Mayadhana and his son Raja Simha I. vigorously repulsed the attacks of the Portuguese ; of Raja Simha II., Mahawansa says : " As a lion bursts into a herd of elephants, or as flakes of wool are swept away by the wind, so was the

enemy seized by fear and fled before the dauntless king."

The Portuguese were never able to establish themselves in the interior ; their only established possessions were the fortresses of Negambo, Colombo, Galle, Battikaloa, and Trincomali, with the land immediately adjoining these settlements. They operated with some success against **Extent of Portuguese Power** the Tamil kingdom, which occupied the northern extremity of the island, and a small strip of land upon the east coast. The capital of Jafna was stormed in 1560, and the sacred tooth fell into the hands of the Portuguese. In vain did the King of Pegu offer 400,000 gold pieces for the relic. The Portuguese valued the destruction of that fragment of bone at a higher price ; it was pounded in a mortar by the Archbishop of Goa, Dom Gaspar, burnt in the fire, and the ashes thrown into the river. Tooth worship was, however, not extirpated by this means ; in no long time a second " tooth " appeared in Kandy, which was said to have been hidden and buried during a Portuguese invasion, while the conquerors were said to have destroyed only an imitation of the real tooth. On the first conquest of Jafna, the Portuguese contented themselves with depriving the Sultan of the island of Mannar and of all his treasures, and imposing a heavy tribute upon him. In 1617, the town was again stormed upon the reported outbreak of hostilities against the Christians ; the Sultan was beheaded and his land declared Portuguese territory.

The story of the destruction of Buddha's tooth is typical of the religious fanaticism of the Portuguese. Every ship **Portuguese Religious Fanaticism** brought, together with soldiers greedy for plunder, bands of monks who were anxious to spread Christianity by any means in their power. Their greatest success was the conversion of a Singhalese king to the one true Church. " The King Dharma Pauli Raja embraced the Christian religion, and was baptised under the name of Don Juan Pandaura ; many nobles of Kotta were

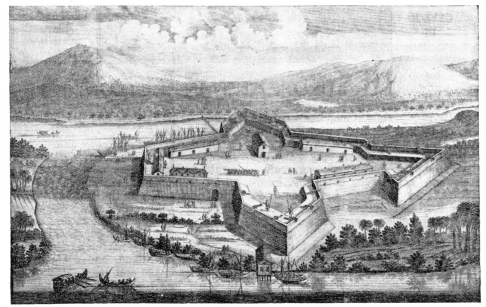

BATTIKALAO, ONE OF THE EARLY PORTUGUESE STRONGHOLDS IN CEYLON

Battikaloa, now the capital of the eastern province in Ceylon, is situated on an island in a salt water lake, 30 miles long and from two to five miles wide ; the old Dutch fort, seen in the picture, now does service as a prison.

converted with him. From this time onward the wives of the nobles, and also those of the lower castes, such as the barbers, fishers, humawas, and chalyas, became Christians, and lived with the Christians for the sake of the Portuguese money."

This apostate king appointed Philip II. of Spain and Portugal his heir, and from that time the Portuguese kings have added to their many titles that of Lord of Ceylon. The soil was well prepared for the conversion of the Singhalese to Christianity. The old religion had degenerated to the lowest possible point ; Raja Simha, the worshipper of Siva, had persecuted his Buddhist subjects. Repeated importations of foreign monks had been unable to check the decay of Singhalese Buddhism ; the people had grown utterly indifferent to religious questions. Within the Portuguese districts members of the lower castes could exist only by keeping on good terms with their masters, and consequently the people came over to the Catholic Church in numbers.

Religious Condition of Ceylon

High-sounding Portuguese names are still to be found among the modern Singhalese, the descendants of converts who adopted the family names of their masters upon their change of faith. The Portuguese exemplified their own interpretation of Christianity by practising inhuman extortion upon every subject within their domains. In this manner they sought to indemnify themselves for the comparatively small profits accruing from their trade. The cultivation of the most valuable product of the island, cinnamon, was retarded by the bitter hatred of the foreigners, and confined to narrow districts in the immediate neighbourhood of the fortified settlements of Colombo and Galle. Spices "were collected sword in hand and exported under the guns of the fortresses." Trade rapidly decreased, and the receipts failed to balance the expenditure of the Portuguese during 150 years of unbroken war. The decay of Portuguese trade in Ceylon was but one of the many phenomena apparent upon the decline of Portugal, which was absorbed by the Spanish monarchy in 1580. The spirit of enterprise which had inspired the country during the fifteenth century and at the outset of the sixteenth had faded ; its power was wasted by constant wars in deadly climates, the people were impoverished, and the oppression of the Inquisition lay upon all minds.

Decay of Portuguese Power

1382

THE EUROPEANS IN CEYLON

Portugal's career as a colonial Power was at an end. Her place in Ceylon was taken by the Dutch, who had now all but achieved their deliverance from Spain.

In 1602 Joris van Spilbergen landed in the island with two ships to conclude an alliance with the angry Singhalese king against the Portuguese ; the king sent two ambassadors " into their beautiful land," and persuaded the people to come to Ceylon with many ships. In the meanwhile, the two Powers concluded a convention in 1609 for the expulsion of the Portuguese from the island, though **Beginning of Dutch Influence** neither the feeble king Vimila Dhamma Surya I. (1592–1620) nor the Dutch felt themselves strong enough for immediate action. The war was not prosecuted with any energy until the time of Raja Simha II. ; the Dutch then captured one Portuguese fortress after another. Ultimately, in 1658, after an armistice of ten years, Colombo and Jafna fell, and the Portuguese were definitely ousted by the Dutch.

The new nationality conducted their policy in a wholly different spirit. They were primarily merchants, and their chief object was to avoid any possible disturbance to their trade. They had originally agreed to send an embassy to the king at Kandy every year. The king treated these with contempt and scorn ; on different occasions the ambassadors **The Dutch Policy of Peace** were beaten, imprisoned, and even put to death, outrages which the Dutch patiently bore. On one occasion only, during the reign of Kirti Sri Raja Simha, did they attempt a punitive expedition with Malay soldiers ; Kandy was captured, and the king was forced to flee, taking with him the tooth of Buddha. Sickness and famine, however, broke out among the troops, and their line of retreat was cut off ; many soldiers succumbed to the attacks of the mountaineers, while others were scattered and lost their way in the inhospitable forests.

Raja Simha II. was succeeded by a number of weak rulers who favoured the

AUDIENCE GRANTED BY THE KING OF CEYLON TO GERARD HULST IN 1656

Inset in top of the picture is a portrait of the Dutch general, Gerard Hulst, who is described as the " First Counsellor, and Director Generall of ye Indies, Comander in Chief of all the Sea and Land Forces sent to Ceylon, and the Coast of the Indies." The united arms of the Singhalese and the Dutch expelled the Portuguese from the island.

1383

THE BARBARIC EXECUTION OF A USURPER
In the reign of Raja Simha, a usurper had himself proclaimed King ; Raja Simha enticed him to his court, had him buried to the elbows and killed by his attendants, who threw wooden balls at his victim. Our illustration is from an old engraving in an early history.

from 1747 to 1780, that Buddhism was purified of its hollow formalities and revived ; two embassies brought over each a chapter of ten monks, the first under the high-priest Upali, from Siam. The religious toleration of the Dutch and the English has since enabled Buddhism to extend its area and regain some of its power in Ceylon, though at the same time the doctrine has been largely modified by the worship of Brahman gods and Dravidian demons.

The Dutch at first derived great profit from their trade in the products of Ceylon.

monks, though they were unable to improve the position of the order. Sri Wira Parakkama Narinda, from 1701 to 1734, built the Dalada Maligawa, a temple yet in existence, to enshrine the sacred tooth, and decorated its outer walls with thirty-two histories of the birth of Buddha ; but under his successor, Vijaya Raja Simha, from 1734 to 1747, the monks had entirely disappeared. The doctrine itself had degenerated into a mixture of Hinduism, devil worship, and Buddhist conventionalities. The connection of the island with Southern India—a large number of the rulers of Kandy married princesses from Madura — had enabled the Brahman gods to gain the pre-eminence in Ceylon ; their images were carried in procession in company with the statues of Buddha, and when a king built a Buddhist shrine he erected with it a temple dedicated to Siva or Vishnu. It was not until the time of Kirti Sri Raja Simha,

The cinnamon plantations captured from the Portuguese were not increased ; but the careful cultivation of the plants raised the value of the bark to an unprecedented height, and high prices were maintained by a strict monopoly. These measures, however, eventually led to the decay of the trade. The high prices attracted the rivalry of other plantations upon other islands. An army of subordinate officials

DUTCH FORCES TAKING THE ISLE OF MANNAR
An incident in the struggle for supremacy in Ceylon before 1658 when the Dutch finally expelled the Portuguese, against whom they had allied themselves with the Singhalese.

DEPOSITION OF THE KING OF KANDY BY THE BRITISH IN 1815

The British assumed complete sovereignty of Ceylon in 1815, when they deported Wikrama Raja Singha, King of Kandy, whose excesses had culminated in the massacre of some native merchants who were British subjects.

swallowed up a large proportion of the profit, and dishonesty was increased by the scanty salaries paid. The cinnamon trade, which originally brought such high profits, at length scarcely succeeded in paying its expenses.

The trade of Ceylon suffered from the decline of Holland as a sea-power. The capture of the Portuguese possessions marks the zenith of Dutch influence, and Dutch trade was at that time five times greater than that of England. While, however, the struggle for Colombo and Jafna was in progress, England dealt a deadly stroke at her rival; in 1651-60 the Navigation Acts were passed, which prevented foreign ships from carrying goods between England and her colonies. In the year 1792 the proportion of trade in the hands of these rivals was as two to five. When Holland became a virtual dependency of the French Republic during the European wars at the close of the eighteenth century, Great Britain took from the Dutch not only their trading fleet,

H. C. White Co.
COLOMBO HARBOUR, CEYLON

which was valued at £10,000,000, but also all their colonies at the Cape, in Malacca, in Cochin, in the Moluccas, etc. The occupation of Ceylon was not a difficult task.

The British Governor of Madras sent an expedition which promptly captured Trincomali, a position of considerable naval importance. The capitulation of Colombo, the Dutch capital, which surrendered without striking a blow, effectively substituted British for Dutch throughout the island—which, unlike many other British conquests of the time, was not restored at the Peace of Amiens in 1802, when, on the contrary, it was formally annexed to the British Crown. For the time, the native rulers in the interior were not dispossessed. But the

savage excesses of the monarch, Wikrama Raja Singha of Kandy, culminated in the massacre of some native merchants who were British subjects; with the inevitable result. The king was easily captured and deported to Madras, and in March, 1815, the chiefs by formal treaty accepted the British supremacy.

Since that date Ceylon has had "no history." The island is ruled as a British Crown Colony, and its notable events have been mainly of commercial interest. The first was the successful development of the country as a great coffee producer; the second was the destruction of the coffee plantation by a fungus which all efforts failed

Underwood & Underwood, London
QUEEN STREET, COLOMBO

to eradicate, about 1870, followed by the development of tea-growing, which has proved a not inefficient substitute. For the rest, the rule of Ceylon has followed the lines of other British Crown Colonies where a large dark-skinned population is governed by a handful of British. EMIL SCHMIDT

FURTHER INDIA

THE LAND, ITS PEOPLES, AND GENERAL EARLY HISTORY

FURTHER INDIA, otherwise known as Indo-China, forms the most easterly of the three great projections southward from Asia. Equal in area to the south of Nearer India—830,586 square miles—it is bounded by China on the north, by India on the north-west ; the western boundary in all its length is formed by the east coast of the Sea of Bengal, its southern boundary is the sea between the mainland and the islands of Java and Borneo, while the China Sea washes its eastern shores. The course of its civilisation has been inspired by impulses derived not from over seas, but from the two civilised countries of India and China.

The superficial configuration of Further India is controlled by parallel mountain ranges running for the most part from north to south, which, beginning in the mountain country between Eastern Tibet and Yunnan, Kwangsi and Kwangtung, the southern provinces of China, to the north of the twenty-fifth degree of latitude, **Mountains of the Peninsula** diverge southward. At the roots of these mountains, in gorges often 3,000 feet deep, run those four mighty rivers which rise in Tibet, afterward diverging fan-wise to hurry on to the different seas. From its passage through the mountains eastward the Yangtse Kiang naturally forms the most important line of communication in the Celestial Empire. The Brahmaputra turns back westward through the broad valley of Assam to the Ganges delta. Only the Salwen and Mekong, running southward, can be said properly to belong to the peninsula of Indo-China. Between these rivers flow parallel streams, the sources of which begin at a point somewhat to the south of the spot where the main streams pass the gorges ; of these the most westward is the Irawaddi, which rises in the mountain land to the east of Assam. The greater part of its course is navigable ; with its tributaries it facilitates communication with Yunnan, passing through the fruitful plains of Chittagong and Arakan, and forming one of the greatest deltas in the world at its mouth in the Gulf of Pegu.

From this river the Salwen, eastward, is divided by no greater obstacle than a low-lying range of hills running north and **The Great Rivers of Indo-China** south, which eventually turns it away from the narrow coast district of Tennasserim and directs its course to Central Further India. Between the Salwen and the Mekong flows the Menam, the main river of Siam, the whole course of which falls within Indo-China, since its sources do not extend beyond the twentieth degree of latitude north. Beyond is the Mekong, rising in Tibet, the delta of which extends eastward into the China Sea. All these streams have fruitful deltas, and plains upon their banks, but navigation on any large scale is excluded by the rapids and shallows immediately above their mouths. The mountain chain running from north to south forms a sharp line of demarcation to the east of the Mekong between Central and Eastern Further India, Cochin-China, Annam, and

1387

Tonquin. The Songka, or Red River, is the only stream flowing northward in Tonquin, a district generally narrow which forms the eastern third of Indo-China ; it is, however, more navigable than the central rivers, and forms the most convenient route of access to Yunnan and its mineral wealth. The climate is that

Physical Features of Indo-China of a tropical Asiatic district under the monsoons. In the alluvial plains of the valleys and deltas all natural growths flourish with inexhaustible fertility, and from an early age these have been the points of departure for Indo-Chinese civilisation. The highlands further to the north are less richly dowered by Nature, and have retained for thousands of years their influence upon tribal formation. Here from a remote antiquity was the home of powerful half-barbaric tribes who were driven out by upheavals among the restless nomadic hordes of Central Asia or attracted by the riches of the southern lowlands, which they repeatedly invaded, bringing infusions of new blood and valuable material for the work of civilisation.

Hence even at the present day racial stocks displaying anthropological and ethnological differences can be plainly recognised. As direct descendants of the earliest inhabitants we have three races belonging to different anthropological groups—the Nigritic, Malay, and Indonesian types. The Nigritic people, who are related to the inhabitants of the Andaman Islands, and to the Aëtas of the Philippines, are now known as Sakai and Semangs, and inhabit small districts within the peninsula of Malacca. The Malays are identical with the inhabitants of the islands, to which they were expelled at a comparatively late period. Tribes which have maintained their purity of blood also occupy certain districts in the Malay peninsula ; while others, mixed

Races of Further India with later invaders, occupy extensive tracts in the lowlands of Siam and Annam ; their original settlements seem to have been the lowlands of Indo-China. On the other hand, the highlands were inhabited by Indonesians, whose nearest relations are now to be found in the Indonesian Archipelago, in the Philippines, Borneo, Sumatra, etc. The modern representatives of the Indonesian race within Indo-China are the Nagas on the

frontier between Assam and Burma ; the Selongs, in the Mergui archipelago ; the Moi—half-wild tribes between the Mekong and the coast of Assam and between Yunnan and Cochin-China ; the Kui, in South-eastern Siam and North-western Cambodia ; and the Mons or Talaings in the deltas of the Burmese rivers, formerly distributed throughout Lower Burma.

The highlands, which extend further northward from Eastern Tibet to the southern provinces of China, were in antiquity inhabited by a powerful race closely allied to the Indonesians, who may be generally comprehended in the tribal families of the Thai. From this point repeated invasions took place into the lowlands at a later period. About 1250 this people was settled in the principality of Xieng-Mai. Under Râma Khomheng in 1283 the more southerly kingdom of Sukhodaya is mentioned in inscriptions. Driven westward by the resistance of the Brahman kings of Cambodia, the Thai are found in possession of the lower Menam about 1350.

Early Kings of Further India The descendants of these immigrants after fusion with the former inhabitants of the district form the chief element in the population of those states of Further India which reached any high degree of culture.

It is impossible to decide whether the Cham are an early branch of the Thai or whether they originated from the Indonesians ; they found the Malays settled in the lowlands and borrowed their language, which is closely related to the different Malay dialects of the present day ; at the same time their physical characteristics display marked divergences from the Malay type and approach more nearly to the Indonesian. The first glimmer of historical information shows them as the settled people of a kingdom which embraced South Tonquin, Annam, and a great part of Central Further India. A second wave of migration advancing within our era brought the Khmers into the fruitful land ; here they, too, mixed with the population in possession, the Malays, and Indonesians—hence the wavy hair of the Kui—and raised their State of Cambodia to high prosperity at the expense of the Champa kingdom. By later invasions of the Thai their district was reduced to its present limits, the smaller State of Cambodia and Southern Cochin-China.

From this cradle of nations new races advanced east and south and expelled the Moi, the Malays, and Khmers from their settlements ; these were the Annamese. At the present day they are settled from the delta of Tonquin to Southern Cochin-China, and have been strongly modified by infusions of Chinese blood, while their civilisation is almost entirely Chinese. Probably the same wave brought a second stream of the Thai forward about the same date, the Lao race in the mountains of what is now North Siam, and a third tribe, the Burmese, who are linguistically related to the Tibetans ; these tribes advanced from the mountain land at the east of Tibet to the lower courses of the Irawaddi, where they settled, driving to the coast the Mons, who show linguistic affinities with the Annamese. About 1000 A.D. they were followed by the Shan, now settled in the mountain districts of Upper Burma, who still call themselves Thai, or Free, and further to the east by the Siamese, who overthrew the supremacy **Migrations and Conflicts** of the former Khmer immigrants in Cambodia and formed a highly prosperous kingdom of their own. The physical characteristics of all these tribes show that they are not free from fusion with other races.

The prehistoric period of Further India is shrouded in darkness, though a few vague and general indications may be derived from the sciences of comparative philology and anthropology. These indications alike point to early racial commixture and fusion. From a philological point of view, several primordial groups stand out in isolation. The dialects of the dark inhabitants of the peninsula at the present day are as yet but little known ; but the special characteristics of the Malay group of languages show that this branch diverged from the original stem in a remote antiquity. The remaining dialects of the people of Further India belong to the isolating family of languages, and point to the existence at an extremely early age of two distinct tribes, which may be designated as Tibeto-Burmese and Thai-Chinese, according to their modern distribution.

We have no means of deciding where the first ancestors of these groups may have dwelt. We can venture to assert only that the separation of these primitive peoples, with whom we are concerned in the history of Further India, took place in the north. During the later history of Indo-China, the Thai preserved their racial purity, as they do at the present day in the mountainous frontier between Further India and China. Philological evidence **Cradle of the Races** points to the fact that an early bifurcation of the Thai formed the tribes of Mon-Annam, which were driven into their present remote habitations by the invasions in later centuries of the Thai. They were then known as Mons and Annamites. The Cham also broke away from the Thai at an early period, and were strongly influenced by the Malay population, with whom they came into contact, both in respect of language and physical structure. Within recent and historical times they were followed by the Khmers, the Laos, Shans, and Siamese.

Upon the dates and the history of these ancient racial movements we have no information whatever. Chinese histories refer, indeed, to an embassy sent from Indo-China, probably from Tonquin, in the year 1110 B.C. to the Imperial Chinese court of the Chau. In 214 B.C. and 109 A.D., Chinese generals founded dynasties of their own in Tonquin. Upon the general history of those ages we have no other information. The wild imagination of the natives has so transformed their legends that though these go back to the creation of the world, they give us no historical material of any value whatever. It is not until the first centuries of our era that the general darkness is somewhat relieved. On the north frontier and in the east we find a restless movement and a process of struggle, with varying success, between the Chinese and the native races ; while in the south and west Hindu civilisation is everywhere victorious. The most important source of our knowledge upon **Light on Early Indo-China** the affairs of Further India in those ages is Ptolemy's description of the world, dating from the first half of the second century A.D. The larger part of the south was occupied by the Champa kingdom of the Chams, with its capital at Champapura. To the east and north-east were settled the Khmers, who, according to an ancient tradition of Cambodia, had advanced southwards from their northern settlements and come into connection with the Chams. Ptolemy, however, also informs us that at his time the coast-line of Further India was inhabited throughout its length by the Sindoi or Hindus. As their importance in Indo-China was at that time great enough for the Alexandrine geographer to describe them as a race of wide distribution, the advance of Hindu civilisation must have taken place at least some centuries previously. The introduction of Brahman civilisation was a victory for merely a few representatives of a higher culture. The physical characteristics of the population of Further India were but little influenced by this new infusion. The movement can hardly have begun before the period at which the Brahmans colonised Orissa. From this point Brahmanism apparently made its way to Indo-China by sea. On the one hand, the Brahmans did not advance along the land route, long hidden and leading through the Ganges delta and Assam, until the second half of the present millennium, at which time Brahmanism had long since fallen into decay in Indo-China. On the other hand, a proof of the fact that the colonisation was of transmarine origin is the predominance of Hinduism upon the coast. The movement to Indo-China cannot have started from Southern India for the reason that at that period Brahmanism had taken but little hold on the south, and the transmission of their civilisation from those shores is therefore extremely improbable. It was not until a much later period that communication between the two countries began, the results of which are apparent in the Dravidian influences visible in the later temple buildings of Indo-China. Further evidence for the northern origin of Indo-Chinese Brahmanism is found in the names of the more important towns of early Indonesia, which are almost entirely borrowed from the Sanscrit names of the towns in the Ganges district, and also from the desire of the Indonesian rulers to retrace their origin to the mythical sun and moon dynasties of Madhya-desa. The maritime route led straight to Burma, but Indian civilisation at the moment found that district less favourable to its development than that of the great and more hospitable Champa kingdom in the central south. The Gulf of Ligor and the coast and banks of the great rivers of

Brahmanism in the Peninsula (side note)

Evidences of Brahman Influence (side note)

Cambodia seem to have been the central points of Brahman influence. This influence was less important in the eastern part of the peninsula of Further India, which was both further from the Brahman starting-point, and more subject to Chinese civilisation. From Upper Burma to Cochin-China countless temple ruins are to be found at the present day, with rich ornamental sculptures and Sanscrit inscriptions, bearing evidence of the force of Brahman influence in earlier ages.

Every year important discoveries are made, especially in those districts which the French have opened up. Most of the traditional names of the kings of Cambodia are to be read in inscriptions in their Sanscrit form from the third century A.D. to 1108. At a later period within this district Sanscrit writing gave way to the native Khmer script. Inscribed memorials, carvings, and building generally, make it clear that Siva and his son, Ganesa, the god with the elephant head, were the most widely distributed of the Brahman gods. The images and symbols of these gods are far more numerous than those of the other figures of Hindu mythology. At the same time Vishnu was highly venerated. The most important and beautiful Brahman temples of Further India are dedicated to this god, instances being the temples of Angkor Thom and of Angkor Wat, built, as we learn from the evidence of the inscriptions, in 825.

Gods of Further India (side note)

At the time when the early exponents of Brahmanism advanced to China, Buddhism had also taken root in their native land, being considered then merely a special variant of the belief in the old gods. Hence, with the transmission of Brahmanism, the seeds of Buddhism were undoubtedly sown in Indo-China. As Buddha himself was received into the cult of Vishnu as being the incarnation of this god, so, during the flourishing period of Brahmanism in Champa and Cambodia, his images were erected and worshipped within the temples dedicated to Siva or Vishnu.

Buddhism advanced to Indo-China by two routes. The first of these led straight from India and Ceylon to the opposite coast. According to the tradition, Buddhaghosha, in the fifth century A.D., after making his translation of the sacred scriptures into Pali, introduced the doctrine of Buddha into the country, starting from the island of Ceylon. Resemblances between the script of Cambodia and the Pali of Ceylon testify to the contact of the civilisation and religion of these two countries. Subsequently, however, the northern or Sanscrit developments of Buddhism had advanced to Further India by way of Central and Eastern Asia.

The doctrine in this form was first transmitted to the vigorous and half-barbaric tribes of the mountainous highlands, who seem to have accepted it readily. At any rate, the Thai races—Laos, Shans, and Siamese—who migrated southward at a later period, were undoubtedly zealous Buddhists. Their advance about the end of the first and second centuries A.D. implies a definite retrogression on the part of Brahmanism in Indo-China. The Brahman gods decay, and the temples sink into ruins. Upon their sites arise buildings which, in their poverty of decoration and artistic conception, correspond to the

Decay of Brahmanism in Further India humility of Buddhist theology and metaphysics. In Cambodia alone did Brahmanism maintain its position for a time, as is evidenced by buildings and inscriptions from the sixth to the thirteenth centuries. About the year 700 the northern type of Buddhism made an unobtrusive entrance, and King Jayawarman V., who

reigned from 968 to 1002 undertook reforms on its behalf. But it was not until 1295 that the schools fell into the hands of the Buddhists, and Buddhism did not become the State religion in Cambodia before 1320.

Buddhism Increases its Influence At that date, the Southern, or Pali, Buddhism had also found adherents in the country. Brahmanism, however, had been very deeply rooted, as is proved by the numerous Sanscrit words borrowed by the modern languages of Further India, and also by many special practices which have persisted to the present day. Vishnu, Siva, and Ganesa, though no longer worshipped as gods, were honoured as heroes, and their images in bronze and stone decorated the temples side by side with the images of Buddha, as, for instance, in the temple of Wat Bot Phram at Bangkok. Vishnu remains one of the heraldic devices on the royal banner of Siam, and the kings of this empire show special favour to the Brahmans in their districts who cling to the old beliefs. They alone are allowed to prepare holy water, and play a predominant part in many palace ceremonies. The aristocracy of Cambodia still lays claim to certain privileges which remind us of those possessed by the Kshatriyas, or Rajputs, in the Brahman caste system.

A STRETCH OF THE VALLEY OF THE IRAWADDI IN BURMA
The Irawaddi is the main highway of commerce in Burma, and its many-mouthed delta makes a prolific rice field.

EAST FRONT OF THE GREAT SHIVE DAGON PAGODA AT RANGOON

This picture can but imperfectly convey an idea of the splendour of the magnificent edifice, which, for the light elegance of its contour, and the happy combination of its several parts, may be fairly said to challenge for beauty any other of its class in India. The building is composed entirely of teak-wood, and the most unwearied pains have not been spared upon the profusion of rich carved work which ornaments it. The whole is one mass of the richest gilding, with the exception of the three roofs, which are silvered. The carved work is so highly executed as to resemble alto-rilievo.

COUNTRIES OF FURTHER INDIA
BURMA AND THE MALAY PENINSULA

FROM the times when, thanks to Ptolemy, a more definite light is thrown upon the affairs of Further India the general history of Indo-China appears characterised by a tripartite division corresponding to the three main geographical districts of the peninsula ; we have to-day the western district, facing the Indian Ocean, the central district, watered by the rivers of the Salwen, Menam, and Mekong, and the eastern district, most easily accessible from China and facing the Chinese Sea.

The earliest sources of Burmese history are of Chinese origin. From the Chinese annals we hear of struggles with the inhabitants of the north-west of Further India during the first century B.C. In these struggles the old capital of Tagong ceased to exist, and further Chinese incursions took place between 166 and 241 A.D.

Burma Before Our Era The earlier history of the country rests solely upon vague tradition. These traditions enable us dimly to observe the persistence of an incessant struggle between petty kingdoms which rise to power and again disappear.

From this constant change a number of larger and more tenacious bodies politic originate. Such is the state of Arakan on the northern coast, which was colonised from Burma, but strongly influenced by India by reason of its neighbourhood to that country. Under its king, Gaw-Laya, it held the predominance over Bengal, Pagan, Pegu, and Siam about 1138, and about 1450 it advanced from Sandoweh, beyond its central point of Akyab, to Chittagong. On the south we have the state of Maiaya Desa, so called after the principal tribe, and—more important than either of the foregoing—the two states of Burma and Pegu. The history of these latter is the history of an incessant struggle between two races—the Burmese, who

advanced from the north, and the native Mons.

The earliest mythology of the Burmese speaks of Prome in the fifth century A.D. as the capital of a primordial kingdom. At a later period certain rebels emigrated from Prome and founded Pagan, which became the central point of a new kingdom, and flourished from the seventh **The Early Burmese Dynasties** to the ninth centuries. About 1060 it was sufficiently powerful to conquer, under the leadership of Anuruddha, or Anorat azo, the Talaing kingdom of Sadou, but was destroyed about 1300 by the dynasty of Panja. The period during which Tagong was the capital of the old Burmese kingdom coincides with the distribution of Indian civilisation by the Brahmans. According to Brahman legends, Tagong on the Irawaddi was founded by King Abhiraja about 500 years before our era. At any rate, the rulers of Tagong were entirely subject to the influence of foreign civilisation. Tradition has preserved long lists of names belonging to different dynasties, in which there is an attempt to establish an original connection with the royal families of early India. Individual members of these lists are still celebrated as mighty heroes in Burmese popular songs.

The scanty substratum of historical truth that can first be derived from the native legends displays the first thousand **Chinese Aggression in Burma** years of our era as an age of restless movement, and of struggles fought out between the individual states, and also against the Singhalese, and in particular the Chinese, who attempted to reduce Burma under their supremacy when they were not themselves occupied by internal disturbances. At a later period Chinese incursions were repeated, and as late as 1284 fierce battles against these powerful neighbours took place. It was not until

1305 that the Burmese ruler Minti succeeded in shaking off the dominion of China, until the time of Shan supremacy in that country. The darkness in which the details of Burmese history are veiled begins to disperse in the second half of the fourteenth century. The character of the development, however, remains unchanged; bloody wars between the two chief races, the Burmese and the Mons, brave and cruel rulers alternating with

SURRENDER OF RANGOON TO THE BRITISH
During the viceroyalty of Lord Dalhousie the British took Rangoon on April 14, 1852, after a blockade and assault by Commodore Lambert.

weaklings, and a general state of upheaval which affected the little states of the west, and even the kingdom of Central Indo-China.

In the year 1364, King Satomenchin, lord of the land of Sagoin and Panja, founded the Burmese capital of Ava, the classical Ratnapura, which for a long time was to be the central point of the history of the country. His successor, Mengyitsauke, increased his kingdom by

the conquest of Prome. He and the following kings defeated both the Arakanese in 1413 and later, and the Chinese in 1424, 1449, and 1477. The centre of power then shifted from Ava to Pegu, the ruler of which, Mentara, after subduing Burma and Arakan in 1540, then stormed Ayuthia, the capital of Siam, in spite of a most vigorous defence, and thus became paramount over the great kingdom in Central Indo-China in 1544. The Siamese repeatedly revolted, although their efforts were forcibly suppressed, and soon succeeded in freeing themselves from the supremacy of the Pegu king, Burankri Naunchan, who reigned from 1551 to 1581. Burma remained dependent upon Pegu for a longer period. Attempts to shake off the foreign yoke failed in 1585; Ava became a provincial town, and was reduced to ruin by neglect.

At the outset of the seventeenth century the forces of Pegu were expelled by Nyaung Mendarah; Ava was restored as the capital of Burma in 1601, while Pegu and the northern Shan states in the neighbourhood were subjugated. In 1636, however, Pegu freed itself from Ava, which its rulers then subdued, and Ava became the capital of the two united states. The balance of fortune and power continued to oscillate between these states. In the second half of the seventeenth century Pegu was predominant; the turn of Burma came at the outset of the eighteenth century. However, between 1740 and 1752 Burma suffered several severe defeats, and again became subject to Pegu. When Burma finally threw off the yoke of Pegu in 1753, the last section of her history as an independent state begins.

Europeans had set foot upon the soil of Indo-China several centuries previously; Malacca had been conquered by Albuquerque in 1511, and had become a stronghold of Portuguese influence in the Malay Archipelago; trading stations had also been founded on the north and west coasts of Further India, but the development

BURMESE HORSE AND FOOT SOLDIERS FIFTY YEARS AGO

of these was hindered by the continual struggles between Pegu and Burma. Upon occasion Portuguese knights and soldiers fought on one or the other side. Adventurers, both Portuguese and Spanish, gained a temporary reputation at the cost of a miserable end. However, European relations with Further India went no further than this. At a later period the English and the Dutch also founded settlements on the Burmese coast, but were collectively expelled in consequence of their tactless behaviour to the Burmese officials. It was not until the middle of the eighteenth century that the English, in return for the help which they gave to

SACRED WHITE ELEPHANT OUTSIDE THE PALACE AT AMARAPURA
Amarapura, literally "the city of the gods," a few miles from Mandalay, was the capital of Burma before 1860.

KING MENG DAN MENG
The well-meaning but incompetent ruler of Burma, who, in 1857, changed the capital from Amarapura to Mandalay.

Alompra, the Burmese liberator, obtained permission to found a factory on the island of Negraïs, at the mouth of the Bassein River, which carried on a considerable trade until October, 1759.

In 1740 Burma was overrun by Beinga-Della of Pegu, and the royal family was utterly exterminated. In 1753, however, Alompra collected a number of adherents in the village of Mozzobo. In a parable apparently emanating from Buddhaghosha we read the following contemptuous statement : " Of the twenty-one castes, nineteen can be released from their sins by good works ; but the huntsmen and fishers, though they visit the pagoda, hear the law, and keep the five commandments until the end of their lives, can never be released from their sins."

Castes Beyond Salvation Alompra drove out the Governor of Pegu and the brother of its king, Aporaza, who appeared in 1754 before Ava with a fleet. In 1755 he advanced upon Pegu and gained possession of the hostile capital in 1757. In memory of the victory of Synyangong on April 21, 1755, Rangoon was founded, a town which rapidly rose to great commercial importance by reason of its favourable geographical situation.

Pegu, which had struggled for so many centuries with Burma for predominance, ceased to exist in 1757. From that date Burma, which, by the occupation of Mergui and Tenasserim, even encroached upon Siam, was indisputably the first power in the west of the peninsula of Further India. After the death of Alompra, May 15th, 1760, his successor, Namdoji Prau, was confronted with the task of quelling revolts, repelling the attacks of the Chinese, who declined to tolerate the growth of this new Power on their southern frontier, and incorporating those petty states of Western Indo-China which had retained their independence. Shembaun (1763–66), the second successor of Alompra, successfully defended his empire against the Chinese, almost destroying their army under General Chien Lang before Ava ; in 1771 he temporarily conquered Siam and subdued Assam, which had hitherto maintained its independence both against India and Indo-China. Alompra's third son, the sixth king of the dynasty of 1757, Bhodau Phra, meaning royal grandfather, a brave ruler, though cruel and capricious, founded Amarapura as a new capital in 1783, and obliged

AN AUDIENCE WITH MENG DAN MENG
The King of Burma receiving the leaders of the Mission from the Governor-General of India at Amarapura in 1855.

1396

all the inhabitants of Ava to emigrate thither.

He suppressed revolts in Pegu with bloodthirsty severity, most cruelly persecuted the Buddhist doctrine, and, in 1874, incorporated Arakan, which he had captured by treachery, with his kingdom. Thus upon his death, in 1819, Burma had reached the zenith of its greatness and power. Phagyi-dau, the grandson and successor of Bhodau Phra, returned to residence in the capital of Ava. He inherited the capricious and irresponsible character of his father without any of his high talent. His exaggerated estimate of his own powers led to the first war with England from 1824 to 1826. By the peace of Yandabo, February 24th, 1826, Burma was deprived of most of its power, compelled to pay an indemnity of £1,000,000, to conclude a commercial treaty, and to receive a British Resident, and was confined to the basin of the Irawaddy ; its possessions now hardly extending beyond the delta of that river, including Rangoon. However, the rulers of the country had been taught nothing by the severe punishment which they had received. In 1837 Phagyi-dau, having become totally insane, was deposed and

Trouble with India

H. C. White Co.
A SCENE IN MANDALAY
The city of Mandalay was from 1860 to 1885 the capital of the Burmese kingdom and the residence of the king.

placed in confinement. His successor, Tharawadi, who was no less autocratic and short-sighted, declined to recognise the convention of Yandabo. The English missionaries were so badly treated that they were forced to evacuate the country, and the British Resident was withdrawn in 1840 in consequence of the insolent treatment which he had experienced.

In 1845 Tharawadi also went mad, and was deposed by his son Pagan Meng ; hostilities, however, still continued. British captains were insulted and payment of the indemnities demanded was refused. Burma was wilfully provoking a new war with England. The war came in 1852. In rapid succession, though at a price of considerable loss, the British troops captured Martaban on April 5, Rangoon, Bassein, Prome, and finally Pegu on November 21. On December 20, Lord Dalhousie proclaimed a new frontier line declaring Lower Burma, or Pegu, British territory. This was a fatal blow to Burmese independence, as the country was cut off from the coast and from communications by sea, and deprived of its most fruitful rice territory. This peace,

British Take Lower Burma

H. C. White Co.
BY THE TURTLE POND AT MANDALAY
The turtle is held in great veneration by the Burmese.

so favourable to England, placed her in complete possession of what had been the east coast of Burma on the Sea of Bengal. The rest of the native kingdom was placed in a position of entire dependency upon British India, the maintenance of good relations with England being thus indispensable. This, however, was a condition impossible of fulfilment by the Burmese rulers.

Pagan Meng was deposed in 1853 and succeeded by Meng dan Meng, a well-meaning ruler, benevolent to his subjects ; he was, however, wholly unable to grasp the situation, as is obvious from the fact that eighteen months after the incorporation of Pegu he sent an embassy to Calcutta requesting the restoration of the territory taken from the kingdom. For a long time he declined to sign the convention confirming the loss of Pegu. At the same time, under this king, who removed his capital from Amarapura to Mandalay in 1857, highly profitable relations were begun between Burma and British India. In 1862 Arakan, Martaban, Pegu, and Tenasserim were united into " British Burma" under Arthur Phayre as Chief Commissioner, and in 1874 Queda in Malacca was voluntarily ceded by its prince, and united to Tenasserim. In 1871 Italy, and in 1873 France, concluded commercial treaties with Burma, which manifested its interest in a definite connection with Europe by the despatch of ambassadors in 1872, 1874, and 1877.

Meng dan Meng died on October 1st, 1878, and was succeeded by Thebaw, a king of the type of Phagyi dau and Tharawadi. After his accession relations between the British and Burmese Governments became seriously strained. The king signalised the opening of his reign by massacring many of his nearest relatives,

BURMESE MAN AND WOMAN

Edwards

and things came to such a pass that it was no longer possible for the British envoy to remain in Mandalay. The crisis arrived in 1885, when a dispute arose between the king and a British mercantile company, on whom he had inflicted an impossible fine, threatening at the same time to confiscate their property in the event of non-payment. An ultimatum was sent to him by the British Government in October, 1885, and, on his failure to comply with it, preparations were made for the occupation of Mandalay. Within less than a fortnight of the declaration of hostilities, the capital was taken on the 28th of November and the king made prisoner. However, desultory fighting continued for a long time, and it was several years before the dacoits were finally put down and the country pacified. Upper and Lower Burma were made a division of the Indian Empire under a Lieutenant - Governor, and in 1886 the Burmese Shan States were incorporated in British India.

MALAY PENINSULA

The long tongue of land which curls out on the south-west of Indo-China is the Malay Peninsula. Of this, the north-western portion is part of Tenasserim, one of the provinces of Burma which was annexed to British India in the time of Lord Amherst. Another portion of the peninsula belongs to Siam. The general title is not unusually restricted to the remaining portion, otherwise described inclusively as Malacca.

The ethnology and early history of the region demand no detailed treatment here. We should merely be repeating what has already been said in the account of the Malay Archipelago. Even its more modern history requires but very brief notice. The value of Malaccan ports from their position on trade routes was recognised as soon as Europeans arrived in the Indian waters ; and Albuquerque himself was prompt to establish a Portuguese settlement at the town of Malacca, which gives its name to the whole territory. When the Dutch displaced the Portuguese in the archipelago, they displaced them also on the peninsula ; the petty native states, however, still subsisted. The Dutch possessions followed the regular course during the Napoleonic wars, when they fell into the hands of the British, but were ultimately restored at the peace.

During the British occupation of Java, Sir Stamford Raffles detected the immense potentialities of a station at Singapore, which, owing to his representations, was purchased from the Raja of Johore in 1819. Penang and the present-day Province Wellesley had been similarly acquired in 1785 and 1798.

In 1824 the British received the Dutch settlements of Malacca in exchange for those on Sumatra. For the time the " Straits Settlements " remained under the control of the Indian Government, but they were converted into a Crown colony in 1867 ; and since 1875, the native principalities have all accepted the

position of protectorates in relation to the Government at Singapore. Not many years after its acquisition, that town had become the British capital, in place of Penang, which had previously held that position. So great has its prosperity been, that the population has risen from about 10,000 to not very far short of 200,000 at the present day.

THE PRINCE OF WALES VISITING THE ARAKAN PAGODA

The Arakan Pagoda, the famous shrine at Mandalay, contains a great brass sitting image of Buddha, under a seven-roofed canopy with massive pillars and gorgeous mosaic ceiling.

VIEWS IN THE ROYAL PALACE OF BANGKOK

The picture at the top of the page gives a general view of the royal palace, and the bottom picture on the left is the throne room, which, with its pictures and chandelier, seems to partake of the magnificence of Louis XIV. rather than of a semi-barbaric potentate. The two pictures in the middle are views taken in the palace grounds, many of the buildings in which follow the Italian rather than the Oriental style. The last picture—that on the bottom right—is the Hall of Audience.

CHAMPA, CAMBODIA AND SIAM

IN Central Further India three kingdoms have successively secured predominance : Champa, Cambodia, and Siam. Our knowledge, however, of the early history of Central Indo-China is confined to the most general outlines.

This is especially true of Champa, the oldest of the three states. The earliest intelligible accounts display the Cham as a powerful people. At the time of its greatest prosperity, near the middle of the first century A.D., Champa was about the size of the modern Cambodia, though at different periods it also extended over Cochin-China, Annam, and even to Southern Tonquin. At the time of Ptolemy the civilisation was Brahman, early Sanscrit inscriptions covering the period from the third to the eleventh century A.D. ; from that date inscriptions are written in Champa, a special dialect strongly influenced by Sanscrit elements. The religion of the country was, as everywhere in Further India, chiefly Siva worship or Lingam ; scarce a trace of Buddhism is to be discovered during that period, and it was not until the downfall of the Champa kingdom that Buddhism became more deeply rooted in the district.

Wars with the Chinese, who were extending their supremacy over Tonquin, Annam, and Cochin-China, and driving out the Cham from those districts, occupy the period from the fourth to the tenth centuries of our era. The Champa were also forced to struggle with the Khmers, who had entered the country from the north according to the early traditions of Cambodia, and were settled in the north-east of the Champa kingdom in the days of Ptolemy. As early as the seventh century they pushed their way like a

SIVA, THE DESTROYER
Cambodians are nominally Buddhists, but they really follow a debased Buddhism, and their chief deity is Siva, the Hindu god who is commonly known as the destroyer of life.

wedge between the Champa kingdom and the states of Annam and Cochin-China, which were subject to China. We find them in full possession of Brahman civilisation ; the earliest written records of the Khmer state of Cambodia are in Sanscrit and belong to the third century ; in 626 this inscription mentions a King Isinawarman, whose three predecessors, Rudrawarman, Bhawawarman, and Mahendrawarman, can be inferred from the oldest Buddhist inscription but one, of the year 667 ; from the first of these kings the list of rulers is continued with but scanty interruption until the year 1108. A reliable eye-witness, the Chinese pilgrim Hiuen Tsang, visited the two states of Cambodia and Champa in the years 631–33, and mentions t h e i r towns Dewarawati, Chamapura, and Champapura. At this period Cambodia was a state of equal power to the earlier Champa kingdom. Even then, however, a dangerous movement became perceptible upon the northern frontier. From the Chinese frontier mountains, tribes of the Thai advanced southward to the borders of Cambodia. A branch of these immigrants, the Lao, settled upon the eighteenth degree of latitude in 547, and founded a state with the capital of Labong ; at a later period other smaller kingdoms of the Thai were formed. At the outset of the seventh century the Lao—in Chinese annals Ai-Lao—made a vigorous advance upon Cambodia. There, however, their power was broken.

Legend associates the defeat of the Thai with the name of the king, Phra Ruang ; the chronology dates from his government, the first year of which, 638 A.D., still forms a chronological starting-point throughout the whole of Central

Further India. The defeated enemy were absorbed into the local civilisation and adopted the writing and the laws of Cambodia. However, their youthful strength could not thus be permanently constrained; in the year 959 A.D. The Thai freed themselves, as is unanimously related by the early records of Cambodia and Siam. Driven on, perhaps, by the movement of the Khitan, who had invaded China in 937, they pressed on under their king, also known as Phra Ruang, to the south, and founded an independent kingdom at the expense of the Khmer state ; this was the nucleus from which was formed the principality of Xieng-Mai about 1250, and the more modern Siam at a somewhat later date. Like a flash in the darkness Kublai Khan, the Chinese Governor of Mangu, burst upon the Thai in 1253–54 ; the kingdom of Namchao, founded by a Thai tribe, was shattered, and the Shan were driven to their present habitations. The Thai kingdom of Sukhodaya on the river Menam, which extended from Ligor to Wingchau and to the great Lake of Cambodia under the rule of Râma Khomheng, suffered but little. The Thai of Siam continued their advance, hemming in the Cham and pressing hard upon the Khmer ; at the end of the thirteenth century they had already reached the mouth of the Menam. Siam had then practically attained its present extension. The Champa kingdom had dwindled to a small district in the south, and Cambodia had been driven south-east-ward. The first period of modern Siamese history begins with King Ramathibodi, who ascended the throne in 1344, and rapidly extended the kingdom by conquest over a large part of Cambodia, and as far as

KING OF CAMBODIA IN 1863
In 1863, Cambodia became a protectorate of France, and though nominally a monarchy, it is now practically a French province.

PEASANT WOMAN OF CAMBODIA

the Malacca peninsula on the south-west. As the centre of gravity in the kingdom had thus changed, the capital of Chaliang was removed further south in 1350 to Ayuthia, which was erected upon the ruins of the old Daona. Cambodia was again attacked and conquered in the years 1353 and 1357 ; the newly-founded capital was peopled with the prisoners, and the weakened neighbour kingdom was forced to cede the province of Chantabum to Siam. The successors to the great Phra-Utong were busied with the task of checking their northern neighbours, of restraining the aggression of Champa, which had sunk to the position of a piratical state, of bringing Malacca under the supremacy of Siam, and of punishing a revolt in Cambodia by the complete destruction of the capital town ; the Khmer were, consequently, removed to the swampy lowlands on the coast. A number of less important rulers then came to the throne, who had much difficulty in maintaining the power of the empire, and under them came that first contact with the European world which has so deeply influenced the modern history of Indo-China. In 1511 King Borommaraja, while re-conquering the revolted province of Malacca, came into contact with the Portuguese, who had occupied the town and fortress of Malacca in the same year ; relations profitable to both parties were begun between the Powers, and a commercial treaty was concluded. With this exception Siam remained for the moment untouched by European influence. The domestic history of the country is characterised by disturbances, quarrels for the succession, and the rule of favourites and women.

So long as peace continued abroad, the weakness of the kingdom passed unnoticed. It collapsed, however, incontinently when the powerful Pegu turned against it after securing the predominance in Burma ; King Mentara invaded the country with a large force, and the inhabitants of Cambodia seized the opportunity of joining in the military operations. Notwithstanding a desperate resistance, the capital of Ayuthia surrendered in 1544, and Siam became a tributary vassal state of Pegu. Hardly had the country begun to recover from these disasters, and to think of its lost independence, when a new invasion by Mentara in 1547 checked its aspirations. The capital, defended by

the present day he is honoured as the great national hero of Siam. In 1564 he utterly defeated the forces of Pegu, and in 1566 peopled the somewhat deserted capital with the prisoners. In the north he reduced the Lao under his power in the two following years, and in the year 1569 he secured his recognition by China as the legitimate King of Siam.

The high ambitions of Phra Naret were directed to extending the Siamese power over the whole of Indo-China. His first task was to shatter Pegu, the previous oppressor of his fatherland. For this campaign the King of Cambodia offered his help ; but when the Siamese troops had marched to Pegu, he treacherously

THE PYRAMID AND PAGODA AT PNOM-PENH, THE CAPITAL OF CAMBODIA

Portuguese knights, resisted all efforts at capture, and Mentara returned home without accomplishing his purpose. In 1556, however, Ayuthia was stormed by Chumigren, the successor of Mentara, and almost the whole population was carried into captivity ; Siam then became a province of Pegu.

Chumigren was so short-sighted as to set up the brother-in-law of the last King of Siam as Governor of the country ; he was a capable man, who transmitted his strong patriotism and love of independence to his highly-gifted son, Phra Naret, who was in power from 1558 to 1593. With him begins the second great popular movement in modern Siamese history ; and even at

invaded the undefended land of his ally. He was beaten back, but the war of Phra Naret with Pegu proved long and arduous in consequence, and it was not until 1579 that the struggle ended with the complete subjugation of Pegu to the power of Siam. Vengeance was now taken upon the ruler of Cambodia for his treachery ; in 1583 he was defeated and captured, and his capital of Lawek was utterly destroyed. In 1587 the outbreak of disturbances in Pegu and Cambodia necessitated the presence of Phra Naret ; when, however, after punishing the instigators of the movement, he proposed in 1593 to conquer the kingdom of Ava, or Burma, his victorious career was suddenly cut short by death.

1403

THE GREAT TOWER OF THE PAGODA
OF WAT-CHING AT BANGKOK

The reign of this great king was followed
by more than a century and a half of weak
rulers, grievous confusion, bloody conflicts
about the succession—in 1627 the house
of Phra Naret was exterminated, and the
Minister, Kalahom, founded a new dynasty
under the title of Phra Chau Phra-satthong
—revolts among the people in the provinces, especially in 1615, and embarrassments abroad. Only upon one occasion did it appear as if Siam had any chance
of advancing to higher prosperity.

In the year 1656 a Venetian adventurer
of Cephallenia, by name Constantine
Phaulkon—in Siamese, Phra Klang ; in
French, M. Constance—entered the country. By his cleverness and capacity he
gained the favour of the reigning king,
Narai, who heaped honours upon him and
appointed him to responsible positions,
ultimately giving him almost unlimited
power in every department of governmental business. Permission was given
to the Dutch, the English, the Portuguese,
and the French to found trading settlements. Communication was improved by
the scientific construction of roads and
canals, and the prosperity of the country
rapidly increased. The French received
special favour from Phaulkon ; in 1663

they were allowed to build a Catholic
church in Ayuthia and to erect a mission
under Lamotte Lambert. King Louis
XIV. and Pope Clement X. sent an
embassy to Siam in 1673 to further
the prosperity of Christianity, a friendly
movement answered in like manner
by Phaulkon in 1684. In 1685, with
Chevalier de Chaumont as ambassador,
a fleet left France, and stations at
Bangkok and Mergui were granted under
a convention in 1687 ; these places
the French fortified, but the encroachments of the garrison under the command
of Volantz du Bruant and des Farges soon
aroused popular animosity. So far-reaching an organisation had been too rapidly
initiated ; Phaulkon fell a victim to a
popular revolt, formed by the mandarins
Phra Phet Ratscha, Wisuta Songtong,
and others, and was put to death in 1689 ;
the reforms he had introduced were, as
far as possible, abolished, the French were
expelled in 1690, and the missions and
native Christians were subjected to severe
oppression. Under the weak rulers
who succeeded—Phra Phet Racha, from
1689 to 1700, succeeded by his sons
and grandsons—the power of Siam
rapidly decayed. Once again the

RICHLY CARVED TOWERS OF THE PAGODA
OF WAT-CHING AT BANGKOK

deepest humiliation was to come from the west. In the neighbouring kingdom of Burma, Alompra had led his people from victory to victory, and had overthrown his hereditary enemy of Pegu. He now proposed to conquer Siam, but after advancing almost to Ayuthia without meeting resistance, he died suddenly in 1760. However, his successor, Shembuan, again invaded the country in 1766 ; in 1767 the capital of Siam was captured and burnt, and the king, who was wounded, perished in the flames.

The fall of the capital and the death of the king left the country at the mercy of the conqueror, who, however, placed but a scanty garrison in occupation.

Burmese, who could not forget or forgive the loss of Siam. He became insane, and was murdered in a popular revolt. Cambodia as a separate state loses all importance from this time.

The position of Phaya Tak was taken in 1782 by his Prime Minister, Chakri, the ancestor of the present dynasty. At that period a French bishop, Béhaine, had gained complete influence over the successor to the throne of the neighbouring kingdom of Annam, and France began to interfere more decisively in the domestic affairs of Eastern Indo-China. The growth of European influence and the action of ecclesiastical ambassadors excited the apprehension of the natives ;

PAGODA AT MOUNT PHRABAT, SIAM, WHERE BUDDHA'S FOOTPRINT IS PRESERVED

Upon the north, where the strength of the Thai was, as ever, concentrated chiefly on their native soil, a Siamese governor was appointed, by name Phaya Tak, a Chinese by birth. He gathered as many men capable of bearing arms as he could, drove back the Burmese, and secured recognition by China after the extinction of the dynasty of 1627. As Ayuthia had been utterly destroyed, the capital was transferred to Bangkok, at the mouth of the Menam, in 1678, which rapidly rose to a great commercial town. This success brought power ; in the same year Phaya Tak subdued Cambodia and the smaller southern states and also the Laos in the North ; in 1777 he defeated the

in Siam the new king and his successors— Pierusing until 1809 ; Phendingkang, from 1809 to 1824 ; Crom Chiat, or Kroma Mom Chit, from 1824 to 1851—manifested their ill-feeling to the foreigners. Embarrassments were constantly placed in the way of the missions and decrees hostile to the Christian religion were repeatedly promulgated. It was not until the years 1840–50 that the French bishop, D. J. B. Pallegoix, to whom the education of the Crown Prince of Siam had been entrusted, succeeded in securing full religious toleration from the prince upon his accession in April, 1851.

Ever since the brilliant career of Phaulkon a certain alarmed astonishment had been the prevailing spirit with which Siam regarded France. The young ruler, Chou Fa-Mongkut, a member of that branch of the ruling house which had been expelled in 1824, attempted in 1851 to enter into closer relations with the Emperor Napoleon through his ambassadors and under his brother and successor, Somdet Phra Paramindr Maha Mongkut (1852–68), and a commercial treaty was concluded with France in 1856, with Britain in 1855, with Germany in 1862, and with Austria in 1858. Peaceful relations with France continued during the reign of King Paramindr Maha Chulalongkorn, who ascended the throne of Siam at the age of fifteen, on October 1st, 1868, and took the power from the hands of his trusted Minister Chau Phraya Sri Suriyawongse on November 16th, 1873. In 1884 France obtained a protectorate over Annam, and the British secured possession of the whole of Burma in 1886, Siam being the only important state of Further India which retained its independence. On May 8th, 1874, the constitution was re-organised, the legislative power being exercised by the king in concert with the great State Council and the Cabinet of Ministers. With the advance of Great Britain and France to her western and eastern boundaries respectively, Siam became an object of increasing interest to Europe. The two European Powers were actually in contact to the north of Siam on the acquisition by

KING MONGKUT OF SIAM AND HIS QUEEN
This king ruled from 1851 to 1868 and was remarkably progressive; he knew Latin and English.

THE "SECOND" KING OF SIAM
King Mongkut's younger brother was crowned as second king, and held this office until his death, in 1885, when the post was abolished.

Britain of the Burmese Shan states of Kyaing Hung and Kyaing Chaing, over which, however, China had claimed a nominal suzerainty. Both, moreover, cast covetous eyes on the trade of Siam, of which England possessed about ninety per cent., while France held only a very small fraction. The latter Power in particular was anxious to extend her dominions; her colonial party cherished the dream of incorporating the whole of Siam in their empire, and were determined, at any rate, to push their frontier up to the Mekong River. The leading statesmen in both countries were anxious to come to an agreement both about Siam itself and the creation of a buffer state on the north, the English proposing to cede Kyaing Hung to China and Kyaing Chaing to Siam, with a reversion to themselves in case either China or Siam parted with these states. Negotiations were opened between the French Ambassador in London and the British Government as early as 1889; but though they were broken off and renewed several times, nothing had been settled when hostilities broke out between the French and Siamese early in 1893. Whether rightly or wrongly, the French accused the Siamese of invading Annam, and announced their intention of extending their frontier to the Mekong. After a certain amount of desultory fighting, during which the French occupied one or two posts on the Mekong, two French gunboats forced their way up to Bangkok, and the French

THE ROYAL HOUSE OF SIAM

The two centre pictures represent King Chulalongkorn I. of Siam in uniform; on the lower right he appears in his religious ceremonial costume, and at the top of the page he is dressed as an English gentleman with his sons in Eton suits, while the lady at the bottom left is his first queen.

Group by W. & D. Downey, London

Government proceeded to dictate terms to Siam. These they subsequently enforced by a short blockade of the Menam. The principal demand of the French was the cession of all Siamese territory on the left bank of the Mekong. including a great portion of the province of Luang Prabang, and this was eventually embodied in the treaty of peace, **War between** which was signed on October **Siam** 3rd, 1893. Negotiations were **and France** at the same time being conducted between England and France with a view to the delimitation of their frontier and the creation of a buffer state to the north. But, unfortunately, these for the time came to nought, France being allowed to incorporate the land east of the Mekong to which Great Britain had a reversion in addition to the Siamese territory proper. In January, 1896, however, the two countries came to an agreement by which they guaranteed the independence of the Menam valley, which contains by far the larger part of the population and trade of Siam, though the authority of the king over the parts not included in the agreement was not intended by any means to be impaired. The chief cause of friction between England and France was thereby removed, though the Mekong alone separates their empires and the north of Siam. The treaty of 1893 has been followed by a more recent one between France and

Siam, by which further territorial concessions have been made to France in the west of the Lower Mekong.

Siam has thus enjoyed peace and has been steadily developing since 1893. Although her territory has been considerably diminished, she has full autonomy and is in a stronger position than she has held for a long time past. By employing European advisers and assistants in nearly all the Government departments, she has made considerable progress in various branches of administration. Her finances have been put on a much more secure basis, and her revenue is gradually increasing, while the corruption that was so prevalent a short time ago has been in great measure put down. The administration of justice and education has advanced steadily, the police force has been reorganised, and a system of provincial gendarmerie has been established. The railways have been gradually **Present** expanding, in particular the **Progress** main line to the north, which **in Siam** is destined to connect Bangkok with Chiengmai; but the interior of the country is still largely undeveloped, and when communications are further opened up in the matter of roads, railways, and canals, it will undoubtedly prove quite a rich one. Lower Siam produces excellent rice in increasing quantities, and the teak forests in the north are of great commercial value.

An Amazon Guard · A rope dancer · An actress
SOME OF THE QUAINT TYPES AND COSTUMES OF SIAM

TONQUIN, ANNAM AND COCHIN-CHINA

FROM an early period the history of Eastern Further India, which is naturally conjoined to China by the configuration of the continent, has been inseparably bound up with that powerful empire which developed a civilisation at an unusually early period. Early reports speak of an embassy from Tonquin to the Imperial Court in the second millennium before our era, and of the foundation of Chinese dynasties in that district in 214 B.C. and 109 A.D. Chinese civilisation, however, which was bound to expand, did not stop at Tonquin. China had already established herself in Annam and Cochin-China, and had made considerable progress when the Brahman movement began to advance northward from Cambodia. There the earlier civilisation was predominant, and in a large degree determined the nature of the development of Annam. The forerunners of Brahmanism made no great progress, except in Cochin-China, **The Chinese Influence in Indo-China** and left but few traces in Annam, and practically none in Tonquin. From that remote epoch when the first dynasties were founded in Tonquin, China for more than a thousand years — until 968—firmly established herself in Eastern Indo-China, though her influence varied with the fortunes of Chinese history at large.

When China proper was in difficulties from internal disturbances, changes of dynasties, or the attack of powerful foes, she exercised little more than a shadowy predominance. Thus during the years 222–618 her powers in Annam were greatly limited, and the local governors availed themselves of the embarassments of the empire to make themselves almost independent. At other periods China governed Eastern Further India with a firmer hand. Thus in the first half century A.D. revolts were suppressed in Cochin-China—which also made itself independent for a short period in 263—and after the powerful Tang dynasty had gained the Chinese throne China once again brought the larger part of Annam and Cochin-China into close dependence upon herself.

In the tenth century, when China was again shattered by internal convulsions, the movements for independence in Annam were again victorious, and their success was permanent from the year 968 to 981. **Chinese Dynasty in Annam** During that period one of the Chinese governors, by name Li, founded in Annam the dynasty known by his name (1010–1225); Tonquin threw off the Chinese yoke in 1164, as did Cochin-China in 1166. China again reduced the rebellious provinces, but only for a time; the emperor, Kublai Khan, subdued Tonquin and also Annam and Cambodia. However, the two last-named states speedily recovered their independence, and Tonquin drove the Chinese out of the country in 1288.

In the fourteenth and at the beginning of the fifteenth century China again secured a footing in Eastern Further India; under the Ming dynasty Annam became tributary to China in 1368, and Tonquin with Cochin-China became a Chinese province; then during the years 1418-27 the Nationalist movement in these states became so strong that the Chinese lost all semblance of power. The leader of this movement, Le Lo, was the founder of the Le dynasty, which ruled for a long period in Annam and Tonquin, with the capital town Hanoi, founded in 1427; by embassies and presents of homage, he made a formal recognition of Chinese supremacy, but henceforward China could no longer interfere in the domestic affairs of **European Advance to Indo-China** Annam. The European advance to the east of Further India produced for the moment more important consequences in this district than in the south and west. Since 1511 Portuguese, and afterwards Dutch, factories had been founded, and from 1610 missions and small native Christian congregations existed. The country and its rulers were at first indifferent,

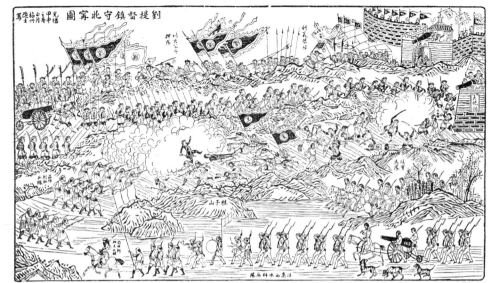

THE FRENCH WAR IN TONQUIN IN 1884: VICTORY OF GENERAL MILLOT AT BACNINH
This spirited picture of the battle, in which 25 Frenchmen were killed, is from a drawing by a Chinese artist.

and afterwards generally hostile to all foreigners; trade ceased almost entirely in the eighteenth century, while the missions and Christian congregations were regarded with suspicion, often bitterly persecuted, and ultimately forced to continue a doubtful existence in secret.

The powerful rulers of the house of Le were succeeded by a succession of weaker princes in the sixteenth century. Under them some parts of Annam became independent in 1558, and the Le dynasty would

have collapsed entirely without the assistance of skilled officials, who became so important that they secured, in 1545, the position of hereditary Minister, much like the Peshwas in the Mahratta States. Nguyen Hoang—Tien Wuong until 1614—in Cochin-China broke away from these officials, and from the nominal ruler in 1570, and became the ancestor of the present ruler of Annam. His successors increased their kingdom by incorporating the remnants of Champa and of Southern

CAPTURE OF HAI-FONG, TONQUIN: AN INCIDENT IN THE FRENCH OPERATIONS OF 1873

1410

Cambodia—the six provinces of the modern lower Cochin-China—and were resident in Huë. These changes caused a considerable degree of complication in the political affairs of Eastern Indo-China during the seventeenth and most of the eighteenth centuries. China claimed a formal supremacy, though she exercised no actual interference. The Le dynasty continued to be the nominal rulers of Annam ; in reality, however, Annam with Cochin-China and Tonquin had become two separate states, which were often involved in furious struggles against one another. The actual rulers of Annam were the descendants of Nguyen Hoang, and in Tonquin the house of Trigne.

European relations with the country had entirely ceased in the eighteenth

southern portion of the kingdom of his ancestors. He sent his son to France with the bishop in 1787, and on November 18th secured the conclusion of an offensive and defensive alliance from Louis XVI. ; by this arrangement France was to receive the Gulf and the Peninsula of Turon, while Nguyen Angne was to be helped by France to conquer the rest of Annam. The execution of this compact on the part of France was largely hindered by the French Revolution ; however, Nguyen Angne, who was supported by the Bishop Adrian, secured the assistance of many French officers, who drilled his troops in European fashion, and conducted the military operations. He was then able between the years 1792 and 1799 to subdue, not only Annam and the Tay Son, but also, in 1802, Tonquin, which

A CHARACTERISTIC SCENE IN HANOI, THE CAPITAL CITY OF TONQUIN

century ; an English attempt under Catchpoole, in 1702, to settle in the island of Pulo Condore came to an end in 1704 with the murder of the settlers by the natives, and the destruction of the factory. It was not until the end of the eighteenth century that Annam came closely into connection with France.

A general rising incited by three brothers of low birth, the Tay Son, entirely transformed the political situation of Annam in 1755 ; the old dynasties of the Le, and the mayors of the palace of the Trigne, entirely disappeared, while the Nguyen family became almost extinct. Only the grandson of the last king of this family, by name Nguyen Angne, escaped to Siam, where he was educated by a French bishop ; he then recovered the most

had meanwhile thrown off the rule of the Tay Son and secured the predominance in Cambodia.

The kingdom had long become a mere shadow of that larger empire which had existed at the time of the emigration of the Siam Thais. Since 1583, when Phra Naret had dipped his feet in the blood of its king, who was beheaded before him, the kingdom had been forced to submit to Siam. The misery of the country was increased by continuous disturbances at home and entanglements abroad with Siam, the Laos, and Annam ; the kings continually retreated before their powerful neighbour, and finally transferred their capital to Saigon on the coast, which occupied the site of the town known to Arrian as Thinai. An attempt on the part of

MAN AND WOMAN OF ANNAM

Cambodia to avail itself of the Siamese disasters in the war with the Burmese, Alompra, came to nothing ; in 1794 the vassal ruler, Somrath Phra Marai, who was set up by Siam, ceded Battambong and Siemrat to his patron in return. From 1806 onwards the impoverished country paid tribute both to Siam and Annam ; it held two seals, one from each of the two neighbouring states, and the kings of Cambodia did homage to each of these Powers.

Thanks to his French auxiliaries, Nguyen Angne proved brilliantly successful, and henceforward to his title of Emperor or King of Annam he added the royal title of " Gia long "—that is, the man favoured by fortune. Once in power, he became suspicious of the foreigners, whose importance he understood better than any other ruler in Further India. While removing his favour, he made no exhibition of open hostility. His Minister of ecclesiastical affairs is said to have had translated into Annamese for the king's benefit, about 1788, a somewhat immoral novel, a fact which throws much light upon the morality and the education prevalent in the court of Annam at that period.

His successor, Minhmang (1720-1841), was at first tolerant towards foreigners ; but the political intrigues of the French and Spanish missionaries roused him to

animosity against the Europeans. In 1833 the missionaries were cruelly persecuted ; in 1838 he forbade Europeans to enter his country, and the profession of Christianity was publicly declared a crime as heinous as high treason. In the same year thirty-three French priests fell victims to this decree. Thie utri, 1841-47, the son and successor of Minhmang, relaxed the persecution by merely imprisoning the missionaries, four of whom were liberated in 1843 upon the threats of the French. Generally speaking, however, the oppression continued, and in 1847 France demanded full religious toleration through Commodore Lapierre, which was granted after the fleet of Annam had been destroyed. In the same year the emperor died.

He was succeeded by his son, Tuduk, who was at first well disposed towards the Christians, and reigned until July 17, 1883. Once again the missionaries interfered in a question as to the succession to the throne, and made the young emperor the furious enemy of foreigners and Christians alike. Severe persecutions broke out in 1848 and 1851. France, who considered herself the Power responsible for the Christians in Asia, ultimately sent out ships and troops in September, 1856.

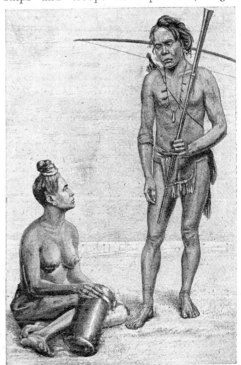

SAVAGE TYPES OF ANNAMESE

Turon was stormed in 1856, but on the morning when the ships sailed away Annam replied with a fresh persecution of the Christians and the murder of the Spanish bishop, Diaz, in 1857. France now made a vigorous effort in co-operation with Spain. On September 1st, 1858, Commodore Charles Rigault de Genouilly again captured Turon and took the town of Saigon in February, 1859. The plan of campaign was then changed ; in 1860 Napoleon III. issued orders to evacuate Annam and to occupy only Cochin-China, the vassal state of Annam. Meanwhile war had broken out with China ; operations were thereby hindered, and were not resumed until after the peace of Pekin. In the beginning of 1861 Vice-Admiral Page destroyed the fortifications on the banks of the Mekong. Admiral Bonard, who had taken over the command in December, 1861, won a victory on January 19th, 1862, at Monglap, conquered the whole province of Saigon, and captured several important towns in Cambodia. Tuduk was forced to conclude

DUY-TAN, THE CHILD KING OF ANNAM
The little King of Annam is the fifth son of the King who was deposed by the French in 1907 for his atrocities. The child of a humble servant of the palace, he is a grave, sweet-faced little creature, who behaved at his Coronation, in 1907, with great dignity, and made a quaint speech to the French Governor-General.

peace on June 15th, at the price of the cession of the three provinces of Saigon, Bienhoa, and Mytho.

Disturbances broke out in December, leading to fresh negotiations, and a definite peace was not concluded until July 15th, 1864. France then returned the above-named provinces, retaining Saigon, and, in spite of the protestations of Siam, undertook a protectorate over Cambodia, a tie which was drawn closer by the convention of June 17th, 1884. The actual ruler is not the king, but the French Resident in Pnom Penh. Fresh outbreaks in Annam necessitated further military operations on the part of France in 1867. The result was the definite loss of those three provinces which now form French Cochin-China.

Meanwhile, a descendant of the Le dynasty, Le Phung, had made himself master of Eastern Tonquin, and of the province of Vac Nigne. However, when Tuduk found himself free to act in 1864, he was cruelly put to death. Even then Tonquin was not pacified. From 1850

GROUP OF ANNAMESE SOLDIERS

War mandarin

A group of soldiers

Civil mandarin

TYPES OF THE SOLDIERS AND OFFICIALS OF COCHIN-CHINA

the great neighbouring empire in the north had been shaken by the Taipings, and it was not until 1865 that the rebels in the southern provinces of Kwangsi and Kwangtung were overpowered. Many of the rebels fled into the province of Annam under Ua Tsong, where, under the " black flag," they disturbed the peace of this much-tried country as banditti and river pirates.

When France established herself in Annam she had other views than the mere extension of her empire. Reports had long previously been in circulation concerning the fabulous natural wealth of the southern provinces of China and of Yunnan in particular. The British and the French were striving to intercept one another in the race for these treasures. Upon the incorporation of Burma, Great Britain gained a water-way, enabling her to advance into the immediate neighbourhood

NATIVE VILLAGE AND TYPICAL LANDSCAPE IN COCHIN-CHINA

of Yunnan. The French were now in possession of the mouth of a great river coming from the north to the Mekong, and proceeded to investigate the possibility of its navigation. For this purpose it proved impracticable. Captain Dontard de Lagrée, from 1866 to 1868, established the fact that the rapids in the immediate neighbourhood of the river mouth formed an impassable obstacle. The Songka, or Red River, in Tonquin offered better prospects. Dupuis, an enterprising Frenchman, fitted out an expedition to this stream at his own expense. In 1870 he advanced up the river in ships as far as Yunnan, and entered into relations with the Chinese mandarins. Hostilities on the part of the Annamese made it necessary to despatch Lieutenant Garnier, in 1873, who, with less than two hundred French troops, subdued in a few months in Tonquin a country populated by a million of inhabitants and twice the size of Belgium.

The French Parliament declined, however, to sanction the results of those successes in Tonquin. The troops were withdrawn, Garnier having been killed on December 31st, 1873, by a treacherous attack of the pirates, and France contented herself with the conclusion of a treaty on March 15th, 1874, obliging Annam to throw open to European trade three additional harbours—Ninh hai at Hai phong, Hanoi, and Thinai or Qui nhon—to grant full religious tolerance, and to apply to France alone for help in suppressing revolts. A commercial treaty was also concluded on August 31st, which, however, was not kept by Annam in spite of its confirmation by that country.

Annam displayed an unvarying spirit of hostility to France, until that Power lost patience. Hanoi was bombarded in 1882, and the French again advanced into Tonquin, where the pirates caused a great deal of trouble, Major Henri Laurent Rivière being killed by an ambuscade on

THE KING OF CAMBODIA IN 1907
King Sisowath, the nominal monarch of Cambodia, but the virtual vassal of France, in full state dress.

May 19th, 1883. By degrees one fortress after another was captured by Rear-Admiral A. A. P. Courbet, including Sontay, which had been occupied by the Chinese. Vao Nigne was also taken by General Charles Theodore Millot in March, 1884. Tuduk, the ruler of Annam, had died in July, 1883, and had been succeeded by his brother, Hiephoa. On August 21st, 1883, by a treaty which was ratified and extended on June 6th, 1884, he was forced to cede further provinces, to recognise the protectorate of France, and to renounce all political connection with other Powers, China included, which had declared in Paris, through the Marquis Tseng in 1882, its refusal to acknowledge the convention of 1874.

In the convention of Tientsin, dated May, 1884, China, which had seriously entertained the project of armed interference in Tonquin, fully recognised the French demands, including the protectorate of Annam and Tonquin. Still she did not withdraw her troops from Langsonin Tonquin, and the struggle continued with varying success for some time, the French suffering considerable losses at the hands of the pirates. Ultimately, British mediation brought about the Peace of London on April 4th, 1885 — confirmed at Tientsin on June 9th —whereby China withdrew all her troops from Tonquin and recognised the French protectorate over these states, which she had ruled, or at any rate claimed, for thousands of years. In May, 1886, the power of the pirates, who were no longer supported by China, was finally shattered. Since April 12th, 1888, Cochin-China, Cambodia, Annam, and Tonquin, to which Laos was added in 1893, have formed practically a single protectorate as " French Indo-China." From that date they cease to have an independent existence, and are absorbed in the French colonial dominion.

EMIL SCHMIDT

BLESSING VASCO DA GAMA'S EXPEDITION TO THE INDIAN OCEAN

Before the great Portuguese navigator sailed for the South Seas his enterprise was blessed at an imposing ceremony in the Basilica de Santa Maria, the Cathedral of Lisbon, his royal patron gracing the occasion by his presence.

INDIAN OCEAN IN HISTORY
THE DRAMA OF A WORLD OF WATERS
AND THE NATIONS ON ITS SHORES

THE INDIAN OCEAN IN EARLY TIMES
THE PRIMITIVE MIGRATIONS

OF all parts of the mighty ocean which encircles the earth, none, unless it be the Mediterranean, seems by its position and shape more adapted to play a part in the history of the world than the Indian Ocean. Just as the Mediterranean basin, so important for the course of the history of the human race, parts the immense mass of the Old World on the west and breaks it up into numerous sections, so the Indian Ocean penetrates the same land mass from the south in the shape of an incomparably vaster and crescent-like gulf, having the continents of Africa and Australia on its two sides, while directly opposite its northern extremity lies the giant Asia. In the number, therefore, of the continents surrounding it, the Indian Ocean is inferior to none of the larger sea-basins—neither to its two great companion oceans in the east and west, nor to the diminutive Mediterranean in the north; each of them is bounded by three continents.

The frame in which the Indian Ocean is set shows a rich variety of configuration. Only the west side—the east coast, that is, of Africa—is massy and unbroken, except for the huge island of Madagascar and some groups of coastal islands. By contrast, the eastern and northern coasts appear all the more indented; and yet they are absolutely different in their kind. The east side terminates to the south in the Australian continent, which **Limits of the Indian Ocean** for long ages was able to pass in lonely tranquillity an existence unknown to history, until modern times finally brought it within the range of politics. But Australia is directly connected on the north with a region that has no parallel on the face of the globe for the rich variety of its configuration—the island world, that is, of Indonesia—the Indian Archipelago. This has been the natural " bridge of nations " toward the east from the earliest times to the present day.

The northern shore, also, from its bulk, is unique in its conformation. Southern Asia, as indeed the whole continent, is a land of vast distances. Three immense peninsulas, on a scale of size that recurs nowhere else, jut out into the sea, and the **The Three Great Peninsulas** ocean penetrates the land in gulfs of corresponding breadth and length which attain the dimensions of fair-sized seas. The formation seems at first sight almost too colossal to guarantee to the adjoining part of the sea an active rôle. But on this point we must always bear in mind that the two most important offshoots of the Indian Ocean, the Persian Gulf and the Red Sea, approach to within a short distance of the Mediterranean, the centre of Western civilisation, like two feelers, virtually becoming the eastern continuation of the Mediterranean.

The geometrical axis of the Indian Ocean runs, like that of the other two great oceans, from north to south; it thus follows a direction which at no time and in no place has been strongly marked in the history of mankind. It was by the Red Sea and the Persian Gulf that the Mediterranean peoples approached the Indian Ocean. Thence their path lay south-east to Indonesia, or south-west to the coast of Africa. Similarly, then, the historical axis of the Indian Ocean runs in the direction of the circles of latitude. It is therefore parallel to the great routes by which communications have been maintained between Central Asia and Europe on the one hand, and between Oceania and the Malay Archipelago on the other.

The Indian Ocean is, physically, not a true ocean. It is unbounded only in the direction towards the Antarctic, to which it exposes its full breadth. On the north it is enclosed like an inland sea. The development, therefore, of oceanic phenomena is one-sided and incomplete ; and thus the farther one goes to the north the more apparent is the transition to the character of an inland sea.

The Great Barriers of Water The unbridged and unbroken expanse of the Pacific, and still more that of the Atlantic, have made them both until a quite late epoch, insuperable barriers to mankind. It is only when the means of communication have been highly perfected that, by connecting the nations, they have, to a degree unsuspected before, encouraged the impulse of the human race to expand. The Indian Ocean, from its shape, which is closed on the one side, has never proved a barrier. Its two corner pillars on the south, Australia and South Africa, have never felt the need to form relations one with the other, and for the countries lying to the north it has always been easier to avoid it, or to cross it by hugging the coast or by cautiously creeping from cape to cape. In this way the thoroughfares of the Indian Ocean are strangely unlike those of other seas.

These thoroughfares, so far as they are confined to the sea, resemble chords drawn from point to point of a great semicircle. They cut the circumference of the ocean at the points where the population clusters most densely on the coasts. A regular sheaf of rays issues from Eastern Africa ; one line to Arabia and the Red Sea, a second to India, a third diagonally through the semicircle from Madagascar to the Malay Archipelago. A fourth line connects Ceylon with Indonesia ; another, the Indonesian medley of islands with Australia. But far more important than all these is that great chord which intersects the semicircle, almost parallel to the base, between the Red Sea and the Sunda Sea, and thus cuts all other lines. It is chiefly on this route that the history of the Indian Ocean has been made. Both **Ocean Routes That Have Made History** the ancient and the modern world have used this path. The land routes also which border upon this ocean form a comparatively simple system, although they are naturally less subject to general laws than the maritime routes. In Eastern Africa, in Arabia, and in the Malay Archipelago, the chief land routes have followed the coasts ; it is only in India and the Malay Peninsula that they strike inland. But there are many routes of minor importance, and these run in the most diverse directions. This is only what must be expected in countries of such widely different character as those which enclose the Indian Ocean.

It might be expected that the two deep indentations of the Red Sea and Persian Gulf would make coast routes inconvenient. But this is not the case. Both have entrances so narrow as to be crossed with ease by entire nations and races, and it is easy for the land traveller to pass round the head of either. But in the south the conformation of the land masses is such as to make many parts of them inaccessible. Both Africa and Australia possess a comparatively small coast line, and there are no natural highways to connect the interior of either continent with the sea. The north, however, with the exception of the Arabian peninsula, is somewhat more favourably situated. It is true that the vast peninsula of the Deccan lacks any access to the sea ; but to its base, where India proper lies in its full breadth, the Indus and the Ganges and their enormous river basins form the **Value of Great Indian Rivers** best international highways in the world. If fortune had ever smiled on these river basins sufficiently to allow them to be inhabited by energetic peoples, skilled in seamanship, nothing could have hindered them from making India predominant in the politics of the Indian Ocean and the Pacific, and impressing Indian civilisation upon the whole of that vast area.

This brings us to the salient point in the history of the Indian Ocean generally. The preliminary conditions to historical greatness are already existent, but the adjacent peoples have shown only local and spasmodic inclinations to make full use of them. The native races of this area have contributed little to history in comparison with the foreigners who at one time and another have invaded it. From millennium to millennium this condition has become worse. The importance of the Indian Ocean has declined, while that of the Atlantic and the Pacific has increased. In these last the white race has triumphed over Nature and the inferiors of its own species ; but in the Indian Ocean white men have met, at the best of times, with only a qualified success. They have found the peoples by which this ocean is bordered too immense and too inert for any permanent conquest.

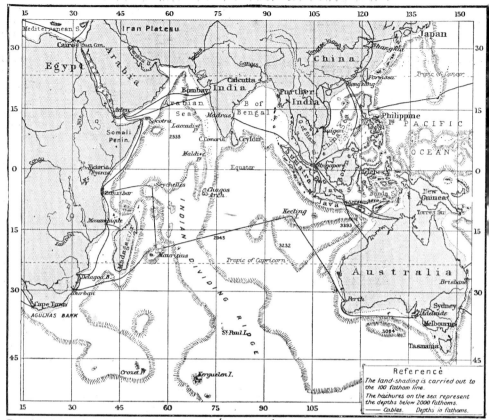

The sea bottom between the coast and the 100 fathom line is called the 'Continental Shelf'

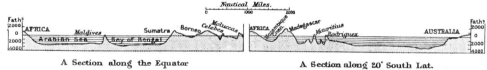

A Section along the Equator   A Section along 20° South Lat.

THE BED OF THE INDIAN OCEAN AND CHINA SEA, SHOWING THE CONTINENTAL SHELF

The remote past of the Indian Ocean is wrapped in the same obscurity as that of most parts of the earth's surface. We are tempted to dwell on the enigma in this case because more than one investigator has been inclined to look for the earliest home of primitive man in one part or another of this ocean. But it is idle to speculate when we have no materials for a conclusion. We must rather take as our starting-point the moment when pressure, exerted from the heart of Asia, drove out the inhabitants of its southern coasts to find a refuge and a new home on the ocean. Supposing this expelled people not to have already inhabited Ceylon, it could only diverge from the direction in which it was pushed, as far as this easily accessible island; any further advance over the surface of the ocean was barred at once by the want of a bridge of islands leading out to it.

On the other hand, the exiles might roam for vast distances toward the south-west or the south-east without let or hindrance, for neither the road to the south-western part of the Old World nor the bridge of islands to the Pacific offered any appreciable obstacles, even for migrating peoples who possessed little knowledge of seamanship. Both paths, indeed, had been trodden by that dark race on its retreat before the wave of Asiatic nations rolling from north to south. Even at the present day we find scanty remnants of it on Ceylon, as in Southern India itself. We find additional traces in Further India or Malacca; indeed, with some certainty,

1419

even in Southern Arabia. But it is far more strongly represented in the Indian Archipelago as far as the Philippines and Melanesia, and even still further in the east. We find it on the largest scale, however, on the continent of Africa, where it forms the chief component element of the population. These migra-

The Early Race Movements tions gave the dark-skinned peoples hardly any occasion for great achievements in seamanship. The passage to Ceylon was simple enough ; and the easterly path with its thickly sown clusters of islands did not require any pretensions to navigation. It is impossible to ascertain whether the early ancestors of the African negroes crossed the ocean on its lateral arms, the Persian Gulf and the Red Sea, or whether they went round them. Even if the negroes on their march to the new home chose the sea route, the few miles of the passage over those narrow arms of the sea were no more able to turn them into a nation of sea-farers than their old homes on the coasts of Asia had served to lure them out on to the open sea. Even in their new home they remained aloof from the ocean and averse from it. Was it the vastness of the spaces in Africa in which they lost themselves, or were nautical skill and love of the sea foreign to the race ? The last alternative would seem to be the true one, for at no time and in no place have members of the negro race performed noteworthy feats at sea. In Africa their efforts were exhausted by the occupation of Madagascar, which was close at hand, and of the coast islands from the main-land.

In the island world of Indonesia and Melanesia even the admixture of Malay blood did not raise the dark-skinned man above the level of coasting navigation. We have, therefore, little to do with him in what follows ; in the sphere of the

Historical Value of Black Races Indian Ocean he is as unim-portant a factor in the history of the world as we shall after-ward find him in the Atlantic Ocean. The lands which he inhabits may still play a part in history ; but he has shown little or no ambition to share in the life of the outer world.

In spite of the small historical import-ance of the black race, its diffusion over the countries round the Indian Ocean is an event of great significance ; it creates

in the island realm of South-east Asia the preliminary conditions for those in-tricate mixtures and blendings the result of which we see in the motley conditions of the population of Indonesia and the Pacific world at the present day. The dark-coloured races have never been numerous enough there to constitute any noticeable check on a wave of nations as it presses on.

Thus, when the Malay stream of nations, giving way before a pressure from north to south, was forced out to the sea from the south-east of the Asiatic continent, it did not touch the zone of Indonesia-Melanesia without influencing the negroid race which it found there ; and it did not leave the country without carrying with it the traces of this probably prolonged con-tact over the entire breadth of the Pacific to the east. The results of this contact vary according to the respective locality and the duration of the reciprocal action. Melanesians and Polynesians are the two ends of the scale : the former is the product of a complete fusion of the two races, the latter seems to have only a

Contact of Primitive Nations negroid tinge. The interme-diate steps are numerous and varied—Micronesians, Alfurs, and Negritos mark only sharply outlined groups in the medley. Indirectly the Australian may be reckoned in, for, in addition to Polynesian influences, Melanesian are not to be rejected.

The Pacific and the Atlantic have each in their turn contributed to develop these ethnic types. If we retain the customary division of the Malay race into an eastern and a western branch, the classification coincides more or less with the region of the two oceans. But while the eastern branch saw its historical task discharged by the occupation of the vast Pacific world, and made hardly any per-ceptible advances into the turmoil of the history of mankind, notwithstanding a skill in seamanship which approached the miraculous, the Western Malays, firmly planted on their native soil of Indonesia, and from the very first efficient and able seamen, presented a different picture. Not only did they advance over the Indian Ocean to Ceylon and Madagascar, but in the majority of the homes which they permanently occupied played a part whose significance is far greater than that of their eastern kinsmen and of nearly all the inhabitants of the Indian Ocean.

They set foot nowhere on the mainland except in the peninsula of Malacca, and are the true children of the ocean ; if they did not succeed in raising themselves to be its acknowledged masters, that is perhaps due less to deficiencies of character and natural ability than to the division and subdivision of their homes over so many islands, and to the position of the Malay Archipelago at the meeting point of two such mighty civilisations as the Chinese and the Indian. It is true that the influence of China was mainly confined to the field of commercial politics ; but this only made the influence of India the wider in its day. This latter reacted with quite unprecedented vigour upon the culture and the spiritual life of the Western Archipelago ; and, although it could not bring the Malay, who was by

temperament far keener, under the yok of religious ideas, and thus bind him t the native soil in the way in which th Hindus were bound, still, under the burn ing rays of Indian philosophy, the politica energy of the insular people was mor prejudicially influenced than we are or dinarily accustomed to suppose. Th

Duration of Ocean History modest share of the India Ocean in the history of mankin goes back to distant ages, abou which we shall probably neve be able to express a definite opinion. I is in its length and breadth prehistoric Long ages must have passed before th historically authenticated relations of th West and the East were formed throug the instrumentality of those same Hamiti peoples who formerly had barred th movement from the East to the West

THE HISTORIC PERIOD DOWN TO ISLAM

THE Indian Ocean has sent out mighty armies of peoples eastward and westward ; but those which went westward have mostly remained strangers to it and kept aloof ; the others, in the east, passed rapidly from its dominion. It has certainly created nations ; where this task faced it on a large scale, as in the Archipelago and in Australia, it has had to share it with its larger neighbours ; while where the task appealed to it on a small scale, as on the coasts of East Africa and on Madagascar, there the result is not commensurate with the dignity and size of the ocean. Again, the political activity of the Indian Ocean has never been prominent. Where growing nations live, as in the western archipelago, on Madagascar, and on the coasts of South and East Arabia, there the great far-reaching empires are wanting ; and where these exist, as in the whole of Southern Asia from the Euphrates on the west to the Brahmaputra on the east, there is no nautical efficiency or

Voyages for Trade Purposes liking for the open sea. What life and movement there has been on the highways of the Indian Ocean is due mainly to commerce. All the nations which ventured out on to the Indian Ocean in times known to history were induced chiefly by commercial objects to make such voyages. The historical rôle of the Indian Ocean must therefore be regarded predominantly from the standpoint of the history of trade. The range

of view is only apparently limited ; ii reality it discloses prospects of remarkabl depth and reveals glimpses of the rise anc fall of nations, such as we never find or an equal scale in the far wider and more richly diversified fields of view presentec by the two other great oceans.

It is impossible to picture to onesel the historical significance of the Indian Ocean without thinking primarily of the weighty part which the Red Sea and the Persian Gulf have been called on tc play within this area. These two northwesterly lateral arms of the ocean are the natural canals and the obvious connecting links between east and west. But even more than the southern approach to the great Mesopotamian plain, whose value would be more clearly realised by us if we possessed greater details about the trade of the Elamites, the ditch-like Red Sea, which reaches close up to the Mediterranean world, has facilitated and maintained this connection. Although in the course of human history there was a long period during which the Red Sea relapsed into a profound tranquillity, yet no proof of its historical value is clearer than the fact that an occurrence so simple as its union with the Mediterranean, which was accomplished between 1859 and 1869, restored to it at one blow its old rôle. Its busy waters even now, when the East has been opened to the widest extent, are the great link of connection between the eastern and the western worlds.

The commerce in the north-west of the Indian Ocean goes back far into remote antiquity. Although the ancient Egyptians, with their invincible predilection for seclusion, never maintained a permanent fleet on the Red Sea, yet they repeatedly tried at the most different periods to bring themselves into direct communication with the countries producing the spices which they used so much and valued so highly—that is to say, with Southern Arabia and the eastern horn of Africa. The last king of the eleventh dynasty, Seanchkara, commissioned Henu to fit out an expedition from Coptos to " Punt " ; a similar task was entrusted to the fleet of Queen Hathepfut about 1490 B.C. on its voyage south. We must certainly regard the Egyptians as the earliest authenticated navigators of the Red Sea and the adjoining parts of the Indian Ocean. Although those isolated expeditions, and even the fleet maintained by Rameses III. (1200–1168), can hardly have served to point out the way to their Punic successors, they are noteworthy as evidence of a nautical spirit in a people which otherwise was so firmly rooted to its own soil.

The magnet, however, which chiefly attracted navigators into this ocean was the peninsula of India. India and the Indian Ocean are two inseparable ideas, as is shown by the two names. And yet this close relationship holds good only in a limited sense. The peninsula to the south of the Himalayas is by its geographical position fitted to rule the surrounding seas more than any other country which bounds the Indian Ocean. Nevertheless, during the course of its history it has never attained a commanding position, from its own unaided strength, at any rate. Yet the peninsula is not so vast as to hinder the thorough development of its latent strength, represented by an excessively dense population; and the unfavourable configuration of its coast line is not the cause of the amazing dearth of historical influence. The fault lies simply and solely in the ethnographical conditions of India.

The Indian Aryans never made a permanent habit of navigation. India never felt the need of seeking the outside world ; but it always was destined to be the goal for the other nations, by land

History of Ocean Commerce

India the Magnet of the Nations

as well as by sea. From its vast treasures it has given to the world more than any other country of the earth, but the world has had to fetch these treasures for itself.

The first attempts at direct maritime communication with India from the west were certainly made by the Phœnicians. Even if we put aside the accounts given by Strabo of their early settlements on the Persian Gulf, and of their emporia on Tylos and Arados, yet their trading voyages on the north-western Indian Ocean go back to the second millennium B.C. ; since at the time of the expedition sent by Hiram and Solomon to Ophir from Eziongeber and Elath, the route to that mysterious land of gold was well known and regularly frequented.

The advance of the Hebrews toward the Indian Ocean is, however, more noteworthy from the historical standpoint. Though at that early period, and down to the Babylonian captivity, they were far from being a commercial nation, and though their political fabric was barely consolidated by the end of that millennium, yet under their keen-sighted King David they already with set purpose secured Edom, the northern extremity of the Red Sea. The brilliant success which attended the friendly alliance of his son Solomon with Hiram, king of Tyre, owing to the above-mentioned expeditions, was only the natural consequences of David's policy.

The Hebrews in Indian Ocean History

There is no better proof of the value which the Hebrews placed on the access to the Indian Ocean than the eagerness with which a whole series of subsequent sovereigns attempted to keep it open. As often as the kingdom of Judah was hard pressed and cut off from the sea, it was always one of the first tasks of its princes to subdue afresh the insubordinate Edomites, or Idumæans, to rebuild the repeatedly destroyed town of Elath, and thus to command the Gulf of Akabah. Judah, humiliated and hemmed in by Sheshonk I., or Shishak, of Egypt during the reign of Rehoboam, showed once more a vigorous expansion in 860 B.C. under Jehoshaphat, who restored Elath and fitted out a new fleet. Then under Jehoram the Idumæans regained their independence, until Uzziah, or Azariah, in the first half of the eighth century, subjugated them for the third time, and rebuilt Elath. Under Ahaz, about 730,

THE FORTIFIED CASTLE OF AKABAH, NEAR THE VILLAGE OF AKABAH
The castle and village of Akabah are 2¼ miles from the head of the Gulf of Akabah, and are supposed to be the site of the Elath of Scripture, the ancient commercial city whence the Jews carried on their trade with India and the East.

the star of Judah on the Indian Ocean paled for ever ; the Idumæans henceforth permanently occupied their ancestral homes.

The loss by the Hebrew nation of its position on the Indian Ocean marks an important epoch in the history of both. In the history of the development of the policy and civilisation of Judah, it signifies the close of the first and only age of united, conscious, and willing efforts at expansion in the direction of the ocean. Being driven back into the interior, Judah was deprived for all succeeding time of the possibility of winning a position in the world as a political unity. For the Indian Ocean, however, that

forced retreat of the Jewish people meant the conclusion of a period when for the first time a nation to which no seaman-like qualities could be attributed learnt and recognised with full consciousness its own value to the history of the world.

With the Phœnicians the case was altogether different. Aiming always at commercial profit without political power, they were deterred by no obstacles from opening up new spheres. Never trusting to force for success, they were past masters of the art of reaching their goal, not by opposing an enemy or a rival, but by utilising him. They had made full use of the Hebrews for this end so long as these latter held a position on the Gulf

THE ISLAND OF GRAIA IN THE GULF OF AKABAH
The Gulf of Akabah is the eastern bifurcation of the northern end of the Red Sea, and is the centre of scenes in sacred history, with Mount Sinai 29 miles from its western shore ; its waters are said to have overwhelmed Pharaoh and his hosts.

of Akabah, and they did not hesitate then for a moment, although from a purely political point of view they were not entirely free agents, to lend the Egyptians the support of their commercial policy. The results of this alliance culminated in the celebrated circumnavigation of Africa under Necho II. in 608 B.C., a feat which throws the most **Phœnician** vivid light on the boldness **Voyage** and skil of the Phœnician **Round Africa** mariners. The trade, which in the last six centuries before the beginning of our present era never completely ceased, either on the Red Sea or the Persian Gulf or the adjacent parts of the Indian Ocean, at no time went beyond that stage of transit trade which it had reached at an early time. Transmitted by the most varied nationalities, it remained for that reason insignificant, being carried on from one intermediate station to another. No change was effected in this respect when Darius, son of Hystaspes, completed the canal begun by Rameses II., from the Delta to the Red Sea, or when Ptolemy II., Philadelphos (284–247), restored the work which had meantime fallen into ruin. What difference did it make that Nebuchadnezzar II. founded Teredon at the mouth of the Euphrates, primarily for trading purposes, and improved the channels of the Euphrates and Tigris for navigation by the construction of numerous, windings ? His improvements were ruined by the rulers of the family of the Achæmenids. Besides this, since one world empire after another enslaved Western Asia as far as the Nile, the Phœnicians had disappeared from the Indian Ocean, thus inflicting a loss to the wholesale commerce which the inhabitants of Southern Arabia, with their still very deficient means of navigation, were, in spite of all their efforts, quite unable to replace. Even the Indian campaign of Alexander the Great, vast as is its historical import-**Greek** ance, did not immediately **Invasion** bear the fruits, so far as mari-**of India** time trade went, which the conqueror had endeavoured to obtain. Egyptian Alexandria itself developed only some centuries after his death into that which it ought to have become immediately after its foundation—the focus, that is, for the trade between India and the Mediterranean, and consequently the emporium for the combined trade of the

ancient world. But Alexander's own short maritime excursion into the regions of the mouths of the Indus, which symbolised his annexation of the ocean ; further, the celebrated expedition of Nearchus from the Indus to the mouths of the Euphrates ; then the attempt of the king to open once more the long-neglected route from the Persian Gulf round Arabia ; his plan for the circumnavigation of Africa ; finally, the improvement which he made in the navigation up to Babylon, and the founding of the port of Charax at the mouth of the Tigris—all this bears eloquent testimony to the importance which Alexander attributed to the Indian Ocean, and to the part which the newly opened-up sea was intended to play in the future schemes of the conqueror. The early death of the monarch brought these plans to an abrupt end.

Nevertheless, the magnificently displayed activity of the Macedonian ruler was not altogether barren of the results which had been expected from it ; on the contrary, its subsequent effects drew India and the Indian Ocean out from **Results of** the gloom of Oriental seclusion **Alexander's** into the full light of Hellen-**Expedition** istic culture. Babylon, indeed, which, after the removal of the Seleucid capital to Antioch rapidly succumbed to the newly found rival, Seleuceia or Ctesiphon, did not become the political, intellectual, or commercial centre of the civilised world at that time. But while, before Alexander, India was known to the Greeks from the meagre accounts of a few travellers, after that brilliant epoch the maritime communication with the East continued uninterruptedly for nearly a thousand years. Favoured by the far-seeing policy of the Ptolemies, which culminated in the construction of the canal to the Pelusiac arm of the Nile, in the founding of ports on the Red Sea, and in securing the old route to Coptos, the intercourse of the West with India now rose above the stage of transit trade practised for so many centuries : it became direct, and in its still modest dimensions formed the intermediate step to international commerce on a larger scale. The year 30 B.C., when Egypt was proclaimed a Roman province, introduced quite new conditions of communication over the Indian Ocean. The way to India, so rich in treasures, now lay open and free to a nation whose material requirements, in spite of all politic self-restraint, had increased enormously. The Romans therefore made full and comprehensive use of the newly opened road. Yet even under these altered circumstances their intercourse with the East would not have gone far beyond the earlier stage had not the new rulers by the utilisation of the monsoons profitably employed a new power which at once enabled them to renounce for ever the hitherto traditional coasting navigation.

The discovery of this phenomenon, peculiar to the northern Indian Ocean, which was made about the middle of the first century A.D., is ascribed to the Greek navigator Hippalus, after whom, indeed, the south-west monsoon has been called. On the one hand, this for the first time rendered real voyages on the high seas possible, and, on the other hand, the regular alternation of the two opposite winds compelled the traders to adopt a regulated system of navigation, which, besides, was too convenient to be abandoned. In the succeeding period Indian **Indian Envoys in Rome** embassies are no longer a rarity in Rome, and the Arabian Sea was traversed to a degree hitherto unknown. Alexandria also now realised the intentions of its founder. One fact alone filled the hearts of the Roman economists with deep concern—that this brisk trade did not swell the national revenue. Even then the Indian trade displayed the characteristic peculiarity that the exports were not balanced by any imports. Pliny, besides Strabo, makes the observation, and under Tiberius the Senate seriously considered by what measures it could stem the constant outflow of Roman gold to the East.

From the earliest times of which we have any authentic information the Indian Ocean has never served any purpose other than that of being a road to India, the eagerly sought-for goal of the West. As might be expected from the scanty resources, the results were meagre, and they did not become important until coasting navigation was abandoned. From that moment the aspect of the Indian Ocean changed. India ceased to be the goal of navigators and explorers alternately. Ceylon and the Golden Chersonese, or Malacca, were now reached from the West, and after the second half of the first century A.D. the merchants of the Roman

Empire penetrated as far as Kattigara. Whether we are to identify this place, as Von Richthofen supposes, with Tonquin, or, as others maintain, with Canton, there is no doubt that the Romans who reached Kattigara came into contact with the Chinese. So, for the first time in the period of authenticated history, this **Coming of the Chinese** people is drawn into the affairs of the Indian Ocean, where it was afterwards to play so prominent a rôle.

The efforts of the Chinese people at sea have already been discussed. Chinese navigation, so far as it touched the Indian Ocean, presents the peculiar feature of always advancing toward the west, until it came into contact with that of the western peoples. This contact is what it required, but it avoided any further progress or overlapping. Accordingly, in the fourteen to eighteen centuries during which we have to consider the Chinese intercourse on the Indian Ocean, that ocean has witnessed a drama such as no other sea can show.

If the western nations limit the area of their voyages, the Chinese, in conformity with their undeniable commercial spirit, follow them with their merchantmen into more western regions ; but if enterprising captains of Western Asia or Europe push further toward the east, the son of the Middle Kingdom gives way without demur. This was the case in the first centuries of the relations between West and East, and the dawn of modern times has seen the same course of events.

These movements take place almost rhythmically. They follow one another with a regularity which tempts one to arrange in harmony with them the relations of the Chinese toward the Indian Ocean. The whole character of the Chinese deterred them from navigating it on their own initiative. They required the stimulus given by the circumstance that **Chinese Commercial Voyages** the mariners of Western Asia, about the year 250 A.D. at the latest, gradually discontinued voyages to Kattigara and contented themselves with seeking nearer ports. The threatened loss of trade compelled the Chinese to follow the barbarians to the West. In the middle of the fourth century A.D. we find them at Penang in the Malacca Straits. Toward the end of that century they reached for the first time Ceylon, the only point outside the region of their native ocean which had any great attraction for them. In Ceylon, however, they saw the germs of that Buddhist doctrine which exercised the most powerful formative influence on their own civilisation. Not content with this goal, which they again and again strove to reach, they came by the middle

Extent of Chinese Voyages of the fifth century as far as the Persian Gulf and the town of Hira on the Euphrates; later, we find them, if we may believe Edrisi, even at Aden and other ports of the Red Sea. The expeditions of the Chinese to Persia and Mesopotamia ended about the year 700, while their ships did not withdraw from Ceylon, which, in this interval, had developed into a flourishing emporium between East and West, until the middle of the eighth century.

The seven centuries in which we first notice the pendulum-like oscillations of Chinese maritime enterprise saw considerable changes in the powers of Western Asia, by whom the trade with China was conducted. Here, too, as always in history, the Chinese were the permanent factor. Apart from the people known in later times under the name of the Malays, who, by sharing in the voyages to Ceylon, became important competitors with them in the second period, the Chinese were for the whole time the undisputed bearers of the trade directed toward the West. But in the West there were far-reaching revolutions. There the Greco-Roman trader was being ousted more and more by nations which, although long settled on the borders of the Indian Ocean, had only just turned their attention to sea traffic.

In the first place we must here mention the Indians themselves, who then, perhaps for the first time in the course of their history, so uneventful in foreign policy, ventured to any large extent upon the sea. We may form our own opinions as to their share in the expeditions to Malacca and the Archipelago, but there is

Attitude of the Indians no doubt that they did not regard passively the splendid development of Western trade which was taking place at their own gates.

By far the greater part of this trade passed into the hands of Persia, after the powerful dynasty of the Sassanids (227–651) had raised that kingdom to the rank of a great Power. But Persia commanded only one of the two sea routes leading from India to the West—that across the

Persian Gulf. Of this it soon gained absolute possession; and the monopoly remained for a long time in its hands, for neither the Indians nor the vigorous inhabitants of the kingdom of Hira (210–614) had any other route available.

Like the Persian ships themselves, the Indian and Arabian merchantmen sailed to Ceylon, where they received the wares brought there by Chinese junks, more especially silk, cloves, aloes-wood, and sandal-wood, in order to carry them directly across the Persian Gulf. On the other hand, the Persian dominion did not extend, either at the time of the Sassanids or later, over the second route to the West, that of the Red Sea. The traces, therefore, of Rome's former command of the seas were preserved here the longest. The far-famed city of Berenice Troglodytice flourished down to the fourth century; and even in the days of Justinian the ships of the East Roman Empire sailed yearly from Klisma and the ancient Elath to India. Owing to the unusually firm

Strength of Persian Trade position of the Persians in the Euphrates valley all attempts to break through their monopoly of the maritime trade on this, the shortest, route were always futile. The Red Sea presented itself as the only avenue of approach to the Far East. The small shipping industry of Klisma and Elath was quite unable to meet the immense requirements of the luxurious Byzantine court as well as those of the civilised world of the Mediterranean. Justinian looked for and found allies geographically more favoured in the Ethiopians of the friendly Axumitic kingdom, whose position at the entrance of the Indian Ocean as well as at that of the Red Sea naturally suggested the transit trade.

The attempt, nevertheless, failed. Many Greek merchants, indeed, went down to Adulis, and actually crossed over to India in Ethiopian ships; yet they did not succeed in impairing the Persian monopoly to any appreciable extent. The Persians in the course of centuries had established themselves too firmly in the Indian ports to be ousted by the competition of an unadventurous and uninfluential people from the position which they had laboriously acquired. So far as the Indian Ocean is concerned, the Persians seem rather to have derived fresh strength for further advances from every attack.

FROM MAHOMET TO VASCO DA GAMA

WHAT the western voyage of Columbus was for the Atlantic, or the descent of Balboa and the expedition of Magalhaes for the Pacific, the eastern voyage of Vasco da Gama was for the Indian Ocean— an event, that is, of the most telling importance for all succeeding time. But while those events in the history of the first two oceans are unmatched for their far-reaching influence, the discovery of the way round the Cape does not stand alone in its importance for the Indian Ocean.

The pioneers of Europe found that they had been anticipated by Islam, which in its whole life and being belongs to the Indian Ocean. On a victorious march of incomparable swiftness it bore the flag of the Prophet to the shores of the Atlantic, and it touched the Pacific with its most eastern offshoots ; but only in the region of the Indian Ocean did it attain a vigorous and unhindered development of its strength and, more important still, only there was it able to spread itself over the surface of the ocean.

It is not to be assumed that the Arabs sailed the sea for the first time after the Hegira. Such a view is contradicted not only by the migration by sea of the Ge-ez nations of South Arabia to the highlands of Abyssinia, but by the navigation of the peoples of Hira and Aden, and by many other facts. But at no period before Mahomet do we find in them even an inclination to that deliberate oversea policy which is so characteristic of the Arabian world during the whole age of the caliphs and later.

Four years after the Prophet's death the Neo-Persian kingdom lay shattered on the ground, struck down by the powerful hand of Omar. It seemed almost as if, under the new conditions and in the warlike turmoil of that time, the Indian Ocean would relapse into that state of insignificance from which it had only slowly emerged in the course of the last few centuries ; for at this same time, 641, the rest of Nearer Asia and even Egypt fell a victim to the Mohammedans.

The Indian Ocean thus had become an Arabian Sea ; from Suez and Massowah on the west as far as the Indus delta on the east its waves, at the time of the Ommeiads and the Abbassids, beat on shores over which the caliphs ruled. In this way the whole commerce of West with East, the world commerce of that day, lay in the hands of the Arabs alone. For the first time since the Indian Ocean has played a part in the authenticated history of mankind, the appearance of the Arabs on the scene compels the observer to divide his field of view. In addition to the route from west to east, which hitherto has been exclusively treated, one of the routes which passes through the northern part of the ocean from north to south now claims serious consideration. We have, in fact, to deal with the encroachment of the Arabs on the coast of East Africa. It is on this particular region that the Arab people has longest asserted its capacity to resist the world powers of modern times.

The expansion of the Arabs toward the East during the age of the Caliphate must still be regarded entirely from the standpoint of the reciprocal relations between Eastern and Western Asia. Possessing a large number of the best

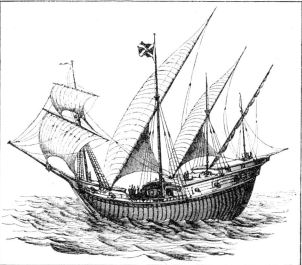

VESSEL OF THE TIME OF VASCO DA GAMA

harbours of the Indian Ocean, among them those which commanded the East Indian trade, the Arabs saw themselves compelled to turn their attention more and more to the sea, and primarily to the eastern ocean. We find Arab fleets on the west coasts of India as early as 637 ; but then it was imperatively necessary to

Arabian Traders in India deprive the Persians, who even after the fall of the Sassanids were a formidable naval power, of the supremacy in the Indian Ocean. The Arabs did not conquer India by the sea route, and failed to drive out of the field the competition of the Persians, in spite of the founding of Basra, or Bassora, and Bagdad, which testifies to their political foresight and their knowledge of the geographical requirements of commerce. For more than two centuries their fleets ploughed the waters of the Indian Ocean in peaceful harmony with the Persian merchantmen. During the first decades of the Caliphate era, this navigation kept to the paths which had been followed from the Sassanid age. It did not go beyond Ceylon ; at that time, indeed, the voyages of the Chinese still extended to the Persian Gulf.

About the year 700, Arabs and Persians, encouraged by improvements in shipbuilding and the knowledge of the compass which they then probably acquired, advanced boldly over the Bay of Bengal and reached the shores of China. In correspondence to this forward movement, and true to their custom of penetrating only so far as was requisite for the maintenance of commercial intercourse, the Chinese at once proceeded to narrow the extent of their voyages more and more.

Although the Chinese held aloof, the Indian Ocean by no means became deserted. For even if the Pacific was closed to the Persians and Arabs in the ensuing period, yet they found in Kalah, on the Strait of Malacca, a place where

Revival of Chinese Voyages the trade with the Chinese could be transacted until these latter once more sought out the old route to Ceylon and the ports of Malabar. This renewed advance of the Chinese is the last of their rhythmic movements on the surface of the Indian Ocean. It began in the second half of the thirteenth century, when Kublai Khan gave a great stimulus to navigation. The ponderous junks of the Chinese, just as in the second age, whose

beginnings lay some 900 years back, once more sailed in large fleets toward the west. Ceylon remained their terminus, as of old, but the powerful and flourishing ports of Calicut and Ormuz became also the objects of their voyages. These were primarily intended for trade, without, however, excluding other enterprises. The Chinese then attempted what they had never previously done on the waters of the Indian Ocean—they actually undertook one voyage of discovery as far as Makdishu, in East Africa, and in the first half of the fifteenth century the monarchs of the Ming dynasty subjugated Ceylon. This was the culminating point of Chinese activity in the Indian Ocean.

By the middle of the fifteenth century China disappeared again from the Indian Ocean, and this time permanently. The attempts repeatedly made by the Chinese during a period of more than one thousand years to remain in touch with the nations of the West bore but little fruit, either for the West or for the East.

On the other hand, the Malay people, which is characterised more than any

Malays the Sailors of the East other in the Eastern Hemisphere by nautical spirit and capacity, began at this time to emerge from its previous obscurity. The voyages which the Malays had undertaken at that early period, when the Chinese for the first time advanced far beyond the Straits of Malacca towards the west, were certainly not the first in their history ; but we possess no exact information on the subject. We can, however, trace with tolerable clearness how the Western Archipelago, and Java in particular, early came into certain relations with India. Thither Brahmanism and Buddhism had both found their way.

It was only at the moment when the Malays, from a correct appreciation of the narrowness of their political and economic basis, withdrew from the island-world to the long since abandoned mainland that they acquired strength and opportunity to affect the destinies of their seas. The founding of Singapore from the old empire of Menangkabau in 1160 is in fact the starting-point of their power, which, in the course of the next centuries, extended to a large part of Indonesia, and found its most conspicuous expression in the prosperity of Malacca, founded in 1252, through which for many centuries the whole commerce from west to east passed.

An unkind dispensation ordained that the Malays should not succeed in developing on a larger scale their hereditary nautical abilities. Hardly were they prepared for a more comprehensive oversea policy, when the era dawned which revolutionised all the existing conditions on the Indian Ocean—the era of its opening up by the Europeans from west to east. Even before this, piracy had been greatly esteemed by the Malays, and it became henceforth their almost exclusive occupation ; by this involuntary step the Malays relinquished any historical rôle in the higher sense.

Only one feat on a larger scale was performed by the Malays within the limits of the Indian Ocean ; this was their settlement of the large island of Madagascar. This migration from their original homes in the Indian Archipelago is mainly prehistoric ; the dates assigned to it vary between the first and the twelfth centuries A.D. The western coasts of the ocean even at this gloomy period did not share the fate of the east side, which continued to be a complete blank so far as history is concerned.

Settlement of Africa by Arabs

Although the Greek traders finally kept aloof, yet the Arabs, who had early sailed from their emporiums in Yemen to the south, did not cease until past the second century A.D. to navigate energetically the east coast of Africa, even far below the equator. Before the advent of the Prophet their voyages were directed exclusively to commercial objects. But fully a century after the Hegira the connection with the south, which was formerly only loose, was drawn tighter ; where previously simple factories had existed, one fortified town after another now sprang up. Round these towns were grouped kingdoms, of small size, it is true, but nevertheless able largely to influence and change the nationality and customs, the religion and type, of the settled population. Makdichu and Barawa. Malindi and Mombasa, but especially Kilwa-Kisiwani, which flourished for many years, were the centres of these states, by whose maintenance for fully nine hundred years the Arab nation has given the most brilliant proof of historical strength and permanence.

Down to modern times the shape of the Indian Ocean was completely misrepresented. It was imagined to be an inland sea, a long, narrow channel, which, joining the Red Sea, formed, as it were, a prolongation of the Mediterranean turned toward the south. While the north shore of this marvellous basin is represented by the south coast of Asia, it was supposed that the boundary on the south was **Mistakes of Early Cartographers** supplied by the continent of Africa. The east coast of Africa was twisted round in early maps, and made to run due east and west at its southern extremity, and to join the south of Asia somewhere in the Far East.

This erroneous conception became momentous for the history of mankind when it was perpetuated by Ptolemy, whose cosmographic system was the main source of the geographical knowledge of the early Middle Ages. The Arabs, the direct heirs of the great geographer, adopted without criticism his facts and his blunders, and thus accepted the tradition that the Indian Ocean was an inland sea, although the direction of the Somali and Zanzibar coast must have been familiar to them.

The Indian Ocean in this Ptolemaic shape became important for the history of the human race in two ways. The one part of its rôle ended in the political achievements of the Arabs on the east coast of Africa, of which the extent was perhaps conditioned not only by the causes already mentioned, but also by the very natural desire of the conquerors to keep in touch with the mother country. Apart from these settlements the Indian Ocean is important for the fable of the " Terra Australis," the unknown southern land, with which it was associated. The idea of this continent, mainly derived from Ptolemy, who gave the name of the Ethiopian Australia to the supposed southern shore of his land-girdled Indian Ocean, was taken up by the Arabs, who gave the **Misled by Ptolemy's Mistake** unknown land the name of the Sendsh coast. Then, partly through the agency of the Arabs, partly directly, the myth was adopted into the geography of the scholastics, and at the close of a troublous, but in many respects sterile, period remained as a problem which the Middle Ages had acquired no claim to solve.

Although it was a mere fancy to think of the Indian Ocean as an inland sea, still its influence in history has practically corresponded to its imagined character. It proved an insuperable barrier between the imperfect civilisations which bordered on it. In early times, it was simply avoided by a détour; later, men sailed along the coasts from harbour to harbour, or let themselves be driven by the monsoon eastward or westward. The direction of the circles of latitude is almost **Paths of Trade** the only historical axis of the ancient Indian Ocean which comes before us. With the exception of the voyages to Sendsh and Sofala, the whole intercourse takes this direction, from the enterprises of the Phœnicians in the second millennium B.C., down past the Greeks and Romans, the Persians and the Arabs, to the last expeditions of the Chinese, whose aim was Ceylon, in the middle of the fifteenth century A.D. One-sided as was this intercourse—except for a few journeys undertaken by the Chinese from religious motives and the warlike expeditions of the Arabs against India, which stand by themselves, it was invariably devoted to purposes of trade—it showed itself important for the development of the civilisation of mankind.

In this exchange of the products of civilisation between the East and the West the latter was always the recipient, the former the giver. And for the last third of the period which we have surveyed the exchange was effected merely by the agency of West Asiatic peoples, by the Persians, and more particularly by the Arabs. At the moment when the latter swept forward from insignificance into the position of a political and intellectual world-power, the old direct connection between the sphere of Mediterranean culture and that of South and East Asia was snapped. Whether it is a question of obtaining rare spices, dyes, or luxuries, or of the introduction of the Indian system of numerals, or of the widening of the knowledge of medicine and mathematics, of geography and astronomy, the result is always the same; the nations that command the Red Sea and the Persian Gulf are inevitably the agents. The Indian Ocean after the seventh or eighth century bears the stamp of a purely Asiatic sea, with possibly a faint African admixture.

Like the Pacific, the Indian Ocean was entirely removed from the field of vision of the western civilised nations; it required to be rediscovered and opened up **Indian Ocean Re-discovered by White Races** no less than its great and virgin neighbours. That the opening up of the two oceans took place about the same time, simultaneously also with the lifting of the gloom which rested on the Atlantic, was partly the result of accidents, but was much more due to the internal development of the western nations. But in each of the oceans the work of exploration ran a different course; for this diversity the facts of physical geography are responsible.

A SCENE ON THE SHORES OF THE RED SEA

THE INDIAN OCEAN IN MODERN TIMES
THE COMING OF THE EUROPEANS

TO the men of to-day the difference between the physical and the historical ocean is no longer familiar. As the waves of the one ocean mingle freely with those of the other, so the currents of world commerce, and also of world history, flow unchecked from one to the other. Both, indeed, move on specially favoured paths, but these paths encircle the whole globe ; they cross the sea in the direction which each man chooses, the essential feature of true international commerce.

Four hundred years have sped since this change in the character of the oceans—not in men's ideas about them—was completed ; a short span of time compared with the millenniums that preceded. They have brought infinitely much to the Atlantic as well as to the Pacific, to each certainly more than to the Indian Ocean ; nevertheless, the sum total of the historical importance of the two former is not **The Era of Oceanic Discovery** greater than that of the latter. In their case also, a new era begins with the European voyages of discovery. One is tempted at first sight to say that the opposition of the maritime nations to the white invader has been more determined than that of nations living inland or neglecting the use of the sea. But such a generalisation must be qualified by exceptions so important as to rob it of nearly all its value. It is true that the Aztecs and Peruvians succumbed to the onslaught of the whites still more feebly than the Indians ; but China, in spite of many storms, still stands unshaken in any respect. On the other side, the opposition was nowhere slighter than from the Polynesians ; the distribution of a sparse population over an immense area from the very first prevented any war being waged. Again, the geographical conditions of India and Indonesia are similar on both the east and west ; yet their dealings with the white races have been of the most different description. So far as the Indies are concerned, we must abandon the idea

of treating the ocean as an important influence on the course of history. It is in the facts of religious and political development that we must seek for the reason why, in India proper, native civilisation succumbed to the slightest shock from without, while in Indonesia it found a safe refuge. The Arabs at the time **Allured by India's Riches** when Vasco da Gama, after his memorable voyage to Calicut, set foot on the soil of India, represented the dominant religion of the Indian Ocean, and possessed the monopoly of commercial intercourse so far as it connected the Indian world with the West. Not merely did the fabulous prosperity of Cairo and Alexandria, the power of Venice, Genoa, and Pisa, of Barcelona and Florence, the splendour, in short, of the Mediterranean world of those times, rise and fall with this trade, but the economic life of Northern Europe as far as Germany and Flanders was materially affected by it. The whole West, indeed, between 1200 and 1500 lay under the spell of the trade with India.

At the moment of the landing of Vasco da Gama, the Arabs recognised the desperate danger which threatened their supremacy. In the succeeding period their resistance to the intruders was more obstinate and lasting than that offered by the natives of India, who were unfamiliar with the sea. Even the Ottoman Turks, who in 1517 by the conquest of Egypt had entered upon the heritage of the Mamelukes, knew perfectly well that Egypt was **The Orient Against the Occident** worthless to them unless they possessed complete liberty of movement on the Indian Ocean. This truth was, however, first brought home to them by the Venetians and Genoese, who lost their main source of prosperity with the interruption of the Levantine trade. The attempts, accordingly, of the Turks to regain that liberty of movement were less persistent than would have been desirable in the interests of all the Mediterranean states.

Far from overthrowing the power of the Portuguese, they were unable even to break through the blockade of the Red Sea, which the new-comers maintained for some decades. The Red Sea, therefore, relapsed temporarily into the condition of a backwater; at the same **The Turk's** time the heavy hand of the **Destroying** Turk, spreading death every-**Hand** where, fell on its northern exit.

From the fifteenth to the nineteenth century the Indian Ocean by no means served the purpose of a common thoroughfare. The Portuguese for more than a century regarded it as their own sea. For while the famous Bull of Alexander VI., limiting Spanish enterprise to the lands and seas west of the Azores, had been withdrawn in the very year when it was issued, still Portugal and Spain had, within a few years of this abortive attempt at demarcation, come to an agreement in which the principle of the Papal judgment was recognised; and the New World was partitioned between these, the two greatest maritime and colonising Powers of the age, by the tracing of an imaginary frontier to the west of the Cape Verde Islands.

The post-Columbian age did away with this, as with so many other ideas. In colonial history between 1600 and 1850 we hear of no considerable region, except the sea of Central America, which was more obstinately contested than the border lands and islands of the Indian Ocean. And as if it were not enough that the European nations should rush forward to secure for themselves the heritage of Portugal, the Arabs from Maskat stepped vigorously on the scene after 1660, and after eighty years of war wrested once more the central coast of East Africa from the detested European.

This international competition ends at the moment when the political equilibrium was disturbed in favour of England, under whose dominion it was now destined to pass for the whole succeeding period. This disturbance was produced by an event which in its later developments has controlled the whole subsequent history of the ocean and the surrounding countries—the first acquisition of territory in India by Britain. If we bear in mind that from 1498 to past the middle of the eighteenth century the political activity of the European Powers was spent on the founding of mere factory colonies, which could not secure to any of the participating nations a broad economic basis or any supremacy, we may see in Robert Clive's decisive victory at Plassey, on June 23rd, 1757, the beginning of a new era both for India and for the Indian Ocean.

THE BRITISH ASCENDANCY IN THE INDIAN OCEAN

THE age which started with the victory of Plassey was inaugurated, first by the Peace of Paris of February 10th, 1763, when that very France, to which a Dupleix had opened out such glittering prospects, renounced for ever the possession of India and consequently the supremacy in the Indian Ocean; and next by the dissolution of the French East India Company in 1770. In this way the only European rival whom England had then to consider was finally driven from the field. England could now look to the realisation of her aim, which was to impress on the Indian Ocean the stamp of a British sea—of a central sea, that is, round which the Asiatic, African, and Australian branches of the British world-empire might cluster. Gigantic as this conception must have appeared to the eighteenth century, yet it was actually realised a hundred years after the withdrawal of the French from India. Immediately before the opening of the Suez Canal England did not, it is true, possess all the shores of the Indian Ocean; but there was no power which could dispute her supremacy single-handed.

The historical importance of the Indian Ocean culminates during those hundred years from the fact that then it was mainly sought and won for its own sake; it was only after the opening up of East Asia that it sank more and more into the position of a thoroughfare. The activity of its indigenous population, although it was not less vigorous than in the foregoing age, recedes into the background **Indian** compared with that of the in-**Ocean** vaders from outside. The **Highway** theatre of events lay now, as earlier, exclusively on the west coast of the ocean, and it ended in the founding and growth of the sultanate of Zanzibar, the keystone to the fabric of politics and civilisation raised by the Arabs in the Indian Ocean. Hardly was the structure completed, when it cracked in every joint. While the ocean previously had been a remote gulf, with one single approach far down at the Cape, it was brought, through the artificial strait of Suez, far nearer to the section of mankind which required expansion ; and in place of the Latin nations, which, dogged as they were, had grown weary from the colonising work of centuries, the fresh and resolute Teutonic races stepped forward. The Moslem bulwark, laboriously reared by the work of a thousand years at the eastern entrance to the Dark Continent, rapidly fell to the ground.

The establishment of her position in India has marked out for Great Britain a definite road by which to maintain communications with her Australian colonies ; she must endeavour to protect the approach at all possible points, as well as to command the surface of the adjacent sea. The Portuguese and Dutch, even the French, had already tried to do so. The Portuguese had laid their hands on numerous parts of the west coast of Africa, from Madeira and Arguin in the north as far as Benguela in the south, **Guarding the Road to India** and had also made bases on the east coast from Sofala to Makdishu and Socotra. The Dutch, with better discernment, made the southern extremities of Africa and India, the Cape of Good Hope (1602 and 1652), and Ceylon (1602–1796) the centre of their system of defence, and at the same time took care to occupy Mauritius (1598–1710) and Delagoa Bay (1721). For France finally the islands, Madagascar and its neighbours, were intended to protect the road to India, at least in the south of the Indian Ocean.

The British were far from following in these steps directly after the beginning of their Indian sovereignty ; on the contrary, for decades St. Helena was still reckoned as a sufficient base on the long route round the Cape. Even the first occupation of Cape Colony (1795–1802), which was merely the result of jealousy of the French, had not yet opened the eyes of English Ministers to the value of South Africa for the Indian Ocean ; they would hardly otherwise have given it back to the Batavian Republic. It was only the agitation of keen-sighted politicians like Lord Wellesley, who as far back as 1798 had clearly expressed his opinion that India was untenable without the Cape, and still more the attacks on the British colonial empire executed or planned by Napoleon I., which brought about the resolution to secure it.

Great Britain, therefore, in 1806, rapidly anticipating Napoleon's intention of occupying the Cape, planted her foot once more, and this time finally, on South Africa. This step decided the whole further course of events on the Indian Ocean. **Britain's Premier Position** Great Britain is now supreme not only at the apex of the great inland sea, but also at the corner pillars at its base. In this way she has not only acquired an impregnable defensive position, but she, beyond all other nations, is in the position to guide the destinies of the Indian Ocean.

Napoleon's expedition to Egypt, which undoubtedly would have attained the desired end had France been a match for England by sea, must be considered as comparatively the most eventful of these operations. But its results were very different from what had been anticipated. It reminded England of the vulnerable point in her position ; and from this time British policy was naturally guided by the hope of securing the Red Sea.

Great events cast their shadows before even in the history of the seas. The plan of cutting the isthmus of Suez was mooted during Napoleon's stay in Egypt, and was never again allowed to drop. The repose in which the Red Sea had been left for three hundred years was rudely shattered now that the interest of Europe was concentrated on it. It became apparent that direct communications were to be reopened between the Mediterranean and the Far East. Once more the attention of the colonial Powers was concentrated on the north-west corner of the Indian Ocean. In 1839 the British occupied Aden, the emporium at the entrance of the Red Sea which had flourished in the old days of sailing-ships. At the moment **Influence of the Suez Canal** when the construction of the canal could no longer be prevented, she firmly planted herself on Perim in the straits of Bab el Mandeb in 1857, and almost at the same time included in her dominion the Persian Gulf.

The expedition of Napoleon had shown Great Britain how insecure her Indian possessions were, so soon as France or any other Power set foot in Egypt. Accordingly, after the battle of the Pyramids, on July 21st, 1798, the chief object of her

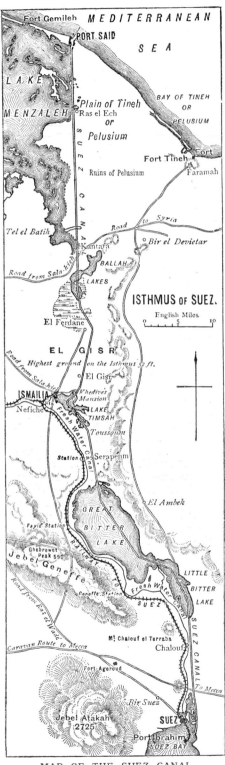

Fort Gemileh MEDITERRANEAN
PORT SAID
SEA

LAKE
BAY OF TINEH
Plain of Tineh   OR
MENZALEH Ras el Ech   PELUSIUM
or
Pelusium
Fort Tineh
Fort
Ruins of Pelusium   Faramah

Tel el Batih
Road   to Syria
Bir el Devietar
Kantara
BALLAH
Road from Sala
LAKES

ISTHMUS OF SUEZ.
El Ferdane   English Miles

EL GISR
Highest ground on the Isthmus 52 ft.
El Gisr
ISMAILIA   Khedive's Mansion
Neficheh   LAKE TIMSAH
Toussoum
Station   Serapeum

El Ambek
GREAT
Fayid Station   BITTER
LAKE
Ghebrewet
Peak 590
Jebel Geneffe   LITTLE
Geneffe Station   BITTER
Fresh Water   LAKE
SUEZ

Caravan Route to Mecca
M. Chalouf el Terraba
Chalouf

Fort Ageroud
To Mecca

Bir Suez
Jebel Atakah   SUEZ
2725
Port Ibrahim
SUEZ BAY

MAP OF THE SUEZ CANAL

Indian policy was necessarily to prevent such a contingency, or even any political and economic strengthening of the country. There was no difficulty in carrying out this purpose so long as the plan of the Suez Canal was still only in the germ, and the British continued to hold the undisputed sovereignty of the seas which they had won during the Revolutionary and Napoleonic wars.

But later, as the plan of the canal assumed more definite shape, and the other Powers, who had gained strength in the interval, once more advanced on the seas, this sovereignty became more difficult, but at the same time more important. Lord Ellenborough was therefore justified in saying that England, if she wished to secure the supremacy of the world, must stand with one foot in India and the other in Egypt. Lord Palmerston privately informed Count Ferdinand de Lesseps that if England was allowed to occupy Egypt permanently with an army and to superintend the traffic in the canal, he and England would be willing to aid the enterprise in every way; but it was found possible to complete the canal in 1869 without this great concession. British policy, however, soon found the means of making the canal a source of strength instead of weakness to her Colonial Empire. In 1875, Lord Beaconsfield seized the opportunity of the Khedive Ismail's pecuniary embarrassments to purchase his shares in the canal. The rebellion of Arabi Pasha afforded an unexpected opportunity of taking a still further step. Half against the will of the Ministry of the moment, the British crushed the revolt and, in 1882, effected the occupation of Egypt. The great problem was thus solved; the way to the Indian Ocean as well as to the Pacific had become a British road. But at the same time the occupation of the old country of the Pharaohs brought Great Britain face to face with a new task, that of flanking the Indian Ocean by an Africa which should be British from Cape Town to the Nile.

The opening of the new waterway brought with it also a mass of new results for mankind in general and for the Indian Ocean and the Mediterranean in particular. This latter now not only developed itself into one of the most crowded thoroughfares, but awoke slowly to a new life of its own, which in its most vigorous form stirred the Italians to oversea expansion.

But still more wide were the effects of the completion of the Suez Canal on the Indian Ocean and the commerce of the world. The numerous routes which ran from the Cape of Good Hope to the north and north-west were suddenly deserted, except by a few sailing-ships. On the other hand, the few routes which traversed the new commercial highway in the first years after its opening have been multiplied and differentiated; there are, at the present day, numbers of trunk lines which converge upon Port Said and diverge again from Aden eastward.

provinces must naturally have forced itself upon men's minds, especially since between them, on the south coast of the Gulf of Aden, on the Zambesi, on the Nyassa, and in the important Zanzibar Archipelago, at the same time or a little later, opportunities were offered for the expansion of the British power. The magnificent idea of an Africa which, on its eastern side at all events, shall be British from the Cape to the mouths of the Nile loses some of its audacity under these circumstances; but it has been keenly taken up, and has already ap-

PORT SAID AT THE MEDITERRANEAN ENTRANCE OF THE SUEZ CANAL

Inset is a portrait of Ferdinand de Lesseps, the distinguished Frenchman, to whom we owe the great artificial waterway that shortens the road to India and the East. Photo of De Lesseps by Elliot & Fry.

The opening up of Australia and Madagascar has done something to restore the importance of the older routes. But old and new alike have the Pacific for their ultimate objective. The Indian Ocean at the present day has again become an anteroom to its larger neighbour.

Great Britain endeavoured in other ways to retrieve the losses which she had thus sustained. In 1866 she acquired British East Africa, a territory precisely equidistant between Cape Colony and Egypt. The idea of a junction of these three

proached its realisation. This idea played its part in causing the masters of Egypt to give Mahdism its well-deserved quietus on September 2nd, 1898, before Omdurman. In realising it, the British have crushed the Matabele empire, and have moved their frontiers far beyond the Zambesi to the north. For its sake they are constructing through Africa a railroad system which not only testifies to economic sagacity, but by means of its northern branches—the Nile Valley and the Uganda railways—makes England independent of

1435

the Red Sea and the Arabian Gulf in the event of these being blocked by a hostile fleet. In fact, combined with other motives, it led also to the defeat of the Boers. The Boers, it is true, were more African than the negroes, since they have struggled, like these at least, to reach the sea, and so far could not disturb Great Britain by sea ; but as a land power she was bound to remain defective on the Indian Ocean so long as the Boer states existed.

During the last thirty or fifty years the north and north-west of the Indian Ocean have also attained an increased importance as the thoroughfare to the East at the moment when East Asia, violently roused from its lengthened seclusion, was opened to the enterprise of the European. Here, too, Britain was victorious. At the first dawn of this period—1824—she laid her grasp upon the Straits of Malacca, with Singapore, Malacca, and Pulo Penang. Since that time the Indian Ocean, so far as it comes into the question of modern world commerce, bears in that part, notwithstanding the extensive possessions of the Dutch, a British stamp.

In conclusion, the last act of this drama lies mostly in the womb of time. It brings us into contact with a nation which has often occupied our attention on the Pacific, but which apparently has no right to meet us here—the Russians. And yet their appearance on the Pacific implies their movement toward the Indian Ocean. If Russia wishes not to be stifled in the enormous expanse of her Asiatic possessions, if she wishes to guide the unwieldy mass, she must force a way to the nearest sea ; her East Asiatic coast is in every respect insufficient, and, above all, too remote. Hence comes that onward movement, during the last decades, toward the south, towards Mesopotamia and the Persian Gulf, which in our days so often assumes tangible form in the question of the Western Asiatic railways and of a Russian harbour on that gulf. The British have here a far more difficult position than anywhere else on the coasts of the Indian Ocean. In the Archipelago the power of Holland is broken up over infinite islands great and small ; in East Africa England's colonial possessions lie firmly riveted round and behind the territories of the Portuguese, Germans, and Italians. But here she sees herself confined between the sea and an antagonist whose ponderous mass presses slowly, but with irresistible power, toward the south. For the moment, the Anglo-Russian agreement of 1907 has recognised the British position ; but it may be that a struggle is only deferred.

KARL WEULE

Photochrome Co.
THE SUEZ CANAL WHERE IT OPENS INTO THE GREAT BITTER LAKE

CENTRAL ASIA

TURKESTAN, TIBET, AFGHANISTAN AND BALUCHISTAN

THE COUNTRIES AND THE PEOPLES

NATURE OF THE LAND

IN comparatively recent times the vast highlands of Asia, with their glittering ramparts of eternal snow, their pasture grounds, their bleak deserts and verdant oases, were regarded with awe by the civilised nations of Europe. It seemed that science, in harmony with the religion and the myths of so many peoples, had succeeded in demonstrating by almost irrefragable proofs that Central Asia was the primitive home of mankind, the cradle whence even our own forefathers were sent out in the pride of youth to find eventually a new home in Europe, while other brothers of our race descended into India, that sun-steeped land of marvels. The truth is still to seek, but it has been shown that Central Asia possesses, so far as we know, no better claim than many other regions of the earth to be considered the cradle of the human race. But Central Asia deserves, even at the present day, the most serious attention of scientific inquirers. Around this citadel of the world lay clustered in a wide semicircle the ancient countries of civilisation, Babylonia, China, and India ; even the beginnings of Egyptian culture point to Asia. All who believe in a common fountain-head of these higher civilisations must look for it in Middle Asia, or must assume that the germs of higher forms of

Asia the Fountain of Civilisation

life were carried through that region in consequence of migrations or of trading expeditions.

Central Asia is the most continental region of the world. In a geographical sense Middle or Central Asia comprises the self-contained interior of Asia : in a historical sense Siberia and the plains of Western Asia and Europe form an appendage of this vast expanse. Central Asia, in the more restricted sense, is the arid plateau, without any outlet, which is divided by immense chains of mountains stretching from east to west into distinct regions—Tibet, Turkestan, and Mongolia.

The World's Greatest Plateau

But this bleak and desolate region has not remained unaltered in the course of thousands of years. In the Tertiary Period, which perhaps saw man develop into the most distinctive form of living creature on the earth, a sea was rolling where now the barren wastes of the Gobi desert and the basin of the Tarim extend : new mountains were upraised and mighty masses subsided. When the sea disappeared, and Central Asia acquired its present configuration, a long time must have elapsed before the land was changed into the sterile steppe which we know at the present day. The Ice Age, which filled Siberia with immense glaciers, hardly affected that transformation. The

THE GREAT MOUNTAINS OF TIBET: "THE ROOF OF THE WORLD"
The illustration conveys some idea of the grandeur of Tibet's scenery; in the distance is a permanent barrier of ice-bound mountain tops high in the region of eternal snows, and in the foreground is a natural stone Hindu temple.

inhabitants of Central Asia, therefore, at the close of the Glacial Period, which must provisionally form the starting-point of historical investigation in this field, were still living in a comparatively well-watered and favoured region, which later became by slow degrees mere steppe and desert. On the other hand, the elevated character of the country has not changed; and this produces even in the southern parts a temperate and almost cold climate, and has in this way exercised a lasting influence on the inhabitants.

Central Asia in the restricted sense is partly bounded, partly intersected, by numerous chains of mountains, which by their trend from east to west are of great importance for the character and history of the country, and divide it into several distinct sections. On the south, the immense wall of the Himalayas divides the cold plateau of Tibet so sharply from the sultry plains of India that the two countries, notwithstanding their close proximity, have exercised little influence on each other and have never entered into close political relations. Farther to the north the Kuen Lun, with its offshoots, divides Tibet from

The Great Mountain Chains

the desolate plain of the Tarim, which in its turn is cut off on the north by the Tian Shan. All three ranges meet toward the west in an immense group of mountains, the centre of which is formed by the Pamirs, so that on this side Central Asia is quite separated from the Turanian lowlands.

Even the rest of the high plateau of Central Asia, the Gobi desert with the surrounding steppes, is bounded by a vast circle of mountain ranges, of which the most important are the Altai on the west, and the Sayansk and Yablonoi Mountains on the north. Beyond the Altai stretch the lowlands of Siberia, which are separated from the plains of Eastern Europe only by the Ural range. On the north-east, however, a chaos of mountains bars the way and fills up the greater part of Eastern Siberia. In this direction, therefore, the migratory spirit of Central Asiatic tribes found least scope. The mountain ranges on the west were never any permanent check on the movements of the nomads, who found in the plains of Turkestan and Western Siberia room for expansion and growth of power. Toward the south the Himalayas blocked their advance; but on the east, China, although partially protected by highlands, lay open to the attacks of the peoples of the steppes.

Thus the trend due east and west, which characterises the lie of the mountain ranges, is clearly noticeable in the migratory movements of the nations.

It is thus a most significant fact that the chain of the Kuen Lun, which runs right through the heart of Central Asia, stretches with its offshoots and parallel ranges, the Altyn Tagh and Nanshan, as far as the middle Hoangho—that is to say, into the most fertile districts of China. Along these lines of mountains, especially on the north side, extends a strip of fertile and more or less well-watered land, which enables the husbandman to make a home there and opens a road to the basin of the Tarim through the horrors of the desert. The importance of this district, the modern province of Kansu, for the civilisation and history of the country is incalculable. It was here that the persevering and stolid Chinaman first waged war with the nomads, built a rampart of fortified towns and agricultural colonies

across the pasture lands of the unruly Central Asiatics, and thus discovered the key to the political supremacy over the whole interior of Asia; but this road must have been taken in far earlier times by those who first brought the manners and customs of the West and East into contact, even if the people which first introduced civilisation into China did not follow that course in their migration. An advance to Tibet or to Northern Siberia was difficult or impossible for the nomad hordes of Central Asia; their movements, from economic reasons, had to be directed mainly eastward or westward; they followed, therefore, the same paths as trade. It was not until a late period that Buddhism by its pilgrimages produced in Central Asia an important movement from north to south. If the history of the surrounding countries is unintelligible without a clear knowledge of Central Asia and its peoples, that of the region of the steppes in the interior of Asia is still more so without reference to the civilised countries which border it, to China on the east, the area

The Paths of Early Settlement

A TYPICAL SCENE IN BARREN AND INHOSPITABLE TIBET

Sterility and ruggedness are the chief characteristics of a great part of Tibet, the mountains barring passage and the soil supporting with difficulty the sparse animal life that tries to win sustenance from its vegetation.

of Mediterranean civilisation on the west, and India on the south.

India, which was repeatedly overrun by hordes of Central Asiatic nomads, for a long period exercised little influence generally on the steppe region, and almost none politically, since the barrier of the Himalayas was a deterrent from military enterprises, and, apart from **Religion** this, the natural features of **Stronger than** Tibet offered no attraction **Warfare** to a conqueror. The attempt made in 1337 by Mohammed Shah Tughlak to push on victoriously from India to China was foiled by the Himalayas and was not subsequently imitated. But here, as in so many cases, the spirit has been mightier than the sword. Northern India, that great seminary of religious and philosophic thought, gradually made its influence felt in Central Asia, and by Buddhist propaganda revolutionised the lives and opinions of the nomads. It was, of course, a case of scattered seeds, which were carried across the mountains and struck root independently, and we must not imagine any permanent union of Indian philosophy with the nomad culture of the steppes.

China stood in a quite different position towards Central Asia. The highlands of Western China offered, it is true, some protection against the inroads of the nomads ; but it did not always prove sufficient. The policy, which the Chinese often adopted, of playing off the nomads one against the other, and of settling various tribes as border-guards within the natural ramparts of the empire, sometimes led to the result that these guardians asserted their independence or made common cause with their kinsmen of Central Asia. The weapons with which China fought the peoples of the steppes were, at all times, not so much **Victory** the warlike spirit of her sons **of China's** or the inaccessibility of the **Culture** country as the highly advanced civilisation which rendered it possible for an extremely dense population to live on the fertile soil. The country might submit, partially or altogether, but the bands of the conquerors soon disappeared among the overwhelming numbers of the conquered, and their barbarian strength could not withstand the example of a higher culture. The civilised countries of Western Asia were better protected than China against the tide of restless nomads. Between the Caspian Sea and the Hiamlayas rise the mountains of Chorasan and Afghanistan. Eastward of these, the fertile districts of the Oxus and the Jaxartes, where agricultural colonies and fortified towns could grow up, formed a vanguard of civilisation. But between the Caspian and the Black Sea the Caucasus rises like a bulwark built for the purpose, and cuts off Western Asia from the steppes of Southern Russia, that ancient arena of nomadic hordes. So long as the natural boundaries were maintained, the fertile plains of Western Asia were safe from the raids and invasions of the nomads. But the people of Iran, which guarded civilisation there, succumbed at length to the attack. The nomads found homes to their liking in the steppes which abound in Iran, Syria, and Asia Minor, and consequently preserved their individuality far longer than in China, and were only partially absorbed by the peoples they had conquered. **Central** We have thus an explanation **Asiatic** of the great difference between **Influence** East and West. China was never more than nominally subject to the nomads, and it finally crippled their power by a systematic colonisation of the steppes ; while the ancient civilisation of Western Asia sank beneath the repeated onslaught of the nomad horsemen, and the country became for a long time an appendage of Central Asia.

Europe, the eastern steppes of which merge into those of South-west Siberia without any well-defined boundaries, was never able to ward off the attacks made from Central Asia. The Huns advanced to the Atlantic, the Avars and Magyars invaded France, the Mongols reached Eastern Germany, and the Ottoman wave spent itself against the walls of Vienna. Europe still harbours in the Magyars, the Turks, and numerous Finnish and Mongolian tribes the remnants of these inhabitants of the heart of Asia. Western Europe, however, with its moist climate, its deficiency in wide tracts of pasture ground, and its national strength and civilisation, suffered no permanent injury, but was able to accept the inheritance of West Asiatic culture.

THE SPRING CARNIVAL AT A TIBETAN MONASTERY: MONKS IMPERSONATING DEMONS OF THEIR MYTHOLOGY

PEOPLES OF
CENTRAL ASIA

NATIVES OF THE COUNTRY OF THE KHAIBAR PASS

WIVES OF A TARTAR GOVERNOR   A WOMAN OF YARKAND

A CAMP OF NOMADS ON A MOUNTAIN PLATEAU IN TIBET

MONGOLS OF THE GOBI DESERT WEALTHY MONGOL TRADER

TARTAR TRADING-WOMEN FROM THE PLAINS OF TIBET

KIRGHIZ NOMADS: 1 FAMILY OF A SULTAN; 2, WEDDING PARTY

INDOOR AND OUTDOOR COSTUMES OF LADIES OF KABUL

TAJIKS, PERSIAN-SPEAKING VILLAGERS OF EASTERN AFGHANISTAN

GHILZAI CHIEFTAIN WITH TRIBESMEN AND HAZARA PEASANTS OF GHAZNI

Frith

BALUCHIS, A PEOPLE OF MIXED ARYAN AND TARTAR DESCENT

PREDATORY TRIBESMEN OF THE BOLAN PASS IN BALUCHISTAN

THE PRIMITIVE PEOPLES OF CENTRAL ASIA

IF we suppose that the original home of mankind lay somewhere in the south-east of Asia, as the discovery of the supposed " missing link " by E. Dubois in Java in 1892 rendered probable, then the rest of the globe may have been early populated from this source. But we cannot speak definitely on this point. It has been shown that man was a contemporary of the mammoth in Siberia. An attempt at a connected historical account must start provisionally with the end of the Glacial Period, since from that time onward no extensive changes of climate or of the earth's surface have taken place. The increasing desiccation of Central Asia is, for instance, important in itself, but cannot be compared with the stupendous phenomenon of the Ice Age.

Two main types, which recur in Europe, are represented among the peoples of Central Asia and Siberia in varying combinations. There is a dolichocephalic, or long-skulled, race, which was **Where the** perhaps originally allied to the **Short-heads** negro, but has acquired in the **Predominate** north a light complexion and partly also fair hair, and a short-skulled or brachycephalic race, also comparatively light-complexioned, whose purest representatives we may at present find among the Mongols and Northern Chinese. Besides these, a pigmy race may have been sparsely distributed, as prehistoric discoveries in Europe and early accounts from China and Japan attest ; but this gradually disappeared among the others, and attained no importance for civilisation. The relation of the long-headed tribes to the short-headed has become all the more important. At the present day the short head is predominant in Central Asia ; but that is a result which has been preceded by many stages of evolution.

According to all appearances, long-headed races filled the North of Europe and Asia at the close of the Ice Age, and they certainly predominated in both continents, with the exception of certain regions of Central Asia. The remnants of these dolichocephalic peoples in Asia are probably the Ainos in Yezo and Saghalin, the Yenissei-Ostiaks who have preserved their ancient tongue in the midst of tribes speaking a Mongolian and Finno-Ugrian language, and other fragments of nationalities in Siberia. **Distribution** In the south the long-heads **of the** are again predominant in the **Early Races** mixed population of Tibet. Many of these primitive dolichocephalic nations have developed in Northern Europe, and partly in Northern Asia, under the influence of the climate, into fair-haired and blue-eyed men ; among the Siberians and the inhabitants of Central Asia large numbers of these can still be found. Probably long heads and also a dark skin are the peculiarities common to primitive man.

Granted that the fair-skinned races were developed under the influence of the climate, the short-headed race is perhaps a variety which is explicable by the relaxation of the struggle for existence which growing civilisation induced. We may find parallels in the domestic animals, in which the same fundamental cause leads to all sorts of changes—to gigantic or diminutive growth, to wool-like hair or different coloured hair, and so on. A short-headed race developed in Asia in early times, and in the course of history occupied the greater part of that continent as well as large districts of Europe. Innermost Asia may possibly have been the primitive home of this race. It cannot at present be definitely settled whether it **The Home** grew up in Tibet, or in Mon-**of Primitive** golia, or, lastly, farther west in **Mankind** Turkestan and even Iran. The beginnings of a higher civilisation seem to start from this race. The first gleam of credible historical knowledge shows to us in the west and east of Asia, in Babylonia and China respectively, a brachycephalic people as the representatives of civilisations which are so closely related in their main features that they suggest with almost overwhelming force a former connection between these peoples, or, at least, their manners and customs. That civilisation was based on agriculture by means of the plough, and on stock-breeding ; that is, on the same foundation as our modern farming. These are by no means obvious achievements which must

Civilisation and Early Husbandry necessarily have been made by every progressive people. The contrary is proved by the instance of the civilised nations of America, who were ignorant of the plough or beasts of draught, and adhered to the use of the mattock, although in other respects their husbandry stood on a high level. In Eastern as well as Western Asia wheat was originally the chief cereal.

Even stock-breeding, which at first was almost exclusively cattle-breeding, shows similar features in both regions. In ancient Babylonia, as in China even to-day, cattle were used exclusively for drawing burdens and for food, and no use was made of their milk. In this respect the two civilised peoples are sharply differentiated from the nomads, who later interrupted the connection between East and West, for the existence of the wandering herdsman depended mainly on the milk of his herds. Horse-breeding appears to have been already practised at the time when the two civilisations were still in contact or arose in a common original home. Here, again, a peculiarity appears. The horse is not ridden, but is used only for draught, and nothing is known of the value of mare's milk, the favourite drink of the Scythians and Mongols.

Another peculiarity common to both the ancient civilised peoples is their acquaintance with copper and bronze, so that we may regard the short-headed races as inventors of metal-working. This fact is important for Europe. There

Ancient Knowledge of Metals also short-headed tribes, following the range of the Alps, migrated in early times from the East, and spread the knowledge of casting bronze as far as Britain. Another similar stream of civilisation reached Southern Siberia, where the rich copper mines and gold mines of the Altai favoured the growth of a peculiar bronze culture.

Supposing that the original home of civilisation did not lie in Central Asia, still the union of the two most ancient civilisations must somehow have been produced by this region.

This much, therefore, can be stated with tolerable certainty, that an ancient civilisation depending on agriculture, stock-breeding, and the knowledge of bronze whose representatives were peoples of a short-headed race, developed in Central Asia or its western frontiers. Under the influence of this civilisation the population increased, so that emigration and colonisation were possible in various directions. In this way tribes of the northern as well as of the southern long-headed race may have been influenced and won over to this higher civilisation. This first period ends roughly with the close of the fourth millennium B.C.

The view that agriculture is older than nomadism contradicts the traditional idea which makes the stages of subsistence by natural products, of cattle-breeding, and of agriculture, follow one after another as regular steps in development. But this theory, which so long stood in the way of a sound comprehension of the most ancient questions of civilisation, is now

The First Domestication of Animals no longer accepted. The oldest agricultural peoples, who broke up the ground with the plough, were also the first cattle-breeders. This does not imply that men tamed oxen and horses from the very first with the conscious intention of using them as beasts of draught. Comparative ethnology teaches us that even now primitive peoples, who tame all sorts of animals, first do so to make pets or companions of them before they think of turning the animals to any profitable use. This does not exclude the possibility that religious conceptions may have first prompted them to domesticate animals.

So long as the breeding of cattle and subsequently of horses continued to be closely bound up with agriculture, and so long as the milk of the female animals was not used there could be no idea of nomadism. It was the use of milk that first enabled whole nations to depend on the possession of flocks and herds for their existence, without reducing their stock by excessive slaughtering. This food first made the arid tracts of steppe habitable and actual sources of prosperity and power. But the nature of their homes and pastures forces these people to make continual and systematic migrations, and thus stamps on the whole sphere of

their material civilisation a trait of mobility and uncertainty, while it marks
their character with a mixture of unrest
and aggressiveness which from time to
time recurs prominently in history. This
new economic form of nomadism cannot
have arisen suddenly ; it assumes the
breeding of such animals as secrete a
continuous and large quantity of milk.
This is, again, a result of long custom ;
for the female animals of themselves give
only as much milk as is necessary for the
early nourishment of their young ones,
after which time the supply dries up.

The laborious and tedious breeding of
milk-giving breeds of cows and soon
afterwards of mares, was not accomplished
by the short-headed civilised nations—
among whom the Chinese to the present
day despise milk—but apparently by
long-headed tribes. We now see Aryan-
speaking nomads in the north and Semitic-
speaking nomads in the south appear on
the scene as economic and political powers.
The civilisation of China still remained
uninfluenced by them ; from which it
seems to follow that nomadism originated
The Rise on the steppes of Western Asia
of Early and Eastern Europe, not in Cen-
Nomadism tral Asia. In Babylonia, the old
empire of Sumerian civilisation
had been overthrown by Semitic nomads
before the year 3000 B.C. After that date
the conquerors and conquered gradually
amalgamated and appeared next in
history as Babylonians. Other Semites
as migratory herdsmen kept to that way
of life, of which the oldest narratives in
the Bible draw so pleasing a picture.

Still more momentous was the first
appearance in history of the Aryan nomads.
The old dispute as to the origin of the
Aryans cannot be answered, because the
whole problem has been put so wrongly.
Two totally distinct questions have been
jumbled together—namely, what was the
origin of the blond, or at least light-
coloured, dolichocephalic peoples, the
majority of whom now employ Aryan
dialects, and what was the starting-point of
the Aryan language ? Of the first question we have already spoken. The fair-
skinned, dolichocephalic peoples are a
race of men which has developed under
the influence of the cool climate out of the
long-headed tribes originally spread over
the whole of Europe and the greater part
of Asia. The original Aryan language,
on the other hand, may have begun, as

some good linguists maintain, in the lowlands of Eastern Europe. It is easy to
draw the inference that precisely this
beginning of a nomadic way of life, and
the necessary migrations, go far to
explain the extraordinary dissemination
of Aryan dialects.

The great historical events with which
the Aryan nomads appear on the scene
Wave of are the conquest and the
Nomad Aryanisation of Iran and India.
Migration The wave of nations may have
rolled in the third millennium
B.C. from Eastern Europe over the
Turanian steppe to the south and have first
flooded Eastern Iran, until an outlet was
made through the valley of Kabul, through
which a part of the Aryans flowed into
India.

A large number of the nomads remained
behind in the steppes of Eastern Europe
and Western Siberia, where they were
known to the earliest Greek authorities
as Scythians. Probably all the nomad
tribes of the great lowlands of Asia and
Europe were comprised under the name
" Scythians " in the wider sense, and
among them probably were represented
peoples speaking a non-Aryan language.

The Scythians long showed no wish to
penetrate into the mountainous civilised
country of the Balkan peninsula, or to
push on over the Caucasus into the region
of the Assyrio-Babylonian civilisation. Iran
was protected by their own kinsmen, who
gradually settled there. On the other
hand, they certainly spread widely toward
the east, perhaps beyond the Altai, where
other tribes gradually imitated them in
their way of life. Numerous blond nomads
are found at a subsequent period in West-
Central Asia.

The horse was employed at first by the
nomads to draw their waggons, until they
acquired the art of riding, and by that
means enormously increased their mobility.
Place of It cannot yet be decided with
the Horse complete certainty whether the
in History Aryans of India on their migrations were acquainted with
riding. It is indisputable that the Scythians by Homeric times were a nation
of horsemen. The nomad tribes became
acquainted with iron at a later period than
the settled civilised nations. The Iranian
Massagetæ in the modern Turkestan,
when they fought their battles against the
Persians in the time of Cyrus, were
familiar with only copper and gold.

Both these metals were obtained from the mines in the Altai, and probably also from the old mining district of the Caucasus. The great Aryan migrations completely interrupted the connection between the old civilisations of the East and West, if such connection still existed. The Chinese nation has continued its independent development, although it has

The Parting of Two Civilisations by no means remained quite stiff and impervious to external influences. Any stimulus that reached China later on the long and dangerous road through the nomad regions of Central Asia, or by sea round Further India, was far too weak to produce deep results. The Chinese nation had to concentrate all its energies on external policy, to keep off the nomads who thronged round its frontiers, or to absorb them, and finally to separate them and pacify them by a well-devised system of throwing out agricultural colonies.

The men with whom the Chinese had to struggle were not migratory herdsmen of Aryan language, but members of the short-headed race or the Mongolian stock, as it is called, after a victorious people which appeared late on the scene. The earliest history of China records nothing as yet of struggles with nomads, but only of the conquest of the forces of Nature and at most of collisions with aborigines, who were at the early hunting stage. However incredible and indefinite in detail these earliest traditions may be, yet the absence of all accounts of nomad invasions, which subsequently were every-day occurrences, and could hardly have been forgotten in an artificial construction of history, is a very significant feature.

It cannot yet be shown whether the nomads of Central Asia had a Bronze Age of a duration worth mentioning, or whether they passed immediately from the Stone Age to the Iron Age. The

Blending of Nationality and Language latter alternative is more probable in the case of most tribes of Central Asia, apart from the old Bronze region in Southern Siberia and its adjoining districts. In Central Asia itself the growth of nomadism with its warlike propensities and its mobility greatly favoured the mixture of nationalities. We find a proof of this in the language. While in earlier times the Aryan language spread in the west under the influence of nomad life, at a later period the Mongolian and Finnish-Ugrian group of languages prevailed in Central Asia and far in the direction of Siberia and Europe. The characteristics of the boundless plains, in which the nations combine and blend like clouds of dust, are reflected in the facts of history. In the gorges of the few mountains a people may possibly preserve its individuality. But any nations that have developed without disturbance for a time will at last inevitably be dislodged, destroyed, and absorbed in another nationality, only to share with this in its turn a similar fate. Small tribes carry others along with them, increase like an avalanche, and finally give their name to an enormous nationality composed of most heterogeneous elements. Peoples before whom the world trembled burst like soap-bubbles, and disappear from the pages of history without leaving a trace behind.

The result is that the population of Central Asia becomes more and more homogeneous from the point of view of language and ethnology, and that the national names designate less and less distinct groups of humanity.

Fusion of Races in Central Asia New differences are created only by the degree of civilisation and by the mixture with other races on the edge of the steppe region of Central Asia. Such racial mixtures were naturally formed first where the Aryan nomads adjoined the Mongolian, and where subsequently Iranian agriculturists gained a footing on the pasture lands of Turkestan. The Aryan race lost much ground here from the point of view of language, but from that of anthropology it exercised great influence on the Mongolian peoples. The old long-skulled race is often mixed with the Mongolian in Siberia. On the other hand, the linguistic affinity of the Mongols with the Tibetans and with the inhabitants of Further India has nothing to do with these more recent occurrences, but may point to a very early connection, which cannot for the moment be more accurately determined. A significant trace of this connection is the name of heaven and the god of heaven— Chinese, *tien*, Bureyatic, *tengri*, Altaic, *tengere*, which crops up as *tangaroa* in Polynesia, and was clearly brought there by the Malayan wave of nations from Southern Asia.   HEINRICH SCHURTZ.

EARLY HISTORY OF CENTRAL ASIA
ANCIENT TURKESTAN AND THE EARLY NOMADS

THE nation of Mongolian nomads which first formed a constitutional unit, and harassed Eastern Asia for many centuries, were known to Chinese authorities as the Hiung nu. The similarity of this name with that of the Huns, who later flooded Europe and heralded the great migration of nations, has long been noticed, and Joseph de Guignes (1721–1800), the first real student of the history of Central Asia, declared the Huns to be kinsmen or descendants of the Hiung nu. This conjecture has in recent times been corroborated by convincing proofs. We may therefore designate the old Hiung nu by the indisputably more correct name of Huns. They appear in the Indian epics as Huna, in the Avesta as Hunavo, in Greek accounts as Phunoi and Unoi. Linguistically the nation was most akin to the later Turks. The kingdom of the Huns **The First Hun Kingdom** was formed in the modern Mongolia about 1200 B.C., apparently under the influence of a Chinese exile of high rank, who created out of the scattered hordes the beginnings of constitutional unity on the model of his own country. In the preceding century some of these hordes had made inroads on China, but were unable to achieve great results. After the unification of the Huns, and especially after the beginning of the Chau dynasty in China in 1122 B.C., which marks the beginning of the Chinese feudal system, the danger became greater. The scantiness of our sources of information prevents us from deciding whether any connection existed between the wars against the nomads and the growth of the feudal system of partitioning the land.

The first ruler of the Chau dynasty, Wu Wang, had still maintained friendly relations with the Huns, who certainly feared the power of the empire, which had gained fresh strength under his government, and tried to buy his goodwill

by presents. As the imperial power decayed, the attacks were renewed with increased vigour. Northern Shansi was laid waste in 910. Some decades later the Huns must have been driven out from the heart of Shansi, where they had established themselves, by an army under **Invasion of China by the Huns** the personal command of the emperor. There was a recurrence of similar events. There was apparently pasture land enough in China at that time to attract the nomads to a long sojourn, just as afterwards small hordes of nomads frequently settled in the interior of China.

About 700 B.C. the Huns advanced to Shantung; in 650 B.C. they devastated Pechili, and there was a succession of attacks on the country, disintegrated by feudalism, and incapable of any combined resistance, until at last the ruler of the Chin Empire, known as Shih Huang-ti (246–210 B.C.), once more transformed, in 220 B.C., China into a real united state, enormously increased his power by the conquest of Southern China, and proceeded to take prompt and decided steps against the nomads. A powerful army drove out the Huns from the country of Ordo within the northern bend of the Hoang-ho, which was an important position as the rendezvous for nomad invaders. The new possessions were protected by military colonies, and China proper was defended against the attacks of predatory hordes by the **The Great Wall of China** gigantic rampart of the Great Wall. Portions of the Great Wall already existed on the frontiers of some earlier feudal states. Shih Huang-ti connected them so as to form a continuous line of defence, which stretched from the shore of the Yellow Sea to the port of Kansu; if it had been kept in repair and efficiently defended, it would certainly have checked the inroads of the Huns. During the first period it served its purpose to some extent. It was due to the Great Wall that the attacks of the Huns were now directed against another quarter, and remote regions of Asia indirectly felt the mighty shock. But the chaotic condition into which China relapsed immediately after the death of Shih Huang-ti soon spoilt

Growth of Hun Power the purpose of the stupendous erection. It was then that the power of the Huns was acquiring new strength under vigorous leaders. Our first comparatively accurate account of the constitution of the Huns dates from the period subsequent to the death of Shih Huang-ti. The eyes of the Chinese were then turned with anxious attention to the increasing power of their nomad neighbours.

The new growth of the Hun Empire began under the rule of Mete, whose father, Tuman or Deuman, had already extended his power from Northern Mongolia to Kansu. Mete, who would have been excluded from the legitimate succession, murdered his father with the help of a devoted army, and was soon able to reanimate the old warlike spirit of his people. He found the territory of the Huns shut in by powerful neighbours on two sides. On the east the Tunghu or Wu hwan, Tungusian tribes akin to the Koreans, had founded a powerful realm and felt themselves so superior to the Huns that they took advantage of the usurpation to claim a high price for their neutrality. On the south-west, on the Altyn in Tagh, were settled the Yue-tshi, a nomad people of Tibetan stock, who were the connecting link of the trade of China and the West, and were perhaps identical with the old Issedones. The Tunghu, deceived by the apparent compliance of Mete, were first attacked and dispersed in 209 B.C. ; they withdrew to the highlands of modern Manchuria. A part of the Sien-pē Tartars, or Tungusians, a

Neighbours of the Early Huns people living further to the east, who also suffered from the attacks of the Huns, migrated to Korea and Japan. On the east the sea fixed an impassable limit to further shiftings of the position of nations ; but on the west, where the Huns now hurled themselves against the Yue-tshi, the movement had room to spread more widely. The Yue-tshi first retreated before the advance of their assailants only into more remote regions of their own country, to the basin of the Tarim, in 177 B.C. After the death of Mete, in 170, they attempted to recover their old territory, but suffered a second crushing defeat from his successor, which produced a division of the nation in 165 B.C. The smaller part found homes south of the Nanshan range ; but the bulk of the people, the " Great Yue-tshi," did not turn southward, but followed the natural trend of the country westward. Driven out from the Tarim basin, they crossed the Tianshan Mountains and sought refuge in the pasture lands on the confines of Europe and Asia, the old arena of the Scythian nomads. On the Issik-kul they came across a shepherd people of Iranian stock, the She, who were compelled to fly before the overwhelming invasion into Ferghana.

Meanwhile the Huns had succeeded in conquering a part of North-west China and East Siberia. The vanquished tribes were not dislodged or made tributary, but to some degree absorbed, since the women were distributed among the conquerors, and the young men were enrolled

Domestic Life of The Huns in the army. In their life and customs the Huns appear as a people who depended for their existence on cattle-breeding, hunting, and to some extent agriculture, but gave the fullest play to their warlike propensities. The place of honour was given to the young and efficient warriors, and old age was despised. No one was reckoned to have reached full manhood until he had slain at least one foe. The method of fighting which afterward decided the battles of the Western Huns and Mongols—the charge of mounted archers, the feigned flight, and the storm of arrows which laid low the unsuspecting pursuer—was already developed among the ancient Huns, as well as the division of the army into two wings. This military system was maintained in times of peace also. The ruler, or *Shenyu,* who to some degree commanded the centre, had two supreme officials, the Tuchi, or Duchi, under him, one of whom was over the eastern, the other over the western, wing or division of the army and the country. The trend from west to east in the geographical configuration of Asia is again recognisable in this arrangement, which was also adopted by the later great nomad empires. The Tuchi and a number of other high officials could be chosen only

A VIEW ON "THE ROOF OF THE WORLD": CHARACTERISTIC SCENERY IN THE PAMIR MOUNTAINS, CENTRAL ASIA

from the kinsmen of the Shenyu, who, with some few other families, had the virtual government of the empire in their hands.

After the death of Mete, in 170 B.C., the power of the Huns increased at first. The Yue-tshi were completely beaten, and the Usun, one of the fair-haired nomad tribes of Central Asia, were driven from their homes in Kansu to the west, where, following on the steps of the Yue-tshi, they caused these latter to fly before them from the Issik-Kul farther southward. The sphere of the Mongolian language and race was thus considerably extended by the Huns. The growing power of the Hun empire was most dangerous to China, the frontiers of which were perpetually ravaged, and seemed still more threatened, since the Tibetan nomads, who were settled in the western mountains, now began to form alliances with the Huns, and to undertake their raids on a mutual understanding.

Tibetans and Huns Unite

It was of no use merely to repel these attacks. If the Chinese wished to free themselves from their oppressors, they were compelled to advance along the old road from Kansu to the Tarim basin, take up strong positions there, separate the southern nomad countries from the northern, and at the same time obtain possession of the indispensable bases and halting-places of the Hun armies to the south of the desert of Gobi. In this way the Western trade also, which had previously depended for its prosperity on the caprice of the nomads, was certain to come under the influences of China. The energetic Emperor Wu Ti (140–87) staked everything on the execution of this colossal plan, entered into alliances with the Yue-tshi and Usun, by this means threatened the Huns in the rear, and finally forced them by successful engagements to retire to the north of Mongolia in 120 B.C. The first step in the advance westward was thus taken, and a new era inaugurated in the foreign policy of China.

Chinese Take the Offensive

The Hun empire still maintained its position in the north for some time, and even considerably extended its power toward the west, but the old sovereignty was a thing of the past. The attacks on the neighbouring peoples and disputes for the crown began to disorganise the constitution, until finally, about 50 B.C., the empire broke up into a southern and a northern part, of which the first recognised the Chinese suzerainty, while the northern still maintained its independence.

Transitory successes could no longer check the fall of the Hun power, for the Chinese could now play off the southern Huns successfully against the northern Huns, and instigate other nomad tribes against the northern empire, which was encircled by enemies. The northern Hun empire finally, in 84 A.D., succumbed to the attacks, in which even Siberian tribes, and especially the Sien pē Tartars, formerly the victims of the Huns, but now grown strong enough for a new conflict, took part. Some of the Huns fled westward, where they were destined yet to attain great prosperity ; the rest were scattered, or were absorbed in the Sien pē, who now possessed the greater portion of Mongolia.

The southern Huns held out longer, at one time as subjects and allies of the Chinese, at another as their opponents, or as supporters of pretenders to the throne. But after 142 A.D. there was an end to the southern empire of the Huns, though not to the influence of the people on the destinies of China. The Huns, who had familiarised themselves with the Chinese civilisation, gradually began to exert a political influence, and finally emperors of Hun origin for a time sat on the throne of the Celestial Empire, or on those of the fragments into which it broke up. But they no longer ruled as nomad princes ; they had become genuine Chinese in act and thought.

Division of the Hun Empire

The nomadic element in the west of Central Asia was of earlier origin than that in the east, and large migrations of nomad peoples had taken place far earlier there than elsewhere. Some thousand years before the founding of the empire of the Huns, migratory tribes of Aryans had occupied Iran and India. But there the movements met with a certain check. The Iranians did not succeed in penetrating westward into the lowlands of Babylonia ; on the contrary, they saw themselves restricted to their new home, and by the influence of the inhabitants who had settled before them, as well as of the ancient civilisation of the country watered by the Tigris and Euphrates, they were gradually brought

ON THE GREAT RIVER OF WEST-CENTRAL ASIA: THE OXUS, OR AMU DARIA, LOOKING EAST, NEAR KHOJAILI

over to a settled life, without immediately losing the warlike virtues of their old pastoral existence.

The mixed Iranian people, which was formed from the Aryan immigrants and the aboriginal population, thus became a bulwark of Western Asia against any further inroads of nomads. The shock of invading hordes was checked by **Checking** the resistance of a people cling-**the Wave of** ing more closely to the soil. **Invasion** The Iranians were not pushed further toward Western Asia by vast bodies of men pressing after them, but the great movement of the nations came to a stop. When the Medes and the Persians obtained the sovereignty over the whole of Western Asia, they were already under the spell of the existing Western civilisation, and were unable to give any Iranian character to the newly conquered countries.

It thus follows that the Aryan nomads of Western Asia generally are hardly spoken of for more than a thousand years. The Assyrio-Babylonian records know nothing of them, and no news of them has reached the Chinese. There were, no doubt, numerous battles and movements of nations, but these last were not on the imposing scale of the migration to India and Iran. The arrival of brachycephalic nomad tribes in Central Asia proper must gradually have made its influence felt, with the effect that the Scythian hordes— nomads of Aryan stock — which had pushed far toward the east, were partly absorbed, partly driven back upon the west, where the shocks of their attack continued, wave upon wave.

The last consequence of the mightiest onslaught was the invasion of Asia Minor by the Cimmerians about the year 700 B.C. These were a nomad people of Thracian stock, who pastured their flocks north of the Danube. After them pressed on the Scythians, who again were expelled by the Sarmatians. The first cause of the movement may perhaps be **Asia Minor** attributed to the westward **the Arena of** advance of the Huns, who had **Race Conflict** long since founded an empire, and clearly pressed on not only against China, but also toward the west. The Cimmerians threatened Assyria from Asia Minor and Armenia, and by so doing came into contact with the Medes, who were pressing on from the east.

The period of more certain history, which begins with the founding of the Medo-Persian Empire, shows us at once the settled Iranians at war with the nomads. An incorrect idea, which is explained by the failure of the Greek historians to understand the conditions of Persia, and Eastern Persia in particular, represents the Persians as the aggressors, who coveted the territory of the nomad herdsmen. In reality, the half mythical expedition of Cyrus against the Massagetæ in 530 B.C., and the well-authenticated march of Darius against the Scythians in 515 B.C., were only attempts to attack the ever-restless neighbours in their own country, and by this means to secure the frontiers. The expedition of Darius in particular was probably based on the plan of attacking the nomad tribes by a sweeping flank movement, and of thus preventing their retreat and finally subjugating them.

The Persian Empire was too short-lived to complete so colossal an undertaking, which would have required the dogged patience of the Chinese. The attempt of Darius, which effectively secured the lower line of the Danube for the Persians, was not repeated. The Scythians, on the other hand, realised the weak **Brief Life** points in the Persian Empire, **of Persian** as is proved by their somewhat **Empire** later plan of attacking Persian territory by way of the Caucasian isthmus, for which they tried to obtain the aid of the Spartans, who were intended to make a simultaneous invasion of Asia Minor.

The system of colonisation, which alone promised permanent results, seems to have been prosecuted all the more vigorously from Eastern Iran, and the fact that the majority of the nomads were of Iranian stock, like the Persians, facilitated the movement. It is probable that in quite early times on the Oxus and Jaxartes —that is to say, in Bactria and Sogdiana— states possessing an Iranian civilisation were developed, which were afterward politically united with Persia, although they can hardly have remained in permanent and complete dependence. By the expedition of Alexander the Great in 327 B.C. they were more closely united with the new world-empire of that monarch, and the foundation was laid for a Greco-Iranian civilised state, the Bactrian Empire, which was developed in the Seleucid period about 250 B.C. and showed a considerable vitality. This empire, like the ancient Iranian Bactria, was a bulwark against the onset of the nomads. It

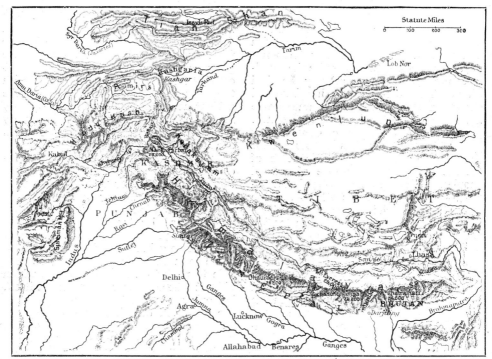

THE GREAT MOUNTAIN SYSTEMS IN AND AROUND TIBET

showed itself a match for the migratory Iranian tribes, and it was only the impact of a non-Aryan shepherd people from Central Asia that for the first time shook once more the strong rampart which guarded Western Asia and India. This new tide of nations, which set in about 160 B.C., was certainly, even if indirectly, due to the Huns.

The nomad tribe of the Usun had abandoned its home on the borders of China and had retreated westward away from the sphere of the power of the Huns, as related above. Since it followed the roads which led away along the Tian Shan and finally crossed that range, it reached the Issik-Kul, where the Yue-tshi, its predecessors on the same path, had won homes for themselves. These latter were now compelled to give way; but they did not again advance westward, where warlike Scythian tribes barred the way, but turned southward against the Bactrian Empire, the internal disruption of which would have been well known to them as neighbours. The result was that Northern Bactria, the country on the Oxus and Jaxartes, fell easily into their hands, while the rest of the Greek state south of the Hindu Kush maintained its position for the time.

The Parthian kingdom, which successfully undertook the defence of the frontiers against the nomads, had grown up since 250 B.C. in Western and Central Iran. But if Iran was closed to the Yue-tshi, they did not allow the road to India, which from all time had possessed a magic attraction for every conquering people, to be permanently blocked. The southern part of the Bactrian Empire stood for some hundred years more. Then, about 25 B.C., Kozulo Kadphises, who had reunited the Yue-tshi after their division into five clans, subdued the modern Afghanistan. This immediately opened the road to the Indian possessions of the Bactrian Empire.

About the year 10 A.D. Kozulo's successor, Huemo Kadphises, or Kadaphes, advanced into North-western India, and thus laid the foundation of the Indo-Scythian Empire. The Yue-tshi now appear in history as Indo-Scythians. They have frequently been confused at a later date with the White Huns, or Ephtalites, with whom they are absolutely unconnected. Undeniably, the fact that Bactria as far as the borders of Central Asia was then united with large portions of India under one rule did much to make Indian influence, especially the Buddhism then flourishing in India, felt far away northward. India generally entered into closer and more direct relations with Central Asia. Fifty years after the founding of the Indo-Scythian Empire the Buddhist propaganda had already reached China. This empire of the Yue-tshi showed a stubborn vitality, and broke up only in the year 579 A.D.

Relations of India with Central Asia A large part of Central Asia first acquires importance for the history and culture of mankind on the appearance of nomad peoples, and as the fountain-head of a disintegrating force; on the other hand, the Tarim basin, which is also called East Turkestan or High Tartary, claims the attention of the historian much earlier and in another sense. By far the greater part of the plain lying between the Tian Shan, the Pamirs, and the Kuen Lun is emphatically a region of steppe and desert. But the mountain streams, the largest of which unite in the River Tarim and the Lob Nor, create a series of fertile oases, which support a considerable permanent population, and form a chain of trading posts along the foot of the mountains. In all probability the oases were more numerous in early times, and the intermediate barren stretches less desolate. The Tarim basin could thus form in ancient days the bridge between the civilisation of Eastern and Western Asia, even if it was not an international highway, and saw at the same time a higher civilisation develop in its fertile regions. The key to many problems of the prehistoric period lies under the burning sands of Eastern Turkestan.

The ancient trade communications through the Tarim basin are certainly to be regarded as a relic of the former connection with civilisation, which was maintained notwithstanding the increasing poverty of the soil and the appearance of barbarous nomad tribes. The nomad, as such, is not inclined to amass the heavy goods which the town merchant stores in his vaults. His chief wealth lies in his flocks and herds, which again depend for their numbers on the possession of the requisite pasture land. Even in the Tarim basin the real traders were thus always to be found among the settled inhabitants of the oases.

Wealth of the Nomad

The earliest recorded trade which passed through the Tarim basin and brought Eastern and Western Asia into some sort of communication was the silk trade. The breeding of silkworms, if Chinese tradition does not err, was practised by that people from very ancient times. The Chinese themselves seem to have attached no especial importance to the silk trade with the West, as is shown by the silence of the ancient accounts. The trade accordingly must have been conducted chiefly by foreigners, who were eager to obtain in exchange the highly valued product of China, while it was long a matter of indifference to the Chinese, who were aware that they could very well dispense with the goods received in return.

The imagination of the West was all the more excited by the mysterious Eastern land which produced the costly silk, and attempts to gain further information were made from early times. Herodotus was able to refer to a book of travels, which did not indeed throw light on China itself, but only on the route of the silk trade and the condition of things in the valley of Tarim; this was the Arimaspeia of Aristeas, which appeared in the seventh century B.C., soon after the Cimmerian irruption. This narrative, notwithstanding its romantic dress, was probably based on actual explorations and travels. The Issedones, whom Aristeas professes to have reached, were an actual people, and their homes probably lay in the Tarim basin. The western neighbours of the Issedones were the Massagetæ—that is, the Iranian nomads, who pastured their herds in Western Turkestan. The name of the Issedones may be of Iranian origin, and have been given to the people, who styled themselves otherwise, by the merchants, who were mainly Iranians. We thus see why Chinese records do not mention the name.

The Home of the Silk Trade

The Issedones were probably a branch of the Tibetan stock, which once spread further northward than now. They are possibly identical with, or at least allied to, the later Yue-tshi, who were expelled by the Huns from their homes in the Tarim basin. But the population of that region can hardly have been homogeneous at the time of Aristeas. The Tibetan Issedones, who are occasionally called Scythians, were far more probably a nomad people, who exercised sovereignty over the country of the oases; but the remnants of the representatives of an earlier civilisation may well have settled

ON THE GREAT TRADE ROUTE OF CENTRAL ASIA

The long commercial highway of Central Asia, running right across the southern part of Western Turkestan and through the Tarim basin in Eastern Turkestan, is a road unparalleled for its length and difficulties. It has changed its course many times in history as robber nomads gained supremacy in the various districts, and a laborious and difficult route has always been preferred to the best road if the latter involved risk of robberies, exorbitant tolls, and other vexatious imposts in these oases, precisely as in modern times the towns of Eastern Turkestan are inhabited by a very mixed population. Long-skulled Iranians, who came into the country as traders, or immigrated as agriculturists, may well have mixed here in early times with the permanently settled short-skulled inhabitants and with the tribes of the Tibetan nomads.

Battles of the Nomads The Arimaspes, a warlike tribe of nomads who seem to have made frequent inroads into the Tarim basin, are mentioned by Aristeas as northern neighbours of the Issedones. By this title he undoubtedly means the Huns, whom we have already seen as invaders of China. In the second century B.C. they also fundamentally altered the conditions of Eastern Turkestan by driving the Yue-tshi westward. The settled population of the oases probably was little influenced by these movements. Aristeas gives noteworthy accounts of the battles of the Arimaspes with the " griffins," the guardians of the gold, who lived to the north of them. These " griffins " are certainly the nations on the Altai, the representatives of the old bronze culture of Southern Siberia, and the builders of those tombs in which great quantities of gold ornaments have recently been found.

Thus the picture of the activity of the warlike nation of the ancient Huns, that leaven of the nomad peoples, is complete on every side. On the east the indefatigable sons of the desert continually advanced against the rich plains of China ; on the south they directed their raids against the representatives of the transit trade of Central Asia, the Tibetan nomads, and the inhabitants of the oases in the Tarim basin ; and on the north they harassed the industrious tribes of the Altai with their expeditions. The great Hun campaign, which finally convulsed Europe to its centre, was only a

Preludes to the Shock of Europe gigantic continuation of these earlier struggles for power and booty. While Aristeas has exhaustively described the Issedones and Arimaspes, he appears to confound the Chinese with the Hyperboreans, the peaceful people on the uttermost border of the world ; at any rate, his account of the Hyperboreans as reported by Herodotus almost coincides with the later descriptions of the Seres. The towns and trading settlements in

the Tarim basin, which Aristeas mentions, can partially be identified with still existing modern localities. This is impossible in the case of many, as may be concluded from the great number of towns buried beneath the sand which have been recently explored by Sven Hedin. Further aids toward identification are supplied by the accounts of the Macedonian merchant Maës, or Titianus, who enables us to fix the stations on the East Asiatic trade route in the first century A.D. This road led from Samarkand to Ferghana, whence the " Stone Tower " and the valley of the Kisil Su were reached, at the entrance of which an important trading town lay in the territory of Kasia. This was certainly the modern Kashgar, for which natural advantages of situation have secured uninterruptedly since ancient times a foremost position among the cities of the Tarim basin. The " Scythian Issedon " may be represented by the modern Kuchar, the most important mart of the Turkish tribes settled to the north in the Tian Shan ; Asmira may be the present Hami. The first Chinese trading

Ancient Towns Under Modern Names town in the district of Kansu which was reached by the caravans coming from the west, the modern Su chau, is identified with the ancient Drosache.

The larger centres of trade, from a political point of view, enjoyed certainly some share of independence, although they did not venture on any very stringent measures against the nomads from fear of interruption to commerce. The different vicissitudes in the relations of the nomads to the dwellers in the country and the towns will have been repeated on a small scale in the Tarim basin ; at one time brute force, at another the refinements of civilisation, gained the day. The connection with India, the beginnings of which are obscure, was of great importance to this civilisation. In this way Eastern Turkestan became the bridge on which Indian manners and customs, and, above all, Indian religion, passed both to China and the rest of Central Asia, in order, in course of time, to work great revolutions in the character and habits of the Central Asiatic peoples.

The trade which moved on the long commercial highway of Central Asia, a road unparalleled for its length and difficulties, could not always be prosecuted with unvarying uniformity. External influences and internal commotions produced the inevitable result that the traffic became brisker at one time, and at another flagged or almost died away, and that the character of the trade altered. In fact, so far as we can survey the conditions generally, we see continual changes occurring. The routes along which the main bulk of trade passes are changed, the customs of commerce are altered; and finally even the wares which East and West exchange are not always the same, but new ones are added to the old.

It is quite in accordance with the nature of commercial intercourse that it always seeks out paths for itself along the line of least resistance. A somewhat difficult and laborious route is preferred to the best road, if the latter involves risk and cost from repeated robberies, exorbitant tolls,

tshi, who possibly are to be identified with the Issedones, the Huns had the northern highway through the Tarim basin in their power, while in the south Tibetan nomads, the Khiang, commanded the roads. It appears from the account furnished in the year 122 B.C. by Chang-kien to his emperor, Wu Ti, after an **Chinese** inquiry into the roads leading **Commercial** to the west and the possibilities **Enquiry** of trade, that traffic then went quite in the south through Szechuen and Tsaidam to the southern border of the Tarim basin, while in the north the Huns and in the centre the Khiang barred the roads. These unfavourable conditions largely contributed to the result that the Chinese abandoned their former policy of indifference toward the peoples of the steppe.

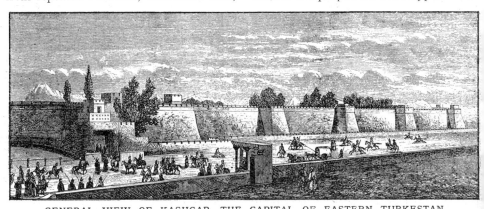

GENERAL VIEW OF KASHGAR, THE CAPITAL OF EASTERN TURKESTAN

The old town of Kashgar, which dates from 1513, is surrounded by a high clay wall; the new town, of which the above is a view, is also surrounded by massive clay walls and dates from 1838. The population is about 50,000.

and other vexatious imposts. In Central Asia, where, on the one hand, different routes were available for the trade between Eastern and Western Asia, and, on the other hand, the nomads were always ready to plunder the merchants directly by brigandage or indirectly by tolls, commerce clearly changed its roads **Shifting of** more frequently than the **the Paths** extant accounts give us to **of Commerce** understand. The supremacy of the Huns in the north doubtless largely contributed toward the result that the northern routes were deserted and the traffic restricted to the roads in the Tarim basin. The wars of the Arimaspes with the Issedones may well have partly aimed at securing to the former the monopoly of trade. After the expulsion of the Yue-

There must also have been changes in the customs of trade. Over vast distances trade can be prosecuted in two ways: either one tribe hands on the goods to another by a system of frontier trade, until they finally reach their farthest destination after various exchanges, or the members of one or more peoples adopt the carrying trade as a profession and traverse the whole distance with their wares. It is, of course, conceivable that for part of the distance caravan trade was usual, and for the other transit trade. On the Central Asiatic routes both methods may have been popular, according to circumstances. The transit trade is, however, certainly older than the caravan system on a large scale. Whether it actually in places, as early Western accounts report, took the simple form of

1461

' dumb trade," or whether customs had been ascribed to the half mythical Seres which were observed elsewhere in intercourse with primitive nations, can no longer be ascertained.

It is in accordance with the whole attitude of China to the outer world that the Chinese did not engage in the carrying trade until late, while, on the contrary, the merchants of Iranian stock were continually exerting themselves to obtain the caravan trade over the whole distance. The opponents of the direct traffic between east and west were naturally the nomads ; above all, the Huns, who preferred to make the roads a desert rather than to lose the high profits obtainable from the transit trade. The laboriousness and insecurity of the traffic produced the result that large emporia grew up in different places, which served also as markets for the surrounding tribes ; such were Samarkand in Western and Kashgar in Eastern Turkestan.

Rise of Trade Centres

China, as we have seen, originally had little need for commerce with the outer world. Foreigners came to the Middle Kingdom in order to purchase the valued Chinese wares, but the Chinese themselves were quite satisfied to take in exchange all kinds of foreign products, with which they could easily dispense in case of need. The state of affairs could not permanently remain so favourable for China. The constant large exportations inevitably led to the growth of a sort of export industry ; that is to say, silk, lacquer, etc., were produced in greater quantities than the home Chinese market required.

If the export trade suddenly stopped, the consequences to China were serious. Besides this, China became gradually accustomed to certain foreign commodities, with which it could not dispense, especially to the spices, drugs, etc., of India and Arabia. Thus any dislocation of trade was severely felt. Such a result ensued when the Huns overthrew the Yue-tshi and barred the valley of the Tarim, while uncivilised Tibetan hordes rendered the roads dangerous in the south. It was an intolerable situation that the Huns should be able to cut off trade communications entirely or to cripple them by excessively high tolls, and the Chinese were inevitably driven to reprisals so soon as an energetic ruler governed them.

Importance of China's Export Trade

Other considerations prompted an advance into the basin of the Tarim. It was recognised in China that the menacing growth of the power of the nomads could be checked only by the occupation of a strong position in their rear and the division of the steppe region into two sections by a strongly fortified military road. Even in this case the old trade route through the Tarim basin suggested itself as the natural line of direction for the advance, while the trading towns naturally formed suitable bases of operations.

The Emperor Wu Ti, about 125 B.C., tried, therefore, to reopen the trade route of Central Asia, and at the same time to crush the enormously increased power of the Huns. An effort was made to gain for this object the alliance of the hereditary enemies of the Huns, the Yue-tshi, who had just conquered Northern Bactria and Sogdiana, and thus were masters of the western extremity of the Tarim roads. Wu Ti sent to them his general, Chang kien ; but, being taken prisoner on the way by the Huns, he did not reach the Yue-tshi until ten years later, and returned to China after an absence of thirteen years. He had been unable to accomplish his chief object of concluding an alliance with the Yue-tshi and arranging a combined attack on the Huns, since the successes of the Yue-tshi in Bactria had given a new, and for China an unfavourable, turn to the future policy of that people. In compensation he brought back to China a store of information about the Western countries and India. The consequent attempts of Wu Ti to establish communications with India through Tibet were a failure. On the other hand, the war against the Huns was now vigorously prosecuted, and the old trade road was intentionally made the base of operations. The Yumen Pass was occupied and secured by military colonies, while the power of the Huns was weakened by repeated blows and ousted from the Tarim basin. Trade revived, but with the difference that now even Chinese caravans and embassies went westward and there formed political connections, especially with the people of the An hsi or Ansi, probably the Parthians. The most easterly point of the Parthian Empire appears then to have been Margiana, or Merv, the Mu lu of Chinese accounts. The Chinese, therefore, certainly advanced so far. Many petty states of the Tarim basin,

Wars to Reopen Trade

and possibly of the countries lying farther to the west, entered into closer political union with the east, and partially recognised the suzerainty of China. It was not, however, before the year 108 B.C. that the immediate possessions of China were extended to the Lob Nor—that is to say, to the eastern boundary of the basin of the Tarim—and secured by fortifications. Chinese troops later advanced to Kashgar in 101 B.C. But the dominion of China in the Tarim basin was never firmly established, although alliances were frequently concluded with the Usun against the Huns. The power of the latter was still too strong to allow the petty states of Eastern Turkestan and the Uigurians any permanent connection with China. The

deposed the new sovereign, who, rightly or not, was accused of cruel tyranny, and put him to death. A Chinese army then appeared, killed the usurper in turn, and placed on the throne a new monarch, approved by China, who appears also to have asserted his power. The influence of China in the Tarim valley gradually diminished. At the beginning of the first century A.D. the power of Yarkand grew so strong that its king, in 33 A.D., claimed the suzerainty of the entire basin of the Tarim, after his request to be recognised by China as Governor of Eastern Turkestan had been refused. The prayers of the other oppressed minor states and the commercial blockade maintained by the king of Yarkand ought to have forced

AN UNDERGROUND WATER-MILL NEAR BOKHARA IN RUSSIAN TURKESTAN

influence of the Huns on the valley of the Tarim and the Western trade rose or fell according to their successes or reverses in their struggle with China.

But the other nomad tribes of Central Asia also interfered in the affairs of those parts. The childless sovereign of the small kingdom of Yarkand had destined a son of the king of the Usun to succeed him. The inhabitants of Yarkand, after the death of their monarch, with the consent of the Chinese Emperor Hsuan Ti, summoned this prince from China, where he was being educated, and in 64 B.C. placed him on the throne, thus hoping to secure for themselves the protection of the Usun and of the Chinese. But the brother of the late king, with the help of the Huns,

Shi Tsu to take vigorous action. The war with Yarkand, however, was left mainly to the Huns, who harassed the new kingdom in the Tarim basin for decades, with varying success.

The second great advance of the Chinese towards the West did not begin until 72 A.D. The wish to open up communications with the West was then stimulated by the introduction of the Buddhist teaching, which had entered China through the Tarim basin. A deputation which Ming Ti, the second emperor of the later or Eastern Han dynasty, had himself sent to the Yue-tshi had returned in 65 A.D., and brought back detailed information about Buddhism. The emperor, in consequence, was induced to erect a statue of Buddha

1463

in his capital, and to show peculiar favour to the new doctrine, without, however, giving it preference over the doctrines of Confucius. The chief cause, however, of the renewed advance westward was doubtless the circumstance that the South Huns had once more combined with **United Action by the Two Hun Nations** the North Huns to block the traffic, and had completely disorganised the sufficiently unsatisfactory conditions already existing in the Tarim basin. Various Chinese armies marched against the Huns in the year 72, one of which, under the command of the general Pan Chau, followed the old trade route to the Tarim basin. The appearance of this renowned commander and diplomatist immediately secured the victory of Chinese influence among the petty states, which had all suffered under the insecurity of trade and the military policy of the Huns.

This time the Chinese were not content with the easily-acquired spoil. They had heard, meanwhile, that a mighty empire of Ta-tsin, the Roman world-empire, lay in the west. The remarkable magnetic force exercised on each other by great states, which lies at the root of their conditions of existence and compels them gradually to absorb all petty intervening states and to form a well-defined frontier, began to assert its power here, although its complete triumph was prevented by the immensity of the distance to be traversed. The Chinese never obtained accurate knowledge of the Roman Empire. Probably they were partly acquainted with the eastern half only, and thought Antioch the capital of the Empire. The name Fu lin for the Roman Empire, which subsequently occurs, seems to be derived from Bethlehem, and thus to point to the Christian faith of the later Romans.

The campaign of Pan Chau, which took him nearly to the confines of Roman influence, dates some decades after the conquest of the Tarim basin. Pan Chau crossed the range of mountains to the west, traversed the territory of the Yuetshi, and finally, in 102 A.D., reached the Caspian Sea, whence he sent explorers further to the west in order to prepare for an attack on the Roman Empire. The unfavourable report, however, which he received and his advanced age forced him to return to China, where he died shortly after.

The political importance of his conquest was considerable, but could hardly be lasting. The numerous petty states, which, at the sight of his army, had sought the protection of China, had no choice but to make terms with their other powerful neighbours, now that China ceased to lend them assistance. The revenue from tribute, gifts, and tolls which China drew from the western countries was far from being sufficient to cover the great outgoings. And the traditional Chinese policy, which would hear nothing of any expansion of the old boundaries and attached little importance to the promotion of trade, now reasserted itself. There was, as early as 120 A.D., a feeling in favour of abandoning all possessions beyond **Decay of Chinese Influence** the Yumen Pass, and it was due to the advice of a son of Pan Chau that the military road, at least as far as the Tarim basin, was retained. The disorders which soon afterward broke out in China completely checked any vigorous foreign policy, while maritime commerce diminished the importance of the overland trade. The petty states in the Tarim basin for many years subsequently led a quiet existence, influenced by India more than by China.

SAND MOUNTAINS NEAR THE OASIS OF SA-CHAN IN CHINESE TURKESTAN

TURKESTAN IN THE EARLY MIDDLE AGES
AND THE RISE AND FALL OF THE NOMAD NATIONS

THE advance of the Chinese toward the West, in spite of the bold plan of Pan Chau to attack the Roman Empire, inflicted no injury upon civilisation, but, on the whole, was beneficial to it. Far more momentous was the turn of events when the nomad hordes of Central Asia sought an outlet in Western Asia and Europe. Northern India had already fallen into the hands of the Yue-tshi, and the hour was approaching when a great part of Europe also would tremble beneath the scourge of the yellow races of the steppes. The main body of the Huns, when their star had set in Mongolia, hurled themselves against the civilised nations of the West. The consequences which the onslaught of the Huns, and, in close connection with it, the advance of other Asiatic nomads, had for Europe, do not come into the history of Central Asia ; but it is worth our while to glance at the development of

Progress Before the Hun Exodus Asiatic affairs up to the emigration of the Huns. The western civilised world had long escaped any dangerous attacks from the nomad peoples of Asia and Europe, perhaps because the nomads of East Europe became gradually more settled and paid more attention to agriculture. The Alani, who are identical with the Aorsi of earlier accounts, seem to have been the most influential nation. Probably this is to be regarded only as a collective name for the nomad tribes, who occupied the region from the Black Sea to the Sea of Aral, and were composed partly of the remains of Irano-Scythians, partly of Ural-Altaians. The proper bearers of the name were settled in the first century B.C. to the north of the Caucasus, where they fought against Pompey in the year 65 B.C. ; they then spread themselves further over the steppe, and appear to have ruled, for a time at least, over most of the nomad tribes of the region of Pontus and the Caspian. There were frequent but unimportant contests with the Romans. According to Chinese records, a part of the country of the Alani

belonged for a time to Sogdiana, a fact which argues armed complications on that frontier. Attacks through the Caucasian gate on Persian and Roman territory occurred several times, but there was no immense migration until the advance of

The First March of Hun Nomads the Western Huns. The first march of Hun nomads towards the West took place about the middle of the first century B.C., when the Hun empire was thrown into the most violent confusion by internal seditions. Several rulers tried simultaneously to usurp the power, and waged bitter war on each other. When at last one of the pretenders, Huhanyé, appeared to be victorious, his own brother, the " Viceroy of the East," rose against him. This Chichi, as he now called himself, expelled his brother from the capital, but then turned to the west ; and since he could not hold the whole empire, founded an independent power, which he gradually extended further westward. The circumstance that a prince in Sogdiana called in his help against the Usun enabled him to transfer the seat of his power to the region of the Sea of Aral. Part of the Alani in that district were perhaps already subject to the Huns. The wars with the Chinese in the Tarim basin ended with the death of Chichi, in 36 B.C., and greatly weakened the Hun power.

Their power did not revive until, in the year 90 A.D., another Hun prince with a large part of his people marched westward and joined the earlier emigrants. This migration was due to the complete collapse of the empire of the Eastern

Second Migration Westward Huns. In both of these migrations it was the most warlike and strongest part of the population which turned westward. The West Huns, therefore, were the picked men of their traditionally war-loving and adventurous race. Their people can hardly have remained unmixed during its migrations, but it probably incorporated the bravest

1465

men from the conquered tribes. In this way a new nationality might well be developed, whose thirst for wars would prove fateful for even distant regions, so soon as an occasion should arise when this concentrated energy could find an outlet. The Chinese, after the advantages gained in the west by the advance of Pan Chau had been mostly relin-

Conflict Between Huns and Chinese quished, had, at the beginning of the second century A.D., to face new contests with the Huns and their Uigurian allies in the Tarim basin. After the middle of the century the West Huns disappear from the horizon of the Chinese, a fact which suggests that the warlike nomads, finally renouncing any plans for the reconquest of their old homes in Mongolia, turned their attention in other directions. For two centuries more they seem to have been content with minor hostilities, until at last, in 350 A.D., the avalanche began to roll. The Huns attacked the Alani first, killed their king, and brought the people partly under their power, and partly forced them in panic further to the west. The great steppe of Eastern Europe and Siberia was thus opened to the Huns and the direction of their further advance suggested. That the storm of conquest did not sweep down on Persia, the fertile plains of which certainly aroused the greed of the marauders, was due to the awe with which the still powerful Neo-Persian empire of the Sassanids inspired the nomads.

The appearance of the Huns would not have had nearly so great an influence on Europe had it not been that the Roman Empire was already beginning to decay and that the Germanic races were in confusion and disorder. The convulsions which shook Europe when the Huns, under the leadership of Balamir, in 375, invaded the Danubian countries do not concern the history of Asia. It is unlikely that all the Huns and Alani took

The Huns Convulse Europe part in the movement toward the west; on the contrary, the Hun supremacy was still maintained in the region of Pontus and the Caspian. For when, after the death of Attila, in 453, their European empire broke up, the rest of the people withdrew once more to the east, and found a refuge there in the old homes of the Huns and Alani. The sovereignty of those regions devolved on Attila's favourite son Irnach. In the sixth century the empire gradually disintegrated into petty states, whose princes frequently interfered in the wars between Persia and Byzantium, or took up arms against each other. In 558 an army of Huns advanced to the gates of Constantinople. As the power of the Huns broke up, the separate elements of which this heterogeneous nation of warriors was composed recovered individual importance, until finally even the name of Huns disappeared from history.

The same fate befell another very mixed branch of the Hun nation, the White Huns, or Hephtalites, who had firmly planted themselves in the modern Khiva and, after 420, made vigorous attacks on Persia. The Sassanid king, Peroz, fell in battle against them in 484. The year 531 saw the last fights with these Huns, some of whom were destined to reappear under a new name and mixed with other nations as Kharismians.

After the disruption of the great Hun Empire in Central Asia and the retreat of most of the Huns to the west, the major part of Mongolia had fallen to the Sien

Mongolia After the Hun Empire pē, since the Chinese had neither the wish nor the power to hold the immense region of the steppes. This Tungusian nation came originally from the modern Manchuria, and, by its advance to the west, during which it probably absorbed the remnants of the Huns and other inhabitants of the steppes, it introduced a new ingredient into the hotchpotch of nations in the pasture-lands of Mongolia. Like all nomad peoples the Sien pē broke up into a number of petty states, which usually had their own political systems, but were occasionally united under an energetic ruler, and then constituted a formidable power, which soon made its influence felt in China and the Tarim basin.

Some such rapid rise of the Sien pē occurred about 150 A.D., when Tun shih huai placed himself at the head of one of their tribes and soon extended his power far over the adjacent peoples. This new nomad empire was hardly inferior in size to the earlier Hun empire, and comprised roughly the same countries, because then, as formerly, the line of least resistance lay due east and west. Even the division of their gigantic territory into a central kingdom with an eastern and a western province was once more adopted by the Sien pē.

Since it was virtually the personality of the ruler which kept the empire together, the power of the Sien pē was considerably diminished by the death of their first prince, in 190, and would certainly have given way to the influence of China had not this danger been averted by the overthrow of the Han dynasty in China in 220, and by the disorders which subsequently ensued. The Sien pē were thus able to realise for a moment the great ambition of the ruling nomad tribes—namely, to bring under their control the Western trade. Like the Huns before them, they had, for this purpose, to come to terms with the Tibetan nomads in the south of the Tarim basin.

During the civil wars in China several hordes of the Sien pē found a welcome opportunity of migrating into that country, where they either served as mercenaries or founded independent states. The most powerful of these tribes were the To ba. Between 338 and 376 the house of To ba ruled the state of Tai in Northern Shansi. In 386 Kuei, who belonged to that dynasty, founded there the Northern Wei, which expanded farther and farther over Northern China, until it practically covered the

A KURD OF TURKESTAN

also a member of the house of To ba, Governor of Hohsi after 394, declared himself King of Hsi ping in 397, and formed the state of Nan Liang, which was conquered in 414 by the prince of Hsi Chin. The To ba had soon become Chinese in life and thought, and they were forced to confront their kinsmen, the nomads of the steppes, entirely in the spirit of the traditional policy of China.

The condition of Mongolia had changed in the course of time. The empire of the Sien pē crumbled away after the strongest and most numerous hordes had migrated to China, and its place was taken by a new one under the rule of the Yen Yen, a mixed people, which apparently had incorporated fragments of primitive Siberian peoples, but linguistically belonged to the Turko-Tartar race. In the early stages of their history the Yen Yen appear to have acquired so invidious a reputation for barbarity and vice that they aroused disgust even among their nomad neighbours, who certainly were not fastidious in this respect. The emperors of the Wei dynasty long held this refractory people in check. The Yen Yen ultimately established their power at the close of the fourth century by the subjugation of the industrious tribes of the Altai range ; they proceeded further to the west and obtained possession of the Central Asiatic trade

KALMUCK WOMEN OF TURKESTAN

same area as the Wei of the Three Kingdoms. In 534 Pei Wei broke up into the Eastern Tung and the Western Wei, which were overthrown in 550 and 557. Wu ku,

routes, and extended their influence over Mongolia as far as the frontiers of Korea. The ruler to whom they owed this rapid rise was Talun. From the name of his successor, Tatara, is said to be derived the designation " Tartars," which in time has become usual for the peoples of the Turko-Mongolian stock. The To ba in Northern China soon saw them-

Struggles for Trade Routes selves involved in arduous wars with the new nomad empire, but in the end proved fully a match for it. After the Yen Yen, in 425 and on many subsequent occasions, had received heavy reverses in their attacks on China, and had been pursued into their own territory, the Pei Wei, according to the time-honoured Chinese policy, extended their influence once more along the old trade route to the west, and thus sapped the very foundations of the opposition of the nomads. Alliances with the two other empires, into which China was then divided, those of the Sung and the Liang, brought little advantage to the Yen Yen ; they were repeatedly defeated, and were unable to regain the command of the trade routes, although in the year 471 they reduced the kingdoms of Kashgar and Khotan to great straits. The Yen Yen were not completely overthrown by the Chinese. It was not until the middle of the sixth century that their kingdom, weakened by internal dissensions, fell before the onslaught of the Turks. A great part of the people followed the example of the Huns and fled to the west. The Avars, who soon afterward appeared as conquerors in East Europe, are probably identical with the Yen Yen. Like the remnants of the Yen Yen in Central Asia, the Avars finally disappeared altogether, or were absorbed by the other nations.

When we see these nomad empires attaining such gigantic size and then completely disappearing, we may easily forget that Central Asia was not

Before Central Asia Became a Desert exclusively a region where wandering hordes fed their flocks and herds, but that it offered homes and food to more or less settled peoples. It has already been shown how flourishing and comparatively civilised settlements developed in the Tarim basin, owing to its favourable position for the trade between East and West, and became the centres of small states. But there were trade routes even further north which led

to the west, and at the foot of the mountains lay districts which were adapted for agriculture. Still further away towered the Altai, with its rich mines, the focus of a primitive civilisation, which, in spite of countless raids by nomads, was still vigorous.

It is certain that numerous towns and permanently settled nations were to be found from the Tian Shan to the Altai. Political power, however, lay mostly in the hands of the nomads, who stamped their character on the constitution of the country, and thus do not appear even in the earliest records as true disseminators of culture. The Uigurians were long the most important nation of this region ; they formed the nucleus of the nine Oghuz, or hordes, to which the Tongra, Sukit, Adiz, Sap, etc., belonged. A distinction was made between a northern branch of the Uigurians, which was settled on the Selenga and subsequently spread to the sources of the Yenissei, and a southern branch in the south and east of the Tian Shan. While the northern Uigurians, called by the Chinese Kao che, or Thin le,

Rise of Mixed Civilisations did not attain any high degree of civilisation, the southern Uigurians, whose country was touched or traversed by the most important trade routes from west to east, were not unaffected by the civilised nations. A remarkable mixture of civilisations, which had a momentous influence on the life of the other nomad peoples, was developed in the towns of the southern Uigurians.

The supremacy of the Yen Yen in Mongolia was broken by the Turks, a nation which significantly became powerful on the Altai. The Turks, it is true, do not belong at all to the old representatives of civilisation of Yenissean stock on the Altai ; they were genuine nomads of Mongolian descent, probably one of those fragments of the great Hun people, which gradually increased again in numbers and importance. But the mineral wealth of the Altai doubtless furnished a source of power, which they knew how to use, whether they themselves mined and smelted, or entrusted this work to their subjects, the old settled inhabitants.

The term " our smiths " which the Yen Yen applied to the Turks on the outbreak of the war, was probably only a deliberate taunt, and not in accordance with facts. It must be observed, however, that among the nomads of Central Asia the trade of the smith was held in high esteem, quite otherwise than, for example, among the nomad tribes of North Africa ; and that in Mongolian tradition even the legendary national hero, Genghis Khan, appears as a smith. At any rate, the superior armament of breastplates, helmets, swords, and lances, and the marvellous " singing arrows," rendered possible by the rich mines, contributed greatly toward securing for the originally not very numerous Turks the victory over their opponents.

The national legend of the Turks traces the descent of the nation from a boy whom a she-wolf suckled. This tradition,

the northern Uigurians with the Yen Yen offered to the Turks a welcome opportunity of further advances. At the first contest of the two peoples, in 490, the Turks made no movement, but when, in the year 536, a Uigurian army marched eastward, and in so doing touched Turkish territory, the ruling chief of the Turks, Tu myn, attacked and conquered them, and incorporated into his people the whole tribe of 50,000 Yurtes. The ease with which this amalgamation was effected betokens the close affinity which existed between the peoples on the boundless steppes of Central Asia. Tu myn was now in a position to defy the Yen Yen, whose power had long

Reproduced by permission from Dr. Sven Hedin's "Central Asia."

REMNANT OF A PERISHED CIVILISATION IN THE SAND WASTES OF CENTRAL ASIA

Dr. Sven Hedin's excavations have thrown a flood of light upon the former prosperity of the Tarim basin. Where there are now wastes of sand, which can be traversed with difficulty by riding animals, once stood waving fields, green forests, and smiling villages. Under this clay ruin Dr. Hedin found cart-wheels, coins, and domestic vessels.

which recalls the story of Romulus and Romus, refers, like it, to totemistic customs, for a golden wolf-head was the badge of Turkish warriors. The scanty Chinese accounts represent the Turks as a branch of the Aschin Huns, who, after their expulsion from China by the Wei dynasty, placed themselves under the protection of the Yen Yen, and were allotted in 439 settlements on the southern slopes of the Altai. Few traces of Chinese civilisation seem to have been retained by them ; on the other hand, they appear to have acquired some culture from the Uigurians, to which fact the adoption of the Uigurian script points. The feuds of

been tottering, and he did so after the prince of the Yen Yen had contemptuously rejected him as a suitor for the hand of one of his daughters. In the year 552 the overthrow of the empire of the Yen Yen was complete, and the Turks now assumed the headship of the Central Asiatic nomads, whose conditions on the whole were little altered by this change of rulers.

Since the traditional policy of aggression against China was rendered hopeless by the now firmly-consolidated power of that state, the Turks turned toward the west, along the road which the Huns had pointed out to all succeeding peoples ;

even Uigurian armies had penetrated to the Volga in 463. Their first success was the subjugation of Sogdiana, where the descendants of the Yue-tshi still maintained their supremacy, and an advance had been made toward the Tarim basin. By the year 437 nine states existed in Sogdiana which were ruled by princes of the dynasty of the Can-wu. **Campaigns of the Nomad Turks** The most important of them was Samarkand. In Tashkent, Ferghana, and Kharismia other dynasties occupied the thrones. The conquest of Sogdiana, the petty states of which, however, had hardly disappeared, gave the Turkish conquerors an interest in the Western trade, especially in the export of silk from Sogdiana, which was then hindered by the Persians, probably because in Persia itself the breeding of silkworms was a prevalent industry, and also because silk was obtained from China by the sea route. The attempt to win the desired object from the Persians by diplomacy led to a long series of hostile complications.

The Turks then, in 569, determined to enter into direct communication with the Byzantines, who must have been equally interested in breaking the Persian trading monopoly. A Turkish embassy arrived at Constantinople, in consequence of which Zimarch went to the capital of the Turkish Great Khan in the Altai with a commission from Justin II., the Byzantine Emperor. We possess his detailed account of the journey, and of the battles of the Turks against the " White Huns " and the Persians, at some of which he was present. We learn from him also that the west of the Tarim basin then fell into the power of the Turks. Later, the Byzantines also, in spite of their cautious policy, were hard pressed by the Turks, since with the period of the Turkish power generally a fresh flood of Central Asiatic tribes poured over Western Asia and Europe. The Khazars, **Turks in Touch with Byzantium** who advanced in 626 to East Europe, were a detached fragment of the Turkish nation. As might be expected, attacks were made on China so soon as any opportunity presented itself.

China now adopted her successful policy of sowing seeds of dissension among the nomads. The Turkish Empire, like the earlier empires, split up into three portions, an eastern and a western province, which were governed by a viceroy, and the

centre, which, both in peace and war, was under the command of the supreme ruler. The Chinese, about the year 600, succeeded in weakening permanently the power of the Turks by dividing the empire into an eastern and a western part.

In the year 630 the Chinese armies won a brilliant victory over the eastern Turks, in which the khan, Kin Li, was captured; thus Chinese influence was again extended to Sogdiana. The eastern empire then broke up into a number of weak and petty states ; but part of the Turks migrated to China, where settlements were assigned to them in order that they might serve as a frontier guard against other nomad tribes. The people, which had not forgotten its old fame, became in Chinese territory once more so strong that, in 681, under Qutluq, it was able to shake off the Chinese rule and spread its influence over Mongolia. The power of the Turks grew still stronger under Me chun, the brother and successor of Qutluq, who skilfully availed himself of the disputes for the Chinese throne. Once more the Turkish Empire became a mighty power. Even **Turks Again in the Ascendant** the western Turks seem temporarily to have been subjugated, and the Turkish supremacy was re-established in Sogdiana, where the petty states of the Yue-tshi still existed.

After Me chun's death, Kultegin, the commander of the army, a nephew of the dead man, murdered the lawful heir, his cousin, and placed his own brother Me ki lien on the throne. We have accurate accounts of these events from the inscriptions on the grave-pillars of Orkhon. The east Turkish Empire still kept its position as a formidable power. But its decline began, and the end was produced by a coalition of the Uigurians and Chinese in the year 745. From that date the Turks almost disappear from the history of Central Asia. The fall of the Turkish power was hastened by the advance of the Arabs, who in the meantime had conquered Persia and penetrated to Sogdiana, where some of the princes sought help from the Turks and fought with chequered success against their new oppressors. In 712 the Arabs won a brilliant victory over the allied Sogdians and Turks, the latter probably being led by Kultegin. In the year 730, however, they met with a severe defeat at Samarkand from the same antagonists. The necessity of defending themselves on different sides certainly helped to effect the rapid fall of the east Turkish Empire.

The western Turks, soon after their separation from the eastern empire, had been forced to acknowledge a sort of suzerainty of Persia. In 620, however, they felt themselves strong enough to extend their empire—which must have lain between the Altai and the Sea of Aral—and to invade Persia and Sogdiana. Turkish mercenaries or allies played a momentous part in the contests for the Persian throne at that time. All the conquered territory, indeed, was very loosely united, as is invariably the case with nomad empires, and when occasion offered it was the more easily broken up again, since the nomad is never so closely attached to his country as the agriculturist. Instances occur where entire nations crossed the **Turks in Western Asia** steppes of Central Asia in their fullest extent, in order to escape the yoke of a hated conqueror and to seek protection perhaps on the Chinese frontier. The western Turks then had command of the northern trade routes of Central Asia so far as they passed through the Uigurian country. Since the Chinese favoured the southern roads through the Tarim basin, Turks and Uigurians combined and, in 639, invaded the petty states of that district, attacked Hami, which was occupied by the Chinese, and thus compelled China to act on the defensive. These disorders lasted for a long time, but finally ended in favour of the Chinese. Soon afterwards the advance of the Arabs through Persia was felt by the western Turks, while the Chinese armies pressed on threateningly from the east. The result was the almost complete fall of the power of the western Turks, whose inheritance passed for a short period to the Tibetans, who had become powerful in the interval.

It was not until the year 700 that the empire revived, only to find itself soon afterwards entangled in bitter wars with the Arabs. It was more affected by remarkable factions at the court and within **The Turks and Arabs at War** the tribal federation, the true cause of which, whether ethnic, social, or political, cannot be discovered. There was a black and a yellow party, which often fought furiously together, and put forward their own candidates whenever the succession to the throne was disputed. The complete overthrow of the empire was effected in 760 by the Qarluk, a tribe of the Turko-Mongolian race living to the west of the Altai range. The remnants appear in later history as Ghuzes.

In Central Asia the place of the Turks as the dominant people was taken by the nomad Uigurians, who were then called Hoei He. Their chief opponents were the Kirghiz in South-western Siberia, who now for the first time came forward as a powerful people and tried to enter into direct relations with China. In alliance with the Chinese they shattered the Uigurian supremacy in the year 830. The question at issue seems once more to have been the command of the trading communications with the west. The Kirghiz then appeared as the connecting agents, who conducted Arabian caravans to China with armed escorts through the hostile Uigurian territory. The Kirghiz never founded an empire of equal extent with that of the Huns or Turks. The Uigurian empire was always restricted to a limited area.

Later, in the tenth and eleventh centuries, the nation of the Khitan, which was mainly of Tungusian stock, extended its rule from Manchuria over a large part of the steppes of Central Asia, until the Mongols founded a new world-empire in that region.

ON THE GOBI DESERT, WHICH THE CHINESE APTLY TERM 'THE SEA OF SAND.'

TWO VIEWS OF A CHARACTERISTIC TIBETAN TOWN OF ANCIENT DATE

These views of a Tibetan town show the general practice of building the Lamaite monasteries upon the crests of the ridges, while on the face of the hill-side are the cave-like dwellings in which the peasant laity find their homes.

RISE AND FALL OF THE OLD EMPIRE OF TIBET

TIBET for a long period was little affected by the enormous revolutions that convulsed Central Asia, and in any case it was only its frontier that felt them. These frontier tribes of Tibet were formerly further removed from the centre. On the south, the Himalayas always formed a strong barrier, but to the north Tibetans were settled as far as the Tarim basin, and even a great part of South-eastern China was filled with Tibetan tribes, which were only gradually absorbed by the Chinese population. Tibet proper lay completely off the main track. The routes of trade and culture did not traverse the country ; and the desolate plateau, scorched by intolerable summer heats and lashed by winter snowstorms, did not allure the neighbouring nomads to daring raids, which might at least have interrupted the stereotyped monotony of existence, and **The Slow Advance of Tibet** have created movement and life. The achievements of civilisation were slow in permeating this region, and it was long before the seeds of progress sprang up from the barren ground.

Originally all Tibetan peoples must have lived that life of mere hunters which appears to be the lowest grade of human existence. Tibet, in spite of its desolation, was adapted for this mode of life. However poor it might be in edible wild plants, it teemed with beasts of the chase, which even now cover the country in immense herds. The agricultural life, which originated with the short-skulled race, was followed only in the advanced posts of the Tibetan people, where they settled in the Tarim basin on the trading route, and found in the oases suitable tracts of country at their disposal. The **Growing Power of Tibet** reason why it did not spread further toward Tibet is mainly that the only districts at all adapted for agriculture lay far to the south, in the upper valleys of the Brahmaputra and the Indus. Any germs of culture that developed in these southern tracts were brought from India, and, naturally, not until the Aryan inhabitants of India had created a civilisa-

tion of their own. This circumstance helps to explain the slow advance of civilisation in Tibet as well as the far reaching influence of India on what was once purely a Central Asiatic region.

What the inhabitants of Northern and Central Tibet derived from Central Asia **Lessons in Social Progress** was not the old agricultural life, but the newer social economy of the nomad tribes It must remain a moot point whether Tibetans were in this mere recipients, or whether by the domestication of the yak they did not materially add to the number of useful animals. The wild yak is spread so far to the north that a tribe of Turko-Mongolian or even Aryan race may have made the first attempts at breeding them. In any case, the waggon was hardly known in Tibet as a means of transport, but animals, and especially the yak, were exclusively used to carry burdens. The introduction of nomadic habits gave the Tibetans, especially those of the north, a greater mobility, allowed an increase of population, and gradually taught them the warlike, marauding life peculiar to all nomads. It would seem that the bow also, which is not the national weapon in Tibet, was introduced from the north.

The Tibetan tribes may have waged little wars on each other, and also on the nomad peoples of Mongolian race living to the north, but no historically important struggles took place until the growing power of Tibet sought its booty among the settled nations. The roads to the south and west were completely barred, but, in compensation, the great commer- **Growing Power of Tibet** cial route on the north, with its trading stations and oases, was exposed to attack, and on the north-east the riches of China itself presented a goal for profitable raids. In Mongolia the mighty empire of the Huns had already been formed out of small tribes, which combined for such marauding expeditions. In Tibet, where the conditions were far less favourable, the political unification of the separate hordes began far later and was less successful. Occasionally, indeed, some frontier tribes had an opportunity of interfering in the internal affairs of China. A doubtful account states that Tibetan auxiliaries appeared in the Chinese service in 1123 B.C., but **Growth of Political Unity** no large empire appears to have been formed until the advent of Buddhism, which, with its proselytising power, levelled the barriers between rival tribes, and first stimulated national union.

The Tibetan history, the Book of the Kings, which appeared only comparatively late under the influence of Chinese models, contains a legendary account of the prehistoric period, which, naturally, is untrustworthy in its details, but shows the sources from which the Tibetans themselves derived their civilisation. According to this there appeared, in the first century B.C., in the country to the south of the modern Lhasa, a marvellously endowed child, whom the wild natives soon regarded as their heaven-sent leader. This child, an invention clearly on the model of the infant Dalai-Lamas of a later age, was a direct descendant of Buddha. He founded a kingdom, the subjects of which were gradually raised by his successors to higher grades of culture, precisely in the way in which Chinese legend traces the progress of civilisation. Under the seventh monarch, in the second century A.D., smelting, the use of the plough, and irrigation were discovered. In the fifth century the fields were enclosed, articles of clothing were made from leather, and walnut-trees were planted. Soon afterward the yak was crossed with the ox, and mules were bred.

Although the legend does not acknowledge any direct introduction of Indian civilisation into Tibet, still the fact that the centre of culture lay in the vicinity of the Indian frontier, and that the genealogy of the royal house was traced **Civilisation Inspired by India** from Buddha, points unmistakably to this source. The widening dissemination of Buddhist doctrine in India had fired a missionary zeal there, which brought the new faith, and in its train a higher civilisation, over the dreaded barrier of the Himalayan snows. From the West, also, where the Buddhist doctrine spread as far as the Tarim basin, Tibet felt the same influence, and when the new faith struck root even in China, Tibet, as the connecting link between China and Central Asia on the one side, and India on the other, suddenly acquired a new importance ; and finally, after the decay of Buddhism in the Indian mother country, Tibet became the peculiar home and sanctuary of the northern worshippers of Buddha.

While in Southern Tibet a small civilised state gradually developed, which depended for its power and prosperity on agriculture, the northern nomads had also begun to organise themselves, and in so doing may have been influenced by the example of the neighbouring Chinese constitution, and of the nomad kingdoms in Central Asia. The north-eastern tribes, called by the Chinese Ti, played, on a small scale, in the first century after the Christian era, the rôle of the Central Asiatics, since they figured at one time as enemies, at another as allies, of the Chinese kingdoms and their claimants. Tibetan chieftains even appear as rulers of small Chinese states in the same way as Hun and Turkish princes usurped the **Rise of Tibetan Empire** thrones of the isolated kingdoms. The Khiang, who lived to the south-east of the Tarim basin and menaced trade communications with the west, were another branch of the Tibetan race. No real empire was established until, in the course of the sixth century B.C., the civilised state in the south brought the northern nomads · also under its influence. A power was created which had a large share in the further political development of Central Asia. Almost impregnable in its own country, it held a menacing position on the south-west frontier of China and on the trade routes which crossed the Tarim basin. The shifting fortunes of the Turkish empires offered ample opportunities of interference.

The empire first aroused the attention of the Chinese in the year 589. With what deliberate purpose the Tibetan rulers endeavoured to advance their civilisation by Indian influence is shown by the embassy to India in 632, which resulted in a more accurate knowledge of the Buddhist religion and in the invention of a script formed after the Indian model. Even then Lhasa was the capital of the empire and the focus of religious life. The relations of the new empire with China were friendly at first; but very soon the pretext for war was given by an incident of a kind not unusual in the history of Central Asiatic kingdoms : the request of the Tibetan monarch for the hand of a Chinese princess was insultingly refused. Since, however, the king obtained his wish in the end, the campaign cannot have resulted so favourably for the Chinese as their historians would have us believe. But the Tibetan preferred to turn his arms for the future against the Tarim basin, where there was a state of anarchy which offered greater prospects of successful conquest ; and by the year 680 the power of Tibet extended as far as the Tian Shan. A combined attack of the Chinese and Turks in 692 had indeed the momentary effect of driving back the Tibetans ; but they returned to the attack, and pressed on in 715 as far as Ferghana, after they had concluded an alliance with the Arabs. During the whole of the eighth century Tibet remained the leading power in the south of Central Asia, and a formidable enemy of China,

Tibet at the Height of Its Power the capital of which was actually stormed and plundered by the Tibetans in the year 763. It was not until 820 that a permanent peace was concluded between Tibet and China, and a pillar with an inscription was erected in Lhasa to commemorate the event.

In the course of the ninth century the power of Tibet rapidly diminished. The Uigurians seized the borderland on the north, and Hsia successfully took over the duty of guarding the frontier against the decaying empire. This kingdom—more accurately Hsi Hsia, or Western Hsia—had been formed in 884, at the time of the Tang dynasty, on the upper course of the Hoang-ho. The royal house was descended from the Toba dynasty of Pei Wē, which had been destroyed in North China in 557 ; but Tangutes, near kinsmen of the Tibetans, formed the picked warriors of the people. In 1032 the state made itself completely independent of the northern Sung dynasty, which ruled in Southern China, and subsequently maintained its position, since it allied itself at one time with the Sung, at another with the Khitan, and later with the Kin, who were supreme in Northern China. The independent position of the country was outwardly demonstrated—and this is a feature which frequently recurs in Central Asia—by the invention of a new script, which was mainly based on the ancient Chinese signs. We have only brief records of the wars of the Hsia kingdom. An invasion by the Tibetans, in

Enervating Influence of Buddhism 1076, ended in their precipitate retreat, the result, it is said, of a superstitious panic which seized the army. In 1227, the Hsia kingdom was annihilated by the Mongols. The fall of the political power of Tibet must be ultimately traced to the fact that Buddhism then permeated the country, crippled the secular power, and effected a thorough spiritual revolution in the minds of the people. Buddhism soon assumed a peculiar character in that isolated land. The priests of Tibet showed little appreciation of the more subtle theological and philosophical disputes and doctrines of their Indian or Chinese co-religionists. But all the more important was the influence of the originally Shamanistic national religion, which exalted the Buddhist clergy and monks into magicians and ascribed to them all the various arts of a degraded mysticism. This is the explanation of the commanding position which the Buddhist priesthood was able to acquire in Tibet, and of the chaos of superstitious ideas which gradually spread thence over Central Asia.

After the end of the ninth century Tibet led a quiet existence, which in no respect excited the attention of its neighbours. In the year 1015 alone an armed quarrel with China caused a short interruption of this tranquillity. Relations with China had again slightly improved the culture of the country. After the entry of the Chinese princess already mentioned, the knowledge had been acquired of making wine from rice or barley, of erecting water-mills, and of weaving stuffs. Chinese

Under the Heel of China artisans also had come into the country, and the sons of the best families were frequently sent to China to be educated. Tibetan civilisation, which had been at first entirely subject to Indian influence, took more and more a Chinese stamp, until finally the storm of the Mongols swept over the land of Tibet, and brought the country into a still more intimate political union with China.

LAMAS WORSHIPPING BEFORE THE HOLY OF HOLIES IN A TIBETAN TEMPLE

The monastery of Kum-Bum, in Tibet, once the residence of the Dalai-Lama, was founded in 1360, and now contains some three thousand monks. Before the Holy of Holies are six cloth-covered columns, each of which has on its upper part a "skirt" of pleated cloth and the floor is covered with prayer-boards. These, having been in constant use for centuries, have been worn into deep grooves by the lamas doing penance. Before worshipping, the lama removes his outer garments and his shoes, then he bows, and throws himself prostrate on the praying-boards. The lama wearing the "Roman" helmet is of a higher caste than the others, and carries a prayer-bell in one hand.

EARLY CIVILISATION OF CENTRAL ASIA

THE example of Tibet shows how closely the progress of civilisation is connected with religious propaganda, and how the wish to spread their own peculiar creed can be the chief cause why members of a more highly civilised people venture to be the apostles of culture in the most remote and most uninviting regions of the world. But this is not a unique phenomenon in Central Asia. However greatly the trade between East and West promoted the civilisation of Central Asia, it cannot be disputed that the most strenuous work in the cause of culture was done by those who, as preachers of the different world-religions, penetrated into the heart of Asia, or marched toward the east on the great commercial roads. Religious zeal alone created that endurance and self-denial which all must possess who attempt to sow in backward nations the seeds of a higher culture and of nobler modes of life. It is an important fact

Results of Mission Work that, among the civilised countries which border upon Central Asia, China alone produced no world-religion, properly so-called, and sent out no missionaries apart from Buddhists. In consequence of this, the Chinese never succeeded in firmly attaching the Central Asiatics to themselves until they finally found, in their encouragement of the Buddhist teaching, an inestimable aid in taming the wild nomad hordes.

The original "religion" of the Central Asiatics was doubtless that simple mysticism which, under various forms, is to be found in all primitive peoples. The chief duties of the wizard priests, who are revered as possessors of mystic powers,

Oases as Sites of Ancient Civilisation consist in averting evil influences and in healing diseases. That belief in one supreme divinity, which is usually found in such cases, has only a subordinate significance and has little influence on the spiritual life. The characteristic form of lower mysticism among the Northern and Central Asiatics is Shamanism. The shaman, or sorcerer, works himself up to a frenzy by beating a drum or by other

similar methods, and then enters into communication with the spirit world, about the nature of which very different ideas, partly influenced by the civilised religions, prevail among the various nations. Even where a higher form of religion has already penetrated, Shamanism usually

Perverted Forms of Religions remains for a long time as a popular national custom; in fact, it stamps a peculiar local character on these religions. In the eyes of the nomads of Central Asia, all priests were a kind of shamans, from whom cures, prophecies, and miracles might be expected. This led to perverted forms of the original religious doctrines, from which neither Buddhists nor Nestorians were exempt.

Every higher form of religion is based on written records and has its sacred books. It thus follows that writing, the first great step towards culture, spreads most quickly in the train of a religious propaganda. Art also follows in the steps of religion. Images of deities and saints, or temples erected in their honour, form part of the indispensable equipment of the missionaries, and announce the victory of the new doctrine. It is thus conceivable that the position of Central Asia between important spheres of civilisation and foci of religious doctrines must certainly have led to a marvellous mixture of influences, among which the original racial characteristics were still discernible.

We must not forget in this connection that the oases of Central Asia were themselves the sites of an ancient civilisation, but that this civilisation, after the

Oases as Sites of Ancient Civilisation irruption of warlike nomad peoples, rested on so narrow a foundation that it could not have made any continuous progress without the stimulating example of other civilisations. The blending of religions and civilisations was accelerated by the fact that rival doctrines did not make their appearances successively, but that the majority of them began to strike root in Central Asia side by side, during the centuries preceding and following the

Christian Era. Buddhism appeared the earliest on the scene, and also exercised the greatest influence on Central Asia. Zoroastrian sun-worship was not vigorously disseminated until 250 A.D., when, under the Sassanids, its priests were stimulated to undertake the work of missionaries by the renascence of Iranian **Rivalry** life and thought; but con**of Four** currently Christianity began to **Religions** enlist supporters. Neither of these religions was completely victorious until finally Islam gained the supremacy in one part of that region, while Buddhism, disseminated from Tibet, held the field in the east. The earlier Buddhism of Eastern Turkestan, which was directly connected with India, entirely disappeared.

We are tolerably well informed from literary sources as to the religious conditions of Central Asia. Our knowledge has been widened by recent archæological investigations in Central Asia, which have yielded a rich harvest of results, notably in the Tarim basin, and give us a vivid idea of the influence exercised by the various civilisations and doctrines. The British excavations in the western valley of the Tarim have brought to light, in addition to Indo-Buddhist, Chinese, and Persian antiquities and inscriptions, rude copper images, which probably served Shamanistic purposes, and may have come from the old civilised province of the Altai, where Shamanism exists even at the present day.

The importance of Buddhism for the west of Central Asia was felt chiefly before the Mongol period. The activity of Buddhist missionaries outside the confines of India could not be vigorously exerted until the new religion had taken firm root in its native country. The period of the great Asoka of Magadha (263–226 B.C.) marks both the victory of Buddhism in Northern India and the extension of the political and **Foreign** religious influences toward the **Missions of** north-west. Kashmir, the bridge **Buddhism** to Central Asia, recognised the suzerainty of Asoka. Even though Buddhism was unable to gain a firm footing there, and was driven to wage frequent struggles with remnants of the old native snake-worship and a repressed Brahmanism, still access had been obtained to the civilised oases of the Tarim basin, where the new religion quickly found ready acceptance.

In externals this Buddhism was, it must be admitted, no result of purely Indian culture. In the first place, the Iranians had encroached upon India and left traces of their nationality on the manners and customs of the people; but after the age of Alexander the Great an offshoot of Hellenistic civilisation existed in Bactria, which exercised an effective influence on art and culture both in the Tarim basin and in North-western India. Where the missionary zeal of Buddhism appeared at this time, it was accompanied and permeated by the elements of Greek art. This Greco-Buddhist art and culture of North-west India found a new home in the Tarim basin. Here, too, the difference between the more ancient western form of Buddhism and the more modern eastern form, which took its shape in Tibet, is clearly defined. Generally speaking, Indians of pure race preached the new faith, and their labours led naturally enough to a wide diffusion of the Indian language, since a knowledge of Sanscrit was necessary for the comprehension of the sacred books. A large non-religious **Connecting** immigration also probably took **Link** place. The influence of India **with India** apparently first made itself felt in Khotan, where a son of Asoka is said to have founded a dynasty. Khotan, owing to its geographical position, has generally formed the connecting link between Central Asia and India, and shows in its civilisation abundant traces of Indian influences. A large number of Buddhist shrines and monasteries were to be found in Khotan. The densely populated oasis, helped by its religious importance, repeatedly obtained great power, although it could not keep it permanently, since, as the gate to the trade route from India and the southern road from the West to the East, it appeared a valuable prize to all conquering tribes of Central Asia. From Khotan Buddhism spread further over the Tarim basin and its northern boundary. The clearest proof of this is found in the numerous cave temples constructed on the Indian model, as well as in the products of Greco-Buddhist art, which modern explorations have brought to light, especially in the western part of Eastern Turkestan. It was certainly the settled portions of the nation, which were steeped in the ancient civilisation, that most eagerly adopted this higher form of religion. The nomads were

ASSEMBLING OF THE GUESTS AT A NESTORIAN WEDDING PARTY

The Nestorians were the first Christian sect to make headway among the nations of Asia, and at one time they attained considerable importance, but, cut off from their headquarters, they and their doctrines became degraded.

less satisfied with it. The counsellor of a Turkish prince candidly stated his opinion that neither the building of towns nor of Buddhist temples was advantageous to the nomads, since it was opposed to their traditional mode of life and would break their spirit. This opinion was justified ; for in reality it was Buddhism which, thanks to the crafty support of the Chinese, finally destroyed the savage bravery of the Central Asiatics.

The second great religion, Zoroastrianism, had naturally its chief sphere of expansion in Western Turkestan, which repeatedly stood completely under Iranian influence. Following the line of the trade routes, which were chiefly frequented by Persian merchants, it forced its way farther to the East, without being able to win for itself there any considerable position as compared with Buddhism. Zoroastrianism spread also among the western nomads, especially the Scythians of Iranian **Religion of Zoroaster** stock, and left some remarkable traces behind. The ancient Slavonic mythology, with its contrast between deities of light and deities of darkness, seems to have been influenced by the Iranian sun-worship ; so, too, were the ideas of the heathen Turkish tribes on the Altai, according to which the human race held the middle place between the powers of light and of darkness. Among several nations, such as the Uigurians, Buddhism and Zoroastrianism for a time counterbalanced each other. We cannot now decide whether their domestic dissensions, which were numerous and important, especially among the Turks, had also a religious tinge. Even before the Iranian sun-worship **Coming of Christianity** acquired fresh powers of winning adherents at the beginning of the Sassanid period, the missionaries of Christianity had already traversed Iran and set foot in Central Asia. The revival of Zoroastrianism must partly be regarded as a reaction against the irresistible advance of Christianity, so unacceptable to the true Iranians. It was not indeed the great united Christian Church that broke down the Iranian barriers by her emissaries, but a branch separated from the parent stem, that of the Nestorians, whom we have already seen, in like manner, as the first introducers of the faith into China. That sect planted the seeds of Western civilisation far away toward the East, but in their isolation they soon became degenerate, since they were thrown upon their own resources, and were unable to keep up any constant communications with the West.

The Nestorian Church, nevertheless, attained for a time to great prosperity. At the beginning of the Mongol period, when the Western Church began to concern herself about her estranged sister in the East, it did not appear hopeless to think of converting the Mongol rulers, and thus to assure the victory of Christianity over its rivals, of whom Islam had long been the most dangerous. There were Christian communities and even small states with Christian princes in China after the seventh century. Here,

Nestorian Power in Asia perhaps, lay originally the half-legendary realm of Prester John, the discovery of which was one of the motives for the Portuguese explorations, until it was thought to have been found in Abyssinia. Besides the Nestorians, missionaries of the Manichæans found their way to China about the year 1000.

The prospects of the older forms of religion in Western Central Asia were completely, even if not immediately, destroyed by the advance of Islam. It was its appearance late on the scene, full of fresh ideals, that secured it the victory over the other faiths which were honeycombed by Shamanist influences and had degenerated in their isolation. In the decisive contest for the conversion of the Mongolian chieftains, which secured spiritual supremacy for the successful religion, Islam was finally victorious in the West.

The struggle, nevertheless, lasted for centuries. At the beginning of the eighth century the Arabs had already become lords of Western Central Asia, and had then advanced on their victorious career to the Tarim basin. Khotan, the chief seat of the Buddhists, had resisted attacks for twenty-five years. Among the inhabitants of Eastern Turkestan the traditions of these religious wars found a concrete expression in the legendary hero, Ordan Padjah, whose marvellous deeds are supposed to have decided the victory of Islam. The new doctrine did not triumph until, in the tenth century, Satuk,

Islam in Asia the Turkish ruler of Kashgar, adopted it, and conquered a large part of the Tarim basin and even of Western Turkestan. After his death, in 1037, the power of the new empire rapidly diminished.

Religious differences gradually acquired a certain ethnic importance, even for the nomad tribes of Central Asia. The Turko-Tartar branch now comprised mainly the Central Asiatics won over for Islam, while the Mongolian branch contained the adherents of the Buddhist creed; but originally both branches were quite closely related, or, more correctly speaking, were of common origin and only in part altered by admixture of foreign blood. Among the Uigurians in particular Islam found at a comparatively early period numerous believers, by the side of whom, however, the representatives of other religions long maintained their position.

The mixture of religions, to which, in the West, Hellenic mythology may have slightly contributed, corresponded to the mixture of civilisation, which found its most permanent expression in the native script and styles of art. Modern excavations in Turkestan have furnished more exact information on the point, especially as to the existence of a style which has grown up out of Indian, Greek, and Persian influences.

If this mixed style betrays the effort made to rise from mere imitation of foreign forms to a certain individuality, the tendency appears still more clearly in the fact that Central Asia produced, in addition to foreign methods of writing,

Ancient Art and Writing a large number of peculiar scripts, which were naturally suggested by already existing models, but nevertheless possess distinctive features of their own. The Chinese script seems least of all to have served as a model, since its defects, as contrasted with the syllabic and alphabetic scripts of the other civilised nations, were too vividly prominent. The influence of the Indian scripts was greater, especially in the Tarim basin. On the other hand, the Persian Pehlevi script had been adopted by the Uigurians, probably through the medium of the Yue-tshi, and the Turkish tribes in their turn learnt it from them. After that, through the influence of the Nestorian missionaries, the use of the Syrian script was extended, and this soon served as a model for new native systems. The Mongols and the Manchus used varieties of the same script. The number of foreign and native scripts in Central Asia during the eighth and ninth centuries seems, as numerous discoveries prove, to have been unusually large. This circumstance points at once to a certain incoherency in the prevailing civilisation, and to the fact that the Central Asiatic culture was local, and at the same time highly susceptible to foreign influences.　　HEINRICH SCHURTZ.

THE MEDIÆVAL HISTORY OF CENTRAL ASIA

THE GREAT MONGOL EMPIRE

THE efforts of civilisation and religion to tame the barbarous people of Central Asia continued for many centuries. Temples of Buddha, Zoroastrian seats of culture, Christian churches, and Moslem mosques arose in the oases ; industries flourished, trade brought foreign merchants into the country, and those who aimed at a refinement of manners and customs and a nobler standard of life were amply provided with brilliant models. Of the nomads a less favourable account must be given ; and yet among many of them the higher forms of religion had struck root. Skilled writers were to be found among them, and the allurements of civilised life made considerable impression. The road which was destined to lead these tribes out of their ancient barbarism had already often been trodden ;

Nomad Lust of Pillage the forces of civilisation seemed pressing on victoriously in every direction. Then once more the nomad spirit rallied itself to strike a blow more formidable than any which had previously fallen. The effort was successful, and as the result of it a region once prosperous and progressive lay for generations at the mercy of races whose guiding instincts were the joy of battle and the lust of pillage. The world glowed with a blood-red light in the Mongol age. Twice—first under Genghis Khan and his immediate successors, and secondly under Timur—the hordes of horsemen burst over the civilised countries of Asia and Europe ; twice they swept on like a storm-cloud, as if they wished to crush every country and convert it into pasture for their flocks. And so thoroughly was the work of ravage and murder done that to the present day desolate tracks show the traces of their destructive fury. These were the last great eruptions of the Central Asiatic volcano. Civilisation con-

quered, and the hordes of the wide steppes were no longer a danger at which it needed to tremble. That which now struck at the civilised world was once more the full power of the nomads of Central Asia welded together for a time by a master hand. The new people which suddenly appeared on the scene, and, although hardly known

Gigantic Armies of the Nomads or noticed before, now advanced with gigantic armies, in reality dealt only the first blow, and represented the vanguard of hosts which grew larger and larger, like an avalanche. The vanguard gave its name to the hosts who followed, and rekindled in them the wild enthusiasm for war, which had died away, owing to the intercourse with civilisation. But the personality of some individual is always of paramount value.

The Mongols play so small a part in the earlier history of Central Asia that we may fairly doubt whether in their case we are dealing with a race whose roots stretch far back into the past. The original home of the Mongols lay, so far as can be ascertained, on the northern edge of the Central Asiatic steppe, in the region of Lake Baikal. Now, it was this same northern edge which was the home of the most important nomad states, and was the true cradle of the conquering pastoral peoples. It was there that the Huns held their own

The Death and Birth of Nations until the last, and the centre of the Turkish power lay there. The nomad population of that region was mainly due to the disruption of the older nationalities, and contained remnants of all earlier inhabitants. The Mongols in particular rose from the remains of the Turkish people, which again was a mixture of Hun and other stocks.

It was no mere accident that this people rekindled the ancient nomad love of war and rapine. In their remote homes they had been the least softened by civilisation or tamed by religious influence, and they had most stubbornly preserved their warlike traditions.

The Mongolian horde had begun to make a name for itself in Central Asia at the beginning of the twelfth century A.D. The conditions of that period were favourable to its rise, as there was no great power in Central Asia at the time. The Kin, or Nu-chi, who in 1125 had conquered and dislodged the Khitan, were the most powerful in the eastern parts of the country ; both peoples were of Tungusian stock, and a part of North China recognised their suzerainty. The Mongols seem to have been tributary to the Nu-chi. In the west the power of the Hakas had greatly weakened ; the Uigurians and some Tartar hordes, such as the partially Christianised Kerait, led an independent life. Yesukai, the father of Genghis Khan, first brought a number of nomad tribes under his rule, and thus aroused the distrust of the Nu-chi, who, in 1135, and again in 1147, made futile efforts to nip in the bud the growing world-power.

Growth of New World Power

Little is known of the other exploits of Yesukai. His empire seemed ready to collapse as quickly as it had risen. On Yesukai's death, in 1175, his son Temujin was only twenty, or, according to some accounts, twelve years old. This was a sufficient reason for the subjugated hordes to revolt from him ; so that the new ruler, who was under his mother's guardianship, had scarcely more left him than the original parent tribe. But an iron will animated the youth. He rallied his adherents and fought with Ong Khan, or Wang, the rival ruler chosen by the other hordes, a battle which at once put an end to any further spreading of the revolt, while a year later he won a brilliant victory over the insurgents, who renewed their attack. He thoroughly vindicated his power as a monarch by his barbarous punishment of the rebel leaders. Some tribes now sought the friendship of the conqueror, others plotted against him or openly attacked him ; but, in the midst of unceasing wars, his power steadily increased. He defeated the Naiman, the Kerait, who were at first his allies, and other tribes, in a series of campaigns ; until, in the year 1206, he was able to hold on

Founder of the Mongol Empire

the banks of the Onon, a tributary of the Amur, a great review and council, at which he saw the greater part of the nomad fighting strength collected round him. Here, at the wish of his followers, he assumed the name of Genghis Khan, or " perfect warrior." It now seemed time to adopt a bolder policy and to carry his victorious arms into the adjoining civilised countries. A pretext for further wars was afforded by the machinations of the Naiman prince Kushlek, who had dealt the deathblow to the empire of the Kara Khitai in 1201 ; he was compelled to fly for refuge to the Nu-chi. The Kirghiz, and after them the Uigurians, in 1209, voluntarily submitted in the meantime. The war with the Nu-chi, after some unimportant skirmishes, broke out in the year 1211 ; and in it the Khitans, who had been subjugated by the Nu-chi, lent valuable aid to the Mongols. Genghis Khan's chief object was to gain possession of Northern China, the best part of the Nu-chi Empire. Hsuan Tsung, the emperor of the Nu-chi, finally fled to the south in 1214, and was thus entirely cut off from his northern resources. Yen King, the capital, which roughly corresponds to the present Peking, now fell into the hands of the Mongols ; but the war ended only in 1234 with the overthrow of the Kin dynasty, seven years after the death of Genghis Khan. It was fortunate for the Nu-chi that they could place in the field against the Mongols the forces of half of China, and could fall back on the strongly fortified Chinese towns. The Mongols learnt gradually in the school of necessity the art of conducting sieges, in which they were destined later to perform great feats at the cost of the civilised peoples who were hard pressed by them. The employment of gunpowder in siege warfare was already familiar to the Chinese, who could teach many other lessons in this branch of warfare, where scientific knowledge was more important than impetuous valour.

Mongol Methods of Warfare

During the wars between the Mongols and the Nu-chi, the Khan Kushlek had journeyed to Turkestan, had formed an alliance there with Kutb ed-din Mohammed, the sultan of the Kharismians, and was on the point of building an empire in Western Central Asia with his help. The interference of the Kharismians on behalf of Kushlek may be attributed partly to trade jealousy. Genghis Khan had certainly tried to bring the trade over the northern roads, but encountered the distinct opposition of the rulers of Turkestan, of whom the most powerful was the Sultan of Kharismia or Chwarizm. Mohammed, who was master of Kashgar, and therefore of the southern roads, had ordered the envoys of Genghis Khan, who wished to conclude a sort of commercial treaty, to be put to death on the spot. The prince of Turkestan could not but have been aware of his power. It seemed as if the Kharismians would be the successors of the enfeebled Seljuks in their dominion over Western Asia and in their protectorate over the Caliphs of Bagdad. As always happens in such cases, a considerable part of the Kharismian power rested on the wealth which they derived from the possession of the Central Asiatic and Indian trade roads. But now this power, and all the covetous dreams which were connected with it, received an overwhelming shock from the onslaught of the Mongols. First of all, Kushlek, who had raised a considerable army, was completely defeated and slain during the rout in 1218. The Mongol forces then swept on against Kharismia, which at that time comprised a great portion of Turkestan and Persia, besides the modern Khiva. Bokhara, the garrison of which offered only a feeble resistance, was plundered and burnt; Otrara, on the middle Syr Daria, the proper border fortress facing Central Asia, held out longer, but finally fell into the hands of Genghis Khan, as did Khojend, Uzgent, and other fortified towns. The main army turned toward Samarkand, which soon surrendered, but had to pay for the sins of its ruler by a terrible massacre.

The resistance of the Sultan Mohammed was now broken : he did not venture on

MAIL-CLAD MONGOL WARRIOR
Showing chain armour and fighting weapons of a Mongol officer in Tamerlane's army.

a battle in the open field, but fled through Persia from town to town, continually pursued by the Mongol troops, only to die at last in misery on an island of the Caspian Sea. The greater part of Persia submitted to the Mongols in 1220. A counter-blow dealt by Mohammed's son, Jelal ed-din Mankburni, temporarily repulsed the troops of Genghis Khan. Nevertheless, the appearance of the Mongol sovereign in person forced the Kharismian to fly to India ; various revolted towns, Herat among them, were relentlessly massacred and burnt. The Mongols pressed on toward the Indus and laid waste Peshawar, Lahore, and Malikpur.

Thus the old path of conquest to India had been already trodden when Genghis Khan took the first steps on the beaten road which leads from the plains of Western Siberia to Europe. Pretexts for a campaign, which was first directed against the nomad tribes in the north of the Caucasus, were soon forthcoming. When, therefore, the Russians from Kieff appeared in the field as allies of these peoples, Mongol and European troops for the first time, in 1233, faced each other in battle. The Russians, who were victorious at the outset, were finally beaten, and the Grand Duke of Kieff himself was taken prisoner. The Mongols, however, to guard against whose attacks even Constantinople had been more strongly fortified, did not follow up their victory. In the year 1224 Genghis Khan planned a campaign in person against India, but was induced by a portent, or more probably by the exhaustion of his war-worn army, to retire to Karakoram, the former capital of the Christian Kerait, which had now become the centre of the Mongol Empire. In the previous year he had organised in the steppe of South Siberia with his whole army a gigantic battue, an enormously exaggerated example of the method of hunting familiar to the nomads of Central Asia, both as a sport and as a means of livelihood.

In the meantime the war in China had continued. Even the West Chinese Empire of the Hsia, with its partly Tibetan population, had been drawn into the whirlpool, and had been wasted in the years 1209 and 1217. Now, after losing Ordos, its northern province, it suffered a still more sweeping devastation at the hands of the Mongols from 1223 to 1226, until in 1227 the last prince of the dynasty was captured and the country completely conquered by the generals of Genghis Khan. The Kin, or Nu-chi, in Northern China, on the other hand, still resisted, until 1234, the attacks of the Mongols, whose best general, Mogli, died in 1225. Genghis Khan survived his general only two years. He died in 1227 in a town on the Upper Hoang-ho, whether from natural causes or poisoned by one of his wives is uncertain. In his person passed away the most genuine representative of the wild, untameable nomads of Central Asia, who, in the old Hun fashion, had built up for himself a giant empire over dead bodies and ruined cities. A thirst for power and a savage joy in destruction were the guiding motives of his policy. The need of professing any nobler aims, even as a specious pretext for his campaigns, was absolutely unfelt by him. And yet he was not wanting in those traits of rough honesty and magnanimity which are redeeming points in the heroes of nomadism; indeed, a certain receptivity of civilisation is apparent in him. The lesson which all the savage commanders of Central Asia learned in the end was destined to be revealed in him, and, above all, in his descendants. Civilisation, downtrodden and bleeding from a thousand wounds, showed itself the stronger in the spiritual contest, and crushed the obstinate pride of the princes of the steppes, until at last they humbly did homage in chapels and temples to the ideals of the civilised world, and painfully accustomed their mail-clad hands to hold the pen.

It was the successors of Genghis Khan who submitted to these influences; but already by the side of the gloomy, blood-stained figure of the first Mongol monarch a man had appeared whom the powerful nomad prince seemed to have chosen as a representative and advocate of civilisation. This was Ili Chutsai, or Yeliu Chutsai, a scion of the royal house of the Kin, a Tungusian, acquainted with Chinese culture. The motive that induced Genghis Khan to bring this member of a hostile family to his court, and soon to entrust him with the complete internal administration, was certainly less the wish to promote the culture of his Mongol subjects than the effort to organise his empire, and especially his revenue, on the model of China.

This succeeded so well that Ili Chutsai continued to hold his high position under the successors of Genghis Khan until his death. But it reflects far more honour on him that he regarded himself at the same time as the advocate of an advanced civilisation, that he boldly opposed the cruel commands of the monarch, protected the oppressed, and, wherever he could, preserved the monuments of art from destruction. He devoted his own property to these objects, or employed it in collecting archives and inscriptions. A number of these latter and a few musical instruments composed the whole wealth which he was found to possess, when calumniators suspected his official administration. In Genghis Khan and his Minister we see the embodiment, side by side, of two great and antagonistic principles—barbarous despotism and civilised self-restraint. These two men seem an epitome of the whole history of Central Asia. It is difficult to ascertain the extent of the Mongol Empire on the death of Genghis Khan; it was still an incompleted structure. The steppes of Mongolia and South-West Siberia were the immediate possessions of the new ruling nation, or were governed, as the country of the Uigurians was, by native rulers in complete subjection to the conqueror. Turkestan might rank as conquered, whereas in Persia the Mongol power was still insecurely established, and North-West India had been raided rather than really subjugated. In China the empire of the Western Hsia was completely annexed; the Nu-chi, on the contrary, still offered stubborn resistance in the provinces on the Lower Hoang-ho. The extent of the Mongol influence towards the south is the most

Death of Genghis Khan

Civilising Influence on The Mongols

Extent of the Mongol Empire

uncertain. No large campaigns were undertaken in the Tarim basin or in Tibet; but probably a number at least of the states in the oases of Eastern Turkestan voluntarily submitted. Many of these petty states were probably subject to the suzerainty of the Uigurians, the Kerait, and other nations, and shared their fate; others, like Kashgar, had been already conquered in the wars against the Kharismians.

The constitution of the Mongol Empire was organised throughout on a military footing, and, from this aspect, was a mere renewal of the ancient Central Asiatic system which obtained among the Huns and Turks. All men capable of bearing arms in the different tribes were enrolled by tens, hundreds, or thousands. The army recruited its ranks from the young men of the subjugated districts, who were distributed among the existing troops, or, if the country had voluntarily surrendered, formed distinct regiments. Standards of yak-tails or horse-tails, of which the most important were the nine-tailed Mongol ensign, and the banner of the Khan made of four black horse-tails, were equally in accordance with Central Asiatic custom. The nine-tailed flag denoted the nine great divisions, or army corps, into which the Mongol levies were distributed. Genghis Khan regulated the internal affairs of his people by a series of laws, most of which were derived from traditions and earlier precedents, and were still suitable to the nomad life. The

MONGOL HELMET

A Mongolian helmet of the 14th century in the collection of the Tsar of Russia.

MONGOLIAN ARMS

Specimens of weapons, tunic, and helmet of the Mongolian period in the Russian Imperial collection.

attitude which he maintained toward religion is noteworthy. On the one side there is the evident wish to elevate the traditional Shamanistic creed by laying greater stress on the belief in the existence of a divine being; on the other side it is recommended that consideration be shown to all other religions and to their priests. Public offices, however, were not to be entrusted to the priests. Generally speaking, the enactments of Genghis Khan are principally concerned with military matters; at the same time they regulate family life in a very simple fashion, define the close time for game, and make universal regulations of certain Mongol customs—such as, for instance, the slaughtering of animals by slitting up the body, the prohibition of bathing, and so on. In his latter days Genghis Khan displayed some leaning toward Buddhism, but showed otherwise that indifferent toleration of the various religions which is everywhere characteristic of the Mongols. Religious zeal, the excuse for so many cruelties, never prompted the massacres perpetrated by them.

The great nobles of the Mongol Empire met in solemn deliberation in 1227 on the banks of the River Kerulen, in the northern steppe. Genghis Khan by his will had nominated as his successor his third son, Ogdai, or Ogotai Khan, who soon afterwards, at a great imperial diet at Karakoram, received the homage of his subjects. Since Ogdai still conceded considerable powers to Ili Chutsai, his father's first

1485

Minister, the latter was able to continue the internal development of the empire, to organise thoroughly the system of taxation, and to draw up lists of the men liable to military service; thus laying a firm foundation, which enabled the Mongol monarchs to extract the maximum of profit from the subjugated civilised countries without pursuing a policy of crushing them completely. The conquering power of the united nomad peoples made bold advance under Ogdai. Persia, where the Kharismian Jelal ed-din had recovered a part of his inheritance, was once more, in 1231, subjugated, and the unfortunate prince was compelled to seek refuge among the western mountains, where he was murdered by Kurdish robbers. Ogdai himself directed his attention against China, where the empire of the Kin was struggling for existence with failing strength. The provinces of Pechili, Shantung, Shansi, and Liaotung were then already in the possession of the Mongols. The Kin held their own only to the south of the Hoang-ho in Shensi and Honan. Tuli, the youngest brother of Ogdai, was commander-in-chief of the Mongols in most of the later battles. The siege of the capital, Kaifongfu, at which the beleaguered Chinese employed powder with great effect, was unsuccessfully attempted in the year 1232. But subsequently an alliance was negotiated between the Mongols and the Chinese Empire of the southern Sung, which quickly crushed the resistance of the Kin. In the year 1234 the last emperor of the Nu-chi was defeated by a combined army of Mongols and Chinese. Shensi fell to the Mongols, Honan principally to the Sung, although misunderstandings already arose between the allies which were premonitions of subsequent events.

Operations Against China and Persia

The conquest of North China was of paramount importance to the Mongols. Chinese civilisation was the first with which they had any lasting intercourse, and thus the political institutions of China served in many respects as models for the wild people of the steppes, while the Uigurian civilisation, which had originally been imitated, sank into the background. The ancient power of China in transforming and absorbing the peoples of the steppe gradually asserted itself more strongly. The further the Mongols penetrated into the Middle Kingdom, the more Chinese they became, until at last the disruption of the gigantic world-empire into the districts of Central Asia on the one side and of China on the other was inevitable.

Mongols Who Became Chinese

The forces which were set free by the overthrow of the Kin were destined to extend the Mongol Empire towards the west. The Mongol hordes under the command of Batu swept on after 1235 against Europe, where the protection of the frontiers lay in the hands of the Russian princes. Riazan was captured on December 21st, 1237, and on February 14th, 1238, fell Vladimir on the Kliasma. The Russian chiefs had to submit to the suzerainty of the Mongols, while Kieff was destroyed on December 6th, 1240. Poland was now ravaged, Duke Boleslav V., the Modest— or the Chaste—was forced by Sandomir to take refuge in Hungary, and a mixed army of Poles and Germans under Henry II. of Lower Silesia was annihilated at Liegnitz on April 9th, 1241.

There, at the edge of the steppe region, the western march of Paidar, or Peta, and his Mongols ended. They turned to Hungary, which Batu himself had already invaded in March, 1241. There was imminent danger that these Mongols would establish themselves firmly in the Hungarian steppe, and that Hungary would now, as on several previous occasions, become the nest of predatory swarms of nomads, who would perpetually harass Europe. The Magyars suffered the very fate which their forefathers had inflicted on so many prosperous countries. The Mongols seemed, in the summer and autumn of 1241, to have formed the intention of making room for themselves and of exterminating the inhabitants. However, on the tidings of the death of the Great Khan, Ogdai, which occurred at Karakoram on December 11th, 1241, they resolved, in the spring of 1242, to withdraw through Kumania to Russia.

Menace to Central Europe

The expansive power of the Mongol Empire was even then immense. While war was being waged in Europe, Ogdai's armies threatened Irak and Asia Minor. Like Turkish armies earlier and later, the Mongols used the road through Armenia, and repeatedly attempted to attack Bagdad. Simultaneously there began in China the attack on the kingdom of the southern Sung, whose princes, in blind infatuation, had helped to destroy the bulwark of their power, the empire of the Kin. The troops of the Sung held for a long time the lines of the middle Hoang-ho and of the Wei-ho by dint of hard fighting ; at the same time the contest was raging in Szechuen on the upper Yangtse Kiang, during which, at the siege of Lu-cheng, a strong Mongol army was almost totally destroyed. There also the death of Ogdai temporarily put an end to the operations. The Great Khan had bequeathed the empire to one of his grandsons, a minor ; but in 1241 the first wife of Ogdai, Nai ma chen, or Jurakina, usurped the regency in his place. Ili Chutsai, the aged chancellor of the first two Great Khans, who wished to secure to the defrauded heir his rights, died suddenly. The empress now succeeded in carrying at a great imperial diet, or *kurultai*, the nomination of her son Kuyuk Khan as sovereign, in 1246. Thus ended an interregnum which had greatly impaired the aggressive powers of the Mongols. It is this which partly explains why in many places, especially when confronting the western states of Europe, the policy of conquest, notwithstanding all sorts of threatening preparations, was abandoned. Besides this, envoys of the Pope had appeared at the diet, in order to ask the Mongols to abstain from further expeditions against the Christians. It is true that they had irritated the self-conscious sovereigns of a world-empire. Nevertheless, the common hostility of the Christians and the Mongols to the Mohammedans seemed to offer the basis for an understanding, especially in Syria, where Crusaders and Mongols were forced to stand by one another. Indeed, finally there appeared some prospect of converting even the Mongol dynasty to Christianity, and of thus winning a mighty triumph for the Church.

Attempt to Christianise the Mongols

Kuyuk turned his attention principally to the east, and attacked Korea, which at the same time might form a bridge to Japan. He died, however, in the year 1248, and Mangu Khan, a son of Tuli and grandson of Genghis Khan, came to the throne in 1251, although only after long deliberations by the great nobles. The gigantic extent of the Mongol Empire of that day is shown by the length of time required to summon and assemble the great councils of the realm. The decay of the unwieldy structure was only a question of time. Mangu himself took the first step towards it when he nominated his brother Kublai Governor-General in China, and thus placed his destined successor under the immediate influence of Chinese civilisation. The Mongol dynasty was fated to become Chinese at no very distant date.

For the time being, however, the frontiers of the empire continued to expand under Mangu. Tibet, hitherto protected by its situation, was attacked, and, as Marco Polo testifies, was completely devastated. A second advance, under the leadership of Hulagu, against Irak and Syria was momentous in results. The war was first waged with the Assassins, whose eastern or Persian branch was almost exterminated. The Mongol arms were then turned against Bagdad, which the feeble resistance of the ruling caliph failed to save. A frightful massacre almost exterminated the whole population of this religious capital of the Islam world. The hostility then evinced by the Mongols to the Mohammedan faith strengthened the hope that the Mongols would let themselves be won over to Christianity. Christians did, indeed, obtain a favoured position at the Great Khan's court ; but Mangu regarded baptism and other rites merely as a sort of convenient magic formula. The behaviour of the unorthodox Nestorian and Armenian priests could not but confirm him in this belief. The Mongol princes must have had very hazy notions as to the inner meaning of the various religions, the ceremonies of which they occasionally observed.

The Many Wars of the Mongols

After a great part of Syria and Asia Minor had been ravaged, the attention of the Mongol sovereign was once more directed to the dominions of the southern Sung, which were now vigorously attacked for some successive years. Kublai, who had satisfactorily averted the disfavour which threatened him, conquered the western border-lands of the Chinese Empire, Szechuen and Yunnan, and, by advancing his armies as far as Tonquin and Cochin China, surrounded Southern China on all sides. Once more the death of the Great Khan temporarily brought the operations to a standstill. Mangu died in the year 1259, and all the Mongol leaders went off to the Tartar steppe to attend the imperial diet.

Death of Mangu Khan

The first of these pictures shows the ruins of the tomb of the wives of Timur, or Tamerlane, while the centre picture is that of the mosque at Samarkand containing the remains of the great emperor, and the third shows the tomb itself. Timur's sarcophagus is the dark one, cracked across the top, and is made from an immense block of jade.

MEMORIALS OF TAMERLANE IN HIS ANCIENT CAPITAL

THE LATER MONGOL EMPIRES

The fall of the gigantic empire could no longer be delayed. It was due not merely to the enormous size of the Mongol state, and the impossibility of preserving the unity of the realm in the face of such immense distances. Still more destructive was the influence of the different civilisations which everywhere forced their way, as it were, through the layer of sand spread over them by the storm-wind of the desert : a spiritual revolution was at work.

If Kublai was on the point of being transformed into a civilised Chinese, the western governors felt themselves surrounded by the civilisations of Western Asia and Europe, while the ancient and genuine Mongol spirit in its primitive barbarism was to be found only in the steppes of Central Asia. The force of the geographical position, which had first called to life the earlier states and civilisations, made itself again irresistibly felt ; out of the provinces of the **Mongols in Touch with Civilisation** Mongol world-empire were formed once more national states under the rule of dynasties of Mongol origin. The way in which the fall would take place depended on the point to which the centre of gravity of the empire should be shifted. If toward the east, then the west would at once wrench itself free ; if toward the civilised countries of the west, it would be a natural consequence that China should attain independence under a Mongol ruler.

In 1260 the choice of the Mongols fell on Kublai Khan ; by this election the centre of gravity was shifted toward the east. Kublai still, indeed, was reckoned the supreme lord of all Mongols ; but in truth he ruled only the eastern steppe districts of Central Asia and the parts of China hitherto conquered. Iran and the possessions in Syria and Asia Minor fell to his brother Hulagu ; in Kipchak, the steppe country of West Siberia and the adjoining European regions, the descendants of Batu ruled, and other Mongol dynasties were being formed in Turkestan.

Chinese civilisation now triumphed in the main eastern empire. What conquering energy still existed among the Mongol people was employed on the subjugation of the empire of the southern Sung and on futile attacks against Japan, after the disorders in Mongolia, which followed on the change of sovereigns, had **Dangers of Extended Empire** been quieted. Serious operations against the Sung were not begun until the year 1267, and twelve years elapsed before the final resistance of the Southern Chinese was ended. But while Kublai thus won the dominion over the whole of China, he was threatened by the danger of losing his possessions in Central Asia through rebellious Mongol princes. At Karakoram, in the years 1260 to 1264, appeared a rival emperor, Alipuko, or Arikbuga. A grandson of Ogdai, Kaidu by name, rebelled, and held out till his death, in 1301. Baian, however, to whom the victory over the Sung is chiefly to be ascribed, brought Mongolia, with the old capital, Karakoram, once more into the possession of his master. Kublai himself resided from the first in Peking, and thus announced that he was more Chinese than Mongol. The histories of China have recognised this fact, since, after 1280, they treat the Mongol reigning house of Kublai as a genuine Chinese dynasty. The further destinies of this dynasty accordingly belong to the history of Central Asia in a very restricted degree, especially after the death, in 1294, of Kublai whose name had testified to some sort of imaginary cohesion between the **Crumbling World Power** various fragments of the Mongol Empire. Anyone who has tried to pass a fair judgment on the crumbling world-empire, and asks what its effect on the civilisation of mankind was, will, as he turns over the records of that blood-stained period, be filled first with a feeling of abhorrence, and of despair of any progress or of any results of higher culture. Is it always the destiny of the nations which are laboriously struggling forward to succumb to the onslaught of rude barbarians, whose dull senses are intoxicated with battle and booty until they are maddened with an aimless and hideous lust for murder?

On no page of history does the old cruelty of nature and destiny stare us so derisively in the face. But it has been already stated that there existed counter influences to all that evil and mischief, which were able to mitigate the terrible impression. The storm did not only wreak destruction; it purified the atmosphere. It was the Mongols who first put an end to the sect of murderers, the Assassins—a conspicuous but not an isolated example of this purifying power. Far higher value must be attached to the fact that once again, although for a brief period and under the supreme command of a barbarous people, all the civilised countries of the Old World enjoyed free intercourse with each other; all the roads were temporarily open, and representatives of every nation appeared at the court of Karakoram. Chinese artisans were settled there; Persian and Armenian merchants met the envoys of the Pope and other Western Powers; a goldsmith from Paris constructed for Mangu the chief ornament of his court, a silver tree; there were numerous Arabs in the service of the Khan, and Buddhist priests laid the civilisation of India at his feet. These representatives of different civilisations must have reacted on each other. For the isolated kingdom of China in particular the Mongol age marked the influx of new and stimulating ideas. Arabian writings were frequently translated into Chinese; Persian astronomers and mathematicians came into the country; daring European travellers also found many opportunities to communicate their knowledge. The keen zest for learning exhibited by the better part of the Mongols seemed to communicate itself to the Chinese, and for a period to overcome the stiff conservatism of the old self-centred civilised nation. While the history of the Eastern Mongol Empire was gradually becoming a chapter of Chinese history, an Iranian state was developing in the west under a Mongol dynasty, which it is usual henceforth to designate as the dynasty of the Ilkhans. Hulagu, who in Mangu's time had consolidated the conquest in Persia, and had

Compensations for War and Bloodshed

Mongol Patronage of Learning

added other parts of Western Asia to them, must be reckoned as an independent sovereign after the accession of Kublai, although a semblance of dependence was preserved. After the capture of Bagdad, Hulagu had conquered some of the petty Mohammedan princes, and thus put himself on good terms with the Christians in Armenia and Palestine. But when an Egyptian army inflicted a heavy defeat on his general, Ketboga, not far from Tiberias, in 1260, the Mongol advance was checked in that direction also. The attempts of Hulagu to reconquer Syria led to frightful massacres, but had not been crowned with any real success when he died, in 1265.

His successor, Abaka, was in consequence restricted to Persia and Irak, thus realising the idea of an Iranian empire under a Mongol dynasty. The irony of fate willed that Abaka should be forced immediately, according to the old Iranian policy, to take measures for protecting his realm against his own countrymen, the Mongols of Kipchak, who threatened to invade the land through the Caucasian gate from Derbend, and had already come to an understanding with the Egyptians, the arch foes of Abaka. Nothing shows more clearly how complete the fall of the Mongol Empire then was. War now began on the other frontier of Iran, towards Turkestan, which had long been threatened, since the Mongols of Jagatai invaded Khorasan, and were only driven out of Persia by Abaka's victory at Herat. A final attempt to recover Syria ended, however, in the defeat of Abaka at Emesa in 1281.

Mongol Against Mongol

In that same year Abaka died, and with his successor the transformation of the dynasty seemed to be completed. The prince, originally a baptised Christian, and brother of the deceased, openly adopted the Mohammedan religion under the name of Ahmed, and thus snapped the last bond of union with his unruly Central Asiatic brethren. This step was, however, premature. The Christians of Armenia and Georgia, the mainstay of the empire, were roused to ominous excitement, and the Mongols could not make up their minds so quickly to abandon their hatred of Islam and its followers. Rebellions ensued, the leaders of which called in the help of the far-off Great Khan, Kublai. Ahmed was deposed, and his nephew Argun gained the sovereignty. Then followed a period of disturbances and renewed fighting in Syria, which was favourable to the Mongols, especially in the time of the Ilkhan Ghazan (1295–1304), but ended later in repeated disasters. Under Ghazan, who henceforward helped Islam to victory, the empire of the Ilkhans temporarily acquired new power; but a reconciliation with the Mohammedan world was not effected, and the zeal of the Christians for the Mongol dynasty soon cooled. Under the successors of Ghazan the empire became disorganised, but the semblance at least of unity was kept up until the death of the Ilkhan Abu Said Bahadur in 1335. The disruption then began which repeated on a small scale the fate of the Mongolian world-empire. The provinces became independent, and the Ilkhan retained a mere shadow of dignity without any real power. In 1336, round Bagdad, under sheikh Hasan Busurg, the emir of the Jelair, who died in 1356, was formed the empire of the Ilkhani, which acquired fresh power, but finally was destroyed in the struggle with the Mozaffarids and Timur between 1393 and 1405. In 1410 died the last of the Ilkhani but one, Ahmed ben Owais, as a prisoner of the Turkoman Prince Kara Yusuf. The dynasties which had been formed in the steppe regions of West Siberia and Turkestan were better able to maintain their individuality than the Mongol princes of China and Iran; it was from these districts that the second great advance of the Mongols under Timur started. In Turkestan arose the empire of Jagatai, which took its name from one of the sons of Genghis Khan, and at the time of its greatest prosperity comprised all the countries on the Oxus

THE GREAT TIMUR, OR TAMERLANE
The Mongol empire-builder who had the greater part of Asia at his feet at the end of the fourteenth century; but whose empire soon broke up.
From the miniature in the Bodleian Library.

and Jaxartes, as well as the greatest part of the Tarim basin. The prevailing religion in these regions was Islam; sectarians of that faith had there offered the Mongols in 1232 a more obstinate resistance than the native princes had previously done. At an early period one of the Mongol sovereigns had gone over to the teaching of Mahomet, although the bulk of the people had not followed his example.

Since there were no external enemies left, the natural effect was that the Mongols soon fought among themselves. Disputes as to the succession, and rebellions were endless; the legitimate reigning dynasty of the line of Genghis Khan sank into the background after 1358, and a government by a mayor of the palace took its place, which obviously could not remain uncontested in the hands of any one family. Some provinces became absolutely independent; for example, Kashgar, which was the most powerful state in those parts in 1369, when Timur first appeared on the scene. The Mongol dynasty of the Shaibanids, though temporarily overthrown, did not disappear; but after the fall of Timur's dynasty in 1494 soon raised itself again to the throne of Samarkand and Bokhara, which it held in the male line until 1599, and in the female until 1868. The kingdom of Kipchak—the Golden Horde—which, roughly speaking, comprised the lowlands of Western Siberia and Eastern Europe, showed greater stability than the Jagatai. A more vigorous foreign policy was both possible and necessary there, and helped to bind the Mongols closely together. The command of Russia, that land of constant ferment, the wars with Poland and Byzantium and the raids over the Caucasus into Western Asia, kept alive the old warlike ardour of the conquest-loving nation. The countries which later formed the kingdom of Kipchak were first partly subdued by Juji, the eldest son of Genghis Khan, and then were completely brought under the dominion of the Mongols by his son Batu.

The expedition of Batu to Central Europe ended the period of great conquests in the west. The Mongols were **Mongol Conquests in the West** unable to hold their position in Hungary and Poland, which were both attacked again in 1254, and Russia alone remained completely in their hands. Batu, who died in 1256, had been practically an independent ruler. He was succeeded, without opposition from the Great Khan, Kublai, by his younger brother Berkai, who was soon involved in contests with the Iranian sovereign of the Mongols, Abaka.

The highest civilisation in the kingdom of Kipchak was then found in the Crimea. The towns of the Crimea had flourished since ancient times, and had increased in prosperity under the Mongols ; the country had maintained its intercourse with Byzantium and Southern Europe. The influence of this advanced culture was noticeable in the Mongolian princes. Many of them, in spite of their soldier-like roughness, appreciated scientific pursuits, tried to draw learned men to their court, and showed towards the representatives of the different religions that tolerance which is perhaps the most pleasing trait in the Mongol character. It must be admitted that the hopes which were so often entertained of winning the Mongol princes completely over to one definite religion were long unrealised.

The history of the kingdom of Kipchak is full of constant wars against all neighbours on the west and the south, and of dynastic disputes and insurrections at home. Part of it belongs to the course of Russian history. The Mongol age does not imply for Russia a brief and bloody **Mongol Influence on Russia** interlude, as it does for most other Western countries ; on the contrary, the nomads of the steppes seem for a time to have associated so much with the native population that at the present day indelible traces of that affinity are left on the national Russian character. A still closer amalgamation was partly prevented by the circumstance that finally the dynasty of Kipchak in the time of Uzbeg, from 1312 to 1340, went over to Islam, and thus repelled the Christian Russians in the same way as the Persian Mongols offended the Armenians and Georgians.

After 1360 the kingdom was filled with disturbances, and it was only the union of the White and the Blue Hordes by Toktamish, in 1378, and the invasion of Timur, from 1391 to 1395, that temporarily restored order ; but with the result that, after the death of Toktamish in 1406, the disorders increased and the power of the kingdom continually diminished. In the fifteenth century the Crimea, with the adjoining parts of Southern Russia, was all that remained of the once mighty realm of Kipchak. In the year 1502 the " Golden Horde " died out, and the kingdom completely broke up.

The Nogai, a branch of the Mongol Jujis, formed in 1466 a kingdom round Astrakhan, which fell before the attacks of the Grand Duke of Moscow. Further to the north arose in 1438 the Khanate of Kasan ; and in the Crimea a small Mongol state, founded in 1420 with the help of Turkey, to which it agreed to pay tribute, held its own until its incorpora- **Split of the Empire under Kublai Khan** tion with Russia in the year 1783. With the split of the Mongol Empire in the time of Kublai the era of the great conquests was virtually closed, although raids and border wars still lasted for a long time. The subjugation of Southern China brought the eastern Mongols completely under the influence of Chinese civilisation. The more westerly of the Mongol states did not show any further power of similar expansion. The most striking proof of this stagnation is the fact that no attempt was made to conquer India, although the gates to this country, so alluring to every great Asiatic conqueror, were in Mongol hands, and although the Mongols had already traversed the Punjab in the time of Genghis Khan. A fresh and powerful impulse, which united a part of the ancient Mongol power once more under one ruler, was needed in order to reach this last goal.

It seems at first sight strange that the new tide of conquest flowed from Turkestan, from the kingdom of Jagatai ; that is to say, from the Mongol state which was most rent by internal wars and showed the least energetic foreign policy. But these dissensions were actually a proof that the ancient Mongol love of fighting

ONE OF THE MANY BATTLES BETWEEN THE MONGOLS AND THE TURKS

This reproduction of an old woodcut illustrates the methods of warfare practised by Timur and his hordes; one Mongol warrior may be seen just after decapitating his fallen foe, and another is in the act of cutting off the nose of an enemy. The original inscription quaintly adds that "the man who had his nose cut off, lost it on the field."

was all-powerful there, and that the forces and impulses of nomadism had remained there unimpaired. The nomad tribes of Turkestan, who, long before the time of Genghis Khan, had repeatedly made victorious inroads into Iran and India, supplied the most splendid material to a leader who knew how to mould them into a loyal and devoted army. While Mongolia proper, which had spread its armies over half the globe, was now poor in men and no longer a theatre for great enterprises, Turkestan had every claim to become the foremost power of the nomad world. All that was required was a master

will. Civilisation may have tried her arts on the forefathers of Timur, that true child of the desert, who was born, the son of a Turki general, on April 8, 1336. They had lived for some hundred years or so as the feudal lords of the small district of Kash, in the very heart of the civilised world of Turkestan, to the south of the prosperous town of Samarkand. But Timur's character shows barely a trace of these influences. In his relations to his native soil he is true to the nomad bent. The little country of Kash served him indeed as a starting-point for his first operations, but he soon shook himself free from it, and fought like a soldier of fortune, whose true home is among the moving tents of his camp—who to-day has under him a mighty army recruited or impressed from every nation, and to-morrow with a few faithful followers is seeking a precarious refuge in the mountain gorges or the desert. The vivid contrasts, so usual among nomads, between harshness and magnanimity, between cruel contempt for the life of strangers and desperate grief for his kinsmen and his friends, are repeated in Timur. Like a true Mongol, he was indifferent in religious questions; but—and this one evil trait he learnt from the civilised peoples—he could play the Mohammedan fanatic when it served his purpose.

Character of the Great Tamerlane

In the year 1358 the realm of Jagatai was in the most desperate disorder. The khan, Buyan Kuli, had become a mere puppet in the hands of his mayors of the palace; but even the family which ruled in his place saw itself in this same year deprived of all influence by a general revolt of the vassal princes, and the kingdom broke up into its separate provinces. In the wars which these new principalities continually waged on one another, Kutb ed-din Amir Timur, as a nephew of the reigning prince of Kash, found opportunities of gaining distinction, and used them to the full.

The first attempts to reconstitute the State under a different rule started in Kashgar, the prince of which, Toghluk Timur—descended from Jagatai in the sixth degree—appears to have extended his influence as far as the Altai Mountains. In the years 1359 and 1360 the armies of Kashgar advanced victoriously to Western Turkestan; Timur found it politic to join them, and he contrived that after the fall of his uncle the principality of Kash should come to his share. But it must have soon been obvious that there was not much to gain in this way. He soon reappeared in the field, but this time as an ally of the emir Hosain, who, as a descendant of the family of the mayors of the palace, had held out in Kabul and now reasserted his claims to the supreme power. In the year 1360 the two allies experienced the most strange vicissitudes, being at one time victors, at another fugitives and even prisoners. But after years of fighting, fortune inclined to their side; a change of sovereigns in Kashgar gave them breathing time, and in 1363 they were able to enthrone as khan at Samarkand a new puppet of the family of Jagatai, Kabul Sultan.

It is not surprising that Timur now tried to put aside his overlord Hosain; but he met with an overwhelming defeat in 1366. He contrived, however, to obtain the forgiveness of Hosain in 1367 and to regain his influence. After better preparations, another attempt succeeded in 1369. Hosain was captured and executed, and a council of the realm nominated Timur to be supreme Great Khan. The nominal sovereignty of the descendants of Genghis Khan was not terminated for some time. Suyurghatmish was succeeded in 1388–1397 by his son Mahmud as Khan of Transoxania.

The new "Lord of the World" began with West Turkestan for his sole possession, and even of that territory parts remained to be conquered. Yusuf Beg of Kharismia, which then comprised Khiva and Bokhara, defied Timur continually, and was not completely defeated

TIMUR IN COUNCIL WITH HIS WISE MEN
Reproduced from an original drawing by a Persian artist.

until 1379. Kamar ed-din of Kashgar, in spite of campaigns in 1375 and 1376, could never be completely vanquished. It was only when West Turkestan was entirely subjugated that the great wars and raids of Timur, fraught with such consequences for civilisation, began with an attack on Persia, which then, like Jagatai at an earlier time, was broken up into several independent principalities.

The separate states could not resist the united power of Turkestan. Khorasan and Herat, the ancient bulwarks of Iran against the nomads, were the first to succumb before the attack of Timur (1381). In the years 1386–7 the Mongol army fought with Armenia, the Turkomans, and the Ilkhani of Bagdad. The year 1388 saw the terrible overthrow of the Iranian national states of the Mozaffarids, which had been formed in Farsistan, the ancient Persis, Kirman, and Kurdistan, and the complete destruction of Ispahan, the capital of Persia. The invasion of Turkestan by the ungrateful Khan Toktamish of Kipchak called Timur away from Persia in 1388–91. He was then completely occupied with the subjugation of the Tarim basin. In 1392 he reappeared in Persia, and laid the country waste, since most of the dethroned princes, even the Mozaffarids, had partially regained their dominions. The race of the Mozaffarids was this time exterminated. In 1393 Armenia and Kurdistan were occupied once more.

It was most unfortunate for the subjugated countries that Timur by his love of conquest was always allured from vanquished regions to other parts of his territories. The native princes then found opportunities to recover their dominions for a time ; whereupon Timur would retaliate. Timur's imagination revelled in horrors ; he aimed at striking terror far and wide. He delighted in raising towers of skulls or building gigantic monuments of corpses and living prisoners.

Delight in Barbaric Cruelty

A momentous campaign in India called Timur away from Persia on this particular occasion. The influence of the Mongols seems to have been asserted here

TIMUR IN STATE, SEATED ON HIS THRONE
From the Persian illuminated manuscript Tuzuk-i Timur, or "Memoirs of Timur."

and there in Northern India on the east side of the Indus. Independent border tribes impeded, as now, the communications between Afghanistan and the valley of the Indus. Beyond the Indus lay Mohammedan states. In 1398 part of the border tribes were conquered after a laborious campaign under the personal command of Timur. Meanwhile a grandson of Timur, Pir Mohammed, captured Multan after a six months' siege, and the combined forces then advanced before Delhi. The city fell into the hands of Timur after a bloody battle. The conqueror then marched beyond the Ganges, and returned to Samarkand in 1399 laden with immense booty.

The attacks on the West were now at once renewed. In 1399 Timur was in Georgia which he cruelly devastated ; but his eyes were already fixed on Asia Minor where the Osmans—or Ottomans—had founded their empire, and on Syria, which

1405

was under Egyptian rule. The Osman war began in the year 1400 with the siege of the city of Sivas, which resisted so long that Timur, after taking it, desisted for the time from further operations in that quarter. He advanced instead against the feebly-defended Syria, the northern part of which, including Damascus, fell into his hands. Bagdad also, where Ahmed ibn Owais had established himself, was captured. The storm then broke on the heads of the Osmans. In the middle of 1402, the Turkish army was defeated near Angora by the forces of Timur. Sultan Bajazet I. himself was taken prisoner, and Asia Minor totally laid waste. Faraj of Egypt, who feared a similar fate, acknowledged the supremacy of Timur.

Thus Tamerlane, the "lame" Timur, had again united the three chief western portions of the Mongol world-empire,

TIMUR IN AUDIENCE WITH A MONGOL PRINCE
After the original Persian drawing.

Jagatai, Kipchak, and Persia, and widened their frontiers still more. When he once more convened a great council of the realm at Samarkand, in the year 1404, he explained to his magnates that only one great undertaking was left him, the conquest of China. But this time a kindly

China Spared by the Death of Tamerlane fate spared the prosperous Chinese Empire. An army of 200,000 men was already in the field, when death cut short the conqueror's plans on February 18th. He died of fever at the age of sixty-nine years. The spirit of boundless ambition and conquest was once more embodied in him ; but it died with him, and the down-trodden seeds of culture were free to spring up again if life was still in them. The age of the great nomad empires definitely closed with Timur, but not before it had produced endless misery and had rent the ancient civilisation of Western Asia to shreds.

Timur's empire had been held together only by the personality of its ruler, and it crumbled away even in his hands so soon as his attention was too closely riveted in any one direction. The term empire is almost too pretentious for this political structure, which merits rather the name of military despotism. The national basis was almost entirely replaced by the purely military. The body that took the field was not a levy from defined districts, but recruited or impressed followers of the individual leaders. Every campaign was an undertaking at the common cost, the supreme command being in the hands of Timur. The troops were not paid by Timur, but by the generals, who looked to recoup themselves with interest. If by so doing they amassed excessive wealth, Timur simply ordained that all sections of the army should be strengthened. Every leader was then forced to employ his fortune in enlisting more soldiers. Such an army could naturally be kept on foot only so long as it was fighting. It would soon have eaten itself away in peace time. Thus, behind Timur's unbridled lust for war, which entirely corresponded to his character, there was a compelling force from which he could not, with safety to himself, withdraw. He possessed an army ready to hand only so long as he waged war and obtained booty, and, so long only as this army remained loyal to him, he was lord of a gigantic empire. He was confronted by the national rulers, whose existence was more firmly rooted in the soil, but who were seldom able to face the rushing torrent of his enormous hosts.

With the death of Timur these opposing forces were certain soon to regain the upper hand. No course was left to the descendants of the mighty conqueror but to submit to them or to give a national tinge to their own policy, a course for which the earlier Mongol dynasties furnished a precedent. For the moment, indeed, the army, the invincible weapon of Timur, was still available, and its leaders were ready to continue the previous system, although there was no longer a master mind to lead them. Above all, it was intended that the expedition against China, which promised such ample booty, should be entrusted to a board of generals, and the question as to Timur's successor be left temporarily in abeyance. But the dispute about the inheritance, which at once broke out, brought these plans to an abrupt close.

The wars about the succession lasted four years. At first it seemed as if Timur's grandson, Khalil, would inherit the empire; but Shah Ruch, a son of the conqueror, born in 1378, asserted his claim in Persia. In 1409 the well-meaning and peaceful Khalil was deposed, and Timur's empire, which already seemed likely to break up into the two states of Turkestan and Persia, was again united under Shah Ruch. But it was no longer the old empire. The larger states, which had outwardly submitted to the scimitar of the lord of the world, Kipchak, Egypt, the Ottoman empire, the Turkoman states of Armenia, and the majority of the Indian possessions, were irretrievably lost now that Timur was dead. Only West Turkestan, the Iranian highlands, and a

The Empire After the Death of Timur part of the Punjab were still retained by his successors. Shah Ruch was not the man to contemplate a continuance of the old policy of war and conquest. The only recourse left to him was to bring the national forces of his states into his service; in other words, to recognise the Iranian people with their culture and to help them. It was chiefly due to the prudence with which he pursued this object that he was able to maintain the

TIMUR IN TIMES OF PEACE
The great conqueror travelling through his dominions.

remnant of the empire for many years until his death in 1447.

His arch-foes were the Turkomans in Armenia and Azerbijan, wild hordes of Central Asiatic nomads, who had planted themselves there on the old military route of the Turkish and Mongol invaders and had formed a predatory state in the old Hun style. There were fragments of all the migratory tribes, who at one time were divided by internecine feuds, at another were united into a formidable military power by the prospect of booty.

The headship of the hordes rested at first with the Turkoman tribe of the " Black Sheep " under its chief Kara Yusuf, who brought Mesopotamia and Bagdad into his power, and gravely menaced Persia. The sudden death of Kara Yusuf, in 1420, freed Shah Ruch from his most formidable antagonist. Azerbijan was now definitely taken from the Turkomans.

But any hope that the Iranised house of Timur would retain at least Persia and Turkestan was ended by the disorders ensuing on the death of Shah Ruch. A stormy period, in which parricide and

1497

fratricide were not infrequent, shook the empire for years, and while the descendants of Timur tried to exterminate each other, the swarms of Turkomans, at whose head the horde of the " White Sheep " now stood, poured afresh over the Persian frontier. Abul Kasim Barbar Bahadur, a grandson of Shah Ruch, held his own in Khorasan until 1457; then, while West Persia was already lost to the Turkomans, Sultan Abu Said, a grand-nephew of Shah Ruch, usurped the power in 1459. But in the year 1467 he found himself forced to fight with Uzun Hasan, the leader of the Ak Koinlo. The heir of Timur was defeated and killed in 1468 ; the larger part

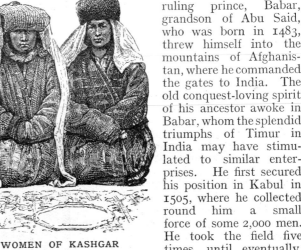

WOMEN OF KASHGAR

of his Persian possessions fell to the Turkoman. Complete disorder then reigned in Turkestan, until, in 1500, Mohammed Shaibani, of the family of Genghis Khan, and his Uzbegs, who represented the nomad spirit as modified by Iranian civilisation, became masters of the country. The Uzbeg dynasties of the Shaibanids, Janids, and Mangites possessed, down to 1868, the various kingdoms into which the country again broke up almost precisely as before the Mongol age.

A Timurid dynasty had held its own in Ferghana. Driven thence by the Uzbeg leader Shaibek Khan, the ruling prince, Babar, grandson of Abu Said, who was born in 1483, threw himself into the mountains of Afghanistan, where he commanded the gates to India. The old conquest-loving spirit of his ancestor awoke in Babar, whom the splendid triumphs of Timur in India may have stimulated to similar enterprises. He first secured his position in Kabul in 1505, where he collected round him a small force of some 2,000 men. He took the field five times, until eventually, in 1526, he succeeded in defeating Ibrahim of Delhi and thus bringing under his sway the most powerful of the five great Mohammedan dominions which then existed in India. When he died, in the year 1530, the last and intellectually the foremost conqueror of Mongolian stock, he had founded a stable empire, that of the " Great Moguls," whose history has already been narrated.

HEINRICH SCHURTZ

RUINS OF THE ANCIENT TOWN OF KASHGAR IN EASTERN TURKESTAN

MODERN HISTORY OF CENTRAL ASIA
TIBET, THE LAND OF THE LAMAS
By Dr. H. Schurtz & Francis H. Skrine

THE world was still trembling before the warlike hosts of Central Asia when those forces were gathering strength which eventually succeeded in taming and rendering harmless the wild spirits of the nomads. These forces were Chinese civilisation and eastern Buddhism, whose influences can be understood only by a survey of the more recent history of Tibet, the theocratic state par excellence of Eastern Asia. The teaching of Buddha had long lost its power in the Indian mother country when it acquired Eastern Central Asia, beginning with Tibet. Mongol Buddhism was not rooted in Indian civilisation, but in the fantastically developed monastic and ecclesiastical system of the lonely Tibetan highlands, which had cut themselves completely off from the plains of India when the Buddhist teaching died away in those parts.

For this reason the more recent eastern Buddhism of Central Asia is sharply differentiated from the earlier western form, which once was so important for the culture of a wide area. The older form had stood in close connection with the plains of the Indus and Ganges valleys ; yet the missionaries in the time of Asoka, when the Buddhism of India was at its zenith, had passed through Kashmir, scaled the southern mountain **Tardy Success of Buddhism** walls of Central Asia, and carried their sacred books, their script, and their civilisation directly to the Tarim basin, and thence northward to the Uigurians and eastward to China. The new teaching had at the time met with hardly any response among the Mongols and the other eastern nomads ; in Tibet it first began slowly to gain a footing. In the course of time the whole western mission field was once more lost.

Christian and Zoroastrian emissaries had worked in opposition to the Buddhist priests until the doctrine of Islam, grand in its simplicity, which has always exercised a marvellously enthralling influence over semi-civilised peoples, drove out all other forms of religion. Besides this, the Buddhism of Central Asia had **Triumph of Islam** lost any support in India, owing to the victory of the Brahmanic teaching, and was dependent entirely upon its own strength. The term " simplicity " is indeed only to be applied with reserve to Islam, which reached Central Asia through Persia. An Islamite mysticism developed under the influence of Iranian intellectual life, which was hardly inferior to the Buddhist in profundity and love of the marvellous, but was for that precise reason capable of ousting and replacing the former. In its ultimate meaning, the victory of the Mohammedan teaching signifies the supremacy of West Asiatic culture over the Indian. And this victory was natural, for Western Asia marches with the steppes of Central Asia for some distance and is closely connected with them by old trade-routes, while the bonds of intercourse between India and the heart of Asia have never been strong.

The later eastern dissemination of the Buddhist faith over Central Asia would have been inconceivable but for the circumstance that even in China Buddhism reckoned numerous followers, and that the Chinese of set purpose favoured a doctrine so gentle and so much opposed to military brutality. But that Tibet, of all others, should become the holy land of Buddhism had been the object of the efforts of Genghis Khan, who, indeed, as a true Mongol, tried to employ for his own purposes the " magic powers " of all

A GROUP OF TYPICAL LAMA PRIESTS

dynasty, remained as an independent ecclesiastical state, and could then for more than a century continue its unaided development under the successors of Pasépa. While in China the Buddhist papacy of the Tibetan chief Lama was no longer recognised, or remained without influence, the activity of Tibetan missionaries was, on the contrary, successfully continued. Tibet could not fail to become the religious centre for these efforts.

religions, without adopting any one of them exclusively. It was, after all, a very natural result that Tibet took, so far as religion was concerned, the place of India in the eyes of Central Asia ; men were accustomed to look for the home of Buddhism in the South, and, since India seceded, Tibet, which was always full of mystery, offered a welcome substitute.

At first, indeed, the growing reputation of Tibet for sanctity did not shield it from disastrous attacks: under the first Mogul princes it was mercilessly plundered and laid waste. But perhaps these lamentable events, by which the temporal kingdom of Tibet was overthrown, were the contributory cause that henceforth the spiritual power came forward and undertook the protection of the country with better prospect of success.

Kublai Khan took account of the altered conditions when he promoted the Lama Pasépa, who was a member of a noble Tibetan family, to be the supreme head of all Lamas in his realm, and thus shifted the centre of gravity of the Buddhist hierarchy to Tibet. In reality by so doing he conferred on the Lama the temporal power also over the country. On the complete disruption of the Mongol Empire, Tibet, which was not claimed by the Chinese Mongol

The Buddhist doctrine of a new birth made men regard the chief Lamas as reincarnations of great saints, or, indeed, as Buddhas themselves. Ultimately a belief gained ground that the Great Lama remained always the same, and immediately after his death was reincarnated in a child, who without demur was regarded and reverenced as Great Lama ; the first regeneration of this kind is said to have occurred in the year 1399. At the beginning of the fifteenth century there was still no idea of strict religious government. The reincarnated Great Lama had by no means met with universal recognition, and many years elapsed before he attained any great authority. Most of the monasteries, in which religious life and learning were centred, probably led a very independent existence. China, where the new reigning house of the Ming was threatened

THE ABBOT OF A GREAT LAMAITE MONASTERY IN TIBET

from the side of Mongolia by the Mongol dynasty driven out in 1368, then turned her attention again to Tibet. The religious influence of Tibet on the nomads of Central Asia was not to be under-estimated. Halima, one of the most esteemed Tibetan Lamas, was brought to the Chinese imperial court, overwhelmed with pompous titles, and entrusted with the spiritual supremacy in Tibet, on the condition that a small tribute was paid yearly. Tibet was thus more closely linked to China, and the conversion and civilisation of the Central Asiatic nomads by emissaries from the holy land were encouraged in accordance with the Chinese policy.

Edwards

YOUNG LAMAS AND BALES OF TEA FROM CHINA

The Buddhist Reformation, which took place about the middle of the fifteenth century, is a noteworthy counterpart of the Reformation of Luther, which began only a little later. In Tibet also the immediate cause of the movement was found in the depravity of the priesthood and the adulteration of the pure faith with popular superstitions of a Shamanistic origin, though the national questions which played an important part in Europe were hardly noticeable there. Tsong ko pa (1419-1478) founded the new sect of the "Yellow Lamas," which the followers of the old sect opposed under the name of "Red Lamas." The yellow sect remained victorious in Tibet proper, while the red sect held its own in Ladak and elsewhere.

Tsong ko pa was the real founder of the Tibetan hierarchy in the form which it has retained up to the present day. He nominated one of his pupils to be Dalai-Lama, a second to be Panchan-Lama ; both would undergo a perpetual process of rebirth and hold permanently the spiritual headship. Tibet was partitioned between them, but the Dalai-Lama received the greater half, and gradually drove the Panchan-Lama into the background. It was long before the Chinese paid attention to the new order of things in Tibet, although under certain circumstances it might produce serious results. A Chinese embassy, accompanied by a small army, appeared at the court of the Dalai-Lama in the year 1522, in order to invite him to the imperial court. When the prince of the Church declined and was concealed by his subjects, attempts were made to carry him off by force, but they resulted in complete failure. The Chinese Emperor Wu Tsung died at this crisis, and his succcessor, Shi Tsung, who

Edwards

TIBETAN SOLDIERS ARMED WITH OLD FLINTLOCKS

favoured Taoism, did not continue the plans against Tibet.

The third reincarnated Dalai-Lama, So nam, gave himself out for a " living Buddha," and as such won wide recognition. He travelled into Mongolia, where, being received with the deepest reverence, **" The Living Buddha "** he came forward as a mediator between a Mongol prince and the Chinese. The victory then of the yellow sect was decisive in the north also ; countless Mongol pilgrims went yearly to Lhasa, and Buddhist monasteries were founded in great numbers. In China the propitious influence of the Tibetan high-priest was noticeable in the increasing peacefulness of the nomads of the steppe. Shi Tsu, the first emperor of the Manchu dynasty, which had ousted the house of the Ming after 1644, fully appreciated that fact, and acknowledged the presents of Tibetan envoys with a flattering invitation to the Dalai-Lama to come to Peking. The invitation was accepted·this time ; the Great Lama appeared in the year 1653 at the court of the Manchu dynasty, where he was the centre of universal respect, was invested with magnificent titles, and was finally escorted to his home by a guard commanded by an imperial prince. But this triumph of the " living Buddha " was soon followed by a humiliation. Since at the death of each Dalai-Lama the office passed to a child, who was considered to be his reincarnation, the government every time rested for many years in the hands of regents, who were naturally tempted to keep their power even when the Dalai-Lama came to manhood, or, what was still simpler, never to allow the boy to live beyond a certain age. The regency was held by temporal princes, in whom we must simply see the successors of those old Tibetan rulers, who for a time had made Tibet a powerful state, but then had been more and more driven back by the hierarchy. As temporal protectors of the priesthood, and supported doubtless by large possessions of land, they had learned how to maintain a certain position.

Finally, when the reins of power slipped from the hands of the decrepit fifth **Temporal Power Restored** Dalai-Lama, the reigning Tipa, or king, Sang Kiu, saw that the moment had arrived to replace the spiritual supremacy, which might be nominally retained, by a temporal. When the Great Lama died in 1682, the Tipa concealed his death, and was then in fact lord of Tibet. The alteration was soon noticed by the surrounding countries. The Tipa placed

TIBETAN HORSEMEN ON NATIVE PONIES AND ARMED WITH SPEARS AND GUNS

A LAMAITE DIGNITARY ENTERING COLONEL YOUNGHUSBAND'S CAMP
Colonel Younghusband conducted a mission from the Government of India to Lhasa, which was entered on August 3, 1904. The treaty of Lhasa, signed on September 7, brought Tibet within the British sphere of influence.

a Kalmuck prince, Kaldan, educated in Tibet as a Lama, at the head of this tribe, and the Kalmucks or Eleutes helped him in return to repel an attack of the Nepalese, a powerful nation of mountaineers, who were dangerous neighbours of the holy land.

The prince of the Eleutes now extended his power on a secret understanding with **Trouble with China** the Tipa, and ventured to attack China, where the fact had been realised with great dissatisfaction that the influence for peace exercised by Tibet on the nomads of the steppes was completely changed. A Chinese Lama, who had been sent to the Dalai-Lama, had not been allowed to see him. When, then, the Eleutian prince, after a defeat, declared to his lord that he had begun the war with China simply and solely at the wish of the Dalai-Lama, the terrified Tipa acknowledged, in answer to a peremptory letter of the emperor Sheng Tsu, or Kang hsi, that the fifth incarnation of the Dalai-Lama was long since dead, and that the deceased had been reincarnated in a boy ; the death had been hushed up and the sixth incarnation not publicly acknowledged, in order to avoid disturbances. The news of these events spread rapidly, and, although China took no further steps, considerably lessened the power of the Tipa. He began in the year 1705 a fresh war against a Tibetan chieftain, but was defeated and slain.

The victorious prince, La tsang, had already instated a new Dalai-Lama. But he was not recognised by China and was replaced by another, whom La tsang undertook to protect. Another Dalai-Lama, who appeared in Mongolia and claimed to be the real sixth incarnation, was also rejected by the Chinese Government, and was recognised only as a saint of inferior rank. The bad example of the **Attempt to Seize the Dalai-Lama** Tipa Sang Kiu had, however, produced its result : the Zungarian prince Zagan-Araptan, successor to Kaldan, who had seen what power in politics and religion the protector of the Dalai-Lama could exert, invaded Tibet with an army in 1717, in order to seize the Buddhist pope. Potala, near Lhasa, where the Dalai-Lama resided with the Khan La tsang, was stormed, and the Khan killed, but the Great Lama was kept in a place of safety. China no longer hesitated to check by

1503

force this dangerous turn of events, which might lead to a new invasion of the Middle Kingdom by the nomads. A Chinese army and a Mongolian levy pushed into Tibet, but the united troops were outflanked and cut to pieces by the Zungarians on the River Kola. The dejection which the Chinese and Mongols felt at this reverse led to the proposal that Tibet should be left to itself, and that a new Dalai-Lama should be appointed in another district. Emperor Kang hsi, however, insisted on renewing the campaign with increased forces. The attempt was successful this time ; the Zungarians evacuated the country in the year 1720, and Kang hsi was then able to effect the necessary closer union of Tibet with China. For the future two Chinese residents, for whom the necessary respect was ensured by a considerable armed force, undertook the protection of the Dalai-Lama in place of the native temporal kings.

Defeat of Mongols and Chinese

The reverence felt for this living Buddha diminished, however, considerably in China when the Dalai-Lama, who was staying in Peking on a visit, died like any ordinary man, of smallpox. The small feudal princes of Tibet at first still retained some power ; but after repeated disturbances they were completely subordinated to the Dalai-Lama—that is to say, to the Chinese governors—in the year 1750. The internal administration of the country, with which China generally interfered very little, was now entirely organised on an ecclesiastical system, since every local governor was given a Lama as colleague, who jointly with him managed the affairs of the inhabitants.

Although the Dalai-Lama was again recognised as supreme, there could be no idea of any actually permanent rule of the "living Buddha," since a new Dalai-Lama was always raised to his high dignity in tender infancy and imperatively required an adviser. For all foreign affairs the Chinese regents undertook this post ; for home affairs a sort of new temporal monarchy was founded, since the "Rajah" of Lhasa usually conducted the government until the Dalai-Lama attained his majority. A strange fatality afterward willed that the Dalai-Lama hardly ever attained the required age of twenty years, but usually died just before, and then was always reincarnated in a

The Lama a Political Puppet

child. In this way the Chinese influence also lost ground. Tibet detached itself more and more completely on every side, and has remained down to the present day one of the most mysterious and isolated countries in the world. When, in 1792, a new invasion of the Nepalese was repulsed with the aid of Chinese troops, the frontier towards India was almost entirely barred. A safeguard against the influences of civilisation was also found in the Himalayan state of Bhutan, lying south of Lhasa, which is a miniature Tibet with a dual government, temporal and spiritual, and an equally intense aversion from any influences from the outside world.

Foreigners were once received with open arms in Tibet. A Jesuit mission gained a footing there in the seventeenth century, and Lhasa was the seat of a group of Capuchins between 1725 and 1760. In 1774 Warren Hastings despatched a special envoy thither, in the person of his friend, George Bogle, who had a friendly reception, and concluded a treaty of peace and amity with Tibet. In 1811 Dr. Manning was entertained by the Dalai-Lama. The intense dislike of all foreigners, which was rampant in China, was fatal to our relations with Tibet. A veil fell on the mysterious land, and would-be explorers were ignominiously turned back from the frontier. In 1886 an attempt to establish commercial intercourse was made by the Government of India. It was defeated by the jealousy of Peking. As is always the case with Oriental races, the Lamas misconstrued our reluctance to enforce reciprocity of trade. They intermeddled in the affairs of Sikkim, a petty frontier state under British tutelage. In 1888 a British expeditionary force retaliated by crossing the Jeylap Pass, north of Darjiling. Tibetan opposition was brushed aside, and if Lord Lansdowne, then Viceroy of India, had not recalled his victorious troops they would have occupied Lhasa. Negotiations continued with Peking, and in March, 1890, the Senior Amban at Lhasa arrived in Calcutta with full power to conclude a commercial treaty. After three years' parleying a Convention was ratified by China, which provided for the demarcation of the Anglo-Tibetan frontier and the creation of a trade mart at Yatung. It remained a dead letter, remonstrance being met by tactics which have proved effectual for half a century.

Closing the Door of Tibet

THE APPROACH TO LHASA, SHOWING THE CONFIGURATION OF THE COUNTRY
Colonel Younghusband's force reached Gyangtse on April 11, 1904, and numerous engagements took place there during the succeeding three months. The monastery was finally taken and opposition broken on July 7.

The Lamas pleaded a *non possumus* on the score that they could not resist the Emperor's will, while the Peking Council ascribed the embargo laid on European traders to the jealousy of the Lhasa junta.

Lord Curzon of Kedleston, who became Viceroy of India in 1899, was not inclined to regard such recalcitrance with equanimity. In July, 1903, he despatched an armed mission, with orders to force its way to Lhasa. Our inveterate foe, the Dalai-Lama, fled to Mongolia, and his ill-armed troops were routed with great slaughter. The occupation of Lhasa on August 3rd, 1904, added nothing to the knowledge of Tibet acquired by stealthy visits of Indian explorers; but on September 7th a provisional treaty was concluded with the Tashi-Lama, who has superseded his colleague. As ratified by the Convention of Peking of April 27th, 1906, it provides for the erection of boundary pillars between Tibet and Sikkim, and the establishment of three trade centres on the frontier. Great Britain disavowed any wish to intervene in Tibetan affairs, while the Lamas promised not to alienate territory to a foreign Power. Pending the liquidation of a war indemnity of £166,000, the occupation by Great Britain of the Chumbi Valley, between Sikkim and Bhutan, was conceded.

A TRAVELLER'S FIRST SIGHT OF LHASA
BY PERCEVAL LANDON

This vivid word picture of a first sight of the "strange and lovely city" of the Dalai-Lama is perhaps the finest description of one of the rarest experiences enjoyed by any traveller of our time. It is taken from Mr. Landon's admirable work "Lhasa," by permission of Messrs. Hurst & Blackett, Ltd.

LHASA would remain Lhasa were it but a cluster of hovels on the sand. But the sheer magnificence of the unexpected sight which met our unprepared eyes was to us almost a thing incredible. There is nothing missing from this splendid spectacle— architecture, forest trees, wide green places, rivers, streams, and mountains, all lie before one as one looks down from the height upon Lhasa stretching out at our feet. The dark forbidding spurs and ravines of the valley of the Kyi Chu, up which we had come, interlock one with another and had promised nothing of all this. The beauty of Lhasa is doubled by its utter unexpectedness. . . . There was nothing to promise us this city of gigantic palace and golden roof, these wild stretches of woodland, these acres of close-cropped grazing land and marshy grass, ringed or delimited by high trees or lazy streamlets of brown transparent water over which the branches almost met.

BETWEEN the palace on our left and the town a mile away in front of us there is this arcadian luxuriance interposing a mile-wide belt of green. Round the outlying fringes of the town itself and creeping up between the houses of the village, at the foot of the Potala, there are trees—trees numerous in themselves to give Lhasa a reputation as a garden city. But in this stretch of green, unspoiled by house or temple, and roadless save for one diverging highway, Lhasa has a feature which no other town on earth can rival.

IT is all a part of that splendid religious pride which has been the making, and may yet prove the undoing, of Tibet. It was right that there should be a belt of nature undefiled encircling the palace of the incarnate god and king, and there the belt is, investing the Potala even inside the loop of the Ling-kor with something of the isolation which guards from the outer world the whole of this strange and lovely town. Between and over the glades and woodlands the city of Lhasa itself peeps, an adobe stretch of narrow streets and flat-topped houses crowned here and there with a blaze of golden roofs or gilded cupolas.

BUT there is no time to look at this ; a man can have no eye for anything but the huge upstanding mass of the Potala palace to his left. It drags the eye of the mind like a loadstone, for indeed sheer bulk and magnificent audacity could do no more in architecture than they have done in this huge palace temple of the Grand Lama. Simplicity has wrought a marvel in stone, 900 ft. in length and towering 70 ft. higher than the golden cross of St. Paul's Cathedral. The Potala would dominate London—Lhasa it simply eclipses. By European standards it is impossible to judge this building ; there is nothing there to which comparison can be made. Perhaps in the austerity of its huge curtains of blank, unveiled, unornamented wall, and in the flat, unabashed slants of its tremendous south-eastern face there is a suggestion of the massive grandeur of Egyptian work ; but the contrast of colour and surroundings, to which no small part of the magnificence of the sight is due, Egypt cannot boast.

THE vivid white stretches of the buttressing curtains of stone, each a wilderness of close-ranked windows, and the home of the hundreds of crimson-clad dwarfs who sun themselves at the distant stairheads, strike a clean and harmonious note in the sea of green which washes up their base. Once a year the walls of the Potala are washed with white, and no one can gainsay the effect ; but there is yet the full chord of colour to be sounded. The central building of the palace, the Phodang Marpo, the private home of the incarnate divinity himself, stands out four-square upon and between the wide-supporting bulks of masonry a rich red crimson, and, most perfect touch of all, over it against the sky the glittering golden roofs—a note of glory added with the infinite taste and the sparing hand of the old illuminator—recompose the colour scheme from end to end, a sequence of green in three shades, of white, of maroon, of gold, and of pale blue. The brown yak-hair curtain, 80 ft. in height and 25 ft. across, hangs like a tress of hair down the very centre of the central sanctuary, hiding the central recess. Such is the Potala.

The Potala, seen from the north, though far from commonplace, is not so striking as the view from the south.

Potala, illustrated in Kircher's "China Illustrata," 1670

Palace of the Kings of Tibet in the time of the old empire

General view of the wonderful Potala, or palace of the Dalai-Lama, as seen from the south.

SCENES IN THE STRANGE AND LOVELY CITY OF LHASA

VIEWS IN SAMARKAND, THE CAPITAL OF EASTERN TURKESTAN
At the top on the right is the Shah Zindeh Mosque, the finest Moslem building in Central Asia, and on its left is the main street in Samarkand. From the conspicuous tower in the centre picture criminals have been thrown to their destruction, and the lowest picture gives a general view of the citadel or fortress of Samarkand from the exterior.

EASTERN OR CHINESE TURKESTAN

WHEN the flood-tide of Mongol conquest ebbed, the home of the new world conquerors sank rapidly from its dazzling height. The sparsely peopled country had given up its best resources, and needed a long time to regain its strength. It was always a point of honour with the senior or Chinese branch of the Mongol dynasty to preserve the cradle of their race, with its old capital, Karakoram. This endeavour also harmonised with the traditional Chinese policy, which always aimed at exerting some influence over the restless nations of the steppe, and must have been adopted by the Mongol sovereigns when they had transformed themselves more and more into genuine Chinese. Kublai Khan had repeatedly suppressed rebellions in Mongolia and become master of the country; his successor, Timur, brought the whole country for a time under his influence. At the period of the Mongol supremacy in China the Buddhist propaganda, of which Tibet **Chinese Favour for Buddhism** was the centre, seems to have shown great activity, being favoured by the Chinese emperors, who were mostly attracted by Buddhism. The circumstance that the Mongols, who had immigrated into China and were again driven out by the Ming, were streaming back to their old home could not fail to help this change.

When the Mongol dynasty was fighting for its existence against the Ming, the Mongols of Central Asia rendered feeble and ambiguous aid. After his complete defeat in 1368, Shun Ti, the Mongol emperor, fled to Shang tu in the north, and soon afterwards died. His son and successor, Biliktu (1370-1378), removed his court once more to Karakoram. Since all the Mongol foreign territories had long since been lost, the sole remnant of the empire left him was the pasture country on the north of the Gobi, which had been the starting-point of the power of his house. There was still the possibility that a new storm might be slowly gathering there, whose bursting would bring disaster on more civilised countries.

But the loss of China, which, to a large extent, was due to the lack of union between the generals and the princes, had not taught the Mongols wisdom. The smaller the remnants of their empire became, the more furiously they fought **Fighting for a Falling Empire** for each shred, until finally complete disintegration set in. The emperor of the Ming seized this opportunity to subjugate Eastern Mongolia. The kingdom of Altyn Khan, to the north-west of the Gobi, remained as the last relic of the Mongolian power.

The more modern attempts to found a great Power in Central Asia, and then in the true Hun fashion to attack the civilised nations, were no longer initiated by the Mongols, whose character had been altered by the tribal disintegration and the awakening zeal for the exercise of the Buddhist religion. Their place was taken by the tribes to the south and south-west of the desert of Gobi, whose country was now partly known as Zungaria. The contemplative doctrines of Buddhism had not gained ground here so quickly, since many of the nomads had been won over to Islam, which is less dangerous to the warlike spirit. From the chaos of peoples in Central Asia a new branch of that Mongolian race of which the Mongols were only a division had detached itself to the south of the Gobi— the Eleutes, or Kalmucks, who, after 1630, had shaken off the Mongol yoke, and had already extended their influence as far as China.

Under its Khan, Kaldan, this people seized Kashgar, destroyed the Mongol Empire of the Altyn Khan, and towards **A New Mongol Race** the end of the seventeenth century threatened China. At the same time Kaldan tried to employ the religious power of Tibet in his own interest by declaring that the Dalai-Lama had raised him to his high position; the temporal prince of Tibet, Sang Kiu, supported him secretly. The Mongols suffered severely under the attacks of the Eleutes, and China's influence in Central Asia dwindled considerably, until eventually the Manchu Emperor, Kang hsi, determined in the year 1696 on a great campaign against Kaldan. Kaldan was forced to retreat further and further. Since his scheme for the support of his claims by the Dalai-Lama seemed not to work satisfactorily, he now went over to Islam, which had many followers in the west of his dominions ; but his death, which occurred soon afterwards, cut these plans short. The military power of the nomad world, which had been again concentrated in Zungaria as a focus, was not extinguished by this event. Zagan-Araptan, the successor of Kaldan, subjugated most of the towns of the Tarim basin and extended his dominions in other directions. He then formed the plan of sending an army to Tibet to assume by force the protection of the Dalai-Lama, and in this way to make full use of the influence of the religious puppet for his own purposes. The attempt met with unexpected success, but drove the Chinese to adopt more decided measures. The expulsion of the Eleutes from Tibet in 1720 was the result. The Zungarian empire remained, nevertheless, for some time a dangerous neighbour of the other Central Asiatic tribes and of the Chinese. Finally, however, China employed dynastic quarrels and internal wars to excuse the destruction of the last great nomad empire of Central Asia, and thus, it seems, to terminate for ever the age of the great wars between the nomad races of Central Africa and the civilised peoples. Eastern Turkestan, which had been in the hands of the Kalmucks, in 1757 fell to the Chinese.

It was not the first time that the Chinese had taken possession of the Tarim basin, commanded the trade roads of Central Asia, and divided the nomad tribes in the north from those in the south ; but this time the effect was different and more permanent. The perpetually turbulent nomad tribes could not be really subdued until they were shut in and surrounded on both sides—until the strong fortresses of civilisation bounded the illimitable horizon of the steppe. The first steps toward this condition had meanwhile been taken by the advance of Russia ; the frontier towards Siberia had been already determined, and any

From Buddha to Islam

Cordon Round the Nomads

movement of the Mongols toward the north and the north-west was made impossible. In the south-west Russia only gradually succeeded in acquiring Turkestan. Here, too, the Chinese position was so weak that the Tarim basin was temporarily lost. When, however, the khanates of Turkestan were occupied by the Russians, China also soon recovered what she had lost.

The expansion of the power of Russia, which in the long run presents dangers to China itself, has therefore admirably supported the Chinese policy, which has always been directed towards the subjugation of the nomad nations of Central Asia. But this very policy employed not only the old method of colonisation and of pitting one nomad prince against another, but also the newer method of encouraging Buddhism. The Manchurian dynasty in this respect has entirely followed the example of the Ming, and the result is simply astonishing. " Buddhist doctrines," says Nikolai von Prschevalskij, " are more deeply rooted in Mongolia than in almost any other part of the world. Buddhism, whose highest ideal is indolent contemplation, entirely suits the natural disposition of the Mongol, and has created a terrible asceticism, which deters the nomad from any progress, and tempts him to seek the goal of human existence in misty and abstract ideas as to the Deity and the life beyond the grave." The ordinary good-tempered indolence of the nomads is left, but in the place of outbursts of martial fury, which affected individuals as well as nations, a continual slow dissipation of energy in religious observances, prayers, and pilgrimages has appeared. In this light the pilgrimages to Tibet or to famous Mongolian sanctuaries are substitutes for the old predatory and warlike expeditions.

All the less important for the spiritual life of the Central Asiatics is the Buddhist teaching, whose primitive form is so instinct with spirituality and thought. The Tibetan form of religion is itself quite debased, and has been merely outwardly introduced into Mongolia, where even the priests as a whole do not understand the Tibetan sacred writings and formulæ, but use them in ignorance as an obscure system of magic. This branch of Buddhism shows a certain independence only in so far as centres of the faith are found in Mongolia, especially the town of Urga,

Why Buddhism Attracts the Nomads

THE BAZAAR IN MODERN KASHGAR, CAPITAL OF EASTERN TURKESTAN

The old town of Kashgar stood on one of the head streams of the Tarim at the junction of several important and ancient trade routes, and the place has thus attained great eminence as a commercial and social centre.

whose *Kutuchta*, or high-priest, ranks directly after the two highest Tibetan Lamas, and, like these, is always reincarnated. As a rule, almost every Buddhist monastery possesses a " Gegan," or reincarnated saint. But the priests have in their influence taken the place of the old tribal chieftains. They are treated with unbounded respect, and the wealth of the country is collected in their sanctuaries. In the border districts toward Islam stand fortified Buddhist monasteries, where the inhabitants seek refuge from marauding or insurrectionary Mohammedans.

While the Buddhist religion thus showed its marvellous ability to restrain the wild Central Asiatics, and while the region of nomadism was more and more encroached upon by Chinese colonies, another and ancient aid to the progress of civilisation, the commerce and international communication on the high-roads of the heart of Asia, leading from east to west, had gradually lost most of its significance. **Decline of Land Traffic** Even in the Mongol age wars broke out for the possession of these roads. The attack of Genghis Khan on the Kharismians was due partly to reasons of commercial policy. But the discovery of the sea route to the East Indies, which soon led to the appearance of European ships in Chinese harbours, could not fail to reduce the already much diminished overland trade to insignificant proportions. It was no longer a profitable undertaking to make the immense journey through insecure districts with valuable wares. **Tea Trade an Aid to Civilisation** The great caravan traffic was suspended, and in its place was left merely a transit trade from station to station, which had no bearing upon civilisation. The overland trade, especially the export of tea, revived only in one previously neglected place— namely, in the north of Mongolia, where the frontiers of the two civilised empires, Russia and China, touch each other. This route contributed distinctly to the pacification of the Mongol tribes, who now obtained good pay for transporting tea through the steppes, and acquired an interest in the prosperity of the trade.

The Chinese policy, notwithstanding all the improvement in the outlook, still met with many obstacles in Central Asia, the chief causes of which were the adherents to Islam in Zungaria, the Tarim basin, and the western provinces of China. Where Islam had once gained a footing it could not be ousted by the more accommodating Buddhism. But the influence which the doctrines of Mohammed exercised on the warlike spirit, the industry, and the energy of its followers, had to be considered, and it required care and tact on the part of Chinese officials to avoid dangerous outbreaks of the masses, whom the new faith had brought into a closer unity. In spite of all this there were often sanguinary and temporarily successful insurrections of the **Later Revolts in Central Asia** Dungans, in which the last of the embers of the old warlike spirit of Central Asia glowed afresh. In the Tarim basin an Islamite revolt had already raged from 1825 to 1828. About the middle of the nineteenth century, the descendants of the dynasty which had been driven out of the western Tarim basin by the Chinese at the close of the Eleutian war, in 1757, tried to win back their territory after they had already made small expeditions over the Chinese

from Khokand, Yakub Bey distinguished himself more and more as a general, until he entirely deprived the incapable Buzurg Khan of his command, and sent him back to Ferghana. In the year 1868 the greater part of the Tarim basin was in the possession of the new ruler, who styled himself, after 1870, " Atalik Ghazi," meaning, defender of the faith.

These successes would have been impossible had not a simultaneous revolt of the Mohammedans in Western China and Zungaria reduced the Chinese Government to dire straits. It was fortunate for China, which was in addition weakened by the Taiping insurrection, that the insurgents attained no great results and did not combine in a general attack on

THE WALLED TRADING TOWN OF YARKAND IN EASTERN TURKESTAN
The favourable position of Yarkand made it the chief trading centre with North India across the Karakoram Pass.

frontier. The first campaign failed through the resistance of the towns of Kashgar and Yarkand.

An Islamite revolt under the leadership of Rasch ed-din Khodja prepared the ground, in 1862, for further operations. An auxiliary force from Khokand, under Mohammed Yakub Bey, took part in a new invasion, which was led by Buzurg Khan, then a pretender. This time the Dungan soldiers of the Chinese mutinied, and seized Yarkand and Khotan, while simultaneously bands of Kirghiz robbers swept by and besieged Kashgar in 1864 ; when they had taken the town, Buzurg Khan deprived them of their booty. During the subsequent wars with the Chinese and the Dungan insurgents, who refused to submit to the Mohammedans

the tottering Celestial Kingdom. Still less did they think of making common cause with Yakub Bey, to whom they were, on the contrary, hostile, or even with the Taipings and the disaffected Buddhist Mongols. The great Dungan insurrection was thus, after all, only a chain of local risings, involving terrible bloodshed and widespread devastation. The Chinese took refuge in the towns, some of which **Local Risings Against the Chinese** gave way before the attacks of the surrounding Dungans, while others held out and thus became important bases for the reconquest of the country; this was especially the case in Kansu, the highroad from China to the Tarim basin, where the insurrection broke out in 1862. In 1869 a Dungan army once more

A BAND OF COURT MUSICIANS TO THE RULER OF KASHGAR

advanced and pillaged as far as Ordos ; and again, in 1873, towns in Southern Mongolia were attacked and destroyed. The conduct of the war on both sides was pitiable.

After 1872 the Chinese began once more to take the offensive and to reconquer Kansu. When this object was attained, after some years of fighting, the fate of Yakub Bey was practically sealed. In the meantime he had been deprived of the support of his fellow-tribesmen and co-religionists in Western Turkestan by the advance of the Russians. In 1878, the year following the sudden death of Yakub, which put an end to all organised resistance, the Tarim basin fell again into the hands of the Chinese, and, together with the districts on the Tianshan, was constituted a separate province in 1884. Here, too, China touches almost everywhere on the territory of the civilised nations, Russia and England, since the last ill-defined border country, the highlands of the Pamirs, has been distributed among the three Powers by the Anglo-Russian agreement of 1895. The trade in the Tarim basin has improved since England has devoted her attention to the communications with India, and has stimulated a considerable caravan traffic. Russia, on the other side, is anxious to revive the old routes to Western Turkestan. The fact that the population of the Tarim basin and that of many parts of Western China profess the Mohammedan faith is a permanent danger to the Chinese —the Dungans again rebelled in 1894— which can be obviated in course of time only by an extensive settlement of Chinese colonists in these districts.

THE NATIVE GUARD OF HONOUR AT THE PALACE IN KASHGAR

1513

SCENES IN THE CAPITAL OF RUSSIA'S VASSAL STATE OF BOKHARA

Bokhara has fallen from its position as principal native state of Central Asia, and the palace of its Amir, shown in the pictures at the top and left bottom corner of the page, though striking in character, is in a somewhat dilapidated condition. A photograph of the Amir is also given, and on his left is a view of the tomb of a saint, while the interior of one of Bokhara's many bazaars is shown in the fifth photograph.

WESTERN TURKESTAN

AFTER the Mongol onslaught the population of Turkestan had gradually divided into three groups. The first of these consisted of the Sarts, the settled agricultural section of the people, the inhabitants of the towns, oases, and riparian districts. These represent to us the relics of the oldest elements of culture, which had been Iranised in course of time, and, owing to large Persian immigrations, had acquired also a physical likeness to the Persians. This peculiarity was intensified by the importation of Persian slaves, and thus the inevitable admixture of brachycephalic nomads was counterbalanced. The Sarts had long abandoned their old faith, and that of Islam was universally adopted. They showed no capacity for political organisation.

The Three Peoples of Turkestan By the second group, the Uzbegs, on the contrary, we are to understand half-settled Turko-Tartars, in whom, notwithstanding an admixture of Iranian blood and a smattering of higher culture, the military temper of the nomad is predominant. This large section of the people, which sprang up during the nomad conquests, first ventured to lay claim to the supremacy, and finally usurped the power of the Mongol dynasties. The movement was really started in the Tarim basin, where, even in the time of Timur, the Kashgarians, who were never completely subjugated, had repeatedly tried to subjugate Western Turkestan.

A third group of inhabitants of Turkestan is composed of genuine nomads, whose chief pasture-lands lie partly in the north and partly to the west of the Amu Daria, toward the Caspian Sea and Khorasan. In the north the people of the Kirghiz—the Cossacks—had lived since early times, and had been driven out only for a short time and from a few regions by roving bands of other nomads ; in the west the Turkomans, predatory hordes who controlled the communications between Persia and the states of Turkestan, had risen from the fragments of nomad tribes.

The rule of the house of Timur in Turkestan ended in 1494. This revolution originated in an attack of several Timurid princes on Mohammed Shaibek Khan, the leader of the Uzbegs, who seem then to have had their homes on the upper Jaxartes and in the borderlands of Eastern Turkestan. The attack **End of the House of Timur** led to a complete defeat of the Timurids, and in consequence they lost their possessions in Masenderan and Khorasan. It seemed as if the whole of Persia would be conquered by Shaibek ; but at that very time the Iranian people had been roused to fresh vitality under the leadership of Ismail el-Safi, and Shaibek with his army fell before this new power in 1510.

Under Shaibek's successors, the Shaibanids, Turkestan still remained for a time a united empire, but then broke up, as had been the case in the later period of the Timurids, and yet earlier under the princes of the Yue chi, into a number of independent states, whose position and size were prescribed by geographical conditions. The purely nomad countries in this way became, for the most part, independent. The people of the Kirghiz, who inhabited the steppe to the north of the Aral Sea and Lake Balkash, had submitted only partially to the house of Timur and the Uzbegs. The decline of the empire of Kipchak gave these nomads an increasing degree of liberty, until, in the sixteenth century, two empires were formed in the South-western Siberian steppes—that of the Ulu Mongol and that of the Kirghiz proper, or Cossacks, under **The Two Empires of the Steppes** the Khan Arslan, who brought numerous other nomad tribes of Central Asia under his rule. The Kirghiz Empire prevented the Uzbegs from encroaching further to the north, but subsequently it broke up—that is to say, the nation of the Kirghiz divided itself into several hordes. In the eighteenth century we find the Southern Kirghiz, who were comparatively the most highly civilised and were partly settled forming a state in the region of Tashkent

TEKKE TURKOMANS OF THE MERV OASIS
A fierce nomad tribe dwelling in the fertile oases of Western or Russian Turkestan.

They subsequently commanded the middle course of the Syr Daria. The purely nomadic elements of the people formed the Great, the Middle, and the Small Horde. Among the Kirghiz there lingered a trace of the old warlike and predatory spirit of the Central Asiatics, which the surrounding nations must have often felt to their prejudice.

At the beginning of the eighteenth century there was formed a league of the Zungarians, the Bashkirs, the Kalmucks of the Volga, and those Cossacks who were already settled in Siberia as Russian advance guards, which reduced the Kirghiz to such straits that in 1719 they vainly appealed to Russia to interfere. Turkestan, the capital of the Middle Horde, lying on the right bank of the Syr Daria, was taken by the Zungarians. Part of the Kirghiz submitted, the others retreated toward the south. Soon, however, they advanced again and won back their country, though only to fall more and more under the influence of Russia.

The two towns of Turkestan and Tashkent were in the Middle Ages commonly

TURKESTAN SARTS
The Sarts represent the oldest culture of Turkestan.

regarded as forming a part of the province which went by the name of Maurennahar, and included the civilised parts of the province of Western Turkestan. Their relations with the nomads were of a fluctuating character. If the power of the Kirghiz diminished, then they or their Uzbeg princes were practically independent, but if it again increased, then they were more or less subject to nomad rule. For the time being they were attached to the Uzbeg empires. The Zungarians possessed Turkestan in 1723, but after 1741 the Kirghiz were again masters of the town. In the year 1780, Yunus Khoja, of Tashkent, inflicted so crushing a defeat on the Kirghiz of the Great Horde, and inspired such terror by the massacre of several thousand prisoners, that they acknowledged him as their supreme lord. Maurennahar, owing to the nature of its soil, is divided into different regions, from which in the course of history corresponding states have been developed : Khiva, the district on the lower course of the Amu Daria ; Bokhara, that on the middle course of the same stream with the valley of the Zarafshan, and the upper valley of the Syr Daria. In addition to these the country on the upper Amu Daria often formed a separate state : but this last region soon fell under the influence of Afghanistan, when a stronger empire was formed in the south. The middle and lower course of the Syr Daria were so much under the influence of purely nomad tribes that no powerful states could have been formed there. Not infrequently the upper valley of the

RUINS OF ANCIENT MERV, WHICH WAS A TOWN BEFORE THE TIME OF ALEXANDER

Zarafshan, with its capital Samarkand, detached itself from the region of Bokhara and constituted a separate state.

Of these states, Khiva had been at first seized by the Persians after the defeat and death of Shaibek Khan. But since the Persians soon made themselves unpopular with the strictly Sunnite inhabitants of the country by favouring the Shiite propaganda, an insurrection broke out in 1515, headed by the Uzbeg Prince Ilbars; with the help of his brothers he gradually drove out the Persians from all the towns in the country, and made successful attacks on Khorasán. Further developments in that direction were checked by the Turkoman tribes, who even then regarded the steppe on the

IN THE MAIN STREET OF MERV

borders of Persia and Khiva as their exclusive property.

Since the brothers of Ilbars had firmly established themselves in different towns as feudal lords, there could be no idea of any close union after the death of the first monarch. It was not until the feuds between the various vassal princes had somewhat calmed down, and the Turkomans were pacified, that the Uzbegs of Khiva, with those of Bokhara, could renew their attacks on the territory of Persia. The Safavid Tamasp I. of Persia finally had no other resource than to ally himself by marriage with the royal family of Khiva, and to purchase with a large sum a treaty which ensured peace for his frontiers.

THE OLD FORTRESS OF MERV, ON THE RIVER MURGHAB

Fresh disorders in China ended with the almost entire extermination of the descendants of Ilbars by Din Mohammed Sultan, who divided the country among the members of his family, and was proclaimed Khan in 1549. He took from the Khan of Bokhara the town of Merv, that ancient outpost of Persian culture, and made it **Struggle** his capital. After his death, **for Possession** however, in 1553, Merv soon **of Merv** lapsed to the Persians. The Khan of Bokhara, Abd Allah, repeatedly interfered in the ensuing disorders, until, in 1578, he succeeded in making himself master of the whole realm. It was not, until 1598, that one of the expelled princes was able to seize the greater part of the country.

Nor was this the last time that Khiva was harassed by civil wars. Princes of the reigning house were allotted towns, which they governed almost independently, relying sometimes on the Uzbegs, sometimes on the Turkomans, the Naiman, the Kirghiz, or the Uigurians, the remnants of whom were living in Khivan territory. Towards the middle of the seventeenth century, when Abul Ghazi I. Bahadur distinguished himself as prince (1644–1663) and as historian of the descendants of Genghis, the Kalmucks extended their rule over the Kirghiz steppe as far as Khiva. The struggles with these new antagonists, and renewed wars with Bokhara, filled up the succeeding decades. Then a more peaceful period set in; the Khan, who resided in Urgenj, or Khiva, was really only the most powerful of the numerous vassal princes, who lived in various towns, and sometimes fought out their petty feuds among themselves.

The characteristic feature of the history of Turkestan in modern times is this pettiness. In the eighteenth century the Kirghiz of the Small Horde got the upper hand in Khiva, until, in 1792, an Uzbeg chieftain founded a new dynasty, which **Period** lasted until 1873. Bokhara, **of Petty** the central province of Western **Feuds** Turkestan, also played no further important part in the world's history. At first the descendants of Shaibek Khan established themselves here; one of these, Obaid Allah (1533–1539), waged war with Persia, if we may apply such a term to his marauding expeditions. The most important of the Shaibanids, Abd Allah II. (1556–1598),

attempted with better success to reach a higher stage of civilisation. In the year 1559 a dynasty from Astrakhan came to the throne, having migrated back again from the Khanate of Astrakhan to Transoxiana in 1554. The Khanates of Balkh and of Samarkand soon completely severed themselves from Bokhara, the political downfall of which became still more complete when Nadir Shah of Persia, in the year 1737, took vengeance for the constant raids on his frontiers by a victorious campaign.

A new Uzbeg dynasty, that of the Mangites, which also boasted of Mongol descent, drove out the house of Astrakhan and occupied the throne of Bokhara until 1868. Ferghana, or the Khanate of Khokand, was the country where the Timurids had held their own for the longest period. It then fell into the power of the Shaibanids and house of Astrakhan, but won in 1700 complete independence, which it preserved until 1876.

Owing to the geographical position of Ferghana, the Persian power, which Khiva and Bokhara were always forced to respect, **Ferghana** was unimportant in those parts, **a Point** but in return the affairs of **of Peril** Eastern Turkestan and the Kirghiz steppe demanded continual attention; for example, the campaign of Yakub Khan, who temporarily drove the Chinese out of the Tarim basin, was initiated from Ferghana. In the year 1814, Khokand, which was then gaining strength, conquered the southern Kirghiz steppe with the towns of Tashkent and Turkestan, and thus exasperated the jealousy which Bokhara had always felt towards Khokand since the rise of the Mangite dynasty. Khokand was finally conquered in 1841 by Nasr Allah of Bokhara (1827–1860), and, notwithstanding, frequent rebellions, it continued in this subjection until the appearance of the Russians in Central Asia.

On the whole the Uzbeg period was for Turkestan an age of petty struggles, which shows little genuine progress in civilisation. A nomadic spirit was predominant in the population, which showed itself in ceaseless raids upon Persia. The international traffic, which had once brought prosperity to Turkestan, was diverted into other channels, and the formerly wealthy cities showed but the shadow of their earlier magnificence.

THE RUSSIAN ADVANCE IN CENTRAL ASIA

THE period of Russia's active forward movement in Central Asia—as distinct from her progress in the regions dealt with in our Siberian section—dates from the close of the Napoleonic wars. Russia, in effect, opened a sweeping movement against the nomad hordes, primarily of the Kirghiz steppe. But this led to the necessity of subjugating the steppe country in general, and the acquisition of a firm foothold on its western margin. So step by step the troops pushed forward. Every fresh advance of the line made the nomads more desperate. When they saw their freedom of movement curtailed and their pasturages cut off, they broke out in revolt; and Russia's answer to revolt was invariably an extension of the fortress cordons. But for a long time it was impossible to carry out the plan systematically, since large tracts of the steppe were not suited for permanent settlements. The Russian lines of defence had therefore to rest on the rivers; in the year **Russia on the Borders of Turkestan** 1847 the southern frontier line ran from the lower Syr Daria to the River Chu, and thence to the Ili. But it was impossible to halt at this stage. Hitherto the struggle had been with the Kirghiz and the other nomad hordes, but now the sphere of the power of Turkestan was entered. If the Khanates had been consolidated states, with which a well-defined boundary could have been arranged, the advance would have been perhaps checked for a long time there, as was actually the case on the Chinese frontier, with the exception of the districts on the Amur. But these countries were only centres of power with an ill-defined sphere of influence, which expanded or contracted according to the energy of the ruler and the accidents of fortune.

The first collision was with Khiva, since on the west, between the Aral and the Caspian Seas, a frontier secure against the predatory nomads who were willing to act as subjects of Khiva could be obtained only by the occupation of the Khanate proper. In the year 1839 General Perovsky started from Orenburg, but after losing a quarter of his army and 10,400 camels from snowstorms on the steppe, he was compelled to return without having set eyes on the troops of Allah-Kuli Khan. On the other side, the first conflicts with Khokand occurred in **Russian Fortresses Increase** the year 1850, when the men of Khokand, and the Kirghiz who were subject to them, tried to drive back the Russians from the lower Syr Daria, with the sole result that the number of Russian fortresses was increased. Fort Perovsk was built in 1853 as the most advanced post. After a long period of quiet caused by the Crimean War the upper Chu valley was occupied from the Ili district in spite of Khokand. The town of Turkestan fell on June 23rd, 1864, and Chimkent on October 4th.

In the meantime, however, a war had broken out between Bokhara and Khokand, and when the Russians, under Michael Tschernajev, took possession of Tashkent also in June, 1865, which the Bokharans already regarded as a certain prize, a war between Russia and Bokhara was the natural consequence. After an uneventful campaign, the Bokharan army was totally defeated by the Russians on May 20th, 1866, near Irjar; and immediately afterwards General Romanovski marched against the Khanate of Khokand now a dependency of Bokhara, and took the town of Khojent. The territory on the Syr Daria, which had been previously administered from Orenburg, was united **Attempt to Repel Russia** in 1867 with the possessions on the Ili (Semirihansk) into a general government of Turkestan until 1878. Mozaffar-ed-din of Bokhara, who had been compelled to abandon Khokand, now made vain efforts to conclude an alliance with it against the Russians. Khiva also refused to help him when, urged by the fanaticism of his people, he once more made preparations to attack the new Russian territory from Samarkand. But before he had raised his sword, it was struck out of his hand ; General Kaufmann unexpectedly advanced on Samarkand, defeated the superior forces of the Bokharans, and entered the old capital of Timur on May 14th, 1868.

The humbled Khan of Bokhara was forced to abandon the Zarafshan valley with Samarkand, and so lost one of his best provinces. It was, in the end, an advantage for Bokhara that Russia in this way obtained a well-defined boundary in the civilised country. This is the only explanation why there was no complete subjugation, and why the reigning house was left in possession of some, even if very restricted, powers. Russia subsequently went so far as to support the Emir of Bokhara, who died in November, 1885, and his son Seyyid Abd-ul-Ahad against insurrections of his subjects.

Russian Advance in Bokhara

By their advance into Turkestan the Russians had entered on the region which since earliest times had commanded the Central Asiatic trade and the roads through the Tarim basin. Although this trade had greatly fallen off, it still appeared to be an important source of wealth and political influence. Russia had early tried to establish communications with Yarkand. The revolt of the Dungans and the successes of Yakub Bey in the Tarim basin during the 'sixties had prevented any direct intercourse with China, which was bound to be the final object of Russian policy ; the Russians were obliged to content themselves with occupying Kuljar,

the terminus of the northern road, in 1871, and with requiring Yakub Bey to conclude a commercial treaty in 1872. Even then the diplomatic rivalry with the British, who anxiously watched the advance of the Russian power in Central Asia, and with the still independent states of Turkestan, was in full swing. While the Russians were busy in diverting the trade of the Tarim basin to their possessions, the British were renewing the old connection between India and that region. Everywhere, in Khokand, Bokhara, and Khiva, British gold was pitted against Russian bayonets. Gradually, also, China, which after prodigious efforts had suppressed the revolts of her subjects in the Tarim basin, appeared on the scene as a great Power, with whom definite frontiers could be arranged. Kuljar was restored to the Chinese at their own wish.

Meanwhile, in the west, the struggle with Khiva had begun afresh, since Seyyid Mohammed Rahim Khan was neither willing nor able to hinder the incursions of the Kirghiz and Turkomans into Russian territory. In spring, 1873, the Khanate was attacked simultaneously from the Caspian Sea and several other directions. The Khan was not deposed, but was forced, on August 12th, to abandon the right bank and the delta of the Amu Daria, and to become a vassal of Russia. Soon afterwards the days of the Khanate of Khokand were also numbered ; a revolt, which, in 1875, caused the prince Khudayar

Renewed Struggle for Khiva

RUSSIAN EXPEDITION TO KHIVA IN 1873 CROSSING THE RIVER OXUS

INTERVIEW OF RUSSIAN GENERAL WITH THE KHAN OF KHIVA

The illustration is from a drawing by a Russian officer, and represents the interview of the Russian general with Seyyid Mohammed Rahim Khan to arrange terms of peace after the campaign during the summer of 1873.

the Eastern question in Europe was to frighten England by advancing to the gates of India. Both military men and civilians thought that, at the least, an advance was the only means of neutralising hypothetical British intrigues with the native princes of Central Asia. Accordingly, the Turkomans were attacked, at first by a series of small campaigns, but, that proving unsuccessful, larger schemes were framed, and attempts were made to reach the chain of oases which were the real centre of Turkoman power, either from the mouth of the Atrek, or from Krasnovodsk at the foot of the mountains on the Persian frontier.

to seek flight, furnished the Russians with a welcome pretext for interference. Finally, on March 3rd, 1876, all that was left of the Khanate of Khokand was incorporated with the Russian Empire as the province of Ferghana. A condition of things which promised to be stable was thus established in the northern and eastern parts of Turkestan ; in front of the Russian territory, the nomad inhabitants of which might be considered as subjugated, lay the Khanates of Khiva and Bokhara, both subject to Russian influence, as a secure belt of frontier, whose complete incorporation into the dominions of the Tsar could be of little importance.

Buffers to Nomad Aggression

The situation was different in the west, in the steppes between the Caspian Sea and the Amu Daria. Here marauding Turkoman tribes still roamed without let or hindrance ; and their nominal suzerain, the Khan of Khiva, was, after his humiliation by Russia, less capable than ever of holding them in check. To subdue them was possible only if the southern frontier were pushed forward to the southern margin of the steppe and the Persian sphere of influence. But there was a two-fold inducement for undertaking this laborious enterprise. It was not merely a question of abating the nuisance of Turkoman marauders ; Russian statesmen considered the new move as a check to England. The military party avowed their belief that the surest way of settling

mountains on the Persian frontier.

The first undertaking of this kind failed in the year 1879. But a year later a new expedition started under the command of General Michael Skobeleff. This time a railway was built simultaneously with the advance of the troops—the first portion of the subsequent Transcaspian Railway, which has now reached Samarkand and opened a new road to international traffic. The fate of the Turkomans was soon sealed. On January 24th, 1881, their strongest fortress, Geok-Tepe, was taken after a heroic defence, and soon afterward the subjugation of the northern, or Tekke, Turkomans was complete.

In this same year a frontier treaty with Persia made the fact clear that Russia had as her neighbour on that side a state possessing a tolerable degree of culture. Toward the south-east, on the other hand, the advance of the Russians did not stop until it reached the borders of Afghanistan.

Russian Advance in the South

There was no necessity for further wars against the nomads : the Turkomans of Merv tendered their submission under diplomatic and military pressure. In spite of this the Russians were soon active in the country to the south of Merv ; and in 1885 their advanced posts came into collison with the Afghans on the River Kushk, a battle being fought in which the Afghans were defeated. The blame for this collision has been thrown by some on England ; it is alleged that the Afghan were instigated to prevent Russia from acquiring that firm position in the south of the steppe country which was a political necessity for her. Others have accused the Foreign Office at St. Petersburg of having deliberately forced on a breach with Afghanistan.

The trouble would seem to be that **Collision of Russians and Afghans** the hand of the Russian Government was forced by the zeal of frontier generals. The questions at issue were settled by a Boundary Commission in 1886–1887, which fixed the frontier between Afghanistan and Asiatic Russia. In 1895 the delimitation of British and Russian spheres of influence was advanced yet another step by the partition of the mountainous Pamir region, which separates Northeastern Afghanistan from the Tarim basin. Since 1886 the influence of Russia within her allotted sphere has been materially increased by the extension of the Transcaspian Railway, which has brought districts long desolate within the range of Russian commerce, and completely assured the military supremacy of its possessors.

The one notable event in recent years has been the Anglo-Russian Agreement of 1907, which in the main is concerned with Persia, but recognises Afghanistan as within the specifically British sphere of interest.

If we look back on what Russia has done in Turkestan we shall see that there is room for conjecture as to her ultimate policy. Her advance might be explained solely by the causes which have induced the peaceful Chinese Empire to occupy the Tarim basin on the verge of the Central Asiatic steppes were it not that evidence exists to suggest some motive beyond the mere desire of obtaining security from the raids of nomad tribes. The first plan for a Russian invasion of India was framed as long ago as 1791; and plans are said to have been considered at various dates since then, notably in 1800, 1855, and 1876. These plans have usually been formed with the idea of influencing the European situation to the advantage of Russia by locking up British troops in India and inducing Great Britain to take a more conciliatory attitude. In all such plans the occupation of Afghanistan has been an essential feature, and no pains have been spared to detach that country from its dependence on Great Britain. An attempt of this kind in 1878, immediately after the Treaty of Berlin, was so far successful that the Afghans declared war on England. But Russia took no steps to **Russia's Afghan Policy** assist the Afghans when they had been drawn into the war; and since that time Russian influence in Afghanistan has suffered a check. The foreign policy of Russia at the present time looks towards the Persian Gulf rather than towards India. The possession of the mouth of the Euphrates would give Russia one of those outlets for the trade of her empire which it has always been her prime anxiety and endeavour to secure.

HEINRICH SCHURTZ

RUSSIAN TROOPS ENTERING THE CITY OF KHIVA ON JUNE 10, 1873

AFGHANISTAN AND BALUCHISTAN

By Angus Hamilton & Arthur D. Innes

THE dominant physical feature of Afghanistan is the Hindu Kush, together with that extension which radiates from the Tirogkhoi plateau and the stupendous peaks of the Koh-i-Baba. But everywhere the orology is of a very rugged character. Its natural divisions may be said to be as follow: The basin of the Kabul river, including its tributaries, the Logar, Panjsher and Kunar rivers; the tableland valleys of the Ghilzai country from Ghazni to Kandahar, including the Argandab, the Tarnak, and the Arghesan; the tributary valleys of the Indus—viz., Kurram, Khost, Dawar, Gomul, Zobe, and Bori; the valley of the Helmund; the basin of the Hamun lake; the valley of the Hari Rud; the valley of the Murghab and the tributary valleys of the Oxus — viz., the Maimana, Balkh, Khulm, Kunduz and Kokcha rivers.

While the general elevation of Afghanistan is considerable and opposed to the **Elevation of the Country** mountain systems, there is but little plain, save the belt between the northern slope of the Hindu Kush and the Oxus, as well as towards the south-west in the wide stretch of desert levels forming the western border. The main natural difficulty is presented by the water question. If the Oxus and the Indus are excluded, as shared by Russia and India respectively, the Helmund is the only river of any magnitude, although there are numerous small streams which yield important tribute to the irrigation systems of the country-side.

The following are the principal hydrographic divisions: the Kabul river and its tributaries, the Indus affluents, the basin of the Oxus, the basin of the Helmund, and the basin of the Hari Rud.

To this outline of the physical and territorial conditions of the country must be added an ethnographic summary of the various racial divisions which, since the incorporation of the Khanates with the dominions of the Amir of Afghanistan, present a very confused study. The Afghans proper are settled principally in the Kandahar country, extending into Seistan and to the borders of the Herat valley. **The Afghan Races** Eastward they spread across the Afghan border into the Toba highlands north of the Khojak, where they are represented by Achakzai and Sudozai clans. They exist in the Kabul districts as Barakzai, the Amir's clan, and as Mahmundzai, or Mohmands, and Yusufzai. They occupy the hills north of the Kabul river, Bajor, Swat, Buner, and part of the Peshawar plains.

After the Afghans come the Pathans, who, recognised in many instances as being of Indian origin, inhabit the hilly regions along the immediate British border. The Afridi, Jowaki and Orakzai clans hold the highlands immediately south of the Khaibar and Peshawar; the Turis of the Kurram, the Dawaris of Tochi, and the Waziris of Waziristan filling up the intervening Pathan hills north of the Gomul. In the Kohat district the Khattak and Bangash clans are Pathan, so that Pathans are found on both sides of the border.

The Ghilzai, reckoned as a Pathan, but connected also with the Afghan, is another racial unit. This tribe ranks as second to none in the military strength of Afghanistan, and in commercial enterprise. Underlying these elements in Afghan ethnography, there is the Tajik, who, representing the original Persian possessor of the soil, still speaks his mother tongue. There are pure Persians in Afghanistan, **Races of Alien Origin** such as the Kizil Bashis of Kabul, and the Naoshirwan of Kharan. The Tajiks are the cultivators in the rural districts, the shopkeepers and clerks in the towns; while they are slaves of the Pathan in Afghanistan no less than the Hindkis are in the plains of the Indus. Next in importance to the Tajik is the Hazara, who speaks a dialect of Persian, and belongs to the Shiah sect of Mohammedans. The Hazaras occupy the highlands of the Upper Helmund valley, spreading through the country between Kabul and Herat, as well as into a strip of territory on the frontier slopes of the Hindu Kush. In the western provinces they are known as Hazaras, Jamshidis, Taimanis, and Ferozkhois. They are pure Mongols, and intermixed with no other races, while they preserve their language and characteristics from the influence of environment. Last of all there are the Uzbegs and the Turkomans, so that the Afghan tribes represent no single people, but a number of racial communities, each possessed of separate interests, and, in great measure, of a separate national entity.

Lying between Persia, on the one hand, and on the other the mountain passes through which, from time immemorial, all invaders have penetrated to the Punjab and the plains of Hindustan, Afghanistan to-day fulfils the functions of a buffer state between the British and the Russian powers in Central Asia, while in the past Afghan territory has given dynasties on the one side to Persia, and on the other to Delhi, and has formed a part now of one empire, now of the other, and again has formed a state or a group of states more or less independent of both.

YAKUB KHAN

The son of Sher Ali, whom he succeeded; under pressure of British arms he signed the treaty of Gandamak.

Thus Mahmud, the great Ghaznavid, issued from the fortress-city of Ghazni; Babar, the founder of the Mogul Empire, was lord of Kabul when he began his career of conquest. Like all outlying provinces of all Oriental empires, the Afghan tribesmen rendered obedience to their suzerain only when they were aware that he could spare an army to coerce recalcitrants; their subjection was always insubstantial. They owned the might of Nadir Shah, but when he died, the Abdali chief, Ahmed Khan, assumed independence and the royal title of Shah, at Kandahar, and established the " Durani " dynasty at Kabul, changing his tribal name for superstitious reasons.

Ahmed Shah led a series of incursions into India; in the greatest of them he temporarily shattered the Mahratta power at Panipat, while the British were making themselves masters of Bengal. But he did not seek to establish an Indian Empire, though the Duranis were owned as masters of the Punjab until the Sikhs freed themselves from the Afghan yoke, and created a dominion of their own under Ranjit Singh. When Mornington arrived as Governor-General in India, men believed that the power of Zeman Shah at Kabul was a menace to Hindustan.

But his might was less than it seemed. In 1801 Zeman Shah was deposed and blinded, and his brother set up in his place, as Shah Shuja, by a group of the Barakzai family, who in reality held the reins of power, though they preferred to assume the position of Ministers. A few years later the Indian Government thought it worth while to seek Shah Shuja's friendship. Little enough came of this move at the time, for Shah Shuja was deposed in his turn in 1810, and betook himself to safe quarters in British territory, whence he made periodical and futile attempts to recover his throne.

For thirty years the Barakzais in Afghanistan and the Sikh Maharaja of Lahore were in constant rivalry, with the practical result that Ranjit Singh wrested from the Afghans one after another of their positions in the Punjab, and incorporated in his own domain Multan, Peshawar, and Kashmir. For these successes he was partly indebted to the internal dissensions of Afghanistan. The titular kings were disposed to resent the supremacy of the Barakzai brotherhood;

A Tajik chief of Pesh Bolak   A Mohmand chief of Dakka   Khugiani chief of Murkhi Kheyl

Nimcha, or a convert to Moslemism   Barakzai chief of Bezoot   An Ummer Kheyl chief of Darunta

Tajik chief of the Kunar Valley   Mohmand chief of Lalpura   A Barakzai, a relative of the Amir

FAMILIAR TYPES OF THE INHABITANTS OF AFGHANISTAN

there was a period of fierce strife and bloodshed, at the end of which the king remained in possession of Herat, while the vizirate and effective dominion passed to a younger Barakzai, Dost Mohammed.

In 1836 Persia was assuming an aggressive attitude towards Afghanistan. Dost Mohammed, somewhat suspicious of the British on one side, perceived on the other that Russia was at the back of Persia. He made overtures to the British, which were rejected. Lord Auckland's Government became possessed with the idea that the only security lay in placing on the throne at Kabul a ruler who would be in effect a puppet of the British; and the Governor-General resolved to reinstate Shah Shuja. In carrying out this programme, no very serious resistance was encountered ; a few white troops and a considerable force of Hindustani sepoys restored the Durani. Dost Mohammed, after vindicating his character as a valiant warrior, surrendered himself, and was placed under honourable surveillance in British territory. British forces remained at Kabul, to maintain the Government they had set up.

The result was what might have been anticipated. Little more than two years had elapsed since the restoration when a riot at Kabul developed into a general insurrection in November, 1841. At Kandahar the British garrison more than held its own ; at Jellalabad a small force maintained a successful defence. But Ghazni was forced to yield before long, and the whole of the large Kabul force, after some of the chiefs had been murdered and others surrendered to the rebels as hostages, was cut to pieces. Retribution followed as a

Bourne & Shepherd, India

HABIBULLA, AMIR OF AFGHANISTAN
Habibulla succeeded his father in 1901, and though at first cold towards British overtures, has now ratified the friendship that prevailed under his predecessor.

matter of course. But the British had awakened to the fact that no politic end could be served by a military occupation. Having definitely vindicated their military supremacy, they reinstated their quondam antagonist, Dost Mohammed, under his old title of Amir.

That very shrewd ruler bore no grudge against the British. In fact, he realised that they had no desire to possess themselves of Afghanistan, whereas Persia was obviously hankering to recover at least Herat. It was from the west that aggression was to be feared ; therefore he recognised his own best interests in cultivating British goodwill. To the day of his death he continued consistently loyal. The Afghan tribesmen remembered the British occupation vindictively, and with an especial hatred towards the Hindustani sepoys. Nevertheless, Dost Mohammed held them in check, even when the sanguinary engagements of the second Sikh war (1848-9) seemed to offer a chance of striking a damaging blow. Later, in 1855, a definite treaty was made between the Dost and the British, which was viewed with dislike by some of the ablest Indian officials, but bore invaluable fruit in the complete quiescence of Afghanistan in 1857, when the Hindustani regiments mutinied against the British Raj. In the interval the Afghan ruler had successfully resisted a Persian attempt on Herat, and British troops had intervened effectively on the Persian Gulf.

So long as Afghanistan showed no signs of being drawn into dangerously close relations with Russia, the Indian Government maintained a policy of non-intervention, which was very unsatisfactory

THE AMIR OF AFGHANISTAN RECEIVING AN AFRIDI DEPUTATION AT KABUL

THE AMIR TESTING A MAXIM GUN DURING THE ARMY MANŒUVRES

to statesmen of the " forward " school. In pursuance of that policy, the British did not interfere in the period of anarchy which followed the death of Dost Mohammed in 1863. His actual successor was a younger son, Sher Ali, who soon found his brothers in arms against him. It was not until 1868 that he appeared to be securely established at Kabul. In 1870 the Amir met the Viceroy of India, Lord Mayo, in durbar at Ambela, when the principle of British non-intervention was clearly enunciated. In the following year his throne was shaken by the revolt of his son, Yakub Khan ; he began to show signs of yielding to Russian influences. In 1878 he received a Russian mission at

the Resident, Sir Louis Cavagnari, with his staff and guard were cut to pieces.

A month later the British had successfully reoccupied Kabul ; Yakub Khan abdicated, and placed himself in their hands. But in July of the following year his brother, Ayub Khan, roused a number of the tribes to join in a *jehad*, or holy war, against the British. Defeating General Burrows on July 27, he at once invested Kandahar. His success was brief. General Roberts, after achieving in August his famous march from Kabul to Kandahar in twenty-two days, completely crushed Ayub in a decisive battle. Abdurrahman, another nephew of Sher Ali, was recognised by the British as Amir. As in 1843, after

THE TOWN AND FORTRESS OF HERAT, THE GATEWAY TO AFGHANISTAN AND INDIA
Herat, on the River Hari-Rud, was founded by Alexander the Great, who seems to have recognised its strategic importance ; it is the capital of Western Afghanistan, is well fortified, and has a population estimated at 45,000.

Kabul. The British Viceroy, Lord Lytton, promptly demanded that a British mission should be received ; when Sher Ali failed to accede to his demands, the second Afghan War—that of 1878-80—began.

Resistance was crushed decisively, and Sher Ali, flying from Kabul, died at Mazar-Sharif in February, 1879, his son, Yakub Khan, being proclaimed Amir. The treaty of Gandamak, on May 26, 1879, gave the British control of a series of the mountain passes, and provided that " scientific frontier " which it had been their main object to secure. But the new arrangements involved the establishment of a British Residency at Kabul, to exercise a controlling influence over the Amir. In September there was a rising in Kabul, and

an aggressive fit, the Indian Government reverted to its normal policy, and in 1881 withdrew its forces from Afghanistan.

Abdurrahman proved himself a ruler of great power and ability, crushing revolts with swift and merciless energy. Whatever suspicions may have been from time to time entertained as to his policy, and however grievances against the British, justifiable or otherwise, may have rankled in his mind, he remained effectively loyal to the British connection, aware, like Dost Mohammed, that the British much preferred maintaining his country as an independent state to bringing it under their own direct dominion, while he could rely upon their resisting any attempt on the part of Russia to absorb

A MODERN FORT AT KABUL, CROWNING A LOW HILL

GENERAL VIEW OF THE CITY OF KABUL

A SCENE IN THE AMIR'S PALACE AT KABUL

IN THE CAPITAL CITY OF AFGHANISTAN

it. When the Powers proposed a definite delimitation of boundaries, and a collision occurred between Russian and Afghan forces, known as the Panjdeh incident, the Amir showed genuine statesmanship in refusing to make much of what might easily have been construed into a *casus belli*. The delimitation was duly carried out, and ratified by a treaty signed at St. Petersburg in 1887.

Delimitation of Afghan Frontiers

The Afghanistan which Abdurrahman left is divided into five provinces—Kabul, Herat, Kandahar, Afghan Turkestan and Badakshan; and two territories—Kafiristan and Wakhan. Kandahar includes Seistan and the basin of the Helmund; Herat the basin of the Hari-Rud and North-western Afghanistan; Afghan Turkestan the former khanates Andkhui, Maimana, Balkh, and Khulm; the province of Badakshan administers the territory of Wakhan and the regions of the Upper Oxus. Kabul, Herat, and Kandahar are the centres of their respective provinces; Tashkurgan and Mazar-i-Sharif of Afghan Turkestan and Faizabad of Badakshan.

This division of Afghanistan into settled provinces is due to Dost Mohammed, who despatched an expedition under his son for the purpose of subjecting the various independent territories that existed in those days in the regions south of the Oxus. By the success which attended these operations, the Afghan dominions were pushed out to the banks of the Oxus and the Murghab. It was Abdurrahman, however, who split the territory thus secured into the divisions of Afghan Turkestan and Badakshan, with which change a considerable improvement upon the previous anarchy and misrule was obtained.

Under Dost Mohammed, as also in the reign of Sher Ali, the utmost confusion prevailed in every department of government. The chiefs of the various tribes were both independent and ambitious, and not infrequently defied the authority of the Amir at Kabul. The period of greatest confusion may be said to have closed with the civil war of 1863-9, from which Sher Ali emerged triumphant. Founding a despotic sovereignty over the tribes, Sher Ali laid the foundations upon which Abdurrahman so successfully reared his autocracy. One by one Abdurrahman suppressed the turbulent Sirdars, thus paving the way to the solidarity which distinguished his own position. In addition, he reformed the Government and its methods. He put a stop to corruption in the public offices, and forbade the acceptance of bribes or the sale of appointments. Beginning at the bottom, he built up a civil and military machinery which, before he appeared, may be said to have been non-existent. On the military side he re-organised the army and introduced modern

Progress Under a Despot

SOLDIERS OF AFGHANISTAN WHO ESCORTED THE BRITISH MISSION

In November of 1904 a British Mission from the Indian Government, under Mr. Louis Dane, the Indian Foreign Secretary, proceeded by way of Peshawar to Kabul to discuss Indo-Afghan questions with the Amir Habibulla.

MIR MAHMUD KHAN, OF KELAT, AND HIS RETINUE

Mir Mahmud Khan succeeded upon his father's abdication in 1893, and is head of the loose confederancy of chiefs in the native state of Kelat in Baluchistan; as a dependency of India the state has a British political agent resident in Kelat.

weapons and Western drill; on the civil side he established financial and political control, and set up an even-handed, if rough and ready, form of justice. The final touch to his edifice was the creation of a Cabinet, the recasting of the provincial methods of administration, and a reform of the laws. The improvements proceeding from these changes have made Afghanistan a firmly constructed, well-ordered, and financially sound state. Occupying 300,000 square miles, with a population of six millions, and a revenue of £2,000,000 sterling a year, with an army estimated at 150,000 on a peace footing, the present state of the country is an effective illustration of the excellence of Abdurrahman's reign.

The death of Abdurrahman caused some anxiety. It was felt that the disappearance of so vigorous a ruler might be followed by a period of turbulence and con-

Fears that Were Not Fulfilled tests over the succession. Happily, the Amir's son, Habibulla, was accepted by the tribes quietly and without disturbance. The new Amir has continued on the old lines; his authority has not been challenged, and he has shown himself not less loyal to the British connection than his father. There has been no trouble with

Russia, while the peace of the border has been well maintained. The relations between the Amir and the Indian Government, at first distant, were improved by the result of the Dane Mission, and thoroughly cemented by the Amir's visit to India in 1907.

BALUCHISTAN

Between Afghanistan and the Ocean, its eastern boundary marching with Sindh, lies the territory known as Baluchistan. The country is mountainous, and on the western or Persian side is largely desert.

Its barren character has rendered it unattractive to conquering kings and khans, and exceedingly ill-adapted for the passage of large armies. The invaders of India have habitually preferred to penetrate the northern passes rather than those of Baluchistan.

The population is composed of two quite distinct races—the Brahuis, whom ethnologists incline to associate with the Dravidian peoples of India, and the Baluchis, who are probably of Iranian stock. The prevailing religion is Mohammedanism—Sunni, not Shi-ite. The country has never acquired the dignity of an organised state. Some chieftain has usually been vaguely recognised as paramount, and, in his turn, has been more or less a tributary of Persia or of Kabul. In short, Baluchistan can hardly be said to have had a history of its own, at least until it came in contact with the British Government in India.

A century ago the British were beginning to investigate the Indus and to open relations with Sindh and with Afghanistan. Incidentally, some knowledge of Baluchistan began to be acquired. Then, as now, the chief authority was recognised as lying with the Khan of Kelat. When the British plunged into their ill-starred Afghan venture of 1838–9, Ranjit Singh's refusal to allow their army passage to the Khaibar Pass and Peshawar, compelled them to make Kandahar instead of Kabul their immediate objective, and to advance through Sindh and Baluchistan by way of the Bolan Pass. The reigning Khan of Kelat rendered no assistance, and was accused of deliberate and designed obstruction. Hence Kelat itself was incidentally attacked and seized, and was again temporarily occupied in 1841.

From the time of Ellenborough to that of Lord Lytton, British policy beyond Sindh and the Punjab was controlled by the principle of " masterly inactivity." But the Government of Disraeli and his Viceroy, Lord Lytton, adopted the doctrines of the " forward " school and the theory of a " scientific frontier." Military opinion, with Russia in view, has been practically unanimous in maintaining that the mountains of the north-west should be made absolutely impassable to the invader. Through the Bolan Pass the mountains can be penetrated. Quetta commands the Bolan Pass. An important step, therefore, was taken when, in 1877, Lord Lytton secured by treaty the right of occupying Quetta.

Ten years later the Khan of Kelat assented to the definite annexation of the Quetta territory by the British. A military railway—a triumph of engineering skill—has secured through communication with the great outpost, which is looked upon as virtually impregnable ; and, politically speaking, the district now forms a part of British India. On the other hand, the Khan of Kelat, by practically becoming a British feudatory, has found his own position secured against rivalry, and consequently exercises over the tribes an authority of a much more definite character than in the past. It has followed that a certain responsibility for his behaviour attaches to the British Government, the consciousness of which was exemplified in 1893 by the deposition of the Khan for misconduct, and the establishment of his own son in his place.

KOHAT, BRITISH POST ON THE FRONTIERS OF BALUCHISTAN, AFGHANISTAN AND PERSIA

Chinese Turkestan

AREA AND POPULATION. The area of Chinese Turkestan is about 555,000 square miles, and the population is estimated at about 1,200,000. The chief towns are Yarkand (75,000), Kashgar (50,000) and Khotan (40,000).

GOVERNMENT. The country is a dependency of China and is under the Viceroy of the Province of Kansu, who resides at Lan-chau. There is also a governor at Ti-hiva, and the active administration is exercised through Chinese officials residing at Urumtsi.

INDUSTRY AND COMMERCE. In the favoured districts, such as around Yarkand and Kashgar, the soil is productive, and cereals, vegetables, and fruits are grown. Wool, cotton and silk are also native products, and jade is worked. The trade route to China is the line of least natural resistance; there are three difficult passes from Chinese Turkestan into Russian Turkestan, and two into India—the Karakoram Pass (18,500 feet) and the Kilik Pass (15,800 feet). In 1906-7 the value of trade with India was £158,000. There are British and Russian consuls in Kashgar.

Russian Turkestan

AREA AND POPULATION. The area of the whole territory is 1,366,456 square miles, and the population (partly estimated) is 9,901,597. The chief towns are: Tashkend, 156,414; Samarkand, 54,900; Maghilan, 45,000; Khojent, 30,076; Khokand, 82,054; Namangan, 61,906; Andijan, 46,680; Khiva, 12,000; Bokhara, 60,000; Karshi, 35,000.

GOVERNMENT. The Governor-General of Russian Turkestan resides in Tashkend; and each province, which is under a military governor, is divided into districts administered by army officers, and these again are portioned into pristis, or subdivisions. Local affairs are controlled by popularly elected village councils. The government of the two Khanates—Bokhara and Khiva—is a despotism of the native khans under the guidance of Russian Residents.

INDUSTRY AND COMMERCE. The country is fertile, and agriculture flourishes. Millet, wheat, barley, and rice are the chief cereals, and cotton has been developed until the raw cotton exported has reached the value of £10,000,000 annually. Grapes, fruits, and vegetables are grown in great variety; and wine and brandy are manufactured. There is considerable mineral wealth, including gold, copper, lead, silver, coal, and gems such as turquoises and beryls.

Tibet

AREA AND POPULATION. The area of Tibet is 463,200 square miles. There is no certainty regarding the number of the population; estimates range from 1,500 000 to 6,500,000, and the lower figure is probably the more nearly correct. Lhasa, the capital, and the seat of the theocratic government, contains from 15,000 to 20,000 inhabitants, two-thirds of whom are monks.

GOVERNMENT. Tibet is a dependency of China, and Chinese authority is represented by two officials termed *ambans*, who have charge of foreign and military affairs respectively. The civil and religious administration is in the hand of Tibetans—that is to say, of the Lamait hierarchy. The titular head of the Govern ment is the Dalai-Lama.

INDUSTRY AND COMMERCE. The differer altitudes and climates of Tibet give grea variety to its produce. Cereals are grown an in some favoured districts certain fruits including peaches and grapes. The chie domestic animal is the yak, which is ofte crossed with Indian cattle, and there are als sheep, buffaloes, pigs and camels. Spinning weaving and knitting of wool may be describe as the primitive industries, and in the depart ment of minerals, gold, salt, and borax ar worked to some extent. There is no foreig industrial enterprise in the country. Th foreign trade of Tibet is with China and wit India. In the year 1906-7 the total trade wit India was about £234,000, the chief exports t India being wool, borax, salt, living anima and musk, and the chief imports therefror cotton and woollen goods, grain and coral.

Baluchistan

AREA AND POPULATION. Baluchistan has a area of 132,315 square miles and a populatio (partly estimated) of 909,000. British Balu chistan has an area of 45,804 square miles an a population of 308,246.

BRITISH BALUCHISTAN. British Baluchistan wa incorporated with British India in 1887, an was divided into two districts—Quetta-Pishi and Thal-Chotiali. Other areas under dire British administration are Zhob, Bolan an Chagai.

NATIVE STATE OF BALUCHISTAN. Native Balu chistan comprises the states of Kelat and La Bela. The Khan of Kelat is head of th tribal chiefs in his district, which has an are of 71,593 square miles and a populatio estimated at 471,000. Las Bela is a sma state near the Sind frontier and has an area c 6,441 square miles and a population of 56,00

GOVERNMENT. The Chief Commissioner fc British Baluchistan—at present Colonel Sir A H. McMahon—is also Governor-General Agent for the native states, conducts th relations between the Governor-General c India and the Khan, and also exercises gener political supervision over the whole district.

INDUSTRY AND COMMERCE. The country i mountainous and generally rugged and barrer and the climate is subject to extremes c temperature. The agricultural products ar wheat, barley, millet, lucerne, rice, maize potatoes, grapes, apricots, peaches, apples dates and melons. The chief domesti animals are camels, horses, oxen and donkey Coal is the only mineral that is worked, b iron, lead, asbestos and chromite have bee found. The chief exports are mustard, rap raw wool, and food grains. The importanc of Baluchistan is that it commands the trad routes between India and Persia.

Afghanistan

AREA AND POPULATION. The area of Afghan stan is about 250,000 square miles, and i population is estimated at 5,000,000. Th capital is Kabul, with a population of abo 150,000, and the chief commercial centre

Kandahar with 30,000 inhabitants; the other important towns are Herat with 12,000 and Tashkurgan with 17,000.

GOVERNMENT. The ruler of Afghanistan is the Amir, Habibulla Khan, whose full name and title is Siraj-ul-millat-wad-din Amir Habibulla Khan, G.C.M.G. The form of government is a despotic monarchy, and the power of the ruler depends upon his personality. There are four provinces—Kabul, Turkestan, Herat, and Kandahar, each under a *naib* or governor. The system of justice is largely feudal, exaction is common and oppressive, and there is no purity in administration. The former Amir, Abdurrahman Khan, established a civil and military system which was a great improvement upon the chaotic state of affairs before his time. By treaty agreement, Afghanistan has no foreign relations with any Power except the Government of India.

INDUSTRY AND COMMERCE. The people are good agriculturists and have good irrigation. Many cereals are grown—wheat, barley, lentils, rice, millet, maize and dal—and there are generally two crops a year. There are also many fruits. Clothes and carpets of silk, wool, and hair are manufactured, and large quantities of wool are sent to Persia and Russia. The exports to India are chiefly raw wool and living animals, hides, skins and drugs. During the Indian fiscal year 1906-7 the Afghan-Indian trade reached the value of £1,330,000.

GREAT DATES IN THE HISTORY OF CENTRAL ASIA

B.C.	
331	Alexander the Great passes through Central Asia in the course of his great [march to India
210	Huns conquer China
A.D.	
90	Huns expelled from China [Goths
376	Huns invade Hungary and drive out the
445-450	Attila, the " Scourge of God," ravages the Western Roman Empire [Aetius
451	Battle of Chalons, and defeat of Attila by
639	Buddhism introduced into Tibet
1206	Genghis Khan reigns from 1206 to 1207, and embraces in his empire all Central Asia as well as Persia and China
1224	Batou, the grandson of Genghis Khan, at the head of his " Golden Horde "— the name given to his Mongolian Tartars—establishes an empire in Kajatchak or Kibzak, now South-east Russia
1252	The " Golden Horde " invades Russia and makes Alexander Newski Grand Duke
1278	Tibet visited by Marco Polo
1370	Timur, or Tamerlane, who reigned from 1370 to 1400, conquered Persia, invaded India, and broke the power of the Turks in Asia Minor
1481	Battle of Bielawisch, at which Ivan III. of Russia crushes the Golden Horde, or Mongolian Tartars
1505	Bokhara, or Sogdiana, subdued by the Uzbek Tartars, its present holders
15 25	Babar, first Mogul Emperor of India, conquers Kabul; after his death, Afghanistan is divided between India
1661	Jesuits visit Tibet [and Persia
1672	Great migration of the Tartar tribe of Kalmucks, who were expelled from China and settled on the Volga and returned in 1771
1747	Ahmed Shah makes Afghanistan independent, and reigns till 1773
1760	Kashgaria, or Eastern Turkestan, subdued by China
1771	Return to Western China of the Kalmucks, thousands perishing during the long march through Central Asia
1774	Visit of Bogle and Hamilton to Tibet
1826	Beginning of a series of unsuccessful insurrections in Kashgaria against China
1838	Restoration of Shah Shuja by British in Afghanistan.
1839	Expedition sent against Khiva by Nicholas of Russia; perished in the cold
1841	British disaster at Kabul; third Afghan War.
1855	Treaty of Britain with Dost Mohammed
1865	The Province of Russian Turkestan created by decree of the Tsar
1866	Mohammed Yakub Beg, during an insurrection in Kashgaria, makes himself ruler, and, in 1867, sends envoys to London
1866	Russian War in Turkestan, and successive defeats of the native armies
1867	Temporary peace between Russia and Turkestan
1868	Renewal of hostilities between Russia and Turkestan. Samarkand captured and secured by treaty
1873	Khiva taken by the Russians. Political and commercial treaty between Russia and Turkestan
1877	China ends the insurrection in Kashgaria by defeating Mohammed Yakub Beg, who was afterwards assassinated, and by capturing Kashgar
1878-80	Third Afghan War; Abdurrahman becomes Amir
1885	Anglo-Russian agreement regarding Afghanistan
1887	Quetta and surrounding territories annexed to British territories
1888	Central Asian railway from the Caspian to Samarkand opened
1889	The Zhob Valley in Baluchistan annexed by Britain at the request of the chiefs
1893	Treaty of Commerce between Great Britain and Tibet. Amir of Turkestan visits Russia, and again in 1898
1895-6	Mohammedan rebellion in Tibet
1895	Explorations and discoveries by Dr. Sven Hedin
1900	Death of the Amir of Afghanistan; succeeded by his son, Habibulla
1903	Expedition under Colonel Younghusband sent to Tibet by Indian Government
1904	After opposition by the Tibetans and their defeat, British force enters Lhasa on August 3rd, and the Treaty of Lhasa is signed on September 7th
1907	Visit of the Amir of Afghanistan to India.

CENTRAL ASIA IN OUR OWN TIME
BY FRANCIS H. SKRINE

CENTRAL ASIA, in its present aspect, demonstrates the influence of environment on the fortunes of the human race. The cradle of our civilisation and religions has lost all political importance. It is a mere geographical expression, connoting 2,600,000 square miles of sparsely-peopled territory lying between Siberia and the vast mountain system which has determined the physical and social evolution of the continent.

The south-western boundary of Central Asia is defined by the plateau of Northern Persia, which skirts the Caspian Sea, continuing the Taurus range of Asia Minor. Its spurs mingle with those of the Kopet Dagh mountains, which are connected with the Caucasus by a submarine ridge whose summits are 150 feet under the surface of the water, and which stretches between Baku and Krasnovodsk, on the Caspian. At the north-western **Boundaries of Central Asia** angle of Afghanistan the Kopet Dagh meets the Alpine system of Asia, which stretches in an unbroken line to Bering's Straits. Its central citadel is a labyrinth of snowy peaks and profound valleys, known as the Pamirs, in which converge the boundaries of the British, Russian, and Chinese empires. Here the Hindu Kush joins hands with the Alai Tagh, which projects a network of lower peaks westwards, forming the Russian provinces of Samarkand and Ferghana, and the Khanate of Bokhara. From the Pamirs stretch eastwards the Kuen Lun Mountains, which bifurcate into the Altyn Tagh and Akka Tagh, separating Chinese Turkestan from Tibet. South-eastwards is the Karakoram range, under which Kashmir nestles ; and thence the mightier Himalayas extend in a graceful curve, marking the northern boundary of Hindustan. Between them and the Akka Tagh is Tibet—a pear-shaped plateau whose lower extremity rests on the Karakoram. Its

eastern marches are roughly defined by a tangle of curved ranges separating it from China. North of the Akka Tagh is a sandy waste, dotted with oases, known as Eastern or Chinese Turkestan, which melts eastwards into the Gobi Desert.

Harking back to the Pamirs plateau, we find it joined on the north-east by the **The Mountain Systems** Tian Shan, or Celestial Mountains, which rise abruptly from the Gobi Desert, and throw out a spur westwards, in the Alexanrovskii and Kara Tau Mountains. To the north-east they are continued by the Ala Tau and Altai ranges, separated by the Zungarian depression, 300 miles in width.

The Central Asian system is the loftiest on the globe's surface. Reckoning only mountains of a greater altitude than 23,000 feet, we have : Mount Kaufmann, in the Ali Plateau, 23,000 ; Mustagh Ata, in the Pamirs, 25,797 ; Akka Tagh, 25,340 ; Aling Gangri, 24,000 ; Kamet, 25,543 ; Gurla Mandlata, 25,934 ; Dhawalgiri, 26,825 ; Mount Everest, 29,002 ; Kanchanjunga, 28,133 ; Donkia, 23,994 ; and Udu, 24,750.

The mountains which stretch in parallel ranges from the Caspian Sea to Central China and the Polar Ocean have had a determining effect on civilisation. On their eastern flank Tibet, with an average elevation of 15,000 feet, proved an insuperable barrier to the migratory **Mountains and Civilisation** instinct of our race. Few and difficult are the breaches in this giant wall, which is penetrable by large bodies of men only in the Suleiman range at its western extremity. Northwards lay the habitat of our remote ancestors, the Aryans. Balkh is now believed to have been the metropolis of these mysterious races. The ruins of the " Mother of Cities," and birthplace of Zoroaster, cover thirty square miles of

North-western Afghanistan. Through easy passes in the Suleimans, the great bulk of these Aryans sought the sunlit plains of India, while other waves of emigration reached Europe by way of Siberia and the Caucasus. Far to the north-east, again, Zungaria, broken by the Tarbagatai Mountain, was the chief outlet for Mongolian hordes, who poured through the depression to bring half the world to heel.

Flood of Peoples into India

Why did the aboriginal inhabitants of Central Asia burst through trammels imposed by Nature ? The answer is to be found in tremendous geological changes which desiccated their habitat and compelled them to seek pastures new. Northwards of the mountain chains starting from the Caspian, the lowlands of Turkestan stretch to the Arctic Ocean. They are divided into two zones by a ridge which never exceeds 1,000 feet in height, extending from the Urals to the Altai range. This is the watershed of the Siberian rivers. The whole area between this gentle elevation and the southern mountain spurs was once an ocean bed. Comparatively recent changes of level, with a corresponding revolution in climatic conditions, have left it a sandy desert studded with salt lakes. The Caspian is the largest of the world's inland seas. It has an area of 180,000 square miles, and is 85 feet lower than ocean-level. The Sea of Aral covers 24,500 square miles, 243 feet above the Caspian. Eastwards is Lake Balkash, extending over 12,800 square miles, and lying 900 feet above the ocean. All have shrunk considerably, and all contain denizens common in Polar seas. Seals abound in the Caspian and Lake Balkash, and the former supplies mankind with isinglass and caviar from the Polar sturgeon. This vast upheaval has changed the face of Asia and the current of history. Rivers rising on the southern and eastern slopes of the vast central water-shed find their way to the Indian and Pacific Oceans, and their alluvial deposit has formed and fertilised the plain of India, Burma, Siam, and China. Those which spring from immense glaciers on the northern side have gradually lost their velocity. In their upper reaches they excel the Nile in vivifying power ; but they feed mere inland lakes, or are absorbed by thirsty sand. The Amu

Inland Seas of the Great Plateau

Daria, or Oxus, springs from glaciers in the Pamirs, and penetrates the Turkoman Desert at Kilif. Up to this point it has many tributaries, among them four rivers which made Balkh a centre of dense population. In its lower course the Amu Daria enriches Khiva, and now finds an outlet in Aral. Between 500 B.C. and 600 of our era it turned abruptly westward 110 miles south of the inland sea, and discharged into the Caspian after a devious course of 600 miles. Its old bed, known as the Uzboi, is still clearly marked, and Russian engineers of the pre-railway era contemplated diverting its current into ancient channels.

The Tejend, Murghab, and Zarafshan, which give fertility to the oases and valleys of Russian Turkestan, once joined the Amu Daria. Owing to changes in level and the needs in irrigation, they now disappear in the Turkoman Desert. The Syr Daria, or Jaxartes, known in upper reaches as the Naryn, rises in the Tian Shan Mountains, and finds the Aral Sea after a course of 1,500 miles. Russian Ferghana, watered by the Syr Daria and its tributaries, is the most fertile valley in Central Asia. Eastwards, and parallel with these mightier rivers, flows the Chu, which is born in the Tian Shan range, to waste its waters in Siberian steppes. The Ili, issuing from the same mountains, pours a flood of wealth into Russian Kulja, and discharges into Lake Balkash. In Chinese Turkestan population clings to oases formed by the River Tarim and its confluents. It rises in the Tian Shan range and, flowing eastward, is lost in the Gobi Desert.

Rivers of Central Asia

The historical interest of Central Asia is confined to its riverine territories, which have been the scenes of many of history's most tragic episodes. Soil overspread by their waters possesses unequalled fertility. Desert sands and upland valleys alike are streaked with deposits of loess, so styled from a Tertiary product found in the Rhine valley. It is a friable yellow loam, which is carried far and wide by the wind, and sometimes covers the subsoil to an immense depth. Loess ranks first among the causes of China's dense population. In Central Asia irrigated loess yields two, and sometimes three, bountiful crops in a single year. Strabo, who wrote shortly before

AMONG THE PEAKS OF THE PAMIRS, 12,000 FEET ABOVE THE SEA

ONE OF THE SNOW-COVERED PAMIR RANGES IN EASTERN TURKESTAN

ANOTHER VIEW AMONG THE WILD AND ROCKY PEAKS OF HIGH ASIA

IN THE PAMIRS, THE CHIEF MOUNTAINS OF CENTRAL ASIA

the birth of Christ, tells us that the Mero oasis boasted vines yielding clusters three feet in diameter. The Zarafshan, literally "gold-spreading," owes its name to the agricultural wealth which it pours into Samarkand and Bokhara.

The climate of this immense tract varies with latitude and height above sea-level. Its northern steppes have a rainfall of eleven inches, confined to June and July, and the same extremes of heat and cold as are presented by Mid-Siberia. The desert, sparsely studded with oases, does not belong to the Sahara type made familiar to us by records of African exploration. In some parts the surface is so firm that a horse's hoofs ring on it as on a macadamised road. Elsewhere the loose sand is lashed by the wind into ridges resembling petrified waves. An intense stillness broods over these wastes, and a boundless horizon seen through the clear air shimmering in heat or broken by mirages. During the spring rains, averaging four inches, the mingled sand and loess is carpeted with the flowers of bulbous plants, long grass, and tufts of reed.

Where the Desert Blossoms Water is alone needed to cover the sand with perennial verdure. It is found almost everywhere at a depth of thirty feet, and primitive wells are frequently met with. Vegetation is scanty save during six weeks following the spring rainfall. Large tracts are, however, covered with the Camel's Thorn—which can be assimilated only by the Ship of the Desert—stunted tamarisks, and a knotty shrub termed saxaul (*halyoxyon ammodendron*), which is prized as fuel, and is even more valuable as a means of binding the billowy sand.

The oases, formed by irrigation, sustain a constant battle with encroaching desert. Upland valleys enjoy a heavier rainfall and the climate of Southern Europe, with wider thermometric ranges due to continental conditions. Tibet, in the same latitude, is swept by storms and cursed by an Arctic climate. Cut off from the outer world by desert and mountain, Central Asia has developed a fauna and flora of its own. Explorers reckon five species of mammals, nine of birds, and fourteen of fish which are not found elsewhere. Tigers are encountered as far north as the Ala Tau range ; bears, wolves, and wild boar abound in the forests which still cover large tracts of upland. Herds of wild asses, antelope, and

deer roam over the desert. Loftier plateaus are the habitat of wild camels, horses, and yaks.

The human denizens of Central Asia reflect every stage of the world's civilisation. The Kirghiz, numbering about 2,500,000, wander in the steppes of Northern Turkestan. They dwell in **Peoples of Central Asia** circular tents of dark grey felt, styled kibitkas, which they tapestry with brilliant carpets. The Kirghiz are a keen-witted and poetical race, and their barbarism is mitigated by a dash of chivalry. The strong arm of Russian conquest has compelled them to desist from the forays which broke the monotony of tending cattle ; but they are inveterate nomads, defying all attempts to introduce education among them or a taste for sedentary life. Government is exercised by hereditary khans. The personal equation is everything, and the chief who derogates is lost. The " Black " Kirghiz, 324,000 strong, range the mountains encircling Lake Issik-kul, on the eastern flank of Russian Turkestan. Their language proves them a very ancient offshoot of the great Turkish family. The Uzbegs are another stem of the race which quitted the Gobi Desert to enter on a career of world-conquest. They are sturdier and more clumsily built than the Kirghiz, with high cheek-bones, ruddy complexions, and dark auburn hair. Uzbegs formed the penultimate wave of conquest which swept over Central Asia. The ruling dynasties of Bokhara and Khiva belong to one of their 72 clans. They are haughty fanatics, despising commerce and the urban population among whom they live. Unlike their kinsfolk, the Kirghiz, Uzbegs have taken kindly to sedentary life. The grossness of their manners is mitigated by a touch of the inborn dignity which characterises unadulterated Asmaulis.

Migration Caused by Droughts The Turkomans belong to a branch of the Turkish family which dwell in Mid-Siberia and the Altai Mountains. Long before the Christian Era, the desiccation of their pastures compelled them to migrate southwards. Following, probably, the ancient course of the Oxus, they spread over the desert which still bears their name. Until the era of Russian conquest their tribal organisation was retained intact. The Yomud Turkomans feed their flocks and herds in the desert south of Aral, taking shelter in the valleys of North-western Persia during the winter months. The Tekkes have absorbed many minor clans in a struggle for existence. About half a century ago they took possession of the Merv oasis and a fertile strip fringing the Kopet Dagh Mountains.

A Race of Tamed Barbarians From these points of vantage they harried Northern Persia and Afghanistan, selling their inhabitants into hopeless slavery at Bokhara and Khiva. Between 1881 and 1884 these hornets' nests were extirpated by Russia. The Turkomans have lost their passion for rapine, and sullenly settled down as agriculturists and cattle-breeders. The horses, which once carried tribesmen incredible distances on forays, are no longer raised. Brilliant and durable carpets were formerly woven by their womenfolk ; but this industry has been well-nigh killed by imported coal-tar dyes.

Sart is the generic term employed by Russians for the sedentary population of Central Asia ; but it includes a variety of ethnological types. Tajiks predominate in urban centres. They descend from Aryan aborigines, from Persian immigrants, or alliances between Uzbegs and imported slaves. The Tajiks are a tall, well-favoured race, with clear olive complexions and black hair and eyes. As each tide of conquest swept over Central Asia they bowed their necks and acquired all the vices bred by slavery. They are intelligent, polished, and laborious, but their faithlessness is as notorious as their want of courage. The languages spoken by this motley human horde are Chagatay, a dialect of Turki, and Tajiki, which is a corrupt form of Persian. In Russian Turkestan the conquerors have not committed the blunder of forcing a knowledge of their vernacular on subject races. Religion has played a great part in moulding the destinies of Central

Waves of Religious Conquest Asia. In the eighth century the entire territory succumbed to Islamic conquest. Five hundred years later a wave of mysticism swept over Asia, which was probably a reflex action of the Crusades. This revival has left indelible traces on social life and thought. Uzbegs, Turkomans and the bulk of dwellers in cities are ardent Sunnis, adhering to Mohammed's traditionary teachings. These are rejected

by Shias, who also champion the clair to succesion as Caliph of the Prophe son-in-law Ali, and the latter's son Hasan and Husayn. The rival sec detest each other cordially. Many Sar of Persian descent are crypto-Shia: but overt nonconformity is forbidden l Uzbeg fanaticism. Islam has never tak€ root among the Kirghiz, whose invetera nomadism resists all attempts to instru or civilise.

The Russian possessions in Centr Asia result from a law which compe an organised government in contact wi barbaric tribes to extend the area of i conquests until they reach the sea, a impenetrable mountain range, or tl boundaries of a state strong enough ` be mistress at home. The Russo-Chine: frontier is defined by mountain chair connecting the Caspian and Polar sea The last rectification of frontier toc place in 1882, when five-sixths of Kulj which had been occupied during tl anarchy of the Taiping Rebellion, wa retroceded to China. In the same yea Russia surrendered to Persia certa

Russian and British Influences valleys watered by the Riv Atrek, on the Caspian's soutl eastern shore ; while the Sha resigned his shadowy clain to suzerainty over Tekke Turkoman: The spheres of British and Russia influence were defined by the mixe Boundary Commissions of 1885 and 189 Afghanistan is admitted to lie within tl orbit of British India, whose approach€ are now defended by solemn treatie Thus, Russia has, of her own free wil placed limits on her expansion soutl wards, and she is free to pursue the task (civilising her vast possessions in Centr Asia. They include the following province

—	Area. Sq. miles.	Population.
Akmolinsk ..	229,609	682,608
Semipalatinsk	184,631	684,59c
Turgai	176,219	453,41€
Semirechensk ..	152,280	987,863
Syr Darja ..	194,853	1,478,398
Ferghana	86,000	1,572,214
Samarkand	26,627	860,02
Transcaspian Territory	214,237	382,487
Bokhara	79,000	2,000,00c
Khiva	23,000	800,00c
Total	1,366,456	9,901,597

The first three are under the Governo General of the Steppes, whose hea€

A VILLAGE ON THE SHORES OF LAKE BALKASH

ON THE ASIATIC SHORE OF THE CASPIAN SEA

NEAR KRASNOVODSK, THE PRINCIPAL TRANSCASPIAN TOWN

SCENES ON THE CASPIAN SEA AND LAKE BALKASH

quarters are Omsk, which has 37,376 inhabitants. Though their soil and climate are essentially Siberian, they are always reckoned as part of Central Asia. Northern Akmolensk is a continuation of the Black Earth zone of Southern Russia, producing cereals, potatoes, and livestock ; the southern half is known as the Hungry Steppe. Semipalatinsk is more fertile, and 20,000 ounces of gold are extracted annually from its sand and gravel deposits. Turgai has emerged from the ocean in comparatively recent ages. Its surface is covered with half-fossilised shells and aquatic plants. The population is wholly nomad Kirghiz, whose herds of cattle are decimated by blizzards during an Arctic winter. Semirechensk possesses vast unexploited treasures of coal and iron, and its eastern valleys, adjoining Chinese Kulja, rank among the most fertile tracts in the world.

Three-fourths of Syr Daria is trackless desert, affording pasture to Turkoman tribes after the spring rains. It is bisected by a highland region watered by tributaries of the river which gives the province its name. The Governor-General of Turkestan resides at Tashkent, a Russianised city containing 155,673 inhabitants. Ferghana, watered by upper reaches of the Syr Daria is as productive as Russian Kulja. For countless centuries it was the main artery of caravan traffic between Europe and China, and supports a relatively dense population. Kokan (81,673), Na Mangan (62,000), Andisan (47,627), and Marghilan (36,490), are centres of trade and of Moslem fanaticism. The province of Samarkand owes its amazing fertility to the River Zarafshan ; and vast mineral wealth is stored up in the eastern valleys. Its world-famous capital is a mere shadow of departed grandeur.

District of Syr Daria

Samarkand has been deprived by the Transcaspian railway of its ancient importance as a starting-point of caravan traffic, and its population has sunk to 50,000. The shade of Timur still seems to brood over the metropolis from which he ruled the world from Russia to the Persian Gulf, from Constantinople to the Ganges. His sepulchre's fluted dome soars high above the leafy forest which enshrouds Samarkand, and its citizens speak of him as *the* Amir. His glorious tombs and mosques, once radiant with enamelled tiles, have been brought to the ver[y] of collapse by earthquakes and centuri[es] of neglect. Nine-tenths of the Tran[s]caspian territory is a desert over whi[ch] Turkomans wander in spring and winte[r.] Its settled population is concentrated [in] Merv and smaller oases watered by t[he] Murghab and Tejend, or occupy the Ato[ck] a fertile belt on the northe[rn] slope of the Kopet Dagh. E[m]bedded in Russian territory a[re] Bokhara and Khiva, known [as] the Khanates, the sole relics of the Islam[ic] dominion established by Mahome[t's] all-conquering successors. Bokhara co[n]sists of a mountainous tract unfit f[or] cultivation, a central plateau watered [by] the Zarafshan, cool, healthy, and dense[ly] peopled, and lowlands subject to encroac[h]ments by the desert sand. The arab[le] area does not exceed 8,000 square mil[es,] and the pressure of population is beginni[ng] to be felt. The capital is a walled ci[ty] with 65,000 inhabitants. It was once [a] busy centre of trade and manufacture, b[ut] both have suffered from Russian compe[ti]tion. Unlike Samarkand, Bokhara is [a] focus of Oriental learning. Thousands [of] students imbibe useless lore and a stro[ng] leaven of fanaticism in its well-endow[ed] colleges. Booksellers' shops abound, b[ut] the libraries, which were formerly Bo[k]hara's chief pride, have succumbed [to] neglect and conflagrations.

Khanates of Russian Turkestan

The government is a despotism, te[m]pered by priestly influence and the tact[ful] guidance of a Russian Resident. It [is] wielded by the Amir, who belongs to t[he] leading Uzbeg clan. Internal order [is] maintained by an armed rabble of 11,0[00] soldiers. In its days of independen[ce] Bokhara was a theocracy, as thoroug[h] going as Calvin's rule in Gene[va.] Uniformity was enforced by a rigid censo[r]ship of morals, and Tajiks, who secre[tly] clung to Shia dogma, suffered unt[old] oppression. Punishments were atrociou[sly] cruel ; prisons were hotbeds [of] disease ; slavery was rampa[nt] in its worst form, and agric[ul]ture groaned under manifo[ld] exactions. The sinister features of nati[ve] rule have been softened by Russi[an] influence, and though Uzbegs and Mul[lahs] may regret the loss of complete autono[my] it is not felt by the masses. Prior to [its] conquest in 1873, Khiva was a yet mo[re] barbarous replica of Bokhara. It consi[sts] of an oasis of 5,210 square miles, fertilis[ed]

Slavery Under a Theocracy

y the Oxus, and 17,800 square miles of
esert. No standing army is maintained,
nd 2,000 naukars, or royal servants, suffice
or purposes of state and police. Both
hanates are divided into districts, administered by a Beg, which are again
arcelled out into Amlaks, or groups of
illages, severally represented by their Aksakal, or greybeard. The
ympathy Russian character is well
etween People equipped for the task of
nd Officials governing Asiatics. Chris-
anity, which is very vital in all classes
home, has checked the growth of racial
ride and caste feeling. For 240 years
ussia lay under the heel of Tartar hordes,
hose blood flows in the veins of many
ling families. The inbred sympathy
hich links European Russians with their
siatic fellow-subjects was seen in a full
easure during the period of conquest.
he Tsar has had many servants in the
ast who are worthy to rank with our
unros, Elphinstones, and Lawrences. No
ipassable gulf yawns between rulers and
led. Children of the soil are eligible for
e highest posts, and such friction as
ists is bred by religious prejudices.

In administering this enormous terri-
ory, Russia distinguishes between nomad
ibes and the denizens of fertile valleys
ho have long enjoyed a certain degree of
vilisation. The Turkomans are governed
patriarchal fashion ; their tribal organi-
tion has been destroyed, and a *starshina*,
mayor, elected by each Aul, or group of
ibitkas, has replaced the chieftain whose
chests were blindly obeyed during forays.
especting nought but superior force, they
ive learnt to revere the District Officer,
ho sternly represses tendencies to revert
ancient misdoings. On the other hand,
habitants of Samarkand, Ferghana, and
ussian Kulja retain their social, and much
their legal, mechanism intact. Indi-
enous institutions have not been trampled
oon, nor does a half-educated proletariat
ussian preach racial discord and fill
ule in the minds of the masses with
entral Asia the daydream of political independence. Each province is
ider a military governor, who is subordin-
e in professional details to the Minister of
ar at St. Petersburg. It is divided into
stricts, which are administered by army
ficers responsible for executive govern-
ent and the collection of revenue. The
strict, again, is portioned out into Pristas,
subdivisions, under executive chiefs.

The Volost, or group of 25 villages, is the
next unit. Villages, averaging 100 houses,
or kibitkas, are officially represented by
starshinas, who are elected by the people,
subject to the district chief's veto. A
complete separation has been effected
between executive and judicial functions.
Crimes are reported by the starshina to
the volostnoi, and ultimately to a Judge
of First Instance, stationed at the district
headquarters. This officer holds a local
investigation, and prepares the case for
trial by a Judge of the Peace under
Russian criminal law. Both are subordinate to the Minister of Justice at St.
Petersburg, and every penal suit runs
through a gamut of appeals involving a
great waste of time. Civil suits between
natives are also tried by the Judge of the
Peace under Mohammedan law, interpreted by a Qazi. If either party be a
Russian, the case is judged in the light of
Russian law, which is gradually superseding
the incoherent mass of dicta and tradition
current in Mohammedan courts. The
Transcaspian territory, inhabited mainly
by Turkomans, has received a peculiar
Patriarchal legal system from General
Tribunals of Kuropatkin, who is still re-
Central Asia membered as an enlightened
Governor-General. A com-
mission of five judges sits at the capital,
Askabad, as a Court of Appeal. Under it
are district courts, consisting of the chief,
aided by five " Popular " Judges, who are
selected from the personnel of the Courts
of First Instance. These latter hold
sessions weekly at the headquarters of each
Volost, for the trial of petty cases. They
are composed of five "Candidate" Judges,
elected by villagers in the several volosts.
This simple system is much appreciated,
and perjury, which is the bane of superior
courts throughout the East, rarely occurs
in these patriarchal tribunals.

Under Moslem rule the State was theoretically sole landlord, although huge areas
had been ceded to generals and Court
favourites, or set apart for the maintenance of mosques and colleges. When
the Russians took possession of conquered provinces they depended on
officers of the former régime for information on land revenue. The inequalities and injustice of these statistics
have not yet been removed. Taxation
on land ranges between 2s. and
3s. 4d. per acre, the maximum being
charged for irrigated fields. A house tax

is levied on heads of families, whether settled or nomad. The average incidence is twelve shillings and sixpence—about 5 per cent. on the household's income. Every starshina is responsible for the amount assessed on his village. There is a tax of one-fortieth on the value of goods sold, from which Russians are exempt. Small duties are paid on tobacco, matches, and kerosene ; and nomads are charged head-money for the right of grazing their cattle on Russian territory. Data are wanting for an estimate of the cost of Russian rule in Asia ; but it is known to be far in excess of revenue. The garrison consists of 213 infantry battalions and 91 squadrons of cavalry, 58 companies of fortress artillery, and 109 of engineers, who are employed on the State railways. The aggregate strength is 130,250 men, who are cantoned at Merv, Samarkand, and other centres o population.

Irrigation and transport are the chief problems presented by Central Asia. A vast upheaval of the soil has dislocated the ancient fluvial system, and rainfall has shrunk owing to the disappearance of forests. Hence the wholesale **Water Worth its Weight in Silver** emigration of the aboriginal inhabitants to Europe, India, and Egypt. Those who remained battled successfully with an adverse environment, and stupendous irrigation works remain to attest their indomitable energy. Near Samarkand there is a chain of wells 420 feet deep, connected by tunnels in which a man can stand upright. The loess, deluged with water from an arik, or distributory, yields two, and sometimes three, harvests in the year. The critical weeks are those which follow the melting of mountain snows. Water is then worth its weight in silver, and it must be so apportioned that every plot may receive its just quota. The task is complicated by ancient royal grants and fierce disputes between inhabitants of upland valleys and villages on a lower level. Russia wisely leaves the management of such delicate operations in native hands. Irrigation is supervised by elected overseers, termed aksakal, and village mirabs, " Lords of the Water," who are remunerated with a fixed proportion of the crops. The area irrigated in Russian Turkestan is nearly 50,000 square miles.

Agriculture, conducted by means of the most primitive appliances, gives results which our scientific farmers might envy.

In Southern Turkestan the poor ma staple food is giant millet, which yields tw hundredfold. Spring and winter, whe and barley and rice are largely cultivate Cotton has developed enormously sir the introduction of American seed in 18: Russia depends wholly on Turkestan the raw material worked up in **Agricultural Produce of Turkestan** mills of Moscow and Pol centres. The yearly export 663,820,000 lb., valued £10,000,000. Viticulture pursued on a large scale in Samarkar In October the environs are knee-deep luscious grapes, and the output sometim reaches 26 tons per acre. The bulk is e ported in the form of raisins ; but wi equal to superior Burgundy, is sold at s pence a bottle. The only limit to t production of wine and brandy is t enormous cost of imported bottles, cor and casks. Every fruit and vegetal known in temperate or semi-tropi climates is raised in the utmost perfectic The future of Central Asia is bound in the irrigation question. It is matter of vital necessity to bring ba the spacious days of Timur by exten ing the means of water supply. C the Tsar's private domains, near Me great results have been achieved by storing one of the great anicuts destroy by Bokharan invaders in 1784. B scientific irrigation is still in its infanc Innumerable streams run to waste in t belt of loess which fringes the mountai The seven rivers of Semirechensk plou their way into the desert by deeply-c channels. With the aid of science a capital the oases would be delivered fro their incubus of sand-encroachment, a Central Asia would again support a den and prosperous population.

Greater progress has been made in t matter of transport. For 2,500 yea Central Asia was the main artery of cor merce between the East and West. Chine **Passing of Primitive Transport** teas, silks, and spices we carried on horse and camel-ba across its passes and desert Internal traffic was restricte to goods of small bulk but considerab value. A revolution has been wroug by the State railways constructed duri the decade ending with 1904. Krasnovods on the Caspian, is linked with Tashke by a line 1,164 miles in length ; and branch of 204 miles has opened up th Ferghana Valley. Another, 193 mil ng, runs south of Merv to Kushinsk on ᴉe Afghan frontier. The Central Asian ᴉd Trans-Siberian systems are united by railway 1,175 miles in length between ᴿenburg and Tashkent. The whole net-ork of 2,758 miles was intended to serve ᴿategic purposes ; but these considera-ᴼns have given way to the imperious demands of commerce. Cara-

ailway ystem of entral Asia
vans no longer bring from China the tea which is con-sumed in every hut and ᴮitka. The produce of Indian and Ceylon ᴵrdens comes by sea to Batum, whence it distributed in the interior by railways ᴵllowing ancient trade routes. Nor is the ᴵdirect gain less considerable. The cruel ᴵaste of animal life has ceased ; and ᴮdder, once consumed by millions of ᴿeatures engaged in transport, is more ᴿofitably employed. Though the long ᴼlation of Central Asia has been broken, is by no means in close contact with the ᴵrrents of modern activity. A branch ᴵilway between the Orenburg-Tashkent ᴵne and Kulja is sorely needed. The ᴿussian terminus at Kushinsk and that ᴵ our Indian system at Chaman, beyond ᴸandahar, are separated by 425 miles of ᴵlly country offering no serious obstacle ᴼ the engineers. If this gap were bridged ᴸondon would be brought within a week's ᴼurney of Karachi. The Persian Gulf is ᴮarely 700 miles from the nearest station ᴵn the Transcaspian Railway ; and ᴿussia's perennial quest of a warm-water ᴼrt might thus find an outlet to the ᴵdian Ocean. The genius of her people ᴼrbids her to aim at maritime supremacy. ᴮstablished on the Persian Gulf, she would ᴮ more vulnerable to naval attack. When ᴿoundless prejudices disappear Great ᴿitain and Russia will perceive that there ᴮ no cause for political or economic rivalry ᴮtween them, and they will pursue the ᴵsk of civilising Asia hand in hand. ᴼmmerce has responded to the stimulus given by improved means

teady ᴮommercial xpansion
of transit. It embraces raw materials of considerable bulk, but many native industries ᴵave suffered from Russian competition. ᴵfter the Franco-Prussian War of 1870-1, ᴸuropean Russia was invaded by a horde ᴵ German manufacturers, eager to profit ᴮy the iron wall of protection which girds ᴵe empire. Their velvets, drill, broad-ᴵoth, damask, and brocades have ousted ᴵe beautiful silk stuffs produced by

Bokharan looms. Coal-tar dyes have lowered the value of Turkoman carpets ; bounty-fed beet-sugar undersells the pro-duct of the cane : Russian yarns are exclusively employed in such cotton manufactures as survive. Central Asia is essentially a chintz-consuming country. The ever-changing taste for this gaudy fabric is watched and catered for by Russo-German mill-owners.

Before the era of conquest a thriving trade was carried on between India and the Khanates. It has been ruined by protection and the absence of British consular agencies east of Baku. The Indian colonies at Bokhara and other trade centres confine themselves to dealing in tea or opium, and lending money at usurious interest. A lucrative field is open to British capital in the export of lamb-skins, known as " Astrachan," which are a speciality of Central Asia. Its mineral wealth has hardly been touched. Kerosene oil is imported from Baku, although extensive deposits exist in the Transcaspian territory. Alluvial gold is mined in Semipalatinsk, and coal to some extent in Semirechensk. The

Immense Latent Wealth
Zarafshan Valley—and, indeed, the whole mountainous area—abound in useful and precious metals. The principle of laisser-faire, which Russians adopt in dealing with religion, extends to education. In the northern provinces about 1·5 per cent. of the population is undergoing some sort of instruction. Elsewhere the Government schools barely suffice to provide a small modicum of Russian, required in candi-dates for inferior offices. Indigenous edu-cation is more vital. Every mosque has its primary school, which gives elementary instruction in theology and the vernacular. Promising lads are drafted into richly-endowed Madrissas, where they undergo a severe training in Arabic literature. These colleges are hotbeds of mysticism and Pharisaic pride.

A serious rising, which took place at Andijan, in Ferghana in 1898, was fomented by adepts in theology termed Ishans. But the danger of a religious war is no longer acute. Islam in Asia is rapidly losing its militant character. Its professors have learnt from the Russo-Japanese War that Europe may be met on equal terms by employing its own weapons ; and they are eager to assimilate all that is valuable in our civilisation.

KRASNOVODSK STATION, THE CASPIAN SEA TERMINUS

RIVERS FREQUENTLY OVERFLOW THEIR BANKS AND FLOOD THE LINE

A TYPICAL TRANSCASPIAN RAILWAY STATION

ON THE TRANSCASPIAN RAILWAY, RUSSIA'S IRON ROAD IN CENTRAL AS

Attempts to foster Russian colonisation
ve met with small success. Fourteen per
nt. of the population of Semirechensk
: European immigrants or Cossacks,
rose children thrive in the cool valleys
Kulja. Military settlements planted in
e Transcaspian territory have failed
ing to the colonists' predilection for
ong drink. European races seem to be
apable of taking root in the continent
rich gave them birth. Their dominion
Asia must be preserved by a constant
eam of temporary immigrants.
Russian rule has conferred untold bless-
;s on subject races. The canker of
very has been cured, and many a
ober's lair exterminated. The fanaticism
d cruelty of native rule has given
rce to a just and gentle administration.
digenous industries have, indeed, suc-
mbed to European competition ; monu-
ents of a glorious past are in hopeless
cay, and its gorgeous colouring has
led from Oriental life. Such are the
awbacks attaching to aggressive civilisa-
n ; and they are seen at Delhi or Cairo,
well as in Samarkand. British India
hat has given Russia many a hint
ssia for the government of Asiatics ;
s Done and, on the whole, it may be
admitted that the model has
en improved on. So diverse are the
nditions encountered that no com-
rison between the two systems can be
rly drawn.
The area of Russian Central Asia is
arly equal to that of India. Its popula-
n is less than 10,000,000, even allowing
· the concealment of their womenfolk
dulged in by Mohammedans, while that
India is nearly 300,000,000. Turkestan
s no predatory classes to be a perpetual
orn in the administrator's side. Over-
pulation has not brought with it a long
ain of famine and disease. Political dis-
ntent is not fostered by a horde of
iefless lawyers and starving literates.
eligious fanaticism is subsiding, and the
rrent of sympathy between man and
an is unchecked by the artificial barriers
caste. There are, indeed, many ob-
acles in the path of Russia as a
vilising power ; and they are attacked
a spirit which should appeal with
ecial force to the fellow-countrymen of
ve and Hastings, of George Stevenson
d Brunel. A frank understanding
tween the two Empires will make the
mense force let loose in Asia's awakening

serve the true interests of humanity.
Eastern, or Chinese, Turkestan has strong
physical and ethnological affinities with
Russian Central Asia. Until 1758 its oases
were the seats of Mohammedan Khanates
formed in the dissolution of Genghis Khan's
overgrown empire. They were overwhelmed by the tide of Chinese expansion,
Chinese and constituted a province
Central styled Hsin King, or the New
Asia Dominion. In 1864 the garrison, perforce neglected by Peking
during the terrible Taiping Rebellion,
mutinied against its officers. A soldier
of fortune named Yakub Beg seized the
opportunity of establishing himself as
ruler of the outlying province. The
moment was opportune for empire-build-
ing. China was bleeding from every vein ;
Russia was occupied in subduing the
Khanates. Yakub Khan's appeal to our
Government for recognition was welcomed
in London and Calcutta, which were
hypnotised by the chimera of a Russian
invasion of India. Had fate been propitious
this able adventurer might have founded
an empire as extensive as Persia. He
reckoned without the recuperative power
and the sleuth-hound determination of
China. In 1877 he was overwhelmed by
a Celestial army, and Eastern Turkestan
was regained. In 1871 Russian troops
occupied Kulja, which had fallen into a
state of complete anarchy, but, eleven
years later, China was strong enough to
demand its retrocession. Good relations
were essential to Russia's deep-laid scheme
of expansion. The eastern portion of
Kulja, 23,750 square miles in area, was
surrendered ; while 4,357 square miles
were incorporated in Semirechensk.
This was the only instance in which
Russia has retraced her steps in Central
Asia.

Eastern Turkestan is bounded on the
north by Zungaria and the Altai Mountains, southward by the highlands of
Boundaries Kashmir and Tibet. Towards
of Chinese the east it merges in the Gobi
Turkestan Desert and spurs of the Altyn
and Akka Tagh, which bisect
the province. Its western marches are
sharply defined by the Tian Shan range
and the hills of Kashmir. Its area is
440,000 square miles ; but its population
is confined to Kulja, and a ring of oases
watered by the Tarim and its tributaries,
which rise in the environing mountains,
to lose themselves in a fringe of salt lakes

A HUNTER OF THE KIRGHIZ STEPPES

From the painting by Vassilli Verestchagin, photographed by Braun, Clement et Cie.

led Lob Nor. In one of these green
ots stands Yarkand, a decayed town of
,000 inhabitants. Another is com-
anded by Kashgar, a walled city with a
pulation of 120,000, the seat of govern-
ent of an influential Russian Consul-
neral, and a British Commercial Agent
der the Resident in Kashmir. Khotan,
ties of in the south, is cultivated
stern like a garden. The valleys
rkestan of Kulja, fertilised by the
river Ili, were once a main
enue of international trade. The centre
Chinese Turkestan is the Lakshan
pression, below sea-level, and geographic-
y the heart of Asia. The climate is
cessively dry, with extremes of heat and
ld. The province suffers still more than
ussian Central Asia from the isolation
posed by natural barriers. Communica-
n with the West is hampered by the Tian
an and Pamirs, whose passes exceed
,000 feet in altitude. Those toward India
e still more difficult. Eastwards it is cut
f from China by the Gobi Desert, once a
eat centre of population, and by a
dalus of mountain ranges. The popula-
n, estimated at 1,000,000, are akin to
e sedentary inhabitants of Western
rkestan. They are nominally Moham-
edans, but have lost the religious zeal
ich characterised their ancestors.
rality is at the lowest ebb, and disease
rampant.

Administration is conducted by a
vernor-General, *Futai*, and two depu-
s, *Tao Tai*, who reside at Kashgar and
Kulja. Below these functionaries are
strict Magistrates, *Chow Kuan*, known
" Ambans " to the West. All these
e members of the mandarinate. Being
norant of the Tajiki and Turki vernacu-
s, they are dependent on venal inter-
eters. An unpaid hierarchy of native
icials is responsible for revenue and
lice functions. Begs are in charge of
wns ; ming-bashis, yiz-bashis, and
theds om-bashis represent thousands,
Official hundreds, and tens of the popu-
rruption lation. The whole system of
government is utterly rotten,
r every vice of a corrupt bureaucracy
creases directly with the distance of
tlying provinces from Peking. Public
ices are sold to the highest bidder,
d able men who cannot afford to pur-
ase are unemployed. Though taxation
on a most oppressive scale, a mere
ction of the sums wrung from hapless

traders and peasants reaches the Imperial
exchequer. Every collector of revenue
retains the lion's share, and it is hardly
surprising that Turkestan should cost
China £30,000 a year while fortunes are
amassed by officials of every grade.
Agriculture is burdened with tithes, *Yung
Lin*, levied in kind. Oil-presses, rice-mills,
and transfers of land are heavily taxed.
Goods sold in the bazaars pay a twentieth
to the State, and mines are subject to a
royalty of 33 per cent. Criminal justice
is in the hands of the Chow Kuan and his
satellite, the Beg. When a fine can be
levied, the worst offender escapes personal
punishment. Homicide is punished by
decapitation, which is carried out after
the sentence has been confirmed at
Peking. Murders, however, are generally
hushed up, for the District Chief who
reports is liable to fine. Severe scourging,
a portable pillory, termed kang, or an
iron bar permanently riveted to the
culprit's body are penalties awarded to
robbers and housebreakers. The gaols
are dens as atrocious as those of Bokhara
and Khiva before the Russian conquest.
Barbarous Eastern Turkestan lies at the
Criminal mercy of Russia. Its army, com-
Penalties manded by an unpaid general,
or *Teetai*, consists of 3,000 horsemen and 4,500 foot soldiers, on paper ; but
the actual strength is 2,300. It is a rabble,
whose discipline and weapons are beneath
contempt.

Agriculture depends wholly on irrigation, which, a century ago, was the most
highly-developed system of Central Asia.
It suffers from the blight of misgovernment. Native officers decline to supply
water unless they are heavily bribed ;
forced labour employed in repairing the
canals and distributories is paid for at
half the current rates, or not paid at all.
The vast public works bequeathed by a
happier age are rapidly decaying. The
crops raised are identical with those of
Russian Turkestan. Cereals, cotton,
hemp, tobacco, and fruit are produced in
great abundance ; but the export of grain
is seriously hampered by a monopoly
surreptitiously claimed by Chinese officials.
The province contains immense mineral
wealth. Alluvial gold was mined in the
Khotan district until the industry was
killed by exorbitant royalties. In the
mountainous tracts deposits of copper,
lead, coal, and naphtha are met with, but
every species of metal is imported from

Western Turkestan; and the hills are stripped of their forest clothing to serve as fuel.

Despite the oppression under which they groan, the inhabitants of this province have not lost the technical skill which rendered them famous throughout Central Asia. Fabrics of gold and silver thread and coloured cotton goods are produced in Kashgar. Khotan is renowned for its cottage-made silks, but cocoon disease has lowered the quality of the raw material.

The transport question is a determining issue in the matter of foreign trade. Turkestan is hemmed in by lofty mountain walls and a trackless desert. Intercourse with the outer world is maintained by caravans of ponies, which work on the "double load" system. Each train of animals carries its burdens to the end of a stage, and then returns for fresh ones. Over-driving, starvation, and cruel usage are universal. The province is closely connected with Western Turkestan by ethnical affinities and the influence of the Russian Consul-General at Kashgar.

Commerce in Eastern Turkestan Chintzes, calicoes, beet sugar, kerosene oil, and metals are brought thither through the Terek, Turgat, and Alaman Passes. Communication with India is still more difficult. The Karakoram defiles are open only between July and November, and the journey to Peshawar occupies two months.

In longcloths, handkerchiefs, and coarse drills Manchester holds its own against Russian competition. English broadcloths, however, have been superseded by silk velvet exported from Germany,

The Tibetan plateau, with an area of 700,000 square miles, is the result of an upheaval which must have occurred at a more recent date than the cataclysmic change which raised Turkestan from the ocean. Northwards it marches with the province just described; its southern boundary is defined by the Himalayas. On the east it is separated from China by a tangle of curved mountain ranges. Kashmir occupies its western confines. Tibet consists of three distinct regions. The northern plateau, known as Chang Tang, averages 500 miles in width and 15,500 feet in altitude. It is dotted with salt lakes, destitute of wood and waters, swept at all seasons by terrific storms, and cursed with an Arctic winter. This in-

hospitable tract is separated from tl Himalayas by an immense trough, styl Bodyul, the name by which the who country is known in China. This valley the main seat of population. Here t Brahmaputra, called Yarro Tsanpo in i upper reaches, and the Indus rise in clo proximity. Mysterious Lhasa stan 11,600 feet above sea-level on

Physical Features of Tibet confluent of the Tsanpo, a1 Shigatse, the second capital, situated on the main rive Bodyul has a severe climate, but hea\ crops of wheat and barley are raised l terrace cultivation. The eastern mounta system is covered with forest, but shelte many a pleasant valley producing ever thing that the semi-tropical zone can fu nish. A lofty watershed which travers this region is the source of the Salwe river, which fertilises Burma, the Mekon on which Siam depends, the Hwang and Yangtse Kiang, to which Chi owes her dense population.

The keynote of Tibetan history struck by its profound isolation. Acce from the north is barred by a dou mountain wall and the Chang Ta plateau. Tibet can never be broug within the orbit of Russian influenc Westwards the mountains of Ladak a Kashmir are impenetrable for considerab bodies of men. Those of the Himalay are hardly less formidable. Darjiling within a fortnight's march of Lhas but there are three passes of 16,000 fe which might be defended by a handful resolute troops against an army. T eastern highlands were thrice a highwa of Chinese invasion. They are st traversed by caravans and a host pilgrims bound for holy Lhasa. But t huge expanse of broken country, with i watershed 16,000 feet in height, wou baffle all the resources of Europe science. The portal designated by Natu is at the extreme south-easterly corn

Portal of Forbidden Land of Tibet. It is a belt of fores clad mountains, 200 miles width, through which t Brahmaputra ploughs its w into Assam. This unknown land is he against all comers by savage Abor a Mishmi tribes, who enjoy free access British India while they guard th fortresses from exploration.

Save in its eastern valleys, Tibet po sesses a very restricted flora. Nine-tent of its territory is far above forest lev ut three or four varieties of shrub, including an indigenous willow, are found in sheltered positions. During its brief summer this northern plateau is dotted with patches of wiry grass, which afford food to immense herds of deer and antelope. The yak feeds in summer on pastures 17,000 feet above the sea, descending to the valleys on winter's approach. This link between the ox and sheep has been domesticated, and carries packs over the highest passes at the rate of twenty miles a day. Its long, silky wool is the raw material of Tibetan clothing and a staple article of transport. The mineral wealth of this secluded country defies calculation. Gold is probably more abundant than in any other region. Despite excessive royalties it is extracted at Thok Talung, in Western Tibet, and the lake region, 16,300 feet above sea-level. The mines, if the word applies to mere surface scratchings, have, from time immemorial, yielded vast wealth to the Peking treasury. Gold is even more plentiful in the northern mountains; and in the highlands eastwards it is found in the shape of small nuggets under twenty feet of gravel. Silver, copper, lead, and mercury mines are worked there in a primitive fashion.

Tibet is inhabited by a Mongolian race numbering about 6,000,000, but the population is confined to the great southern valley and the eastern mountain system. The Tibetans are clumsily built, but possess great physical strength. They are light-hearted folk, passionately fond of dancing and childish games. Their bravery was proved during two invasions from British India, but priestly despotism has robbed them of initiative and implanted many slavish vices in their character. Both sexes are clad in a flowing robe with a high collar, and long boots with cloth tops. Violet is the colour affected by males, while blue distinguishes females, who also display a band of coloured stuff attached to their backs covered with quaint silver ornaments. The men are expert blacksmiths, and have the instinct for art which is the mark of Mongolian races. Polyandry is the rule where land is scarce; elsewhere polygamy prevails among the wealthier classes. Morals have no existence. Religion has proved a determining force in the formation of the national character. About 640 A.D. Buddhism was grafted by wandering missionaries on an archaic form of demon-worship suggested by the fearful storm which rages in their elevated valleys. About the year 1390 the creed of Buddha underwent a revival; but its spirit was antithetic to the Reformation. Lamaism slowly took shape, its cardinal doctrines being the occurrence of infant incarnations of Buddha, and the superior efficacy of elaborate ceremony as distinguished from good deeds. This belief favoured the growth of a hierarchy in the strictest sense. At its apex are two *avatar* Popes, in the person of the Dalai-Lama, whose abode is Lhasa, and the Tashi-Lama, ruling at Shigatse. Below them are orders closely resembling the cardinals and bishops of the West. Nearly every family dedicates at least one of its members to the priesthood. Two-thirds of the 30,000 inhabitants of Lhasa are monks; and the clusters of solid, white-fronted houses which are scattered over Bodyul and the eastern valleys are invariably dominated by monasteries. The clergy, as a body, are dissolute, avaricious, and tyrannical; but their behests are blindly obeyed by the people. Libraries are found in every monastery. The Tibetan language is losing its monosyllabic character. It has an ancient literature, consisting mainly of translations from the Sanscrit Tantras. These text-books reflect the degradation which Hinduism has suffered by the rise of sects which worship the Female Principle as a means of gaining transcendental power.

Government is on a theocratic basis, public policy being shaped by oracular utterances interpreted by the priesthood. There is a secular arm, in the person of the Desi Gyalpo, who acts as regent during the Dalai-Lama's minority. Executive power is wielded by a Nomokan, " King of Law," selected by infant incarnation from the chief of the four great monasteries. Like the Lama Popes, these great functionaries are believed to be avatars of Buddha. The King of Law is assisted by a council of five inferior Lamas, who are in charge of judicial, revenue, provincial, foreign, and religious departments. Tibet is divided into four provinces—Nari, U, Tsang, and Khem, each larger than an average European state, which are administered by Kablons, or governors. The